EUROPEAN FRANCHISING
Law and Practice in the European Community
Volume 1

EUROPEAN FRANCHISING
Law and Practice in the European Community
Volume 1

Edited by
MARK ABELL, LLB

Partner, Field Fisher Waterhouse,
Solicitors, London

In association with Ernst & Young
and the Royal Bank of Scotland

WATERLOW PUBLISHERS

First edition 1991
© Waterlow Publishers 1991

Waterlow Publishers
50 Fetter Lane
London EC4A 1AA
A division of Maxwell Legal Services plc

ISBN 0 08 040868 0 (Volume 1)
       0 08 040871 0 (2-volume set)

British Library Cataloguing in Publication Data

European franchising.
  I. Abell, Mark
  658.8708

This book has been produced in association with:

Field Fisher Waterhouse,
41 Vine Street,
London EC3N 2AA
(071-481 4841)

Ernst & Young,
7 Rolls Buildings,
Fetter Lane,
London EC4A 1NH
(071-928 2000)

The Royal Bank of Scotland,
42 St Andrew Square,
Edinburgh EH2 2YE
(031-556 8555)

Typesetting by Avonset, Midsomer Norton, Bath.
Printed in Great Britain by BPCC-Wheatons Ltd, Exeter.

Dedicated with much love
to
Mum, Dad and my darling wife Shizuka

M.A.

VOLUME 1

Contents

VOLUME 2

Contents

Foreword

By the RT HON SIR LEON BRITTAN, QC
Vice-President of the European Commission

In pursuing the goals of economic growth, job creation and consumer satisfaction, the Community's competition policy encourages industrial and commercial innovation, such as franchising, in an open, competitive European market. Franchise agreements have developed considerably in the Community during recent years. They constitute a new form of distribution of both goods and services under which an agreement is concluded between two economically independent undertakings, which governs the use of names, trade marks and particular techniques in the marketing of goods and services in premises of uniform appearance.

Franchising systems may contribute to the establishment of a unified European market. They facilitate cross-frontier development, as they are normally based on the leverage which an established name or idea can give a relatively small investment to enable the product or service involved to spread quickly, far and wide. In the light of the growing importance of franchising the European Commission has established a block exemption regulation for certain forms of franchise agreements, covering all economic sectors and including those where specific block exemptions have been adopted (motor vehicles, beer, service stations). This is because franchise agreements are considered to be different in nature from, for example, selective distribution or exclusive purchasing agreements.

Regulation (EEC) No 4087/88 constitutes a key element of the legislation designed to establish the internal market through prevention of substantial market partitionings and other restrictions. The Commission has made determined use of its prerogatives for the purpose of opening up the internal market in this important area well before 1992.

Franchise agreements generally have a positive effect on competition and are capable of stimulating economic activity in various ways. They normally improve distribution of goods or the provision of services by enabling franchisors to establish an extensive network of retail stores without the need for major investments, which may assist the entry of new competitors on to the market, in particular small and medium-sized undertakings, thus increasing inter-brand competition. They also enable independent traders to establish outlets more rapidly and with a greater chance of success than if they had to do so without the franchisor's experience and assistance. They are therefore able to compete more effectively with major distribution undertakings. Further, they allow consumers and other end users a fair share of the resulting benefits, as they combine the advantage of uniformity normally associated with a system of branches owned by one single enterprise, with the drive to succeed that is usually characteristic of independent entrepreneurs running their own business.

However, franchising agreements can also restrict competition if they include provisions which are normally prohibited under Article 85(1) of the EEC Treaty, such as the granting of exclusive territories to the franchisees. These restrictions may, however, be accepted, under the conditions of Article 85(3) in view of the benefits which the system yields in terms of improved and rationalised distribution, advantages which are passed on to consumers who can buy a wide range of products in uniform outlets, which ensure a constant quality of the goods and services, assisted by personnel qualified in giving advice on up-to-date products and product configurations. All the more an exemption may be justified where the market is competitive, where numerous other outlets selling competing products, and where the network does not have a large market share.

The unity of the common market must, at all times, be our aim and we must preserve it from any form of market sharing which would lead to absolute territorial protection for enterprises. Market sharing must not be allowed to replace competition. Franchising, which can restrict competition to a certain extent, may however, under certain conditions, be encouraged as a commercial phenomenon particularly well-suited to the challenges of the Single European Market. The combination of a franchisor's idea and a franchisee's enterprise could boost economic activity and employment, while enlarging the range of goods and services on offer to the public. Franchising makes products and services available to a wide public and does not stop at local or national frontiers. Economic growth, employment creation and consumer satisfaction are goals we all share. The development of the common market in Europe and new technologies and methods of selling goods and services should come together as a catalyst for industrial and commercial developments. To this end the Commission has given an important incentive to the Community-based entrepreneurs who want to market their products through franchising systems, by adopting Regulation (EEC) No 4087/88, thus establishing the necessary legal framework along the lines of which these entrepreneurs can set up their networks and compete effectively within an open internal market.

I hope that this publication will be of great assistance to those parties interested in franchising within the EC and wish it every success.

August 1991

Introduction

By MARK ABELL

The European Community is comprised of twelve countries, has a population of over 342,000,000 and covers over 2,363,000 square kilometres. It has come a long way since it was first created in the 1950's. However, it has still further to go before it becomes an economically, culturally and politically unified whole.

Franchising is an increasingly potent force in the European Community and upon the basis of present trends is expected to grow in importance, someday possibly reaching the levels which it has already achieved in the United States. It is however currently at very different stages of development in each of the twelve Member States. The economic north/south divide is very evident. Its legal regulation and the relevant commercial taxation and intellectual property laws differ substantially in each Member State. The availability of finance and the form such finance takes, likewise differs markedly.

The book is a 'living' testament to the existence of the single market. It is truly a European product, being comprised of several components from each Member State. It is also, however, proof of the inherent difficulties which still exist within the single market. As co-author and editor of the work, I have visited and worked on the text of this book in six of the twelve Member States. The contributors have exposed me to the rich variety of attitudes and lifestyles within the Community. Some of them have lived up to their national stereotypes, while others have totally disproved them.

The contrasting world views of the various nationalities have been very evident. The very different ways of working and doing business that exist in each Member State have also frequently surfaced. Basic concepts of how and when things should be done differ at alarmingly basic levels. Language has also proved itself to be a definite barrier, despite the increasing linguistic sophistication of the European professional classes.

The European Community is a complex socio-economic tapestry, with a weft and a warp of differences and similarities that makes the existence of the single market possible, but at the same time makes the successful exploitation of it a very substantial challenge.

Much has been written on the European Community and the single market. Much has likewise been written on international franchising. There are some works on franchising within certain parts of the European Community and others upon certain aspects of franchising within the EC. This however is the first multi-disciplinary book on franchising in the European Community.

It was originally conceived out of my personal experiences of advising both franchisors entering the European Community from outside and those moving from one Member State to another. It was given further shape by my experiences advising developers and sub-franchisors upon the importation of franchise systems from other Member States and from outside of the EC. I have found that obtaining full and reliable intelligence quickly and in an easily digestable form on franchising in the EC is a very difficult task. I hope this book will help to overcome that difficulty for franchisors and their professional advisors in the future.

The first volume deals with the European Community as a single unit, explaining in turn its history and structure, the drive towards full integration in 1992, the impact of the so-called 1992 reforms on various aspects of franchising, the availability of finance, the future of the EC and a series of relevant case studies.

The second volume deals with each Member State in turn, focusing upon a general introduction to the country, an analysis of the national market, national law, accounting and taxation requirements and the availability of finance.

The contributors were chosen from a broad multi-disciplinary background on the premise that a worthwhile text such as this could only be properly written by professionals drawn from all relevant fields. Were such a text written solely by (say) lawyers or consultants, it would inevitably result in an unbalanced view of the issue being reviewed. The individual contributors were chosen on the basis of their proven knowledge and experience of franchising within their given area of expertise. The chapters in this book are therefore not merely academic accounts of what should be — they are tempered by real experience of the problematic issues involved.

The writing and editing of this book has taken some three years from its first inception to its eventual appearance on the bookshelf. During that time I have received so much help and so very many kindnesses that it is impossible to mention them all. For this I apologise. Nevertheless, those who deserve a particular mention include Ron Campbell of the Royal Bank of Scotland, Andy Pollock of DPRS and Brian Smith of Ernst & Young for the support they gave me during the early stages of the project; Janice Salt for all of her hard work as administrator, sub-editor, diplomat, secretary and general factotum and her husband Jeff for allowing her to devote so much extra time to the project; Kate Thompson for all of her hard work in typing the text, likewise to Amelia Plaza, Lesley Connolly and Ruth Wilkinson; Mark Antingham for all of the late nights and long weekends he put into the sub-editing; Michelle Hugill for her help in writing Chapter 3 of Volume 1; Amanda Hughes, John Wolf, Richard Baldock and Andrew Lafferty for their hard work in assisting with the research and proofing; to my partners in Field Fisher

Waterhouse, especially John Nelson-Jones, for their support in this venture and to Max for entertaining me during those many boring hours of proof reading.

Above all, I must give very special thanks to my dear wife Shizuka, who has sacrificed so very many evenings, weekends and holidays to allow me to work on this book. Without her active support and enthusiasm this book would never have been started, let alone finished. I am a very lucky man indeed.

August 1991 Mark Abell

The Role of the European Franchise Federation – An Introduction

By TON VERVOORT
Chairman, European Franchise Federation

Ask ten people at random in your local main street, 'What is franchising?' The chances are that not more than one or two will come up with a satisfactory answer. Whether you are in France or Germany, Italy or Holland, you will find the general public is not familiar with franchising in spite of the fact that in any European country 10 to 15% of all retail outlets are owned by franchisees.

European franchisees together realise an annual turnover equivalent to some £3.5 billion sterling. Few citizens are aware that in many shopping centres every second or third shop is owned by an independent entrepreneur, while the name on the shopfront can be found on identical stores all over the country. One may ponder why the average citizen is so unfamiliar with franchising.

We like to think that the main reason is that to a large extent franchising in Europe developed smoothly, with few mishaps serious enough to make the headlines. While in practically every European country there has been the odd profiteer who launched a 'get rich quick' advertising campaign without having any tangible benefit to offer, fortunately these incidents were few and far between.

At an early stage franchisors in every country of the European Community resolved to rally their interests. National franchise associations were founded, their main objective being to further *bona fide* franchising, and to see to it that the franchisee was offered a fair deal. National franchise associations also act as liaison between legislators and the franchise community. Most associations drafted a code of ethical conduct for franchising, member franchisors being required to abide by the code.

Some 20 years ago the national franchise associations formed the European Franchise Federation (EFF) in order to further the interests of their members with the European Commission, to co-ordinate the activities of the franchise associations in other countries and to exchange information with their fellow members. Also, with a view to the international expansion of franchising, the member countries agreed to one European Code of Ethics for Franchising which was presented to 'Brussels' and issued as an official publication in 1982. (Improved and with valuable additions, the second version will be ready for publication in all European languages by December 1991).

The European Code of Ethics is but one of the benefits of the fact that franchisors' interests have been entrusted to organisations they support and sustain themselves. These associations represent the franchising community nationally, while the EFF is the voice of European franchisors and franchisees. This is of increasing importance as the open market is becoming a reality.

International co-operation emphatically proved its value when the European Commission found in the mid-eighties that in fact franchise contracts were on strained terms with Article 85(1) of the Treaty of Rome (on concerted practices). Since franchising offered opportunities for development to small and medium-sized undertakings, the Commission prepared to draft a regulation which, under cetain conditions, would exempt franchise contracts from Article 85(1). The EFF was able to inform the Commission fully of the ins and outs of franchising and of the terms in franchise contracts that were essential to make franchising work and ensure that the franchisors could indeed further the development of their franchisees' undertakings; in fact, to prove to the Commission that a certain degree of 'concerted practice' is essential to the success of franchising.

As they did in the past, the EFF and the national associations will continue to make it their business to guard against legislation or competition that may impede further positive development of franchising (national or multi-national) by self-regulation and by providing information to all concerned. Undoubtedly the national associations, each in their own country, as well as the European Franchise Federation, fulfill an important role in furthering the development of franchising in the Europe of today and even more so in the years to come.

Hilversum, July 1991   A. Vervoort

Editor's Note

The terminology used in international franchising to describe the parties involved and the types of agreement used is confusing to say the least. In an attempt to overcome this problem Alexander S Konigsberg, then Vice-Chairman of the International Franchising Committee of the International Bar Association (IBA) published a lexicon in 1989 entitled: *International Franchising: Commonly Used Terms – Volume 1*.

In accordance with this lexicon, in this book the following terms have these meanings:

(1) *A master franchise agreement*
A relationship whereby a franchisor grants to another party, described as a 'sub-franchisor', the right to itself open franchise outlets and to franchise third parties described as 'sub-franchisees' to open franchise outlets within a specified or exclusive territory.

(2) *A development agreement*
An agreement pursuant to which a franchisor grants exclusive rights to a party described as the 'developer' to develop a territory by such party itself opening a number of franchise outlets.

(3) *A sub-franchise agreement*
An agreement by which a sub-franchisor grants a franchise to a sub-franchisee.

(4) *Franchisor*
The ultimate proprietor of the franchise.

(5) *Sub-Franchisor*
A party to a master franchise agreement as described in (1) above.

(6) *Developer*
A party to a development agreement as described in (2) above.

(7) *Franchisee*
A unit franchisee taking a franchise directly from the franchisor.

(8) *Sub-franchisee*
A party who takes a franchise from a sub-franchisor under a sub-franchise agreement.

It is hoped that use of this terminology in this book will not only help avoid confusing the reader, but will also encourage its common usage by the international franchising community.

Editor

List of Contributors

MARK ABELL (Editor) is a partner in the London City law firm of Field Fisher Waterhouse and leads the firm's franchise and licensing team.

Mark has written numerous articles in journals such as the *Law Society's Gazette*, *Franchise World*, *Business Franchise Magazine*, *The European Intellectual Property Law Review* and the *International Financial Law Review*. He has also lectured widely on franchising and licensing both in the UK and abroad at academic institutions such as Queen Mary and Westfield College, London and McGeorge University in Austria, government organisations such as the European Patent Office in Munich and commercial organisations such as the Confederation of British Industry and the Japan Franchise Association in Tokyo. He has also lectured on behalf of the World Intellectual Property Organisation (WIPO), an arm of the United Nations, on franchising and technology transfer and is a member of the Licensing Executives Society and Secretary of the International Lawyers Association's Franchise Commission (UIA). He is also a member of the Editorial Board of, and a regular contributor to, the legal periodicals, *Patent World*, *Trademark World*, and *Copyright World*.

Mark is also the co-author, with his partner, John Nelson-Jones, of the chapter on franchising in *International Business Transactions* published by Kluwer, and author of the chapter on know-how licensing in the EC in the same publication. Two leading textbooks, *The Franchise Option – A Legal Guide* and *The International Franchise Option*, both by Mark Abell, are published by Waterlow Publishers.

Field Fisher Waterhouse has been actively involved in franchising and licensing for over 30 years and boasts a wide spectrum of international and domestic franchising and licensing expertise in all relevant legal disciplines.

JOHN N. ADAMS, Professor of Commercial Law, University of Kent and Director of the Common Law Institute of Intellectual Property, is both a practising barrister and an academic lawyer. He has written numerous articles which have been published in leading periodicals in the United Kingdom and in the United States. His books include *Franchising* (Third Edition 1990), *Commercial Hiring and Leasing* (1989), *Merchandising Intellectual Property* (1987) and *Understanding Contract Law* (1987). He has also edited the Intellectual Property volume of the fifth edition of the *Encyclopaedia of Forms ands Precedents*, and has contributed to or edited other sections of the *Encyclopaedia of Forms and Precedents*, Halsbury's Laws and Atkins' *Court Forms*. He is a frequent speaker at conferences. As Director of the Common Law Institute of Intellectual Property, he is responsible for promoting research into various aspects of intellectual property law.

JAMES H. AMOS, JR is Vice-President International of I Can't Believe It's Yogurt in Dallas, Texas, a franchisor of soft-serve frozen yogurt.

Upon graduating from the University of Missouri at Columbia, Missouri, Jim established a career pattern of leadership, serving eight years, prior to resigning as a Captain, in the United States Marine Corps. He is a veteran of two combat tours in Vietnam where he received 16 decorations including the Purple Heart.

Previous positions have included National Director of Franchising for Arby's Inc., a fast-food franchise and Executive Vice-President of Insty Prints, a franchisor of commercial quick print and copy centers. In his present position of Vice-President International, of I Can't Believe It's Yogurt, Jim developed the international division, negotiating all phases of master franchise agreements in 25 countries worldwide and positioning I Can't Believe It's Yogurt as one of the fastest growing international franchisors.

MARK ANTINGHAM is a solicitor working in the International and Financial Department of Field Fisher Waterhouse, London. His practice is comprised mainly of intellectual property, particularly franchising, trade marks and technology licensing. In addition to this he also advises a wide spectrum of both UK and international companies on general commercial matters.

ZYGMUNT AUSTER is a partner in the Copenhagen law firm of Plesner & Lunoe, practising in commercial law. The majority of Zygmunt's practice involves taxation and intellectual property law, both contentious and non-contentious.

Since 1990 Zygmunt has also been involved in joint venture and other activities in Eastern Europe, particularly Poland.

ROBERTO BALDI has his own law office in Milan which deals with all areas of commercial and international law, specialising in distributorship, franchising and commercial agency.

Roberto is a prolific author with some 100 articles on commercial and international law, including franchising, to his credit. He has contributed to a book and written papers in Italian,

French, Spanish, German and English. He is a former visiting Professor at the University of Milan and the University of Modern Languages, where he taught courses in commercial law including franchising.

He is a member of the Milan Bar Association of which he is a one-time counsel member. He is also a former member and Head of the Italian Delegation to the Commission Consultative des Barreaux de la Communauté Européenne, a former counsel member of the International Bar Association of Italian Speaking Lawyers and of the Club International du Droit de la Distribution Commerciale.

CRAIG BAYLIS is a solicitor and partner in Field Fisher Waterhouse, London. He acts for a large number of substantial corporate clients, advising upon environmentally related issues.

HANS BEEJTINK is the partner who co-ordinates the Moret, Ernst & Young franchise team in Amsterdam. This team specialises in setting up information systems for franchise chains, and other aspects of franchising such as the franchise agreement, consultancy, etc.

Hans graduated from the University of Amsterdam, where he studied business administration, and after that qualified as a certified public accountant. He worked for seven years as a management consultant and for more than seven years as an accountant. He became a partner in Moret, Ernst & Young in 1983.

Moret, Ernst & Young is one of the Netherlands' leading accounting firms.

CHRISTA BREUCHA-SCHMIDBERGER works in the Stuttgart office of Ernst & Young.

GERARD COLL is a partner in the Dublin law firm of Eugene F. Collins & Son. He studied law at University College, Dublin (BCL 1978), the Law Society of Ireland (Solicitor, 1982) and at the University of Amsterdam (Dip. EI. 1982). Gerard is a member of the International Bar Association; the Association Internationale des Jeunes Avocats and of the Company and Commercial Law Committee of the Law Society of Ireland and is a lecturer on company law in the Law Society School.

GUNTER ERDMANN qualified as a lawyer in 1978 and practices as a partner in Wenke, Erdmann & Partner in Hamburg. Gunter's work involves him in advising on a wide selection of corporate and commercial law, particularly those areas involving industrial corporate law, competition law, trade marks, acquisitions and both domestic and international franchising.

Gunter is widely published in the area of franchising. His publications include *The Business Idea: Requirements of Sound Franchising, Chances in Franchising, How to Test a Franchise Offer* (Verlag Norman Rentrop 90/91) and *The Joining up of Agreements in International Franchising.* Gunter has also spoken at various venues upon franchising, including the second forum on franchise law in Germany in 1990. He is a subscribing member of the German Franchise Association.

CONCEPCION FERNANDEZ was born at Cartagena, Spain, in 1963; and is a senior associate of Bufete Cuatrecasas, Barcelona. She was educated at the University of Zaragoza (Law Degree, 1986) and the Free University of Brussels (European Law Degree, 1987). She held a NATO International Fellowship 1987-1989, and is a member of the Barcelona Bar Association and the International Association of Jurists.

Concepción was resident member in Brussels in another Spanish law firm before joining Bufete Cuatrecasas, where she is responsible for the EC law team in its Barcelona office. She contributed to several works on Franchising and on Licensing, as well as to the Spanish edition of Bellamy & Child, *Common Market Law of Competition*.

RUTH FINLAY is a solicitor in the Litigation Department of Eugene F. Collins & Son, Dublin. Ruth studied law at University College, Dublin (BCL 1983) and the Law Society of Ireland (Solicitor 1986). After qualifying she spent two years abroad, with Allen, Allen & Hemsley, Solicitors, Sydney, and Baker McKenzie, Chicago, specialising in trade mark litigation and prosecution with both firms before returning to Eugene F. Collins & Son in 1989. She is a member of the European Communities Trade Mark Practitioners Association.

DENISE FRANKLIN is a member of the Massachusetts Bar and Federal Bar of the District of Massachusetts. She practised environmental insurance law in Boston at Brown, Rudnick, Freed & Gesmer. She is currently an Environmental Legal Advisor to Field Fisher Waterhouse in London.

DAVID GAGE works in the Paris office of Ernst & Young.

MAITRE OLIVIER GAST is an Advocate at the Paris Bar. He is the founder of the Gast business consultancy with offices in Paris, Brussels, Milan and Barcelona. He is Founder-President of the European University of Franchising at Colmar and president of the Franchising Committee of the Union Internationale des Avocats.

He has written more than 150 articles on the subject of franchising law, EEC law, competition law and modern business, published in legal journals as well as magazines designed for business people. He is the author of several books: *How to Negotiate a Franchise* (1983), *A Guide to International Franchising* (1985), *European Competition and Franchise Law Procedures* (1989) and *Franchising in Brasil* (1990).

He is the inventor of the 'rule of 3/2', acknowledged as a significant contribution to the improvement of franchising in Europe.

He is a well known speaker at international conferences and specialises in franchising and EEC competition law. In 1981 he spoke in Japan on the occasion of the 10th anniversary of the Japanese Franchising Association as well as at the International Franchising Association Congress in Acapulco in 1984. He is technical advisor to many franchising associations throughout the world and Advocate for the Fédération Française de la Franchise.

To recognise his work, the French Minister of Commerce and Craftmanship, M. François Doubin, awarded him the Silver Ribbon of French Franchising in October 1988. Finally, in June 1989 he was entrusted by the Minister of Commerce with the task of writing the final draft of the decree implementing the 1989 Law on franchising.

GASPARE INSAUDO is a manager in the retail section of Ernst & Young's Milan Office.

ALBINO JACINTO is a partner in the Lisbon office of Ernst & Young.

MARK JANMAAT is a franchise consultant at EFC-International BV in the Netherlands. Mark has substantial experience of working in various sectors of Dutch industry. His activities at EFC focus on the internationalisation of franchising and he has spoken at various international seminars throughout Europe. EFC has been actively involved in franchising for over 20 years and is the only full-service franchise consultancy in the Netherlands.

BERNARD JEFFCOTE is an international tax partner with Ernst & Young, London. He is now Partner in Charge of tax education in Europe for Ernst & Young and a member of the International Tax Group of specialist partners and managers from the UK and overseas who practice together in the London office.

ERIC P. A. KEYZER is a partner in the Amsterdam office of the law firm Loeff, Claeys, Verbeke (one of the largest in continental Europe) and leads the Amsterdam Intellectual Property and Competition Law Department.

Eric Keyzer has written several articles and papers on franchising, commercial distribution and agency, which have appeared in English and French journals and books. He has lectured in particular on Dutch and EC aspects of franchising, licensing, transfer of technology, distribution and agency, both in the Netherlands and abroad, at academic institutions such as the University of Groningen and McGeorge School of Law in Austria as well as at seminars in the Netherlands, France, Spain and the USA.

He is a member of the Benelux Licensing Executives Society, AIPPI, and the Ligue Internationale du Droit de la Concurrence, and is also active in the Franchise Commission of the Association Internationale des Jeunes Avocats (AIJA). He is a co-author of *Dutch Business Law*, published by Kluwer, and of *Règles et Usages en Affaires aux Pays-Bas*. He was an assistant professor at Leiden University from 1977 to 1979 and in 1979 was admitted to the Amsterdam Bar.

LOUIS LAFILI is a partner in the Brussels firm of Lafili & Van Crombrugghe. He graduated from the University of Louvain with a Degree in Law in 1972 and further graduated from the University of Nancy with a Diplôme d'Etudes Françaises.

He has had various texts published on subjects such as arbitration, company law, agency and distribution, joint ventures and contracts. He has reported in international conferences on environmental law, mining law, fair trade practices, bankruptcy law, company law, directors' liability, agency and distribution, pharmaceutical products and European law.

Louis' main area of practice is in corporate law and he is active in various ICC arbitration cases as arbitrator or counsel. He speaks six European languages.

ANTHONY LANDES is a senior solicitor with Field Fisher Waterhouse in London. He is a fluent Swedish speaker and has practised as an English solicitor in Stockholm. In addition to franchising, he has substantial experience of international commercial law with an emphasis on intellectual property, particularly sponsorship and computer-related work.

ANDREW LITTLE is a partner in Field Fisher Waterhouse in London and for several years was Legal Counsel and Vice-President of Holiday Inns International. Andrew has had a wealth of experience in private practice and the hotel and franchising industries throughout Europe. In addition to providing legal advice, he has been heavily involved in commercial negotiations and the practical and financial arrangements for the successful development and management of hotel and other projects.

ANGUS MACMILLAN is manager of the International Unit of the Royal Bank of Scotland's Franchise and Licensing Department based in Edinburgh, and has worked in various branches and departments throughout his career with the Bank. He is an Associate of the Institute of Bankers in Scotland.

Much of Angus' time is spent representing the Bank at franchise conventions and exhibitions both in the UK and overseas and he has developed a large span of contacts throughout the franchising industry as a result. He has written numerous articles on international franchising for the specialist franchise magazines as well as publications aimed at international development, and he is also a regular speaker at franchise seminars and conferences.

The International Unit of the Royal Bank's Franchise and Licensing Department was formed following the forging of a strategic alliance with Banco Santander of Spain in 1988. Thereafter Angus assisted in setting up a franchise department in Banco Santander's head office in Madrid, based on the Royal Bank's operations in the UK. As a consequence, the two banks' franchise departments work very closely together, the aim being to develop a joint capability across Europe.

JOHN McSTAY is the marketing partner in the Dublin office of Ernst & Young.

CESAR BESSA MONTEIRO graduated in law from the Lisbon School of Law in 1966 and was admitted to the Portuguese Bar in 1969. He was secretary to the Lisbon Delegation of the Portuguese Bar Association from 1981-83 and was Vice President of the same Association from 1984 to 1986.

He has held many other prominent posts, including a directorship of the Portuguese Group of the International Association for the Protection of Industrial Property (AIPPI), a member of the Ethics Committee of the Portuguese Association of Industrial Property Consultants, the International Federation of Industrial Property Consultants and of the United States Trade Marks Association. He has also been a reporter at various influential intellectual property conferences throughout the world.

His writing activities include various publications; *Doing Business in Portugal* (Common Market Reports, Commerce Clearing House Inc, Chicago, Illinois 1986), *Patents throughout the World* and *Trade Marks throughout the world* (Trade Activities Inc. New York) and a book on the legal aspects of doing business in Western Europe (West Publishing Co.).

Cesar is a partner in the Lisbon firm of Veiga Gomes, Bessa Monteiro.

NIKOS MOUSTAKIS is a manager in the Athens office of Ernst & Young.

MICHAEL PANAJOTOPOULOS graduated from the European School of Management (Paris, Oxford, Berlin) with a Master's degree specialising in franchising. Prior to that he studied business administration in Germany.

Michael, who speaks five European languages, has worked in the Franchise and Licensing Department of the Royal Bank of Scotland, concentrating upon the European side of the Bank's business. Michael has also written numerous articles in commercial journals such as *Le Droit du Chef D'Entreprise* (France) and *Business Franchise Magazine* (UK).

HELEN PAPACONSTANTINOU is a partner in the Athens law firm of Michael G. Papaconstantinou.

Helen studied law at the London School of Economics (LLB), Harvard Law School (LLM) and the Université Libre de Bruxelles (PhD). She is a member of the Athens Bar and the New York Bar.

She has written several articles in Greek and foreign journals regrading commercial, corporate and European Community matters. She is the author of the Greek chapter in international publications such as *Mergers and Acquisitions in Europe* (Gee & Co. (Publishers) Ltd) and *Commercial Agency and Distribution Agreements*, published on behalf of AIJA by Graham and Trotman.

Both the firm and Helen Papaconstantinou personally have been actively involved in franchising and licensing and have considerable experience in this field.

DR JEREMY PHILLIPS, Editor of *Managing Intellectual Property*, is an intellectual property consultant who has acted extensively in all aspects of intellectual property law.

Jeremy has held academic posts in Dublin, Durham and London in which he developed an interest in teaching and research relating to all aspects of intellectual property. A member of the Editorial Board of *European Intellectual Property Review*, he was Editor of *Trade Mark World* for nearly two years before establishing a new journal, *Managing Intellectual Property*, published by Euromoney Publications. He has spoken at conferences around the world on trade mark and licencing-related issues and chaired the first ever trade mark conference to be held in Moscow. Jeremy has written numerous books on intellectual property, including a standard introductory text for students.

ENRIC PICAÑOL, born in Barcelona, Spain in 1952, is a partner at Bufete Cuatrecasas, Barcelona, responsible for its International Division. He was educated at the University of Barcelona (Law Degree, 1976; Economics and Business Degree, 1977); University of London, LSE (Masters of Laws, 1983); and International Faculty of Comparative Law, Strasbourg (Diplomé 3ème cycle, 1976). He is a member of the Editorial Board, *Revista Jurídica de Catalunya*, and *European Business Law Review*. He is a member of the Barcelona Bar Association, IBA and ASIL.

Enric has written numerous articles in journals such as *Revista Jurídica de Catalunya*, *Revista de Instituciones Europeas*, *Legal Issues of European Integration*, Butterworth's *Journal of International Banking and Financial Law*, *International Financial Law Review*, and *European Business Law Review*. He is author of the Spanish edition of Bellamy & Child, *Common Market Law of Competition*. Enric was lecturer in Private International Law at the Faculty of Laws of the University of Barcelona. He has also lectured at the Barcelona Bar Association, at McGeorge School of Law, at University College London, and other academic and commercial institutions, such as the London Chamber of Commerce and the Confederation of Spanish Industry.

NICOLE VAN RANST graduated from the University of Ghent with a degree in Law in 1986.

She joined the Brussels law firm of Lafili & Van Crombrugghe in 1986, where her main area of practice is international commercial law. She is registered with the Brussels Bar Association, and has a particular interest in franchising.

Nicole is a member of the International Association of Young Lawyers, Vlaams Pleitgenootschap, Jeune Barreau and L'Union des Avocats Européens. She has had various articles published on agency, distributorship and franchise agreements and has written reports for several international conferances on bankruptcy law, company law and securities.

DEBBIE REEVES is a senior manager in the London office of Ernst & Young and is a member of the firm's retail and franchise group.

Debbie specialises in the retailing, manufacturing and high-tech sectors. In addition to her audit clients, she has been involved in franchise feasibility studies for a wide range of companies and many special investigations arising from acquisitions, disposals, the raising of finance and fraud. She lectures internally at Ernst & Young and has written several franchise articles and a course for the University of Stirling MBA in Retailing and Wholesaling.

Ernst & Young's franchise group is made up of specialists across a wide range of disciplines who are able to undertake a complete 'one stop' service from the feasibility study and launch through to follow-up advice and on-going support. Ernst & Young act for a number of the world's leading franchisors.

GRAHAM ROSE is manager of the Franchise and Licensing Department at the Royal Bank of Scotland, and has spent all his career with the Bank. He is an Associate of the Institute of Bankers in Scotland. As well as having day-to-day responsibility for the Royal Bank's franchising activities, he maintains a wide range of contacts within the franchise sector, and frequently represents the Bank at franchise conventions and exhibitions.

Graham has written various articles on different aspects of franchising for specialist publications such as *Franchise World* and *Business Franchise Magazine*, and is regularly invited to speak on franchising at seminars and conferences.

NICK ROSE is a litigation partner in Field Fisher Waterhouse in London and a leading member of the Franchise and Licensing team. He has wide experience of franchising disputes on both a domestic and international basis. He has written extensively upon intellectual property and dispute resolution. He has also lectured at a number of places in Europe on dispute resolution, in the context of both licensing and franchise disputes.

ALEX SCHMITT is managing partner in the Luxembourg law firm Bonn & Schmitt.

A graduate of Harvard Law School and of Brussels' University Law School, Alex Schmitt was first admitted to the Brussels Bar, and, after working several years as an associate with law firms in Brussels and New York, joined the Luxembourg Bar in 1983. He specializes in banking, international finance and corporate law. Mr Schmitt is also lecturing on Luxembourg law at the Law School of the University of Brussels. He is the Luxembourg correspondent to a number of international banking law journals, and has published a considerable number of articles on various aspects of commercial and banking law.

DR BRIAN SMITH is Ernst & Young's principal franchising consultant. He has over 26 years experience in the industry both as franchisee and franchisor. This experience included 15 years as Managing Director of ServiceMaster Ltd, where he was responsible for that company's operations and expansion in Europe. He also negotiated and had approved ServiceMaster's standard form of contract with the EC to clear the way for the establishment of a European network.

Brian is a founder member and past Chairman of the British Franchise Association and has lectured extensively on franchising. He has an MSc in Business Administration and a PhD in Management.

Brian has had first-hand experience in operations in foreign markets, having established a European network where he was managing director of a Swiss holding company and managing director of company-owned operations in Germany (a greenfield site), France and the UK. He has developed master licence-holders in a number of other foreign markets.

PETER STAERMOSE is a partner in Ernst & Young's Copenhagen office.

PROFESSOR JOHN STANWORTH is Director of the Future of Work Research Group at the London Management Centre, Polytechnic of Central London. He began his career as a scientist working in manufacturing industry and has, over the last 20 years, emerged as a leading expert in the field of small business research and training.

He has over 100 publications to his credit and has been involved in more than 30 radio and television interviews. His most recent work, entitled *Work 2000 – the Future for Industry, Employment and Society*, is based on a programme of interviews with top decision-makers and opinion leaders.

Professor Stanworth has a history of research into franchising going back to the mid-1970s and has briefed front-bench politicians of both major British parties on issues relating to franchising.

JOAQUIN VELASCO is a partner in the Madrid office of Ernst & Young.

WIM VERGEYLEN is a consultant in the Brussels office of Ernst & Young.

MARK WEBSTER is a partner with Knightsbridge Communications Ltd in London. The company specialises in providing a wide range of marketing and communications solutions to business needs, with clients in the UK, Europe, the US and Japan.

Mark started his career concentrating on corporate advertising and promotion, but his specific experience is in the information technology arena, where development and expansion has been rapid and widespread, leading to new marketing techniques and increased opportunities. Mark has considerable experience of co-ordinating Pan-European marketing campaigns, and sees enormous potential for companies who make the effort to get it right.

SIAN WILLIAMS is a chartered accountant who trained in UK taxation and is now a member of Ernst & Young's International Tax Group.

MARTIN WILSON was educated in Geneva, London and Paris and is a member of Field Fisher Waterhouse's Commercial Litigation Department in London. He advises a wide range of corporate clients on litigation problems and has a special interest and expertise in franchising.

PART ONE

INTRODUCTION
TO THE
EUROPEAN COMMUNITY

CHAPTER 1

Members of the European Community

By MARK ABELL

The European Community (EC) has an area of 2,363,000 square kilometres. It stretches as far east as Rhodes (Greece) (28°E), as far west as Ireland (10°W), as far north as the Shetland Islands (62°N) and as far south as Crete (35°N). Twelve nations of Europe are at present members of the EC: France, Germany, United Kingdom, Denmark, the Netherlands, Belgium, Luxembourg, Spain, Portugal, Italy, Greece and Ireland.

The EC had a population in 1987 of 342,000,000 inhabitants, with a population density of 145 persons per square kilometre.

The EC's gross national product for 1988 was PPS 4,464,000 million (approx. US$5,066 bn). (PPS stands for Purchasing Power Standard, a unit representing an identical volume of goods and services for each country).

DENMARK

Denmark is situated in northern Europe between the North Sea and the Baltic Sea. It has an area of 43,075 square kilometres. The main peninsula of the country, Jutland, is joined to the continent of Europe by a 68 kilometre border with Germany. The rest of the country is made up of numerous islands. The former colonies of the Faroe Islands, out in the North Atlantic, and Greenland are now independent.

Denmark had a population in 1989 of 5,119,200. Copenhagen is the capital. There are 1,000,000 inhabitants of the city. Danish is the national language.

Denmark has a temperate climate throughout the year. February is the coldest month of the year. The average temperature at that time is −0.4°C. July is the warmest month with the average temperature of 16°C.

The economy of Denmark relies on industry and agriculture. The country's scarcity of domestic raw materials means that it has to import heavily to ensure production. This in turn leads to a large amount of exports in order to make payments. In 1985 Danish industry accounted for 75% of the nation's exports, agricultural goods accounted for 17% and fishing accounted for 4%. Industrial goods produced in Denmark include machinery, ships and chemicals. Agricultural goods include meat products and dairy produce.

The currency unit in Denmark is the Danish Krone (Dkr). The country's gross national product in 1989 was 765,400 million Krone.

IRELAND

The island of Ireland is situated in the extreme north west of the continent of Europe. The total area of the island is 84,421 square kilometres (32,595 square miles). The Republic of Ireland (or Eire) consists of 70,282 square kilometres (27,136 square miles) and Northern Ireland, independent from the Republic, comprises 14,139 square kilometres (5,459 square miles).

The Republic of Ireland had a population in 1987 of 3,510,000. The capital city is Dublin. The two official languages of Ireland are Irish, which is the national language, and English. Irish is a Celtic language closely related to Scottish Gaelic.

The climate of Ireland is dominated by the surrounding seas. The average temperature in January and February, (the coldest months) is 6°C. The average temperature in July and August (the warmest months) is 15°C. Ireland consists of four provinces, Connaught, Leinster, Munster and Ulster. Six of Ulster's counties form Northern Ireland. Until 1921 Eire was part of the United Kingdom.

The economy of Ireland relies on agriculture and industry. 15% of the Country's workforce is employed in agriculture. Livestock, barley and wheat are the major exports. The main components of the manufacturing industry in Ireland are food processing and mechanical engineering.

The local currency is the Irish Punt or pound (£I). Ireland's 1989 gross national product was £I 20,619m. The country's exports amount to almost 65% of the GNP.

SPAIN

Spain is situated on the Iberian Peninsula. It shares a common border with France at the north east of the peninsula and with Portugal in the west. The mountains of the Pyrenees have traditionally kept Spain isolated from the rest of Europe. The Bay of Biscay in the north, the seas to the east and south and Portugal to the west define the rest of Spain's borders. The country has an area of 504,810 square kilometres.

Spain had a population in 1987 of 38,800,000 inhabitants. Its capital city is Madrid. The national language is Spanish. Basque, Catalan and Galician are also spoken.

Geographically the country's northern section, extending from the Atlantic to the Mediterranean, is highly mountainous. South of this area is a vast, dry central plateau surrounded by mountain ranges and the coastline.

The economy of Spain relies on industry, mining, agriculture and forestry. Industrial production includes machinery, chemicals, steel and textiles. Agricultural goods include fruit and vegetables, potatoes, cattle and wine. There has been recent growth through investment at new industrial sites. Tourism is also important.

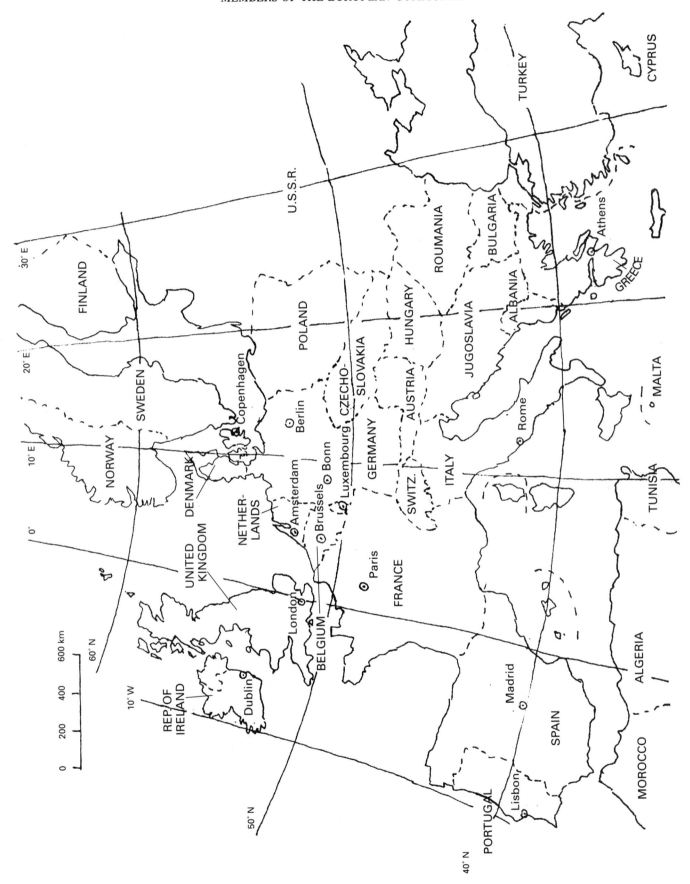

Spain was, in the Middle Ages, one of the greatest international powers, with a large empire. During the period from the end of the Spanish Civil War in the late 1930s until the death of Franco the country was governed by a right-wing military dictatorship. It is now a parliamentary democracy, the present constitution dating from 1978.

Spain's currency is the Spanish Peseta. The value of the country's 1988 exports was 4,693 billion Pesetas (40.470 billion US dollars). The 1988 gross domestic product was 34,500 billion Pesetas ($354 bn).

FRANCE

France is located directly in the centre of the western area of continental Europe. It shares land frontiers with six other nations, Belgium, Luxembourg, Germany, Switzerland, Italy and Spain.

France had a population in 1989 of 56,100,000 inhabitants. Its capital city is Paris. The national language is French.

The country has an area of 544,000 square kilometres. 144,000km are covered by forest, and 314,000km are in agricultural use.

The climate in France is temperate. The average temperature in Paris is 11.5°C, although it is considerably higher in the South of France.

France ranks as the fourth largest market economy in the world. It ranks fourth among world exporters. The French economy relies on industry and agriculture. The country is the world's fourth largest producer of cars. France's industrial production also includes aircraft, textiles and chemicals. The nation also is a big agricultural producer, fourth in the world for beef products, sixth for wheat, and second for sugar-beet and wine.

The currency unit is the French Franc (FF). The 1989 gross national product was FF5,289 billion (880 billion US dollars).

BELGIUM

Belgium is a constitutional monarchy located between France, Germany, Luxembourg and the Netherlands. It has an area of 30,550 square kilometres. Its capital city is Brussels. Antwerp, Ghent and Bruges are other major cities.

Belgium had a population in 1989 of 9.9 million, of which 1 million reside in Brussels.

The country has three national languages, Flemish, French and German. Flemish is a Dutch dialect. English is frequently understood and spoken.

Belgium has a temperate climate. The coldest month is January, with an average temperature of 2.6°C, and the hottest is July with an average temperature of 17.1°C.

The country is divided into three regions. The Dutch-speaking region, called Flanders, is in the north of the country, and the French-speaking region, called Wallonia, is in the south. The Brussels region is the third and is officially bilingual. German-speaking cantons exist in the Eastern part of the country and are included in the Wallonia region.

The economy of Belgium relies mainly on industry. Major industrial exports include steel, cobalt and machinery. Glass cutting, diamond cutting and textile industries are also important.

Belgium is a member of Benelux, the economic union between the low countries of Luxembourg, the Netherlands and Belgium

The Belgian Franc (BF) is the country's currency. Belgium's 1985 gross national product was BF4,787,000 million. Exports accounted for nearly 66% of the GNP.

PORTUGAL

Portugal is the westernmost country of the European continent. Its rectangular-shaped territory is bordered on two sides by the Atlantic Ocean and on the others by Spain. It has an area of 92,326 square kilometres.

Portugal had a population in 1989 of just over 10,000,000 inhabitants. Its capital city is Lisbon. The national language is Portuguese.

The country has several distinctive regions. Minho is the mountainous northern province. The Douro province, just south of Minho, is world renowned for its wines, particularly port. The Algarve is the country's southernmost province. A growing tourist industry is developing there because of its scenic beauty.

Portugal was, in the Middle Ages and after, a major world power with a large empire.

Portugal's economy relies on agriculture and tourism. Its agricultural production includes wine, textiles, fish, leather goods and olive oil.

The currency unit is the Portugese escudo (Esc). Portugal's 1988 gross national product was Esc 6002.3 billion.

THE NETHERLANDS

The Netherlands is a constitutional monarchy located to the west of Germany and to the north of Belgium. It has an area of 41,160 square kilometres. Its capital city is Amsterdam, but the administrative centre is in the Hague. The Netherlands is popularly known as 'Holland'. This name strictly applies only to the two north-western provinces of the country, North and South Holland, which played an important role in the country's history.

The Netherlands has a population of 14.9 million.

Dutch is the national language. English is very widely spoken also.

The climate in the Netherlands is temperate. The average temperature in January is 1.7°C. The average temperature in July is 17°C.

Approximately half of the country lies below sea level. Dykes and pumps are required to keep the land dry. The Netherlands is divided into two main regions, the Low Netherlands which are those areas which would be regularly flooded by the sea without dykes and pumps, and the High Netherlands, the area which is high enough to escape flooding.

The Netherlands has traditionally been an international trading nation and formerly had a substantial empire.

The economy of the Netherlands relies on industry, commerce and horticulture. Six million people constitute the working population of the country. From this group, 67% are employed in the services sector, 28% are employed in commerce and 5% are employed in agriculture. The main industrial production is in light machinery, chemicals, textiles and shipbuilding. Dutch farms produce flower bulbs and blooms, cattle, vegetables and fruit.

The Netherlands is a member of Benelux, the economic union between the Low countries of Europe.

The Netherlands currency is the Guilder, also known as the Florin (Fl). The 1983 gross national product was 283.50 billion Guilders.

ITALY

Italy is located in south central Europe. It shares borders with France, Switzerland, Austria and Yugoslavia. Its coastline stretches around four different seas, the Ligurian, the Tyrrhenian, the Ionian and the Adriatic. It contained 57,500,000 inhabitants in 1989. The capital city is Rome. The national language is Italian.

The climate generally experienced is Mediterranean, with mild, wet winters and hot, dry summers. Maximum temperatures in Milan average 5°C in January and 28°C in August.

Formerly the centre of the Roman Empire, Italy was, until the Rissorgimento and its unification under Generalissimo Garibaldi in the later part of the nineteenth century, a collection of independent principalities.

The Italian economy relies on tourism, industry and agriculture. Machinery, motor vehicles, textiles and chemicals are the main industrial products. Agricultural crops include wheat, rice, citrus fruit, grapes, olives and wine.

The currency unit is the Italian Lira. Italy's 1989 gross national product was equal to 752 billion U.S. dollars.

GREECE

Greece is located in the far south-east of Europe. It is the eastern and southernmost EC member state. It shares borders with Albania, Yugoslavia, Bulgaria and Turkey. Its area consists of 131,990 square kilometres. The heavily indented coastline stretches for 15,000 kilometres.

Greece had a population in 1987 of 9,850,000 inhabitants. The capital city is Athens. Greek is the national language. The average temperature in Athens is 9°C in winter and 30°C in summer.

Greece is often called the 'cradle of western civilisation', and once exerted a strong influence over the rest of Europe. The Greek empire predated that of Rome by several hundred years. In the 1960s, Greece was a right-wing military dictatorship. It is now a parliamentary democracy.

The Greek economy relies on shipping, tourism, industry, agriculture and mining. Industrial production includes textiles (mainly cotton), chemicals and food processing. Agricultural goods include wheat, corn (maize), olives, raisins, wine grapes, citrus fruit and tobacco. Mining production is in lead, zinc, and iron ore.

The currency unit is the Greek Drachma (Dr). Greece's 1986 gross national product was Dr 4,928,000 million.

GERMANY

Germany lies in the centre of Europe. It shares a common border with Denmark in the north, towards eastern Europe it borders Poland and Czechoslovakia, to the south it borders the Alpine countries of Austria and Switzerland, and towards the west it borders France, Belgium, Luxembourg and the Netherlands. Since World War II, Germany had been divided into two states, the Federal Republic of Germany and the German Democratic Republic. Today the Federal Republic of Germany is one sovereign state that encompasses all of the country. The two Germanies united into one nation in October 1990. The country now has an area of 357,041 square kilometres.

Germany has a population of 78.4 million inhabitants. The capital city is to be Berlin, which is also the largest city with a population of 3,352,000. The national language is German.

Until unification under Bismark in the late part of the nineteenth century, Germany was a collection of independent principalities. Political jealousies, the depression of the 1930s and the rise of Hitler and the Nazis gave rise to two world wars and exerted an overwhelming influence over Europe's political future.

There are three main regions of country, the North German Plain, the Central German Uplands and the Alpine Foothills. Germany's climate is temperate. The coldest month of the year is January, where temperatures range from 1.5°C to −6°C. July is the hottest month of the year, where average temperatures can range between 17°C and 20°C.

Germany is one of the world's major industrial countries. Agriculture is also an important part of the economy. German industrial products include steel, machinery, vehicles, chemicals and textiles. Agricultural goods include cattle, potatoes, grain, sugar-beet and fruit.

The currency unit of Germany is the Deutschemark (DM). The preliminary figure for the 1989 gross national product for the united Germany is DM 2,255 billion.

UNITED KINGDOM

The United Kingdom is located off the north west coast of Europe. It is composed of the island of Great Britain (England, Wales and Scotland) and Northern Ireland. The United Kingdom overall has an area of 244,100 square kilometres. England has an area of 130,363 square kilometres. Scotland has an area of 78,772 square kilometres, Wales an area of 20,845 square kilometres. Northern Ireland is located on the island of Ireland, west of Great Britain. It has an area of 14,120 square kilometres.

The United Kingdom had an overall population in 1989 of 57,200,000 inhabitants. The capital city is London. England has a population of 46,221,000 inhabitants. The national language is English. Scotland has a population of 5,196,000 inhabitants. Its capital city is Edinburgh, the national languages are English and Gaelic. Wales has a population of 2,077,000 inhabitants; its capital city is Cardiff, and the national languages are English and Welsh. Northern Ireland has a population of 1,537,000 inhabitants, its capital city is Belfast and the national language is English.

Britain's Empire, which was finally replaced by the Commonwealth after the Second World War, was one on which the 'sun never set', covering a large portion of the globe.

The economy of England relies on agriculture, industry and mining. The major crops produced are barley, wheat, livestock and dairy products. The chief English exports are machinery, vehicles, chemicals and textiles. Large deposits of oil, natural gas, coal, iron ore and china clay are also important.

The economy of Scotland relies on agriculture, mining and whisky distilling. The major crops are barley, oats, potatoes; livestock includes cattle, sheep and pigs. The shipbuilding, engineering, textile and linen industries are important.

The currency unit for all of the United Kingdom is the pound sterling (£). The gross national product of the United Kingdom for 1989 was 663 billion US dollars.

LUXEMBOURG

The Grand Duchy of Luxembourg is an independent sovereign state located between Belgium, France and Germany. It has an area of 2,587 square kilometres. It is only 82km long and 58km wide.

Luxembourg has a population of 370,000 inhabitants. 100,000 of them live in Luxembourg City, the capital, and its surrounding area.

The language of the country is Luxembourgish, a Mosel-Frankish dialect. French and German are also recognised languages. English is widely spoken in major city centres.

Luxembourg enjoys a temperate climate without extremes. The average temperature in January is −2°C. In July it is 18°C.

The country is divided into two clearly defined regions. In the north is 'Oesling', the uplands of the Ardennes. It's a hilly region with a high point of 547 metres. The south and centre are referred to as the 'Good Land'. They consist of farmland and woods, with the highest point being 420 metres.

The economy of Luxembourg relies on industry and agriculture. In the far south west of the country lies the iron ore mining district. In this area, an important steel industry exists. Chemicals, rubber and fertilisers are also produced. Agriculturally, the country relies on crop production and dairy products. Wine-growing plays a minor role in Luxembourg's economy.

Luxembourg is economically tied to Belgium and the Netherlands as a member of the Benelux union.

Luxembourg has its own currency, the Luxembourg Franc, which is freely interchangeable with the Belgian Franc. The gross national product in 1989 was 262.8 billion francs, when its foreign trade represented nearly 75% of GNP.

CHAPTER 2

Creation of the European Community

By MARK ABELL

In 1950 in an attempt to recover from the devastation of the Second World War, France and Germany began negotiations for economic integration. The aim was to pool their coal and steel resources under common institutions. On 25 July 1952 France, Germany, Benelux (Belgium, the Netherlands and Luxembourg) and Italy created the European Coal and Steel Community (ECSC) under the Treaty of Paris.

This first tentative step towards European Union was carefully restricted to basic commodities in one specific economic sector. However, it soon became apparant that transnational co-operation could be of great benefit across the whole economic spectrum. In June 1955 at the Messina Conference, despite the earlier failure of efforts to establish an Agricultural Community and a European Defence Community, it was decided by the foreign ministers of the six ECSC member states that there was a definite need for a united Europe with common institutions and a common market. As a result of the Messina Conference the Brussels Conference was held under the chairmanship of Belgium's Foreign Minister Paul-Henri Spaak and it led to the so-called Spaak Report, released in April 1956. The Spaak Report contained detailed proposals for the establishment of a European Community and a European Atomic Energy Community. These proposals became the basis for future negotiations and treaties establishing the European Economic Community (EEC) and Euratom were ratified in Rome on 25 March 1957, becoming effective on 1 January 1958.

The six original member states were joined by the United Kingdom, Ireland and Denmark after 10 years of painfully slow negotiations. The Treaty of Accession formally took effect on 1 January 1973.

The Treaty of Accession of Greece took effect on 1 January 1981, and Spain and Portugal became members on 1 January 1986.

On 1 July 1987 the Single European Act (SEA) took effect. This Act is a treaty to advance the member states of what is now the European Community (EC) towards a full European Union. It aims at removing all remaining legal, political, fiscal and technical barriers to the free movements of people, services, goods and capital (see Chapters 8, 9 and 10). It therefore by necessity amends several provisions of the Treaty of Rome.

THE TREATY OF ROME

The Treaty of Rome is the basic constitutional document of the EC and comprises six parts, four annexes, 13 Protocols and two conventions together with a Final Act covering both the EEC and European Treaties, with nine annexed Declarations. The six parts of the treaty are as follows:

		Articles
Part 1	Principles of the Community	1–8C
Part 2	Foundations of the Community	9–84
Part 3	Policy of the Community	85–130T
Part 4	The Association of Overseas Countries and Territories	131–136A
Part 5	Institutions of the Community	137–209
Part 6	General and Final Provisions	210–248

1. Principles

The task of the Community is declared in Article 2 as:

'Establishing a common market and progressively approximating the economic policies of Member States, to promote throughout the Community a harmonious development of economic activities, a continuous and balanced expansion, an increase in stability, an accelerated raising of the standard of living and closer relations between the States belonging to it'.

Its general activities are stated in article 3 to include:

'(a) the elimination, as between Member States, of customs duties and of quantitive restrictions on the import and export of goods, and of all other measures having equivalent effect;

(b) the establishment of a common customs tariff and of a common commercial policy towards third countries;

(c) the abolition, as between Member States, of obstacles to freedom of movement for persons, services and capital;

(d) the adoption of a common policy in the sphere of agriculture;

(e) the adoption of a common policy in the sphere of transport;

(f) the institution of a system ensuring that competition in the common market is not distorted;

(g) the application of procedures by which the economic policies of Member States can be co-ordinated and disequilibria in their balances of payments remedied;

(h) the approximation of the laws of Member States to the extent required for the proper functioning of the common market;

(i) the creation of European Social Fund in order to improve employment opportunities for workers and to contribute to the raising of their standard of living;

(j) the establishment of a European Investment Bank to facilitate the economic expansion of the Community by opening up fresh resources;

(k) the association of the overseas countries and territories in order to increase trade and to promote jointly economic and social development.'

Article 4 of the Treaty provides for the establishment of an Assembly, a Council, a Commission (acting with assistance of an advisory Economic and Social Committee) and a Court of Justice, each with distinct limits on their powers.

The duty of member states to take all appropriate measures is contained in Article 5, while Article 6 provides for the close co-ordination of economic policies, and Article 7 provides against any discrimination, on grounds of nationality.

Article 8 provides for a series of transitional periods for the creation of a truly common market, whilst Article 8A contains the reference to that magic date, 31 December 1992, by which the internal market must:

'Comprise an area without internal frontiers in which the free movement of goods, persons, services and capital is assured . . .'

In accordance with Article 8B:

'The Council, acting by a qualified majority on a proposal from the Commission, shall determine the guidelines and conditions necessary to ensure balanced progress in all the sectors concerned.'

Differences in development are, however, allowed for by Article 8C.

2. Foundations

The main aim of the Treaty of Rome is the creation of a customs union — that is, the removal of all tariff and quantitative restrictions, and the application of a common external tarriff.

This part of the Treaty contains provisions which are designed to give effect to this aim and introduce the concept of the free circulation of goods within the Common Market.

The controversial Common Agricultural Policy (CAP) is established by Article 38, the objectives of which are:

'(a) To increase agricultural productivity by promoting technical progress and by ensuring the rational development of agricultural production and the optimum utilisation of the factors of production, in particular labour;
(b) Thus to ensure a fair standard of living for the agricultural community, in particular by increasing the individual earnings of persons engaged in agriculture.
(c) To stabilise markets;
(d) To assure the availability of supplies;
(e) To ensure that supplies reach consumers at reasonable prices.' (Article 39(1))

The next section of the Treaty provides for the free movement of persons, services and capital (see Chapter 10).

Article 48 provides that workers must be allowed to move freely throughout the Market (save for reasons of public policy, public security, or public health).

The right of establishment (that is, the abolition of restrictions on the freedom of the establishment on nationals of one member state in the territory of another) is provided for in Article 52, whilst Article 59 provides for freedom to supply services and Article 67 removes restrictions on the movement of capital. A common transport policy is provided for in Article 74 (see Chapters 10, 11 and 12).

3. Policy

Title I of this part of the Treaty contains the so-called 'Common Rules'.

The rule of competition is contained in the infamous Articles 85 and 86 and form the base of the Community's antitrust policy (see Chapters 26 to 30).

Article 91 allows the Commission to take action against dumping of goods into the EC by non-member states (see Chapter 37).

Article 92 provides against state aid which distorts or threatens to distort competition, whilst Articles 95, 96 and 97 seek to abolish tax-based discrimination and harmonise indirect taxation in all member states.

The approximation of laws affecting the establishment or functioning of the EC is provided for in Article 100. Articles 100A and 100B provide for the methodology to be used to achieve this.

The second title in this Section of the Treaty of Rome is concerned with economic policy, whilst Title III deals with social policy (see Chapter 22). Title IV provides for a European Investment Bank (see Chapter 34), whilst the issue of Economic and Social Cohesion is addressed by Title V (see Chapter 22). Research and Development provisions are found in Title VI and Environmental provisions in Title VII (see Chapter 21).

4. The Association of Overseas Countries and Territories

This section of the Treaty provides for special relations with non-member states which have had special relationships with Belgium, France, Italy, the Netherlands and the United Kingdom.

5. Institutions

Title I of Part 5 of the Treaty of Rome provides for the creation of single institutions for the EC, namely the Assembly (or European Parliament as it is more commonly known), the Council, the Commission, the Economic and Social Committee and the European Court of Justice. These are described in detail in Chapter 3 below.

Title II details budgetary provisions for the EC. The way in which the EC is financed has changed over the years and is now based upon a mixture of agricultural levies, customs duties and contributions from the budgets of the member states.

The Audit Board established under Article 206 is responsible for examining the EC's revenue and expenditure.

6. General and Final Provisions

This section of the Treaty deals with miscellaneous matters such as the legal personality and functioning of the Community, safeguards, external relations, Treaty commitments on member states, Final Provisions, Annexure, Protocols, Conventions and Declarations.

CHAPTER 3

The Institutions of the European Community

By MARK ABELL

Introduction

According to the Treaties there are four Community institutions, namely the Council, the Commission, the European Parliament and the Court of Justice of the European Communities (ECJ). All four institutions are now common to all three communities.

The Court and Parliament (or Assembly as it used to be called) have been common to all three Communities from their outset. A decision was taken to that effect when the EEC and Euratom Treaties came into existence (see the Convention on Certain Institutions Common to the European Communities, annexed to the Rome Treaties). There have been a single Commission and single Council since 1967 as a result of the Treaty Establishing a Single Council and a Single Commission of the European Communities (Merger Treaty) which was signed on 8 April 1965 and which came into force on 1 July 1967.

The Single European Act (SEA), which came into force on 1 July 1987, contains certain provisions which alter the relations between the Community institutions and the way in which they operate. It has also, for the first time, given Community recognition to the European Council and made provision for the establishment of a Court of First Instance (CFT) to be attached to the ECJ.

The Commission of the European Communities

The Commission of the European Communities, which is based mainly in Brussels, can be regarded as the executive body of the European Community. However its powers are wider than might at first sight be expected of such an executive body. The Commission acts as the guardian of the Treaties and can supervise the activities of the member states. It has a specific role within the EC legislative process. It also has the power to apply EC law to individuals or firms in certain areas, for example, competition.

Composition

The composition of the Commission is laid down by the Merger Treaty. A Commissioner must be a national of a member state and there must be one national from each member state and no more than two from one State (Article 10(1), Merger Treaty). In practice the Commission consists of seventeen Commissioners, two from each of the larger member states (France, Italy, Germany, Spain and the UK) and one from each of the smaller member states (Belgium, Denmark, Ireland, Luxembourg, the Netherlands, Greece and Portugal). Commissioners are appointed by common accord of the governments of the member states for a renewable term of four years (Article 11, Merger Treaty). The whole Commission is replaced at one time. It should be noted here that the term 'Commission' commonly denotes the full Commission as well as the Commissioners.

The Commission is clearly intended to be an independent body, and Article 10(2) of the Merger Treaty states that 'the Members of the Commission shall, in the general interest of the Communities, be completely independent in the performance of their duties'. It constitutes a collective body; its powers are vested equally in each Member and each Member is jointly responsible for the measures taken by the Commission.

Most Commissioners are professional politicians and continue to pursue their political careers when they leave the Commission. However they do not take, and are not permitted (Article 10, Merger Treaty) to take, instructions from the national governments of the states in which they are domiciled or from any other states or bodies. In this respect the Commission differs from the Council of Ministers, whose members clearly represent the interests of the member states. The allegiance of the Commissioners is owed to the Community. A Commissioner cannot be dismissed, but may be compulsorily retired for serious misconduct or failure in his duties (Article 13, Merger Treaty). It is also possible for the whole Commission to be removed by a vote of censure in the European Parliament (Article 144 EEC).

The president of the Commission is appointed for a two year term (Article 14, Merger Treaty) and, save where the whole Commission is replaced, the Commission shall be consulted as to the appointment of the president. The two year term is renewable and in practice a president remains, if he desires, for the whole period of the Commission.

The Commission is divided into twenty-three departments called Directorates-General (DGs), each one covering a different area of community law. For example DG IV deals with competition and DG XV with financial services. Each DG is headed by a Director-General, who is in turn responsible to the particular Commissioner having the responsibility for the subject covered by the DG. A full list of all the Directorates General appears at the end of this chapter.

The Commissioners are assisted in their work by a group of staff, called a *cabinet*. A Commissioner appoints his own *cabinet*, not necessarily from amongst Commission officials.

The Commission as the guardian of the Treaties

It is up to the Commission to ensure that the provisions of the Treaties and the decisions of the institutions are properly implemented. It is therefore provided with specific enforcement provisions under all three Treaties. Under Article 38 ECSC the Commission can issue a decision (which is binding on the member state concerned) holding that a member state has breached its Treaty obligations. The decision will only come before the ECJ if the member state concerned takes annulment proceedings. If the member state fails to comply with the decision, it may incur financial penalties under Article 38. However, as yet no financial penalty has been imposed on a member state under that Article.

The applicable enforcement provisions under the other treaties are Articles 169-171 EC and Articles 141-143 of the Euratom Treaty. These provisions are identical. The Commission delivers an opinion, which is not binding (Article 189), and, if the member state fails to abide by it, the Commission may take action before the ECJ. The Commission has a discretion as to whether to take a member state to the ECJ. The current attitude of the Commission is to take a member state in breach of its obligations to the ECJ unless there are good reasons not to.

The Commission has certain specific enforcement powers in the area of state aids (Article 93(2)). It can issue a legally binding decision to a member state in breach of the Treaty provisions on state aids and if the member state concerned fails to comply with the decision within the prescribed time limit, the Commission may take it to the ECJ.

The Commission also has certain supervisory powers over individuals, traders and undertakings, particularly in the field of competition (see Chapters 26 and 27). Under the ECSC the Commission alone administers competition rules (Articles 65(4) and 66(1) ECSC). Under the EEC Treaty the Commission has wide powers (Regulation No. 17 of the Council of 6 February 1962, implementing Articles 85 and 86 of the Treaty (OJ (1962) 13/204)) to invoke the competition rules contained in Articles 85 and 86 (see Chapter 30). It has the power to prosecute cases and adopt decisions requiring the termination of infringements of the competition rules. It also has wide investigative powers (contained in Regulation 17 – see Chapter 30 below) whereby it can, for example, compel companies to disclose information and submit to an on-the-spot investigation. Where firms are found to be in breach of the competition rules the Commission can impose penalties in the form of fines of up to 10% of the undertaking's worldwide turnover. Under the EC Treaty the Commission's powers in the field of competition are not exclusive, as it is open to an individual undertaking to invoke EEC competition rules against another undertaking before a national court.

The legislative capacity of the Commission

In the ECSC the forms of legislation defined (Article 14) are limited to acts of the Commission. This does not mean that the Council has no role under the ECSC but rather that the Commission has the basic law-making power. Under Article 14 the Commission has the power to take decisions, make recommendations or deliver opinions.

The EEC Treaty lays down broadly the areas in which the Community is to develop policy, leaving most of the basic decisions on policy formulation to be taken later. Most substantive decisions must be taken by the Council (leaving control with the member states). However, the Commission has a certain amount of legislative power expressly conferred on it by the Treaty; for example, under Articles 33(7) and 13(2) EEC it has the power to issue directives, and under Article 90(3) EEC it can issue directives or decisions.

The most important legislative role of the Commission is in proposing legislation. This is a very important role, as it is the only body which can propose legislation. The Council has no such power. It can only act on Commission proposals, and, where the Council wishes to amend a Commission proposal, unanimity is required (Article 149(1) EEC). The Commission retains an element of control over how the Council acts and in reality it can stop the Council from acting by withdrawing its proposal. Since the introduction of the co-operation procedure under the SEA (see below) the Commission still maintains an important role, as it decides which of the Parliament's amendments are put before the Council (although, acting unanimously, the Council can override the Commission).

The Commission enacts binding legislation in exercise of powers delegated to it by the Council. In practice the Council delegates wide implementing powers to the Commission, particularly in connection with the common policies (eg commercial policy, agriculture, fisheries, the environment) and more recently it has done so in connection with the completion of the internal market. When implementing secondary legislation the Commission is required to consult committees consisting of member states' representatives. Three procedures now exist and these involve different sorts of committees.

The most widely used committee system is the management committee. The management committees have existed since 1962 and they are particularly useful where the Commission's powers involve a certain amount of discretion. Under this system the Commission submits its implementing measure to the appropriate management committee, which gives its opinion by qualified majority. The Commission is not bound by the committee's decision, but should it decide to bring the legislation into force despite an adverse opinion, it must inform the Council, which has one month to take alternative action (by qualified majority). If, on the other hand, the Commission acts in line with the committee's opinion or if the committee fails to reach a qualified majority, the Commission's decision is final and there is no appeal to the Council.

The other types of committees are advisory committees, which the SEA recommended should be used for measures relating to the completion of the internal market, and regulatory committees. Where the advisory committee system applies, the Commission will listen to the opinions and representations of the member states but merely has to inform the committee of its actions. The regulatory committees work in a similar way to the management committees, but with greater scope for appeals to the Council.

The Commission has no power to sub-delegate powers conferred on it by the Council. However, the Council itself can and does delegate powers directly to member states.

The Economic and Social Committee

The Economic and Social Committee (ESC) in its present form came about as a result of the merger (see Article 5 of the Merger Treaty) of the ESCs set up under both the EEC and Euratom Treaties. There is also a separate consultative committee (not considered here) which exists under the ECSC Treaty (Article 18 ECSC).

The ESC is a consultative and advisory body which provides a means whereby the views of various economic and social interest groups can be made known to the Council and Commission. The ESC is technically not a Community institution (not being mentioned in Article 4 of the EEC Treaty). However it fulfils an important function and merits serious consideration.

Articles 193 to 195 EEC and 165S to 167 Euratom govern the composition and appointment of the ESC; they require, *inter alia*, certain categories of economic and social activity to be represented and the composition of the Committee to take account of the need to ensure adequate representation of the various categories of such activity.

The ESC consists of 189 members representing employers, workers and other groups on matters such as transport, employment, trade and agriculture. There are different numbers of representatives from different member states, depending upon the size of the member state. The Members are appointed by the governments of the member states.

The ESC must be consulted by the Council and Commission where the Treaty so provides (Article 198 EEC) and may be consulted where the Council or Commission considers it appropriate (Article 198 EEC). In addition the ESC also puts forward its views on its own initiative. It is only since 1972 that the ESC has had its own right of initiative. (Article 196 EEC states that the ESC is only to be convened at the request of the Council or Commission; however, it was decided in October 1972 at the meeting of the Heads of State or of Government in Paris that the ESC should have its own right of initiative). This means the ESC can deliver opinions on its own initiative. Where both the Parliament and the ESC are to be consulted there is no general rule as to which is consulted first (Gregg Myles, *EEC Brief* Vol. 1). What usually happens is that both bodies are consulted simultaneously (*ibid*).

The opinions of the ESC are published in the *Official Journal* and the ESC produces an Annual Report which contains a list of its opinions and other information.

The Council of the European Communities

The Council of the European Communities or Council of Ministers is the primary law-making body of the Communities. Under the ECSC decision-making power is placed mainly in the hands of the Commission, with major decisions requiring the consent of the Council of Ministers. When acting under the EEC and Euratom Treaties it is the Council of Ministers which takes the key decisions and (except in special cases) it can only act on a proposal from the Commission.

It should be emphasised that the Council of Ministers must not be confused with the Council of Europe, which is not an institution of the European Community at all. The Council of Europe was established in 1949 and now has 21 member states (including all the member states of the European Community). Its function is merely to provide a forum for discussion; its institutions, namely a Committee of Ministers and a Consultative Assembly, do not have the same decision-making powers as the Council of Ministers of the European Community. It was the Council of Europe which was responsible for drawing up the European Convention on Human Rights and Fundamental Freedoms, which was signed in 1950. As a result of the Convention the European Commission of Human Rights and the European Court of Human Rights were established.

Composition

The Council of Ministers consists of one representative from each member state. Article 2 of the Merger Treaty states that:

'The Council shall consist of representatives of the member states. Each Government shall delegate to it one of its members.'

The Council varies in composition depending upon what is being discussed. For example, if discussing agricultural matters it will consist of Ministers of Agriculture. When general matters are being discussed, member states are normally represented by their Foreign Ministers. Such meetings are usually referred to as the 'General Council'. It is possible for two or more Council meetings to be taking place at the same time. Given the precise drafting of Article 2 of the Merger Treaty, the Council should technically consist of Ministers. However, some countries have sent top civil servants to represent them at Council meetings.

The Presidency of the Council rotates, at six-monthly intervals, between the member governments. The Merger Treaty (Article 2) lays down the order in which the different member states hold the office of President. It contains two cycles so that member states do not always occupy the same part of the year. It is the responsibility of the President to convene Council meetings either on his own initiative or at the request of the Commission (Article 3, Merger Treaty).

The President draws up the agenda for Council meetings and therefore has a certain amount of control in deciding what is discussed. The President, however, does not have total control, as other members can express their wishes as to what is discussed and the agenda can be amended if agreed unanimously.

Role of the Council

Under the EEC Treaty Article 145 states that the Council's function is to ensure that the objectives set out in the Treaty are attained. In order to facilitate this, it is given the power to take decisions and to ensure the co-ordination of the general economic policies of the member states. To decide upon the precise powers conferred on the Council, it is necessary to look at the Treaty provisions with regard to specific policy areas. The Treaty will specify which institution has which power. Generally, under the EEC Treaty most legislative power is conferred on the Council.

Voting

The Treaty provisions also specify the way in which the Council should operate. In some instances it will be required to act unanimously, for example under Articles 43(2) and 100 EEC, or to consult the Parliament, for example under Article 43 EEC. It is therefore necesary to look at each Treaty provision separately. The Council is required to act by a majority unless the Treaty provides otherwise (Article 148(1) EEC). In practice many provisions require a qualified majority with only a few allowing for voting by a simple majority. Qualified majority voting is a system of weighted voting, although the proportions of votes are not exactly proportionate to the population size of the member states. Article 148(2) EEC defines a qualified majority and lays down the following weighting for the votes of the member states:

Germany	10
France	10
Italy	10
United Kingdom	10
Spain	8
Greece	5
Netherlands	5
Portugal	5
Belgium	5
Denmark	3
Ireland	3
Luxembourg	2

The total number of votes is 76 and a qualified majority is 54. The use of qualified majority voting prevents two big member states from having a blocking power and means that the big countries alone cannot now out-vote the smaller. Prior to the accession of Spain and Portugal in 1986, two big member states could act together as a blocking minority. In short, no more than one big state could be out-voted.

Majority voting is not used in all cases where the Treaty makes provision for it and by convention, it will not be used to push through a measure where important interests of a member state are at stake. This has arisen as a result of the Luxembourg Accords of 1966, which ended the French 'empty chair policy'. (From the middle of 1965 until January 1966 the French boycotted Council meetings, partly as a protest against the introduction of qualified majority voting at the commencement of the third stage of the establishment of the Common Market.) The Luxembourg Accords record the terms of an agreement between the member states whereby they will try to reach agreement where important interests are at stake rather than use majority voting. In addition, France recorded its view that, where it considered very important matters were at stake, the discussion must be continued until unanimous agreement was reached. In practice the French view prevailed and when there was an important national interest at stake discussions continued until unanimity was reached (albeit with abstentions).

The SEA has amended the EEC Treaty to increase the number of occasions which allow for qualified majority voting; for example, Article 100A EEC allows for the adoption of legislation by a qualified majority for the purposes of achieving the internal market by the end of 1992. The member states unanimously agreed to the amendment. Although it would still be possible for the Council to adopt measures by unanimity, it makes it politically very difficult for a member state to insist on unanimity under the Luxembourg Accords. It is noteworthy that even in the year before the SEA came into force, much legislation was enacted by way of qualified majority.

A further important change occurred in December 1986 when the Council amended its rules of procedure to enable a member state or the Commission to request voting proceedings to be commenced. Prior to the amendment it was up to the member state holding the Presidency to start voting proceedings.

COREPER

The Council is assisted in its work by a Committee of Permanent Representatives based in Brussels, known as COREPER. It consists of the Permanent Representatives (ambassadors) of the member states to the Communities. The role of COREPER has been confirmed by the Merger Treaty (Article 4). It is responsible for preparing the work of the Council and carrying out the tasks assigned to it by the Council. COREPER is assisted by expert working groups, usually consisting of national civil servants representing the particular issue under discussion. The working groups may substantially amend Commission proposals and in practice precise details of many of the texts of the Council are decided upon by working groups. Once a working group has discussed the details of the Commission proposal, then it is passed on to COREPER and from there it goes to the Council.

The European Council

The European Council came about following the decision of the Heads of State or of Government, meeting in Paris in December 1974, to meet regularly together with their foreign ministers and the President and one of the Vice-Presidents of the Commission. Until the SEA, the European Council was not referred to in the Treaties, but it is mentioned in Article 2 of the SEA, giving it official recognition in Community law. Article 2 provides that the European Council shall meet at least twice a year; it shall be attended by the Heads of State or of Government of the member states and the President of the Commission of the EC; and that they shall be assisted by the Ministers for Foreign Affairs and by a Member of the Commission.

The SEA makes no mention of the powers of the European Council. It does not generally legislate. It will discuss both Community matters and political co-operation and will indicate general political decisions. The enactment of legislation is left to the proper machinery. What usually occurs in practice is that the Commission proposes legislation based on the instructions or decisions of the European Council.

The European Parliament

The European Parliament, formerly known as the European Assembly, does not have any formal law-making powers. Yet it still has an important role to play as a Community institution. The significance of the European Parliament has increased since the first direct elections were held in 1979. In addition its advisory and supervisory powers have been enhanced by the SEA, most notably through the introduction of the co-operation procedure (see below).

Although the Treaties provide that the member states can decide where the institutions are to be located (Articles 216 EEC, 77 ECSC and 189 Euratom), they have not as yet fixed permanent seats for any of them. Plenary sessions of the Parliament are held in Strasbourg and Committee meetings in Brussels, with the Secretariat being located in Luxembourg.

Composition and structure

Originally members of the European Parliament came from national parliaments, but Article 138(3) EEC always envisaged that the Parliament would ultimately be directly elected. As already noted, the first direct elections to the European Parliament were held in 1979 and have been held every five years since then. There are currently 518 members of the European Parliament (MEPs). The allocation of seats, which is not strictly proportional to population size, is as follows:

Germany	81
France	81
Italy	81
United Kingdom	81
Spain	60
Netherlands	25
Belgium	24
Greece	24
Portugal	24
Denmark	16
Ireland	15
Luxembourg	6

There is no uniform electoral system and until one is adopted, each member state is free to choose its own electoral system (see Article 7(2) of the Act providing for direct eletions – annexed to Council Decision 76/787 OJ 1976 L278/1). The electoral systems vary from one member state to another; some use the same system as for national elections and others have a special system. The 'first-past-the post' system used by the United Kingdom (with the exception of Northern Ireland), unlike the system in other member states, does not involve any element of proportionality.

MEPs sit in political as opposed to national groups. The Socialist Party, with 180 MEPs, is currently the largest group. There is a well established system of parliamentary committees which carry out much of the work of the Parliament. The committees prepare reports on specific issues; they work closely with the Commission and also consult the Council and other representatives of interested groups. Matters coming before the Parliament are usually discussed by the appropriate committee first and the committee report will then form the basis of the debate in Parliament. It is the committees which usually prepare the Parliament's opinions on the Commission's proposals to the Council.

Role of the Parliament

The EEC and Euratom Treaties provide many instances where there is a requirement to consult the Parliament on Commission proposals. Provision has also been made for optional consultation at the request of the Council and in practice the Parliament is consulted on all major matters. Where there is express Treaty provision for the Parliament to be consulted and it is not in fact consulted, then it has the right to complain.

The duty imposed on the Council is to consult the Parliament, but there is no duty on it or the Commission to take any notice of the Parliament. Since the case of *Roquette v. Council* (Case 138/79, [1980] ECR 3333) it would appear that the meaning of 'consultation' goes beyond merely requesting an opinion and in fact requires the Council to inform the Parliament and wait for a reply. It is, however, submitted (notably by T.C. Hartley in *The Foundations of European Community Law*) that if the Parliament were deliberately obstructive, the Council could go ahead without waiting for an opinion. Where the Parliament has given its opinion and the proposal is subsequently amended, if the final text is 'substantially identical' to that which was submitted to the Parliament, then it is not necessary for there to be further consultation (*Chemiefarma v. Commission*, Case 41/69, [1970] ECR 661, paragraphs 68 and 69).

The co-operation procedure

The co-operation procedure, which was introduced by the SEA (Articles 6 and 7 SEA), applies for some (but not all) cases where the Parliament is to be consulted and in particular to many of the measures being introduced as part of the 1992 programme. Under the co-operation procedure the Parliament has to be consulted twice. The co-operation procedure can be found in Article 149(2) EEC (as amended by the SEA).

Under the co-operation procedure the Commission prepares a proposal and submits it to the Council in the same way as it does as part of the usual legislative process. The Council will then consult the Parliament, which may suggest amendments to the Commission's proposal. It will then send its opinion back to the Council. Instead of taking a final decision at that stage, if the co-operation procedure applies, the Council is required to adopt, by qualified majority, a common position. There is no time limit imposed on the Council for the adoption of its common position. Once a common position has been adopted, it is sent back to the Parliament for the second time, together with the Council's statement of reasons which led to the adoption of its common position and a statement of the Commission's position. The Parliament then has three months in which to act. The Parliament may do one of four things:

(i)   It may approve the common position (by a majority of votes cast); or

(ii) Fail to adopt a position within the three-month time limit; or

(iii) Reject the Council's common position. This requires an absolute majority of the MEPs (not a majority of the MEPs present); or

(iv) Amend the Council's common position, again by an absolute majority.

If the Parliament approves the common position or takes no position within the three-month time limit, the Council simply adopts the proposal. If the Parliament rejects the Council's common position, the Council can still adopt the measure but only if it acts unanimously.

If the Parliament amends the proposal, the matter is referred back to the Commission. It is then up to the Commission to decide whether or not to accept any of the amendments made by the Parliament; a one month time limit applies. The proposal is then sent to the Council for its second reading. The Council has three months in which to act. There are four possibilities open to the Council; it can:

(i) accept the proposal as amended by the Commission, by qualified majority; or

(ii) adopt the amendments proposed by the Parliament (ie those amendments not incorporated by the Commission); in this case unanimity is required; or

(iii) adopt its own amendments, again unanimity is required; or

(iv) fail to act within the three month period (subject to a possible one month extension granted by the Parliament) so that then the Commission proposal lapses.

The co-operation procedure allows the Parliament to have a greater role in the legislative process, although the final word still rests with the Council.

Budgetary powers

The Parliament holds a strong position in the complicated Community budgetary procedure. The Commission drafts a preliminary budget based on estimates received from the institutions. This in turn is forwarded to the Council for it to formulate the draft budget. It is not until the Council has decided upon the contents of the draft budget that the Parliament becomes involved.

The powers of the Parliament differ depending upon the type of expenditure involved. The Parliament has the last word on non-compulsory expenditure, that is expenditure not required by the Treaties or Community law. In the case of compulsory expenditure, it can propose modifications. As long as the Parliament does not increase expenditure, such modifications are deemed to be accepted by the Council unless, acting by qualified majority, it rejects them.

Parliament has the right to reject the Budget as a whole. It has exercised this right in the past, for example, it happened for the first time in December 1979 when it threw out the draft budget for 1980.

Other powers

The Parliament can require the entire Commission to resign by passing a motion of censure, by a two-thirds majority (Article 144 EEC, 24 ECSC, and 114 Euratom). This power has never been used and, even if it were, it would be open to the Council of Ministers to re-appoint the same Commissioners.

The Parliament is given the express power to put questions to the Commission (Article 140 EEC, 23 ECSC, and 110 Euratom). It makes use of this power and replies are published in the Official Journal.

The European Court of Justice

The ECSC Court of Justice was replaced in 1958 by a single Court of Justice of the European Communities (ECJ). It is the duty of the ECJ to ensure that in the interpretation and application of the Treaties the law is observed (Articles 164 EEC, 136 Euratom, and 31 ECSC).

The ECJ, which sits in Luxembourg, consists of 13 judges, one from each member state plus an additional one, to make an odd number. The appointment of the additional judge rotates among the larger member states. The judges are appointed by mutual agreement of the member states. They are chosen for their independence and judicial competence (Articles 167 EEC, 32 ECSC, and 139 Euratom). Judges hold office for a six year term, which can be renewed. During the term they cannot be removed by the member states, but provisions exist whereby the Judges and Advocates-General theoretically can, by a unanimous vote, dismiss one of their number if they consider him no longer competent to hold office (see Article 6 of the Statute of the Court of Justice of the EEC and the Statute of the Court of Justice of Euratom). The appointments of the judges are staggered so that not all terms expire at the same time.

The judges of the ECJ are assisted by 6 Advocates-General and a Registrar. In practice four Advocates-General come from the four big member states and two from other member states. The Advocates-General make reasoned submissions to the Court in order to assist the Court (Article 166 EEC, 32(a) ECSC and 138 Euratom). The Advocate-General assigned to a case will, together with his legal secretary, research the issues involved and once the parties have given their submissions to the Court, then the Advocate-General delivers his opinion. The judges will consider the opinion of the Advocate-General. It is not, however, binding on the Court. The opinion of the Advocate-General will appear in the law reports alongside the Court's judgment. It should be noted that the Court gives a single judgment in the name of the Court. It is not therefore possible to attribute any particular views to any one Judge.

Under the Treaties the ECJ is empowered (Article 165 EEC, 137 Euratom and 32 ECSC as amended by the Convention on Certain Institutions of Commission to the European Communities 1957) to make use of chambers of three or five judges to deal with certain categories of case. More extensive use of chambers has been made in recent years, within the limits of the present legislative restrictions which, for example, provide that all cases brought by a member state or a Community institution must still be heard by the full Court (Article 32 ECSC, 165 EEC and 165 Euratom). The quorum for a full Court is seven.

THE CO-OPERATION PROCEDURE

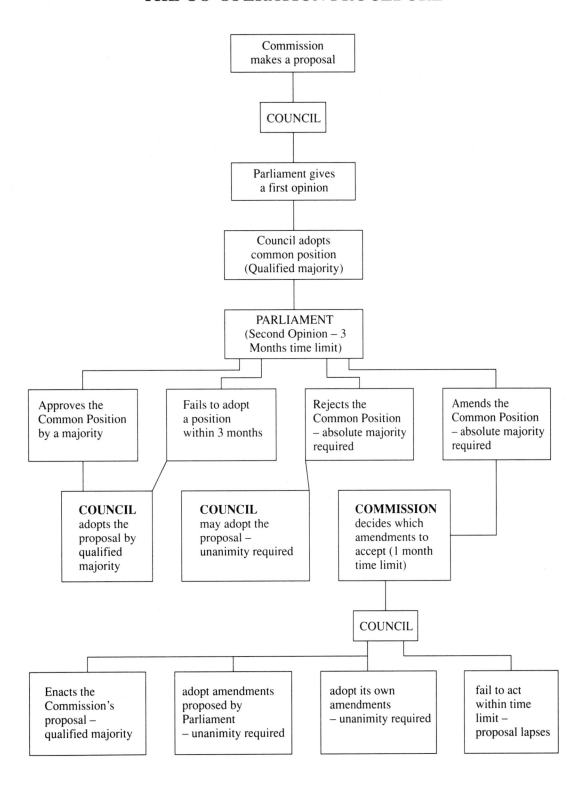

Commission
makes a proposal

COUNCIL

Parliament gives
a first opinion

Council adopts
common position
(Qualified majority)

PARLIAMENT
(Second Opinion – 3
Months time limit)

Approves the
Common Position
by a majority

Fails to adopt
a position
within 3 months

Rejects the
Common Position
– absolute majority
required

Amends the
Common Position
– absolute majority
required

COUNCIL
adopts the
proposal by
qualified
majority

COUNCIL
may adopt the
proposal –
unanimity required

COMMISSION
decides which
amendments to
accept (1 month
time limit)

COUNCIL

Enacts the
Commission's
proposal –
qualified majority

adopt amendments
proposed by
Parliament
– unanimity required

adopt its own
amendments
– unanimity required

fail to act
within time
limit –
proposal lapses

The jurisdiction of the ECJ is derived from the Treaties. It may be called upon to give opinions or rulings pursuant to a request from one of the other institutions, on matters such as the Community's competence to enter into international agreements. However, the ECJ devotes a far greater proportion of its time to giving judgments. Cases coming before the ECJ fall into two broad categories, direct actions and preliminary rulings, which are referred to the ECJ by national courts.

Direct actions

There are a number of different ways in which a member state, Community institution or even an individual can commence proceedings before the ECJ.

All three treaties contain provisions (Articles 169-171 EEC, 88 ECSC and 141-142 Euratom) whereby Community Law can be enforced directly against a member state. Essentially these provisions allow the Commission to institute proceedings against a member state which has failed to fulfil one of its Treaty obligations (Articles 169 EEC, 141 Euratom and 88 ECSC) or under the EEC and Euratom Treaties, for one member state to take action against another member state where it feels that the other member state has failed to fulfil one of its Treaty obligations (Articles 170 EEC and 142 Euratom). It is quite rare for one member state to take action against another. This is mainly for political reasons. It is, however, not uncommon for the Commission to bring proceedings against a member state, for example, for failing to implement a Community Directive.

The ECJ also has the power (Articles 173 and 174 EEC and 146 and 147 Euratom) to review the legality of acts of the Council or Commission (action for annulment). Actions may be brought before the ECJ by a member state, a Community Institution and in some instances by a natural or legal person (certain conditions must be satisfied). The grounds upon which an action for annulment may be founded are stated in Article 173 EEC as:

(i)   lack of competence;
(ii)   infringement of an essential procedural requirement;
(iii) infringement of the Treaty or any rule of law relating to its application; and
(iv)   misuse of powers.

The provisions in this respect of the EEC and Euratom Treaties are identical.

A direct action may also be brought against the Council or the Commission for a failure to act (Articles 175 EEC and 148 Euratom, which are identical, and 35 ECSC). Such an action may be brought by a member state, a Community institution or a natural or legal person where the institution concerned has failed to adopt an act which would have been of direct and individual concern to him. It should be noted that failure to act refers to the failure on the part of the Council or Commission to take action which is required of it under the Treaty.

Other direct actions which may be brought by either member states or individuals include actions for damages for non-contractual liability (Articles 178, 215(2) EEC) for loss suffered as a result of a Community action.

Finally the ECJ has jurisdiction in disputes involving employees of the Community institutions ('staff cases'). (Article 179 EEC, 152 Euratom) and in matters involving the European Investment Bank (Article 180 EEC).

Preliminary rulings

Under Article 177 EEC courts or tribunals of the member states may refer questions on the interpretation and validity of Community law to the ECJ. In such cases the ECJ is limited to giving its interpretation on the question of Community law and has no jurisdiction with respect to the application of the law to the facts of the case. A national court or tribunal has the option to refer a case to the ECJ where it considers that a decision on the interpretation of EEC law is necessary in order to enable it to render a judgment. However, where the national court is a court from which there is no right of appeal it must refer the question to the ECJ. In some instances the national court may request a question of EEC law to be referred to the ECJ following a request from one of the parties, although the national court is in no way obliged to grant such a request. When a national court requests a preliminary ruling the proceedings are usually suspended until the ruling is given. The ruling of the ECJ is binding on the court which referred the question and in practice may have wider implications throughout the Community. Unlike direct actions, cases brought under Article 177 are commenced and completed in national courts.

The Court of First Instance

The legal position of the ECJ was altered by the SEA. The SEA (Articles 4, 11 and 75) changed all three Treaties by providing the Council with the power to create a Court of First Instance (CFI). The new Article 168A of the EEC Treaty, and its equivalent identically worded provisions in the ECSC and Euratom Treaties (Articles 32E and 45 ECSC and 140A and 160 Euratom) empower the Council to establish a court to be attached to the Court of Justice. The CFI is not therefore to be regarded as a new institution or as an autonomous body (T. Millet, *The Court of First Instance of the European Communities* at p.7).

The creation of the CFI has introduced a 'hierarchy of judicial institutions at the Community level' (Phil Fennell, *The Court of First Instance*, Eur. Access 1990 1, pp 11–12).

The CFI was established by a Council Decision of 24th October 1988 (OJ 1988 L 319/1) and commenced work in Luxembourg in September 1989. It was created primarily to relieve the ECJ of its increasing caseload and as a result of the persistence of the ECJ in drawing the attention of the Council of Ministers to the need for institutional reform in this area (see Phil Fennell op. cit.)

The CFI consists of 12 members, (Article 2(1) of the Council Decision), one coming from each member state. It does not have Advocates-General as such. However, the members of the CFI 'may be called upon to perform the task of an Advocate General' (Article 2(3) Council Decision). The requirements for holding office as a member or judge of the CFI and the conditions of appointment are very similar to those applicable to the ECJ (see Article 168A(3) EEC and the equivalent provisions in the ECSC and Euratom Treaties).

The CFI is required to sit in chambers of three or five judges but may sit in plenary session in particularly important cases (Article 2(4) of the Council Decision). This situation is the converse of that which applies to the ECJ.

The CFI does not, as yet, have its own rules of procedure and must apply the Rules of the ECJ until its own rules are adopted. It is thought that the CFI rules will be closely modelled on the ECJ Rules (see further 'A court of first instance at last in session', NLJ 140 (1990) 524-527).

Jurisdiction

There was much debate as to which categories of cases would be assigned to the CFI. A certain amount of opposition was encountered to some suggestions. For example, France and the Commission opposed the transfer of anti-dumping cases to the CFI; as a compromise the Council provided in Article 3(3) of the Decision for the question to be re-examined in two years time.

Article 168A limits the jurisdiction of the CFI by specifically excluding certain cases. It states:

'That court shall not be competent to hear and determine actions brought by member states or by Community institutions or questions referred for a preliminary ruling under Article 177.'

It also further limits the jurisdiction of the CFI to 'certain classes of action or proceedings brought by natural or legal persons'.

The jurisdiction conferred on the CFI is set out in Article 3 of the Decision. Article 3(1) states that the CFI shall exercise at first instance the jurisdiction conferred on the ECJ by the Treaties and implementing legislation in four categories of cases:

(i) staff cases referred to in Article 179 EEC and 152 Euratom;
(ii) actions brought against the Commission under Articles 33(2) and 35 ECSC by undertakings or associations of undertakings concerning individual acts relating to the application of Article 50 ECSC (financial levies) and Articles 57 to 66 ECSC (production, prices, agreements and concentrations);
(iii) actions brought against a Community institution by natural or legal persons under Article 173(2) EEC and Article 175(3) EEC relating to the implementation of the competition rules applicable to undertakings;
(iv) claims for damages caused by the action or failure to act which is the subject of one of the above categories of action.

It is clear from the wording of Article 3 that the jurisdiction conferred on the CFI is exclusive, and that with respect to the categories of cases defined therein, there is no option but to bring the case in the first instance before the CFI. The jurisdiction preserves the principle of the 'lawful judge', according to which a citizen should know in advance who will be his judge (see T. Millett - *supra*).

Appeals to the ECJ

Article 168A provides that appeal lies against a decision of the CFI on a point of law only. More specifically the grounds of appeal are set out in Article 51 of the Statute of the Court (added by Article 5 of the Council Decision establishing the CFI). They are:

(i) lack of competence of the CFI;
(ii) breach of procedure before the CFI which adversely affects the interests of the appellant;
(iii) infringement of Community law by the CFI.

An appeal must be lodged within two months of the notification of the decision appealed against (Article 49 of the Statute of the Court).

The right to appeal to the ECJ is not restricted to the parties to the action but includes in addition any party intervening in the proceedings before the CFI, provided that, if not a member state or a Community Institution, the intervening party can show that the decision of the CFI has directly affected him (Article 49 of the Statute of the Court). It is also possible for member states and Community Institutions, which did not intervene in the proceedings before the CFI, to appeal (Article 49 of the Statute of the Court), but if they do so, they may be ordered to pay the appellant's costs. When exercising a right of appeal, interveners, member states and Community Institutions cannot raise new grounds of appeal. Their right is limited to supporting the submissions of one of the parties.

On hearing an appeal from the CFI, if the ECJ finds that it is well founded, then it has two options; it can either refer it back to the CFI or give final judgment itself (Article 54 of the Statute of the Court). Where a case is referred back to the CFI, the CFI is bound by the decision of the ECJ (Article 54 of the Statute of the Court).

It is too early to assess the extent to which the CFI will relieve the ECJ of its increasing caseload. Much depends upon the number of appeals that are made to the ECJ from the CFI. However, it is undeniable that with a Community of twelve member states a CFI is certainly needed. Now that the CFI is in operation it is always possible to extend the categories of cases with which it deals (within the confines of Article 168A) without the need to amend the Treaties.

Conclusion

The activities of the Community institutions are governed by the constraints imposed on them by the Treaties. In recent years, as the Community has grown the institutions have appeared more powerful. However, in reality, the institutions have not become any more powerful in themselves but their respective roles and functions have to some extent altered *inter se*. The Parliament gained significance with the advent of direct elections in 1979 and more recently its powers have been enhanced by the introduction of the co-operation procedure through the SEA. The nature of the ECJ has changed, also as a result of the SEA, which enabled the CFI to be established. What will be the full effect of the CFI remains to be seen. The importance of the Commission lies in its independence and political neutrality. Its role as a Community institution should not be under-estimated. While it is the Council of Ministers which is the primary law-making body and decision-maker, the Commission is still able to influence policy. The Commission makes full use of the powers conferred on it and of its extensive opportunities to influence the development of the European Community.

ANNEX

The 23 Directorates-General (DGs) of the European Commission

DG 1:   External relations
DG II: Economic and financial affairs
DG III: Internal market and industrial affairs
DG IV: Competition
DG V: Employment, industrial relations and social affairs
DG VI: Agriculture
DG VII: Transport
DG VIII: Development
DG IX: Personnel and administration
DG X: Information, communication and culture
DG XI: Environment, nuclear safety and civil protection
DG XII: Science, research and development
DG XIII: Telecommunications, information industries and innovation
DG XIV: Fisheries
DG XV: Financial institutions and company law
DG XVI: Regional policy
DG XVII: Energy
DG XVIII: Credit and investments
DG XIX: Budgets
DG XX: Financial control
DG XXI: Customs union and indirect taxation
DG XXII: Co-ordination of structural policies
DG XXIII: Enterprise policy, distributive trades, tourism and co-operatives

PART TWO

*FRANCHISING
IN THE
EUROPEAN COMMUNITY*

CHAPTER 4

A Strategy for the European Community

By DR. BRIAN A. SMITH

Introduction to The European Community

Entering foreign markets is somehow an emotive issue. Franchisors and other businesses who have ventured abroad will generally agree that they have taken greater risks without the care and consideration which would normally be standard in the home market. An easy assumption and one which is frequently made is that because someone speaks your mother tongue as well as their own, they are good business people. The franchisor considering entering the European Community or expanding within it should have an understanding not only of the differences in languages to be overcome, the different currencies to cope with, and the unusual food to eat, but also the nuances of a country or regional culture which, for the first time visitor, is nigh on impossible. Within the European Community a common currency, to make things easier, may take a few years to achieve, but a common language may take a decade and a common culture centuries, if ever. For these reasons the following chapter aims to outline the main differences between each of the European member states to help the franchisor build a strategy for franchising in Europe and outlines the steps to setting this up successfully.

Background

There were originally three Communities in Europe, each set up by a separate treaty: The European Coal and Steel Community, The European Economic Community and the European Atomic Energy Community. All are now commonly known as the European Community consisting of 325 million people in 12 countries, or member states, where the temperatures range from -3 degrees to $+33$ degrees centigrade, where 11 currencies are used and 9 languages are spoken within 14 main cultures embracing numerous sub-cultures with individual regional variations spread over 2,363,000 sq.km. A market which seems certain to grow even larger. The recent 'Eurobarometer', the official survey of public opinion in the European Community, reveals that 71% of non-German EC citizens support German unification. Membership of the EC is considered a good thing for a united Germany by 76% of all East Germans. The wishes of the majority were realised, and a further 16.6 million people have joined the EC. In the interim, after full unification, the EC industrial authorities face the problem of how they will enforce the Community's competition rules as West German companies go for a share of the East German market.

The member states of the Community are: the Federal Republic of Germany, The Netherlands, France, Spain, Denmark, Belgium, the Grand Duchy of Luxembourg, Italy, the Republic of Ireland, Portugal, Greece and the United Kingdom. Details of the size, population, language and currency of each of these countries is given in Appendix 1 of this chapter.

The Single European Act

In 1985 the European Community agreed the Single European Act which committed the 12 member states to establishing a Single European Market by 31 December 1992. This lengthy process will culminate in the abolition of frontier controls and formalities for goods crossing the borders of any of the member states, freedom of access of citizens to the financial services of each member state, liberalisation of capital movements by freeing the legislative and restrictive practices of the capital markets of each member state, freedom of access to all member states and equal access to the professional activities within the Community, freedom to compete for government contracts throughout the Community, harmonisation of requirements for public and private transport, patent protection, removal of fiscal barriers and, therefore, no internal economic frontiers.

ECU

As well as the above advantages to the Community, a European Currency Unit (ECU) was created in 1979 to serve as a basis for determining the European Monetary System exchange rate parities and settling transactions between central banks, which swap 20% of their gold and dollar reserves for ECUs. The European Community countries maintain the value of their own currencies against the ECU under the terms of the exchange rate mechanism (ERM). The ECU is a weighted basket of currencies containing a specified proportion of the currency of 10 of the member states, weighting being decided by the relative importance of each member state's GNP and its trade within the Community. As there is no central bank for creating, issuing or managing ECUs, they can only be obtained from commercial banks where the ECU is 'bundled or unbundled' from its component national currencies. Commercial use of the ECU is still very limited. There is a movement among some politicians and business leaders for greater use of the ECU or the creation of a true European currency. The UK has joined the ERM fairly recently and the pound, therefore, no longer floats freely against the ECU. Because of its composite character, the ECU is far less volatile against individual currencies than they are against each other, providing benefits to both investor and borrower. Despite this, the ECU is adopted far more by international financial markets than by businesses.

Demographics

Recent estimates indicate that the European Community experienced a growth rate in population (births minus deaths plus net migration) of 3.9 per thousand in 1988 of which 1.8 per thousand came from net migration. Luxembourg's high population growth is almost entirely attributable to immigration, while Ireland's declining population is a result of a very high rate of emigration. Italy has Europe's lowest birthrate with Spain, Greece and Germany not far behind.

Overall, Europe will have to rely on immigration to maintain its current population. Only Irish women bear more than two children, all other countries produce well below the considered replacement level of two. So the rising natural growth rate recorded is more a result of a demographic bulge (currently large numbers of women of child bearing age) rather than a self sustaining population.

The demographic significance of these figures will become more apparent as time passes. For example, according to Professor Charles Handy in his book 'The Age of Unreason', within 5 years there will be 580,000 fewer younger Britons between the age of 16-19 in the UK because of the big drop in the birth rate in the early 1970s. This demographic transition is not confined to the UK but is happening right across Europe.

With improved health and economic success, death rates have dropped at the same time as birth rates have declined because of contraception and abortion. The average birth rate of 1.9 (1.4 in Germany) has now dropped below the generation replacement level which requires on average 2.1 children from every child bearing woman. Europe's annual population growth rate, already the lowest in the world, is projected to decline from 0.8% in 1950 to 0.25% by the year 2000. This reduction in the younger generation suggests that by the year 2040 one in five Europeans will be a pensioner and one in ten of those will be 75 years old.

Culture

Accepting that there are many cultures within the EC, it is perhaps worthwhile looking briefly at what is generally accepted to be the most basic difference, even if it is an over simplification — the North-South divide.

Social distance and self expression where northern self-restraint meets southern spontaneity can be difficult for both parties. To be greeted by a male friend from the south in the Italian traditional 'abbraccio' (embrace) can initially be embarrassing for the northerner whilst a drawing away can be insulting to the southerner.

Formality in negotiation varies too. Northerners like to get to the point quickly. A southern businessman will tend to indulge in what the northerner considers 'small talk' or general topics. Attitudes towards authority vary too. The Northerner considers he may do as he wishes provided it is not expressly forbidden. In France and Spain you may only do it if the government says you can.

More basically, it has been said that the northern protestant tradition is of 'living to work' whilst southern catholics work to live, although some experts say this divergence is reducing. In the north the authority tends to be vested with the office; in the south it is ascribed to the person.

On a more practical note, for example, Germans have a high regard for punctuality. Being 15 minutes late is likely to be considered an insult. Keeping a delivery date is a matter of honour with the Germans. Conversely, to the Frenchman the rigid, rule based inflexible approach of the Germans in a meeting is perceived as weakness in being unable to change strategy or tactics to cater for the needs of the client.

There will always be differences in culture but the move, both physical and mental, in bringing together the Community will continue with increased understanding and acceptance.

KEY STEPS TO FRANCHISING IN EUROPE

A prerequisite to success in the international market is success in the home market. A needed product or service which consumers are willing to buy through a franchised distribution system where both the franchisee and the franchisor are adequately compensated for their time and investment is the key to success. If the formula has not worked or if any of these parties have failed to be satisfied in the home market, then the venture is unlikely to succeed in a foreign market. The decision to go abroad must be based on sound business reasons and be part of a planned programme of expansion. The most common reason given by franchisors who have entered foreign markets is a response to an unsolicited approach from a national or intermediary in the overseas country. The most frequently quoted reason given for failure in a foreign market is the poor choice and judgement of local partner. It is not difficult to see the relationship between this and the former statement. A change of strategy or direction in any organisation requires the investment of time, of management resources and of money. Usually all three are in limited supply and one truism which is rarely contradicted is that 'It always takes longer and costs more than was originally considered'. This will almost certainly be the case when franchising abroad. It is essential to ensure that the home operation is sound and has available the management and financial resources necessary to expand overseas. Consideration should be given to the implications of travel between the home and target market both in terms of cost and time. Will communications be a problem? Are the necessary language skills available? Is the trade or service mark registered?

An internal strategic audit addressing these and other relevant issues and which measures the availability of financial and management resources will focus attention and lead to plans which can be effected with the minimum amount of surprise or disappointment.

Having established that both the desire and the resources to enter the common market exist, two key questions for the franchisor are:

Which of the twelve countries should be first?

What form should the franchisor operation take in the selected country?

The formulation of a European Community franchising strategy can only properly be achieved on a one-to-one basis with the company concerned. A corporate strategy is unique to the company and no book method can take account of the company and its culture, its hopes and aspirations and the interface with the twelve member states that combine to make the European Community. The removal of the barriers detailed above is a major achievement. However, as discussed earlier, there are 12 countries and 9 languages which basically means 12 sections or sub strategies. There are few, if any, companies who have the resources to move into the EC en masse and give the support and training necessary even to the most basic master franchise arrangement. A number of companies have, of course, tried. At best, there is a presence with unhappy master franchises and unhappy franchisors. At worst, there are expensive disputes, loss of presence and a considerably reduced value in the trade name of the franchisor.

There are several factors to take into account when deciding which of the European Community countries to enter. Although the Community has a larger population than either the USA or the USSR, different languages, complex cultures and differing regional identities require them to be treated as individual countries when considering a marketing strategy. A chemist shop in the UK can sell a wide range of products which would require a prescription from a doctor in Greece. The UK has a very high percentage of home ownership whereas Germany does not. Englishmen go shopping, Italian men do not. These, and numerous other examples reinforce the need to research each country separately.

One of the almost universal benefits in franchising to all parties — the franchisor, the franchisee and the end consumer — is the economies of scale that can be derived from growing the network. The larger the number of franchisees, the greater the buying power, the more effective the marketing and the more convenience to the consumer. Experience in international franchising indicates that it is much more desirable and profitable to have depth in one market than a superficial, and costly presence in many.

Most franchises can be measured in terms of a critical mass. This is the number of average successful franchisees required in the network to support the franchisor's overheads and give an acceptable return on investment.

An examination of the twelve member states of the European Community shows populations ranging from Luxembourg at 373,000 with two languages to 78,500,000 in Germany with one language. The concentration and distribution of the population and the geography of a country may well be major factors and be sufficient to reduce the choice regarding both the country and the form.

Questions should be asked concerning each country relative to culture, climate, social structure, standard of living, regional differences, spending patterns, degrees of affluence and poverty, spending priorities, shopping habits, market trends, consumer preferences, attitudes and values, religious beliefs, dietary customs, eating habits, housing, retail and commercial property, leisure patterns. More specific to franchising will be attitudes to self employment. Is franchising an accepted method of distribution? Will franchisees be available? Will franchisees be able to fund the franchise? How well does the financial community understand franchising? What is the government's attitude towards franchising at the local and national level?

Dependent on the type of franchise, greater or lesser importance will be attached to the questions and their answers. More specific questions will relate to each individual franchise, particularly the availability of any specialised equipment, materials, products and any other supplies. Are they reliably available at an accepted cost and to the standard required? If importation of items is necessary, what will be the cost in transport? Are there problems in shipment? Will they attract customs duty or other taxes?

Is property available of sufficient size? Can you purchase property or is it leased? What is the process of obtaining premises? Is a premium (key money) a consideration? What planning permissions are required? Are these easily obtained? Do local builders have access to the required materials? Do they meet their time targets? Are the costs commensurate?

Are all of these things compatible to the franchisee and the franchisor in both the short term and the long term?

In market research, the methodology can so easily influence the answers that care needs to be taken.

Good research depends on knowing:

- *What to ask.* Posing the question in as neutral a way as possible without suggesting the answer.
- *Who to ask.* Quantitative information can often be obtained from official sources. In the absence of official information, knowledgeable observers with non-vested interests may be hard to find.
- *When to ask.* Timing between the hours in a day or season of the year can radically affect the results.
- *How to ask.* Information seeking questions can so easily appear to be judgemental, particularly in commercial situations.

Once the market research has been completed and the country selected, the next question is to decide what form the franchisor organisation should take. There are a number of organisational structures which can be considered when franchising outside the home territory and each may have its place in a European Community strategy.

The commonest forms are:

- Franchising direct from the home country.
- Operating a wholly owned subsidiary company or branch within the selected country which functions as the franchisor.
- Setting up a joint venture operation with a local partner (individual or firm) which acts as the franchisor.
- Appointing one or more Master Franchise holders for the country or region with authority to subfranchise.

Research will indicate which countries could benefit from the total company owned operation. Financial modelling and the monitoring of results will indicate how viable this is and the possible timing. Inevitably, it is extremely unlikely that all twelve member states will fall into the same category. Joint ventures may be a consideration where local skills and knowledge are needed. Direct franchising or master franchises may be the choice where the market is considered to be too small to support a complete franchisor organisation. With a well established European base, complete direct help can be supplied to the master franchise and control and support to the franchisees can not only be monitored but also strengthened and visible.

Direct Franchising

Direct franchising can be attractive when the target country is geographically close, the language and customs are similar and the franchisees can be managed and served effectively from the existing franchisor's headquarters. Direct franchising may also be a choice when the market is limited and only likely to support a few franchisees.

Direct franchising is attractive because income from franchisees does not have to be shared with a partner, common systems and manuals can be used and only minimal increases in overheads will be incurred. The franchisor has direct contact and can exercise greater and more direct control of all aspects of the franchise.

Within the European Community, direct franchising between member states is likely to find more acceptance than with countries outside the Community. Third countries will have to be concerned with the legality of their contract in a member state and its acceptance within the member state and to franchisees. Taxes may be a consideration particularly if there is a withholding tax on management fees. There will also be concern for exchange rates and the ability to transfer funds outside the EC with minimum charges. Finally, careful consideration should be given to the feelings of the franchisees who may perceive a franchisor in another country in an unattractive light.

Appointing one or several franchisees to cover specified areas through multiple outlets without the right to sub franchise in a country is a variation of direct franchising and may more readily be applied to the larger type of franchised business.

Subsidiary Company

The only guaranteed way to establish a controlled and directed franchise which meets all the criteria of the home market within the EC is by the establishment of a subsidiary company owned by the franchisor. Some basic research will identify the most appropriate country or countries to enter and which would show the best return. A strong and successful franchise operation within a member state which is owned by the franchisor is the most powerful way of showing commitment and belief in the business. However, the totally owned subsidiary company is the option which requires the greatest commitment and investment. The franchisor assumes all the risks and responsibilities and conversely enjoys all the rewards.

The ability completely to control, direct and protect the franchise within a country has advantages and allows the franchisor to develop experience and understanding of operating in the country which can be exploited in other markets. The decision to operate in this way must not be taken lightly. Once the process of setting up a company has started, costs will be incurred which will have to be written off if the decision is reversed. Management resources will need to be totally committed to the venture. Local staff will have to be recruited and trained. The target country should be thoroughly researched to ensure that critical mass can be reached comfortably with adequate margins to allow for errors and miscalculations. The company owned franchise business does have other advantages. A training centre in Europe for both internal and external management as well as for franchisees and a warehousing and distribution centre for products and materials throughout the EC can more easily be set up. This can be on either a short term basis until local supplies are established or on a more permanent basis where economies of scale are obtained. The company operation can serve as a control centre for European operations and provide a career path for management. It should be a model for other member states to follow in whatever form.

Joint Venture

A joint venture franchise operation commonly entails the franchisor and a local partner (company or individual) setting up a company within the target country. This company is appointed or licensed by the franchisor to be responsible for all franchise operations within the country and an exclusive long term (twenty years or more is common) agreement is signed.

The joint venture will be more readily accepted in the member state having both local and foreign ownership. Partners are likely to be easier to find than a master franchise holder as the foreign franchisor also has an investment and longer term commitment. This is also perceived as increasing the chance of success and usually means a more rapid establishment of the franchise bringing together the knowledge and experience of the franchisor with the local knowledge and commitment of the member state's partner.

Whilst the benefits of a joint venture are considerable, the setting up and subsequent operation is not without its difficulties and risks. The initial decisions as to who will have control and what proportion of investment and in what form each party's contribution will take, are major decisions for both parties. A shared vision and common goals regarding market penetration and timing are as essential as agreeing the distribution of subsequent profits. The initial and on-going fee structure will need a considerable amount of thought and financial modelling. Fees from franchisees to the joint venture company and on to the franchisor are an obligation and not subject to the profitability or otherwise of the individual operation. However, a fee structure which compensates the franchisor whilst increasing the losses and problems of the joint venture company cannot be in the interests of anyone. Consequently, the franchisor may be faced with a situation whereby royalties are reduced in return for the equity participation in the joint venture company.

It is recommended that clear lines of responsibility and decision making are agreed and committed to a policy document to ensure decisions can be made without delay or recriminations. Whilst negotiations will take time, both parties need to feel satisfied, believe in the venture and have confidence in each other.

Master Franchise

A master franchise agreement is frequently the preferred choice of foreign franchisors seeking entry into the European Community – particularly where language, cultures and customs differ. It requires the minimum commitment in terms of management resources and finance. The franchisor will usually sell the franchise rights, including the rights to sub franchise to an individual or company for an initial fee. On-going management service fees as a percentage of total sales are common and an agreement to purchase equipment and consumables used in the business may also be built into the contract. The obligations of the franchisor may include training and the supply of manuals and sample promotional and other materials plus on-going training for the master franchise holder's staff and, possibly, franchisees. These latter arrangements commonly require the travel and living expenses to be paid for by the master franchise holder.

The master franchise agreement provides a means for a franchisor to expand with little, if any, cost and the ability to recover that cost fairly quickly and, indeed, to show a profit. The purchaser of the master agreement will usually seek an exclusive arrangement. This in essence means the franchisor agrees not to appoint anyone else in the territory. The franchisor effectively leaves the control and operation of the business in the hands of the master franchise holder who may or may not exploit the opportunity. The master franchise holder will need to invest in testing and piloting the franchise and in building an organisation to grow and develop the business.

Wherever, whenever and however the franchisor establishes a presence in Europe, a pilot operation will need to be established to prove the concept, fine tune the systems and ensure the format works. With the well-developed communication and technological transfer systems in existence today there is very little in the Western world which is completely new. However, the franchisor may need to educate both consumers and prospective franchisees in the specific benefits of the services or products being offered and the franchise distribution system is likely to need marketing in a way that appeals to the local population. The product or service and the way it is marketed and positioned will need to be tailored to suit the local or regional differences in language, culture and taste.

Starting a franchise operation in the European Community will require an investment in time, money and management resources. A great deal of work and effort is needed to adapt a franchise for a foreign country. Once the decision is made to go, in whatever form, the work begins.

The location has to be agreed, suitable premises found and furnished, local staff recruited and trained.

Manuals need translating, training materials need translating and adapting. Videos may need translating and converting to one of the European systems. Equipment, products and materials need adapting, sourcing, testing and converting. Promotional materials – point of sale, direct mail, sales portfolios and advertising – will need to be created, adapted or translated, usually a combination of all three. Accounting systems will need similar treatment and should be checked by professional accountants who understand franchising to ensure they comply with legislation and customs. Administrative procedures will need to be developed or tuned to local situations. Insurance, self-employment regulations, tax registration, reporting and ordering processes will need attention and the relevant financial and legal expertise consulted. The franchise agreement may need adaptation by experienced local franchise lawyers as will leasing agreements. Knowledge will be needed concerning local building and planning regulations both internal and external.

A critical path or flow chart will help in ensuring control and the right order. The establishment of the pilot operation should be an early priority as this will serve as a model to prove the concept and test existing programmes as well as to develop new ways more suited to the market where appropriate. Here the manuals can be tested for completeness, the promotional programmes confirmed and the financial models proven as accurate. From the pilot operation, the final touches can be put to the fee structure, the training programme, the franchisee profile, the pricing policy, the franchise offer and the management structure. Operational support can be identified and developed.

Initially, the pioneering of a franchise in the European Community will probably be carried out by managers from the home country.

- Be prepared and willing to hand operational responsibility over to local partners.
- Be prepared to continue to invest and endeavour to build teams in each new market who can relate to opposite numbers in different countries.
- The sharing of common problems and their solutions will help in developing a strong team spirit which creates the family partnership spirit so unique in franchising at all levels and in all countries where it is practised.

Conclusion

Whichever method of franchising system is chosen the different culture and attitudes in each Member State of the European Community concerning money, work, government's role, leadership, honour and social values, ways of thinking, business etiquette and personal communication must be taken into account. The continuing improvements in communication in television, video and the cinema, faster travel and educational exchange are helping to lessen the culture shock. It is, however, still there and success in franchising in the EC will very much depend on understanding varying cultures and business attitudes and accepting and adapting to them.

ANNEX 1

The 12 Member States

The Federal Republic of Germany
Area	357,000 sq km
Population	78,500,000
Density of Population	220 per sq km
Capital	Berlin
Language	German
Currency	Deutsche Mark

The Federal Republic has one of the world's strongest economies and its citizens enjoy an extremely high standard of living. The country is generally noted for its precision, quality and high standards. There are strict codes and standards maintained by a number of official organisations such as the Craft Guilds (Handwerkskammer).

The Netherlands
Area	41,785 sq km
Population	14,760,000
Density of Population	353.2 per sq km
Capital	Amsterdam
Language	Dutch
Currency	Florin or Guilder

A member of the Benelux Economic Union (with Belgium and Luxembourg) as well as the EC.

France
Area	547,026 sq km
Population	55,870,000
Density of Population	102.1 per sq km
Capital	Paris
Language	French
Currency	French Franc

One of the original members of the European Community and the member state covering the largest area.

Spain
Area	504,782 sq km
Population	38,980,000
Density of Population	77.2 per sq km
Capital	Madrid
Language	Spanish
Currency	Peseta

Spain, together with Greece and Portugal, has been granted an extension beyond 1992 in which to harmonise some of its rules and regulations to conform with the rest of the European Community.

Denmark
Area	43,069 sq km
Population	5,132,000
Density of Population	119.2 per sq km
Capital	Copenhagen
Language	Danish
Currency	Kroner

A high standard of living with a well educated workforce and highly efficient transport and communications.

Belgium
Area	30,513 sq km
Population	9,930,000
Density of Population	325.4 per sq km
Capital	Brussels
Languages	French/Flemish
Currency	Belgian Franc

A member of the Benelux Economic Union (with the Netherlands and Luxembourg) as well as an original member of the EC. The main Community Institutions are situated in Brussels.

The Grand Duchy of Luxembourg
Area	2,586 sq km
Population	370,000
Density of Population	143.1 per sq km
Capital	Luxembourg
Languages	French, German
Currency	Luxembourg Franc

This is the smallest of the Community countries but only in size. It has the best employment record, the richest people, low inflation, a huge budgetary surplus and the lowest public debt. A member of the Benelux Economic Union (with Belgium and the Netherlands).

Italy
Area	301,225 sq km
Population	57,440,000
Density of Population	190.7 per sq km
Capital	Rome
Language	Italian
Currency	Lire

A country of considerable contrast between the relatively rich industrial north and a considerably poorer south.

Republic of Ireland
Area	70,283 sq km
Population	3,544,000
Density of Population	50.4 per sq km
Capital	Dublin
Language	English
Currency	Punt (Irish pound)

Although English is the common language, there are considerable cultural differences between the United Kingdom and the Republic of Ireland.

Portugal
Area	92,082 sq km
Population	10,410,000
Density of Population	113.1 per sq km
Capital	Lisbon
Language	Portuguese
Currency	Escudo

Like Spain and Greece, Portugal has an extended period beyond 1992 in which to harmonise some of its rules and regulations with the other 9 countries.

Greece

Area	131,944 sq km
Population	10,020,000
Density of Population	75.9 per sq km
Capital	Athens
Language	Greek (modern)
Currency	Drachma

As a newer Member, Greece, as well as Spain and Portugal, has an extended period in which to harmonise some of its rules and regulations with the rest of the Community.

United Kingdom

Area	244,100 sq km
Population	57,065,000
Density of Population	233.4 per sq km
Capital	London
Language	English
Currency	Pound (Sterling)

A country used frequently by the Americans as a platform for entry into Europe.

CHAPTER 5

Franchising and the Franchise Relationship in the European Community

By PROFESSOR JOHN STANWORTH

INTRODUCTION

In Europe the era following the Second World War was characterised by a fascination with size. In one country after another, 'corporatist' policies saw State planners, big business and big unions developing economic strategies based, almost inevitably, on the premise that large size yielded economies of scale, efficiency and wealth. In the late 1960's, however, politicians and economic planners began to wake up to the fact that *small* businesses were not merely a remnant of the first industrial revolution, doomed to extinction in the near future, but rather, large and small enterprises co-existed in a dynamic but symbiotic relationship of inter-dependence.

Since that time, the importance of the smaller business has become increasingly well understood. Scase and Goffee in their recent book, *Entrepreneurship in Europe*, describe the small business entrepreneur in Europe as the 'popular hero' of our time. With unemployment in the EC over the last decade at its highest levels since the 1930's and technological advance in the large firm sector often leading to at best 'jobless growth', politicians across the political spectrum have been increasingly looking to smaller businesses to create both jobs and wealth.

However, the interest within the EC in small businesses is not restricted to politicians and economic planners. As Scase and Goffee put it:

'on the other hand, changes in the broader ideological and cultural fabric of Western European countries have heightened people's expectations of independence and self-fulfilment (whilst), on the other hand, developments in technology and management practices have brought about tighter forms of employee control' (1987; 5).

The tighter monitoring and control of so many jobs now appears at variance with growing desires for independence and autonomy, leading many people to start up their own businesses in an attempt to fulfil these ambitions. Although self-employment is a very demanding role and no business is completely free of external constraints, the personal involvement which so many crave is at least partially satisfied:

'Although most proprietors work long hours they are, nonetheless, free from the managerial control of others. Indeed, many see their businesses as extensions of their own personalities; by contrast, most employees feel constrained at work and are forced to shape their personalities according to the needs of their employer's businesses' (Scase & Goffee, 1987; 5).

Even though it would be wrong to understate the historical, cultural and political differences existing between the different EC member states, the desire for independence, autonomy and self-fulfilment appears very broadly based and transcends national boundaries with astonishing ease and determination (Collins, Moore & Unwalla, 1964; Golby & Johns, 1971; Stanworth & Curran, 1973; Kets de Vries, 1977; Scase & Goffee, 1987).

The proportions of self-employed in various economies nonetheless vary quite substantially, as the following table demonstrates:

TABLE 1   **Percentage of Civilian Self-Employment other than in Agriculture in Selected Societies, 1979**

	%
Italy	19.1
Japan	18.7
Australia	11.9
France	10.0
Federal Republic of Germany	9.0
United States	7.3
United Kingdom	6.5
Sweden	4.3

Source: P. Ganguly & G. Bannock, *UK Small Business Statistics and International Comparisons*, Harper & Row, 1985

In the 1960's, Britain's relatively low dependence upon small enterprises for jobs, products and services was frequently interpreted as a sign of a *mature advanced economy* and policies were devised to actually aid the process of economic concentration. Since then, this view has been reversed. Bannock, Research Director on the Bolton Committee on small firms, for instance, put the case as follows:

'If small firms . . . were outmoded and a sign of technological and economic immaturity, why were they more numerous and important in all other advanced industrial societies, including the United States and Germany, which were more advanced than the UK? If competing abroad and faster growth required . . . concentration . . . into bigger units, how was it that Japan and Italy could sustain exceptionally rapid growth in exports and output with a much bigger proportion of output in small firms than other countries?' (Bannock, 1981: 50).

Since then, the growing desire for autonomy, the encouragement and assertion of values based on enterprise by EC governments, plus the stimulus to self-employment which recession tends to bring, have all acted to increase the numbers taking up this employment option. An indication of the strength of the trend is given by statistics for the UK, where self-employment increased by 32 per cent between

1979 and 1984 to a figure of 2.5 million or 10 per cent of the workforce. The figure has since grown further to around 12 per cent.

FRANCHISING AND THE STRENGTHS OF COMBINING SMALL & LARGE SCALE

The conventional small firm population within the EC has, to date, been somewhat less successful than might have been hoped in terms of jobs and wealth creation. Two observations are particularly relevant here:

'It is a characteristic that of those new firms starting in business perhaps half will cease to trade within three years and the vast majority of those which remain in business will have ceased to exhibit any increase in employment once they are more than three or four years old.' (Storey, 1987: 152)

As Storey points out, not only do most small firms have a high initial risk of failure, most of those which do succeed create relatively few jobs. In fact, approximately 2 out of every 3 small businesses in Britain employ no-one but the owner (Curran, 1987). The reasons for the failure to survive and grow are many. Small businesses are often chronically under-capitalised from the outset. Business ideas are not properly market-tested. Pricing policies are flawed and financial control is often almost non-existent. All of these factors indicate that most small businessmen need outside help in getting established.

A major problem here is lack of knowledge and guidance where the small business is concerned. EC member-state governments and others have tried to help but with limited success. Professor David Birch of the Massachusetts Institute of Technology in his much quoted (and also much misquoted) report on *The Job Generation Process* has made the point:

'It is no wonder that efforts to stem the tide of job decline have been so frustrating. . . . The firms that such efforts much reach are the most difficult to work with. They are volatile. The very spirit that gives them their vitality and job generating powers is the same spirit that makes them unpromising partners for the development administrator.' (Birch, 1979: 20)

Small businesses mistrust government and bureaucracy, no matter how well-meaning. But franchising can and does embrace a link between the small business and the expertise and specialisation that come with size, in a way that national governments have failed to achieve. A point made by both Storey and Birch is that EC and national government aid is spread widely and thinly over large numbers of small businessmen (who essentially select themselves for the role of entrepreneur, no matter how unsuited). In the franchise situation, in addition to other inherent advantages, there is a selection process which, whilst not perfect, weeds out many unsuitable candidates. Thus, it would appear that franchising is a method of 'cloning' success by duplicating a format based on established 'best practice'.

The underlying strength of franchising, combined with the EC-wide drive for self-employment opportunities, goes a long way towards explaining the ready internationalisation of many franchises (both within and without the Common Market). The American fast food giants come most obviously to mind here, but there are outstanding European examples too. For instance, the Benetton fashion company has used franchising to spearhead its growth across Europe. Britain's own Body Shop, set up by Anita Roddick in 1976, is now established in around 30 different countries and has been described as Britain's most successful retailer abroad, outpacing giants such as Marks and Spencer and Mothercare.

INTERNATIONAL MARKETS

The internationalisation of franchising generally continues unabated, both within and without the European Community, led principally by American franchise companies. In 1986, over 350 American business format franchisors operated over 30,000 foreign outlets covering most countries of the world. No figures showing what percentage of these are within the EC are available. In an increasing number of EC member states, the shift from manufacturing to services, the process of urbanisation, rising disposable incomes and expanding consumer markets provide similar conditions to those which fuelled the earlier franchising surge in the United States.

There are a number of ways in which the EC markets (or 'market' following 1992) can be penetrated:

'. . . franchising directly to individuals, company-owned operations, joint ventures or master franchises. Many franchisors use more than one method in conducting foreign operations but the most popular, cheapest and fastest method is the master license technique' (US Department of Commerce, 1986: 8).

Under the master franchise or subfranchisor technique, a master franchise, or subfranchisor receives the right to develop the franchisor's system in a specific country or region. The US Department of Commerce claims that the problems facing 'franchise companies in accomplishing international transactions are relatively less formidable than those of other service sectors' (US Department of Commerce, 1986: 9). The heaviest foreign concentrations of American franchise outlets are in Canada (9,031); Japan (7,366); Continental Europe (4,844 – especially France, West Germany, the Netherlands and Belgium); the United Kingdom (2,415); followed by Australia, Asia, the Caribbean, Africa, Mexico and South America.

Europe

Totally reliable and comprehensive data on the scale and distribution of franchising in the EEC is simply not available at present. Probably the two most cited sources are those which form the basis of the statistics in Table 2, i.e. the European Franchise Federation figures and the Euromonitor Report, *Franchising in the European Economy: Trends and Forecasts 1980-1990*.

Figures from these separate sources often bear little comparison, e.g., those for Sweden, UK and Germany illustrate quite clearly the stark inadequacy and the conflicting nature of the data in this field. Nonetheless, the figures in general serve to illustrate the reasonably substantial scale of this form of business activity in Europe and few would disagree that it appears set for fairly substantial expansion between now the the end of this century.

Euromonitor claims that Italy, the United Kingdom and Sweden are expected to show the strongest growth in franchising and that France, Belgium and the Netherlands will grow more slowly but that they 'already have a more mature franchise industry than the former countries'. However, it might be argued that the recent figures issued by the European Franchise Association do not completely support this latter claim.

The main areas of franchise development in Europe to date have been retailing, fast food, hotels, car hire and servicing plus domestic and industrial service areas. Considerable potential now exists in the rapidly growing 'business services' sector where printing, office and despatch services still have great potential.

TABLE 2 **Business Format Franchising in the European Economy, 1988***
(Source: European Franchise Association, 1989).

Country	Number of franchisors	Number of franchisee outlets	Franchise sales in billion ECU (unless otherwise stated)
Austria	30	1,363	N.A.
	—	—	—
Belgium (1987)	77	4,045	2.85
	(135)	(4,500)	(3.0 bn$)
Denmark	8	25	N.A.
	—	—	—
France	675	29,698	13.15
	(680)	(38,000)	(15.5 bn$)
Italy	197	11,500	4,500 (bn Lire)
	(99)	(9,000)	(3.8 bn$)
Netherlands	248	8,332	5.4
	(390)	(8,500)	(7.0 bn$)
Norway	120	850	0.5
	—	—	—
Portugal	—	—	—
	(100)	(1,100)	(0.39 bn$)
Sweden	44	752	0.4
	(110)	(3,000)	(1.0 bn$)
UK	270	20,000	3.8 (bn£)
	(520)	(30,000)	(5.0 bn$)
West Germany	180	9,000	4.8
	(400)	(26,000)	(2.8 bn$)
Denmark, Greece, Spain & Norway	—	—	—
	(675)	(10,000)	(1.3 bn$)
Totals:	1,849	85,565	—
	(3,109)	(130,100)	(39.79 bn$)

*Sales of Automobiles, Trucks & Soft Drink Bottlers & Hotels excluded.

The figures presented in brackets above are forecasts for 1988 contained in the Euromonitor publication, *Franchising in the European Economy: Trends and Forecasts 1980-1990*, 1987. As can be seen, there are certain obvious obstacles to direct comparisons with the European Franchise Association (EFA) figures. The latter do not include Portugal, Greece or Spain, whereas the former do. Euromonitor amalgamate figures for Denmark, Greece, Spain and Norway, like the EFA. Also, sales turnover figures are presented in different currencies. Finally, whereas the EFA presents data on number of franchised *outlets*, Euromonitor figures in the same column refer to numbers of *franchisees*. Given that some franchisees may be expected to be multi-outlet holders, we would expect numbers of franchisees to be lower than numbers of franchised outlets, which they are plainly not.

FAILURE RATES

One of the hottest debates in the field of franchising in the EEC over the years has been the true level of franchise failure rates. The argument is that failure rates amongst franchised businesses are 'vastly' lower than those for conventional independent businesses. However, many of the people who write in this area in truth understand little about the specialist field of assessing business failure rates.

On the issue of franchise failure rates, be they in the EC or elsewhere, there are a number of points that need to be kept in mind. Firstly, there are good reasons why a franchised business outlet *should* stand a better chance of success than a conventional one, particularly at the start-up stage. After all, what is a franchisee buying into if not a tried and tested business format?

Conventional small businesses, on the other hand, are very vulnerable in their early days. Many people who set up on their own do so in a haphazard manner with a minimum of planning. Their basic business idea may be flawed, sales projections may be hopelessly over-optimistic, the business may be under-capitalised from the outset, financial control mechanisms may be non-existent, and so on.

When a person buys into a franchise, on the other hand, there should have been some assessment of their suitability to run a business *per se* and they should know the capital requirements required to become successfully established. If you cannot raise sufficient fundfing, you should not be allowed across the starting line.

That is the theory and much of the time that is how things turn out. Nonetheless, myths concerning success rates continue to survive and often enjoy the status of industry 'folklore'. In the EC this is largely due to the complete lack of real figures on failure rates. Most of the people who write on this issue present figures which are highly dubious. Most worrying of all, they are usually unaware of either the origins or the inaccuracy of the figures they use. It is therefore not possible here to comment specifically on failures in the EC. However, it is useful to examine the situation in the USA, if only to show how dangerous it can be to rely on incorrect figures.

The publishers' press release which accompanied the publication of one book on franchising recently said: 'It is reckoned that as many as 90 per cent of all new businessses fail, whereas 90 per cent of new franchises succeed.' The origin of claims such as these appears to be a publication by the International Franchise Association (IFA) entitled *Franchising: the Odds-On Favourite* which claimed that: 'Even if the actual franchise failure rate were eight times greater than reported, it would still pay an investor to be franchised rather than start an independent small business.'

The IFA admitted that their figures excluded 'illegitimate fringe' activities surrounding the field of franchising which would have altered the picture somewhat. But, even so, errors in their researchers' methodology and interpretation of official statistics on conventional small businesses were so gross as to attract the attention of academic researchers of some note, working for the American Small Business Administration (SBA), which was itself involved in funding individual entry into franchising at that time.

The SBA was able to induce the IFA to act in accordance with their researchers' recommendation that:

'. . . the International Franchise Association withdraw from circulation all copies of the book *Franchising: the Odds-On Favourite* . . . The book presents grossly inaccurate data on failure rates and would be very misleading to potential franchisees' (Ozanne and Hunt, 1971).

Nonetheless, these figures entered the public arena with greater force than their withdrawal. They, and figures like them, continue to circulate and potentially mislead. The most accurate and honest statement that can be made on the issue of comparative failure rates is that made by Janet Housden in her own book on franchising in 1984, where she said:

'It has breen claimed that as well as helping in the creation of new businesses, franchising substantially reduces the subsequent rate of failure in such businesses. . . . No firm evidence has yet been produced to support this contention, but it seems reasonable to assume that franchised outlets of a reputable system are less likely to fail than independently-owned outlets, because of the franchisor's vested interest'. (Housden, 1984).

Our knowledge in this field in the European Community and the USA is advancing slowly. The researchers (above) who were working for the SBA in the early 1970's conducted an in-depth study of American fast-food franchising and estimated that, during the two-year period 1969–70, the failure rate was somewhere between 6.7 and 20.1 per cent of all fast-food *franchise systems* (franchisors). *Franchisee* failure rates were about one-third that level. Lest these statistics appear confusing, although the rate of franchise system failure was quite high, many of the failures occurred amongst smaller systems with relatively few franchisees.

The problems with calculating failure rates are many. The key ones, however, are: poor response rates to research questionnaires; the fact that 'ethical' franchisors are more likely to reply than 'unethical' ones; systems that have failed and disappeared are unlikely to reply and it is difficult to distinguish between *turnover* rates and *failure* rates. If a franchise system is doing badly, franchisees may sell-out to other investors due to low profit (or loss) figures, but outlets continue in existence and may not register as individual franchisee failures.

Recent advances in methods of calculating survival rates amongst conventional small businesses indicate that these are probably rather higher than had previously been imagined – about 40 out of every 100 new firms probably survive the first ten years (this will vary somewhat with the business sector involved). Also, if we look at, say, the British Franchise Association's own figures for 1986 (again based on very low response rate research), and if we aggregate outlet closures and those changing hands, we get a failure rate figure for the year of around 10 per cent.

THE FRANCHISE RELATIONSHIP

Franchising offers a promising chemistry for combining the economies of scale enjoyed by the franchisor with the flexibility of the franchisee to exploit local market situations. But who is the franchisee, what are his or her background and motives in taking a franchise, and how do such socio-economic factors influence the successful running of a franchise operation? Until recently, very little was known about such questions and the key to understanding the nerve-centre of franchising – the franchise relationship – was shrouded in mystery and reliant, at best, upon anecdotal evidence. However, more recently research has illuminated discussion in this area.

The relationship between franchisor and franchisee is a delicate one requiring careful management given the franchisor's interest in protecting his trade name and public image, on the one hand, and the franchisee's motivation for independence, on the other. The franchisor's interest in closely monitoring the activities of franchised outlets stems from a desire to ensure that standards of service and efficiency are maintained. These interests clash potentially with the franchisee's role as a *self-employed small businessman* with its norms of *independence and autonomy*.

At one extreme, the franchised small business could be viewed as an emerging form of independent small business now common throughout most advanced industrial societies whose distinguishing characteristic is its overt and close association with another, usually larger, enterprise. This association, it could be said, is little different except in degree and the explicit form it takes to that now found between many small businesses and other firms with whom they do business. In an increasingly interdependent economy such as the European Community, a close association such as this may be seen simply as a reflection of the fact that 'no firm is an island entire of itself' in a modern economy. Adopting a view at the opposite extreme, it might be argued that the franchised enterprise is, in reality, simply a *managed* outlet featuring in the corporate marketing strategy of another truly independent business – that of the franchisor (Rubin, 1978: 225).

In recent research by the author in the European Community to clarify this issue, the franchised small enterprise was first examined in terms of its formal independence, that is, in terms of its contractual and legal aspects and then in terms of the operational dimension. The latter concerned day-to-day relations. After all, all social and business relations develop a repertoire of behaviours additional to those prescribed in any contract. Real life relations turn on a subtle balance of negotiations and either party may choose to ignore or depart from contractually prescribed patterns of conduct, possibly with the open or tacit approval, or at least the reluctant acceptance, of the other party to the transaction. In other words, the description of the formal level of association between franchisor and franchisee prompts the question: *what actually happens in practice* ?

Two major in-depth research projects addressing these issues have been conducted in the UK in recent times at the Polytechnic of Central London. The first was based on 3 of the 8 companies which founded the British Franchise Association in 1977 — Wimpy International (fast food), Dyno-Rod (drain cleaning and hygiene services) and ServiceMaster (carpet, upholstery and allied cleaning services). This research involved tape-recorded face-to-face interviews with 13 key franchisor executives plus 51 franchisees. An additional 114 franchisees and 207 potential franchisees completed written questionnaires.

In the second project, 4 companies were studied — Home Tune (mobile car tuning), Prontaprint (high speed printing services), Servowarm (central heating installation and servicing) and Ziebart (vehicle rust-proofing). The research involved 15 tape-recorded face-to-face interviews with franchisor executives and 80 with franchisees. An additional 135 franchisees completed written questionnaires. The two projects, between them, involved over 400 franchise respondents: 28 franchisors and 380 franchisees.

It would be wrong to generalise from the results of specifically British research to the other eleven member states. However, bearing in mind the lack of any such research in the other countries, it is useful to examine the figures to set the US figures in perspective and to illustrate some of the differences and similarities that can arise.

General socio-economic characteristics of franchisees

A detailed analysis of the socio-economic characteristics of franchisees in the latter study (Stanworth, 1984) suggested that the most remarkable finding was the very high level of experience of prior self-employment. Given this it is worthwhile comparing, where possible, experiences of franchising with conventional self-employment and homing in on the franchisor-franchisee relationship given that franchisees expectations of self-employment were grounded in practical and real situations.

Age

As appears the case for conventional small businessmen, franchisees were most likely to take up their franchised businesses when they were in their 20's or 30's (Boswell, 1973; Mayer & Goldstein, 1961). Approximately 35% set up in their 30's compared to 30% in their 20's and 23% in their 40's. There appeared little support for any suggestion that franchisees enter their business ventures at notably different stages in their careers than conventional small businessmen. In fact, the evidence is that the type of business (business sector) is more important here than whether it is franchised or not.

For instance, in the most expensive of the 4 franchises in the second project (Prontaprint) only 17% started up in their 20's, compared with 45% from the lowest entry cost franchise (Home Tune). The franchise with the highest percentage setting up in their 40's (Servowarm) also had the highest percentage of previously self-employed (53%) for whom franchising was their second or subsequent attempt at self-employment.

Thus, where distinct patterns did emerge, they appeared to be explained by a variety of factors, such as capital requirements and previous career histories. Also, it is worth remarking on the sheer spread of ages of incoming franchisees. In the second research project (data on this issue is not available for the first), 3 out of the 4 franchises had recruited franchisees in their 60's.

Marital status

The value of assistance from a spouse to the successful running of a small business is becoming increasingly realised. There are several ways in which this can come about, either inside the business or even outside it (e.g., by supplementing the family income). Only one of the franchises formally required a prospective franchisee's spouse to take part in the interview process but, in the others, it was not uncommon for the spouse to attend at least one of the interviews.

Nearly 90% of the franchisees were married and nearly 70% had spouses involved to a greater or lesser extent in the day-to-day running of their franchise. In the home-based franchises (Home Tune, Servowarm and ServiceMaster), the figure was in the region of 70 − 80% whilst the others averaged around 50%. In the conventional small businesses, it has been noted that there is a tendency for wives to withdraw from the business as it expands (Goffee & Scase, 1980). However, this did not appear the case with franchise businesses. In all, a third of spouses had employment outside the franchise but more than half of these helped in the franchise as well.

Education

Ozanne and Hunt (1971), in the US, noted an 'unexpectedly high level of formal education amongst their study of fast food franchisees with only 10% not completing high school at one extreme and a similar proportion obtaining post-graduate qualifications at the other. In the current study, both projects showed half of the franchisees as having had either a selective state or private education, thus rendering them characteristically different from the population as a whole.

There was a distinct pattern (and positive correlation) linking buy-in cost of the franchise to likelihood of (1) having attended a selective state school, (2) having had a private education and (3) having left school with some form of qualification. As might be expected, those with manual worker fathers were the most likely to have attended a non-selective state school and to have left without any formal qualifications. Those from upper white collar backgrounds were the most likely to have left school with qualifications, although they were more likely to have attended non-selective state schools than those whose fathers were self-employed.

Nearly two-thirds of franchisees undertook some form of college education after leaving school. This was usually on a part-time basis in the case of the low-cost franchise, Home Tune, but most commonly full-time in the case of the highest cost franchise, Prontaprint. Franchisees who had attended grammar schools were more than three times as likely to have subsequently studied full-time as those who attended non-selective state schools.

PRE-ENTRY ADVICE

It is a conventional wisdom that many people who stage an entry into business do so with a minimum of planning and advice and their general approach is essentially haphazard (Mayer & Goldstein, 1961; Thackray, 1980). In some respects, the franchisees in the current research replicated this – in both projects, only one-fifth investigated more than one franchise opportunity.

However, the level of pre-entry investigation undertaken by franchisees appeared related to a number of factors. First was the level of franchise investment required – 38% of Prontaprint respondents and 31% from DynoRod considered more than one franchise opportunity whereas for Home Tune and ServiceMaster the figures were only 11% and 13% respectively. There was, however, a remarkable change over time. For instance, of the Home Tune respondents who had taken their franchises during the two years prior to interview, over 40% had considered more than one franchise, indicating a general trend towards greater awareness.

Respondents who bought existing franchise outlets were less likely than those setting up from scratch to consider other franchises. It is, however, possible that these people were more concerned to buy an on-going business than they were to buy a franchise per se and they may thus have considered other business propositions, albeit non-franchised.

In the case of all four franchises in the second project, between 70 – 90% sought professional advice from a third party. Again the distribution was as might be expected with respondents from the higher investment figure franchisees being more likely to seek advice. The most important source of advice was solicitors (56%) followed by bank managers (48%) and accountants (40%). Less than 10% sought advice from other professional sources. There was some evidence that, when individual franchises were experiencing serious trading difficulties, incoming franchisees were considerably less likely to have taken third party advice which appeared to be linked to lower levels of encouragement to do so by franchisors.

The tendency for prospective franchisees to seek third party advice appeared to be increasing over time. However, less than 20% of the franchisees studied felt that their advisers had

been very knowledgeable about franchising – more than 60% felt that they were definitely not knowledgeable. By far the most knowledgeable and reliable advice came from a non-professional source – existing franchisees. Over 95% of those reporting on this question felt that they had been supplied with accurate information. The source of advice was regarded as essentially neutral with most being given neither encouragement nor discouragement.

The importance of the bank manager to franchisees did not stop at advice. The first of the two projects being reported here showed that 45% obtained funding assistance from the clearing banks when starting up. The second project, some time later, indicated that this figure had risen to over 50%. In fact, 42% claimed to have raised over one-quarter of their total start-up requirements from the clearing banks and, of these 25% claimed to have raised over half.

PRIOR WORK EXPERIENCE AND FRANCHISEE PROFITABILITY

At the time of entry into franchising, franchisees from the various companies varied considerably in terms of previous educational background (see discussion earlier) and work experience. Once again, the level of capital investment required to enter the respective franchises correlated quite closely with certain franchise characteristics. For instance, in the second project, nearly 35% of Prontaprint franchisees had degrees or degree level professional qualifications compared with 7% in the case of Home Tune. The spread of occupational posts held prior to entry into franchising reflected this with Home Tune respondents being far more likely to have been involved in manual work than Prontaprint respondents (in the first project, the same contrast was apparent between ServiceMaster and Dyno-Rod respondents).

However, many respondents had been upwardly socially mobile. If we compare occupations held *immediately before* entry into franchising with respondents *main* career occupations, the proportion of manual workers falls by one-fifth, bringing the Home Tune figure down to 35% and the second project average to 18.8%.

While franchisors seldom made specific reference to the desired educational attainments of franchisees, this was not so with regard to prior work experience. This was seen as an important consideration, if often for what might be regarded as negative reasons. Prior experience in the operational line of the franchise was often seen as undesirable. Franchisor-executives tended to prefer people from outside their industry with no preconceived ideas or bad habits which might interfere with the franchisor's training programme or contaminate other franchisees.

Research into fast food franchisees in the US indicates that those *with* prior experience tend to be at least modestly more successful (Ozanne & Hunt, 1971). This research also pointed to a link between income levels achieved in previous employment and success as a franchisee. The UK research intended to investigate both these relationships further but found this exceedingly difficult for a number of reasons.

Firstly, although response rates had been generally very good for research of its kind, the non-response rates on questions relating to profit ranged from 45% − 70% (of those who answered all the other questions). Also, a fairly high proportion of the franchisees studied were in the early years of their existence as franchisees (the median period was 2.5 to 5.5 years).

Another attempt to yield data in this area − asking respondents to register levels of satisfaction with their profitability − yielded fairly high blanket levels of satisfaction which once again ruled out the possibility of detailed sub-group analysis (60% were 'fairly satisfied' or 'very satisfied'). Nearly 80% of respondents were willing to state levels of income taken from their franchise in the year before interview and this data was compared with official statistics on earnings levels for employees in the occupational groups of which the franchisees had previously been members. The resulting analysis indicated that one-third were drawing less than they might have received as employees. However, it is quite possible that, in the relatively early years of establishing a business, many franchisees were deliberately retaining as much money in the business as possible. Also, this form of analysis makes no allowance for the fringe benefits associated with self-employment, nor some of the non-monetary rewards and satisfactions.

As was mentioned earlier, one of the most interesting observations to emerge from the research was the high proportion of franchisees with prior experience of self-employment. The figures here were both high and consistent (see Table 3 below). The figures for respondents with previous first-hand experience of self-employment were between 33% and 36% aggregate for both projects and the figure for those with either direct experience or second-hand exposure via one or more parents was exactly 55% on each occasion. The first of these figures is corroborated by American research (Ozanne & Hunt, 1971) and appears likely to hold on a much wider cross-cultural basis. Given that such a large proportion came from this background, additional interest was focused on the issue of the franchisor-franchisee relationship − on the accommodation of the franchisor's desire for standardisation and control and the franchisee's quest for independence and autonomy.

TABLE 3   History of previous self-employment amongst Franchisees and Fathers

	Franchisees PSE*	Fathers PSE	Both PSE	Franchisees or Father PSE
	%	%	%	%
FRANCHISE				
Home Tune	23.9	35.2	7.0	52.1
Prontaprint	32.8	35.9	15.6	53.1
Servowarm	53.1	37.5	25.0	65.6
Ziebart	33.3	43.8	18.8	58.3
ServiceMaster	16.1	16.1	0.0	32.2
Dyno-Rod	35.5	25.8	12.0	48.4
Wimpy	48.1	44.2	19.2	73.1

* PSE: *Previously Self-Employed* Note: Row totals do not equal 100%

ENTERPRISE, AUTONOMY AND THE FRANCHISE RELATIONSHIP

Formal Independence

Data on the formal level of independence was obtained through an analysis of franchise contracts. These were found to be characteristically detailed and comprehensive in specifying the nature of the relationship between franchisee and franchisor. In terms of franchisee independence, some of the provisions appeared to circumscribe closely the franchisee's freedom of action as a businessman. One stipulated, for example, that the franchisee:

'Will conduct his franchised . . . business in all respects as shall be *laid down by the Company from time to time in the Manual or otherwise.* The franchisee will keep the copy of the Manual in his possession up to date with all variations thereto which the Company may make.'

This form of contract has been extensively criticised in the American literature (Hunt, 1972: 36) since it involves, in effect, the franchisee's commitment to an open-ended agreement:

'Since the provisions of the operating manual can be changed at the prerogative of the franchisor, the franchisees find themselves in the tenuous position of being bound to a contract that can be modified *unilaterally* by the franchisor.' (Hunt, 1972: 36-37)

Contracts were also explicit in relation to restrictions on the franchisee's right to dispose of his franchised business. Sometimes the franchisor claimed the right of first refusal to purchase and required that written permission must be given before the outlet could be sold to another person. The franchisor also often insisted on being informed of all the confidential details of any transaction − valuation of the premises, etc. − intended to result in the sale of an outlet. In one of the franchises under study, the franchisor was entitled to 10 per cent of the sale price of the franchise when it changed hands.

Of course, obligations were also imposed on the franchisor. But given that the contract is drawn up by the franchisor, it has the character of a *contract of adhesion* rather than a *contract of negotiation* (Hunt, 1972: 37). That is, rather than being the end result of a process of bargaining between parties, it is offered by one of the parties (the franchisor) on a take-it-or-leave-it basis. Franchisors are very reluctant to vary their standard contract to suit individual franchisees.

On the other hand, franchisors admitted that they did sometimes vary certain aspects of the contract for a new franchisee particularly with regard to size of territory and, to a lesser extent, by modifying requirements on minimum capital required or other starting costs. One fifth of the franchisees interviewed claimed that they renegotiated the territory they were originally offered.

Over time, contracts were judged by franchisees to have become more comprehensively prescriptive and more strictly enforced and all franchisors reported enforcement problems. Yet there were also indications that franchisors tried to tread lightly concerning contracts. For instance, no franchisor reported frequent mention of the contract in their relations with franchisees and over 80 per cent of the interviewed sample of franchisee respondents claimed that their franchisor never mentioned the contract to them in everyday relations.

Just over half of the franchisees believed that the contract favoured the franchisor while almost 40 per cent thought it about neutral between the two parties. Only six per cent, on the other hand, were convinced that the contract was weighted in favour of franchisees. Despite these findings almost 60 per cent of franchisees stated that there was no section of the contract they felt should be altered. Although most franchisor respondents believed that they strictly enforced the contract, franchisees — those over whom the contract was allegedly being enforced — did not accept this view. Less than a quarter of franchisees reported feeling that the contract was 'very strictly' or 'fairly strictly' enforced.

In other words, at the formal level, relations between the franchisor and franchisee might be described as implicitly one-sided since the contract is drawn up on a virtually non-negotiable basis by the franchisor and put to the franchisee on a take-it-or-leave-it bases. But the findings also hint strongly that consideration of franchisor-franchisee relations solely at the formal level is misleading.

Findings from both franchisors and franchisees suggest that the contract, although central in a formal sense to their relations, is not permitted a similarly explicit position in their day-to-day relations. For instance, franchisors not infrequently had to pursue franchisees for their monthly statements or royalty payments, but this rarely involved an explicit reference to the franchisee's contractual obligations. Instead, the appeal was usually framed in terms of the need for administrative efficiency and couched in the form of an informal, personal plea for co-operation from the franchisee.

Operational Independence

The above discussion suggests that there is what might be termed an operational realm in franchisor-franchisee relations which is not necessarily revealed by an analysis of contractual relations. It may be suggested that this is no less than might be expected given that no contract can fully define everyday relations and, more important, a contract of adhesion essentially embodies one party's view of how it would like relations to be patterned. In practice, all kinds of other influences will push and pull relations into other patterns.

At the operational day-to-day level, franchisors and franchisees in the second project were questioned in detail on who they felt was responsible for certain key aspects of the outlet's operations. As Table 4 indicates, franchisors and franchisees were in broad agreement on the division of responsibilities on seven key aspects of outlet decision-making. Franchisors claimed responsibility for control over the product/service mix and pricing while franchisees claimed control over hours of opening, employment of

personnel, bookkeeping, service quality standards and local advertising.

However, these findings cannot be accepted as a total consensus of views. As the percentages in Table 4 indicate, there were sizeable minorities holding contrary views on some of these aspects and especially on quality control and product/service mix changes. Thus, almost 20 per cent of franchisees felt that they had equal say in product/service mix additions, deletions or alterations and somewhat surprisingly a further 26 per cent believed they had *most* influence.

TABLE 4 **Franchisor and Franchisee views on Control over Operational Elements of the Franchised Outlet**

Operational element	Franchisors' views (n=15)	% Agreeing with view
Additions/Deletions to Produce/Service	Mainly or Totally the Decision of the Franchisor	93.3
Responsibility for Pricing	Mainly or Totally the Decision of the Franchisor	80.0
Hours of Operation	Mainly or Totally the Decision of the Franchisee	66.6*
Employment of Staff/Staff Wage Levels	Mainly or Totally the Decision of the Franchisee	60.0/ 93.3
Quality of Service to the Customer	Mainly or Totally the Decision of the Franchisee	46.7
Book-keeping	Mainly or Totally the Decision of the Franchisee	73.3
Local Advertising	Mainly or Totally the Decision of the Franchisee	33.3**

Operational Element	Franchisees' View (n=215)	% Agreeing with view
Additions/Deletions to Produce/Service	Mainly or Totally the Decision of the Franchisor	55.3
Responsibility for Pricing	Mainly or Totally the Decision of the Franchisor	62.8
Hours of Operation	Mainly or Totally the Decision of the Franchisee	78.1
Employment of Staff/Staff Wage Levels	Mainly or Totally the Decision of the Franchisee	93.5/ 88.4
Quality of Service to the Customer	Mainly or Totally the Decision of the Franchisee	74.4
Book-keeping	Mainly or Totally the Decision of the Franchisee	85.1
Local Advertising	Mainly or Totally the Decision of the Franchisee	91.6

 * One franchisor claimed total responsibility for hours of operation which were precisely defined in the franchisor-franchisee contract
** Eight of the 15 franchisors interviewed claimed that responsibility for local advertising was equally distributed between franchisor and franchisee

Franchisor-Franchisee Communications

Another aspect of the franchisee's operational freedom was measured by day-to-day contact with the franchisor. Almost 35 per cent of franchisees reported contact with their franchisor as occurring at least once a week. For the remaining franchisees for whom information is available, the typical frequency of contact with their franchisor was once a month. Three-quarters reported that they, rather than the franchisor, initiated these contacts in the majority of instances. Their replies indicated that they were generally using the franchisor as a resource in these contacts, that is, seeking solutions to technical and other operating problems. In other words, a high proportion of franchisor-franchisee contacts were initiated by franchisees rather than by franchisors positively supervising franchisees.

Franchisees reported a relatively low level of franchisor representative visits to their outlets. Less than 10 per cent were visited more frequently than once a fortnight and 18 per cent claimed they were never visited. The typical reported frequency was monthly or bi-monthly. These figures hardly betoken close supervision by franchisors and correlate well with franchisees' declared preferences on the frequency of franchisor visits. They also correlate with the replies of franchisee respondents in the face-to-face interviews of whom almost two-thirds felt that the level of assistance from their franchisor was about right. This did not mean that franchisees were uncritical of franchisors on the quality of assistance provided. Among those franchisees who had been operating their franchise for over a year, 17 per cent rated the assistance provided as 'poor' or 'very poor' while a further 34 per cent rated it as only 'adequate'. However, these findings have to be balanced against the almost 50 per cent who rated assistance provided by the franchisor as 'good' or 'very good'. Over time the level of approval tended to rise since most franchisees were more satisfied at the time of interview than they had been in their first six months of operation.

Assistance is not the same as supervision and franchisees in the face-to-face interviews were asked whether they would prefer more or less supervision from their franchisor. Only 5 per cent felt they were over-supervised while over 80 per cent felt the level was about right. Indeed, 12 per cent would have liked more supervision than they were currently receiving. Keeping in mind the adage that it is impossible to please all the people all the time, it does seem from these findings and those in the preceding paragraphs, that franchisors have achieved a reasonable compromise between being perceived as providing too little assistance and over-supervising. Given that three of the franchisors had around 100 outlets each at the time, this might be accepted as constituting a high level of effective franchisee management by franchisors.

Control

Franchisors did indicate problems in maintaining what they felt was a satisfactory level of control over franchisees. Franchisor respondents in two of the franchises mentioned problems in getting franchisees to make proper and full financial returns on time and these problems tended to be greater with longer established franchisees. Marketing was also a problem because all franchisors put great emphasis on this aspect but often felt that franchisees were very deficient in marketing skills. All the franchisors had instituted methods of detecting evasion in the form of incorrect financial information or franchisees purchasing supplies from non-approved sources. Finally, since maintaining the franchise's national image is crucial to its success, quality control at the outlet is a permanent problem – a single franchisee's failure here could do enormous damage to the franchise's reputation.

Commenting on the disadvantages of franchising from their point of view, it was the above issues that predominated in franchisors' replies. They conceded that *the franchise relationship inevitably meant a loss of control compared to the conventionally managed outlet*. It also required a more persuasive style of management since franchisors were well aware that attempts to control franchisees too closely were likely to be counter-productive. (This did not, of course, prevent them from exerting very close control over particular franchisees from time to time even to the point of terminating the contract if necessary but this was relatively rare).

Representation

Indications of tension in the operational realm from the franchisees' viewpoint are perhaps most clearly exemplified in the formation of franchisees' associations. The latter can take two forms. The first is the joint consultative committee set up by the franchisor for an exchange of views between franchisees and between franchisor and franchisees, over which the franchisor exerts sufficient control to ensure the association's activities broadly serve his interests. The second is an independent association freely founded and controlled by franchisees in a particular franchise with the aim of increasing their bargaining power vis-a-vis the franchisor and to act as a vehicle for exchanging ideas and information among franchisees. The first variety is often established to prevent the emergence of the second. Some franchisors freely expressed the view that the completely independent franchise association was too similar to a trade union, challenging franchisor authority and power.

Latent forces pushing franchisees into an independent association to protect their interests in relations with the franchisor are recognised on both sides of the franchising industry. A minority of franchisor respondents saw the emergence of such associations as inevitable. Forty per cent of all franchisees in the study thought franchisees should have a national association while a further 17 per cent were uncertain. However, in relation to their own franchise, franchisees were very much less enthusiastic or even sceptical of what such an association might achieve.

Research which formed a part of the present project, investigated franchisor-franchisee joint committees and independent franchise associations in four franchise companies from among the total of seven studied in the two projects. The response of one franchisor whose franchisees had formed an independent association (to which over 90 per cent of the franchisees belonged) was that it was 'unneces-sary' and caused 'hindrance and delays' in dealing with franchisees. Franchisee members, on the other hand, plainly saw the association's main aim as serving their interests particularly with regard to the standard contract which the franchisor had unilaterally changed to be more restrictive from the franchisees' viewpoint.

Some franchisees believed the effect of the association had been to achieve a more favourable contract than would have otherwise been the case. Some also believed that the subsequent restoration of a more amicable relationship between franchisees and franchisor was helped by the activities of the association. The franchisor may well have adapted his behaviour at the operational level to take into account the threat posed by the franchisees' association but this is, of course, not easy to demonstrate. It does show, however, how occurrences at the operational level may 'feed back' to the formal level.

CONCLUSIONS

The research upon which this chapter is based takes us forward from an earlier state of reliance upon anecdotes and hunches in our attempts at understanding some of the socio-economic processes involved in franchising. Perhaps not surprisingly, reality presents us with a rather more complex picture than existed previously.

One conclusion that can be drawn from the research data is that franchisees do not appear to differ greatly in terms of background and motivation to the conventional small businessman. He/she comes from a similar background (though is often rather better educated) and often has earlier links with the world of self-employment. In fact, the actions of many who bought franchises were motivated by an interest in self-employment generally as much as franchising per se. Further, the differences between various franchises was quite substantial. That is, the capital requirements of entry had a substantial influence upon the kinds of people entering different franchises.

Franchising appears a good avenue into self-employment for certain kinds of people in particular. Amongst these are people whose previous employment in no way lends itself to self-employment. For instance, an ex-print worker, garage mechanic or restaurant manager may well feel able to 'clone' a business they have previously worked for. However, someone coming out of the armed forces or a professionally trained production manager or designer from a large company may feel less well equipped to turn their previous experience into a business. Nonetheless, they do have skills which can intertwine with those of a franchisor to build a complete business operation.

Because most of the franchises under study had been recruiting franchisees quite actively in the years immediately preceding the research, many of the individuals participating had only been franchisees for a modest period of time: 2 – 5 years was typical. Given the rapid growth of franchising in recent years, this situation appears fairly common. The result

of this is that there is little data available upon which to plot long-term trends in franchisee profitability. In addition, a strong reliance on borrowed finance in the early days plus marked variations in the initial capital requirements of the various franchises makes any assessment of success complex and difficult.

Views expressed by many franchisors tended to add weight to American research claims of a relationship between success as a franchisee and success in previous employment. However, all the franchisors were able to point to stark exceptions to this general rule. Others claimed that franchisee recruitment strategies based solely upon this view could even be counter-productive on occasions in a franchise such as Dyno-Rod where the franchisee's employees were likely to be tough manual workers. The social and communications gaps likely to result from recruiting exclusively middle class professional franchisees could be considerable.

On the question of the franchisor-franchisee relationship, it was seen that, at the operational level, the franchisee enjoys considerable independence. Franchisors might claim that, by virtue of the authority derived from the contract which forms the basis of the formal level of relations, franchisee pre-rogatives are strictly limited. On the other hand, franchisees are the only decision-makers who, in practice, can effectively make certain decisions. Indeed, it might be doubted whether franchisors would ever *want* to make some of these decisions even if they then claimed the ultimate right to do so. For instance, one of the attractions of franchising for franchisors is *not* having to worry about personnel problems at the outlet level.

In other areas the franchisor's exercise of control is likely to be too remote or too late. Quality control over service to the customer at second hand, for example, is unlikely to be fully effective or when exercised is often an indication that things have already gone wrong. Typically, control is maintained through visits by the franchisor's field officers, but 'dummy' consumers may also be used or an open invitation made to dissatisfied customers on promotional literature or invoices to contact the franchisor's head office. However, as reported earlier, franchisor field representative visits may be infre-quent and responding to consumer complaints means acting after the quality lapse has occurred.

More subtly, relations between franchisors and franchisees which relate to the latters' independence are also influenced by other latent influences. Franchisors need the goodwill of franchisees and attempts to over-supervise or to impose new contractual obligations against the will of franchisees quickly exhausts this goodwill. This may even promote an inde-pendent franchisee association thus increasing franchisee bargaining influence. Franchisors can cope with such an association but they usually prefer not to have to. There is also the threat of seeking external help to which franchisees could resort. For instance, politicians and the mass media offer further resources for franchisees. This is no idle threat for an industry which has shown itself to be very sensitive indeed towards its public image.

'Independence' is a relative notion and it is all too easy to discuss the degree of independence of the small franchised outlet on an implicit but misleading assumption that the conventional small business is unambiguously independent. Historically, the small enterprise, even when it was the typical or basic unit in the economy, operated under severe restrictions on its independence.

Many conventional small firms have much larger firms as their main customers and this may also constitute a severe limitation on independence without affecting the nominal or legal definition of independence. In Britain, for instance, one well-known high street chain store has become notorious for gradually strengthening links between itself and a host of small suppliers to the point where the latter are almost totally dependent on what has become the main buyer of their product. The buyer stipulates product design and quality, delivery and price and the small supplier is strongly discouraged from seeking other customers. The Bolton Report, in Britain, estimated that in manufacturing industry 35 per cent of small firms were dependent on one customer for 25 per cent or more of their business (Bolton Report, 1971: 32). A similar picture emerges from other economies (Storey, 1983).

Many conventional small enterprises are much more independent than the typical franchised outlet but the difference remains a relative one. In other words, rather than a dichotomy we may suggest a continuum of independence with various kinds of small enterprise being located on different points of the continuum. A priori, we need not assume that franchised small businesses are necessarily always located at the least independent end of the continuum.

THE FUTURE

The data presented above does indicate that the franchise relationship, at its best, can indeed result in a mutually beneficial franchisor-franchisee relationship with franchisees feeling self-employed.

However, there are still certain observers inclined towards the view that such feelings of independence are largely subjective. Nearly 20 years ago, Burck (Fortune, 1970) was urging tighter franchise regulations in the US and suggesting that the industry should abandon the 'myth' that a franchise holder is an independent small businessman. More recently, Felstead (1989) has cited cases from German and Danish courts where franchise contracts were deemed to be so tight as to bestow employee status on franchise holders (Arendorff, 1986; Schulz, 1988). Other recent accounts also furnish evidence of contractual rigidities (Kneppers-Heynert), 1989).

The current text has already noted that, 'over time, contracts were judged by franchisees to have become more comprehensively prescriptive and more strictly enforced'. Certain factors at work in the field of franchising might be seen as having the potential to accelerate this process.

First is the formation of national associations of franchisors in the EC. This movement facilitates a forum for the exchange of information, ideas and experiences and the institution-alisation of what, from a franchisors viewpoint, may be seen as 'best practice'.

Second is the development of specialist business services capable of advising and acting for franchisors not only in individual member states but throughout the whole of the EC. Key examples here derive from the fields of law and finance. Prontaprint's successful legal battle (*Franchise World*, March–May 1987) to restrain an ex-franchisee from entering into direct competition with the franchisor would appear to represent an example of increasing legal sophistication on the part of the franchise industry, the lessons of which are likely to be generalised to other franchisors. The French 'University of Franchising' which seeks to train franchising managers is another example of the increasing 'profes-sionalism' of franchising.

Thirdly, the very first quotation in this text cited Scase and Goffee (1987), claiming that in Europe 'developments in technology and management practices have brought about tighter forms of employee control'. Pressures on franchisees to adopt, and be exposed to the franchisor's use of, such technology and practices would appear bound to grow over time. Thus, to an extent at least, the very processes which Scase and Goffee claim are likely to push people in Europe towards wanting to work for themselves, may be acting to actually constrain the independence of franchisees.

Against the above factors, we may be witnessing the growing use of collective strength by franchisees. In the UK recently, the Franchise Advice and Consultancy Trade Organisation has been formed to act as a trade organisation for franchisees (*Franchise World*, January-February 1989). It may be remembered (above) that, amongst the franchisees interviewed in the research reported here, 40 per cent favoured the formation of a national franchisee association, though usually without any great expectations as to what this would achieve.

No doubt the delicate relationship between franchisor and franchisee will continue to evolve and adapt to changing circumstances. However, whatever unforeseen directions the relationship may take in the future, it appears likely to remain a focus of interest for those intrigued by this novel interplay between the forces of small and large size.

ACKNOWLEDGEMENTS

Data presented in this paper is drawn from research projects directed by the author in association with Professor James Curran of Kingston Polytechnic. The field researchers on the projects were Michael Woodmansey and Jensine Hough, both formerly of the Polytechnic of Central London.

REFERENCES

Arendorff, P. A., 'Denmark: Franchising and Employment Contracts', *Journal of International and Distribution Law*, Vol. 1, No. 2, December, 1986

Bannock, G., *The Economics of Small Firms: Return from the Wilderness*, Basil Blackwell, 1981

Bolton, J. (Chairman), *Small Firms, Report of the Committee of Inquiry on Small Firms*, London, HMSO, Cmnd. 4811, 1971

Birch, D. L., *The Job Generation Process*, MIT Study on Neighbourhood and Regional Change, Cambridge, Mass., 1979

Boswell, J., *The Rise and Decline of Small Firms*, George Allen & Unwin, 1973

Burck, C. G., 'Franchising's Troubled Dreamworld', *Fortune*, 1970

Collins, O. F. & Moore, D. G., with Unwalla, D. B., *The Enterprising Man*, East Lansing: Michigan State University Press, 1964

Euromonitor, *Franchising in the European Economy-Trends and Forecasts 1980-1990*, Euromonitor, 1987

Felstead, A., 'Franchising: A Testimony to the 'Enterprise Economy' and 'Economic Restructuring in the 1980's?' in *Farewell to Flexibility? Questions of Restructuring Work and Employment*, (Ed.) Anna Pollert, Basil Blackwell, forthcoming

Franchise World, Franchise Publications, March–May 1987

Franchise World, Franchise Publications, January–February 1989

Ganguly, P. & Bannock, G., *UK Statistics and International Comparisons*, Harper & Row, 1985

Golby, C. W. & Johns, G., 'Attitude & Motivation', *Committee of Inquiry on Small Firms, Research Report No. 7*, HMSO, 1971

Housden, J., *Franchising and Other Business Relationships in Hotel and Catering Services*, Heinemann, 1984

Hunt, S. D., 'The Socio-economic Consequences of the Franchise System of Distribution', *Journal of Marketing*, Vol. 36, 1972

Kets de Vries, M. F. R., 'The Entrepreneurial Personality: A Person at the Crossroads', *Journal of Management Studies*, Vol. 14, 1977

Kneppers-Heynert, E. M., 'Why Franchising?', paper delivered at the *Fifth International Conference on Distribution*, Bocconi University, Milan, 1989

Mayer, K. B. & Goldstein, S., *The First Two Years: Problems of Small Firm Growth and Survival*, Washington: Small Business Administration, 1961

Ozanne, U. B. & Hunt, S. D. *The Economic Effects of Franchising*, Select Committee on Small Business, US Senate, September 1971

Rubin, P., 'The Theory of the Firm and the Structure of Franchise Contract', *Journal of Law and Economics*, Vol. 21, 1978

Scase, R. & Goffee, R., *Entrepreneurship in Europe*, Croom Helm, 1987

Schulz, A., 'Germany: Are Franchisees Salaried Employees?', *Journal of International and Distribution Law*, Vol. 2, No. 3, March, 1988

Stanworth, J. & Curran, J., *Management Motivation in the Smaller Business*, Gower Press, 1973

Stanworth, J., *A Study of Power Relationships & Their Consequences in Franchise Organisations*, Report to the Economic and Social Research Council, 1984, published as *The Franchise Relationship* by Franchise Publications, 1984. (An earlier report, *A Study of Franchising in Britain*, was presented to the Economic & Social Research Council in 1977.)

Storey, D. J. (ed.), *The Small Firm: An International Survey*, Croom Helm, 1983

Storey, D. J., Keasey, K., Watson, R. & Wynarczyn, P., *The Performance of Small Firms*, Croom Helm, 1987

Thackray, J., 'Small US Business Gets Big', *Management Today*, January 1980

US Department of Commerce, *Franchising in the Economy 1986-88*, International Trade Administration, Washington DC, 1988

The Initial Franchise Fee in Franchising Chains in the European Community

By MICHAEL PANAJOTOPOULOS

This chapter is based on a study carried out by the author in France, the UK and Germany amongst approximately 250 franchisors.

The initial franchise fee or up-front fee is the amount of money paid by the franchisee in order to enter a franchise system and includes all the support which enables him to commence trading.

To estimate the amount of the initial franchise fee, it suffices to evaluate the exact cost levied for the initial services the franchisor offers to the franchisee. In a way it is a question of whether or not the initial franchise fee is economically justifiable.

However, initial franchise fees vary according to the different franchises. In Europe, some years ago, when the franchise system was still in its infancy, the franchisors asking for a franchise fee were rather a minority. Nowadays, the tendency has completely changed: nearly all contracts include an initial franchise fee.

Thus, the following questions arise:

- How do the franchisors evaluate the initial franchise fee?
- How do they justify the initial franchise fee to the franchisees?
- How do the franchisees treat their initial franchise fee in their accounting books?

What is an Initial Franchise Fee?
Franchisors interpret the term 'initial franchise fee' in two different ways; the licence fee, and the cost of the franchise package as a whole.

This fact is best described in the *Directory of Franchising* (UK), 1989: 'The majority of (UK) franchisors use the term to cover the start-up costs that new franchisees have to meet to join the franchise and set-up in business. However, some franchisors use the term merely to cover the fee they charge their new franchisees for the right to use their name, trade marks, copyright materials, etc., and for goodwill. Therefore, the amount of the franchise fee quoted can vary dramatically depending in which context it is used.'

However, the initial franchise fee is by no means just the licence fee and/or the cost of the franchise package as a whole. It contains many more elements.

(1) The most obvious part is the *remuneration for the provision of the initial services*. These comprise:

— recruitment of the franchisee;
— marketing services: market studies, local and national advertising campaigns or promotional activities, etc.
— 'merchandising' services (as they are often called in France): site-selection and preparation of trading premises (shopfitting and design, decor, layout of work and service areas, displays and merchandising of goods, development and layout of equipment).
— financial services: cash flow and profit forecasts, arrangements to facilitate the franchisee's access to financial facilities, financial advice.
— initial training and education: on-site or other training, assistance, operational manual.

Obviously, it would be prudent for the franchisor to periodically review the fee to reflect inflationary pressures on overhead expenses.

(2) Another component of the initial franchise fee is what can be called the *intangible assets* of the franchise: the right to use and benefit from the brand name, the know-how and the goodwill. They allow the franchisee to 'acquire' clients from one day to the next (the ones attracted by the brand name) and to have products/services available to be sold.

The intangible assets also comprise a '*right to the franchise*': the franchisor conveys a 'good' for the duration of the contract, this good having an indisputable economic value. At the same time, the initial franchise fee carries the notion of a *competitive advantage*.

It is suggested that the 'right to the franchise' must include *a right of automatic renewal*, or '*right of priority*'. The latter is generally calculated on the cumulated (real or forecasted) turnover during the period of the contract.

(3) Another right, the *right of reservation*, where there is a preliminary contract, before the actual franchise agreement, is directly linked to the initial franchise fee, without necessarily being part of it.

(4) A frequently ignored aspect of the initial franchise fee is its *security function* guaranteeing the proper execution of the contract by the franchisee. This means that if a franchisee delays or cancels the opening of his franchised business, he loses his initial franchise fee. On the other hand, the franchisor, having received the payment in advance, can be obliged by the franchisee to provide the anticipated services. Thus, the obligations arising from the initial franchise fee have a reciprocal character. This 'security' can act as a guarantee for the franchisor in several cases, such as:

— failure of the franchisee within the first months of opening;
— liquidation of the franchisee's assets.
— the franchisee leaves the chain before the end of the contract having obtained all the know-how.

Consequently, the initial franchise fee constitutes for both parties an obligation in the legal sense of the word.

(5) In the term initial franchise fee we can also often find the notion of *territorial exclusivity*. The initial franchise fee

can vary in certain cases according to the conceded territory and the potential market. At a first stage it has to be defined whether this exclusivity concerns just the brand or also the supplies. We can analyse the exclusivity during the contract as the renunciation by the franchisor of the direct exploitation of the existing clientele in a predefined zone. It comprises the totality of rights and the services mentioned in the contract. This means that the initial franchise fee is an intangible and temporary right which comes into force with each new contract and at each renewal of the contract. The value of the right to the franchise is established on the day of the signature of the contract and corresponds to x years of exclusivity. This way of perceiving the initial fee allows one to solve the question of the clientele at the end of the contract: the clients 'belong' to the franchisor only.

(6) To the other elements of the initial franchise fee it is appropriate to add what the French Chambre Nationale des Conseillers Financiers has called 'growth-margin of a franchise'. This margin should finance the development of the chain by permitting the franchisor to cover more quickly his intangible investment of putting the franchise package together and of financing the recruitment of his franchisees as well as the initial assistance. Two principles can be applied to calculate this margin:

— put the margin equal to zero for the first franchise, then raise it in the course of time to reflect the growing strength of the franchise (progressive margin);
— it should never be such as to result in an initial franchise fee that is difficult to pay with the cash flow of a one-year operation of the best pilot of the franchisor.

Although some experts claim that there is *no legal justification* for the initial franchise fee, others believe that it results form the responsibility of the franchisor with regard to the brand.

(7) Last but not least, the psychological aspect of the initial franchise fee: a franchise provides the security of a proven system. The franchisor/franchisee relationship places the latter in a position where he delegates problematic situations. Also, a franchise chain resembles a 'family', which does not only operate within the professional field. Therefore, we can say that the payment of the initial franchise fee corresponds to the acquisition of *psychological security*.

On the other hand, the initial franchise fee allows us to test the motivation of franchise-candidates or, in other words, guarantee the quality of new franchisees.

Despite the many different constituents of the initial franchise fee mentioned above, a great number of franchise experts interviewed around Europe believe that often franchisors ask for a fixed amount of money which depends on what their competitors ask and on what the franchisees are prepared to pay. This fact can be called the *market-acceptability* of the initial franchise fee. Nevertheless, the franchisor's objective should be to make profit from making other businesses work, not just from selling franchises. The objective can best be assured by keeping the initial investment as modest as possible.

The elements of the initial franchise fee mentioned here may overlap and are not necessarily mutually exclusive.

THE RESEARCH

The questions posed to the franchisors were the following:
(1) How would you define the initial franchise fee?
(2) What is the amount of your initial franchise fee?
(3) How was the initial franchise fee calculated?
(4) In what account do your franchisees normally keep record of the initial franchise fee?
(5) Has your initial franchise fee changed since it was first established?

Definition of the initial franchise fee (first question: 'How would you define the initial franchise fee?'):

The franchisors asked considered the initial franchise fee as a payment for:

In France:
(1) the transfer of know-how	32%
(2) the benefit of the image of the brand	25%
(3) the access to the franchise chain	18%
(4) initial services	15%
(5) the costs of the franchisor	7%
(6) the signature of the contract	4%

Other less frequent answers were: 'selection of the franchisee', 'training', 'a financial potential', 'a part of the turnover of the franchisor', and 'a mutual commitment'.

In the UK:
(1) the initial service	33%
(2) training/education	30%
(3) the (right to use a) name/image	24%
(4) the costs of the franchisor	16%
(5) the know-how	13%
(6) an exclusive territory	11%

Other less frequent answers were: 'a financial potential', 'the contract', 'access to the chain', 'selection of the franchisee', 'commission', and 'advertising'.

In Germany:
(1) the know-how	36%
(2=) the initial services	14%
(2=) the advertising	14%
(2=) an exclusive territory	14%
(3=) the training	11%
(3=) the system/concept	11%
(3=) equipment	11%

Other less frequent answers were: 'entrance fee', 'image/name', 'licence fee', 'potential turnover'.

(The total of percentages is not 100% because most franchisors gave more than one answer).

It should be stressed that the answers (1) to (6) correspond to the statements of the franchisors. Thus, the answers (1) and (4) for Britain and (4) and (5) for France, express different perceptions of the franchisors but can be considered as being identical.

The obvious interpretation is that for British franchisors the initial franchise fee represents something rather **tangible** (initial services and training), whereas for the French it is mostly **intangible** (know-how transfer, image and access to the franchise). It is surprising that Germans, although they may mean it indirectly, do not mention the word 'costs'. Interestingly, 9 per cent of British franchisors consider the initial franchise fee as a payment for a licence, whereas the Germans hardly ever referred to this element and the French did not mention it at all.

Amount of the initial franchise fee (second question: 'What is the amout of your initial franchise fee?'):
The answers to this question prove that whether or not franchisors ask for an initial franchise fee depends to a great extent on 'market acceptability'. Both in France and in Britain, where franchising is now widely accepted, more than 90 per cent of franchisors ask for an initial franchise fee (results of this study: 98 per cent for Britain and 91 per cent for France). In contrast, German franchising, despite its recent development, has not yet convinced (mainly the banks and economic authorities) that it is a serious alternative to conventional trade forms: only slightly more than two thirds of German franchisors ask for an initial franchise fee.

Some franchisors replied with a range of possible amounts for the initial franchise fee, these amounts depending on different factors. In such cases, the average of the ranges was calculated for the purpose of this study.

In the case of a hotel the initial franchise fee depended on the number of rooms; this particular case was not included in the calculation for the following table.

The initial franchise fees in Europe according to the franchisors (figures in ECU 1990)

	France ECU	*Britain* ECU	*Germany* ECU
average	11,100	12,497	8,985
maximum	45,000	37,500	37,500
minimum	1,875	3,750	500

The average initial franchise fee in France seems to be slightly lower than in Britain, although the time-lag of one year between the two surveys (inflation rate!) and the random factor should explain the difference. Taking also into consideration that the German survey was the last to be carried out, the initial franchise fee in Germany seems to be substantially lower than in the other two countries.

Contrary to the French situation where there seems to be a preference for the amount of 7,500 ECU (22 per cent of franchises) in Britain there is just a 'normal' concentration of 80 per cent of the fees between 3,750 ECU and 15,000 ECU.

The comparatively high maximum fee in France represents a hotel.

Calculation of the initial franchise fee (third question: 'How was the initial franchise fee calculated?'):
The franchisors claim to base the calculation of the initial franchise fee on the following factors:

In France:

costs of the franchisor	24%
cost of establishing the franchisee's business	14%
market acceptability (level of fees the market will bear)	14%
'technical assistance'	12%
initial training	8%
population of the territory	6%
forecast turnover of the franchise	5%
image of the brand-name	3%
launch advertising	2%
site selection	2%
cost of the selection of the franchisee	1%

14 per cent of French franchisors answered 'did not know' or 'did not want to answer'.

In the UK:

costs of the franchisor	33%
market acceptability	23%
cost of setting-up the franchisee's business	23%
initial training	21%
equipment	11%
launch advertising	4%
image of the brand-name	4%
territory	3%
cost of the franchise contract	1%

7.5 per cent of British franchisors answered 'did not know' or 'did not want to answer'.

In Germany:

costs	36%
initial services	24%
market acceptability	16%
potential turnover	16%
lump fee	16%
exclusive territory	8%
contract	4%
supplies	4%
profit	4%
advertising	4%

12 per cent of German franchisors answered 'did not know' or 'did not want to answer'.

The percentages indicated above correspond to the answers of the franchisors. However, for their interpretation, it should be taken into account that:

— many franchisors found it difficult to explain the calculation of their initial franchise fee and
— this question produces a delicate psychological situation for the franchisor (who feels obliged to give a serious impression and 'cannot' (does not want) to admit that there is

no scientific calculation behind his initial franchise fee. (Since all conversations were 'face to face', I can personally confirm this difficulty.) These observations were most obvious in France.

Accounting treatment of the initial franchise fee from the franchisee's point of view (fourth question: 'In what account do your franchisees normally keep record of the initial franchise fee?')

The items for training, market research, initial advertising and promotion, and stock should be expensed in the period the expenditure is incurred. Outfitting of premises will be capitalised as for fixed assets and written off over their useful lives. Payment for know-how and patents may be capitalised as an intangible asset and written off over its useful life. Purchased goodwill should be written off in the year it is incurred or amortised over its useful life' (KPMG Peat Marwick McLintock).

The answers of the franchisors to the fourth question were:

In France (original answers with approximate translation in English where necessary):

frais d'établissement (establishment costs)	15%
investissements (investments)	10%
frais généraux (general costs)	8%
redevance initiale forfaitaire (initial lump-sum fee)	6%
immobilisations (property costs)	5%
investissements amortissables	
investissements immateriels	
fonds de commerce	3%
immobilisations incorporelles	
charges d'exploitation (operating costs)	2%
honoraires (fees)	
concessions	
fournitures (supplies)	1%
publicité (advertising)	
amortissements (depreciation)	

In the UK:

capital	35%
profit & loss	13%
initial franchise fee	13%
management services fee	5%
general accounts	3%
goodwill	1%
legal fees	1%

In Germany (original answers with approximate translation in English where necessary):

Investitionen (investments)	31%
Werbekosten (advertising costs)	15%
Gründungskosten (establishment costs)	15%
Betriebskosten (operating costs)	15%
Anfangskapital (initial capital)	8%
Einstiegskosten (entrance costs)	8%
Geschäftskonto (company account)	8%
Goodwill	8%
Kosten (costs)	8%

Approximately one quarter of the franchisors in France and Britain did not know how their franchisees booked the initial franchise fee in their accounts. This percentage was 42% in Germany.

Clearly, having regard to the number of answers, there seems to be less confusion about how to book the initial franchise fee in the UK.

We can conclude that in all three countries the franchisors do not split the initial franchise fee into its different elements as advised by the experts and use one account only. (Only in 2–3 cases in each country was a differentiated accounting procedure mentioned.)

Again, the answers represent the answers of franchisors. It may well be (it is actually very probable according to some franchisors' statements) that when it comes to accounting, the franchisee company's accountant will do his job the way it should be done.

Development of the initial franchisee fee (fifth question: 'Has your initial franchise fee changed since it was first established?'):

Half of British franchisors have not yet changed their initial franchise fee, whereas the other half have done so. The equivalent percentages in France were 56% and 44% respectively. In Germany, only 20% of franchisors have changed their initial franchise fee since they first introduced it. This can be explained by the well-known price stability but also by the low acceptance of franchising in this country in comparison to its western neighbours.

In the case of a fee change all British and German franchisors had increased their fee, contrary to the French for whom the figures were:

increase: 83%   decrease: 11%   variation: 6%

The development of the initial franchise fee very often depended on the inflation rate and the market acceptability.

The (in the author's opinion) high percentage of non-change of the initial franchise fee can be explained by the fact that at franchise exhibitions, where this survey took place, many franchise companies are still only beginning their franchise development.

Clearly, in France, where a profit element in the initial franchise fee is not considered unethical, some franchisors seem to have had to readjust a 'too high' fee during their development. Their British and German counterparts seem to be more cautious and are therefore able – when they change it – to increase their initial franchise fee.

A final comment

A statistical analysis of the French data of this survey showed that there is no statistical correlation between the initial franchise fee and the following:

— the age of the franchise;
— the turnover of the franchise chain;
— the number of franchisees in the franchise chain.

The conclusion would therefore be that – despite the consideration of costs – the initial franchise fee is to a certain degree a psychological figure depending to a great extent on the level which the market will bear.

Whatever conclusion the individual reader draws from this survey, he or she should not judge initial franchise fees as 'expensive' or 'cheap' simply by considering the amounts. Only when the relation between performance and counter-performance of the franchise-partnership is fully considered, can such an evaluation be permitted.

CHAPTER 7

The Structure of International Franchising within the European Community — A Statistical Analysis

By MARK ABELL

As indicated in Chapter 5 above, there are few statistics of franchising in the EC available. It was therefore thought appropriate to conduct a survey of franchisors in the European Community to investigate their approach to the Single Market and their perception of the role and importance of franchising in it. Questionnaires were sent out in October and November 1990.

The questionnaire was sent to 1,281 franchisors in 10 member states listed in Appendix 19 (it was not possible to locate the addresses of franchisors in Greece, or to locate franchisors based in Luxembourg). They were located by using a variety of sources including the membership lists of the relevant franchise associations. 316 (i.e. 25 per cent) answered the questionnaire. A further 32 franchisors (i.e. 2.5 per cent) answered the questionnaires too late to be included in the results of this survey. In some member states such as the United Kingdom, the Netherlands and France, the return rate was much higher, whilst there was a very low rate of return from Denmark and no answers at all were received from Eire. Of those franchisors who responded, 125 (i.e. 39 per cent) were in the retail sector, 166 (i.e. 52 per cent) were in the service sector and 30 (i.e. 9 per cent) were in the fast food sector.

On a member state basis, the breakdown is as follows:

Belgium	Number	Percentage
Product:	7/10	70
Service:	3/10	30
Fast Food:	0/10	0

Denmark	Number	Percentage
Product:	2/3	66.6
Service:	1/3	33.3
Fast Food:	0/3	0.0

France	Number	Percentage
Product:	47/78	60.2
Service:	29/78	37.2
Fast Food:	2/78	2.6

Germany	Number	Percentage
Product:	9/36	25.0
Service:	26/36	42.3
Fast Food:	1/36	2.7

Italy	Number	Percentage
Product:	2/6	33.3
Service:	4/6	66.6
Fast Food:	0/6	0

The Netherlands	Number	Percentage
Product:	13/42	30.9
Service:	24/42	57.1
Fast Food:	5/42	11.9

Portugal	Number	Percentage
Product:	6/9	66.6
Service:	2/9	22.2
Fast Food:	1/9	11.1

Spain	Number	Percentage
Product:	12/26	46.1
Service:	8/26	30.8
Fast Food:	6/26	23.1

United Kingdom	Number	Percentage
Product:	23/106	21.7
Service:	69/106	65.1
Fast Food:	14/106	13.2

The full results of the survey are detailed at the end of this Chapter.

It should be noted that certain franchisors seemed to misunderstand parts of the questionnaire. For example, when answering questions 9, 10, 15 and 16, a small number of franchisors failed to list the order of their preferences and merely answered 'yes' or 'no'.

Other franchisors failed to answer all of the questions. These have been included in the results of the survey and account for any small inconsistencies to be found herein.

In analysing the figures, regard has been had firstly to the actual number of franchisors carrying out a particular activity (such as exporting its concept abroad) and secondly to the percentage of the national franchise industry that this figure represents. This second figure tends to indicate the degree to which national franchisors are 'international' in their corporate thinkings. However, too much reliance should not be placed upon the figures especially for countries which had a low return rate such as Denmark. The figures should be taken merely as an indicator of trends within the European Community.

The survey suggests that the UK (41 franchises) is the biggest EC exporter of franchises followed by France (37 franchises) and Germany (15 franchises), with Denmark (1 franchise) being the smallest exporter (Question 2).

These figures, expressed as a percentage of those franchisors who answered the questionnaire indicate that Belgium (50%), Italy (66.7%) and Portugal (66%) are the largest exporters.

In terms of the three sectors, product and service franchises are in general terms relatively equally balanced, although fast-food franchises seem to be less frequently exported.

As regards future plans for international development by franchisors that to date have no international operation, France (36), the UK (41), The Netherlands (20), Germany (16) and Spain (15), have the greatest number of franchisors, whilst Denmark (1) has the lowest number (Question 3).

Predictably, the overwhelming trend is for EC franchisors to export their franchises to other EC member states. France (36), Germany (11), the UK, (29) and The Netherlands (11) have exported the greatest number of franchises to other EC member states (Question 4). Percentage wise, Italy (66.7%) is the greatest exporter.

This trend is buttressed by the fact that of those franchisors who at present have no foreign operations the vast majority intend to open their first foreign franchise in another EC member state. Only in Germany (4), France (2), UK, (1) and Spain (1) did franchisors intend to open their first foreign franchise outside of the EC (Question 5).

Further, the majority of franchisors have or intend to have outlets in other EC countries — 76% in the UK, 84.6% in France, 66.6% in Germany, 73% in Spain, 88.8% in Portugal, 100% in Italy, 80% in Belgium, 66.6% in The Netherlands and 33.3% in Denmark (Question 6).

Opening outlets in other countries is predictably seen as more necessary in the better developed franchise markets such as France (41 within two years; 20 within five years; 2 within ten years), Germany (12 within two years; 9 within five years; 3 within ten years), The Netherlands (22 within two years; 8 within five years; 1 within ten years) and the UK (52 within two years; 22 within five years; 7 within ten years). Most franchisors seem to recognise the need to exploit the Single Market by 1996. (Question 7).

Most franchisors saw opening an outlet in another EC country as a high or medium priority (Question 8), particularly in Belgium (40% high; 50% medium; 10% low), France (53.8% high; 42.3 medium; 3.1% low) and Germany (19.4 high; 63.8% medium; 13.8% low), (despite the obvious opportunities in the Eastern part of Germany). Surprisingly, UK franchisors are somewhat less committed to international expansion (28.3% high; 21.6% medium; 37.7% low), whilst Italian franchisors seem to be the least committed (33.3% high; 16.7% medium; 50% low).

The appointment of a sub-franchisor/master franchisee seems to be the most popular first choice for international expansion, particularly amongst German franchisors (72.2%), UK franchisors (52.3%) and Portuguese franchisors (77.7%). Direct franchising should, it is often suggested, become more common in the Single Market. This is certainly borne out by the responses from Italy where 41.7% stated it to be their preferred first choice. It is also popular in Spain where 23% and Belgium where 30% stated it to be their preferred first choice. It is suggested that this may well be because the preferred target country is both geographically and culturally close to the franchisor's member state. For example, as regards Italy, France or Spain; Spain — Portugal, France or Italy; and Belgium — France, Luxembourg or The Netherlands (Question 9).

This suggestion is partly borne out by the responses to Question 10. Out of the Spanish franchisors who responded to the questionnaire, the preferred EC country to enter first was 42.3% Portugal, 26.9% France and 26.9% Italy. In Belgium 40% preferred France, 10% The Netherlands and 10% Luxembourg. In Italy 50% preferred France. In choosing the preferred target member state franchisors seem to take account of the country's geographical/cultural proximity and the state of its economy.

Most franchisors (Question 11) seem to think that they are more likely to enter another member state because they are approached by a potential partner, rather than as a result of a planned campaign. The notable exception to this is Germany, where 52.7% thought a planned campaign more likely compared to 22.2% which thought an approach by a potential partner to be more likely. The rest of the German franchisors who answered the questionnaire expressed no opinion.

Most franchisors (Question 12) thought that the Single Market was relevant to franchising with the Dutch being the most sceptical (33.3% thought that it was not relevant).

Likewise, most franchisors (Question 13), thought that 1992 and the Single Market was relevant to their own particular franchise business, although again the Dutch (42.8% answered 'no') were the least convinced followed by the Italians (33.3% answered 'no') and the UK, (33.9% answered 'no').

The multiplicity of languages within the EC could quite easily create an invisible barrier to the success of the Single Market. The need to speak the language of the target member state (Question 14) is perceived by the majority of franchisors to be very important, although this opinion is held by fewer German franchisors (25%) and UK franchisors (36.7%) than other franchisors (e.g. 80% in Belgium). Whether or not the reason for this is the importance of a third language such as English is not known.

Lawyers, consultants, accountants and bankers in the franchisors' member state are generally perceived not to be well-equipped to help franchisors enter into other member states. This is particularly so in Portugal (77.7% of franchisors) and Italy (66.7% of the franchisors). Not all franchisors felt able to comment on this question. (Question 15).

The biggest problem in trying to open up an outlet in another EC member state is generally perceived to be the opportunity to meet suitable partners. This is particularly so in Portugal (88.8%), Germany (52.7%), UK (38.6%) and France (32%) (Question 16).

Finance was perceived as the biggest problem by most franchisors in Italy (66.7%) but not by any Portuguese or Danish franchisors and by only 4.7% in the UK.

The market differences were perceived as the biggest problem by most Dutch franchisors (52.3%), by 33% in the UK, 38.8% in Germany, 30% in Belgium, 33.3% in Denmark and 24.3% in France. This, it is suggested, reflects a fairly realistic view of the Single Market.

The biggest advantage of opening up an outlet in another EC member state is perceived to be increased profit by most franchisors, whilst increased prestige is seen as being the biggest advantage by another large group of franchisors (Question 17).

Surprisingly, the majority of franchisors who responded to the questionnaire believe that franchising should be regulated by law; 88.8% in Portugal, 57.6% in Spain, 85.7% in The Netherlands, 100% in Denmark, 65% in the UK, 66.7% in France, 69.4% in Germany and 50% in Belgium. This stand is directly opposite to the view of all national franchise associations (except for the French) and the European Franchise Federation. Only in Italy did the majority of franchisors answering the questionnaire think that franchising should not be regulated by law (83.3%). (Question 18).

If franchising were to be regulated by law, the vast majority of franchisors answering the questionnaire would prefer it to be regulated by the EC Commission rather than individual member states (Question 19).

Finally, the vast majority of franchisors answering the questionnaire believe that franchising is going to be an important economic force in the Single Market (Question 20). Only Italy, France, UK, and Spain have a small number of doubters.

In conclusion, the results of this survey are a useful indicator of the general trends in European Franchising. Viewed in the context of other market and industry knowledge, they will hopefully be of use to those involved in franchising in the EC but are not a definitive irrefutable statement.

The figures suggest that franchising will continue to grow as a method of trade between EC member states and that franchisors are far more interested in exporting their concepts to other parts of the European Community than to North America and other markets.

Franchisors are fairly confident about the importance of franchising within the Single Market, but surprisingly seem to believe that legal regulation by the EC Commission rather than voluntary regulation is in the best interests of their industry.

FRANCHISING AND 1992 QUESTIONNAIRE

1 Is your franchise a service, product or fast-food franchise?
Service/Product/Fast-food

2 Do you have outlets in other countries?
Yes/No

3 If not, do you intend to have outlets in other countries?
Yes/No/N.A.

4 Do you have outlets in other EC countries?
Yes/No/N.A.

5 If you have no outlets in other countries but intend to open one in the future, is the first one likely to be in the EC or not?
EC/Non-EC/N.A.

6 Do you have or intend to have outlets in other EC countries?
Yes/No

7 If yes, when will you open one — in the next two, five or ten years?
Two/Five/Ten years

8 Is opening an outlet in another EC country a high, medium or low priority?
High/Medium/Low

9 How would you prefer to enter another EC country? (Please number preferences 1—6)
Master franchise/Subsidiary/Joint venture/
Direct franchising/Buying a competitor in the country/
Other

10 Please state in order of preference the EC countries you would like to enter. (Please number countries 1—12 in order of preference)
[1st, 2nd, 3rd and 4th choices invited]

11 If you enter another EC country, is it likely to be because of a planned campaign or because a potential partner approaches you?
Planned campaign/Approach by potential partner

12 In your opinion, is 1992 and the single market relevant to franchising?
Yes/No

13 How important is speaking the language of a member state you wish to enter?
Very important/Important/Unimportant

15 Do you think that the lawyers, consultants, accountants and bankers in your country are properly equipped to help you enter another EC country?
Yes/No/Undecided

16 What is the biggest problem in trying to open up an outlet in another EC country? (Please number 1—4 in order of difficulty)
Language/Finance/Market differences/
Opportunity to meet suitable partners

17 What is the biggest advantage of opening up an outlet in another EC country? (Please number 1—6 in order of advantage)
[1st, 2nd, 3rd, 4th, 5th and 6th choices invited]
Keeping ahead of competition at home/
Attacking market of potential competitors/
Economy of scale/Other

18 Should franchising be regulated by law?
Yes/No/Don't know

19 If franchising is regulated by law, should it be by the EC Commission or by individual member state governments?
EC/member state/Don't know

20 In your opinion, is franchising going to be an important economic force in the single market?
Yes/No/Don't know

LIST OF ABBREVIATIONS

Industry Type

TL	Total
S	Service
F	Fast food
P	Product

Problems

Lang	Language
Fin	Finance
MD	Market differences
Opp	Opportunity to meet suitable partners

Preferred Mode of Entry

MF	Master franchise
Sub	Subsidiary
JV	Joint venture
DF	Direct franchising
Buy	Buying a competitor in the country

Advantages

Inc Prof	Increased profit
Inc Pres	Increased prestige
K Ahead	Keeping ahead of competition at home
Econ	Economy of scale
Others	Others

Countries

GB	Great Britain (United Kingdom)
F	France
E	Spain
P	Portugal
I	Italy
GR	Greece

D	Germany
DK	Denmark
L	Luxembourg
NL	Netherlands
B	Belgium
EIR	Republic of Ireland

FRANCHISING AND 1992

Country: United Kingdom (GB)

Type	Resp	TL = 106 N	TL = 106 %	S = 69 N	S = 69 %	P = 23 N	P = 23 %	F = 14 N	F = 14 %
QUESTION 1	S	69	65.1	N/A	N/A	N/A	N/A	N/A	N/A
	P	23	21.7	N/A	N/A	N/A	N/A	N/A	N/A
	F	14	13.2	N/A	N/A	N/A	N/A	N/A	N/A
QUESTION 2	Yes	41	38.6	26	37.6	10	43.5	8	57.1
	No	62	58.5	43	62.3	13	56.5	6	42.9
QUESTION 3	Yes	41	38.6	31	44.9	6	26.1	4	28.6
	No	20	18.8	11	15.9	7	30.4	2	14.3
	N/A	44	41.5	26	37.6	10	43.5	8	57.1
QUESTION 4	Yes	29	27.4	17	24.6	7	30.4	5	35.7
	No	15	14.2	9	13.0	3	13.0	3	21.4
	N/A	62	58.5	43	62.3	13	56.5	6	42.9
QUESTION 5	EC	42	39.6	33	47.8	5	21.7	4	28.6
	Non-EC	1	0.9	0	0.0	1	4.3	0	0.0
	N/A	62	58.4	35	50.7	17	73.9	10	71.4
QUESTION 6	Yes	81	76.4	56	81.1	15	65.2	10	71.4
	No	23	21.6	11	15.9	8	34.8	4	28.6
QUESTION 7	2 Years	52	49.0	34	49.2	11	47.8	7	50.0
	5 Years	22	20.7	17	24.6	3	13.0	2	14.2
	10 Years	7	6.6	5	7.2	1	4.3	1	7.1
QUESTION 8	High	30	28.3	19	27.5	7	30.4	4	28.5
	Medium	23	21.6	16	23.1	4	17.3	3	21.4
	Low	40	37.7	26	37.6	8	34.7	6	42.8

Type		TL = 106		S = 69		P = 23		F = 14	
	Resp	N	%	N	%	N	%	N	%
QUESTION 9	MF	55.5	52.3	42.5	61.5	10	43.4	3	21.4
	Sub	5.5	5.1	1.5	2.1	3	13.0	1	7.1
	JV	14.5	13.6	9.5	13.7	3	13.0	2	14.2
	DF	12.5	11.7	7.5	10.8	1	4.3	4	28.5
	Buy	2.0	1.8	1.0	1.4	1	4.3	0	0.0
	Other	2.0	1.8	0.0	0.0	0	0.0	2	14.2
	1st Pref								
QUESTION 10	GB	N/A	N/A	N/A	N/A	N/A	N/A	N/A	N/A
	F	27	25.4	24	34.7	3	13.0	0	0.0
	E	7	6.6	4	5.7	1	4.3	2	14.2
	P	2	1.8	1	1.4	0	0.0	0	0.0
	I	1	0.9	1	1.4	0	0.0	0	0.0
	GR	0	0.0	0	0.0	0	0.0	0	0.0
	D	23	21.6	13	18.8	7	30.4	3	21.4
	DK	0	0.0	0	0.0	0	0.0	0	0.0
	L	0	0.0	0	0.0	0	0.0	0	0.0
	NL	5	4.7	4	5.7	1	4.3	1	7.1
	B	2	1.8	2	2.8	0	0.0	0	0.0
	EIR	17	16.0	8	11.5	4	17.3	5	35.7
	2nd Pref								
QUESTION 10	GB	N/A	N/A	N/A	N/A	N/A	N/A	N/A	N/A
	F	10	9.4	6	8.6	2	8.6	2	14.2
	E	10	9.4	6	8.6	2	8.6	2	14.2
	P	1	0.9	1	1.4	0	0.0	0	0.0
	I	7	6.6	5	7.2	2	8.6	0	0.0
	GR	0	0.0	0	0.0	0	0.0	0	0.0
	D	22	20.7	18	26.0	2	8.6	2	14.2
	DK	1	0.9	1	1.4	0	0.0	0	0.0
	L	0	0.0	0	0.0	0	0.0	0	0.0
	NL	15	14.1	9	13.0	4	17.3	2	14.2
	B	9	8.4	6	8.6	2	8.6	1	7.1
	EIR	3	2.8	2	2.8	1	4.3	0	0.0
	3rd Pref								
QUESTION 10	GB	N/A	N/A	N/A	N/A	N/A	N/A	N/A	N/A
	F	11	10.3	7	10.1	2	8.6	2	14.2
	E	6	5.6	6	8.6	0	0.0	0	0.0
	P	1	0.9	1	1.4	0	0.0	0	0.0
	I	4	3.7	3	4.3	0	0.0	1	7.1
	GR	2	1.8	0	0.0	1	4.3	1	7.1
	D	8	7.5	5	7.2	3	13.0	0	0.0
	DK	4	3.7	3	4.3	1	4.3	0	0.0
	L	3	2.8	3	4.3	0	0.0	0	0.0
	NL	15	14.1	13	18.8	1	4.3	1	7.1
	B	16	15.0	8	11.5	5	21.7	3	21.4
	EIR	4	3.7	2	2.8	2	8.6	0	0.0
	4th Pref								
QUESTION 10	GB	N/A	N/A	N/A	N/A	N/A	N/A	N/A	N/A
	F	6	5.6	7	10.1	1	4.3	0	0.0
	E	3	2.8	6	8.6	1	4.3	0	0.0
	P	3	2.8	1	1.4	0	0.0	0	0.0
	I	9	8.4	3	4.3	1	4.3	0	0.0
	GR	2	1.8	0	0.0	0	0.0	2	14.2
	D	10	9.4	5	7.2	2	8.6	1	7.1
	DK	9	8.4	3	4.3	3	13.0	2	14.2
	L	3	2.8	3	4.3	1	4.3	1	7.1
	NL	6	5.6	13	18.8	2	8.6	1	7.1
	B	9	8.4	8	11.5	1	4.3	0	0.0
	EIR	9	8.4	2	2.8	1	4.3	1	7.1

Type	Resp	TL = 106		S = 69		P = 23		F = 14	
		N	%	N	%	N	%	N	%
QUESTION 11	P1 Cam	57.5	54.2	39.5	57.2	13.5	58.6	4.5	32.1
	Approach	35.5	33.4	23.5	34.0	4.5	19.5	7.5	53.5
QUESTION 12	Yes	86	81.1	60	86.9	17	73.9	9	64.2
	No	16	15.0	9	13.0	4	17.3	3	21.4
QUESTION 13	Yes	69	65.0	47	68.1	14	60.8	8	57.1
	No	36	33.9	22	31.8	8	34.7	6	42.9
QUESTION 14	V Important	39	36.7	28	40.5	7	30.4	4	28.5
	Important	51	48.1	32	46.3	11	47.8	8	57.1
	Unimportant	11	10.3	7	10.1	3	13.0	1	7.1
QUESTION 15	Yes	28	26.4	17	24.6	6	26.0	5	35.7
	No	34	32.0	23	33.3	5	21.7	6	42.9
	Undecided	41	38.6	27	39.1	11	47.8	3	21.4
QUESTION 16	Lang	11	10.3	9	13.0	1	4.3	1	7.1
	Fin	5	4.7	5	7.2	0	0.0	0	0.0
	MD	35	33.0	19	27.5	8	34.7	8	57.1
	Opp	41	38.6	30	43.4	9	39.1	2	14.2
	1st Pref								
QUESTION 17	Inc Prof	51	48.1	32	46.3	12	52.1	7	50.0
	Inc Pres	6	5.6	5	7.2	0	0.0	1	7.1
	K Ahead	11	10.3	10	14.4	1	4.3	0	0.0
	Attack	15	14.1	10	14.4	3	13.0	2	14.2
	Econ	2	1.8	1	1.4	0	0.0	1	7.1
	Others	4	3.7	2	2.8	1	4.3	1	7.1
	2nd Pref								
QUESTION 17	Inc Prof	22	20.7	19	27.5	1	4.3	2	14.2
	Inc Pres	13	12.2	12	17.3	1	4.3	0	0.0
	K Ahead	18	16.9	11	15.9	2	8.6	5	35.7
	Attack	20	18.8	12	17.3	6	26.0	2	14.2
	Econ	3	2.8	3	4.3	0	0.0	0	0.0
	Others	2	1.6	1	1.4	1	4.3	0	0.0
	3rd Pref								
QUESTION 17	Inc Prof	9	8.4	9	13.0	0	0.0	0	0.0
	Inc Pres	11	10.3	6	8.6	2	8.6	3	21.4
	K Ahead	23	21.6	15	21.7	5	21.7	3	21.4
	Attack	17	16.0	13	18.8	1	4.3	3	21.4
	Econ	9	8.4	7	10.1	2	8.6	0	0.0
	Others	0	0.0	0	0.0	0	0.0	0	0.0
	4th Pref								
QUESTION 17	Inc Prof	3	2.8	1	1.4	1	4.3	1	7.1
	Inc Pres	25	23.5	17	24.6	4	17.3	4	28.5
	K Ahead	15	14.1	12	17.3	2	8.6	1	7.1
	Attack	12	11.3	10	14.4	0	0.0	2	14.2
	Econ	10	9.4	6	8.6	3	13.0	1	7.1
	Others	0	0.0	0	0.0	0	0.0	0	0.0
	5th Pref								
QUESTION 17	Inc Prof	1	0.9	1	1.4	0	0.0	0	0.0
	Inc Pres	12	11.3	8	11.5	3	13.0	1	7.1
	K Ahead	2	1.8	2	2.8	0	0.0	0	0.0
	Attack	7	6.6	4	5.7	2	8.6	1	7.1
	Econ	37	34.9	27	39.1	4	17.3	6	42.8
	Others	4	3.7	3	4.3	1	4.3	0	0.0

Type	Resp	TL = 106 N	TL = 106 %	S = 69 N	S = 69 %	P = 23 N	P = 23 %	F = 14 N	F = 14 %
QUESTION 17	**6th Pref**								
	Inc Prof	0	0.0	0	0.0	0	0.0	0	0.0
	Inc Pres	2	1.8	2	2.8	0	0.0	0	0.0
	K Ahead	0	0.0	0	0.0	0	0.0	0	0.0
	Attack	2	1.8	1	1.4	1	4.3	0	0.0
	Econ	2	1.8	1	1.4	1	4.3	0	0.0
	Others	57	53.7	41	59.4	8	34.7	8	57.1
QUESTION 18	Yes	69	65.0	45	65.2	14	60.9	10	71.4
	No	25	23.5	14	20.2	9	39.1	2	14.3
	Don't Know	10	9.4	8	11.5	0	0.0	2	14.3
QUESTION 19	EC	64	60.4	41	59.4	14	60.9	9	64.3
	MS	28	26.4	19	27.5	4	17.4	5	35.7
	Don't Know	14	13.2	9	13.0	5	21.7	0	0.0
QUESTION 20	Yes	89	83.9	58	84.0	21	91.3	10	71.4
	No	6	5.6	5	7.2	0	0.0	1	7.1
	Don't Know	9	8.4	4	5.7	2	8.6	3	21.4

FRANCHISING AND 1992

Country: France (F)

Type	Resp	TL = 78 N	TL = 78 %	S = 29 N	S = 29 %	P = 47 N	P = 47 %	F = 2 N	F = 2 %
QUESTION 1	S	29	37.1	N/A	N/A	N/A	N/A	N/A	N/A
	P	47	60.2	N/A	N/A	N/A	N/A	N/A	N/A
	F	2	2.5			N/A	N/A	N/A	N/A
QUESTION 2	Yes	37	47.4	12	41.3	24	51.1	1	50.0
	No	40	52.6	17	58.6	23	48.9	1	50.0
QUESTION 3	Yes	36	46.1	13	44.8	21	44.6	1	50.0
	No	7	8.9	2	6.8	1	2.1	0	0.0
	N/A	0	0.0	0	0.0	0	0.0	0	0.0
QUESTION 4	Yes	40	51.3	17	58.6	22	46.8	1	50.0
	No	28	35.9	6	7.6	18	38.2	1	50.0
	N/A	0	0.0	0	0.0	0	0.0	0	0.0
QUESTION 5	EC	40	51.3	15	51.7	24	51.0	1	50.0
	Non-EC	2	2.6	0	0.0	18	38.2	0	0.0
	Other	4	0.0	1	3.4	3	6.3	0	0.0
QUESTION 6	Yes	66	84.6	26	89.6	26	55.3	1	50.0
	No	6	8.9	1	3.4	4	8.5	1	50.0
QUESTION 7	2 Years	44	56.4	15	51.7	29	61.7	0	0.0
	5 Years	14	17.9	8	27.5	6	12.7	0	0.0
	10 Years	2	2.6	1	3.4	0	0.0	1	50.0
QUESTION 8	High	39	50.0	15	51.7	24	51.0	0	0.0
	Medium	36	46.2	13	44.8	21	44.6	2	100.0
	Low	1	1.3	1	3.4	0	0.0	0	0.0

Type	Resp	TL = 78		S = 29		P = 47		F = 2	
		N	%	N	%	N	%	N	%
QUESTION 9	MF	39	50.0	16	55.1	22	46.8	1	50.0
	Sub	13	16.7	2	6.8	10	21.2	1	50.0
	JV	17	21.8	8	27.5	9	19.1	0	0.0
	DF	2	2.6	0	0.0	2	4.2	0	0.0
	Buy	1	1.3	0	0.0	1	2.1	0	0.0
	Other	6	7.7	2	6.8	4	8.5	0	0.0
	1st Pref								
QUESTION 10	GB	6	7.7	2	6.8	4	8.5	0	0.0
	F	3	3.8	1	3.4	2	4.2	0	0.0
	E	18	23.1	6	20.6	12	25.5	0	0.0
	P	2	2.6	0	0.0	2	4.2	0	0.0
	I	6	7.7	1	3.4	5	10.6	0	0.0
	GR	1	1.3	1	3.4	0	0.0	0	0.0
	D	16	20.5	7	24.1	9	19.1	0	0.0
	DK	2	2.5	1	3.4	1	2.1	0	0.0
	L	5	6.4	2	6.8	3	6.3	0	0.0
	NL	4	5.1	1	3.4	2	4.2	1	50.0
	B	13	16.7	8	27.5	5	10.6	0	0.0
	EIR	1	1.3	1	3.4	0	0.0	0	0.0
	2nd Pref								
QUESTION 10	GB	10	12.8	3	10.3	7	14.8	0	0.0
	F	0	0.0	0	0.0	0	0.0	0	0.0
	E	9	11.5	3	10.3	6	12.7	0	0.0
	P	2	2.6	2	6.8	0	0.0	0	0.0
	I	11	14.1	3	10.3	8	17.0	0	0.0
	GR	0	0.0	0	0.0	0	0.0	0	0.0
	D	5	6.4	3	10.3	2	4.2	0	0.0
	DK	0	0.0	0	0.0	0	0.0	0	0.0
	L	5	6.4	3	10.3	1	2.1	1	50.0
	NL	3	3.8	2	6.8	1	2.1	0	0.0
	B	5	6.4	3	10.3	2	4.2	0	0.0
	EIR	0	0.0	0	0.0	0	0.0	0	0.0
	3rd Pref								
QUESTION 10	GB	6	7.6	5	17.2	1	2.1	0	0.0
	F	0	0.0	0	0.0	0	0.0	0	0.0
	E	7	9.0	3	10.3	4	8.5	0	0.0
	P	4	5.1	2	6.8	2	4.2	0	0.0
	I	4	5.1	1	3.4	3	6.3	0	0.0
	GR	1	1.3	1	3.4	0	0.0	0	0.0
	D	8	10.3	2	6.8	6	12.7	0	0.0
	DK	1	1.3	0	0.0	0	0.0	1	50.0
	L	5	6.4	2	6.8	3	6.3	0	0.0
	NL	3	3.8	3	10.3	0	0.0	0	0.0
	B	8	10.2	3	10.3	5	10.6	0	0.0
	EIR	0	0.0	0	0.0	0	0.0	0	0.0
	4th Pref								
QUESTION 10	GB	1	1.3	1	3.4	0	0.0	0	0.0
	F	0	0.0	0	0.0	0	0.0	0	0.0
	E	0	0.0	0	0.0	0	0.0	0	0.0
	P	0	0.0	0	0.0	0	0.0	0	0.0
	I	1	1.3	0	0.0	0	0.0	1	50.0
	GR	3	3.8	1	3.4	2	4.2	0	0.0
	D	0	0.0	0	0.0	0	0.0	0	0.0
	DK	1	1.3	0	0.0	1	2.1	0	0.0
	L	1	1.3	0	0.0	1	2.1	0	0.0
	NL	1	1.3	0	0.0	1	2.1	0	0.0
	B	0	0.0	0	0.0	0	0.0	0	0.0
	EIR	2	2.6	1	3.4	1	2.1	0	0.0

Type	Resp	TL = 78		S = 29		P = 47		F = 2	
		N	%	N	%	N	%	N	%
QUESTION 11	P1 Cam	19	24.4	6	20.6	13	27.6	0	0.0
	Approach	58	74.4	23	79.3	33	70.2	2	100.0
QUESTION 12	Yes	73	93.6	27	93.1	44	93.6	2	100.0
	No	5	6.4	2	6.8	3	6.3	0	0.0
QUESTION 13	Yes	70	89.7	27	93.1	41	87.2	2	100.0
	No	8	10.2	2	6.8	6	12.8	0	0.0
QUESTION 14	V Important	38	48.7	16	55.1	21	44.6	1	50.0
	Important	30	38.5	11	37.9	18	38.2	1	50.0
	Unimportant	4	5.1	2	6.8	2	4.2	0	0.0
QUESTION 15	Yes	35	44.9	10	34.4	24	51.0	1	50.0
	No	36	46.1	16	55.1	19	40.4	1	50.0
	Undecided	0	0.0	0	0.0	0	0.0	0	0.0
QUESTION 16	Lang	15	19.2	6	20.6	8	17.0	1	50.0
	Fin	16	20.5	7	24.1	9	19.1	0	0.0
	MD	16	20.5	6	20.6	10	21.2	0	0.0
	Opp	25	32.1	8	27.5	16	34.0	1	50.0
QUESTION 17	Inc Prof	21	26.9	9	31.0	12	25.5	0	0.0
	Inc Pres	9	11.5	3	10.3	6	12.7	0	0.0
	K Ahead	12	15.4	5	17.2	7	14.8	0	0.0
	Attack	12	15.4	3	10.3	8	17.0	1	50.0
	Econ	3	3.8	0	0.0	2	4.2	1	50.0
	Others	12	15.4	6	20.6	6	12.7	0	0.0
QUESTION 18	Yes	55	70.5	20	68.9	34	72.3	1	50.0
	No	12	15.4	6	20.6	5	10.6	1	50.0
	Don't Know	10	12.8	3	10.3	7	14.8	0	0.0
QUESTION 19	EC	55	70.5	20	68.9	34	72.3	1	50.0
	MS	9	11.5	3	10.3	5	10.6	1	50.0
	Don't Know	13	16.7	6	20.6	7	14.8	0	0.0
QUESTION 20	Yes	66	84.6	26	89.6	39	82.9	1	50.0
	No	3	3.8	2	6.8	1	2.1	0	0.0
	Don't Know	9	11.5	1	3.4	7	14.8	1	50.0

FRANCHISING AND 1992

Country: Spain (E)

Type	Resp	TL = 26		S = 8		P = 12		F = 6	
		N	%	N	%	N	%	N	%
QUESTION 1	S	8	30.8	N/A	N/A	N/A	N/A	N/A	N/A
	P	12	46.1	N/A	N/A	N/A	N/A	N/A	N/A
	F	6	26.9	N/A	N/A	N/A	N/A	N/A	N/A
QUESTION 2	Yes	9	34.5	2	25	4	33.3	3	50.0
	No	15	57.6	6	75	8	66.6	3	50.0
QUESTION 3	Yes	15	57.6	5	62.5	10	83.3	3	50.0
	No	2	7.7	2	25.0	1	8.3	0	0.0
	N/A	2	7.7	0	0.0	0	0.0	2	33.3

Type	Resp	TL = 26		S = 8		P = 12		F = 6	
		N	%	N	%	N	%	N	%
QUESTION 4	Yes	9	34.5	2	25	4	33.3	3	50.0
	No	15	57.6	6	75	8	66.6	3	50.0
	N/A	0	0.0	0	0.0	0	0.0	0	0.0
QUESTION 5	EC	15	57.6	5	62.5	9	75	3	50.0
	Non-EC	1	3.8	0	0.0	2	16.6	0	0.0
	Other	6	23.0	2	25.0	1	8.3	3	50.0
QUESTION 6	Yes	19	73.0	6	75.0	9	75.0	5	83.3
	No	5	19.0	2	25.0	3	12.0	0	0.0
QUESTION 7	2 Years	8	30.8	2	25.0	4	33.3	2	33.3
	5 Years	9	34.5	5	62.5	4	33.3	3	50.0
	10 Years	3	11.5	1	12.5	1	8.3	0	0.0
QUESTION 8	High	8	30.8	3	37.5	4	33.3	1	16.6
	Medium	8	30.8	2	25.0	4	33.3	4	66.6
	Low	5	19.0	2	25.0	4	33.3	0	0.0
QUESTION 9	MF	11	42.3	5	62.5	5	41.6	3	50.0
	Sub	2	7.7	1	12.5	2	16.6	0	0.0
	JV	2	7.7	1	12.5	1	8.3	1	16.6
	DF	6	23.0	1	12.5	3	25.0	1	16.6
	Buy	1	3.8	1	12.5	1	8.3	1	16.6
	Other	2	7.7	0	0.0	2	16.6	0	0.0
	1st Pref								
QUESTION 10	GB	1	2.8	0	0.0	0	0.0	1	16.6
	F	5	19.2	1	12.5	3	25.0	1	16.6
	E	6	23.1	2	25.0	2	16.6	2	33.3
	P	9	34.6	5	62.5	2	16.6	2	33.3
	I	1	3.8	0	0.0	1	8.3	0	0.0
	GR	0	0.0	0	0.0	0	0.0	0	0.0
	D	4	15.4	0	0.0	4	33.3	0	0.0
	DK	0	0.0	0	0.0	0	0.0	0	0.0
	L	0	0.0	0	0.0	0	0.0	0	0.0
	NL	0	0.0	0	0.0	0	0.0	0	0.0
	B	0	0.0	0	0.0	0	0.0	0	0.0
	EIR	0	0.0	0	0.0	0	0.0	0	0.0
	2nd Pref								
QUESTION 10	GB	5	19.0	0	0.0	3	25.0	1	16.6
	F	10	38.4	3	37.5	6	50.0	2	33.3
	E	0	0.0	0	0.0	0	0.0	0	0.0
	P	1	3.8	1	12.5	1	8.3	0	0.0
	I	1	3.8	0	0.0	0	0.0	1	16.6
	GR	0	0.0	0	0.0	0	0.0	0	0.0
	D	2	7.7	1	12.5	0	0.0	0	0.0
	DK	2	7.7	0	0.0	1	8.3	0	0.0
	L	0	0.0	0	0.0	0	0.0	0	0.0
	NL	0	0.0	0	0.0	0	0.0	0	0.0
	B	2	7.7	1	12.5	1	8.3	1	16.6
	EIR	1	3.8	0	0.0	0	0.0	0	0.0
	3rd Pref								
QUESTION 10	GB	1	3.8	0	0.0	1	8.3	1	16.6
	F	1	3.8	0	0.0	1	8.3	0	0.0
	E	1	3.8	0	0.0	1	8.3	0	0.0
	P	2	7.7	1	12.5	1	8.3	0	0.0
	I	5	19.0	0	0.0	3	25.0	1	16.6
	GR	0	0.0	0	0.0	0	0.0	0	0.0

Type	Resp	TL = 26		S = 8		P = 12		F = 6	
		N	%	N	%	N	%	N	%
	3rd Pref *contd*								
QUESTION 10	D	4	15.4	0	0.0	2	16.6	2	33.3
	DK	0	0.0	0	0.0	0	0.0	0	0.0
	L	0	0.0	0	0.0	0	0.0	0	0.0
	NL	2	7.7	2	25.0	1	8.3	0	0.0
	B	2	7.7	0	0.0	1	8.3	1	16.6
	EIR	0	0.0	0	0.0	0	0.0	0	0.0
	4th Pref								
QUESTION 10	GB	0	0.0	0	0.0	0	0.0	1	16.6
	F	2	7.7	1	12.5	1	8.3	1	16.6
	E	0	0.0	0	0.0	0	0.0	0	0.0
	P	1	3.8	0	0.0	1	8.3	0	0.0
	I	1	3.8	0	0.0	1	8.3	0	0.0
	GR	2	7.7	0	0.0	2	16.6	1	16.6
	D	0	0.0	0	0.0	0	0.0	0	0.0
	DK	1	3.8	0	0.0	1	8.3	1	16.6
	L	1	3.8	1	12.5	0	0.0	0	0.0
	NL	2	7.7	1	12.5	1	8.3	0	0.0
	B	0	0.0	0	0.0	0	0.0	0	0.0
	EIR	1	3.8	1	12.5	1	8.3	0	0.0
QUESTION 11	P1 Cam	12	46.1	4	50.0	6	50.0	4	66.6
	Approach	10	38.4	3	37.5	6	50.0	1	16.6
QUESTION 12	Yes	21	80.6	6	75.0	12	100.0	4	66.6
	No	3	11.5	0	0.0	0	0.0	2	33.3
QUESTION 13	Yes	16	61.5	7	87.5	9	75.0	3	50.0
	No	6	23.0	1	12.5	3	25.0	2	33.3
QUESTION 14	V Important	13	50.0	5	62.5	6	50.0	4	66.6
	Important	9	34.5	3	37.5	6	50.0	1	16.6
	Unimportant	2	7.7	0	0.0	0	0.0	1	16.6
QUESTION 15	Yes	5	19.0	2	25.0	4	33.3	1	16.6
	No	14	53.9	5	62.5	5	41.6	3	50.0
	Undecided	5	19.0	1	12.5	3	25.0	2	33.3
QUESTION 16	Lang	10	38.4	3	37.5	6	50.0	3	50.0
	Fin	3	11.5	1	12.5	3	25.0	1	16.6
	MD	5	19.0	2	25.0	3	25.0	0	0.0
	Opp	9	34.5	1	12.5	5	41.6	1	16.6
QUESTION 17	Inc Prof	7	26.9	2	25.0	3	25.0	1	16.6
	Inc Pres	1	3.8	0	0.0	1	8.3	0	0.0
	K Ahead	4	15.4	2	25.0	1	8.3	1	16.6
	Attack	7	26.9	0	0.0	3	25.0	1	16.6
	Econ	5	19.0	2	25.0	4	33.3	2	33.3
	Others	3	11.5	1	12.5	2	16.6	1	16.6
QUESTION 18	Yes	15	57.6	4	50.0	10	83.3	4	66.6
	No	9	34.5	3	37.5	2	16.6	1	16.6
	Don't Know	2	7.7	1	12.5	0	0.0	1	16.6
QUESTION 19	EC	22	84.6	8	100.0	9	75.0	5	83.3
	MS	1	3.8	0	0.0	1	8.3	0	0.0
	Don't Know	3	11.5	0	0.0	2	16.6	1	16.6
QUESTION 20	Yes	21	80.6	7	87.5	12	100.0	4	66.6
	No	1	3.8	0	0.0	0	0.0	1	16.6
	Don't Know	3	11.5	1	12.5	0	0.0	1	16.6

FRANCHISING AND 1992

Country: Portugal (P)

Type	Resp	TL = 9 N	TL = 9 %	S = 2 N	S = 2 %	P = 6 N	P = 6 %	F = 1 N	F = 1 %
QUESTION 1	S	2	22.2	N/A	N/A	N/A	N/A	N/A	N/A
	P	6	66.6	N/A	N/A	N/A	N/A	N/A	N/A
	F	1	11.1	N/A	N/A	N/A	N/A	N/A	N/A
QUESTION 2	Yes	6	66.6	1	50.0	4	66.6	1	100.0
	No	3	33.3	1	50.0	2	33.3	0	0.0
QUESTION 3	Yes	3	33.3	1	50.0	2	33.3	0	0.0
	No	0	0.0	0	0.0	0	0.0	0	0.0
	N/A	6	66.6	1	50.0	4	66.6	1	100.0
QUESTION 4	Yes	6	66.6	1	50.0	4	66.6	0	0.0
	No	3	33.3	0	0.0	2	33.3	0	0.0
	N/A	0	0.0	1	50.0	0	0.0	1	100.0
QUESTION 5	EC	3	33.3	1	50.0	2	33.3	0	0.0
	Non-EC	0	0.0	0	0.0	0	0.0	0	0.0
	Other	6	66.6	1	50.0	4	66.6	1	100.0
QUESTION 6	Yes	8	88.8	2	100.0	6	100.0	0	0.0
	No	0	0.0	0	0.0	0	0.0	0	0.0
QUESTION 7	2 Years	2	22.2	1	50.0	1	16.6	0	0.0
	5 Years	4	44.4	0	0.0	4	66.6	0	0.0
	10 Years	2	22.2	1	50.0	1	16.6	0	0.0
QUESTION 8	High	1	11.1	0	0.0	1	16.6	0	0.0
	Medium	4	44.4	1	50.0	3	50.0	0	0.0
	Low	3	33.3	1	50.0	2	33.3	0	0.0
QUESTION 9	MF	7	77.7	2	100.0	5	83.3	0	0.0
	Sub	0.5	5.5	0	0.0	0	0.0	0	0.0
	JV	3.5	38.8	0	0.0	2	33.3	1	100.0
	DF	1	11.1	0	0.0	1	16.6	0	0.0
	Buy	0	0.0	0	0.0	0	0.0	0	0.0
	Other	0	0.0	0	0.0	0	0.0	0	0.0
	1st Pref								
QUESTION 10	GB	0	0.0	0	0.0	0	0.0	0	0.0
	F	1	11.1	1	50.0	0	0.0	0	0.0
	E	7	77.7	1	50.0	5	83.3	1	100.0
	P	0	0.0	0	0.0	0	0.0	0	0.0
	I	0	0.0	0	0.0	0	0.0	0	0.0
	GR	0	0.0	0	0.0	0	0.0	0	0.0
	D	0	0.0	0	0.0	0	0.0	0	0.0
	DK	0	0.0	0	0.0	0	0.0	0	0.0
	L	0	0.0	0	0.0	0	0.0	0	0.0
	NL	1	11.1	0	0.0	1	16.6	0	0.0
	B	0	0.0	0	0.0	0	0.0	0	0.0
	EIR	0	0.0	0	0.0	0	0.0	0	0.0
	2nd Pref								
QUESTION 10	GB	0	0.0	0	0.0	0	0.0	0	0.0
	F	3	33.3	1	50.0	2	33.3	0	0.0
	E	0	0.0	0	0.0	0	0.0	0	0.0
	P	0	0.0	0	0.0	0	0.0	0	0.0
	I	1	11.1	1	50.0	0	0.0	0	0.0
	GR	0	0.0	0	0.0	0	0.0	0	0.0

Type	Resp	TL = 9		S = 2		P = 6		F = 1	
		N	%	N	%	N	%	N	%
	2nd Pref *contd*								
QUESTION 10	D	4	44.4	0	0.0	2	33.3	1	100.0
	DK	1	11.1	0	0.0	1	16.6	0	0.0
	L	0	0.0	0	0.0	0	0.0	0	0.0
	NL	1	11.1	0	0.0	0	0.0	0	0.0
	B	0	0.0	0	0.0	0	0.0	0	0.0
	EIR	0	0.0	0	0.0	0	0.0	0	0.0
	3rd Pref								
QUESTION 10	GB	4	44.4	1	50.0	3	50.0	0	0.0
	F	1	11.1	0	0.0	0	0.0	0	0.0
	E	0	0.0	0	0.0	0	0.0	0	0.0
	P	0	0.0	0	0.0	0	0.0	0	0.0
	I	0	0.0	0	0.0	0	0.0	0	0.0
	GR	0	0.0	0	0.0	0	0.0	0	0.0
	D	1	11.1	0	0.0	1	16.6	0	0.0
	DK	0	0.0	0	0.0	0	0.0	0	0.0
	L	1	11.1	0	0.0	1	16.6	0	0.0
	NL	0	0.0	0	0.0	0	0.0	0	0.0
	B	1	11.1	1	50.0	0	0.0	0	0.0
	EIR	1	11.1	0	0.0	0	0.0	1	100.0
	4th Pref								
QUESTION 10	GB	2	22.2	0	0.0	1	16.6	0	0.0
	F	2	22.2	0	0.0	2	33.3	0	0.0
	E	0	0.0	0	0.0	0	0.0	0	0.0
	P	0	0.0	0	0.0	0	0.0	0	0.0
	I	1	11.1	0	0.0	1	16.6	0	0.0
	GR	1	11.1	0	0.0	0	0.0	1	100.0
	D	2	22.2	2	100.0	0	0.0	0	0.0
	DK	0	0.0	0	0.0	0	0.0	0	0.0
	L	0	0.0	0	0.0	0	0.0	0	0.0
	NL	0	0.0	0	0.0	0	0.0	0	0.0
	B	1	11.1	0	0.0	1	16.6	0	0.0
	EIR	0	0.0	0	0.0	0	0.0	0	0.0
QUESTION 11	P1 Cam	2	22.2	0	0.0	1	16.6	1	100.0
	Approach	7	77.7	2	100.0	5	83.3	0	0.0
QUESTION 12	Yes	9	100.0	2	100.0	6	100.0	1	100.0
	No	0	0.0	0	0.0	0	0.0	0	0.0
QUESTION 13	Yes	9	100.0	2	100.0	6	100.0	1	100.0
	No	0	0.0	0	0.0	0	0.0	0	0.0
QUESTION 14	V Important	7	77.7	2	100.0	4	66.6	1	100.0
	Important	1	11.1	0	0.0	1	16.6	0	0.0
	Unimportant	1	11.1	0	0.0	1	16.6	0	0.0
QUESTION 15	Yes	2	22.2	1	50.0	1	16.6	0	0.0
	No	7	77.7	1	50.0	5	83.3	1	100.0
	Undecided	0	0.0	0	0.0	0	0.0	0	0.0
QUESTION 16	Lang	0	0.0	0	0.0	0	0.0	0	0.0
	Fin	0	0.0	0	0.0	0	0.0	0	0.0
	MD	1	11.1	0	0.0	1	16.6	0	0.0
	Opp	8	88.8	2	100.0	5	83.3	1	100.0

Type	Resp	TL = 9 N	%	S = 2 N	%	P = 6 N	%	F = 1 N	%
	1st Pref								
QUESTION 17	Inc Prof	6	66.6	2	100.0	3	50.0	0	0.0
	Inc Pres	0	0.0	0	0.0	0	0.0	0	0.0
	K Ahead	3	33.3	0	0.0	2	33.3	1	100.0
	Attack	0	0.0	0	0.0	0	0.0	0	0.0
	Econ	0	0.0	0	0.0	0	0.0	0	0.0
	Others	0	0.0	0	0.0	0	0.0	0	0.0
	2nd Pref								
QUESTION 17	Inc Prof	2	22.2	0	0.0	2	33.3	0	0.0
	Inc Pres	1	11.1	0	0.0	0	0.0	0	0.0
	K Ahead	3	33.3	1	50.0	2	33.3	0	0.0
	Attack	2	22.2	1	50.0	0	0.0	1	100.0
	Econ	0	0.0	0	0.0	0	0.0	0	0.0
	Others	0	0.0	0	0.0	0	0.0	0	0.0
	3rd Pref								
QUESTION 17	Inc Prof	1	11.1	0	0.0	0	0.0	1	100.0
	Inc Pres	5	55.5	1	50.0	4	66.6	0	0.0
	K Ahead	1	11.1	1	50.0	0	0.0	0	0.0
	Attack	0	0.0	0	0.0	0	0.0	0	0.0
	Econ	1	11.1	0	0.0	0	0.0	0	0.0
	Others	0	0.0	0	0.0	0	0.0	0	0.0
	4th Pref								
QUESTION 17	Inc Prof	0	0.0	0	0.0	0	0.0	0	0.0
	Inc Pres	2	22.2	1	50.0	0	0.0	1	100.0
	K Ahead	1	11.1	0	0.0	0	0.0	0	0.0
	Attack	0	0.0	0	0.0	0	0.0	0	0.0
	Econ	5	55.5	1	50.0	4	66.6	0	0.0
	Others	0	0.0	0	0.0	0	0.0	0	0.0
	5th Pref								
QUESTION 17	Inc Prof	0	0.0	0	0.0	0	0.0	0	0.0
	Inc Pres	0	0.0	0	0.0	0	0.0	0	0.0
	K Ahead	0	0.0	0	0.0	0	0.0	0	0.0
	Attack	6	66.6	1	50.0	4	66.6	0	0.0
	Econ	2	22.2	1	50.0	0	0.0	1	100.0
	Others	0	0.0	0	0.0	0	0.0	0	0.0
	6th Pref								
QUESTION 17	Inc Prof	0	0.0	0	0.0	0	0.0	0	0.0
	Inc Pres	0	0.0	0	0.0	0	0.0	0	0.0
	K Ahead	0	0.0	0	0.0	0	0.0	0	0.0
	Attack	0	0.0	0	0.0	0	0.0	0	0.0
	Econ	0	0.0	0	0.0	0	0.0	0	0.0
	Others	9	100.0	2	100.0	4	66.6	1	100.0
QUESTION 18	Yes	8	88.8	2	100.0	5	83.3	1	100.0
	No	1	11.1	0	0.0	1	16.6	0	0.0
	Don't Know	0	0.0	0	0.0	0	0.0	0	0.0
QUESTION 19	EC	9	100.0	2	100.0	6	100.0	1	100.0
	MS	0	0.0	0	0.0	0	0.0	0	0.0
	Don't Know	0	0.0	0	0.0	0	0.0	0	0.0
QUESTION 20	Yes	9	100.0	2	100.0	6	100.0	1	100.0
	No	0	0.0	0	0.0	0	0.0	0	0.0
	Don't Know	0	0.0	0	0.0	0	0.0	0	0.0

FRANCHISING AND 1992

Country: Italy (I)

Type	Resp	TL = 6 N	TL = 6 %	S = 4 N	S = 4 %	P = 2 N	P = 2 %	F = 0 N	F = 0 %
QUESTION 1	S	4	66.6	N/A	N/A	N/A	N/A		
	P	2	33.3	N/A	N/A	N/A	N/A		
	F	0	0.0	N/A	N/A	N/A	N/A		
QUESTION 2	Yes	4	66.6	3	75.0	1	50.0		
	No	2	33.3	1	25.0	1	50.0		
QUESTION 3	Yes	2	33.3	1	25.0	1	50.0		
	No	0	0.0	0	0.0	0	0.0		
	N/A	4	66.6	3	75.0	1	50.0		
QUESTION 4	Yes	4	66.6	3	75.0	1	50.0		
	No	0	0.0	0	0.0	0	0.0		
	N/A	2	33.3	1	25.0	1	50.0		
QUESTION 5	EC	2	33.3	1	25.0	1	50.0		
	Non-EC	0	0.0	0	0.0	0	0.0		
	N/A	4	66.6	3	75.0	1	50.0		
QUESTION 6	Yes	6	100.0	4	100.0	2	100.0		
	No	0	0.0	0	0.0	0	0.0		
QUESTION 7	2 Years	4	66.6	3	75.0	1	50.0		
	5 Years	2	33.3	1	25.0	1	50.0		
	10 Years	0	0.0	0	0.0	0	0.0		
QUESTION 8	High	2	33.3	2	50.0	0	0.0		
	Medium	1	16.7	1	25.0	0	0.0		
	Low	3	50.0	1	25.0	2	100.0		
QUESTION 9	MF	2.5	41.7	2	50.0	1	50.0		
	Sub	1	16.7	0	0.0	1	50.0		
	JV	0	0.0	0	0.0	0	0.0		
	DF	2.5	41.7	2	50.0	0	0.0		
	Buy	0	0.0	0	0.0	0	0.0		
	Other	0	0.0	0	0.0	0	0.0		
	1st Pref								
QUESTION 10	GB	1	16.7	1	25.0	0	0.0		
	F	3	50.0	2	50.0	1	50.0		
	E	0	0.0	0	0.0	0	0.0		
	P	0	0.0	0	0.0	0	0.0		
	I	0	0.0	0	0.0	0	0.0		
	GR	0	0.0	0	0.0	0	0.0		
	D	2	33.3	1	25.0	1	50.0		
	DK	0	0.0	0	0.0	0	0.0		
	L	0	0.0	0	0.0	0	0.0		
	NL	0	0.0	0	0.0	0	0.0		
	B	0	0.0	0	0.0	0	0.0		
	EIR	0	0.0	0	0.0	0	0.0		
	2nd Pref								
QUESTION 10	GB	2	33.3	1	25.0	1	50.0		
	F	1	16.7	1	25.0	0	0.0		
	E	1	16.7	1	25.0	0	0.0		
	P	0	0.0	0	0.0	0	0.0		
	I	0	0.0	0	0.0	0	0.0		
	GR	0	0.0	0	0.0	0	0.0		

Type	Resp	TL = 6 N	%	S = 4 N	%	P = 2 N	%	F = 0 N	%
	2nd Pref *contd*								
QUESTION 10	D	2	33.3	1	25.0	1	50.0		
	DK	0	0.0	0	0.0	0	0.0		
	L	0	0.0	0	0.0	0	0.0		
	NL	0	0.0	0	0.0	0	0.0		
	B	0	0.0	0	0.0	0	0.0		
	EIR	0	0.0	0	0.0	0	0.0		
	3rd Pref								
QUESTION 10	GB	2	33.3	1	25.0	1	50.0		
	F	2	33.3	1	25.0	1	50.0		
	E	1	16.7	1	25.0	0	0.0		
	P	0	0.0	0	0.0	0	0.0		
	I	0	0.0	0	0.0	0	0.0		
	GR	0	0.0	0	0.0	0	0.0		
	D	1	16.7	1	25.0	0	0.0		
	DK	0	0.0	0	0.0	0	0.0		
	L	0	0.0	0	0.0	0	0.0		
	NL	0	0.0	0	0.0	0	0.0		
	B	0	0.0	0	0.0	0	0.0		
	EIR	0	0.0	0	0.0	0	0.0		
	4th Pref								
QUESTION 10	GB	0	0.0	0	0.0	0	0.0		
	F	0	0.0	0	0.0	0	0.0		
	E	4	66.6	2	50.0	2	100.0		
	P	0	0.0	0	0.0	0	0.0		
	I	0	0.0	0	0.0	0	0.0		
	GR	0	0.0	0	0.0	0	0.0		
	D	1	16.7	1	25.0	0	0.0		
	DK	0	0.0	0	0.0	0	0.0		
	L	0	0.0	0	0.0	0	0.0		
	NL	1	16.7	1	25.0	0	0.0		
	B	0	0.0	0	0.0	0	0.0		
	EIR	0	0.0	0	0.0	0	0.0		
QUESTION 11	P1 Cam	1	16.7	1	25.0	0	0.0		
	Approach	5	83.3	3	75.0	2	100.0		
QUESTION 12	Yes	5	83.3	4	100.0	1	50.0		
	No	1	16.7	0	0.0	1	50.0		
QUESTION 13	Yes	4	66.6	3	75.0	1	50.0		
	No	2	33.3	1	25.0	1	50.0		
QUESTION 14	V Important	3	50.0	3	75.0	0	0.0		
	Important	1	16.7	1	25.0	0	0.0		
	Unimportant	2	33.3	0	0.0	2	100.0		
QUESTION 15	Yes	1	16.7	1	25.0	0	0.0		
	No	4	66.6	3	75.0	1	50.0		
	Undecided	1	16.7	0	0.0	1	50.0		
QUESTION 16	Lang	0	0.0	3	75.0	0	0.0		
	Fin	4	66.6	0	0.0	1	50.0		
	MD	0	0.0	1	25.0	0	0.0		
	Opp	2	33.3	0	0.0	1	50.0		

Type	Resp	TL = 6		S = 4		P = 2		F = 0	
		N	%	N	%	N	%	N	%
	1st Pref								
QUESTION 17	Inc Prof	5	83.3	3	75.0	2	100.0		
	Inc Pres	1	16.7	1	25.0	0	0.0		
	K Ahead	0	0.0	0	0.0	0	0.0		
	Attack	0	0.0	0	0.0	0	0.0		
	Econ	0	0.0	0	0.0	0	0.0		
	Others	0	0.0	0	0.0	0	0.0		
	2nd Pref								
QUESTION 17	Inc Prof	1	16.7	1	25.0	0	0.0		
	Inc Pres	4	66.6	2	50.0	2	100.0		
	K Ahead	0	0.0	0	0.0	0	0.0		
	Attack	0	0.0	0	0.0	0	0.0		
	Econ	0	0.0	0	0.0	0	0.0		
	Others	0	0.0	0	0.0	0	0.0		
	3rd Pref								
QUESTION 17	Inc Prof	0	0.0	0	0.0	0	0.0		
	Inc Pres	0	0.0	1	25.0	0	0.0		
	K Ahead	3	50.0	0	0.0	2	100.0		
	Attack	0	0.0	0	0.0	0	0.0		
	Econ	1	16.7	1	25.0	0	0.0		
	Others	0	0.0	0	0.0	0	0.0		
	4th Pref								
QUESTION 17	Inc Prof	0	0.0	0	0.0	0	0.0		
	Inc Pres	0	0.0	0	0.0	0	0.0		
	K Ahead	1	16.7	1	25.0	0	0.0		
	Attack	0	0.0	0	0.0	0	0.0		
	Econ	3	50.0	1	25.0	2	100.0		
	Others	0	0.0	0	0.0	0	0.0		
	5th Pref								
QUESTION 17	Inc Prof	0	0.0	0	0.0	0	0.0		
	Inc Pres	0	0.0	0	0.0	0	0.0		
	K Ahead	0	0.0	0	0.0	0	0.0		
	Attack	4	66.6	1	25.0	2	100.0		
	Econ	0	0.0	0	0.0	0	0.0		
	Others	0	0.0	0	0.0	0	0.0		
	6th Pref								
QUESTION 17	Inc Prof	0	0.0	0	0.0	0	0.0		
	Inc Pres	0	0.0	0	0.0	0	0.0		
	K Ahead	0	0.0	0	0.0	0	0.0		
	Attack	0	0.0	0	0.0	0	0.0		
	Econ	0	0.0	0	0.0	0	0.0		
	Others	4	66.6	1	25.0	0	0.0		
QUESTION 18	Yes	1	16.7	1	25.0	0	0.0		
	No	5	83.3	3	75.0	2	100.0		
	Don't Know	0	0.0	0	0.0	0	0.0		
QUESTION 19	EC	4	66.6	3	75.0	1	50.0		
	MS	2	33.3	1	25.0	1	50.0		
	Don't Know	0	0.0	0	0.0	0	0.0		
QUESTION 20	Yes	3	50.0	2	50.0	1	50.0		
	No	1	16.7	1	25.0	0	0.0		
	Don't Know	2	33.3	1	25.0	1	50.0		

FRANCHISING AND 1992

Country: Germany (D)

Type	Resp	TL = 36 N	TL = 36 %	S = 26 N	S = 26 %	P = 9 N	P = 9 %	F = 1 N	F = 1 %
QUESTION 1	S	26	72.2	N/A	N/A	N/A	N/A	N/A	N/A
	P	9	25.0	N/A	N/A	N/A	N/A	N/A	N/A
	F	1	2.7	N/A	N/A	N/A	N/A	N/A	N/A
QUESTION 2	Yes	15	41.6	12	46.1	3	33.3	0	0.0
	No	21	58.3	14	53.8	6	66.6	1	100.0
QUESTION 3	Yes	16	44.4	11	42.3	4	44.4	1	100.0
	No	4	11.1	2	7.6	2	22.2	0	0.0
	N/A	16	44.4	13	50.0	3	50.0	0	0.0
QUESTION 4	Yes	11	30.5	8	30.7	3	33.3	0	0.0
	No	25	69.4	18	69.2	6	66.6	1	100.0
	N/A	0	0.0	0	0.0	0	0.0	0	0.0
QUESTION 5	EC	24	58.3	16	61.5	4	44.4	1	100.0
	Non-EC	4	11.1	2	7.6	2	22.2	0	0.0
	Other	11	30.5	8	30.7	3	33.3	0	0.0
QUESTION 6	Yes	24	66.6	18	69.2	5	55.5	1	100.0
	No	7	19.4	5	19.2	4	44.4	0	0.0
QUESTION 7	2 Years	12	33.3	10	38.4	2	22.2	0	0.0
	5 Years	9	25.0	6	23.0	2	22.2	1	100.0
	10 Years	3	8.3	2	7.6	1	11.1	0	0.0
QUESTION 8	High	7	19.4	6	23.0	1	11.1	0	0.0
	Medium	23	63.8	15	57.6	7	77.7	1	100.0
	Low	5	13.8	4	15.3	1	11.1	0	0.0
QUESTION 9	MF	26	72.2	18	69.2	7	77.7	1	100.0
	Sub	4	11.1	3	11.5	1	11.1	0	0.0
	JV	2	5.5	2	7.6	1	11.1	0	0.0
	DF	3	8.3	3	11.5	0	0.0	0	0.0
	Buy	1	2.7	0	0.0	0	0.0	0	0.0
	Other	0	0.0	0	0.0	0	0.0	0	0.0
QUESTION 10	**1st Pref**								
	GB	1	2.7	1	3.8	0	0.0	0	0.0
	F	4	11.1	3	11.5	1	11.1	0	0.0
	E	2	5.5	1	3.8	0	0.0	1	100.0
	P	0	0.0	0	0.0	0	0.0	0	0.0
	I	5	13.8	4	15.3	1	11.1	0	0.0
	GR	0	0.0	0	0.0	0	0.0	0	0.0
	D	0	0.0	0	0.0	0	0.0	0	0.0
	DK	1	2.7	0	0.0	0	0.0	0	0.0
	L	0	0.0	0	0.0	0	0.0	0	0.0
	NL	17	47.2	13	50.0	4	44.4	0	0.0
	B	0	0.0	0	0.0	0	0.0	0	0.0
	EIR	0	0.0	0	0.0	0	0.0	0	0.0
QUESTION 10	**2nd Pref**								
	GB	4	11.1	3	11.5	1	11.1	0	0.0
	F	8	22.2	5	19.2	1	11.1	0	0.0
	E	1	2.7	1	3.8	0	0.0	0	0.0
	P	1	2.8	0	0.0	0	0.0	1	100.0
	I	3	8.3	3	11.5	0	0.0	0	0.0
	GR	0	0.0	0	0.0	0	0.0	0	0.0

Type		TL = 36		S = 26		P = 9		F = 1	
	Resp	N	%	N	%	N	%	N	%
	2nd Pref *contd*								
QUESTION 10	D	0	0.0	0	0.0	0	0.0	0	0.0
	DK	1	2.7	1	3.8	0	0.0	0	0.0
	L	5	13.8	3	11.5	2	22.2	0	0.0
	NL	1	2.7	1	3.8	0	0.0	0	0.0
	B	6	16.6	4	15.3	2	22.2	0	0.0
	EIR	0	0.0	0	0.0	0	0.0	0	0.0
	3rd Pref								
QUESTION 10	GB	1	2.7	1	3.8	0	0.0	0	0.0
	F	7	19.4	5	19.2	4	44.4	0	0.0
	E	3	8.3	2	7.6	1	11.1	0	0.0
	P	0	0.0	0	0.0	0	0.0	0	0.0
	I	2	5.5	2	7.6	0	0.0	0	0.0
	GR	0	0.0	0	0.0	0	0.0	0	0.0
	D	0	0.0	0	0.0	0	0.0	0	0.0
	DK	0	0.0	0	0.0	0	0.0	0	0.0
	L	5	13.8	4	15.3	1	11.1	0	0.0
	NL	1	2.7	1	3.8	0	0.0	0	0.0
	B	5	13.8	4	15.3	0	0.0	1	100.0
	EIR	0	0.0	0	0.0	0	0.0	0	0.0
	4th Pref								
QUESTION 10	GB	3	8.3	1	3.8	2	22.2	0	0.0
	F	3	8.3	3	11.5	0	0.0	0	0.0
	E	4	11.1	3	11.5	1	11.1	0	0.0
	P	0	0.0	0	0.0	0	0.0	0	0.0
	I	2	5.5	2	7.6	0	0.0	0	0.0
	GR	0	0.0	0	0.0	0	0.0	0	0.0
	D	0	0.0	0	0.0	0	0.0	0	0.0
	DK	1	2.7	1	3.8	0	0.0	0	0.0
	L	4	11.1	3	11.5	1	11.1	0	0.0
	NL	3	8.3	1	3.8	1	11.1	1	100.0
	B	3	8.3	2	7.6	1	11.1	0	0.0
	EIR	0	0.0	0	0.0	0	0.0	0	0.0
QUESTION 11	P1 Cam	19	52.7	14	53.8	3	33.3	1	100.0
	Approach	8	22.2	7	26.9	3	33.3	0	0.0
QUESTION 12	Yes	30	83.3	23	88.4	6	66.6	1	100.0
	No	5	13.8	3	11.5	2	22.2	0	0.0
QUESTION 13	Yes	29	80.5	22	84.6	6	66.6	1	100.0
	No	7	19.4	4	15.3	3	33.3	0	0.0
QUESTION 14	V Important	9	25.0	7	26.9	2	22.2	0	0.0
	Important	19	52.7	14	53.8	7	77.7	0	0.0
	U Important	7	16.6	5	19.2	0	0.0	1	100.0
QUESTION 15	Yes	5	13.8	5	19.2	3	33.3	0	0.0
	No	20	55.5	15	57.6	5	55.5	0	0.0
	Undecided	8	22.2	6	23.0	1	11.1	1	100.0
QUESTION 16	Lang	4	11.1	3	11.5	1	11.1	0	0.0
	Fin	4	11.1	3	11.5	1	11.1	0	0.0
	MD	12	33.3	6	23.1	6	66.6	0	0.0
	Opp	16	44.4	14	53.8	1	11.1	1	100.0

Type	Resp	TL = 36 N	%	S = 26 N	%	P = 9 N	%	F = 1 N	%
QUESTION 17	**1st Pref**								
	Inc Prof	15	41.6	12	46.1	2	22.2	1	100.0
	Inc Pres	8	22.2	6	23.0	2	22.2	0	0.0
	K Ahead	3	8.3	3	11.5	0	0.0	0	0.0
	Attack	7	19.4	4	15.3	2	22.2	0	0.0
	Econ	2	5.5	1	3.8	1	11.1	0	0.0
	Others	1	2.7	0	0.0	1	11.1	0	0.0
QUESTION 17	**2nd Pref**								
	Inc Prof	5	13.8	4	15.3	1	11.1	0	0.0
	Inc Pres	7	19.4	6	23.0	1	11.1	0	0.0
	K Ahead	12	33.3	7	26.9	2	22.2	0	0.0
	Attack	1	2.7	1	3.8	0	0.0	0	0.0
	Econ	1	2.7	0	0.0	0	0.0	1	100.0
	Others	0	0.0	0	0.0	0	0.0	0	0.0
QUESTION 17	**3rd Pref**								
	Inc Prof	7	19.4	6	23.0	1	11.1	0	0.0
	Inc Pres	2	5.5	1	3.8	1	11.1	0	0.0
	K Ahead	6	16.6	6	23.0	2	22.2	0	0.0
	Attack	3	8.3	2	7.6	0	0.0	1	100.0
	Econ	1	2.7	1	3.8	0	0.0	0	0.0
	Others	0	0.0	0	0.0	0	0.0	0	0.0
QUESTION 17	**4th Pref**								
	Inc Prof	1	2.7	1	3.8	0	0.0	0	0.0
	Inc Pres	6	16.6	4	15.3	1	11.1	1	100.0
	K Ahead	1	2.7	1	3.8	0	0.0	0	0.0
	Attack	8	22.2	7	26.9	1	11.1	0	0.0
	Econ	0	0.0	0	0.0	0	0.0	0	0.0
	Others	0	0.0	0	0.0	0	0.0	0	0.0
QUESTION 17	**5th Pref**								
	Inc Prof	0	0.0	0	0.0	0	0.0	0	0.0
	Inc Pres	0	0.0	0	0.0	0	0.0	0	0.0
	K Ahead	2	5.5	1	3.8	0	0.0	1	100.0
	Attack	0	0.0	0	0.0	0	0.0	0	0.0
	Econ	12	33.3	11	42.3	1	11.1	0	0.0
	Others	0	0.0	0	0.0	0	0.0	0	0.0
QUESTION 17	**6th Pref**								
	Inc Prof	0	0.0	0	0.0	0	0.0	0	0.0
	Inc Pres	0	0.0	0	0.0	0	0.0	0	0.0
	K Ahead	0	0.0	0	0.0	0	0.0	0	0.0
	Attack	0	0.0	0	0.0	0	0.0	0	0.0
	Econ	0	0.0	0	0.0	0	0.0	0	0.0
	Others	19	52.7	12	46.1	1	11.1	1	100.0
QUESTION 18	Yes	25	69.4	17	65.3	7	77.7	1	100.0
	No	6	16.6	5	19.2	1	11.1	0	0.0
	Don't Know	5	13.8	4	15.3	1	11.1	0	0.0
QUESTION 19	EC	27	75.0	21	80.7	5	55.5	1	100.0
	MS	3	8.3	2	7.6	1	11.1	0	0.0
	Don't Know	4	11.1	2	7.6	2	22.2	0	0.0
QUESTION 20	Yes	35	97.2	26	100.0	9	100.0	1	100.0
	No	0	0.0	0	0.0	0	0.0	0	0.0
	Don't Know	0	0.0	0	0.0	0	0.0	0	0.0

FRANCHISING AND 1992

Country: Denmark (DK)

Type	Resp	TL = 3 N	TL = 3 %	S = 1 N	S = 1 %	P = 2 N	P = 2 %	F = 0 N	F = 0 %
QUESTION 1	S	1	33.3	N/A	N/A	N/A	N/A		
	P	2	66.6	N/A	N/A	N/A	N/A		
	F	0	0.0	N/A	N/A	N/A	N/A		
QUESTION 2	Yes	1	66.6	1	100.0	0	0.0		
	No	2	33.3	0	0.0	2	100.0		
QUESTION 3	Yes	0	0.0	0	0.0	0	0.0		
	No	2	66.6	0	0.0	2	100.0		
	N/A	1	33.3	0	0.0	0	0.0		
QUESTION 4	Yes	0	0.0	0	0.0	0	0.0		
	No	3	100.0	1	100.0	2	100.0		
	N/A	0	0.0	0	0.0	0	0.0		
QUESTION 5	EC	0	0.0	0	0.0	0	0.0		
	Non-EC	0	0.0	0	0.0	0	0.0		
	Other	1	33.3	0	0.0	1	50.0		
QUESTION 6	Yes	1	33.3	1	100.0	0	0.0		
	No	2	66.6	0	0.0	2	100.0		
QUESTION 7	2 Years	1	33.3	1	100.0	0	0.0		
	5 Years	0	0.0	0	0.0	0	0.0		
	10 Years	0	0.0	0	0.0	0	0.0		
QUESTION 8	High	0	0.0	0	0.0	0	0.0		
	Medium	1	33.3	1	100.0	0	0.0		
	Low	1	33.3	0	0.0	1	50.0		
QUESTION 9	MF	0	0.0	0	0.0	0	0.0		
	Sub	0	0.0	0	0.0	0	0.0		
	JV	2	66.6	1	100.0	1	50.0		
	DF	0	0.0	0	0.0	0	0.0		
	Buy	0	0.0	0	0.0	0	0.0		
	Other	0	0.0	0	0.0	0	0.0		
	1st Pref								
QUESTION 10	GB	1	33.3	1	100.0	0	0.0		
	F	0	0.0	0	0.0	0	0.0		
	E	0	0.0	0	0.0	0	0.0		
	P	0	0.0	0	0.0	0	0.0		
	I	0	0.0	0	0.0	0	0.0		
	GR	0	0.0	0	0.0	0	0.0		
	D	1	33.3	0	0.0	1	50.0		
	DK	0	0.0	0	0.0	0	0.0		
	L	0	0.0	0	0.0	0	0.0		
	NL	0	0.0	0	0.0	0	0.0		
	B	0	0.0	0	0.0	0	0.0		
	EIR	0	0.0	0	0.0	0	0.0		
	2nd Pref								
QUESTION 10	GB	0	0.0	0	0.0	0	0.0		
	F	0	0.0	0	0.0	0	0.0		
	E	0	0.0	0	0.0	0	0.0		
	P	0	0.0	0	0.0	0	0.0		
	I	0	0.0	0	0.0	0	0.0		
	GR	0	0.0	0	0.0	0	0.0		

Type	Resp	TL = 3		S = 1		P = 2		F = 0	
		N	%	N	%	N	%	N	%
	2nd Pref *contd*								
QUESTION 10	D	0	0.0	0	0.0	0	0.0		
	DK	0	0.0	0	0.0	0	0.0		
	L	0	0.0	0	0.0	0	0.0		
	NL	1	33.3	1	100.0	0	0.0		
	B	0	0.0	0	0.0	0	0.0		
	EIR	0	0.0	0	0.0	0	0.0		
	3rd Pref								
QUESTION 10	GB	0	0.0	0	0.0	0	0.0		
	F	0	0.0	0	0.0	0	0.0		
	E	0	0.0	0	0.0	0	0.0		
	P	0	0.0	0	0.0	0	0.0		
	I	0	0.0	0	0.0	0	0.0		
	GR	0	0.0	0	0.0	0	0.0		
	D	0	0.0	0	0.0	0	0.0		
	DK	0	0.0	0	0.0	0	0.0		
	L	0	0.0	0	0.0	0	0.0		
	NL	0	0.0	0	0.0	0	0.0		
	B	1	33.3	1	100.0	0	0.0		
	EIR	0	0.0	0	0.0	0	0.0		
	4th Pref								
QUESTION 10	GB	0	0.0	0	0.0	0	0.0		
	F	0	0.0	0	0.0	0	0.0		
	E	0	0.0	0	0.0	0	0.0		
	P	0	0.0	0	0.0	0	0.0		
	I	0	0.0	0	0.0	0	0.0		
	GR	0	0.0	0	0.0	0	0.0		
	D	1	33.3	1	100.0	0	0.0		
	DK	0	0.0	0	0.0	0	0.0		
	L	0	0.0	0	0.0	0	0.0		
	NL	0	0.0	0	0.0	0	0.0		
	B	0	0.0	0	0.0	0	0.0		
	EIR	0	0.0	0	0.0	0	0.0		
QUESTION 11	P1 Cam	2	66.6	1	100.0	1	50.0		
	Approach	0	0.0	0	0.0	0	0.0		
QUESTION 12	Yes	3	100.0	1	100.0	2	100.0		
	No	0	0.0	0	0.0	0	0.0		
QUESTION 13	Yes	3	100.0	1	100.0	2	100.0		
	No	0	0.0	0	0.0	0	0.0		
QUESTION 14	V Important	2	66.6	1	100.0	1	50.0		
	Important	0	0.0	0	0.0	0	0.0		
	U Important	0	0.0	0	0.0	0	0.0		
QUESTION 15	Yes	2	66.6	1	100.0	1	50.0		
	No	0	0.0	0	0.0	0	0.0		
	Undecided	0	0.0	0	0.0	0	0.0		
QUESTION 16	Lang	0	0.0	0	0.0	0	0.0		
	Fin	0	0.0	0	0.0	0	0.0		
	MD	1	33.3	1	100.0	0	0.0		
	Opp	1	33.3	0	0.0	1	50.0		

Type	Resp	TL = 3		S = 1		P = 2		F = 0	
		N	%	N	%	N	%	N	%
QUESTION 17	**1st Pref**								
	Inc Prof	0	0.0	0	0.0	0	0.0		
	Inc Pres	0	0.0	0	0.0	0	0.0		
	K Ahead	1	33.3	1	100.0	0	0.0		
	Attack	1	33.3	0	0.0	1	50.0		
	Econ	0	0.0	0	0.0	0	0.0		
	Others	0	0.0	0	0.0	0	0.0		
QUESTION 17	**2nd Pref**								
	Inc Prof	1	33.3	1	100.0	0	0.0		
	Inc Pres	0	0.0	0	0.0	0	0.0		
	K Ahead	0	0.0	0	0.0	0	0.0		
	Attack	0	0.0	0	0.0	0	0.0		
	Econ	0	0.0	0	0.0	0	0.0		
	Others	0	0.0	0	0.0	0	0.0		
QUESTION 17	**3rd Pref**								
	Inc Prof	0	0.0	1	100.0	0	0.0		
	Inc Pres	1	33.3	0	0.0	0	0.0		
	K Ahead	0	0.0	0	0.0	0	0.0		
	Attack	0	0.0	0	0.0	0	0.0		
	Econ	0	0.0	0	0.0	0	0.0		
	Others	0	0.0	0	0.0	0	0.0		
QUESTION 17	**4th Pref**								
	Inc Prof	0	0.0	0	0.0	0	0.0		
	Inc Pres	0	0.0	0	0.0	0	0.0		
	K Ahead	0	0.0	0	0.0	0	0.0		
	Attack	1	33.3	1	100.0	0	0.0		
	Econ	0	0.0	0	0.0	0	0.0		
	Others	0	0.0	0	0.0	0	0.0		
QUESTION 17	**5th Pref**								
	Inc Prof	0	0.0	0	0.0	0	0.0		
	Inc Pres	0	0.0	0	0.0	0	0.0		
	K Ahead	0	0.0	0	0.0	0	0.0		
	Attack	0	0.0	0	0.0	0	0.0		
	Econ	1	33.3	1	100.0	0	0.0		
	Others	0	0.0	0	0.0	0	0.0		
QUESTION 17	**6th Pref**								
	Inc Prof	0	0.0	0	0.0	0	0.0		
	Inc Pres	0	0.0	0	0.0	0	0.0		
	K Ahead	0	0.0	0	0.0	0	0.0		
	Attack	0	0.0	0	0.0	0	0.0		
	Econ	0	0.0	0	0.0	0	0.0		
	Others	1	33.3	1	100.0	0	0.0		
QUESTION 18	Yes	3	33.3	1	100.0	2	100.0		
	No	0	0.0	0	0.0	0	0.0		
	Don't Know	0	0.0	0	0.0	0	0.0		
QUESTION 19	EC	2	66.6	1	100.0	1	50.0		
	MS	1	33.3	0	0.0	1	50.0		
	Don't Know	0	0.0	0	0.0	0	0.0		
QUESTION 20	Yes	3	100.0	1	100.0	2	100.0		
	No	0	0.0	0	0.0	0	0.0		
	Dont' Know	0	0.0	0	0.0	0	0.0		

FRANCHISING AND 1992

Country: The Netherlands (NL)

Type	Resp	TL = 42 N	TL = 42 %	S = 24 N	S = 24 %	P = 13 N	P = 13 %	F = 5 N	F = 5 %
QUESTION 1	S	24	57.1	N/A	N/A	N/A	N/A	N/A	N/A
	P	13	30.9	N/A	N/A	N/A	N/A	N/A	N/A
	F	5	11.9	N/A	N/A	N/A	N/A	N/A	N/A
QUESTION 2	Yes	13	30.9	6	25.0	7	53.8	0	0.0
	No	28	66.6	17	70.8	6	46.1	5	100.0
QUESTION 3	Yes	20	47.6	13	54.1	5	38.4	2	40.0
	No	10	23.8	7	29.1	0	0.0	3	60.0
	N/A	7	16.6	2	8.3	5	38.4	0	0.0
QUESTION 4	Yes	11	26.1	6	25.0	5	38.4	0	0.0
	No	27	64.2	16	66.6	7	53.8	4	80.0
	N/A	2	4.7	1	4.1	1	7.6	0	0.0
QUESTION 5	EC	22	52.3	12	50.0	5	38.4	5	100.0
	Non-EC	0	0.0	0	0.0	0	0.0	0	0.0
	Other	13	30.9	8	33.3	5	38.4	0	0.0
QUESTION 6	Yes	28	66.6	16	66.6	10	76.9	2	40.0
	No	14	33.3	8	33.3	3	23.0	3	60.0
QUESTION 7	2 Years	22	52.3	11	45.8	7	53.8	4	80.0
	5 Years	8	19.0	4	16.6	4	30.7	0	0.0
	10 Years	1	2.3	1	4.1	0	0.0	0	0.0
QUESTION 8	High	10	23.8	8	33.3	1	7.6	1	20.0
	Medium	16	38.0	6	25.0	8	61.5	2	40.0
	Low	6	14.2	2	8.3	2	15.3	2	40.0
QUESTION 9	MF	16	38.0	7	29.1	7	53.8	3	60.0
	Sub	4	9.5	3	12.5	1	7.6	0	0.0
	JV	5	11.9	4	16.6	2	15.3	0	0.0
	DF	6	14.2	3	12.5	2	15.3	2	40.0
	Buy	3	7.1	2	8.3	1	7.6	0	0.0
	Other	0	0.0	0	0.0	0	0.0	0	0.0
	1st Pref								
QUESTION 10	GB	1	2.3	1	4.1	0	0.0	0	0.0
	F	3	7.1	2	8.3	1	7.6	0	0.0
	E	1	2.3	0	0.0	1	7.6	0	0.0
	P	0	0.0	0	0.0	0	0.0	0	0.0
	I	0	0.0	0	0.0	0	0.0	0	0.0
	GR	0	0.0	0	0.0	0	0.0	0	0.0
	D	12	28.5	8	33.3	3	23.0	0	0.0
	DK	0	0.0	0	0.0	0	0.0	0	0.0
	L	1	2.3	1	4.1	0	0.0	0	0.0
	NL	0	0.0	0	0.0	0	0.0	0	0.0
	B	18	42.8	7	29.1	6	46.1	5	100.0
	EIR	0	0.0	0	0.0	0	0.0	0	0.0
	2nd Pref								
QUESTION 10	GB	4	9.5	3	12.5	1	7.6	0	0.0
	F	6	14.2	3	12.5	2	15.3	0	0.0
	E	1	2.3	1	4.1	0	0.0	0	0.0
	P	0	0.0	0	0.0	0	0.0	0	0.0
	I	0	0.0	0	0.0	0	0.0	0	0.0
	GR	0	0.0	0	0.0	0	0.0	0	0.0

Type	Resp	TL = 42		S = 24		P = 13		F = 5	
		N	%	N	%	N	%	N	%
	2nd Pref *contd*								
QUESTION 10	D	5	11.9	2	8.3	1	7.6	1	20.0
	DK	3	7.1	2	8.3	1	7.6	0	0.0
	L	5	11.9	0	0.0	2	15.3	4	80.0
	NL	0	0.0	0	0.0	0	0.0	0	0.0
	B	3	7.1	0	0.0	3	23.0	0	0.0
	EIR	0	0.0	0	0.0	0	0.0	0	0.0
	3rd Pref								
QUESTION 10	GB	6	14.2	2	8.3	5	38.4	0	0.0
	F	1	2.3	1	4.1	0	0.0	0	0.0
	E	2	4.7	1	4.1	1	7.6	0	0.0
	P	1	2.3	0	0.0	1	7.6	0	0.0
	I	4	9.5	1	4.1	1	7.6	0	0.0
	GR	0	0.0	0	0.0	0	0.0	0	0.0
	D	8	7.1	0	0.0	1	7.6	3	60.0
	DK	1	2.3	1	4.1	0	0.0	0	0.0
	L	2	4.7	1	4.1	1	7.6	0	0.0
	NL	0	0.0	0	0.0	0	0.0	0	0.0
	B	0	0.0	0	0.0	0	0.0	0	0.0
	EIR	0	0.0	0	0.0	0	0.0	0	0.0
QUESTION 11	P1 Cam	18	42.8	12	50.0	5	38.4	1	20.0
	Approach	16	38.0	5	20.8	7	53.8	4	80.0
QUESTION 12	Yes	28	66.6	18	75.0	8	61.5	1	20.0
	No	14	33.3	5	20.8	5	38.4	4	80.0
QUESTION 13	Yes	20	47.6	12	50.0	6	46.1	2	40.0
	No	18	42.8	9	37.5	6	46.1	3	60.0
QUESTION 14	V Important	23	54.7	13	54.1	4	40.7	4	80.0
	Important	12	28.5	6	25.0	5	38.4	1	20.0
	U Important	3	7.1	0	0.0	3	23.0	0	0.0
QUESTION 15	Yes	20	47.6	9	37.5	8	61.5	3	60.0
	No	10	23.8	7	29.1	2	15.3	1	20.0
	Undecided	8	19.0	5	20.8	2	15.3	1	20.0
QUESTION 16	Lang	0	0.0	0	0.0	0	0.0	0	0.0
	Fin	4	9.5	1	4.1	0	0.0	3	60.0
	MD	22	52.3	15	62.5	6	46.1	1	20.0
	Opp	11	26.1	3	12.5	7	53.8	0	0.0
	1st Pref								
QUESTION 17	Inc Prof	8	19.0	6	25.0	2	15.3	0	0.0
	Inc Pres	5	11.9	0	0.0	1	7.6	3	60.0
	K Ahead	10	23.8	6	25.0	3	23.0	1	20.0
	Attack	4	9.5	2	8.3	2	15.3	0	0.0
	Econ	7	16.6	4	16.6	2	15.3	1	20.0
	Others	1	2.3	0	0.0	1	7.6	0	0.0
	2nd Pref								
QUESTION 17	Inc Prof	13	30.9	6	25.0	2	15.3	5	100.0
	Inc Pres	5	11.9	3	12.5	2	15.3	0	0.0
	K Ahead	2	4.7	1	4.1	1	7.6	0	0.0
	Attack	2	4.7	1	4.1	1	7.6	0	0.0
	Econ	4	9.5	2	8.3	2	15.3	0	0.0
	Others	0	0.0	0	0.0	0	0.0	0	0.0

Type	Resp	TL = 42		S = 24		P = 13		F = 5	
		N	%	N	%	N	%	N	%
	3rd Pref								
QUESTION 17	Inc Prof	5	11.9	3	12.5	2	15.3	0	0.0
	Inc Pres	3	7.1	3	12.5	0	0.0	0	0.0
	K Ahead	3	7.1	2	8.3	1	7.6	0	0.0
	Attack	9	21.4	3	12.5	1	7.6	5	100.0
	Econ	5	11.9	2	8.3	3	23.0	0	0.0
	Others	0	0.0	0	0.0	0	0.0	0	0.0
	4th Pref								
QUESTION 17	Inc Prof	1	2.3	0	0.0	1	7.6	0	0.0
	Inc Pres	4	9.5	1	4.1	3	23.0	0	0.0
	K Ahead	6	14.2	2	8.3	0	0.0	4	80.0
	Attack	2	4.7	5	20.8	1	7.6	0	0.0
	Econ	6	14.2	4	16.6	1	7.6	1	20.0
	Others	2	4.7	0	0.0	1	7.6	0	0.0
	5th Pref								
QUESTION 17	Inc Prof	1	2.3	1	4.1	1	7.6	0	0.0
	Inc Pres	4	9.5	2	8.3	0	0.0	2	40.0
	K Ahead	0	0.0	1	4.1	1	7.6	0	0.0
	Attack	6	14.2	2	8.3	4	30.7	0	0.0
	Econ	6	14.2	3	12.5	1	7.6	3	60.0
	Others	2	4.7	2	8.3	0	0.0	0	0.0
	6th Pref								
QUESTION 17	Inc Prof	0	0.0	0	0.0	0	0.0	0	0.0
	Inc Pres	3	7.1	2	8.3	1	7.6	0	0.0
	K Ahead	0	0.0	0	0.0	0	0.0	0	0.0
	Attack	0	0.0	0	0.0	0	0.0	0	0.0
	Econ	0	0.0	0	0.0	0	0.0	0	0.0
	Others	17	40.4	7	29.1	6	46.1	5	100.0
QUESTION 18	Yes	36	85.7	21	87.5	11	84.6	5	100.0
	No	0	0.0	0	0.0	0	0.0	0	0.0
	Don't Know	3	7.1	2	8.3	1	7.6	0	0.0
QUESTION 19	EC	37	88.0	22	91.6	11	84.6	5	100.0
	MS	3	7.1	1	4.1	1	7.6	0	0.0
	Don't Know	0	0.0	0	0.0	0	0.0	0	0.0
QUESTION 20	Yes	37	88.0	21	87.5	11	84.6	5	100.0
	No	0	0.0	0	0.0	0	0.0	0	0.0
	Don't Know	4	9.5	2	8.3	1	7.6	0	0.0

FRANCHISING AND 1992

Country: Belgium (B)

Type	Resp	TL = 10		S = 3		P = 7		F = 0	
		N	%	N	%	N	%	N	%
QUESTION 1	S	3	30	N/A	N/A	N/A	N/A		
	P	7	70	N/A	N/A	N/A	N/A		
	F	0	0.0	N/A	N/A	N/A	N/A		
QUESTION 2	Yes	8	80.0	3	100.0	5	71.4		
	No	2	20.0	0	0.0	2	28.5		

Type	Resp	TL = 10 N	%	S = 3 N	%	P = 7 N	%	F = 0 N	%
QUESTION 3	Yes	1	10.0	0	0.0	1	14.2		
	No	1	10.0	0	0.0	1	14.2		
	N/A	8	80.0	3	100.0	5	71.4		
QUESTION 4	Yes	8	80.0	3	100.0	5	71.4		
	No	0	0.0	0	0.0	0	0.0		
	N/A	2	20.0	0	0.0	2	28.5		
QUESTION 5	EC	1	10.0	0	0.0	1	14.2		
	Non-EC	0	0.0	0	0.0	0	0.0		
	N/A	9	90.0	3	100.0	6	85.7		
QUESTION 6	Yes	8	80.0	3	100.0	5	71.4		
	No	0	0.0	0	0.0	0	0.0		
QUESTION 7	2 Years	8	80.0	3	100.0	5	71.4		
	5 Years	0	0.0	0	0.0	0	0.0		
	10 Years	0	0.0	0	0.0	0	0.0		
QUESTION 8	High	4	40.0	2	66.6	2	28.5		
	Medium	5	50.0	1	33.3	4	57.1		
	Low	1	10.0	0	0.0	1	14.2		
QUESTION 9	MF	4.5	45.0	0	0.0	4.5	64.2		
	Sub	1	10.0	0	0.0	1	14.2		
	JV	2.5	25.0	2	66.6	0.5	7.1		
	DF	2	20.0	1	33.3	1	14.2		
	Buy	0	0.0	0	0.0	0	0.0		
	Other	0	0.0	0	0.0	0	0.0		
	1st Pref								
QUESTION 10	GB	0	0.0	0	0.0	0	0.0		
	F	4	40.0	3	100.0	1	14.2		
	E	1	10.0	0	0.0	1	14.2		
	P	0	0.0	0	0.0	0	0.0		
	I	0	0.0	0	0.0	0	0.0		
	GR	0	0.0	0	0.0	0	0.0		
	D	3	30.0	0	0.0	2	28.5		
	DK	0	0.0	0	0.0	0	0.0		
	L	1	10.0	0	0.0	1	14.2		
	NL	1	10.0	0	0.0	2	28.5		
	B	0	0.0	0	0.0	0	0.0		
	EIR	0	0.0	0	0.0	0	0.0		
	2nd Pref								
QUESTION 10	GB	2	20.0	0	0.0	2	28.5		
	F	1	10.0	0	0.0	1	14.2		
	E	4	40.0	3	100.0	1	14.2		
	P	0	0.0	0	0.0	0	0.0		
	I	0	0.0	0	0.0	0	0.0		
	GR	0	0.0	0	0.0	0	0.0		
	D	0	0.0	0	0.0	1	14.2		
	DK	1	10.0	0	0.0	1	14.2		
	L	1	10.0	0	0.0	1	14.2		
	NL	1	10.0	0	0.0	0	0.0		
	B	0	0.0	0	0.0	0	0.0		
	EIR	0	0.0	0	0.0	0	0.0		

Type	Resp	TL = 10		S = 3		P = 7		F = 0	
		N	%	N	%	N	%	N	%
3rd Pref									
QUESTION 10	GB	0	0.0	0	0.0	0	0.0		
	F	1	10.0	0	0.0	1	14.2		
	E	1	10.0	0	0.0	1	14.2		
	P	0	0.0	1	33.3	0	0.0		
	I	2	20.0	0	0.0	1	14.2		
	GR	0	0.0	0	0.0	0	0.0		
	D	2	20.0	2	66.6	0	0.0		
	DK	0	0.0	0	0.0	0	0.0		
	L	1	10.0	0	0.0	1	14.2		
	NL	1	10.0	0	0.0	1	14.2		
	B	0	0.0	0	0.0	0	0.0		
	EIR	0	0.0	0	0.0	0	0.0		
4th Pref									
QUESTION 10	GB	1	10.0	0	0.0	1	14.2		
	F	0	0.0	0	0.0	0	0.0		
	E	1	10.0	0	0.0	1	14.2		
	P	3	30.0	2	66.6	1	14.2		
	I	1	10.0	0	0.0	1	14.2		
	GR	0	0.0	0	0.0	0	0.0		
	D	2	20.0	1	33.3	1	14.2		
	DK	0	0.0	0	0.0	0	0.0		
	L	0	0.0	0	0.0	0	0.0		
	NL	0	0.0	0	0.0	0	0.0		
	B	0	0.0	0	0.0	0	0.0		
	EIR	0	0.0	0	0.0	0	0.0		
QUESTION 11	P1 Cam	4	40.0	2	66.6	2	28.5		
	Approach	4	40.0	1	33.3	3	42.8		
QUESTION 12	Yes	10	100.0	3	100.0	7	100.0		
	No	0	0.0	0	0.0	0	0.0		
QUESTION 13	Yes	9	90.0	3	100.0	6	85.7		
	No	1	10.0	0	0.0	1	14.2		
QUESTION 14	V Important	8	80.0	3	100.0	5	71.4		
	Important	0	0.0	0	0.0	0	0.0		
	U Important	2	20.0	0	0.0	2	28.5		
QUESTION 15	Yes	3	30.0	1	33.3	2	28.5		
	No	5	50.0	2	66.6	3	42.8		
	Undecided	2	20.0	0	0.0	2	28.5		
QUESTION 16	Lang	0	0.0	0	0.0	0	0.0		
	Fin	3	30.0	1	33.3	2	28.5		
	MD	3	30.0	2	66.6	1	14.2		
	Opp	4	40.0	0	0.0	4	57.1		
1st Pref									
QUESTION 17	Inc Prof	5	50.0	0	0.0	5	71.4		
	Inc Pres	0	0.0	0	0.0	0	0.0		
	K Ahead	3	30.0	3	100.0	0	0.0		
	Attack	2	20.0	0	0.0	2	28.5		
	Econ	0	0.0	0	0.0	0	0.0		
	Others	0	0.0	0	0.0	0	0.0		

Type	Resp	TL = 10		S = 3		P = 7		F = 0	
		N	%	N	%	N	%	N	%
	2nd Pref								
QUESTION 17	Inc Prof	3	30.0	1	33.3	2	28.5		
	Inc Pres	3	30.0	0	0.0	3	42.8		
	K Ahead	0	0.0	0	0.0	0	0.0		
	Attack	0	0.0	0	0.0	0	0.0		
	Econ	2	20.0	2	66.6	0	0.0		
	Others	0	0.0	0	0.0	0	0.0		
	3rd Pref								
QUESTION 17	Inc Prof	2	20.0	2	66.6	0	0.0		
	Inc Pres	0	0.0	0	0.0	0	0.0		
	K Ahead	5	50.0	0	0.0	5	71.4		
	Attack	0	0.0	0	0.0	0	0.0		
	Econ	1	10.0	1	33.3	0	0.0		
	Others	0	0.0	0	0.0	0	0.0		
	4th Pref								
QUESTION 17	Inc Prof	0	0.0	0	0.0	0	0.0		
	Inc Pres	3	30.0	1	33.3	2	28.5		
	K Ahead	0	0.0	0	0.0	0	0.0		
	Attack	5	50.0	2	66.6	2	28.5		
	Econ	0	0.0	0	0.0	1	14.2		
	Others	0	0.0	0	0.0	0	0.0		
	5th Pref								
QUESTION 17	Inc Prof	0	0.0	0	0.0	0	0.0		
	Inc Pres	2	20.0	2	66.6	0	0.0		
	K Ahead	0	0.0	0	0.0	0	0.0		
	Attack	1	10.0	1	33.3	1	14.2		
	Econ	5	50.0	0	0.0	4	57.1		
	Others	0	0.0	0	0.0	0	0.0		
	6th Pref								
QUESTION 17	Inc Prof	0	0.0	0	0.0	0	0.0		
	Inc Pres	0	0.0	0	0.0	0	0.0		
	K Ahead	0	0.0	0	0.0	0	0.0		
	Attack	0	0.0	0	0.0	0	0.0		
	Econ	0	0.0	0	0.0	0	0.0		
	Others	8	80.0	3	100.0	5	71.4		
QUESTION 18	Yes	5	50.0	1	33.3	5	71.4		
	No	5	50.0	2	66.6	2	28.5		
	Don't Know	0	0.0	0	0.0	0	0.0		
QUESTION 19	EC	0	90.0	2	66.6	7	100.0		
	MS	0	0.0	0	0.0	0	0.0		
	Don't Know	1	10.0	1	33.3	0	0.0		
QUESTION 20	Yes	10	100.0	3	100.0	7	100.0		
	No	0	0.0	0	0.0	0	0.0		
	Don't Know	0	0.0	0	0.0	0	0.0		

Is franchising going to be an important economic force in the single market? (Question 20)

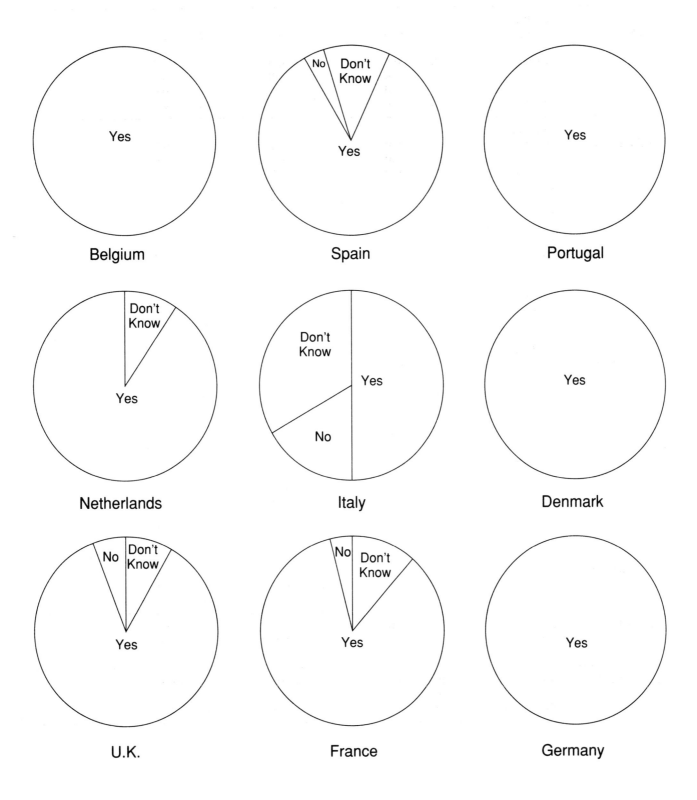

Is opening an outlet in another EC country a high, medium or low priority? (Question 8)

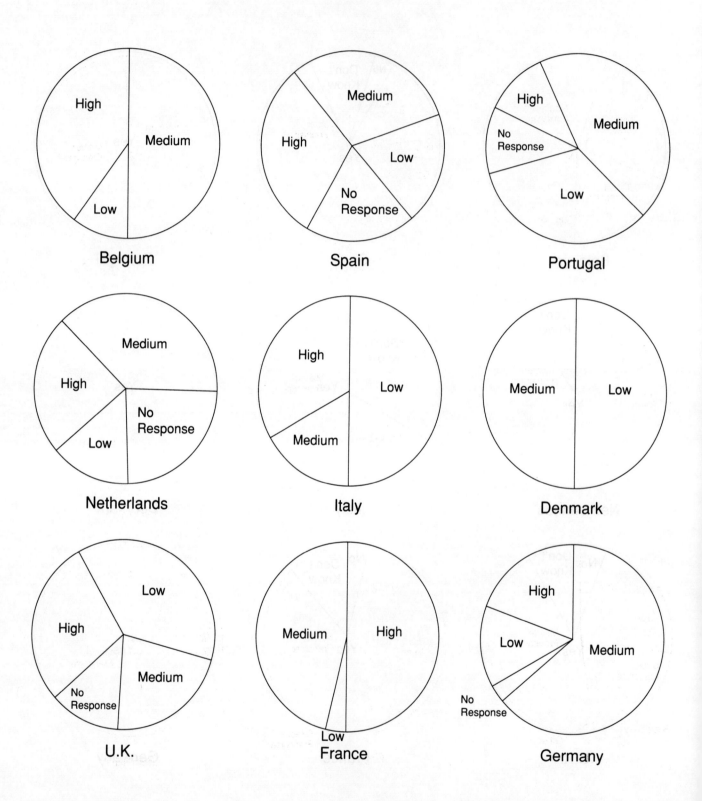

How would you prefer to enter another EC country? (Question 9)

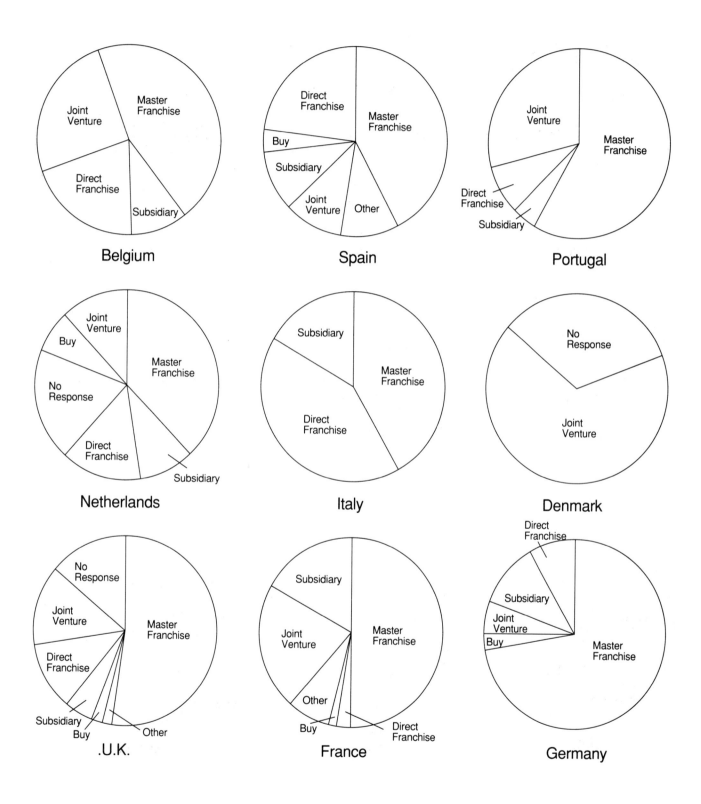

State the EC country you would most prefer to enter. (Question 10)

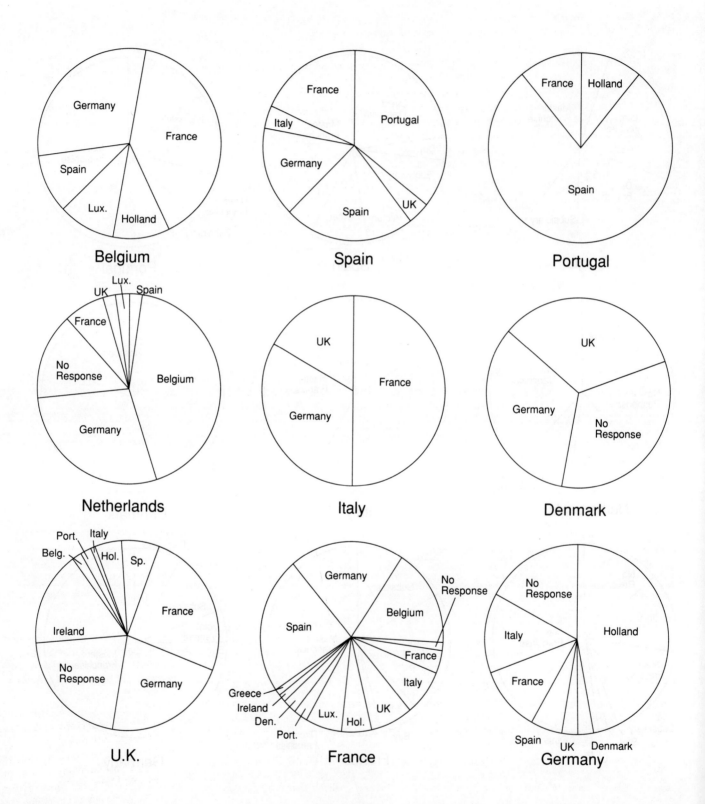

What is the biggest problem in trying to open up an outlet in another EC country? (Question 16)

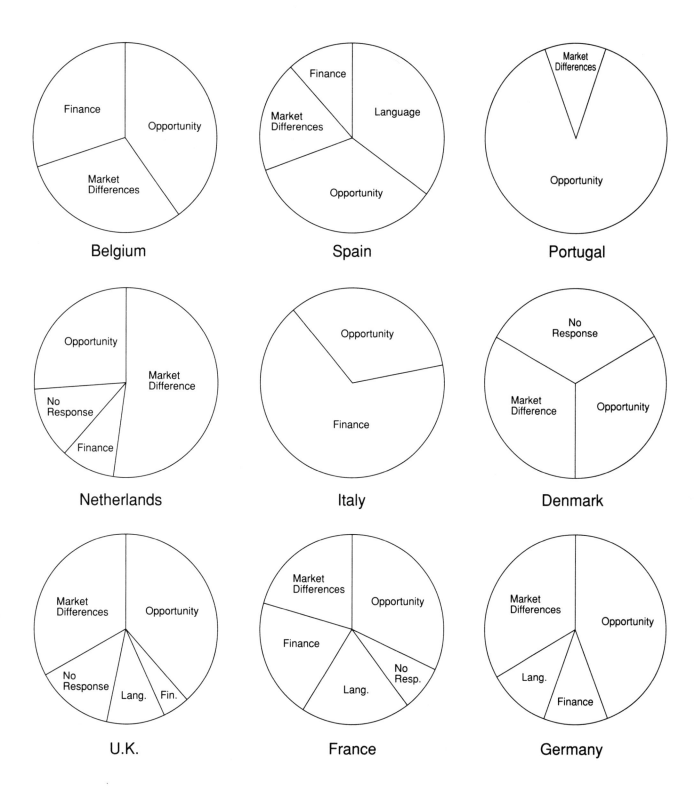

Should Franchising be regulated by law? (Question 18)

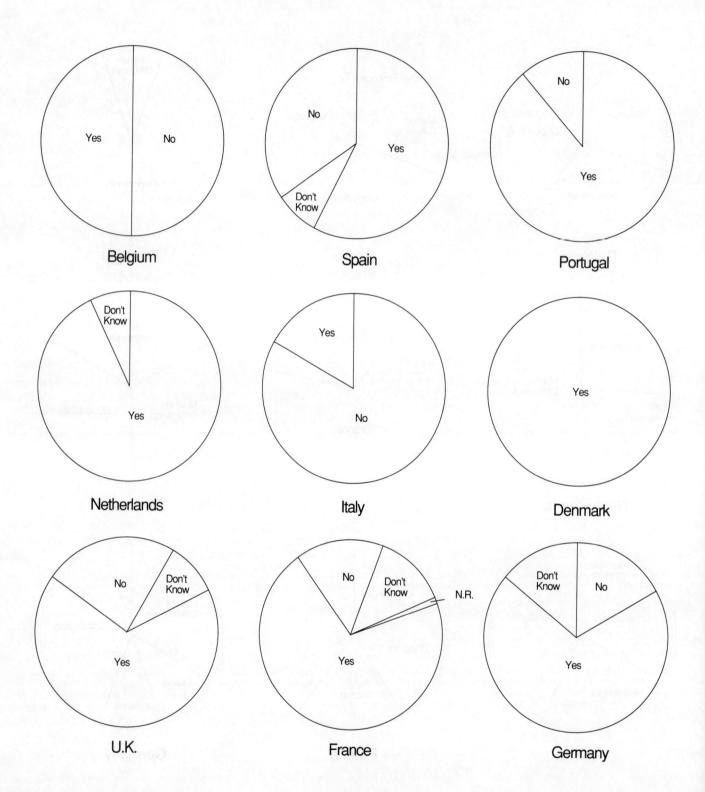

If Franchising is regulated by law, should it be by the EC Commission or by Individual Member State Governments?
(Question 19)

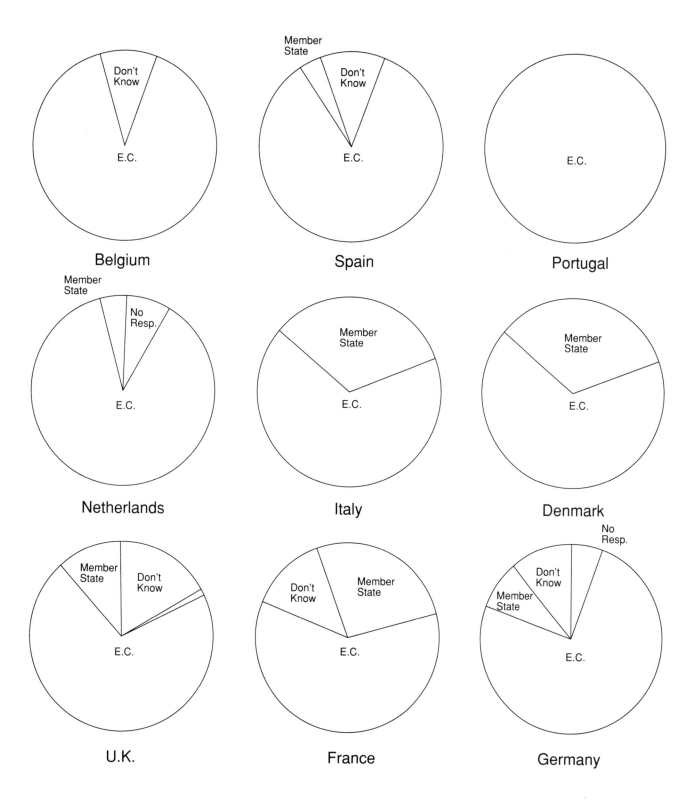

PART THREE

FRANCHISING
IN THE
SINGLE MARKET

CHAPTER 8

Introduction to the Single Market

By MARK ABELL and ANDREW LITTLE

Despite being founded some 40 years ago the European Community remains characterised in economic, political and financial terms by fragmentation and division. Despite the belief of many 'Europeans' in the single market, it still remains an elusive ideal, and the countries of Europe a collection of distinct and diverse markets.

The economies vary sharply not only between each of the 12 member states but also from region to region within each country. The contrasts between the industrial North of Italy and its more traditional agrarian South, the industrial powerhouse of Germany and underdeveloped provincial Portugal are cases in point. A 'two-speed Europe' in which the 'Northern States' (Britain, France, Germany, Benelux Northern Italy and Denmark) reap the benefits of the single market whilst the 'Southern States' (Greece, Spain, Portugal and parts of Italy and Ireland) are left behind has been seen as a distinct possibility.

In political terms Europe has been shaken by two oil crises and severe Asian competition bringing protectionism to the fore. The Gulf Crisis showed the increased influence of the 12 member states when dealing in unison although the temptation of individual states to act unilaterally seemed in certain cases difficult to resist. The member states have shown a marked ability to avoid adopting common policies and this in turn has led to the erection of many conflicting and irreconcilable barriers as regards free movement of goods, taxation and technical standards, to mention only a few. Industrial research while being highly funded is lacking in any uniformity or co-operation between member states leading to the inefficient use of resources, unnecessary duplication and wasteful competition. Thus although the EC's total budget for research is equivalent to that of Japan, in terms of achievements the member states have fallen badly behind.

In financial terms, the absence of a common currency compounds the problems created by the barriers to free movement of capital and the lack of co-ordination within the financial markets.

As a result EC industry has on the whole lagged far behind that of its main competitors in Japan and the United States. This has been most marked in the high technology sector. For example, the EC share of external trade in manufactured goods fell by 1.4% between 1974 and 1985, as against increases of 0.7% for the USA and 5.4% for Japan. In the information technology and office automation sectors the Community's share fell by 2.2% whilst the USA and Japan increased by 3.3% and 5.5% respectively. Investment in the Community in the period 1981-1987 increased by 4% compared with 30% in the USA and 31% in Japan. The highest Community productivity rate in electronic goods is

47% of that of the USA, whilst that of Japan was almost two and a half times the US rate.

The cost of this fragmented 'non-Europe' is therefore considerable and the Cecchini Report *The European Challenge 1992 – The Benefits of A Single Market* (Wildwood House) has calculated that the loss through frontier formalities amounts to 12,000m ECUs annually, whilst the non-harmonisation of technical standards applicable to numerous products costs the companies and consumers approximately 40,000-50,000m ECUs per year. Blatant discrimination in not awarding public procurement contracts by member state governments presents a further cost of 40,000m ECUs annually whilst the limited size of national markets increases the cost of production of EC industry by over 10,000m ECUs.

Despite this however the EC has immense potential with a population of approximately 340 million compared to 244m in the US and 122m in Japan. It has a GDP of ECU 3,669 billion compared with ECU 3,869 billion for the US and ECU 2,058 billion for Japan.

The creation of a single market aims at removing the cost of a 'non-Europe' and requires the removal of all physical, technical and fiscal barriers. It is not merely the anticipated cost saving which will benefit EC industry but also the triggering effect which the barriers' removal is expected to achieve. The reduced costs of goods and the ability to treat the Community as one single market is expected to create a rennaissance in European industry and create a new competitive environment which causes industry to rethink its strategy to take full advantage of the opportunities created by the single market. Economies of scale in production, research and development, distribution and advertising are all seen to be geared to success in the new European age. Industry and commerce will have to strive for a greater degree of efficiency in adopting the best and leanest methods for management and organisation. Failure to perceive and attack the EC as one single market will have dire effects for industry and commerce. It is for this reason that the single market holds so much potential for business format franchising.

The concept of an internal market is not a new one and originates from the Treaty of Rome. However, at the beginning of the 1980s member states became keenly aware that it was far from being realised and a series of Summits in 1982, 1984 and 1985 brought together EC heads of state or government to identify completion of the internal market as a real priority.

The first concrete result of this movement was the EC Commission's White Paper published in 1985 (reference June 1985 (COM) 85) which set out, in 300 proposals (later reduced to 279), the measures which would have to be adopted to achieve successfully a single market. These issues were divided into three headings – the removal of physical barriers, the removal of technical barriers and the removal of fiscal barriers. A timetable specifying the date for implementation of the various proposals was set, with a deadline of 31 December 1992. The White Paper was a brave, ambitious and comprehensive programme the like of which had never been seen before in the history of the development of the Community.

On 14 and 28 February 1986, the Single European Act (SEA) was signed, constituting a revision of the Treaty of Rome and setting in place various mechanisms aimed at achieving the implementation of the White Paper.

The SEA provides a definition of the internal market and endorses the deadline for 1992. The Single Market is defined as '. . . an area without internal frontiers in which the free movement of goods, persons, services and capital is to be ensured . . .'. The date was chosen because, as pointed out by Lord Cockburn (for four years Britain's Senior Commissioner in Brussels and whose brainchild the White Paper was), it was far enough off to allow those concerned time to prepare, but close enough to focus the mind.

The start of 1992 marks the beginning of a new procedure for the approximation of laws in all areas where the White Paper has not been applied. The Council of Ministers will be able to force member states to recognise each other's national laws as equivalent, but the absence of a mandatory deadline has been criticised by a number of eminent 'Europeans'.

Another important measure brought in by the SEA is the substitution for unanimous consent of qualified majority voting in the Council for Ministers, as regards the adoption of proposals relating to completion of the internal market, in particular any matter concerning the approximation of laws. This rule, in principle, circumvents the Luxembourg Compromise Council and the practice of unanimous consent. Henceforth, the members of the Council will be able to override the objections of any one of the member states. The rule is nevertheless ambiguous as the conditions in which it may be used are not clearly specified. Further, the Single European Act contains enough 'safeguard' clauses to allow member states to exempt themselves from modified directives adopted in this manner. In the name of health, safety and public policy or by revoking requirements related to protection of the environment or the working environment, they will be able to avoid the application of a decision they have not approved. It is actually the institutionalisation of a 'two speed' Europe in which directives would not be executed identically everywhere because the economies are too different. The SEA also contains a certain number of provisions modifying the functioning of the Community institutions.

Since 1985, only a limited progress has been made towards the realisation of the White Paper objectives. Though the Commission has struggled to keep up with its main schedule, the Council is lagging behind. Although the Commission had developed draft directives for close to 90% of the items examined in the White Paper by 31 December 1988, only 142

have been adopted by the Council. This slow progress is due in part to the delay by member states in ratifying the SEA, and also to the cumbersome nature of the legislative process. The Council is also reluctant to delegate its executive powers to the Commission. There is still a considerable amount to be done in order to achieve the single market by 1992.

The Commission issues progress reports every year and the fourth progress report was issued in April 1989, although fresh figures were released in January 1990. Following the changes in the original proposals, the Commission's current programme consists of 279 separate proposals. Of these 261 have been presented by the Commission to the Council and 142 have been adopted by the Council, including 10 which have been partially adopted. By the end of 1989 50% of the White Paper measures had been adopted. The speed at which measures have been adopted increased considerably throughout 1988/1989 although the actual implementation of Community measures by the member states in their national laws is significantly behind schedule. Out of 68 directives which had entered into force at the end of October 1989 only 7 had been incorporated into national law in all member states.

It is easy to identify areas where delays have occurred and to point to the inherent sluggishness in the bureaucratic process to implement the programme towards a Single Market. However, now that this programme has commenced and is well under way it is almost inconceivable that it can be stopped, short of the disbandment of some of the basic structures of the EC. Moreover, as 1992 approaches, the process of the implementation of the Single Market is gaining momentum, fueled by a desire in the industries of the individual member states not to lag behind their competitors. The debate within the EC is now over the infrastructure of the Community. The pressure is on to create a federal Europe with centralised decision-making on matters such as the economy, foreign affairs and defence.

These changes provide a unique opportunity for significant growth in business format franchising. By its very nature franchising, with its promotion of well recognised international brand names, is well suited for the development of businesses and service industries across frontiers. The removal of obstacles to the movement of goods and services across frontiers is likely to be particularly beneficial to both franchisors and franchisees. Franchisors should be able to expand their systems internationally far more quickly. Although the cultural and language differences are likely to remain throughout the EC the technical and fiscal barriers which inhibit the free movement of goods and services will reduce.

To franchisees an additional incentive to joining a franchise system will be that the system itself is far more likely to become Pan-European as opposed to remaining purely a domestic system. Furthermore a franchisor in one member state will more easily be able to develop franchised units in other states.

In considering the changes which the Single Market will herald for franchising it may be appropriate to briefly consider the background of franchising in the USA. When examining the reasons why business format franchising was created as a business development system in the USA, and the rapid speed with which it grew, the first cause which often comes to mind is the common culture and language that applies throughout the USA. However, possibly as important is the relatively low level of physical, technical and fiscal barriers between the States in the USA of the sort which the SEA was enacted to break down in Europe. This is notwithstanding the considerable body of franchise law which has developed throughout the USA. A US franchisor coming into Europe is often bewildered and frustrated by the range of the different barriers he has to surmount in order to establish his franchise system throughout individual member states. It is frequently these rather than cultural differences which may prevail amongst the member states which are the real cause for the slow development of a franchise system. A US franchisor compares this with the speed with which he has established his system across the USA.

The effect of the SEA and the implementation of the Single Market has already been recognised in the USA. The cry of 'Fortress Europe' is born out of a fear of the renaissance of European industry and the creation of a competitive environment in which European industry will be able to shrug off the parochial ties which have hitherto fettered its development. The US industrialist and his Japanese counterpart are conscious that their European competitors will be more able to emulate their own levels of efficiency and competitiveness.

Business format franchising has played a very significant part in the US commercial scene; there seems every reason that as the barriers in Europe come down so franchising will similarly play as significant a role in the European business world, and will become an everyday way of business development amongst the member states.

CHAPTER 9

Barriers to a Single Market

By MARK ABELL

As mentioned in Chapter 8 above the White Paper describes in great detail the barriers which need to to be abolished before a Single Market can be achieved within the European Community.

These barriers have an immediate impact upon franchising in the EC and their removal can be expected to have an equally positive effect upon it. Not only do they make it difficult for franchisors to physically move their goods across national boundaries, they also add substantial 'hidden costs', so reducing the overally profitability.

As mentioned above (Chapter 8) the Cecchini Report analyses in great detail these barriers and their effects upon trade. These all apply directly to franchising, for example customs-related costs put a charge on companies equal to a major proportion of their profits from intra-EC trade. Firms in effect pay a penalty dividend (approximately 25% of profits in many sectors) to the National Board of Controllers for the privilege of going 'European'. Smaller companies including many franchisors are to a significant extent debarred from transport activities by administrative costs and regulatory procedures.

A bewildering array of price differences faces consumers of essential services; for example car insurance may vary by as much as 300% between the highest and lowest price countries. Tariffs for telephone services vary approximately 50% from one EC country to another.

The cost of Europe's fragmented market is enormous. EC firms were estimated by the Report to pay approximately ECU 8 billion in administrative costs and delays. Most alarming perhaps to franchisors is the fact that the Report clearly showed that small or middle sized companies pay more as a result of the lack of a Single Market. Customs costs per consignment were found to be up to 30% to 45% higher for companies with under 250 employees than for larger companies. The introduction of a harmonised system of commodity description and coding, the new community tariff (Taric) applying to goods whose description is harmonized and the introduction of the Single Administrative Document (see Chapter 00 below) will hopefully decrease this to some extent. Nevertheless the problem will still remain until all of the barriers are finally pulled down.

PHYSICAL BARRIERS

The existence of national trade quotas, the operation of the Common Agricultural Policy, the collection of VAT and excise duties, health controls, transport controls, statistical controls, immigration controls, security and customs controls all act as effective physical barriers to the creation of a single market. The removal of these barriers seems to be affecting the free movement of both goods and individuals. Free movement of goods will be effected by the introduction of the Single Administrative Document (SAD), the elimination of national trade quotas, the progressive abolishing of road transport quotas and other similar steps. The free movement of individuals (see Chapter 22 below) is hindered by the advent of terrorism and drug trafficking and progress has been somewhat limited. The right of residence in other member states (see Chapter 22 below) is also an important move although this has been particularly difficult for non-active persons, retired persons and students.

TECHNICAL BARRIERS

Technical barriers are the result of differing member state laws and practices which tend to inhibit or indeed prevent trade within the Community.

The vastly different technical regulations and standards in different member states, the unnecessary duplication of testing and certification procedures, (see Chapter 13 below) and the reluctance of government organisations to end discrimination in terms of those companies that are allowed to tender for public procurement contracts (see Chapter 16 below) are examples of technical barriers affecting product based franchises and other businesses. The barriers restricting free banking and insurance services between the member states (see Chapters 23 and 24 below) are examples of technical barriers affecting services.

The EC Commission has adopted two differing approaches to the removal of technical barriers. The first method has its origin in the Cassis De Dijon Case (Case 120/78 *Rewe Zentral AG v Bundesmonopolverwaltung Für Branntwein* [1979] ECR 649) and is known as the 'Mutual Recognition' approach. The second approach is that of harmonisation.

The Cassis De Dijon case clearly indicated that the obstacles to movement within the Community resulting from disparities between national laws relating to the marketing of products must be accepted in so far as those provisions may be recognised as being necessary in order to satisfy mandatory requirements relating to the effectiveness of fiscal supervision, the protection of public health, the fairness of commercial transactions and the defence of the consumer. Where a product is lawfully manufactured and marketed in one member state it should be able to be sold without restriction throughout the community. If products meet the legislative requirements in a member state it is presumed to be of such a standard that it can be resold in other member states even if it does not exactly meet the requirements of the other states. Thus the so called doctrine of mutuality. In the Cassis de Dijon case a liqueur was made and lawfully marketed in France although as it did not contain the minimum amount of alcohol required under German law, it was not allowed to be marketed in Germany by the German authorities. The European Court of Justice ruled the German authorities to be acting unlawfully as a minimum alcohol requirement was not a necessary provision for the protection of public health.

In situations where mutual recognition is not enough, Community rules are necessary to replace the varying legislative provisions of each member state. This harmonisation has been widely used by the Community over the last 25 years although it can be a painfully slow process due to the competing and differing interests involved. As a result the Commission has reduced harmonising legislation to a minimum and where harmonisation is not absolutely necessary the mutual recognition principle applies instead. The harmonisation of technical standards (see Chapter 13 below) means that this approach is becoming easier with time. Whilst services in 1985 represented 58.5% of the value added to the EC economy (compared with only 26% for manufactured goods), services have always taken somewhat of a backseat. The White Paper aims however to redress this imbalance in areas such as banking, insurance and telecommunications which have traditionally been heavily regulated in member states. Differing regulations give rise to significant technical barriers. The White Paper approach is one of applying the rules of the state where the bank (for example) was originally based. Host country rules and control are restricted to the bare minimum so as to avoid barriers arising.

The non-recognition of professional and other qualifications also give rise to technical barriers restricting the free movement of individuals. Progress is slowly being made to remove this barrier. Already doctors, nurses, dentists and midwives throughout EC member states have had their basic training harmonised. Progress has been made in the areas of mining, electricity, gas, oil and water. The directive on a general system for recognition of higher education diplomas bearing on completion of professional education and training of at least three years duration (Directive No 89/48, OJ1989 L 19/16), was adopted in December 1988 and should give considerable impetus to the removal of such barriers.

The removal of discrimination in public procurement has also been stepped up (see Chapter 16 below).

FISCAL BARRIERS

Fiscal barriers are created by differing rates and types of indirect taxation in member states, particularly VAT and Excise duties. Indirect taxes are collected by the member state in which the goods are finally consumed. Export goods are tax free, and the importer pays VAT and Excise duties. The rates of VAT vary from $0 - 38\%$, whilst Excise duties range from a high of 10.5% to a low of 0% per bottle of alcohol. The resulting artificial price differences between member states clearly act to the detriment of consumers and are a significant obstacle to the free movement of goods and open competition.

Their effect upon franchising is obvious. The ability of the franchisor to encourage a uniform approach to pricing is greatly reduced and the administrative burden resulting from cross boarder movement of goods greatly increases.

Proposals for a uniform system of indirect taxation have existed since 1987. However, bearing in mind that the difference between taxation rates of American states do not show any real adverse affect upon trade, it has been deemed only necessary to approximate the rates of indirect taxation within $2.5 - 3\%$. (Further details are given in Chapter 33 below). Excise duty is also seen to be in need of change, with harmonisation and the inter-linking of bonded warehouses to be put into effect together with the abolition of duty-free concessions between member states.

CHAPTER 10

The Basic Freedoms and their Effects on Franchising

By MARK ABELL

(1) FREE MOVEMENT OF GOODS

If a product based franchise is to be able to approach the Single Market properly it must be able to transport its products throughout the Community freely, cheaply and with as little red tape as possible. Those measures leading to the free movement of goods are, therefore, of great importance to franchising, and deserve further consideration.

(a) The Customs Union

The European Community is based both on a customs union between member states which prohibits them from imposing on each other import and export duties and all charges having equivalent effect, and on the adoption of a Common Customs Tariff as regards their dealings with non member states. Goods are defined by the Court of Justice as 'products which can be valued in money and which are capable, as such, of forming the subject of commercial transactions' *(Commission v. Italy* [1968] ECR 423). The term therefore covers all goods which are likely to be dealt with by franchises, but not, for example, currency.

It is important for franchisors from outside the EC to note that products coming from outside the member states are entitled to free circulation if the import formalities have been complied with and any custom duties or charges having equivalent effect which are payable have been levied in the appropriate member state, and if they have not benefited from the total or partial drawback on such duties or charges.

In order to give effect to free movement of goods Council Directive 83/643/EEC (OJ) 1983 L 359/8 (as amended by Directive 87/53/EEC (OJ) 1987 L 24/33) was adopted. As mentioned above the cost of delays at member state boarders has been estimated at 1,000 million ECU. Until all barriers to the free flow of goods between member states are abolished the current measures aim at easing the controls. At present only limited success has been achieved, although the introduction of the Single Administrative Document (SAD) goes a long way to reducing red tape (see Chapter 12 below).

Article 12 of the Treaty of Rome itself also addresses this issue (which has direct effect) and prevents member states from introducing between themselves any new customs duties or charges having equivalent effect and from increasing those already in existence. Customs duties and other charges having equivalent effect on imports have been gradually abolished in accordance with articles 13(2), 14 and 15 of the Treaty of Rome (all of which have direct effect). Article 16 requires the member states to abolish between themselves customs duties and charges having equivalent effect. Article 17(1) provides that articles 9 to 15(1) of the Treaty also apply to customs duties of a fiscal nature.

(b) The Common Customs Tariff (CCT)

The CCT facilitates the easier international movement of goods and so has a direct effect upon franchising within the single market. Despite fears over a 'fortress Europe' developing (see Chapter 37 below), the member states are committed under article 18 of the Treaty of Rome to develop international trade and lower trade barriers by way of entering into agreements based on reciprocity and mutual advantage and aimed at reducing customs duties. This to an extent mirrors the aims of the General Agreement on Tariffs and Trade (GATT) (see Chapter 37 below). Article 29 of the Treaty provides that in striving to achieve the CCT, the Commission must comply with four basic guidelines, namely:

1. The need to promote trade between member states and third countries;
2. Development of conditions of competition in the Community insofar as they lead to an improvement in the competitive capacity of undertakings;
3. The requirements of the Community as regards the supply of raw materials and semi-finished goods; in this connection the Commission will take care to avoid distorting conditions of competition between member states in respect of finished goods;
4. The need to avoid serious disturbances to the economies of member states and to ensure rational development of production and expansion of consumption within the Community.

The CCT was established for industrial products from 1st July 1968 and customs duties between the original six members, Denmark and the United Kingdom were abolished on 1st July 1977. On 1st January 1986 customs duties were abolished between the then nine member states. On 1st March 1986 customs duties were abolished between the ten member states, Spain and Portugal. (This, however, was only in relation to Spanish and Portuguese exports and it will be established in relation to imports on 1st January, 1993).

The aim of the CCT is to verify the exact amount of duty which can be levied on specific goods. In 1988 the rules underwent significant change when on 1st January 1988 the Combined Nomenclature (CN) was adopted. This nomenclature is the same as that used by the EC's main trading partners and was introduced by Regulation (EEC) No. 2658/87. The CN is based upon the International Convention on the Harmonised Commodity Description Coding System, and meets both the requirements of the CCT and of the external trade statistics of the Community. The Community also introduced an integrated Community tariff (Taric) which incorporates various provisions such as tariff quotas which are not included in the CN.

This will greatly reduce franchisors' administrative burden vis a vis imported goods.

Taric is updated in each member state by way of electronic data transfer whilst customs procedures are expedited through the CN project. The most recent CN Commission Regulation (EEC) No. 2886/89 (OJ 1989 L 282/1) runs for some 692 pages and defines general rules and specific provisions for particular goods.

(c) Quantitative Restrictions

Quantitative restrictions on imports and any measures having equivalent effect would greatly reduce the attractiveness of the single market to franchisors. However such restrictions are, as a principle, prohibited between member states (Article 30 of the Treaty of Rome).

Whilst Article 31 (1) requires the member states to refrain from introducing between themselves any new quantitative restrictions or measures having equivalent effect, Article 32(1) provides that member states must refrain from making more restrictive quotas and measures having equivalent effect which existed at the date of the entry into force of the Treaty. In addition, article 32(2) provides that these quotas are to be abolished by the end of the 'transitional period'. Article 33 provides a timetable for the elimination of quantitative restrictions. Article 34 provides that quantitative restrictions on imports and all measures having equivalent effect are prohibited between member states. Member states are committed under article 35 to abolish quantitative restrictions and those having equivalent effect on them stated in the timetable so long as the general economic situation and the situation of the particular economic sector concerned so permits.

Commission Directive 70/50 EEC (1970 OJ No. L13/29) lists the number of measures which have equivalent effect to a quantitative restriction and which need to be abolished. 'Measures' include laws, regulations, administrative provisions, administrative practices and all instruments issuing from a public authority, including recommendations. They do not have to include obstacles to trade such as customs duties, changes having equivalent effect or state aids which are covered by other provisions of the Treaty of Rome.

There are, however, exceptions to the requirements for the free movement of goods. These are found in the case of *Rewe-Zentral AG v Bundesmonopolverwaltung für Branntwein* (commonly referred to as the Cassis de Dijon case (see Chapter 26) ([1979] ECR649) and Article 36 of the Treaty of Rome. They have a substantial impact upon franchising in the Single Market.

In the Cassis de Dijon case it was argued that the liquor manufactured in France could not be sold in Germany under the name Cassis de Dijon as it did not comply with the relevant requirements of German national law. The Court took the view that goods lawfully produced and marketed in one member state must, in principle, be admitted to the market of any other member state.

However, Article 36 lays down a number of exceptions, to which the court in the Cassis de Dijon case added a further three grounds.

Article 36 of the Treaty provides:

'The provisions of article 30 to 34 shall not preclude prohibitions or restrictions on imports, exports or goods in transit justified on grounds of public morality, public policy or public security; the protection of health and life of humans, animals or plants, protection of national treasures possessing artistic historical archeological value or the protection of industrial or commercial property. Such provisions or restrictions shall not, however, constitute a means of arbitrary discrimination or a disguised restriction on trade between member states'

The Cassis de Dijon case provided that there were three other grounds upon which disparities between national law of member states relating to the marketing of products must be accepted. These are the effectiveness of fiscal supervision, the fairness of commercial transactions and the defence of the consumer. The effectiveness of fiscal supervision refers to tax evasion and in the fairness of commercial transactions to fair competition.

This list should not be thought of as being exhaustive. For example, protection of the environment is also recognised by the Court of Justice as an exception by article 100A(4) of the Treaty of Rome.

A franchisor expanding its operation throughout the EC must therefore ensure that its products are not excluded from free movement by Article 36 or the Cassis de Dijon ruling. Failure to do so will make the establishment of a pan-EC franchise extremely difficult if not impossible. The benefits of a single market such as reduced production and administration costs would effectively be denied such a franchisor.

As mentioned above, Article 100 provides for legislative harmonisation as to the manner in which to complete the internal market. The harmonisation of standards (see Chapter 13 below) has also assisted the free movement of goods within the common market as has the opening up of public procurement policy (see Chapter 16 below).

(2) FREE MOVEMENT OF WORKERS

The free movement of workers is governed by Part 2 Title III (Articles 48 − 51) of the Treaty of Rome. This has an obvious impact upon the ease with which a franchisor can expand its operation from member state to member state.

The Treaty basically provides as follows:

1. The abolition of any discrimination based on nationality between workers of the member states as regards employment, remuneration and other conditions of work and employment. There is no general definition of what amounts to a 'worker'. Of particular importance to franchising is the

fact that self-employed persons are excluded by Articles 52 to 58 of the Treaty.

2. The freedom of movement is subject to limitations justified on the grounds of public policy, public security, or public health and entails the right to accept offers of employment made freely within the territory of member states.

3. To stay in a member state for the purpose of employment the worker must act in accordance with the provisions governing the employment of nationals of that state as laid down by law, regulation or administrative action

4. To remain in the territory of a member state after having being employed in that state subject to certain conditions. The position is now governed by Council Regulation (EEC) No. 1612/68 of 16th October 1960 (OJ No. L257/2) — as amended by the Acts of Accession 1979 and 1985 and Council decision 23/101/EEC and the Commission Regulation EEC No. 1251/70 of 29th June 1970 (OJ No. L142/24) and Council Regulation EEC No. 1612/68 and Council Regulation 68/360/EEC of 15th October 1968).

The Fontainebleau European Council of 1984 established an ad hoc Committee on a United Europe (the so-called Adonnino Committee). They submitted reports to provide the Commission with proposals as regards the 'People's Europe', particularly in relation to social rights, education and Community services. These reports were approved by the European Council and led to the adoption of a resolution reducing the checks on individuals crossing the EEC's internal frontiers (OJ No. C159.19.6.1984).

The difficulties of free movement associated with crime, drugs and terrorism have meant that progress has been extremely slow although the eventual aim is to eliminate Police and Customs formalities and replace them with occasional spot checks and temporary special border controls. There is also a proposal to facilitate free movement of workers through an obligation on member states to provide proof of residence through a European Communities Residence Card, although so far negotiations for a general right of residence for a Community citizen have not been concluded.

In relation to individual tax exemptions, a number of Directives have been adopted.

Directive 85/348/EEC amends cancelled Directive 69/169/EEC on the exemption from turnover tax and excise duty of imports and international travel. Directive 85/49/EEC amends cancelled Directive 74/561/EEC on tax reliefs to be allowed on importation of goods in small consignments of a non-commercial character within the Community and Directive 88/331/EEC amends Council Directive 83/181/EEC concerning exception for small consignments from VAT.

Directive 89/48/EEC aims at establishing a general system for the recognition of higher education diplomas awarded on completion of professional education and training of at least three years duration so enabling professional people qualified in one member state to become a member of his or her counterpart profession in another member state without the necessity for re-qualification.

Entitlement to Social Security is also a Pan European right.

(3) FREEDOM OF ESTABLISHMENT AND TO PROVIDE SERVICES

Chapter 2 of Title II of the Treaty of Rome relates to the right of establishment and Chapter 3 to services. A distinction between the two is a difficult one but may be summarised by stating that temporary pursuit of an activity will amount to a service and a degree of permanence will amount to establishment.

Both freedom to provide services and freedom of establishment are vital to franchisors and franchisees operating within the EC. Without both freedoms the scope for exploiting the Single Market and the methods of such exploitation would be severely reduced. For example, without the freedom of establishment a French franchisor could not easily establish a pilot operation in the United Kingdom. As both good practice and the British Franchise Association's rules require the establishment of a pilot operation before the establishment of franchise outlets, the lack of such a freedom would greatly increase the difficulties of the French franchisor. At best the whole process would be considerably slower.

Both the freedom of establishment and freedom to provide services have been implemented principally by Directives which are far too numerous to mention in this text. The SEA has added an extra impetus to the achievement of both freedoms.

The mutual recognition of professional and academic qualifications mentioned above is vital to the freedom of establishment and Council Directive 89/48/EEC on General Assistance for the Recognition of Higher Education Diplomas or on Completion of Professional Education and Training of at Least a Year's Duration (OJ NO. L19/16). This general directive applies to all regulated professions for which University level training of at least 3 years is required and recognition is based upon mutual trust. However, where there are major differences in educational training for the structure of a profession, there is provision for compensatory mechanisms of an non-discriminatory type or an aptitude test. The Directive was due to be adopted by all member states by 4th January 1991.

Article 52 of the Treaty of Rome which concerns the abolition of restrictions to the right of establishment based on nationality, also applies to the setting up of agencies, branches or subsidiaries by nationals of any member states established within the territory of another member state. This is perhaps one of the most important provisions of the Treaty of Rome for franchisors as it gives them full freedom in choosing how to structure the development of the Pan EC Franchise Network.

The widely differing nature of franchised businesses means that there can be no one correct way in which to exploit the single market. The similarities between a drain cleaning business and one engaged in beauty therapy are minimal. What amounts to a good, commercially effective structure for one may be unsuitable for the other. The freedom of establishment gives a far wider choice to franchisors. It gives them the ability to exploit the single market in the manner best suited to their particular business.

Freedom of establishment includes the right to take up and pursue activities as self-employed persons and to set up and manage undertakings, especially companies or firms within the meaning of Article 58 (2) of the Treaty. Establishment allows the national of one member state to pursue his activity in any other member state under the conditions laid down for nationals of that member state by the law of that country. This is, of course, subject to provisions on free movement of capital considered below.

On 18th December 1961, the Council adopted a General Programme on the Abolition of Restrictions on Freedom of Establishment (OJ.1962 2/36). This set out the conditions under which freedom of establishment was to be attained for each type of activity. The programme incorporates rules set out in Article 54 (3) concerning the implementation of freedom of establishment. Priority is given to activities where freedom of establishment makes a valuable contribution to the development of production and trade under this article so that the EC Commissioners effected extensive organisational programmes in the field of EC Company Law (see Chapters 17 and 18 below). Various other directives have also been passed concerning areas such as the food and beverage industry, the film industry and agriculture.

During the transitional period, which ended on 31st December 1969 a few directives were passed, but the push towards freedom of establishment was given a filip by the judgment in the case of *Reyner v. Belgium* ([1974] ECR 631). This held that Article 52 of the Treaty of Rome has direct effect. Under Article 54, a number of directives covering varying occupations such as Doctors, Nurses, Dentists, and Veterinary Surgeons have been issued.

Article 52 therefore imposes an obligation to achieve a specific result, and the fulfilment of that obligation may be made easier by, but is not dependant on, implementation of a programme of progressive measures. If there is no special provision of Community law, the member states are required to take the measures necessary to ensure freedom of establishment. They are also required to bring their existing legislation into line with Community law.

The difference between the right of establishment and the right to provide services is a thin and technical one. The service may be performed without the formality of establishing a physical presence or business, for example, a franchisor based in the United Kingdom granting a sub-franchisor in, say, Spain assistance to provide training. In fact, the word 'services' is used as a catch all term to cover activities not embraced by the provisions for the movement of goods, persons and capital. If the franchisor maintains a permanent presence in a member state in which a service is provided, even if that presence does not take the form of a branch or agency, but rather is merely an office, the enterprise will be subject to the rules on the right of establishment and not those on the provision of services.

The freedom to provide services therefore is of fundamental importance to franchisors operating within the Single Market.

The restrictions to be abolished under Article 59 include all requirements imposed on franchisors and other persons providing a service on the basis of their nationality or the fact that they reside in a member state other than the one in which the service is provided. The prohibition of discrimination applies to both direct and indirect discrimination and extends not only to public authorities, but also to any rules regulating the provision of services. It affects all relationships which have a connection with the Community and includes the freedom for recipients of services to go to another member state to receive the service there. It may be restricted only by provisions that are justified by the general good.

A General Programme for the Abolition of Restriction of Freedom to Provide Services (GPARFPS) – the counter-part of the General Programme for the Abolition of Restriction and Freedom of Establishment mentioned above, was also adopted. The *Van Binsbergen* case ([1974] ECR 1299) held that Article 59 has direct effect and therefore creates individual rights that the national courts must protect, at least in so far as it seeks to abolish discrimination based on nationality.

Article 60 of the Treaty of Rome describes services as being:

'Normally provided for remuneration, in so far as they are not covered by the provisions relating to freedom of movement of goods, capital and persons.

Services shall in particular include:-
(a) activities of an industrial character;
(b) activities of a commercial character;
(c) activities of craftsmen;
(d) activities of the professions.'

Thus, franchisors are, by virtue of Article 59, free to extend their franchise network throughout the twelve member states and then supervise and police it to help ensure its success.

(4) FREE MOVEMENT OF CAPITAL

Article 67 of the Treaty of Rome provides for the abolition, between the member states, of all restrictions on movement of capital belonging to persons resident in member states and any discrimination on the nationality or on the place of residence of the parties or on the place where such capital is invested.

The reason for this is that movement of capital is seen as a significant way of increasing productivity and raising the standard of living within the EC.

Of all of the freedoms necessary for the creation of a Single Market, free movement of capital has probably caused the most problems for member states.

As far as franchisors are concerned, the free movement of capital between the member states is very important. Without it, franchisors based in one member state, say France, would not be able to receive initial franchise fees, service charges, royalties and any other payments such as advertising fund contributions from franchisees in another state, without a great deal of administrative difficulty, if at all.

However, progress towards the liberalisation of capital movements, apart from Directives in 1960 and 1962 has been slow, and in fact has even regressed since several member states have made use of the available safeguard clauses.

In dealing with movement of capital, the Community has had to be aware of other, wider-ranging agreements such as the agreement on the International Monetary Fund (IMF) of July 1st and 22nd 1944, the signatories of which include all of the member states of the EC. This Agreement has the primary objective of co-operation in the currency field and elimination of factors disturbing the international flow of payments. It also contains an obligation to liberalise currency payments.

The Treaty of Rome does not define the term 'Movement of Capital' although this does not create any real problems.

The restrictions to be abolished include in particular, restrictions under currency law or laws regulating foreign trade and exchange in so far as they govern relationships between one member state and another. Thus, domestic provisions on the capital market which only apply to transactions within the member state are not actually effected.

All discrimination based upon nationality and place of residence are to be abolished to the extent necessary to ensure the proper functioning of the Common Market. This provision does not however, have direct affect and the Council is entrusted with the task of adopting the measures necessary to implement it. So long as capital movement has not been liberalised, the member states retain the power to adopt control measures and to enforce compliance with them by means of criminal penalties.

The Council has adopted two implementing Directives, one in 1960 and one in 1962. These Directives cover only restrictions arising from exchange controls and thus the member states continue to have freedom with respect to other restrictions.

The Commission has adopted a further three Directives regulating the conditions affecting the listing of securities on Stock Exchanges, although these are clearly of little relevance to franchising.

In addition to the two safeguard clauses in the Treaty of Rome relating expressly to movements of capital, the member states have access to safeguards by way of Article 107(2) (Protective Measures to Offset Exchange Rate Alterations), Article 108(3) (Authorization by the Commission to Take Protective Measures Against Balance of Payment Difficulties) and Article 109 (Unilateral Protective Action Against the sudden 'Balance of Payments Crisis') to limit the free movement of capital within the Community.

Although Article 107(2) has never been invoked, use has been made of the safeguard clauses in Articles 108(3) and 109.

France was the first member state to have recourse to safeguard measures when in July 1968 the Commission

authorised France to apply certain exchange control measures. These measures were terminated on September 4th 1968, but a wave of speculation against the French Franc in November 1968 caused the Commission to issue, on December 4th 1968 a decision authorising new and more severe exchange control measures affecting certain capital movements. These restrictions have been gradually relaxed but the decision continues in force.

The monetary crisis in February 1973 brought on by the weakness of the US Dollar caused Germany to invoke Article 109 and imposed restrictions on transfers of domestic securities to non-residents, loans and other credits contracted with non-residents, and certain direct investments by one resident in order to counter-speculative movements.

Italy has taken advantage of both Articles 108(3) and Article 109 on several occasions throughout 1974 to 1976 and again in 1981 through to 1982.

When the transitional period for the establishment of the Common Market ended (on December 31st 1969), the economic situation within the EC was deteriorating with inflation rising at an alarming rate and unemployment beginning to take on serious proportions. Speculative dealings on foreign exchange markets further exacerbated these problems. France and Germany's devaluation of their currency made the problems still worse. Thus, in December 1969, it was agreed by the member states' governments that the Council would draw up a plan aimed at the creation of the Economic and Monetary Union and to develop monetary co-operation through the harmonization of economic policies. In March 1970 the Werner Report, published by the Commission, found that:

'Economic and Monetary Union will make it possible to realise an area within which goods and services, people and capital will circulate freely without competitive distortions, without thereby giving rise to structural or regional disequilibrium'.

As a result on March 22nd 1971, the Council adopted a Resolution on the achievement by stages of an Economic and Monetary Union within the Community. The Resolution called for the Union to be introduced by December 31st 1980. Progress was however, slow and the first and second stages were not achieved in time.

However, on March 13th 1979, the European Monetary System was established. Closer co-ordination of the Economic and Monetary Policies of the member states within the EMS was seen as being essential to the achievement of financial integration.

The Resolution of 11 member states (excluding the United Kingdom) in November 1990, to establish a central European bank, the Euro Fed, and put a single European currency in place, hopefully by the year 2000, is the logical extension of the implementation of the free movement of capital within the European Community (see Chapter 34 below).

CHAPTER 11

Franchising, Transport and Communications in the Single Market

By MARK ABELL

As many franchises, particularly those in the retail sector, rely upon the supply of specific 'tied' goods, it is important to appreciate the impact that the Single Market will have upon the various modes of transport used to import and distribute such goods.

The efficiency and harmonisation of the Community's communications infrastructure will therefore have a significant effect upon franchising in the single market.

TRANSPORT

The White Paper commits the Community to creating an integrated transport system that will support and buttress a truly Single Market. There are four main forms of transport:

1. Road Transport

The Commission is committed to cabotage (i.e. allowing non-resident carriers to operate in other member states for the transport of goods and passengers by road), the phasing out of all road transport quotas and establishing the right to provide services for the transport of passengers by road.

However the implementation of these proposals is being considerably hampered by the insistence of certain member states that the financial implications of such measures be carefully considered.

In order to achieve these aims a number of measures have been imposed and/or carried out:

(a) It has been proposed that a regulation be adopted to enable any road hauler established in a member state to carry out a national haulage operation in a different member state – this would be subject to certain conditions. Regulation No. 4059/89 (OJ 1989 L390/3) allows a form of cabotage as from July 1st 1990. This Regulation supplies member states with 15,000 'cabotage permits' each of which is valid for two months. These permits allow non-resident carriers to obtain a permit to carry out haulage operations in other member states. The number of permits will increase each year.

A draft Regulation (OJ 1987 C77/13) also proposes similar measures in respect of the carriage of passengers.

(b) Regulation No. 1841/88 (OJ 1988 L163/1) was adopted by the Council on 21st June 1988. As from 1st January 1991 this Regulation abolished all national bilateral quotas on the carriage of goods by road between member states.

It is also proposed to adopt a regulation concerning the removal of internal restrictions on the carriage of passengers by car or bus (COM (87-89) of 9th April 1987).

2. Rail Transport

The Commission's proposals concerning rail transport are perhaps the most controversial to be made concerning transport policy .

Whilst rail transport is no longer perceived as being a second rate mode of transport, its political status has taken on renewed importance.

The EC Commission intends to create a Community-wide rail transport policy that will integrate existing national rail networks and relax member state monopolies. A draft Directive has been prepared which would initially phase out subsidies and allow private rail operators to compete side-by-side with state-owned operators throughout the Community. Even more radically, the Commission proposes to create one Single European Rail Authority.

The gist of these proposals is that there is a distinction to be made between ownership and management of the rail infrastructure. Enterprises using the infrastructure pay a form of fee in consideration of the use.

Some small degree of harmonisation of matters such as track gauge, signalling facilities and the training of drivers is also proposed.

3. Air Transport

Air transport within the EC comprises of a series of bilateral and multilateral agreements between member states and between air carriers concerning fares, capacity, access etc. Policy comprises two distinct parts.

The first part needs to deal with competition, airfares and passenger sharing. Article 85 and 86 applies to air transport by way of Regulation No. 3975/87 (OJ 1987 L374/1). Regulation No. 3976/87 (OJ 1987 L374/9) permits the passing of the Block Exemptions of which three have so far been adopted, one concerning the joint planning and co-ordination of capacity, sharing of revenue and consultations on tariffs and scheduled air services on slot allocation at airports (Regulation No. 2671/88 (OJ 1988 L239/9)), one on computer reservations systems for air transport services (Regulation No. 2672/88 (OJ 1988 L239/13)), and one on ground handling services such as refuelling, handling of baggage, mail and in-flight catering. (Regulation No. 2673/88 (OJ 1988 L239/17)).

The procedures for the establishment of scheduled airfares on routes between member states are dealt with by Council Directive No. 87/601 (OJ 1987 L374/12).

Bilateral agreements between the air carrier of one member state and that of another concerning passenger sharing are dealt with by Council Directive No. 87/602 (OJ 1987 L374/19).

The second part of the policy is set out by the Commission in its communication to the Council of September 1989. This seeks to establish a pan-EC Air Transport Policy and deals with a number of issues including (l) the criteria and procedures to be adopted by member states regarding the establishment of scheduled airfares (OJ 1989 C258/3), (2) the Regulation of Access by Air Carriers to Scheduled Inter-Community Air Service Routes and on the Sharing of Passenger Capacity Between Air Carriers and Scheduled Air Services Between Member States (OJ 1989 C258/6), (3) the exemption of certain categories of agreements from Article 85 (OJ 1989 C258/12), the mutual recognition of Aviation Personnel Licences (OJ 1990 C10/12), (4) Air Worthiness Requirements and Multiple Route Designation/cabotage.

4. Shipping

In order to ensure freedom of maritime transport both at sea and on inland waterways, the Commission has to date adopted four separate Regulations:

(a) Regulation No. 4055/86 (OJ 1986 L378/1) guarantees the freedom to provide maritime transport between member states and between member states and third countries. It provides for the phasing out of present cargo sharing arrangements and prevents the adoption of any further such arrangements.

(b) Regulation No. 4056/86 (OJ 1986 L378/4) applies Article 85 and Article 86 to maritime transport and provides for certain exemptions.

(c) Regulation No. 4057/86 (OJ 1986 L378/14) seeks to protect Community ship owners against cost cutting practices of ship owners from third countries. It is the first application of anti-dumping concept within the service sector.

(d) Regulation No. 4058/86 (OJ 1986 L378/21) sets out a number of actions that may be taken to safeguard free access to cargos and ocean trades unless such access is restricted by third countries.

The Commission proposes to adopt further measures to protect EC vessels. These include the adoption of the concept of Community Ship Owner (OJ 1989 C263/16) and the adoption of the Community Flag (OJ 1989 C263/11), the prohibition on restrictions on provision of maritime transport services within member states (OJ 1989 C263/17) and measures to improve the effectiveness of state port control in the Community (OJ 1989 C263/15).

TELECOMMUNICATIONS

A more liberal, flexible and competitive approach to telecommunications services and equipment market will also more easily facilitate growth of Pan-EC franchise networks.

The Green Paper on the Development of the Common Market for Telecommunications Services and Equipment ((COM) (87 290)) identifies four different areas which need to be liberalised to promote growth of the Single Market.

Thus whilst national monopolies of special rights in member states will be retained, it will be required not to prejudice the establishment of a general European infrastructure.

The distinction is made between 'basic' or 'reserved' services on the one hand and 'competitive' services on the other. Basic or reserved services will still be subject to national monopolies/special rights. This is restricted to the telephone network. Competitive services, that is all other telecommunication services, will be the preserve of the free market.

The provision of telecommunications equipment will also be liberalised.

The Single Market principle will be applied to telecommunications and harmonization will be encouraged at the same time as liberalization. A number of Directives have been adopted to this end.

All this should make communications between the franchisor and its EC network easier, cheaper and more efficient.

CHAPTER 12

Franchising and the Movement of Goods to, from and within the Single Market

By MARK ABELL

The free movement of goods between member states is central to the plans of any franchisor (other than some dealing exclusively in the provision of services) in establishing a pan-EC franchise network. As goods moving within the European Community are subject to a Community Transit (CT) procedure this procure must be carefully studied and understood by franchisors, sub-franchisors and developers operating within the EC.

The CT procedure aims at:

1. Establishing whether or not goods are in 'free circulation' and entitled to be duty-free or to reduced Intra-Community rates of duty.
2. Controling the movement of goods subject to special measures (e.g. regulation of their destination, exportation etc).
3. Establishing an international transit system within the EC.

The various procedures which comprise CT must be carefully followed by franchisors in order to ensure that their goods enjoy duty-free or reduced rate status. It should also be noted that there are severe penalties imposed upon parties making any false declaration. Exporters bear the burden of ensuring that the CT is complied with, and therefore franchisors operating in more than one member state must take great care to ensure that they are completely familiar with CT procedure.

THE SINGLE ADMINISTRATIVE DOCUMENT

The so-called Single Administrative Document (SAD) is used to comply with CT procedure. It comprises a total of eight copies each with a distinct function.

1. The first copy is for the country of despatch/export and remains at the office of departure so that it can be used for control purposes.
2. The second copy is for statistical use for the country of despatch/export and bears the export declaration for statistical purposes.
3. The third copy is for the consignor/exporter.
4. The fourth copy is for the office of destination and is kept by the customs in the importing member state as evidence that the goods are in free circulation.
5. The fifth copy is returned from the office of destination to customs in the member state of despatch so as to provide evidence that the goods actually reached their destination intact.

6. The sixth copy is used in the importing member state as the customs import declaration.
7. The seventh copy is the import declaration for statistical purposes in the importing member state.
8. The eighth copy is retained by the importer (or his agent) and serves as the VAT copy for goods cleared on location which are not served by the customs computerised entry system.

Copies one to three remain in the exporting member state whilst copies four to eight travel forward with the goods.

Each set of papers is printed on self-copying paper although certain sections are blocked out as they need to be completed upon receipt by the importer.

Customs Notice 484 (July 1987) gives full details on completing the SAD.

Full and Split Use

The SAD is a flexible set of documents and it is not always necessary to use all eight copies and it is possible to obtain from customs' reduced sets for what is known as 'split use'.

The full eight-part set must be completed when the same set is used for despatch, CT and destination purposes, when the export declaration is being pre-entered or when a pre-shipment advice under Simplified Clearance Procedure (SCP) is provided with no other commercial document being used.

If there are a number of consignees for a load it is necessary to ensure that there is a full set for each consignee although it is being used only for despatch or transit purposes.

The availability of split use is aimed at reducing unnecessary paperwork and bureaucracy. The SAD can be divided up into its constitute elements so that only relevant papers may be used for a particular transaction. This may happen for example if a franchisor in one member state is exporting goods to a franchisee in another member state who wishes to complete its own export declarations but to employ an agent to deal with the CT formalities. Whilst it is possible for the franchisor only to complete the appropriate parts of SAD, it is more usual to obtain split sets for each use. For example, copies two and three for export entry and copies one, three, four, five and seven for full CT procedure.

There are six different split use sets of the SAD available from customs:

1. SCP pre-shipment advice and personal shipment declaration (copies two and three).
2. Full entry of exports direct to Non-Community countries (copies two and three).

94

3. Evidence of the community status of the goods only (copies one and four).

4. SCP pre-shipment advice combined with the status declaration (copies one to four).

5. Full pre-entry of exports combined with a status declaration (copies one to four).

6. Export and CT (copies one, two, three, four, five and seven).

Status of Goods

Another dimension to the CT system is that it also indicates whether or not the goods in question have Community Status, and are therefore entitled to free circulation within the Community or have Non-Community Status. Community Status is conferred upon those goods that either originate in an EC member state or having been imported from outside of the Common Market have had customs duty paid on them with no refund having been claimed. Thus consider the situation if an American franchisor ships its products to its sub-franchisor for the UK, Eire and Benelux which is based in the UK. The sub-franchisor can ship them to its franchisees in Belgium without restraint providing the have had all relevant duties paid as they enjoy Community status. Status is indicated by a series of abbreviations which are detailed below:

T1
This applies to both non-EC originating goods which are not in free circulation or subject to a claim to remission or repayment of customs duty and Community originating goods which are subject to an export refund under the Common Agricultural Policy.

T2
This indicates that goods are in free circulation without any subsequent repayment of duty or claim to a Common Agricultural Policy export refund. They are therefore free of customs duty prior to export.

T2ES and T2PT
These apply to goods which are either in free circulation in Spain (ES), Portugal (PT) and are therefore eligible to the appropriate transitional rate of duty granted to the relevant member states upon their excession under the Common Agricultural Policy.

Other CT procedures include T2L (for goods exported to other parts of the EC which do not cross the territory of other member states before they are cleared for import). Form T2M (used to provide evidence of Community Status which is made by EC member state fishing vessels), Article 41 of Regulation EEC 222/77 which provides special arrangements to replace the full CT procedure for Community goods crossing one internal frontier of the Community, Copy Control T5 Form (a special control procedure existing essentially to provide proof that certain goods arrive at a particular destination or are used or disposed of in a particular way).

It is possible to obtain pre-authentication of goods in order to avoid the need for SAD's to be presented to customs at the time of export clearance. In order to effect pre-authentication, full CT documentation is authenticated by exporters themselves using a stamp issued by local customs. This facility is only available to exporters who are also approved for the use of Local Export Control.

When goods are exported by post, customs declarations specific to parcel traffic will normally be required to accompany each package.

When goods are exported to another member state for temporary use and then returned to the member state of origin the SAD can be replaced by a Community Carnet. The restriction upon goods that can be covered and individuals that can use them are detailed in Notice 756/88. The carnet can be used to replace SAD for temporary exports and full details are given in Notice 104.

TIR procedure allows goods which are in sealed containers or road vehicles to cross through a number of EC member states with the minimum of customs interference. Carnets are used for this purpose and the appropriate procedures are contained in customs Notice 464.

When the full CT procedure is being used, the individual signing the SAD form has to give a guarantee to cover any duty or similar charges which may become payable if there is any irregularity during the transit operation. The guarantee can either be a written contract given by a person or organisation such as a bank or insurance company etc., other than the principal in the transit operation, or a cash deposit which would have to be made in each member state involved in the movement. Cash deposits will not be recoverable until the transit operation had been completed to the satisfaction of the customs at the office of departure. There are individual guarantees, comprehensive guarantees and flat rate guarantees.

CHAPTER 13

Franchising and Technical Standards in the Single Market

By MARK ABELL

The diversity of technical standards in the EC is often a source of great difficulty for a franchisor seeking to operate in more than one member state. For example, a franchisor which retails consumer electronics may have to comply with a slightly different set of regulations in each member state. This makes the free flow of goods between different franchisees almost impossible; it also reduces the savings the franchisor can pass on to its franchisees as a result of bulk purchasing. The drive towards harmonisation is therefore of great importance to franchising.

The European Community originally sought to adopt a markedly centralised approach to the task of harmonising technological standards within the EC. This however proved to be impractical due to the sheer size of the task. It was impossible for the Commission to fulfil its stated ambition of laying down standards for each and every product in the common market. Not only was it immensely time consuming but inevitably by the time a set of standards had surfaced from the bureaucratic machinery, it was usually way out of date.

To cut this gordian knot of technicalities, the Council aimed to solve the problem 'at a stroke' by adopting a resolution in 1985 setting out general principles for an entirely new approach to the problem of harmonising standards on a pan-EC basis.

This new approach is essentially deregulatory and means that directives concerning standards tend to specify the essential requirements as regards safety, health, and environmental and consumer protection which must be achieved so as to qualify the products for free movement within the EC. In other words those products which fail to comply with the requirements laid down by directives are denied access to the single market.

The implications for a pan-European franchise are obvious. Full knowledge of and compliance with the common standards are essential.

Inevitably not all goods will be subject to directives, and many will be subject to the principle of mutual recognition instead.

Under the principle of mutual recognition if a product is certified as meeting the standards current in the member state of origin it can be freely traded in any of the other eleven member states without the need for further modification, certification, testing or re-naming. It is therefore of course essential that standards within each member state are acceptable to the other members.

Responsibility for drawing up these European standards rests with three separate bodies namely:

1. CEN – the European Committee for Standardisation;
2. CENLEC – the European Committee for Electro-Technical Standardisation, and

3. ETSI – the European Telecommunications Standards Institute.

The standards laid down by these three bodies are not mandatory. However, if they are not complied with the manufacturer must prove that its products conform to the essential requirements of the relevant directive.

CEN, CENLEC and ETSI work through approximately two hundred different committees comprising technicians, manufacturers, consumers and representatives of EFTA.

Standards developed by these three bodies are the result of a great deal of consultation with the national standards bodies in each member state.

The procedure for ensuring that member states avoid adopting conflicting national standards is laid down in Directive 83/189 (OJ 1983 L 109/8 as amended by No. 88/182 OJ 1988 L81/75). It requires all member states to notify the Commission in writing on a quarterly basis of all relevant technical regulations that are to be passed or amended. All other member states are then given access to this information. In order to try and ensure the success of the drive towards uniformity the Commission published two separate communications in June 1989. The first was entitled, 'A Global Approach to Certification and Testing' and the second was a proposal for a Council decision on the modules for various phases of the conformity assessment procedures to be used in the technical harmonisation directive.

The first communication aims at providing for mutual recognition of certifications whether undertaken by the manufacturers themselves or by third parties (such as testing laboratories). CEN and CENLEC have drafted two sets of voluntary European standards in this regard based upon national standards. It is hoped that these will assist in the continual pro-quality control. The first set of standards (EN 29000) involve techniques which manufacturers can adopt to help ensure quality standards. The second set of standards (EN 45000) concern the standards to be achieved by testing laboratories and inspection and certification bodies. The aim of the Commission is to promote the use of these standards and it is actively encouraging the establishment of a European organisation for certification and testing as one way of doing so.

The Commission is also seeking to establish an accreditation procedure for laboratories and is financing the creating of CERTIFICATE, a new database concerning certification procedures which will be available to manufacturers both inside and outside the EC.

The second communication of the Commission proposes a modular approach to the question which is based on the principle that full certification procedures can be divided into various functions or modules which can then be used in a flexible combination of procedures to ensure appropriate safety levels for specified products. The pieces to this jigsaw include declarations of conformity, type approval and product production quality assurance.

This modular approach allows manufacturers some degree of choice as although the Council set out the procedures and conditions of application considered appropriate for particular directives, the final choice of the specific procedures will be left to the economic operators themselves.

Thus a heavy burden rests upon the European standards bodies in developing a uniform set of standards together with implementation of EC legislation in the national law of member states. This means that it will require a good deal of political will on behalf of all of the member state governments.

CHAPTER 14

Franchising and Product Liability in the Single Market

By MARK ABELL and ANTHONY LANDES

The Commission to the Council of Ministers of the European Communities submitted a draft Product Liability Directive in 1976 and a revised draft in 1979 on liability for defective products and on 25th July 1985 an agreed text of the Directive was adopted, with the requirement that member states implement it in their national laws within three years i.e. by July 1988.

The main aims of the Directive are twofold: to harmonize product liability law within the European Communities, and to increase consumer protection. These aims are illustrated by the following passages from the introduction to the Directive:

'Whereas approximation of the laws of the member states concerning the liability of the producer for damage caused by the defectiveness of his products is necessary because the existing divergencies may distort competition and affect the movement of goods within the Common Market and entail a differing degree of protection of the consumer against damage caused by a defective product to his health or property;

Whereas liability without fault on the part of the producer is the sole means of adequately solving the problem, peculiar to our age of increasing technicality, of a fair apportionment of the risks inherent in modern technological production'.

It is clear that on full implementation of the Directive, the position as regards product liability in all European member states will be comparable to the current position in the US, insofar as the question of product liability of manufacturers and sellers for injuries to extra-contractual or third party users and consumers is concerned.

The Directive is arguably the most significant international initiative on product liability to date. It seeks to introduce strict liability for defective products, and provides for harmonisation of the law in all EC member states. It is therefore of great importance to franchisors in the single market.

Article 1 of the Directive states the essence of the new law with classic brevity. 'The producer shall be liable for damage caused by a defect in his product.' This is the principle of strict liability, namely that the person who suffered the damage does not have to prove negligence. Nor need he have entered into a contract with the producer or supplier. The injured party need only prove injury and causation and is not required to prove fault. Although liability is strict, it is not absolute in that evidence must be brought to show that the product was *defective*. For example, if a television explodes, it is clearly defective, but the American lady who attempted to dry her poodle in a microwave oven, with the result that the poodle disintegrated after 90 seconds, would not recover damages.

The Directive has a direct implication on franchising and in particular the liability of franchisors for the conduct of its sub-franchisors, developers and franchisees.

Despite, in most cases, the franchisor having no direct contact with the consumer, it may be that the franchisor will nevertheless face a claim for damages should the products supplied by the franchisee be defective, on the basis that the franchisor would be regarded as a 'producer' (see below for comment). Thus, the franchisor's liability for the acts and conduct of franchisees with third parties will become increasingly significant in the future. It follows that careful consideration should be given to this area when drafting franchise agreements having specific regard to the fact that when determining whether a product is defective, it will be considered, amongst other circumstances, from the point of view of the consumer.

The basic principles of the Directive are laid down in articles 1 (see above), 2 and 3.

Article 2 states that for the purpose of the Directive, 'product' means all moveable products (with the exception of agricultural products) whilst Article 3 provides that a 'producer' means the manufacturer of a finished product, the producer of any raw material or the manufacturer of a component part and any person who, by putting his name, trademark, or other distinguishing features on the products presents himself as its producer.

The following entities would be regarded as producers.

1. Manufacturer

This includes not only the manufacturer of the finished product (eg a car) but also of the components and raw materials, eg brakes and windscreen. Another type of producer is a processor ie someone who alters the essential characteristics of the product. The mere packaging of goods will not constitute processing but, for example, whoever cooks raw food will be a processor and thus a producer. Therefore a McDonald's sub-franchisee who makes hamburgers under a franchise, processes the various food products that go to make up the hamburger and is strictly liable to the consumer for damage caused if the hamburger is defective.

2. Own brander

A producer is also any person who, by putting its name on the product or by using a trademark or other distinguishing mark in relation to the product, has held itself out to be the producer of the product.

This covers supermarkets and department stores who sell 'own-brand' foods and clothes and would include a franchisor who for example sources soap and cosmetics and then marks them with the name of the franchise before passing them for retail to franchisees. They are strictly liable, even if they did not manufacture the products. Part of the essence of a franchise is the use of the franchisor's name on the product, so at first glance a franchisor appears to be caught by this provision.

3. EC importer

A producer is also any person who imports a product into the European Community for sale, hire, leasing or any form of distribution in the course of his business. This category covers importers into the EC from outside it, but not those who import into a member state from the EC. The EC importer is held strictly liable for any defect in the product, even though it did not manufacture it. This provision applies to franchises where:

(a) the franchisor imports the product from outside the EC (eg Taiwan); or

(b) the franchisee receives the product from a franchisor based outside the EC (eg the US).

Thus an area developer in the UK granting franchises of a US company to franchisees and supplying them with products from the US would be liable for defects in the products.

4. Recordless retailers

The supplier of a defective product is strictly liable if, within a reasonable time, the injured consumer requests it to identify the producer, own-brander or EC importer, and the supplier fails within a reasonable period to do this or to identify his own supplier. Franchisees are specially at risk from this provision. Even if the franchisee did not make the defective product, a franchisee who is unable to supply the necessary information will be held liable just as if it had. It is, therefore, essential for franchisors and, in particular for sub-franchisors/developers and sub-franchisees, to keep accurate records of all those who supply products to them and, where known, of the producer, own-brander or EC importer.

Since a franchisor is included in the EC Directive concept of a 'producer', a franchisor must be aware of its direct responsibility for the franchisee's conduct. It is clear, therefore, that the product liability principles set out in the Directive apply to franchisors both when the franchisor is the manufacturer of the product and when he is not. This highlights the need for caution when the franchisor appoints agents and the extent to which the franchisor's trade marks are permitted for use in the sub-franchisor's/developer's and sub-franchisee's business.

The franchisor *must* have a sufficient degree of control to ensure satisfactory performance by the sub-franchisor/ developer or sub-franchisee who sells products or offers services in accordance with the prescribed methods and procedures of the franchise. The franchisor provides the sub-franchisor/ developer with advertising, promotion, training, financing and other specialised management resources which are in turn passed on to franchisees. The franchisor is, therefore, directly involved in the sub-franchisor/developer or sub-franchisee's business activities. There is no excuse or exemption from liability. A franchisor has to consider the consumer's expectations. It is not the consumer's task to determine whether a franchisor is manufacturing certain products or not.

Even if the consumer is aware that a franchisee is conducting his business by itself, and that a franchisor or sub-franchisor is providing instruction, the consumer expects the franchisor to take responsibility for the products.

A franchisor's prime interest is that its concept will be uniform in all of its business units and its ultimate aim is to ensure its name or trademark will become well established. Consequently, a franchise agreement stipulates precise conditions concerning the manufacture of goods and quality control. In addition, third parties can expect a franchisor to select its franchisees in such a way that the further performance of services will be consistent.

The Directive does not only impose strict liability on those distributors who are supplying defective products, but also, on those who, through the sale of a product under a certain trademark grant the rights of that specific trademark to third parties. Under those circumstances, where a franchisor's name or trademark is involved, the franchisor will always be regarded as the producer. The underlying reason clearly is that by buying under a reputable trademark, the consumer can expect good quality and believes that whenever he buys certain products or orders from a franchisee under the franchisor's name trade name or trademark, he will receive the goods and services as if they were normally manufactured or performed by the franchisor.

Thus, it is clear that depending on the circumstances the franchisor faces a potential claim if the product supplied by a franchisee is defective. It is, therefore, important to consider the defences that are available to franchisors (or franchisees as appropriate) and further the provisions that can be made in the franchise agreement itself to minimise the exposure to a claim.

Defences under the Directive

There are a number of specified defences. Three of these are relevant to franchising.

1. No liability will arise if the franchisor, sub-franchisor, developer, or sub-franchisee can show that the product was not put into circulation. This not only protects franchisors and sub-franchisors who can show the product was not supplied to the franchisee(s), but it also protects franchisors, sub-franchisors, developers and sub-franchisees from liability for injury caused by products stolen from them and products intended solely for internal use.

2. No liability will arise if it is probable that the defect which caused the damage did not exist in the product at the time of supply. This would save a franchisor or sub-franchisor who could prove that the defect did not exist in the product when it supplied it to the sub-franchisee. The defence is also important for products with a short life expectancy or which are known to be damaged by wear and tear or lack of repair.

3. The most controversial defence is the development risks defence: that the the state of scientific and technical knowledge at the relevant time was not such as to enable the existence of the defect to be discovered. For all the publicity devoted to it, this defence will rarely be applicable in franchising. By its nature it principally applies to advanced technological industries such as aerospace and pharmaceuticals.

Contractual terms and notices

Liability to consumers cannot be limited or excluded by any contract term, by any notice or by any other provision. However, it is still possible for businesses to allocate liability amongst themselves by means of contract terms and exclusion clauses. Therefore it is essential that the master franchise, development and franchise agreements deal with the apportionment of liability between the franchisor, sub-franchisor, developer and sub-franchisees for damage caused by any defect in the product. Fairness suggests that:

(a) Where the franchisor insists upon the use of specified material supplied by the franchisor in the processing or manufacture of the product and this material causes the defect, the franchisor should bear liability and indemnify the sub-franchisor, developer and sub-franchisee against it;

(b) Where the sub-franchisor, developer or franchisee manufacturers or processes the product and that manufacture or process causes the defect, the sub-franchisor, developer or sub-franchisee (as the case may be) should assume liability and indemnify the franchisor and other parties against claims;

(c) Where the defect is caused by a product emanating from a third party, it should be up to the franchisor, sub-franchisor, developer or sub-franchisee (whichever is arranging for the supply of the product) to obtain the appropriate indemnity from that supplier.

Nevertheless, it is only to be expected, as a matter of business reality, that the terms finally agreed will reflect the respective bargaining strengths of the parties.

Forum shopping and the enforcement of judgments

By virtue of the Brussels Convention on Judgment and Jurisdiction 1968 (see Chapter 34 below), plaintiffs injured by defective goods may have a choice of a number of different forums — the home state of any of the defendants (eg franchisor, developer or sub-franchisor), the country where the wrongful act was performed, or the country where the damage was caused.

As the Directive will have been implemented slightly differently in each member state, this will undoubtedly lead to 'forum shopping' by potential plaintiffs.

A consumer may, therefore, depending on the circumstances, have a choice of forum as to where to bring proceedings. Clearly, the consumer will select the jurisdiction which is most beneficial to him, and this element should not be disregarded by franchisors planning their franchise relationships in Europe. Further, franchisors should be aware that court decisions can be enforced in all European member

states (Brussels Convention on Enforcement of Court Jurisdiction and Judgment of 1978 — see Chapter 34 below) and several other countries abroad.

Practical advice

The following steps are recommended to limit product liability claims against the franchisor, sub-franchisor, developer and sub-franchisee and to restrict potential conflict between them on any apportionment of liability.

Quality control
The franchisor must exercise careful quality control over any products which it sources and ensure that the franchise agreement places a duty upon the sub-franchisor, developer and sub-franchisee to do likewise.

Advertising safety claims
The franchisor sub-franchisor and developer must be careful to ensure that in its advertising campaigns it does not make any exaggerated safety claims. The franchisor must also ensure that it vets any of the sub-franchisor's and developer's advertising and that they in turn vet the sub-franchisee's local advertising before such advertising is released.

Instructions and warnings
The sub-franchisee must be placed under a duty by the franchise agreement to give appropriate instructions and warnings.

Risk transfer
The franchisor, sub-franchisor and developer must take care to keep detailed records of all producers and suppliers used, and impose through the franchise agreement, a similar duty upon the franchisee.

The franchisor, sub-franchisor and developer must negotiate suitable contract terms with other businesses.

The franchisor, sub-franchisor and developer must avoid making any unnecessary admissions and must incorporate a clause in the franchise agreement obliging the franchisee to do likewise.

Providing for remaining risks
The franchisor, sub-franchisor and developer should take out product liability insurance for itself and its franchisees, with perhaps an appropriate contribution by the franchisees.

The franchisor, sub-franchisor and developer must budget for any uninsured risks and establish a sinking fund to be contributed to by the sub-franchisees.

CONCLUSION

It is clear that as a consequence of the EEC directive on product liability the potential liability faced by franchisors will increase so bringing the position closer to that which currently exists in the US. It is therefore important that franchisors are made aware of the potential liability that they face, and that all efforts are made to minimise the risks.

CHAPTER 15

Franchising and Strict Liability for Services in the Single Market

By MARK ABELL

The basic approach

The EC Draft Directive on strict liability for services is at present very much in the formative stage. Informal proposals have been made, and draft copies have been sent to various industries throughout the European Community. The EC is presently considering replies which have been received. It is, however, safe to assume that the EC will wish to implement the Directive. A Directive dealing with liability for products is already being implemented (see Chapter 14 above) and one for services is an obvious progression to seek to ensure that all businesses, whether dealing in services or products, have the same level of obligations.

The implications for service franchises are substantial and similar to those of the Product Liability Directive for product based franchises. (See Appendix 16 for the text of the existing draft.)

The nub of the Directive is contained in Article 1, which provides that:

'the supplier of a service shall be liable for damage caused by a safety defect in his service'.

The Directive will concentrate upon the meaning of a safety defect and definition will not be strict.

A safety defect is defined as follows:

'A service has a safety defect when it does not provide a degree of safety which may reasonably be expected as regards health and physical integrity of persons and the physical integrity of moveable and immovable property including that forming the object of the service. A service is defective by reason of the fact that there is a safety defect that could be proved.'

This definition provides for an element of 'reasonableness'. It does not however state the test for such reasonableness. For example any person having their fitted carpets cleaned has an expectation that the cleaning will be successfully carried out unless advised to the contrary. But is that a reasonable expectation since most people know that from time to time things go wrong?

At present it is necessary in jurisdictions such as Scotland and England and Wales to prove negligence in the Courts.

Under the proposed draft Directive the Courts would have to consider whether there was a reasonable expectation that no damage would result and who should hold that expectation and by what objective criteria reasonableness should be judged.

Most people in the absence of any warning to the contrary will expect in their absence their carpets to be properly and successfully cleaned. There is, though, an argument that it is not a reasonable expectation but rather an emotive or subjective expectation. Liability under the Directive in the case referred to above would depend on which view the member state courts took. The former would, at least in cases of this sort, impose a form of strict liability whereas the latter would impose a liability akin to that found in England and Wales under the present law of negligence.

Joint and several liability of franchisors

Article 3 of the draft directive provides that:

'Any person who provides a service using the services of a representative or other legally dependent intermediary shall continue to be deemed to be a supplier of services within the meaning of this Directive'.

The implications for franchisors are clear. Franchisors will become liable for defective services provided by their franchisees. The logic of this stance is clearly the same as that which led to the adoption of the Product Liability directive (see Chapter 14 above). The logic is, however, it is suggested, faulty. Manufacturers, importers and branders have the opportunity to exercise a degree of quality control over the goods they handle. So-called 'up-stream' suppliers of services do not. They can train the eventual suppliers to the public, they can police the services, but ultimately they cannot guarantee the services standards to the same extent as can manufacturers, importers and own-branders of physical merchandise.

Of still further concern to franchisors however is the fact that Article 8 provides that suppliers (such as the franchisor and/or sub-franchisor) will be held jointly and severally liable if damage is shown to have resulted from the service concerned.

Article 8 provides:

'1. If, in applying this Directive, several people are liable for a given damage, they shall be jointly liable, without prejudice to the provisions of national law, relating to the law of recourse of one supplier against another.

2. The franchisor, the master franchisee and the franchisee, within the meaning of Commission Regulation (EEC) No 4087/88 of 30 November 1988 on the application of Article 85(3) of the Treaty to categories of franchisor agreements, shall be deemed to be jointly and severally liable within the meaning of paragraph 1.

However, the franchisor and the master franchisee may absolve themselves of liability if they can prove that the damage is due to a product which, on the basis of Regulation (EEC) No 4087/88, they themselves had not been able to supply or impose.'

This gives the plaintiff the ability to use a 'blunderbuss' approach in litigation and join in all possible parties, leaving it to them to apportion any blame and damages between themselves. Alternatively the plaintiff may home in on just the franchisor or master franchisee in the belief that they have more assets with which to satisfy any judgment.

Thus franchising is placed in a unique situation. All other parties in danger of being jointly liable for defective services have the right to prove that they were not at fault and should therefore not be liable. However, franchisors and master franchisees do not have that right. If the franchisee is proved to be liable, the franchisors and master franchisee are automatically jointly and severally liable too.

The only escape is if the damage is due to a product they had not been *able to supply or impose* under the block exemption (not 'had not supplied or imposed'). This escape route is narrow indeed.

Future action

As one would expect, the member state franchise associations and the American IFA have reacted in a very hostile way to the draft Directive. These bodies argue, amongst other things, that the existing law provides sufficient protection for the consumer, particularly the EC Block Exemption's requirement that franchisees indicate their status as an independent undertaking.

The implications for franchisors are obvious. If a strict liability approach is adopted, then franchisors will have to consider seriously taking such steps as are necessary to reduce their risk exposure. However, until the final Directive is adopted it will be impossible to see exactly what action will be sufficient in this regard. If the draft is not substantially changed, comprehensive insurance cover will be vital, although premiums are likely to be high.

The supervision of the franchisee will clearly be imperative. The risk limitation exercises outlined in Chapter 14 above concerning product liability may well suggest other possible approaches to be adopted as regards liability for services also. Hopefully franchising may well be expressly excluded from the Directive. However, this cannot be assumed and will by no means be certain until the Directive is actually adopted.

Franchising and Public Procurement in the Single Market

By MARK ABELL

Public procurement is a term used to cover all purchases by the Central Government of a member state, regional Governments, Nationalised Industries, and Government associated entities, e.g., the armed forces. These purchases cover two particular areas: supply of goods (public supply contracts) and supply of services (public works contracts). The areas covered by such purchases will include energy, transport, hygiene, telecommunications, water, defence, high-technology hardware and software and construction. It is therefore a potential source of substantial work for franchisees operating in these and other related areas.

Most Western European countries tend to adopt protectionist policies by favouring domestic suppliers in their purchasing policies.

In some ways this may tend to favour franchising. For example, whilst a German company may not be awarded a French government contract for say environmental hygiene works, its French sub-franchisor or developer will be in a far better position. However, on the whole such a protectionist policy must reduce the potential scope of work for franchisors. If for example a UK company is granted a master franchise for the UK and Benelux it may find itself discriminated against when tendering for a Dutch government contract.

The reasons for this discrimination are not hard to identify. National Governments often wish to support declining industries within their own country, boost particular areas of high unemployment, compensate communities in environmentally damaged areas and support emerging high tech industries within their own country so that these can compete on a worldwide scale. In addition, the field of defence is a highly strategic one, and Governments generally wish to have their own arms suppliers.

At the moment, only twenty per cent of the total figure for purchases by Public Authorities is subject to open competition throughout the Community, while more than seventy five per cent of the total expenditure is used for purchases from 'National Champions'. It is therefore clear that the existing community law on public procurement is not proving effective and further measures will need to be taken.

The liberation of public procurement policy is bound to effect great savings in the EC (estimated in the Cecchini Report at over 1.25 billion ECU).

One of the prime objectives of the EC is the free movement of goods, services and persons within the Community. Article 30 of the EEC Treaty (see Chapter 12 above) deals with free movement of goods and prohibits quantitative restrictions on imports and all measures having an equivalent effect. This is relevant to the area of public procurement, and in one of the better known cases on this subject, *Procureur Du*

Roi v. *Dassonville* ([1974] ECR 837) the ECJ stated that the obligation to eliminate trade barriers concerned 'all trading rules enacted by member states which are capable of hindering directly or indirectly, actually or potentially, intra-community trade'. The effect of this judgment is that if Governments discriminate against imported goods and services in their purchasing they are hindering intra-community trade and are therefore in breach of Article 30.

This is not the only provision in the Treaty of Rome which affects public procurement. Article 90 prevents member states from using public undertakings in a way which contravenes the EEC Treaty, and it is arguable that protectionist policies which are in breach of the spirit of the EEC Treaty are therefore a breach of Article 19.

Article 7 of the Treaty of Rome is a very broad and general provision which states that 'within the scope of application of this treaty, and without prejudice to any special conditions contained therein, any discrimination on the grounds of nationality shall be prohibited.' This Article is so general that when it is applicable in its own right it has no direct effect. However, in conjunction with other Articles it can give rise to a cause of action. Discrimination can involve either treating similar situations differently or treating different situations similarly.

Articles 52, 53, 59 and 62 in conjunction with Article 7 will have a bearing on public procurement. Articles 52 and 53 EEC require the removal of restrictions on the freedom of establishment of nationals of other member states and the prohibition of the imposition of new restrictions on such freedom, while Articles 59, 60 and 62 achieve the same effect for persons established in one member state providing services for persons established in other member states.

There are seven Directives on public procurement, three concerning public supply contracts and another four concerning public works contracts.

1. PUBLIC SUPPLY CONTRACTS

Directive 70/32 of December 17th 1969 is aimed at preventing discrimination against foreign suppliers by the governments of member states in their purchasing policies. The Directive prevents measures whether legal or matters of administrative practice which prevent the supply of imported products from other member states or grant domestic products a preference or which make the supply of imported products more difficult ie, more expensive than those of domestic products.

In addition to defining and listing the measures which are to be regarded as having an effect equivalent to quantitative restrictions contrary to Article 30 EEC the Directive enumerates certain other types of discrimination which member states are to eliminate. This includes the elimination of any rule by which technical specifications are determined which applies to both domestic and imported products but in fact effectively restricts the free movement of goods between member states to an extent not justified by the necessities of procurement.

The second Directive on public supply contracts was Directive 77/62 which has been subsequently amended by Directive 80/767 and 88/295. This is a more practical and procedural Directive which deals with the co-ordination of procedures for the award of public supply contracts with a view to opening up the Community Market. It has been in force since 1978. Rather than re-enforcing the principle of non-discrimination, as the previous Directive does, it imposes a number of positive obligations on purchasing bodies when awarding the public supply contract.

The basic thrust of the Directive is that all public supply contracts with a value of over 200,000.00 EUA (European Units of Account, now the ECU) must be advertised throughout the EC in the official Journal of the European Community and tenders must be accepted by the lowest or otherwise most effective bidder, irrespective of nationality in the European Community.

However, the scope of Directive 77/62 is very limited. Four major areas of public procurement are not covered by the Directive – transport, energy, water and telecommunications. In addition all small public supply contracts are not caught by the Directive even though these are capable of having an impact on competition. Thirdly, as the Directive is adopted pursuant to article 30 of the Treaty of Rome, goods originating outside the EC do not fall within the scope of the Directive. Also, certain kinds of public supply contracts awarded pursuant to international agreements are not covered by the Directive, nor are certain specifically defined contracts.

Directive 88/295 amends the 1977 Directive in several important particulars. It was drafted pursuant to the Commission's White Paper of June 1985 which highlighted the need for improved application of the directives together with substantial improvement of the directives. Among these suggested improvements to the Directives mentioned in the White Paper was a system of pre-information of interested suppliers; restrictions on the use of single tender procedures; the obligation to use European technical standards and the rationalisation of publication procedures.

The Directive first of all aims to restrict the number of exemptions to the general open tender rule propounded in the 1977 Directive. Some areas of the transport industry will now be covered by the open tender procedure, including harbours and airports. The production, transport and distribution of drinking water or energy or telecommunications services will still be exempted from the open tender procedure, but in all other cases this will become the normal procedure. Contracting authorities will have to justify the use of the restricted and negotiated procedures. They will have to draw up a written Report in such cases and if requested, communicate this to the Commission.

In order to try and reduce the number of exemptions the Directive defines public supply contract as contracts for pecuniary interest concluded in writing involving the purchase, lease, rental or hire purchase with or without an option to buy, of products between a supplier and a public authority.

The monetary threshold limit has also been reduced so that smaller undertakings are also covered by the Directive (from 200,000.00) ECU to 130,000.00 ECU).

Technical specifications must be defined by reference to European standards or harmonisation documents (see above) and time limits from the receipt of tenders are also extended so that foreign contractors are not adversely affected.

Transparency of procedures is also improved as annual pre-information notices must now be published giving details of the probable purchasing requirements of authorities for that year.

There is also a greater obligation of member states to submit details of statistical reports relative to contract awards. The reports must be submitted before October 31 of each year for the preceding year and must contain details of the number of contracts awarded each year by that authority above and below the threshold.

Member states had to adopt the measures necessary to comply with this Directive by January 1st 1989.

2. PUBLIC WORKS CONTRACTS

The legislation on public works has developed parallel to that on public supply contracts.

The first Directive on Public Works was Directive 71/304, adopted in Summer 1971 and applies the basic non-discriminatory principle of Directive 70/32 to public works contracts.

Directive 71/305 does for public works contracts what the 1977 Directive did for public supply contracts. It imposes regulations on the issuing of invitations to tender and award of contracts by public authorities in member states.

Large scale contracts, ie, involving sums of over £400,000.00 must be advertised in the Official Journal of the European Community and all European contractors who are interested must be given equal information on those contracts. If the contracts are to be awarded by selective tender, candidates must be selected on an equal basis without regard for nationality from firms applying to the advertisement, and the contract must be awarded on objective criteria stated to the competing parties in the contract document. The Directive also sets out methods by which the authority awarding the contract can invite interested contractors to demonstrate their technical competence.

This Directive was followed a year later by Directive 72/277 which prescribes the form which notices under Directive 71/305 must take.

The two most recent directives on public works contracts are Directive s 78/669, and 89/440. Directive 78/669 amends Directive 71/305 only in one particular. The value of contracts below which the directive does not apply is expressed in terms of European Units of Account in the original Directive. The 78 Directive changes this to ECUs in line with the parallel Directive on public supply contracts, Directive 77/62. The limit of 1,000,000 units remains the same.

Directive 89/440 does for public works contracts what Directive 88/295 did for public supply contracts. It is an attempt to implement some of the proposals of the White Paper by improving the Directives by limiting the number of exemptions from the open award of contracts procedure.

It gives a specific definition of 'public works contracts' stating them to be contracts for pecuniary interest concluded in writing between a Contractor and a Contracting Authority which has as its object the execution and design of work also exhaustively defined, largely including building and construction work.

The financial threshold of the Directive is changed to 5,000,000 ECU.

Exemptions applying to the areas of transport, energy, water and telecommunications are reduced so that tele-communications are now covered by the Directive and only contracts awarded to carriers by land, air, sea or inland waterway and works contracts awarded by contracting authorities concerning the production, transport and distri-bution of drinking water or reproduction and distribution of energy are exempted from the provisions of the Directive, in addition to secret contracts or high security contracts.

As with Directive 88/295, contracting authorities have to justify the use of restricted and negotiated procedures. There are also procedures for harmonisation of technical speci-fications so as not to prejudice foreign contractors, and extentions of time limit for restricted procedures tenders and negotiated procedures tenders for the same reasons.

3. CONCLUSION

Present public procurement policy emphasises the open award procedure, allows for regular statistical monitoring, requires publication of pre-contractual information notices and generally improves the transparency of contract award procedures. It also reduces the exemptions to the general rule.

However, it has failed to resolve some of the problems, specifically that of remedies for infringement of the directives which is a serious problem. Further legislation will therefore be necessary to resolve the problems of legislation completely within this field.

Despite these problems however the opportunities in the Single Market for franchising have significantly increased as a result of the various Public Procurement Directives. Government agencies have to consider carefully tenders from all sources. The combination of a foreign franchisor's system and a local franchisee's market knowledge may well mean that franchising greatly benefits from the liberalisation of public procurement.

CHAPTER 17

Franchising and European Company Law

By MARK ABELL and MARK ANTINGHAM

INTRODUCTION

There is at present no uniform company law in the twelve member states. Consequently businesses operating in more than one member state are bearing a considerable burden of expense and administrative work due to the necessity of coping with different bodies of law. The Commission's proposals for creating a legal framework facilitating co-operation between commercial undertakings in different member states are contained in a series of directives, draft directives, regulations and proposals for regulations issued by the Council of Ministers and the Commission since 1968. So far there have been eleven directives and two regulations which have been approved by the Council of Ministers.

These Directives have not yet been adopted by all member states. For example only the First, Second, Third, Fourth, Sixth, Seventh and Eighth Directives have so far been implemented by legislation in the United Kingdom. The Companies Act 1989 implemented the Seventh and Eighth Directives.

The 1992 White Paper placed particular emphasis on the need for a Council decision on the proposal for a European Company Statute; this is considered in Chapter 18. This proposal together with the related fifth draft Directive on the structure and management of Public Companies and the ninth and eleventh Directives on groups of companies, as well as the tenth draft Directive on cross border mergers has proved controversial. Political controversy in this area has largely concerned the inclusion of worker participation in the proposals which a number of Governments have been reluctant to endorse. The United Kingdom argues that worker participation and other instances of 'industrial democracy' are not essential for the creation of the single market. The Commission and certain other member states (for example Germany, France and Italy), see such examples of industrial democracy as adding an essential social dimension to the Commission's Programme.

Along with worker participation a second major political issue which arises from a number of these proposals is the extent to which the Community rules should be allowed to override existing national laws of member states. This has been illustrated by problems with merger control regulations. In many member states concern is felt that the proposed Community Rules would be an inadequate safeguard of national interest against overseas bidders, including those from other member states. For example in the United Kingdom the takeover by Switzerland's Nestle Group of Rowntree Mackintosh in 1990 indicated the degree of national sensitivity which can exist in member states when faced with control of a major industrial concern passing to a

'foreign company'. It is likely therefore that the second phase of harmonisation will involve more controversy rather than less.

The individual Directives are considered in turn below.

THE FIRST DIRECTIVE

The First Directive was introduced on the 9th March 1968. It was aimed at harmonising the company laws of member states in three areas: the compulsory disclosure of basic information concerning companies in a readily accessible form; the protection of third parties dealing with companies from any technical limitations on corporate powers and capacity; and the restriction on the nullification of companies after incorporation.

Disclosure of information

Disclosure is one of the most important parts of this Directive, underpinning many of the other Directives. There are a number of documents and other information concerning a company which must be filed on a public register in the member state in which the company is incorporated. This covers documents such as the company's Memorandum and Articles of Association. Copies of the public register have to be freely obtainable by anyone who wishes to have access to such information.

A notice of the receipt of such documentation must be published in a designated official journal by the Government of the member state concerned.

The Directive also provides that all letters, invoices and order forms of companies incorporated within the Community must state:

(a) The registered number of the company.

(b) A statement of that the company is wound up if appropriate.

(c) The amount of the company's issued and paid up share capital.

(d) The 'legal form' of the company (e.g. that it is a private limited company).

(e) The location of the register in which the file on the company is kept, for example, 'registered in England'.

(f) The address of the registered office of the company.

Protection of Third Parties

The 'ultra vires' doctrine provides under English Law that companies are unable to act outside the scope of their expressed authority. This expressed authority is as defined in the 'objects clause' of the Memorandum and Articles. The 'ultra vires' doctrine currently poses a considerable risk to a third party, as an innocent third party even if acting in good faith may be unable to enforce a contract against a company because of this limitation on the company's powers, despite the third party being unaware of this limitation when contracting with the company.

The Directive restricts this doctrine as follows:-

(i) Those obligations which have been incurred by persons acting on behalf of the company prior to the date of the company's incorporation which have not subsequently been ratified by the company are jointly and severally enforceable against those persons who entered the contract in the first place. This is enforceable without limit.

(ii) Third parties who contract with a company may rely on any acts which the company does even if they are not within the capacity of the company unless the third party had notice of such incapacity at the time he entered the contract.

(iii) Any irregularity in the appointment of a person authorised to represent a company of whom details have been registered, shall not adversely effect a third party dealing with that person unless the third party has notice of the irregularity in the appointment.

Nullification

No law of a member state may provide for the nullification or removal from the register of a company after incorporation except by a decision of a Court upon certain specified grounds.

Implementation of the Directive

The Directive has been implemented in all member states except Spain, where a draft law is currently before Parliament.

THE SECOND DIRECTIVE

This was adopted on the 13th December 1976. The Directive is designed to co-ordinate the provision of member state national laws relating to the formation of Public Limited Companies and particularly with regard to the maintenance, increase and reduction of their share capital. The aim was to ensure minimum equivalent levels of protection for both the company and its shareholders.

THE THIRD DIRECTIVE

This aims at protecting the interests of third parties and members of the company following mergers of public companies. It was adopted on the 9th October 1978.

The Third Directive imposes minimum standards for two prescribed methods of asset merger by public companies at a national level. This is by either acquisition or the formation of a new company. The Directive represents the first somewhat tentative steps of the Commission in the field of merger policy. It is the forerunner of the draft Tenth Directive which itself deals with cross border mergers which is dealt with below and the proposed Merger Control Regulation and proposed draft Thirteenth Directive on takeovers. These are important parts of the Commission's 1992 programme.

The two methods are as follows: 'A merger by acquisition' is where one or more companies are wound up without going into liquidation. They then transfer to another company all their assets and liabilities in exchange for the issue to the shareholders of shares in the transferee company and if its appropriate a cash payment not exceeding 10% of the nominal or part value of the shares issued may be made. 'A merger by formation of a new company' occurs where two or more companies are wound up without going into liquidation. Their assets and liabilities are transferred to the new company, with shares in the new company being allocated to the existing companies' shareholders. There may also be a cash payment not exceeding 10% of the par value of the new shares.

THE FOURTH DIRECTIVE

The Fourth Directive contains detailed rules as to the drawing up of the accounts for companies. The Directive has been implemented in all Member states except for Belgium, Italy and Spain.

DRAFT FIFTH DIRECTIVE

This Directive is regarded by the Commission as an important part of the harmonisation programme although in recent years little progress has been made to its final adoption.

It has two key objectives, firstly to impose a distinction between members of the board of directors of public companies who are responsible for management and those who are responsible for supervision by introducing two tier boards. Secondly it will introduce a mandatory system of employee participation in large public companies. The draft has encountered considerable opposition from a number of the member states particularly the United Kingdom due to the proposals for employee participation. If adopted, it may have a considerable effect on franchisors incorporated in the EC.

The system is to operate as follows:

The Two-Tier System

The Directive is based upon the premise that although most member state national laws provide for only one administrative organ in public companies, there is often a de facto distinction between executive and non-executive directors. A legal distinction is therefore required to differentiate between their different functions and responsibilities. The original 1972 draft provided for the compulsory introduction of a two-tier system. Due to the extreme opposition which was encountered the amended 1983 draft acknowledges that the two tier system will in many respects be impractical and a one-tier system may be retained subject to the imposition of certain requirements which will harmonise its function with two-tier structures.

The draft Directive proposes that a company is managed by a management body which is itself under the supervision of the supervisory body with members of the management body being subject to appointment and dismissal by members of the supervisory body. Supervisory body members, and in large companies within the Community members of the management body, are to be appointed for fixed periods which are not to exceed six years. A large company is defined as one which employs in excess of 1,000 employees within the Community, and is therefore unlikely to include many franchisors. Members of the management body are unable without the sanction and authority of the supervisory board to carry out any activity for any other undertaking other than the company itself. In the same way an agreement to which the company is party and in which a member of the management board has an interest has to be authorised by the supervisory board. The company in general meeting must then be informed of such an authorisation having taken place. It is a legal requirement that members of both boards are to carry out their functions in the best interests of the company with regard to the paramount interests of the shareholders and employees. It is also a requirement that even after having vacated office they must preserve confidential information relating to the company which they have learnt during their period with either one of the boards.

At least every three months the management board must submit a progress report to the supervisory board and at any time the supervisory board may request a special report on any aspect of the company's business. The management body is also required to give the supervisory body draft annual accounts and a draft annual report of the company within five months from the end of the company's financial year.

The management board's powers are further limited by a requirement in the draft Directive which places upon them the obligation to obtain the supervisory board's authorisation for decisions which relate either to establishing long term co-operation with other undertakings or the ending of such agreements already in existence. Authorisation must also be obtained for a substantial cut back or extension to the company's activities or a closure of part of the undertaking or for any substantial reorganisation or changes within the company.

The Draft Directive requires that member states must impose joint and several liability on members of both bodies (management and supervisory) in respect of damage that the company suffers as a result of breaches of the law of the member states, acts ultra vires the company's powers as set out in its Memorandum and Articles of Association or statutes as well as in respect of other wrongful acts. This category of 'wrongful acts' is not given further definition but it is likely to encompass such activities as negligence by members of the boards.

It is sufficient that a simple majority of the shareholders in the company can initiate proceedings where damage has been sustained by the company in such a way. Additionally, derivative proceedings can be bought on behalf of and in the name of the company by a shareholder holding at least 5% in nominal value of the company's issued share capital or shares of 100,000 ECU nominal value, whichever is the less. However if the shareholders take such a course and the Court subsequently finds there were no reasonable grounds in the first place for commencing proceedings, the shareholders will be held personally liable in respect of the costs which have been incurred.

The One-Tier System

The one-tier system closely mirrors the management and supervisory bodies of the two tier system by drawing a distinction between executive and non-executive directors. The Company will be managed by executive members who are appointed by the non-executive members of the board. Executive members are supervised by the non-executive members who are obliged to nominate one executive member as having particular responsibility in respect of personnel and employee relations. Similarly, executive members of the company must report to non-executive members every three months and are also responsible for the production of draft accounts and draft annual reports within five months of the ending of the company's financial year. The provisions detailed above concerning the civil liability of the members of management and supervisory bodies in the two-tier system apply with equal effect to executive and non-executive participants in the one-tier system.

Employee Participation

The draft Fifth Directive introduces compulsory employee participation in large company decision making under both the two- and one-tier systems and this has proved to be very controversial. Franchisors should note that franchisees are *not* counted as employees for this purpose; franchisee participation in the affairs of the franchisor company is not envisaged.

Employee Participation in the Two-Tier System

In respect of companies who have this system participation is to be provided for in accordance with one of four alternative schemes. These are summarised as follows:

Scheme 1
This consists of participation in the appointment of members of the supervisory body. Two thirds of the members of the supervisory body are to be appointed by the general meeting of the company whereas a minimum of one third and a maximum of one half are to be appointed by employees of the company.

Scheme 2 — Participation by co-option to the supervisory organ

In this scheme shareholders and employee's representatives may object to the appointment to the supervisory organ of a candidate who has been proposed by that body if they think that he/she is unable to fulfil his/her duties or, that if the appointment went ahead the supervisory body would when regard was had to the relative interests of the company, shareholders and employees, be imbalanced. In this situation the appointment of such a candidate cannot be made unless the objection is declared to be invalid by an independent body which is set up for this purpose under public law.

Scheme 3 — Participation through an employees body

An employees body is entitled to receive from the company's management board/body regular information and participating consultation in all aspects of the company, particularly its competition, progress and prospects and its investment plans. The employees body must be consulted before the supervisory body approves any of the transactions which have been proposed by the management body which are listed above for which the supervisory body's authorisation is required.

Scheme 4 — Participation through collective agreed schemes

Such agreements as these are required to make provision for employee participation or representation in accordance with four principles. These are firstly that relevant members of the supervisory body and the employees representatives are to be elected in accordance with systems of representation which ensure that minorities are protected. Secondly the elections must be by secret ballot, thirdly all employees must be able to participate in the election and fourthly freedom of expression of opinion has to be guaranteed.

Employee Participation in the One-Tier System

In large companies under this system employee participation in the decisions of the administrative body is required in accordance with one of the three schemes (1, 3 and 4) set out above in relation to the two tier system.

THE SIXTH DIRECTIVE

This Directive was adopted on the 17th December 1982 and concerns internal divisions of public companies.

THE SEVENTH DIRECTIVE

This specifies how and in what circumstances consolidated accounts are to be prepared and published by companies with subsidiaries.

The results of these reforms will be to eliminate many present forms of off balance sheet financing currently practised by companies.

THE EIGHTH DIRECTIVE

This relates to auditors' qualifications. Member states are obliged to ensure that auditors are not only independent but that they properly carry out their task of auditing company accounts. Minimum requirements for the education and training of auditors are set out. Member states are to implement the Eighth Directive within the period allowed for implementing the Seventh Directive.

Statutory audits may only be carried out by those approved by relevant authorities in the member states. These may be professional associations. 'Approved persons' can either be individuals who have obtained professional qualifications or they may also be firms of auditors who employ individuals who are 'approved'.

It is also a requirement that auditors must be 'persons of good repute'. This somewhat vague expression means that auditors must not do anything incompatible with their professional integrity.

THE PROPOSED NINTH DIRECTIVE

This represents an extension to the Seventh Directive which in imposing the principle of consolidation of group accounts seeks to lay bare the economic and financial relationships which exists within groups of companies.

THE DRAFT TENTH DIRECTIVE

This Directive is aimed at facilitating cross-border mergers between companies in different member states by harmonising various aspects of the law relating to the protection of shareholders, creditors and employees. As the proposal stands, a two-thirds majority of the members of both companies in favour of the merger will need to be obtained.

THE ELEVENTH DIRECTIVE

The objective of this Directive is to bring branches of foreign incorporated companies into line with the disclosure and related requirements imposed on locally incorporated subsidiaries by the First, Fourth, Seventh and Eighth Directives. This is particularly relevant to franchisors who establish a foreign branch to carry out market research or to control its sub-franchisor or franchisees. The proposals recognise that a branch does not have a separate legal personality and would therefore require disclosure of information concerning the company of which the branch is part including its accounts, which must be drawn up in accordance with the Fourth and Seventh Directives (that is to say in a manner corresponding to Sections 228 — 230 of the UK Companies Act 1985) ie, the company accounts must give a true and fair view of the state of affairs within that company or group of companies.

Branches of companies from other member states

Registration requirements of the First Directive are applied to the following documents in particular. They must register:

1. The address of the branch.
2. Details of the register and registration number of the company in the member state where the company is incorporated.
3. The name of the branch if different from that of the company.
4. The activities carried out by the branch.
5. Details of the persons who are authorised to represent the company.
6. The annual accounts and annual report of the company drawn up and audited in accordance with the Fourth, Seventh and Eighth Directives. For a company which is a subsidiary within the meaning of the Seventh Directive consolidated accounts and the consolidated annual report of the parent undertaking need only be filed.
7. The winding up the branch or the appointment of a liquidator.
8. The branch's closure.

All printed material and letterheads used by the branch have to state in addition to the information stipulated by the First Directive the register and registration number of the company in its member state of incorporation.

Branches from third countries

Compulsory disclosure requirements imposed by Article 3 of the First Directive apply equally to a company not governed by the law of a member state but similar to the types of company to which the First Directive applies. Additional to the information required to be filed by branches of companies from other member states, branches of companies from third countries have also to disclose:

1. The law of the state by which the company is governed.
2. The company's 'legal form', its registered office, its name and objects and the amount of its issued capital. The instruments of its constitution (for example the Memorandum and Articles of Association of the company) and all amendments to these documents must also be filed.
4. The register in which the company is recorded and its registration number.

The individual laws of the member states in which the branch is established may require certified signatures of those who are authorised to represent the company and to accept service of legal documents.

The Directive also provides for the compulsory disclosure of annual accounts and the annual report of the company which must be drawn up in accordance with the Fourth and Seventh Directives. These must also be audited in accordance with the law of the State which governs the company.

A major difficulty with the draft is that is has no definition of the expression 'branch'. The equivalent provision in the UK Companies Act 1985 applies when a company incorporated outside Great Britain 'so establishes a place of business in Great Britain'. This test has not always been easy to apply with there being considerable case law on this point. Clearly if the United Kingdom experience is any measure, the lack of a clearly defined term can create considerable difficulties.

THE MERGER CONTROL REGULATIONS

The Merger Control Regulations were adopted by the Council of Ministers in December 1989. It was due to a number of highly publicised cross border bids that the Merger Control Regulations achieved a priority status in terms of both politics and economics. Recent high profile bids have been, for example, Nestlé for Rowntree Mackintosh and GEC/Siemens for Plessey. A high degree of activity in this field in the late 1980's prompted the Commission to deal with this matter, and focused attention particularly on the great differences in member states on their respective takeover laws and practices.

Companies are not favourably disposed to further controls over the acquisition strategy, in addition to those controls already imposed by respective national laws. There was hope in some quarters that mergers subject to Commission control would not attract domestic law as well. This however, has not been the case. Few mergers are likely to fall within the ambit of the Regulations, although the Commission has reserved the right to intervene in mergers not normally within their scope. Principally mergers with a Community aspect are only subject to Commission control. However the national authorities can intervene on some occasions. Firstly they may intervene in order to protect national security or other, so called 'legitimate' interest and secondly to protect a particular and distinct market.

EC rules may be applicable even when the merger has no Community dimension. There are two occasions when this is the case, the first is where for largely technical reasons a Regulation cannot completely remove the Commission's power to apply existing competition rules which are laid down in Articles 85 and 86. The Commission has therefore reserved the right to intervene on the basis of the existing rules when mergers do not have a Community dimension but where the combined companies would exceed a world wide turnover threshold of 2000,000,000 ECU and a Community threshold of in excess of 100,000,000 ECU. Even where such sums are not involved it is possible for a national court in certain circumstances to apply EC competition rules. Secondly smaller member stats may wish to involve the Commission where they do not have a sophisticated merger control policy of their own.

As already stated the Regulation only applies to mergers which have a 'Community Dimension'. The Regulation will apply to a transaction which will have the direct or indirect effect of bringing together undertakings which together have an aggregate worldwide turnover of more than 5000,000,000 ECU and secondly where the aggregate community wide turnover of at least two of the undertakings concerned is more than 250,000,000 ECU. Turnover thresholds are to be reviewed after four years and the new figures will be decided by a qualified majority.

Merger is defined as the acquisition of direct or indirect control of the target undertaking. It should be remembered that control is not satisfied where as part of the company's financing arrangements banks or other financial institutions acquire shares with a view to resale, as long as they do not exercise the voting rights of those shares.

There is a general principle that mergers will be deemed to be compatible with the EC as long as the merged undertakings' market share does not exceed 25%. Even if it does exceed 25% it may still be deemed to be compatible when all the circumstances, including the parties' market position and choices available to consumers and suppliers, are taken into account together with the effect of international competition.

The fact that a merger is incompatible with the common market does not necessarily mean to say that the Commission will refuse authorisation. There are certain criteria which the Commission will take into account when deciding whether to authorise a merger or not. These can be summarised as follows:

1. Will damage inflicted on competitors be outweighed by improved production and distribution or the promotion of technical or economic progress?

2. Will the merger impose upon the different undertakings restrictions which are not necessary for achieving the merger?

3. Does the merger give the companies concerned an opportunity for eliminating competition in the market place?

DRAFT THIRTEENTH DIRECTIVE ON TAKEOVERS

The Commission believes that whilst takeover bids should in principle be encouraged there should be minimum rules laid down to protect companies from purely speculative financial operations. Rules and regulations have therefore been proposed concerning the conduct of both the target and predatory companies.

DIRECTIVE ON INSIDER TRADING

On the 13th November 1989 the Council adopted a Directive requiring member states to make Insider Dealing unlawful.

The Directive defines Insider Dealing as occurring when a person in connection with a company which has issued shares (this includes a director, shareholder or employee) takes advantage of the knowledge that he has acquired (inside information) by buying and selling shares in that company. Inside information must be unpublicised and obtained purely by virtue of his connection with the company; it must also be information which will have a significant effect on the price it it were made public. Where a company engages in Insider Dealing, the prohibition applies to individuals who took part in the decision to carry out the transaction.

The Directive makes it clear however, that certain activities are not included. These are, for example, the activities of market makers pursuing their normal business of buying and selling shares and transactions which have occurred on the basis of estimates prepared from information available to the public.

With regard to penalties, none have been included, although the Directive does require member states to introduce penalties which are sufficient to promote compliance with its rules. As a result differences in penalties are likely to be observed between member states. It should be noted that the Directive covers not only share but also other debt securities as well as options and futures.

CONCLUSION

Company law is somewhat of an EC political football. Harmonisation of company law will considerably help franchisors with subsidiaries or branches in more than one member state. It will remove many of the anomalies between the company laws of member states and so greatly simplify administration. However, introduction of worker participation would complicate matters and might well discourage some franchisors from setting up branches or subsidiaries within the EC.

The advent of the Societas Europea (see Chapter 18 below) may, however, reduce the importance of harmonisation of member states' law as far as pan-European franchisors are concerned.

Franchising and the European Company (Societas Europea)

By MARK ABELL and MARK ANTINGHAM

The creation of a European company or Societas Europea, to use the 'Euro-ese', has long been seen as necessary to facilitate the proper exploitation of the Single Market.

The potential importance of the Societas Europea to pan-European franchising is considerable. It could enable franchisors to base their head office functions in a company not limited by national constraints. It would not only facilitate easier cross-border policing and support, but also remove many of the problems which beset franchisors operating direct franchises in other member states.

The EC Commission's original proposal for the creation of a Societas Europea (SE) was put forward in 1970, with a revised proposal being produced in 1975. Discussions proceeded at a somewhat slow pace, and the proposal was shelved in 1982. However, the Commission subsequently resurrected it by issuing a new Memorandum in July 1988, for discussion by the member state governments.

The response by the British Government was markedly negative. In August 1988 the Department of Trade and Industry and the Department of Employment issued a consultative document on the proposal and invited the response of all interested parties, in industry and commerce in particular. The responses suggested that the business community did not feel that a European company statute would be needed, and, on the basis of how the proposed company was described in the Memorandum, little use would be made of it. Businesses particularly were concerned about the porposals which would allow for compulsory worker participation. However, the eleven other member states were far more positive and decided that it was worthwhile proceeding with the proposal. Consequently the Commission proposed promulgation of a European Company statute (OJ 124/170), as amended by EC bulletin supplement 4175.

The guiding principle of the proposal is to achieve freedom from the legal and practical constraints placed on firms by the existence of a separate set of rules in each of the 12 member states. The SE will be based on an independent legal order, which will be separate from national systems and which will refer to company law as already harmonised within the European community.

The SE will co-exist with nationally incorporated companies as an alternative business medium, rather than replacing them.

CREATION OF AN SE

Under the proposal a distinction is drawn between public limited companies (Plcs) and companies or firms within the meaning of Article 58 of the EEC Treaty. Two or more Plcs may form an SE by merger, forming a holding company or forming a joint subsidiary, provided that at least two of them have their central administration in different member states. Companies or firms within the meaning of the second paragraph of Article 58 and other legal bodies governed by public or private law which have been formed in accordance with the law of a member state *and* have their registered office and central administration in the Community may set up an SE by forming a joint subsidiary, again provided that at least two of them have their central administration in different member states. Article 58 EEC states as follows:

'Companies or firms formed in accordance with the law of a member state having a registered office, central administration or principal place of business within the community shall, for the purposes of this chapter, be treated in the same way as natural persons who are nationals of other member states.'

Additionally, an existing SE, together with one or more other SEs or together with one or more limited companies incorporated under the laws of a member state and having their registered office and central administration within the community, may form an SE by merging or by forming a holding company. Under Article 3 of the draft statute an SE may also set up one or more subsidiaries. However, an SE which itself is a subsidiary of an SE cannot create a further SE.

It is an essential principle common to all methods of formation that, in order to form the SE, there need to be at least two national companies originating from different member states. The Commission's wish to allow for the creation of large 'Euro-Nationals' capable of challenging large US or Japanese enterprises is evident. Under Article 13 of the statute founder companies have to draw up the instrument of incorporation and the company's statute in accordance with the laws of the state where the SE is to have its registered office. Not only must the registered office of the SE be situated within the EC, but the registered office and the central administration must be located at the same address.

For private limited companies that wish to form an SE via an (assets) merger, they must first of all become Plc's in accordance with their national law.

Formation by Merger

Articles 17 to 30 of the statute provide the details of how this is to be effected. With the formation of an SE by merger, merging companies are to be wound up (without going into liquidation), transferring to the SE all their assets and liabilities. In return their shareholders would receive shares in the SE and a cash payment (if any) not exceeding 10 per cent of the nominal value of the shares so issued. Forming an SE is not therefore a method for evading liabilities *per se*.

The first stage in any merger would be for the boards of the founder companies to draw up draft terms of the merger arrangements. The draft terms would include *inter alia*.

(1) Type, name and registered office of each of the founder companies and of the SE.
(2) The share exchange ratio (and where appropriate the amount of any cash payment).
(3) The date from which transactions by the founder companies would be treated for accounting purposes as being those of the SE.

The draft terms of the merger would then have to be published in the manner prescribed by the laws of each member state in accordance with Article 3 of Directive 68/151/EEC. Publication must take place at least one month before the date of the General Meeting of the shareholders of each founder company which would be called to decide upon it. Various items of information concerning the particulars would have to be disclosed in the publication. This would include, for example, the identities of the founder companies and the conditions which determine, in accordance with Article 25 of the statute, the date on which the merger and formation shall take effect.

Interestingly enough Article 25, dealing with the date on which the simultaneous merger and formation shall take effect, will be determined by the law of the state in which the SE has its registered office. It is perhaps a valid criticism of the proposal that it relies too heavily in terms of 'mechanical detail' on the pre-existing laws of member states for it to be a truly distinct body of law.

The Board of each of the merging companies would have to draw up a detailed written report explaining and justifying the draft terms of merger from both a legal and an economic viewpoint, with particular reference to the share exchange ratio.

The physical conduct of the merger will be supervised by one or more experts acting on behalf of each founder company, but independent of them, examining the draft terms of the merger and drawing up a written report for the shareholders. This statement must at least indicate the methods used in arriving at the proposed share exchange ratio and state whether the methods used are adequate in the circumstances. These experts will be entitled to call for any relevant information required by them to carry out their investigations. This body of independent experts would be appointed or approved by a judicial or administrative authority in the member state in which the company concerned has its registered office. At least one month after the publication of the draft terms of the merger, these, together with the instrument of incorporation of the SE and the statutes if they are a separate instrument, shall be approved by the general meetings of each of the founder companies. The resolutions of the general meetings proving the merger will be subject to the provisions giving effect to Article 7 of EC Directive 78/85(5) in the case of domestic mergers.

Article 23 of the statute gives protection to creditors and debenture holders in the case of a domestic merger. Additionally, there is to be supervision of the legality of mergers under Article 24, where the laws of a member state governing one or more founder companies provide for judicial or administrative preventative supervision of the legality of mergers. Such laws will apply to the companies. Where the laws of a member state governing one or more of the founder companies do not provide for judicial or administrative preventative supervision of the legality of mergers, the national provisions giving effect to Article 16 of Directive 78/85(5)/EEC shall apply to the company or the companies concerned.

Article 28 provides that liability of the members of the Board of the founder companies is governed by the provisions of the national law in the state in which the founder company concerned has its registered office or where appropriate by the terms of regulation. This gives effect to Articles 20 and 21 of Directive 78/88J/EEC.

Formation of an SE Holding Company

Under Article 31 of the draft statute, if an SE is formed as a holding company, all the shares of founder companies shall be transferred to the SE in exchange for shares in the SE.

In this case, founder companies continue to exist. The procedure is as follows. Firstly, the administrative and management board of each founder company draws up draft terms for the formation of the SE holding company. This contains the particulars referred to in Articles 18 and 21, that is to say, those relating to the draft terms of the merger and the supervision of the conduct of the merger. A report is then to be prepared as in the case of Article 20 and the formation of an SE by merger.

Similarly, the provisions of Article 2 in respect of the shareholders' approval for the formation of the holding company by the general meeting of each of the founder companies apply. The provisions of Article 28 as to the liability of board members of the company also apply. Additionally under Article 33 the administrative or management board of each of the founder companies will have an obligation to discuss with representatives of its employees all the legal, economic and employment implications of the formation of the holding company, together with any measures which they propose to deal with the implications which arise.

Formation of a Joint Subsidiary

All legal bodies governed by public or private law are able to use this method of formation. This is regardless of whether or not they are in company form. It is not even a requirement that the 'legal body' carries on a commercial activity or an activity with an ultimate economic purpose. This is a very broad concept, and is based upon that adopted for the European Economic Interest Grouping (EEIG) (see Chapter 19). It is not possible to convert into an SE a company incorporated under national law with branches in a number of member states.

Under Article 34 of the draft statute, if a joint subsidiary is to be formed as an SE, the administrative or management board of each of the founder companies shall draw up terms for the formation of the subsidiary, including the following:

(1) the 'type', name and registered office of the founder companies and of the proposed SE;
(2) The size of the shareholdings of the founder companies in the SE; and
(3) The economic reasons for its formation.

Draft terms of formation and the instrument of incorporation of the SE and its statutes have to be approved by each of the founder companies in accordance with the law which governs it. There are special provisions where a founder company itself is an SE whereby the instruments of incorporation and the statute shall be authorised in accordance with Article 72 of the Treaty of Rome.

An SE may also form a subsidiary. The administrative or management board will draw up the draft terms, which must include the economic reasons for the formation, the name and registered office of the founder company and the instrument of incorporation of the subsidiary or its statute. The instrument of incorporation of the subsidiary or its statute must be approved in accordance with Article 35 of the statute.

Articles 34 and 35 are worded in such a way that the actual decision to set up an SE is not taken by the boards of the founder companies, but by their general meetings. The statute governs the approval of the formation of a joint subsidiary only when one of the parent companies is an SE.

CAPITAL

Not unexpectedly, the capital of the SE must be denominated in the European Currency Unit (ECU) (See Chapter 34). Articles 38 to 60 concern capital, shares and debentures. The minimum capital of an SE is 100,000 ECU. With regard to the issue of shares, at least 25 per cent of their nominal value must be paid up at the time of the company's registration. The remaining consideration must be paid in full by the end of five years from the date on which the company was incorporated or acquired legal personality. It must be borne in mind that under Article 39 shares may not be issued at a price lower than their nominal value.

The amount of the capital may be varied, in accordance with the provisions in Articles 42, 43 and 45. Articles 42 and 43 deal with increase of capital and the authorisation of further increases in capital respectively, whilst Article 45 deals with reduction of capital.

Increase in Capital

Under Article 42 an increase in capital requires the amendment of the company statutes. Where all or part of the consideration for the increase in capital is in a form other than cash, a report on the valuation of the consideration must be submitted to the shareholders of the SE in general meeting. This report is to be prepared by an independent expert

appointed or approved by the Court within the jurisdiction of the country where the SE has its registered office. The expert's report is to be published, and any ensuing increase in the registered capital of the company has to be decided upon by the general meeting. The decision and the amount of the increase in the subscribed capital of the company has to be published in accordance with Article 9.

Under Article 43 capital increases of less than one half of the capital already subscribed to the company can be authorised under the statutes or instrument of incorporation or alternatively at a general meeting.

It is necessary for the management board of the company to register decisions which authorise a future increase in the capital in this way. Where the authorised capital has been fully subscribed or where the period during which the management board is authorised to increase capital (which cannot be for more than five years) has passed, the board has to amend the statutes or articles of the company to indicate the new total capital of the SE.

Reduction of Share Capital

Any reduction in the share capital of the company, except where it occurs pursuant to a court order, must be subject to a decision of the shareholders in general meeting carried out by a majority of at least two-thirds of those who are entitled to vote. The notice convening the general meeting must specify the purpose of the reduction and the way in which it is to be carried out as two of the minimum basic requirements.

It should be noted that a reduction of capital can only be effected by reducing the nominal value of the shares. The nominal subscribed capital may not be reduced to an amount of less than the minimum capital of the company. It is only where losses have been incurred that the general meeting may decide to reduce the capital below the minimum, and in that case the company shall at the same time decide to increase the capital in an amount equal to or higher than the minimum capital of the company.

The transfer of shares and replacement and cancellation of share certificates are governed by the laws of the states in which the registered offices of the SEs are situated.

BOARD STRUCTURE

The European company statute provides for two types of board structure, a two-tier board (a management board and a supervisory board) or a one-tier board, which would be an administrative board. The supervisory board and the management board would have no members in common; the supervisory board would appoint the management board and would be consulted on important, specified issues. The administrative board would have a majority of non-executive members and would delegate management to certain of its members, who would be the executive directors and who would be consulted in the same way as the supervisory board. The European company statute would cover the rights, duties and liability of directors with a few exceptions, including the effects of delegation and of allocation of responsibilities, as these would be the same for executive and non-executive directors.

In respect of governing bodies, the statute is based on national company law and on the amended proposal for a fifth Directive on the structure of public limited companies. It makes provision for a separation of powers between the general meeting of shareholders, which is to decide certain major items of business, and the bodies which manage and represent the SE. Management and representation of the SE is a function of either a management board as a supervisory board, monitoring its activities (the two-tier board system) or of an administrative board (the single-tier system). The SE's founder companies are authorised to choose between the two systems. Detailed rules for each system are laid out in Section 1, Articles 62 to 65 and Section 2 Articles 66 to 68 of the statute. Section 3 rules are common to both one-tier and two-tier board systems. Section 4 contains detailed rules governing the general meetings.

EXISTING CROSS-BORDER STRUCTURES

As already indicated, the aim behind the Commission's proposal for a cross-border corporation by way of the European Company is a good one. Transnational corporate structures within the EEC which are already in existence have been created where businessmen in only two member states, for example, have particular reason for attempting to create a form of cross-border link. This could very much be the case with franchising. An early example of a cross-border link was that formed in 1927 by Unilever, which is essentially an Anglo-Dutch conglomerate with two holding companies, one British, the other Dutch, with provisions in their respective articles of association for common directors, a common operating policy and an equalisation agreement aimed at balancing distributions between shareholders of the two holding companies. The formation of Unilver took place for commercial reasons, it was not intended as a vehicle for escaping from the laws and regulations of either state.

The more recent European trend has been for partnerships to develop as opposed to distinct companies with their feet effectively in two countries. A recent example of an attempt to form what amounts broadly speaking to a partnership on a cross-border basis within the EEC is that between Dunlop and Pirelli. Such partnerships have had a chequered history and it can be argued that where they have failed to survive, there is the possibility that stronger corporate ties might have saved the relationships if this had been possible. With a partnership, if the business climate becomes unfavourable or problems are encountered, the respective partners simply part company and return to their own fields of operation in their own countries. It is therefore arguable that a truly cross-border company would have no choice but to stay together, as the compulsion to make a success out of any problems encountered is directly linked to the ultimate success of the merged firm. Success has favoured companies which have

managed to forge very strong links, for example Iveco Trucks with Fiat, MAN and others.

It is evident that in the franchising field motivation for companies to form a European Company will be due to a realisation that operations in several markets can be dovetailed together. For most franchisors the European Company will simply not be a viable way of doing business. Many franchisors, whilst in theory they may wish to use the SE as an opportunity for expansion, simply do not have the suitability of concept, financial and/or market strength or often the will to join forces with another franchisor, who may also be a competitor. There would however be real benefits where the franchisor wishes to merge several different European subsidiaries.

In terms of franchisors who may wish to take advantage of any such option should it become available, many franchisors would perhaps be working with similar businesses and products, but a different business infrastructure. The existing franchise outlets would be able to exist relatively happily each in its own domestic market with perhaps a combination or one of the brands being franchised in other countries. It is in the areas of joint activity that problems may occur.

MAJOR ISSUES

A European Company governed by the European Company statute would in theory be taxed on an aggregate basis under the tax law of the member state in which its legal headquarters is situated. This would be taxation after adjustments for profits and losses made by its establishments in other member states have been taken into account. In this respect, it would bring most member states into line with the United Kingdom's existing treatment of a company having world-wide activities and would widen the UK position to allow the losses of subsidiaries, whether arising from companies resident in the United Kingdom as in the present situation or within Europe, to be set off against a holding company's profits.

There are also plans for the harmonisation of the tax treatment of mergers, divisions and contributions of assets, transactions and securities and the carrying over of losses. There are no plans as yet to confer other tax advantages on European Companies, as this might be unduly prejudicial to small and medium-sized enterprises not organised on a European basis.

Provisions that could be included in the statute are set out in the draft Fifth Directive (see Chapter 17 above) and include firstly, workers electing between one third and one half of a supervisory board which corresponds to the German model; secondly, workers participating through a separate body representing the employees; and thirdly, collective agreements in a form to be decided within the Company, but subject to specified minimum rights for the workforce.

The statute might also address the relationship between different companies within a single group. Although such groups are the basis of most developed corporate structures, they cannot be easily reconciled with the accepted principle of each company having economic independence and account-ability. If a European Company has nationally incorporated subsidiaries, this question will become acute.

IS A STATUTE NEEDED?

If Europe is compared with the United States as a federal model, it is by no means obvious that the European Community needs an EC company statute. The United States has managed perfectly well without a common company law system, although the laws of most of the fifty states are relatively similar. In the European Community, where common-law and civil-law systems co-exist, it is arguable that Europeans could get by without a common system of company law and that differences relating to European transnational corporate groupings could be settled by the European Courts in the same way as US federal courts regulate inter-state commerce.

It is possible that reorganisation by take-over is in reality a better route to European corporate restructuring than the company statute. It is arguable that in the United States the take-over system has (at least in the long term) worked fairly well to achieve corporate restructuring. As the purpose of take-overs is to facilitate the reorganisation of capital, it would be better for Europe to accord these a more significant role and concentrate on simplifying take-over and merger procedures. This can be done by replacing the current range of 'poison pills' (weighted voting rights etc) and other restrictive rules and provisions which appear in various member states, with an effective set of common rules governing take-overs and mergers. It is unlikely that the European Company statute, even if simple, easy to use and effective, will limit the use of the take-over weapon.

Thirdly, it is arguable that at least in the short term the statute will be used only by truly transnational ventures, so it will have to co-exist, possibly for generations, with existing national law. Thus the applicability of the European Company to franchising will particularly depend on the suitability of two companies in terms of market and financial resources. In purely practical terms, the possibility of co-existence between European company law and national law of the twelve member states will not simplify matters. It will instead present yet another set of rules for lawyers to interpret and yet another source of expense for their clients.

It may be easier to tackle the administrative difficulties and costs of incorporating subsidiaries in various jurisdictions by harmonising national laws around the most flexible models of company law (such as that applying in the UK), rather than to hope to achieve this result by creating a totally new corporate system.

Intense political differences over worker participation have been encountered, which is itself bound up with the current proposals. As it is, the Commission makes worker participation one of the reasons for introducing the statute in the first place. Although the European Parliament seems to favour the principle of worker participation, it seems misguided for the Commission to use it to justify the need for the statute, as US experience demonstrates that worker participation is not an essential requirement for economic success.

THE DIFFICULTIES

From the British point of view proposals for a company statute seem likely to prove impossibly complicated, bearing in mind that domestic UK company law is governed by a century of case law and by two Companies Acts. From a legal point of view it is to be hoped that the statute will be much more concise than traditional UK legislation.

Finalising the European company statute will be pro-longed, acrimonious, difficult and expensive. The Com-mission, for example, believes that a statute based perhaps in part on the European Company proposal put forward in 1970 and revised in 1975 offers the best method of overcoming the obstacles to incorporation between companies across Europe. The new statute could, in the Commission's view, be drawn up quickly, contributing to the creation of the 1992 integrated market. However, it is difficult to see how this result could be achieved without leaving a considerable amount to exiting national laws. If a considerable amount was left to existing national laws, this would negate the advantage that the statute is to cover all aspects of the European Community's company law. The 1975 draft, for example, contains some 274 articles, each with several sub-clauses, and four annexes containing a further 170 paragraphs. After several years of discussion less than a third of the draft had passed a first reading, and even this was achieved by leaving in suspense key contentious issues such as board structure and worker participation. Simplifying the document, as the Commission clearly hopes to do, by reference to harmonisation methods already achieved or under discussion, (for example, as with accounts and mergers) or which could be dealt with under existing national laws (for example, groups, winding up and insol-vency) may prove difficult.

Questions of worker participation, board structure, the limits of the limited liability concept, reductions of capital, the rights of shareholders, the holding of meetings, disclosure duties, procedures for giving and registering security over the company's assets, the choice of location for the European Companies Registry, formulation of a set of procedures for company formation, accounting and auditing policies and a plethora of other issues all have to be addressed. This is clearly a massive task.

There have been frequent attempts to harness a European feeling in the various types of corporate structure which have been outlined above, particularly for major cross-border infrastructure and industrial ventures. Lawyers and accountants concerned with these matters, however, are only too painfully aware of how problematical, time consuming, expensive and ultimately unnatural these corporate hybrids can be.

The long-term interests of all concerned will be best served by a complete and self-sufficient body of European company law emerging. Generally, transnational European corporate groupings are certain to play a major part in developing the internal market. It is hard to imagine that franchising will not throw up its own share of such groupings. It is in the interests of all member states to press for early creation of a flexible, essentially simple and non-doctrinaire legal structure.

FRANCHISING AND THE SE

As already mentioned, the SE would allow franchisors operating in more than one member state the opportunity to restructure their operations in a number of ways.

A franchisor may decide to merge its European subsidiaries to reduce the administrative, and particularly the accounting work. For example, a French franchisor with subsidiaries in Spain and Portugal, each operating direct franchises in their respective member states may decide to merge them into a single SE. The SE may also well prove to be an ideal vehicle through which franchisors operating in adjoining fields, such as for example road haulage and courier services, in different member states could combine to form a truly European operation.

Alternatively the franchisor may go one step further and merge the subsidiaries and itself into an SE. One substantial administrative benefit of this would be to do away with the difficult, tedious and expensive task of producing consolidated accounts of the entire group. The creation of a European HQ would have other obvious advantages associated with economy of scale. The SE will also form an ideal joint venture vehicle for franchisors and their partners.

The SE is undoubtedly going to be of great benefit to some larger franchisors working in more than one EC member state. However, its benefits should not be overstated. They are purely structural and administrative. The comparatively small size of many franchisors may also reduce the potential role of the SE in franchising. The SE will not in any way impact upon many of the difficulties of the single market such as national differences, different languages, different commercial customs and so on.

CHAPTER 19

Franchising and the European Economic Interest Grouping

By PROFESSOR JOHN ADAMS and DR FRANK WOOLDRIDGE

Introduction

An increased awareness of the existence of EEIG's (European Economic Interest Groupings), and their possible utility as a method of co-operation between business organisations and between professional firms within the European Economic Community has become manifest within the past two or three years. The EEIG was much influenced by the French GIE (groupement d'interêt économique), which is widely used as a vehicle for co-operative ventures in France, for example in the construction industry. The GIE is a legal entity separate from its members. It operates under its own name, and has its own directors. Importantly, it can contract as a legal entity with third parties. It was introduced by an Ordinance of 23 September 1967. Article 1 provides (authors' translation): 'Two or more individuals or legal persons may agree between themselves to form for a specific term a *groupement d'interêt économique*. The object of the grouping is to facilitate or develop the economic activities of the members or to improve or increase the profits or benefits of such activities; it is not to make profits for itself.'

The EEIG

The EEIG was created by Council Regulation (EEC) No 2137/85 of 25 July 1985 (Appendix 4). Like the GIE, the EEIG is a partnership-like entity to which companies, firms, natural persons and other legal entities in different member states may belong for the purpose of certain types of cross-frontier activities. Its object is to facilitate or develop the economic activities of its members, and to improve or increase the results of those activities. It is not designed to make profits for itself. The EEIG is differentiated from most forms of co-operation based upon a contractual relationship in so far as (depending on the member state), it may have its own legal personality and, in any case, it has its own independent capacity. The flexibility of the EEIG, its tax transparency, and relative lack of legal restrictions on it, may facilitate its use as a business medium within the Community, especially in relation to joint ventures involving those countries such as France which do not recognise agreements between shareholders about the conduct of a company.

EEIG's and Franchising

It has been contended that in addition to the uses indicated above, the EEIG might prove of use for the purposes of franchise networks. Certainly, it might have a role in relation to the type of franchise operation known as the 'voluntary group or chain'. These have been a feature of the grocery trade in the United Kingdom and some other EEC countries over the last thirty years or so. They are a means of enabling small independent shops to compete more effectively against super-markets. The usual scheme is that a group of wholesalers associate to supply an otherwise independent group of retailers who operate under a common trade name. The fundamental difference between this arrangement and franchising, as it is generally understood, is the informality of the association between the members of the group. They tend to be held together by economic convenience, rather than by contractual ties. By contrast, 'business format' franchising has the following characteristics:

(1) a contractual relationship between the parties under which the franchisor licenses the franchisees to carry on business under a name, mark etc. associated with the franchisor;
(2) control by the franchisor over the way in which the franchisees carry on business;
(3) provision of assistance to the franchisees by the franchisor in running their outlets;
(4) the businesses are however separate: the franchisees provide and risk their own capital.

Although it is difficult to be entirely certain, it would seem possible to exaggerate the potential utility of EEIG's in relation to this type of franchising. It would not seem that GIE's have been employed very extensively in franchising in France, although they have been used for certain purposes. An EEIG (like the GIE) suffers from the limitations that it cannot make profits for itself, and that its activities must be no more than ancillary to those of its members. Furthermore, an EEIG may not exercise a power of management over its members' own activities. This of itself would limit its application in relation to business format franchising. In addition, its members have joint and several unlimited liability for the debts and other liabilities of the grouping. These factors, coupled with the uncertainties inherent in the complex legal regime applicable to such groupings may well tend to discourage formation as well. Furthermore, the legal rules applicable to the groupings do not seem to accord very satisfactorily with the concept of control by the franchisor. Thus, in accordance with Article 12 of the Regulation, no one member may hold the majority of the votes.

However subject to the above reservations EEIG's may have an ancillary role to play in business format franchising. It is evident that as franchisee networks grow in size it will become increasingly necessary to provide them with ancillary services. Groupings might well be used for the purpose of holding trademarks and other intellectual property, though this might complicate structures often set up to optimise tax liability because, as noted above, they are tax transparent.

They might also be used in the same way as in the voluntary group as a means of providing common purchasing, transport, distribution and advertising services for a franchise network. It must be remembered that the activities of some larger groupings might well be subject to Community competition law and that on some occasions negative clearance will have to be asked for or advantage taken of certain existing exemptions when making use of a grouping, although the object of introducing EEIG's is obviously to encourage co-operation between undertakings.

CHAPTER 20

Franchising and Small and Medium-sized Enterprises in the Single Market

By MARK ABELL

Every member state has a different definition of what amounts to a small and medium sized enterprise (SME). Definitions range from companies that employ 50 employees to those that employ 500.

Small and medium sized enterprises are defined by the European Investment Bank as:

'Any firm with a workforce of not more than 500, net fixed assets of not more than ECU 75,000,000, and not more than one third of its capital held by a larger company'.

This definition would account for most franchisors not only in the European Community but throughout the world. On a wider front, this definition means that 95% of all companies within the European Community are small and medium sized enterprises and account for two thirds of employment within the Community.

The Community therefore regards such companies as essential to the success of the Single Market.

As a result, an action programme with a number of projects has been established for SME's. The programme was adopted by the Council in 1986 and has two basic objectives.

The first is to create a favourable environment for SME's by generally improving the social, fiscal and administrative environment in which they operate. The second aim is to positively contribute towards the needs of SME's by improving their access to capital, export markets, training and information.

The Commission Directorate General for Enterprise Policy (DG XXIII) is responsible for implementing this action programme.

There are currently seven projects which aim to assist franchisors and other SME's. These are detailed below:

1. The Business Co-operation Centre and Supporting Computer Network

The Business Co-operation Centre launches and co-ordinates projects for co-operation between firms seeking to engage in technical, commercial, financial or sub-contracting operations. It is backed-up by a supporting computer network which links business advisers established in certain regions or sectors of the European Community and is used to match offers and requests for co-operation between firms. It may be that this could present interesting opportunities for suitable franchisors.

2. European Information Centres

There are a great number of these multi-purpose information centres established throughout the European Community. They aim at supporting Chambers of Commerce, established business consultants and other information outlets by providing information on Community legislation, aid, loans, research programmes and Third Country markets.

3. Euro-Info Bulletin

This is a monthly newsletter published by the European Commission and circulated to the business community.

4. COMETT (Community Action Programme for Education and Training for Technology)

This is a three-year programme launched in 1987 which aims to promote joint projects between universities and enterprises for continuing training for technology.

5. BRITE

This is a community research programme in industrial technologies for Europe.

6. SPRINT

This aims at promoting the transnational development of an infra-structure for innovation and technology transfer. It also aims to promote the fast dissemination of new technologies and their industrial application.

7. Prisma

On 25 January 1991 the Commission established Prisma to improve the range of services offered to enterprises to help them prepare for the single market. SMEs are specifically mentioned in the Notice (91/C 33/05). One of the objects of the initiative is to prepare SMEs for the opening up of public procurement and the removal of safeguards within the ambit of Article 115 EEC by means of technical assistance, in particular for the introduction of better methods for managing production and distribution.

Article 7 of the Notice identifies the following as being eligible for assistance:

'(a) Operating expenditure and facilities for local bodies whose aim it is to set up or develop the following services relating to public procurement:

— selection and distribution of information in a form adapted to the needs and capacities of enterprises on the basis of the TED (Tenders Electronic Daily), and other sources which include more detailed information or information relating to invitations to public tenders in non-member countries or for amounts beneath the thresholds in Community directives,
— information on national quality systems, Community testing and certification standards, legal and procedural obligations in other Member States,
— where appropriate, information on research and development results relating to products intended for public sector markets, information on new market opportunities, exhibitions, seminars

or conferences related to public procurement,
— other support and advice services;

(b) Aids to SMEs for costs related to co-operation with other firms in the field of public tenders; registration and admission to lists of qualified tenderers; translation and other costs related to a response to public tenders outside the area where the firms are located;

(c) Other aids designed to improve competitivity specifically directed towards SMEs located in Objective 1 regions and in sectors for which safeguards are presently authorised under Article 115 of the EEC Treaty.'

These operational programmes are financed jointly by the member states and the EC. Member states wishing to benefit from the programme were invited to present proposals to the EC Commission before 8 August 1991. To date it is not known what the results have been.

One of the greatest problems for small and medium sized enterprises including franchisors is access to risk capital and funding. The European Community currently offers three sources of finance to franchisors and other small and medium sized enterprises.

Community loans are available from the European Investment Bank and through the New Community Financial Instrument. Loans are made available to intermediary financial institutions who submit projects for the loans to the European Investment Bank, which then in turn decides upon eligibility. The intermediary bank or other institution then provides that funding in local currencies for specific projects. The New Community Financial Instrument Loans have been made available for the development of intangible assets such as patent research and development projects and to facilitate capital contributions. It would therefore seem to be available to the more highly technologically geared franchises.

The Venture Consult Scheme seeks to increase access to finance of SME's that are involved in new technologies at the first stage of capital formation.

In addition various grants are available from the Structural Funds – The European Regional Development Fund, The European Social Fund and the Guidance Section of the European Agricultural Guidance and Guarantee Fund.

CHAPTER 21

Franchising and the Environment in the Single Market

By DENISE FRANKLIN, MARK ABELL and CRAIG BAYLIS

Recent highly-publicised environmental disasters have dramatically proven to the world that there needs to be a co-ordinated effort to control activities which affect the environment. The methyl isocyanate gas leak in Bhopal, India killed 2,000 people and injured 200,000 more; the explosion at the Chernobyl nuclear reactor will have lasting effects all over the world as radioactive material from Chernobyl was found to have drifted as far as the USA.

To establish a measure of control in the European Community, the Commission introduced through the Single European Act (SEA) provisions conferring express authority to legislate on environmental matters. Previously, the Commission had created environmental legislation under the broadly stated goals of the Treaty of Rome.

One of the most important provisions of the SEA is a statement contained in Article 130R that 'environmental protection requirements shall be a component of the Community's other policies'. This statement suggests that future EC legislation in other areas must consider environmental issues. That protection of the environment is a matter to be reckoned with represents an important shift away from emphasis on the primacy of economic matters.

A further step towards unified environmental control was the creation of the European Environment Agency in May 1990. Its immediate task is to provide reliable scientific and technical information on the environment to enable the Commission to draft effective legislation. Currently, enforcement of the legislation is left to the member states, although the European Environment Agency may be able to fill that role in the future.

Article 100A of the Treaty of Rome reinforces these objectives and principles by providing for a high level of environmental protection. Although the White Paper does not contain any new initiatives for environmental protection the EC Commission's Fourth Environmental Action Programme states that 'the future competitiveness of community industry and world markets will depend heavily upon its ability to offer goods and services causing no pollution and achieving standards at least as high as its competitors'. A number of steps have already been taken such as the reduction of industrial accidents, management of waste control, the improvement of health and safety of workers and consumers, the classification, containment and control of risks from the development and use of bio-technology, control of noise, water and air pollution and the classification and labelling of dangerous substances. The most significant development was the proposed creation of the European Environmental Agency, the primary role of which will be to collect information to enable the Commission to create effective environ-mental policies and legislation rather than a policing role.

This means that the franchisors operating within the single market will in the future have to pay particular attention to the environmental impact that their business has upon the community. The days of small innocuous fines for pollution in countries such as the United Kingdom are numbered and being subject to international legislation such as that found in Germany will soon become the norm. Franchisors who do not consider this legislation carefully will accordingly find themselves at a severe financial disadvantage.

The Commission has drafted environmental legislation which concerns the control of pollution in areas such as water, waste products, air, chemicals, noise and wildlife and the countryside. Of particular concern to franchise operations are:

(1) the Draft Directive on Civil Liability for Damage Caused by Waste, and
(2) the Environmental Assessment Directive.

Liability for damage caused by waste

The Draft Directive on Civil Liability for Damage Caused by Waste provides that 'producers' are liable to pay the cost of cleaning up damage caused by their waste. A 'producer' is defined as the 'legal person' who generates or has actual control over the waste at the time of the incident. The liability attaching to the producer is born out of the 'polluter pays' principle, which holds that those responsible for pollution should bear the cost of its control and remedy.

This could have severe consequences for franchisors in the EC. For instance, if a franchisee, such as a dry cleaner, were to contribute to the contamination of land, it is possible that the franchisor might be considered the 'producer' for liability purposes. Where a franchisor has significant control over the franchisee, 'legal person' could be read to include the franchisor. This liability could also arise under the common law of agency.

Further, if a franchisee's operations have caused damage to the environment and the franchisee absconds or is insolvent, the liability for contamination will most likely attach to the franchisor. The key issue is how one defines 'legal person' or 'person with actual control' in accordance with the 'polluter pays' principle. In a situation where there is no franchisee able to pay damages, the franchisor could well be liable to pay clean-up costs rather than the alternative — which could leave the government to pay the bill.

In order to ward off potential liabilities, the franchisor might wish to include certain warranties of non-polluting behaviour from the franchisee in the franchise agreement. A franchisor may also want to include a clause in which the franchisee indemnifies the franchisor for any pollution liability attributed to the franchisor. In addition, a franchisor might require that the franchisee takes out insurance against these types of liability.

Since the Draft Directive is not yet in force, parties to the franchise would need to check the national legislation of the franchisee's member state to determine what type of laws currently cover the cost of cleaning up pollution. For example, in the UK liability for the cost of cleaning up pollution will soon attach to the 'owner' of the property. Again, depending how 'owner' is interpreted, this could include the franchisor for the same reasons as discussed above. If the franchisor has taken an intervening lease on the property, as was the practice during the boom years of the 1980's, its liability is even more likely.

Environmental assessment

The other Directive which concerns franchising is the Environmental Assessment Directive. This Directive imposes the obligation on member states of taking information on environmental effects of a project into consideration in their planning consent procedures. An 'assessment' is not a document, but a series of steps toward decision-making. The Directive sets out two annexes of projects which may be needed to produce material, called an 'environmental statement' in the UK, which discusses:

(1) Information on the project,
(2) Information on the site,
(3) Assessment of how the development will change the site environment, and
(4) Mitigating measures taken to ward off damaging environmental effects.

Depending on the franchise concerned, a franchisee may need to conduct an environmental assessment to gain planning permission for the project. The franchise agreement should clearly assign such responsibility to the franchisee together with the cost of the assessment and any additional costs relating to the process.

CHAPTER 22

Franchising and Social Policy in the Single Market

By MARK ABELL

Following the Madrid Summit in June 1989, the European Council voiced the opinion that job development and creation should be given top priority. It agreed to set an agenda which would aim at working towards achieving the social dimension if the Single Market.

However, whilst all the 12 member states agreed upon the need for social progress within the context of the Single Market, there is substantial disagreement on how it should be achieved. This disagreement is basically between the United Kingdom (which believes that such progress must flow naturally out of the Single Market) and the other member states (which believe in a more directed approach).

In 1988, a Commission working party examined the social impact of the Single Market on three specific sectors, namely industries and services, regions, and small and medium-sized enterprises. The survey suggested that there was a risk that small and medium-sized enterprises might be adversely affected by the internal market and suggested that they be carefully monitored by the Commission. Franchising, it is suggested, is one positive way in which small- and medium-sized enterprises can not only avoid being adversely affected by the internal market but positively prosper from it.

The Commission Working Paper entitled *The Social Dimension of the Internal Market* (September 1988) listed over fifty different proposals for initiatives relating to the social dimension. These proposals have been backed by the Economic and Social Committee of the Commission and the European Parliament. The majority of member states are also greatly in favour of them.

Since the publication of that paper a number of initiatives have been put in action.

The 'Framework Directive' to encourage improvements in health and safety at work and three directives relating to minimum requirements, use of work equivalent and versatile protective equipment have been passed (Directives Nos. 89/391 (OJ 1989 L183/1), 89/654 (OJ 1989 L393/1), 89/655 (OJ 1989 L393/13) and 89/695 (OJ 1989 L393/18) respectively). Two further directives on heavy loads and VDUs are also due to be adopted in due course.

A directive on the recognitioin of higher education diplomas has been passed (see Chapter 10 above) and another concerning the levels of education and training is also due to be passed. A further directive has been passed concerning employee participation in companies (see OJ 1989 C263/69). The concept of employee participation is an essential part of supervision and strategic development of companies. There are three models of participation provided for in the European Company, namely participation in membership of the supervisory organ, participation through a body representing the staff and distinct from the governing bodies, and a form of participation to be established by collective agreement (see Chapter 18 above).

The European 'social dialogue' consultations between employee organisations and trade unions were instituted in 1985 and have been relaunched by Jacques Delors, President of the Commission.

There is also a proposed directive to shift the burden of proof in equal pay cases.

However, the greatest initiative regarding the social dimension of the Single Market was adopted at the Strasbourg Summit in December 1989 by all the member states except for the United Kingdom. The Community Charter of Fundamental Social Rights is not legislation but a declaration that, in its own words:

'the member states commit themselves to take such steps that are appropriate to mobilise all resources that may be necessary in order to guarantee the fundamental social rights contained in the Charter . . . the completion of the internal market must offer improvements in the social field for citizens of the European Community, especially in terms of freedom of movement, living and working conditions, social protection, education and training.'

The principal of subsidiarity is to be applied to initiatives contained in the Charter. This means that the Community will only enact rules when it is more efficient to adopt them at a European rather than a national level. The Charter identifies twelve basic rights:

(1) The right to freedom of movement;
(2) Rights in connection with employment and remuneration;
(3) Rights relating to improvement of living and working conditions;
(4) Rights to social protection;
(5) Rights to freedom of association and collective bargaining;
(6) Rights to vocational training;
(7) Rights of men and women to equal treatment;
(8) Rights of workers to information, consultation and participation;
(9) The right to have adequate protection and safety at the workplace;
(10) Rights relating to protection of children and adolescents;
(11) Rights of elderly people; and
(12) Rights of disabled persons.

Despite the vehement dissent of the British Government and the need for unanimity in Council on all matters relating to the rights and interests of employed people, the

Commission adopted an action plan in November 1989 which sets out exactly how it intends to push forward the proposals of the Charter at a European level. The programme contains over forty proposals of which seventeen are for directives. The proposals include the following:

(1) Advising member states on what is an 'equitable wage';

(2) Regulating working time in the interests of health;

(3) Giving employment rights to part-time and fixed-term contract workers;

(4) Providing evidence of an existence of a contract of employment;

(5) Promoting consultation in the event of collective redundancies affecting companies across frontiers;

(6) Achieving more equal treatment of men and women;

(7) Protecting pregnant women in the workplace;

(8) Promoting in companies the development of information, consultation and participation practices, particularly in companies operating across the Community;

(9) Encouraging worker participation in company profit-sharing and share ownership;

(10) Establishment of a European Health and Safety Agency;

(11) A minimum working age and a limit on the hours that can be worked by young people;

(12) Facilitating occupational integration of disabled people; and

(13) Promoting health and safety at work.

Clearly, the Social Charter and the Commission's action programme will impact on franchisees in the European Community. However, until the Council is willing to adopt the proposals in a concrete form, it is difficult to comment upon exactly what that effect will be. Inevitably, however, it seems that franchisors, sub-franchisors, developers and franchisees will have to cope with further regulations as regards their employees.

CHAPTER 23

Franchising and Non-Life Insurance in the Single Market

By MARK ABELL

With the advent of increasing potential liability for franchisors, the availability of cheap and comprehensive insurance throughout the EC is of paramount importance. Product liability, liability for services, liability for environmental pollution and so on mean that franchisors must ensure that they are paying the lowest possible premiums for the fullest possible cover. This situation can only be fulfilled if there is free competition in providing insurance services throughout the whole of the single market.

The European Commission intends with this aim in view to make it possible for insurance companies established in any of the twelve member states to provide their services freely throughout the European Community.

Insurers will be subject to similar controls in each of the member states where they wish to open an office. They will in effect enjoy freedom of establishment and freedom to supply services (see Chapter 10 above). Directive number 88/357 (OJ 1988 L 172/1) on non-life insurance services was supposed to have been in force in most member states by 30th June 1990 (some members have been given more time to implement the more liberal rules of the directive in full). A number of types of insurance contracts were excluded from the scope of the directive, particularly those relating to liability for pharmaceutical products and compulsory insurance for building works. Even these exclusions will disappear in time.

The directive distinguishes between large risks (principally from major industrial companies) and mass risks (i.e. those relating to individuals and small businesses, which will include most franchisees).

Large risks are defined by reference to the nature of the risks including marine, aviation and transport risk or the size of the policy holder (a minimum balance sheet total of ECU 12.4 million or a net turnover of ECU 24 million per annum and/or 500 employees or more. From 1st January 1993 these figures will be approximately halved). Those at risk can be covered by any insurance company throughout the Community, based on home country control.

As regards mass risks however, the insurance companies may remain subject to the various host country rules and controls pending harmonisation.

Insurance undertaking are given an automatic right to start accepting business in the host country once they have furnished the host country authorities the information set out in the directive.

The adoption of this directive means that franchisors and franchisees are now able to shop around and obtain the best possible cover for all corporate risks including product liability and professional indemnity.

As regards the insurance industry however there is still a way to go in particular in relation to motor insurance liberalisation, harmonisation of technical reserves and provision of home country rule for mass risks. A single insurance licensing system is currently being considered by the Commission, which will remove restrictions on the duplication of activities by a company outside its home county through cross-border services and establishment.

CHAPTER 24

Making the most of Franchising in the Single Market

By MARK ABELL

Franchisors must ensure that they make maximum use of the opportunities that the advent of the single market presents to them.

They must ensure that they take advantage of the new and improved facilities available, such as the reduced cost of capital equipment and cheaper and readily available finance. For example the greater choice of insurers and new insurance products at lower premiums will enable them to save substantial amounts (see Chapter 23 above). The increased staff mobility and ease of recruitment in all twelve member states will aid Europeanisation of the franchise (see Chapter 10 above). The availability of training schemes promoted by the Commission will also assist in this. (See Chapter 20.)

The establishment of Pan European telecommunication networks, the greater choice of terminal equipment, a wider choice of suppliers of telecommunication services, reduced transport costs and an increased choice of carriers (see Chapter 11 above) will improve the quality of service and offer substantial advantages to franchisors who are willing to shop around and take advantage of the Single Market.

The opportunities and rights to provide cross-border services based on home country control (particularly as regards financial services) will make the Europeanisation of franchises far simpler. The elimination of physical, technical and fiscal barriers coupled with standardisation and increased opportunities to tender for public procurement contracts offer real opportunities for franchisors wishing to expand their network throughout the European Community. (See Chapters 13 and 16 above.)

Franchisors must also ensure that they take best advantage of various opportunities presented by the various information services of the EC Commission which provide not only information centres but also many relevant and enlightening statistics on industries and services in the Community. The twelve member states also offer similar complimentary services.

The various grants available from the Community and loans from the European Investment Bank could be of great use to franchisors. See Chapter 34 below.

The opportunity of forming a European company (see Chapter 18 above) and/or a European Economic Interest Grouping (see Chapter 19 above) will allow many franchisors to take advantage of the Single Market in the most cost effective and structurally appropriate manner.

The Single Market however also presents threats to franchisors such as the threat of being taken over by a competitor based in another member state. The rapid change within the market also present an immense challenge. Franchisors must keep abreast of these changes, be they legal or technical, in order to survive, let alone exploit, the Single Market.

Consideration of appropriate structures to expand throughout the EC will be necessary. Will centralisation of the management of a pan-European franchise by way of the Societas Europea be necessary or will the establishment of an EEIG to work alongside national sub-franchisors present a more suitable structure? The education of management for the new European business environment, including language and business culture, will also take on a greater degree of importance. Franchisors must meet this challenge to succeed in the Single Market.

Those franchisors who manufacture products will find still further challenges. The wider market must continuously be reviewed ensuring that the purchasing policy is the correct one. Scope for increased capacity and the optimum use of manufacturing capacity must be considered together with the possible economies of scale and the localisation/centralisation of production. New standards may require changes in production (see Chapter 13 above).

All franchisors must try to improve their management knowledge of the European market and adopt the most appropriate marketing techniques. Local sub-franchisors/developers will give franchisors a substantial advantage over non-franchise competitors. Nevertheless, the franchisor itself must understand the situation in each of the relevant member states so that it can co-ordinate the approach being taken by each member state/sub-franchisor/developer.

Distribution of products sold or used by the franchisor must also be carefully considered. For example, would an EEIG be an appropriate vehicle through which to distribute products throughout the Single Market, or is a subsidiary, branch or local distributor/agent more appropriate? What forms of transport should be used for the distribution to ensure that it is most cost effective?

As ever franchisors must strive to ensure that their research and the development of their product or service is given priority.

The possibilities of rationalisation/concentration of activities in areas where the business is strongest or diversification/expansion into less developed member states must of course always be carefully considered and the possibility of mergers, takeovers, joint ventures and various forms of incorporation must be scrutinised.

The Single Market presents franchisors with a very special and unprecedented challenge. For those franchisors who take up this challenge there are likely to be very rich rewards. For those franchisors who ignore the challenge, the future promises something very different.

PART FOUR

FRANCHISING AND THE LAW OF THE EUROPEAN COMMUNITY

EC Intellectual Property Law

By DR JEREMY PHILLIPS

1 THE LEGAL BASIS FOR THE EUROPEAN COMMUNITY'S JURISDICTION OVER INTELLECTUAL PROPERTY

As explained in previous chapters the European Community (EC), originally known as the European Economic Community, currently comprises twelve Member States with several other countries likely join before the year 2000.

The principal free trading bloc within Europe, the EC is committed to the following principles: the establishment of the territories of the EC as a single market; the free movement of goods, services and workers within the territory of the EC; the removal of internal barriers to trade within the single market; the establishment of national laws in individual member states which approximate to or harmonise with each other; the promotion of competition for the supply of goods and services within the EC and the provision of legal means by which all these aims may be implemented and enforced. The constitution of the EC is to be found in the Treaty of Rome.

Intellectual property law is the legal lynchpin which fastens together the components of a franchise. It protects the trade mark, trade names, trade dress and other identificatory indicia of the franchise format; it governs the artwork, design and packaging of goods sold under franchise; it controls the unauthorised use of databases, information, accounting systems and stock inventories; it protects inventions which may lie at the heart of both goods and services franchises. However, while intellectual property is the lynchpin of the franchise, the control of intellectual property rights is fundamental to the effective regulation of the EC's competition policy.

There are various ways that intellectual property rights can be exercised in a way which falls foul of the Treaty of Rome and its subordinate legislation. The following, for example, are objectionable under European competition law:

(1) The use of separate national monopolies in order to divide up the EC into separate markets, for example by licensing party A in France and party B in Belgium to make and sell the same product, with the condition that party A cannot export his goods to Belgium and party B cannot export his to France. The effect of this monopoly is that it prevents party C, an entrepreneur, buying the goods in France where they are cheap and selling them into Belgium where they cost more, or vice-versa.

(2) The use of a monopoly so as to limit the supply of goods which are in demand, in order to force up the price artificially and make maximum profit with minimum effort.

(3) The dividing up of a market with one's licensees/franchisees so as to ensure that each can make a profit without having to compete with the others.

(4) The formation of groupings such as patent pools, in which manufacturers each license each other to make the others' products but all agree to refuse to license those who are not members of the patent pool.

(5) The use of intellectual property rights to maintain a market dominance so that price-fixing between supposed competitors can take place.

The European Commission, which is empowered to enforce EC competition rules, must examine complaints made to it that the domestic laws of member states contravene the provisions of the Treaty of Rome, particularly Article 30 which deals with laws restricting imports. Since many national laws were passed long before the member states formed or joined the EC, it is not surprising that there have been many occasions when pre-EC laws were found to be incompatible with the Treaty. However, post-accession laws have also been found to be in contravention of Article 30.

The Commission must also examine all activities, undertakings and practices which look as if they will distort competition or breach EC policy within the territory of the EC. To this end, all contracts and arrangements must be notified to the Commission, which must examine them for adherence to EC policy. Agreements and practices which fall foul of the competition policy of the EC are unlawful and unenforceable (see Chapter 26 below).

The EC's responsibility is too great to be discharged in every particular case, since it would require the Commission to examine every single contract, licence and commercial practice in order to ascertain its effect. Accordingly there are a number of limitations placed upon the discharge of the Commission's responsibilities (see Chapter 28 below).

(1) Objectionable contract and commercial practices will escape the censure of EC law if they do not distort trade between member states. Thus a market-sharing agreement between two chains of fish and chip shops in North-East England would be regarded as being of largely, if not entirely, parochial effect, while a similar agreement made between two chains of shops on the Netherlands-Germany border could be viewed quite differently.

(2) The effect of objectionable practices and agreements must be capable of being felt within a substantial portion of the market for the goods or services in question. Thus if two small companies, each of whom enjoys no more than a 2 per cent share of the widget market, enter into a market-dividing and patent-pooling arrangement, the overall effect may well be pro-competitive, since it will enable them to compete more

effectively against the market leaders. This principle is difficult to implement since its application depends upon what one regards as the relevant market. Does *Pronuptia* (see Chapter 29 below) for example, enjoy a very large share of the wedding dress market, a small share in the market for dresses of every type, or a miniscule share in the market for clothes of all types? Much technical litigation has been given over to issues of this nature.

(3) Agreements which consist entirely of non-objectionable provisions do not need to be notified to the Commission. The so-called 'block exemptions' under Article 85 of the Treaty (see Chapters 28 and 29 below) are regulations which list the clauses which will not attract the Commission's disapproval. These regulations govern licences of patents (Regulation 2349/84), know-how (Regulation 559/89), research and development agreements (Regulation 418/85) and franchising (Regulation 4087/88). An agreement which potentially overlaps each of these topics (e.g. a franchising agreement which also involves a patent licence and a know-how licence) will enjoy the benefit of block exemption so long as it fits completely within the terms of any one of those exemptions – but it is not possible to go 'cherry-picking', taking some conditions from one exemption, others from another and thus making a block exemption mosaic.

(4) Even agreements which potentially fall within the scope of an investigation under Article 85 need not be investigated if, on a cursory examination of them, it appears that there is no *prima facie* ground for concern. In such a case the Commission may issue a 'comfort letter' to the parties to such an agreement (see Chapter 27 below) to the effect that it is not the Commission's intention to take action against them (on 'comfort letters', properly called 'administrative letters', see V. Korah, 'Comfort Letters – Reflections on the Perfume Cases' (1981) 6 E. L. Rev. 14.). Such 'comfort letters' are not binding and the Commission is not estopped from investigating an agreement in respect of which it has already indicated a general willingness not to investigate. Nor it seems are national courts obliged to respect them, though it is unlikely that there would be many cases in which they would not wish to do so.

Once a practice carried out by one or more party, or a national law, is considered to be in breach of the EC's competition policy, it may be the subject of judicial proceedings which will determine its legality. These proceedings take place before the European Court of Justice (ECJ), which itself is the supreme judicial body of the EC.

There are basically two avenues by which cases involving EC competition policy come before the ECJ. One is when proceedings are instituted before the ECJ by the Commission, usually as a result of an investigation made by it into a practice or state of affairs discovered by it or reported to it. In such proceedings the Commission puts its case, the party or parties involved put theirs and the ECJ, guided but not bound by the considered written opinion of the Advocate General, then makes its ruling. The other route by which the ECJ hears cases is when, in litigation which originates in a member state, a national court is faced with a matter which involves the interpretation of the Treaty of Rome or its subordinate

legislation. In such a situation the national court will stay the proceedings before it and refer the matter to the ECJ. Where this happens, the ECJ simply examines the case on an abstract basis, in terms of hypothetical facts posed by the national court which makes the reference. The finding of fact as to whether those hypothetical facts in fact apply is left to the national court, which hears evidence and makes its decision in the usual way. Once the ECJ has given its decision, it conveys it to the national court in question, which then continues the proceedings. This system of references may seem somewhat cumbersome and inconvenient, but it ensures that national courts all have to apply the same interpretations to EC law, to foster and element of consistency.

The following paragraphs under this heading will examine some of the provisions of the Treaty of Rome as they effect intellectual property generally. Specific issues relating to franchising will be dealt with elsewhere in this book.

1.1 Free movement of goods

Under the Treaty of Rome, Article 30:

'Quantitative restrictions on imports and all measures having equivalent effect shall, without prejudice to the following provisions, be prohibited between Member States.'

What this means is that national governments may not impose or enforce laws which have the effect of keeping out goods made in other member states. In fact, relatively few laws which keep out imports are 'quantitative restrictions on imports' in an express sense, since the member states of the EC are all, at least in theory and largely in practice, committed to free trade rather than protectionism or 'market reserve' (a term which originated in Brazil describing the policy of prohibiting foreign businesses from engaging in specified markets at all). Most national laws which fall foul of Article 30 are those which, while aimed at some other stated object, are 'measures having equivalent effect' within the EC.

All intellectual property rights of a statutory monopoly nature are potentially capable of preventing imports, because the statutory patent, trade mark and copyright monopoly in every member state carries the exclusive right to prohibit the unauthorised importation of protected goods into that State. But intellectual property monopolies are not prohibited; instead they are positively permitted under Article 36 of the Treaty. According to the provisions of Article 36:

'The provisions of Articles 30 to 34 shall not preclude prohibitions or restrictions on imports, exports or goods in transit justified on grounds of public morality, public policy or public security; the protection of health and life of humans, animals and plants; the protection of national treasures possessing artistic, historic or archaeological value; or the protection of industrial or commercial property. Such prohibitions or restrictions shall not, however, constitute a means of arbitrary discrimination or a disguised restriction on trade between Member States.' (emphasis added)

Intellectual property rights are concerned with 'the protection of industrial or commercial property' and thus fall within the scope of the first part of Article 36. An intellectual property right which was arbitrarily discriminatory or which constituted a disguised restriction on trade would not be permitted.

Fortunately, within the EC there is little or no scope for the removal of the protection accorded to national intellectual property rights on the ground of arbitrary discrimination. This is because all member states are members of both the Paris Union (on intellectual property) and the Berne Union (on copyright) whose conventions require that any right which is granted under national law should be available not only to nationals but also, without discrimination, to the nationals of any other Union member state.

The mere fact that the law of one member state recognises a right which does not exist in other member states, as for example where Germany recognises a utility model right while the UK does not, does not constitute a breach of Article 30, in that the same right is available to nationals from all other member states. The undesirable effects of different intellectual property rights being granted in different countries make the matter one for approximation or harmonisation of laws, not the prohibition of one country's law.

Another aspect of the interaction between Articles 30 and 36 is that which requires the adoption of the doctrine of 'exhaustion of rights'. Under this doctrine, once goods have been marketed in the EC with the agreement or consent of the intellectual property rights owner, no intellectual property right may be enforced in any member state so as to restrict the movement of those goods. Accordingly, if the owner of a trade mark registered in France and Germany licenses the sale of goods bearing his mark in France, he cannot then use his German trade mark registration in order to prohibit the importation of those goods into Germany.

To the layman it would seem that, in the instance mentioned above, the trade mark owner has effectively lost his trade mark right in Germany. This is not the case. The Treaty of Rome does not allow the destruction of property rights. According to Article 222:

'This Treaty shall in no way prejudice the rules in Member States governing the system of property ownership'

This would seem to contradict the principle we have derived from Article 30. If an intellectual property right cannot be used, it is effectively suspended — but the Treaty cannot prejudice property rights, of which intellectual property rights are a part. In truth, however, competition law doctrine has resolved this apparent contradiction. Every property right has two aspects, its existence and its exercise. Article 222, which prevents the prejudice of property rights, is referring to the *existence* of those rights, while Articles 30 and 36 are referring to the *exercise* of those rights. The doctrine of 'exhaustion of rights' therefore fits in with both sets of provisions. The trade mark right is preserved by Article 222, but cannot be utilised in specified ways under Article 30.

1.2 Concerted actions between undertakings

Under the Treaty of Rome, Article 85:

(1) The following shall be prohibited as incompatible with the common market: all agreements between undertakings, decisions by associations of undertakings and concerted practices which may affect trade between Member States and which have as their object or effect the prevention, restriction or distortion of competition within the common market, and in particular those which:

(a) directly or indirectly fix purchase or selling prices or any other trading conditions;

(b) limit or control production, markets, technical development, or investment;

(c) share markets or sources of supply;

(d) apply dissimilar conditions to equivalent transactions with other trading parties, thereby placing them at a competitive disadvantage;

(e) make the conclusion of contracts subject to acceptance by the other parties of supplementary obligations which, by their nature or according to commercial usage, have no connection with the subject of such contracts.'

This provision goes right to the heart of intellectual property licensing practice. If you have an intellectual property right and do not wish to exploit it solely yourself, you can license it to others. The licence may be seen as a means of enhancing competition and increasing consumer choice, by enabling a small manufacturer to license others to make his product — or it may the means by which the large and powerful enterprise ties up his closest rivals. Article 85(1) is written in clear language; its draftsmanship is broad. Even if the parties to an agreement or concerted practice do not intend to contravene the Article, they fall within its ambit if the consequence of their activity is that its impact has any of the undesired effects.

What happens if an agreement or concerted practice contravenes Article 85? We see from Article 85(2) that:

'(2) Any agreements or decisions prohibited pursuant to this Article shall be automatically void.'

Since EC law is automatically superior to the domestic law of the member states, this means that a UK court could not enforce a contract which is *prima facie* enforceable under English contract law because, being a prohibited agreement, it is 'automatically void'. Moreover, the parties who engage in activities contrary to Article 85 face fines of great magnitude, which may continue to mount up until the prohibited activity ceases.

The power of the EC to enact the 'block exemptions' in respect of acceptable agreements or categories of agreements derives from Article 85(3), which states:

'(3) The provisions of paragraph 1 may, however, be declared inappplicable in the case of:
— any agreement or category of agreements between undertakings;
— any decision or category of decisions by associations of undertakings;
— any concerted practice or category of concerted practices:
which contributes to improving the production or distribution of goods or to promoting technical or economic progress, while allowing consumers a fair share of the resulting profit, and which does not:

(a) impose on the undertakings concerned restrictions which are not indispensable to the attainment of these objectives;

(b) afford such undertakings the possibility of eliminating competition in respect of a substantial part of the products in question.'

Where an agreement falls within the scope of a block exemption, it will not in principle be void under Article 85(1). The Commission has however reserved to itself in certain circumstances the right to decide that even an agreement which qualifies for inclusion within the terms of a block exemption should not be entitled to rely upon its protection (see Chapter 27 below for further details).

1.3 Abuse of monopoly

Article 85 does not of itself provide sufficient ammunition with which to combat the threat of anticompetitive practices, for it only covers agreements and practices which have as their object or effect the distortion or elimination of competition. The Treaty of Rome, Article 86, overlaps considerably with Article 85 but goes wider (see Chapter 27 below), Article 85 only deals with wrongs done by two or more parties in concert; Article 86 also catches the wrongful individual monopolist. A different provision is needed to make his actions unlawful and to bring him to heel. Under Article 86:

'Any abuse by one or more undertakings of a dominant position within the common market or in a substantial part of it shall be prohibited as incompatible with the common market in so far as it may affect trade between Member States. Such abuse may, in particular, consist in:

(a) directly or indirectly imposing unfair purchase or selling prices or other unfair trading conditions;
(b) limiting production, markets or technical development to the prejudice of consumers.
(c) applying dissimilar conditions to equivalent transactions with other trading parties, thereby placing them at a competitive disadvantage;
(d) making the conclusion of contracts subject to acceptance by the other parties of supplementary obligations which, by their nature or according to commercial usage, have no connection with the subject of such contracts.'

In Article 86 there is no direct equivalent of Article 85(2) which makes agreements void, even though 'an abuse by one or more undertakings of a dominant position' may well be founded upon a contractual arrangement between the two parties who between them hold a dominant position.

1.4 Harmonisation and approximation

Another aspect of the EC's policy of fostering competition is that domestic laws which govern trade should be assimilated as closely as possible to each other, so that local market conditions do not distort trade overall across the territory of the EC. For example, if the UK's copyright laws accorded life-plus-fifty years protection to designs for manufactured articles, while other countries in the EC provided for the same works only the limited term of protection accorded to utility models or industrial designs, there would be an inconsistency within the EC market. Designs would cease to be protected in some countries at one time, in others at a later time, with the result that the free flow of lawfully-manufactured goods would be impeded. A German manufacturer could lawfully produce articles and could sell them to France, but not to the UK – which would be an inconvenience and an inconsistency, as well as a snare to the unwary trader.

The solution to this problem is to seek the approximation or harmonisation of national laws. This may be done under Articles 59 to 66 and 100 of the Treaty of Rome, so as to ensure that differences in national laws do not act as disguised barriers to free trade and to prevent distortion of the internal market. It may also be done under Article 113, within the context of arriving at a common commercial policy in the relations of the EC to non-member states. It has already been done in the case of trade marks, where the Directive on the Approximation of Trade Mark Laws was passed and came into force in 1988. The result of the passage of directives which, by their legal nature, do not take direct legal effect but require separate implementation in each member state, is that as each member state comes to amend its national laws, it will do so in accordance with the principles laid down in the directive. Compliance with a directive does not require each member state to possess identical laws; it requires the achievement of particular ends, leaving the means by which those ends are achieved to be determined by each member state.

1.5 EC-wide protection

Even more radical than the establishment of harmonised national laws in each member state is the establishment of a single law which would cover each member state in exactly the same manner, though its enforcement and interpretation would inevitably depend upon the unique judicial system of each member state.

Currently a proposed Regulation on the European Community trade mark awaits adoption by the EC, though there is some legal doubt as to whether the establishment of a single European Community trade mark can be achieved by a Regulation rather than by an international convention. A draft Community Patent Convention seeks to introduce a single patent to cover the territory of the EC, and the French government has maintained that the same legislative mechanism is necessary for trade marks.

While both a Community trade mark and a Community patent would provide protection upon the territory of individual member states, neither would seek to remove the possibility of opting for national protection instead. This may mean that the potential for inconsistencies to remain within the extent of trading monopolies in the EC will be preserved.

2 TRADE MARKS

Since trade marks (for the purpose of this analysis 'trade mark' includes 'service mark' unless the contrary is apparent) are the most conspicuous features in the relationship of franchisor to franchisee, being in many cases the name by which the franchised goods or services are referred to, they are clearly of great significance in franchising practice.

The fact that a trade mark is an arbitrary name or device cannot be seen as minimising its importance as a means of establishing or preserving a market position or of dividing a market. The truth of this proposition may be seen in relation to a market such as that for soft drinks. Even though the trade mark attached to a soft drink does not affect its physical nature, and even though the expense involved in making soft drinks is very low (raw materials, storage, manufacture and packaging cost little), the ability of a trade mark to attract massive goodwill means that the irrational loyalty of the consumer for the familiar name itself constitutes a major barrier to market entry. This phenomenon can be seen in the success of, for example, the McDonald hamburger, which has obtained and held a significant market share against 'generic' hamburgers of arguably higher quality, and in the preference of shoppers for the acquisition of brand-name cereals for a higher price than the identical 'own brand' product manufactured by the manufacturer of the branded product.

Prima facie any sizeable trade mark licence can be regarded as an agreement which has the effect of distorting or preventing competition within the EC, since it enables the licensee to perform acts which are not open to non-licensees. It is open to the Commission to enact a block exemption on trade mark licences, allowing all trade mark licences which consist entirely of non-objectionable clauses to escape the requirement of notification to the Commission on the ground that they are deemed innocuous under Article 85(3) of the Treaty. To date no Regulation to that effect has been implemented; nor has any draft been circulated. This is because the types of transaction which involve the licensing of a trade mark are widely varied in their legal and commercial nature. They include character merchandising, sponsorship, manufacture under licence, distribution and marketing deals, research and development contracts, technology transfer transactions and franchising. Of these, as has been mentioned above, franchising and research and development contracts have been accorded separate block exemption Regulations of their own; technology transfer transactions are also exempted, to the extent that they fall within the scope of the block exemption for patents or know-how licensing. Accordingly there is relatively little left to regulate. Since, it is submitted, (i) trade mark licences are adequately governed by Articles 85 and 86 of the Treaty of Rome, and (ii) case law has investigated in detail the potentially anti-competitive effect of trade mark licensing, there is no real need for a further exemption which would cover those elements of licensing not already covered.

2.1 Free movement of goods

The supremacy of the Treaty of Rome over national law is unarguable. Be that as it may, though, there is still much strength left in the right granted by national registration. For one thing, the mere fact that one member state's trade mark law may regard a competitior's mark as confusingly similar to

a registered mark, while the law of another member state may not, does not of itself transgress Article 30. Thus the failure of the German Trade Marks Register to accept the registration of a UK company's 'Terrapin' trade mark on the basis of prior registrations by German undertakings of the 'Terra' and 'Terranova' marks was held to be a matter for national law only, it being accepted that what is confusingly similar in one country may not be confusingly similar in another. (*Terrapin (Overseas) Ltd v. Terranova Industrie* (Case 119/75; [1976] ECR 1039). Another example of the power of the national registration is that, after a substantial period of legal uncertainty, it has been agreed that the protection given to national holders of registered trade mark rights is not usurped by the 'doctrine of common origin', the much-criticised notion that if two marks registered in the different member states originally stemmed from the same common origin, the proprietor of neither mark could exercise it against the importation of goods from the other. This doctrine, formulated in the *Hag I* decision (*Van Zuylen Frères v. Hag AG* (Case 192/73; [1974] ECR 731), has now been reversed in *Hag II* (*SA CNL-Sucal NV v. Hag GF AG* (unreported ECJ judgment of 17 October 1990).

Article 30 has been held to require trade-marked goods to be circulated freely within the EC. For this reason an owner of a trade mark in the Netherlands has been prevented from using that registration in order to prohibit the importation from the UK of lawfully-marketed goods in order to exploit a substantial price differential (*Centrafarm BV v. Sterling Drug Inc.* (Case 15/74; [1974] ECR 1147). There are however limits to this freedom. For example, where the product is of a pharmaceutical nature, the owner of a Netherlands trade mark has been held entitled to prohibit its importation from the UK where the product was both repackaged and marketed under a different name (*Centrafarm BV v. American Home Products Corp* (Case 3/78; [1978] ECR 1823). In such a case, Article 36 entitles national laws to protect the integrity and distinctiveness of manufactured pharmaceutical products without being forced to run the risk of being adjudged disguised restrictions upon importation. But where (i) repackaged pharmaceutical goods are not damaged or otherwise tampered with, (ii) the identity of the repackager is clearly established and (iii) the manufacturer is using his trade mark so as to partition the market and (iv) the repackager gives due notice of his intention to repackage before the repackaging, it will not be possible to wield a trade mark right against a repackaging resaler (*Hoffman-La Roche & Co. v. Centrafarm Vertriebsgesellschaft* (Case 102/77; [1978] ECR 1139). Following this it is not surprising that where repackaging consists merely of applying an external wrapping through which the original mark and wrapping are clearly visible, the identification of the repackager being visible also, national trade mark rights may not exclude importation (*Pfizer Inc. v. Eurim-Pharm GmbH* (Case 1/81; [1981] ECR 2913).

It is also well established that the principle of free movement of goods applies only in respect of goods first marketed with the consent of the EC member state trade mark owner; it does not apply to all goods marketed lawfully in other jurisdictions and then imported into the EC. Thus goods lawfully marketed in the US with the consent of US trade mark owner can still be excluded from the territories of the EC by national owners of trade marks. (*EMI Records Ltd. v. CBS UK Ltd.* (Case 51/75; [1976] ECR 811).

2.2 Concerted action between undertakings

The existence of trade mark rights *per se* cannot constitute an infringement of Article 85, but the exercise of such a right, even by assigning or licensing it to a third party, can be an infringement of Article 85 where it has the effect, or is done with the intention, of partitioning the EC into two or more separate markets. Accordingly a trade mark owner who registers a mark in several EC member states and then grants in each state an exclusive licence to sell the trade-marked goods in that territory alone is partitioning the common market; such an agreement is void (*Consten & Grundig v. Commission* (Cases 56 & 58/84 [1966] ECR 299). See also *Tepea v. Commission* (Case 28/77 [1978] ECR 1391).

It is important to note that, while Articles 85 and 86 are at least potentially overlapping, concepts which are inherent in the applicability of the one are not necessarily to be implanted into the other. Thus Article 86 deals with abuse of a 'dominant position', a concept upon which Article 85 is silent; one should not therefore import that concept into Article 85 in order to argue that only an agreement between undertakings who enjoy a dominant position can fall foul of that Article — it is only necessary that those who hold the trade mark rights be capable of excluding competition to an appreciable extent (*Sirena Srl v. Eda Srl* (Case 40/70; [1971] ECR 69).

2.3 Abuse of monopoly

Prima facie, the ability of trade marks to act as a means of creating an abuse of monopoly is strictly limited. This is because a trade mark is only a mark which establishes a link between a particular trader and his goods or services. Goods and services can be marketed regardless of the mark which is applied to them, since the mark is not an integral part of the goods or services themselves. Where a trade mark becomes synonymous with particular goods or services (the author is not aware of any case in which a service mark has been held to be 'generic', but submits that the principle which governs trade marks similarly applies to trade marks) to the extent that it becomes associated with the identity of those goods or services, not with the relationship to the mark's owner, the mark has become so powerful that it is made to shed its power; it becomes a 'generic term' which, since none can reasonably seek to sell goods without using it, all can use. When a mark becomes generic, it may be expunged from almost any national trade mark register.

The exercise of trade mark rights as a means of protecting a dominant position does not seem to have formed the ground upon which either the European Court of Justice has founded any decision or upon which the Commission has instituted any action.

2.4 Harmonisation and approximation

In 1988 the European Commission published the Directive to Approximate the laws of the member states relating to Trade Marks (First Council Directive of 21 December 1988 (89/104/EEC). This Directive requires all member states to amend their domestic law so as to bring it in line with the provisions of the Directive not later than 28 December 1991 (Article 16.1) (though this date may be deferred to 31 December 1992 at the latest) (Article 16.2).

Under the provisions of the Directive, member states must conform to the following norms in respect of all registrable trade marks and service marks (Article 1).

(1) A common definition of a trade mark must be adopted (Article 2). Unlike in the United States, where a distinctive scent has been held registrable, marks must be 'capable of being represented graphically', a definition which does not preclude musical jingles from being registered.

(2) The grounds of registrability should be common (Article 3), even though in practice they will be applied differently by national courts which apply their own criteria of confusion based upon local linguistic and semantic considerations.

(3) Registration will not be allowed where the applicant's mark is identical with or confusingly similar to a mark already registered nationally or as a European Community trade mark, or to a mark which is unregistered but which enjoys the status of a 'well known' mark under Article 6 bis of the Paris Convention (Article 4).

(4) A common set of criteria for infringement will be adopted, each country providing that the unauthorised use of a registered mark on signs, goods and packaging for which the trade mark owner's goods or services are registered or to which they are connected constitutes an infringement. Taking unfair advantage of marks, and making detrimental use of them (presumably this includes most if not all forms of comparative 'knocking' advertising) are also infringing acts (Article 5).

(5) The principle of 'exhaustion of rights' is to govern marks, so that once goods are marketed with the trade mark owner's consent their free circulation may only be restricted if the goods have been changed or impaired after the first marketing of them (Article 7).

(6) Trade marks may be licensed for some or all goods or services for which they are registered, and for all or part of the member state in which they are registered; a licensee in breach of contract may be sued for trade mark infringement (Article 8).

(7) Where there has been five years' continuous unauthorised use of another's mark, by a later registrant for the same trade mark, with the knowledge of the trade mark owner who fails to object to that use, there is to be taken as acquiescence in that use (Article 9). Although the relevant Article in the Directive is headed 'Limitation in consequence of acquiescence', it does not explicitly affect the period of limitation after which it is no longer possible to bring an action for damages, which will remain unchanged in any member state in which an action is brought. It only means that a registered mark

which has been used, unchallenged, for five years in the full knowledge of a prior registrant cannot after that period be declared invalid or made the subject of an injunction.

(8) Where a registered mark is not used for a period of five years and there is no good reason for the non-use, the proprietor of that mark faces revocation of his mark and is unable to rely upon his registration in infringement proceedings (Article 12) or in proceedings to challenge the validity of a later mark (Article 11).

2.5   EC-wide protection

The proposal has been made (amended proposal for a Council Regulation on the Community trade mark, COM (84) 470 final; 84/C 230/01) for a single European Community trade mark (CTM) which would apply, on the basis of a single registration, throughout the territory of the EC. This proposal has been embodied in the form of a Regulation which still awaits adoption, on account of some minor issues which still await settlement, such as the location of the European Community Trade Mark Office and the nature of the legal means by which it should be implemented.

In 1987 four sites for the office were shortlisted - London, Madrid, Munich and the Hague. Munich's claim was aborted because it already houses the European Patent Office (not an EC institution). London's claim has been similarly buried now that the European Bank for Reconstruction and Development has been awarded to her. Luxembourg (not shortlisted) claims that as a matter of EC law, the CTM office is a legal institution which must be located there.

The French have firmly maintained that, by analogy with the Community Patent Convention, there should be a Community Trade Mark Convention, establishing formal treaty relations between the EC member states, rather than a Regulation.

The proposed CTM would not supplant national trade mark systems within member states (Proposed Regulation, Recital, para. 4) but would run in tandem with them. In respect of some marks (e.g. those registered in different countries by different parties and those registered in respect of purely local services) national registration would seem to be the more appropriate form of protection. For others (e.g. fast-moving consumer goods, Europe-wide franchises) a single Europe-wide registration would seem to offer a more convenient mode of protection.

The basic proposal for the CTM is as follows:

(1)   A single trade mark would cover the entire territory of the EC and would be revoked, transferred or surrendered on an EC-wide basis alone (Article 1.2).

(2)   'Any signs . . . which are capable of distinguishing goods or services' are to be registrable (Article 3) (This seems to be rather wider than the required notion of a mark for the purposes of the Directive on approximation);

(3)   Among the categories of unregistrable marks are

'The shape which results from the nature of the goods themselves, or which has some technical consequence; also the shape of the goods where this affects their intrinsic value' (Article 6).

This would seem to suggest that the functional-but-distinctive marks which have won registration in the US will not be registrable as CTMs.

(4)   Registration will be refused where, inter alia, the applicant's mark is identical with or similar to an earlier CTM or an earlier mark registered nationally in one or more member states (Article 7.1), or even a 'sign used in the business world' and which is not registered nationally but which would under national law carry the right to prevent a national trade mark registration (Article 7.2(d)).

(5)   Once a CTM is granted, it can be enforced subject to the principle of exhaustion, in similar fashion to national marks under the Directive on approximation (Article 11).

(6)   Publishers of dictionaries, encyclopaedias and similar works must indicate, when using or listing CTMs, that such words are CTMs so that the risk of imparting the impression that they are generic terms is reduced (Article 9).

(7)   The CTM is governed by the draft Regulation but its infringement is governed, in each member state, by the domestic law governing infringement of nationally-granted marks (Article 12).

(8)   A five-year period of non-use will leave the CTM vulnerable to the sanctions of unenforceability and revocation (Article 13).

(9)   A licensee in breach of his licence by using the CTM after the licence terminates, for unlicensed goods or in breach of quality control, may be sued for CTM infringement (Article 21).

One piece of EC legislation which is already in operation, though sadly ineffective, is the Anti-Counterfeit Regulation (Regulation No. 3842/86 of 1 December 1986 Laying Down Measures to Prohibit the Release for Free Circulation of Counterfeit Goods). This Regulation lays down the conditions under which the customs authorities of member states may intervene in order to seize goods suspected of being counterfeit, as well as measures which may be taken to dispose of the goods if they are indeed counterfeit. For the purpose of this Regulation (Article 1.2), counterfeit means:

' . . . bearing without authorisation a trade mark which is identical to a trade mark validly registered in respect of such goods in or for the Member State in which the goods are entered for free circulation or which cannot be distinguished in its essential aspects from such a trade mark and which thereby infringes the rights of the owner of the trade mark in question under the law of the Member State.'

This definition is itself criticised by trade mark owners on the ground that if a mark is fraudulently put on goods for which it is not registered, the Regulation will not apply.

Under the Regulation, in each member state a trade mark owner may lodge a written application with the competent authority (i.e. the customs administrators), declaring that he has valid grounds for suspecting that the importation of counterfeit goods in contemplated (Regulation 3842/86, Article 3.1). The trade mark owner must furnish the authority with enough information to enable him to identify the goods, together with proof that he is the trade mark owner (Regulation 3842/86, Article 3.2). The customs authority can then seize the goods on entry to the country (Regulation 3842/86, Article 5), following which the trade mark owner has ten days to show that the goods are indeed counterfeit; if he cannot, the goods will be released for free circulation (Regulation 3842/86, Article 6), but if he can, they will be destroyed or otherwise disposed of (Regulation 3842/86, Article 7). This Regulation is compatible with the Community Trade Mark system, on a *mutatis mutandis* basis (Regulation 3842/86, Article 10).

While almost all member states have now adapted their national legislation in response to this Regulation, which entered into force on 1 January 1988, it has been of little comfort to trade mark owners. This is because, apart from the expenses incurred under national laws passed in compliance with the Regulation, there is the inconvenient paperwork and provision of information which must be dealt with before the customs authorities can act. Since most infringers do not provide precise information relating to their consignments of counterfeit goods for the benefit of the trade mark owners, the Regulation remains little used.

2.6 International protection

There is no single convention providing for the international registration of trade marks. The following should however be noted.

(i) The Paris Convention
Signed in 1883, and revised at regular intervals (a major revision is expected to emanate from the diplomatic conference taking place in the summer of 1991), the Paris Convention for the Protection of Industrial Property provides for the reciprocal recognition by each signatory of the status of industrial property applications emanating from any other signatory (Article 2). The number of signatories is now around 100. Each year in the January issue of *Industrial Property* the World Intellectual Property Organisation (WIPO) publishes a state-of-the-art table of each of the treaties and conventions administered by it, listing the state of accessions and ratifications by each country. This list is updated by information published each month in *Industrial Property*.

The Convention also provides, *inter alia*, that members should provide protection against acts of unfair competition (Articles 1 and 10bis) and that special recognition should be given to well-known marks (*marques notoires*) in countries in which they have not yet been registered (Article 6bis). In countries in which a unitary approach renders international conventions directly applicable as national law, these provisions are important. However, in countries such as the UK, where international conventions have no legal force under domestic law unless and until they are enacted by Parliament or another legislative source, their impact has been minimal.

(ii) The Madrid Agreement of 1891
By the terms of the Madrid Agreement provision is made for a streamlined system by which the owner of a trade mark

registration in his own country can apply through an administrative procedure to an office of the World Intellectual Property Organisation through which his application may be forwarded to a maximum of twenty-seven further countries Current signatories to the Madrid Agreement are (in alphabetical order) Algeria, Austria, Belgium, China, Czechoslovakia, Egypt, France, Germany, Hungary, Italy, Luxembourg, Morocco, North Korea, the Netherlands, Portugal, Roumania, Spain, Switzerland, Tunisia, USSR, Vietnam and Yugoslavia. Once the application is forwarded, national trade mark offices may object to its registration. If they do not, it is registered by default twelve months after it has been forwarded.

The attractions of an application through the Madrid Agreement rather than through a multiplicity of national filings are (i) economy, it being cheaper to use this means than to file nationally, and to renew trade marks granted under the Agreement, (ii) simplicity and (iii) the ability to obtain a trade mark registration by default after only one year from its being forwarded to national trade mark offices, if such an international application is forwarded and no objection to registration has been raised within the limitation period. The disadvantages are that (i) if an applicant's domestic trade mark is invalidated, his international trade marks are also undermined, (ii) the selection of countries available is poor, since it excludes the entire continent of America north and south, Japan, Scandinavia and the UK, (iii) French is the sole official language of the Agreement's application system and (iv) the length of time it can take for an applicant from an examination-based trade mark system to derive any benefit from the Agreement, since it is necessary first to obtain a domestic registration – which may take some years – before filing for international protection. This Agreement is likely to be superseded within fifteen or twenty years by the Madrid Protocol of 1989, once it comes into force.

(iii) The Nice Agreement of 1952
Under this Agreement the signatory states adopt the same standard of classification of trade mark and service mark registrations. There are 42 arbitrary classifications, 34 for trade marks and 8 for service marks. Where different countries share the same classification system it is easier to ascertain whether a particular mark has been registered for a particular set of goods or services.

(iv) The Madrid Protocol of 1989
The 1989 Protocol would appear at first blush to be a Protocol to the 1891 Madrid Agreement; it is however a separate international agreement which stands quite independently of the 1891 Agreement. It seeks to provide, as does the Madrid Agreement, a scheme for international registration, but it differs from the 1891 Arrangement in the following particulars: (i) it allows for an international application to be made on the basis of a domestic application, not a domestic registration; (ii) the national offices to which the application is forwarded will have two years in which to raise objection to it; (iii) the languages of the Protocol will be French and

English; (iv) renewal fees will be chargeable at the same level as the level adopted nationally by each signatory state.

It is too early to know whether the Protocol will be a success, but the indications are that it will eventually supplant the Agreement. The two systems are completely self-contained, but the Protocol contains provision for revision of the two systems' relationship to each other.

When eventually the European Community Trade Mark is in operation, it will be possible to designate the European Community Trade Mark Office as a destination for an international mark filed under the Protocol, but not under the Agreement.

3 PATENTS

The same principles which govern competition by means of trade mark exploitation also govern the use of patents. The relevance of patents to the typical franchise has hitherto been small, though it may grow through the use of 'grant-back' clauses which require the franchisee who is a licensee of patented or other proprietary knowledge to license its use by the franchisor and indeed by all other franchisees.

3.1 Free movement of goods

The use of a patent right as a means of preventing the import into one member state of a product made with the patent owner's consent in another is prohibited as being in conflict with the principle of free movement of goods. The use of national laws to secure such an end is contrary to Article 30 of the Treaty of Rome (*Centrafarm BV v. Sterling Drug Inc.* (Case 15/74; [1974] ECR 1147)). This principle applies where goods are put on to the market in a country both where the product is patentable and where it is not (*Merck & Co. v. Stephar BV* (Case 187/80; [1981] ECR 2063)).

However it is open to national laws to prohibit conduct which would otherwise be permitted − for example manufacturing under an expired patent − where the manufactured product is identical (or virtually so) and its manufacturer is liable under national law for slavish imitation, so long as the slavish imitation remedy is open to any party and not merely to nationals (*Industrie Diensten Groep v. A. Beele Handelmaatchappij BV* (Case 6/81; [1982] ECR 707)).

Case law has also revealed that where a product is made under a compulsory licence under the national law of one member state, the compulsory licence stipulating that the licensee can manufacture and sell in that country alone, the licensee cannot argue that the product as made and sold by him has been marketed with the consent of the patent owner. In such a case the principle of exhaustion of rights will not apply and the holder of a national patent right will be able to enforce it against goods manufactured under a compulsory licence but in breach of its terms (*Pharmon BV v. Hoechst AG* (Case 19/84; [1985] ECR 2281)).

3.2 Concerted action between undertakings

Patent licences are not *per se* contrary to Article 85 of the Treaty of Rome, but where they contain terms which are objectionable as being restrictive of competition and which are not necessary for protecting the specific object of the patent, they will be struck down as being in breach of Article 85 (*Windsurfing International Inc v. Commission* (Case 193/83; [1986] ECR 611), striking down a patent licence which included a 'no-challenge' clause and an obligation to use non-patented items).

Since patent licences are, from a legal point of view if not a commercial one, a relatively homogeneous collection of contracts, it has proved possible for the EC to promulgate a 'Block Exemption' which enables the parties to a patent licence to avoid the necessity of notifying it to the Commission if it complies with the exemption's terms (Regulation on the application of Article 85(3) of the Treaty to certain categories of patent licensing agreements, no. 2349/84, of 23 July 1984).

Simply put, Regulation 2349/84 views the obligations which are typically found within patent licences as falling within one of three distinct categories; there are terms which are always unobjectionable, those which are sometimes objectionable and those which are always objectionable. These three categories are usually called the white list, the grey list and the black list respectively. The grey list is not in fact a list; it is those terms which are neither stated to be generally unrestrictive of competition or those which are so restrictive.

The 'white list' (reg. 2349/84, Article 2) consists of obligations upon the licensee to do such unobjectionable things as to purchase goods or a service only from a specified source which is necessary for the technically satisfactory exploitation of the patent; not to grant sublicences or assign the patent; to pay a minimum royalty or to mark the patentee's name on manufactured goods. The licensee may of course have the whip hand, in which case the terms of the licence may be dictated by him. In such a case, an obligation upon the licensor to grant the licensee the same terms as he grants to a subsequent licensee (i.e. more favourable terms) is acceptable.

The 'black list', contained in Article 3, prevents the parties to a patent licence from enjoying the benefits of the regulation where:

(1) The licensee is prohibited from challenging the validity of any patent or other industrial property right belonging to or associated with the licensor − although there are no objections to a clause which provides for automatic termination of a licence in the event of a validity challenge;

(2) The licence runs for a longer duration than the patent rights it covers − unless the licensee has a right to terminate the licence which he must be able to exercise at least once a year;

(3) Either party is restricted from competing with the other;

(4) The licensee is required to pay royalties on goods not manufactured under the licensor's intellectual property rights;

(5) There is a quantitative restriction upon the extent to which the licensee may use the licensed invention;

(6)   Either party is restricted in its ability to fix prices or discounts in respect of products manufactured under the licence;

(7)   Either party is restricted as to the customers he may deal with or to whom he may distribute goods;

(8)   A requirement that the licensee assign in whole or in part any rights in granted patents for improvements or in applications for such patents;

(9)   The licensee is required to accept further licences or goods which he does not want − unless they are technically necessary for his manufacture under the licence;

(10)   The licensee is required not to put licensed products into those parts of the market for which another licensee has been licensed (an exclusive territory clause);

(11)   The licensee is entitled to put licensed products into those parts of the market for which another licensee has been licensed but does not do so as a result of a concerted practice between the two licensees;

(12)   One or both parties refuse to meet demand from users or resellers who wish to remarket the manufactured goods in other EC territories − unless there is an 'objectively justified reason' for so doing.

(13)   One or both parties are required to make it difficult for users or resellers to obtain goods from other resellers, especially by means of the exercise of industrial property rights.

As to the 'grey list', Article 4 provides that the benefit of Regulation 2349/84 will apply in respect of patent licences containing only obligations which do not fall within the 'black list', even though they are not all included in the 'white list', so long as those licences are notified to the Commission for its approval. This notification must be carried out in accordance with Regulation 1699/75. If the Commission does not oppose exemption within six months, the licence is taken to be acceptable to it.

3.3   Abuse of monopoly

While the application of Article 86 so as to prevent the owner of one or more patents exploiting them in the way he chooses to do so has not yet been the subject of a decision of the ECJ, the principle that the abusive exercise of patent rights falls within its ambit is beyond doubt.

3.4   Harmonisation and approximation

The approximation of patent laws within the EC has not been a prime concern of the EC, since much of the necessary work on this subject was done for it by the European Patent Convention (EPC). Under this Convention, provision is made for a unified and centralised system for examining patent applications and granting patents in the Convention's member states. The workings of the EPC are discussed at 3.6 below.

So far as the bringing together of the law of EC member states is concerned, the EPC required each of its members to adopt common criteria of patentability; if they did not do so, the European Patent Office (EPO) would be unable to examine an application and determine its patentability in a multitude of countries with unique patentability criteria.

At the time of writing, of EC member states only the Republic of Ireland and Portugal have failed to join the EPC. The other countries share common laws governing the criteria of patentability, the maximum duration of the patent grant and sundry other matters. Laws relating to licence-of-right schemes, compulsory licences in the case of non-use or government need, to the ownership of inventions as between employers and employees and to the substance of infringement and enforcement still fall within the purview of domestic legislation.

3.5   EC-wide protection

A draft Community Patent Convention (CPC) has been in the pipeline since as long ago as 1975 (The Community Patent Convention, Luxembourg, 15 December 1975); the 1975 draft, as modified by protocols on the settlement of infringement and validity litigation and the function, status, privileges and immunities of the Common Appeal Court (COPAC), has been superseded by the Council Agreement Relating to Community Patents of 15 December 1989 (Agreement 89/695). Political problems and uncertainties in Denmark and the Republic of Ireland have been largely responsible for the delays in implementing the Community patent, which remains inoperable until the first day of the third month following the ratification of the Convention by the last EC member state. (Agreement 89/595, Article 10). The Convention will not come into effect if the last member state to sign it is not a signatory to the EPC, in which case the CPC will come into force on the date of accession of that state to the EPC.

Designed to fit in with the European Patent Convention (discussed at 3.6 below), the Community patent will provide unitary territorial protection by means of a single patent grant covering all EC member states. Application for a Community patent will be made to the European Patent Office. An applicant seeking protection in all EPC countries can simply designate the EC as a single destination for the patent grant, in exactly the same way as it is at present possible to designate a single member state.

Once granted, a Community patent can be enforced by means of infringement proceedings before 'Community Patent Courts' (effectively the national court in each country which already deals with patent litigation). From each such court there lies an appeal to the Common Appeal Court (COPAC), to ensure that consistency − if not actually achieved − is at least attempted. Note that COPAC does not have jurisdiction to hear and decide matters arising out of the interpretation of the provisions on jurisdiction in the CPC and its attendant protocols: these matters are dealt with by the ECJ on a reference from a designated court listed in Article 3.2 of Agreement 89/695. Designated courts include the House of Lords as well as 'the courts of the Contracting States when ruling on appeals', which presumably includes the Court of Appeal.

The Community patent will not replace or render obsolete the national patent systems, though it will make those systems less attractive for applicants seeking international patent protection and ultimately more expensive and less efficient for those who seek only national protection. If an applicant obtains both a Community patent and a national patent in respect of the same invention, it is the former which prevails (CPC, Article 75).

The CPC provides for the doctrine of 'exhaustion of rights' to apply automatically to Community patents (CPC, Article 28). It also provides that the 'exhaustion of rights' doctrine will not apply where a national court, applying domestic law, grants a compulsory licence to another to use that patent; compulsory licences may be granted by national courts, but only in respect of the territory over which they exercise jurisdiction (CPC, Article 45).

Two proposed modifications of existing patent protection within the EC should be briefly noted, though neither is of great relevance to the franchise industries currently in operation. One is a proposed Regulation which would extend the life of pharmaceutical patents, so that instead of there being merely a twenty-year period of protection from the date of application, a period of sixteen years from grant would apply (Proposal for a Council Regulation concerning the creation of a supplementary protection certificate for medicinal products, Com (90) 101 final - SYN 255, 11 April 1990). The second is a proposed Directive on the protection of biotechnological inventions, which would increase the scope for patenting biotechnological inventions, many of which fall outside the apparent scope of the patent system – or indeed outside any legal system of protection at all (Proposal for a Council Directive on the Legal Protection of Biotechnological Inventions, Com (88) 496 final – SYN 158, 17 October 1988.)

3.6 International protection

The Paris Convention (see section 2.6(i) above), to which some 101 countries are signatory, provides the basis for international patent protection by stipulating (i) minimum levels of protection for industrial property, (ii) the reciprocal treatment in each signatory state of industrial property rights applications originating from other signatory states and (iii) the establishment of 'priority periods' during which a person from one signatory state can claim in a foreign country in which he subsequently files for patent, trade mark or design protection the priority date of his own previous domestic application.

Building on this, the industrial countries and the developing nations are well on the way to a truly international system for obtaining patents. In particular it is necessary to note the following.

(i) The Patent Co-operation Treaty
Under the Patent Co-operation Treaty (PCT) (concluded in Washington in 1970) it is possible to file a single application which will be processed by the World Intellectual Property Organisation in Geneva. There are at present 47 signatories to the PCT. WIPO provides search and examination of applications which are then channelled to designated signatory states for approval. This system is of value both to industrially significant countries, for whom the PCT offers convenience, some economy of scale and the payment of fees on a more belated basis than would be the case for national or EPC filings, and also to smaller jurisdictions, where the value of examination is recognised but the establishment and maintenance of a fully-fledged patent office examination department is too costly or not feasible.

The EPC and CPC are fully compatible with the PCT, which means that it is possible for a PCT applicant to designate the entire territory of the EC as the destination of his patent, or to make a selection of European countries of his choice.

(ii) The European Patent Convention
The Convention on the Grant of European Patents, concluded in 1973, provides for the establishment of a European Patent Office (EPO) and for the introduction of a centralised application and grant system for the national patent systems of its signatory states, in addition to the national application systems which preceded it. The EPO is based in Munich with a Search Office in the Hague.

Under the EPC a single patent application may be made to the EPO, which will examine it for novelty and inventive step. If the application is accepted, it will proceed to grant and will take effect in as many countries of the EPC as the applicant has designated. Currently there are fourteen signatories to the EPC (in alphabetical order): Austria, Belgium, Denmark, France, Germany, Greece, Italy, Liechtenstein, Luxembourg, the Netherlands, Spain, Sweden, Switzerland and the United Kingdom. A patent for Liechtenstein may not be obtained except in conjunction with a patent for Switzerland.

In terms of office charges, EPO fees are fixed on the basis that it should always be cheaper to apply to three or more countries via the EPO. Of course, office charges are only one small part of an applicant's expenses, the other costs relating to professional services of patent agents, patent attorneys, translators, searchers etc. This being so, the overall saving may be very small.

The EPO's standard of search and examination has generally been highly regarded, though the office has been criticised for being too slow and over-technical in many aspects of its work. The rate of increase of filings at the EPO has substantially exceeded early predictions and shows no sign of abating. The EPO was originally intended to process a maximum of 40,000 patents annually. If one includes PCT applications channelled through the EPO, the 1988 figure was nearly 60,000. This is placing great pressure on EPO staff, with the result that, in respect of some areas of patent applications, the EPO subcontracts its examination work to the under-employed national patent offices of signatory states.

A patent granted at the EPO takes effect as a bundle of national patents. Renewal fees are paid to national patent offices. EPC patents are enforced following the same criteria – and by the same courts – as are ordinary national patents. The duration of an EPC patent is a maximum of twenty years from the date of the first application.

If a patent application is rejected by the EPO, it cannot be resurrected as a national patent application in any of the EPC countries. For this reason, if an applicant is advised that his application is a weak one, he may well wish to apply through separate national patent offices on the basis that, while he may lose three or four of his applications, the others may well succeed.

Once the EPO has processed an application which has been accepted, there is a nine-month period during which opposition proceedings may be brought. Post-grant oppositions can be costly and keenly-contested. Once the nine-month opposition period expires, an EPC patent can only be challenged through the national courts.

(iii) The African Organisation for Industrial Property (OAPI)

OAPI is the better-known French acronym for the Organisation Africaine pour la Propriété Industrielle, a group of countries which have fused their territories together for patenting purposes and which operate through a single patent office in Yaoundé, Cameroon. Although the OAPI makes the possibility of seeking a patent in French-speaking Africa a more attractive one, the number of OAPI patents filed and granted is still very small on account of the lack of industrial and economic development in the region as a whole.

(iv) The African Regional Industrial Property Office (ARIPO)

Modelled more closely upon the EPC than OAPI is ARIPO, a group of largely English-speaking countries which propose to allow the central filing of patents in Harare, Zimbabwe, in respect of designated countries. To date the number of Members of ARIPO is not uninpressive, but the number of countries which have actually adjusted their internal patent laws to make them compatible with the ARIPO system is small. Until Nigeria and South Africa are members of ARIPO, its significance is likely to remain strictly limited.

4. UTILITY MODELS

There is no protection of utility models under UK law, but many other countries, of which the most prominent is Germany, have flourishing utility model (or 'petty patent') systems. The utility model or *Gebrauchsmüster* in Germany provides protection for a maximum of ten years in respect of inventions which are perhaps of doubtful patentability and in respect of which instant protection is needed. One may register a utility model in Germany without the formalities of search and examination (only if there is to be infringement litigation are search and examination requisites); protection follows registration.

Many countries in the world have utility model systems, but there is relatively little homogeneity between them in comparison with patent or design registration systems. Examination of annual statistics published by WIPO shows that while, in most countries, the number of patent applications by foreign applicants greatly exceeds the number made by

national applicants, the exact opposite is true for utility model protection. This would seem to suggest that those countries which operate such systems provide a strong 'back yard' protection for their own industries and businesses.

4.1 Free movement of goods

The same principles which govern patents and trade marks govern utility model protection so far as Articles 30 to 36 of the Treaty of Rome are concerned. There has been no litigation concerning utility models which has been referred to the ECJ on this, or any other ground of incompatibility with EC competition rules.

4.2 Concerted action between undertakings

The same principles will apply as govern trade marks and patents. Although the duration of utility model protection is less than that of patents, its commercial value as a means of influencing the market is much the same. It is for this reason that the patent 'block exemption' applies equally to utility models and to French *certificats d'utilité* as it does to patents (Regulation 2349/84, Article 10).

4.3 Abuse of monopoly

The same principles will apply as govern trade marks and patents, but they may be applied a little more leniently to utility models where, on account of the lower degree of protection offered within individual member states, it is more difficult in practice to abuse one's position of dominance.

4.4 Harmonisation and approximation

The EC has not yet made any formal proposal for a directive on utility models. Since those countries which do not have them are relatively unfamiliar with their use, and since they do not in general seem to have offered major problems requiring solution within the field of distortion of the internal market or trade between member states, it is unlikely that moves towards harmonisation or approximation will be made in the near future.

4.5 EC-wide protection

No proposal for a Regulation on a Community utility model has been put forward.

4.6 International protection

Other than in terms of the very general recognition given to all forms of industrial property under the Paris Convention, there is little specific reference to utility models under international law (but see Paris Convention, Articles 4, 5 and 11). Nor has there been any move towards an international treaty on them, since most countries in the world have no such legal device and have expressed no immediate interest in introducing them.

5 COPYRIGHT

While trade marks underpin the essence of the franchise, copyright provides protection for a variety of elements which are vital to its success, such as proprietary software, menus, labels, product designs, recipes and manuals. It is therefore important to understand how the benefit of copyright can be obtained. Unlike patents and trade marks, copyright protects works upon their creation and in general without the need to fulfil any requirements of deposit and registration.

While the monopoly provided by copyright protection is extensive (generally in the region of life plus fifty years for authors' works, fifty years for works which incorporate them), the protection afforded by copyright is weak. Only actual copying is prohibited, leaving it open to any person who has independently designed or created in his own words or style a work previously conceived by another to use it without fear of legal reprisal. Perhaps because of the inherent weakness of the copyright monopoly and perhaps because of the principle of market substitutability (i.e. If you can't use one copyright work, you can always create your own to fit the tastes of the same market), the EC has not been anxious to restrict the ability of the individual copyright owner to obtain maximum benefits from his monopoly. Only where the copyright owner is a collecting society which takes assignments of rights from a whole class of authors or copyright owners and then administers those rights collectively in a small and vulnerable market, or where the copyright owner is a large-scale manufacturer whose industrial copyrights are wielded with patent-like force, is the Commission moved to intervene.

5.1 Free movement of goods and services

Neither the principle of free movement of goods and services nor the principle of exhaustion of rights would seem to entitle a cable television programme distributor to intercept a transmission from one country in which it is lawfully broadcast with the copyright owner's consent and then to show it on the cable network of another (*Coditel SA v. Cine-Vog SA* (Case 262/81; [1982] ECR 3381).

The principle of free movement of goods has however been upheld where gramophone records have been lawfully made in one country, where collecting society royalties are low, but imported into another where collecting society royalties are high. In such a case no exercise of national copyright law is possible (*Musik-Vertrieb-Membran GmbH & K-tel International v. GEMA* (Cases 55 & 57/80; [1981] ECR 147).

5.2 Concerted action between undertakings

Assignments and exclusive licences to exploit copyright works are not automatically to be regarded as falling within the ambit of Article 85 of the Treaty of Rome (*Coditel SA v. Cine-Vog SA* (Case 262/81; [1982] ECR 3381). However, where a distribution agreement is used by a copyright owner to keep prices up and the copyright owner severs supplies of copyright-protected goods to dealers who resell at lower prices, Article 85 will render such practices void (*Deutsche*

Grammophon Gesellschaft mbH v. Metro-SB-Grossmarkte GmbH (Case 78/70; [1971] ECR 487)

5.3 Abuse of monopoly

The ECJ has taken a fairly sympathetic view of the copyright owner's ability to enforce his copyright without falling foul of Article 86, so long as that exploitation is not based upon arbitrary, unfair or capricious criteria of discrimination. Accordingly, where a collecting society licensed a discotheque to play records, the performance and mechanical reproduction royalties being calculated as a percentage of the discotheque's turnover, there is no *per se* abuse of monopoly by the collecting society under Article 86, but any royalty collection scheme which discriminates against the discotheque's imporation of records originating from outside the country may well contravene Articles 30 and 86 (*Basset v. SACEM* (Case no. 402/85; [1983] 3 CMLR 183). An even clearer example of the ECJ's tolerance of the exploitation of copyright monopolies may be found in *Volvo v. Erik Veng*, a case which, since it deals with copyright in an industrial design, is dealt with at paragraph 6.3 below.

In contrast with the ECJ's tolerant view of the exercise of copyright, the Commission has come close to destroying the monopoly nature of the right, effectively forcing parties to award compulsory licences on fair terms. One such Commission decision, involving the monopoly enjoyed by the Ford Motor Company in its corrosion panels, resulted in the copyright owner being required to grant licences to manufacture spare parts at a royalty rate pitched around the industry norm (this case may well have been decided differently in the light of the *Volvo* case, in which the ECJ took the opposite view). The Commission issued a Statement of Objections on 7 November 1985, seeking interim measures against Ford. The motor company acted in response to the objections in order to avoid the proceedings. In another decision (*Magill TV Guides v. ITV, BBC and RTE* (OJ No. L 78, 21 March 1989)), the Commission has required three broadcasting authorities which publish weekly television programme guides to grant copyright licences in their schedules of forthcoming programmes to independent publishers of weekly television programme guides. This decision is currently being appealed to the ECJ, which is expected to overrule it in keeping with the *Volvo* principle.

5.4 Harmonisation and approximation

Consideration of harmonisation of copyright laws within the member states started as long ago as 1976 with the 'Dietz Report' (A. Dietz, *Copyright in the European Community* 1976; English edition 1978), but no real progress has been made, since the copyright cultures of the member states are so diverse and so many disparate legal notions are employed at national levels. For all that, the EC member states' laws already have broadly the same effect: they protect much the same type of works, in much the same way. Licensing of copyright in all areas of the EC has been heavily influenced by (i) EC competition law and (ii) US drafting practice, with the result that there is a great deal of similarity in practice.

An EC Green Paper was published in 1988 (*Copyright and the Challenge of Technology* (88 (Com) 172)). The Green Paper concentrated principally upon the new technologies, and has been criticised by civil lawyers on account of its bias towards pragmatism. A further reform proposal came in the form of a proposed Directive on software protection (*Proposal for a Council Directive on the Legal Protection of Computer Programs* (Com (88) 816 final - SYN 183)). This proposal too has received a controversial reception because of its permissive attitude towards the copying of the interfaces which enable computer programs to relate to each other. Neither proposal is likely to lead to law reform before the end of 1992 at the very earliest.

5.5   EC-wide protection

Since all EC member states are members of the Berne Union and the Universal Copyright Convention, there is more or less absolute EC-wide protection for all works created in EC member states or by EC nationals wherever they create their works. The term of protection is different in each country, however, but the mere fact of a different copyright term does not mean that there is a distortion of the internal market — even if it means that a work is protected in one country and in the public domain in another (*EMI v. Patricia Import und Export* (OJ No. C62, 11 March 1989).

5.6   International protection

The Berne Union and the Universal Copyright Convention (UCC) provide for the establishment of minimum norms of copyright protection to be adopted by all signatory states and for reciprocity of protection to be granted to nationals of signatory states. This protection is given, in the case of Berne, on the understanding that there are no formalities necessary for protection to be granted under national law and, in the case of the UCC, on the assumption that any national formalities are taken to be complied with, in respect of published works, so long as the work in question hails from another signatory state and bears the © sign (or the word 'copyright') together with the copyright owner's name and the year of first publication.

The major limitation of the Berne Union and the Universal Copyright Convention is that they only cover authors' works. Works such as sound and video recordings, films, typographical editions of works, television and cable transmissions and performers' rights do not fall within their scope. Numerous other conventions exist under the administration of WIPO, covering these 'neighbouring' rights — but most of them do not have many signatories.

6   DESIGNS

Designs come in two forms — registered and unregistered. The notion of registration of designs is common within the international community and is well understood within the EC. Unregistered designs, such as those recognised by the UK law, are in a kind of judicial limbo: they live within a copyright law (Copyright, Designs and Patents Act 1988, Part III) but are not copyright. This is explicit in the Act itself. If unregistered designs were covered by copyright, the UK would be obliged under the Berne Convention to grant in the UK the protection of unregistered design law to nationals of countries in which British unregistered designs would not enjoy copyright protection. Their true preserve is that of industrial designs under the Paris Convention. Under this heading it will be assumed that both registered and unregistered design rights will be treated as being of equivalent effect so far as EC competition law is concerned.

6.1   Free movement of goods

Design rights under national laws can certainly be used in order to prevent a lawfully made product bearing a design from being imported into another EC member state in which that design is covered by legal protection (*Keurkoop v. Nancy Kean Gifts BV* (Case No. 144/81; [1982] ECR 2853)). The opposite would have been the case if the product was originally put on to the market with the design right owner's permission or consent.

6.2   Concerted action between undertakings

It is believed that there are no grounds for distinguishing design right licences and concerted actions from those involving other intellectual property rights. However, as is also the case with utility models, the lower degree of protection enjoyed by designs will mean that the application of the law to the facts may result in a more tolerant attitude being taken towards restrictive activities involving designs.

Regulation 2349/84, which provides 'block exemption' relief for patent and utility model licences which are *prima facie* unobjectionable, does not extend to designs, whether registered or not (Article 10).

6.3   Abuse of monopoly

The mere fact that a design right is exercised does not of itself constitute an infringement of Article 86 of the Treaty of Rome. Nor does a refusal to grant even a licence to manufacture on payment of reasonable royalties, at least where the design owner is a motor manufacturer (*Volvo AB v. Erik Veng (UK) Ltd.* (Case No. 238/87; [1989] 4 CMLR 122).

6.4   Harmonisation and approximation

The need for harmonisation has been agreed to exist both on the part of industry and by the Commission, but no proposal or draft directive has yet been published.

6.5   EC-wide protection

No proposal for a signle EC design right has yet been tabled. At present, therefore, there is no single means of obtaining EC-wide protection.

6.6 International protection

As with patents and trade marks, the Paris Convention imposes upon its signatory states an obligation to protect industrial designs by whatever means each state prefers. Article 5 quinquies simply states that 'Industrial designs shall be protected in all the countries of the union'. States must also offer reciprocity in respect of the designs generated by nationals of other signatory states.

7 PLANT VARIETIES

Separate protection for plant varieties is provided outside of the patent system by a number of countries, including some member states of the EC. The basic principle is that, where plant variety protection is available under the terms of the UPOV Convention (Convention for the Protection of New Varieties of Plants, 1961), it should be available as an alternative to patent protection, not in addition to it. For this reason the European Patent Convention and the national patent laws of all EPC countries expressly exclude plant varieties from patent protection.

7.1 Free movement of goods and concerted action between undertakings

The ECJ has held that there are no defining characteristics of plant variety rights which require them to be treated, for the purposes of Article 85 of the Treaty of Rome, any differently from other intellectual property rights. If this is the case, it seems unfortunate that the patent 'block exemption' does not extend to plant variety rights licences the convenience it gives to licences of utility models and patent rights (Regulations 2349/84, Article 10).

In practice the ECJ seems to take a more lenient view of restrictive and anticompetitive clauses with regard to plant varieties than it does with other intellectual property rights. Thus the ECJ has permitted a licence which imposed an export ban upon a licensee, on the ground that such a ban would enable the producer to select licensed growers. (*Louis Erauw-Jacquery Sprl v. La Hesbignonne Société Cooperative* (Case No. 27/87; [1988] 4 CMLR 586); however in the same case a minimum price-fixing clause could not be justified upon the same ground.

7.2 Abuse of monopoly

It is believed that plant variety rights will be treated no differently from other intellectual property rights in this matter.

7.3 Harmonisation and approximation

No proposals for the assimilation of national laws have yet been tabled. Given that this is still a relatively new area of law in which national experience has yet to bear fruit, it is unlikely that harmonisation of law in this field will be accorded any priority.

7.4 International protection

The UPOV Convention of 1961 established that plant varieties protection should be available to ratifying states as an alternative to the protection granted by patents for inventions. In fact, some countries which are signatory to the UPOV Convention and which operate plant variety protection systems do also grant patents for inventions for plant varieties which fulfil the criteria of patentability, e.g. the United States following the Chakrabarty case (*Diamond v. Chakrabarty* (1980) 206 USPQ 193).

The UPOV Convention also provides for the reciprocity of legal protection as between nationals and companies of the various signatory states.

8 TRADE SECRETS AND CONFIDENTIAL INFORMATION

Where no other form of intellectual property right is available, it is possible to rely upon the fact that one possesses information which is of commercial value and which one can disclose on a limited basis to those whom one restricts from communicating that information to others or from using it without permission. Into this category falls information which enables a licensee of intellectual property rights to succeed in putting them into effect, avoiding the expense and inconvenience of empirical experimentation of his own.

It is possible to protect information through the law of contract, by stipulating that certain information may not be disclosed except with the licensor's permission and that certain specified consequences will stem from a wrongful disclosure. Since a wrongful disclosure will almost inevitably result in a loss of trust between franchisor and franchisee, the termination of the franchise is generally regarded as an acceptable option open to the franchisor, notwithstanding the investment which the latter may have made in his licensed business.

8.1 Free movement of goods

There have been no ECJ decisions on the status of trade secrets or other confidential information in relation to their impact upon the free flow of goods. This is not surprising since the national rules which protect secrecy in EC member states tend to do so in relation to *processes*, while what is covered by Article 30 of the Treaty of Rome is the flow of *products*. Since the processes in question have not been put on to the market, it is surely impossible to say that principles of 'exhaustion of rights' apply in respect of products marketed through the use of such secrets.

Where a product is put on to a market in a member state of the EC on the terms it may only be leased, not purchased, and where one of the conditions of the lease is that the product may not be opened up for inspection — as could easily happen in respect of a franchised service for achieving a technical result such as unblocking a drain or tuning a car — the effect of national laws enforcing such a secret may depend upon the interpretation of the notion of 'putting a product on the market'. If the act of leasing is regarded as one of putting a product on to the market, then the secret may be itself regarded as 'exhausted'; but if, as seems quite possible, the mechanism by which the product achieves its technical end is a matter of indifference to customers, it would seem reasonable to expect that the secret will be capable of further protection under Article 36, even if it entails the quantitive restriction of the import of goods under Article 30.

8.2 Concerted action between undertakings

In principle there seems no reason why know-how and trade secrecy licences should not be subjected to Article 85 of the Treaty of Rome in the same way as any other intellectual property licences. This would seem to be implicit from the fact that know-how is given the benefit of a 'block exemption' in respect of acceptable licences (Regulation No. 556/89 on the application of Article 85(3) to certain categories of know-how licensing agreements; see Chapter 29 below).

For the purposes of the know-how exemption (Regulation 556/89) know-how is defined briefly and succinctly as 'a body of technical information that is secret, substantial and identified in any appropriate form' (Regulation 556/89, Article 1.7). From this it is clear that elements of franchise agreements, such as the contents of manuals and of training programmes, should be clearly and explicitly identified as secret in the basic contract.

The format of Regulation 556/89 is similar to that which gives exemption to patent licences, in that there is a 'white list', a 'black list' and a 'grey list'. Licences which consist entirely of 'white list' obligations enjoy the benefit of avoiding notification to the Commission.

8.3 Abuse of monopoly

Although Article 86 of the Treaty of Rome, by its very width, can be regarded as encompassing trade secrets and know-how, it is difficult to know how it would be brought to bear against a dominant party whose market strength was derived from one or more trade secrets.

8.4 Harmonisation and approximation

Although the category of items protected by trade secrecy law includes know-how, which is the subject of a 'block exemption', no suggestion has been made that individual member states should be required to approximate their laws on trade secrecy. In jurisprudential terms, different states draw their laws on secrecy protection from different juridical sources, but in practical terms there is little substantive difference between their laws. Secrets are protected because of their value and their significance; the vast majority of secrets are protected by the law of contract, which specifies the extent of protection required by the party which discloses the secret to another. In practice, confidentiality clauses and disclosure agreements are much the same throughout the EC.

8.5 EC-wide protection

To date there have been no formal moves to provide a single law on Europe-wide trade secrets. Nor has there been any pressure placed upon the European Commission to do so. Reform in this area is unlikely.

8.6 International protection

There is no international system for the protection of trade secrets or confidential information. There is not even any explicit mention of know-how or trade secrets in the Paris Convention, but members of the Paris Union, including all EC member states, are obliged to protect parties against unfair competition (Paris Convention, Articles 1 and 10bis), which could be said to include trade secrecy.

An Introduction to the Relevant Competition Law of the European Community

By MARK ABELL

1. BASIC PROVISIONS

In order to help ensure the full integration of the twelve member states, the Treaty of Rome provides against any agreements or practices that prevent free competition throughout the Common Market. These provisions (as mentioned in Chapter 2 above) are contained in Articles 85 to 94.

The provisions which are exercised most are Articles 85 and 86. Article 85 focuses on agreements and practices that prevent, restrict or distort competition between member states, whilst Article 86 concentrates upon abuse of a dominant position.

It is Article 85 that is of most importance to franchisors in the EC, and it is therefore considered in considerable detail below.

2. ARTICLE 85

Article 85 of the Treaty of Rome provides:

'(1) The following shall be prohibited as incompatible with the Common Market:

All agreements between undertakings, decisions by associations of undertakings and concerted practices which may affect trade between member states and which have as their object or effect the prevention, restriction or distortion of competition within the common market, and in particular those which:

(a) directly or indirectly fix purchase or selling prices or any other trading conditions

(b) limit or control production, markets, technical development, or investment;

(c) share markets or sources of supply;

(d) apply dissimilar conditions to equivalent transactions with other trading parties, thereby placing them at a competitive disadvantage; and

(e) make the conclusion of contracts subject to acceptance by the other parties of supplementary obligations which, by their nature or according to commercial usage, have no connection with the subject of such contracts.

(2) Any agreements or decisions prohibited pursuant to this Article shall be automatically void.

(3) The provisions of paragraph 1 may, however, be declared inapplicable in the case of:

(a) any agreement or category of agreements between undertakings;

(b) any decision or category of decisions by associations of undertakings;

(c) any concerted practice or category of concerted practices

which contributes to improving the production or distribution of goods or to promoting technical or economic progress, while allowing consumers a fair share of the resulting benefit, and which does not:

(a) impose on the undertakings concerned restrictions which are not indispensable to the attainment of these objectives;

(b) afford such undertakings the possibility of eliminating competition in respect of a substantial part of the products in question.'

3. ARTICLE 85(1)

This Article is primarily concerned with the economic effect of franchising and other agreements on trade between the member states rather than their particular legal form. It is, therefore, futile for lawyers to try and draft their way around its provisions without changing the commercial and economic effect of the agreement.

Thus, it is necessary to carefully consider the provisions of the Article and whether or not franchising agreements are 'sui generis' contrary to them or not.

Undertakings are not defined by Article 85 but by the Commission's decision in *Polypropylene* (OJ [1986] L230/11; [1988] 4CMLR 347) where it was stated that the concept of an undertaking is not identical with the question of legal personality for the purposes of fiscal or company law and that it may refer to any entity engaged in commercial activity.

Both franchisors and franchisees are, therefore, undertakings. However, the proximity of their economic relationship means that it should nevertheless be asked whether or not they come within Article 85(1).

The basic question is whether or not the franchisor and franchisee can be regarded as a single economic unit. In the case of *Beguelin Import* v. *GL Import Export* (Case 22/71 [1971] ECR 949 [1972] CMLR 81) the Court was of the opinion that Article 85 did not apply to an agreement between a parent company and its subsidiary on the basis that there was 'no economic independence'. On this criterion, given the independence of the franchisee to conduct its affairs as it wishes, within the discipline of the franchise system it must be assumed that the franchisor and franchisees are separate undertakings.

Given that the franchisor and the franchisees are separate undertakings it is important to consider whether or not any agreements, decisions or concerted practices prevent, restrict or distort competition.

Clearly a franchise agreement would come within the Article, but it is necessary to look much deeper into the complex franchise relationship to identify other areas of agreement or co-operation that may have an effect on competition. An agreement does not have to be written. As evidenced by the decision in *ACF Chemiefarma NV* v. *Commission* (Case 41/69 [1970] ECR 661) even a so-called 'gentleman's agreement' may be held to be an agreement. Likewise in the case of *Re Stichting Sigarettenindustrie Agreements* (OJ [1982] L232/1 [1982] 3CMLR 702] even a 'simple understanding' can amount to an agreement within the terms of Article 85. Thus a franchisor will contravene the Article if, for example, although the franchise agreement permits the franchisee to decide its own pricing structure, it comes to an informal, oral agreement with one or more franchisees to fix prices. Likewise if the franchisor adopts a policy of granting 'de facto' exclusive territory Article 85 (1) will be contravened.

Similarly, the establishment of a franchisee association will qualify as an agreement within the meaning of Article 85, on behalf of its members (*Heintz Van Landearyck* v. *Commission* (Case 209/78 [1980] ECR 3125 [1981] 3 CMLR 134). Caution must, therefore, be exercised when drafting the constitution of a franchisee association. This alone, however, may not be enough to avoid contravention of Article 85. Any decisions by the association may also cause problems, for example a decision by members to adopt a particular pricing structure. As a result, the association could be held liable by the Commission (see *AROW* v. *BNIC,* OJ 1982 L379/1; [1982] 2 CMLR 240).

It should also be appreciated that the Commission is more likely to find it easier to conclude that the decision of a franchisee association is anti-competitive than to prove a concerted practice.

The question of concerted practices potentially creates substantial problems for franchise networks under Article 85. In the case of *ICI* v. *Commission* (Commonly called the *Dyestuffs* Case) (Case 48/69 [1972] ECR 619 [1972] CMLR 557) concerted practices were described as:

a form of coordination between undertakings which, without having reached the stage where an agreement properly so-called has been concluded, knowingly substitutes practical cooperation between them for the risks of competition'.

In *Suiker Unie* v. *Commission* (the *Sugar Cartel* Case) (Case 40/73 etc [1975] ECR 1663, [1976] 1CMLR 295) they were further described as:

'any direct or indirect contact between such operators, the object or effect whereof is either to influence the conduct on the market of an actual or potential competitor or to disclose to such a competitor the course of conduct which they themselves have decided to adopt or contemplate adopting on the market'.

It is, therefore easy to imagine how the common interests of the members of a franchise network could lead them into concerted practices.

However, as the Court stated quite clearly in *Compagnie Royale Astwienne des Mines SA* and *Rheinzink GmbH* v. *Commission* (Cases 29,30/83 [1984] ECR 1679, [1985] 1CMLR 688) mere parallel behaviour is not sufficient proof of a concerted practice. Moreover, *Dyestuffs* and other cases suggest that the economic analysis of the market is fundamental to determining whether or not there are concerted practices. Given the unique character of a franchise network and the need for some degree of uniformity together with the nature of many of the markets that they operate within it is suggested that whilst franchisors should always be cautious of becoming involved in concerted practices with franchisees and franchisees themselves indulging in them, it might not be so great a problem as it may at first appear to be.

Whether a franchise agreement has as its object or effect the distortion of competition is a matter that deserves careful consideration. The two words are independent of each other and in the case of *VdS* v. *Commission* the Court held that if the agreement's object was to restrict competition it was unnecessary to show that it also had an ani-competitive effect (Case 45/85 [1988] 4CMLR 264). This followed the earlier case of *Société Technique Minière* v. *Maschinenbau Ulm* (Case 56/65 [1966] ECR 235, [1966] CMLR 357) which stated that it was first necessary to consider the object of the agreement and then its effect. In considering the effect of the agreement account should be taken of the competition that would exist in the absence of the disputed agreement, the parties' market shares, whether or not it is part of a network (such as a franchise network) and its effects on parallel imports.

If the object of an agreement is not or cannot objectively be proved to be preventative, restrictive or distortive of competition then an in depth market analysis of the effects will be necessary, as such an examination of an agreement's effect cannot be carried on

'in isolation from . . . the factual or legal circumstances causing it to prevent restrict or distort competition'

(*Brasserie de Haecht* v. *Wilkin* (Case 23/67 [1967] ECR 407, [1968] CMLR 26)

In the cases of *Consten and Grundig* (Case 56 and 58/64 *Consten and Grundig* v. *Commission* [1966] ECR 299) the Court established the basic principle that agreements which prohibit exports within the Common Market of their nature restrict competition within the meaning of Article 85(1) irrespective of the actual facts.

Thus there are two different types of agreement, those that do not necessarily restrict competition and those that of their nature do. This gives rise to two different approaches, the 'per se' approach outlined in *Consten and Grundig* and endorsed in the *Maize Seed* Case (Case 258/78 *Nungesser v Commission* [1981] ECR 45) and the 'Rule of Reason' approach, laid out in *Brasserie de Haecht* and endorsed in the *Metro* Cases (Case 26/76 *Metro* v. *Commission* (No 1) [1977] ECR 1875 and Case 75/84 *Metro* v. *Commission* (No 2) [1986] ECR 3021), by which an agreement does not fall foul of Article 85 if its restrictions are reasonable in terms of both time and scope.

The *Pronuptia* Case (*Pronuptia de Paris GmbH* v. *Pronuptia de Paris Irmgard Schillgalis* (Case 161/84 [1986] 1 ECR 353) held that franchising agreements are not per se anti-competitive and whether or not they are depends upon their contents (see Chapter 27 below). In paragraph 14 the Court stated:

'It should next be observed that the compatibility of distribution franchise agreements with Article 85(1) cannot be assessed in the abstract but depends on the clauses contained in such contracts. In order to give a fully useful response to the national court this Court will consider those contracts which have a content similar to that described above.'

There is, it is suggested, a very strong argument for suggesting that franchise agreements, sui generis, have neither the object nor effect of preventing, restricting or distorting competition. Indeed, to the contrary, franchising tends to increase competition. Even the Commission itself has recognised this by stating in Recital 7 of Regulation 4087/88 that:

'Franchise agreements . . . normally improve the distribution of goods and/or services as they give franchisors the possibility of establishing a uniform network with limited investments, which may assist the entry of new competitors on the market particularly in the case of small and medium sized undertakings thus increasing interbrand competition. They also allow independent traders to set up outlets more rapidly and with a higher chance of success than if they had to do so without the franchisor's experience and assistance. They have, therefore, the possibilities of competing more efficiently with large distribution undertakings.'

This matter is discussed in more detail in Chapter 27 below.

The effect of agreements, decisions and concerted practices on interstate trade is of considerable importance when considering Article 85. It has important political overtones for the member states as it affects exactly where decisions concerning competition law are made. The Courts have adopted a liberal approach to the question of interstate trade.

Where an agreement prevents sales from one member state into another the clause has obvious effect. However, matters are not always so simple and it is important to carefully consider the Court's approaches.

In *Commercial Solvents* v. *Community* (Cases 6,7/73 [1974] ECR 223, [1974] 1 CMLR 309) the Courts considered interstate trade was affected if the structure of competition within the Common Market was altered.

However, the test outlined in the *Société Technique Minière* Case (see above) has been used more frequently. In this case the Court considered that Article 85 applied only if it were:

possible to foresee with a sufficient degree of probability on the basis of a set of objective factors of law or of fact that the agreement in question may have an influence, direct or indirect, actual or potential, on the pattern of trade between member states'.

This judgement has been subsequently refined to a substantial degree.

The *Windsurfing* Case (*Windsurfing International Inc* v. *Commission* – Case 193/83 [1986] 3 CMLR 489) held that if any one part of an agreement affects trade between member states it all does. This means that even though the restrictions themselves do not affect interstate trade, they become subject to Article 85.

Further whilst there is no suggestion that there need be any decrease in interstate trade, the *Consten and Grundig* Cases (see above) state that the test is satisfied where an increase results.

It is important to note that, as evidenced by *Re Vacuum Interrupters Ltd* (OJ 1977 148/32, [1977] 1 CMLR 67) the parties may be in the same member state but still affect trade between member states.

In *Pronuptia* (see above) it was held that those clauses effecting partitioning of markets in a distribution franchise agreement are 'per se' capable of affecting trade between member states, even though the parties are in one member state, insofar as they prevent the franchisees from setting up themselves in other member states.

Those undertakings situated close to member state borders are particularly at risk on this issue (*Re Industrial Timber* [1976] 1 CMLR D11) .

Finally, franchisors should appreciate that an agreement relating to trade outside of the EC may still be subject to the provisions of Article 85. (*Aluminium Products* OJ 1985 L92/1 [1987] 3 CMLR 813).

4. ARTICLE 85(2)

Agreements, decisions and concerted practices unlawful under Article 85(1) are void. No declaration is required and as provided in Regulation 17/62 Article 1 this provision of Article 85(2) applies regardless of whether or not a decision to that effect has been taken.

Article 85(2) could, therefore, be used by a franchisee as a defence in an action by a franchisor to enforce an agreement which contravenes Article 85(1). Once a franchise agreement has been found to be illegal it is void and so has an effect on all past and future effects of the agreement.

Although a franchise agreement contains provisions contravening Article 85(l) it will not necessarily mean that the entire agreement is null and void.

The Courts will tend to adopt the so-called 'blue-pencil' approach and delete only the offending provisions (*Consten and Grundig-Verkaufs GmbH* v. *EEC Commission* – Case 56/64 [1966] ECR 299). However, if the provisions cannot be separated from the agreement or fundamentally changes its nature by the deletion, the whole agreement will be found void and unenforceable (*Electric Massage Instruments* Landgericht, Mannheim, – Case No 70 (kart) 88/64 January 22, 1965).

A franchisor which is party to an agreement which is void under Article 85(2) is likely to be fined up to ECU 200 million.

5. ARTICLE 85(3)

Simply because a franchise agreement contains provisions which are prohibited under Article 85(1) does not mean that those provisions are necessarily void.

Article 85(3) expressly provides that an agreement, decision or concerted practice can be granted an exemption if it satisfies four independent conditions.

The first condition is a positive one. The agreement must contribute something of objective benefit to the community such as improving distribution or helping economic progress, both of which are often achieved by franchise networks.

The second condition is also a positive one. It requires the agreement to offer consumers a fair share of the resulting benefit.

The third condition is a negative one and provides that only essential restrictions are permitted.

The fourth condition, again a negative one, is that the agreement does not enable the elimination of any substantial competition.

Article 85(3) is widely drawn and on the whole fairly liberally interpreted. The Commission has identified a number of practices which it believes to be dramatically opposed to a single market, such as market sharing, price fixing and the prevention of exports between member states. These are unlikely to be accepted under Article 85(3). However, other restrictions are likely to be viewed with a reasonable degree of tolerance by the Commission.

6. TYPES OF EXEMPTION

There are three ways in which a franchise agreement can seek to take advantage of Article 85(3), applying for individual exemption, taking advantage of the 'de minimis' exemption and drafting it to come within the franchising block exemption (Regulation EC 4087/88).

The individual and the franchise block exemption are dealt with in detail in Chapter 27 below.

The de minimis exemption is contained in the Commission's notice of 3rd September 1986 (86/231/02). This notice deals with agreements of minor importance between small and medium sized undertakings, which do not have an appreciable impact upon market conditions.

It allows agreements, which may otherwise fall foul of Article 85(1), by providing exemption from it.

The notice sets quantitative criteria to define the term 'appreciable impact' so that undertakings are better able to decide whether the arrangements have an appreciable effect on market conditions.

Paragraph 7 of the notice states that:

'The Commission holds the view that agreements between undertakings engaged in the production or distribution of goods or in the provision of services generally do not fall under the prohibition of Article 85(1) if:

— the goods or services which are the subject of the agreement (hereinafter referred to as 'the contract products') together with the participating undertakings' other goods or services which are considered by users to be equivalent in view of their characteristics, price and intended use, do not represent more than 5% of the total market for such goods or services (hereinafter referred to as 'products') in the area of the common market affected by the agreement and
— the aggregate annual turnover of the participating undertaking does not exceed 200 million ECU.'

However, these yardsticks are not inflexible and Paragraph 8 states that:

'The Commission also holds the view that the said agreements do not fall under the prohibition of Article 85(1) if the above mentioned market share or turnover is exceeded by not more than one tenth during two successive financial years.'

This exemption is extremely useful in so far as it 'legalises' thousands of agreements between small undertakings that would, usually through ignorance, never have been notified to the Commission.

However, it is in some ways divisive and should be relied on only with the greatest reluctance.

The problem is that in order to know whether or not the goods or services represent 'more than 5% of the total market . . . in the area of the common market affected . . .' one must have a clear idea of what the market is and what area of the common market is affected.

Paragraph 11 states that:

'The relevant products market includes besides the contract products any other products which are identical or equivalent to them. This rule applies to the products of the participating undertakings as well as to the market for such products. The products in question must be interchangeable. Whether or not this is the case must be judged from the vantage point of the user, normally taking the characteristics, price and intended use of the goods together. In certain cases, however, products can form a separate market on the basis of their characteristics, their price or their intended use alone. This is true especially where consumer preferences have developed.'

As the market has in one case been adjudged to be as narrow as the spare parts for a cash register, one must be very cautious about making such an assessment.

Paragraph 13 states that:

'The relevant geographical market is the area within the Community in which the agreement produces its effects. This area will be the whole common market where the contract products are regularly bought and sold in all member states. Where the contract products cannot be bought and sold in a part of the common market, or are bought and sold only in limited quanititaties or at irregular intervals in such a part, that part should be disregarded.'

Indeed, paragraph 14 provides that:

'The relevant geographical market will be narrower than the whole common market in particular where:

— the nature and characteristics of the contract product, e.g. high transport costs in relation to the value of the product, restrict its mobility, or

— movement of the contract product within the common market is hindered by barriers to entry to national markets resulting from State intervention, such as quantitative restrictions, severe taxation differentials and non-tariff barriers, e.g. type approvals or safety standard certification. In such cases the national territory may have to be considered as the relevant geographical market. However, this will only be justified if the existing barriers to entry cannot be overcome by reasonable effort and at an acceptable cost.'

Thus judging what the relevant area of the common market is will also present difficulties.

Moreover, the agreement may come with the 'de minimis' exemption in its early days, but as the enterprises become more successful and their turnover and market share gradually increases, it is likely that it will creep out of the exemption without being noticed. Ideally the companies involved should continuously review their position, but in practice this rarely happens. As a result companies can have an extremely unpleasant surprise when a dispute arises and the other party claims that certain restrictions (or indeed the whole agreement) is void for want of notification.

It should also be noted that paragraph 6 of the notice states that:

'This Notice is without prejudice to the competence of national courts to apply Article 85(1) on the basis of their own jurisdiction, although it constitutes a factor which such courts may take into account when deciding a pending case. It is also without prejudice to any interpretation which may be given by the Court of Justice of the European Communities.'

7. PROCEDURE

Until Regulation 17 was issued on 6th February 1962 Article 85 was enforced by the authorities of each member state.

Regulation 17, (as described in detail in Chapter 30 below) aims to ensure the uniform application of the competition rules and concerns itself with supervisory and administrative matters. One aspect of this is providing for the notification of agreements, decisions and concerted practices to the Commission for negative clearance, a comfort letter, exemption or to take advantage of a block exemption's opposition procedure.

Under Regulation 27 (see below) every party to an agreement has the right to submit an application to the Commission. Any party exercising this right must notify the other parties to the agreement so that they can protect their own interests. Notification is effected on Form A/B (see below).

Thirteen copies of the form and its annexures must be filed (one for the Commission and one for each member state). Three copies of any relevant agreement and one copy of any other supporting documents must also be filed together with appropriate information required by the form.

The purpose of the Form is stated in the accompanying notes to be

'to allow undertakings, or associations of undertakings, wherever situated to apply to the Commission for negative clearance for arrangements or behaviour, or to notify such arrangements and apply to have them exempted from the prohibition of Article 85(1) of the Treaty by virtue of Article 85(3)'

To be valid, applications for negative clearance in respect of Article 85, notification to obtain an exemption and notifications claiming the benefit of an opposition procedure must be made on Form A/B (by virtue of Article 4 of Commission Regulation No. 27).

The form consists of a single sheet calling for the identity of the applicant(s) and of any other parties. This must be supplemented by further information given under the headings and references detailed below. For preference the paper used should be A4(21 x 29.7 cm — the same size as the form) but must not be bigger. Leave a margin of at least 25mm or one inch on the left-hand side of the page and, if both sides are used, on the right-hand side of the reverse.

The accompanying note stresses that:

'It is important that applicants give all the relevant facts. Although the Commission has the right to seek further information from applicants or third parties, and is obliged to publish a summary of the application before granting negative clearance or exemption under Article 83(3), it will usually base its decision on the information provided by the applicant. Any decision taken on the basis of incomplete information could be without effect in the case of a negative clearance, or voidable in that of an exemption. For the same reason, it is also important to inform the Commission of any material changes to your arrangements made after your application or notification.'

The note also recites the provisions of Article 15(1)(a) of Regulation No. 17 which reads:

'The Commission may by decision impose on undertakings or associations of undertakings fines of from 100 to 5,000 units of account where, intentionally or negligently, they supply incorrect or misleading information in an application pursuant to Article 2 or in a notification pursuant to Articles 4 or 5.'

The key words here are 'incorrect or misleading information'. However, it often remains a matter of judgement how must detail is relevant; the Commission accepts estimates where accurate information is not readily available in order to facilitate notifications; and the Commission calls for opinions as well as facts.

The application or notification is registered in the Registry of the Directorate-General for Competition (DG IV). The date of receipt by the Commission (or the date of posting if sent by registered post) is the effective date of the submission. The application or notification may be considered invalid if it is incomplete or not on the obligatory form.

'If the Commission intends to grant the application, it is obliged (by Article 19(3) of Regulation No. 17) to publish a summary and invite comments from third parties. Subsequently, a preliminary draft decision has to be submitted to and discussed with the Advisory Committee on Restrictive Practices and Dominant Positions composed of officials of the member states competent in the matter of restrictive practices and monopolies (Article 10 of Regulation No. 17) — they will already have received a copy of the application or notification. Only then, and providing nothing has happened to change the Commission's intention, can it adopt a decision.'

Article 214 of the Treaty and Articles 20 and 21 of Regulation No. 17 require the Commission and member states not to disclose information of the kind covered by the obligation of professional secrecy. On the other hand, Article 19 of the Regulation requires the Commission to publish a summary of the application, should it intend to grant it, before taking the relevant decision. In this publication, the Commission '. . . shall have regard to the legitimate interest of undertakings in the protection of their business secrets' (Article 19(3)). In this connection, if one believes that one's interests would be harmed if any of the information one is asked to supply were to be published or otherwise divulged to other parties, all such information should be put in a second annex with each page clearly marked 'Business Secrets'; in the principal annex, under any affected heading state 'see second annex' or 'also see second annex'; in the second annex repeat the affected heading(s) and reference(s) and give the information one does not wish to have published, together with the reasons for this. Do not overlook the fact that the Commission may have to publish a summary of the application.

Before publishing an Article 19(3) notice, the Commission will show the undertakings concerned a copy of the proposed text.

The application requires the following information:

1. Brief description
Give a brief description of the arrangements or behaviour (nature, purpose, date(s) and duration) − (full details are requested below).

2. Market
The nature of the goods or services affected by the arrangements or behaviour (including the customs tariff heading number according to the CCC Nomenclature or the Community's Common Customs Tariff or the Nimexe code if known − specifying which). A brief description of the structure of the market (or markets) for these goods or services − e.g. who sells in it, who buys in it, its geographical extent, the turnover in it, how competitive it is, whether it is easy for new suppliers to enter the market, whether there are substitute products. If one is notifying a standard contract (e.g. a contract appointing dealers), say how many agreements are expected to be concluded. If any studies of the market are known, it would be helpful to refer to them.

3. Fuller details of the party or parties
3.1 Do any of the parties form part of a group of companies? A group relationship is deemed to exist where a firm:

— owns more than half the capital or business assets, or
— has the power to exercise more than half the voting rights, or
— has the power to appoint more than half the members of the supervisory board, board of directors or bodies legally representative the undertaking, or
— has the right to manage the affairs of another.
If the answer is yes, it is necessary to give:

— the name and address of the ultimate parent company,
— a brief description of the business of the group (and, if possible, one copy of the last set of group accounts),
— the name and address of any other company in the group competing in a market affected by the arrangements or in any related market, that is to say any other company competing directly or indirectly with the parties ('relevant associated company').

3.2 The most recently available turnover of each of the parties and, as the case may be, of the group of which it forms part (it helps also if one provides a copy of the last set of accounts).

3.3 The sales or turnover of each party in the goods or services affected by the arrangements in the Community and worldwide. If the turnover in the Community is material (say more than a 5% market share), one should also give figures for each member state, and for previous years (in order to show any significant trends), and give each party's sales targets for the future. Provide the same figures for any relevant associated company. (Under this heading, in particular, a best estimate might be all that can readily be supplied).

3.4 In relation to the market (or markets) for the goods or services described at 2 above, give, for each of the sales or turnover figures in 3.3, an estimate of the market share it represents.

3.5 If a party has a substantial interest falling short of control (more than 25%) in some other company competing in a market affected by the arrangements, or if some other such company has a substantial interest in one's own company, give its name and address and brief details.

4. Full details of the arrangements
4.1 If the contents are reduced to writing give a brief description of the purpose of the arrangements and attach three copies of the text (except that the technical descriptions often contained in know-how agreements may be omitted; in such cases, however, indicate parts omitted).

If the contents are not, or are only partially, reduced to writing, one must give a full description.

4.2 Detail any provision contained in the arrangements which may restrict the parties in their freedom to take independent commercial decisions, for example regarding:

— buying or selling prices, discounts or other trading conditions;
— the quantities of goods to be manufactured or distributed or services to be offered;
— technical development or investment;
— the choice of markets or sources of supply;
— purchases from or sales to third parties;
— whether to apply similar terms for the supply of equivalent goods or services;
— whether to offer different goods or services separately or together.

(If one is claiming the benefit of an opposition procedure, it is necessary to identify particularly in this list the restrictions that exceed those automatically exempted by the relevant regulation).

4.3 State between which member states trade may be affected by the arrangements, and whether trade between the Community and any third countries is affected.

5. *Reasons for negative clearance*
If applying for negative clearance state, under the reference:

5.1 Why, i.e. state which provision or effects of the arrangements or behaviour might, it is thought, raise questions of compatibility with the Community's rules of competition. The object of this sub-heading is to give the Commission the clearest possible idea of any doubts that exist about arrangements or behaviour that one wishes to have resolved by a negative clearance decision.

Then, under the following two references, give a statement of the relevant facts and reasons as to why it is considered Articles 85(1) or 86 are inapplicable, i.e.:

5.2 Why the arrangements do not have the object or effect of preventing, restricting or distorting competition within the common market to any appreciable extent, or why the undertaking does not have or its behaviour does not abuse a dominant position; and/or

5.3 Why the arrangements or behaviour are not such as may affect trade between member states to any appreciable extent.

6. *Reasons for exemption under Article 85(3)*
If one is notifying the arrangements, even if only as a precaution, in order to obtain an exemption under Article 85(3), one should explain how:

6.1 The arrangements contribute to improving production or distribution, and/or promoting technical or economic progress.

6.2 A proper share of the benefits arising from such improvement or progress accrues to consumers.

6.3 All restrictive provisions of the arrangements are indispensible to the attainment of the aims set out under 6.1 above (if claiming the benefit of an opposition procedure, it is particularly important to identify and justify restrictions that exceed those automatically exempted by the relevant Regulation); and

6.4 The arrangements do not eliminate competition in respect of a substantial part of the goods or services concerned.

7. *Other information*
7.1 Mention any earlier proceedings or informal contacts, of which one is aware, with the Commission and any earlier proceedings with any national authorities or courts concerning these or any related arrangements.

7.2 Give any other information presently available that might be helpful in allowing the Commission to appreciate whether there are any restrictions contained in the arrangements, or any benefits that might justify them.

7.3 State whether it is intended to produce further supporting facts or arguments not yet available and, if so, on which points.

7.4 State, with reasons, the urgency of the application or notification.

7.1 Negative Clearance
Article 2 of Regulation 17 provides that:

'Upon application by the undertakings or associations of undertakings concerned, the Commission may certify that, on the basis of the facts in its possession, there are no grounds under Article 85(1) or Article 86 of the Treaty for action on its part in respect of an agreement, decision or practice'.

If a franchisor is in doubt as to the legality of its agreement (which is say drafted outside of the terms of the block exemption) it can apply for negative clearance. If the application is successful the Commission decides that it will not challenge the agreement under Article 85(1). However, great care must be taken by the franchisor when preparing the documents supporting the application as the clearance applies only on the facts notified to the Commission. Thus if the franchisor, either intentionally or inadvertantly, omits to disclose all of the relevant facts or a subsequent change the negative clearance may not be effective. The Commission will publish notification of any request for negative clearance in the Official Journal and invites comments from interested third parties, laying down a time limit of usually thirty days. At the same time the Commission will take the advice of the 'Advisory Committee on Restrictive Practices and Dominant Positions'. If it is decided to grant negative clearance a formal decision is published in the Official Journal.

This procedure takes anything up to a year and so in order to streamline matters, the Commission can, if the notifying party has indicated in Form A/B his willingness to accept one, issue an informal comfort letter instead. If this route is to be followed the 'provisional letter' (as it is sometimes called) is published pursuant to Article 19(3) Regulation 17 to give notice to third parties. Following this, if no third party comments are received, the comfort letter will be issued indicating that there is no need for the Commission to take action on the agreement and that the file will be considered closed, there being no need for a formal decision under Article 6 of Regulation 17. However, it is important to note that a comfort letter does not have the status of a decision and is *not* binding on any national court. Its value is restricted entirely to that of evidence (*Anne Marty S.A.* v. *Estée Lauder S.A.* – Case No 37/79 [1981] ECR 2481).

A franchisor wilfully or negligently giving false, incomplete or misleading information to the Commission can, under Article 15 of Regulation 17, be fined from 100 ECU to 5,000 ECU.

The advantage of being granted a negative clearance is that it enables the franchisor to find out (apparently before it is even entered into) whether or not its agreement offends Article 85(1) .

7.2 Individual Exemptions
The procedural requirements are laid down in Regulation 17 Articles 4 and 5.

The application, the same as that for negative clearance, is made on Form A/B which requires as much detailed information as possible. This is important as immunity from fines is limited to activity described in the notification.

7.3 The Block Exemption

In order to take advantage of the Block Exemption's Opposition Procedure a franchise agreement must be notified on Form A/B making specific mention of Article 6 of Regulation 4087/88. This is dealt with in detail in Chapter 27 below.

7.4 Failure to Notify

Failure to notify an agreement, decision or concerted practice is not illegal. However, notification does protect the franchisor from the possible imposition of a fine for violating Article 85(1), as under Article 15(5) Regulation 17 fines cannot be imposed for actions taking place after notification. Notification also fixes the date as of which an exemption decision takes effect (Article 6 Regulation 17) and may, therefore, determine the date from which a franchise agreement contravening Article 85(1) will be considered null and void.

7.5 Post Notification Amendment

A franchisor which notifies its franchise agreement to the Commission under Article 85(3) may during discussions with the Commission find that it cannot benefit from the Block Exemption's Opposition Procedure and does not come within Article 85(3). In such circumstances the franchisor can amend the notified agreement in accordance with the Commission's observations to accord with the provisions of Article 85(3) (see Chapter 22 – *Computerland* etc.) Failure by the franchisor to so modify the agreement will of course lead to the imposition of a fine and the unenforceability of the agreement.

8. DURATION, CONDITIONS AND REVOCATION OF EXEMPTION

Exemptions granted under Article 85(3) are valid only for a specified period (usually five to ten years). After the expiry of the stated period the situation is reassessed, and if there have been no changes the exemption is usually extended.

Exemptions may also be granted subject to various conditions. The parties to the agreement are entitled to express their opinions on any such conditions, but the powers of the Commission are fairly wide. These conditions may be anything from mere updating requirements such as in the *ACEC – Barliet* Case decision of July 17, 1968 (OJ C201 August 12, 1968) to restrictions upon certain commercial practices such as in the *Synthetic Fibres* Case decision of July 4, 1984 (OJ C207, August 2, 1984).

The Commission also has the power to revoke or modify an exemption if the factual situation has changed, a condition of the exemption is breached, the exemption was granted on false information or was fraudulently obtained or the exemption is abused. Failure to desist from a prohibited practice subjects the breaching party to a possible fine.

9. ARTICLE 86

Article 86 of the Treaty of Rome provides:

'Any abuse by one or more undertakings of a dominant position within the common market or in a substantial part of it shall be prohibited as incompatible with the common market in so far as it may affect trade between Member States. Such abuse may, in particular, consist in:

(a) directly or indirectly unfair purchase or selling prices or unfair trading conditions;

(b) limiting production, markets or technical development to the prejudice of consumers;

(c) applying dissimilar conditions to equivalent transactions with other trading parties, thereby placing them at a competitive disadvantage;

(d) making the conclusion of contracts subject to acceptance by the other parties of supplementary obligations which, by their nature or according to commercial usage, have no connection with the subject of such contracts.'

It is important to note that the list is not exhaustive and that it has been applied to several abuses not specifically mentioned.

The term undertaking has the same meaning as in Article 85 (see above), as does the phrase 'effect on inter-state trade'.

The term 'dominant position' is one which necessitates a detailed economic analysis of the relevant market as regards product, geography and time/seasons.

If a dominant position is established it must be decided whether or not it exists in a 'substantial part of the common market'.

Clearly Article 86 is of most importance to large multinationals established in the EC such as Roche, IBM and United Brands. Although it has not to date been used against franchisors it would be wrong to suppose that due to their size franchisors do not fall within Article 86. The important issue is not size but market power, as was illustrated by the *Hugin* Case (OJ 1978 L22/78 [1978] 3 CMLR 345). In this case Hugin, the cash register manufacturer, refused to supply its spare parts to the UK supermarket chain Liptons. Hugin's market share of cash registers was 12-14%, but its share of the spare parts market for its machines was 100%. The Commission found there to be a breach of Article 86 by Hugin, although on appeal the court overruled the Commission's decision on the ground that there was no effect on inter-state trade, although it upheld the finding of dominance.

The case of *BBI v. Boosey and Hawkes*: Interim measures (OJ 1987 L 286/36, [1988] 4 CMLR 67) also illustrates the applicability of Article 86 to small enterprises. Boosey & Hawkes, the musical instrument manufacturer had worldwide turnover of £38 million in 1985, and was found to be dominating the market for 'British-style brass bands' – in which its market share was 80-90%. Franchisors dealing in a limited market could therefore easily find themselves involved in a dispute under Article 86.

However, once dominance has been established it is necessary to consider whether or not there has been any abuse. In order to decide whether or not behaviour is legitimate or abusive the European court and the Commission have developed the concept of 'objective justification'. This approach entails investigating behaviour which prima facie appears to be abusive, such a refusal to supply to see whether or not there are reasons which on an objective basis justify it.

Merely because there is no specific clause in the franchise agreement which could lead to a conclusion that there is abuse of a dominant position does not mean that a franchisor is safe from Article 86. Concerted practices between the franchsior and its franchisees, or indeed between two rival franchise chains could amount to an abuse of a dominant position.

In the case of *Coca-Cola* (press release, 9 January 1990) the Commission found, following an investigation started in 1987, that Coca-Cola held a dominant position in the Italian drink market and abused that position by granting fidelity rebates to large distribution chains as a reward for selling only Coca-Cola. Following the investigation Coca-Cola has now given the Commission a formal undertaking that insofar as its agreements with large distributors in the EC are concerned, it will not introduce the following provisions:

(a) A customer rebate or other advantage on condition that it does not purchase other Cola flavoured beverages;

(b) Rebates on condition that customers achieve certain purchasing targets of Coca-Cola defined with each customer individually;

(c) Tying provisions that render rebates conditional upon the customer's purchase of one or more additional beverages produced by the Coca-Cola Corporation.

The Treatment of Franchising by the Law of the European Community

By MARK ABELL

The effect of EC law on franchising is best dealt with by considering firstly the case law, secondly the Commission decisions upon applications for individual exemption and thirdly the so-called franchise block exemption (Regulation 4087/88).

1. THE *PRONUPTIA* CASE

In this celebrated case the franchisor, Pronuptia de Paris GmbH of Frankfurt am Main, a subsidiary of the French company bearing the same name, was engaged in litigation with its franchisee Mrs Irmgard Schillgalis of Hamburg. Mrs Schillgalis had three outlets in Hamburg, Oldenburg and Hanover, and the dispute concerned arrears of fees based on the franchisee's sales figures for 1978 to 1980.

The French parent company of the franchisor distributes under the name 'Pronuptia de Paris' wedding dresses and other clothes worn at weddings. Distribution of these products in the Federal Republic of Germany was carried out in part through shops run directly by its subsidiary and in part through shops belonging to independent retailers tied to the subsidiary by franchise agreements, executed in its name by the subsidiary acting both on behalf of the parent company and on its own behalf.

The terms of the three agreements all dated 24th February 1980 were for practical purposes identical.

The main terms of the three agreements submitted to the court for consideration are summarised in paragraph 1.2 of the judgment as follows:

'The franchisor:

— grants to the franchisee the exclusive right to use the mark Pronuptia de Paris for sale of its products and services for a particular territory outlined in a map attached to the agreement, as well as the right to advertise in that territory.
— agrees not to open another Pronuptia shop in the territory in question and not to provide any product or service to third parties in that territory.
— agrees to assist the franchisee in the commercial and promotional aspects of his business, in the setting up and designing of the shop, in the training of personnel, sales techniques, in fashion and product advice, sales, marketing, and generally in all respects in which, in the experience of the franchisor, it could contribute towards the improvement of the turnover and profitability of the franchisee.

The franchisee, who remains the sole proprietor of its business and bears the associated risks, is required:

— to use the name Pronuptia de Paris and sell merchandise under that name only in the shop specified in the agreement. The shop must be arranged and decorated principally for sale of wedding related products, according to the directions of the franchisor, with the purpose of protecting the worth of the mark used by the Pronuptia distribution chain. The shop may not be transferred to another site or redesigned without the franchisor's approval.
— to purchase from the franchisor 80 per cent of its requirements of wedding dresses and accessories as well as a proportion to be determined by the franchisor himself of cocktail dresses and formal wear and to obtain the remainder only from suppliers approved by the franchisor.
— to pay to the franchisor, in consideration of the benefits provided, an initial payment for the contract territory of 15,000 DM and, for the duration of the contract, a royalty equalling 10 per cent of the turnover realised by the sale of both Pronuptia products and all other merchandise; evening dresses purchased from suppliers other than Pronuptia are not, however, included in this figure.
— to take account, without prejudice to its freedom to fix its own retail prices, of the recommended resale prices proposed by the franchisor.
— to advertise in the licensed territory only with the consent of the franchisor and in any case to make such advertising conform to that carried out on a national or international level by the franchisor, to disseminate as conscientiously as possible the catalogues and other promotional aids supplied by the franchisor, and generally to use the commercial methods communicated by the franchisor to the franchisee.
— to make its principal objective the sale of wedding articles.
— not to transfer to third parties the rights and obligations arising out of the contract nor to sell the business without prior agreement of the franchisor, it being understood that the franchisor will grant his approval if the transfer is required for health reasons and the new contracting party can establish that he is solvent and prove that he is not in any form whatever a competitor of the franchisor'.

The first instance court ruled that the franchisee must pay 158,502DM arrears of royalties due on its turnover in the years 1978-1980. The franchisee appealed against this judgement to the Oberlandesgericht, Frankfurt am Main, claiming it was not required to pay the arrears because the agreement infringed Article 85(1) of the Treaty and did not benefit from the group exemption for exclusive dealing agreements provided by Regulation 67/67. In a judgement of 2nd December 1982, the Oberlandesgericht accepted the franchisee's arguments. It found that the reciprocal obligations of exclusivity constituted restrictions on competition within the Common Market, since the franchisor could not supply any other business in the contract territory and the franchisee could only purchase and resell other merchandise from other member states in a very limited way. Since no exemption under Article 85(3) applied to them, held the Oberlandesgericht, these agreements must be considered void under Article 85(2). With respect to the issue of exemption, the Oberlandesgericht considered in particular that it was not necessary for it to decide if franchise agreements are in principle excluded from the application of Regulation 67/67. In fact, according to the Oberlandesgericht, the agreements at issue in any event involved undertakings going beyond the scope of Article 1 of the regulation and constituted restrictions on competition not covered by Article 2.

The franchisor applied for review of this judgement to the Bundesgerichtshof, requesting reinstatement of the first instance court's judgement. The Bundesgerichtshof concluded that its judgement on the application depended on an interpretation of Community law.

The European Court was set the following questions by the Bundesgerichtshof:

1. Is Article 85(1) of the EEC Treaty applicable to franchise agreements such as the contracts between the parties, which have as their object the establishment of a special distribution system whereby the franchisor provides to the franchisee, in addition to goods, certain trade names, trade marks, merchandising material and services?

2. If the first question is answered in the affirmative: Is Regulation no. 67/67/EEC of the Commission of 22nd March 1967 on the application of Article 85(3) of the Treaty to certain categories of exclusive dealing agreements (block exemption) applicable to such contracts?

3. If the second question is answered in the affirmative:

(a) Is Regulation no. 67/67/EEC still applicable if several undertakings which, though legally independent, are bound together by commercial ties and form a single economic entity for the purposes of the contract participate on one side of the agreement?

(b) Does Regulation no. 67/67/EEC, and in particular Article 2(2)(c) thereof, apply to an obligation on the part of the franchisee to advertise solely with the prior agreement of the franchisor and in a manner that is in keeping with the latter's advertising, using the publicity material supplied by him, and in general to use the same business methods? Is it relevant in this connection that the franchisor's publicity material contains price recommendations which are not binding?

(c) Does Regulation no. 67/67/EEC, and in particular Articles 1(1)(b), 2(1)(a) and 2(b) thereof, apply to an obligation on the part of the franchisee to confine the sale of the contract goods exclusively or at least for the most part to particular business premises specially adapted for the purpose?

(d) Does Regulation 67/67/EEC, and in particular Article 1(1)(b) thereof, apply to an obligation on the part of a franchisee – who is bound to purchase most of his supplies from the franchisor – to make the rest of his purchases of goods covered by the contract solely from suppliers approved by the franchisor?

(e) Does Regulation no. 67/67/EEC sanction an obligation on the franchisor to give the franchisee commercial, advertising and professional support?

The court's judgement in *Pronuptia* was the first directly concerned with distribution franchises and so attracted a great deal of attention from the franchising community.

It stated very clearly that certain restrictions upon the franchisees were prohibited under Article 85(1).

However, it also recognised in paragraph 15 that:

'In a distribution franchise system such as this, an enterprise which has established itself as a distributor in a market and which has thus been able to perfect a range of commercial methods gives independent businessmen the chance, at a price, of establishing themselves in other markets by using its mark and the commercial methods that created the franchisor's success. More than just a method of distribution, this is a manner of exploiting financially a body of knowledge, without investing the franchisor's own capital. At the same time this system gives businessmen who lack the necessary experience access to methods which they could otherwise only acquire after prolonged effort and research and allows them also to profit from the reputation of the mark. Distribution franchise agreements are thus different from either dealership agreements or those binding approved resellers appointed under a system of selective distribution which involve neither use of a single mark nor application of uniform commercial methods nor payment of royalties in consideration of the advantages thus conferred. Such a system, which permits the franchisor to take advantage of his success, is not itself restrictive of competition. For it to function two conditions must be satisfied.'

It therefore also found that ancillary restrictions necessary to ensure that the franchisor did not have to run the risk that its

'know-how and assistance might benefit competitors even indirectly' (paragraph 16).

are not prohibited by Article 85(1).

The court considered that:

'the franchisor must be able to take the measures necessary for maintaining the identity and reputation of the network bearing his business name or symbol.' (paragraph 17).

and that

'provisions which establish the means of control necessary for that purpose do not contribute restrictions on competition for the purposes of Article 85(1).' (paragraph 17).

The final judgement of the court was that:

'1.(a) The compatibility of distribution franchise agreements with Article 85(1) depends on the clauses contained in the contracts and on the economic context in which they have been included.

(b) Clauses that are indispensible to prevent the know-how and assistance provided to the franchisee by the franchisor from benefiting the franchisor's competitors do not constitute restrictions of competition within the meaning of Article 85(1).

(c) Clauses which implement the control indispensible for preservation of the identity and the reputation of the system symbolised by the trade mark also do not constitute restrictions of competition within the meaning of Article 85(1).

(d) Clauses which effect a division of markets between the franchisor and franchisee or between franchisees constitute restrictions of competition within the meaning of Article 85(1).

(e) The fact that the franchisor has transmitted suggested prices to the franchisees does not constitute a restriction of competition, on condition that there has not been a concerted practice between franchisor and franchisees or between franchisees regarding putting these prices into effect.

(f) Distribution franchise agreements which contain clauses effecting a division of markets between franchisor and franchisee or between franchisees are capable of affecting trade between member states.

2. Regulation 67/67 is not applicable to distribution franchise agreements such as those which have been considered in this proceeding.'

2. APPLICATION FOR INDIVIDUAL EXEMPTION UNDER ARTICLE 85.3

Following the European Court's decision in *Pronuptia* and the resulting anxiety experienced by franchisors in the EC, the Commission was determined to adopt a considered approach towards franchise agreements.

It, therefore, turned its attention to franchise agreements which had been notified under Article 85(3). At that time it only had experience of one 'production franchise' and in order to use its powers to adopt a block exemption (Regulation 19/65) it required more experience.

2.1 PRODUCT FRANCHISES

Campari

The *Campari Agreement* (O.J. 1978 L70/69; [1978] CMLR 397) (see Appendix 8) granted franchisees a territorially exclusive right to use the Campari trade mark to promote the Campari drink manufactured using local wines and a 'secret recipe' of herbs provided by the franchisor.

The agreement contained a number of restrictions scrutinised by the Commission.

1. Exclusivity and active sales
Exclusivity and a restriction on actively seeking sales outside the territory were held to restrict competition. However, exclusivity was exempted on the grounds that it enabled the franchisee to make a proper return on its investment. The restriction on active sales was likewise exempted on the ground that it assisted in the concentration of effort by each franchisee.

2. Restriction on handling competing products
This restriction was held to restrict competition, but was exempted as it aimed to decentralise the alcohol's production and rationalise distribution.

3. Obligation to supply only the original Italian made product to duty free shops
This restriction was held to be justified as the outlets served an international customer base that would want to obtain a uniform product.

4. Obligation to produce only in plants capable of guaranteeing quality
This obligation was cleared as it did not go beyond a legitimate interest in quality control by the franchisor.

5. Obligation to apply know-how
This obligation was cleared as being a proper concern of the franchisor.

6. Tie-in of the secret recipe of herbs
Likewise this obligation was perceived to be a necessary one and was therefore cleared.

Moosehead

The agreement between Moosehead Breweries Limited and Whitbread and Company plc comprised a marketing and technical agreement; the trade mark user agreement and a trade mark assignment agreement, collectively referred to by the Commission as the 'Agreement' (OJ 1990 L100/33) (see Appendix 8 below).

Under the agreement, Moosehead granted to Whitbread the sole and exclusive right to produce, promote, market and sell beer manufactured for sale under the name 'Moosehead' in the United Kingdom, using Moosehead's secret know-how in exchange for a royalty. There were various provisions regarding quality control restrictions upon sales outside of the territory and non-competition clauses.

The part of the agreement which is of most interest to franchisors is that which concerns trade marks and know-how. Under the agreement, Whitbread agreed to sell the product only under the trade mark 'Moosehead' and to use the trade mark Moosehead only on or in relation to the product. The property rights in the trade mark in the United Kingdom were assigned to Whitbread and Moosehead jointly. This assignment was intended to give Whitbread a strong guarantee of its right to use the trade mark during the term of the agreement. Moosehead granted under the agreement to Whitbread the exclusive licence to use the trade mark in relation to the product in the territory during the term of the agreement. Moosehead agreed not to register or use without the consent of Whitbread any trade mark which resembles or may easily be confused with the Moosehead trade mark in the territory. Whitbread undertook similar obligations.

Most importantly, Whitbread acknowledged the title of Moosehead to the trade mark and the validity of the registration of Moosehead as proprietor. Whitbread undertook to observe all conditions which may be prescribed by the terms of the registration of the trade mark and also not to do anything which would or might invalidate such registration or title or apply to vary or cancel any registration of the marks. On termination of the agreement, Whitbread agreed to reassign the trade marks to Moosehead.

The Commission cleared the various restrictions and granted the parties negative clearance.

Of most importance to franchisors are the Commission's comments in Clause 15(4) of the decision concerning the trade mark non-challenge clause. The Commission stated:

'(a) In general terms the trade mark non-challenge clause can refer to the ownership and/or the validity of the trade mark;

— the ownership of a trade mark may in particular be challenged on grounds of the prior use and prior registration of an identical trade mark.

A clause in an exclusive trade mark licence agreement obliging the licensee not to challenge the *ownership* of a trademark as specified in the above paragraph does not constitute a restriction of competition within the meanings of Article 85(1). Whether or not the licensor or licensee has the ownership of a trade mark, the use or it by any other party is prevented in any event, and competition would thus *not* be affected.

— the *validity* of a trade mark may be contested on any ground under national law, and in particular on the grounds that it is generic or descriptive in nature. In such an event, should the challenge be upheld, a trade mark may fall within the public domain and may thereafter be used without restriction by the licensee and any other party.

Such a clause may constitute a restriction of competition within the meaning of Article 85(1), because it may contribute to the maintenance of a trade mark that would be an unjustified barrier to entry into a given market.

Moreover, in order for any restriction of competition to fall under Article 85(1), it must be appreciable. The ownership of a trade mark only gives the holder the exclusive right to sell products under that name. Other parties are free to sell the products in question under a different trade mark or name. Only where the use of a well-known trade mark would be an important advantage to any company entering or competing in any given market, the absence of which therefore constitutes a significant barrier to entry, would this clause which impedes the licensee to challenge the validity of the trade mark, constitute an appreciable restriction of competition within the meaning of Article 85(1).

(b) In the present case, Whitbread is unable to challenge both the ownership and the validity of the trade marks.

As far as the validity of the trade marks is concerned, it must be noted that the trade mark is comparatively new to the lager market in the territory. The maintenance of the Moosehead licence will thus *not* constitute an appreciable barrier to entry to any other company entering or competing in the beer market in the United Kingdom. Accordingly, the Commission considers that the trade mark non-challenge clauses included in the agreement, in so far as it concerns its validity, does not constitute an appreciable restriction and does not fall under Article 85(1). Furthermore, in so far as this clause concerns ownership, it does not constitute a restriction of competition within the meaning of Article 85(1) for the reasons stated above.'

Thus the Commission seems to have adopted a 'rule of reason' test rather than the automatic infringement test (see Chapter 26 above). It suggests that a restriction of competition must be appreciable to fall foul of Article 85(1). No-challenge clauses affecting a well-known trade mark will amount to an appreciable effect, but the same clauses affecting little known trade marks will not. The important thing to remember is that such an inoffensive clause will gradually become offensive as the trade mark becomes better known. The effects of this ruling clearly go much further than just product franchises.

2.2 BUSINESS FORMAT FRANCHISES

Whilst the Campari case contained many of the restrictions and obligations common to business format franchise agreements its use to the Commission as a source of experience of franchise agreements was somewhat limited.

As the Court recognised in paragraph 13 of the *Pronuptia* judgement:

'Franchise agreements, whose legality has not hitherto been considered by this Court, present enormous diversity. From the arguments before the Court, it is necessary to distinguish between different types of franchise, particularly service franchise agreements, by which the franchisee offers services under the sign and the trade name, or indeed the trade mark, of the franchisor and complies with the franchisor's directives; production franchise agreements by which the franchisee himself manufactures, according to the instructions of the franchisor, products which he sells under the franchisor's trade mark; and finally, distribution franchise agreements by which the franchisee restricts himself to the sale of certain products in a shop carrying the mark of the franchisor. The Court will only consider this third type of agreement which conforms to that expressly referred to in the question from the national court.'

The Commission, at this time, still had no experience of distribution and service franchises. It therefore spent time and energy considering the notified agreements of Pronuptia, Yves Rocher, Computerland, ServiceMaster and Charles Jourdan, so as to gain sufficient experience of franchising to enable it to adopt a block exemption. (See Appendix 8 below for copies of these decisions).

A summary of the Commission's decision on key clauses is given, in tabular form, below. In all five cases exemptions rather than negative clearances were given. The clauses which the Commission considered to be anti-competitive involved sharing the market between the franchisor and the franchisees – something which always makes the Commission very uncomfortable. As Professor Valentine Korah comments (in 'Franchising and the EEC Competition Rules Regulation 4087/88'):

'. . . a national court could have enforced the territorial protection. It is the Community Courts' judgement in *Pronuptia* rather than the Commission's decisions that creates law. The judgement in *Pronuptia*, at paragraph 27, did state that the economic context of the agreement is relevant. If, however, the Commission was prepared to grant an individual exemption, there cannot have been much pressure on the franchisors to request a clearance rather than an exemption'.

As a result of the *Pronuptia* decision however national courts are far less likely to hold that franchise agreements containing such provisions fall outside of Article 85(1).

Although the Commission adopted the same general approach there are noticeable differences between the different decisions. The differences are presumably due to either differences in the terms of the agreements or the franchisors' respective positions in the market.

Nevertheless the Court's decision in *Pronuptia* enabled the Commission to clear the clauses which aim to enable the franchisor to maintain the identity and the reputation of its name and other intellectual property rights and to protect its know-how, in all five applications.

Having gained this experience of franchise agreements the Commission was able to adopt Regulation 4087/88, the so-called Franchise Block Exemption.

3. EC REGULATION 4087/88

The opinion of the Advocate General Mr Pieter Verloren van Themaat which precedes the actual *Pronuptia* judgement stated clearly that:

'Block exemption for franchise agreements is desirable' (para. 4.3)

Taking this lead, and with experience of franchise agreements obtained from considering the applications for individual exemption detailed above, the Commission adopted EC Regulation 4087/88 on 30 November 1988. The text (which appears in Appendix 9 below) was published in the Official Journal on 28th December 1988 (OJ 1988 L359/46). It came into force on 1 February 1989 and applies for a period of ten years.

The Regulation was warmly welcomed by the franchising community as it is basically sympathetic towards franchising, recognising its contribution towards the stimulation of competition. In the recitals it acknowledges that franchises

'normally improve the distribution of goods and/or the provision of services as they give franchisors the possibility of establishing a uniform network with limited investment which may assist the entry of new competitors into the market, particularly in the case of small and medium sized undertakings thus increasing interbrand competition and allowing independent traders to set up outlets more rapidly and with a higher chance of success than if they do so without the franchisor's experience and assistance'.

Structure and form of the Regulation

The recitals describe both the aim of the Regulation and the Commission's understanding of what amounts to a franchise agreement. Recital (3) shows that the Commission, like the European Court in *Pronuptia*, believes that:

'Several types of franchise can be distinguished according to their object: industrial franchise concerns the manufacturing of goods,

distribution franchise concerns the sale of goods, and service franchise concerns the supply of services.'

In recital (4) the Commission boldly states that:

'It is possible on the basis of the experience of the Commission to define categories of franchise agreements which fall under Article 85(1) but can normally be regarded as satisfying the conditions laid down in Article 85(3). This is the case for franchise agreements whereby one of the parties supplies goods or provides services to end users. On the other hand, industrial franchise agreements should not be covered by this Regulation. Such agreements, which usually govern relationship between producers, present different characteristics than the other types of franchise. They consist of manufacturing licences based on patents and/or technical know-how, combined with trade-mark licences. Some of them may benefit from other block exemptions if they fulfill the necessary conditions.'

It therefore decided in recital(5) that:

'This Regulation covers franchise agreements between two undertakings, the franchisor and the franchisee, for the retailing of goods or the provision of services to end users, or a combination of these activities, such as the processing or adaptation of goods to fit specific needs of their customers. It also covers cases where the relationship between franchisor and franchisee is made through a third undertaking, the master franchisee. It does not cover wholesale franchise agreements because of the lack of experience of the Commission in that field.'

The Commission believes that franchise agreements can fall foul of Article 85(1) and affect intra-Community trade (recital (6)) but recitals (7) and (8) detail the benefits of franchising as not only improving the distribution of goods and/or services but also the fact that:

'As a rule, franchise agreements also allow consumers and other end users a fair share of the resulting benefit, as they combine the advantage of a uniform network with the existence of traders personally interested in the efficient operation of their business. The homogeneity of the network and the constant co-operation between the franchisor and the franchisees ensures a constant quality of the products and services. The favourable effect of franchising on interbrand competition and the fact that consumers are free to deal with any franchisee in the network guarantees that a reasonable part of the resulting benefits will be passed on to the consumers.'

The Commission acknowledges in the recitals the need to identify those provisions restrictive on competition which may be included in franchise agreements and in recital (9) states that:

'This Regulation must define the obligations restrictive of competition which may be included in franchise agreements. This is the case in particular for the granting of an exclusive territory to the franchisees combined with the prohibition on actively seeking customers outside that territory, which allows them to concentrate their efforts on their allotted territory. The same applies to the granting of an exclusive territory to a master franchisee combined with the obligation not to conclude franchise agreements with third parties outside that territory. Where the franchisees sell or use in the process of providing services, goods manufactured by the franchisor or according to its instructions and or bearing its trade mark, an obligation on the franchisees not to sell, or use in the process of the provision of services, competing goods, makes it possible to establish a coherent network which is identified with the franchised goods. However, this obligation should only be accepted with respect to the goods which form the essential subject matter of the franchise. It should notably not relate to accessories or spare parts for these goods.'

The desirability of listing allowable restrictions in the Regulation is stated in recital (12) which provides that:

'The Regulation must specify the conditions which must be satisfied for the exemption to apply. To guarantee that competition is not eliminated for a substantial part of the goods which are the subject of the franchise, it is necessary that parallel imports remain possible. Therefore, cross deliveries between franchisees should always be possible. Furthermore, where a franchise network is combined with another distribution system, franchisees should be free to obtain supplies from authorised distributors. To better inform consumers, thereby helping to ensure that they receive a fair share of the resulting benefits, it must be provided that the franchisee shall be obliged to indicate its status as an independent undertaking, by any appropriate means which does not jeopardise the common identity of the franchised network. Furthermore, where the franchisees have to honour guarantees for the franchisor's goods, this obligation should also apply to goods supplied by the franchisor, other franchisees or other agreed dealers.'

The recitals also acknowledge the need to specify restrictions which may not be included in franchise agreements in Recital (13), and states that

'This applies in particular to market sharing between manufacturers to clauses unduly limiting the franchisees choice of supplies or customers and to cases where the franchisee is restricted in determining its prices. However, the franchisor should be free to recommend prices to the franchisees, where it is not prohibited by national laws and to the extent that it does not lead to concerted practices for the effective application of these prices.'

Recital (14) describes the need for an opposition procedure for 'agreements which are not automatically covered by the exemption because they contain provisions that are not expressly exempted by the Regulation and not expressly excluded from exemptions'.

The need for the Commission to retain the power to withdraw exemption from individual agreements if it deems it necessary to do so is expressly stated in recital (15).

The Regulation comprises nine Articles which can be divided into six separate parts, as follows:

(1) Article 1:   Exemption and Definitions
(2) Article 2:   The exempted provisions
(3) Article 3:   The 'Whitelisted' provisions which can be imposed
(4) Article 4:   The Compulsory provisions
(5) Article 5:   The 'Blacklisted' provisions which cannot be imposed
(6) Articles 6, 7, 8 & 9:   Procedural matters including the Commission's power to oppose and/or dispute the exemption and the opposition procedure which can be used by franchisors which are in doubt as to whether or not their agreement comes within the terms of the Regulation

Summary of Restrictions allowed

In brief the block exemption allows the following restrictions to be imposed by the franchisor on the franchisee.

Territorial exclusivity

Exclusivity is desirable from the standpoint of both franchisor and franchisee. The Regulation recognises this and allows three types of exclusivity. The franchisor can agree:

(a) not to appoint another franchisee in the contract territory;

(b) not to exploit the franchise itself or to market the goods and services which are the subject of the franchise in the contract territory;

(c) not to sell its goods to third parties in the contract territory.

As in the Patent Block Exemption and the Know-How Block Exemption the Commission draws an uneasy distinction between passive and active selling (see Chapter 28 below) which is hard to justify on a strictly commercial basis.

Non-Competition

The Regulation allows three types of non-competition clauses:

(a) The franchisee may be required not to compete directly or indirectly in a similar business in the territory in competition with a member of the franchise network for a reasonable period of up to one year (it should be noted that one year will not always be seen by the Commission as being reasonable).

(b) The franchisee may be required not to acquire financial interests in the capital of a competing undertaking sufficient to give him the power to influence its economic conduct.

(c) The franchisor may impose a customer restriction by requiring the franchisee to sell only to end users and other franchisees where these goods are not sold through other channels by the manufacturer or with his consent.

Location

The Block Exemption allows two types of location clauses:

(a) The franchisee may be compelled to obtain the franchisor's consent to any change in the location of the premises. (However, if the franchisor unreasonably refuses consent, i.e. for reasons other than for protecting its industrial/intellectual property rights and maintaining the common identity and reputation of the network, the benefit of the Block Exemption can be withdrawn.)

(b) The franchisee may be required to exploit the franchise only from the premises.

Quality Controls

'White' clauses permitting the imposition of quality controls include:

(a) The application of the franchisor's commercial methods and use of the licensed intellectual property rights.

(b) Compliance with the franchisor's standards as regards equipment, premises and transport.

(c) Co-operating with any inspection by the franchisor.

(d) Refraining from assigning any rights or obligations.

The Definitions

Article 1(1) and (2) exempts from Article 85(1) EEC those provisions which are detailed in Article 2, whilst Article 1(3) contains the Regulation's definitions.

These definitions are of great importance and should be carefully considered.

'Franchise means a package of industrial or intellectual property rights relating to trade marks, trade names, shop signs, utility models, designs, copyrights, know-how or patents, to be exploited for the resale of goods or the provision of services to end users.'

These resemble the definitions found in *Pronuptia*.

'Franchise Agreement means an agreement whereby one undertaking, the franchisor, grants the other, the franchisee, in exchange for direct or indirect financial consideration, the right to exploit a franchise for the purposes of marketing specified types of goods and/or services; it includes at least obligations relating to:

— the use of a common name or shop sign and and a uniform presentation of contract premises and/or means of transport.
— the communication by the franchisor to the franchisee of know-how.
— the continuing provision by the franchisor to the franchisee of commercial or technical assistance during the life of the agreements.'

The need for there to be know-how communicated is very important, as it excludes from the Regulation those so-called franchises which are in fact only a trade mark licence.

The financial consideration can be either direct or indirect and presumably be structured as the franchisor requires to comprise upfront fees, continuing/periodic fees or even product mark-up.

The earlier drafts of the Regulation were narrower containing the words 'for resale' rather than 'for the purpose of marketing' — so excluding methods of supply such as agency or hire.

The Regulation likewise shows the Commission's appreciation of the fact that franchising is more than merely a way of distributing goods manufactured by the franchisor.

The three requirements concerning use of a common name etc., communication of know-how and continuing assistance are cumulative. Earlier drafts had the word 'and' inserted after each sentence, and this is still so in the French version. The German version, however, like the English does not include the word 'and'. Nevertheless it is unlikely that a franchise which has no know-how and under which the franchisor gives no continuing assistance would be able to take advantage of the block exemption.

The exclusion of wholesale franchises from the Regulation by the use of the term 'end users' is to be regretted as there seems to be no logical reason for it. It has been suggested (by Valentine Korah — 'Franchising and the EEC Competition Rules Regulation 4087/88') that the reason for this is to exclude multiple levels of trade franchises and that it makes it unlikely that master franchise agreements will be able to take advantage of the Regulation. Certainly it does prevent 'pyramiding' and similar multi-level marketing techniques popular in the USA but it is doubtful that this alone will mean that master franchises will rarely come within the regulation. This would be likely only where the sub-franchisor buys products for resale to franchisees. Service franchises and those which do not tie in the franchisor's own products will not be affected adversely by this provision.

Master Franchise Agreement is defined in Article 1(3)(c) as

'an agreement whereby one undertaking, the franchisor, grants the other, the master franchisee, in exchange of direct or indirect financial consideration, the right to exploit a franchise for the purposes of concluding franchise agreements with third parties, the franchisees'

It should be noted that the exclusion of tripartite agreements means that master franchise agreements can only be bipartite.

'Franchisor's goods means goods produced by the franchisor or according to its instructions, and/or bearing the franchisor's name or trade mark.'

'Contract premises is defined so as to cover both static franchises and mobile ones. It means the premises used for the exploitation of the franchise or, when the franchise is exploited outside those premises, the base from which the franchisee operates the means of transport used for the exploitation of the franchise.'

'Know-how — the definition of know-how is one of the most important parts of the Regulation, bearing in mind that the know-how on many franchises is fairly low level. It means a package of non-patented practical information, resulting from experience and testing by the franchisor, which is secret, substantial and identified.'

'Secret means that the know-how, as a body or in the precise configuration and assembly of its components, is not generally known or easily accessible; it is not limited in the narrow sense that the individual component of the know-how should be totally unknown or unobtainable outside the franchisor's business.'

'Substantial means that the know-how includes information which is of importance for the sale of goods or the provision of services to end users, and in particular for the presentation of goods for sale, the processing of goods in connection with the provision of services, methods of dealing with customers, and administration and financial management; the know-how must be useful for the franchisee by being capable, at the date of conclusion of the agreement, of improving the competitive position of the franchisee, in particular by improving the franchisee's performance or helping it to enter a new market.'

'Identified means that the know-how must be described in a sufficiently comprehensive manner so as to make it possible to verify that it fulfils the criteria of secrecy and substantiality; the description of the know-how can either be set out in the franchise agreement or in a separate document or recorded in any other appropriate form.'

The need for the practical information which comprises the know-how to result from experience and testing means that only established business formats can take advantage of the exemption. If the franchisor is a large corporation already having an annual turnover of over 2000 million ECU (i.e. is not able to take advantage of the de minimis exemption), and creates a new business concept, totally divorced from its existing business (for example a brewery creating a hotel concept) it may not be able to take advantage of the block exemption. If, however, one accepts the suggestion of the Court in *Pronuptia* that the franchise will not come within Article 85(1) until the network is widespread this may not be a problem. It should, however, be noted that if this were the case it would not be an attractive commercial proposition for the franchisee either.

As in the recitals definition of a franchise agreement the Regulation's drafting is far from clear and it is not made clear whether the requirement for secrecy, substance and identification is alternative or collective. That is to say does know-how have to be secret, substantial and identified or is it sufficient for it to be secret or substantial or identified?

Bearing in mind the economic nature of franchising, it would seem to be collective. This should not, however, present problems for proper business format franchises. The definition of 'secret' fairly reflects the degree of secrecy that any franchise can expect of the franchisor's know-how. Each element may not be secret in itself (anyone can make a hamburger or design self service facilities), but the compound of the elements is secret for example, there is only one MacDonalds!

Likewise, the definition of 'substantial' should create no problems for a proper business format franchise. The advantage over competitors and importance in regards to the provision of the goods or services are basic commercial requirements for any proper franchise.

If the franchisee is already in the market it should help improve his competitiveness. If the franchisee is not already in the market it should help him to enter it.

The need for the know-how to be identified will usually be satisfied by the franchisor's manual, which may not merely be restricted to a written text but also include sound and video recordings, computer programs and other documentation. Again this will present no problem for a 'proper' business format franchise, it will, however, prevent mere trademark licences on distribution networks taking advantage of the Regulation.

These definitions are, in summary, fairly broad and recognise the basic elements of business format franchising.

When considering whether or not a franchise agreement can take advantage of the regulation the first step must be to ensure that it comes within these defined terms.

Mandatory Restrictions

Assuming that the franchise comes within the definitions, the agreement must contain one or more of the mandatory restrictions contained in Article 1. As stated above, Article 1 exempts those franchise agreements which include one or more of these listed restrictions.

'The exemption provided for in Article 1 shall apply to the following restrictions of competition.

(a) an obligation on the franchisor, in a defined area of the common market, the contract territory, not to:

— grant the right to exploit all or part of the franchise to third parties.
— itself exploit the franchise, or itself market the goods or services which are the subject matter of the franchise under a similar formula.
— itself supply the franchisor's goods to third parties.

(b) an obligation on the master franchisee not to conclude a franchise agreement with third parties outside its contract territory.

(c) on obligation on the franchisee to exploit the franchise only from the contract premises.

(d) an obligation on the franchisee to refrain, outside the contract territory, from seeking customers for the goods or the services which are the subject matter of the franchise.

(e) an obligation on the franchisee not to manufacture, sell or use in the course of the provision of services, goods competing with the franchisor's goods which are the subject matter of the franchise. Where the subject matter of the franchise is the sale or use in the course of the provision of services both certain types of goods and spare parts or accessories therefor, that obligation may not be imposed in respect of these spare parts or accessories.'

It is important to note that it does *not* exempt those agreements which include similar but lesser or narrower restrictions. Thus, for example, if only partial exclusivity is granted to the franchisee, with no location clause, restriction on adverse sales or restriction on suppliers the block exemption *cannot* be taken advantage of.

Exactly why this should be is not clear; perhaps the suggestion is that lesser but similar restrictions do not offend Article 85(1) and therefore do not need to be exempted.

Exclusivity

As evidenced by the *Pronuptia* case and the subsequent grants of individual exemption the EC authorities' attitude towards exclusivity is somewhat complicated. The European Court stated in paragraph [27] 1 of the *Pronuptia* judgement that:

'The compatibility of distribution franchise agreements with Article 85(1) depends on the clauses contained in the agreements and on the economic context in which they are included.'

This implies that until the franchise network is widespread the grant of exclusivity is unlikely to prevent, restrict or distort competition and will therefore not offend Article 85(1).

In *ServiceMaster*, however, the Commission felt unable to grant negative clearance as although the network was not then widespread, it was likely to become so in the near future.

This apparent adoption of the so-called Rule of Reason, so often used in the USA, demands some very fine judgement by the parties to an agreement, when they are deciding whether or not they need apply for exemption.

The block exemption eases this difficulty to some degree by allowing the grant of exclusivity in various ways. These have previously been approved by way of individual exemptions granted by the Commission.

Although there is no specific statement, the three restrictions would deem to be in the alternative. Bearing in mind that lesser restrictions do not benefit from the exemption this is a matter of some considerable importance, which will, no doubt, be clarified by the Commission in due course.

Master Franchise Restrictions

This restriction is, of course, commonly found in a master franchise agreement, and is commercially desirable to ensure a structured and regularised approach to the market. Under a sub-franchise agreement between the sub-franchisor (master franchisee in the Commission's terminology) and the sub-franchisee the restrictions contained in Article 2(a) could, of course, be imposed upon the sub-franchisor.

Location Clause

This should be differentiated from Article 3(2)(i) (see below) which states that a restraint on changing the location of an outlet does not offend Article 85(1).

Active sales restraint

This provision highlights the Commission's dilemma caught as it is between on the one hand the desire to achieve a truly single market, free of artificial barriers and on the other the reluctant acceptance of the need for some degree of protection. The resulting distinction between active sales (where the franchisor actively seeks to attract customers) and passive sales (where the franchisor merely sells to customers who approach it) is extremely artificial. Imagine, for example, a Paris based French language fashion magazine. A fashion retail franchisor has a number of exclusive franchisees in North East France and Belgium. A French franchisee can place advertisements in the fashion magazine advertising its presence. The magazine will be sold all over Europe. Belgian customers may be attracted by the lower prices, and the idea of shopping in France and so purchase goods from that franchisee rather than one in, say, Antwerp in Belgium. The franchisee is not actively seeking business from Belgium. The magazine is French, and if the franchisee were to refrain from advertising in any magazine which was sold in other member states it would be placed in an impossible position. The advert must, therefore, amount to a passive sales technique in Belgium. How does this differ from active sales techniques? Further, such a distinction is extremely hard to enforce in practical commercial terms.

Tie-ins

In other words, the franchisee can be required to buy only the franchisor's goods *but not* only from the franchisor (see black clauses – Article 4 below).

The exemption of spare parts and accessories is important to note, but should always be considered in conjunction with Articles 2(a); 2(d); 3(1)(e) and (f) (none of which distinguish between spare parts and accessories) on the one hand and the franchisor's goods on the other. As neither word is defined one must carefully consider their meanings. Is ice an accessory to a coke? Is a straw an accessory to a milkshake? The restriction seems to be somewhat artificial and unnecessary.

Conditionally cleared restrictions

Article 3(1) permits restrictions:

'Insofar as they are necessary to protect the franchisor's industrial or intellectual property rights or to maintain the common identity and reputation of the franchised network:

These 'whitelisted' obligations include quality control tie-ins, non-competition customer restrictions, advertising and other miscellaneous matters. They are all exempted conditionally upon the terms set out above, and so require a good deal of examination as regards the necessity for them.

'Article 3 shall apply notwithstanding the presence of any of the following obligations on the franchisee, insofar as they are necessary to protect the franchisor's industrial or intellectual property rights or to maintain the common identity and reputation of the franchised network:

(a) to sell, or use in the course of the provision of services, exclusively goods matching minimum objective quality specifications laid down by the franchisor.

(b) to sell, or use in the course of the provision of services, goods which are manufactured only by the franchisor or by third parties designated by it, where it is impracticable, owing to the nature of the goods which are the subject matter of the franchise, to apply objective quality specifications.

(c) not to engage, directly or indirectly, in any similar business in a territory where it would compete with a member of the franchised network, including the franchisor; the franchisee may be held to this obligation after termination of the agreement, for a reasonable period which may not exceed one year, in the territory where it has exploited the franchise.

(d) not to acquire financial interests in the capital of a competing undertaking, which would give the franchisee the power to influence the economic conduct of such undertaking.

(e) to sell the goods which are the subject matter of the franchise only to end users, to other franchisees and to resellers within other channels of distribution supplied by the manufacturer of these goods or with its consent.

(f) to use its best endeavours to sell the goods or provide the services that are the subject matter of the franchise; to offer for sale a minimum range of goods, achieve a minimum turnover, plan its orders in advance, keep minimum stocks and provide customer and warranty services.

(g) to pay to the franchisor a specified proportion of its revenue for advertising and itself carry out advertising for the nature of which it shall obtain the franchisor's approval.'

Quality control

Such restrictions are clearly necessary to enable the franchise network to function in an appropriate commercial manner. It is also possible to set down such specifications for spare parts and accessories which are sold or used in the course of providing services.

This is further buttressed by the subsequent article.

Tie-in

The real problem here is that it is uncertain exactly what constitutes impracticality. This must surely be a question of fact but without any guidance from the Commission or the Court it is somewhat unsatisfactory.

The exemptions given to Computerland and Service Master give a limited indication of what might be acceptable and it is suggested that the majority of properly constituted business format franchises will not have any problems on this count.

It should always be borne in mind, however, that any such restrictions which are not necessary will fall foul of the blacklist in Article 5(b) (see below).

Non-competition

This provision again allows the grant of exclusivity to franchisees by permitting restrictions to be placed upon their peers, so long as such restrictions are necessary to protect the franchisor's industrial or intellectual property or to maintain the common identity and reputation of the network. Proving such necessity to the Commission may well prove to be more difficult than it would at first seem. The argument for such necessity will usually be that too intense a degree of intrabrand competition could lower the network's standards and make it difficult for new franchisees to become established. The success of such an argument will, it seems, inevitably depend upon the facts of the particular case particularly the nature of the franchise business, competition in the market and the prior knowledge of new franchisees.

The post-term restriction is good news for the franchisor, as it will enable it to take over a franchisee's business following termination of the franchise agreement. Such restriction is not, however, intended to entirely preclude a franchisee from competing with the franchisor in the future. It would appear that it aims to allow the franchisor to take back the goodwill of the franchise vested in a particular outlet. The restriction is, therefore, only allowed for 'a reasonable period which may not exceed one year in the territory where it has exploited the franchise'.

It would seem that the Commission did not consider whether such competition would include the power to influence the economic conduct of an undertaking allowed during the term by 3(1)(d). If it does then it could mean that the franchisee must divest itself of such an interest which is lawfully held during the term of the agreement.

The restriction is far narrower than the *Pronuptia* judgment which did not prescribe a time limit. If a longer period is required by the franchisor it may, therefore, be possible to successfully apply for negative clearance or individual exemption. It may even be possible to apply through the Regulation's opposition procedure (see below).

Influence over a competitor

This provision is a product of the Commission's concern on the one hand to encourage small and medium sized businesses to expand and on the other to protect the franchisor's legitimate interests.

Interestingly, a lesser provision in the Service Master agreement restricting the franchisee from engaging in a competing business (other than through the acquisition of not more than 5% of the Capital of a publicly quoted company) was cleared as not infringing Article 85(1).

Customer restriction

This restriction links in with Article 4(a)(see below), which requires all agreements taking advantage of the regulation to be able to cross supply/source with other franchisees and distributors. The aim of this is to ensure that there is no price discrimination between franchisees/other distributors.

Subject to this the restriction seeks to prevent the establishment of other parallel distribution channels which are not sanctioned by the franchisor. It is suggested that this restriction extends to spare parts and accessories (see clause 2(e) above).

Miscellaneous restrictions

These restrictions are all vitally important to a franchise as they permit the franchisor to ensure that the network operates on a commercially viable basis.

These clauses were endorsed by the Commission in both *Computerland* (at paragraph 23(iv)16) and *ServiceMaster* (at paragraph 16).

Advertising

The Commission recognises that one of the great advantages of franchising to the franchisee is the resulting access to collective advertising on a regional, national and international level. Without an advertising levy the market penetration of many franchises would be at a far lower level. This freedom is, however, tempered by the requirement elsewhere in the regulation (Article 5(e) below) that franchisees are able to determine their own prices.

Advertising levies paid/calculated in some other way are also likely to be acceptable to the Commission (this list is not exhaustive).

Local advertising is also seen as necessarily being subject to the franchisor's control to protect its legitimate interests.

Article 3(2) – Unconditionally cleared restrictions

The clearance given to the following restrictions is not conditional upon the need to protect the franchisor's intellectual property rights etc. However, it is interesting to note that in the original drafts these restrictions were also stated to be conditionally allowed as are those contained in Article 3(1).

The reason for this late change of heart is not clear to the author, but is nevertheless welcomed.

Article 3(2) provides that

'Article 1 shall apply notwithstanding the presence of any of the following obligations on the franchisee:

(a) not to disclose to third parties the know-how provided by the franchisor; the franchisee may be held to this obligation after termination of the agreement.

(b) to communicate to the franchisor any experience gained in exploiting the franchise and to other franchisees, non-exclusive know-how resulting from that experience.

(c) to inform the franchisor of infringements of licensed industrial or intellectual property rights, to take legal action against infringers or to assist the franchisor in any legal actions against infringers.

(d) not to use know-how licensed by the franchisor for purposes other than the exploitation of the franchise; the franchisee may be held to this obligation after termination of the agreement.

(e) to attend or have its staff attend training course arranged by the franchisor.

(f) to apply the commercial methods devised by the franchisor, including any subsequent modification thereof, and use the licensed industrial or intellectual property rights.

(g) to comply with the franchisor's standards for the equipment and presentation of the contract premises and/or means of support.

(h) to allow the franchisor to carry out checks of the contract premises and/or means of transport, including the goods sold and the services provided, and the inventory and accounts of the franchisee.

(i) not without the franchisor's consent to change the location of the contract premises.

(j) not without the franchisor's consent to assign the rights and obligations under the franchise agreement.'

Article 3(3), however, exempts these restrictions from article 85(1) in the event that they may fall within it.

Confidentiality

The Commission is always willing to recognise the need for confidentiality in relationships such as franchising. The post term requirement is commercially very important and unlike the restriction on competing is not restricted to a maximum of one year. Indeed there is not even a restriction on the obligation to the time during which the know-how is not in the public domain.

Improvements

This obligation is similar to that allowed by the Commission in *ServiceMaster*, where it stated [para. 14]

'The franchisee's obligation to communicate to Service Master any improvements he makes in the operation of the business. Their grant back obligation is made on a non-exclusive and reciprocal basis. It will improve the efficiency of the Service Master franchise network by creating a free interchange of improvements between all franchisees'.

Bearing in mind the fact that, according to John Love's book *Behind the Golden Arches*, all of the successful innovations of MacDonalds originated from franchises (whilst those of the franchisor failed badly), such a requirement would seem to be essential to the proper functioning of a network.

Infringements

The policing requirement is clearly to the good of both the franchisor and franchisees alike. The likelihood of franchisees locating an infringer, especially with an international

franchise are much greater than the franchisor finding it. Similarly logistically it may be far easier for the franchisee rather than the franchisor to take any necessary legal action.

Use of know-how

The clause affords additional protection to the franchisor's know-how not only during the term of the agreement but also post term – without any time limit. Thus although a former franchisee can compete with the franchisor after the expiry of a reasonable period not exceeding one year (Article 3(1)(c) above), it must compete without recourse to the franchisor's know-how. The difficulty of enforcing such a restriction is of course compounded by the low level nature of much franchising know-how – although the franchisor's method of stock control may be unique it may not differ so very much from normal trade practices. In such a case proving use of the franlchisor's know-how will inevitably be difficult and depend entirely on the facts of the case.

Training

This is essential for the success of franchising networks and shows some degree of appreciation of the dynamics of franchising by the Commission.

Methods

The Commission has accepted the necessity for such tight control in both Pronuptia and various individual exemptions, notably ServiceMaster and Yves Rocher.

Standards

This restriction is again one which is fundamental to the success of franchising.

Location

This should be distinguished from Article 2(c) which allows the obligation to sell only from the franchised premises. If the franchisor unreasonably refuses its consent it is possible that consent may be withdrawn under Article 8(c) (see below).

Non-assignment

This is fundamental to the franchisee's control of the network and was accepted by the Commission in Service Master.

Article 4. — Compulsory provisions

In Article 4 the Regulation is stated to apply only if the following provisions are contained in the franchise agreement:

'The exemption provided for in Article 1 shall apply on condition that:

(a) the franchisee is free to obtain the goods that are the subject matter of the franchisee from other franchisees; where such goods are also distributed through another network of authorised distributors, the franchisee must be free to obtain the goods from the latter.

(b) where the franchisor obliges the franchisee to honour guarantees for the franchisor's goods, that obligation shall apply in respect of such goods supplied by any member of the franchised network or other distributors which give a similar guarantee, in the common market.

(c) the franchisee is obliged to indicate its status as an independent undertaking; this indication shall however not interfere with the common identity of the franchised network resulting in particular from the common name or shop sign and uniform appearance of the contract premises and/or means of transport.'

The need for these provisions is explained in recital (12) as follows:

'The Regulation must specify the conditions which must be satisfied for the exemption to apply. To guarantee that competition is not eliminated for a substantial part of the goods which are the subject of the franchise, it is necessary that parallel imports remain possible. Therefore, cross deliveries between franchisees should always be possible. Furthermore, where a franchise network is combined with another distribution system, franchisees should be free to obtain supplies from authorised distributors. To better inform customers, thereby helping to ensure that they receive a fair share of the resulting benefits, it must be provided that the franchisee shall be obliged to indicate its status as an independent undertaking, by any appropriate means which does not jeopardise the common identity of the franchised network. Furthermore, where the franchisees have to honour guarantees for the franchisor's goods, this obligation should also apply to goods supplied by the franchisor, other franchisees or other agreed dealers.'

It is unlikely that even individual exemptions will be given if the provisions are not included in an agreement according to one Commission official.

The *Pronuptia* case stated in clause 21

'Thanks to the control exercised by the franchisor over the selection of goods offered by the franchisee, the public can find at each franchisee's shop merchandise of the same quality. It can be impractical in certain cases, such as the field of fashion goods, to formulate objective quality specifications. Enforcing such specifications can also, because of the large number of franchisees, impose too great a cost on the franchisor. A clause prescribing that the franchisee can only sell products provided by the franchisor or by suppliers selected by him must, in these circumstances, be considered necessary for the protection of the reputation of the network. It must not however, operate to prevent the franchisee from obtaining the products from other franchisees.'

The result of the Commission's adoption of this approach is that it is impossible for the franchisor to adopt different pricing policies in different member states, so working against the single market.

The stance taken on guarantees follows the Commission's long-standing conviction that improper use of guarantee systems can substantially interfere with interstate trade and so prevent the creation of a true single market.

The requirement for disclosure of the franchisee's status was a late addition to the regulation. It is in no way arduous and one would expect franchisors in any event to insist on such a provision to restrict their liability to third parties for the franchisee's acts and omissions.

The Blacklist

Recital 13 of the Regulation emphasises the need for this blacklist. It states:

'The Regulation must also specify restrictions which may not be included in franchise agreements if these are to benefit from the exemption granted by the Regulation, by virtue of the fact that such provisions are restrictions falling under Article 85(1) for which there is no general presumption that they will lead to the positive effects required by Article 85(3). This applies in particular to market sharing between competing manufacturers, to clauses unduly limiting the franchisee's choice of suppliers or customers, and to cases where the franchisee is restricted in determining its prices. However, the franchisor should be free to recommend prices to the franchisees, where it is not prohibited by national laws and to the extent that it does not lead to concerted practices for the effective application of these prices.'

The recital does not, however, give any reason for the inclusion of particular clauses.

Valentine Korah suggests in 'Franchising and the EEC Competition Rules: Regulation 4087/88' that:

'It may possibly be argued that a blacklist clause that does not restrict competition does not prevent the application of the exemption, but this is far from clear. It is based on the belief that the Commission should not prevent the application of the regulation to transactions which the Commission states are desirable, unless the ancillary provisions restrict competition.

Such a conclusion cannot be derived from the words of the legislation. Recital 13 does not state that the listed clauses do infringe article 85(1), but only that there is no generally positive presumption about such clauses. Article 1(2) of the empowering regulation, No. 19/65 provides:

The Regulation shall define the categories of agreements to which it applies and shall specify in particular:

(a) the restrictions or clauses which must not be contained in the agreements;
(b) the clauses which must be contained in the agreements, or the other conditions which must be satisfied.

It empowers the Commission to blacklist clauses even if they do not infringe Article 85(1). One would have to argue, therefore, either that the Commission has purported to list the provisions on the basis that they do infringe, and that if one can convince a court that they do not, then the reason for the list is gone and with it the consequences. Alternatively, one might argue that regulation 19/65 was made under Article 87 of the Treaty, which provides for legislation only to implement the competition rules. There is no case law to support either proposition.'

It would, therefore, seem that the blacklist may not be as deadly as it at first seems. However, to challenge its validity would be a mammoth task. It is likely that franchisor's will prefer to adopt more commercially fruitful approaches than expend vast amounts on legal fees.

The provisions blacklisted are as follows:

'The exemption granted by Article 1 shall not apply where:

(a) undertakings producing goods or providing services which are identical or are considered by users as equivalent in view of their characteristics, price and intended use, enter into franchise agreements in respect of such goods or services.

(b) without prejudice to Article 2(e) and Article 3(1)(b), the franchisee is prevented from obtaining supplies of goods of a quality equivalent to those offered by the franchisor.

(c) without prejudice to Article 2(e), the franchisee is obliged to sell, or use in the process of providing services, goods manufactured by the franchisor or third parties designated by the franchisor and the franchisor refuses, for reasons other than protecting the franchisor's industrial or intellectual property rights, or maintaining the common identity and reputation of the franchised network, to designate as authorised manufacturers third parties proposed by the franchisee.

(d) the franchisee is prevented from continuing to use the licensed know-how after termination of the agreement where the know-how has become generally known or easily accessible, other than by breach of an obligation by the franchisee.

(e) the franchisee is restricted by the franchisor, directly or indirectly, in the determination of sale prices for the goods or services which are the subject matter of the franchise, without prejudice to the possibility for the franchisor of recommending sale prices.

(f) the franchisor prohibits the franchisee from challenging the validity of the industrial or intellectual property rights which form part of the franchise, without prejudice to the possibility for the franchisor of terminating the agreement in such a case.

(g) franchisees are obliged not to supply within the common market the goods or services which are the subject matter of the franchise to end users because of their place of residence.'

Market sharing

The concept of market sharing is anathema to the Commission and so its inclusion in the blacklist comes as no surprise.

The clause will, as suggested by M de Cockborne of the EC Commission ((1989) *Journal of International Franchising and Distribution Law* 101), most likely apply as between a franchisor and a sub-franchisor.

Tie-ins

These blacklisted provisions are very much a mixed bag. Article 5(6) is unlikely to have much effect on properly constituted business format franchises in practice as it is difficult to imagine any tie required by a responsible franchisor that could not be justified under Aricle 2(e) or cleared under Article 3(1)(b).

Article 5(c), however, is somewhat cumbersome and could well necessitate the franchisor to instigate a procedure for approving supplies of spare parts and accessories put forward by the franchisees, unless they are proved to be necessary to protect the franchisor's intellectual property rights and the like.

Post-term use of know-how

The Commission reflects in blacklist item (d) its dislike of any restrictions upon an individual's right to make his own living. However, in doing so it creates a potential problem for the franchisor. It only needs one franchisee to place the know-how in the public domain and the franchisor is severely compromised. It must then rely solely upon its intellectual property rights, name and reputation. More importantly, of course, if the know-how is placed in the public domain the franchisor may no longer be able to claim the protection of the block exemption as the know-how will no longer be secret as defined in Article 1(g). This underlines the importance of the franchisor continually developing and refining its know-how.

Resale price maintenance

This clause also casts light upon the Commission's long-standing prejudices. Price maintenance is anathema to the Commission and will not be tolerated − be it maximum or minimum price maintenance.

No challenge

It is no surprise that this clause is included in the blacklist, but one must question its commercial value bearing in mind the franchisor's right to terminate. This means that a franchisee will only challenge the rights if it wishes to end its involvement in the franchise − which will not always be the case.

The franchisor may wish to try and obtain further protection for the rights following the lead set by Computerland which had the franchisee acknowledge in the agreement the value and goodwill of the rights.

Customer discrimination

Whilst market sharing is condoned by the Commission in Article 2, the blacklist prohibits customer sharing. The concept of residence is potentially problematic and may require interpretation by the Commission or the Court in due course.

THE OPPOSITION PROCEDURE

The opposition procedure contained in Articles 6 and 7 is a device adopted by the Commission to lessen its work load and at the same time give franchisors a quicker response and greater degree of certainty as regards their agreements.

The rationale for the procedure is summarised in Recital 14 which states that:

'Agreements which are not automatically covered by the exemption because they contain provisions that are not expressly exempted by the Regulation and not expressly excluded from exemption may nonetheless generally be presumed to be eligible for application of Article 85(3). It will be possible for the Commission rapidly to establish whether this is the case for a particular agreement. Such agreements should therefore be deemed to be covered by the exemption provided for in this Regulation where they are notified to the Commission and the Commission does not oppose the application of the exemption within a specified period of time.'

The opposition procedure is available to agreements which satisfy the requirements of Articles 4 and 5.

Such agreements must be notified to the Commission and if not opposed within a period of six months can take advantage of the block exemption.

Examination of the Commission's 15th, 16th and 17th reports on competition policy indicates why it favours this approach. In 1988 it managed to grant only ten individual exemptions – a larger number than in any previous year. All of these made heavy demands upon the Commission's resources. By comparison in 1985 it received 14 notifications under various opposition procedures, of which nine were invalid, one was opposed and four were valid.

In 1986 there were 32 notifications under the opposition procedure and in 1987 a further four. A further four occurred in 1988.

The attraction for the franchisor is that if it has any doubts about the agreement's compatibility with the block exemption it can notify it to the Commission without the usual long wait for a decision. This notification is likely to result in an actual exemption rather than merely a comfort letter (see above).

However, the procedure is not without problems and Valentine Korah ('Franchising and the EEC Competition Rules: Regulation 4087/88') suggests that the 'vires' for it is open to question. Professor Korah argues that Regulation 19/65 (under which the regulation is made) does not expressly provide for the Commission to have any discretion once the group exemption has been adopted. She also quotes the Deringer Report (Doc. 104/1960–1961) which questioned the validity of a provision that agreements should become provisionally valid if notified to the Commission in the absence of opposition within six months.

On a more practical level there are problems as regards the exact status of an agreement that has been notified under the opposition procedure less than six months previously. It may be unlikely that disputes over the agreement will arise at such an early stage, but on a purely commercial basis it can create problems. How can franchisees (and indeed the franchisor) be expected to commit substantial time, effort and money when the agreement may have to be substantially rewritten? It is suggested that such periods of uncertainty are inevitable in any notification system and that six months is far preferable to the much longer delays experienced with applications for clearance and individual exemptions under Article 85(3).

Applications under the opposition procedure are made on form A/B, and must make particular mention of Article 6 of the Regulation.

In practice application will usually be made at the same time for negative clearance, individual exemption and perhaps a comfort letter (see above).

Opposition to the application by the Commission will be in writing, as will any withdrawal of its opposition.

It would appear that there is no mechanism by which a third party can complain about the exemption of an agreement under the opposition procedure, although under Article 6(5) and (6) member states are allowed three months within which they can require the Commission to oppose exemption and such opposition can then only be withdrawn with the member state's consent. If a third party wishes to prevent exemption, therefore, it must first of all have intelligence of the application (which is not a matter of public record).

As there is no decision given by the Commission (it is automatic after six months) there is no 'act' against which a third party can complain. Thus the only route is for the third party to complain to its national Office of Fair Trading or other regulatory authority and request it to notify the Commission of its opposition to exemption. The need for prior intelligence and three-month time limit for member state opposition, however, makes this somewhat unlikely.

SUMMARY

The adoption of the Franchise Block Exemption was without doubt a very positive step for franchising in the European Community. It in many ways signified its 'coming-of-age' as a way of doing business within, and between, the twelve member states.

The Regulation is not however all that franchisors might have wanted, and whereas the *Pronuptia* decision was, on the whole, a fairly liberal one, the Commission chose what is in many ways a far more conservative approach.

Whereas the court cleared many clauses on the ground that they do not infringe Article 85(1) as they are needed to protect the uniformity and reputation of the franchise network the Commission requires (in Article 3(1)) that they must be justified on that ground.

Such clauses include those imposing quality control, tie-ins, non-competition, customer restrictions, best endeavours and advertising requirements.

The court also took a more liberal view on other issues too. For example, whereas the regulation permits post-term competition restrictions only for a reasonable period not exceeding one year, the court did not think it necessary to stipulate a maximum time limit, so long as the restriction's duration was reasonable.

It would, however, be wrong to regard the *Pronuptia* decision as more liberal in every aspect. Whereas the court was willing to allow tie-ins only if less restrictive measures would not work, the regulation conditionally exempts tie-ins if the aim is to achieve uniform quality.

Although perhaps not as sympathetic as the court's decision in *Pronuptia*, Regulation 4087/88 follows its lead. It might however have been better if the Commission had adopted a very different approach, based more upon economic conditions, that is to say the interbrand and intrabrand competition. Such an approach would mean that franchise networks would usually be able to take advantage of the block exemption during their early days; only when they had acquired a notable market share would they have to consider the need to apply for individual exemption.

STRATEGIC APPROACH TO EC LAW

It is clearly important for franchisors in the European Community to confront the competition law issues in order to assist the ultimate success of their networks. Failure to be sensitive to the issues involved may result not only in the imposition of substantial fines, but also in the destruction of the entire contractual base of the network.

The following is a suggested modus operandii for deciding which approach to take on the EC anti-trust issues.

(1) Can the franchise agreement be drafted so as to both come within Regulation 4087/88 and satisfy the commercial needs of the Franchisor? − if so, take advantage of the franchise block exemption.

(2) If (1) is not possible, what is the worldwide turnover of the parties and the market share? If the aggregate annual turnover of the participating undertakings does not exceed 200 million ECU and the goods or services do not represent more than five per cent of the total market for such goods or services in the area of the Common Market affected by the agreement, it will be able to take advantage of the 'de minimis' exemption. Great care should be taken however

not to 'creep' outside of the exemption in the future (see above).

(3) If (1) and (2) are not possible can the franchise agreement be drafted so as to be commercially acceptable and possibly come within the block exemption? If so, notify the agreement under Article 6(1) of Regulation 4087/88, the so-called 'Opposition Procedure' (in reality this is usually done in conjunction with an application for individual exemption and possibly negative clearance also).

(4) If the Opposition Procedure is not available apply for negative clearance and/or individual exemption under Article 85(3).

ANNEX 1

ANALYSIS OF PROVISIONS IN PRONUPTIA, YVES ROCHER, COMPUTERLAND SERVICEMASTER AND CHARLES JOURDAN AGREEMENTS

Clause	Pronuptia	Yves Rocher	Computerland	ServiceMaster	Charles Jourdan
1. Exclusivity					
(a) *Provisions*	Exclusive territory	Exclusive territory	Exclusive territory	Restriction on setting up outlets outside of the territory	Franchisees and corner franchisees have limited exclusivity
	Operation only from approved premises	Operation only from approved premises	Restriction on opening second shop	Restriction on active sales promotion outside of the territory	Only franchised outlet in the territory (although competing franchise corner retailers and traditional retailers exist in the territory)
	Franchisee receives 10% of any mail order sales by franchisor in the territory	Franchisor retained mail order sale rights	Satellite shops allowed outside of the territory		Operation only from approved outlets
(b) *Market*	Substantial inter-brand competition. Most competition did not operate through franchises	Concentrated	Market share less than 5% (3.3% of retail sales in EC in 1986)	6% market share in UK and under 5% in Common Market as a whole	Less than 10% in France and approximately 2% in the Common Market as a whole
	No market share figure	In France franchisor supplied 15% of any product and 7.5% of cosmetics as a whole	Competed with retail networks supplied directly by the manufacturers *plus* other franchisee's satellite shops	Growth expected	
			Exclusive territory was small	Strong interbrand competition	

Clause	Pronuptia	Yves Rocher	Computerland	ServiceMaster	Charles Jourdan
(c) Decision	Restricts competition. Exempted under Article 85(3)	Restricts competition. Exempted under Article 85(3)	Restricts competition. Exempted under Article 85(3)	Restricts competition. Exempted under Article 85(3)	Provision against corner franchisees cleared. Provisions affecting other franchisees restrict competition. Exempted under Article 85(3)

2. Post-term restriction on competition

	Pronuptia	Yves Rocher	Computerland	ServiceMaster	Charles Jourdan
(a) Provision	Not to compete with other franchisees during the term of the agreement and for one year after termination.	Not to compete with other franchisees during the term of the agreement and for one year after termination within its former territory	Not to compete with other franchisees during the term of the agreement and for one year after termination within 10 kilometres of the former franchisee's outlet	Not to actively solicit sales from outside the territory during the term of the agreement and not to compete with other franchisees for one year after termination in the former franchisees territory, and for two years elsewhere	No post-term restrictions
(b) Decision	Cleared	Cleared	Cleared	Cleared	N/A

3. Cross Supplies

	Pronuptia	Yves Rocher	Computerland	ServiceMaster	Charles Jourdan
(a) Provision	Right for franchisees to purchase from other franchisees and other suppliers	Right for franchisees to purchase from other franchisees and other suppliers	Franchisees allowed to buy from franchisor (which operated a central purchasing system). Allowed to buy from other vendors	Equipment to be used had to be approved by franchisor. Certain chemicals had to be purchased from the franchisor or from nominated suppliers or other franchisees	Right for franchisees to buy from or sell to other distributors provided their principal activity did not become that of a wholesaler
(b) Decision	Inserted at Commission's request	Inserted at Commission's request	Cleared	Cleared	Inserted at Commission's request

4. Retail Price Maintenance

	Pronuptia	Yves Rocher	Computerland	ServiceMaster	Charles Jourdan
(a) Provision	Franchisees allowed to set their own retail prices	Franchisees allowed to set their own retail prices	Franchisee obliged to use advertising material made or approved by the franchisor	N/A	N/A
(b) Decision	Inserted at Commission's request	Inserted at Commission's request	Cleared, as aim is to maintain quality control not to interfere with franchisee's right to determine its own prices	N/A	N/A

ANNEX 2

CLAUSES OF FRANCHISE AGREEMENTS AFFECTED BY THE FRANCHISING BLOCK EXEMPTION – COMMISSION REGULATION (EEC) NO. 4087/88

The block exemption details what provisions must, can and cannot be incorporated into franchise agreements.

The table details these in what is hopefully an easily understandable form in the left-hand column and gives examples of relevant clauses which might commonly be found in franchise agreements in the right-hand column. (It should be borne in mind that these clauses are only examples and that every franchise will have different requirements and hence slightly different provisions in its agreement.) The clauses given in Article 5 are examples of *prohibited* clauses.

1. Article 2

Exempted restrictions

The Franchisor

The franchisor can agree with the franchisee not to do any of the following in the contract Territory:

Not to grant the franchise to another franchisee.

Not to compete with the franchisee.

Not itself to supply competing goods to any third parties.

The franchisor hereby grants to the franchisee the exclusive right to carry on the business in the Territory for the duration of this agreement and agrees not to compete with the franchisee in any way nor to supply directly the Goods to third parties in the Territory during the duration of this Agreement.

The Master Franchisee

The master franchisee/area developer may agree not to grant franchises outside of the contract Territory.

The master franchisee shall have the right to operate the services within the Territory through wholly owned limited liability companies or through franchising the business to third parties within the Territory. The master franchisee shall not be permitted to actively carry on the business outside of the Territory through wholly owned limited liability companies or through sub-franchises granted to third parties.

The Franchisee

A franchisee may agree:
(a) Only to run the franchise from named premises.

(b) Not to solicit custom from outside the contract territory.

(c) Not to manufacture, sell or use in the course of providing services competing goods (although spare parts are not covered by this exemption).

The franchisee shall operate the business only from the Premises.

The franchisee shall not solicit customers for the franchise from without the Territory, although nothing shall prevent him from meeting the orders of unsolicited customers from outside of the Territory.

The franchisor shall at no time during the continuance of this Agreement and any extension and/or variation thereof engage in or seek to engage in the manufacture sale or use of goods which compete with the Goods, (save that this shall not apply to any provision of spare parts for repair of the Goods).

2. Article 3.1

Conditionally permitted obligations of franchisees

The following obligations can be imposed upon the franchisees, only in so far as is necessary to protect the franchisor's industrial/intellectual property rights or maintain the common identity and reputation of the franchise network.

Comply with quality specifications laid down for goods used/sold.

To tie in goods manufactured by the franchisor or by third parties where quality specifications are not possible due to the nature of the goods.

The franchisee shall only use such Goods in the carrying out of the services as shall meet the minimum technical specifications laid out in schedule 1 hereto.

In order to maintain the high standards of reliability and uniformity of business and to enable the franchisees and other franchisees to enjoy the benefit of bulk purchase supply to the franchisees, during the term of this Agreement the franchisee shall purchase the Goods specified in Schedule 1 hereto from the franchisor, other franchisees and such third parties as are indicated in Schedule II.

Non-competition clauses during and post-term against both franchisor and any other franchisees in a territory where it would compete with the network (the post-term restrictions can last for up to one year).

The franchisee shall not be engaged, interested or concerned in any business in the Territory or any other territory granted by the Franchisor to another franchisee which may compete with the services or any part of them and during the term or up to one year after the termination of the Agreement including any financial interest in such business which may enable it to influence such business's conduct.

Pay a fixed proportion of revenue as an advertising fee and ensure that all advertising has prior approval of the franchisor.

The franchisee will pay to the franchisor on the first day of every month an Advertising Fee equivalent to 5% of the previous month's gross turnover which monies the franchisor shall use for its national Advertising Budget. In addition to the Advertising Fee, the franchisee shall undertake such local advertising/promotion described in the manual as the franchisor in its reasonable discretion deems necessary in order to properly market the services in the franchisee's locality. All such advertising and promotions must have the prior written consent of the franchisor. In no circumstances will the franchisee undertake any national advertising.

Only to re-sell to end-users, other franchisees and other retailers supplied by the manufacturer or with his consent.

The franchisee shall sell the Goods only to other franchisees and end-users. It shall at no time sell the goods to wholesalers.

Use best endeavours to sell the Goods/provide the Services and offer a minimum range of goods for sale; achieve minimum turnover; plan orders in advance; keep minimum stocks and provide the customer with warranty services.

The franchisee shall during the first year of this Agreement achieve a minimum turnover of £60,000 and thereafter a minimum turnover of £100,000 for the second year which will thereafter increase each subsequent year pro rata with any increase in the retail price index published in the United Kingdom or any index which shall at any time replace the said retail price index. In any event the franchisee shall use its best endeavours to promote the services in the Territory and shall at all times maintain a minimum stock of the Goods so as to enable it to properly meet such demand and carry out appropriate guarantee and warranty work.

3 Article 3.2

Unconditionally permitted obligations of the franchisee

The following obligations can be imposed on the franchisee:

Confidentiality of know-how, during and after the term of the Agreement.

The franchisee will not furnish any information as to the know-how, the methods of operation, publicity, profits, financial affairs, present or future plans or policies of the franchisor or any other information relating to the operation of the franchisor either during the term of the Agreement or at any time after its termination.

The non-exclusive licensing back of any improvements that the franchisee may make.

The franchisee will immediately notify the franchisor of any improvements in the Goods which it makes and upon the request of the franchisor shall grant the franchisor a non-exclusive licence without cost which licence will enable the franchisor to sub-licence the improvements to third parties.

To inform the franchisor of any intellectual property right infringements and take any action against infringers or assist the franchisor to do so.

The franchisee shall immediately inform the franchisor of any infringement of the marks as soon as it shall become aware of the same and any such steps as may be necessary against the infringers to preserve the franchisor's rights shall be taken by the franchisee as directed by the franchisor. The costs of doing so shall be borne entirely by the franchisor.

Comply with the franchisor's standards for Equipment, Transport and Premises.

The franchisee shall ensure that all transport and equipment used by it, in connection with the Business, shall be in such mechanical condition and decorated in such manner as the franchisor shall, from time to time, require.

The franchisee shall ensure that the Premises are, at all times, decorated in such manner and by such signs, insignia and marks as the franchisor shall, from time to time, require.

Only to use the know-how licensed under the Agreement in the exploitation of the franchise during the term of the Agreement and following the termination not to use it in any way at all.

The franchisor shall at all times during the currency of the Agreement, use the know-how licensed to it by the franchisor hereunder only in order to carry out the services in accordance with this Agreement, and after the expiration of the Term or any earlier termination thereof shall not use the know-how.

Allow the franchisor to carry out spot checks of the Premises/Transport including inventory and accounts.

The franchisee shall, at all times, permit the franchisor and any person authorised by the franchisor to visit the Premises and inspect the Equipment and Goods to ensure that they are in a fit state of repair and condition.

The franchisee shall permit the franchisor and any person authorised by it to enter at all reasonable times and upon reasonable notice upon the Premises and inspect all books of account, vouchers and other supporting documentation and correspondence.

Attend or have staff attend training courses arranged by the franchisor.

The franchisor shall, from time to time at the expense of the franchisee, provide the franchisee and his senior staff with such training as the franchisor thinks fit at such place or places in the United Kingdom, as the franchisor may require. The franchisee shall ensure that it and his relevant staff attend such training sessions as and when required.

Not to change location of Premises without the franchisor's consent.

The franchisee shall carry out the Business from the Premises and shall not change the location of the Premises or assign all or part of them to a third party without the prior written consent of the franchisor.

To apply the commercial methods (and any modification thereof) and the licensed industrial/intellectual property rights.

The franchisee shall carry out the Business using the Marks at all times in a manner deemed appropriate by the franchisor.

The franchisee shall carry on the Business in strict accordance with the contents of the Manual as amended from time to time.

Not to assign the rights and obligations under the Franchise Agreement without the franchisor's consent.

The franchisee shall not have the right to assign his rights or obligations under this Agreement but shall have the right at any time to sell the Business with the prior written consent of the franchisor and subject to the conditions listed below. . . .

4. Article 4

Compulsory conditions

These provisions must be contained in any agreement that seeks to take advantage of the Block Exemption.

The franchisee must be able to obtain its goods from other franchisees and any other authorised distributors.	In order to maintain the high standards of reliability and uniformity of business and to enable the franchisees and other franchisees to enjoy the benefit of bulk purchase supply to the franchisees, during the term of this Agreement the franchisee shall purchase the Goods specified in Schedule 1 hereto from the franchisor, other franchisees and such third parties as are indicated in Schedule II.
If there are guarantees to be honoured, the franchisee must honour guarantees on all goods distributed by any franchisee or any distributor which may give a similar guarantee in the Common Market.	The franchisee shall honour all current guarantees on Goods in the Territory regardless of the Goods' origin.
The franchisee must indicate its independent status.	The franchisee shall clearly indicate on all literature and correspondence and by way of a prominently displayed notice board at the Premises the fact that it is an independent franchisee of the franchisor and is in no other way connected with it.

5. Article 5

Prohibited conditions

These provisions must not be contained in any agreement that seeks to take advantage of the Block Exemption. The clauses below are examples of prohibited provisions.

Agreements between competing manufacturers/suppliers of identical or similar services.	Non-applicable.
Prohibitions on alternative sourcing of supplies (without prejudice to Article 3.1 above).	The franchisee shall source the Goods only from the franchisor regardless of the quality, availability and pricing policy of alternate supplies.

If only approved suppliers are permitted in order to preserve quality, reputation, etc. of the franchise *and* the franchisor refuses for reasons other than protecting intellectual property rights, etc.	The franchisee will source the Goods directly from the franchisor or such other parties as the franchisor shall in its complete discretion without limitation, approve. (NB. It is not the clause but the franchisor's actions under it that are prohibited.)
Prohibition of the franchisee using know-how of the franchisor after the termination of the franchise agreement when such know-how has come into the public domain by means other than the franchisee's breach.	The franchisee undertakes not at any time after the termination of this Agreement by whatever means to use the know-how regardless of whether or not it might reasonably be deemed to be within the public domain.
The franchisee is not free to determine its own sales prices (although the franchisor can recommend prices).	The franchise shall ensure that at all times it does not charge less than the minimum sale price detailed in Schedule 1 hereto.
Prevent the franchisee challenging the intellectual/industrial property rights of the franchisor (without prejudice to the franchisor's ability to terminate in such a case).	The franchisee shall at no time seek to challenge the franchisor's rights to the property in the marks.
Discriminating against the supply to end-users on the basis of their place of residence.	The franchisee shall undertake not to supply Goods to purchasers the place of residence of which lies outside of the Territory.

It should be noted that:

(1) Any agreement that fulfils the conditions of Article 4 can take advantage of the Block Exemption even though it contains restrictions on competition which are not covered by Articles 2 and 3 but do not come within Article 5, provided they are notified and not opposed within 6 months of such notification.

(2) Under Article 8 the Commission can withdraw the benefit of the Block Exemption if an agreement, although ostensibly complying with it, has effects incompatible with Article 85(3).

CHAPTER 28

The Know-How Block Exemption

By MARK ABELL

It is quite likely that some franchisors will wish to license their manufacturing know-how to parties in the EC, so as to better ensure supply of their products to their franchisees in the member states. The export of ice cream, for example, from the USA to the EC is not only costly, but takes up valuable management/administrative time. Licensing an Irish or French dairy, for example, to manufacture the ice cream could be a very attractive commercial possibility in such circumstances.

It is quite likely that any agreement licensing the transfer of know-how from one party to another will contain restrictions that are contrary to Article 85 of the EEC Treaty. The know-how block exemption (Regulation EEC 556/89 summarised below; full text in Appendix 10), like the franchise block exemption, is an attempt to reduce the Commission's work-load and facilitate easier licensing of know-how in the EC by granting automatic exemption from Article 85 to agreements which comply with its terms. The patent block exemption (Regulation EEC 2349/84) is very similar to Regulation EEC 556/89 and shares the same objectives, but has largely been eclipsed by the latter and is therefore not considered here.

The definitions contained in the know-how regulation are of great importance and deserve careful consideration. 'Know-how' is defined as a body of technical information which is secret, substantial and identified in some appropriate form.

It seems to have been assumed by the Commission that the term 'technical information' is self-explanatory and it is not defined in the Regulation: but other key words which describe that information are described in some detail in the Article and therefore require close consideration.

The purpose of the insistence upon the know-how being identifiable, secret and substantial (as stated in Article 1.3) is to avoid the drafting of 'sham' agreements the aim of which, rather than licensing know-how, is to carve up the EC market.

The real significance of the know-how Regulation lies in the fact that it covers not only 'pure' know-how licensing agreements but also 'mixed' know-how and patent licensing agreements. Both 'pure' and 'mixed' agreements may contain ancillary provisions relating to trade marks or other industrial or intellectual property rights and must be between only *two* parties.

The restriction of the exemption to bilateral agreements only must be borne in mind, and whereas a parent company and its subsidiary will be considered one party, joint ventures are perceived to be separate entities and thus know-how licensing agreements between two companies and their joint venture will not be able to take advantage of the block exemption, as stated in Article 5.1(2).

For the know-how block exemption to apply to the licensing agreement, it must contain one or more of the right obligations specified in Article 1.1, which basically concern restrictions upon the licensee's and licensor's exploitation of know-how by area and/or time, trade mark usage and quantity. These time limits must be carefully adhered to and include not only those stated below, but also what are described as 'lesser restrictions' (such as agreeing to licence only one other person in the territory). The restrictions are specified in detail in Annex 3 below. The clauses are divided into black clauses (forbidden) and grey clauses (permissible in certain circumstances).

Restraints on manufacture or use and on active selling can be imposed (under Article 1.2) for a period not exceeding 10 years from the date of signature of the first licence agreement entered into in respect of the same technology, whilst a restraint on passive selling can run for a period not exceeding 5 years from the date of signature of the first licence agreement entered into by the licensor within the EC in respect of the same technology.

These first six restrictions are all stated to relate to the 'same technology', which Article 1.7(8) defines as meaning 'the technology as licensed to the first licensee and enhanced by any improvements made thereto subsequently irrespective of whether and to what extent such improvements are exploited by the parties or other licensees and irrespective of whether the technology is protected by necessary patents in any member states.'

The important point to note here is that it is not possible to extend the protection period by holding up an improvement as an entirely new piece of technology. If the technology is substantially improved, then in order to obtain a further period of exemption it will be necessary to enter into a new licence agreement. The problem in such cases will of course be identifying the know-how and proving that it is substantial in its own right, separate from the original technology licensed.

In the previous draft of the Regulation the maximum period that the restriction could be imposed for was 7 years and it is only due to a great deal of lobbying by interested parties that it has been increased in the final draft to 10 years. The initial seven-year period over which protection could be granted was only cautiously welcomed as, although it represented a clear recognition of the fact that a stream of know-how can amount to intellectual property deserving protection, it was felt that it was unnecessarily short and should be more in line with the ten-year period recognised by the Commission in the case of *Boussis Interpane* (15.12.86, OJ 1987 L50, 19.2.87). The Commission has accepted this point but still feels able to allow prohibition of passive sales for a period of only up to 5 years.

The know-how block exemption may well become very important to draftsmen preparing know-how licenses within the EC. Its provisions are complex and require careful consideration, but it amounts to an EC green light for the use of know-how licensing as an aggressive tool to exploit the post-1992 single market, and hence provides a useful addition to a franchisors' options in the EC.

ANNEX 1

THE KNOW-HOW BLOCK EXEMPTION SUMMARISED (EC REGULATION 556/89)

Article 1.1 (Permitted length of restrictions)

Article	Restriction	Period	Comments/Effect
1.1(1)	An obligation on the licensor not to licence other undertakings to exploit the licensed technology in the licensed territory.	Not exceeding for each territory 10 years from the date of signature of the first licence agreement entered into by the licensor for that territory in respect of the same technology *or* the life of any *necessary* patents.	Provides for imposition of sole territory (in which the licensor will not compete with the licensee).
1.1(2)	An obligation on the licensor not to exploit the licensed technology in the licensed territory himself.	Not exceeding for each territory 10 years from the date of signature of the first licence agreement entered into by the licensor for that territory in respect of the same technology *or* the life of any *necessary* patents.	Provides for exclusivity (in which no-one will compete with the licensee). In order to take advantage of this exemption the licensee must manufacture or prepare to manufacture the licensed product by itself of through a connected undertaking or subcontractor.
1.1(3)	An obligation on the licensee not to exploit the licensed technology in territories within the Common Market which are reserved for the licensor.	Not exceeding for each territory 10 years from the date of signature of the first licence agreement entered into by the licensor for that territory in respect of the same technology *or* the life of any *necessary* patents.	Allows licensor to retain exclusive areas. In order to take advantage of the exemption the licensor must manufacture or prepare to manufacture the licensed product by itself or through a connected undertaking or sub-contractor.
1.1(4)	An obligation on the licensee not to manufacture or use the licensed product, or use the licensed process, in territories within the Common Market which are licensed to other licensees.	Not exceeding ten years from the date of signature of the first licence agreement entered into by the licensor within the EC in respect of the same technology or the life of any necessary patent.	This is essential as it allows the granting of exclusive territories to other licensees.
1.1(5)	An obligation on the licensee not to pursue an active policy of putting the licensed product on the market in the territories within the Common Market which are licensed to other licensees, and in particular not to engage in advertising specifically aimed at those territories or to establish any branch or maintain any distribution depot there.	Not exceeding ten years from the date of signature of the first licence agreement entered into by the licensor within the EC in respect of the same technology *or* the life of any *necessary* patent.	This permits a restriction upon active sales (as contrasted with passive sales). In order to take advantage of this exemption the licensee must manufacture or prepare to manufacture the licensed product by itself or through a connected undertaking or sub-contractor.

Article	Restriction	Period	Comments/Effect
1.1(6)	An obligation on the licensee not to put the licensed product on the market in the territories licensed to other licensees within the Common Market.	Not exceeding five years from the date of the signature of the first licence agreement entered into by the licensor within the EC in respect of the same technology.	This permits a restriction upon passive sales. In order to take advantage of this exemption the licensee must manufacture or prepare to manufacture the licensed product by itself or through a connected undertaking or sub-contractor.
1.1(7)	An obligation on the licensee to use only the licensor's trademark or the get-up determined by the licensor to distinguish the licensed product during the term of the agreement, provided that the licensee is not prevented from identifying himself as the manufacturer of the licensed products.	Duration of the Agreement.	This 'own use' quantitative restriction enables the licensor to retain some control over the licensed product and to prevent any flooding of the market. By implication this may also restrict potential parallel imports of the product to other territories.

Article 2 (Permitted Provisions)

Article	Summary	Suggested clause	Comments
2(1)	Confidentiality of know-how both during and post-term.	Both during the term and after its expiration the licensee shall use its best endeavours to preserve the secrecy of all confidential information, keeping it protected against loss, theft or damage, ensuring that such know-how is still secret and is not used by it, or its employees, officers or agents except in accordance with this agreement.	This is clearly essential. Without such a clause the licensor could not consider licensing its know-how.
2(2)	Not to sub-licence or assign.	The licensee shall not sub-licence or assign the benefit of this licence to any third party.	The licensor must be able to control its own know-how.
2(3)	In so far as know-how is still secret, not to exploit it post-term.	(See Article 2(1) above).	The problem here, as always with know-how, is enforcement and proving that the know-how is still secret.
2(4)	Non-exclusive grant back to the licensor of any improvements provided that the licensee itself is able to exploit them and that the licensor has no greater right to use them than the licensee.	If the licensee shall devise an improvement it shall disclose to the licensor the nature and means of making use of it and will grant to the licensor a non-exclusive licence to use and sub-licence the use of the improvement anywhere except within the territory.	This is in line with the Commission's general approach to grant backs and does not allow exclusive grant backs that would be restrictive on trade.

Article	Summary	Suggested clause	Comments
2(5)	The imposition of minimum quality specifications.	In order to ensure the satisfactory exploitation of the know-how the licensee shall ensure that all of the products manufactured by it comply with the minimum quality specifications contained in Schedule 1 hereto.	These must be set by objective standards as provided in the *Windsurfing* case. It is therefore not sufficient for the licence to provide that quality must be 'up to the licensor's reasonable demands', consent not to be 'unreasonably withheld'. This is further complicated by the fact that despite the removal of technical barriers in accord with the Single European Act, member states still have differing technical requirements in many areas. There is also a question as to whether or not any 'tie-ins' permitted by this provision would be allowable under each member state's law — there would certainly seem to be a clash with UK law in the form of the Patent Act (see Article 3(3)).
2(6)	To assist the licensor in policing the know-how *but* without prejudice to the licensee's right to challenge the validity of any patents licensed, which is also preserved by Article 32(4).	The licensee shall (without prejudice to its inalienable right to challenge the validity of the know-how or patents and the licensor's proprietorship thereof) immediately notify the licensor of any actual or potential infringement of the know-how or patents and assist the licensor in the prevention of any such infringement in any such reasonable manner as the licensor requires at the licensor's sole cost.	This provision is clearly important from the licensor's point of view as it enables it to police the know-how more easily in other member states.
2(7)	Despite the know-how becoming public knowledge (other than by the acts of the licensor) to provide for the continued payment of royalties under the agreement.	The licensee shall pay the licensor royalties for the duration of the term notwithstanding that the know-how has become public knowledge, unless such public knowledge results directly from the act of the licensor.	This is clear evidence of the Commission's intention not to interfere with the commercial bargain struck by the parties and should be read together with Article 7(7) which provides that the Commission can withdraw the benefit of the block exemption if the agreement is incompatible with Article 85(3) of the Treaty of Rome because the period for which the licensee is obliged to continue paying royalties after the know-how has become publicly known by the action of third parties substantially exceeds the lead time acquired because of the head start in production and marketing and this obligation is detrimental to competition in the market. But see Article 3(5) below.

Article	Summary	Suggested clause	Comments
2(8)	Obligation to restrict exploitation of know-how to certain fields.	The licensee shall use the know-how only for the manufacture, use, sale and distribution of the products in the territory.	Although 'use sharing' is allowed, it should be noted that customer sharing is *not* permitted (see Article 3(7)).
2(9)	Minimum royalties and production targets are allowed.	In each year of the term licensee shall pay to the licensor by way of royalties a sum of no less than . . . (the minimum royalty) and if the total royalties paid in any one year shall be less than the minimum royalty, the licensee shall, within 14 days of the year end, pay the licensor the balance due.	It is essential to take note of Article 7(8) if the parties were already competitors before the grant of the licence, as if the targets effectively prevent the licensee using competing technologies the Commission have the power to withdraw the benefit of the Block Exemption.
2(10)	Not to discriminate between different licensees by providing that the licensee be granted any more favourable terms granted to later licensees.	If the licensor shall enter into an agreement to licence the know-how to a third party in the EC and such licence shall contain terms more favourable to that third party than the terms of the Agreement are to the licensee, then the licensor shall forthwith agree to vary the terms of the agreement so as they are no less favourable than the terms granted to the third party.	This enables licensees to retain their competitiveness with later licensees who obtain say a lower royalty rate. The licensor may well seek to resist such a clause.
2(11)	To mark the licensed products with the licensor's name.	The licensee shall affix to a conspicuous part of the products it manufactures a durable label indicating that it is manufactured under licence from the licensor.	This is essential to the licensor who wishes to establish its name/marks in the licensee's territory and so build up a degree of goodwill in the products on its own behalf. This market penetration will be central to any sales drive it makes on its own behalf after the expiry of the license agreement.
2(12)	Not to use the know-how to construct facilities for third parties and so effectively breach the confidentiality obligation.	The licensee (without prejudice to its right to increase its own manufacturing capacity or set up additional facilities for its own use on normal commercial terms) shall under no circumstances use the know-how to construct facilities for third parties.	Such an action would clearly be against the spirit of most licensing agreements and amount to a breach of confidentiality.

Article 3 (Prohibited Provisions)

Article	Summary	Typical prohibited clause	Comments
3(1)	Post-term non-use restrictions where the know-how has become public knowledge.	The licensee shall, following the end of the term or earlier termination of the agreement, in no way utilise the know-how, including such of it which has entered into the public domain, in its business.	It must, however, be noted that the licensee cannot take advantage of this clause merely by breaching the confidentiality clauses, as it is expressly stated not to apply when the public knowledge is due to such a breach. In effect this merely lays down the limitations of Article 2(3).

Article	Summary	Typical prohibited clause	Comments
3(2)	Obligations imposed upon the licensee to assign to or exclusively licence to the licensor use of any improvements it makes are not acceptable. This does not apply to the licensing of improvements which are not severable from the original know-how. Post-term use bans are also not permissible in so far as the improvements are severable from the licensor's know-how.	The licensee shall assign to or exclusively license the licensor to use any improvements that it makes, and following the termination of the agreements the licensee shall not use such improvements in its business.	This should be read together with Article 2(4) and aims at allowing the licensee to enjoy the benefits of its own improvements providing that they are severable from the original know-how. Although this is fine in theory, it is likely to be somewhat difficult to apply in practice and will necessitate very careful description of the original know-how in the licence agreement by the draftsman.
3(3)	Requiring the licensee at the time the agreement is entered into to accept quality specifications or further licenses or tied goods/services unless they are necessary for a technically satisfactory exploitation of the licensed technology or for ensuring standards.	The licensee shall ensure that all of the products manufactured by it comply with whatever minimum quality specifications the licensor shall in its full and sole discretion decide, regardless of whether or not such standards might reasonably be considered necessary by the licensee.	This really amounts to a refinement of Article 2(5) and clearly establishes its limits.
3(4)	Non-challenge of secrecy and patents – but this is without prejudice in the licensor's right to terminate in the event of such a challenge and is therefore not so severe a restriction.	The licensee shall in no circumstances whatsoever seek in any way to challenge the licensor's interest in the know-how and patents.	This prohibited restriction also appears in the patent block exemption and is in accordance with the Commission's general approach to non-challenge provisions (article 2(6)).
3(5)	Royalties charged on goods/services which are not entirely or partially produced by means of the licensed technology.	The licensee shall also pay to the licensor an additional royalty based upon 0.5% of the invoice value of delivery services used to transport the products to their purchasers.	This is aimed at preventing licensors collecting royalties on incidental know-how how over which the licensor does not have any legitimate right, and in general the restriction is perfectly acceptable. However, it does create problems for certain fields of technology in which quite legitimately the royalty will be calculated by reference to the amount of water or electricity used in the process, and effectively means that such a licence could not take advantage of the block exemption. Royalties also cannot be charged on know-how which has become public knowledge due to the licensor's actions.
3(6)	Customers that can be served by the licensor.	The licensor shall in no circumstances make sales of the products (be they active or passive) to wholesalers or to consumers working in the (specified) industry.	This again underlines the Commission's approach that any market sharing must be on the basis of geographical territory rather than 'users', so facilitating 'passive' sales (see Article 2(8)).

Article	Summary	Typical prohibited clause	Comments
3(7)	Quantity of products manufactured or sold.	The licensee shall not manufacture more products than the quota detailed in Schedule 2 hereto and shall restrict such manufacture to the plant.	Such restrictions are perceived as unnecessary and unacceptable restrictions on competition (see Article 1(1)(8) and Article 4(2)).
3(8)	Prices.	The licensee shall sell the products only at the prices stipulated by the licensor from time to time.	This is of course to be expected, as price fixing in whatever guise it takes, is anathema to the Commission.
3(9)	Regulation of R&D, production/use of competing products and their distribution. This is without prejudice to the licensee having to use its best endeavours to exploit the licensed technology and the licensor's right to terminate the licensee's exclusivity and the passing on to it of improvements. The licensor can also demand evidence that the licensee is not abusing the licence by using the know-how to produce goods/ services other than those licensed.	The licensee shall refrain from competing in any way whatsoever with the licensor or the licencees and their agents in respect of research and development, production or the use of competing products and their distribution.	This prevents a total bar on the licensee handling competing goods and carrying on competing R&D, but still provides the licensor with considerable protection.
3(10)	Automatic prolongation of a licence by the inclusion of the licensor's improvements unless the licensee has the right to refuse the improvements or to terminate at the end of the initial term and at least every three years thereafter.	The term of this agreement shall be for a period of 10 years from the date of its execution or the date of communication by the licensee to the licensor of any improvements, whichever is the longer.	This avoids a licensee being trapped in a licence in perpetuity and the resulting anticompetitive implications.
3(11)	The time limits contained in 1(2) and 1(4) are extended by an agreement not to licence or exploit the same technology in the territory.	The licensor shall not licence any undertaking other than the licensee to exploit the know-how within the territory for a period of 15 years from the date of the Agreement.	This is the corollary of Article 1(2) and (4).
3(12)	Passive selling to users or residents in other territories and making it difficult for such users/resellers to obtain the products from other licensees.	The licensee shall not sell or distribute the products to any party with its place of business outside of the territory.	This again makes the distinction between passive and active selling in an attempt to balance competitiveness with the licensee's need for some protection (see Article 1(1)(5) and 1(1)(6)).

Exclusive Distribution and Supply Agreements

By MARK ABELL

Exclusive distribution and supply agreements and selective distribution agreements are subject to Article 85 of the Treaty of Rome in the same way as franchise agreements. They are also able to take advantage of the 'de-minimis' exemption (see Chapter 26 above) and to apply for individual exemption under Article 85(3) (see Chapter 31 below).

In addition to these options there are also Block Exemptions on exclusive distribution and exclusive supply.

As franchisors may well find it necessary to enter into exclusive distribution and supply agreements in order to ensure the success of their franchise network they should be aware of the restrictions placed upon such agreements.

These Block Exemptions are reasonably liberal and it is advisable to try and ensure that such agreements come within their ambit.

EXCLUSIVE DISTRIBUTION – REGULATION 1983/83

The first Block Exemption on exclusive distribution agreements was published in 1967 (Regulation EEC 67/1967). After being extended twice, this exemption expired on 30th June 1983 and was replaced on 1st July 1983 by two new Block Exemptions giving effect to exclusive distribution agreements and exclusive purchasing agreements (see Appendix 11 below).

Regulation 67/67 aimed at omitting the appointment of exclusive distributors who could be tied on an exclusive basis to a particular supplier and who obtained a degree of territorial protection. However, the Commission decided to allow exclusive territories only subject to the distributor being allowed to passively sell outside of its territory. The Block Exemption stated that inter-brand competition must be allowed and that horizontal reciprocal exclusive dealing arrangements were not permitted at all.

However, with the benefit of experience the Commission became aware of a number of shortcomings of this Regulation. It tended to allow too great a degree of restriction upon inter-brand competition and did not exclude non-reciprocal horizontal agreements. Further, case law (Case 47/76 *De Norre* v. *Concordia* – [1977] ECR 65 [1977] 1 CMLR 378) suggested that the Regulation was far too lenient towards exclusive purchasing agreements. After some discussion, the two new regulations were adopted in 1983. It was decided to adopt two separate regulations as the problem with exclusive distribution is the degree of exclusivity that can be afforded to the distributor. The basis of exclusive purchasing agreements is that the exclusivity of supply closes the outlet to other brands.

Regulation 1983/83 applies to agreements made from 1984 onwards.

As with the Franchise Block Exemption (see Chapter 27 above) the exclusive distribution Block Exemption contains a White list and a Black list. However, it does not contain an opposition procedure as is the case with the Franchise Block Exemption.

The Block Exemption applies to agreements which grant exclusivity to a distributor. Article 1 of the Regulation provides for restriction upon a supplier not to supply any other parties who will resell goods to consumers in the territory.

It is important to note that the Block Exemption is only available to bilateral agreements (although it is worth noting that terms which imply an economic connection between the parties are likely to lead to them being regarded as single undertakings).

It is also important to note that the Regulation is only available where the goods are supplied for resale. This immediately raises the problem of how the term 'resale' is defined. Goods such as foodstuffs and cosmetics are repackaged or diluted before being sold on. Case law suggests that this comes within the definition of 'resale'. However, in the case of *Campari* (OJ 1975 L70/69 [1978] 2 CMLR 397) (Appendix 7) the Commission decided that there was no resale in this case. A mix of various herbs and flavourings was sold by Campari to firms which added them to local wines and then sold them on under the Campari mark. This was deemed not to qualify as resale (although in fact it was granted an individual exemption under Article 85(3)).

The Block Exemption permits the appointment of an exclusive distributor for all of the Common Market or for a number of parts of it. The territory granted can also include countries that are not members of the EC. It also applies to undertakings within the same member state, although it is not possible to appoint more than one distributor within a particular territory and stay within the Regulation and exclusivity must be geographical and not based upon types of customer.

Apart from exclusivity no other obligation or restriction can be imposed upon the supplier.

No restriction or non-competition can be imposed upon the distributor other than an obligation not to manufacture or distribute competing goods, the obligation to obtain the goods exclusively from the supplier and an obligation not to actively seek customers outside the territory (thus allowing passive sales outside of the territory).

The White list of obligations which can be imposed upon the distributor includes the following:

— to purchase whole ranges of goods and/or minimum quantities

— to sell the goods under specified trademarks or packaged in a specified manner

— to actively promote sales of the goods through advertising, maintaining minimum stock, providing customer guarantee services and employing specialised/technically trained staff. The Regulation specifically identifies these provisions as being in the White list so as to avoid any possible confusion.

The Black list is contained in Article 3. This specifies four circumstances in which it is impossible to take advantage of the Block Exemption. Two conditions deal with inter-brand conditions and the other two with intra-brand competition.

If there is a horizontal reciprocal exclusive distribution agreement i.e. a market-sharing agreement which has been dressed up to have the appearance of being an exclusive distribution agreement it will fall foul of the Block Exemption.

Likewise, exemption is not available to non-reciprocal exclusive distribution systems unless at least one of them has a turnover of less than 100,000,000 ECU. This is so that manufacturers do not restrict competition by co-operating in the distribution of their goods. However, in the case of small firms, it is considered that the pro-competitive effects outweigh the anti-competitive effects.

Where users are able to obtain the contract goods only from the exclusive distributor in his territory and have no other alternative source of supply from outside the territory, advantage of the Regulation cannot be taken.

Likewise, it is not available when either or both of the parties to the agreement endeavour to make it difficult for other users or intermediaries to obtain the goods inside or if there is no other supplier within the Common Market, from other sources outside of the Common Market. This is particularly so when intellectual property rights such as trademarks are used to this effect.

The remaining articles of the Regulation are basically procedural and Article 4 defines the term 'connected undertakings', and Article 5 describes how to calculate the turnover of companies. Article 6 provides for the withdrawal of the benefit under the Block Exemption and Article 7, various transitional matters. Article 9 provides that the Regulation applies to concerted practices as well as to agreements and Article 10 provides that the Regulation will expire at the end of 1997.

EXCLUSIVE PURCHASING AGREEMENTS

Regulation EC 1984/83 is in many respects similar to EC Regulation 1983/83. It should however be noted that in Article 3(c) the exemption is not available where exclusive purchasing obligations are agreed for more than one type of goods where the goods are connected by a natural or commercial usage. Article 3(d) provides that the Block

Exemption is not available to agreements which are concluded for either an indefinite duration or for a period of more than five years.

The Regulation also contains special provisions for the supply of beer and petrol (Title II and Title III respectively).

SELECTIVE DISTRIBUTION AGREEMENTS

Selective distribution agreements, where the supplier wishes to restrict distribution to undertakings which satisfy his own criteria laid down by it are somewhat akin to franchises, although they will probably be mutually exclusive. Nevertheless, some selective distribution networks, such as that of BMW cars, are commonly referred to as 'franchises'.

It is therefore worth quickly considering this alternative approach to the market.

There is no Block Exemption for selective distribution agreements. However, on a number of occasions the court has held that a producer may operate a selective distribution system without infringing Article 85(1). The distributor participating in the selective distribution network may be able to take advantage of the Exclusive Distribution Block Exemption described above (see *Hasselblad* (OJ [1982] L161/18), upheld on appeal Case 107/82 [1984] 1 CMLR 325)).

Alternatively, in the Metro 1 case (Case 26/76 *SB-Grossmarkte Metro GmbH & Co v. Commission* ([1977] ECR 1875, [1978] 2CMLR 1) an electronic manufacturer (SABA) operating a selective distribution system was granted negative clearance of part of the system on the basis that it tended to enhance inter-brand competition. Metro appealed against this decision as it wished to participate in the distribution network. It was however, rejected as the Court confirmed that provided the sellers are chosen on the basis of objective criteria of a qualitative nature and that the conditions were uniformly laid down and enforced, they were acceptable.

However, it must be stressed that this approach is available only where the goods are of such a type that it is legitimate to restrict the number of outlets that handle them (e.g. expensive perfumes and prestige automobiles). It is only in the case of such goods that non-price competition as upheld in Metro 1 is objectively justifiable.

It is also important to bear in mind that the basic criteria upon which outlets are chosen must be qualitative and not quantitative.

Nevertheless, the Commission has ruled that an obligation to establish a certain number of outlets was not necessarily quantitative. It is also important to note that it is not possible under the Metro doctrine to limit the number of retail outlets that can be opened. Thus, the supplier can seek to ensure certain standards by ensuring that only a certain type of distributor participates in the network, but cannot partition or control the market in any way. This contrasts remarkably with franchising agreements, and thus makes franchising far more attractive a proposition for many suppliers in the EC.

Discrimination against parties that fit the established criteria is not permitted as is the case with restrictions that are no longer necessary to maintain the quality standards.

Restrictions on horizontal sales between distributors, as with franchising, will not be accepted by the Commission.

Despite all of these rulings however, if it appears from the economic context that the network is anti-competitive, it will fall foul of Article 85(1).

Individual exemption has been granted to a number of selective distribution systems such as Omega, Yves St Laurent perfumes and BMW. However, it was refused to Peugeot (OJ 1986 L295/19) due to the Commission's concern over the possible prevention of export of right-hand drive cars. However, Commission Regulation EEC No. 23/85 of 12th December 1984 deals specifically with vehicle distribution and servicing agreements.

CHAPTER 30

Franchising and Anti-Trust Procedure in the European Community

By NICK ROSE

INTRODUCTION

It is unlikely that a franchisor will ever need to take action in the European Commission or the European Court. However, it may well be that the franchisor will face a challenge from a sub-franchisor or developer or unit franchisee in proceedings before the European Commission or the European Court. Provisions of the franchise agreement may be challenged on the basis that they are anti-competitive and are outside the scope of the provisions set out in the block exemption. Such a challenge may arise in the following circumstances:

1. If the sub-franchisor developer/unit franchisee wishes to terminate the franchise agreement and continue its business independently.

2. Alternatively, as a defence to, for example, an action for non-payment of royalties a 'Euro-defence' could be raised seeking to argue that elements of the franchise agreement infringe Article 85. An example of a 'Euro-defence' being raised is the case of *Pronuptia* in 1986 (see Chapter 27 above). The French franchisor Pronuptia de Paris, a supplier of wedding dresses and accessories, sued a unit franchisee in the German Courts, a Mrs. Schillgalis of Hamburg, for outstanding royalties. The franchisee raised a 'Euro-defence' on the basis she was not obliged to pay the outstanding monies as the relevant franchise agreements infringed Article 85(1). Eventually the case was referred to the European Court and certain provisions were held to be prohibited under Article 85. The following comments are relevant to the *Pronuptia* case:

(i) The underlying approach taken by the European Court was to consider first of all whether the Agreement was likely in general to be anti-competitive in the light of the fundamental aims of the Treaty to increase competition. Generally, if the answer is 'no' then any clauses inherent in the successful operation of the Agreement will fall outside Article 85(1). If the legitimate objective of increasing competition is achieved then the ancillary restraints necessary to support the objective will not be anti-competitive.

(ii) In this case, given the likelihood of cross-border sales between Pronuptia retailers the Court feared that the Pronuptia system would give rise to a *de facto* market partitioning unless Pronuptia franchisees were permitted to open shops in other member states. Although the Court ruled that the exclusive territorial restrictions were within Article 85(1) the main result of this case was to take out of the ambit of Article 85 (1) ancillary restrictions necessary to the efficacy of commercial agreements which are designed to increase competition.

(iii) Despite the Block Exemption such challenges may still arise as elements of a Franchise Agreement, or a Franchisor's 'restricted practice' may still be challenged as in the *Pronuptia* case.

3. If the franchisor fails to give proper support to a sub-franchisor/developer/unit franchisee, as the franchisor's business will often be in direct competition, then the sub-franchisor/area developer/unit franchisee could argue that the franchisor's failure to comply with its obligations under the terms of the franchise agreement was similarly anti-competitive.

The Commission has the power to withdraw the benefit of the Block Exemption from the franchisor. This could be the precursor to a 'Euro-defence' in proceedings against a franchisee. The following scenario may occur:

(i) A franchisee sends a complaint to the Commission.
(ii) The Commission withdraws the benefit of the Block Exemption.
(iii) The Commission may then take action against the franchisor or, alternatively, in any national proceedings commenced by the franchisor, for example, for unpaid royalties, a Euro-defence is raised by the franchisee, reinforced by the withdrawal of the benefit of the Block Exemption.

A lack of support from a franchisor may for example arise when the franchisor's business is sold and the purchaser of the business will not have the same (or any) commitment to the franchise network as the original franchisor. The sub-franchisor/developer/unit franchisee may find itself in a network with an uncommitted franchisor or, even worse, a franchisor who does not understand the business fully. If the franchisor is still operating its own shops then the franchisor's outlets will be in direct competition with the sub-franchisor/developer/ unit franchisee. If the franchisor is failing to fulfil its obligations under the Franchise Agreement, for example by failing to provide an updated operating manual, advertising support, entries in trade journals, to train staff, to supply stationery and other relevant materials, then the businesses of the sub-franchisor/ developer/unit franchisee will inevitably suffer. The franchisor being in competition with the franchise network may be able to stifle or restrict competition through its lack of support, and in such a case the sub-franchisor/developer/unit franchisee, if sued for outstanding royalties, may raise a 'Euro-defence' to the effect that the franchise agreement is anti-competitive.

4. In addition to raising a 'Euro-defence' in national proceedings, sub-franchisors/developers/unit franchisees may also wish to take the initiative and challenge the Franchise

Agreement before the European Commission seeking an investigation of the operation of the franchisor. It is therefore important to examine the powers of investigation of the European Commission for alleged infringement of EC Competition Rules. Tactically this may be perceived to be of some benefit to sub-franchisors/developers/unit franchisees in order to improve their negotiating position with Franchisors in any dispute.

The European Commission's powers apply equally to all member states. The purpose of competition law (or 'anti-trust' law as it is referred to in the United States) is to control in the public interest the actual or potential market power of business firms.

Before examining the Commission's powers of investigation it is important to note some important provisions of the Treaty of Rome.

PROVISIONS COMMON TO SEVERAL INSTITUTIONS

Under Article 189 the European Council and the Commission may make regulations, issue directives, take decisions, make recommendations or deliver opinions.

A regulation has general application and is binding in its entirety and directly applicable in all member states.

A directive is binding, as to the results to be achieved, upon each member state to which it is addressed, but leaves to the national authorities the choice of form and method.

A decision is binding in its entirety upon those to whom it is addressed.

Recommendations and opinions have no binding force.

Under Article 192 decisions of the Council or of the Commission which impose an obligation on a party to pay a sum of money are automatically enforceable within all member states.

Enforcement is covered by the rules of civil procedure in force in the state in the territory of which it is carried out. The order for its enforcement is appended to the decision, to be enforced without any formality other than verification of the authenticity of the decision by the national authority which the Government of each member state designates for the purpose and makes known to the Commission and to the European Court.

Articles 85 and 86 are dealt with in chapter 26.

A. THE COMMISSION'S POWERS

Outline of the Commission's procedures

Regulation 17
Article 87 states that within three years of the entry into force of the Treaty the Council should adopt any appropriate regulations or directives to give effect to the principles set out in Articles 85 and 86. Accordingly, in 1962 the Council introduced Regulation 17 to implement Articles 85 and 86 (Appendix 12).

The important provisions of Regulation 17 are as follows:

Article 3 – termination of infringements. The Commission may, either upon application by a third party or upon its own initiative, find that there is an infringement of Article 85 or 86 of the Treaty and it may by decision require the undertakings or associations of undertakings concerned to bring such infringement to an end. Either member states or any legal party with a legitimate interest may make an application (in the form of a 'Complaint') to the Commission to investigate whether there is an infringement of Article 85 or 86. Before making a decision the Commission may address to the undertakings concerned recommendations for termination of the infringement. In practice Article 86 is of no relevance generally to franchises.

Article 11 – request for information. This entitles the Commission to obtain all necessary information from the Governments and competent authorities of the member states and from undertakings and associations of undertakings, in order to carry out an investigation.

Article 13 – at the request of the Commission the competent authorities of member states shall undertake the investigations which the Commission considers to be necessary under Article 14(1), or which is ordered by a decision pursuant to Article 14(3).

Article 14 sets out the investigating powers of the Commission which will be dealt with in more detail below.

Article 15 relates to the fines which may be imposed by the Commission.

Article 16 gives the Commission the power to impose by decision on undertakings or associations of undertakings periodic penalty payments in order to compel them, for example, to put an end to any infringement of Article 85 or 86 in accordance with a decision taken under Article 3.

Article 17 gives the European Court of Justice unlimited jurisdiction to review decisions of the Commission whereby the Commission has fixed a fine or a periodic penalty payment.

Article 19 – this contains express provisions for the undertakings or associations of undertakings having a right to be heard on matters to which the Commission has taken objection.

Under Regulation 17 the Commission also has the power to grant negative clearance to an agreement or to give an exemption to a particular agreement or practice.

The procedure of the Commission is essentially an administrative one. The Commission will first of all investigate the facts and will then either take no action or will make known its objections to the undertakings concerned. After receiving a response from the undertakings to the objections the Commission will take any decision necessary in the circumstances of the case.

1. Notification and complaints

The Commission may commence proceedings, or carry out an investigation, following its own initiative or after receiving a complaint made by a third party. Strategic use can be made of this procedure by any party wishing to improve either the terms of the franchise agreement with the franchisor or to force the franchisor to comply with its obligations under the franchise agreement in order to prevent any restricted practice. Investigations by the Commission are usually very slow and it will often take at least 18 months for the Commission to make any decision after receiving a complaint from a third party.

Litigation will usually have the effect of terminating the franchise relationship. However, by making a complaint to the Commission it is unlikely that the relationship between the franchisor and the sub-franchisors/developers/unit franchisees will deteriorate to such an extent that the Agreement will be terminated. During the lengthy period of time in which the Commission will investigate the complaint there will be pressure on the franchisor to improve its practices or perhaps re-negotiate the terms of its franchise agreement to the benefit of the other party.

The Commission may be notified of a suspected infringement of the competition rules in a number of ways:

(i) by receiving a complaint from a third party which would initiate the Commission's formal complaint procedure;

(ii) a number of agreements are voluntarily notified to the Commission whereby the parties to the agreement will seek a comfort letter from the Commission or an exemption under Article 85(3);

(iii) the Commission will regularly peruse trade journals, questions and answers in the European Parliament and consider the activities of various undertakings which may be the subject of proceedings or investigation by national anti-trust authorities.

Franchisors should be wary of any careless publicity as to their practices, which may be outside the scope of the Block Exemption, as such publicity may be drawn to the attention of the Commission. The Complaint could equally be made by a developer against the practice of its sub-franchisor or by a unit franchisee against a sub-franchisor. Examples of the terms of a franchise agreement which will be outside the scope of a Block Exemption are set out in Article 5 and are dealt with in Chapter 27.

2. Investigation

Whether it acts on its own initiative, or commences proceedings following a complaint from a third party, the Commission will then proceed with a fact finding stage. The Commission has two main investigatory powers:

(i) a right of request for information; and

(ii) a right of inspection of company documents such as accounts and business records.

(i) Request for information

(a) The Commission must first of all give all undertakings the opportunity to comply with a request for information voluntarily. If the undertaking fails to comply with the request then the Commission may take a decision ordering the relevant information to be given.

(b) These procedures are set out in Article 11 of Regulation 17. Franchisors/sub-Franchisors/Developers should beware that if they do voluntarily comply with a request for information then full and frank disclosure must be made failing which a penalty can be imposed by the Commission for intentionally or negligently supplying incorrect information.

(c) If a request for information is received by a franchisor the safest course might be to wait for the Commission to exercise its powers under the second stage of its procedure and make a decision ordering the necessary information to be disclosed under Article 11(5). The Commission will specify, in the decision, what information is required, a strict time limit will be imposed, penalties for non-compliance will be indicated as well as the right to have the decision reviewed by the European Court of Justice. It may be easier for the franchisor to comply with such a decision than attempt voluntarily to provide full and frank disclosure as the decision will be more precise in its scope.

(d) Franchisors should take legal advice when answering either a request for information or in complying with a decision from the Commission, as careful thought and time must be given to any answer.

The supply of incorrect or incomplete information will often reinforce the Commission's suspicions of anti-competitive behaviour.

(e) It is important to note the Commission can require production of documents located in offices outside the EEC.

(ii) Right of inspection

(a) The Commission may carry out on the spot investigations which can be ordered by decision of the Commission or authorisation can be given to the Commission's inspectors. Article 14 of Regulation 17 sets out the Commission's powers of inspection. There is no requirement that the undertaking should first of all be given the opportunity to permit inspection voluntarily. The power to order an inspection has led to what is now known as the Commission's 'dawn raids'.

(b) It is not necessary for an inspection to be announced in advance to an undertaking, and they can be carried out by surprise. If an inspector arrives at premises requesting admission, and the franchisor does not co-operate, no penalty can be imposed. However, the Commission may then issue a decision under Article 14(3) compelling the franchisor to submit to an inspection and penalties may then be imposed in the event of non-compliance.

(c) In the case of *CdF Chemie* v. *Commission* [1987] 3 CMLR 716 the European Court decided that national authorities should be informed in advance of an impending investigation in accordance with Article 14(2). However, the advance notice can be simply a telephone call to the national authority shortly before the inspection takes place.

(d) In the past the majority of inspections were made without a decision, a mandate having been given to an inspector and advance notice given to the relevant undertakings. Unannounced inspections ('the dawn raids') have become much more frequent since about 1980. The reasons for this change in attitude are two-fold: voluntary co-operation by undertakings has diminished; and the Commission became increasingly concerned that substantial cartels were operating which could not be detected by investigation after advance notice had been given as evidence was being concealed or destroyed. The practice of 'dawn-raids' was tested in the case of National Panasonic following a dawn raid by two Commission officials accompanied by an official of the Office of Fair Trading. The case was taken to the European Court of Justice on the basis that the right of privacy granted by Article 8(1) of the European Convention on Human Rights had been breached. However, the European Court held that the Convention had not been breached and that Article 8(2) which gives primacy to 'national security, public safety and economic well-being' applied to competition law.

(e) An example may relate to, say, suspected price fixing in a fast food chain. If the franchisee refers the terms of the Franchise Agreement to the Commission then before or after investigating the relevant facts, the Commission may be so concerned as to the franchisor's practice that the Commission may decide that a dawn raid is necessary in order to inspect the franchisor's operation. In practice most dawn raids occur as a result of the Commission's determination to eliminate cartels partitioning markets.

(f) If a franchisor is ever submitted to a dawn raid by the Commission then it should do the following:

(i) Read carefully the 'Explanatory Memorandum' attached to the inspector's warrant which will define the inspector's power and the franchisor's rights.

(ii) Produce the specific documents which will usually be set out in the warrant.

(iii) Provide copies of any relevant documents requested by the inspector.

(iv) Answer any questions by the inspector who will be entitled to seek an oral explanation of any documents or aspects of the franchisor's operation.

(v) Keep a record of what is said as the answers may provide evidence produced by the Commission in relation to any subsequent proceedings.

(vi) The franchisor is also entitled to have a lawyer present during the inspection and the franchisor should contact its solicitors without delay upon arrival of the inspector.

(iii) Commercial confidentiality

There is, of course, a conflict between the duty of the Commission to allow undertakings to comment on the effect of their arrangements when investigating all possible breaches of Article 85, and the concern of all companies that the confidentiality of commercial information should be maintained.

Articles 20 and 21 of Regulation 17 require the Commission and member states not to disclose any information of the kind covered by the obligation of professional secrecy. When the Commission publishes details in the Official Journal of any decisions, exemptions or applications for negative clearance, it will omit, or indicate with dots, any confidential or price sensitive information. Accounts of royalty payments, for example, should be treated as confidential.

3. Statement of objections

Before completing its investigation, if the Commission is pursuing a complaint received from a third party, the Commission will usually give the third party the right to respond in writing to any replies or information given by the undertaking under investigation. After a full exchange of written comments from both sides the Commission will conclude its investigation and pursue any one of the following options:

1. If the Commission considers that there is sufficient evidence to indicate an infringement by the undertaking then the Commission will serve a Statement of Objections on the undertaking concerned. The Statement of Objections will set out in written form the Commission's case and will set out each aspect of the undertaking's business which the Commission considers may infringe Article 85. The undertaking will usually be given a fixed time limit in which to respond.

2. If the Commission is convinced that there is no evidence indicating an infringement then the Commission will advise the third party that no formal procedure will be opened in relation to the complaint. If the Commission commenced an investigation under its own initiative the Commission will simply advise the undertaking that no further action will be taken.

3. Alternatively, the Commission may pursue an informal settlement. It may indicate to the undertaking that, although no formal proceedings will be issued, certain terms of the agreement between the parties or certain aspects of the undertaking's business operation should be revised as a means of resolving the dispute.

4. Party's right to reply and to be heard

After receiving a Statement of Objections the undertaking will have the opportunity of replying in writing or of seeking an oral hearing which will be a relatively informal affair.

5. Interim measures

In the case of *Cameron Care Limited* v. *Commission* (Case 792/79R [1980] ECR 119) the European Court held that the Commission has power to take interim measures when, pending a final decision being taken by the Commission, the practice of certain undertakings may injure the interests of some member states causing damage to other undertakings. The European Court held that, whilst enquiries are being carried out, no irreparable damage should be caused to the undertakings and so the Commission may pass interim, but essential, safeguards.

Any interim measures must be temporary and must merely preserve the status quo. Any party who is the subject of such interim measures has the right to apply to the European Court of Justice for emergency review. In order to obtain interim measures the following points should be noted:

(i) the applicant must have a 'really strong prima facie case';
(ii) the Commission will act primarily on the evidence presented by the applicant rather than the evidence obtained by their own enquiries;
(iii) the applicant may be required to provide an indemnity in respect of the costs of the person against whom interim measures are adopted if no infringement is ultimately found;

(iv) the Commission may act on its own initiative if a firm's conduct has the effect of injuring the interests of some member state, causes damage to other firms or jeopardises the Community's competition policy.

An example can be found in the Ford Werker case. Ford Germany sought to prevent the export by German distributors to the United Kingdom of right hand drive Ford motor cars manufactured in Germany. Ford Germany's purpose was to maintain a higher selling price in the United Kingdom. The Commission imposed interim measures, and Ford was instructed to withdraw a circular sent to its German distributors informing them that orders by them for right hand drive cars would not be accepted. A periodical penalty payment of 1,000 ECU per day was imposed by way of enforcement. The European Court replaced the Commission's decision with measures which froze imports into the United Kingdom from Germany at pre-circular levels, until a full hearing of the appeal against the interim measures could be heard by the European Court. The European Court overturned the Commission's interim measures because the Commission's decision demonstrated no infringement of the Treaty under Articles 85 and 86 but the principle of the Commission having power to impose interim measures was not disputed by the Court.

6. Decisions and penalties

After the oral hearing and/or the written reply from the undertaking the Commission will then take a final decision as to whether the franchisor has infringed Article 85. Before taking a final decision the Commmission will consult the Advisory Committee on Restrictive Practices and Monopolies. The Commission's draft decision, together with a written opinion of the Advisory Committee, will then be passed to the Commissioners who will then take the final decision and notify it to the undertaking. All decisions are published in the Official Journal. Various penalties can be imposed.

(a) Cease and Desist orders

These orders play a central role in EC law where infringements are found of Article 85 or 86 and the Commission may require firms to terminate the agreements or practices forthwith. If the conduct has already ceased then the Commission may simply declare that the infringement had taken place at an earlier stage.

(b) Orders requiring specific conduct

Article 3(1) of Regulation 17 permits the Commission to require firms in breach of the Treaty to bring the infringement to an end by taking positive measures, for example, the restoration of a minimum quantity of supplies. The Commission will endeavour to regulate future market behaviour by such an order.

(c) Fines

The Commission may fine the franchisor/sub-franchisor/developer or franchisee for a breach of Article 85, the maximum fine being one million units of account or 10 per cent of the previous year's turnover whichever is greater.

If a franchisor receives a decision by the Commission ordering it to terminate an agreement or conduct forthwith, if the undertaking fails to comply, the Commission may order it to pay fines of up to one thousand units of account per day (approximately £600.00) until the order is complied with, or a sum not exceeding 10% of the turnover of an undertaking in the previous financial year whichever is the greater.

(d) Failure to comply

If the franchisor does not comply with any decision of the Commission this would undoubtedly lead to a second decision of the Commission attracting further fines and/or periodic penalty payments. The Commission can avoid the necessity of the second decision by the imposition of periodic penalty payments in its original decision.

In addition, or alternatively, the Commission may under Article 16 impose daily periodical penalty payments of 50 to 1,000 ECUs for the duration of any such breaches. The limitation period for imposition of fines and penalties is fixed at three years for procedural infringements, and five years for all others, time running in each case from the date on which the infringement commenced.

The prerequisite for the imposition of fines is intentional or negligent infringement of the competition rules, although the Commission usually condemns the conduct as 'at least negligent'.

(e) Review of decisions of the Commission

Historically under Article 173 it has been possible for recipients of decisions of the Commission to bring an action to have various 'acts' of the Commission annulled by the European Court of Justice ('ECJ'). Not only decisions but other 'acts' can be challenged under Article 173. In *IBM* v. *EC Commission* it was held that any act capable of affecting the interests of the applicant by bringing about a change in his legal position could be challenged. This may include comfort letters because they can put an end to the provisional validity of an old agreement. However, anti-trust cases involve a great deal of factual assessment and in dealing with such cases the ECJ has always taken a very long time to reach a judgment inevitably increasing the delay in giving judgment in other cases.

The possibilities for seeking a speedy review of decisions of the Commission has now been significantly increased by the establishment of a Court of First Instance of the European Communities ('CFI').

The Single European Act provided for the establishment of the CFI to be attached to the ECJ and on 25th September, 1989, the CFI was inaugurated in Luxembourg. This should ease the burden of the ECJ and allow for a quicker and better administration of justice. The CFI consists of 12 members appointed by common accord of the Governments of the member states for six years and they are re-appointable. There will be a renewal of six members every three years. The CFI will sit in divisions of three or five judges. The CFI will have jurisdiction in three areas:

(i) disputes between the Community and its servants;

(ii) applications for judicial review of acts of the Commission or for failure to act by the Commission and in some circumstances for damages in relation to the implementation of the competition rules applicable to undertakings;

(iii) applications for judicial review against the Commission of the Coal and Steel Community.

The first public hearing before the CFI took place on 14th December, 1989.

Any decision of the Commission after an investigation into a franchise network or a franchise agreement can therefore be reviewed by the CFI and although appeal on points of law to the ECJ is available the decision of the CFI will be final and conclusive as to the facts. An appeal on a point of law shall only lie on three grounds, namely a lack of competence of the CFI, breach of procedure before the CFI or infringement of community law by the CFI. Appeals can be lodged against final decisions of the CFI and various other decisions such as the disposal of any procedural issue concerning a plea of lack of jurisdiction. The normal time limit for appeal is two months from the date on which the decision has been notified except in the case of a decision dismissing an application to intervene in proceedings before the CFI in which case the time limit will be two weeks from the date of notification.

If the ECJ allows an appeal then it must quash the decision of the CFI. It may give final judgment in the matter or refer the case back to the CFI for judgment in which case the CFI will be bound by the ruling of the ECJ on any issue of law.

B. SHOULD A SUB-FRANCHISOR/ AREA DEVELOPER/UNIT FRANCHISEE COMPLAIN TO THE COMMISSION OR PROCEED BEFORE THE NATIONAL COURTS?

All national courts of the member states are under a duty to give effect to the rights created by Article 85 and any sub-franchisor/developer/unit franchisee who wishes to complain about any aspect of the franchise agreement or of the franchisor's business operation, should consider very carefully whether he can persuade the national court that the agreement in dispute is prohibited by Article 85 or complain to the Commission.

1. Article 85: a sword and a shield

Before considering in detail the relevant merits of bringing a complaint to the Commission or proceeding before the national courts it should be noted that Article 85 can be used as a sword as well as a shield.

(1) A sword
(a) In the UK, for example, an action can be taken in the English courts for damages for breach of Articles 85 and 86. (Confirmed by the House of Lords in *Garden Cottage Foods* v. *Milk Marketing Board* [1984] AC 130).

(b) Furthermore, in the UK the remedy of an injunction is available to prevent infringements of Articles 85 and 86 if the sub-franchisor/area developer/unit franchisee is able to persuade the national courts that its business would suffer irrevocable prejudice if the anti-competitive practice of the franchisor continued.

An injunction was given in the case of *Cutsforth* v. *Mansfield Inns Limited* [1986] 1 All ER 577. Mr. Cutsforth and others supplied jukeboxes and video games machines to public houses. Mansfield Inns took over the tied houses within the relevant area and introduced a new policy under which only certain approved suppliers could be used. Mr. Cutsforth no longer appeared on the approved list. Mr. Cutsforth successfully applied for an interim injunction requiring Mansfield Inns not to interfere in any way in the arrangements between Cutsforth and his customers. The High Court in London held that the agreement extending Mansfield Inns's control of beer supplies to enable it to also control the supply of coin operated games equipment went outside the block exemption (which applies to beer supply arrangements) and therefore infringed Article 85.

This can be easily translated into a franchising scenario. A brewery is in a position not dissimilar to that of a franchisor in being able to dictate to the Landlord (the equivalent to a franchisee) the beers and other beverages to serve to customers. Similarly a brewery can insist on its trade marks being used by the Landlord. If a Franchise Agreement includes 'tie-ins', for example, the franchisee is prevented from obtaining supplies of a quality equivalent to those offered by the franchisor then the franchisee could seek an injunction if the franchisee could show that its business would suffer irreparable harm. In practice it is unlikely that the franchisee will be able to obtain an interlocutory injunction as damages will normally be an adequate remedy in anti-trust cases. The franchisee would have to show that there was an immediate danger to his livelihood. The House of Lords confirmed in the *Garden Cottage* case that any infringement of Article 85 would constitute a breach of statutory duty for which damages can be awarded.

The internal position in other member states is far from clear and a Directive from the Commission would be welcomed in order to harmonise the remedies available in national Courts for infringement of Community law.

(2) A shield
Community law can be used as a defence in any proceedings brought by a franchisor, for example for outstanding royalties, as a defendant may allege that Article 85 has been breached. This is what is known as a 'Euro defence'. The Euro defence has not yet been tested at a full trial in the UK and generally only in interlocutory proceedings. Normally Euro defences have not fared particularly well in the UK Courts. An example which is of interest to Franchisors is the case of *Dymond* v. *Britton* where a patentee sued its exclusive licensee for non payment of royalties and the licensee served a Defence alleging the licence infringed Article 85 (1). The patentee applied for Summary Judgment at an early stage in the proceedings on the basis that the licensee had no valid

defence. The Court reluctantly recognised that the Euro defence was at the very least an arguable defence and expressed regret at not being able to give summary judgment at the Preliminary Hearing thus allowing the defendant to defend the case at trial.

2. Options available to the National Courts

Before turning to the difficult question of pursuing a complaint before the Commission or presenting an action in the national courts, any party must consider whether an effective remedy will be available from the national courts. In the *SABAM* case (Case 127/73) [1974] ECR 5 the European Court stated that national courts are not necessarily exempt from giving judgment when an agreement or practice before it has been considered by the Commission or indeed if the Commission has initiated a procedure pursuant to Regulation 17 (Article 3). The national courts will have the following options:

(i) staying the proceedings before it pending a decision from the Commission or

(ii) allowing the proceedings to continue and considering whether the act complained of is, or is not, capable of having an effect on competition in the European market.

(iii) referring any issue of interpretation of European law by way of a preliminary ruling under Article 177 of the Treaty of Rome.

3, The choice between a complaint to the Commission or national proceedings

The following factors are particularly relevant:

1. *Urgency.* If an urgent remedy is needed an application for an injunction in the national courts (assuming damages will not be an adequate remedy) will usually provide a more speedy and effective remedy than bringing a complaint to the European Commission and subsequently applying for interim measures to be taken by the Commission. The Commission has often been reluctant and slow to impose interim measures.

2. *Costs.* Although national litigation is expensive in the Courts a successful Plaintiff will usually recover his costs from the Defendants, whereas an unsuccessful Plaintiff would normally have to pay the costs of both sides. In Commission proceedings the costs are not recoverable, each party will pay its own costs. The plaintiff must therefore carry out a thorough assessment of the strength of his case and the likely length of proceedings.

3. *Damages.* If the claimant has suffered loss this would favour proceedings in the national courts. The Commission, unlike national courts, cannot award damages for past losses and can only impose a fine. However, if a favourable decision is obtained it would then be open to the claimant to commence a domestic action claiming damages. There will inevitably be a lengthy delay, until the Commission decision is obtained and the domestic action can then be commenced, but at least the claimant will be supported by a Commission decision in

its favour confirming that the relevant agreement or practice has breached Article 85.

4. *Continuing Relationship.* In a franchise relationship the Commission proceedings should assist in a negotiated settlement. The Commission, if it is unhappy about any aspect of the Franchise Agreement, will often suggest a modification of the terms of the Agreement or of the franchisor's practices. National litigation usually leads to a total breakdown in relations.

5. *Prospects of success.* Subject to the speed with which a remedy may be required to an urgent problem, it would probably be easier to establish a good case before the Commission of a breach of Article 85 than before most national Courts given the Commission's strict views on anti-competitive practices and the wariness of some national Courts to apply EEC law with direct effect.

6. *Delay.* Account must be taken of the likely lengthy delays which will be involved as the Commission is often very slow to react and the complaint will find itself in a queue of complaints to be determined according to the size of the case. In the case of most franchise agreements any complaint is likely to be seen as a relatively small matter and the fact finding stage may take up to 18 months or even two years to conclude.

7. *Stay of proceedings.* There will usually be little benefit in pursuing both the Commission route and the domestic route. If the complaint is made to the Commission it is likely that the national courts will stay the domestic proceedings pending a decision by the Commission.

4. Conflict between EEC Law and National Law

National competition laws are confined to the operation and activities of domestic firms in a domestic market. The application of Article 85 deals, in theory at least, only with adverse effects on trade between member states.

The Commission will usually take a very broad view as to whether any agreement can have a potentially adverse effect on trade between member states and so in practice the inter-state trade requirement is now of little real significance. EEC rules in practice can apply to purely domestic matters. The complainant only needs to show the potential effect on trade between member states. If, for example, the unit franchisee, who is bringing the complaint, wishes to sell its products or provide its services to any other member state then the unit franchisee should be able to show the potential effect on trade between member states without any difficulty if there is any potential inhibition on cross-border sales.

The franchisor may therefore be subjected to two different forms of investigation of the same conduct at the same time. In the UK the franchisor may be investigated by the Director General of Fair Trading under the national Competition Act as well as by the European Commission. In such a case the following principles apply:

1. If the Commission takes a positive decision this will be binding and take effect in each member state and the domestic undertaking will be bound by it whatever the outcome of the

investigation by the national authorities. The authorities must enforce the Commission ruling irrespective of the domestic law.

2. A comfort letter provided by the Commission merely expresses the Commission's intention not to proceed with infringement proceedings. It has no effect on the enforcement of national law.

3. Where the requirements of Article 85 or 86 are not met then the national authorities will have a free hand to apply solely national law.

C. THE CONFLICT BETWEEN PROTECTION OF TRADE MARKS, THE FREE MOVEMENT OF GOODS AND ANTI-TRUST LAW

1. Trade marks

The franchisor's trade marks are of course fundamental to the operation of its network. The franchisor will need to take speedy and effective action against any unauthorised use of its trade marks by a sub-franchisor/developer/unit franchisee after the termination of an agreement, and in contravention of any non-competition clause. Furthermore, both the franchisor, and its sub-franchisors, developers and unit franchisees must all be prepared to take immediate and effective action against any third party who may infringe its trade marks in order to protect the industrial property rights of the whole network.

Unfortunately, the European Court of Justice has shown itself less than sympathetic to trade marks and to other intellectual property rights. There is a constant conflict between the protection of intellectual property rights (with its associated monopolies), and EC competition law (which seeks to eliminate monopolies) and the law on the free movement of goods.

2. Free movement of goods

The Treaty of Rome establishes the principle of free movement of goods. Article 30 states that quantitative restrictions on imports and all measures having equivalent effect shall, without prejudice to subsequent provisions, be prohibited between member states.

Article 36 states that the provisions of Articles 30–34 shall not preclude prohibitions or restrictions on imports, exports or goods in transit justified on the grounds of public policy and various other grounds including protection of industrial and commercial property. However, such prohibition shall not constitute a means of arbitrary discrimination or a disguised restriction on trade between member states.

Almost any measure which hinders imports to any significant extent will be generally treated as equivalent to a quantitative restriction. However, such restriction may be justified if it is to protect an industrial property, such as a trade mark, as long as it is not discriminatory or unduly restrictive.

It is a basic principle of EEC law that, once goods have been released into free circulation in one member state, they should enjoy unrestricted entry into the markets of every other member state.

3. Exhaustion of rights

A trade mark owner cannot prevent the importation of goods previously marketed within the EEC with his consent or with the consent of a connected party such as a licensee, subsidiary, parent or sister company. In the Centrafarm case the European Court held that it was inconsistent with the rules on the free movement of goods for the holder of a trade mark to prohibit the marketing in one member state of goods which have been put on the market in another member state by the proprietor with his consent.

A trade mark owner is entitled to protect his exclusive right to use the trade mark, for the purpose of putting products protected by the trade mark into circulation for the first time. The trade mark owner is only entitled to protection against competitors wishing to take advantage of the status and reputation of the trade mark by selling products illegally bearing that trade mark before the trade mark has been circulated in the Common Market for the first time.

The European Court will not therefore allow a trade mark owner to rely on the exclusiveness of a trade mark right with a view to prohibiting the marketing in another member state under an identical trade mark after the trade mark has been marketed in another member state either with the owner's consent or with the consent of a licensed party such as a franchisee.

The trade mark owner should also note that he cannot prevent the movement of goods with the same trade mark if the mark is derived from a common origin.

Article 30 only applies to trade between member states and does not apply when a trade mark owner seeks to prohibit the importation of goods, which infringe the owner's trade mark, from outside the EEC. The European Court will, in such circumstances, enforce the trade mark owner's rights.

4. Unfair competition

The European Court has approved the fact that the Paris Convention for the Protection of Industrial Property is applied to all member states to assure effective protection against unfair competition. The European Court will permit national laws to prohibit slavish imitation of products and that all undertakings should be entitled to effective protection against unfair competition in the form of blatant and unfair copying. There would be no contravention of Article 30 in such circumstances. The European Court will consider the consumer's interests and the fact that the consumer needs to be protected against unfair competition in this form.

5. What is the connection between protection of trade marks and competition law?

As discussed above, Article 85 can provide a defence to an action for infringement of an intellectual property right taken by a franchisor if, and only if, the franchisor is seeking to enforce an agreement prohibited under Article 85. There must be a connection between the right to protect the trade mark, the infringement action and a prohibited agreement, or practice, if an alleged breach of Article 85 is to provide the basis of a defence.

In the absence of any allegation of a breach of Article 85, in relation to the franchise agreement or franchisor's practice, the most appropriate defence to an action for trade mark infringement is likely to relate to the partitioning of the Common Market and the free movement of goods, being the preserve of Article 30.

However, in some instances Article 85 can provide a defence to an action for a trade mark infringement when none would exist under Article 30. If a unit franchisee, as the owner of trade mark rights, seeks to prevent imports from a non-member state into the Community, on the grounds that the products infringe its mark, the defendant may argue that the inability to import the products into the Community will indirectly affect trade within the Community and, if there is going to be a restriction on trade between member states, then the doctrine under Article 85 may apply provided there is a connection with a prohibited agreement (in this case the unit franchisee's franchise agreement).

A unit franchisee will be licensed to use the franchisor's trade mark. However, the franchisee cannot use its trade mark rights obtained as a result of the franchise agreement, to restrict parallel imports from one member state into another member state of goods using the same trade mark. The franchisor cannot open an outlet in all member states, granting exclusive trade mark rights and at the same time seek to prevent parallel imports of the product to those member states. This would be seen by the Commission and the European Court as a division of the market. The sub-franchisor/developer/franchisee cannot bring a trade mark infringement suit (pursuant to the licence of trade mark rights in an Agreement) which has the object or effect of dividing the market. In such a case the importer may well have a defence under Article 85(1) as well as under Articles 30 to 36 of the Treaty. The importer would have to show evidence of continuing collusion between the parties to divide markets.

CONCLUSION

In summary the franchisor should note the following practical points:

1. Avoid the inclusion of any terms in a franchise agreement outside the scope of the Block Exemption or if this is not commercially viable take advantage of the de minimis exemption (see Chapter 26 above), or apply for negative clearance or individual exemption (see Chapter 26 above). This will reduce the chances of proceedings being brought either in the national courts or before the Commission.

2. Any terms included in the franchise agreement which fall foul of Article 85 may also provide sub-franchisors/developers/unit franchisees with a legitimate defence in domestic proceedings to an action for recovery of outstanding royalties or other payments.

3. The franchisor should be wary of the Commission's power to initiate its own investigations into the franchisor and its network so the franchisor should avoid any restricted concerted practices, as well as any illegal terms in the Franchise Agreement. The franchisor should be careful to avoid any careless publicity. In the event that the Commission does commence any investigation, either by making a request for information or a 'dawn-raid' the franchisor should take legal advice immediately to make sure that the correct procedures are followed and full compliance is made with the Commission's request or decision.

4. In the case of parallel imports from a country outside the EEC it may be preferable for a franchisor, as the trade mark owner, to commence an infringement action against the importer who will not be able to rely on a defence under Article 30 or Article 85. In any action commenced by a sub-franchisor/developer/unit franchisee the importer may have a defence under Article 85 on the grounds that the party seeking to enforce the trade mark rights will be relying on a prohibited Agreement as the potential prohibition of the imported goods may restrict trade between member states.

5. Finally, a mention of Article 86 of the Rome Treaty. This provides that any 'abuse by one or more undertakings of a dominant position within the Common Market or in a substantial part of it should be prohibited as incompatible with the Common Market insofar as it may affect trade between member states'.

Examples of abuses are charging customers unfair prices or imposing upon them unfair trading conditions. The central issue in the application of Article 86 is whether the firm in question has a dominant position or market power. Assessing market power is a complicated task and all competitive forces should be taken into account.

A dominant position relates to a position of economic strength enjoyed by an undertaking which enables it to prevent effective competition being maintained on the relevant market by affording it the power to behave to an appreciable extent independently of its competitors, customers and ultimately of its consumers (the European Court of Justice in *United Brands* – Case 27/76).

Therefore any franchisor who potentially has a dominant position or market power should take care not to abuse its position in the market. The franchisor need not fear actually being in a 'dominant position'. It is the potential abuse of its dominant position which should justify caution in its practices. Therefore a franchisor with a dominant position in the market should take care in relation to the imposition of 'tie-ins', for example the forced purchasing of goods by franchisees.

CHAPTER 31

Franchising and the Convention on the Law Applicable to Contractual Obligations

By MARK ABELL

The Convention on the Law Applicable to Contractual Obligations (Appendix 13) is potentially of immense importance to all franchisors doing business in or with the European Community.

It focuses upon private international law and although a child of the European Commission and subject to the authoritative interpretation of the European Court in Luxembourg, its impact is universal. The Convention affects not only domestic member state contracts and inter-member state contracts but also international contracts. Once it is incorporated into member state law (it is already adopted into English law by way of the Contracts (Applicable Law) Act 1990) courts will have to observe it when deciding conflicts between laws of other countries, whether or not Members of the EC, and its own laws.

Article 1 of the Convention provides that:

'The rules of the Convention shall apply to contractual obligations in any situation involving a choice between the laws of the different countries'.

A number of contracts and specific issues are expressly excluded from the scope of the Convention under Article 1(2) namely:

(a) questions involving the status or legal capacity of natural persons, without prejudice to Article 11;

(b) contractual obligations relating to:

— wills and succession,
— rights in property arising out of a matrimonial relationship,
— rights and duties arising out of a family relationship, parentage, marriage or affinity, including maintenance obligations in respect of children who are not legitimate;

(c) obligations arising under bills of exchange, cheques, and promissory notes and other negotiable instruments to the extent that the obligations under such other negotiable instruments arise out of their negotiable character;

(d) arbitration agreements and agreements on the choice of court;

(e) questions governed by the law of companies and other bodies corporate or unincorporated such as the creation, by registration or otherwise, legal capacity, internal organisation, or winding-up of companies and other bodies corporate or unincorporated and the personal liability of officers and members as such for the obligations of the company or body;

(f) the question whether an agent is able to bind a principal, or an organ to bind a company or body corporate or unincorporated, to a third party;

(g) the constitution of trusts and the relationship between settlers, trustees and beneficiaries;

(h) evidence and procedure, without prejudice to Article 14.

The policy underlying the Convention is to give the parties to agreements the freedom to choose the applicable law, either when concluding the contract or by later agreement. Consider for example, once the Convention is in force where there is, for example, a dispute between an American franchisor and a German sub-franchisor. If the Franchise Agreement has been drafted so as such a dispute is subject to arbitration in London, previously this would be sufficient to suggest that English law was the governing law of the Agreement. However under the Convention the applicable law is that of the party making 'the characteristic performance', namely the franchisee's country — Germany. For this reason it will be necessary to ensure that all franchise agreements expressly state what the choice of law will be and not merely what the venue of the arbitration or court hearing will be.

The aim of the Convention is to enhance legal certainty, but it would appear that this has not been achieved in every respect. For example Article 4(2) provides that if a contract, in which no choice of law is made by the parties, is to be performed by a branch office, the applicable law will be that of the country where the branch office is situated. This could lead to considerable uncertainty where a multinational franchisor has a number of branches throughout the European Community and uses Master Franchise Agreements which leave it open to the franchisor to use any of its EC branch offices or subsidiaries for the performance of its obligations.

The Convention does not however, enable parties to a franchise agreement to escape the impact of 'mandatory rules' such as Article 85 and Article 86 of the Treaty of Rome (see Chapter 27 above).

Thus, the master franchise agreement between an American franchisor and a Belgian sub-franchisor will be subject to Article 85 and Article 86, even if the parties have agreed that it should be governed by the law of the United States.

Article 7(2) safeguards the application of mandatory rules of the country where the court is situated, irrespective of the law applicable to the contract.

Article 7(2) which has been excluded from the English Statute enacting the Convention, provides that the mandatory rules of another country 'with which the situation has a close connection' (whatever this means) will prevail over the law governing the contract if the law of the other country so requires. Thus, for example, U.S. laws concerning anti-trust embargoes' freezing of assets and restrictions of resale to certain countries would be affected by this provision. It would seem that this is likely to be a source of substantial dispute in international contracts in general, if not in franchising in particular.

The Convention provides in Article 6 that a rule of the law of any country otherwise applicable may be refused by the court if it is manifestly incompatible with the court's public policy. This includes competition rules of the EC and the principle of free movement of goods, freedom of services, and freedom of establishment (see Chapter 12 above). Attempts to breach such Community public policy would not be enforceable by the courts of the member states. Despite this homogenity however, there is still a considerable difference between the treatment of foreign public policy in the Common Law courts of the United Kingdom and Eire on the one hand and the Civil Law courts of the other ten EC member states on the other. Both would refuse the application of penal and revenue laws of foreign countries but treat differently foreign exchange control regulations not covered by an international convention. In common law countries, such foreign exchange control regulations, foreign trade restrictions and price regulations have been considered in situations where a civil law approach would have refused to do so.

The consumers in the EC are protected by monetary rules of their own member states.

The original aim of the European Commission was to create a uniform commercial code for the European Community, but this proved to be impossible. Instead, the United Nations Convention on Contracts for International Sales was considered to be an alternative. This Convention is another attempt by the Community to further homogenise a complicated area of law. Its effects upon franchising in the European Community are potentially great, but it would seem that it can be substantially limited by proper drafting of franchise documentation.

CHAPTER 32

Franchise Disputes and the Enforcement of Judgments in the European Community

By NICK ROSE

Any franchisor in the EC who is in the process of establishing, or has established, a network of sub-franchisors, developers and unit franchisees within the EC will need an effective procedure to resolve cross border disputes. The franchisor should therefore be aware of its ability to sue any sub-franchisor/developer/unit franchisee in another member state of the European Community and to enforce judgments obtained in one member state in another member state where the assets of the defendant to the litigation may be located.

Similarly, a franchisor located outside the EC may establish a network located within the EC and knowledge of the arrangements for the reciprocal enforcement of judgments within EC member states is essential.

For example, a French franchisor may have sub-franchisors in Germany, Holland and the UK. The sub-franchisors in turn will have unit franchisees.

The French franchisor must make sure that there is a provision in its franchise agreement with the sub-franchisors that, in the event of a unit franchise breaching any of its obligations, if the sub-franchisor does not take effective action against the unit franchisee then the franchisor may take action direct against the unit franchisee. If, in this example, a unit franchisee in Germany fails to maintain adequate quality control or is failing to pay the appropriate level of royalties, and the sub-franchisor is failing to enforce its rights properly against the unit franchisee, the French franchisor must take action. Should the franchisor sue in France? If so, can a French judgment be enforced against the unit franchisee's assets in Germany? Alternatively, should the franchisor sue locally in Germany? Will German law prevail? Does the franchise agreement provide for a jurisdiction of a particular member state to resolve all disputes between the parties? If the franchise agreement does refer all disputes to a particular jurisdiction, can the franchisor still sue the unit franchisee in another member state?

All of these questions need to be addressed and sometimes with a degree of urgency particularly if the franchisor's intellectual property rights are being challenged, for example, by a former unit franchisee (now trading independently) or by an independent third party abusing the trade marks of the franchise network.

Franchisors increasingly may have outlets in two or more member states or the franchisor may have a sub-franchisor/developer who in turn will have outlets in two or more member states. A cross border dispute resolution process between outlets in different member states will be important and knowledge of the 1968 Brussels Convention will not only assist in the drafting of the relevant franchise agreements but will also help to answer some of the above questions to enable the use by the franchisor of the correct jurisdiction within his network when taking action.

THE BRUSSELS CONVENTION

Following the 1968 Brussels Convention franchise disputes may now be resolved more readily within the EC, as a judgment in one member state can be enforced in the other member states who have acceded to the Brussels Convention. Disputes will often be adjudicated in one country, yet the relief sought may only be exercisable in another country where the defendant's assets are located. The purpose of the Convention was to enable a party to effectively obtain the relief granted by its national courts and to introduce a machinery of enforcement which, as far as possible, respects no national boundaries.

A classic example of a dispute involving a franchisor and a franchisee in a different member state is the case of *Pronuptia* decided in 1986 (see Chapter 27 above). This involved a French franchisor Pronuptia de Paris and a German franchisee in Hamburg, Mrs. Schillgalis. Pronuptia supplied wedding dresses and accessories. The franchisee refused to pay certain monies on the grounds that the relevant franchise agreements infringed Article 85(1). Under three agreements Pronuptia had granted the franchisee the exclusive right to use the mark 'Pronuptia de Paris' in the Hamburg, Oldenburg and Hanover areas, and had also agreed not to open a shop itself in each area, nor to supply any third party in each area with Pronuptia products or services.

Under Article 177 of the EEC Treaty the German courts referred the case to the European Court. The Court decided that certain 'restrictive' provisions fell outside the scope of Article 85(1) but held that certain provisions which gave rise to 'absolute territorial protection' did restrict competition and fell within the scope of Article 85(1). The case is typical of an 'international' franchise dispute although the decision of the Court preceded the Block Exemption on Franchise Agreements.

The member states which are now signatories to the Convention are as follows:

France
Germany
Italy
Belgium
The Netherlands
Luxembourg
United Kingdom
Ireland
Denmark
Spain
Greece

All of these countries now have provisions within their national law based upon the 1968 Brussels Convention whereby any judgment in any of the other member states may be automatically enforced within their own jurisdiction. Portugal is expected to accede to the Convention in due course.

The object of the 1968 Convention

It will first be necessary to consider the nature of the 1968 Convention. Article 220 of the Treaty of Rome required member states to enter into negotiations with each other with a view to securing, for the benefit of their nationals, a simplification of formalities governing the reciprocal recognition and enforcement of judgments of courts and other tribunals. As a result, the key feature of the Brussels Convention is that judgments obtained in one of the Contracting States become exportable to other Contracting States with the minimum of formalities and conditions and with the scope for challenge of the judgment in a receiving country being very limited.

The Convention was originally signed in Brussels on 27th September, 1968. The Convention was followed by the 1971 Protocol on convention interpretation by the European Court. It was not until 1978 that the United Kingdom, along with Denmark and Ireland, signed the 1968 Accession Convention which came into force on 1st January, 1987, and thus the UK became a Contracting State to the Convention.

The object of the 1968 Convention is to bring enforcement of judgments into line with the European Community's ideal of harmonisation. The basic functions of the Convention are:

(1) to standardise the conditions in which the courts of the EC states have jurisdiction on civil matters over claims against parties who are domiciled in the EC (and in a few cases who are not); and

(2) to enable all judgments of EC courts against non-EC domiciled parties to be recognised and enforced in other EC states.

The difficulty in seeking effective and easy enforcement lay in the complexity and diversity of national laws. Although bilateral enforcement treaties did exist between individual member states these were largely divergent and incomplete. The Convention therefore sought a simplification and unification of recognition and enforcement conditions and procedures.

The Civil Jurisdiction and Judgments Act 1982, which came into force in the UK on the 1st January, 1987, provides one example of how a member state has applied the provision of the Convention and brought into play one single set of rules governing the enforcement of foreign judgments. This Act contains the necessary provisions to achieve the aims and objects of the Brussels Convention and is typical of similar national legislation passed in the other Contracting States.

Interpretation

Section 3 of the Civil Jurisdiction and Judgments Act ('the Act') provides that 'Any question as to the meaning or effect of any provision of the Convention shall, if not referred to the European Court in accordance with the 1971 Protocol, be determined in accordance with the principles laid down by any relevant decision of the European Court.' It further provides that judicial notice will be taken of any decision or opinion expressed by the European Court on any question arising out of the Convention. Similar legislation has been passed in the other Contracting States.

The European Court is therefore competent to determine questions of interpretation in the UK and in all Contracting States.

ESSENTIAL PRE-CONDITIONS FOR RECOGNITION AND ENFORCEMENT OF A JUDGMENT IN ANY CONTRACTING STATE

1. All franchise disputes will satisfy the first precondition that the subject matter of the judgment must be civil and commercial.

2. There must be the existence of a judgment which will include any decree, order or writ of execution, including an order for costs, in any national court. The Convention applies to money or non-money judgments. Any injunction awarded by a national court will be enforced in any other Contracting State unless the injunction was obtained in the course of ex parte proceedings, whereby the defendant would not have received notice of the application and would not be represented at the hearing. For example, urgent applications, where secrecy is required, are made ex parte, the defendant is not notified of the hearing but is usually given the opportunity at a later date to put his case and apply to discharge the injunction. An example would be in the case where the franchisor had evidence of a franchisee making secret profits and not disclosing his true weekly turnover. The franchisor may fear the franchisee's ability to destroy or falsify the relevant documents, such as the cash book, if the franchisee received notice of a court hearing, and so the franchisor may apply for an injunction ex parte to freeze the franchisee's bank accounts and obtain delivery up of all its financial and book-keeping documents.

3. The judgment must be of a 'court or tribunal'.

4. The foreign judgment should not be defective under the judgment state's law.

JURISDICTION

Grounds of jurisdiction

The grounds of jurisdiction can be divided into five categories:

(i) Jurisdiction based upon the situation of the defendant's domicile.

(ii) Jurisdiction based upon submission to the jurisdiction by the defendant.

(iii) Exclusive jurisdiction arising either from the terms of an agreement nominating the jurisdiction of one Contracting State to deal with disputes between the parties or alternatively exclusive jurisdiction arising in various stipulated circumstances which will be examined in more detail below.

(iv) Special jurisdiction for example in matters relating to a tort whereby jurisdiction will be in the courts of the country in which the harmful event occurred.

(v) Special rules apply to jurisdiction in matters relating to insurance and consumer contracts but these are outside the scope of this chapter.

Each of these grounds will now be examined in turn.

1. Domicile

The domicile of the defendant constitutes the principal jurisdictional factor for Convention purposes and so it is essential to determine its meaning.

A. Domicile of individuals

There is no Convention definition of domicile. There are differences in national law meanings of domicile and these remain, since the drafters of the Convention were anxious to avoid placing too many difficulties in the path of adoption of the Convention by member states and unification of the relevant laws.

Article 51 lays down Convention choice of law rules for determination of an individual's domicile as follows:

In order to determine whether a party is domiciled in a Contracting State whose courts are seized of the matter, the court shall apply its internal law.

If a party is not domiciled in a state whose courts are seized of the matter, then, in order to determine whether the party is domiciled in another Contracting State, the court shall apply the law of that state.

The main purpose of this rule is to avoid the occurrence of positive and negative conflicts of jurisdiction.

Problems can arise under this rule. For example, the courts of, say, France, applying the latter's domicile concept, may decide that a sub-franchisor/developer/franchisee was domiciled not in France but in, say, Germany and that the French courts were not, therefore, entitled to exercise jurisdiction under the Convention and so the franchisor might then try to bring the proceedings in Germany. If, however, although domiciled in Germany under France's concept, the sub-franchisor/developer/franchisee was held by German courts not to be domiciled in Germany by the latter's own concept, but in France or, alternatively, in The Netherlands, then the franchisor would then be unable to bring proceedings in France or Germany on the basis of situation of domicile in the Contracting State of the forum. If problems arose in The Netherlands regarding domicile a situation could come about that the franchisor would be unable to proceed in France or Germany or The Netherlands or conceivably any other Contracting State.

These problems can be avoided by the inclusion of a jurisdiction clause in a franchise agreement which, under

Article 17, will confer exclusive jurisdiction on the nominated Contracting State.

A brief account of the meaning of domicile for civil jurisdictional purposes under the laws of the original Contracting States will show several differences in relation to the national laws of domicile.

The Netherlands

Domicile is the place in which an individual has his home or effective residence, under Article 10 of the Civil Code 1970. If, therefore, a person's centre of business and professional interests is situated in one place, but he lives with his family in another territory, then the latter will be his domicile.

Italy

Domicile is situated in the place in which an individual has the chief centre of his interests and affairs under Article 43(1) of the Civil Code. As under The Netherlands concept, but in contrast to that of France and Luxembourg, the definition is objective requiring no evidence of intention.

France and Luxembourg

Domicile is the place in which an individual's 'principal establishment' is situated under Article 102 of the Civil Code, as that of his usual residence and the centre of his family, economic and vocational interests. In order to bring about a change of domicile, Article 103 requires the individual to reside in a new place and to form an intention to make the latter his principal establishment.

Belgium

As in France and Luxembourg domicile is an individual's 'principal establishment'. However, in Belgium the place in which the individual's name is entered upon the official population register is deemed to be the principal establishment, subjectively ascertained, under Article 36 of the Judicial Code. The theory is that each person is to have the right to choose his principal establishment and is presumed to know the consequences of registration and the place of registration will take precedence over the individual's principal establishment in the event of any conflict.

Germany

Domicile exists where an individual has a fixed and stable establishment under Article 7 of the Civil Code. Unlike the French and Italian concepts, the establishment required by German law need not be the principal centre of a person's personal or business affairs and the major difference, therefore, between the German and other Contracting States concepts is that under the former, a person may be domiciled in more than one place, or even nowhere at all when he manifests an intention to abandon his existing domicile without establishing a new one.

UK

As regards the UK Section 41 of the Act states that an individual is domiciled in the UK if he is resident in the UK and the nature and circumstances of his residence indicate that he has a substantial connection with the UK. Similar rules apply regarding domicile in a part of the UK. If an individual has been resident in the UK, or a part of the UK, for three months or more then the provisions of domicile will be presumed to be fulfilled unless the contrary is proved.

B. Domicile of companies

This is dealt with separately under the Convention and Article 53 states as follows:

'For the purposes of this Convention, the seat of a company or other legal person or association of natural or legal persons shall be treated as its domicile. However, in order to determine that seat, the court shall apply its rules of private international law.'

The seat of a company is a concept used by continental legal systems which, before 1987, formed no part of UK law. The function of the seat of a company is similar to a concept of the place of incorporation under UK law.

Section 42 of the Act states that the company will have its seat in the UK if and only if it was incorporated or formed under the law of a part of the UK and has its registered office or some other official address in the UK or its central management and control is exercised in the UK.

The following is a brief outline of the original Contracting States laws concerning the meaning of seat.

French law generally adopts the 'real seat' doctrine. This is the place of the company's central management, administration and control, the place in which corporate decisions are taken and general meetings of shareholders and directors meetings are held. It should therefore be relatively easy to ascertain the real seat and the company should be subjected to the law and jurisdiction of the State in which the company actually organises its business activities.

This can be contrasted to a 'statutory seat'. This is the place designated as the company's seat in its Statute or Memorandum and will therefore usually correspond with the place of incorporation. If this doctrine is applied then the statutory seat will overrule the location of the company's central management and control if it is located in a different state from that of a statutory state.

France: since 1966 it has been possible for third parties to resort to a company's statutory seat in France if the statutory seat and the real seat diverge through removal of the real seat to a foreign country.

Germany applies the real seat doctrine.

Italy: Italian courts will follow the real seat doctrine when neither statutory nor real seat is situated in Italy. When either is so situate, however, Italian law will be applied.

Belgium and Luxembourg also apply the real seat approach when the real seat is located there.

The Netherlands. This is the only original Contracting State which will solely be concerned with the statutory seat of a company.

2. Jurisdiction based upon submission by the defendant

Article 18 states that:

'Apart from jurisdiction derived from other provisions of this Convention, a court of a contracting State for whom a defendant enters an appearance shall have jurisdiction. This rule shall not apply where appearance was entered solely to contest the jurisdiction, or where another court has exclusive jurisdiction by virtue of Article 16.'

Therefore regardless of the rules relating to domicile, if a plaintiff issues proceedings in the jurisdiction of a Contracting State in which the defendant is not domiciled, but the defendant nevertheless acknowledges service of the Writ then by submitting to the jurisdiction the Courts of that Contracting State will have jurisdiction.

3. Exclusive jurisdiction

(a) Article 16

Article 16 confers exclusive jurisdiction in certain cases regardless of domicile for example, in proceedings concerned with the registration or validity of patents, trade marks, designs or other similar rights. The courts of the Contracting State in which a deposit or registration has been applied for, has taken place or is under the terms of an international convention deemed to have taken place, will have jurisdiction.

Another example of exclusive jurisdiction under Article 16 will be in proceedings concerning immovable property. In such a case the courts of the Contracting State in which the property is situated will have exclusive jurisdiction.

(b) Article 17

Article 17 states that if the parties, one or more of whom is domiciled in a Contracting State, have agreed that a court or courts of a Contracting State are to have jurisdiction to settle any disputes which have arisen or which may arise in connection with a particular legal relationship, that court or those courts shall have exclusive jurisdiction.

Any such agreement conferring jurisdiction must be in writing or evidenced in writing.

Therefore in any franchise agreement, if jurisdiction is conferred on the courts of any member state then those courts will have exclusive jurisdiction and no disputes between the parties can be litigated in any other jurisdiction.

Businessmen are thus enabled, at the time of concluding contracts, to reduce the risk of jurisdiction disputes recurring at a later stage and to secure the resolution of any dispute in their chosen forum.

It is a precondition of the application of Article 17 that one of the parties to the franchise agreement must be domiciled in a Contracting State. The other party may not be domiciled in an EC country. Where an agreement is concluded by parties, none of whom is domiciled in a Contracting State, but the courts of a Contracting State, for example, France, are nominated in a jurisdiction clause, then the courts of all other Contracting States shall have no jurisdiction over the parties' disputes unless the French courts, being the chosen courts, have declined jurisdiction.

Franchisors should note Article 17(4). If an agreement conferring jurisdiction was concluded for the benefit of only one of the parties, then that party shall have the right to bring proceedings in any other court which has jurisdiction by virtue of the Brussels Convention. The franchisor may be able to show that jurisdiction was conferred on his own local court solely for his benefit. If a franchisor can satisfy the courts on this point then the franchisor may be able to choose an alternative jurisdiction.

4. Special jurisdiction

Article 5 states that a person domiciled in a Contracting State may be sued in another Contracting State in certain situations. Examples are as follows:

(i) In matters relating to a contract, in the courts for the place of performance of the obligation in question.

(ii) In matters relating to tort in the courts for the place where the harmful event has occurred. The infringement of intellectual property rights constitutes a tort and therefore the courts of the country where the infringement (the harmful event) occurred will have jurisdiction.

(iii) In a civil claim for damages based on an act giving rise to criminal proceedings then, to the extent that the court has jurisdiction under its own law to entertain civil proceedings, the court seized of the criminal proceedings will have jurisdiction.

Article 6 also sets out situations in which the courts of a Contracting State may have special jurisdiction regardless of domicile. For example, if the person is one of a number of defendants, then that person may be sued in the courts for the place where any one of the defendants is domiciled. Another example would be in the case of a counterclaim arising from the same contract or facts on which an original claim was based, and the court in which the original claim is pending will have jurisdiction.

Examples of the application of the Jurisdiction Rules

It is always essential for a franchisor to protect its intellectual property rights. If the franchisor has a network in two or more countries in the EEC and wishes to take action to prevent any infringement of its trade marks, the rules relating to jurisdiction will operate as follows:

1. The franchisor may sue the infringer in its country of domicile provided the domicile is in a Contracting State.

2. Alternatively, by virtue of Article 5 the infringer may be sued in the courts of the country where the infringement (the harmful event) occurred. The question then arises: what is the harmful event? The harmful act may be the application of the trade mark to goods (in one Contracting State) and the importation of the goods bearing the infringing trade mark (into another Contracting State). It can be argued that the harmful act will be both the importation (probably by a distributor) and the application of the trade marks by the manufacturer. However, any action against the manufacturer in respect of the application of the infringing trade mark to the goods will have to be issued in the jurisdiction of the manufacturer unless the manufacturer was a party to the importation of the goods into the distributor's jurisdiction.

3. In the case of *Handelskwekerij G J Bier BV* v. *Mines de Potasse d'Alsace* (Case 21/76 [1977] 1 CMLR 284) the European Court held that jurisdiction may be conferred on the courts of the country where both the harmful act was perpetrated and where the damage was suffered. For example, if a franchisor in the UK wished to take action for infringement of its trade marks and the act of infringement took place in France the franchisor could commence proceedings in the UK if the franchisor was able to show actual financial loss incurred in the UK and a direct connection between the economic loss and the infringing act.

However, in such a case if the English courts did accept jurisdiction the question of infringement would have to be decided according to French law because the infringing act took place in France. The relevant law will be the law relating to the rights recognised in the jurisdiction where the harmful act occurred.

4. In any proceedings concerning the registration or validity of trade marks the courts of the Contracting State in which, for example, the registration of the trade marks has been applied for will have exclusive jurisdiction by virtue of Article 16.

An exception to this rule will be proceedings relating to the Community Patent which, when it is implemented, will be valid for the whole Community.

The franchisor should therefore commence any action for infringement of its trade mark in the country where the rights are registered even if the defendant may not be domiciled in that Contracting State and even if the harmful act of infringement occurred in another Contracting State. If the franchisor commenced an infringement action in the jurisdiction where the harmful act occurred, and if the defendant challenged the validity of the trade mark, this challenge would have to be referred to the courts in the country where the trade marks were registered thereby causing a substantial increase in the likely costs and a potential duplication of the litigation.

RECOGNITION

The essential principle is that any judgment given in a Contracting State will be recognised by the other Contracting States without any special procedure being required (Article 26 paragraph 1).

The scope for challenging the jurisdiction of the original court is extremely limited.

Article 28 of the Convention lays down certain rules in respect of recognition:

(a) in considering an allegation of lack of jurisdiction the national courts are bound by the findings of fact upon which the original court based its jurisdiction;

(b) a judgment will not be recognised if it conflicts with the jurisdictional rules under Articles 7-12a of the Convention (insurance), 13-15 (consumer contracts) or Articles 16 and 17 (exclusive jurisdiction);

(c) the jurisdiction of the court of the Contracting State in which the judgment was given may not be reviewed subject to (b) above.

In general the grounds upon which the judgment can be challenged are procedural rather than substantial. The following are four possible grounds where a judgment in a franchise dispute may not be recognised in the UK and they are as follows:

(a) if such recognition is contrary to public policy in the UK;

(b) where the judgment was given in default of appearance by the defendant, who was not duly served with the document which commenced the proceedings in sufficient time to enable him to arrange for his defence;

(c) if the judgment is irreconcilable with the judgment given in a dispute between the same parties in the UK;

(d) if the judgment is irreconcilable with an earlier recognisable judgment given in a non-Contracting State involving the same cause of action between the same parties.

ENFORCEMENT

Article 31 provides that the judgment of a Contracting State, enforceable in that Contracting State, is enforceable in any other Contracting State if, on the application of any interested party, it is registered in the Contracting State where enforcement is sought.

Outside the UK an application for enforcement of a judgment must be made and in all the Contracting States will involve the making of an 'Order authorising enforcement' of the foreign judgment – known as the 'formule executoire' – in accordance with Article 31.

The precise manner of giving expression for authorisation is a matter for the national procedure of each enforcement state. Some states require a separate order to be made following an ex parte application and in other states a copy of the judgment is merely stamped in order to register it.

In the UK the application for registration must be made to the High Court in England or Northern Ireland and in Scotland to the Court of Session. The reasonable costs or expenses incidental to its registration shall be recuperable as if they were sums recoverable under the judgment.

Interest on the judgment debt depends on the law of the Contracting State in which the judgment was issued. The rate and the date of interest will be fixed by the foreign judgment court. Although both the Convention and the Act are silent on this point, it seems clear that the judgment must be registered in the currency in which it was given.

In addition to the essential preconditions for the recognition of judgments described above, Article 31 provides for certain additional positive preconditions for the actual registration of a judgment in a Contracting State and an enforcement order. They are as follows:

(i) The foreign judgment must be enforceable in the judgment state.

A judgment will still be enforceable even if it is subsequently varied, superseded or cancelled by a final judgment of a court of the judgment state, provided it is enforceable for the time being in the judgment state. For example, if an appeal has been lodged in the judgment state, and therefore the judgment at least provisionally cannot be enforced in the judgment state, then the judgment cannot be enforced in any other Contracting State in which the defendant's assets may be located. A translation of the judgment (if necessary) should also be lodged in the registering court.

If there is a dispute in the judgment state as to whether or not the judgment has been satisfied, then the judgment is unlikely to be enforced in the UK.

(ii) The applicant for enforcement must be 'an interested party'.

(iii) Certain documents must be produced and evidence showing that the foreign judgment was served on the defendant.

PRACTICAL PROCEDURE FOR REGISTRATION AND ENFORCEMENT UNDER THE 1968 CONVENTION

The procedural rules for registration and enforcement will vary in each Contracting State. However, in each Contracting State the registration procedures to be followed are really only formalities which the plaintiff must follow to enforce the judgment. There cannot be any review of the judgment itself. As an example, procedural rules in the UK are set out below:

(1) Registration

1. The application for registration must be made ex parte, that is to say without notice to the defendant, supported by an affidavit stating the following:

(i) whether the judgment provides for the payment of a sum or sums of money;

(ii) whether interest is recoverable on the judgment in accordance with the law of the state in which the judgment was given and, if so, the rate of interest, the date from which it is recoverable and the date on which it ceases to accrue;

(iii) an address within the jurisdiction for service of process on the Applicant and the name and the usual or last known address or place of business of the person against whom the judgment was given;

(iv) to the best information and belief of the deponent:

    (a) the grounds on which the right to enforce the judgment is vested in the Applicant; and

    (b) as the case may require either that at the date of the application the judgment has not been satisfied or the part or amount in respect of which it remains unsatisfied.

2. There must be exhibited to the affidavit:

(i) the judgment (or a certified copy) together with documents showing that the judgment has been served and is enforceable;

(ii) in the case of a judgment in default of a defence being served by the defendant, then the original or certified copy of the document which establishes the defendant being served with the documents commencing proceedings;

(iii) if the Applicant is in receipt of some form of financial assistance in the proceedings then the relevant document should be lodged;

(iv) a certified English translation must be lodged.

The UK court must then give its decision without delay following this procedure. Registration can only be refused by the UK court for one of the reasons specified in Articles 27 or 28. The court must notify the decision to the Applicant without delay and, if enforcement is authorised by the court, then the Applicant must draw up the court order. The court will state a period within which an appeal may be made against the order and must notify the Applicant and execution will not be issued until that period has expired.

A Notice of Registration may then be served on the judgment debtor by delivering it to him personally or sending it to him at his usual or last known address or place of business.

(2) Appeals and stage of execution

If enforcement is authorised the judgment debtor can appeal against the decision within one month of service of the notice. The period will extend to two months where the judgment debtor is domiciled in a Contracting State other than the UK.

A UK court will stay proceedings where it is notified that an appeal has been lodged against the judgment in the country where the judgment was given or where the time for such an appeal has not yet expired.

During the above one month/two months time period specified for an appeal to the High Court in the UK, no enforcement other than protective measures can take place. The judgment debtor can, in certain circumstances, apply for an order freezing a defendant's assets or restraining any continuing infringement of its intellectual property rights.

CONCLUSION

The long-term effect of the 1968 Convention may well be seen as being the most important step towards a single system of European Law. In practical terms its effect is to provide a successful plaintiff in the court of a foreign Contracting State with a far simpler and a less expensive method of successfully enforcing a judgment against assets situated in other Contracting States.

Franchisors who pursue litigation against a developer/sub-francisor/unit franchisee for example, for non-payment of royalties or failure to give a proper account of profits should be able to enforce judgments within the EEC relatively easily. Furthermore, as injunctions can be enforced franchisors should be able to take urgent action and enforce the injunction if the sub-franchisor/developer/unit franchisee is located in the jurisdiction of another Contracting State.

If the franchise agreement contains an arbitration clause, and not a jurisdiction clause, arbitration awards are also automatically enforceable in the majority of member states of the EC being parties to the New York Convention. Arbitration awards are automatically enforceable in the courts of signatories to that Convention.

The Brussels Convention is a significant step in the overall process of European unity. The Convention may not provide for all events and circumstances within the area of its operation but this is a realistic reflection on the current state of European integration — social, political, legal and economic — as a whole.

Franchisors attempting to enforce judgments against recalcitrant sub-franchisors/developers/unit franchisees in another Contracting State may find the rules and procedures complex and, at times, fairly baffling. Franchisors can rest assured that Members of Parliament in the UK also had great difficulty understanding the legislation and the following are examples of statements made during the course of the Act's progress through Parliament, before the doctrine of the Convention was finally approved:

'I have been trying to read the Bill over the last day or two. Great stretches of it remain a complete mystery to me . . . I do not remember an occasion where I have been faced with a more daunting task in addressing this House than this afternoon, because of the nature of the Bill . . . Lord Lloyd of Kilgerran actually understands only two clauses of this Bill . . . I would go further and say that the measure gives to the word 'Complexity' a new dimension.'

and

'The more I read, the more I was grateful to my Right Honourable and Learned Friends the Lord Chancellor and the Lord Advocate for undertaking the introduction of this mind-boggling myriad of legal complexity . . . I can confirm that my own constituents are not discussing the Bill's detailed provisions in the pubs, the clubs and on the streets.'

PART FIVE

FRANCHISING
AND
FINANCE

Overview of Taxation in the EC

By SIAN WILLIAMS and BERNARD JEFFCOTE

1. TAX HARMONISATION WITHIN THE EC

Tax harmonisation, of both direct and indirect taxes, within the EC is one of the financial measures which must be taken to achieve fair competition for businesses operating within the EC. Understandably so, it is also an issue of extreme political sensitivity.

In June 1990, political agreement was reached by the EC Council to introduce three longstanding proposals in relation to direct taxation within the Community. Limited progress has also been made in the area of indirect taxes.

The implementation of measures affecting taxation is a particularly difficult area because although most European legislation can, following the Single European Act, become law by a qualified majority, unanimity by all 12 member states, is still required on taxation matters.

Direct taxes

Given the extreme diversity of corporate tax regimes currently in force in the various member states, it is not surprising that progress towards harmonisation has been slow. The reasons for this diversity are historic and generally reflect the difference in economic and social structures of the member states. Recent tax reforms undertaken in a number of countries, for example the UK, Germany and Holland have reduced the disparities in the rates of corporate tax, and further, the three EC Directives on direct taxation were formally adopted by the EC Council in July 1990. The intention is to implement these by 1 January 1992. The measures cover the following areas:

— Withholding taxes on dividends between 'parent' and 'subsidiary' companies in EC member states.
— The tax treatment of cross border mergers, divisions of companies and transfers of assets between member states.
— Arbitration procedures between EC member states.

These will have some impact on removing the differences between tax systems; however, fundamental differences will still remain.

With one exception, all countries operate a 'global' system whereby corporate taxes are levied on resident corporations on worldwide profits. The exception is France which taxes its residents on profits arising in France only; this is known as a territorial system. Thus income or profits derived from a foreign branch of a French company are excluded from the basis of taxation. By contrast all countries limit the taxation of non-resident companies to income or profits derived from activities or sources in their jurisdiction.

Perhaps the most important differences in tax systems arise from the method of taxation of companies' profits both at the corporate and shareholder level. Some countries, for example the Netherlands and Luxembourg, tax profits twice so far as individual shareholders are concerned; that is once at the company level and again at the shareholder level. At the other end of the spectrum, Germany and Italy have eliminated this double taxation by granting a credit to shareholders for the full corporate tax paid by the company on the profits out of which the dividends are paid. Greece achieves the same result by a different method; that is, by allowing the dividend as a deduction in arriving at the profit liable to corporate tax. The other countries fall somewhere in the middle, in that an individual can only deduct a part of the corporate tax paid on the profits out of which the dividend is paid against his tax liability on the dividend. So far as dividends paid to resident corporate shareholders are concerned, all of the countries have implemented measures to avoid double taxation either by granting a credit to the parent company for the tax paid by the subsidiary or by granting full or partial exemption from tax in respect of the dividend.

For the taxation of distributions to non-resident shareholders, all countries, with the exception of Ireland and the UK, levy a withholding tax on dividends paid to such shareholders. In the case of dividends derived by non-resident parent companies, the rate of withholding tax levied will depend on the terms of a double taxation treaty between the country concerned and the shareholder's country of residence. Most treaties concluded between EC member states and other major countries usually provide for a reduction in the rate of withholding tax to 5 per cent on dividends paid to a non-resident parent.

The EC Directive on the tax treatment of dividends between 'subsidiaries' and 'parent' companies provides that no withholding tax should be applied to dividends distributed by a company in one member state to a company in another member state which owns at least 25% of the paying company's share capital.

Agreement to the Directive was reached between member states after granting derogations to Germany, Greece and Portugal:

— Germany is allowed to charge a 5% withholding tax from 1 January 1992 until 30 June, 1996 provided the rate of tax on distributed profits is at least 11% less than the tax on undistributed profits.
— Greece has a derogation without a time limit, enabling it to charge withholding tax for so long as it does not charge corporation tax on distributed profits, although it is specifically stated that the rate of withholding tax must not exceed the rate provided for in existing treaties.

— Subject to existing tax treaties, Portugal is permitted to charge a withholding tax not exceeding 15% for the first five years and 10% for the following three years: the derogation also allows for a review at the end of the eight year period with a view to the possible extension of the duration of the 10% charge.

Corporate tax rates are frequently used in the comparison of tax systems, however too much emphasis on tax rates can be misleading. Although some convergence of corporate tax rates has already been achieved, the tax base of each country must also be considered.

It is often the case that a reduction in the tax rate will be accompanied by a widening of the tax base, typically by a reduction in allowable tax expenditure. This has assumed even greater significance following the plethora of tax reforms in the last couple of years which have generally reduced the tax rates in the EC and indeed in several non EC States. However, closer examination of the tax reforms in most of the countries concerned reveals that although the statutory rates have been reduced, the reduction or removal of many tax reliefs result in a lesser decrease in the effective rates of tax than the reduction in statutory rates would suggest. In some situations the effective tax rate is actually increased due to the widening of the tax base. The 1984 reforms in the UK were an example of a reduction in the nominal tax rate which was matched by an increase in the effective tax rate due to reduced capital allowances.

The rules for calculating taxable income differ greatly within the EC, particularly with regard to capital gains. The Directive on mergers within the EC goes some way towards eliminating these differences.

The Directive deals primarily with EC mergers whereby two companies are joined together without formal takeover or liquidation. It is a form of merger largely unknown in the UK and therefore usually referred to by its French term of 'fusion'. The Directive provides a form of rollover relief in these circumstances.

Possibly one of the major reasons for the diversity of tax systems in the EC, apart from economic and social factors, is the fact that, in reality, the member states are competitors. The tax system is therefore a method of attracting foreign investors and capital.

Some countries achieve this by granting favourable tax treatment to companies operating in underdeveloped or industrial regions. Examples of this can be found in France, Germany, Italy and the UK. Such incentives include: tax holidays (France); accelerated depreciation (Germany); and complete exemption from tax (Italy). Other countries are known for their favourable tax systems for holding companies (Luxembourg), intermediary companies for the receipt of royalties, dividends, and interest (the Netherlands) and co-ordination centres (Belgium).

In addition to the above Directives which have been formally agreed by the EC Council, the EC Commission has recently agreed on two additional proposals for achieving a single market, which are being presented to the EC Council.

The first proposed Directive would require member states to eliminate by 1 January 1993 their tax at source on royalties and interest payments between parents and subsidiary corporations. Delayed effective dates would be granted to Portugal and Greece to cushion the effect of the proposal on their national budgets. The present situation shows wide differences among the taxes imposed by the member states. The withholding tax on royalties varies from 0% to 33⅓% and the withholding tax on interest from 0% to 48.4%.

The second proposal concerns the single market requirement that losses must be deductible even if incurred by a branch or subsidiary in a member state other than in which the head office is located. The Commission proposes a choice between two different methods: one method is the imputation or tax credit method, and the other is the deduction of losses incurred by permanent establishments situated abroad and the reincorporation of subsequent profits to the extent of amounts previously deducted. Member states are free to choose a method and will almost certainly opt for the method that most closely corresponds to their current national practice. A choice is not provided for subsidiaries; the only allowable method is the deduction of losses and the future reincorporation of subsequent profits.

These proposals are currently intended only to eliminate double taxation situations within the single market, but member states are allowed to extend the proposed measures to branches and subsidiaries located outside the EC.

The desire of the European Commission to harmonise corporate taxes in the EC is understandable, particularly if the free market in goods and capital is to be achieved post 1992. Failure to achieve harmonisation may result in a concentration of activity in one member state with a low tax base, to the detriment of countries with a high tax base. Although standard rates of corporate tax are more uniform than before, effective rates remain diverse. The real challenge for businesses within the EC is to understand fully the effective tax rates on their individual and diverse activities.

Indirect tax

VAT is a European tax which is imposed in each EC country (other than Portugal, where it is in the process of being introduced). The method of operation of VAT is laid down by Community Directives and is broadly similar in all countries. What so far has not been harmonised, are the rates of tax and this has caused little difficulty so far, as tax can usually be levied in the country of consumption at its rates and border controls ensure collection of the appropriate tax where the goods or services are purchased in another member state.

The proposed free movement of goods and people in the Single European Market, will mean that border collection cannot happen. If nothing is done, cross-border shopping will ensue, with those countries with low VAT rates benefiting to the detriment of those with high rates.

At present VAT rates, categories and bands are widely different. For example Denmark applies a single rate of 22% to all taxable goods and services, whilst countries such as Belgium operate five bands ranging from 6% to 34%. In

Britain and Ireland certain goods such as books and childrens clothes are totally exempt from tax. As a result significant distortions in the cost of goods arises, for example in Ireland VAT on cars is so high that a basic family car costs more than a luxury estate car in Belgium.

To avoid this cross-border shopping the Commission has made four proposals:

(a) That there will be only two rates of VAT in any member state.

(b) The rate of tax on a specified and restricted range of goods – food, energy products, water, pharmaceuticals, books, newspapers and periodicals, and passenger transport – must be in the range of 4% to 9%.

(c) All other goods and services will be charged at between 14% and 20%.

(d) Excise duties throughout the Community will be exactly the same.

The 5% – 6% variation in VAT rates was thought not to lead to cross-border shopping, based on the US experience of Sales Tax variances between neighbouring states.

These proposals were deemed politically unacceptable, the primary objections coming from Denmark and Ireland who were faced with reducing high rates of indirect taxation and thereby incurring a significant revenue loss, and from the UK who resisted the attempt to charge VAT on goods that were previously exempt.

The most recent proposals include a VAT floor of 15% on most goods and services, plus a wide band of 0–9% for a list of goods which have historically been subject to preferential treatment in the member states.

In December 1990 the EC Council approved an interim VAT system which provides that VAT will continue to be paid in the destination country but the chargeable event will be the acquisition by the importing company rather than the border crossing. Consequently, both controls and payments at the border can be eliminated. To prevent fraud, companies will have to provide tax authorities with quarterly reports listing the total value of their trade with clients in other member states and their clients' VAT numbers.

The interim system will be replaced by a permanent system based on the payment of VAT in the member state in which the goods originate. This new system will apply only within the single market, however. VAT payment in the destination country will continue to apply for trade with other countries.

Excise duties

The key difference between excise duties and VAT is that the former are only levied once. The proposal to align duties throughout the Community brings with it additional horrendous political and economic problems for the individual member states and as a result the Commission's initial proposals have had to be rethought.

At present trade distortions are avoided by exporting goods duty free, and therefore borders have been of critical importance for regulating trade.

Originally, the Commission suggested that the excise rates should be harmonised. However, opposition came from countries where high rates are imposed on beers, wines and spirits for social and health reasons and countries where the wines and spirits are produced which were in favour of maintaining low rates. This would mean that the UK would have to take 60 pence off a bottle of wine and Germany would be obliged to put 9 pence duty onto a bottle, on which at present no excise is levied. The result was an agreement for rates to be aligned, with a Community wide minimum rate and no maximum rate. However the latest proposals contain objectives for the excise rates to be standardised.

2. TAX PLANNING FOR AN EC FRANCHISE NETWORK FOR BOTH MEMBER STATE FRANCHISORS AND NON-EC FRANCHISORS

This section considers a number of broad aspects of taxation which may apply generally to franchising, whether in EC or non EC countries. An understanding of the taxation implications of franchise operations around the world is an important advantage to both franchisor and franchisee. Taxation can be a substantial expense and unless judicious tax planning is undertaken the return from a franchise may be significantly eroded.

Generally, the taxation of a franchising operation is no different from any other business. However, a particular feature is the payment of fees from franchisee to franchisor. These may take the form of an initial fee followed by a series of recurring payments. The terms of the franchise agreement are frequently relied on to determine the tax status of these payments so they must be carefully worded. Clearly, the franchisee will wish to maximise the deductibility of payments from taxable income, the franchisor to minimise any tax liability arising on receipt.

The choice of an advantageous structure will require detailed examination of the tax system prevailing in the relevant jurisdictions as well as consideration of the type of entity most suited to the franchising operation. Cross border activities within the EC may benefit from the inclusion of new entities such as the European Economic Interest Groupings and Societas Europea, the tax treatment of which is covered later in this chapter.

While every attempt has been made to ensure the accuracy of the contents of this chapter it should be borne in mind that it will provide general guidance only, and further professional advice should be sought on specific matters.

Initial fees

A franchisee will generally prefer that initial fees are deductible or, at worst, depreciable for tax purposes. The nature and description of the fee will usually determine the treatment that is appropriate. Fees paid for tangible assets, such as plant and property, will usually but not always, be depreciable, as will payment for know how. Payments for the right to operate in a particular territory are subject to more variable treatment; in the UK for example. they will usually be regarded as goodwill, which is neither deductible nor depreciable for tax purposes; in other countries, such as Canada, the Netherlands and Switzerland, such payments are generally depreciable. The US usually allows them to be deducted or amortised over the franchise period.

Expenditure on normal trading items, such as an initial stock of raw materials, consumables or goods for resale will generally constitute a normal trading expense and will therefore be deductible, although the deduction may be deferred until the goods are sold.

Clearly the franchisor will prefer to minimise his tax liability on any receipts. In some circumstances, receipts can be treated as capital proceeds subject to privileged rates of taxation. However depending on the volume of business undertaken, it is likely that most fees will generally be regarded as trading income. Payments received for know how are also likely to be considered revenue; however receipts allocated to the right to operate in a particular territory or goodwill may be considered capital.

Recurring fees

The treatment of recurring fees is relatively straightforward. They are generally regarded as revenue expenses by the franchisee and trading income by the franchisor. A complication which arises particularly in respect of recurring fees, but also applies to initial fees, is that the country in which the franchisee resides may apply a withholding tax deduction to those payments. It is therefore important to try to seek protection under the terms of a double taxation agreement or treaty between the franchisor's home country and the franchisee's country.

Since franchising implies a mixed contract involving typical licence agreement clauses as well as elements of supply or service contracts, each element must follow its own tax treatment.

Franchisors from treaty countries should carefully distinguish within agreements whether the fees to be paid by the franchisee relate to royalties or to other services. The concept of a royalty frequently accords to the OECD double tax treaty model.

Relationship between the franchisor and franchisee

The relationship between the franchisor and franchisee will usually be one of independence. However, if related parties are involved, domestic tax authorities may be able to query the level of fees which are paid on the basis that they are not at arm's length. Should any payments be considered excessive, they are unlikely to be deductible for tax purposes and could be held to be a distribution by the franchisee. Transfer pricing problems of this nature can be avoided if prices to related parties are set at the same level as those to independent third parties.

In some countries the existence of a relationship between two parties can be sufficient to completely change the way in which the payment is regarded for tax purposes. For example in the UK a payment for know how (which is normally depreciable) to a related party is deemed by legislation to be a payment for goodwill (which is not depreciable).

Even when a franchisor and franchisee are independent, problems can occur when a franchisor rents property to a franchisee. Many countries reserve the right to tax income from real estate situated within their borders, therefore a franchisor may have a foreign tax liability on such rentals. If there is no rental but a correspondingly high franchise fee, some Revenue authorities may seek to reclassify part of the fee as rental if this would increase the tax due.

Generally however, a franchisor will not have a taxable presence in a country simply because independent franchisees are operating in or are resident in that country. Where a franchisor does have a taxable presence, agreement will need to be obtained from the appropriate Revenue authorities to the division of the franchisor's profit between Head Office and the foreign country operations.

Particular considerations for the franchisor

When considering the international tax implications of the franchise business the franchisor will seek to combine the following to achieve optimum results:

(i) Minimum tax exposure in the country in which a franchise has been granted.
This is largely a question of ensuring that the franchisor has minimal or preferably no presence in that country.

(ii) Minimum withholding taxes.
Exposure to withholding taxes can be minimised if a favourable double taxation agreement exists between the franchisee's country and the country of the franchisor. If a suitable double taxation treaty does not exist it may be appropriate to establish an intermediary company to which the franchisor licences the relevant rights and which in turn licences those rights to the franchisee. The intermediary would need to be based in a country which has a favourable regime regarding withholding taxes and taxes on royalties generally. Traditionally, The Netherlands has been regarded as suitable for this purpose as it imposes no withholding tax on royalties and provides a favourable treatment for royalties passed through from a franchisee to an ultimate franchisor. The Netherlands also has an extensive network of double taxation agreements most of which provide for low and zero withholding taxes on royalties. In some countries Revenue authorities have sought to limit the extent to which relief can be obtained by 'treaty shopping' i.e., by contending that the intermediary is not the beneficial owner of the royalties received. There is a tendency for new double tax treaties to contain provisions directed against 'treaty shopping' arrangements. It is essential to obtain current advice before seeking to set up sub-franchising companies in apparently suitable countries.

(iii) Minimum or deferred home country taxes

The traditional method of long term deferral of income is to establish a network of subsidiaries around the world to operate in certain countries with a view to gathering profits there and ultimately dividending them back to the franchisor or parent company. There are a number of alternative structures which may be adopted in order to minimise dividend withholding taxes but the success of each depends on the location of the operating companies and the ultimate recipient company.

(iv) Maximum use of foreign tax credits

It can be difficult to ensure that maximum relief is obtained for foreign country tax suffered. In the US, relief via credit or deduction is given in respect of foreign taxes paid on foreign source income and capital gains whether or not the US has a tax treaty with the foreign country.

However, it can be difficult for US corporations to utilise foreign tax credits fully, due to the low US rates of corporate tax. A common approach in the US to reducing foreign withholding taxes is to license franchisee rights to a corporation in a favourable treaty country. The US tax authorities' attempts to eliminate back-to-back licensing companies have generally been limited to inbound situations and have not been applied to US licensors. However, treaty shopping through intermediary corporations by US groups is becoming more restricted.

Also, the UK Revenue are looking very closely at 'dividend mixer' companies whose purpose is to average tax suffered in high and low tax regimes to maximise UK relief for foreign tax.

(v) Minimum excise duties

An EC franchisor will not have many options in regard to relief from duty since these reliefs are generally targeted at those importers manufacturing and re-exporting goods outside the Community. He should be aware however that duty reliefs are available where imported goods are rejected by the importer because they do not comply with the conditions of the contract, or where goods have to be exported for repair and subsequently reimported.

It is, perhaps, more valuable for the franchisor to consider administrative and cashflow saving options such as the following:

Duty and VAT deferment

A scheme is operated by Customs and Excise where duty and VAT (collected by Customs at the time of importation as if it were a duty) does not have to be paid up front on each consignment of imported goods. Instead, a special guarantee is set up through the importer's bank and amounts are not actually deducted from his account until the fifteenth day after the month in which the importation takes place. This is an absolutely standard facility and one which all regular importers should take advantage of.

Customs warehousing

Warehousing is advantageous to importers which need to store imported goods, prior to sale. A customs warehouse is, effectively, outside the customs territory of the EC and duty and other taxes only become liable when the product is removed from the warehouse for sale.

Period entry

Period entry is of value to importers regularly bringing in a wide variety of products, in considerable quantities. Essentially, period entry entails the approval by Customs of your own computer system which is able to complete a customs declaration and forward the data by floppy disc, tape or electronic data interchange. Period entry can deliver the following advantages; reduced customs clearance costs, improved customs entry accuracy, reduced documentation, administration, customs clearance queries and problems.

CROSS BORDER CO-OPERATION

European Economic Interest Groupings (EEIGs)

Although there are some advantages to the EEIG over other cross border entities, so far few have been set up. To some extent this can be explained by the fact that the EEIG is a relatively new concept; however, the uncertainties surrounding the tax treatment of an EEIG particularly in an international context are also a major disincentive.

Direct taxes

The basis for the tax treatment of an EEIG is set out in Article 40 of the Regulation enabling EEIGs, which provides that the profits or losses resulting from the activities of a Grouping shall be taxable only in the hands of its members.

Article 40 is not as straightforward as it appears as it does not specify who may charge the tax. The result is that three territories may seek to charge tax: the territory in which the EEIG has its official address, any other territory in which the grouping may have an office, and the territory of residence of the members. The Regulation offers no alleviation of the triple charge. Nor does it suggest how the administration of one territory will enforce direct tax liabilities against an EEIG member in another territory.

There is also the question of the measurement of profit. Most member states require cross border dealings between connected parties to be on an arm's length basis. This could result in the member state in which the EEIG is situated seeking to impute a profit to the activities of the Grouping, i.e., on a cost plus basis, and to tax the member on that profit even though the members simply contributed on a cost sharing basis.

Indirect taxes

For VAT purposes it appears that the EEIG will be regarded as a business entity in any member state in which it has economic activity. It will be entitled to recover VAT input tax incurred, but will have to charge output tax on the services it supplies to the members. Where the member is in the EC, depending on the nature of the services, the services should either be zero rated or tax chargeable but recoverable by the member.

International considerations

It is likely that, in practice, the greatest difficulties of applying the tax rules in relation to EEIGs will arise where there is an international dimension. There will be problems principally when reconciling the separate legal personality of an EEIG with the limited application of the fiscal transparency concept to EEIGs. Difficulties in applying double tax treaties in relation to EEIGs can also apply, as illustrated below.

Where an EEIG takes part in cross border transactions, which double tax treaties will be relevant?

— Those between the third country and the members of the EEIG?
— Or that between the third country and the country of 'residence' or registration of the EEIG?

In the absence of international agreement on this, the terms of all relevant double tax treaties will need to be examined. One example of the problems that may arise is when an EEIG has to deduct withholding tax. As an EEIG is not a taxpayer, treaty relief may often not be available, since treaties usually only apply to payment between residents of the contracting states and 'resident' usually means a resident liable to tax.

Societas Europea (SE)

The European company or Societas Europea (SE), is intended to enable firms established in the Community to choose an appropriate structure for co-operation on a scale required by the Community-wide market. It is intended to help them be competitive with firms from outside the Community.

On the tax side, the effect of the Commission's proposal is to remove the congenital handicap of multinationals being subject to different national tax laws. For tax purposes, the SE will be subject to the laws of the country where it has its head office.

Where an SE has a permanent establishment in other member states, any losses incurred by those establishments may be allowed to be set off against the profits of the SE. In other words, there is a consolidation of profits and losses across frontiers.

This consolidation of an SE's tax liability under the laws of the country where it has its head office will be an advantage for multinational companies. This will be particularly useful to US multinationals which will be able, for example, to use any loss incurred by a Belgian permanent establishment against the profit of its German parent SE. This will reduce the German tax payable and therefore the amount of German tax credit. This reduction could be a useful way to reduce the amount of foreign tax credits available for use against US tax due on the US multinational parent.

CHAPTER 34

Banking and Finance in the European Community

By GRAHAM ROSE and ANGUS MACMILLAN

1. CAPITAL MOVEMENTS

The EEC Treaty envisaged the free movement of capital within the Community as an essential complement to the free movement of goods, people and services. But progress on removing controls has varied between member states.

The UK, Germany, the Netherlands and Denmark have abolished exchange controls earlier than the other EC countries.

The Single European Act states that 'the internal market shall comprise an area without internal frontiers in which the free movement of goods, persons, services and capital is ensured in accordance with the provision of this Treaty'. Efficient and competitive financial markets are essential for the achievement of a genuine single market. That requires full freedom for capital movements, as well as wider-ranging liberalisation in the financial services field.

A directive removing controls from all capital movements within the Community was adopted in June 1988. It applies to most member states from 1 July 1990. However, Spain, Ireland, Greece and Portugal have until the end of 1992 to comply fully with its terms and, in view of the particular difficulties the requirements may pose for countries with less developed financial markets, Greece and Portugal may be permitted a further extension to 1995 if the Council of Ministers so decides.

The new directive also looks forward to the prospect of liberalisation beyond the Community. Member states have also declared their intention to free capital movements to and from non-Community countries.

The Community has also combined the two existing facilities for medium-term financial assistance for member states in balance of payments difficulties. Loans up to 16 billion ECU in total can be made, normally financed by market borrowing. Member states experiencing balance of payments difficulties as a result of freeing capital movements will be eligible for loans under this facility.

The economic benefits are forecast to be that the opening of national financial markets will enhance competition and choice in financial services within the Community. It should therefore lead to a more efficient and less costly channelling of savings into investment. Savers will be offered a wider range of financial assets, and borrowers will have access to more diverse and cheaper financing – particularly in countries which currently have extensive restrictions.

As barriers to the provision of financial services throughout the Community are dismantled, the financial sector will be exposed to new competitive pressures. The effect of these changes should be to strengthen the Community economy generally as well as increase efficiency in the financial sector.

2. IMPEDIMENTS TO FREE TRADE

Member state subsidies

The EEC Treaty establishes the fundamental principle that aid, in whatever form, granted by member state governments is incompatible with the concept of a common market if it distorts competition in trade within the Community. Articles 92–94 of the EEC Treaty lay down the mechanism for regulating such aid. In brief, governments must notify aid proposals or amendments to the Commission. The Commission examines the justification for the aid from the Community viewpoint (for example, it considers whether the aid would contribute to agreed EC objectives, and whether any benefit outweighs the potential cost in distorting competition). The Commission then issues a decision on whether the aid can be granted.

The Commission's future work on state aids is aimed at improving transparency and control. As part of this process the Commission has prepared an inventory of the budget resources which member states use for state subsidies. This will give the Commission a much better base on which to judge the extent to which it has been able to regulate existing support, and enable it to identify and take action against subsidies which are being granted without approval.

For further details on state aids see Volume 2, 'Investment Incentives', in the section on each member state.

Language and culture

Emerging cross-border transactions in Europe emphasise the paramount importance of communications in the service industries in general, and in financial services in particular. Although English is becoming the financial language of the world, there are still many problems associated with cultural and language difficulties which make market integration in Europe a more delicate process than in the US or Japanese markets.

Currencies and central banks

One of the key strengths of the US market is clearly the use of a common denominator: the dollar. For Europe to have a common currency and a common Central Bank is essential. However, impatient as we may be to see a European Central Bank; we must realise that gradual progress in this direction is more likely than dramatic moves.

Competition and anti-trust legislation

The issue of concentration of power and market share in the EC is a very complex one. For example, it might be necessary to accept that the creation of financial groups on a European scale could lead, in smaller countries, to the consolidation of groups with huge domestic market shares (see above).

Merger control

Merger controls and regulations in EC countries suffer from two weaknesses: they are often imprecise and they are not harmonised. So far the Commission has put forward proposals for regulations which give it some control over mergers. Unfortunately, these do not replace national regulations, but create a further level of supervision (see above).

Accounting principles

Another area of harmonisation that is critical to the creation of an integrated market is accounting. One of the strengths of the US market is the famous US GAAP (Generally Accepted Accounting Principles), which provide for a homogeneous treatment of transactions throughout the country. A typical example of this is the treatment of goodwill, which can impact on a merger or an acquisition to such an extent that it creates intra-EC distortions. The same applies to foreign exchange, amortisations, calculation of equity, treatment of reserves and pension commitments, to name just a few (see above).

Legal systems

Mentioning the problem of legal systems is like opening Pandora's box. It is to be hoped that the magnitude of national differences, which will give work to international lawyers for decades to come, will not discourage those who have tried actively to push the concept of the 'Societas Europa' without which an integrated market will look like a patchwork (see above).

Capital adequacy

The financial services industry is by definition providing services based on public trust in its ability to meet its commitments. In this respect specific regulations, such as the BIS capital adequacy rules and the European Banking Licence Directive, are critical.

Industry supervision

The financial services industry has always been the focus of many kinds of supervisory organisations. There are currently substantial differences, even in the principles established by those organisations, in the way in which they protect the investor, regulate industry or supervise the institutions.

3. INSTITUTIONAL FINANCE

If retail financial services have been transformed by increasing computerisation, recent trends in institutional finance have been equally dramatic.

The evolution of our society has been dominated by an increasing interconnection and interdependence which has now reached a true level of globalisation. European integration of financial services will create a fully integrated ensemble – the EC – within this wider global financial world where Japan, the US and other countries also play major roles. Europe, as an integrated market, already exists in the minds of those who operate in the international capital markets, and 1992 will not insulate the EC from strong competitive pressure from Japanese and American financial institutions. In this context, the main question is how European financial institutions will be able to become or remain major players in the global markets. 'Project 1992' in this respect is an opportunity, but also a challenge, since non-European competitors have been looking at Europe as an integrated market well in advance of most European institutions.

The securitisation process, that is to say, increasing reliance on stocks and shares as a means of finance, was only marginally affected by the October 1987 crash. Those who expected a return to traditional lending have been disappointed. The process will be further enhanced by the free distribution of securities within the EC as a result of the integration of the market. This raises strategic issues for those institutions which have relied on traditional banking products as a source of finance. Recent acquisitions of brokers and merchant banks are a sign of the increased awareness on the part of commercial banks and insurance companies of the need to combine corporate finance activities with specialised services in the field of securities. As far as continental Europe is concerned, the 'universal' banking structure is probably responsible for the erosion of European leadership in favour of mainly Japanese and American institutions. On the other hand, Japanese securities houses are both retail and institutional, and US houses are themselves now moving towards wider concepts.

The institutionalisation of capital markets represents a major challenge for Europeans. Financial assets are increasingly owned by individuals through specialist institutions such as portfolio managers, mutual funds, pension funds and so on. An integrated EC capital market is bound to increase this trend, particularly in countries where it remains comparatively under-developed.

At the major institutional level, the prospect of 1992 again promises to bring differential changes to different types of financial enterprises.

Strategic choices: products

With the exception of those who can afford, or at least believe they can afford, a global strategy which includes all the products within their areas, many financial institutions will have to make choices of strategic significance, and therefore very difficult ones on what services they are going to offer. These institutions are presumably considering the following basic premises.

Start from your roots
Most of the errors committed in the last few years in the financial services market have been the result of strategic

choices which led some institutions into businesses which were not part of their culture. The most obvious case is the number of ambitious plans made by commercial banks to enter investment banking, and by brokers to become bankers. Lessons from these experiences have to be drawn.

Seek complementaries

Rather than going outside your natural habitat (both geographically and in products), the seeking of complementary areas of development is critical. Regional strategies, ie banks going into mortgage or leasing businesses, are natural moves. Why not explore them first?

Exploit strengths

Everybody has strengths – location, management, distribution, creativity. An analysis of these strengths and the building-up of a strategy to develop them are essential.

Define objectives clearly

The need for focus implies that objectives need to be clearly defined. Strategic initiatives are often so vague that they are impossible to implement.

Implementation problems: internal growth or acquisitions?

A presence in the integrated European market can be implemented either by internal growth or by acquisitions.

In many cases, the answer to the strategic decision is simple: do it. The necessary presence in a market can always be gained first by opening a representative office or a branch, or setting up a company, to prepare the ground. This requires capital and, more importantly, people. One result of 'Project 1992' will be to increase the demand for good entrepreneurs, with international experience.

The acquisition route can have several motivations, such as acquiring a larger market share at once, or gaining local management, or doing things at speed, or avoiding entry barriers to a market. Acquisitions in the financial sector are delicate, but happen every day.

The obstacles to an acquisition strategy can be of a different nature, and scale.

(1) *Nationalism.* National authorities or managements often remain very sensitive to acquisition by foreign entities. Even if the new rules make it difficult to oppose acquisitions by EC institutions, the truth, in practice, is that financial institutions are politically sensitive. Regulatory differences make the acquisitions procedure in some countries more difficult than in others.

(2) *Defensive strategy.* Several defence strategies have been developed which can make an acquisition very difficult, if not impossible in some countries, mainly involving some form of 'poison pill' or defensive cross-shareholdings.

(3) *Scarcity value* means a proactive attitude is necessary. Often institutions are asking for 'something for sale', which is a poor and dangerous strategy.

The opportunity for acquisitions is real, however, and regardless of the difficulties noted above, transactions which make sense for both parties and are correctly priced are announced almost every day.

Consolidation is the trend in the United States. When inter-state banking rules were changed, a flow of mergers and acquisitions started immediately. Consolidation in the banking industry is now firmly underway: even 'unfriendly' transactions are happening, without opposition from the various state or federal authorities. A major consolidation of the European financial services industry is on its way and is likely to change the financial map of the EC.

Size is critical in retail finance, and an acquisition is often the fastest way to reach the critical mass. It will sometimes be necessary to find innovative methods, such as the exchange of subsidiaries, giving each party to a deal access to the other's market.

Brain power and motivation in sophisticated markets are the key to success. This is particularly true in private banking, asset management and corporate finance. Acquisitions in this field are more delicate than in others; they are, however, means of obtaining management participation, especially for an ambitious and stimulating project.

Growth in Europe is likely to boost the acquisition market. 'Project 1992' includes elements which should create growth and enable Europe to regain some of its previously lost world market share. Similarities of strategic problems make the dialogue between the leaders of the financial institutions much easier. Since most European financial institutions have the same problems and ambitions, link-ups and cross-shareholding ideas are much easier to develop.

Professional advice makes things happen. Europe has now started to focus on all the above issues and professional advice is there to assist managements to implement an acquisition strategy. Merger and acquisition specialists can help to realise and implement projects.

THE EUROPEAN BANKING SYSTEM

There is no European banking system as such. However, existing independent national regulatory systems will be replaced by the mutual recognition of other member states' standards. These standards will be based on EC directives. This new approach will call for a significant increase in co-ordination of regulation between national authorities.

The EC banking legislation will not apply to the central banks of member states, Post Office Giro institutions, and certain specified institutions peculiar to particular member states.

Certain basic principles will apply to the new European banking system.

(1) *Single licence.* Institutions will generally require authorisation for their operations only in the member state in which their registered head office is situated (the 'home state'). An institution which holds such an authorisation will be able to provide services and open branches in another member state (the 'host state'). In principle, home state authorisation will be sufficient; further authorisation in the host state will not be required.

(2) *Home state control.* Both initial authorisation and continuing prudential supervision will be carried out by home state authorities. The host state will have only a complementary role to play, principally in the supply to the home state authorities of information relating to the activities in its territory of institutions authorised by the home state.

(3) *Mutual recognition.* Member states are required to recognise each others' supervisory and authorisation standards.

(4) *Common minimum standards.* EC directives will establish common minimum standards for authorisation and continuing supervision. These standards will aim to achieve a proper standard of protection for depositors and investors and to create the conditions for a competitive EC-wide financial serrvices market. Common minimum standards are necessary to prevent an institution from putting consumers at risk by obtaining EC-wide authorisation in a state with low regulatory standards.

(5) *Additional national standards.* A member state will generally be able to impose stricter national rules than the common EC rules. However, rules which discriminate against institutions from other member states will be unlawful. In addition, a member state which applies stricter or additional standards of authorisation will not be able to prevent firms authorised in other member states from establishing branches in its territory or providing cross-border services. Clearly, this may make member states less inclined to impose standards which are significantly stricter than those laid down in EC directives. There is a risk of a movement towards the lowest common denominator of regulation.

(6) *Continuing national regulation.* In all areas which are not expressly dealt with by EC legislation, member states will remain free to adopt whatever rules they wish, again so long as these do not conflict with EC law.

Main banks

The data in this table ranks the banks in this survey under three headings (capital, assets, and pre-tax profits) all in absolute figures arrived at by converting the national currency into US dollars.

Bank	Country	Capital US$m	Assets US$m	Pre-tax profits US$m
Crédit Agricole	France	11,802	241,992	1,266
Barclays Bank	UK	10,715	204,907	1,111
National Westminster	UK	9.761	186,559	649
Deutsche Bank	Germany	8,462	202,263	2,081
Union Bank of Switzerland	Switzer.	8,150	113,854	784
Compagnie Financière de Paribas	France	7,926	138,668	1,225
Banque Nationale de Paris	France	6,177	231,463	918
Swiss Bank Corporation	Switzer.	6,153	105,090	647

Bank	Country	Capital US$m	Assets US$m	Pre-tax profits US$m
Crédit Lyonnais	France	5,617	210,727	940
Société Générale	France	5,528	164,741	1,013
Dresdner Bank	Germany	5,405	147,001	796
Rabobank Nederland	Netherl's	5,336	90,016	670
Groupe des Caisses d'Epargne Ecureuil	France	5,180	152,722	626
Crédit Suisse	Switzer.	4,898	88,926	678
Banco Bilbao Vizcaya	Spain	4,691	69,986	1,286
Cariplo–Cassa di Risparmio delle P. Lombarde	Italy	4,513	82,103	961
Midland Bank	UK	4,372	100,320	989
Banca Nazionale del Lavoro	Italy	4,153	100,967	−(106)
Abbey National	UK	3,940	59,732	804
Commerzbank	Germany	3,803	112,825	623
Skandinaviska Enskilda Banken	Sweden	3,708	58,718	735
Instituto Bancario San Paolo di Torino	Italy	3,697	107,403	986
Algemene Bank N'land	Netherl's	3,576	90,411	514
Lloyds Bank	UK	3,521	92,392	−(1,148)
Banesto–Banco Español de Credito	Spain	3,485	39,362	468
Amro Bank	Netherl's	3,465	93,824	499
Banca Commerciale Italiana	Italy	3,415	88,594	559
Banca di Monte dei Paschi di Siena	Italy	3,402	75,694	473
Instituto Mobiliare Italiano	Italy	3,199	27,004	533
TSB Group	UK	3,135	42,511	259
West LB	Germany	3,059	104,508	294
NMB Postbank Group	Netherl's	2,753	84,194	455
Banco Central	Spain	2,702	40,511	614
Union Bank of Finland	Finland	2,686	36,362	201
DG Bank	Germany	2,650	109,168	322
Svenska Handelsbanken	Sweden	2,636	44,218	635
Bayer. Hypo. Wech. Bank	Germany	2,619	90,129	409
PKbanken	Sweden	2,594	50,117	515
Groupe des Banques Populaires	France	2,570	64,701	289
Credito Italiano	Italy	2,491	75,233	316
Bayerische Vereinsbank	Germany	2,464	102,191	420
Kreditanstalt für Wiederaufbau	Germany	2,395	64,693	79
Royal Bank of Scotland	UK	2,258	45,772	381

Bank	Country	Capital US$m	Assets US$m	Pre-tax profits US$m
Generale Bank	Belgium	2,123	67,637	107
Banca di Roma	Italy	2,075	64,472	162
Banco Santander	Spain	2,029	41,266	741
Bayer. Landesbank	Germany	1,947	90,855	330
Kansallis Osake Pankki	Finland	1,925	37,033	49
CIC Group	France	1,898	74,725	387
Banque Indosuez	France	1,838	55,316	328

Who owns the EC's banks

Ownership	Number in top 50	Average assets $bn	Average pre-tax profits $m
Private companies	2	62.98	364
Public companies	40	93.12	603
Co-operatives	5	121.37	488
State-owned	3	135.36	521

Figures relate to fiscal year 1989.
Source: The Banker, October 1990.

5. THE EUROPEAN MONETARY SYSTEM (EMS)

The EMS came into existence on 12 March 1979, following agreement between Heads of Government in December 1978. Each member state is now a member of the EMS.

The European Currency Unit (ECU)

The ECU (European Currency Unit) is the central element of the EMS. Its value is calculated as a basket of set amounts of Community currencies, broadly reflecting the relative GNP of the member states, their trade and their currencies' importance for short-term finance at the time the amounts are fixed. All Community currencies are now included in the ECU.

By agreement, these amounts must be reviewed every five years (or at the request of any member state, if the weight of any currency has changed by more than 25 per cent since the last revision).

The Exchange Rate Mechanism (ERM)

Each member state which participates in the EMS exchange rate mechanism has a central rate against the ECU. These central rates can be realigned, if necessary, by mutual agreement of the participants. From these ECU central rates, bilateral central rates are calculated for each currency against each of the other participants. Margins of ±2.25% (±6% for

the lira and peseta) are used to set 'floor' and 'ceiling' rates from the bilateral central rates and these are the limits within which central banks are obliged to maintain the value of their currency.

Hence central banks have an unlimited obligation to intervene in the foreign currency markets in Community currencies. The central banks participating in the ERM open to each other unlimited credit lines in their own currencies for a short period for this purpose. Each currency has a 'divergence indicator' which compares its movement against its ECU central rate with its maximum permitted movement. The divergence indicator therefore acts as an early warning signal as the currency approaches its floor or ceiling. When a currency crosses its divergence threshold, the member state is expected to take corrective measures. In practice, currencies seldom reach their threshold before the maximum divergence in bilateral rates has been reached.

Greece and Portugal do not yet participate in the ERM.

European Monetary Co-operation Fund (EMCF)

The EMCF administers the exchange rate mechanism and intervention mechanism of the EMS. It issues ECU to the EMS central banks, in exchange for deposits by them of 20 per cent of their gold and dollar reserves. (These exchanges are purely notional: gold and dollars do not change hands and the central banks continue to earn interest on their dollar deposits.) These ECUs can then be used, within agreed limits, for settling the debts incurred by central banks in the operation of the EMS.

European Monetary Union

European Monetary Union (EMU) has been agreed as an objective by all EC member states except the United Kingdom. The failure of the British government to agree with the other member states caused substantial damage to European unity, but did not lessen the resolve of the other eleven member states, who have put their names to a 1994 starting date for the next phase of EMU and have laid down the conditions for its achievement.

The next stage of EMU entails the setting of the EuroFed, the planned Federal Central Bank, which should begin operations on 1 January 1994, provided that certain conditions are met. These conditions are the finishing of the EC single market programme, the largest possible number of (but not necessary all) EC currencies in the Exchange Rate Mechanism (ERM) (see above) and parliamentary ratification of an EMU treaty.

This would in turn entail secondary legislation ensuring freedom from national political influence for individuals seconded from national central banks sitting on the EuroFed Board and preventing individual governments from printing money to cover their deficits. By 1997, there should be a review of the progress of a Monetary Union, and in particular on macroeconomic convergence 'to enable the decision to move to stage three to be taken within a reasonable period'. Exactly when a single currency will emerge is difficult to say as yet, although M. Jacques Délors, the Commission President, has optimistically pronounced that the EC could give itself a single currency before the year 2000.

6. SETTLEMENT OF EUROPEAN INDEBTEDNESS

Settlements of international indebtedness are similar in the different European Community countries, the only difference being the national exchange control regulations, all of which will disappear in the near future.

Foreign currency accounts

If a company regularly receives and makes payments in foreign currencies, it could benefit by opening accounts in those currencies. The sale proceeds could then be used to meet any expenses incurred in that currency overseas, thus eliminating the exchange risk and at the same time making savings on foreign exchange commissions.

International payment services

Through correspondent banks or local subsidiaries, a credit institution can arrange for money to be sent abroad by cable, telex, mail, bankers draft or SWIFT (Society for World-wide Inter-bank Financial Telecommunications). SWIFT is a sophisticated network for the rapid and accurate transmission of international payments. It is operated by major banks world-wide.

Documentary credits

Banks issue documentary credits for customers engaged in importing and merchanting transactions and handle documentary credits in favour of exporting companies. A documentary credit is a banker's undertaking that, provided the terms and conditions of the credit are complied with, the beneficiary will receive payment for the transaction. It can be the safest and fastest method of obtaining payment. There are several types of credit available according to a company's requirements, the terms of the contract, or the documentary requirements of the importer.

Documentary collections

The documents relating to a company's exported goods are delivered to a bank, which then forwards them to a correspondent bank in the buyer's country. These documents are then only released to the buyer against the terms specified in the company's instructions to its bank.

Tender, performance and other bonds

Overseas trade buyers often demand that exporters provide bonds or guarantees stating that they will comply with the terms of the contract or pay compensation for any loss resulting from the failure to do so. It should be mentioned that bonds represent binding obligations against their issuer and do not guarantee trade debts.

7. FINANCE FOR EUROPEAN TRADE

(1) *Overdrafts or loans* are usually arranged through local bank branches subject to normal lending criteria and should be available in the local currency as well as in foreign currency.

(2) *Euro-currency loans* can be provided in all major currencies and each loan can be tailored to individual needs. Loans are available for periods from 1 to 5 years or more. Foreign currency earnings in the same currency or currencies can be used to fund repayment of the loan. This will reduce exposure to exchange rate fluctuations as well as eliminating the need to buy and sell foreign currency. Of course, if there is no matching income in the relevant currency, exchange rate implications must be considered.

(3) *Acceptance credits.* This facility allows importers and exporters to obtain finance by means of bills of exchange drawn on their bank. The bills, once accepted by the bank, can be discounted in the money market, for instance the London money market, at rates which are generally finer than those available on overdraft.

(4) *Export finance.* Banks provide different forms of export credit facilities under various schemes supported by governments and other organisations. For instance, in the UK short-term export finance is available through a range of schemes operated by the banks. These schemes provide credit insurance and associated finance packages to suit most exporters selling on credit terms of up to 180 days. Finance made available to the exporter is normally 100 per cent of the credit-insured value of the invoice.

(5) *Forfaiting.* Companies are often required, when bidding for export contracts, to include a financing package. In this case, forfaiting can be of assistance. It is the discounting of bills of exchange or promissory notes, at a fixed rate of interest throughout, without recourse to the exporter.

(6) *Leasing.* Companies which are subject to corporation tax may also wish to consider leasing as a means of financing foreign plant and equipment to be used in their trade. This type of finance is provided on flexible and competitive terms with regard to repayment profile and interest charged, compared with other sources of medium-term funding.

(7) *Factoring.* Domestic factoring may be of particular interest to importers who find that they are having to pay their overseas suppliers before they receive payment from their debtors.

Off-shore funding – franchise/licence fees

This is an important issue and one should consider the most effective way of receiving payment of funds such as royalties. For instance, it may be worthwhile for the franchisor to organise a structure whereby the licence is owned by an off-shore company, so that the income accruing does not attract the tax of the company's home country. Such a company could be the parent of the 'local' trading company (for company-owned outlets) and a 'local' franchisor should sub-franchising be envisaged. In Jersey, for example, the tax authorities have recently introduced the concept of the 'exempt company', ie one which does not attract Jersey tax at the standard rate, only an annual payment of £500. To qualify for such status companies must be incorporated in Jersey but owned by non-residents of the island and controlled outside it. Various conditions, of course, have to be complied with in this respect, and guidance should be obtained before committing oneself to this route.

8. GRANTS AND LOANS IN THE EC

This section is not exhaustive but gives a general guide to the financial assistance available in the EC. Each individual company should research the possibility of financial assistance based on its specific case.

(a) EC structural funds

The Community structural funds, administered by the Commission, are intended to support investment in infrastructure, industry and agriculture in the less developed regions of the community. There are five priority objectives for the funds, as follows:

(1) Promoting the development and structural adjustment of the regions where development is lagging behind;
(2) Converting the regions seriously affected by industrial decline;
(3) Combating long-term unemployment;
(4) Facilitating the occupational integration of young people;
(5) With a view to the reform of the common agricultural policy:
    (a) Speeding up the adjustment of agricultural structures, and
    (b) Promoting the development of rural areas.

There are three funds, and aligned to these are a number of programmes. The European Social Fund (ESF) and the European Agricultural Guidance and Guarantee Fund (FEOGA) were established under the EEC Treaty. The European Regional Development Fund (ERDF) was set up in 1975, and is intended for the development and structural adjustment of less developed and declining industrial regions.

(b) European Investment Bank loans

The European Investment Bank (EIB) lends to both private and public sectors. Loans are for capital investment in industry, infrastructure and energy, helping to further a European Community objective. Direct EIB loans normally begin at about 1.35 million ECU and can be for up to half the gross investment cost of a project, at medium-long-term, fixed or floating rates. EIB finance for small-scale industry ventures is possible through intermediary institutions. Loans may be in the currency of the borrowers' preference. Companies might consider negotiating a loan in a cocktail of currencies to match their receivables. Interest rates are close to what it costs the bank to borrow on capital markets. There are no arrangement fees and the bank takes no profit.

(c) Innovation loans and venture capital funding

Earlier Commission proposals to back a scheme of loans for innovation in small and medium-sized companies have faded away with the growth of venture capital schemes and the formation of the European Venture Capital Association. Two schemes in particular – the *Venture Consort* pilot scheme and *Eurotech Capital*, aim to stimulate technological development across Europe.

(d) Information, innovation and technology transfer

The Directorate-General for Telecommunications, Information Industries and Innovation has contributed funds towards work on the dissemination of information and the establishment of the Euronet-Diane network over the past few years. Funding has also been available for a number of feasibility studies, pilot projects and actual projects undertaken by organisations, in the member states, in the field of information, database provision, etc.

(e) Research, Development and Demonstration Fund

The opportunities to secure shared cost contracts under the Community's R & D programmes are many and varied. It is worth noting that the Community's contribution to a successful application under one of its R & D programmes is up to 50 per cent of eligible costs. However, as schemes are often over-subscribed, it is essential to ensure that an application for funding is technically good.

(f) EURATOM loans

EURATOM loans are administered by the Commission with the object of reducing the Community's external dependence on energy supplies by the promotion of the use of nuclear energy. These decisions empower the Commission to raise loans on behalf of the European Atomic Energy Community (EURATOM), the proceeds of which are for on-lending to finance investment projects involving the industrial generation of nuclear based electricity and industrial fuel-cycle installations.

(g) Transport and infrastructure funds

Efforts to establish a transport infrastructure programme for the Community have come up against many difficulties, despite the fact that suggestions for such a programme were first raised several years ago. It should be stressed that national governments play a predominant role in the choice of projects and it is, therefore, vital for a project promoter to gain the support of the relevant Transport Ministry at the outset.

(h) MEDIA 1992

This programme has the overall objective of enabling the national audio-visual industry to make the most of the opportunities to be offered by the Single European Market. MEDIA 1992 comprises a range of projects and pilot schemes falling within the four groups – distribution, production, training and finance.

(i) ESF

Provides funding to organisations running schemes for vocational training and job creation. Public authorities must provide at least as much funding as that sought from the ESF. Individual companies can apply, but they must obtain some funding from a public authority to be eligible for a grant.

(j) FEOGA

Helps finance agricultural, fishing, infrastructure and social policy, and much goes directly to support farming in less favoured or environmentally sensitive areas and to modernise infrastructure.

In addition there are also IMPs (Integrated Mediterranean Programmes), aligned to the structural funds, with three major objectives – development, adaptation and support; and PEDIP, a special five-year programme aimed at improving productivity and quality and developing Portuguese industry.

9. THE INTEGRATION OF FINANCIAL MARKETS IN THE EUROPEAN COMMUNITY

European obstacles to be removed by 1992

Three sets of non-tariff barriers are to be removed in order that the internal market can be accomplished.

(1) *Physical barriers.* This set of barriers covers mainly controls at customs and health and safety standards which differ from one country to another. It is an area which is unlikely to affect financial services in an age of computerised transactions.

(2) *Technical barriers.* This concept covers a much wider area, and will influence considerably the financial services industry. The main objective of removing such barriers is to ensure the free marketability of products and services within the Community. The various regulatory regimes can be grouped mainly around three sets of regulations – exchange controls, supervisory recognition and regulatory approvals.

(3) *Fiscal barriers.* These include the need for a complex revision of VAT rates, excise duties and other indirect taxes. They also apply to the very delicate question of the taxation of securities, both from an income tax and capital gains tax point of view. Untangling the jungle of withholding taxes and double taxation treaties is obviously of major importance.

In a nutshell, the whole 'Project 1992' requires the elimination of artificial obstacles to the circulation of capital.

Conclusion

The European integrated financial market is happening now and will soon be a reality. Those who doubt this should look closely at the seriousness of the strategies being put in place by the financial institutions.

If not all Europeans are preparing for it, the US and Japanese financial institutions certainly are. There is a totally different perspective from these institutions; they look at Europe as a whole, while Europeans look at it with borders and barriers. It is obvious that they will be very active in the implementation of the integrated market and some of them will occupy leadership positions in it.

Restructuring in the financial services industry is inevitable for business reasons and is being accelerated by the approach of 1992. Even if political hurdles slow the process, they will not stop the consolidation of European financial markets.

'Europe 1992' is not so much a threat as a challenge and an opportunity for European institutions to become powerful players in the global capital markets. The economic objective of the single market is growth and the recapturing of lost market share: this will support a global recovery in the financial services industry of Europe. Its effects upon franchising in the European Community are obvious. Wider availability of flexible, pan-EC financing will assist vigorous and widespread growth. The harmonisation of financial institutions will also greatly reduce the administrative burden presently imposed upon pan-EC franchisors by the differing procedures imposed in each member state.

10. ALLIANCES AMONG BANKS

(1) The Inter-Alpha Group of Banks

Inter-Alpha is an association consisting of prominent European banks. Its origins date from 1971 and, since then, the membership has expanded to the present level broadly in line with the development of the EC. All the constituent banks have a common commitment to providing their customers with comprehensive financial services throughout Europe, and Inter-Alpha plays an important role in helping them to achieve this objective. Whilst there have been numerous examples of joint group co-operation, it is fully understood that each bank should retain its autonomy and independence. The Group at present consists of:

Kredietbank	(Belgium)
Privatbanken	(Denmark)
Crédit Commercial de France	(France)
BHF Bank	(Germany)
National Bank of Greece	(Greece)
Allied Irish Bank	(Ireland)
Instituto Bancario San Paolo Di Torino	(Italy)
NMB Bank	(The Netherlands)
Banco Espirito Santo & Commercial de Lisboa	(Portugal)
Banco Bilbao Vizcaya	(Spain)
The Royal Bank of Scotland	(UK)

The Group has no hierarchical structure and is linked only by a loosely worded 'agreement'. The Group functions primarily through the Steering Committee, which comprises two members from the executive of each bank, and meets formally three times each year and determines the general policy for the Group. The responsibility for implementing such a policy rests with the permanent co-ordinating Committee, which meets four times a year.

(2) Unico-Banking Group

Unico Banking Group, founded in 1977, is an Association of seven major European Co-operative Banks. The member banks share a common strength in that all of them have a dense office network in their respective countries. In Europe alone, the member banks' combined network comprises some 37,000 offices.

The members of the Group are:

Andelsbanken Danebank	(Denmark)
Cera Spaarbank	(Belgium)
Crédit Agricole	(France)
DG Bank	
(Deutsche Genossenschaftsbank)	(Germany)
Genossenschaftliche Zentral Bank AG	
(GZB-Vienna)	(Austria)
Okobank Osuuspankkien	
Keskuspankki Oy	(Finland)
Rabobank Nederland	(The Netherlands)

In most countries, the origin of the local Co-operative Bank goes back to agriculture. Over the years, however, a shift to other sectors of the economy has taken place. Medium and small-sized companies have become a major target group of the Unico Banks.

At present, Unico Member Banks have offices on all Continents. Since its establishment Unico Banking Group has created two funds, the Unico Investment Fund and the Unico Equity Fund. In 1981, the Group decided to expand its international service potential by establishing Unico Trading Company.

(3) The Euro-Partners Co-operation Group

The Euro-Partners Co-operation Group originates from the agreement concluded in Frankfurt-am-Main on 14 October, 1970 between Commerzbank (Germany) and Crédit Lyonnais (France). Banca de Roma (Italy) joined the Group on January 11, 1971, while Banco Hispano-Americano (Spain) became its fourth partner on October 16, 1973.

The purpose of the Co-operation Group is to combine the financial potential and know-how of the Euro-Partners in order to offer customers with business in the other countries of the four Banks financial services just like those at home.

Joint services include a common loan programme called Transcredit.

Today, a staff of roughly 100,000 in more than 5,000 branches and agencies are at the service of the Euro-Partners' clientele. In addition, there are some 170 outlets in all continents, including more than 100 subsidiaries and affiliated companies.

(4) ABECOR

ABECOR (Associated Banks of Europe Corporation SA) was founded in 1974 in Brussels. It is an association of eight member banks which have agreed to co-operate with each other whilst retaining their individual autonomy. Its members are:

ABN Bank (Algemene Bank Nederland)	(The Netherlands)
BBL (Banque Bruxelles Lambert)	(Belgium)
BIL (Banque Internationale à Luxembourg)	(Luxembourg)
BNP (Banque Nationale de Paris)	(France)
Barclays Bank	(United Kingdom)
Hypo Bank (Bayerische Hypotheken- und Wechsel-Bank)	(Germany)
Dresdner Bank	(Germany)
Österreichische Länderbank	(Austria)
Associated Member:	
Banque de la Société Financière Européenne	(France)

ABECOR has a world-wide network of some 11,000 offices and about 300,000 staff. The ABECOR secretariat, located in Brussels, acts as a co-ordinating body under the auspices of a Steering Committee and an Executive Committee. The Secretariat is comprised of a Secretary-General and two officials seconded from the member banks.

(5) EBIC

EBIC (European Banks' International Company SA) is a group of banks servicing its shareholders. People from the member banks meet in order to exchange views and opinions on professional topics. The member banks are:

AMRO Bank	(The Netherlands)
Banca Commerciale Italiana	(Italy)
Creditanstalt Bankverein	(Austria)
Deutsche Bank	(Germany)
Generale Bank	(Belgium)
Midland Bank	(United Kingdom)
Société Générale	(France)

11. COMMERCIAL ASPECTS OF FRANCHISING WHICH MAKE IT ATTRACTIVE TO EC BANKS

There are strategic advantages for the lending banker when helping the development of a franchise operation. These advantages can be briefly summarised as follows:

(1) *Speading of the bank's risk.* In this case the bank spreads its risk by lending small amounts of capital to a large number of separate businesses – the franchisees who have taken on the proven concept. However, the bank must closely

monitor its exposure to any one franchise company and closely follow the progress of the franchisor. This means that a company considering franchising should already have a proven, profitable business with a distinctive trading style which lends itself to replication and expansion by way of franchising. Furthermore, the company wanting to become a franchisor has to prove that its concept is successful elsewhere. The pilot operations should prove profitable during at least one or two years in order for the prospective franchisor to start franchising. It is imperative that there is a sufficient profit margin for both franchisor and franchisee.

(2) *Safer lending.* It can be shown that a franchisee in a proven franchise operation has a far better chance of being successful than a businessman starting on his own as an independent. This is due to the advantages of using a proven and tested method of doing business. A franchisee is usually more highly motivated than an employee and often has useful local knowledge. Franchisees receive the benefit of the bulk purchasing and negotiating power which the franchisor has arranged on behalf of all the franchisees in the network. There are sometimes territorial guarantees to ensure that no other franchisee is set up within a defined area around the franchisee's business address.

(3) *Central marketing approach.* By entering into a relationship with the franchisor of a well-structured, well-funded and ethical franchise, it is possible for a lending banker to obtain an introduction to many franchisees requiring financing. The franchisor finds it very attractive to deal with a 'central point of contact at the bank'.

Many European banks, after having considered these basic attractive aspects of franchising, have appointed franchise managers or have set up specific franchise departments. The objectives of these are:

(1) To assess available franchises and to negotiate, if appropriate, financial packages with the financial directors of suitable franchise companies.

(2) To advise prospective franchisors as regards the suitability of their business to be franchised and how to go about the same as well as giving them introductions to franchise associations, solicitors, accountants and consultants.

(3) To provide guidance and recommendations to their branches and regional Advances Departments in respect of franchisor and franchisee lending propositions.

PART SIX

MARKETING
AND
ADVERTISING

CHAPTER 35

Marketing and Advertising in a Single Market in Europe

By MARK WEBSTER

Franchises, like other businesses, rely on successful marketing and advertising to increase and sustain their sales. The creation of an advertising fund in many franchises imposes a heavy burden upon the franchisor to 'get it right'. This burden − and the rewards of success − will greatly increase in the Single Market.

The changes to be brought about by the creation of the Single Market in 1992 will have profound consequences for all those concerned with the marketing of goods and services. So fundamental and so far-reaching are the implications of the creation of the Single Market that no company, big or small, can remain unaffected. Each marketing manager will therefore be faced with developing a strategy which seeks to capitalise on the opportunities that the Single Market will bring, and to counter the threats that it will present.

1992 − THE OPPORTUNITIES

As indicated in Chapter 1, there are twelve countries in the European Community with a total population of over 340 million, that is six times the size of the UK, more than one third larger than the population of the USA, and more than one and a half times the population of Japan. The EC countries enjoy a combined GDP of well over $4,000 billion. Thus there will be a market which is larger than any other in the world, a market which is socially and politically stable and, by 1992, it will be increasingly accessible commercially.

Most member state, and indeed many non-member state companies are now aware that 1992 − used not so much as a single date but more as a shorthand for the complex change itself − is a major significant issue for business planning. Companies are aware of the broad nature of the impending changes, and now the cry is for more specific information: 'What does it mean for my business this year and next?' And the principal role in assessing the consequences for a consumer goods company rest inevitably with those who lead the marketing team.

Good marketing stewardship is the anticipation and management of change. The period between now and the end of 1992 (the target date) is likely to see the biggest change that most marketing managers will experience in their lifetime. If we just remind ourselves of the simple definition of marketing as having the right products, in the right place, at the right time, at the right price, sold at a profit − then we can comprehend the impact of that change.

THE NEW DEMOGRAPHICS

The map of Europe is in the process of being re-drawn. The opening of the Channel Tunnel, the falling away of old frontiers, the demolition of the Iron Curtain, the concentration of wealth in a limited area: all of these require a re-assessment by companies of their new geographic position vis-à-vis their market.

For many years, sophisticated marketeers have been able to locate their target consumers by reference to their buying behaviour as well as where they live. We have seen, for example, the increased accumulation of disposable income in the south-east of England, and we have seen how this has attracted an increasing level of premium, innovative products and services. How will this look five years on? With the Channel Tunnel open and high-speed road and rail links crossing frontiers of diminishing importance, the distribution map of that part of Europe will change dramatically. Where will the centre of the new Europe be in consumer marketing terms?

To master the new demographics one must redraw the map, not based on old nation-states, but based on where the people you can reach in five years, and most want to trade with, are concentrated.

THE EUROBRAND AUDIT

Each brand, product or service marketed by a company should be classified for its potential volume and profitability in Europe as distinct from one country alone. In order to do this, each company must devise its own system of carrying out a 'Eurobrand' audit. The objective should be to designate each product in their range into one of four groups as follows: Eurostar, Europlayer, National Star, National Player. The criteria for classifying products in each position must be decided by the company. Here are a few suggestions:

Eurostar

This product either enjoys a strong position in Europe now or, on judgement, has the potential to take such a position. It is probably a national star already or sold in at least four European countries with volume and/or profit equal to the current domestic base business. The product (or product category) may soon require major investment, e.g. its own sales force in Europe, or a joint venture or acquisition to extend further into Europe. It should have an offensive strategy. There will be few Eurostars in the portfolio.

Europlayer

This product is either now on sale in Europe, or has the potential to be sold. It is possibly sold in one or more

European countries with volume and/or profits of over 25 per cent of the domestic business, but it is thought unlikely ever to be a Eurostar.

National Star

This product is a major volume and profit earner in the domestic market, and is No. 1 or No. 2 in its category. It has only marginal exports to other European countries at the moment. Such products, which will be relatively few in any one company or business unit, should be considered as a possible Europlayer. If not, the company should look at possible European competitors, and start to devise a defensive strategy.

National Player

This product contributes to the company's volume, profit and overheads. On judgement, it has little or no potential in Europe but is likely to be at competitive risk from new Europlayers. It should build a defensive strategy or possibly may be a candidate for divestment.

The Eurobrand audit requires significant marketing input and needs constant updating in the light of changing trends and habits.

EUROPEAN LEAGUE TABLE

Whether it is decided to follow an offensive or defensive strategy, a key ground rule is to carry out a competitor analysis for each consumer category in which the company operates. This needs to be done in each EC country in order to construct a European league table. Such a table may well have two divisions, for example, Division I: leading companies; Division II: secondary companies.

On a country-by-country basis, we have either to obtain or to estimate the size of the relevant markets in volume and value, market shares and brand positioning. Based on an analysis of their product, packaging and advertising, what do we believe to be the market positions and competitive advantage of each of our major European competitors?

As of now, the competitive structure of many consumer markets will probably vary significantly across the EC. Each country is likely to have different market leaders and players and their markets will probably require different kinds of positioning strategies. If some competitors are operating in several different countries, their market share will be substantially different in each country.

Once we have established the European league table, an attempt should be made to estimate likely trends over the next five to ten years, given the new conditions in the Single Market. This involves an attempt to estimate a number of factors. These will include changes in our source of supply, changes in technology which may involve raw materials and capital equipment for processing, and any likely new entrants to the category. All of these estimates will help towards

conclusions on the level of probable competition in the future and the consequent profit margins that can be anticipated. Obviously, little of this information is ready-to-hand, but requires investigation and analysis. Is it, therefore, really necessary? Suffice it to say that, if companies don't do it, it is fairly certain that there will be competitors from other major European countries who will do so.

Marketing and advertising in Europe is an extremely broad subject and there are many aspects and issues which are important and relevant. The following are a selection of the more obvious.

'EUROBRANDING'

This term encapsulates the thought that it may now be possible to sell the same product across the EC, given that there is increasing homogenisation in European countries, and that, from 1992, there will be the same rules affecting all products in the same category in all countries. It is an example of 'globalisation of markets', in which companies like McDonald's, Coca-Cola and Levis are often cited as being indicative of a worldwide trend. Of course, the standardisation of marketing consumer products across 340 million consumers provides a gleam in the eye of many advertising and marketing people. The economics of scale coming from such standardisation are potentially considerable.

The other side of the coin is argued quite as convincingly. The essence of marketing is to react to the actual needs of the consumer, and this means taking into account local characteristics, preferences and perceptions. The convenience of instant coffee is attractive to UK tea drinkers, but the French still prefer the taste of ground coffee. Nova, as a brand name for a car, signifies newness to English speakers but means that it 'does not go' (*no va*) in Spanish!

In some EC countries commercial TV is not yet available for marketing, whereas it is possible with peak-time TV spots to reach a very large percentage of the UK population quite quickly. Vacuum cleaners are almost universal in Northern Europe but domestic cleaning is achieved by other means in the South. There is a great danger, however, in polarising, and thereby simplifying the debate to one of European integration verses national responsiveness. The real question is *not* whether to standardise or not to standardise. Rather it is: what opportunity is there to create a competitive advantage given the new market situation?

Up to now, Europe has been approached on a country-by-country basis with little economic or business leverage available from an integrated approach. The 1992 phenomenon signals that this is changing, and that there will be increasing advantages for Eurobranding. There will not be a 1992 revolution but rather an evolution where increasing rewards will go to companies who have got the balance right between standardisation and national responsiveness across Europe.

The Eurobrand issue may be summed up in the adaptation of a slogan: 'think European, act local'.

WILL THERE BE A 'EURO-CONSUMER'?

There is a lot of debate about whether or not a Euro-consumer exists or is likely to emerge as a result of the Single Market. Each of the major European countries have numerous consumer segmentation studies which have been carried out over the past decade and already some research companies are conducting European-wide consumer studies. Overall, there are a number of general findings:

(1) There are many *similarities* between countries, even in countries as diverse as Spain and Denmark.

(2) Often the *differences* between consumer groups within one country are much greater than any difference between countries themselves.

(3) The youth in each country have more in common now than ever before. They drink the same drinks, wear the same clothes, eat the same hamburgers and soon will be watching the same TV programmes. They hold similar attitudes – they are often rebellious; in general, they've got spare spending money, they are highly fashion and peer-group conscious and do not want to do things in the way their parents did. But this is the same as youth in the 1970's, 1960's and 1950's. It is how they settle down as they become older that is more important.

For these are likely to be the 'Euro-consumers' of the future, and this is where international planners and researchers will be able to track and identify emerging Euro-opportunities. The gradual 'greying' of Europe might well have more serious implications than the 'greening'. Demographically Northern Europe is ageing; thus the moving up the age scale of the 'baby-boomers' will affect both style and content of European products across the board.

BUSINESS COMMUNICATION

On the other hand, in the business community, where buying decisions are mostly based on professional motives, and where professions are practised reasonably uniformly across borders, a Euro-approach to planning is relatively easy to adopt in comparison with consumers. Those who have been involved in international business-to-business work can tell you that a French CAD/CAM engineer talks exactly the same language as his Danish colleague. The Danish engineer also knows that the French engineer is equally keen to learn about the latest in CAD technology. And furthermore it is more than likely that the newest CAD innovation could boost the French company's bottom line as well as improve the Danish company's profit.

If the 'think European, act local' theme has a natural arena to succeed, it is in business-to-business advertising, where the discerning professional buyers can more naturally focus on your clear-cut business proposition, as well as 'see through' any weaknesses or lack of focus which will show up under scrutiny.

NEW CHALLENGES

There are changes already happening within the manufacturing, distribution and selling process and they directly affect the way that advertising is developed in the future. Pan-European brands will demand a more international approach. Emergence of the new demographics will also challenge national boundaries in favour of regions represented by, for instance, prevalence of wealth or particular common consumer habits. The emergence of new international media will also bring new challenges even to purely national advertisers. No longer will discounting, for instance, be purely on a national level.

Advertising is often described as the 'cherry on the cake' in the marketing process – it is the final communication point with the end user. Within the Single Market, therefore, many of the changes in advertising decisions will follow on from the changes in marketing strategy. Some changes, however, will stem from alterations in media structure and ownership in Europe.

Advertisers and their agencies must gear themselves for these changes. Over the last decade, advertising professionals have been split between those who believe in globalisation to different degrees and those who tend to think only nationally. Not surprisingly, the former has been actively supported by the large multi-national agencies, while the latter viewpoint has tended to be followed by agencies with no major representation outside their domestic base. Within the new Europe, however, the demands likely to be placed on agencies to offer an international service are likely to be much more pressing. As manufacturers and service companies reorganise themselves on a more central or regional basis, agencies will be expected to fall into line with this restructuring.

NEW ADVERTISING OPPORTUNITIES

The emerging target markets across Europe will provide some new long-term opportunities for market segmentation, product positioning and for overall advertising.

From another perspective – that of product categories – there are already examples of pan-European advertising approaches. Current examples of these product sectors are major fast-moving consumer goods – detergents, household cleaners, toiletries and confectionery. Some durable markets, particularly high-tech products, television and hi-fi are already pan-European. The international appeal of upmarket brands in drink, clothing and cigarettes has also been highlighted.

However, the Single Market is likely to see the growth of some other common product sectors which are currently not so clear. Healthy eating, for instance, is a universal trend across Europe. Even the Southern Europe markets are becoming much more conscious of avoiding products which are likely to cause premature heart disease or obesity. Inevitably, over the next decade, consumer tastes are likely to become more continental in terms of eating habits and home-based products.

Both these areas should be carefully monitored by marketing organisations and suitable strategies developed. The areas where differences between countries are most marked and are likely to remain so are in the purely domestic categories. In small appliances, for example, electric kettles until very recently were a relatively unknown phenomenon in Holland, whereas coffee-makers, which are in virtually every Dutch household, are still very limited in the UK. Ice-cream makers are a very popular product in the Mediterranean countries, but are relatively unknown in the north of Europe. Clearly pan-European campaigns for such products could be totally wasteful. Of course, advertising can change some of these habits but this is not likely to happen very rapidly.

NEW CREATIVE STANCE

It's a well-known advertising cliché that international campaigns tend to aim for the lowest common denominator rather than ideas which are relevant to each country. The completion of the Single Market is unlikely to change entrenched views about this. Languages will still be tied to nationalities, cultural differences will still remain, senses of humour will also vary across the European map. At their peril do advertisers and agencies ignore this. The major challenge will be to develop international campaigns which to consumers simply don't look like international campaigns. The re-organisation which is happening behind the scenes in terms of pan-European joint ventures, mergers and acquisitions simply shouldn't show when it comes to communicating with consumers.

Equally there is a danger that the stronger countries in advertising terms – such as the UK – will try to export themselves just as the Americans did in the late 60s and the early 70s on the basis that their higher standards should work well in other countries. However, this could be dangerous. UK advertising is often seen as an entertainment source, and contains lots of whimsy, plagiarism and understated humour, while German advertising tends to concentrate on the facts and often lacks emotion. French advertising, on the other hand, tends to be highly emotional and, more often than not, full of sexual innuendo. Italian advertising is passionate.

Whilst risking these generalisations, it would be a mistake to fail to recognise the appeal that each of these different approaches has in their home market. They are all tried and tested routes.

However, there are successful examples of common strategies being used across the whole of Europe but of separate creative ideas as a means of implementing these strategies being adapted for each country. This more sensible approach should continue. Again: think European – but act local.

NEW MEDIA

There are some very major changes which are taking place in the media world. Many of these are technology-led – such as

satellite TV – others are based on the continuing battle between 'media barons' to acquire major international footholds in media ownership. Both of these are happening coincidentally with the Single Market rather than as a result of specific Brussels directives. However, they are all part of the process of opening up European boundaries.

By 1992, the nature of the media and the media planning and buying process will have been transformed. There are several factors which will influence media advertising opportunities in the European Community, some of which are a direct result of the liberalisation of the market, while others, such as technological developments will be bringing about enormous changes. As it is, this technological revolution is helping to expand and implement the opportunities afforded to advertisers by the creation of a Single Market.

New liberalised markets

Markets all over Europe are becoming more liberal and increasingly commercial. New private channels are emerging, Tele 5 in Germany, a new commercial state-owned channel in Denmark, more national channels in Spain. TV channels are offering more flexibility in programming – there is more variability in spot lengths and availability – and the contractors are generally adopting a more commercial attitude to developing audiences for TV. However, in this new climate, TV advertising efficiency is threatened by the proliferation of brands using TV, and the increase in airtime availability.

New opportunities

These alternative methods of communicating to the consumer are becoming increasingly interesting with the possibility of implementation across a Single Market. As media costs have risen during the 1980s, the less traditional forms of communication are becoming more attractive.

Consumer promotions are a case in point. 1992 brings closer the time when TV consumer promotions can be developed, at least as formats, for the Single Market. At the moment, most sponsored promotions are developed as projects for one national market and then, if successful, exported to other markets. But on-screen consumer product placement is becoming common in a number of European Community markets, particularly Italy and France. Sponsorship started with televised events but has now extended into drama, quiz/game shows, documentaries and some light entertainment areas, and there will be even greater scope with the increasing number of programme hours being made available with the development of, for example, satellite TV. It will, of course, be vital to identify the correct sponsor vehicle for a brand and the following questions must be considered:

— Is the sponsorship activity consonant with the brand's values?
— Is the promotion visible to consumers/customers?
— Is the promotion merchandisable beyond the TV activity itself?

— Is the project controllable?
— Will the project generate positive trade and employee reaction?
— Can the benefits to the brand be evaluated?

If there is a positive answer to all these questions, then TV consumer promotions can be considered as a possible component of a total, multinational media strategy.

MEDIA RESEARCH

With this increasingly pan-European media activity, both of a traditional and of a more innovative nature, it becomes even more vital to obtain reliable audience research for the Single Market. However, there is no consistent cross-frontier media research available to compare with the comprehensive surveys which cover most individual EC countries. All countries, except Greece and Portugal, have metered audience measurement for television, but a TV rating, for instance, is measured differently in every market. Each survey differs in its definition of viewing/reading occasions, its methodology and its reporting.

Clearly a lot of work needs to be done to standardise practice in order to formulate more sophisticated media planning. For example, there will need to be a set of standard Single Market demographic definitions, a Single Market brand/advertisement classification system, standard audience definitions for viewing, listening and reading, and standard calculation methods for ratings, reach and frequency.

While such harmonised data will facilitate co-ordinated schedules right across the Single Market, knowledge still needs to be acquired in the following areas: measurement of time-shifted viewing, the true extent and influence of 'zapping' (changing channels to avoid commercials) and 'zipping' (fast-forwarding through commercials), advertising efficiency in terms of impact, awareness and liking, assessing accurately the contribution made by each medium in a multi-media campaign, and measuring the value of brand exposures via sponsor messages, product placement and consumer promotions on television and in print. The International Media Council is currently trying to develop these areas of media research and will need the backing and co-operation of all interested parties.

SATELLITE BROADCASTING

There are three types of satellite — low, medium and high power — also known as Direct Broadcast to Home (DBH). Each covers different geographical areas — footprints — depending on the size of the satellite receiving dish and the position of the satellite in the sky. A new generation of medium and high powered satellites would allow viewers to receive signals directly (hence the name Direct Broadcast to Home) with a small privately owned dish, thus eliminating the need for cable which has been slow to develop.

In the future, more and more direct broadcast satellites will be launched, offering more choice of programmes for viewers. Clearly this technology will revolutionise consumer viewing and the range of consumer communication for the advertiser across Europe.

A 'BELOW-THE-LINE' PERSPECTIVE

Sales promotion, trade and direct marketing will play an essential role in marketing in the Single Market, just as they do in any market.

At the very least, they are vital complementary activities to media advertising investment. As consumers continue to develop wider tastes and needs, as they demand more choice and as the traditional media which address them become more fragmented, so the need for a co-ordinated approach and strategy becomes vital. A brand or product must be heard as one voice, speaking not only on television, in press or posters, but also through the mail, the trade and from the shelf. The consumer must be able to hear the message clearly, amidst the clamour which is seeking his or her attention.

In the Single Market, this clamour will not only be more strident, it will also be more diverse. This is not to say, however, that sales promotion, trade marketing and direct marketing are mere ancillaries to media advertising. They can be, and often are, stand-alone techniques. Frequently they are effective opening moves, where budget limitations exist or where a certain amount of testing or exploration is required. It may be necessary to stimulate trade support and distribution, or ensure that consumer sampling is in hand before heavy investment is made in media advertising.

It is likely that some markets will be so tightly definable that the ability of direct promotion to target precisely on the prospect will make this the single most effective weapon.

These techniques have one thing in common. They each involve themselves far more in the actual consumer purchase decision than does advertising or public relations — they are designed to have a much more immediate 'buy-ME' effect. Sales promotion sets out to offer an incentive or added value device at the point of a sale. Direct marketing closes the gap between producer and consumer by setting out to develop a personal dialogue, often eliciting an immediate sale and invariably seeking further response.

Thus these techniques are close to the sharp end of the marketing ship, often closely interwoven with sales force effort. They tend towards the tactical rather than the strategic. But, in the new Europe, they will require careful co-ordination as part of the overall communications plan.

LOOKING TO THE FUTURE

As with all changes being brought about by the Single Market, advertising and sales promotion trends are difficult to predict. But they are already happening, they are big and fast and will inevitably continue — far beyond the Single Market target date of 1992 and well into the next century.

Both amongst consumers and within product groups, common threads are starting to emerge around Europe. Each of these has to be monitored in turn. However, this presents a further difficulty — the problem of incompatible statistical data between each EC country. For instance, socio-economic groups are not necessarily all described in the same way. Age groups are broken down differently. Over the next few years, research companies and analysts must gear themselves up to cope with such inadequacies and become sensitive to the opportunities and pitfalls.

Marketing organisations are already starting to audit these new opportunities. While their strategies are drawn up, advertising and sales promotion in their roles as the ultimate communication point must also adapt to the changes that are currently taking place behind the scenes. However, changes in advertising and promotional approach should only move at a rate which their consumer targets can fully accept and understand. Otherwise, size and convenience will override the need for relevance and appeal.

It would be ironic if the 'new' Europe fails to recognise the changes that have already happened in the US. There the move has been away from size and homogenity into segmentation — for instance in ethnic and niche marketing. The lesson for Europeans, is, if you want to be big don't be obvious.

NEGOTIATING THE REGULATIONS

Over the years every member state of the EC has accumulated a mass of legislation to protect the consumer or to satisfy pressure groups. That regulation has hemmed in the sales and marketing of products and services with a complex maze of rules and restrictions governing almost every aspect of the relationship between producer and consumer. This legal jungle which is the European consumer market is not unified now and very probably will not be for many years to come, although the legislative machinery is moving in that direction and the lists of amendments issued from Brussels seem never-ending. It is the duty of every manufacturer and trader to ensure that the latest of the directives relating to their product groups is noted and the action required by it taken. This information is readily available from government sources such as the 1992 Group of the UK Department of Trade and Industry.

Despite Brussels' best efforts, finding common denominators of taste and acceptance in the general public is difficult enough. Legally it is virtually impossible. What is perfectly acceptable in the UK (premium promotions, for instance) is often not permitted in other seemingly liberal markets such as Denmark and Germany. In certain countries even prizes are taxable, and give-aways can't be given. These simple examples don't even approach the complexity of the legislation surrounding certain restricted products such as tobacco and alcohol.

So while much of the legislation is set to change, the attitudes within each member nation will no doubt persist for years to come. Much of the local legislation is part and parcel of national identity and national politics and will therefore be obstinately intractable. The key to negotiating this maze is caution and diplomacy, and the recommendation is to seek local advice.

In summary, the essential issues in preparing a marketing strategy for a business are:

— Focus on the new environment and understand it both geographically and from a consumer standpoint.
— Master the ground rules which the market brings with it.
— Have an understanding for the differences in personality and approach of the nationalities involved.
— Conduct a Euro-audit to see how your product or service compares, to capitalise on strengths and reduce exposure to weaknesses.
— Identify and prioritise new market opportunities which will emerge by virtue of the Single Market's growth.
— Identify the necessary resources needed internally to carry through the new tasks, and review the service agencies supporting the marketing drive.
— Set up a Single Market unit to ensure that your response to the opportunities is co-ordinated throughout the business.

WHAT WILL IT MEAN TO THE FRANCHISEE?

While the overall picture is undoubtedly complex, confusing and full of pitfalls, Europe 1992 offers very real opportunities for those who are forward-thinking enough to take them. Local advice, local knowledge and a global overview to integrate all the localities are probably the most necessary tools for a European strategy. Franching is well placed to fulfil these requirements. There are however some key points:

(1) Never assume that because it worked in one country it will necessarily work in another.

(2) Always ensure that all legislation, both EC and local, is taken into account — especially where it covers advertising and promotion, packaging and consumer rights.

(3) Always take local advice — particularly in matters of public taste and acceptance and national pride.

(4) Always ensure that your advisors on marketing and advertising are fully conversant with advertising and marketing codes of practice in the countries you wish to cover and that they employ relevant nationals to carry out translation and negotiation with the media.

(5) Consider the possibility that in bringing in goods or services from other EC states you may have to adapt to reposition the marketing strategy, the packaging and maybe the manufacturing methods in order to comply with local legislation and tastes.

(6) Finally, think European — act local.

The Regulation of the Media in the Single Market

By MARK ABELL

The importance of successful advertising by franchisors in the Single Market has been underlined in the previous Chapter. The Europeanisation of the media through which much of this advertising is disseminated and the advent of new technology in the media, notably satellite and cable television, has not gone unnoticed by the Commission.

Three principal initiatives have been taken.

In 1984 a Green Paper 'Television Without Frontiers' (Green Paper on the establishment of a Common Market in Broadcasting, particularly Satellite and Cable Broadcasting COM 8430 (June 14th 1984)) contained their initial response to the situation.

This Green Paper advocated the removal of all obstacles to cross-border broadcasting and the harmonisation of broadcasting regulations in the Common Market. As a result of this Green Paper a draft Broadcasting Directive was published in 1986 and later modified in 1988 (Draft Directive on The Co-ordination of Laws, Regulations and Administrative Provisions Relating to Broadcasting Activities (COM 86/146, OJ 1986 C 179/4 modified COM (88) 154, OJ 1988 C 110/3).

Following a Council Meeting in March 1989 agreement was reached on most of the issues involved and the Directive was passed later that year.

The second initiative of the Commission was to issue, in 1986, a programme on Community Broadcasting Production under the name of MEDIA and a few years later initiated a programme for the co-ordinated introduction of High Definition Television (HDTV) (Communication on Action in Favour of European Audio Visual Productions, COM (86) 255; Proposal for a Cancelled Decision on High Definition Television, COM (88) 659).

A third initiative is the involvement of member states in the negotiation, through the Council of Europe of trans-border broadcasting. This convention takes an approach not dissimilar to that adopted by the Directive and aims at encouraging cross-border television broadcasting subject to minimum standards.

THE BROADCASTING DIRECTIVE

The Directive (No. 89/552, OJ1989 L298/23) aims to promote freedom of broadcasting throughout the twelve member states and embodies the principle that any programme which is legally produced in a member state should be freely broadcastable anywhere in the Community. It regulates programme content, and most importantly as far as franchisors are concerned advertising and sponsorship. It also covers a number of other miscellaneous points.

The member states have until 3rd October 1991 to ensure that their laws, regulations and administrative procedures comply with its terms.

Any broadcast which complies with the minimum standards laid down in the Directive may be freely received and transmitted between member states, although individual member states are not prevented from laying down still stricter guidelines.

The responsibility for ensuring that broadcasts comply with these standards lies with the member state from which the broadcasts are made. However, a degree of extraterritoriality has been introduced by making member states responsible to secure compliance with the standards by all broadcasts received within their jurisdiction. Thus, a member state may have to take action as regards broadcasts from non-EC member states. In practical terms this could mean that sanctions are taken against any franchisor or other company advertising through such an offending broadcast, even though the broadcast originates from outside of the EC.

Programme content

There are requirements regarding programme content, although these are of no great importance to franchisors.

It is worth noting however that the 'local content' requirement for programmes being broadcast has been strongly objected to by the U.S.A. on the grounds that it offends GATT.

Advertising

The restrictions placed on advertising are clearly of prime importance to franchisors who are aiming at pan-European advertising coverage.

Advertising is heavily controlled, particularly that in relation to products such as pharmaceuticals and alcohol, whilst tobacco product advertising is totally banned.

Advertising must not include racial, sexual or national discrimination and must be offensive to neither religious nor political beliefs. It should not encourage behaviour perceived to be prejudicial to health, safety or environmental protection, nor must it pose a moral or physical danger to children.

The actual form of advertising is also strictly regulated as is the amount of transmission time which can be dedicated to it. For example, as regards TV films lasting for more than three quarters of an hour, a commercial break is only allowed once every 45 minutes. Other programmes of more than 20 minutes duration may have a commercial break only once every 20 minutes, although advertising is not allowed to interrupt programmes of less than 30 minutes duration if they are news, current affairs, documentaries or childrens' programmes. If such programmes are more than 30 minutes, then the 20 minute rule takes effect.

As regards the transmission time dedicated to advertising, only 15% of daily transmission time or 20% if direct offers to the public are included are allowed providing that block advertising does not exceed 15% and direct offer advertising does not exceed 1 hour per day. Spot advertising must not exceed more than 12 minutes every hour.

Exactly what amounts to an advertisement is carefully dealt with by the Directive. An announcement clearly amounts to advertising although background signage and bill-board advertising seem to be excluded from the definition. Thus if a franchisor advertises products at a sports stadium from which events are televised, these would not come within the ambit of the Directive.

Sponsorship

Sponsorship is a fast growing industry in the European Community. Sponsorship of programmes is authorised under the Directive subject to restrictions imposed by Article 12. These restrictions include clearly identifying sponsored programming, ensuring that the programme content and scheduling is not influenced by the sponsor and so effecting editorial independence, ensuring that sponsorship does not encourage the purchase or rental of products or services of the sponsor or any third party. Sponsorship is not permitted in relation to news and current affairs programmes nor by the manufacturers or sellers of tobacco and certain medical products.

THE CONVENTION

The Convention on trans-border broadcasting has been adopted by 23 Members of the Council of Europe and its provisions become binding upon each member only once it has been signed. Ten member nations, including the United Kingdom have signed. Other nations, which are not members, can also sign. Eastern Block countries such as Hungary and Poland for example, have indicated an interest. Signatories to the Convention, guarantee freedom of reception and retransmission in their jurisdiction of television programme services which comply with the Convention requirements. It is important to note that the Convention expressly states that member nations who are also EC members have a primary obligation amongst themselves to comply with the Directive. Thus the Convention requirements only take priority over the Directive in relation to EC originating broadcasts which are received in a member nation which is not a member of the EC.

CONCLUSION

Before embarking upon television/radio advertising campaigns, franchisors must pay great attention to the controls exerted by the Directive and the Convention. It is important also to ensure that careful attention is paid to the national rules of each member state which will receive the broadcasts.

PART SEVEN

THE FUTURE OF FRANCHISING IN THE EUROPEAN COMMUNITY

CHAPTER 37

Fortress Europe?

By MARK ABELL

The future of franchising in the European Community to a great extent depends upon the future of the European Community itself. There can be no doubt that the European Community is here to stay. What is not so certain however is how the Single Market will develop, how the Community's relationship with the outside world will develop and exactly what member states the European Community will comprise of in the future. The future of franchising will to no small extent depend upon whether the widespread fears of a 'fortress Europe' are realised or not. The introduction of franchise systems from the United States, Canada, Australia, Japan and other non-EC member states into the single market will have an enormous effect on the development of franchising in the EC. If barriers are erected to make entry into the EC difficult for such foreign franchisors, the growth of franchising in the single market will undoubtedly be retarded.

It is therefore necessary to examine the development of the European Community's international commercial policy and the development of the Community itself as regards to geographical neighbours.

EC INTERNATIONAL COMMERCIAL POLICY

There is no doubt that the establishment of the internal market will have a significant impact upon the external trading policy of the Community. The debate which began during 1988 continues. Will the Community become an inward looking protectionist Fortress Europe, using existing and possibly new trade measures to impede trade between the Community and third countries? Alternatively, will it adopt a more liberal trading position and become, as described in the Commission's press release dated October 1988, 'The Europe World Partner' in international trade? Innumerable public statements have been made from both sides of this debate.

In June 1988 the member states Heads of Government declared:

'the internal market should not close in on itself. In conformity with the provisions of GATT, the Community should be open to third countries, and must negotiate with those countries where necessary, to ensure access to their markets for Community exports. It will seek to preserve the balance of advantages accorded while respecting the unity and the identity of the internal market of the Community'.

The US Secretary, C. William Verity, stated just four months later that the US would monitor the European Community plans to create a single market to ensure it did not create new barriers to the US and other foreign companies and added:

'the architects in the single market were increasingly under seige. Backsliding, narrow international interest and protectionism may grow as 1992 approaches.'

Fears of the evolution of a Fortress Europe have noticeably subsided over the last 18 months, but nevertheless still exist and are a force to be reckoned with in international commercial policy. This is likely to continue to be so some time after 1993. The EC policy to third countries will evolve slowly, and no matter what statements are made either way, the accessibility of the single market to third countries is likely to be a matter of evolution rather than a definite trade policy. The parliamentary report on EC antidumping policy released in November 1990 suggests that the long-term rationale for antidumping measures (see below) will become increasingly tenuous as companies become more global in their structure. Dumping, in simple terms, is the practice of selling goods on a foreign market at less than the cost of production. This global trend, it suggests, undermines the whole notion of 'domestic' industry, and it urges EC policy makers to create a global competition policy which is suitable to the new economic realities.

The EC international trading policy is based on the General Agreement on Tariffs and Trade (GATT) and the OECD.

GATT came into force on 1st January 1948. The aim was to try and avoid recreating the economic crisis that led to the second world war. The preliminary negotiations took place between the United States and the United Kingdom whilst the war was still in progress and were later extended after the war to include a number of other countries.

In November 1947 the Havana Conference led to the formulation of the Havana Charter. The ambitious plans to create an international trade organisation contained in the Charter never actually came about due to the United States' reluctance to ratify it. Nevertheless the Charter did give birth to GATT which is a multi-lateral treaty to which over 90 nations, accounting for well over 80% of world trade, subscribe.

Its basic objective is an open, liberal and competitive trading system so as to provide a framework of certainty and predictability in world markets. GATT is the only multi-lateral agreement involved in effecting this.

December 1990 saw the end of the GATT Uruguay round. EC policy on a number of trade issues on the Uruguay agenda had become clearer during 1990. It seems that agricultural policy is proving to be the bone of contention in international trade relations during 1991.

Internally it is the Commission that makes proposals in relation to the EC commercial policy and administers it, often jointly with the Council. However the Council retains considerable powers (see Chapter 3 above).

There is as yet no completed common EC commercial policy.

However during the Uruguay negotiations the Commission has stated that experience of GATT:

'shows that in those multi-lateral negotiations designed to liberalise market access progress is achieved because all the participants exchange ''concessions'' so everyone achieves a balance of advantages from the negotiations. . . . it will be premature . . to grant non member countries [of the European Community] automatic and unilateral access to the benefit of the internal liberalisation process until such new agreement exists. . . .' (Press Release 19 October 1988)

It therefore seems to be certain that the concept of reciprocity will be the key factor in European Community commercial policy. The effect that it will have upon franchisors will therefore depend to a great extent upon the franchisor's home jurisdiction. One thing is for certain, if the EC does build walls against foreign companies, franchising is likely to be one of the best ways of breaking through those walls for some businesses. The appointment of local sub-franchisors and developers will often mean that non EC franchisors can still successfully exploit the single market. Such ability is likely to depend to a great extent on the nature of the franchise. Product-based, importing franchises will find the walls most difficult to surmount, while service-based franchises are likely to find few problems.

However it would be wrong to believe that the European Community will shun co-operation with third countries unless there is complete reciprocity.

The Commission press statement dated 19th October 1988 gives weight to this conclusion. It states that:

'[the Commission] reserves the right to make access to the benefits of 1992 for non member countries' firms, conditional upon a guarantee of similar opportunities or at least non discriminatory opportunities – in those firms' own countries . . . the Community will offer free access to 1992 benefits for firms from countries whose market is already open or which are prepared to open up their market of their own volition or through bilateral or multi-lateral agreements. It does not mean that all partners must make the same concessions or even that the Community will insist upon concessions from all its partners. For example, it will not ask developing countries to make concessions that are beyond their means. Nor does reciprocity mean that the Community will ask its partners to adopt legislation identical to its own. Nor does it mean that the Community is seeking sectoral reciprocity based on comparative trade levels, this being a concept whose introduction into the United States legislation has been fought by the Community'.

The EC Commission continued to say that:

'non Community firms will benefit in the same way as the Community's own firms from the fact that instead of facing twelve different national markets, each with their own set of red tape, they will be able to operate in a unified market of 320 million consumers [now 340 million] with a single set of laws, standards and testing procedures'.

The EC Commission has however refused US demands that the American National Standards Institute (ANSI) be represented on the technical committees of CENELEC (see Chapter 13 above). Nevertheless the Commission has agreed to put into effect a mutual exchange programme between the two bodies in order to try and ensure some common ground as regards testing and certification.

The attitude of individual member states to trading relations with third countries will be heavily influenced by their experiences of the lowering of barriers to create the single market. The Commission's 350 page report issued in November 1990, entitled 'European Economy – The Impact of the Internal Market' suggests that experiences will vary considerably from member state to member state.

The Report was compiled by the Commission after extensive research in co-operation with each of the twelve member states. Whereas previous reports were limited to forecasting and speculation, this Report is claimed to be based upon heavyweight factual research.

The Report recognises the North–South divide between the twelve member states. Whilst the Single Market is encouraging Northern companies to integrate their highly sophisticated economies further without having to move into new sectors, companies from Southern Europe are faced with a daunting choice. They must either tackle their Northern 'rivals' by breaking into whole new areas of industry, or consolidate their hold over traditional labour-intensive industries such as textiles and footwear, and dramatically upgrade their quality in order to fend off Third World competition.

The hardest choice is faced by Greece and Portugal, whilst Spain has already made inroads into the Northern-dominated world of electronics.

The Commission is, however, adamant that fears that free trade and fierce competition will provoke massive industrial and social upheaval within the Community are unfounded. In the words of Henning Christophersen, European Commissioner for Macro-Economic Policy 'The fear of massive transfer of economic activities between the geographic zones is exaggerated.'

Nevertheless, given the anxieties that many EC member states feel about the opening of their markets to other member states, it is easy to see that there will be some considerable pressure to resist competition by third countries by whatever means are available.

As regards franchising there are three major issues which will affect franchisors, particularly foreign franchisors, within the European Community. These are dumping, origin and the right of establishment. These are each considered in some detail below.

1. ANTI-DUMPING POLICY AND FRANCHISING

Retail franchises in particular are under constant pressure to reduce production costs, and so increase the competitiveness of their franchisees. The lower labour costs in Asia and Eastern Europe mean that it is, commercially speaking, often better to have the goods manufactured in such countries and to then import them into member states. They then enjoy free circulation inside the Community (see Chapter 12).

In the race to depress their manufacturing costs and hence attract greater volumes of business many Asian and Eastern European countries have found, and in the future will continue to find themselves accused of offending the provisions of the General Agreement on Tariffs and Trade (GATT) concerning anti-dumping. This can have grave effects for the importing franchisor/sub-franchisor/developer, upsetting its pricing structure and involving it in many time consuming investigations. Franchisors/sub-franchisors, and developers that import goods into the EC must therefore become acquainted with the basic principles involved. If the walls of a Fortress Europe do rise, then these franchises will undoubtedly suffer as a consequence.

GATT's basic objective is an open, liberal and competitive trading system so as to provide a framework of certainty and predictability in world markets. It is the only multilateral agreement involved in effecting this.

Members of GATT recognise that dumping is to be condemned if it:

'causes or threatens material injury to an established industry in the territory of a contracting party or materially retards the establishment of a domestic industry.' (Article VI of GATT).

Article VI lays down the basic principles of Anti-Dumping, but like all documents that deal only with principles fails to give details of how the principles should be put into effect. It is silent upon how evidence of alleged dumping should be obtained.

Within the EC the concept of dumping and the actions which may be taken to counteract it are contained in Council Regulation EEC No. 2423/88 – (formerly No. 217/84) ('Protection against dumped or subsidised imports from countries not members of the EEC') (referred to as 'the Regulation'). These rules transcend national laws and bind all twelve member states of the European Community. They aim to protect the single market and are a cornerstone of the post 1992 'Fortress-Europe' that non-European member states are so preoccupied with. When compared with the anti-dumping laws of other jurisdictions, such as the USA, the similarity of approach can easily be seen as they derive from the provisions of GATT Article VI.

More detailed than the GATT code, the Regulation describes the rules and procedures upon which the Community's Anti-Dumping measures are to be taken. It must be emphasised, however, that the Regulation does not provide a full account of EC Anti-Dumping practice and procedure – which is far less straightforward than the simplicity of the Regulation might indicate.

A complaint of dumping must first be initiated by a complaint to the Commission from EC industry that feels it is suffering from dumping practices. The complaint is carefully considered by the Commission. If it feels that the complaint has merit it will issue notice of the commencement of a dumping investigation. The dumping investigation is carried out by the Commission. The Council of Ministers and the Advisory Council are also involved.

The dumping calculation

In order to be able to judge whether or not they are in danger of becoming subject to an anti-dumping action, franchisors must familiarise themselves with the basic elements of the dumping calculation.

In essence the EC may impose a duty on any product where:

(a) its export price (simply put the price paid by the franchisor or franchisee to the exporter less expenses of importation) is less than its so-called 'normal value' (roughly speaking the ex-factory price of the goods in the country of manufacture), and

(b) the sale of that product in the importing country is causing injury to local industry.

The aim of the Regulation is to counteract the effect of products sold at an 'unfair' low price by raising the selling price within the EC. This is done by imposing a tariff upon their importation (in addition to any normal tariff which may be applied to all such products regardless of dumping).

The dumping margin

The concept and principles of dumping are set out under Article 2 of the Regulation. The essence of the dumping investigation is the calculation of a 'dumping margin' defined as:

'the amount by which the normal value exceeds the export price'

In effect, 'normal value' means domestic price or a price which is equivalent to domestic price.

The preferred basis for determining 'normal value' is the price paid or payable for the like product in the exporting country or country of origin. This domestic market price is however disregarded in certain circumstances of which the most important is domestic sales being made at a price below the cost of production over an extended period of time and in substantial quantities, in which case 'normal value' is constructed by adding the cost of production and a reasonable profit margin .

Where the exporter and importer are associated, the 'export price' is the actual export price at which the imported product is first re-sold to an independent buyer, less all costs incurred between importation and re-sale, including all duties and taxes and a reasonable profit margin .

The Community Authorities make comparisons between 'normal value and export price' at ex-factory level, having taken into account permissible allowances.

The dumping margin is generally expressed as a percentage on the basis of the CIF export prices of the products. The formula used to calculated the percentage is:

$$\frac{\text{normal value} - \text{export price}}{\text{CIF export price (duty paid)}} = \frac{\text{dumping margin}}{\text{EC frontier}}$$

Injury

Calculation of a dumping margin alone is not sufficient to enable the Commission to impose a dumping duty upon imports into the Community. It must first show that the dumped imports are causing or threatening to cause material injury to a Community industry, or materially retarding the establishment of such an industry. This accords with the GATT Article VI requirement that dumping 'causes or threatens material injury' to local industry.

It is calculated by taking into account various socio-economic and statistical factors.

'Community industry' means all Community manufacturers or those who account for a major proportion of the Community production of imports which are identical or similar to the dumped products.

As in all areas of dumping, the Commission has wide discretion when reaching its conclusions on injury. In practice once it is found that dumping has occurred it will generally find that dumping has caused injury. Findings of 'no injury' have however occasionally been made, and the question of whether or not injury has been caused is increasingly an important one in dumping cases.

Of perhaps greatest practical importance is the fact that the dumping duty imposed can be no more than the level of injury suffered. Thus if a dumping margin of 50% is found against an exporter, but injury is calculated as being only 25%, the dumping duty imposed can be no more than 25%. The basis for this is that the duty is meant to remove the threat to local industry not to exact penal remedies against companies guilty of dumping.

Community interest

Before anti-dumping duties can be imposed it is also necessary for the Commission to show that the imposition of such duties is in the interests of the Community. This includes matters such as consumer interests and the interests of importers.

However generally the third area of investigation has become merged with questions of injury.

Remedies

Once an Anti-Dumping duty has been calculated by the Commission it is published in the Official Journal as a provisional duty which takes effect for a limited period of up to six months. The duty is not actually collected but the Importer must provide a guarantee that it will be paid if it is later decided that it should be collected.

Up to six months after the announcement of provisional duties, these are reassessed and imposed as definitive duties. It is unusual for provisional duties to differ significantly from definitive duties. It is however open to the defendants to further argue their case to try and reduce the duty imposed.

A duty may be imposed in one of a number of ways by for example ad valorem duty (i.e. a fixed percentage of the CIF price before payment of customs duty), specific duty (i.e. a fixed amount per unit imported), or a duty on an amount equal to the difference between the price at the Community frontier and a fixed price established by the Commission. Ad valorem duty is the most common.

In general terms duties cannot be imposed retroactively although there are certain limited exceptions. Such exceptions include circumstances in which a previously given undertaking has been violated. In such circumstances retroactivity can only be for ninety days prior to the provisional duties.

A decision whether or not to impose definitive duty is taken by a vote of the Council in which each member state has a certain number of votes.

Duration of duties

In basic terms the definitive duties lapse five years after the date on which they entered into force or were last modified or confirmed.

It is important to note therefore that if after for example three years a company applies for the removal of the dumping duty, but fails to achieve this, the duties will run for five years from the date of the review i.e. three years longer than they otherwise would have done if no application had been made!

Further, there is the so-called 'sunset provision' by which public notice is given of the imminent expiration of dumping duties so that interested parties can if necessary apply for their extension. Such an application is only granted after extensive investigation by the Commission in a way similar to the original one. The imposition of an anti-dumping duty can therefore cause long-term difficulties for a franchise necessitating resourcing possibly from within the EC.

An alternative to accepting duties is for the exporter to give an undertaking to the Commission to increase its prices and so to remove the dumping factor. Undertakings have of late become less popular with the Commission as they are easily breached and more difficult to monitor.

The ECs approach to anti-dumping may however soon change as in November 1990 the European parliament called for more transparent, fairer policies which are subject to more democratic controls. It has laid down a number of suggested guidelines; nevertheless, it views EC anti-dumping procedure as far fairer than that of the US.

The impact on franchising

The temptation for an importing franchisor, sub-franchisor or developer may be to persuade the exporter to reduce its prices still further so that the increase in duty does not affect the gross consumer purchase price. This would however amount to 'Double Dumping' which is forbidden under the Regulation. Another temptation for some franchisors would be to import only the components and assemble them in the EC. This however may well fall foul of the Regulation as so-called 'Component Dumping'. In order to avoid component dumping a 40% local content requirement must be complied with.

To date dumping investigations within the EC have tended to be restricted to heavy industrial products, chemicals and consumer electronics. This does not however set any precedent for the future. Clearly those franchises which are most at risk are 'distribution franchises' dealing in goods manufactured in cheaper markets such as the Far East and Eastern Europe or aggressive expanding countries such as Japan. It should however be borne in mind that Services (in the form of shipping (see Chapter 11 above)) have also been subject to dumping actions.

Franchisors should therefore always be aware that any price advantage it obtains in the Single Market as a result of products being manufactured overseas may be short lived. If the viability of a franchise were to rest solely upon these lower manufacturing costs, then the franchisor should consider its future in the EC, and the possibility of a dumping action being launched against its supplier very carefully indeed.

The problem might best be illustrated by a hypothetical golf accessory retail franchise from, say, Canada. The franchisor selects stock entirely from Hong Kong and Taiwan, and arranges for its German and British sub-franchisors to buy the clubs and bags directly from Hong Kong and Taiwanese manufacturers. The sub-franchisors make a profit of 20% on the sale of the clubs. This is their main source of income. The low prices give the franchise a tremendous price advantage over shops selling European manuufactured clubs, and as a result the Hong Kong and Taiwanese clubs (and therefore the franchise) begin to take a progressively higher market share. The British club manufacturers find it impossible to meet the Taiwanese and Hong Kong prices for sustained periods and eventually file a formal complaint of dumping to the EC Commission. The Commission investigates the allegations, and being satisfied that there is a prima facie case initiates an anti-dumping investigation against the Hong Kong and Taiwanese manufacturers.

As a result of the investigation an additional duty of 30% is placed upon the clubs.

The sub-franchisors are then placed in a commercially disastrous position. In order to avoid the disintegration of the whole chain the franchisor must either radically change the franchise concept, its financial gearing, or its source of products. In any event the franchise is bound to suffer a severe set-back.

2. ORIGIN

The question of the origin of products is also an important one for franchising in the EC as it essentially affects the right to free movement within the Single Market.

The question of origin can be divided into three basic elements. Firstly rules of origin relating to specific products, secondly the rules relating to origin of products exported to the Community from third countries and thirdly origin of products assembled in the Community.

When two or more countries are concerned in the manufacture of a product Regulation No. 802/68 (OJ1968 L 141/1, Eng. Spec. Ed. P165), (Appendix 15, Part 5), provides that the place of origin is where the 'last substantial

process operation is carried out'. It is a general rule of trade and can be used more or less restrictively as the case may be. However, as regards certain products the Community has more specific regulations in relation to origin, for example, televisions, radio receivers, integrated circuits and photo-copiers. There is also a draft proposal for printed circuit boards.

As regards products exported to the Community the question of origin will determine how they are treated by relevant anti-dumping duties or quantitative restrictions.

As regards the origin of products which are imported to the Community as a component and then assembled in a member state the general principle remains the 'last substantial procedure or operation'. However, this is not always easy to determine, as evidenced by the dispute between France and the United Kingdom over Nissan motor vehicles assembled at the Nissan plant in Washington, Tyneside in the United Kingdom. France unilaterally imposed a quantitative restric-tion on the import of Japanese cars and contended that the Nissan vehicles assembled in the United Kingdom came within this quota. The dispute was finally settled only after intervention by the Commission. The fear is that the trend will be to require greater local content before products, such as for example films, can enjoy the advantages of the Single Market. The public procurement directives, for example, contain certain local content requirements.

Clearly, the free movement of goods imported by franchisors or their sub-franchisors/developers into the EC is a matter of great importance, and will greatly affect the future of foreign franchisors in the Single Market. If, for example, an ice cream franchisor sets up a manufacturing plant in Southern Ireland (using imported products) to supply its sub-franchisors throughout the Single Market, any restriction upon the freedom of movement of the ice cream manufactured in Southern Ireland would have disastrous effects upon the entire franchise network. The high transport costs incurred in importing ice cream direct from the United States to each individual member state would be prohibitive and make the product uncompetitive on the grounds of price. The capital expenditure necessary to establish the Southern Irish factory would also severely damage the profitability of the franchise if it turned out to be more or less a white elephant, capable of supplying only some of the member states, or in the worse case only Eire itself.

3. RIGHT OF ESTABLISHMENT

The availability of the right of establishment (see Chapter 10 above) to third countries is of far less importance to franchisors than to other businesses that deal with their affairs in other countries through subsidiaries. Nevertheless, unless franchisors from third countries enjoy the right of establish-ment in the Community, their options as regards the struc-turing of their operations in the European Community are noticeably reduced.

Article 58 of the Treaty of Rome provides that free access to the Single Market is available to:

'. . . companies or firms formed in accordance with the law of a member state as having their registered office, central administration or principal place of business within the Community'.

Thus a sub-franchisor which is in effect the subsidiary of a third country parent franchisor, and which is already established in the EC should be treated in exactly the same way as a French, German, Danish or Spanish franchisor.

However, although certain member states such as the United Kingdom, the Netherlands and Luxembourg take this view of Article 58, others, such as France, take a far more restrictive view. France places conditions on third country companies establishing themselves within the national territory and has even tried to rely upon this restrictive view to prevent the acquisition of a French company by a company of another member state which happened to have third country shareholders.

There would seem to be no easy solution to this divergence of views upon Article 58, and it will have to be resolved either by the European Court of Justice or by a Community-level initiative to harmonise member state rules.

CONCLUSION

At midnight on 31 December 1992, the walls of a Fortress Europe will not suddenly spring into place. There will be no sudden changes which will irrevocably increase the obstacles to non-EC franchisors doing business in the Community. Nevertheless, franchisors are not immune from the global economic climate; they will continue to be affected by the EC's international and internal economic policies. The same is true for EC-based franchisors. Thus when planning their strategy for the Single Market, franchisors must take account of wider economic issues.

The Growth of the European Community and its Effect on Franchising

By MARK ABELL and ANGUS MACMILLAN

INTRODUCTION

Europe comprises three major trading blocks – the European Community, the European Free Trade Association (EFTA) and Eastern Europe (COMECON). Recent developments in both Western and Eastern Europe are resulting in a fundamental reappraisal of both the internal operation of these groups and the external relationships which they have with one another. A period of relative stability is being followed by one of radical change, which is altering the political and economic face of Europe more than at any time since the end of the Second World War.

EUROPEAN FREE TRADE ASSOCIATION

EFTA comprises six member countries – Finland, Sweden, Norway, Iceland, Switzerland and Austria. The Association was originally set up in 1959 by the Stockholm Convention and at that time included both the United Kingdom and Denmark within its membership. The Association was set up in response to the European Economic Community, to offer its members the opportunity to gain the benefits of an economic association, without involving any political co-operation or joint economic policies.

EFTA's approach to integration has been described as 'minimalist'. It was devised to show that political integration was not a sine qua non of economic integration, nor did political integration necessarily flow from economic integration.

The aim of the organisation was similar to the fundamental aims of the Common Market, namely to reduce tariff barriers between member countries and so produce a region of free trade. However, it did not have any of the political implications inherent in the EC. Because of the different, less all embracing, aims, which flowed from the different value system of the EFTA countries, the institutional structure is less invasive. It is based on two principles. Firstly, the principle of subsidiarity, which requires that a higher-level institutional body should never be allowed to make a decision that a lower level body could make just as well. Secondly, the system was developed in order to allow different communities to develop differently which in turn meant tolerating differences between countries and not imposing common, group wide, institutions, standards or policies. This included allowing each member state to maintain its own tariff policy, rather than imposing a common external tariff.

One sector which EFTA did not try to include within the general thrust of internal tariff reduction was agriculture. In all countries, administered support prices had long replaced market determined ones. In these circumstances it was clear that free trade would not provide an optimal solution. Nor did EFTA seek to go down the route of the EC in developing a form of Common Agricultural Policy. Not only would this not have fitted with the overall philosophy aimed at minimising centralised intervention, the model from the EC may not have given too much encouragement to follow this example.

Though the membership of EFTA has varied somewhat over time – most notably with the departure of the UK and Denmark to join the EC – the grouping has provided a dynamic source of growth for its members within a framework which provides a stark contrast to the EC in terms of intervention and regulation. In addition, the organisation has allowed the development of bilateral links between EFTA and the EC, to such an extent that the two blocs are each other's largest trading partners, with annual business in excess of US$210billion.

However, the EC's drive towards a single market is forcing EFTA to reappraise its relationship with the Community, a reappraisal made all the more imperative by the decision in July 1989 by Austria to seek full membership to the EC. EFTA countries are worried that the developments following 1992 in the EC may squeeze them out of the Community's markets.

Following the EFTA (Luxembourg) initiative in 1984, both the EC and EFTA are looking to create a European Economic Space (EES), a single economic and commercial market which covers all 18 countries and 370 million people. Central to this development would be the extension of the EC's four fundamental freedoms for the cross border movement of goods, capital, services and persons. Brussels also sees it as necessary that EFTA give up some independence and adopt existing Community legislation on such issues as competition, public procurement and technical standards which flow from the 'four freedoms'. Exceptions would be negotiated when there were issues of deep national interest.

Negotiations are underway. So far a number of steps have been taken. In 1988 it was agreed that there would be both mutual notification of proposed new standards and the reciprocal recognition of tests, results and certificates. The SAD (see Chapter 12 above) can be used for transporting goods between the two blocks, and a common transit procedure adopted, together with an abandonment of export restrictions and an agreement on the definition of a product's origin. The 1988 Lugano Convention reflects the provisions of the Brussels Convention on the enforcement of judgments (see Chapter 31 above), whilst co-operation on environmental issues (see Chapter 21 above), transparency on state aids and increased co-operation on Research and Development programmes have also been put in place.

The timetable was originally aiming for agreement to be reached by the end of 1990. However, the target was not met and it remains to be seen how willing EFTA countries will be to accept the imposition of wide-ranging Community law of which they have had no hand in development.

Furthermore, Austria's application suggests that EFTA may have a problem in maintaining internal cohesion.

In October 1990 the Norwegian Government collapsed when one of its components, the Centre Party, refused to accept the plan to relax restrictions on foreign ownership of Norwegian property, industry, banks and other financial institutions. The removal of these restrictions was one of the demands of the European Community in its negotiations with the six members of EFTA for the European Economic Space. In Sweden, the Social Democratic Government tried to add credibility to a feeble emergency economic package by pledging that Sweden would join the EC.

It would seem that all six EFTA countries are suffering more and more from the pulling power of the single European market and from the fear of being marginalised when it is in full operation. The Finns, now free of the tight rein that Moscow kept upon their foreign policy since the Second World War, intend to 'stick to the process of the EFTA – EC negotiations to see where that process leads' whilst Iceland has accused Sweden of 'betraying the EFTA process'.

It is not only a fear that Americans and Japanese will consider it better to invest in the EC member states rather than in countries on its periphery. Even their own businessmen seem to be afraid of losing out and in Sweden for example, there has been a heavy drain of capital into the EC since restrictions on the movement of capital were lifted a year ago.

The strength of the European currencies, pegged together within the Exchange Rate Mechanism, (see Chapter 34 above) set against the vulnerability of the EFTA nations minor currencies is yet another problem.

The question being asked in the six EFTA member states seems to be 'if we have to accept so many EC rules to achieve the level paying field required for fair competition, why not go the whole hog and join?'

It seems that even Switzerland, despite its decentralised government and long independent traditions, is now considering the possibility of EC membership.

EASTERN EUROPE

Alongside the major development inherent in the move towards the single internal market, there have been changes in Eastern Europe of an even more fundamental nature and exhibiting a pace which is nothing short of breath-taking. Emanating from the Gorbachov policy of Glasnost in the USSR, the drive for greater political and economic freedom in the Eastern European countries has rapidly developed a momentum which is both unstoppable and irreversible.

It was both the pace of change and direction and the extent of that change which left commentators in the West and politicians in the East astonished. The political changes are the most obvious, but they imply economic developments which are no less revolutionary.

The nature and the extent of the economic change will vary considerably from country to country, while the impact on EC and EFTA members will be equally varied. The change brought about by the unification of Germany has been the most rapid and most radical, while those East European countries, with already serious debt and economic problems, will find the changes hardest to make.

Eastern Europe has a number of advantages. The population is generally well educated and relatively skilled, certainly compared with, say, Latin America and even with Portugal, within the EC. It also has a much more egalitarian distribution of income and wealth, minimising the internal conflicts which typify some other developing middle income countries. Meanwhile, though debt in Eastern Europe is high, it is, with the exception of Poland and, perhaps, Hungary, much more bearable than in some other countries. Low labour costs and geographical proximity will also make East Europe attractive, to the extent that investment both from individual countries and from the EC as an entity, may be diverted to the East, away from the Mediterranean countries within the Community. This could have notable effects on trade with the EC (see Chapter 37 above).

The countries also present a great potential for growth, as markets are introduced into their economies. This explosion of economic liberalism is offering companies in both the East and the West an unimagined opportunity for trade.

Against this, however, the countries of the East do have a less developed infrastructure. This results in poorer economies, and growth is almost inevitable given the low base. Trade must increase. However, since Eastern Europe's total value of imports in 1988 was just over US$100bn – only two-thirds of the level of the UK – growth in business may be rapid in percentage terms, but the actual scale may remain small for some time to come. Eastern Europe therefore presents interesting but complex opportunities for franchisors.

Opportunities for individual countries vary. In the most advantageous position is Germany which stands to gain substantially, in the long run, though short-term uncertainty is tending to cause vulnerability. In addition, both Norway and Austria are expecting to improve trade links.

Several of the Eastern European countries, particularly Hungary, Czechoslovakia and Poland, would like to see their future inextricably linked with that of the present twelve EC member states. Franchisors intending to invest in Eastern Europe are therefore likely to think it prudent to establish operations in the EC first.

INCREASING EC MEMBERSHIP

The Italian presidency in the last three months of 1990 saw the United Kingdom eventually succumb to membership of the Exchange Rate Mechanism (see Chapter 34 above). It also saw eleven of the EC member states (excluding the United

Kingdom) agree a time table for moving to the next stage of Economic and Monetary Union (EMU – see Chapter 34 above). By 1st January 1994 the next phase of EMU will have begun with the setting up of the EuroFed, a Pan EC Central Bank, subject to certain conditions including the finishing of the EC Single Market, the largest possible number of EC currencies in the Exchange Rate Mechanism and Parliamentary ratification of an EMU treaty. A single currency could well be in place by the year 2000.

A more fundamental question which will have to be answered relates to membership of the EC. There is growing pressure on the EC to open its doors to EFTA and Eastern European countries alike. However, the EC, like any club, must be selective as regards its membership. If this is not so, then it will cease to exist as an effective force.

The fact that the European flag happens to have twelve stars is a historical accident. It had twelve stars when there were just six members. There is no cultural, historical or geographical reason that justifies Greece being a member but not Czechoslovakia, or Portugal being a member and not Hungary. The twelve present members are members because they are members. Arguments concerning membership are not arguments of principle but of practicality. In the case of both ETFA and Eastern European countries the argument is that such expansion would weaken the existing Community. 'Maybe in ten to fifteen years, for Czechoslovakia and Hungary' is, according to the Financial Times (25th October 1990) the conventional Eurocratic wisdom.

To say that membership will be available to those who meet the membership criteria is not a real answer to the question. The criteria are only what the present twelve member states wish to make them. To allow Spain, Portugal and Greece into the Community was a strategic political decision based partly on geography, culture and history, but also on the wish to reinforce new democracies. In order to score this political goal, a great number of concessions and allowances were made for their relative economic weaknesses over long transitional periods. To do the same for Hungary, Czechoslovakia and Poland would be far more costly and difficult.

Nevertheless the choice may be between deepening the Community or alternatively widening it.

THE EFFECTS ON FRANCHISING

Austria, Sweden and Switzerland all have organised franchise associations and some banks offer specific finance for franchising in these countries, recognising it as a tried and tested business medium. Finland, Iceland and Norway however do not have any substantial experience of franchising.

The Eastern European countries, with some small but notable exceptions, have no experience of franchising whatsoever.

The future of franchising in the EC is of course inextricably tied with future membership of the European Community and its relationship with Eastern Europe and EFTA.

At present the EC is an excellent platform from which franchisors can venture into Eastern Europe and EFTA. This by itself encourages the growth of franchising in the EC, which with the advantages offered by the Single Market is a prudent first step for non European Franchisors desiring to establish their concept in 'Greater Europe'.

If the membership of the EC does increase, the likely effect upon franchising in the Community will be a complex one.

The increased geographical spread of the Community can only increase its importance in world trade and therefore its desirability to non-EC Franchisors.

If the new members are countries such as Switzerland, Austria or Sweden with an existing franchise 'industry', the growth is likely to encourage franchising both into and out of the new member states within the Community.

If the new members are 'advanced' economies with little or no experience of franchising, such as Norway and Finland, the growth is, it is suggested, likely to have little medium effect. These markets are small and geographically remote. The relative lack of franchising in Greece and Portugal to date suggests that such markets will take time to mature in terms of franchising. Growth of franchising is likely in existing less developed national markets such as Greece, before new member states with a similarly underdeveloped franchise market.

If new member states are found in Eastern Europe a whole host of new opportunities and problems will present themselves to franchisors in the EC.

The lack of infrastructure, need for quick, low capital risk growth of small and medium sized businesses and the many unknown factors of the national markets which have been unexploited for so long will present a host of exciting opportunities for franchisors in the EC. However, as stated above, the membership of such nations will inevitably retard the growth and development of the Single Market and the EC's economy across the board. Not only will it divert the political will which is now so tightly focused on creating a true single market amongst the twelve member states, it will also cost a great deal in terms of financial and other resources that would otherwise have been used to further develop the quality of the Single Market in the existing twelve member states. Franchising in the Single Market will therefore still have to contend with various remaining barriers; as a result its growth may, to some degree, be impeded. The trend may well be to exploit what are perceived to be the most rewarding markets based on a coefficient of potential rewards and difficulties, rather than a desire to establish a truly Pan-EC franchise network.

Enlarged EC membership would increase still further the advantages of franchising within the single market, in terms of geographical coverage of franchise networks. It would also however dilute the single market and hence withhold many of the future advantages of the single market for some time to come.

CHAPTER 39

The Future Development of Franchising in the European Community

By MARK ABELL

INTRODUCTION

The greatest debate on the international franchise scene is the degree and type of regulation that franchising should be subjected to. The debate rages between two directly opposite camps, those who see any form of franchise specific regulation as being pejorative and against the best interests of franchising, and those who believe that the most important matter to be dealt with is the protection of would-be franchisees from the sharp practices of suspect or bogus Franchisors.

The Anti-Regulation lobby puts forward self-regulation by national franchise associations as being a solution to the problem. As Mr Brian Smart, Executive Director of the British Franchise Association, said at a seminar sponsored by Field Fisher Waterhouse and the Union Internationale Des Avocats (UIA) in October 1990, 'Franchise Associations must seek to impose the highest possible standards upon their members. This is far more effective than imposing a legal minimum standard which will, in any event be evaded by bogus franchisors, one way or the other'.

The pro-regulation camp's response to this is that only compulsory standards are properly adhered to. At best, voluntary standards will have little or no effect until franchisors are forced, through commercial or legal pressures to become members of the association, and compliance with voluntary standards is a term of membership.

There are in effect two areas that require consideration as regards regulation, be it voluntary or statutory.

The first area is the sale of franchises. It is important that the potential franchisee receives full, frank and relevant information concerning the franchise.

The second area is that concerning the rights and obligations of the franchisor and the franchisee respectively. It is in general the former area that is causing the most excitement in the European Community at present.

An examination of the regulatory systems in some other jurisdictions provides the best way of obtaining a perspective on the options currently facing the ELC.

THE UNITED STATES

The United States regulatory system is of course, always held up as the 'bête noire' of the franchising industry.

Franchise sales regulation in the United States has two parts: disclosure and registration. Disclosure is required under the Fair Trade Commission or 'FTC Rule' which applies in all 50 states. Registration is required only in certain states. This section provides a summary of the general disclosure requirements that apply in the United States, with comments on typical practices there.

What must be disclosed and when?

The FTC Rule applies in all 50 states and sets the minimum standards for disclosure to prospective franchisees. The FTC Rule requires that certain information be given to prospective franchisees in a standard form, which may be either the 'FTC Format' or the 'Uniform Franchise Offering Circular (UFOC) Format.' There are slight differences between the two formats, but only the UFOC Format is accepted by the states that require franchise registration. Most US franchisors therefore use the UFOC format.

The information required to be disclosed is discussed in detail below. The purpose of the FTC Rule was to address problems of non-disclosure and misrepresentation of material facts in connection with sales of franchises. It is a violation of the FTC Rule for a Franchisor or franchise sales broker to:

— fail to furnish prospective Franchisees with the basic Disclosure Document in the manner and within the time periods established in the rule.
— make any representations about actual or potential sales, income or profits except in the manner permitted under the rule.
— make any claim or representation (such as in advertising or other written or oral statements) that is inconsistent with the information required to be disclosed in the Disclosure Document.
— fail to furnish prospective Franchisees, within the time periods established in the rule, with copies of the standard Franchise Agreements and the final agreements to be signed by the parties.
— fail to return refunds or deposits identified as refundable in the basic Disclosure Document.'

State laws that regulate franchise disclosure generally provide that it is unlawful:

— to offer or sell any franchise in the state without having first provided the prospective Franchisee with a copy of the offering circular registered with the state, within the time periods specified under the state law.
— wilfully to make any untrue statement of a material fact or wilfully to omit to state any material fact required to be stated in the offering circular, or fail to notify the state of any material change.
— to offer or sell a franchise by means of any written or oral communication which includes an untrue statement of a material fact or which omits to state a material fact necessary in order to make the statements made, in the light of the circumstances under which they were made, not misleading.'

What subjects are covered in the disclosure document?

The following is a summary of the items required to be disclosed under the UFOC Format:

1. Franchisor and any predecessors
This item contains a general description and brief history of the Franchisor and the franchise offered.

2. Identity and Business Experience of Persons Affiliated with the Franchisor; Franchise Brokers
Directors, officers and other executives who will have management responsibility for the Franchisor's operations relating to franchises are listed. Each person's business experience for at least the preceding 5 years must be listed.

3. Litigation
Pending and completed litigation that involves claims against the Franchisor relating to violation of securities laws, fraud, unfair or deceptive practices, and other comparable allegations must be described for the preceding 10-year period. The disposition of each case (including general terms of settlements) must be included.

4. Bankruptcy
The bankruptcy history for the preceding 15-year period of the Franchisor, its predecessor(s) and current officers and general partners must be disclosed.

5. Franchisee's initial franchise fee or other initial payment
This item sets forth requirements for payment of the initial franchise fee and also describes the Franchisor's use of proceeds from initial fees.

6. Other fees
This section is divided between 'recurring fees' and 'non-recurring fees'. Recurring fees are the operating and advertising fees. Non-recurring fees are other fees that the Franchisee must pay from time to time under the Franchise Agreement.

Most US franchisors list all types of fees that the franchisee may be required to pay, whether or not the fees will be paid to the franchisor. Some of the fees typically listed are paid to the franchisor (e.g., renewal and transfer fees, interest on late payments, training deposits), while some are paid to third parties as a result of the franchisee's obligations under the Franchise Agreement (e.g., insurance, warranty reimbursement, expenses associated with training).

7. Franchisee's initial investment
This item must include a chart that sets forth the various expenditures the franchisee must make in order to open for business, estimates of the franchisee expenses, and lists of vendors or other persons to whom the franchisee will need to pay money. Most franchisors add explanatory notes to the chart.

8. Obligations of franchisee to purchase or lease from designated sources
If there are any items required to be purchased by franchisees that are available from only one source these must be disclosed. Items that are optional for use in the franchise may, as a practical matter, be available from only one source, but if there is no requirement to purchase them, it is not necessary to disclose designated sources of optional items.

9. Obligations of franchisee to purchase or lease in accordance with specifications or from approved suppliers
Most US franchisors require franchisees to use and sell only approved goods in the franchised business, including equipment, parts and supplies. Many franchisors approve goods for use in the franchise by reference to brand names. Some franchisors have specific procedures for approval of suppliers, particularly in the food business. Except in the case of a product franchise (such as 'Baskin-Robbins Ice Cream'), most US franchisors do not require franchisees to purchase goods from the franchisor or its affiliates. However, all items must meet the applicable standards and specifications established by the franchisor.

A few franchisors now reserve the right to approve providers of services. This could include management services, advertising agencies, accountants, etc. The franchisor may require such service providers to execute confidentiality and non-competition agreements relating to information they may receive in the course of working for franchisees.

10. Financing arrangements
If the franchisor or any affiliate offers financing arrangements to franchisees, detailed disclosure of the terms of the financing must be included.

11. Obligations of franchisor; other supervision, assistance or services
This section lists the specific services to be provided by the franchisor before and after opening of the franchise. It also contains page and section references to the Franchise Agreement.

In addition, the training programmes and training personnel of the franchisor must be described. Other types of assistance offered by the franchisor (such as site assistance) are also listed in this item.

12. Exclusive area or territory
The Disclosure Document must state whether or not the franchisee will have any exclusive territorial rights, and the conditions attached to those rights.

13. Trademarks, service marks, tradenames, logotypes & commercial symbols
The Disclosure Document must list the primary names, marks, and logos used in connection with the franchise and the status of their registration at federal and state levels. If there are any restrictions on their use (such as settlement agreements in connection with trademark disputes), these restrictions must be disclosed.

14. Patents and copyrights
If there are any patents or copyrights material to the franchise, these must be disclosed. Most franchisors note in this item that operating manuals, advertising materials, or

other publications used in connection with the franchise are copyrighted (or, if not copyrighted, treated as confidential).

15. Obligation of franchisee to participate in the actual operation of the franchise business

The Disclosure Document must state whether the franchisee must personally operate the business, and whether the franchisor recommends that the franchisee personally operate the business.

16. Restrictions on goods and services offered by the franchisee

This item includes not only restrictions on approved goods or services, but also customer or territorial restrictions imposed on the franchisee.

17. Renewal, termination, repurchase, modification and assignment of the franchise agreement and related information

This is the infamous provision in which, typically, the exact language of the Franchise Agreement and ancillary agreements (which are attached to the Disclosure Document) concerning the subjects listed is simply repeated.

18. Arrangement with public figures

If a public figure is used in connection with selling franchises, certain information must be disclosed. This does not apply if a public figure is only used in connection with advertising the goods and services offered by franchisees.

19. Actual, average, projected or forecasted franchise sales, profits or earnings

Prior to 1989, there were numerous complicated requirements for disclosing 'earnings claims'. Item 19 has been considerably simplified, and many franchisors are now beginning to offer information about sales, profits, and earnings.

20. Information regarding franchises of the franchisor

Statistical data about the number of franchises, the states in which they are located, and the history of terminations and non-renewals are included here. In addition, a list of all franchisees is attached as an exhibit to the document.

21. Financial statements

The audited financial statements for the previous three fiscal years of the franchisor must be attached.

22. Contracts

All contracts to be executed by the franchisee in connection with the purchase of the franchise must be attached as exhibits.

23. Acknowledgment of receipt and state addenda

A form to be dated and signed by each prospective franchisee is found at the last page of the Disclosure Documents. The form is detached and retained by the franchisor to prove compliance with the disclosure requirements. Many franchisors also incorporate 'state changes' in a separate addendum to the Disclosure Document, and use a separate receipt form to indicate that the franchisee who is a resident of a registration state has received the proper state-specific Disclosure Document.

Arduous though these statutory regulations may be, it is difficult to believe that the imposition of such regulations in the EC would inevitably lead to the repression of franchising and lead to its dying away. America, despite its 'over regulation' of franchising is by far and away the most developed franchise market, and arguably the market that holds the greatest financial rewards for franchisors.

JAPAN

The regulation of franchising does not necessarily have to be as comprehensive or as heavy-handed as that seen in America. The Japanese situation offers an alternative approach.

The Fair Trade Commission guidelines of 1983 require disclosure by franchisors of six basic categories of information:

1. The amount of the initial franchise fee and any conditions as regards refunds
2. The term, renewal and termination conditions
3. The availability of any compensation for losses of the franchise
4. The conditions concerning the supply of goods, expected sales turnover, and expected earnings.
5. The nature of management assistance, including the allocation of related costs.
6. The nature of the continuing payment of fees, including the terms of payment.

In addition the Retailers Law requires retail franchisors to make full disclosure as regards:-

1. Name and address of the franchisor and its representatives (if any)
2. The initial deposit
3. Conditions or methods of sale of the goods
4. Trademarks to be used
5. Term, renewal and termination conditions
6. Date of commencement of the franchise system
7. Nature and level of continuing fees
8. Any requirement concerning the shop's structure, design and layout
9. The degree and type of management assistance to be provided to the franchisee.

The regulating governing body, the Ministry of International Trade and Industry (MITI) has no power to compel compliance or punish non compliance, other than public declaration of the failure to comply.

As a result of the lack of enforceability and various other factors, the Japan Franchise Association has formulated its own voluntary disclosure code in conjunction with MITI. The scheme requires a greater degree of disclosure than the Retail Law and FT guidelines and is based on the US example. To date over 30% of franchisors accounting for 60% of all franchisee outlets participate in the scheme.

This hybrid scheme of both statutory and voluntary regulation is unlikely, it is suggested, to be of any real use in the EC.

THE EUROPEAN FRANCHISE FEDERATION CODE OF ETHICS

The European Franchise Federation (EFF) was established on 23rd September 1972 and is comprised of national franchise associations or federations in Europe. At present its members are Belgium, Denmark, France, Italy, the Netherlands, the United Kingdom and West Germany.

The EFF proclaims its aims in the preface to the European Code of Ethics for franchising as:

'among others, the ongoing unbiased and scientific study of franchising in every respect, the co-ordination of its members' actions, the promotion of the franchise industry in general and of its members' interests in particular.'

The Code of Ethics is intended to lay down a single code of conduct for the Common Market, which is adopted by its members which undertake not to delete or amend it in any way. However, the preamble does provide that national requirements may necessitate certain other clauses or provisions and, providing these do not conflict with or detract from the Code and are attached to the Code in a separate document, permission to do this will not be withheld by the EFF.

Exactly what that will mean in practice remains to be seen. It would take a committed (if not naive) 'European' optimist to believe that it will lead to a truly uniform approach being taken by each member. With the best will in the world Franchise Associations have vested interests that are not only commercial but also national.

Nevertheless, the Code is potentially of great importance to franchisors, as is the arbitration system established by the EFF for franchise disputes.

Guiding principles

The guideline principles of the Code are expressed to be as follows:

'The Franchisor is the initiator of a franchise network, composed of itself and its Individual Franchisees, of which the Franchisor is the long-term guardian.

2.1 The obligations of the franchisor:
(a) Before starting its franchise network, the Franchisor shall have operated a business concept with success, for a reasonable time and in at least one pilot unit;
(b) The Franchisor shall be the owner, or have legal rights to the use, of its network's trade name, trade mark or other distinguishing identification;

(c) The Franchisor shall provide the Individual Franchisee with initial training and continuing commercial and/or technical assistance during the entire life of the agreement.

2.2 The obligations of the individual franchisee:
(a) The Individual Franchisee shall devote his best endeavours to the growth of the franchised business and to the maintenance of the common identity and reputation of the franchise network;
(b) The Individual Franchisees shall supply the Franchisor with verifiable operating data to facilitate the determination of performance and the financial statements necessary for effective management guidance, and allow the Franchisor, and/or its agents, to have access to the individual Franchisee's premises and records at the Franchisor's request and at reasonable times;
(c) The Individual Franchisees shall not disclose to third parties the know-how provided by the Franchisor, neither during nor after termination of the agreement.

2.3 The ongoing obligations of both parties
(a) Parties shall exercise fairness in their dealings with each other. The Franchisor shall give written notice to its Individual Franchisees of any contractual breach and, where appropriate, grant reasonable time to remedy default;
(b) Parties should resolve complaints, grievances and disputes with good faith and goodwill through fair and reasonable direct communication and negotiation.'

Recruitment, advertising and disclosure

The issues of Recruitement, Advertising and Disclosure, selection of Individual Franchisee, the franchise agreement and status of sub-franchisors are also addressed by the guidelines, as follows:

'(a) Advertising for the recruitment of Individual Franchisees shall be free of ambiguity and misleading statements;
(b) Any recruitment, advertising and publicity material, which contains direct or indirect references to results, figures or earnings to be expected by Individual Franchisees, should be objective and capable of verification;
(c) In order to allow prospective Individual Franchisees to enter into any binding contract with full knowledge, they shall be given a copy of the present Code of Ethics as well as full and accurate written disclosure of all information material to the franchise relationship, within a reasonable time prior to the execution of these binding documents;
(d) If a Franchisor imposes a Pre-contract on a candidate Individual Franchisee, the following principles should be respected:

— Prior to the signing of any Pre-contract, the candidate Individual Franchisee should be given written information on its purpose and on any consideration he may be required to pay to the Franchisor to cover the latter's actual expenses, incurred during and with respect to the Pre-contract phase; if the Franchise agreement is executed, the said consideration should be reimbursed by the Franchisor or set off against an Individual Franchisee possible entry fee to be paid by the Individual Franchisee;
— the Pre-contract shall define its term and include a termination clause;
— the Franchisor can impose non-competition and secrecy clauses to protect its know-how and identity.

Selection of individual franchisees

A Franchisor should select and accept as Individual Franchisees only those who, upon reasonable investigation, possess the basic skills, education, personal qualities and financial resources sufficient to carry on the franchised business.

The Franchise Agreement

(a) The agreement shall reflect the interests of the members of the franchised network in protecting the Franchisor's industrial or intellectual property rights and in maintaining the common identity and reputation of the franchised network:

— all agreements and all contractual arrangements in connection with the franchise relationship should be written in the official language of the country the Individual Franchisee is established in, and signed agreements shall be given immediately to the Individual Franchisee.
— the Franchise agreement should comply with both the letter and spirit of National law, of European Community law and of this Code of Ethics.

(b) The Franchise agreement shall set forth clearly the respective obligations and responsibilities of the parties and all other material terms of the relationship, in fairness and free of ambiguity;

(c) The essential minimum terms of the agreement shall be the following:

— the rights granted to the Franchisor;
— the rights granted to the Individual Franchisee;
— the goods and/or services to be provided to the Individual Franchisee;
— the obligations of the Franchisor;
— the obligations of the Individual Franchisee;
— the duration of the agreement which should be long enough to allow the Individual Franchisee to amortise his initial franchise investments;
— the basis for renewal, if any, of the agreement;
— the terms upon which the Individual Franchisee may sell or transfer the franchised business and the Franchisor's possible preemption rights in this respect;
— provisions relevant to the use by the Individual Franchisee of the Franchisor's distinctive signs, trade name, trade mark, service mark, store sign, logo or other distinguishing identification;
— the Franchisor's right to adapt the franchise system to new or changed methods;
— provisions for termination of the agreement;
— provisions for surrendering promptly upon termination of the franchise agreement any tangible and intangible property belonging to the Franchisor or other owner thereof.

Master franchisee

This Code considers a Master Franchisee to be a Franchisee in its franchise relationship with its Franchisor. In this relationship with the individual Franchisees, established within the franchise territory, granted the Master Franchisee by the Franchisor, the Master Franchisee performs, where appropriate and at its sole risk, the duties of its Franchisor, for the time and within the limits granted the Master Franchisee by the latter. The provisions of the present Code should be interpreted in this sense.'

As master franchisees and sub-franchisees play an important role in franchising within the EC, it is essential that their role should be made clear.

Exactly how this is interpreted by each Member States' franchise association is yet to be seen.

The British Franchise Association is currently reviewing its own disclosure requirements in the light of the European Code of Ethics.

The approach initially proposed to be taken is that there will be a general obligation placed upon the Franchisor to make full and frank disclosure of relevant facts to potential franchisees. It is also suggested that there will be a format by which disclosure will take place.

This format will not however, be compulsory, although Franchisors must be able to justify their approach if it differs from the BFA's model.

It has not yet been decided by the BFA what the model will contain, but a draft is currently being considered by the membership.

THE FRENCH APPROACH

The attitude towards regulation in France is very different to that exhibited in other EC Member States. From an anti-regulatory stance ten years ago, the French Franchise Federation (FFF) eventually decided that it was in the best interests of French franchising to have statutory regulation as regards Disclosure to potential franchisees.

As a result, the so-called 'Loi Doubin', was adopted by the French legislature and eventually put into effect by way of statutory instrument (see Appendix 17).

France is the biggest franchise market in the European Community. It represents over 15% of the French commercial sector — approximately 60,000 companies representing a total annual turnover of 700 billion francs, and an annual payroll of 30 billion francs.

The first step towards the adoption of legislation was taken by the eminent French lawyer, Olivier Gast, when in 1985 he drafted an Act to regulate franchising and 'any type of contract the purpose of which is to raise initial funds from executive investors for an intangible consideration which is neither commercially feasible nor operable'.

The aim of this draft, was to ensure that franchising relationships were regulated without the necessity of policing the actual franchisor-franchisee relationship on a continuing basis. This aim has been incorporated in the Loi Doubin. The French therefore have adopted a principle whereby the contract is legally enforceable between the parties provided they are given adequate prior disclosure. It is perceived that there is no need to complicate the dealings of the parties to the contract by over regulation. Freedom of contract must be preserved but must be enlightened. The act requires the party deemed to be the stronger (i.e., the franchisor) to provide to the other (i.e., the franchisee) with specified information enabling the latter to enter into the contract in full possession of the relevant facts.

It is important to note that the Loi Doubin is not a 'franchise law', but is in fact of much broader application.

Paragraph 1 of Section 1 (see Appendix 17 below) states clearly that it applies to:-

'all contracts entered into in the parties' mutual interests which entail authorisation of use by one of the parties to the other of its trade name, trade mark or trade signs'.

It therefore covers not only franchise contracts but also distributorship, dealership, partnership and trade mark licence contracts, voluntary chains, associations, co-operatives and so on, so long as the criteria of Paragraph 1 of Section 1 are met, that is to say provided there is a commitment of exclusivity or quasi-exclusivity in carrying on the business.

The reason for this is obvious, the so-called 'jam sandwich syndrome'. If you apply pressure, the jam tends to ooze out at the sides. If only franchises were regulated, the less salubrious franchisors would merely re-catagorise their businesses as distributorships or dealerships, and so try to effectively avoid the statutory disclosure requirement.

The information must be supplied in writing with the proposed contract, at least 20 days before the contract is signed (Sl, para. 4) or at least 20 days before any payment is made (this alternative usually applies in the case of a preliminary exclusive-territory contract). In the latter event, para. 3 of Sl of the Act contains special provisions relative to the services rendered in consideration of such payment and the parties' reciprocal obligations, in the event of default.

Finally, para. 2 of Sl provides that the contents of the document is spelled out by decree. However, Parliament laid down guidelines by specifying that the information provided shall relate inter alia to 'the firm's age and experience, the conditions of and prospects of growth of the market involved, the size of the operators' network, the term and terms of renewal, cancellation and assignment of contract and the scope of the exclusive Provisions.

The implementing decree was issued on 4 April 1991. It basically imposes a duty of disclosure.

The information provided in the disclosure document must be 'in good faith' and enable the Disclosee to contract 'in full knowledge of the circumstances'. The twinning of these two concepts may cause some difficulty. Incorrect information may be given in good faith but will not enable the Disclosee to contract 'in full knowledge of the circumstances'.

The way out of the difficulties presented by this dilemma, according to Maître Gast, is to ensure that the Disclosee receives as much information as possible.

The problem with this advice is that there is a danger that the Disclosee will be given so much information that it will not be able to see the wood for the trees, so defeating the whole object of the Act.

However, although a surplus of information may be confusing, too little may amount to a breach of the law. Given a choice between the two, franchisors are likely to tend to be safer rather than sorry. If any information is not disclosed, full reasons for the non-disclosure must be given.

One of the burden's necessarily imposed by the Loi Doubin is the need for Disclosers to continuously update the disclosure document. Failure to do this will mean that the information is not given in good faith and therefore amounts to a breach of the law.

The firm French opinion is that the Loi Doubin is necessary to ensure ethical conduct in franchising. Ethical franchisors, they argue, have nothing to fear from its disclosure requirements. Even before the Act was adopted, franchisors often gave disclosure of the details of their networks.

From now on, the disclosure document supplied will have to comply with minimum legal requirements that will not cause any real difficulty for ethical franchisors. Any minor inconvenience resulting from this legal duty is far outweighed by the advantages to be gained from an 'industry wide image of trustworthiness and honesty'.

THE EUROPEAN COMMISSION APPROACH

The passing of the Loi Doubin has, it is fair to say, caused some friction between French and other national franchise associations. The fear is that the EC Commission will follow the French lead and decide to adopt either a regulation, or more likely, a directive imposing disclosure requirements upon franchisors throughout the EC.

Certainly it would seem to make sense that if there is to be statutory regulation of disclosure requirements, it should be on an EC rather than a national basis. Certainly this is the view expressed by the majority of franchisors who responded to the questionnaire described in Chapter 7 above. In this way, the European Community would be able to avoid the complex web of federal and state laws that cause so many problems for franchisors in the United States. This, it is suggested, is vital for the establishment for a truly Single Market of which franchisors can take full advantage without becoming weighed down by a heavy burden of differing EC Member State regulations.

The Commission's view

Directorate General IV (Competition) and Directorate General XXIII (Enterprise Policy) are the organs of the Commission that are concerned with franchising. DG IV drafted the franchise Block Exemption — (see Chapter 27 above).

The Commission has had substantial contact with the European Franchise Federation and has, it seems, been persuaded that the Federation's Code of Ethics, if properly applied, is a suitable tool with which to regulate franchising in the EC. The attitude of the Commission is that the preferred way to harmonise the control of franchising in the different member states is to deregulate rather than to regulate, wherever possible.

This approach is of course popular with the franchise associations in the member states and gives added importance to the European Franchise Federation's Code of Ethics.

However the French 'Loi Doubin' has made such harmonisation through deregulation somewhat difficult and although no formal regulation of franchising is being planned by the Commission to date, it is by no means bound always to be so.

Possible future developments

Indeed it is possible that in the future the Commission may deem it appropriate to regulate not only the sale of franchises but also the contractual relationship between the parties. There is precedent for such an approach to be found in EC Directive 86/653/EC concerning self-employed commercial agents (see Appendix 18 below). This is concerned, not with Article 85 (Competition) but Article 117 (Social Policy). This Article is concerned with improvement of living standards and working conditions. It is therefore worthwhile examining this Directive as it may well suggest a possible future approach to franchising if the Commission deem it necessary to regulate the contractual relationship.

A commercial agent is defined by the Directive as a person who is a self-employed intermediary and has continuing authority to negotiate the sale or purchase of goods, and concludes those transactions on behalf of and in the name of his principal. Certain classes of persons are excluded from this definition such as an officer of a company, a partner, a receiver, legal advisors, an unpaid commercial agent, persons working on a commodity exchange or in a commodity market, an agent for overseas government and administrators, an individual wholly or mainly engaged with those of commercial agents and in particular who is engaged in the business of selling goods from mail order catalogues to consumers. Commercial agents or distributors who purchase on their own account and in their own name (as principals) are also excluded. The Directive does not apply to the provision of services.

The Commercial Agents Directive regulates four areas of the contractual relationship, namely, rights and obligations, remuneration, termination and compensation.

1, Rights and obligations

The agent has a general duty to act 'dutifully and in good faith' and a specific duty to make proper efforts to negotiate such business as his principal has entrusted to him and to comply with all reasonable instructions from his principal.

The principal has a similar duty of good faith including a duty to provide necessary information and documentation for the performance of the agent's duties. In particular, the principal must further:

'1.1 Give notice to the agent within a reasonable time once he anticipates that the volume of transactions will be significantly lower than that which the agent could normally have expected.

1.2 Give written notice as above of his acceptance or refusal or of any non-execution of a transaction which the agent has procured for the principal, or of the delivery of any goods under such a transaction.'

Any attempt to contract out of the above provisions will be void.

This general duty of good faith, could well be imposed upon franchisors and franchisees to good effect. Certainly no franchise network will last for long without mutual good faith. To impose it as a legal duty in a franchise agreement could have some very positive benefits for franchising in general. It would also be of great benefit to franchisors and franchisees alike who suffer at the hands of franchisees/franchisors who do not act in good faith. No doubt many would say that existing laws already afford sufficient protection and that another Euro-law would merely complicate an already satisfactory system.

2. Remuneration of agents

The Commercial Agents Directive imposes a general duty to pay the agreed remuneration, or if none, that customarily paid to agents in the area in which the agent operates and the area in which his office is situated or, if there is no customary practice, that which is reasonable in all the circumstances.

There are detailed regulations relating to the payment of commission, notably:

'2.1 During the period of the agency contract: On repeat orders from customers acquired by the agent, even if those orders were not placed through the agents. Where the agent has an exclusive right to act on behalf of the principal in a specific geographical area or in relation to a specific group of customers.

2.2 After the conclusion of the agency contract: If the transaction was mainly a result of the agent's efforts during the period of the agency contract and was entered into within a reasonable period after it, or the order of the third party reached the principal or agent before the agency contract ended.

2.3 When the principal has, or should have, carried out the transaction or, if earlier, the third party has completed his part of the transaction. It is payable not later than the last day of the month next following the end of the quarter in which it became due.'

The right to commission can only be extinguished if it is established that no contract between the third party and the principal will be completed; and that fact is due to a reason for which the principal is not to blame.

The principal must provide a statement of commission due and also provide all necessary information, including extracts from the principal's books, in order for the agent to check the amount of commission payable.

Any term in an agreement that is less favourable to the agent will be void.

Any attempt to regulate the service charge, royalty or other initial and continuing fee paid by franchisees to franchisors would be totally unacceptable. It would in effect, make many franchises unworkable. The calculation of such fees by the franchisor is (or at least should be) a very delicate matter, and the calculations can only be based upon the experience of the franchisor in its particular sector. The differences between a high street retail franchise such as for example, Tie Rack or Body Shop, a service franchise such as for example Hypro-mat (the French car wash franchise – see Chapter 43) or Service Master (see Chapter 42) and an 'investment' franchise, such as Holiday Inn, are enormous.

3. Termination of the agency contract

The Directive imposes a right for each party to receive from the other a signed written contract at any time, including any terms agreed after the conclusion of the agency contract.

Minimum notice periods for either party are one month for the first year, two months for the second, three months for the third and subsequent years. If a fixed period contract is converted into an indefinite period contract by continued performance by both parties after the end of the fixed period, the time from which the notice period is calculated shall run from the commencement of the fixed period.

The general contract law regarding repudiation for a breach of contract or frustration is not affected by the recommendations.

Any regulations concerning the termination of a franchise agreement would no doubt be welcomed by franchisees. It would however inevitably work against the interests of the franchisees as a whole. The franchisor acts as a form of trustee for the franchisees' collective interests. If a maverick franchisee misbehaves, the franchisor has a commercial and moral if not legal duty, to restrain the franchisee from such behaviour as soon as possible. Such unchecked behaviour will most likely soon cause substantial damage to the image of the franchise as a whole and therefore in turn to the interests of each individual franchisee.

However, the imposition of any automatic right of renewal on the terms of the then current franchise agreement providing there is no substituting breach and has been no recurring breach, may be worth considering. There can be no real objection to such a renewal (for a second term only – not in perpetuity) if the franchisee is conducting its business in a proper manner in accordance with the franchise agreement. This would go some way to preventing less scrupulous franchisors abusing franchisees for their own ends.

For example, a business needing an injection of cash may see Initial Franchise Fees as an easy way of obtaining the needed cash. Once it has received the money and successfully used it to solve its liquidity or cash flow problems, it may well wish to ditch the franchisee by simply refusing to renew the franchise agreement. The franchisee however has made a real commitment to the franchise and should, it is submitted, be allowed to renew the agreement for at least one more term. Naturally this situation can be avoided by ensuring that the franchise agreement expressly gives the franchisee this right. In practice however, this does not always happen, and an implied legal right would 'plug this gap'. It would certainly not hinder any ethical franchisors. It might also be argued that in order to ensure that such a rule was not circumvented by franchisors granting short-term franchises, a minimum length of franchise be imposed.

Likewise, it may be that there should be an implied right for every franchisee to sell its business to a third party, subject to the franchisor's preemptive right of purchase and approval of any third party.

However, the right of sale to a third party alone is not sufficient. If there is only six months of the franchise agreement left to run the market price will be negligible, and the franchisee will not be able to realise its true capital investment. The right of sale must include the automatic granting to the purchaser of a new franchise agreement. Thus, a franchisee with six months left to run of a seven-year term agreement could sell a new seven-year term agreement (on the then current franchise terms) to the third party. As the franchisor has the right to approve such a potential purchaser, there can be no objection to such an implied right. Such a clause is essential to enable the franchisee to realise a profit on its capital investment in the franchise.

4. Compensation

The Commercial Agents Directive provides that compensation will be payable by the principal and take into account losses, liabilities, costs and expenses he has incurred, including any commission he would have earned;

(a) When the principal discharges the agency contract except by reason of any breach by the agent entitling the principal to terminate the contract under the general law; or

(b) If the agent discharges the contract by reason of breach by the principal or by reason of age, infirmity or illness of the agent in consequence of which he cannot reasonably be required to continue his activities or by frustration of the contract including the death of the agent.

Compensation is not payable if the agent has assigned his rights and duties to another person nor if he has failed to give written notice to the principal before the end of one year following termination of the contract.

The idea of compensation having to be paid by the franchisor to the franchisee would certainly be fiercely resisted by franchisors and would, it is suggested, serve no real purpose other than to substantially retard the development of pan-European Community franchises.

In any event, if the franchisee is allowed to sell its business at a market value as suggested above, compensation would not be an issue.

Any term contained in a commercial agency agreement is void under the Directive if it is inconsistent with any of the Directive's provisions for the protection of the agent. Such a term is essential for any Directive that seeks to regulate contractual relationships.

The guiding principles of the European Code of Ethics for Franchising (see above) might also be incorporated in such a franchise Directive.

Whether or not the EC Commission decides to focus upon the rights and duties of franchisors and franchisees in the Community there would certainly seem to be a number of issues worthy of consideration and which could be approached by them in a manner with which they are already familiar.

Certainly, an obligation placed upon the franchisor and franchisee to act towards each other 'dutifully and in good faith' would not be out of place.

CONCLUSION

The future of franchising in the European Community would, in a commercial sense, seem to be secure. It is likely to play a significant role in enabling small and medium sized companies take advantage of the single market.

Exactly how, or indeed if, franchising will be regulated is still far from certain although it seems likely that, at least in the short to medium term the trend will be for member states not to regulate franchising by statute (with the exception of France of course). The Commission likewise seems to be willing to give voluntary regulation a chance to succeed. However, the failure of such voluntary regulation will surely lead to the Commission taking steps in the direction already taken by the French.

It seems therefore that the future regulation of franchising in the European Community is largely, for the time being, in the hands of the franchisors.

PART EIGHT

CASE STUDIES

CHAPTER 40

I Can't Believe It's Yogurt!

By JAMES AMOS

BACKGROUND

In January 1978, Julie and Bill Brice were students at Southern Methodist University in Dallas, Texas, USA. They had grown up in a secure home with a close-knit Dallas family. Their father, Bill Brice, Sr., a successful lawyer and businessman, felt that one way of determining their business acumen was to give them a go at running a small business.

It happened that a client of the Brice law firm had a couple of small yogurt stores he wanted to sell. Today, it is a legend in the world of business format franchising how Bill and Julie Brice invested $10,000 of their college tuition money into a concept with the improbable name of 'I Can't Believe It's Yogurt!'

The business acumen of Bill and Julie Brice resulted in a multi-million dollar international dream come true. With 13 years in business behind them they have seen their company grow 40 to 50 per cent a year since 1983 when franchising began. From those first two stores, I Can't Believe It's Yogurt! has grown to over 400 domestic locations, service on board American Airlines, frozen offerings in hypermarkets and nearly 100 kiosks or free-standing machines in hospitals, schools, theme parks and government cafeterias.

In 1989, the decision to develop international markets was made. In one year, nine master franchise agreements were signed covering sixteen countries. While it may not have been the most strategic time to consider globalisation, clearly, the corporate competencies and strategic fit to effect geographic expansion were at hand.

Macroeconomically, roughly one-third of US corporate profits are generated by international business. American competitiveness abroad has a tremendous direct effect on domestic employment levels and on the economic health of the nation. Every billion dollar's worth of exports creates about 25,000 new jobs. In fact, in the past five years nearly five million new jobs created in manufacturing in the US were export related. In addition, most US business leaders believe that growth potential of the domestic market in the United States is levelling off. A US Congressional study of industrial competitiveness from the Office of Technology Assessment reported that 'where a global market exists, firms operating on a worldwide basis may have advantages over those that restrict themselves to a domestic market'.

ICBIY AND THE EC

With all of this, Europe clearly was changing the rules for international trade. Centuries of institutionalised trade barriers appeared to be being swept away with a unified European market consisting of 342 million consumers and 12 member states with nine languages. The EC would change commercial, financial, legal, tax and other business areas so much so that US companies could not sit idly by and ignore them. Even a company as small as I Can't Believe It's Yogurt! could recognise that the process of integrating European communities into a truly single market by removing physical, technical and fiscal barriers to the movement of goods, services, capital, and people was a significant step towards creating a global economy and thus global markets.

Along with all this opportunity, as trade barriers fall it appears that a plethora of new regulations might emerge in their place and undermine the potential for growth within the EC. 'Fortress Europe' became a fear once 1992 was a reality.

Consequently, I Can't Believe It's Yogurt! put its toe into international waters in October of 1989 by attending the Anuga Food Show in Cologne, Germany. After all, with all of the motivation to enter Europe, if the European taste for what was a decidedly different yogurt product was not positive, there would be no market. Happily in five and a half days we fed 36,000 people our frozen yogurt and evoked interest from 19 different countries. It appeared our product not only would be accepted but had the same market potential, if not greater, than had been displayed in the US.

Now came the time for more strategic planning as well as tactical application. Bill and Julie Brice, Rick Postle, the Chief Operating Officer and Jim Amos huddled together to determine our options.

There are at least half a dozen ways of structuring international agreements, the most obvious being joint ventures and master franchise agreements. We felt that a joint venture concept would narrow our possibilities as we would have to expend domestic dollars for expansion. On the other hand, a master franchise concept might allow us to expand with greater breadth while reducing dramatically the capital outlay for growth. The group concurred and we set about creating a profile of our master partner. That profile would drive our international development not only in the EC but in the Pacific Rim and the Middle East. We decided that we would want a partner that had the vision and the desire to seek disproportionate market share within their country. Therefore, they would have to want not only market dominance, but have the financial capability to educate the consumer and advertise in their market. Consequently, we would want to grant exclusive rights to that partner to penetrate their market with all phases of product development.

It should be pointed out that relationship development then became the driving force behind the selection of a master franchise partner. It became obvious that there were numerous candidates in almost every country with the financial wherewithal to penetrate their markets. However, we soon learned that regardless of the structure of the agreement or indeed the legal documents supporting that agreement, it was the relationship that would drive the documents, not vice-versa. This concept is often overlooked in domestic business format franchising and if the selection of the franchisee is important in domestic growth, it is absolutely imperative in international growth. We at I Can't Believe It's Yogurt! have been patient until we have had the profile of the candidate that was a strategic fit for us. We have walked away from agreements because we believe that in some instances no agreement is better than one based on the wrong relationship.

Mutual advantage is the key to selecting the proper partner. The right partner will have integrity and the company or group represented will display a co-operative culture. A proper matching of strengths, weaknesses and motivation is necessary where your strength should be the weakness of the partner. In general, this means labour, raw materials and an expanding market merges with technology, know-how, marketing and management expertise to maximise business opportunity. 'Chemistry' is the glue that keeps things working but it is in fact an intangible that is often defined as trust. The result is an implicit understanding that both partners will live up to the unwritten terms of the agreement.

As it happens, we allowed market demand to drive our development, meaning we reacted to the greatest pressure. While we now have master franchise agreements covering 16 countries, in Europe we are represented in the United Kingdom, Sweden, Norway, Finland, Belgium, Luxembourg and the Netherlands, with agreements pending in France, Germany, Greece and Spain. Our goal is to have representation throughout the EC. However, each member state still has well-established industrial, health, safety and environmental standards that act as formidable non-tariff trade barriers. Products often require different testing and certification procedures in each EC country. As a result, it's often necessary to maintain separate production lines for each market. We are not aggressive where there may be limited demand for the product. Obviously, when and if 'essential requirements' are set as standards within the EC, this will not only create larger markets but also lower costs.

One of the most difficult obstacles to development has been the differing testing and certification requirements from country to country. We have not only avoided markets with onerous bureaucratic requirements but also those that have proven to have no basis at all in reality or logic. As an example, Germany requires an importer of yogurt to classify some of its product by colour, as if that had any bearing at all on what is classified as yogurt. What is all the more frustrating, is that some German frozen yogurt manufacturers produce a product that is pasteurised with yogurt culture present. The end result is a product that is called frozen yogurt but has absolutely no live culture. At best, it is ice cream but certainly not frozen yogurt. France and Italy also have onerous qualifying requirements. Hopefully, if the

intent is to establish broad 'essential requirements' to meet basic health, safety and environmental needs, then all member states will have to comply with the standards to these essential requirements.

There have been many other considerations that we have had to monitor as we continue expanding into the EC. For instance, how will 1992 affect our current EC markets? Will EC integration affect our corporate and management structure in the US and internationally? If so, in what way? How should our information flows be managed? Have we planned strategically for the eventuality that progress towards integration is slowed? What should be our legal and tax structure? Should we establish closer relations with the European Commission in Brussels?

This clearly is an ongoing process and while it may seem cumbersome and not quite relevant, business people who are complacent about how 1992 will affect their business should think again. The EC's new controls on mergers as an example, may even affect business between two non-EC based companies (see Chapter 17 above).

Finally, at the risk of stating the obvious, the essential ingredient for conducting international business, whether it is in the EC or elsewhere, is people – people who are 'geocentric' in attitude, thinking in world terms and seeing opportunities, not constraints. Flexibility, resourcefulness, a positive attitude, curiosity, emotional stability and motivation are attributes that Lennie Copeland and Lewis Griggs tout in their book *Going International*. They are right! International work inflicts stress. No matter how well you strategise and plan, you must have the right people carrying the ball. The competence of the players as it relates to cultural savvy and business skills will ultimately determine the end results.

At any rate, companies new to European business in 1992, will need to examine each of the three principal areas of their company to determine a strategy for entering the single European Market:

(1) Marketing, including customers, distribution and pricing.

(2) Production, including supplies, product range and processing technology costs.

(3) Infrastructure, which includes organisation for human resources, financial resources and information technologies.

As artificial competitive advantages disappear, national champion companies will no longer be granted state aid. Monopoly power will disappear and major joint ventures will increase between European partners. The new harmonised standards will encourage multinational firms in Europe which will make it more difficult for small to medium-sized businesses to survive market forces such as pricing policy. As Europe regulates itself into an integrated economy and new harmonious standards apply, it could become increasingly more difficult for American companies to do business in the EC.

At I Can't Believe It's Yogurt! we feel that we have made the correct decision to enter the EC in a timely fashion. As Napoleon once mused, 'Ground I can recover, time I can never retrieve.'

CHAPTER 41
Interlink Express

By MARK ABELL

THE FRANCHISE

Interlink Express Plc is engaged in the provision of overnight delivery and collection services through a network of franchise depots in Great Britain, Northern Ireland and the Republic of Ireland.

It provides four main services all of which involve overnight delivery. The company does not provide 3-day delivery and is therefore significantly different to any of its competitors who provide a selection of services rather than just an overnight one. Competitors include, for example, Securicor, Federal Express, Parceline, TNT, Post Office, British Rail, Nextday and other express parcel operators.

The four services offered are:

1. Interlink Express Parcels — a parcel delivery service
2. Interlink Express Freight — a delivery service for freight up to 350 kilogrammes per item
3. Interlink Data Mail — a delivery service for business mail documents and other small items not exceeding 5 kilogrammes
4. Interloft Express — a pigeon-carrying service with birds carried in special boxes.

All services are offered on a next-day basis or with timed delivery options.

Interlink began life in the early 1980's when the current Chairman, Mr Richard Gabriel, saw the opportunity for an overnight parcels delivery service.

The company results at June 1988 showed a turnover of £31.4 million and a pretax profit of £5.8 million with an approximate 10,600 consignments handled each night.

It is important to note that in the Interlink franchise, it is the franchisor who collects the income from customers and then pays on a share of it to the unit franchisees.

INTERNATIONALISATION

In 1986 the company decided that the advent of 1992 meant that they must expand into other EC member states. They undertook a substantial amount of research into what seemed to be two extremes in terms of other EC member states, Germany, which is physically a large nation and The Netherlands which is one of the smallest EC member states.

Interlink is a very customer-orientated operation and believes that in order to give its franchisees a chance of an increased income, the delivery network had to be expanded throughout Europe. In addition, Interlink was only too aware that its competitors were also looking at Europe. Moreover, potential European competitors were preparing to enter the United Kingdom as were those from the United States. Federal Express was already in the market and UPS was expected to follow shortly thereafter.

The initial thinking was that to enter into a co-operation agreement with already established delivery services in the other member states would not be viable as this would probably result in compromising the 'Interlink Philosophy' of high-quality customer service. It was decided that the best approach would be to set up a Master Corporation almost identical to the UK, operation in another member state and once that had been established to then link it in to that existing in the United Kingdom.

One of the main problems of setting up in another country was the fact that on day one of operations at least thirty or forty outlets were needed. This meant substantially deferred profit and high negative cash flow would be encountered. This was understood and accepted.

The research undertaken in Holland and West Germany was highly structured and very professional, being undertaken by very experienced consultants. This research lead Interlink to believe that although there would be problems in any new market, it was best to go to a market where problems were more containable.

IRISH REPUBLIC

Whilst contemplating entry into Holland or Germany, an opportunity presented itself in Southern Ireland. An existing courier company became insolvent and its agents were looking for a new courier network with which to become involved. This was an opportunity which Interlink felt it could not turn down.

Southern Ireland was, after some initial research, seen as not being a soft option for expansion. The infrastructure is extremely poor and the competition within the transport industry extremely severe. On the other hand, the English language reduced a large number of difficulties as did the ease of physical communication with Ireland. It is possible to reach Dublin from a whole range of local airports throughout the United Kingdom.

The Irish operation, after a lot of hard work, became very successful. It started with 10 outlets and now has 26 which is more than all of the other competitors put together. It delivers between 2,500 – 3,000 parcels per night (approximately 10% of the load in the United Kingdom) which is very high for Southern Ireland. It began in July 1986 but for the financial year 1990, it is expected to turn over approximately 3.5 million Irish Pounds.

The development of the franchise in Ireland was assisted by a number of advantages.

To begin with, the approach of the Irish to business and the general lifestyle meant that the franchisees seem to experience no problem in starting from 'scratch'. Franchisees generally accepted advice and instructions that they were given.

The transport law in Southern Ireland did not create any problem for systems such as Interlink which operates a 'central hub system'.

Further, the franchisees and management collected both a need and an enthusiasm for the Interlink concept.

Irish law, being very similar to that of England and Wales, meant that the franchise agreement needed only minimal adaptation and meant that legal expenses were lower and management time spent upon considering the amendments much less.

Further, there was already some existing traffic with Southern Ireland which could be absorbed into the franchise system.

The costs in Southern Ireland were fairly small and there was no need for investment in high technology.

Possibly the most significant factor in the success of the operation was that it was possible to recruit highly-motivated and committed management from the outset which enabled the system to be adapted to the needs of the local market without too much difficulty where the law and market conditions permitted.

The disadvantages were that just before the start of the Interlink franchise in Southern Ireland, a prominent member of the Southern Irish government was involved in a financial scandal involving franchising. As a result, franchising had a very poor reputation in Eire at that time. It was also extremely difficult to recruit franchisees due to their lack of investment funds and the difficulty in selling an idea such as Interlink, which for all its success, depends upon the support of the franchisor and having a successful network. More than in any other form of franchise, the franchisees depend on each other for their mutual success. A quick and efficient collection is of no use if ultimate delivery is slow and inefficient.

The structure of the franchise was that an Irish subsidiary, Interlink Ireland Limited, was set up with a £100 share capital. It was a 100% subsidiary of Interlink Express Plc which provided the necessary financial guarantees etc., for the company. These guarantees were happily accepted by suppliers in Ireland due to the close cultural links of the U.K.

In order to try and ensure the success of the franchise, Interlink made sure that it paid both its franchisees and suppliers as quickly as possible. This resulted in an increased negative cash flow but soon filled any credibility gap that may have previously existed.

WEST GERMANY

In 1987, Interlink undertook still further research of the Dutch and German markets. At the same time it also investigated the possibility of entering the North American market. All relevant aspects including franchise law, transport law, geography, market conditions and the like were carefully examined. As a result, in 1988 it was decided to establish a network in West Germany. The financial and managerial restraints meant that it was only possible to concentrate on one country at a time.

Once the decision to enter West Germany had been made, still further indepth research was undertaken which involved the drawing up of business plans and feasibility studies. A highly respected firm of consultants was used for this task.

In March 1988, following the Irish example, a local franchise manager was recruited in Germany, and as with the Irish franchise manager he was sent to the United Kingdom for training in the franchise operation.

The competition in West Germany was extremely high although it was considered that it was a potentially very profitable market (which contrasts with the expectations of Southern Ireland which due to low population was considered to be at best marginal).

Legal problems were experienced as regards franchising and as regards regulation of transportation. The approach of the German population towards franchising, self-employment and personal motivation was substantially different to that in the United Kingdom and Southern Ireland. Further, franchisees demanded the use of high technology from the start. The Irish experience of a willingness to start from scratch was not repeated in West Germany.

The conduct of the operation was the same as that used in Southern Ireland. A West German subsidiary was incorporated with the shares being held entirely by a Dutch holding company which was in turn held by Interlink Express Plc.

The West German network fell upon substantial operational problems and as a result, Interlink folded the operation and withdrew from Germany. There seem to have been many reasons for the failure of the operation, but three are particularly noticeable. Firstly, insufficient managerial control was exercised by Interlink over its subsidiary. It seems that the amount of time and commitment needed was severely underestimated. Secondly, recruitment of suitable staff seems to have been difficult. Thirdly, an understanding of, but lack of appreciation of the cultural differences between the United Kingdom and Germany created problems.

FUTURE DEVELOPMENTS

Interlink Express Plc is still convinced that in order to survive and prosper, it must establish itself in the other EC member states. In view of its German and Irish experiences, it has now adopted a different approach to the Single Market. Instead of attempting to move itself into each member state in turn, it has tried to locate existing delivery networks in other member states with which Interlink has some degree of synergy and common interest, and then operating with those networks to give transborder coverage. At present, it is operating in this way in Holland, Belgium and Luxembourg and is about to enter Spain and Italy. These arrangements are proving to be successful. However, the company would still prefer to repeat the approach taken in Ireland and West Germany as it believes this to be in the long term interests of the company. However, financial and managerial restraints mean that this is not possible at present.

The lessons to be learnt from Interlink Express Plc's experience seem to be that there is no substitute for indepth research into potential markets, but research alone will not ensure success. Proper structuring and use of managerial resources is essential as is a realistic understanding of the psychology of local nationals and the way in which it will impact upon the franchise business.

CHAPTER 42

ServiceMaster in Europe

By DR. BRIAN A. SMITH

ServiceMaster has the world's largest network of independent franchise businesses engaged in professional cleaning services for homes and offices. Today there are almost 5,000 ServiceMaster businesses operating worldwide and over 250 in the United Kingdom.

ServiceMaster offers four types of franchise in the United Kingdom

— on location carpet and furniture cleaning;
— furniture repair service;
— office cleaning;
— maid service.

In the United States there is also a lawn care franchise and a woodworm pest control franchise. All the ServiceMaster franchises are what is commonly termed mobile franchises in that the franchisee does not, initially, have to buy or maintain shop, office or commercial premises. In the beginning most of the franchisees operate from home, although of course as the business grows it may be preferable to take on a small office and storage accommodation.

ServiceMaster is a unique company. In both 1984 and 1989 it was at the top of the Service 500 listing in Fortune Magazine. In 1984, then called ServiceMaster Industries, it was quoted as 'the most profitable company among the service 500 over the last 10 years, indeed the jewel among all 1,000 in the service and industrial lists combined was ServiceMaster. Its return on stockholder's equity averaged an exotic 30.1%. Servicemaster is in the mundane business of providing housekeeping and other factotum services. . . .' (Fortune Magazine 1984). In 1989 Fortune Magazine said 'the shiningest star of the Group is also somewhat unorthodox. ServiceMaster, of suburban Chicago, headed the 1984 list and leads the 1989 version as well with an average return on equity for the decade of − wow! − 63.7%. Back-to-back championships attest, in this case, to the power of religion. The company selects a biblical quotation for each annual report and reiterates there the company's first objective ''To honour God in all we do.'' The name ServiceMaster connotes ''Masters of Service'' as well as ''service to the Master'' ' (Fortune Magazine 1989). There is no question that ServiceMaster is an extremely profitable company.

ServiceMaster is unique in another way too and that is in the philosophy of the company. ServiceMaster believes that the philosophy of a company determines the character and nature of the business it conducts and the climate of the company is created by the concepts of management and life that govern its policies and practices. The philosophy of ServiceMaster and the words used to express that philosophy have been carefully conceived, nurtured and refined through years of thought, work and commitment. These are expressed in four objectives.

— To honour God in all we do;
— to help people develop;
— to pursue excellence; and
— to grow profitably.

These objectives were further expanded on by the then Chairman of the company in 1983.

'To honour God in all we do − our company recognises God's sovereignty in all areas of our business. Our objective is to apply consistently the principles, standards and values of the Bible in our business attitudes and actions.

To help people develop − our company believes that people grow with the challenge and opportunity for achievement and requires an individual to stretch. Employees will be encouraged to expand their abilities and potential through the company's educational and training programmes and education available outside the company. In recruiting, developing and training employees the company will provide an equal opportunity for all.

To pursue excellence − our company accepts the responsibility continually to seek better methods, to render current and new services to its customers at better value. Our trade marks and service marks stand for excellence. We are committed to continue serving each of our customers with a pursuit of excellence.

To grow profitably − our company sees growth and revenue while maintaining adequate profit both as the material means of achieving the other purposes and as a measurement of the company's value to its customers, employees and shareholders. Our company is committed to use profit with a sense of stewardship and responsibility to employees and customers while providing a means for profitable investing. We are also determined to share these benefits of free enterprise system domestically and throughout the world.'

More recently ServiceMaster has expressed its vision as 'to be an ever expanding and vital market vehicle for use by God to work in the lives of people as they serve and contribute to others.'

The history of ServiceMaster in the USA goes back to 1929 when a gentleman called Marion E. Wade founded a carpet and furniture mothproofing business. As fitted carpets were becoming more popular Mr Wade was one of the first men to recognise the need for an efficient method of cleaning carpeting in-situ whereas previously all carpeting had to be taken away to be cleaned.

In 1947 the company was incorporated as Wade Wenger & Associates and the business moved more and more away from mothproofing into the on-location carpet cleaning business, and special chemicals and equipment were developed for this purpose.

In 1952 the company signed its first franchise agreement in America and in 1958 the first foreign agreement was signed with a gentleman called Raymond Crouch who bought, for £5,000, the exclusive rights to operate the ServiceMaster Carpet and Upholstery cleaning business throughout Western Europe. Raymond Crouch was an entrepreneur operating a family carpet wholesaling business. He had the foresight to recognise that demand for fitted carpets would continually grow in the UK. These would require an efficient and effective method of cleaning, without the risks associated with plant cleaning – shrinkage and colour bleeding.

The turnover of the US company in 1958 is not known but in 1963 the turnover in America was $3.4m and net income $128,433. In 1989 ServiceMaster Worldwide had a turnover of $1.6 billion and a net income of $68m.

Raymond Crouch appointed a general manager and set up a carpet cleaning operation in Hammersmith Road, London. The uniqueness of the system, the special chemicals and equipment was attractive not only to the user but also to carpet retailers who were selling the fitted carpets and to the carpet manufacturers. They were happy to recommend a system which could safely be used on fitted carpets and which overcame all the major objections current at that time, that such fitted carpets could not be cleaned effectively on the floor.

These manufacturers endorsements contributed further to the growth of the company. This unique service, like most unique services, commanded a high price, because demand was relatively low and the service was in scarce supply. The owners of expensive fitted furnishings were willing to pay a premium price. Not only was the service new but franchising was new too in the UK at that time. In fact only one franchise existed, as we know franchising today, and that was Wimpy, the hamburger chain.

ServiceMaster in the UK had to overcome two difficulties in finding franchisees.

(i) The service of on-location carpet cleaning was new and untested outside London.

(ii) The franchise system of doing business was virtually unknown and suspect.

Nevertheless about six franchises were established in the first two years.

The carpet manufacturing industry in England in the early 1960's was extremely strong and exporting all over the world. It was not long before suppliers of carpet, or those closely connected with the supply chain heard of ServiceMaster and sought to establish this unique system in their country. Following the ServiceMaster US pattern of Master Franchise Co-ordinators, agreements were set up overseas. The first of these was in 1961 in Sweden, followed by France, Austria, Eire, Holland, Switzerland, Yugoslavia and even in the Middle East.

In 1974 ServiceMaster in Europe had 126 franchisees in 13 countries.

- UK   61
- Austria   2
- Denmark   1
- Finland   10
- France   12
- Holland   1
- Germany   2
- Ireland   2
- Italy   1
- Norway   2
- Sweden   14
- Switzerland 16
- Yugoslavia   1
- Portugal   1

The demand for the service was considerable. ServiceMaster's European franchisees' reputation rapidly spread through the 'carpet supply network' and providing the price was acceptable distance was no object. A crew would regularly drive from Helsinki in Finland to Moscow in Russia. A unique, albeit mundane, service commanding a high price with no competition was obviously attractive to potential franchisees.

The growth was rapid and uncontrolled. Some master licence holders went the franchise route – Finland, Switzerland, whilst others ran very large cleaning businesses.

There was no business format franchise such as we know it today, incorporating the marketing, financial and administrative control functions of running the business. It was the lack of these and perhaps the lack of the ability to train and control such a diverse group involving some 11 languages and different cultures, that gradually led to a decline in the European operations. As competition grew and increased locally, so the European master franchisors found that they could obtain chemicals and equipment locally, reducing their costs. With increasing competition, prices came down or did not increase to cope with inflation, making the business far less profitable than it had previously been.

The growth in these early years was not planned although determined efforts were made to fill gaps in countries where ServiceMaster was not represented. However, the unfortunate perception the franchisees had of ServiceMaster was that of a machinery and equipment supplier. As times got harder the collection of fees became more difficult. There was no standard franchise agreement, sometimes the agreements were drawn up in the country where the franchisor was located and sometimes in the UK.

In 1976, ServiceMaster Industries Incorporated, the American parent company, bought the rights in Europe and set up two wholly owned company operations in the United Kingdom and Switzerland. The Swiss operation was the holding company which was established to run all European operations. The UK company ran the UK operation which was considerably larger. This changeover was seen by a number of the European master co-ordinators as an opportunity to break their ties with ServiceMaster. Occasionally the business was transferred within the country to another Master franchise coordinator. By 1982 ServiceMaster was represented in only 4 countries. Two operating franchisees in Sweden, one in Germany, one in Belgium, two or three in Finland. Meanwhile ServiceMaster continued to grow in the USA, new opportunities developed, new franchises were introduced and management and other resources were concentrated on building these new businesses, rather than developing in Europe. In 1986, a change in international responsibilities led to renewed consideration of opportunities in Europe.

A new team was set up specifically to develop a strategy for Europe and once approved to put that strategy into operation. Market potential models were developed, taking into account market comparisons, family units, income, the head of the household, GNP as a ratio to the USA, percentage of disposable income spent on furnishing services and the percentage of disposable income spent on new carpets and furniture, etc. Western Europe was graded by size of market and the opportunity presented by ServiceMaster. It was also recognised that an agreement would be needed that would be universal wherever possible. Obviously one that could be used throughout the Common Market was a good starting point.

On June 3, 1987, ServiceMaster Limited, the UK company, notified the EEC Commission of its standard form of Service Franchise Agreement for use in all the member states of the EEC. ServiceMaster applied for a negative clearance or alternatively an exemption under the competition rules of the EEC Treaty. A notice accordingly appeared in the Official Journal of the European Community inviting comments from interested parties.

ServiceMaster UK was chosen to submit the agreement as this agreement was, with minor modifications, being effectively used in the United Kingdom. Extracts from this are as follows:

'ServiceMaster Limited (England) is a wholly owned subsidiary of ServiceMaster Operations AG (Switzerland) which in its turn is largely owned by the ServiceMaster Company Limited Partnership (US company). ServiceMaster Switzerland owns, besides ServiceMaster Limited, a subsidiary in the Federal Republic of Germany, ServiceMaster Operations Germany GmbH, and a subsidiary in France, ServiceMaster SARL.

The business of the ServiceMaster Group is the provision of services in the health care, educational, industrial, residential and commercial markets. The services provided relate to the management and performance of housekeeping, plant maintenance, food service, laundry and linen, material usage and handling, pest control, cleaning and auxiliary services, as well as lawn care services.

Some of the services are performed with products or equipment manufactured and designed by ServiceMaster.'

This notice also included details of ServiceMaster operations at that time – at the end of 1987 ServiceMaster had 3,700 franchise licenses in operation worldwide. In the EEC there were 245 ServiceMaster franchise licenses, the majority located in the United Kingdom. ServiceMaster stated its intention to establish a European network of franchise licenses. In 1987 the total network turnover for ServiceMaster Group amounted to 1,790m ECU.

'The EEC operation at present principally within the United Kingdom had a turnover of about 24m ECU. Revenues from franchise services consisting of initial franchise fees, monthly fees based on franchisees' volume of business and income received from the sale of products and equipment to franchisees.

The notified franchise agreement concerns the provision of housekeeping, cleaning and maintenance services to both commercial and domestic customers according to the franchisor's methods and on an ancillary basis the supply of goods directly linked to the provision of these services. The franchisor has established a substantial know-how in the provision of these services and the method of conducting and marketing the business are secret and the exclusive property of ServiceMaster. ServiceMaster is also the owner of trade marks associated with the product employed in the operation of the business. The ServiceMaster franchise system is based on the use by all franchisees of the ServieeMaster name and know-how relating to the provision of these services and on a continuous commercial and technical assistance provided by ServiceMaster to the franchisees.

The franchisees are proprietors of their business which they operate for their own account and at their own risk. In exchange for the right to exploit a ServiceMaster franchise, franchisees have to make various financial contributions, and are bound by obligations aimed at preserving the uniformity and quality standards of the system.

The market of the services affected by the notified franchise agreement is a fragmented market since it concerns a variety of services and a variety of customers. The market is highly competitive. There are a large number of firms of varying size supplying the services of housekeeping, cleaning and maintenance to both commercial and domestic customers. It is relatively easy for new suppliers to enter the market since these services require no sophisticated equipment.

The market share of ServiceMaster in the EEC is at present below 5%. ServiceMaster operates principally in the United Kingdom where it holds a market share of 6%. However, ServiceMaster is developing its franchise network with the intention to expand throughout the EEC. Also ServiceMaster consider that its market share will increase in the near future throughout the EEC and possibly exceed 5%.

In the United States and Canada, ServiceMaster holds a strong position in the service markets in question. This is particularly shown by the number of its franchisees in that market, 2,137 at the end of 1987 and its recent acquisitions of two other US service companies Terminex and American Food Management.'

Following observations made by the Commission, ServiceMaster accepted to make a certain number of amendments to its originally notified franchise agreement. At the same time ServiceMaster prepared separate agreements for commercial customers and domestic customers. These agreements are, however, identical as regards the clauses to be considered on the EEC competition rules. ServiceMaster communicated the amended franchise agreements on May 10, 1988. The relevant features of these amended agreements follow.

i Selection of the franchisees. In order to be admitted to the ServiceMaster franchise network the applicant must meet the ServiceMaster standards with respect to business experience and financial status, and must complete a training programme organised by ServiceMaster.

ii The franchisee has the right to use in its business the ServiceMaster know-how, trade name, trade mark and copyright. In addition to these rights ServiceMaster supplies the franchisees with an operational manual containing details of ServiceMaster methods of operation and thereafter with continuous commercial, technical and administrative assistance. ServiceMaster further provides the franchisees with advice on location and installation of any business premises.

iii The franchisee agrees to use the ServiceMaster methods of operation and to comply with all instructions with regard to the franchisors' standard for the equipment and general appearance of the business premises and with regard to standard and quality of the service to be provided.

iv Franchisees may not at any time use the know-how and intellectual copyright licence for purposes other than the exploitation of the franchise.

v The franchisee agrees to respect before and after the termination of the agreement the confidentiality of all information and know-how received from Service-Master and to impose a similar obligation on his employees.

vi The franchisee must report to ServiceMaster any improvements in the method of business he makes and permit ServiceMaster and all other franchisees of the ServiceMaster network to use these improvements without any payment being made. In his turn he will benefit from the interchange of improvements made by other franchisees.

vii On termination of the agreement the franchisee must cease using the trade name, trade mark and other signs of ServiceMaster and return any material received from ServiceMaster. The franchisee must further cease using the information and know- how concerning the ServiceMaster system unless the whole of the system as a package has fallen into the public domain.

viii The franchisee may only provide the ServiceMaster services from the premises agreed upon by ServiceMaster.

ix The franchisee is prohibited from setting up premises in the territories of other franchisees.

x With regard to ServiceMaster itself the franchisee has only a non-exclusive right to use the ServiceMaster know-how and intellectual copyright within the territory.

xi ServiceMaster reserves the right to compete itself or appoint other franchisees within the territory of each franchisee; however, ServiceMaster intends to use this right only in the case of bad performance of a franchisee, or in the case of the size of the allocated territory which requires the appointment of a further franchisee. Also ServiceMaster reserves the right to enter into contract with customers who prefer negotiating their cleaning and maintenance contract on a national or even EEC basis rather than on a local basis. In such cases the franchisees can be required to carry out the services to be provided under these contracts.

xii The franchisees remain free to enter into contract with all other customers not requiring a national or EEC type of maintenance contract.

xiii With regard to other franchisees, each franchisee benefits from a limited territorial protection. All other franchisees are under an obligation not to actively seek customers outside their own territory. However the provision of services to non-solicited customers outside the territory is permitted.

xiv The franchisee agrees to use their best endeavours to promote and increase the turnover of the ServiceMaster business in his territory. He must devote the necessary time and attention to that business during the hours of operation of the business and during such other hours are as necessary to perform the administrative, marketing, promotion and accounting functions required in the conduct of the business.

xv The franchisee must acquire such cleaning and other equipment as shall be required for the operation of the business. This equipment must be approved by ServiceMaster.

The franchisee must further purchase certain chemicals used in the operation of the business from ServiceMaster or suppliers nominated or approved of by ServiceMaster. Provided the franchisee can find suppliers able to provide the required equipment and chemicals, which satisfy certain objective criteria, ServiceMaster's approval will not be withheld. For example the criteria used for chemicals are safety, non-toxicity, high degradability, and effectiveness. The franchisee is also free to obtain the equipment or chemicals from other ServiceMaster franchisees.

xvi In principal the franchisee must concentrate on his primary business of providing services rather than acting as a retailer of goods. However, with the prior written consent of ServiceMaster, which will take into account the need for uniformity in the operation of the franchise system, the franchisee may, from time to time, sell homecare products to the customer for whom he provides services. The franchisee may also sell homecare products to other ServiceMaster franchisees.

xvii Advertising can be done by either ServiceMaster or the franchisee. For the advertising done by ServiceMaster the franchisee has to pay a monthly fee calculated on his gross sales income less VAT. Advertising by the franchisee is subject to ServiceMaster's approval. ServiceMaster leaves the franchisees free in the determination of their prices for the supply of services or homecare products, but it may recommend prices to them.

xviii In exchange for the right to operate a ServiceMaster franchise the franchisees must pay an initial franchisee fee and subsequently a monthly fee calculated on their gross sales income less VAT. The franchisee must submit regular financial statements and ServiceMaster is allowed into the premises during working hours in order to inspect the aspects of the operation.

xix During the term of the agreement the franchisee may acquire a financial interest in the capital of a competing company provided it is a publicly quoted company and the capital provided does not exceed 5% of the issued shares. The acquisition of financial interests in non-competing companies is completely unrestricted.

xx After the termination of the agreement the franchisee may not for a period of one year, be engaged in a business competing with a ServiceMaster franchise system within a territory in which he has provided services prior to the termination of the agreement. Outside these territories the franchisee may not for a period one year solicit customers who were, during the period of two years, prior to the termination of the agreement, customers of the ex-franchisee.

xxi Assignment of the agreement or sale of the business to third parties must be consented to by ServiceMaster. ServiceMaster's approval will not be withheld if the proposed purchase of the business fulfils the selection conditions applicable to all franchisees and is not a competing business of ServiceMaster. The duration of the agreement is five years, with the possibility to renew the agreement for periods of each time five years.

'The Commission proposes to adopt a favourable decision towards the ServiceMaster franchise agreement described above. Before doing so it invites interested third parties to submit any observations they may have.'

The above notice was duly posted and ServiceMaster were eventually granted the exemption in accordance with the notice.

In developing a European strategy it was obviously important to consider major markets and any problems there may possibly be in entering them. A plan was put together which combined direct or wholly owned company operations, joint ventures, and master franchise coordinators. Existing operations were brought into the plan, and attempts were made to revive contacts with ex-ServiceMaster operations in certain countries.

A brief examination of Western Europe quickly indicates the major areas of population as the United Kingdom, West Germany, France, Italy and Spain. An examination of income and GNP makes West Germany and France the obvious choices, all else being equal.

In the business that ServiceMaster is in, cleaning, there are considerable barriers to entering Germany in the form of the Handwerkskammer, or German Guild Association. In the middle ages tradesmen tended to band together throughout Europe and form Guilds or Livery companies, but whereas in most countries these have fallen into disuse or only have a traditional role, in Germany they continue, and it is part of Germany's strength that they do so. The training and apprenticeship provided by the German Guilds to their apprentices, so they eventually become Masters or Meisters, contributes, in no small way, to the success and reputation of that country for its precision and technical efficiency. However, they do pose a barrier to newcomers and in particular the Cleaning Guild or Gebäudereinigung has very successfully prevented numerous European cleaning companies from obtaining a foothold in the German market. The primary objection the Guilds have to newcomers is that they do not meet the high standards considered necessary and that consumers may not get the service expected or may be put at risk through faulty workmanship. It was decided to establish a ServiceMaster company in Germany, ServiceMaster Operations GmbH and to tackle this problem head-on.

Headquarters were established near Dusseldorf and the whole process of preparing the business for franchising in Germany commenced. Translating the manuals, importing chemicals and equipment, establishing the Corporation, etc.

It was established that the European Managing Director did meet the requirements of the Guild. However what had to be proven was that ServiceMaster could, through its intensive training, manuals, expertise and knowledge, set up franchisees who would not harm the reputation of the Guild or its members. This was not a fast process and in fact it took something in excess of 18 months. However, eventually success was achieved and this was acknowledged by the Chief Executive Officer of ServiceMaster in the shareholders' meeting held on May 8, 1989. In response to a question 'are you making progress in Europe' the answer was 'we are but slowly. We reached a new milestone last year when we got the necessary approval for our franchising in Germany, so we look for the good future of business there'. A number of franchisees have since been established in business in Gerrnany and all should be set well to expand in the future.

In addition to establishing a company in Germany, companies were also established in Spain and France and the necessary preparations were put in hand.

Developing a European strategy, as is shown by ServiceMaster, requires a considerable investment in terms of people, money and time. It is to ServiceMaster's credit that they entered the European market with that commitment.

The current position is best summed up, once again by the Chief Executive of ServiceMaster in the shareholders' meeting of May 4, 1990, when he said 'We have a good business in the United Kingdom, we have a growing and developing business in Gerrnany but a lot is happening in Europe and I do not think that anybody has all the answers yet as to what is going to happen in that multiple market place. It is really 25 different markets, with 25 different languages and 25 different cultures and even the unification that you hear about under the common market is not going to change those characteristics'.

CHAPTER 43

Hypromat France

By MARK ABELL and MARTIN WILSON

1. HISTORY

Hypromat France was set up in 1973. At the outset, the Company's activities were limited to the distribution of single and multiple car-wash units manufactured in Switzerland for use by the automobile industry (garages and car dealers).

Up until 1985, Hypromat France devoted itself to developing the quality and technical viability of its product; resulting in multiple lane car wash centres based upon self-service high-pressure water hoses operating 24 hours a day.

Faced with the rapid growth in the market in 1986, the Company developed prefabricated and pre-equipped centres. The structure of the centres was designed specially for use by Hypromat France and now forms a vital part of the Company's franchise package. The original single lane model therefore soon became a fully automated model with between 2 and 8 lanes.

It was also in 1986 that the franchising concept was introduced to ensure the growth of the product. At the same time, Hypromat France bought its logo, the 'Blue Elephant'.

By 1989, as a result of a strong brand image and an aggressive sales campaign, Hypromat France had added 100 further car-wash centres to its existing network of 300 centres, of which 40 were run by two subsidiaries of the Company. Today, Hypromat France is a Company which can be said to have successfully used the franchising system as a means of integrating the production, marketing and sales of its product in seven EC Member States.

2. ACTIVITIES

(a) Product

The product is a self-service car-wash centre suitable for all types of vehicle and equipped with high-pressure water hoses. Each centre is designed with at least two lanes, one covered and one uncovered for larger vehicles such as lorries and boats.

The water is treated and a detergent is added containing no chemical additives and which is more than 90% bio-degradable.

Proprietory rights in the structure of the centre, the water treatment system and the trademark itself are protected in the most appropriate way.

(b) The 'Blue Elephant' franchise

The 'Blue Elephant' franchise is a strictly regulated venture between Hypromat France (the Franchisor) and its

Franchisees. The proper operation of each centre is ensured by the strict contractual provisions. The franchisee's package incorporates the following elements:

(i) acquisition of the company's technical expertise, experience and use of the Hypromat logo;

(ii) the provision of know-how;

(iii) property and user-rights in respect of the promotional signs; the trademark ('Blue Elephant'), brand-names, Hyprolav and Hyprobril products, and logos, etc.

According to Hypromat France, consumers today have proved to be very loyal to the brand and the 'Elephant Bleu' logo which is widely recognised, constitutes a guarantee of quality and service.

3. ADVERTISING AND PR

Publicity and promotion are fundamental to the success of Hypromat's European franchise network. Public awareness of its activities and logo are very high and must remain so if the product is to succeed. The franchisees take charge of the local advertising of their centre and Hypromat takes responsibility for advertising on a national level (radio, press, television etc.). The national advertising budget is financed by the franchise fees and was increased from 2 million to 5 million francs between 1988 and 1989. Apart from advertising, Hypromat has undertaken promotional activities such as participation in charitable events, attendance at conferences and sponsoring motor sports. Where possible, these are based upon the active participation of its franchisees.

Further, given that Hypromat is aiming to recruit its clients on an impulse purchase basis, its potential market must be able to react immediately to the sight of the logo by the side of the road. Awareness of the brand is therefore vital.

4. THE MARKET

Hypromat carries out extensive research into the market and its competitors in each target EC member state. The constant growth in the number of cars within the European Community reflects the growing importance attributed by consumers to their cars. The car is the average consumer's second largest expense and the percentage of most European consumers' budget allocated to their car is constantly rising in parallel with the standard of living.

Hypromat identified two areas of indirect competition:

(a) 30% of the car-wash market in France and 50% of the car-wash market in Europe is devoted to the brush-based washing method. According to Hypromat, this method no longer satisfies consumers' requirements and, in terms of technical development, has already peaked. The disadvantages of this system are that only average sized cars can be washed, the washing quality is mediocre and car bodies and accessories are often damaged or scratched.

(b) 50% of car owners in France and 40% of car owners in the European Community wash their cars by hand. Many of these non-consumers do so simply because they enjoy washing their cars. Hypromat France envisage that European legislation to protect the environment will soon lead to the prohibition or restriction of this practice.

The future is very promising for high-pressure hoses. While eliminating the disadvantages of brush-based cleaning and hand-washing, they allow the consumer complete independence. The system may be used for all types of vehicle. Evidence of the product's ease of use is provided by the fact that 40% of Hypromat centre's clients are women — an achievement which few would have previously thought possible in the car-wash market.

The appearance on the market of direct competition has encouraged the company's optimism in relation to the future of high-pressure, self-service car-washing.

Competitors currently on the market in France are Hydrostar, Karcher, Carwash, Auto Smart, WAP, France Lavage. Hypromat controls more centres than all of its competitors put together and represents 10% of the car wash-market. The Company now runs more than 400 centres of which 250 are franchised.

No other competitor has yet managed to establish itself significantly on a European level. Hypromat France is therefore entering a new and undeveloped market. This enables it to take its time and conduct extensive research before establishing itself in a new country.

5. ESTABLISHMENT IN EUROPE

In general, Hypromat has opted for the establishment of a subsidiary in each EC country. Each subsidiary is fully owned by the parent company. To date, the subsidiary companies are Hypromat Portugal, Hypromat Spain and Hypromat UK.

Each subsidiary purchases the car-wash centres from Hypromat France and then sells them on to the franchisees. In addition to this distribution function, the franchisor must prove and establish its know-how by means of pilot centres' in each country. The subsidiary eventually takes over control of the operation of the centres belonging to the network.

Hypromat subscribes to the principle that Europe has already long been a single economic entity and as a result the organisation of its franchise network should be based upon the simple Franchisor-Franchisee formula. As a result, Hypromat signs franchise agreements directly with local franchisees.

The franchise agreement varies in respect of each European country and is regulated by French law incorporating a French jurisdiction clause. A certified translation in the language of the relevant country accompanies the French contract.

There is only one exception to this rule: the Benelux countries are controlled by a Master Franchisee who is financially independent of Hypromat France. The reason for this difference in approach is that Hypromat envisaged some difficulty in simultaneously establishing itself in the three Benelux countries given the existence of wide cultural and linguistic differences within a relatively small market.

Hypromat takes the view that although the word 'franchise' is usually considered to be synonymous with standardisation, the legal, social and economic reality is that each country requires the adaptation of the product to its market. The product is therefore not of a uniform nature. Hypromat has observed that there are wide differences in habits of consumers even within single countries. For instance, in Northern France, car owners wash their cars more often when it is raining and in the winter. In Southern France, the most popular time for a car-wash is in the Summer and cars are rarely washed on rainy days. Further, the versatility of the product allows each consumer a measure of independence. This is vital given that each country's consumers show marked differences of approach in the use of the product. The simplicity of the concept makes allowances for this and is therefore universally exportable.

Due to the fact that Hypromat uses a degree of technical sophistication in respect of electronics, electricity, telecommunication and water treatment methods, it is fundamentally important that the company and its product should be able to adapt to local requirements.

The Manual, which serves to transfer the franchisor's know-how is always altered in accordance with the specifications of each country and is not only translated, but also adapted to allow for such factors as different communication support systems and the obligation imposed in some countries for the Manual to be translated into two languages. All of this clearly illustrates the need for every aspect of the franchise to be adaptable from the product to the Manual. Hypromat appears to have succeeded in this and, with its new research and development department is likely to ensure that it continues to do so.

In the future, Hypromat plans to establish itself right across Europe as a leader in its field. Plans to expand towards the other side of the Atlantic will be considered in five years time.

APPENDICES

APPENDIX 1

Selected Articles from EEC Treaty

Introductory note

The articles printed have been selected for their relevance to franchising, the maintenance of competition and the free flow of goods and services across national boundaries.

The text is as amended by subsequent enactments, notably the Merger Treaty of ECSC and EURATOM, the accession treaties with the countries joining the EEC after the original Six and the Single European Act of 1986.

Table of Articles printed

Article 1

By this Treaty, the High Contracting Parties establish among themselves a EUROPEAN ECONOMIC COMMUNITY.

Article 2

The Community shall have as its task, by establishing a common market and progressively approximating the economic policies of member states, to promote throughout the Community a harmonious development of economic activities, a continuous and balanced expansion, an increase in stability, an accelerated raising of the standard of living and closer relations between the states belonging to it.

Article 3

For the purposes set out in Article 2, the activities of the Community shall include, as provided in this Treaty and in accordance with the timetable set out therein

(a) the elimination, as between member states, of customs duties and of quantitative restrictions on the import and export of goods, and of all other measures having equivalent effect;

(b) the establishment of a common customs tariff and of a common commercial policy towards third countries;

(c) the abolition, as between member states, of obstacles to freedom of movement for persons, services and capital;

(d) the adoption of a common policy in the sphere of agriculture;

(e) the adoption of a common policy in the sphere of transport;

(f) the institution of a system ensuring that competition in the common market is not distorted;

(g) the application of procedures by which the economic policies of member states can be co-ordinated and disequilibria in their balances of payments remedied;

(h) the approximation of the laws of member states to the extent required for the proper functioning of the common market;

(i) the creation of a European Social Fund in order to improve employment opportunities for workers and to contribute to the raising of their standard of living;

(j) the establishment of a European Investment Bank to facilitate the economic expansion of the Community by opening up fresh resources;

(k) the association of the overseas countries and territories in order to increase trade and to promote jointly economic and social development.

Article 4

1. The tasks entrusted to the Community shall be carried out by the following institutions:

a European Parliament,
a Council,
a Commission,
a Court of Justice.

Each institution shall act within the limits of the powers conferred upon it by this Treaty.

2. The Council and the Commission shall be assisted by an Economic and Social Committee acting in an advisory capacity.

3. The audit shall be carried out by a Court of Auditors acting within the limits of the powers conferred upon it by this Treaty.*

Article 5

Member states shall take all appropriate measures, whether general or particular, to ensure fulfilment of the obligations arising out of this Treaty or resulting from action taken by the institutions of the Community. They shall facilitate the achievement of the Community's tasks.

They shall abstain from any measure which could jeopardise the attainment of the objectives of this Treaty.

Article 6

1. Member states shall, in close co-operation with the institutions of the Community, co-ordinate their respective economic policies to the extent necessary to attain the objectives of this Treaty.

2. The institutions of the Community shall take care not to prejudice the internal and external financial stability of the member states.

Article 7

Within the scope of application of this Treaty, and without prejudice to any special provisions contained therein, any discrimination on grounds of nationality shall be prohibited.

The Council may, on a proposal from the Commission and in co-operation with the European Parliament, adopt, by a qualified majority, rules designed to prohibit such discrimination.**

Article 8

1. The common market shall be progressively established during a transitional period of twelve years.

This transitional period shall be divided into three stages of four years each; the length of each stage may be altered in accordance with the provisions set out below.

2. To each stage there shall be assigned a set of actions to be initiated and carried through concurrently.

3. Transition from the first to the second stage shall be conditional upon a finding that the objectives specifically laid down in this Treaty for the first stage have in fact been attained in substance and that, subject to the exceptions and procedures provided for in this Treaty, the obligations have been fulfilled.

This finding shall be made at the end of the fourth year by the Council, acting unanimously on a report from the Commission. A member state may not, however, prevent unanimity by relying upon the non-fulfilment of its own obligations. Failing unanimity, the first stage shall automatically be extended for one year.

At the end of the fifth year, the Council shall make its finding under the same conditions. Failing unanimity, the first stage shall automatically be extended for a further year.

At the end of the sixth year, the Council shall make its finding, acting by a qualified majority on a report from the Commission.

4. Within one month of the last-mentioned vote any member state which voted with the minority or, if the required majority was not obtained, any member state shall be entitled to call upon the Council to appoint an arbitration board whose decision shall be binding upon all member states and upon the institutions of the Community. The arbitration board shall consist of three members appointed by the Council acting unanimously on a proposal from the Commission.

If the Council has not appointed the members of the arbitration board within one month of being called upon to do so, they shall be appointed by the Court of Justice within a further period of one month.

The arbitration board shall elect its own chairman.

The board shall make its award within six months of the date of the Council vote referred to in the last subparagraph of paragraph 3.

5. The second and third stages may not be extended or curtailed except by a decision of the Council, acting unanimously on a proposal from the Commission.

6. Nothing in the preceding paragraphs shall cause the transitional period to last more than fifteen years after the entry into force of this Treaty.

7. Save for the exceptions or derogations provided for in this Treaty, the expiry of the transitional period shall constitute the latest date by which all the rules laid down must enter into force and all the measures required for establishing the common market must be implemented.

Article 8a*

The Community shall adopt measures with the aim of progressively establishing the internal market over a period expiring on 31 December 1992, in accordance with the provisions of this Article and of Articles 8b, 8c, 28, 57(2), 58, 70(1), 84, 99, 100a and 100b and without prejudice to the other provisions of this Treaty.

The internal market shall comprise an area without internal frontiers in which the free movement of goods, persons, services and capital is ensured in accordance with the provisions of this Treaty.

Article 8b**

The Commision shall report to the Council before 31 December 1988 and again before 31 December 1990 on the progress made towards achieving the internal market within the time limit fixed in Article 8a.

The Council, acting by a qualified majority on a proposal from the Commission, shall determine the guidelines and conditions necessary to ensure balanced progress in all the sectors concerned.

Article 8c***

When drawing up its proposals with a view to achieving the objectives set out in Article 8a, the Commission shall take into account the extent of the effort that certain economies showing differences in development will have to sustain during the period of establishment of the internal market and it may propose appropriate provisions.

---

* Paragraph 3 added by Article 11 of the Treaty amending Certain Financial Provisions.
** Second paragraph as amended by Article 6(2) of the SEA.

* Aricle added by Article 13 of the SEA.
** Article added by Article 14 of the SEA.
*** Article added by Article 15 of the SEA.

If these provisions take the form of derogations, they must be of a temporary nature and must cause the least possible disturbance to the functioning of the common market.

Article 30
Quantitative restrictions on imports and all measures having equivalent effect shall, without prejudice to the following provisions, be prohibited between member states.

Article 31
Member states shall refrain from introducing between themselves any new quantitative restrictions or measures having equivalent effect.

This obligation shall, however, relate only to the degree of liberalisation attained in pursuance of the decisions of the Council of the Organisation for European Economic Co-operation of 14 January 1955. Member states shall supply the Commission, not later than six months after the entry into force of this Treaty, with lists of the products liberalised by them in pursuance of these decisions. These lists shall be consolidated between member states.

Article 32
In their trade with one another member states shall refrain from making more restrictive the quotas and measures having equivalent effect existing at the date of the entry into force of this Treaty.

These quotas shall be abolished by the end of the transitional period at the latest. During that period, they shall be progressively abolished in accordance with the following provisions.

Article 33
1. One year after the entry into force of this Treaty, each member state shall convert any bilateral quotas open to any other member states into global quotas open without discrimination to all other member states.

On the same date, member states shall increase the aggregate of the global quotas so established in such a manner as to bring about an increase of not less than 20 per cent in their total value as compared with the preceding year. The global quota for each product, however, shall be increased by not less than 10 per cent.

The quotas shall be increased annually in accordance with the same rules and in the same proportions in relation to the preceding year.

The fourth increase shall take place at the end of the fourth year after the entry into force of this Treaty; the fifth, one year after the beginning of the second stage.

2. Where, in the case of a product which has not been liberalised, the global quota does not amount to 3 per cent of the national production of the state concerned, a quota equal to not less than 3 per cent of such national production shall be introduced not later than one year after the entry into force of this Treaty. This quota shall be raised to 4 per cent at the end of the second year, and to 5 per cent at the end of the third. Thereafter, the member state concerned shall increase the quota by not less than 15 per cent annually.

Where there is no such national production, the Commission shall take a decision establishing an appropriate quota.

3. At the end of the tenth year, each quota shall be equal to not less than 20 per cent of the national production.

4. If the Commission finds by means of a decision that during two successive years the imports of any product have been below the level of the quota opened, this global quota shall not be taken into account in calculating the total value of the global quotas. In such case, the member state shall abolish quota restrictions on the product concerned.

5. In the case of quotas representing more than 20 per cent of the national production of the product concerned, the Council may, acting by a qualified majority on a proposal from the Commission, reduce the minimum percentage of 10 per cent laid down in paragraph 1. This alteration shall not, however, affect the obligation to increase the total value of global quotas by 20 per cent annually.

6. Member states which have exceeded their obligations as regards the degree of liberalisation attained in pursuance of the decisions of the Council of the Organisation for European Economic Co-operation of 14 January 1955 shall be entitled, when calculating the annual total increase of 20 per cent provided for in paragraph 1, to take into account the amount of imports liberalised by autonomous action. Such calculation shall be submitted to the Commission for its prior approval.

7. The Commission shall issue directives establishing the procedure and timetable in accordance with which member states shall abolish, as between themselves, any measures in existence when this Treaty enters into force which have an effect equivalent to quotas.

8. If the Commission finds that the application of the provisions of this Article, and in particular of the provisions concerning percentages, makes it impossible to ensure that the abolition of quotas provided for in the second paragraph of Article 32 is carried out progressively, the Council may, on a proposal from the Commission, acting unanimously during the first stage and by a qualified majority thereafter, amend the procedure laid down in this Article and may, in particular, increase the percentages fixed.

Article 34
1. Quantitative restrictions on exports, and all measures having equivalent effect, shall be prohibited between member states.

2. Member states shall, by the end of the first stage at the latest, abolish all quantitative restrictions on exports and any measures having equivalent effect which are in existence when this Treaty enters into force.

Article 35
The member states declare their readiness to abolish quantitative restrictions on imports from and exports to other member states more rapidly than is provided for in the preceding Articles, if their general economic situation and the situation of the economic sector concerned so permit.

To this end, the Commission shall make recommendations to the member states concerned.

Article 36
The provisions of Articles 30 to 34 shall not preclude prohibitions or restrictions on imports, exports or goods in transit justified on grounds of public morality, public policy or public security; the protection of health and life of humans, animals or plants; the protection of national treasures possessing artistic, historic or archaeological value; or the protection of industrial and commercial property. Such prohibitions or restrictions shall not, however, constitute a means of arbitrary discrimination or a disguised restriction on trade between member states.

Article 37
1. Member states shall progressively adjust any state monopolies of a commercial character so as to ensure that when the

transitional period has ended no discrimination regarding the conditions under which goods are procured and marketed exists between nationals of member states.

The provisions of this Article shall apply to any body through which a member state, in law or in fact, either directly or indirectly supervises, determines or appreciably influences imports or exports between member states. These provisions shall likewise apply to monopolies delegated by the state to others.

2. Member states shall refrain from introducing any new measure which is contrary to the principles laid down in paragraph 1 or which restricts the scope of the Articles dealing with the abolition of customs duties and quantitative restrictions between member states.

3. The time table for the measures referred to in paragraph 1 shall be harmonised with the abolition of quantitative restrictions on the same products provided for in Articles 30 to 34.

If a product is subject to a state monopoly of a commercial character in only one or some member states, the Commission may authorise the other member states to apply protective measures until the adjustment provided for in paragraph 1 has been effected; the Commission shall determine the conditions and details of such measures.

4. If a state monopoly of a commercial character has rules which are designed to make it easier to dispose of agricultural products or obtain for them the best return, steps should be taken in applying the rules contained in this Article to ensure equivalent safeguards for the employment and standard of living of the producers concerned, account being taken of the adjustments that will be possible and the specialisation that will be needed with the passage of time.

5. The obligations on member states shall be binding only in so far as they are compatible with existing international agreements.

6. With effect from the first stage the Commission shall make recommendations as to the manner in which and the timetable according to which the adjustment provided for in this Article shall be carried out.

Article 85

1. The following shall be prohibited as incompatible with the common market: all agreements between undertakings, decisions by associations of undertakings and concerted practices which may affect trade between member states and which have as their object or effect the prevention, restriction or distortion of competition within the common market, and in particular those which:

(a) directly or indirectly fix purchase or selling prices or any other trading conditions;

(b) limit or control production, markets, technical development, or investment;

(c) share markets or sources of supply;

(d) apply dissimilar conditions to equivalent transactions with other trading parties, thereby placing them at a competitive disadvantage;

(e) make the conclusion of contracts subject to acceptance by the other parties of supplementary obligations which, by their nature or according to commercial usage, have no connection with the subject of such contracts.

2. Any agreements or decisions prohibited pursuant to this Article shall be automaticlly void.

3. The provisions of paragraph 1 may, however, be declared inapplicable in the case of:

— any agreement or category of agreements between undertakings;

— any decision or category of decisions by associations of undertakings;

— any concerted practice or category of concerted practices;

which contributes to improving the production or distribution of goods or to promoting technical or economic progress, while allowing consumers a fair share of the resulting benefit, and which does not:

(a) impose on the undertakings concerned restrictions which are not indispensable to the attainment of these objectives;

(b) afford such undertakings the possibility of eliminating competition in respect of a substantial part of the products in question.

Article 86

Any abuse by one or more undertakings of a dominant position within the common market or in a substantial part of it shall be prohibited as incompatible with the common market in so far as it may affect trade between member states.

Such abuse may, in particular, consist in:

(a) directly, or indirectly imposing unfair purchase or selling prices or other unfair trading conditions;

(b) limiting production, markets or technical development to the prejudice of consumers;

(c) applying dissimilar conditions to equivalent transactions with other trading parties, thereby placing them at a competitive disadvantage;

(d) making the conclusion of contracts subject to acceptance by the other parties of supplementary obligations which, by their nature or according to commercial usage, have no connection with the subject of such contracts.

. . .

Article 91

1. If during the transitional period, the Commission, on application by a member state or by any other interested party, finds that dumping is being practised within the common market, it shall address recommendations to the person or persons with whom such practices originate for the purpose of putting an end to them.

Should the practices continue, the Commission shall authorise the injured member state to take protective measures, the conditions and details of which the Commission shall determine.

2. As soon as this Treaty enters into force, products which originate in or are in free circulation in one member state and which have been exported to another member state shall, on reimportation, be admitted into the territory of the first-mentioned state free of all customs duties, quantitative restrictions or measures having equivalent effect. The Commission shall lay down appropriate rules for the application of this paragraph.

Article 100

The Council shall, acting unanimously on a proposal from the Commission, issue directives for the approximation of such provisions laid down by law, regulation or administrative action in member states as directly affect the establishment or functioning of the common market.

The European Parliament and the Economic and Social Committee shall be consulted in the case of directives whose implementation would, in one or more member states, involve the amendment of legislation.

Article 100a*

1. By way of derogation from Article 100 and save where otherwise provided in this Treaty, the following provisions shall apply for the achievement of the objectives set out in Article 8a. The Council shall, acting by a qualified majority on a proposal from the Commission in co-operation with the European Parliament and after consulting the Economic and Social Committee, adopt the measures for the approximation of the provisions laid down by law, regulation or administrative action in member states which have as their object the establishment and functioning of the internal market.

2. Paragraph 1 shall not apply to fiscal provisions, to those relating to the free movement of persons nor to those relating to the rights and interests of employed persons.

3. The Commission, in its proposals envisaged in paragraph 1 concerning health, safety, environmental protection and consumer protection, will take as a base a high level of protection.

4. If, after the adoption of a harmonisation measure by the Council acting by a qualified majority, a member state deems it necessary to apply national provisions on grounds of major needs referred to in Article 36, or relating to protection of the environment or the working environment, it shall notify the Commission of these provisions.

The Commission shall confirm the provisions involved after having verified that they are not a means of arbitrary discrimination or a disguised restriction on trade between member states.

By way of derogation from the procedure laid down in Articles 169 and 170, the Commission or any member state may bring the matter directly before the Court of Justice if it considers that another member state is making improper use of the powers provided for in this Article.

5. The harmonisation measures referred to above shall, in appropriate cases, include a safeguard clause authorising the member states to take, for one or more of the non-economic reasons referred to in Article 36, provisional measures subject to a Community control procedure.

Article 100b*

1. During 1992, the Commission shall, together with each member state, draw up an inventory of national laws, regulations and administrative provisions which fall under Article 100a and which have not been harmonised pursuant to that Article.

The Council, acting in accordance with the provisions of Article 100a, may decide that the provisions in force in a member state must be recognised as being equivalent to those applied by another member state.

2. The provisions of Article 100a(4) shall apply by analogy.

3. The Commission shall draw up the inventory referred to in the first subparagraph of paragraph 1 and shall submit appropriate proposals in good time to allow the Council to act before the end of 1992.

Article 101

Where the Commission finds that a difference between the provisions laid down by law, regulation or administrative action in member states is distorting the conditions of competition in the common market and that the resultant distortion needs to be eliminated, it shall consult the member states concerned.

If such consultation does not result in an agreement eliminating the distortion in question, the Council shall, on a proposal from

* Articles added by Article 19 of the SEA.

the Commission, acting unanimously during the first stage and by a qualified majority thereafter, issue the necessary directives. The Commission and the Council may take any other appropriate measures provided for in this Treaty.

Article 102

1. Where there is reason to fear that the adoption or amendment of a provision laid down by law, regulation or administrative action may cause distortion within the meaning of Article 101, a member state desiring to proceed therewith shall consult the Commission. After consulting the member states, the Commission shall recommend to the states concerned such measures as may be appropriate to avoid the distortion in question.

2. If a state desiring to introduce or amend its own provisions does not comply with the recommendation addressed to it by the Commission, other member states shall not be required, in pursuance of Article 101, to amend their own provisions in order to eliminate such distortion. If the member state which has ignored the recommendation of the Commission causes distortion detrimental only to itself, the provisions of Article 101 shall not apply.

. . .

Article 117

Member states agree upon the need to promote improved working conditions and an improved standard of living for workers, so as to make possible their harmonisation while the improvement is being maintained.

They believe that such a development will ensue not only from the functioning of the common market, which will favour the harmonisation of social systems, but also from the procedures provided for in this Treaty and from the approximation of provisions laid down by law, regulation or administrative action.

Article 118

Without prejudice to the other provisions of this Treaty and in conformity with its general objectives, the Commission shall have the task of promoting close co-operation between member states in the social field, particularly in matters relating to:

— employment;
— labour law and working conditions;
— basic and advanced vocational training;
— social security;
— prevention of occupational accidents and diseases;
— occupational hygiene;
— the right of association, and collective bargaining between employers and workers.

To this end, the Commission shall act in close contact with member states by making studies, delivering opinions and arranging consultations both on problems arising at national level and on those of concern to international organisations.

Before delivering the opinions provided for in this Article, the Commission shall consult the Economic and Social Committee.

Article 118a*

1. Member states shall pay particular attention to encouraging improvements, especially in the working environment, as regards the health and safety of workers, and shall set as their objective the harmonisation of conditions in this area, while maintaining the improvements made.

* Article added by Article 21 of the SEA.

2. In order to help achieve the objective laid down in the first paragraph, the Council, acting by a qualified majority on a proposal from the Commission, in co-operation with the European Parliament and after consulting the Economic and Social Committee, shall adopt, by means of directives, minimum requirements for gradual implementation, having regard to the conditions and technical rules obtaining in each of the member states.

Such directives shall avoid imposing administrative, financial and legal constraints in a way which would hold back the creation and development of small and medium-sized undertakings.

3. The provisions adopted pursuant to this Article shall not prevent any member state from maintaining or introducing more stringent measures for the protection of working conditions compatible with this Treaty.

The Commission shall endeavour to develop the dialogue between management and labour at European level which would, if the two sides consider it desirable, lead to relations based on agreement.

Article 118b*

The Commission shall endeavour to develop the dialogue between management and labour at European level which could, if the two sides consider it desirable, lead to relations based on agreement.

* Article added by Article 22 of the SEA.

Council Directive

of 25 July 1985
on the approximation of the laws, regulations and administrative provisions of the member states concerning liability for defective
products
(85/374/EEC) — (OJ 1985 L210/27)

The Council of the European Communities

Having regard to the Treaty establishing the European Economic Community, and in particular Article 100 thereof,

Having regard to the proposal from the Commission*,

Having regard to the opinion of the European Parliament**,

Having regard to the opinion of the Economic and Social Committee***,

Whereas approximation of the laws of the member states concerning the liability of the producer for damage caused by the defectiveness of his products is necessary because the existing divergences may distort competition and affect the movement of goods within the common market and entail a differing degree of protection of the consumer against damage caused by a defective product to his health or property;

Whereas liability without fault on the part of the producer is the sole means of adequately solving the problem, peculiar to our age of increasing technicality, of a fair apportionment of the risks inherent in modern technological production;

Whereas liability without fault should apply only to movables which have been industrially produced; whereas, as a result, it is appropriate to exclude liability for agricultural products and game, except where they have undergone a processing of an industrial nature which could cause a defect in these products; whereas the liability provided for in this Directive should also apply to movables which are used in the construction of immovables or are installed in immovables;

Whereas protection of the consumer requires that all producers involved in the production process should be made liable, in so far as their finished product, component part or any raw material supplied by them was defective; whereas, for the same reason, liability should extend to importers of products into the Community and to persons who present themselves as producers by affixing their name, trade mark or other distinguishing freature or who supply a product the producer of which cannot be identified;

Whereas, in situations where several persons are liable for the same damage, the protection of the consumer requires that the injured person should be able to claim full compensation for the damage from any one of them;

Whereas, to protect the physical well-being and property of the consumer, the defectiveness of the product should be determined by reference not to its fitness for use but to the lack of the safety which the public at large is entitled to expect; whereas the safety is assessed by excluding any misuse of the product not reasonable under the circumstances;

Whereas a fair apportionment of risk between the injured person and the producer implies that the producer should be able to free himself from liability if he furnishes proof as to the existence of certain exonerating circumstances;

Whereas the protection of the consumer requires that the liability of the producer remains unaffected by acts or omissions

* OJ No. C 241, 14.10.1976, p. 9 and OJ No. C 271, 26.10.1979, p.3.
** OJ No. C 127, 21.5.1979, p. 61.
*** OJ No. C 144, 7.5.1979, p. 15.

of other persons having contributed to cause the damage; whereas, however, the contributory negligence of the injured person may be taken into account to reduce or disallow such liability;

Whereas the protection of the consumer requires compensation for death and personal injury as well as compensation for damage to property; whereas the latter should nevertheless be limited to goods for private use or consumption and be subject to a deduction of a lower threshold of a fixed amount in order to avoid litigation in an excessive number of cases; whereas the Directive should not prejudice compensation for pain and suffering and other non-material damages payable, where appropriate, under the law applicable to the case;

Whereas a uniform period of limitation for the bringing of action for compensation is in the interest both of the injured person and of the producer;

Whereas products age in the course of time, higher safety standards are developed and the state of science and technology progresses; whereas, therefore, it would not be reasonable to make the producer liable for an unlimited period for the defectiveness of his product; whereas, therefore, liability should expire after a reasonable length of time, without prejudice to claims pending at law;

Whereas, to achieve effective protection of consumers, no contractual derogation should be permitted as regards the liability of the producer in relation to the injured person;

Whereas under the legal systems of the member states an injured party may have a claim for damages based on grounds of contractual liability or on grounds of non-contractual liability other than that provided for in this Directive; in so far as these provisions also serve to attain the objective of effective protection of consumers, they should remain unaffected by this Directive; whereas, in so far as effective protection of consumers in the sector of pharmaceutical products is already also attained in a member state under a special liability system, claims based on this system should similarly remain possible;

Whereas, to the extent that liability for nuclear injury or damage is already covered in all member states by adequate special rules, it has been possible to exclude damage of this type from the scope of this Directive;

Whereas, since the exclusion of primary agricultural products and game from the scope of this Directive may be felt, in certain member states, in view of what is expected for the protection of consumers, to restrict unduly such protection, it should be possible for a member state to extend liability to such products;

Whereas, for similar reasons, the possibility offered to a producer to free himself from liability if he proves that the state of scientific and technical knowledge at the time when he put the product into circulation was not such as to enable the existence of a defect to be discovered may be felt in certain member states to restrict unduly the protection of the consumer; whereas it should therefore be possible for a member state to maintain in its legislation or to provide by new legislation that this exonerating circumstance is not admitted; whereas, in the case of new legislation, making use of this derogation should, however, be subject to a Community stand-still procedure, in order to raise, if possible, the level of protection in a uniform manner throughout the Community;

Whereas, taking into account the legal traditions in most of the member states, it is inappropriate to set any financial ceiling on the producer's liability without fault; whereras; in so far as there are, however, differing traditions, it seems possible to admit that a member state may derogate from the principle of unlimited liability by providing a limit for the total liability of the producer for damage resulting from a death or personal injury and caused by identical items with the same defect, provided that this limit is established at a level sufficiently high to guarantee adequate protection of the consumer and the correct functioning of the common market;

Whereas the harmonisation resulting from this cannot be total at the present stage, but opens the way towards greater harmonisation; whereas it is therefore necessary that the Council receive at regular intervals, reports from the Commission on the application of this Directive, accompanied, as the case may be, by appropriate proposals;

Whereas it is particularly important in this respect that a re-examination be carried out of those parts of the Directive relating to the derogations open to the member states, at the expiry of a period of sufficient length to gather practical experience on the effects of these derogations on the protection of consumers and on the functioning of the common market.

Has adopted this Directive:

Article 1

The producer shall be liable for damage caused by a defect in his product.

Article 2

For the purpose of this Directive 'product' means all movables, with the exception of primary agricultural products and game, even though incorporated into another movable or into an immovable. 'Primary agricultural products' means the products of the soil, of stock-farming and of fisheries, excluding products which have undergone initial processing. 'Product' includes electricity.

Article 3

1. 'Producer' means the manufacturer of a finished product, the producer of any raw material or the manufacturer of a component part and any person who, by putting his name, trade mark or other distinguishing feature on the product presents himself as its producer.

2. Without prejudice to the liability of the producer, any person who imports into the Community a product for sale, hire, leasing or any form of distribution in the course of his business shall be deemed to be a producer within the meaning of this Directive and shall be responsible as a producer.

3. Where the producer of the product cannot be identified, each supplier of the product shall be treated as its producer unless he informs the injured person, within a reasonable time, of the identity of the producer or of the person who supplied him with the product. The same shall apply, in the case of an imported product, if this product does not indicate the identity of the importer referred to in paragraph 2, even if the name of the producer is indicated.

Article 4

The injured person shall be required to prove the damage, the defect and the causal relationship between defect and damage.

Article 5

Where, as a result of the provisions of this Directive, two or more persons are liable for the same damage, they shall be liable jointly and severally, without prejudice to the provisions of national law concerning the rights of contribution or recourse.

Article 6

1. A product is defective when it does not provide the safety which a person is entitled to expect, taking all circumstances into account, including:

(a) the presentation of the product;
(b) the use to which it could reasonably be expected that the product would be put;
(c) the time when the product was put into circulation.

2. A product shall not be considered defective for the sole reason that a better product is subsequently put into circulation.

Article 7

The producer shall not be liable as a result of this Directive if he proves:

(a) that he did not put the product into circulation; or
(b) that, having regard to the circumstances, it is probable that the defect which caused the damage did not exist at the time when the product was put into circulation by him or that this defect came into being afterwards; or
(c) that the product was neither manufactured by him for sale or any form of distribution for economic purpose not manufactured or distributed by him in the course of his business; or
(d) that the defect is due to compliance of the product with mandatory regulations issued by the public authorities; or
(e) that the state of scientific and technical knowledge at the time when he put the product into circulation was not such as to enable the existence of the defect to be discovered; or
(f) in the case of a manufacturer of a component, that the defect is attributable to the design of the product in which the component has been fitted or to the instructions given by the manufacturer of the product.

Article 8

1. Without prejudice to the provisions of national law concerning the right of contribution or recourse, the liability of the producer shall not be reduced when the damage is caused both by a defect in product and by the act or omission of a third party.

2. The liability of the producer may be reduced or disallowed when, having regard to all the circumstances, the damage is caused both by a defect in the product and by the fault of the injured person or any person for whom the injured person is responsible.

Article 9

For the purpose of Article 1, 'damage' means:

(a) damage caused by death or by personal injuries;
(b) damage to, or destruction of, any item of property other than the defective product itself, with a lower threshold of 500 ECU, provided that the item of property:
    (i) is of a type ordinarily intended for private use or consumption, and

(ii) was used by the injured person mainly for his own private use or consumption.

This Article shall be without prejudice to national provisions relating to non-material damage.

Article 10

1. Member states shall provide in their legislation that a limitation period of three years shall apply to proceedings for the recovery of damages as provided for in this Directive. The limitation period shall begin to run from the day on which the plaintiff became aware, or should reasonably have become aware, of the damage, the defect and the identity of the producer.

2. The laws of member states regulating suspension or interruption of the limitation period shall not be affected by this Directive.

Article 11

Member states shall provide in their legislation that the rights conferred upon the injured person persuant to this Directive shall be extinguished upon the expiry of a period of 10 years from the date on which the producer put into circulation the actual product which caused the damage, unless the injured person has in the meantime instituted proceedings against the producer.

Article 12

The liability of the producer arising from this Directive may not, in relation to the injured person, be limited or excluded by a provision limiting his liability or exempting him from liability.

Article 13

This Directive shall not affect any rights which an injured person may have according to the rules of the law of contractual or non-contractual liability of a special liability system existing at the moment when this Directive is notified.

Article 14

This Directive shall not apply to injury or damage arising from nuclear accidents and covered by international conventions ratified by the member states.

Article 15

1. Each member state may:

(a) by way of derogation from Article 2, provide in its legislation that within the meaning of Article 1 of this Directive 'product' also means primary agricultural products and game;
(b) by way of derogation from Article 7 (e), maintain or, subject to the procedure set out in paragraph 2 of this Article, provide in this legislation that the producer shall be liable even if he proves that the state of scientific and technical knowledge at the time when he put the product into circulation was not such as to enable the existence of a defect to be discovered.

2. A member state wishing to introduce the measure specified in paragraph 1(b) shall communicate the text of the proposed measure to the Commission. The Commission shall inform the other member states thereof.

The Member state concerned shall hold the proposed measure in abeyance for nine months after the Commission is informed and provided that in the meantime the Commission has not submitted to the Council a proposal amending this Directive on the relevant matter. However, if within three months of receiving the said information, the Commission does not advise the member states concerned that it intends submitting such a proposal to the Council, the member state may take the proposed measure immediately.

If the Commission does submit to the Council such a proposal amending this Directive within the aforementioned nine months, the member state concerned shall hold the proposed measure in abeyance for a further period of 18 months from the date on which the proposal is submitted.

3. Ten years after the date of notification of this Directive, the Commission shall submit to the Council a report on the effect that rulings by the courts as to the application of Article 7(e) and of paragraph 1(b) of this Article have on consumer protection and the functioning of the common market. In the light of this report the Council, acting on a proposal from the Commission and pursuant to the terms of Article 100 of the Treaty, shall decide whether to repeal Article 7(e).

Article 16

1. Any member state may provide that a producer's total liability for damage resulting from a death or personal injury and caused by identical items with the same defect shall be limited to an amount which may not be less than 70 million ECU.

2. Ten years after the date of notification of this Directive, the Commission shall submit to the Council a report on the effect on consumer protection and the functioning of the common market of the implementation of the financial limit on liability by those member states which have used the option provided for in paragraph 1. In the light of this report the Council, acting on a proposal from the Commission and pursuant to the terms of Article 100 of the Treaty, shall decide whether to repeal paragraph 1.

Article 17

This Directive shall not apply to products put into circulation before the date on which the provisions referred to in Article 19 enter into force.

Article 18

1. For the purposes of this Directive, the ECU shall be that defined by Regulation (EEC) No. 3180/78*, as amended by Regulation (EEC) No. 2626/84**. The equivalent national currency shall initially be calculated at the rate obtaining on the date of adoption of this Directive.

2. Every five years the Council, acting on a proposal from the Commissioin, shall examine and, if need by, revise the amounts in this Directive, in the light of economic and monetary trends in the Community.

Article 19

1. Member states shall bring into force, not later than three years from the date of notification of this Directive, the laws, regulations and administrative provisions necessary to comply with this Directive. They shall forthwith inform the Commission thereof***.

2. The procedure set out in Article 15(2) shall apply from the date of notification of this Directive.

Article 20

Member states shall communicate to the Commission the texts of the main provisions of national law which they subsequently adopt in the field governed by this Directive.

* OJ No. L379, 30.12.1978, p. 1.
** OJ No. L247, 16.9.1984, p. 1.
*** This Directive was notified to the member states on 30 July 1985.

Article 21
Every five years the Commission shall present a report to the Council on the application of this Directive and, if necessary, shall submit appropriate proposals to it.

Article 22
This Directive is addressed to the member states.

Done at Brussels, 25 July 1985.

For the Council
The President
J. POOS

Proposal for a Council Regulation on the Statute for a European Company

COM(89) 268 final – SYN 218
(Submitted by the Commission to the Council on 25 August 1989)
(89/C 263/07)

The Council of the European Communities

Having regard to the Treaty establishing the European Economic Community, and in particular Article 100a thereof,
Having regard to the proposal from the Commission,
In co-operation with the European Parliament,
Having regard to the opinion of the Economic and Social Committee,

Whereas the completion of the internal market within the period set by Article 8a of the Treaty, and the improvement it must bring about in the economic and social situation throughout the Community, mean not only that barriers to trade must be removed, but also that the structures of production must be adapted to the Community dimension; for this purpose it is essential that companies whose business is not limited to satisfying purely local needs should be able to plan and carry out the reorganisation of their business on a Community scale;

Whereas such reorganisation presupposes that existing companies from different member states have the option of combining their potential by means of mergers; whereas such operations can be carried out only with due regard to the competition rules of the Treaty;

Whereas restructuring and co-operation operations involving companies from different member states give rise to legal and psychological difficulties and tax problems; whereas the approximation of member states' company law by means of directives based on Article 54 of the Treaty can overcome some of these difficulties; whereas such approximation does not, however, remove the need for companies governed by different legal systems to choose a form of company governed by a particular national law;

Whereas the legal framework in which business still has to be carried on in Europe, being still based entirely on national laws, thus no longer corresponds to the economic framework in which it must develop if the objectives set out in Article 8a of the Treaty are to be achieved; whereas this situation forms a considerable obstacle to the creation of groups consisting of companies from different member states;

Whereas it is essential to ensure as far as possible that the economic unit and the legal unit of business in Europe coincide; whereas for this purpose provision should be made for creating, side by side with companies governed by a particular national law, companies formed and carrying on business under the law created by a Community regulation directly applicable to all member states;

Whereas the provisions of such a regulation will permit the creation and management of companies with a European dimension, free from the obstacles arising from the disparity and the limited territorial application of national company laws;

Whereas such a regulation forms part of the national legal systems and contributes to their approximation, thus constituting a measure relating to the approximation of the laws of the member states with a view to the establishment and functioning of the internal market;

Whereas the Statute for a European company (SE) is among the measures to be adopted by the Council before 1992 listed on the Commission's White Paper on completing the internal market, approved by the European Council of June 1985 in Milan; whereas the European Council of 1987 in Brussels expressed the wish to see such a Statute created swiftly;

Whereas since the presentation by the Commission in 1970 of a proposal for a Regulation on the Statute for a European company, amended in 1975, work on the approximation of national company law has made substantial progress, so that on those points where the functioning of a European company does not need uniform Community rules, reference may be made to the law governing public companies in the member state where it has its registered office;

Whereas, without prejudice to any economic needs that may arise in the future, if the essential objective of the legal rules governing a European company is to be attained, it must be possible at least to create such a company as a means of enabling companies from different member states to merge or to create a holding company; and of enabling companies and other legal bodies carrying on an economic activity, and governed by the laws of different member states, to form a joint subsidiary;

Whereas the European company itself must take the form of a public company limited by shares, this being the form most suited, in terms of both financing and management, to the needs of a company carrying on business on a European scale; whereas in order to ensure that such companies are of reasonable size, a minimum capital should be set which will provide them with sufficient assets without making it difficult for small and medium-sized businesses to form a European company;

Whereas a European company must be efficiently managed and properly supervised; whereas it must be borne in mind that there are at present in the Community two different systems of administration of public companies; whereas, although a European company should be allowed to choose between the two systems, the respective responsibilities of those responsible for management and those responsible for supervision should be clearly defined;

Whereas, having regard to the approximation effected by the Fourth Council Directive 78/660/EEC* and the Seventh Council Directive**, as last amended in both cases by the Act of Accession of Spain and Portugal, on annual accounts and consolidated accounts, the provisions of those directives can be made applicable to European companies and such companies may choose between the options offered by those provisions;

Whereas under the rules and general principles of private international law, where one undertaking controls another governed by a different legal system, its ensuing rights and obligations as regards the protection of minority shareholders and third parties are governed by the law governing the controlled undertaking, without prejudice to the obligations imposed on the

---

* OJ No. L222, 14.8.1978, p.11.
** OJ No. L193, 18.7.1983, p.1.

controlling undertaking by its own law, for example the requirement to draw up consolidated accounts;

Whereas, without prejudice to the consequences of any later co-ordination of the law of the member states, specific rules for the European company are not at present required in this field; whereas the rules and general principles of private international law should therefore be applied both in cases where the European company exercises contrtol and in cases where it is the controlled company;

Whereas the rule thus applicable in the case where the European company is controlled by another undertaking should be specified, and for this purpose reference should be made to the law governing public companies in the state where the European company has its registered office;

Whereas for purposes of taxation the SE must be made subject to the legislation of the state in which it is resident; whereas provision should be made for deduction of losses incurred by the SE's permanent establishments abroad; whereas in order to avoid any discrimination against other firms carrying on cross-border business, similar provisions will be proposed by means of a directive for all other legal forms of business;

Whereas each member state must be required to apply in respect of infringements of the provisions of this Regulation the sanction applicable to public limited companies governed by its law;

Whereas the rules on the involvement of employees in the European company are contained in Directive . . . based on Article 54 of the Treaty, and its provisions thus form an indissociable complement to this Regulation and must be applied concomitantly;

Whereas, on matters not covered by this Regulation, the provisions of the law of the member states and of Community law are applicable, for example on:

— social security and employment law,
— taxation and competition law,
— intellectual property law,
— insolvency law;

Whereas the application of this Regulation must be deferred so as to enable each member state to incorporate into its national law the provisions of the above-mentioned Directive and to set up in advance the necessary machinery for the formation and operation of European companies having their registered office in its territory, so that the Regulation and the Directive may be applied concomitantly,

Has adopted this Regulation:

TITLE 1

GENERAL PROVISIONS

Article 1
(Form of the European company (SE))
1. Companies may be formed throughout the Community in the form of a European public limited company (Societas Europea, 'SE') on the conditions and in the manner set out in this Regulation.
2. The capital of the SE shall be divided into shares. The liability of the shareholders for the debts and obligations of the company shall be limited to the amount subscribed by them.

3. The SE shall be a commercial company whatever the object of its undertaking.
4. The SE shall have legal personality.

Article 2
(Formation)
1. Public limited companies formed under the law of a member state and having their registered office and central administration within the Community may form an SE by merging or by forming a holding company, provided at least two of them have their central administration in different member states.
2. Companies or firms within the meaning of the second paragraph of Article 58 of the Treaty and other legal bodies governed by public or private law which have been formed in accordance with the law of a member state and have their registered office and central administration in the Community may set up an SE by forming a joint subsidiary, provided that at least two of them have their central adminstration in different member states.

Article 3
(Formation with participation of an SE)
1. An SE together with one or more other SEs or together with one of more limited companies incorporated under the laws of a member state and having their registered office and central administration within the Community may form an SE by merging or by forming a holding company.
2. An SE together with one or more other SEs, or together with one or more companies or legal bodies within the meaning of Article 2(2), may set up an SE by forming a joint subsidiary.
3. An SE may itself form one or more subsidiaries in the form of an SE. Such a subsidiary may not, however, itself establish a subsidiary in the form of an SE.

Article 4
(Minimum capital)
1. Subject to paragraphs 2 and 3, the capital of an SE shall amount to not less than ECU 100,000.
2. Where an SE carries on the business of a credit institution it shall be subject to the minimum capital requirements laid down by the laws of the member state in which it has its registered office in accordance with Article . . . of Council Directive . . . *.
3. Where an SE carries on the business of an insurance undertaking it shall be subject to the minimum capital requirements laid down by the laws of the member state in which it has its registered office.

Article 5
(Registered office of SE)
The registered office of an SE shall be situated at the place specified in its statutes. Such place shall be within the Community. It shall be the same as the place where the SE has its central administration.

Article 6
(Controlled and controlling undertakings)
1. A 'controlled undertaking' means any undertaking in which a natural or legal person:

* Second Council Directive on the taking up and pursuit of the business of credit institutions.

(a) has a majority of the shareholders' or members' voting rights; or

(b) has the right to appoint or remove a majority of the members of the administrative, management or supervisory board, and is at the same time a shareholder in, or member of, that undertaking; or

(c) is a shareholder or member and alone controls, pursuant to an agreement entered into with other shareholders or members of the undertaking, a majority of the shareholders' or members' voting rights.

2. For the purposes of paragraph 1, the controlling undertaking's rights as regards voting, appointment and removal shall include the rights of any other controlled undertaking and those of any person or body acting in his or its own name but on behalf of the controlling undertaking or of any other controlled undertaking.

Article 7
(Scope of the Regulation)

1. Matters covered by this Regulation, but not expressly mentioned herein, shall be governed:

(a) by the general principles upon which this Regulation is based;

(b) if those general principles do not provide a solution to the problem, by the law applying to public limited companies in the state in which the SE has its registered office.

2. Where a state comprises several territorial units, each of which has its own rules of law applicable to the matters referred to in paragraph 1, each territorial unit shall be considered a state for the purposes of identifying the law applicable under paragraph 1(b).

3. In matters which are not covered by this Regulation, Community law and the law of the member states shall apply to the SE.

4. In each member state and subject to the express provisions of this Regulation, an SE shall have the same rights, powers and obligations as a public limited company incorporated under national law.

Article 8
(Registration)

1. Every SE shall be registered in the state in which it has its registered office in a register designated by the law of that state in accordance with Article 3 of the Directive 68/151/EEC*.

2. Where an SE has a branch in a member state other than in which it has its registered office, the branch shall be registered in that other member state under the procedures laid down in the laws of that member state in accordance with Article . . . of Council Directive . . . **.

Article 9
(Publication of documents)

Publication of the documents and particulars concerning the SE which must be published under this Regulation shall be effected in the manner laid down in the laws of each member state in accordance with Article 3 of Directive 68/151/EEC.

* OJ No. L26, 31.1.1977, p.1.
** OJ No. L61, 5.3.1977, p.26.

Article 10
(Notice in the OJ)

1. Notice that an SE has been formed, stating the number, date and place of registration and the date and place of publication and the title of the publication shall be published for information purposes in the *Official Journal of the European Communities* after the publication referred to in Article 9. The same shall be done where a liquidation is terminated.

2. The member states shall ensure that the particulars referred to in paragraph 1 are forwarded to the Official Publications Office of the European Communities within one month of the disclosure referred to in Article 9.

Article 11
(Documents of SE)

Letters, order forms and similar documents shall state legibly:

(a) the name of the SE, preceded or followed by the initials 'SE' unless those initials already form part of the name;

(b) the place of the register in which the SE is registered in accordance with Article 8(1), and the number of the SE's entry in that register;

(c) the address of the SE's registered office;

(d) the amount of capital issued and paid up;

(e) the SE's VAT number;

(f) the fact that the SE is in liquidation if that is so.

Any branch of the SE, when registered in accordance with Article 8(2), must give the above particulars, together with those relating to its own registration, on the documents referred to in the first paragraph emanating from that branch.

TITLE II

FORMATION

Section 1

General

Article 12
(Founder companies)

The founder companies of an SE for the purposes of this Title are the companies, firms and other legal bodies which may form an SE by the means of formation provided for in Articles 2 and 3.

Article 13
(Instrument of incorporation and statutes of the SE)

The founder companies shall draw up the instrument of incorporation and the statutes, if the statutes are a separate instrument, in the forms required for the formation of public limited companies by the law of the state in which the SE is to have its registered office.

Article 14
(Experts; verification)

The provisions of national law concerning the examination of consideration other than cash, adopted in the state in which the SE is to have its registered office, pursuant to Article 10 of Directive 77/91/EEC*, shall apply.

* OJ No. L26, 31.1.1977, p.1.

Article 15
(Supervision of formation)

The procedure for ensuring that the requirements of this Regulation and, where appropriate, of applicable national law, are complied with in regard to the formation of an SE and its statutes shall be those provided in respect of public limited companies under the law of the state in which the SE is to have its registered office. Member states shall take the measures necessary to ensure that such procedures are effective.

Article 16
(Legal personality)

The SE shall have legal personality as from the date set by the law of the state in which it is to have its registered office.

Section 2

Formation by merger

Article 17
(Definition)

1. In the formation of an SE by merger, the merging companies shall be wound up without going into liquidation and transfer to the SE all their assets and liabilities in exchange for the issue to their shareholders of shares in the SE and a cash payment, if any, not exceeding 10 per cent of the nominal value of the shares so issued or, where there is no nominal value, of their accounting par value.

2. A company may participate in the formation of an SE by merger even if it is in liquidation, provided it has not yet begun to distribute its assets to the shareholders.

3. The rights of the employees of each of the merging companies shall be protected in accordance with the provisions of national law giving effect to Directive 77/187/EEC*.

Article 18
(Draft terms of merger)

1. The administrative or management board of the founder companies shall draw up draft terms of merger. The draft terms of merger shall include the following particulars:

(a) the type, name and registered office of each of the founder companies and of the SE;

(b) the share exchange ratio and, where appropriate, the amount of any cash payment;

(c) the terms relating to the allotment of shares of the SE;

(d) the date from which the holding of shares of the SE entitles their holders to participate in profits and any special conditions affecting that entitlement;

(e) the date from which transactions by the founder companies will be treated for accounting purposes as being those of the SE;

(f) the rights conferred by the SE on the holders of shares to which special rights are attached and on the holders of securities other than shares, or the measures proposed concerning them;

(g) any special advantage granted to the experts appointed under Article 21(1) or to members of the administrative, management, supervisory or controlling bodies of the founder companies.

2. The draft terms of merger shall be drawn up and certified in due legal form if the law of the member state in which any of the founder companies has its registered office so requires.

3. The law of the member state requiring that the draft terms of merger be drawn up and certified in due legal form shall determine the person or authority competent to do so. Where the laws of several member states in which the founder companies have their registered offices require the draft terms of merger to be drawn up and certified in due legal form, this may be done by any person or authority competent under the law of one of those member states.

Article 19
(Publication of the draft terms of merger)

1. For each of the founder companies, the draft terms of merger shall be made public in the manner prescribed by the laws of each member state in accordance with Article 3 of Directive 68/151/EEC at least one month before the date of the general meeting called to decide thereon.

2. For each of the founder companies, the publication of the draft terms of merger referred to in paragraph 1, effected in accordance with Article 3(4) of Directive 68/151/EEC shall contain at least the following particulars:

(a) the type, name and registered office of the founder companies;

(b) the register in which the documents and particulars referred to in Article 3(2) of Directive 68/151/EEC are filed in respect of each founder company, and the number of the entry in that register;

(c) the conditions which determine, in accordance with Article 25, the date on which the merger and formation shall take effect.

3. The publication shall also specify the arrangements made in accordance with the provisios of national law giving effect to Articles 13, 14 and 15 of Directive 78/855/EEC* and with Article 23 of this Regulation for the exercise of the rights of the creditors of the founder companies.

Article 20
(Board's report)

The administrative or management board of each of the merging companies shall draw up a detailed written report explaining and justifying the draft terms of merger from the legal and economic point of view and, in particular, the share exchange ratio.

The report shall also indicate any special valuation difficulties which have arisen.

Article 21
(Supervision of the conduct of the merger)

1. One or more experts, acting on behalf of each founder company but independent of them, appointed or approved by a judicial or administrative authority in the member state in which the company concerned has its registered office, shall examine the draft terms of merger and draw up a written report for the shareholders.

2. In the report referred to in paragraph 1 the experts must state whether, in their opinion, the share exchange ratio is fair and reasonable. The statement must at least:

(a) indicate the method(s) used in arriving at the proposed share exchange ratio;

(b) state whether the method(s) used are adequate in the circumstances, the values arrived at using each method and an

* OJ No. L61, 5.3.1977, p.26.

* OJ No. L295, 20.10.1978, p.36.

option on the relative importance attributed to such methods in arriving at the value decided on.

The report shall also indicate any special valuation difficulties which have arisen.

3. Each expert shall be entitled to obtain from the merging companies all relevant information and documents and to carry out all necessary investigations.

4. Where the law of all the member states in which the founder companies have their registered office make provision for one or more independent experts to be appointed for all the founder companies such appointments may be made, at the joint request of those companies, by a judicial or administrative authority in any of the member states. In such cases the law of the member state of the appointing authority shall determine the content of the expert's report.

Article 22
(Approval of the merger by general meetings)

1. The draft terms of the merger and the instrument of incorporation of the SE and, if the statutes are a separate instrument, its statutes shall be approved by the general meeting of each of the founder companies. The resolution of the general meeting approving the merger shall be subject to the provisions giving effect to Article 7 of Directive 78/855/EEC in the case of domestic mergers.

2. For each of the founder companies, the provisions of national law adopted in accordance with Article 11 of Directive 78/855/EEC shall apply to the information to be provided to shareholders before the date of the general meeting called to approve the merger.

Article 23
(Protection of creditors)

The following provisions of the national law to which the founder companies are subject shall apply:

(a) the provisions relating to the protection of the interests of creditors and debenture holders of the companies in the case of a domestic merger;

(b) the provisions relating to the protection of the interests of holders of securities, other than shares, which carry special rights, provided that where the SE is being formed by the merger of public limited companies:

— the law of the State in which each of the companies has its registered office shall determine whether a meeting of the holders of such securities may approve a change in their rights,

— the law of the state in which the SE is to have its registered office shall determine whether the holders of such securities are entitled to require the SE to redeem their securities.

Article 24
(Supervision of the legality of mergers)

1. Where the laws of a member state governing one or more founder companies provide for judicial or administrative preventative supervision of the legality of mergers those laws shall apply to those companies.

2. Where the laws of a member state governing one or more founder companies do not provide for judicial or administrative preventative supervision of the legality of mergers, or where such supervision does not extend to all the legal acts required for a merger, the national provisions giving effect to Article 16 of Directive 78/855/EEC shall apply to the company or companies concerned. Where those laws provide for a merger contract to be concluded following the decisions of the general meeting held concerning the merger, that contract shall be concluded by all the companies involved in the operation. Article 18(3) shall apply.

3. Where the laws of the state in which the SE is to have its registered office and the laws governing one or more of the founder companies provide for judicial or administrative preventative supervision of the legality of mergers, such supervision shall be carried out first in respect of the SE. The supervision may be carried out in respect of the founder companies only when it can be shown that such supervision has been carried out in respect of the SE in accordance with Article 15.

4. Where the laws governing one or more of the founder companies taking part in the merger provide for judicial or administrative preventative supervision of the legality of the mergers whereas the laws governing one or more of the other founder companies taking part in the merger do not, such supervision shall be carried out on the basis of the documents drawn up and certified in due legal form referred to in Article 16 of Directive 78/855/EEC.

Article 25
(Effective date)

The date on which the merger and the simultaneous formation of the SE takes effect shall be determined by the law of the state in which the SE has its registered office. That date must be after all necessary supervision has been carried out and, where appropriate, the certified documents referred to in Article 24 have been drawn up for each of the founder companies.

Article 26
(Publicity)

For each of the founder companies, the merger must be publicised in the manner prescribed by national law, in accordance with Article 3 of Directive 68/151/EEC.

Article 27
(Effects of the merger)

A merger shall have the following consequences *ipso jure* and simultaneously:

(a) the transfer, both as between the founder companies and the SE and as regards third parties, of all the assets and liabilities of the founder companies to the SE;

(b) the shareholders of the founder companies become shareholders of the SE;

(c) the founder companies cease to exist.

Article 28
(Liability of board members)

The liability of members of the administrative or the management board of founder companies and of such companies' experts shall be governed by the provisions of national law giving effect to Article 20 and 21 of Directive 78/855/EEC in the state in which the founder company concerned has its registered office or, where appropriate, by this Regulation.

However, in the case of an appointment under Article 21(4), the liability of the expert or experts shall be governed by the law of the member state of the judicial or administrative authority which appointed them.

Article 29
(Nullity)

The question of the nullity of a merger that has taken effect pursuant to Article 25 shall be governed by the national law of the company concerned but a merger may be declared null and void only where there has been no judicial or administrative preventative supervision of its legaltity or where there is no certified documentation where such supervision or the drawing up of such documentation is laid down by the laws of the member state governing the relevant company. However, where the laws of the state in which the SE has its registered office do not provide for a merger to be declared null and void on such grounds, no such nullity may be declared.

Article 30
(Merger: Shareholdings between fellow founder companies)
Articles 17–29 shall also apply where one of the founder companies holds all or part of the shares of another founder company. In such a case, shares in founder companies which come into the possession of the SE as part of the assets of a founder company shall be cancelled.

Section 3

Formation of an SE holding company

Article 31
(Definition)
1. If an SE is formed as a holding company, all the shares of the founder companies shall be transferred to the SE in exchange for shares in the SE.
2. The founder companies shall continue to exist. Any provisions of the laws of the states in which the founder companies have their registered office, requiring that a company be wound up if all its shares come to be held by one person shall not apply.

Article 32
(Draft terms of formation)
1. The administrative or management board of the founder companies shall draw up draft terms for the formation of an SE holding company containing the particulars referred to in Article 18(1)(a), (b) and (c) and Article 21 and shall prepare the report provided for in Article 20.
2. The provisions of Article 21 shall apply to the supervision of the formation of the holding company in respect of each founder company.
3. The provisions of Article 22 shall apply to the approval of the formation of the holding company by the general meeting of each of the founder companies.
4. The provisions of Article 28 on the liability of board members shall apply.
5. The formation of an SE holding company may be declared null and void only for failure to supervise the formation of the holding company in accordance with Article 29.
6. For the purposes of applying the provisions of Article 2 on formation by merger, merger shall be read as formation of an SE holding company.

Article 33
(Matters affecting employees)
The administrative or management board of each of the founder companies shall discuss with the representatives of its employees the legal, economic and employment implications of the formation of an SE holding company for the employees and any measures proposed to deal with them.

Section 4

Formation of a joint subsidiary

Article 34
(Draft terms of formation)
If a joint subsidiary is formed in the form of an SE, the administrative or the management board of each of the founder companies shall draw up draft terms for the formation of the subsidiary including the following particulars:

(a) the type, name and registered office of the founder companies and of the proposed SE;
(b) the size of the shareholdings of the founder companies in the SE;
(c) the economic reasons for the formation.

Article 35
(Approval of the formation)
1. The draft terms of formation and the instrument of incorporation of the SE and its statutes, if the statutes are a separate instrument, its statutes shall be approved by each of the founder companies in accordance with the law which governs it.
2. Founder companies incorporated under national law shall be subject to all the provisions governing their participation in the formation of a subsidiary in the form of a public limited company under national law.
3. Where a founder company itself has the form of an SE, the following provisions shall apply:

(a) the instrument of incorporation and the statutes shall be authorised in accordance with Article 72 of the Regulation;
(b) if the decision on the participation of the SE in the formation of the subsidiary falls within the matters to be decided by the general meeting, the instrument of incorporation and the statutes must also be approved by the general meeting.

Section 5

Formation of a subsidiary by an SE

Article 36
(Draft terms of formation)
If an SE forms a subsidiary in the form of an SE, the administrative or management board shall draw up draft terms for the formation of the subsidiary. Those draft terms shall include the following particulars:

(a) the name of the registered office of the founder company and the instrument of incorporation of the subsidiary or its statutes are a separate instrument;
(b) the economic reasons for the formation.

Article 37
(Approval of the formation)
The instrument of incorporation of the subsidiary or its statutes, if the statutes are a separate instrument, shall be approved in accordance with Article 35(3).

TITLE III

CAPITAL – SHARES – DEBENTURES

Article 38
(Capital of the SE)
1. The capital of the SE shall be denominated in ECU.

2. The capital of the SE shall be divided into shares denominated in ECU. Shares issued for a consideration must be paid up at the time the company is registered in the Register referred to in Article 8(1) to the extent of not less than 25 per cent of their nominal value. However, where shares are issued for a consideration other than cash at the time the company is registered, that consideration must be transferred to the company in full within five years of the date on which the company was incorporated or acquired legal personality.

3. The subscribed capital may be formed only of assets capable of economic assessment. However, an undertaking to perform work or to supply services may not form part of these assets.

Article 39
1. Shares may not be issued at a price lower than their nominal value.

2. Professional intermediaries who undertake to place shares may be charged less than the total price of the shares for which they subscribe in the course of such a transaction.

Article 40
All shareholders in like circumstances shall be treated in a like manner.

Article 41
Subject to the provisions relating to the reduction of subscribed capital, the shareholders may not be released from the obligation to pay up their contributions.

Article 42
(Increase in capital)
1. The capital of the SE may be increased by the subscription of new capital. An increase in capital shall require amendment of the statutes. Shares issued for a consideration in the course of an increase in subscribed capital must be paid up to not less than 25 per cent of their nominal value. Where provision is made for an issue premium, it must be paid in full.

2. Where all or part of the consideration for the increase in capital is in a form other than cash, a report on the valuation of the consideration shall be submitted to the general meeting. The report shall be prepared and signed by one or more experts independent of the SE and appointed or approved by the court within whose jurisdiction the registered office of the SE is situated.

3. The expert's report shall be published in accordance with Article 9.

4. Any increase in subscribed capital must be decided upon by the general meeting. Both this decision and the increase in the subscribed capital shall be published in accordance with Article 9.

5. Where the capital is increased by the capitalisation of available reserves, the new shares shall be distributed amongst the shareholders in proportion to their existing shareholdings.

However, in its decision on the increase in capital, the general meeting may decide that some or all of the new shares shall be distributed amongst the employees of the SE.

Article 43
(Authorisation of future increase in capital)
1. The statutes or instrument of incorporation or the general meeting, the decision of which must be published in accordance with Article 9, may authorise an increase in the subscribed capital, provided that such increase shall not exceed one-half of the capital already subscribed.

2. Where appropriate, the increase in the subscribed capital up to the maximum authorised under paragraph 1 shall be decided by the administrative or the management board. The power of such body in this respect shall be for a maximum period of five years, and may be renewed one or more times by the general meeting, each time for a period not exceeding five years.

3. The administrative or the management board must register decisions authorising a future increase in capital.

The administrative or the management board must register, and publicise in accordance with Article 9, all issues of shares up to the maximum authorised capital limits and the consideration furnished for those shares. In addition, the board shall report each year in the notes on the accounts on the use it has made of the authorisation.

4. Where the authorised capital has been fully subscribed or where the period referred to in paragraph 2 has elapsed with only part of the authorised capital having been subscribed, the administrative or the management board shall amend the statutes to indicate the new total capital.

Where the authorisation to increase capital has not been used, the administrative or the management board shall decide to delete the authorisation clause referred to in paragraph 1. The board shall register such decisions.

5. Where an increase in capital is not fully subscribed, the capital shall be increased by the amount of the subscriptions received only if the conditions of the issue so provide.

Article 44
(Subscription rights of shareholders)
1. Whenever capital is increased by consideration in cash, the shares must be offered on a pre-emptive basis to shareholders in proportion to the capital represented by their shares.

2. Any offer of subscription on a pre-emptive basis and the period within which this right must be exercised shall be published in accordance with Article 9. However, it may be provided that such publication is not required where all the shares of the SE are registered. In such case, all the shareholders must be informed in writing. The right of pre-emption must be exercised within a period which shall not be less than 14 days from the date of publication of the offer or from the date of dispatch of the letters to the shareholders.

3. The right of pre-emption may not be restricted or withdrawn by the statutes or the instrument of incorporation. This may, however, be done by decision of the general meeting. The administrative or the management board shall be required to present to such a meeting a written report indicating the reasons for restriction or withdrawal of the right of pre-emption and justifying the proposed issue price. The decision shall require at least a two-thirds majority of the votes attaching to the securities represented or to the subscribed capital represented. The decision shall be published in accordance with Article 9.

4. The statutes, the instrument of incorporation, or the general meeting, acting in accordance with the rules for a quorum, a majority and publication set out in paragraph 3, may give the power to restrict or withdraw the right of pre-emption to the administrative or the management board which is empowered to decide on an increase in subscribed capital within the limits of the authorised capital. This power may not be granted for a longer period than the power for which provision is made in Article 43(2).

5. Shareholders may obtain copies of the reports referred to in paragraph 3 free of charge from the day on which notice of the general meeting is given. A statement to that effect shall be made in the notice convening the general meeting.

Article 45
(Reduction of capital)

1. Any reduction in the subscribed capital, except under a court order, must be subject at least to a decision of the general meeting acting in accordance with the rules for a quorum and a majority laid down in Article 44(3). Such decision shall be published in accordance with Article 9.

The notice convening the general meeting must specify at least the purpose of the reduction and the way in which it is to be carried out.

2. Where there are several classes of shares, the decision of the general meeting concerning a reduction in the subscribed capital shall be subject to a separate vote, at least for each class of shareholders whose rights are affected by the transaction.

3. A reduction of capital shall be effected by reducing the nominal value of the shares. However, the nominal subscribed capital may not be reduced to an amount less than the minimum capital. Only where losses have been incurred may the general meeting decide to reduce the capital below the minimum capital, and in that case it shall at the same time decide to increase the capital to an amount equal to or higher than the minimum capital.

4. Where the subscribed capital is reduced in order to adjust it to the diminished value of the company following losses, and, as a result of the reduction, assets exceed liabilities, the difference shall be entered in a reserve. This reserve may not be used for the distribution of dividends or for the granting of other benefits to shareholders.

Article 46
(Protection of creditors in the event of reduction of capital)

1. In the event of a reduction in the subscribed capital, the creditors whose claims antedate the publication of the decision to make the reduction shall be entitled at least to have the right to obtain security for claims which have not fallen due by the date of that publication.

The conditions for the exercise of this right shall be governed by the law of the state where the company has its registered office.

2. The reduction shall be void or no payment may be made for the benefit of the shareholders until the creditors have obtained satisfaction or the court within whose jurisdiction the registered office of the SE is situated, has decided that their application should not be acceded to.

3. Paragraphs 1 and 2 shall apply where the reduction in the subscribed capital is brought about by the total or partial waiving of the payment of the balance of the shareholders' contributions.

They shall not apply to reductions in the subscribed capital for the purpose of adjusting it to the real value of the company following losses.

Article 47

The subscribed capital may not be reduced to an amount less than the minimum capital laid down in accordance with Article 4. However, such a reduction may be made if it is also provided that the decision to reduce the subscribed capital may take effect only when the subscribed capital is increased to an amount at least equal to the prescribed minimum.

Article 48
(Own shares)

1. The subscription for shares of the SE by the SE itself, third parties acting on its behalf or undertakings controlled by it within the meaning of Article 6 or in which it holds a majority of the shares is prohibited.

2. If shares of the SE have been subscribed for by a person acting in his own name, but on behalf of the SE, the subscriber shall be deemed to have subscribed for them for his own account.

3. The founder companies of the SE, by which or in the name of which the statutes or the instrument of incorporation of the SE were signed or in the case of an increase in the subscribed capital, the members of the administrative or the management board, shall be liable to pay for shares subscribed in contravention of this Article.

Article 49

1. The acquisition of shares of the SE by the SE itself, third parties acting on its behalf or undertakings controlled by it within the meaning of Article 6 or in which it holds a majority of the shares is prohibited.

2. Paragraph 1 shall not apply to:

(a) the acquisition by the SE or third parties acting on its behalf of shares of the SE for the purpose of distributing them to the employees of the SE;

(b) shares acquired in carrying out a decision to reduce capital;

(c) shares acquired as a result of a universal transfer of assets;

(d) fully paid-up shares acquired free of charge, or by banks and other financial institutions as purchasing commission;

(e) shares acquired by virtue of a legal obligation or resulting from a court ruling for the protection of minority shareholders, in the event, particularly, of a merger, a change in the company's object or form, transfer abroad of the registered office, or the introduction of restrictions on the transfer of shares;

(f) shares acquired from a shareholder in the event of failure to pay them up;

(g) shares acquired in order to indemnity minority shareholders in controlled companies;

(h) fully paid-up shares acquired under a sale enforced by a court order for the payment of a debt owed to the company by the owner of the shares.

3. Shares acquired in the cases listed in paragraph 2(c) to (h) above must, however, be disposed of within not more than three years of their acquisition unless the nominal value of the shares acquired, including shares the SE may have acquired directly or indirectly, does not exceed 10 per cent of the subscribed capital.

4. If the shares are not disposed of within the period laid down in paragraph 3 they must be cancelled.

5. The SE may not accept its own shares as security or acquire any rights of usufruct or other beneficial rights over them.

6. An SE may not advance funds, nor make loans, nor provide security, with a view to the acquisition of its shares by a third party.

7. Paragraph 6 shall not apply to transactions concluded by banks and other financial institutions in the normal course of business, nor to transactions effected with a view to the acquisition of shares by or for the employees of the SE or a controlled company. However, these transactions may not have the effect of reducing the net assets of the SE below the amount of its subscribed capital plus the reserves which by law or under the statutes may not be distributed.

8. Shares acquired in contravention of paragraph 1 shall be disposed of within six months of their acquisition.

9. If an undertaking comes under the control of the SE or if a majority of its shares are acquired by such an SE, and it holds shares in the SE, the undertaking shall dispose of the shares in the SE within 18 months from the date of its coming under the control of the SE or from the date when the SE acquired a majority of its shares.

If an SE acquires its own shares by way of universal transfer of assets or if an undertaking which is controlled by the SE or the majority of whose shares are held by the SE acquires shares of the SE in this manner, such shares shall be disposed of within the same period.

10. Shares acquired by the SE pursuant to paragraph 2(a) shall, if they have not been distributed to the employees within 12 months of being acquired, be disposed of within the following six months.

11. No rights may be exercised in respect of the shares referred to in paragraphs 8, 9 and 10 until they have been disposed of or distributed to the employees.

Article 50
(Disclosure of holdings)

Holdings of the SE in other companies shall be disclosed in accordance with the provisions of national law giving effect to Directive 88/627/EEC*.

Article 51
(Indivisibility of shares)

The rights attached to a share shall be indivisible. Where a share is owned jointly by more than one person, the rights attached to it may be exercised only through a common representative.

Article 52
(Rights conferred by shares)

1. Shares may carry different rights in respect of the distribution of the profits and assets of the company. Payment of fixed interest may be neither made nor promised to shareholders.

2. Non-voting shares shall be issued subject to the following conditions:

(a) their total nominal value shall not exceed one half of the capital;

(b) they must carry all the rights of a shareholder other than the right to vote, except that the right to subscribe for new shares may be limited by the statutes or by resolution of the general meeting to non-voting shares. In addition they must confer special advantages;

(c) they shall not be included in a computing a quorum or majority required by this Regulation or the statutes of the company.

The above shall be without prejudice to paragraph 5.

3. Any other restriction or extension of voting rights, such as shares carrying multiple voting rights, is prohibited.

4. Shares carrying the same rights shall form a class.

5. Where there are several classes of shares, any decision of the general meeting which adversely affects the rights of a particular class of shareholders shall be subject to a separate vote at least for each class of shareholder whose rights are affected by the transaction. The provisions governing an amendment of the statutes shall apply as regards the convening of meetings and the required quorum and majority to the holders of the shares of the class concerned.

Article 53
(Issue of bearer and registered shares)

1. Shares may be in either bearer or registered form. The statutes may entitle shareholders to request conversion of their bearer shares into registered shares or vice-versa.

2. An SE which issues registered shares shall keep an alphabetical register of all shareholders, together with their addresses and the number and class of shares they hold. The register shall be open for public inspection on request at the registered office of the SE.

Article 54
(Issue and transfer of shares)

The laws of the State in which the SE has its registered office shall govern the issue, replacement and cancellation of share certificates, and the transfer of shares.

Article 55
(Publication requirements for obtaining stock exchange listing and for offering securities to the public)

1. The provisions of national law giving effect to Directive 80/390/EEC*, shall apply to the listing particulars to be published for the admission of securities of the SE to official stock exchange listing.

2. The provisions of national law giving effect to Directive 89/298/EEC** shall apply to the prospectus to be published where securities are offered to the public.

Article 56
(Issue of debentures)

The SE may issue debentures.

Article 57
(Body of debenture holders)

The laws of the State in which the SE has its registered office shall apply to the body of debenture holders.

Article 58
(Debentures convertible into shares)

1. Articles 43 and 44 shall apply to the issue of debentures convertible into shares.

2. The laws of the state in which the SE has its registered office shall apply to the conditions and procedure for the exercise of conversion or subscription rights.

3. As long as convertible debentures are outstanding, the SE may not decide on any amendment of the statutes affecting the rights of the holders of such debentures except where less than five per cent of the convertible debentures is still outstanding and their holders have the opportunity to exercise their conversion or subscription rights in good time before the amendment takes effect or if the body of convertible debenture holders has approved the proposed amendment. In the latter case, a higher percentage may be stipulated in the loan conditions.

4. Where conversion or subscription rights attached to convertible debentures have been fully exercised or have been exercised only in part but the period in which they may be

---

* OJ No. L348, 17.12.1988, p.62.

* OJ No. L100, 17.4.1980, p.1.
** OJ No. L124, 5.5.1989, p.8.

exercised has expired the management or the administrative board shall alter the statutes to show the new amount of capital. Where subscription or conversion rights are not exercised within the prescribed period, the management or the administrative board, shall delete from the statutes the clause concerning the issue of convertible debentures.

Such amendments to the statutes shall be published in accordance with Article 9.

Article 59
(Participating debentures)

1. The general meeting may, by a resolution which meets the requirements for altering the statutes, decide to issue debentures carrying the right to share in profits. Such debentures shall be issued for cash and shall carry rights determined wholly or partly by reference to the profits of the SE.

2. Article 58(3) shall apply, *mutatis mutandis*, to participating debentures.

Article 60
(Other securities)

The SE shall not issue to persons who are not shareholders of the SE other securities carrying a right to participate in the profits of assets of the SE.

TITLE IV
GOVERNING BODIES

Article 61

The statutes of the SE shall provide for the company to have as its governing bodies the general meeting of shareholders and either a management board and a supervisory board (two-tier system) or an administrative board (one-tier system).

Section 1
Two-tier system

Sub-section 1
Management board

Article 62
(Functions of the management board; Appointment of members)

1. The SE shall be managed and represented by a management board under the supervision of a supervisory board.

2. The members of the management board shall be appointed by the supervisory board, which may remove them at any time.

3. No person may at the same time be a member of the management board and the supervisory board of the same SE.

4. The number of members of the management board shall be laid down in the statutes of the SE.

5. The rules of procedure of the management board shall be adopted by the supervisory board, after obtaining the views of the management board.

Sub-section 2
Supervisory board

Article 63
(Functions of the supervisory board; Appointment of members)

1. The supervisory board may not participate in the management of the company nor represent it in dealings with third parties. However, it shall represent the company with members of the management board.

2. Subject to the measures adopted to give effect to Article 4 of the Council Directive . . . (completing the Statute in respect of the involvement of employees in SEs) members of the supervisory board shall be appointed by the general meeting.

Article 64
(Right to information)

1. At least once every three months, the management board shall report to the supervisory board on the management and progress of the company's affairs, including undertakings controlled by it, and on the company's situation and prospects.

2. The management board shall inform the chairman of the supervisory board without delay of all matters of importance, including any event occurring in the company or in undertakings controlled by it which may have an appreciable effect on the SE.

3. The supervisory board may at any time require the management board to provide information or a special report on any matter concerning the company or undertakings controlled by it.

4. The supervisory board shall be entitled to undertake all investigations necessary for the performance of its duties. It may appoint one or more of its members to pursue such investigations on its behalf and may call in the help of experts.

5. Any member of the supervisory board may, through the chairman of that board, require the management board to provide the supervisory board with any information necessary for the performance of its duties.

6. Each member of the supervisory board shall be entitled to examine all reports, documents and information and the results of enquiries and inspections obtained under the preceding paragraphs.

Article 65
(Rules of procedure, calling of meetings)

1. The supervisory board shall adopt its rules of procedure and shall elect a chairman and one or more vice-chairmen from among its members.

2. The chairman may call a meeting of the supervisory board on his own initiative and shall do so at the request of a member of the supervisory board or of a member of the management board.

Section 2
The one-tier system

Article 66
(The administrative board; Appointment of members)

1. The SE shall be managed and represented by an administrative board. The board shall be composed of at least three members. It shall adopt its rules of procedure and shall elect a chairman and one or more vice-chairmen from among its members.

2. The management of the SE shall be delegated by the administrative board to one or more of its members. The executive members shall be fewer in number than the other members of the board. The delegation of management responsibilities to an executive member of the administrative board may be revoked by the board at any time.

3. Subject to the measures adopted to give effect to Article 4 of Council Directive . . . (completing the Statute in respect of the involvement of employees in SEs) members of the administrative board shall be appointed by the general meeting.

Article 67
(Right to information)

1. The administrative board shall meet at least once every three months to discuss the management and progress of the company's affairs, including undertakings controlled by it and the company's situation and prospects.

2. Each member shall inform the chairman of the administrative board without delay of all matters of importance, including any event occurring in the company or in undertakings controlled by it which may have an appreciable effect on the SE.

3. Any member of the administrative board may request the chairman to call a meeting of that board to discuss particular aspects of the company. If the request has not been complied with within 15 days, a meeting of the administrative board may be called by one third of its members.

4. Each member of the administrative board shall be entitled to examine all reports, documents and information supplied to the board concerning the matters referred to in paragraphs 1 and 3.

Section 3

Rules common to the one-tier and two-tier board systems

Article 68
(Term of office)

1. Members of the governing bodies shall be appointed for a period laid down in the statutes not exceeding six years.

However, the first members of the supervisory board or of the administrative board, who are to be appointed by the shareholders shall be appointed by the instrument of incorporation of the SE for a period not exceeding three years.

2. Board members may be reappointed.

Article 69
(Conditions of membership)

1. Where the statutes of the SE allow a legal person or company to be a member of a board, that legal person or company shall designate a natural person to represent it in the performance of its duties on the board. The representative shall be subject to the same conditions and obligations as if he were personally a member. Publication under Article 9 shall refer both to the representative and to the legal person or company represented. The legal person or company shall be jointly and severally liable without limitation for obligations arising from the acts of its representative.

2. No person may be a board member who:

— under the law applicable to him, or
— as a result of a judicial or administrative decision delivered or recognised in a member state,

is disqualified from serving on an administrative, supervisory or management board.

3. The statutes may lay down special conditions of eligibility for members representing the shareholders.

4. Notwithstanding the rule laid down in Article 94(2), the statutes of the SE may provide voting procedures for the appointment of members of the administrative board by the general meeting such that one or more members and their alternates may be appointed by a minority of the shareholders.

Article 70
(Vacancies)

The statutes of the SE may provide for the appointment of alternate members to vacancies. Such appointments may be terminated at any time by the appointment of a full member.

Article 71
(Power of representation)

1. Where the management board is composed of more than one member, or where the management of the company is delegated to more than one member of the administrative board, those members have authority to represent the company collectively only in dealings with third parties. However, the statutes of the SE may provide that a member of the relevant board shall have authority to represent the SE alone or together with one or more other members of the board or together with a person who has been given general authority to represent the company under paragraph 2.

2. The administrative board or, as the case may be, the management board with the approval of the supervisory board, may confer a general authority to represent the company on one or more persons. Such authority may be revoked at any time, in the same way, by the board which granted it.

3. Acts performed by those having authority to represent the company under paragraphs 1 and 2 shall bind the company vis-à-vis third parties, even where the acts in question are not in accordance with the objects of the company, providing they do not exceed the powers conferred by this Regulation.

Article 72
(Operations requiring prior authorisation)

1. The implementation of decisions on:

(a) the closure or transfer of establishments or of substantial parts thereof;
(b) substantial reduction, extension or alteration of the activities of the SE;
(c) substantial organisational changes within the SE;
(d) the establishment of co-operation with other undertakings which is both long-term and of importance to the activities of the SE, or the termination thereof;
(e) the setting up of a subsidiary or of a holding company,

may be effected by the management board only following prior authorisation of the supervisory board or by the administrative board as a whole.

Implementation may not be delegated to the executive members of the administrative board.

Acts done in breach of the above provisions may not be relied upon against third parties, unless the SE can prove that the third party was aware of the breach.

2. The statutes of the SE may provide that paragraph 1 shall also apply to other types of decisions.

Article 73
(Conflicts of interest)

1. Any transaction in which a board member has an interest conflicting with the interests of the SE, shall require the prior authorisation of the supervisory board or the administrative board.

2. The statutes of the SE may provide that paragraph 1 shall not apply to routine transactions concluded on normal terms and conditions.

3. A member to whom paragraph 1 applies shall be entitled to be heard before a decision on the authorisation is made but may not take part in the deliberations of the relevant board when it makes its decision.

4. Authorisations given under paragraph 1 during any financial year shall be communicated to the shareholders not later than at the first general meeting following the end of the financial year in question.

5. Failure to obtain authorisation may not be relied upon against third parties, unless the SE can prove that the third party was aware of the need for, and lack of, such authorisation.

Article 74
(Rights and obligations)

1. Each member of a board of the SE shall have the same rights and obligations, without prejudice to:

(a) any internal allocation of responsibilities between the members of the board, and the provisions of the board's rules of procedure governing the taking of decisions in the event of a tied vote;

(b) the provisions concerning the delegation of management responsibilities to executive members.

(2) All board members shall carry out their functions in the interests of the SE, having regard in particular to the interests of the shareholders and the employees.

3. All board members shall exercise a proper discretion in respect of information of a confidential nature concerning the SE. This duty shall continue to apply even after they have ceased to hold office.

Article 75
(Removal of members)

1. Members of the supervisory board or the administrative board may be dismissed at any time by the same body, persons or groups of persons who under this Regulation or the statutes of the SE have the power to appoint them.

2. In addition, members of the supervisory board or the administrative board may be dismissed on proper grounds by the court within whose jurisdiction the registered office of the SE is situated in proceedings brought by the general meeting of the shareholders, the representatives of the employees, the supervisory board or the administrative board. Such proceedings may also be brought by one or more shareholders who together hold 10 per cent of the capital of the SE.

Article 76
(Quorum, majority)

1. Unless the statutes of the SE require a higher quorum, a board shall not conduct business validly unless at least half of its members take part in the deliberations.

2. Members who are absent may take part in decisions by authorising a member who is present to represent them. No member may represent more than one absent member.

3. Unless the statutes of the SE provide for a larger majority, decisions shall be taken by a majority of the members present or represented.

4. Under terms laid down in the statutes of the SE a board may also take decisions by procedures under which the members vote in writing, by telex, telegram or telephone or by any other means of telecommunication, provided that all members are informed of the proposed voting procedure and no member objects to the use of that procedure.

Article 77
(Civil liability)

1. Members of the administrative board, the management board or the supervisory board, shall be liable to the SE for any damage sustained by the company as a result of wrongful acts committed in carrying out their duties.

2. Where the board concerned is composed of more than one member, all the members shall be jointly and severally liable without limit. However, a member may be relieved of liability if he can prove that no fault is attributable to him personally. Such relief may not be claimed by a member on the sole ground that the act giving rise to liability did not come within the sphere of responsibilities delegated to him.

Article 78
(Proceedings on behalf of the company)

1. The administrative board or the supervisory board, may institute proceedings on the company's behalf to establish liability.

2. Such proceedings must be brought if the general meeting so decides. The general meeting may appoint a special representative for this purpose. For such a decision, the statutes may not prescribe a majority greater than an absolute majority of the votes attached to the capital represented.

3. Such proceedings on behalf of the company may also be brought by one or more shareholders who together hold 10 per cent of the capital of the SE.

4. Such proceedings may be brought by any creditor of the SE who can show that he cannot obtain satisfaction of his claim on the company.

Article 79
(Waiver of proceedings on behalf of the company)

1. The SE may waive its right to institute proceedings on the company's behalf to establish liability. Such a waiver shall require an express resolution of the general meeting taken in the knowledge of the wrongful act giving rise to damage for the company. However, such a resolution may not be passed if it is opposed by shareholders whose holdings amount to the figure referred to in Article 75.

2. Paragraph 1 shall also apply to any compromise relating to such proceedings agreed between the company and a board member.

Article 80
(Limitation of actions)

No proceedings on the company's behalf to establish liability may be instituted more than five years after the act giving rise to damage.

Section 4

General meeting

Article 81
(Competence)

The following matters shall be resolved by the general meeting:

(a) Increases or reductions in subscribed or authorised capital;

(b) issues of debentures convertible into shares or carrying subscription rights and of debentures carrying the right to share in the profits;

(c) the appointment or removal of members of the administrative board or of the supervisory board, who represent the shareholders;

(d) the institution of proceedings on the company's behalf for negligence or misconduct by board members;

(e) the appointment or dismissal of auditors;

(f) approval of the annual accounts;

(g) appropriation of the profit or loss for the year;

(h) amendment of the statutes;

(i) winding up and appointment of liquidators;

(j) transformation;

(k) merger of the SE with another company;

(l) transfer of assets.

Article 82
(Holding of general meeting)

1. A general meeting shall be held at least once a year. However, the first general meeting may be held at any time in the 18 months following the incorporation of the SE.

2. A general meeting may be called at any time by the management board or the administrative board.

Article 83
(Meeting called by minority shareholders)

1. It shall be provided that one or more shareholders who satisfy the conditions set out in Article 75 may request the SE to call the general meeting and to settle the agenda therefor.

2. If, following a request made under paragraph 1, no action has been taken within a month, the court within whose jurisdiction the registered office of the SE is situated may order the calling of a general meeting or authorise either the shareholders who have requested it or their representative to call the meeting.

Article 84
(Methods of calling meetings)

1. (a) The general meeting shall be called by a notice published either in the national gazette specified by the legislation of the state of the registered office in accordance with Article 3(4) of Directive 68/151/EEC or in one or more large-circulation newspapers.

(b) However, where all the shares in an SE are registered or where all its shareholders are known, the general meeting may be called by any means of communication addressed to all the shareholders.

2. The notice calling the general meeting shall contain the following particulars, at least:

(a) the name and the registered office of the SE;

(b) the place and date of the meeting;

(c) the type of general meeting (ordinary, extraordinary or special);

(d) a statement of the formalities, if any, prescribed by the statutes for attendance at the general meeting and for the exercise of the right to vote;

(e) any provisions of the statutes which require the shareholder, where he appoints an agent, to appoint a person who falls within certain specified categories of persons;

(f) the agenda showing the subjects to be discussed and the proposals for resolutions.

3. The period between the date of first publication of the notice in accordance with paragraph 1(a), or the date of dispatch of the first communication as mentioned in paragraph 1(b), and the date of the opening of the general meeting shall be not less than 30 days.

Article 85

1. One or more shareholders who satisfy the requirements laid down in Article 75 may request that one or more additional items be included on the agenda of a general meeting of which notice has already been given.

2. Requests for inclusion of additional agenda items shall be sent to the SE within seven days of the first publication of the notice calling the general meeting in accordance with Article 84(1)(a) or the dispatch of the first communication calling the general meeting by the means mentioned in Article 84(1)(b).

3. Items whose inclusion in the agenda has been requested under paragraph 2, shall be communicated or published in the same way as the notice of meeting, not less than seven days before the meeting.

Article 86
(Attendance at general meeting)

Every shareholder who has complied with the formalities prescribed by the statutes shall be entitled to attend the general meeting. However, the statutes may prohibit shareholders having no voting rights from attending the meeting.

Article 87
(Proxies)

1. Every shareholder shall be entitled to appoint a person to represent him at the general meeting.

2. The law of the member state where the registered office of the SE is situated or the statutes may restrict the choice of representative to one or more specified categories of persons, but a shareholder may not be prevented from appointing another shareholder to represent him.

3. The appointment shall be made in writing and shall be retained for the period mentioned in Article 99(4).

Article 88

1. Where the proxies appointed are persons acting in a professional capacity, the provisions of Article 87 and the following provisions shall apply:

(a) the appointment shall relate to only one meeting, but it shall be valid for successive meetings with the same agenda, without prejudice to paragraph 2;

(b) the appointment shall be revocable;

(c) all the shareholders whose names and addresses are known shall be invited, either in writing or by publication in one or more large-circulation newspapers, to appoint the person in question as their proxy;

(d) the invitation to appoint the person in question as a proxy shall contain at least the following information:

— the agenda showing the subjects for discussion and the proposals for resolutions;

— an indication that the documents mentioned in Article 89 are available to shareholders who ask for them,

— a request for instructions concerning the exercise of the right to vote in respect of each item on the agenda;

— a statement of the way in which the proxy will exercise the right to vote in the absence of any instructions from the shareholder;

(e) the right to vote shall be exercised in accordance with the shareholders' instructions, or in the absence of such instructions in accordance with the statement made to the shareholder. However, the proxy may depart from the shareholders' instructions or the statement made to the shareholder by reason of circumstances unknown when the instructions were given or the invitation to appoint a proxy issued, where voting in accordance with instructions or the statement would be liable to prejudice the shareholder's interests. The proxy shall forthwith inform the shareholder and explain the reasons for this action.

2. Notwithstanding paragraph 1(a), a proxy may be appointed for a specified period not exceeding 15 months. In this case the information indicated in paragraph 1(d) shall be given to all shareholders referred to in paragraph 1(c) before any general meeting.

Article 89
(Availability of accounts)
The annual accounts and, where appropriate, the consolidated accounts, the proposed appropriation of profits or treatment of loss where it does not appear in the annual accounts, the annual report and the opinion of the persons responsible for auditing the accounts shall be available to every shareholder at the latest from the date of dispatch or publication of the notice of general meeting called to adopt the annual accounts and to decide on the appropriation of profits or treatment of loss. Every shareholder shall be able to obtain a copy of these documents free of charge upon request. From the same date, the report of the persons responsible for auditing the accounts shall be available to any shareholder wishing to consult it at the registered office of the SE.

Article 90
(Right to information)
1. Every shareholder who so requests at a general meeting shall be entitled to obtain information on the affairs of the company arising from items on the agenda or concerning matters on which the general meeting may take a decision in accordance with Article 91(2).
2. The management board or the executive members of the administrative board shall supply this information.
3. The communication of information may be refused only where:

(a) it would be likely to be seriously prejudicial to the company or a controlled company; or
(b) its disclosure would be incompatible with a legal obligation of confidentiality.

4. A shareholder to whom information is refused may require that his question and the grounds for refusal shall be entered in the minutes of the general meeting.
5. A shareholder to whom information is refused may challenge the validity of the refusal in the court within whose jurisdiction the registered office of the SE is situated. Application to the court shall be made within two weeks of the closure of the general meeting.

Article 91
(Decisions; Agenda)
1. The general meeting shall not pass any resolution concerning items which have not been communicated or published in accordance with Article 84(2)(f) or Article 85(3).
2. Paragraph 1 shall not apply when all the shareholders are present in person or by proxy at the general meeting and no shareholder objects to the matter in question being discussed.

Article 92
(Voting rights)
1. A shareholder's voting rights shall be proportionate to the fraction of the subscribed capital which his shares represent.
2. The statutes may authorise:

(a) restriction or exclusion of voting rights in respect of shares which carry special advantages;
(b) restriction of votes in respect of shares allotted to the same shareholder, provided the restriction applies at least to all shareholders of the same class.

3. The right to vote may not be exercised:

(a) where a call made by the company has not been paid;
(b) on shares held by the SE itself or by one of its subsidiaries.

4. The law of the state where the registered office of the SE is situated shall govern the exercise of voting rights in cases of succession, usufruct, pledge of shares, or failure to notify substantial holdings.

Article 93
(Conflict of interest)
Neither a shareholder or his representative shall exercise the right to vote attached to his shares or to shares belonging to third persons who were the subject matter of the resolution where the subject matter of the resolution relates to:

(a) the assertion of claims by the SE against the shareholder;
(b) the commencement of legal proceedings to establish the liability of that shareholder to the company in accordance with Article 78;
(c) waiver of the right to bring proceedings to establish the liability of that shareholder to the company in accordance with Article 79.

Article 94
(Required majority)
1. Resolutions of the general meeting shall require at least an absolute majority of the votes attached to the subscribed capital present or represented unless a greater majority is prescribed by this Regulation.
2. However, as regards the appointment or dismissal of members of the administrative board, the management board or the supervisory board, the statutes may not require a majority greater than that mentioned in paragraph 1.

Article 95
(Amendment of statutes)
1. A resolution of the general meeting shall be required for any amendment of the statutes of the instrument of incorporation.
2. However, the statutes may provide that the administrative board or the management board may amend the statutes or the instrument of incorporation where the amendment merely implements a resolution already passed by the general meeting, or by the board itself by virtue of an authorisation given by the general meeting, by the statutes, or by the instrument of incorporation.

Article 96
1. The complete text of the amendment of the statutes or of the instrument of incorporation which is to be put before the general meeting shall be set out in the notice of meeting.
2. However, the statutes may provide that the complete text of the amendment mentioned in paragraph 1 may be obtained by any shareholder free of charge upon request.

Article 97

1. A majority of not less than two thirds of votes attached to subscribed capital represented at the meeting shall be required for the passing by the general meeting of resolutions amending the statutes or the instrument of incorporation.

2. However, the statutes may provide that where at least one-half of the subscribed capital is represented, a simple majority of the votes in paragraph 1 shall suffice.

3. Resolutions of the general meeting which would have the effect of increasing the liabilities of the shareholders shall require in any event the approval of all the shareholders involved.

4. A resolution amending the statutes or the instrument of incorporation shall be made public in accordance with Article 9.

Article 98

(Separate vote of each class of shareholder)

1. Where there are several classes of shares, any resolution of the general meeting shall require a separate vote at least for each class of shareholders whose rights are affected by the resolution.

2. Where a resolution of the general meeting requires the majority of votes specified in Article 97(1) and (2), that majority shall also be required for the separate vote of each class of shareholders whose rights are affected by the resolution.

Article 99

(Minutes)

1. Minutes shall be drawn up for every meeting of the general meeting.

2. The minutes shall contain the following particulars, at least:

(a) the place and date of the meeting,
(b) the resolutions passed;
(c) the result of the voting.

3. There shall be annexed to the minutes:

(a) the attendance list;
(b) the documents relating to the calling of the general meeting.

4. The minutes and the documents annexed thereto shall be retained for at least three years. A copy of the minutes and the documents annexed thereto may be obtained by any shareholder, free of charge, upon request.

Article 100

(Appeal against resolutions of general meeting)

1. Resolutions of the general meeting may be declared invalid as infringing the provisions of this Regulation or of the company's statutes, in the following manner.

2. An action for such a declaration may be brought by any shareholder or any person having a legitimate interest, provided he can show that he has an interest in having the infringed provision observed and that the resolution of the general meeting may have been altered or influenced by the infringement.

3. The action for such a declaration shall be brought within three months of the closure of the general meeting, before the court within whose jurisdiction the registered office of the SE is situated. It shall be taken against the SE.

4. The procedure in the action for such a declaration shall be governed by the law of the place where the SE has its registered office.

5. The decision declaring the resolution void shall be published in accordance with Article 9.

6. The declaration that a resolution is void may no longer be made by the court if that resolution has been replaced by another taken in conformity with this Regulation and the statutes of the SE. The court may, on its own initiative, grant the time necessary to enable the general meeting to pass such a new resolution.

TITLE V

ANNUAL ACCOUNTS AND CONSOLIDATED ACCOUNTS

Section 1

Annual accounts

Sub-section 1

Preparation of annual accounts

Article 101

1. The SE shall draw up annual accounts comprising the balance sheet, the profit and loss account and the notes on the accounts. These documents shall constitute a composite whole.

2. The annual accounts of the SE shall be drawn up in accordance with the provisions of Directive 78/660/EEC subject to paragraph 3 of this Article.

3. (a) Articles 1, 2(5), final sentence, 2(6), 4(1), final sentence, 4(2), final sentence, 4(3)(b), final sentence, 4(4), final sentence, 5, 43(2), 45(1)(b), final sentence, 54, 55 and 62 of Directive 78/660/EEC shall not apply.

(b) For the purpose of drawing up the annual accounts, the provisions of Articles 2, 3, 4, 6 and 7 of Directive 78/660/EEC shall apply. The SE may avail itself of the option provided for in Article 6 of that Directive.

(c) For the presentation of the balance sheet, the SE may choose between the layouts prescribed by Articles 9 and 10 of Directive 78/660/EEC. It may avail itself of the options provided for in Articles 9, 10, 11, 18, final sentence, 20(2) and 21, final sentence, of that Directive.

(d) For the presentation of the profit and loss account, the SE may choose between the layouts prescribed by Articles 23 to 26 of Directive 78/660/EEC. It may avail itself of the options provided for in Articles 27 and 30 of that Directive.

(e) The items shown in the annual accounts shall be valued in accordance with the principles laid down in Article 31 of Directive 78/660/EEC. They shall be valued on the basis of the principle of purchase price or production cost according to the provisions of Articles 34 to 42 of that Directive.

However, the SE may choose to apply one of the three alternative valuation methods provided for in Article 33 of that Directive. If the SE avails itself of that possibility, it shall ensure that the method applied is consistent with the principles laid down in that Article. Details of the method applied shall be given in the annex thereto.

The SE may avail itself of the options provided for in Articles 34(1), 36, 37(1) and (2), 39(1)(c) and (2) and 40(1) of that Directive.

(f) In addition to the information required under other provisions of Directive 78/660/EEC, the notes on the accounts must include the information provided for in Article 43 of that Directive at least. The SE may avail itself of the options provided for in Articles 44 and 45(1) and (2) of that Directive.

Sub-section 2

Preparation of the annual report

Article 102

1. The SE shall drawn up an annual report which must include at least a fair review of the development of the company's business and of its position.

2. The annual report shall also include the information provided for in Article 46 of Directive 78/660/EEC.

Sub-section 3

Auditing

Article 103

1. The annual accounts of the SE shall be audited by one or more persons authorised to do so in a member state in accordance with the provisions of Directive 84/253/EEC*. Those persons shall also verify that the annual report is consistent with the annual accounts for the same financial year.

2. If the SE meets the criteria laid down in Article 11 of Directive 78/660/EEC, it shall not be required to have its accounts audited. In such cases, members of the administrative board or the management board shall be subject to the sanctions applicable to public limited liability companies in the state in which the SE has its registered office where the annual accounts or annual reports are not drawn up in accordance with the provisions of this section.

Sub-section 4

Publication

Article 104

1. The annual accounts, duly approved, and the annual report and audit report shall be published as laid down in accordance with Article 3 of Directive 68/151/EEC by the laws of the member state in which the SE has its registered office.

2. The SE may avail itself of the options provided for in Article 47 of Directive 78/660/EEC.

3. Articles 48, 49 and 50 of Directive 78/660/EEC shall apply to the SE.

Sub-section 5

Final provisions

Article 105

Articles 56 to 61 of Directive 78/660/EEC shall apply to the SE. The SE may avail itself of the options provided for in those Articles.

Section 2

Consolidated accounts

Sub-section 1

Conditions for the preparation of consolidated accounts

Article 106

1. Where the SE is a parent undertaking within the meaning of Article 1(1) and (2) of Directive 83/349/EEC, it shall be required

---

* OJ No. L 126, 12.5.1984, p.20.

to draw up consolidated accounts and a consolidated annual report in accordance with the provisions of that Directive.

2. Articles 1(1)(c) last sentence, 1(d)(bb), last sentence, 1(d), second and third subparagraphs, 4 and 5 of Directive 83/349/EEC shall not apply.

3. The SE may avail itself of the options provided for in Articles 1, 6, 12 and 15 of Directive 83/349/EEC.

Article 107

1. Where the SE is a parent undertaking within the meaning of Article 1(1) and (2) of Directive 83/349/EEC and is at the same time a subsidiary undertaking of a parent undertaking governed by the law of a member state, it shall be exempt from the obligation to draw up consolidated accounts subject to the conditions laid down in Articles 7 and 8 of that Directive. Article 10 of that Directive shall apply.

2. Articles 7(1)(b), second subparagraph, 8(1), last sentence, 8(2) and (3), and 9 of that Directive shall not apply.

3. The exemption provided for in paragraph 1 shall not apply where the securities of the SE have been admitted to official listing on a stock exchange established in a member state.

Article 108

1. Where the SE is a parent undertaking within the meaning of Article 1(1) and (2) of Directive 83/349/EEC and is at the same time a subsidiary undertaking of a parent undertaking which is not governed by the law of a member state, it shall be exempt from the obligation to draw up consolidated accounts subject to the conditions laid down in Article 11 of that Directive.

2. Article 8(1), second sentence, 8(2) and (3), and 10 of that Directive shall not apply.

3. The exemption provided for in paragraph 1 shall not apply where the securities of the SE have been admitted to official listing on a stock exchange established in a member state.

Sub-section 2

The preparation of consolidated accounts

Article 109

1. The consolidated accounts shall comprise the consolidated balance sheet, the consolidated profit and loss account and the notes on the accounts. These documents shall constitute a composite whole.

2. The consolidated accounts shall be drawn up in accordance with the provisions of Directive 83/349/EEC subject to paragraph 3 of this Article.

3. (a) Articles 16(5), final sentence, 16(6), 33(2)(c), first sentence, 33(3), final sentence, 34, point 12, final sentence, and point 13, final sentence, 35(1)(b), second sentence, 40, 41(5) and 48 Directive 83/349/EEC shall not apply.

(b) The SE may avail itself of the options provided for in Articles 17(2), 19(1)(b), 20, 26(1)(c), final sentence, 26(2), 27(2), 28, second sentence, 29(2)(a), second sentence, 29(5), final sentence, 30(2), 32, 33(2)(d) and 35(1) of Directive 83/349/EEC.

Sub-section 3

Preparation of the consolidated annual report

Article 110

1. The consolidated annual report shall include at least a fair review of the development of the company's business and the

position of the undertakings included in the consolidation taken as a whole.

2. The consolidated annual report shall also include the information provided for in Article 36 of Directive 83/349/EEC. The SE may avail itself of the option provided for in the final sentence of paragraph 2(d) of that Article.

Sub-section 4

Auditing of the consolidated accounts

Article 111

The consolidated accounts shall be audited by one or more persons authorised to do so in a member state in accordance with the provisions of Directive 84/253/EEC. Those persons shall also verify that the consolidated annual report is consistent with the consolidated accounts for the financial year in question.

Sub-section 5

Publication

Article 112

1. The consolidated accounts, duly approved, and the consolidated annual report, together with the audit report, shall be published as laid down in accordance with Article 3 of Directive 68/151/EEC by the laws of the member state in which the SE has its registered office.

2. Article 38(3), (4) and (6) of Directive 83/349/EEC shall not apply.

3. The management board and the executive members of the administrative board shall be liable to the sanctions provided for (. . .) if the consolidated accounts and consolidated annual report are not published.

Section 3

Banks and insurance companies

Article 113

1. SEs which are credit or financial institutions shall comply, as regards the drawing up, auditing and publication of annual accounts and consolidated accounts, with the rules laid down pursuant to Directive 86/635/EEC* by the national law of the state in which the SE has its registered office.

2. SEs which are insurance companies shall comply, as regards the drawing up, auditing and publication of annual accounts and consolidated accounts, with the rules laid down, pursuant to Directive 00 (which, supplementing Directive 78/660/EEC, harmonises the provisions governing the annual accounts and the consolidated accounts of insurance companies, by the national law of the state in which the company has its registered office).

TITLE VI

GROUPS OF COMPANIES

Article 114

1. Where an undertaking controls an SE, that undertaking's consequent rights and obligations relating to the protection of

* OJ No. L372, 31.12.1986, p.1.

minority shareholders and third parties shall be those defined by the law governing public limited companies in the state where the SE has its registered office.

2. Paragraph 1 shall not affect the obligations imposed on the controlling undertaking by the legal system which governs it.

TITLE VII

WINDING UP, LIQUIDATION, INSOLVENCY AND SUSPENSION OF PAYMENTS

Section 1

Winding up

Article 115

An SE may be wound up:

1. upon the expiry of the duration laid down for it in the statutes or the instrument of incorporation;

2. by resolution of the general meeting of shareholders; or

3. by decision of the court of the place where the SE has its registered office:

(a) where the subscribed capital of the company has been reduced below the minimum capital provided for in Article 4;

(b) where the disclosure of annual accounts has not taken place in the SE's last three financial years;

(c) on any ground laid down in the law of the place where the SE has its registered office or provided for in the statutes or the instrument of incorporation.

Article 116

(Winding up by resolution of the general meeting)

1. A resolution of the general meeting of shareholders to wind up the SE on any ground laid down by the statutes or instrument of incorporation shall require at least a simple majority of the votes attached to the subscribed capital represented.

2. In all other cases a resolution of the general meeting of shareholders to wind up the SE shall require at least a two-thirds majority of the votes attached to the subscribed capital represented. The statutes may, however, lay down that, when at least half the subscribed capital is represented, the simple majority referred to in paragraph 1 is sufficient.

Article 117

(Winding up by the court)

1. Winding-up proceedings may be brought in the court of the place where the SE has its registered office by the administrative board, the management board or the supervisory board of the SE, by any shareholder, or by any person with a legitimate interest.

2. Where the SE is able to remove the ground for winding up, the court may grant it a period of time sufficient to allow it to do so.

Article 118

(Publication of winding up)

The winding up shall be published in the manner referred to in Article 9.

Article 119

(Wound-up SE to continue in existence)

1. Where an SE is to be wound up as a result of a resolution to that effect of the general meeting of shareholders or upon the

expiry of its prescribed duration, the general meeting of shareholders may resolve that it is to continue in existence as long as there has been no distribution on the basis of liquidation in accordance with Article 126.

2. The resolution that the company is to continue in existence shall be passed in accordance with Article 116(2), and published in the manner referred to in Article 9.

Section 2

Liquidation

Article 120
(Appointment of liquidators)

1. The winding up of an SE shall entail the liquidation of its assets. The liquidation shall be carried out by one or more liquidators.

2. Liquidators shall be appointed:

(a) by the statutes or instrument of incorporation, or in the manner laid down therein; or

(b) by a resolution of the general meeting of shareholders acting by simple majority of the votes specified in Article 116(1); or

(c) failing an appointment pursuant to (a) or (b), by the court in whose jurisdiction the registered office of the SE is situated on the application of any sharehlder or of the administrative board, the management board or the supervisory board.

3. In the absence of an appointment pursuant to paragraph 2, the duties of liquidator shall be performed by the administrative board or the management board.

4. The general meeting shall determine the remuneration of the liquidators. Where the liquidators are appointed by a court in whose jurisdiction the registered office of the SE is situated, the court shall determine their remuneration.

Article 121
(Removal of liquidators)

The liquidators may be removed before the termination of the liquidation:

(a) where they were appointed in accordance with Article 120(2), (a) and (b) or where Article 120(3) applies, by a decision of the general meeting acting by the simple majority of the votes specified in Article 116(1);

(b) irrespective of the manner of appointment, by a court in whose jurisdiction the registered office of the SE is situated, on petition of any person having a legitimate interest in the matter and showing a proper ground.

Article 122
(Powers of liquidators)

1. The liquidators may take all appropriate steps to liquidate the SE and, in particular, shall terminate transactions pending, collect debts, convert remaining assets into cash where this is necessary for their realisation and to pay the sums owing to creditors. The liquidators may undertake new transactions to the extent necessary for the purposes of the liquidation.

2. The liquidators shall have the power to bind the SE in dealings with third parties and to take legal proceedings on its behalf.

The appointment, termination of office and identity of liquidators shall be published in the manner referred to in Article

9. It must appear from the disclosure whether the liquidators may represent the company alone or must act jointly.

Article 123
(Liability of liquidators)

The rules on the civil liability of members of the administrative board or of the management board of an SE shall also apply to the civil liability of liquidators for wrongful acts committed in carrying out their duties.

Article 124
(Accounting documents)

1. The liquidators shall draw up a statement of the assets and liabilities of the SE on the date the winding up commenced. Any shareholder or creditor of the SE shall be entitled to obtain a copy of this statement free of charge, upon request.

2. The liquidators shall report on their activities to the general meeting each year.

3. The rules concerning the drawing up, auditing and publication of annual accounts or consolidated accounts and the approval of persons responsible for carrying out the statutory audits of those accounts shall apply *mutatis mutandis*.

Article 125
(Information supplied to creditors)

The notice of the winding up of the company provided for in Article 118 shall invite creditors to lodge their claims, and shall indicate the date after which distributions on the basis of liquidation will be made.

An invitation to lodge claims shall also be sent in writing to any creditor known to the company.

Article 126
(Distribution)

1. No distribution on the basis of liquidation may be made to the beneficiaries designated in the statutes or the instrument of incorporation, or failing any such designation to the shareholders, until all creditors of the company have been paid in full and the time-limits indicated in Articles 125 and 127(2) have expired.

2. After the creditors have been paid in full, and anything due to the beneficiaries referred to in paragraph 1 has been distributed, the net assets of the SE shall, except where otherwise stated in the statutes or the instrument of incorporation, be distributed among the shareholders in proportion to the nominal value of their shares.

3. Where the shares issued by the SE have not all been paid up in the same proportion, the amounts paid up shall be repaid. In that case only the remaining net assets shall be distributed in accordance with paragraph 2. If the net assets are not sufficient to repay the amounts paid up, the shareholders shall bear the loss in proportion to the nominal value of their shares.

4. Where a claim on an SE has not yet fallen due or is in dispute or where the creditor is not known, the net assets may be distributed only if adequate security is set aside for the creditor or if the assets remaining after a partial distribution represent sufficient security.

Article 127
(Distribution plan)

1. The liquidator or liquidators shall draw up a plan for the distribution of the net assets of the company pursuant to Article 126 after the date indicated in Article 125.

2. This plan shall be brought to the attention of the general meeting and of any beneficiary designated in the statutes or instrument of incorporation. Any shareholder and any beneficiary may challenge the plan in the court of the place where the SE has its registered office within three months of the date on which it was brought to the attention of the general meeting or of that beneficiary. No distribution may be made until that period has expired.

3. Where there is a challenge it shall be for the court to decide whether and to what extent any partial distribution may be made in the course of the proceedings before the court takes its decision.

Article 128
(Termination of liquidation)

1. The liquidation shall be terminated when the distribution is complete.

2. Where, after the liquidation is terminated, further assets or liabilities of the SE come to light which were previously unknown, or further liquidation measures prove necessary, a court in whose jurisdiction the registered office of the SE is situated shall, on the application of any shareholder or creditor, renew the mandate of the former liquidators or appoint other liquidators.

3. Termination of liquidation and removal of the SE from the register referred to in Article 8(1) shall be published in the manner referred to in Article 9.

4. Following the liquidation, the books and records relating to the liquidation shall be lodged at the register referred to in paragraph 3. Any interested party may examine such books and records.

Section 3

Insolvency and suspension of payments

Article 129
In respect of insolvency and suspension of payments the SE shall be subject to the law of the place where it has its registered office.

Article 130

1. The opening of insolvency or suspension of payments proceedings shall be notified for entry in the register by the person appointed to conduct the proceedings. The entry in the register shall show the following:

(a) the nature of the proceedings, the date of the order, and the court making it;

(b) the date on which payments were suspended, if the court order provides for this;

(c) the name and address of the administrator, trustee, receiver, liquidator or any other person having power to conduct the proceedings, or of each of them where there are more than one;

(d) any other information considered necessary.

2. Where a court finally dismisses an application for the opening of the proceedings referred to in paragraph 1 owing to want of sufficient assets, it shall, either of its own motion or on application by any interested party, order its decision to be noted in the register.

3. Particulars registered pursuant to paragraphs 1 and 2 shall be published in the manner referred to in Article 9.

TITLE VIII
MERGERS

Article 131
(Types of merger)
An SE may merge with other SEs or with other public limited companies incorporated under the law of one of the member states in the following ways:

(a) by forming a new SE;
(b) by the SE taking over one or more public limited companies;
(c) by a public limited company taking over the SE;
(d) by forming a new public limited company.

Article 132
(Applicable law)

1. Where the companies participating in the merger have their registered offices in the same member state, the provisions of national law giving effect to Directive 78/855/EEC shall apply.

2. Where the companies participating in the merger have their registered offices in different member states, the provisions of Title II shall apply *mutatis mutandis*.

TITLE IX
PERMANENT ESTABLISHMENTS

Article 133
1. Where an SE has one or more permanent establishments in a member state or a non-member state, and the aggregation of profits and losses for tax purposes of all such permanent establishments results in a net loss, that loss may be set against the profits of the SE in the state where it is resident for tax purposes.

2. Subsequent profits of the permanent establishments of the SE in another state shall constitute taxable income of the SE in the state in which it is resident for tax purposes, up to the amount of the losses imputed in accordance with paragraph 1.

3. Where a permanent establishment is situated in a member state, the imputable losses under paragraph 1 and the taxable profits under paragraph 2 shall be determined by the laws of that member state.

4. Member states shall be free not to apply the provisions of this Article if they avoid double taxation by allowing the SE to set the tax already paid by its permanent establishments against the tax due from it in respect of the profits realised by those permanent establishments.

TITLE X
SANCTIONS

Article 134
The provisions of national law applicable to the infringement of the rules relating to public limited companies shall apply to the infringement of any of the provisions of this Regulation.

TITLE XI
FINAL PROVISIONS

Article 135
The involvement of employees in the SE shall be defined in accordance with the provisions adopted to give effect to Directive 00 by the member state where the SE has its registered office.

Article 136
An SE may be formed in any member state which has implemented in national law the provisions of Directive 00 (on the involvement of employees in the SE).

Article 137
This regulation shall enter into force on 1 January 1992.
   This regulation shall be binding in its entirety and directly applicable to all member states.

Proposal for a Council Directive complementing the Statute for a European company

with regard to the involvement of employees in the European company
COM(89) 268 final — SYN 219
(Submitted by the Commission to the Council on 25 August 1989) — (89/C 263/08)

The Council of the European Communities

Having regard to the Treaty establishing the European Economic Community, and in particular Article 54 thereof,
   Having regard to the proposal from the Commission,
   In co-operation with the European Parliament,
   Having regard to the opinion of the Economic and Social Committee,
   Whereas in order to attain the objectives set out in Article 8a of the Treaty, Council Regulation No . . . establishes a Statute for a European company (SE);
   Whereas, in order to promote the economic and social objectives of the Community, arrangements should be made for employees to participate in the supervision and strategic development of the SE;
   Whereas the great diversity of rules and practices existing in the member states as regards the manner in which employees' representatives participate in supervision of the decisions of the governing bodies of public limited companies makes it impossible to lay down uniform rules on the involvement of employees in the SE;
   Whereas the laws of the member states should therefore be co-ordinated with a view to making equivalent the safeguards required for the protection of the interests of members and third persons, of public limited companies in each member state, with due regard to the specific characteristics of the operation of such companies having their registered office in its territory; whereas such co-ordination must take account of the fact that an SE is created by a restructuring or co-operation operation involving companies governed by the law of at least two member states;
   Whereas account should be taken of the specific characteristics of the laws of the member states by establishing for the SE a framework comprising several models of participation, and authorising, first, member states to choose the model best corresponding to their national traditions, and, secondly, the management or the administrative board, as the case may be, and the representatives of the employees of the SE or of its founder companies to choose the model most suited to their social environment;
   Whereas the provisions of this Directive form an indissociable complement to the provisions of Regulation No

. . . and it is therefore necessary to ensure that the two sets of provisions are applied concomitantly,

Has adopted this Directive

Article 1
The co-ordination measures prescribed by this Directive shall apply to the laws, regulations and administrative provisions in the member states concerning the involvement of employees in the SE.
   These measures are an essential supplement to Regulation No. . . . on the Statute for a European company.

TITLE 1
MODELS OF PARTICIPATION

Article 2
Member states shall take the necessary measures to enable employees of the SE to participate in the supervision and strategic development of the SE in accordance with the provisions of this Directive.

Article 3
1. Subject to the application of paragraph 5, the participation of SE employees prescribed by Article 2 shall be determined in accordance with one of the models set out in Articles 4, 5 and 6 by means of an agreement concluded between the management boards and the administrative boards of the founder companies and the representatives of the employees of those companies provided for by the laws and practices of the member states. Where no agreement can be reached the management and administrative boards shall choose the model applicable to the SE.
   2. An SE may not be formed unless one of the models referred to in Articles 4, 5 and 6 has been chosen.
   3. Subject to the application of paragraph 5, the chosen model may be replaced by another model in Articles 4, 5 and 6 by an agreement concluded between the management or the administrative board and the representatives of the employees of the SE. This agreement must be submitted for the approval of the general meeting.

4. Each member state shall determine the manner in which the participation models shall be applied for SEs having their registered office in its territory.

5. A member state may restrict the choice of the models referred to in Articles 4, 5 and 6 or make only one of these models compulsory for the SEs having their registered office in its territory.

Section 1

Supervisory board or administrative board

Article 4

The appointment of members of the supervisory board or the administrative board, as the case may be, shall be governed by the following rules:

— at least one-third and not more than one-half of them shall be appointed by the employees of the SE or their representatives in that company, or

— they shall be co-opted by the board. However, the general meeting of shareholders or the representatives of the employees may, on specific grounds, object to the appointment of a particular candidate. In such cases the appointment may not be made until an independent body established under public law has declared the objection inadmissible.

Section 2

Separate body

Article 5

1. A separate body shall represent the employees of the SE. The number of members of that body and the detailed rules governing their election or appointment shall be laid down in the statutes in consultation with the representatives of the employees of the founder companies in accordance with the laws or practices of the member states.

2. The body representing the employees shall have the right:

(a) at least once every three months, to be informed by the management board or the administrative board of the progress of the company's business, including that of undertakings controlled by it, and of its prospects;

(b) where it is necessary for the performance of its duties, to require from the management board or the administrative board a report concerning certain of the company's business or any information or documents;

(c) to be informed and consulted by the management board or the administrative board before any decision referred to in Article 72 of Regulation No. . . . is implemented.

3. Article 74(3) of that Regulation shall apply to members of the separate body.

Section 3

Other models

Article 6

1. Models other than those referred to in Articles 4 and 5 may be established by means of an agreement concluded between the management boards and the administrative boards of the founder companies and the employees or their representatives in those companies.

2. The agreement reached shall provide at least for the employees of the SE or their representatives:

(a) once every three months, to be informed of the progress of the company's business, including that of undertakings controlled by it, and of its prospects;

(b) to be informed and consulted before any decision referred to in Article 72 of Registration No . . . is implemented.

3. Where the agreement provides for a collegiate body representing the employees, that body may require the management board or the administrative board to provide the information necessary for the performance of its duties.

4. The agreement shall provide that the employee's representatives must observe the necessary discretion in relation to any confidential information they hold on the SE. They shall be bound by this obligation even after their duties have ceased.

5. If the law of the state where the SE has its registered office so permits, the agreement may permit the management board or the administrative board of the SE to withhold from the employees or their representatives any information the disclosure of which might seriously jeopardise the interests of the SE or disrupt its projects.

6. The parties to the negotiations may be assisted by experts of their choice at the expense of the founder companies.

7. The agreement may be concluded for a fixed period and re-negotiated upon expiry of that period. However, the agreement concluded shall remain in force until the entry into force of the new agreement.

8. Where the two parties to the negotiations so decide, or where no agreement such as is mentioned in paragraph 1 can be reached, a standard model, provided by the law of the state where the SE has its registered office, shall apply to the SE. This model shall be in conformity with the most advanced national practices and shall ensure for the employees at least the rights of information and consultation provided for by this article.

Section 4

Election of the representatives of the employees of the SE

Article 7

The representatives of the employees of the SE shall be elected in accordance with systems which take into account, in an appropriate manner, the number of staff they represent.

All employees must be able to participate in the vote.

The election shall be conducted in accordance with the laws or practices of the member states.

Article 8

The first members of the supervisory board or the administrative board to be appointed by the employees and the first members of the separate body representing the employees shall be appointed by the representatives of the employees of the founder companies in proportioin to the number of employees they represent and in accordance with the laws or practices of the member states. Those first members shall remain in office until such time as the requirements for electing the representatives of the employees of the SE are satisfied.

Section 5

Article 9

1. The management board or the administrative board of the SE shall provide the representatives of the employees with such financial and material resources as enable them to meet and perform their duties in an appropriate manner.

2. The practical arrangements for making available such financial and material resources shall be settled in consultation with the representatives of the employees of the SE.

Section 6

Representation of employees in the establishments of the SE

Article 10

Save as otherwise provided in this Directive, the status and duties of the representatives of the employees or of the body which represents them, for which provision is made in the establishments of the SE, shall be determined by the laws or practices of the member states.

TITLE 2

EMPLOYEE PARTICIPATION IN THE CAPITAL OR IN THE PROFIT OR LOSS OF THE SE

Section 1

Article 11

Employee participation in the capital or in the profits or losses of the SE may be organised by means of a collective agreement negotiated and concluded by the management boards and the administrative boards of the founder companies, or of the SE when constituted, and the employees or their representatives who are duly authorised to negotiate in those companies.

Section 2

Final provisions

Article 12

1. Member states shall bring into force the laws, regulations and administrative provisions necessary to comply with this Directive by 1 January 1992. They shall immediately communicate the measures taken to the Commission.

The provisions adopted pursuant to the first sub-paragraph shall make express reference to this Directive.

2. Member states shall communicate to the Commission the main provisions of domestic law which they adopt in the field covered by this Directive.

Article 13

This Directive is addressed to the member states.

APPENDIX 4

Council Regulation (EEC) No. 2137/85

of 25 July 1985
on the European Economic Interest Grouping (EEIG)
(OJ 1985 L199/1)

The Council of the European Communities

Having regard to the Treaty establishing the European Economic Community, and in particular Article 235 thereof,

Having regard to the proposal from the Commission*,

Having regard to the opinion of the European Parliament**,

Having regard to the opinion of the Economic and Social Committee***,

Whereas a harmonious development of economic activities and a continuous and balanced expansion throughout the Community depend on the establishment and smooth functioning of a common market offering conditions analogous to those of a national market; whereas to bring about this single market and to increase its unity a legal framework which facilitates the adaptation of their activities to the economic conditions of the Community should be created for natural persons, companies, firms and other legal bodies in particular; whereas to that end it is necessary that those natural persons, companies, firms and other legal bodies should be able to co-operate effectively across frontiers;

Whereas co-operation of this nature can encounter legal, fiscal or psychological difficulties; whereas the creation of an appropriate Community legal instrument in the form of a European Economic Interest Grouping would contribute to the achievement of the above mentioned objectives and therefore proves necessary;

Whereas the Treaty does not provide the necessary powers for the creation of such a legal instrument;

Whereas a grouping's ability to adapt to economic conditions must be guaranteed by the considerable freedom for its members in their contractual relations and the internal organisation of the grouping;

Whereas a grouping differs from a firm or company principally in its purpose, which is only to facilitate or develop the economic activities of its members to enable them to improve their own results; whereas, by reason of that ancillary nature, a grouping's activities must be related to the economic activities of its members but not replace them so that, to that extent, for example, a grouping may not itself, with regard to third parties, practise a profession, the concept of economic activities being interpreted in the widest sense;

Whereas access to grouping form must be made as widely available as possible to natural persons, companies, firms and other legal bodies, in keeping with the aims of this Regulation; whereas this Regulation shall not, however, prejudice the application at national level of legal rules and/or ethical codes concerning the conditions for the pursuit of business and professional activities;

Whereas this Regulation does not itself confer on any person the right to participate in a grouping, even where the conditions it lays down are fulfilled;

Whereas the power provided by this Regulation to prohibit or restrict participation in a grouping on grounds of public interest is without prejudice to the laws of member states which govern the pursuit of activities and which may provide further prohibitions or restrictions or otherwise control or supervise participation in a grouping by any natural person, company, firm or other legal body or any class of them;

Whereas, to enable a grouping to achieve its purpose, it should be endowed with legal capacity and provision should be made for it to be represented *vis-à-vis* third parties by an organ legally separate from its membership;

Whereas the protection of third parties requires widespread publicity; whereas the members of a grouping have unlimited joint and several liability for the grouping's debts and other liabilities, including those relating to tax or social security, without, however, that principle's affecting the freedom to exclude or restrict the liability of one or more of its members in respect of a particular debt or other liability by means of a specific contract between the grouping and a third party;

Whereas matters relating to the status or capacity of natural persons and to the capacity of legal persons are governed by national law;

Whereas the grounds for winding up which are peculiar to the grouping should be specific while referring to national law for its liquidation and the conclusion thereof;

Whereas groupings are subject to national laws relating to insolvency and cessation of payments; whereas such laws may provide other grounds for the winding up of groupings;

Whereas this Regulation provides that the profits or losses resulting from the activities of a grouping shall be taxable only in the hands of its members; whereas it is understood that otherwise national tax laws apply, particularly as regards the apportionment of profits, tax procedures and any obligations imposed by national tax law;

Whereas in matters not covered by this Regulation the laws of the member states and Community law are applicable, for example with regard to:

— social and labour laws,
— competition law,
— intellectual property law;

Whereas the activities of groupings are subject to the provisions of member states' laws on the pursuit and supervision of activities; whereas in the event of abuse or circumvention of the laws of a member state by a grouping or its members that member state may impose appropriate sanctions;

Whereas the member states are free to apply or to adopt any laws, regulations or administrative measures which do not conflict with the scope or objectives of this Regulation;

Whereas this Regulation must enter into force immediately in its entirety; whereas the implementation of some provisions must nevertheless be deferred in order to allow the member states first to set up the necessary machinery for the registration of groupings in their territories and the disclosure of certain matters

* OJ No. C14, 15.2.1974, p.30 and OJ No. C103, 2.8.1978, p.4.
** OJ No. C163, 11.7.1977, p.17.
*** OJ No. C108, 15.5.1975, p.46.

298

relating to groupings; whereas, with effect from the date of implementation of this Regulation, groupings set up may operate without territorial restrictions,

Has adopted this Regulation:

Article 1

1. European Economic Interest Groupings shall be formed upon the terms, in the manner and with the effects laid down in this Regulation.

Accordingly, parties intending to form a grouping must conclude a contract and have the registration provided for in Article 6 carried out.

2. A grouping so formed shall, from the date of its registration as provided for in Article 6, have the capacity, in its own name, to have rights and obligations of all kinds, to make contracts or accomplish other legal acts, and to sue and be sued.

3. The member states shall determine whether or not groupings registered at their registries, pursuant to Article 6, have legal personality.

Article 2

1. Subject to the provisions of this Regulation, the law applicable, on the one hand, to the contract for the formation of a grouping, except as regards matters relating to the status or capacity of natural persons and to the capacity of legal persons and, on the other hand, to the internal organisation of a grouping shall be the internal law of the state in which the official address is situated, as laid down in the contract for the formation of the grouping.

2. Where a state comprises several territorial units, each of which has its own rules of law applicable to the matters referred to in paragraph 1, each territorial unit shall be considered as a state for the purposes of identifying the law applicable under this Article.

Article 3

1. The purpose of a grouping shall be to facilitate or develop the economic activities of its members and to improve or increase the results of those activities; its purpose is not to make profits for itself.

Its activity shall be related to the economic activities of its members and must not be more than ancillary to those activities.

2. Consequently, a grouping may not:

(a) exercise, directly or indirectly, a power of management or supervision over its members' own activities or other the activities of another undertaking, in particular in the fields of personnel, finance and investment;

(b) directly or indirectly, on any basis whatsoever, hold shares of any kind in a member undertaking; the holding of shares in another undertaking shall be possible only in so far as it is necessary for the achievement of the grouping's objects and if it is done on its members' behalf;

(c) employ more than 500 persons;

(d) be used by a company to make a loan to a director of a company, or any person connected with him, when the making of such loans is restricted or controlled under the member states' laws governing companies. Nor must a grouping be used for the transfer of any property between a company and a director, or any person connected with him, except to the extent allowed by the member states' laws governing companies. For the purposes of this provision the making of a loan includes entering into any

transaction or arrangement of similar effect, and property includes moveable and immoveable property;

(e) be a member of another European Economic Interest Grouping.

Article 4

1. Only the following may be members of a grouping:

(a) companies or firms within the meaning of the second paragraph of Article 58 of the Treaty and other legal bodies governed by public or private law, which have been formed in accordance with the law of a member state and which have their registered or statutory office and central administration in the Community; where, under the law of a member state, a company, firm or other legal body is not obliged to have a registered or statutory office, it shall be sufficient for such a company, firm or other legal body to have its central administration in the Community;

(b) natural persons who carry on any industrial, commercial, craft or agricultural activity or who provide professional or other services in the Community.

2. A grouping must comprise at least:

(a) two companies, firms or other legal bodies, within the meaning of paragraph 1, which have their central administrations in different member states, or

(b) two natural persons, within the meaning of paragraph 1, who carry on their principal activities in different member states, or

(c) a company, firm or other legal body within the meaning of paragraph 1 and a natural person, of which the first has its central administration in one member state and the second carries on his principal activity in another member state.

3. A member state may provide that groupings registered at its registries in accordance with Article 6 may have no more than 20 members. For this purpose, that member state may provide that, in accordance with its laws, each member of a legal body formed under its laws, other than a registered company, shall be treated as a separate member of a grouping.

4. Any member state may, on grounds of that state's public interest, prohibit or restrict participation in groupings by certain classes of natural persons, companies, firms, or other legal bodies.

Article 5

A contract for the formation of a grouping shall include at least:

(a) the name of the grouping preceded or followed either by the words 'European Economic Interest Grouping' or by the initials 'EEIG', unless those words or initials already form part of the name;

(b) the official address of the grouping;

(c) the objects for which the grouping is formed;

(d) the name, business name, legal form, permanent address or registered office, and the number and place of registration, if any, of each member of the grouping;

(e) the duration of the grouping, except where this is indefinite.

Article 6

A grouping shall be registered in the State in which it has its official address, at the registry designated pursuant to Article 39(1).

Article 7

A contract for the formation of a grouping shall be filed at the registry referred to in Article 6.

The following documents and particulars must also be filed at that registry:

(a) any amendment to the contract for the formation of a grouping, including any change in the composition of a grouping;

(b) notice of the setting up or closure of any establishment of the grouping;

(c) any judicial decision establishing or declaring the nullity of a grouping, in accordance with Article 15;

(d) notice of the appointment of the manager or managers of a grouping, their names and any other identification particulars required by the law of the member state in which the register is kept, notification that they may act alone or must act jointly, and the termination of any manager's appointment;

(e) notice of a member's assignment of his participation in a grouping or a proportion thereof, in accordance with Article 22(1);

(f) any decision by members ordering or establishing the winding up of a grouping, in accordance with Article 31, or any judicial decision ordering such winding up, in accordance with Articles 31 or 32;

(g) notice of the appointment of the liquidator or liquidators of a grouping, as referred to in Article 35, their names and any other identification particulars required by the law of the member state in which the register is kept, and the termination of any liquidator's appointment;

(h) notice of the conclusion of a grouping's liquidation, as referred to in Article 35(2);

(i) any proposal to transfer the official address, as referred to in Article 14(1);

(j) any clause exempting a new member from the payment of debts and other liabilities which originated prior to his admission, in accordance with Article 26(2).

Article 8

The following must be published, as laid down in Article 39, in the gazette referred to in paragraph 1 of that Article:

(a) the particulars which must be included in the contract for the formation of a grouping, pursuant to Article 5, and any amendments thereto;

(b) the number, date and place of registration as well as notice of the termination of that registration;

(c) the document and particulars referred to in Article 7(b) to (j).

The particulars referred to in (a) and (b) must be published in full. The documents and particulars referred to in (c) may be published either in full or in extract form or by means of a reference to their filing at the registry, in accordance with the national legislation applicable.

Article 9

1. The documents and particulars which must be published pursuant to this Regulation may be relied on by a grouping as against third parties under the conditions laid down by the national law applicable pursuant to Article 3(5) and (7) of Council Directive 68/151/EEC of 9 March 1968 on co-ordination of safeguards which, for the protection of the interests of members and others, are required by member states of companies within the meaning of the second paragraph of Article 58 of the Treaty,

with a view to making such safeguards equivalent throughout the Community*.

2. If activities have been carried on on behalf of a grouping before its registration in accordance with Article 6 and if the grouping does not, after its registration, assume the obligations arising out of such activities, the natural persons, companies, firms or other legal bodies which carried on those activities shall bear unlimited joint and several liability for them.

Article 10

Any grouping establishment situated in a member state other than that in which the official address is situated shall be registered in that state. For the purpose of such registration, a grouping shall file, at the appropriate registry in that member state, copies of the documents which must be filed at the registry of the member state in which the official address is situated, together, if necessary, with a translation which conforms with the practice of the registry where the establishment is registered.

Article 11

Notice that a grouping has been formed or that the liquidation of a grouping has been concluded stating the number, date and place of registration and the date, place and title of publication, shall be given in the *Official Journal of the European Communities* after it has been published in the gazette referred to in Article 39(1).

Article 12

The official address referred to in the contract for the formation of a grouping must be situated in the Community.

The official address must be fixed either:

(a) where the grouping has its central administration, or

(b) where one of the members of the grouping has its central administration or, in the case of a natural person, his principal activity, provided that the grouping carries on an activity there.

Article 13

The official address of a grouping may be transferred within the Community.

When such a transfer does not result in a change in the law applicable pursuant to Article 2, the decision to transfer shall be taken in accordance with the conditions laid down in the contract for the formation of the grouping.

Article 14

1. When the transfer of the official address results in a change in the law applicable pursuant to Article 2, a transfer proposal must be drawn up, filed and published in accordance with the conditions laid down in Articles 7 and 8.

No decision to transfer may be taken for two months after publication of the proposal. Any such decision must be taken by the members of the grouping uninimously. The transfer shall take effect on the date on which the grouping is registered, in accordance with Article 6, at the registry for the new official address. That registration may not be effected until evidence has been produced that the proposal to transfer the official address has been published.

2. The termination of a grouping's registration at the registry for its old official address may not be effected until evidence has been produced that the grouping has been registered at the registry for its new official address.

3. Upon publication of a grouping's new registration the new official address may be relied on as against third parties in

---

* OJ No. L65, 14.3.1968, p.8.

accordance with the conditions referred to in Article 9(1); however, as long as the termination of the grouping's registration at the registry for the old official address has not been published, third parties may continue to rely on the old official address unless the grouping proves that such third parties were aware of the new official address.

4. The laws of a member state may provide that, as regards groupings registered under Article 6 in that member state, the transfer of an official address which would result in a change of the law applicable shall not take effect if, within the two-month period referred to in paragraph 1, a competent authority in that member state opposes it. Such opposition may be based only on grounds of public interest. Review by a judicial authority must be possible.

Article 15

1. Where the law applicable to a grouping by virtue of Article 2 provides for the nullity of that grouping, such nullity must be established or declared by judicial decision. However, the court to which the matter is referred must, where it is possible for the affairs of the grouping to be put in order, allow time to permit that to be done.

2. The nullity of a grouping shall entail its liquidation in accordance with the conditions laid down in Article 35.

3. A decision establishing or declaring the nullity of a grouping may be relied on as against third parties in accordance with the conditions laid down in Article 9(1).

Such a decision shall not of itself affect the validity of liabilities, owed by or to a grouping which originated before it could be relied on as against third parties in accordance with the conditions laid down in the previous subparagraph.

Article 16

1. The organs of a grouping shall be the members acting collectively and the manager or managers.

A contract for the formation of a grouping may provide for other organs; if it does it shall determine their powers.

2. The members of a grouping, acting as a body, may take any decision for the purpose of achieving the objects of the grouping.

Article 17

1. Each member shall have one vote. The contract for the formation of a grouping may, however, give more than one vote to certain members, provided that no one member holds a majority of the votes.

2. A unanimous decision by the members shall be required to:

(a) alter the objects of a grouping;

(b) alter the number of votes allotted to each member;

(c) alter the conditions for the taking of decisions;

(d) extend the duration of a grouping beyond any period fixed in the contract for the formation of the grouping;

(e) alter the contribution by every member or by some members to the grouping's financing;

(f) alter any other obligation of a member, unless otherwise provided by the contract for the formation of the grouping;

(g) make any alteration to the contract for the formation of the grouping not covered by this paragraph, unless otherwise provided by that contract.

3. Except where this Regulation provides that decisions must be taken unanimously, the contract for the formation of a grouping may prescribe the conditions for a quorum and for a majority, in accordance with which the decisions, or some of them, shall be taken. Unless otherwise provided for by the contract, decisions shall be taken unanimously.

4. On the initiative of a manager or at the request of a member, the manager or managers must arrange for the members to be consulted so that the latter can take a decision.

Article 18

Each member shall be entitled to obtain information from the manager or managers concerning the grouping's business and to inspect the grouping's books and business records.

Article 19

1. A grouping shall be managed by one or more natural persons appointed in the contract for the formation of the grouping or by decision of the members.

No person may be a manager of a grouping if:

— by virtue of the law applicable to him, or

— by virtue of the internal law of the state in which the grouping has its official address, or

— following a judicial or administrative decision made or recognised in a member state

he may not belong to the administrative or management body of a company, may not manage an undertaking or may not act as manager of a European Economic Interest Grouping.

2. A member state may, in the case of groupings registered at their registries pursuant to Article 6, provide that legal persons may be managers on condition that such legal persons designate one or more natural persons, whose particulars shall be the subject of the filing provisions of Article 7(d), to represent them.

If a member state exercises this option, it must provide that the representative or representatives shall be liable as if they were themselves managers of the groupings concerned.

The restrictions imposed in paragraph 1 shall also apply to those representatives.

3. The contract for the formation of a grouping or, failing that, a unanimous decision by the members shall determine the conditions for the appointment and removal of the manager or managers and shall lay down their powers.

Article 20

1. Only the manager or, where there are two or more, each of the managers shall represent a grouping in respect of dealings with third parties.

Each of the managers shall bind the grouping as regards third parties when he acts on behalf of the grouping, even where his acts do not fall within the objects of the grouping, unless the grouping proves that the third party knew or could not, under the circumstances, have been unaware that the act fell outside the objects of the grouping; publication of the particulars referred to in Article 5(c) shall not of itself be proof thereof.

No limitation on the powers of the manager or managers, whether deriving from the contract for the formation of the grouping or from a decision by the members, may be relied on as against third parties even if it is published.

2. The contract for the formation of the grouping may provide that the grouping shall be validly bound only by two or more managers acting jointly. Such a clause may be relied on as against third parties in accordance with the conditions referred to in Article 9(1) only if it is published in accordance with Article 8.

Article 21
1. The profits resulting from a grouping's activities shall be deemed to be the profits of the members and shall be apportioned among them in the proportions laid down in the contract for the formation of the grouping or, in the absence of any such provision, in equal shares.
2. The members of a grouping shall contribute to the payment of the amount by which expenditure exceeds income in the proportions laid down in the contract for the formation of the grouping or, in the absence of any such provision, in equal shares.

Article 22
1. Any member of a grouping may assign his participation in the grouping, or a proportion thereof, either to another member or to a third party; the assignment shall not take effect without the unanimous authorisation of the other members.
2. A member of a grouping may use his participation in the grouping as security only after the other members have given their unanimous authorisation, unless otherwise laid down in the contract for the formation of the grouping. The holder of the security may not at any time become a member of the grouping by virtue of that security.

Article 23
No grouping may invite investment by the public.

Article 24
1. The members of a grouping shall have unlimited joint and several liability for its debts and other liabilities of whatever nature. National law shall determine the consequences of such liability.
2. Creditors may not proceed against a member for payment in respect of debts and other liabilities, in accordance with the conditions laid down in paragraph 1, before the liquidation of a grouping is concluded, unless they have first requested the grouping to pay and payment has not been made within an appropriate period.

Article 25
Letters, order forms and similar documents must indicate legibly:

   (a) the name of the grouping preceded or followed either by the words 'European Economic Interest Grouping' or by the initials 'EEIG', unless those words or initials already occur in the name;
   (b) the location of the registry referred to in Article 6, in which the grouping is registered, together with the number of the grouping's entry at the registry;
   (c) the grouping's official address;
   (d) where applicable, that the managers must act jointly;
   (e) where applicable, that the grouping is in liquidation, pursuant to Articles 15, 31, 32 or 36.

Every establishment of a grouping, when registered in accordance with Article 10, must give the above particulars together with those relating to its own registration, on the documents referred to in the first paragraph of this Article uttered by it.

Article 26
1. A decision to admit new members shall be taken unanimously by the members of the grouping.

2. Every new member shall be liable, in accordance with the conditions laid down in Article 24, for the grouping's debts and other liabilities, including those arising out of the grouping's activities before his admission.

He may, however, be exempted by a clause in the contract for the formation of the grouping or in the instrument of admission from the payment of debts and other liabilities which originated before his admission. Such a clause may be relied on as against third parties, under the conditions referred to in Article 9(1), only if it is published in accordance with Article 8.

Article 27
1. A member of a grouping may withdraw in accordance with the conditions laid down in the contract for the formation of a grouping or, in the absence of such conditions, with the unanimous agreement of the other members.

Any member of a grouping may, in addition, withdraw on just and proper grounds.
2. Any member of a grouping may be expelled for the reasons listed in the contract for the formation of the grouping and, in any case, if he seriously fails in his obligations or if he causes or threatens to cause serious disruption in the operation of the grouping.

Such expulsion may occur only by the decision of a court to which joint application has been made by a majority of the other members, unless otherwise provided by the contract for the formation of a grouping.

Article 28
1. A member of a grouping shall cease to belong to it on death or when he no longer complies with the conditions laid down in Article 4(1).

In addition, a member state may provide, for the purposes of its liquidation, winding up, insolvency or cessation of payments laws, that a member shall cease to be a member of any grouping at the moment determined by those laws.
2. In the event of the death of a natural person who is a member of a grouping, no person may become a member in his place except under the conditions laid down in the contract for the formation of the grouping or, failing that, with the unanimous agreement of the remaining members.

Article 29
As soon as a member ceases to belong to a grouping, the manager or managers must inform the other members of that fact; they must also take the steps required as listed in Articles 7 and 8. In addition, any person concerned may take those steps.

Article 30
Except where the contract for the formation of a grouping provides otherwise and without prejudice to the rights acquired by a person under Articles 22(1) or 28(2), a grouping shall continue to exist for the remaining members after a member has ceased to belong to it, in accordance with the conditions laid down in the contract for the formation of the grouping or determined by unanimous decision of the members in question.

Article 31
1. A grouping may be wound up by a decision of its members ordering its winding up. Such a decision shall be taken unanimously, unless otherwise laid down in the contract for the formation of the grouping.

2. A grouping must be wound up by a decision of its members:

(a) noting the expiry of the period fixed in the contract for the formation of the grouping or the existence of any other cause for winding up provided for in the contract, or

(b) noting the accomplishment of the grouping's purpose or the impossibility of pursuing it further.

Where, three months after one of the situations referred to in the first subparagraph has occurred, a members' decision establishing the winding up of the grouping has not been taken, any member may petition the court to order winding up.

3. A grouping must also be wound up by a decision of its members or of the remaining member when the conditions laid down in Article 4(2) are no longer fulfilled.

4. After a grouping has been wound up by decision of its members, the manager or managers must take the steps required as listed in Articles 7 and 8. In addition, any person concerned may take those steps.

Article 32

1. On application by any person concerned or by a competent authority, in the event of the infringement of Articles 3, 12 or 31(3), the court must order a grouping to be wound up, unless its affairs can be and are put in order before the court has delivered a substantive ruling.

2. On applications by a member, the court may order a grouping to be wound up on just and proper grounds.

3. A member state may provide that the court may, on application by a competent authority, order the winding up of a grouping which has its official address in the state to which that authority belongs, wherever the grouping acts in contravention of that state's public interest, if the law of that state provides for such a possibility in respect of registered companies or other legal bodies subject to it.

Article 33

When a member ceases to belong to a grouping for any reason other than the assignment of his rights in accordance with the conditions laid down in Article 22(1), the value of his rights and obligations shall be determined taking into account the assets and liabilities of the grouping as they stand when he ceases to belong to it.

The value of the rights and obligations of a departing member may not be fixed in advance.

Article 34

Without prejudice to Article 37(1), any member who ceases to belong to a grouping shall remain answerable, in accordance with the conditions laid down in Article 24, for the debts and other liabilities arising out of the grouping's activities before he ceased to be a member.

Article 35

1. The winding up of a grouping shall entail its liquidation.

2. The liquidation of a grouping and the conclusion of its liquidation shall be governed by national law.

3. A grouping shall retain its capacity, within the meaning of Article 1(2), until its liquidation is concluded.

4. The liquidator or liquidators shall take the steps required as listed in Articles 7 and 8.

Article 36

Groupings shall be subject to national laws governing insolvency and cessation of payments. The commencement of proceedings against a grouping on grounds of its insolvency or cessation of payments shall not by itself cause the commencement of such proceedings against its members.

Article 37

1. A period of limitation of five years after the publication, pursuant to Article 8, of notice of a member's ceasing to belong to a grouping shall be substituted for any longer period which may be laid down by the relevant national law for actions against that member in connection with debts and other liabilities arising out of the grouping's activities before he ceased to be a member.

2. A period of limitation of five years after the publication, pursuant to Article 8, of notice of the conclusion of the liquidation of a grouping shall be substituted for any longer period which may be laid down by the relevant national law for actions against a member of the grouping in connection with debts and other liabilities arising out of the grouping's activities.

Article 38

Where a grouping carries on any activity in a member state in contravention of that state's public interest, a competent authority of that state may prohibit that activity. Review of that competent authority's decision by a judicial authority shall be possible.

Article 39

1. The member states shall designate the registry or registries responsible for effecting the registration referred to in Articles 6 and 10 and shall lay down the rules governing registration. They shall prescribe the conditions under which the documents referred to in Articles 9 and 10 shall be filed. They shall ensure that the documents and particulars referred to in Article 8 are published in the appropriate official gazette of the member state in which the grouping has its official address, and may prescribe the manner of publication of the documents and particulars referred to in Article 8(c).

The member states shall also ensure that anyone may, at the appropriate registry pursuant to Article 6 or, where appropriate, Article 10, inspect the documents referred to in Article 7 and obtain, in person or by post, full or partial copies thereof.

The member states may provide for the payment of fees in connection with the operations referred to in the preceding subparagraphs; those fees may not, however, exceed the administrative cost thereof.

2. The member states shall ensure that the information to be published in the *Official Journal of the European Communities* pursuant to Article 11 is forwarded to the Office for Official Publications of the European Communities within one month of its publication in the official gazette referred to in paragraph 1.

3. The member states shall provide for appropriate penalties in the event of failure to comply with the provisions of Articles 7, 8 and 10 on disclosure and in the event of failure to comply with Article 25.

Article 40

The profits or losses resulting from the activities of a grouping shall be taxable only in the hands of its members.

Article 41

1. The member states shall take the measures required by virtue of Article 39 before 1 July 1989. They shall immediately communicate them to the Commission.

2. For information purposes, the member states shall inform the Commission of the classes of natural persons, companies,

firms and other legal bodies which they prohibit from participating in groupings pursuant to Article 4(4). The Commission shall inform the other member states.

Article 42

1. Upon the adoption of this Regulation, a Contact Committee shall be set up under the auspices of the Commission. Its function shall be:

(a) to facilitate, without prejudice to Articles 169 and 170 of the Treaty, application of this Regulation through regular consultation dealing in particular with practical problems arising in connection with its application;

(b) to advise the Commission, if necessary, on additions or amendments to this Registration.

2. The Contact Committee shall be composed of representatives of the member states and representatives of the Commission. The chairman shall be a representative of the Commission. The Commission shall provide the secretariat.

3. The Contact Committee shall be convened by its chairman either on his own initiative or at the request of one of its members.

Article 43

This Regulation shall enter into force on the third day following its publication in the *Official Journal of the European Communities*.

It shall apply from 1 July, with the exception of Articles 39, 41 and 42 which shall apply as from the entry into force of the Regulation.

This Regulation shall be binding in its entirety and directly applicable in all member states.

Done at Brussels, 25 July 1985.

For the Council
The President
J. POOS

De Minimis Notice

Commission notice of 3 September 1986 on agreements of minor importance which do not fall under Article 85(1) of the Treaty establishing the European Economic Community*
(86/C231/02)

I

1. The Commission considers it important to facilitate co-operation between undertakings where such co-operation is economically desirable without presenting difficulties from the point of view of competition policy, which is particularly true of co-operation between small and medium-sized undertakings. To this end it published the 'Notice concerning agreements, decisions and concerted practices in the field of co-operation between undertakings'** listing a number of agreements that by their nature cannot be regarded as restraints of competition. Furthermore, in the Notice concerning its assessment of certain subcontracting agreements*** the Commission considered that this type of contract which offers opportunities for development, in particular, to small and medium-sized undertakings is not in itself caught by the prohibition in Article 85(1). By issuing the present Notice, the Commission is taking a further step towards defining the field of application of Article 85(1), in order to facilitate co-operation between small and medium-sized undertakings.

2. In the Commission's opinion, agreements whose effects on trade between member states or on competition are negligible do not fall under the ban on restrictive agreements contained in Article 85(1). Only those agreements are prohibited which have an appreciable impact on market conditions, in that they appreciably alter the market position, in other words the sales or supply possibilities, of third undertakings and of users.

3. In the present Notice the Commission, by setting quantitative criteria and by explaining their application, has given a sufficiently concrete meaning to the concept 'appreciable' for undertakings to be able to judge for themselves whether the agreements they have concluded with other undertakings, being of minor importance, do not fall under Article 85(1). The quantitative definition of 'appreciable' given by the Commission is, however, no absolute yardstick; in fact, in individual cases even agreements between undertakings which exceed these limits may still have only a negligible effect on trade between member states or on competition, and are therefore not caught by Article 85(1).

4. As a result of this Notice, there should no longer be any point in undertakings obtaining negative clearance, as defined by Article 2 of Council Regulation No. 17****, for the agreements covered, nor should it be necessary to have the legal position established through Commission decisions in individual cases; notification with this end in view will no longer be necessary for such agreements. However, if it is doubtful whether in an individual case an agreement appreciably affects trade between member states or competition, the undertakings are free to apply for negative clearance or to notify the agreement.

* The present Notice replaces the Commission notice of 19 December 1977, OJ No. C313, 29.12.1977, p.3.
** OJ No. C75, 29.7.1968, p.3, corrected by OJ No. C84, 28.8.1968, p.14.
*** OJ No. C1, 3.1.1979, p.2.
**** OJ No. 13, 21.2.1962, pp.204/62.

5. In cases covered by the present Notice the Commission, as a general rule, will not open proceedings under Regulation No. 17, either upon application or upon its own initiative. Where, due to exceptional circumstances, an agreement which is covered by the present Notice nevertheless falls under Article 85(1), the Commission will not impose fines. Where undertakings have failed to notify an agreement falling under Article 85(1) because they wrongly assumed, owing to a mistake in calculating their market share or aggregate turnover, that the agreement was covered by the present Notice, the Commission will not consider imposing fines unless the mistake was due to negligence.

6. This Notice is without prejudice to the competence of national courts to apply Article 85(1) on the basis of their own jurisdiction, although it constitutes a factor which such courts may take into account when deciding a pending case. It is also without prejudice to any interpretation which may be given by the Court of Justice of the European Communities.

II

7. The Commission holds the view that agreements between undertakings engaged in the production or distribution of goods or in the provision of services generally do not fall under the prohibition of Article 85(1) if:

— the goods or services which are the subject of the agreement (hereinafter referred to as 'the contract products') together with the participating undertakings' other goods or services which are considered by users to be equivalent in view of their characteristics, price and intended use, do not represent more than 5 per cent of the total market for such goods or services (hereinafter referred to as 'products') in the area of the common market affected by the agreement and
— the aggregate annual turnover of the participating undertakings does not exceed 200 million ECU.

8. The Commission also holds the view that the said agreements do not fall under the prohibition of Article 85(1) if the above mentioned market share or turnover is exceeded by not more than one tenth during two successive financial years.

9. For the purposes of this Notice, participating undertakings are:

(a) undertakings party to the agreement;
(b) undertakings in which a party to the agreement, directly or indirectly,

— owns more than half the capital or business assets or
— has the power to exercise more than half the voting rights, or
— has the power to appoint more than half the members of the supervisory board, board of management or bodies legally representing the undertakings, or
— has the right to manage the affairs;

(c) undertakings which directly or indirectly have in or over a party to the agreement the rights or powers listed in (b).

(d) undertakings in or over which an undertaking referred to in (c) directly or indirectly has the rights or powers listed in (b).

Undertakings in which several undertakings as referred to in (a) to (d) jointly have, directly or indirectly, the rights or powers set out in (b) shall also be considered to be participating undertakings.

10. In order to calculate the market share, it is necessary to determine the relevant market. This implies the definition of the relevant products market and the relevant geographical market.

11. The relevant products market includes besides the contract products any other products which are identical or equivalent to them. This rule applies to the products of the participating undertakings as well as to the market for such products. The products in question must be interchangeable. Whether or not this is the case must be judged from the vantage point of the user, normally taking the characteristics, price and intended use of the goods together. In certain cases, however, products can form a separate market on the basis of their characteristics, their price or their intended use alone. This is true especially where consumer preferences have developed.

12. Where the contract products are components which are incorporated into another product by the participating undertakings, reference should be made to the market for the latter product, provided that the components represent a significant part of it. Where the contract products are components which are sold to third undertakings, reference should be made to the market for the components. In cases where both conditions apply, both markets should be considered separately.

13. The relevant geographical market is the area within the Community in which the agreement produces its effects. This area will be the whole common market where the contract products are regularly bought and sold in all member states.

Where the contract products cannot be bought and sold in a part of the common market, or are bought and sold only in limited quantities or at irregular intervals in such a part, that part should be disregarded.

14. The relevant geographical market will be narrower than the whole common market in particular where:

— the nature and characteristics of the contract product, e.g., high transport costs in relation to the value of the product, restricts its mobility; or
— movement of the contract product within the common market is hindered by barriers to entry to national markets resulting from state intervention, such as quantitative restrictions, severe taxation differentials and non-tariff barriers, e.g., type approvals or safety standard certification. In such cases the national territory may have to be considered as the relevant geographical market. However, this will only be justified if the existing barriers to entry cannot be overcome by reasonable effort and at an acceptable cost.

15. Aggregate turnover includes the turnover in all goods and services, excluding tax, achieved during the last financial year by the participating undertaking. In cases where an undertaking has concluded similar agreements with various other undertakings in the relevant market, the turnover of all participating undertakings should be taken together. The aggregate turnover shall not include dealings between participating undertakings.

16. The present Notice shall not apply where in a relevant market competition is restricted by the cumulative effects of parallel networks of similar agreements established by several manufacturers or dealers.

17. The present Notice is likewise applicable to decisions by associations of undertakings and to concerted practices.

Pronuptia Judgment

Pronuptia de Paris GmbH v. *Pronuptia de Paris Irmgard Schillgallis* (Case 161/84) [1986] 1 CMLR 414

BEFORE THE COURT OF JUSTICE OF THE EUROPEAN COMMUNITIES

(*Presiding,* Lord Mackenzie Stuart CJ; Everling, Bahlmann and Joliet PPC; Koopmans, Due and Galmot JJ.)
Mr Pieter VerLoren van Themaat, *Advocate General.*

29 January 1986

Reference from Germany by the Bundesgerichtschof (Federal Supreme Court) under Article 177 EEC.

Restrictive practices. Franchising. There are at least three distinct types of franchising agreement, each of which should be treated separately for the purposes of EEC restrictive practices law:

   (a) service franchise agreements;
   (b) production franchise agreements; and
   (c) distribution franchise agreements. [13]

Restrictive practices. Franchising. Distribution. Distribution franchising agreements do not *per se* infringe Article 85 EEC, but may do so depending on their content. [14]–[15]

Restrictive practices. Franchising. Distribution. Know-how. One of the two essential conditions for the operation of a distribution franchise system is the ability of the franchisor to communicate his know-how to the franchisees and provide them with the necessary assistance in putting his methods into effect without aiding his competitors. Clauses essential to achieve this are permissible under Article 85(1) EEC, and include:

   (a) prohibition on the franchisee opening a shop in an area where he could be in competition with another franchisee, for the duration of the franchise and a reasonable time thereafter;
   (b) obligation on the franchise not to alienate his shop without the prior approval of the franchisor. [16]

Restrictive practices. Franchising. Distribution. Reputation. The second essential condition for the operation of a distribution franchise system is the ability of the franchisor to preserve the identity and reputation of the network. Clauses which provide a basis for essential control to that end do not restrict competition under Article 85(1) EEC and include an obligation on the franchisee:

   (a) to apply the commercial methods developed by the franchisor and to utilise his know-how;
   (b) to sell contract goods only in premises arranged and decorated according to the franchisor's specifications so as to guarantee a uniform image;
   (c) not to move his shop to another location without the franchisor's approval;
   (d) not to assign the contract without the franchisor's approval;
   (e) to accept the franchisor's consent over the selection of goods offered in the shop;
   (f) to submit all advertising to the franchisor. [17]–[22]

Restrictive practices. Franchising. Distribution. The following clauses in a distribution franchising agreements are not essential for the operation of such a system, are restrictive of competition and thus infringe Article 85(1) EEC: clauses which partition markets between the franchisor and franchisee or between franchisees *inter se*, including an obligation on the franchisee to sell the contract goods only at the location designated in the contract. [23]–[24]

Restrictive practices. Franchising. Distribution. Prices. Clauses in a distribution franchising agreement which restrict the franchisee's ability to fix his own prices freely restrict competition contrary to Article 85(1) EEC. However, for the franchisor merely to recommend prices is acceptable. [25]

Restrictive practices. Franchising. Distribution. Inter-State trade. Market partitioning. Distribution franchising agreements which contain clauses partitioning markets between franchisor and franchisee or between the franchisees *inter se* are *per se* capable of affecting inter-State trade even if they are concluded between enterprises established in the same member-state, in so far as they prevent franchisees setting themselves up in another member-state. [26]

Restrictive practices. Franchising. Distribution. Group exemption. Registration 67/67 does not apply to typical distribution franchising agreements. [34]

The Court *interpreted* Article 85(1) EEC and Regulation 67/67 *in the context of* an international franchising system for the distribution and sale of wedding apparel, the German subsidiary of the French parent running its own shops as well as licensing franchisees in specific territories in Germany to run shops under its supervision, *to the effect that* franchising agreements for the distribution of goods are not *per se* anticompetitive, *that* whether they are or not depends on their clauses, *that* those clauses necessary for the proper use of the franchisor's know-how and for protection of the identity and reputation of the franchisor's mark are acceptable under Article 85(1), *that* clauses which partition markets within the franchise system (intra-brand) are anti-competitive, *and that* Regulation 67/67 does not apply to such distribution franchising agreements.

Dr. Rainer Bechtold, of the Stuttgart Bar, for the plaintiff.
Dr. Eberhard Kolonko, for the defendant.
S. C. Margerie, for the French Government as *amicus curiae.*
Dr. Norbert Koch, Legal Adviser to the EC Commission for the Commission as *amicus curiae.*

The following case was referred to by the Court in its judgment:

1. *Etablissements Consten SA and Grundig-Verkaufs-GmbH* v. *EEC Commission* (56 & 58/64), 13 July 1966; [1966] ECR 299, [1966] CMLR 418. Gaz: 56/64

The following further cases were referred to by the Advocate General:

2. *S.V.P.N.A.S.* v. *Billy,* 19 June 1973 (Tribunal de Grande Instance, Bressuire).
3. *Maje Distribution,* 4 March 1974 (Tribunal Correctionnel, Paris).

307

4. *Morvan* v. *Intercontinents*, 28 April 1978 (Cour d'Appel, Paris).

5. *Telefleurs* v. *Interflora*, 10 May 1978 (Cour d'Appel de Paris): Cahiers de Droit de l'Enterprise No. 6-78.

6. Judgment of 22 April 1982 (Cour d'Appel, Douai): [1982] *Gazette du Palais* (Doctrine) 565.

7. *Felicitas* v. *Georges*, 19 June 1982 (Cour d'Appel, Colmar): [1982] Dalloz Jur. 553.

8. *Meierei-Zentrale*, 23 March 1982 (Bundesgerichtshof): [1982] WuW 781.

9. *GTE. Sylvania Inc* v. *Consumers Union of the United States Inc.*: 441 US 942.

10. *Italy* v. *EEC Council and Commission* (32/65), 13 July 1966: [1966] ECR 389, [1969] CMLR 39. Gaz: 32/65

11. *Société Technique Minière* v. *Maschinenbau Ulm GmbH* (56/65), 30 June 1966: [1966] ECR 235, [1966] CMLR 357. Gaz: 56/65.

12. *Brasserie de Haecht SA* v. *Wilkin* (No. 1) (23/67), 12 December 1967: [1967] ECR 407, [1968] CMLR 26. Gaz: 23/67.

13. *Bräuerei A. Bilger-Söhne GmbH* v. *Jehle* (43/69), 18 March 1970: [1970] ECR 127, [1974] 1 CMLR 382. Gaz: 43/69.

14. *De Norre* v. *NV Brouwerij Concordia* (47/76), 1 February 1977. [1977] ECR 65, [1977] 1 CMLR 378. Gaz: 47/76.

15. *SA Fonderies Roubaix-Wattrelos* v. *Soc. Nouvelles des Fonderies A. Roux* (63/75), 3 February 1976: [1976] ECR 111, [1976] 1 CMLR 538. Gaz: 63/75.

16. *Metro-SB-Grossmärkte GmbH & Co, KG* v. *EC Commission* (26/76), 25 October 1977: [1977] ECR 1875, [1978] 2 CMLR 1 Gaz: 26/76.

17. *L'Oreal NV & L'Oreal SA* v. *De Nieuwe AMCK PVba* (31/80), 11 December 1980: [1980] ECR 3775, [1981] 2 CMLR 235, Gaz: 31/80

18. *SA Lancombe and Cosparfrance Nederland BV* v. *Etos BV and Albert Heijn Supermart BV* (99/79), 10 July 1980: [1980] ECR 2511, [1981] 2 CMLR 164. Gaz: 99/79.

19. *Hasselblad (GB) Ltd* v. *EC Commission* (86/82), 21 February 1984: [1984] ECR 883, [1984] 1 CMLR 559. Gaz: 86/82.

20. *L.C. Nungesser KG and Kurt Eisele* v. *EC Commission* (258/78), 8 June 1982. [1982] ECR 2015, [1983] 1 CMLR 278. Gaz: 258/78

21. *Coditel SA* v. *Cine-Vog Films SA* (No. 2) (262/81), 6 October 1982: [1982] ECR 3381, [1983] 1 CMLR 49. Gaz: 262/81.

Table of Proceedings

Opinion of VerLoren van Themaat A.G., 19 June 1985
Judgment of the European Court of Justice, 28 January 1986
Award of the European Court of Justice, 28 January 1986
Language of the proceedings: German

Opinion of the Advocate General
(Mr Pieter VerLoren van Themaat)

1. Introduction

1.1. *The questions referred by the Bundesgerichtshof*
In a dispute with its French franchisor over the payment of arrears of royalties, a German franchisee successfully pleaded in the appeal court that the franchise agreement in question was void under EEC competition law. According to the appeal court

Article 85 of the EEC Treaty prohibits franchise agreements of the kind at issue in the proceedings, inasmuch as they contain restrictions of competition which are not exempted, under Article 85(3) and Regulation 67/67 of 22 March 1967, from the prohibition laid down in Article 85(1) of the Treaty.

The plaintiff in the main proceedings appealed against the judgment to the Bundesgerichtshof. The Bundesgerichtshof considered that the judgment of the appeal court raised questions of Community law, and therefore, by an order of 15 May 1984, referred a number of questions to the Court of Justice.

According to writers on the subject, distribution systems involving franchise agreements did not gain currency in the member-states until the early 1970s. Systems of that kind developed very quickly, however, and now constitute a significant proportion of distribution systems. Even if, in answering the questions referred, the Court restricts itself to franchise agreements having the characteristics of the agreements at issue, its answers will therefore have repercussions for the validity of tens of thousands of contracts. Furthermore, the importance of the Court's answers to the questions referred is reinforced by the fact that according to the written and oral observations which it presented in these proceedings the Commission has not yet adopted a clear policy in the matter.

The questions referred by the Bundesgerichtshof are as follows:

1. Is Article 85(1) of the EEC Treaty applicable to franchise agreements such as the contracts between the parties, which have as their object the establishment of a special distribution system whereby the franchisor provides to the franchisee, in addition to goods, certain trade names, trade marks, merchandising material and services?

2. If the first question is answered in the affirmative: Is Commission Regulation 67/67 of 22 March 1967 on the application of Article 85(3) of the Treaty to certain categories of exclusive dealing agreements (block exemption) applicable to such contracts?

3. If the second question is answered in the affirmative:

(a) Is Regulation 67/67 still applicable if several undertakings which, though legally independent, are bound together by commercial ties and form a single economic entity for the purposes of the contract participate on one side of the agreement?

(b) Does Regulation 67/67, and in particular Article 2(2)(c) thereof, apply to an obligation on the part of the franchisee to advertise solely with the prior agreement of the franchisor and in a manner that is in keeping with the latter's advertising, using the publicity material supplied by him, and in general to use the same business methods? Is it relevant in this connection that the franchisor's publicity material contains price recommendations which are not binding?

(c) Does Regulation 67/67, and in particular Articles 1(1)(b), 2(1)(a) and 2(2)(b) thereof, apply to an obligation on the part of the franchisee to confine the sale of the contract goods exclusively or at least for the most part to particular business premises specially adapted for the purpose?

(d) Does Regulation 67/67, and in particular Article 1(1)(b) thereof, apply to an obligation on the part of the franchisee – who is bound to purchase most of his supplies from the franchisor – to make the rest of his purchases of goods covered by the contract solely from suppliers approved by the franchisor?

(e) Does Regulation 67/67 sanction an obligation on the franchisor to give the franchisee commercial, advertising and professional support?

1.2 *The main provisions of the contracts entered into by the franchisee concerned*

As appears from the three contracts between the parties in the main proceedings, which were submitted to the Court at its request after the hearing, the franchisor binds itself:

Not to grant to any third party the right to use the trade mark 'Pronuptia de Paris' in the contract territory concerned (Hamburg, Oldenburg and Hannover respectively) (clause 1(1));

Not to open any other Pronuptia shops in the contract territory (clause 1(2));

Not to provide goods or services to third parties in the contract territory (clause 1(2);

To provide commercial assistance to the defendant in advertising, in establishing and stocking her shop, in training staff and with regard to sales techniques, fashions and products, purchasing and marketing and, very generally, to help the defendant to increase her turnover and profits (clause 3(1)).

The franchisee (who according to clause 3(5) remains the sole proprietor of her business, bear the risks of the business herself and her sole enjoyment of the profits) is obliged *inter alia*:

To sell the products covered by the agreement, using the trade name and trade mark Pronuptia de Paris, only in the shop referred to in clause 1, which must be equipped mainly for the sale of bridal fashions, in accordance with the brand image of Pronuptia de Paris (clauses 3(3) and 4(1));

To purchase from the franchisor 80 per cent of wedding dresses and accessories, together with a proportion of cocktail and evening dresses to be set by the defendant (clause 3(6));

To purchase the remaining wedding dresses and accessories and cocktail and evening dresses exclusively from suppliers approved by the franchisor (clause 3(6));

To pay to the franchisor a royalty of 10 per cent on all sales (including sales of articles not supplied by Pronuptia) during the validity of the contract (clause 5(1));

To refrain, during the period of validity of the contract and for one year after its termination, from competing in any way with a Pronuptia shop and in particular from engaging in the specialised sale of wedding dresses and accessories in the Federal Republic of Germany, in West Berlin or in an area where Pronuptia is already represented (clauses 6(6) and 9);

To make the sale of the goods covered by the contract her main objective (clause 6(6));

To carry on business in a specified location and to equip the premises primarily for the sale of bridal wear, in accordance with the image of Pronuptia de Paris and following its instructions (clauses 1(3), 3(3) and 4(1));

To carry on business, and in particular to sell products covered by the contract, under the trade mark and trade name Pronuptia de Paris, only in those premises (clauses 3(3) and 4(1));

To use the trade mark Pronuptia de Paris in her advertising only with the prior approval of the franchisor, to harmonise her advertising with that of Pronuptia, using the advertising material made available by Pronuptia with the recommended prices included therein (clauses 1(1) and 6(1));

To advertise, to distribute advertising material to the best of her abilities and in general to apply the business methods of the franchisor (clause 6(5));

Strictly to respect all industrial and commercial property rights of Pronuptia and to inform Pronuptia immediately of any infringements of those rights by third parties of which she might become aware (clause 14).

Pursuant to clause 6(1), Pronuptia is to recommend to the franchisee appropriate standard prices; both parties are to regard these standard prices as guidelines for retail sale (without prejudice to the franchisee's liberty to set prices herself).

1.3 *Plan of discussion*

As I have already pointed out, the answer to be given by the Court to the questions referred may have repercussions on the validity of other franchise agreements, and on the approach to be adopted by the Commission in this field. In the second part of this opinion I shall therefore make a number of general remarks regarding this system of distribution, which is relatively new to the Community. In particular, I shall examine to what extent a sufficient degree of certainty with regard to the content and legal nature of franchise agreements for the sale of products already exists in legislation, judicial decisions and academic literature, and especially within the trade organisations concerned, so as to enable the Court to deliver a more general ruling. I do not think that the wording of the questions referred by the Bundesgerichtshof prevents that. It precludes the Court only from ruling with regard to franchise agreements which have been current in the Community for a longer period (for example, in the hotel, café and restaurant sector) in relation to the provision of services or to manufacturing.

In the third part of my opinion I shall investigate the similarities and differences between franchise agreements, in particular franchise agreements such as that now at issue, and other distribution systems already current in Community legal practice, especially those which have been discussed in judgments of the Court, such as agency agreements, exclusive distribution or purchasing contracts, selective distribution systems, brewery contracts, and licencing agreements.

I shall also discuss what conclusions may be drawn in this case from previous decisions of the Court.

In the fourth part of my opinion I shall state how, in my view, the questions referred in this case should be answered.

2. General remarks regarding franchise agreements for the distribution of products

2.1 *The development of the franchise system as a new distribution system*

It appears from the already quite extensive literature on the subject, that the franchise system, based on earlier American experience, was introduced into the EEC in the early 1970s. Its subsequent development has however been rapid. In 1969 there were only a few franchise systems in the distribution sector in the Federal Republic of Germany. By 1978 the total number of franchise systems (including arrangements for the provision of services) had risen to 85 (with 11,000 franchisees); in May 1982 there were 200 such systems, with 120,000 franchisees and a total turnover of 100 thousand million DM, of which 65 to 75 thousand million DM was in the retail sector. In France (where franchising also began to develop in the early 1970s) there were more than 300 franchise systems in 1981 and 500 in 1985 (with 25,000 participating shops and 8 per cent of total retail sales). In the Netherlands there were 280 franchise systems in 1983. Similar development took place after 1970 in other member states.

2.2 *Legal characteristics of the franchise system according to academic opinion*

It appears from the literature, and was confirmed by the Commission at the hearing, that none of the member states have specific legislative provisions regarding franchise agreements. Furthermore, no precise definition of franchise agreements in general, or of franchise agreements for the distribution of products in particular, can be drawn from the case law that exists or from the relevant academic writing. The main elements of franchise systems for the distribution of products in all the member states examined seem however to be the following:

(1) although they remain independent and bear their own risks, franchisees are integrated to a considerable extent into the franchisor's distribution network;

(2) marketing strategy is based on a chain effect, brought about by the use, in return for payment, of a common business name, trade mark, sign or symbol, and – in many cases – uniform arrangement of shop premises;

(3) exclusive rights are granted to the franchisee within a defined area and for defined products, and exclusive rights that vary in scope are granted to the franchisor with regard to the supply or selection of the products to be sold by the franchisee. The writers on the subject also seem to be agreed that the term 'franchise agreement', as it is used in Europe, must be understood in a much more restricted sense than the original American term, which applied to many more distribution systems. As will appear from my remarks below, however, recent American literature also uses the term in a more restricted sense.

On the basis of a comparative legal study, Mr E. M. Kneppers-Heynert, in a recent article in the *Bijblad Industriële Eigendom*,[1] arrived at the following general description, which seems to me to be reasonably representative:

Franchising is a contractually governed form of commercial co-operation between independent undertakings, whereby one party, the franchisor, gives one or more other parties, the franchisees, the right to use his trade name or mark and other distinguishing features, in the sale of products or of services. The sale takes place on the basis of an exclusive marketing concept (system or formula) developed by the franchisor; in return, the franchisor receives royalties. The use of those rights by the franchisee is supervised by the franchisor in order to ensure uniform presentation to the public and uniform quality of the goods or services.

The European Code of Ethics for Franchising, drawn up by the European Franchising Federation and the eight national associations of which it is composed (six of them from EEC member states), was submitted to the Court at the hearing. It refers *inter alia* to the following six characteristics of a franchise agreement.[2]

1. 'Ownership [by the franchising firm (the Franchisor)] of a Company Name, a Trade Name, Initials or Symbols (possibly a Trade Mark) of a business or a service, *and* Know-how, which is made available to the franchised firm(s) – the Franchisee(s) . . . [and its] control of a range of Products and/or Services presented in a distinctive and original format, and which must be adopted and used by the franchisee(s), the format being based on a set of specific business techniques which have been previously tested, and which are continually developed and checked as regards their value and efficiency.'

2. 'Implicit in any Franchising Agreement is that there shall be a payment made in one form or another by the Franchisee to the Franchisor in recognition of the service supplied by the Franchisor in providing his name, format, technology and know-how.'

3. 'Franchising is therefore something more than a Sales Agreement or a Concession Agreement or a Licence Contract in that both parties accept important obligations to one another, over and above those established in a conventional trading relationship.'

4. 'The Franchisor will guarantee the validity of its rights over the brand, sign, initials, slogan, etc., and will grant the franchised firms unimpaired enjoyment of any of these which it makes available to them.'

5. 'The Franchisor will select and accept only those franchise candidates who possess the qualifications required by the franchise. All discrimination on the grounds of politics, race, language, religion or sex, will be excluded from the qualifications.'

6. 'The Franchise Contract will specify in particular the points set out below, it being understood that the provisions adopted will be consistent with national or Community law.

The method and conditions of payment of fees and royalties.

The duration of the Contract and the basis for renewal; the time and duration of notice.

The rights of the Franchisor prior to assignment by the Franchisee.

The definition of 'open territorial rights' granted to the Franchisee, including options (if granted) on adjoining territories.

Basis for distribution of the assets affected by the contract, if the Contract is terminated.

Distribution arrangements relative to supply of goods, including responsibility for transport and transport charges.

Terms of payment

Services provided by the Franchsor: Marketing assistance, Promotion, Advertising: Technology & Know-how: Managerial Administrative & Business Advice: Financial & Taxation Advice: Conditions under which these services to be provided and relevant charges: Training.

Obligations of the Franchisee: To provide Accounts & Operating Data: To receive Training and to accept Inspection Procedures.'

With regard to training and assistance the Code of Ethics also contains a large number of specific guidelines, of which only the following seem relevant to the assessment of franchise agreements of the kind referred to in the Code of Ethics in the light of Article 85 of the EEC Treaty:

The Franchisor will assist the Franchisee by providing guidance as to the operating costs and margins that he should be achieving at any given time in his business.

Any non-concurrence [sic] clause applicable after breach or termination of the contract, must be precisely stated and defined in the contract as regards its duration and territorial extent.

2.3 *Case law*

Only in France have the definitions formulated by the trade organisations been more or less adopted by the courts: see Tribunal de Grande Instance de Bressuire, 19 June 1973 (*S.V.P.N.A.S.* v. *Billy*); Tribunal Correctionnel de Paris, 4 March 1974 (*Maje Distribution*); Cour d'Appel de Paris (Fifth Chamber), 28 April 1978 (*Morvan* v. *Intercontinents*); Cour d'Appel de Paris, 10 May 1978 (*Telefleurs* v. *Interflora*[3]); Cour

---

1 [1984] B.I.E. 251.
2 *Translator's note:* What follows is taken from the published English version of the Code.
3 *Cahiers de Droit de l'Entreprise* No. 6–78.

d'Appel de Douai, 22 April 1982[4]; Cour d'Appel de Colmar (First Civil Chamber), 9 June 1982 (*Felicitas* v. *Georges*[5]). In those judgments it is striking that exclusive rights are not always regarded as essential (Cour d'Appel de Colmar and Cour d'Appel de Douai), but permission to use a trade name, signs and symbols and the application of uniform sales methods are so considered. In the absence of legislative definitions, moreover, franchise agreements are assessed exclusively on the basis of the provisions of the agreement at issue.

Within the Community it is only in the judgment of the Bundesgerichtshof of 23 March 1982 (*Meierei-Zentrale*[6]) that I have been able to find a judicial ruling on the competition law aspects of franchise agreements. In that judgment the prohibition of resale price maintenance laid down in section 15 of the Gesetz gegen Wettbewerbsbeschränkungen (German Restraint on Competition Act)[7] was considered applicable to a franchise agreement in which resale prices were fixed. In its 1981 report, *Full-line Sourcing and Tie-In Sales*, however, the British Monopolies and Mergers Commission did take the view that exclusive supply obligations could in certain circumstances be significant from the point of view of competition law.

As I have already pointed out, in the United States the term franchise agreement was initially used in a very wide sense. According to the more recent restricted use of the term (which served as a model for the European development) a franchise is defined as a licence from the owner of a trade mark or trade name permitting another to sell a product or service under that mark or name.[8]

In the United States, as in the United Kingdom, exclusive purchase obligations contained in franchise agreements are not automatically regarded as 'tying arrangements' prohibited by competition law. In appropriate market conditions they may however fall under that prohibition. Since the 1977 *Sylvania*[9] judgment the 'rule of reason' has been applied to vertical territorial restriction clauses in order to ascertain whether there is restriction of competition (in particular horizontal restriction). Contract provisions regarding resale prices are regarded as prohibited *per se* where it appears that the franchisor, not content with mere price recommendations, is attempting one way or another to force the franchisee to apply his suggestions or recommendations. In the *Sylvania* judgment the 'rule of reason' was applied to territorial restrictions on premises, such as those at issue in the Pronuptia case, notwithstanding the resulting restrictions on competition between retailers of Sylvania products. Despite the concomitant restrictions on 'intra-brand' competition, vertical restrictions on competition such as those at issue in the *Sylvania* case were regarded as beneficial for 'inter-brand' competition. Only in certain cases and on the basis of their actual economic consequences may such vertical restrictions of competition be held to be caught by the *per se* prohibition contained in American anti-trust legislation. Having regard to the later American legal practice the decisive question seems to be whether or not there is effective competition with other products on the relevant market. In speaking of the American practice I should point out that in the United States the problem peculiar to the EEC of separate national markets with prices which are often widely divergent does not exist. A single internal market was achieved long ago in the United States, so that the problem of obstacles to parallel imports does not arise.

2.4 *Conclusions*
On the basis of academic opinion and case law in the Community, on the basis of the views of the European Franchising Federation

and on the basis of the most recent American definitions of franchise agreements of the type at issue, I think that the significant distinguishing features of a franchise agreement for the sale of products are the independence of the undertakings involved, the existence of a licence for the use of a company name, trade name, emblem or other symbols, and for know-how in a broad sense, together with a uniform manner of presentation, the usual consideration being the payment of a royalty by the franchisee for the licences granted. In the American case law it seems that the market position of the undertakings concerned and the distinction between the vertical relationship between franchisor and franchisee and the horizontal relationship between each of the franchisees and their competitors are of particular importance in assessing such agreements from the point of view of competition law. Except in extraordinary market conditions, it seems that inter-branch competition is considered more important for the maintenance of effective competition than intra-brand competition. In the United States the imposition of fixed prices by franchisors seems to be regarded as automatically contrary to the prohibition of price agreements, just as it is in the Federal Republic of Germany. For the rest, the judicial practice in the United States and in three of the large member states of the EEC seems to be to judge each agreement on its own merits, taking into account its specific provisions and, in so far as competition aspects are to be dealt with, the specific circumstances of the relevant market. The last-mentioned factor is particularly relevant with regard to the various exclusivity clauses to be found in franchise agreements.

3. Similarities and differences between franchise agreements and other distribution systems considered in previous judgments of the Court

3.1 *Exclusive agents*
Since in the literature and the case law on franchise agreements the fact that the franchisee is an independent undertaking or that he deals in his own name and at his own risk is considered to be an essential characteristic of such agreements, I think, contrary to Pronuptia's contention, that comparison of this new type of agreement with agency agreements as referred to in the Commission communication of 24 December 1962[10] is not relevant to the questions referred by the Bundesgerichtshof. As appears from clause 3(5) of the agreements at issue, they do not differ in that respect from the general picture.

3.2 *Exclusive distribution agreeements*
The contracts in question are similar in more respects to exclusive distribution agreements. In particular the franchisee's exclusive purchase rights laid down in clause 1(1) and (2), and the franchisor's (restricted) exclusive supply rights laid down in clause 3(6) are clearly similar, at first sight, to the characteristics which determine the applicability of Regulation 67/67 of 22 March 1967 on the application of Article 85(3) of the Treaty to certain categories of exclusive dealing agreements. It is not

4 [1982] Gaz. Pal. (Doctrine) 565.
5 [1982] Dall. Jur. 553.
6 [1982] WuW 781.
7 For an English translation of the Restraint of Competition Act see [1982] 1 *Commercial Laws of Europe* 1.
8 Black's Law Dictionary, 5th Edition, 1979; von Kalinowski, *Antitrust Laws and Trade Regulation*, Vol 2, paragraph 6H.01/1981 supplement.
9 441 US 942.
10 JO 2921/62.

surprising, therefore, that in this case the national court raised separate questions on the issue of the applicability of that regulation.

With regard to the first question referred by the national court, regarding the applicability in principle of Article 85 to franchise agreements, I think a particularly relevant analogy may be made with the Court's statement of the problem in its judgment of 13 July 1966 in Case 32/65 (*Italy* v. *EEC Commission*[11]). In particular the third paragraph on page 407 of the Reports[12] may, subject to the differences which I shall discuss later between franchise agreements and 'classical' exclusive distribution agreements, be applied by analogy in answering the first question put by the national court.

In that paragraph it is stated:

'It is not possible either to argue that Article 85 can never apply to an exclusive dealing agreement on the ground that the grantor and the grantee thereof do not compete with each other. For the competition mentioned in Article 85(1) means not only any possible competition between the parties to the agreement, but also any possible competition between one of them and third parties. This must all the more be the case since the parties to such an agreement could attempt, by preventing or limiting the competition of third parties in the product, to set up or preserve to their gain an unjustified advantage detrimental to the consumer or the user, contrary to the general objectives of Article 85. Therefore even if it does not involve an abuse of a dominant position, an agreement between businesses operating at different levels may affect trade between member states and at the same time have as its object or effect the prevention, restriction or distortion of competition and thus fall under the prohibition in Article 85(1). Thus each of Articles 85 and 86 has its own objective and so soon as the particular features of either of them are present they apply indifferently to various types of agreements.'

In the following paragraph the Court refuses to compare exclusive distribution systems with agency agreements and other forms of integration in which a single undertaking incorporates its distribution network into its own organisation (and there is thus no question of agreements between several independent undertakings).

I think the particular importance of the passage quoted lies in the fact that it seems valid *mutatis mutandis* for all bilateral vertical agreements. Furthermore, like the American case law, it appears to treat possible restrictions on horizontal competition as decisive for the application of Article 85(1), rather than the mutual restrictions on their commercial freedom agreed to by the parties to a vertical relationship.

That conclusion is not affected by the Court's statement in the *Consten and Grundig* v. *EEC Commission*[13]) (with regard to the argument that the agreement in question had increased competition between similar products of different brands) that 'although competition between producers is generally more noticeable than that between distributors of products of the same make, it does not thereby follow that an agreement tending to restrict the latter kind of competition should escape the prohibition of Article 85(1) merely because it might increase the former. The Court went on to state that 'for the purpose of applying Article 85(1), there is no need to take account of the concrete effects of an agreement once it appears that it has as its object the prevention, restriction or distortion of competition'.

Closer examination of the *Grundig-Consten* judgment as a whole shows, I think, that there too the Court was particularly

concerned with restrictions of competition between the exclusive distributor and third parties (in that case, parallel importers of products of the same brand), that is, intentional restrictions on horizontal competition. In that respect I refer in particular to the Court's remarks at the bottom of page 342 and the top of page 343 of the Reports.[14] Greater importance is however ascribed also to horizontal 'intra-brand competition', especially where national markets are protected against parallel imports, than is the case in recent American judgments.

The necessary details were set out by the Court in a preliminary ruling of 30 June 1966 in Case 56/65 (*Société Technique Minière* v. *Maschinenbau Ulm*[15]), where it held that 'in order to decide whether an agreement containing a clause "granting an exclusive right of sale" is to be considered as prohibited by reason of its object or of its effect, it is appropriate to take into account in particular the nature and quantity, limited or otherwise, of the products covered by the agreement, the position and importance of the grantor and the concessionaire on the market for the products concerned, the isolated nature of the disputed agreement or, alternatively, its position in a series of agreements, the severity of the clauses intended to protect the exclusive dealership or, alternatively, the opportunities allowed for other commercial competitors in the same products by way of parallel re-exportation and importation.'

3.3 *Brewery contracts*

The exclusive distribution agreements which the Court has been called upon to consider mainly concerned exclusive importers, and according to statements made by the Commission at the hearing that was also generally true of exclusive distribution agreements notified to it. In particular they did not directly concern large numbers of retailers, as is the case here. In that respect the Court's judgments regarding brewery contracts may however be relevant. Building on a passage from the *Maschinenbau Ulm* judgment cited above, in the first *Haecht* judgment (Case 23/67[16]) the Court held with regard to brewery contracts of the kind in question (involving the obligation to purchase from one brewery only) that:

'. . . in order to examine whether it is caught by Article 85(1) an agreement cannot be examined in isolation from the . . . context, that is, from the factual or legal circumstances causing it to prevent, restrict or distort competition. The existence of similar contracts may be taken into consideration for this objective to the extent to which the general body of contracts of this type is capable of restricting the freedom of trade.'

If that paragraph, together with the paragraph which follows it, is applied by analogy to franchise agreements, I think it can be inferred that Article 85(1) is applicable where a franchisor from one member state has such a market position in a second member state that through his subsidiaries, if any, and by means of a number of franchise agreements with independent traders he significantly impedes the access to the market of other producers or wholesalers in that second member state.

It appears from paragraph 5 of the judgment of the Court in Case 43/69 (*Bilger* v. *Jehle*[17]) that in taking into account other

11 [1966] ECR 399, [1969] CMLR 39.
12 Page 63 (CMLR).
13 [1966] ECR 299 at 342, [1966] CMLR 418 at 473.
14 Page 473 (CMLR).
15 [1966] ECR 235 at 250, [1966] CMLR 357 at 375–376.
16 [1967] ECR 487 at 415 [1968] CMLR 26 at 40.
17 [1970] ECR 127, [1974] 1 CMLR 382.

comparable contracts not only contracts concluded by a large number of retailers with the same producer (or wholesaler) should be considered but also similar exclusive supply contracts concluded with other producers from the same *state*. In the case of brewery contracts the combined effects of such contracts between retailers and producers in the same member state may indeed result in partitioning of the market. As far as I have been able to ascertain the Court has until now only had to deal with brewery contracts between a brewery and its commercial clients in a single member state. I think, however, that in principle the partitioning of markets (or other forms of restriction on horizontal competition) may come about as a result of the combined effect of franchise agreements for similar products independently of the place where the producer or wholesaler is established.

On the subject of brewery contracts, I think that the judgment of the Court of 1 February 1977 in Case 47/76 (*De Norre* v. *Brouwerij Concordia*[18]) is also of some relevance to the second question referred by the Bundesgerischtshof in the present case. In that judgment the Court held that in spite of certain differences, recognised by the Court, between such agreements and traditional exclusive distribution agreements, for which Regulation 67/67 was originally enacted, the regulation also applies to brewery contracts, that is, 'agreements to which only two undertakings from one member state only are party, under which one party agrees with the other to purchase only from that other certain goods for resale and which do not display the features set out in Article 3 of Regulation 67/67 of the Commission . . . if, failing exemption, they would fall under the prohibition contained in Article 85(1) of the EEC Treaty'. That ruling was based in particular on a finding that 'agreements such as that in question fulfil the conditions laid down in Article 1(1)(b) of Regulation 67/67, as appears from paragraph 13, and on the previous judgments in the *Roubaix-Wattrelos* case (Case 63/75[19]), as appears from paragraphs 16 to 33.

Again with reference to that judgment, I think that in deciding whether or not it is possible to apply it by analogy in the present case the fact that the judgment is restricted to agreements to which only two undertakings from the same member state are party is not of vital significance. There is nothing in the judgment to indicate that the Court would not have considered Regulation 67/67 to be applicable to a brewery contract between a retailer in one member state and a brewery in another member state.

However, the judgment naturally leaves entirely open the question whether other characteristics of franchise agreements of the kind at issue in these proceedings do indeed militate against the applicability of Regulation 67/67. As I shall argue in more detail in the following part of my opinion, I think that is indeed the case.

3.4 *Selective distribution systems*
In these proceedings Pronuptia has also relied on the judgment of the Court in Case 26/76 (*Metro* v. *Commission*[20]). In paragraph 20 of that judgment the Court held that:

'In the sector covering the production of high quality and technically advanced consumer durables, where a relatively small number of large- and medium-scale producers offer a varied range of items which, or so consumers may consider, are readily interchangeable, the structure of the market does not preclude the existence of a variety of channels of distribution adapted to the peculiar characteristics of the various producers and to the requirements of the various categories of consumers.

On this view the Commission was justified in recognising that selective distribution systems constituted, together with others, an aspect of competition which accords with Article 85(1), provided that resellers are chosen on the basis of objective criteria of a qualitative nature relating to the technical qualifications of the reseller and his staff and the suitability of his trading premises and that such conditions are laid down uniformly for all potential resellers and are not applied in a discriminatory fashion.'

The mere fact that the franchise agreements in question contain not only qualitative but strict quantitative criteria means, in my view, that this last sentence is not applicable by analogy in this case.

The preceding sentence of paragraph 20 is indeed of some indirect relevance to this case, as is the second last sentence of paragraph 21, which reads as follows:

'For specialist wholesalers and retailers the desire to maintain a certain price level, which corresponds to the desire to preserve, in the interests of consumers, the possibility of the continued existence of this channel of distribution in conjunction with new methods of distribution based on a different type of competition policy, forms one of the objectives which may be pursued without necessarily falling under the prohibition contained in Article 85(1), and, if it does fall thereunder, either wholly or in part, coming within the framework of Article 85(3).'

The second sentence of paragragph 22 also seems to me to be of some relevance to the present case. It states that:

'the Commission must ensure that this structural rigidity [of prices, referred to in the preceding sentence] is not reinforced, as might happen if there were an increase in the number of selective distribution networks for marketing the same product.'

Finally, paragraph 24 states which provisions were not considered by the Commission to be restrictive of competition.

In its judgment in Case 31/80 (*L'Oreal* v. *De Neuwe Amck*[21]) the Court held in paragraph 17 that:

'When admission in a selective distribution network is made subject to conditions which go beyond simple objective selection of a qualitative nature and, in particular, when it is based on quantitative criteria, the distribution system falls in principle within the prohibition in Article 85(1), provided that, as the Court observed in its judgment of 30 June 1966 (*Société Technique Minière* v. *Maschinenbau GmbH*), the agreement fulfils certain conditions depending less on its legal nature than on its effects first on 'trade between member states' and secondly on 'competition'.'

The following two paragraphs define those conditions in further detail (according to paragraph 18, regard must be have in particular to the consequences of the agreement in question for the possibility of parallel imports, while paragraph 19 refers *inter alia* to the paragraphs of the first *Haecht* judgment quoted above). In the Lancome case (Case 99/79[22]) The Court had already taken the same position as that expressed in paragraph 17. The paragraphs referred to are also of some relevance to the present case.

---

18 [1977] ECR 65, [1977] 1 CMLR 378.
19 [1976] ECR 111, [1976] 1 CMLR 538.
20 [1977] ECR 1875, [1978] 2 CMLR 1.
21 [1980] ECR 3775, [1981] 2 CMLR 235.
22 [1980] ECR 2511, [1981] 2 CMLR 164.

With regard to the prohibited nature of a premises clause such as that contained in clause 4 of the agreements at issue, the Commission has also relied on paragraph 51 of the judgment of the Court of 21 February 1984 in Case 86/82 (*Hasselblad* v. *EC Commission*[23]). After confirming that quantitative selection criteria are prohibited, that paragraph states that 'Clause 28 of the dealer agreement allowed the applicant in fact to restrict the freedom of dealers, even authorised dealers, to establish their business in a location in which the applicant considers their presence capable of influencing competition between dealers'. Paragraph 52 goes on to confirm that that clause, among others, is prohibited.

3.5 *Licence agreements*

Since licences also play a key rôle in franchise agreements, the judgments of the Court in *Nungesser* (Case 258/78[24]) and *Coditel II* (Case 262/81[25]) are also relevant to this case. In paragraph 58 of the *Nungesser* judgment the Court concluded that 'having regard to the specific nature of the products in question . . . in a case such as the present, the grant of an *open* exclusive licence, that is to say, a licence which does not affect the position of third parties such as parallel importers and licencees for other territories, is not in itself incompatible with Article 85(1) of the Treaty'. In paragraph 61 of the same judgment the Court points out that it had consistently held 'that absolute territorial protection granted to a licensee in order to enable parallel imports to be controlled and prevented results in the artificial maintenance of separate national markets, contrary to the Treaty'. The key importance of that statement is confirmed in paragraph 78.

In the *Coditel II* case the Court held that: 'A contract whereby the owner of the copyright for a film grants an exclusive right to exhibit that film for a specific period in the territory of a member state is not, as such, subject to the prohibitions contained in Article 85 of the Treaty. It is, however, where appropriate, for the national court to ascertain whether, in a given case, the manner in which the exclusive right conferred by that contract is exercised is subject to a situation in the econonic or legal sphere where the object or effect of which is to prevent or restrict the distribution of films or to distort competition on the cinematographic market, regard being had to the specific characteristics of that market.' However, it is stated in paragraph 19 of that judgment, that the exercise of the exclusive right to exhibit a cinematographic film must not give rise *inter alia* to 'the possibility of charging fees which exceed a fair return on investment, or an exclusivity the duration of which is disproportionate. . . .' That paragraph in particular is relevant to the present case, since the basic issue concerns the royalties.

4. Proposed replies to the questions referred

4.1 *General remarks*

All the judgments referred to contain, I think, elements which should be borne in mind in answering the questions referred.

The type of franchise agreement referred to in the questions corresponds, in my view, to the description of franchise agreements contained in the literature and case law reviewed above, inasmuch as the right to the use of the company name and the mark or sign 'Pronuptia de Paris', the provision of know-how in a broad sense and then obligation to arrange the premises in accordance with the image of the franchisor and according to its instructions are central to those agreements (clauses 1(3), 3(1) and (3), 4(1) and 14). The fundamental importance of those factors is confirmed by the licence royalties agreed upon, in the amount of 10 per cent of the franchisee's total turnover (clause 5(1)). Under clause 3(5) of the agreement, however, the franchisee alone bears the risks of his business. From an economic point of view I think it is above all these characteristics which make franchise agreements extraordinarily attractive to franchisors as a new distribution method. To outside observers a shop set up and run in accordance with the contract resembles a subsidiary. Contrary to the case of a subsidiary, however, the franchisor does not have to carry any investment costs. Nor need he conduct any market studies in the place where the shop is to be established, since in the event of inadequate sales (in particular where costs are high and profits low) he bears no risk whatsoever, but is still entitled to the substantial royalty of 10 per cent of total turnover.

It would appear from the rapid development of the new system that it also has advantages for the franchisee; the main advantage is probably the fact that it gives him (usually exclusive) access to products of high quality the market for which is already established. The market for such products may in particular be established where, as in this case and in other franchise systems mentioned by the franchisee, the franchisor already has subsidiaries in other parts of the member state concerned, and the franchise system thus constitutes an extension of a system of subsidiaries which has already stood the test of the market.

For consumers, finally, the presence of a franchise system alongside other distribution systems may have some appeal for the same reasons, but also under the same conditions, as those set out in paragraph 20 of the *Metro* judgment with regard to selective distribution systems. In so far as the admission of franchisees to the system is made subject to quantitative restrictions (for example, by accepting only one franchisee in a defined area, as in this case), I consider, on the basis of the *L'Oreal*, *Lancôme* and *Hasselblad* judgments, that Article 85(1) must be held to be applicable in principle to the agreement in question, if the general conditions developed in the Court's judgments in Cases 32/65, 56 and 58/64, 56/65, 23/67, 43/69, 47/76, 26/76 and 258/78 (cited above) are fulfilled.

I think the following criteria relevant to the assessment of franchise agreements such as those at issue can be drawn from the judgments referred to:

(a) Since the important point for the application of Article 85(1) is, according to all the judgments referred to, the horizontal effects of vertical agreements (for instance the exclusion of certain competitors, such as parallel importers), it seems to me that the question whether or not a franchise agreement results in a fair division of costs and benefits as between franchisor and franchisee is not it itself relevant to the question whether Article 85(1) is applicable. The same is true in principle of specific obligations of the franchisee, such as the obligation of specialisation (clauses 3(3), 4(1) and 6(6)), the obligation to advertise (clauses 1(1) and 6(4) and (5)) and the obligation to set up and run the shop in a particular manner (clauses 3(3) and 4(1)). With regard to such vertical obligations I think Article 85(1) can only apply when it can be shown in a particular case that they cause injury to third parties (competitors, suppliers or purchasers), which will seldom be the case where there are adequate alternative chains of distribution for similar products.

(b) If the main issue is thus the 'horizontal' effects, or more correctly the results of the agreement for third parties, then,

23 [1984] ECR 883, [1984] 1 CMLR 559.
24 [1982] ECR 2015, [1983] 1 CMLR 278.
25 [1982] ECR 3281, [1983] 1 CMLR 49.

according to the judgments of the Court, particular attention must be paid to the questions whether (i) parallel imports remain possible (see for example the *Grundig-Consten, Bilger* and *Nungesser* judgments), (ii) whether, having regard to the market position of the suppliers concerned, access to the market for other suppliers or dealers is restricted (see the quotations from Cases 56/65, 23/67, 43/69, 26/76 and 31/80) and (iii) whether the agreement results in price increases (*Metro* and *Coditel II*) or involves price-fixing by means of contractual obligations or concerted practices on the part of the franchisor, its subsidiaries and its various franchisees.

With regard to this last criterion I am of the view, contrary to the American and German case law referred to, that the Court's judgments regarding resale price maintenance and other forms of price agreement need only be applied in a case where a party is in a position of economic strength on the local markets concerned, or where price maintenance is also applied by competitors. In the light of paragraphs 21 and 22 of the *Metro* judgment I think, too, that the strong upward influence on prices which will most certainly be exerted by the royalty provision in the agreement at issue should only be regarded as a ground for applying Article 85(1) where a franchisor from one member state plays a rôle of price leader or otherwise occupies a position of economic strength in a significant number of local markets in a second member state.

On the basis of those criteria I think it possible to give a sufficiently clear answer to the first question referred by the national court to enable that court to reach a decisioin on the facts of this case. I think a more concrete answer than that proposed by the Commission is desirable.

Since, for the reasons which I shall discuss, I am of the view that Regulation 67/67 is not applicable to franchise agreements such as those here at issue, Question 3 in the order for reference does not as such require an answer. In its judgment the Court might, however, wish to make it clear that obligations such as those referred to in subparagraphs (b), (d) and (e) of Question 3 cannot, except in unusual circumstances, be regarded as restrictions of competition within the meaning of Article 85(1).

4.2 *Answer to the first question*

In the light of the criteria which I have deduced from the judgments of the Court and summarised above, I think clauses 1(1) and (2), 3(3), 4(1), 5(1) and 6(1) and (6) of the agreements are of particular importance for the answer to the first question. Since according to the existing literature and case law, the nature of franchise agreements remains undefined, I would go so far as to suggest that the Court should restrict its answer to the first question asked by the Bundesgerichtshof to franchise agreements with the same content as those concluded between the parties in this case. It would of course be very useful for practitioners if the Court included a summary of those agreements in its judgment. The answer to the first question could in my view be as follows:

Article 85(1) of the EEC Treaty is applicable in franchise agreements such as those concluded between the parties in this case in so far as *inter alia*:

(a) they are concluded between a franchisor from one member state, or its subsidiary as referred to in Question 3(a), and one or more franchisees in one or more other member states, and

(b) by way of its subsidiaries and franchisees in one or more of those other member states or in a significant part of their territory the franchisor has a substantial share of the market for the relevant product;

and either

(c) the agreements prevent or restrict, or are intended to prevent or restrict, parallel imports of the products covered by the contract into the contract territory or exports of those products by the franchisee to other member states.

or

(d) the agreements result – in particular through the establishment of local or regional monopolies for the products covered by the contract, through royalty provisions and contractual provisions or concerted practices with regard to the setting of prices and on account of the absence of effective competition from similar products – in the setting of unreasonably high retail prices, that is to say, prices which could not be charged if effective competition existed, even allowing for the superior quality of the products covered by the contract.

In the wording of this answer I have made it clear that criteria (c) and (d) are to be regarded as alternative criteria. In accordance with the judgments of the Court, criterion (c) places the emphasis on the absolute territorial protection of national markets, which cannot fail to result in significant restriction of horizontal competition unless the market shares involved are negligible. In criterion (d), on the other hand, the accent is placed on the prevention of monopolistic price increases, which as a rule will only be possible when the party concerned has a substantial share of the relevant local or regional markets and where there is no downward influence on prices as a result of other means of distribution for similar products.

4.3 *Answer to the second and third questions*

I agree with the Commission and the French Government that block exemption for franchise agreements is desirable. I consider it particularly desirable having regard to the frequency with which they now occur and their generally beneficial nature; as a rule, it is only in particular market circumstances (in particular, the absence of competing distribution systems) or where they are applied in a particular manner that the intentional or unintentional restriction of competition associated with them may stand in the way of exemption under Article 85(3) of the EEC Treaty.

As a rule franchise agreements will presumably benefit consumers by improving the distribution of products, since they make possible the rapid penetration of new products or products with particular qualities onto discrete local retail markets. It is the task of the Commission first to acquire the necessary experience by adopting a number of individual decisions in representative cases, and then, in a block-exemption regulation in accordance with the four conditions of Article 85(3), to lay down the conditions in which the positive effects of franchise agreements can be attributed a greater weight than the restrictions on competition which may be considered essential to their positive effect.

Like the Commission and the French Government I am also of the view, however, that Regulation 67/67 cannot be considered applicable to franchise agreements such as those now at issue. For me the following considerations were decisive in arriving at that conclusion.

In the first place, it is clear that when Regulation 67/67 was adopted franchise agreements for the distribution of products within the Community were still extremely rare; during the preparation of the regulation, therefore, no consideration could be given to the specific problems which they raise. The problems to which consideration was given in preparing that regulation, and in regard to which sufficient experience had been gained, as required by the fourth recital in the preamble to Regulation

19/65, related in fact only to exclusive importers. Similarly, according to the Commission's answer to a question which I posed at the hearing, during the preparation of the recent block exemptions for exclusive distribution and exclusive purchasing agreements their application to franchise agreements was not advocated by interested parties or by government experts.

Secondly, on the basis of the literature and case law referred to and the views of the franchising organisations mentioned above, I think that franchise agreements are predominantly characterised by the effort, by means of licences for trade names, trade marks, signs or symbols and know-how in a broad sense and by other provisions, to assimilate the commercial practices of the franchisee as closely as possible to those of the franchisor or its subsidiaries. The franchisee, for his part, is entirely responsible for the risks of his business and must pay a royalty, in this case a substantial one, to the franchisor. Exclusive supply and purchase obligations play only a subordinate rôle, and from the point of view of competition policy they can only be assessed in the context of the objective pursued, namely the thorough integration of franchisees in the franchisor's network of uniformly managed retail outlets. In Regulation 67/67, on the other hand, it is licensing agreements which are subordinate in nature.

Thirdly, franchise agreements with the characteristics of those in question also differ substantially from brewery contracts (to which the Court has held Regulation 67/67 to be applicable) inasmuch as they result in the formation of rigid local or regional monopolies for the products concerned. In that regard I refer in particular to clause 1 of the agreements which were submitted. Furthermore, the difference referred to in the previous paragraph between those agreements and exclusive distribution agreements also exists in relation to brewery contracts.

Fourthly, I think that the application of Regulation 67/67 is excluded by Article 3(b) of that regulation. Franchise agreements such as those here at issue give the franchisee absolute territorial protection and make it difficult for dealers to obtain supplies of the products covered by the contract from other dealers within the Common Market. In addition to clause 1, which I have already mentioned, I refer in that regard to clauses 3(3) and (6) and 4(1) of the agreements.

For those four reasons I propose that the Court should answer the second question asked by the national court in the following manner:

Regulation 67/67 on the application of Article 83(3) of the Treaty to certain categories of exclusive dealing agreements is not applicable to franchise agreements with a content similar to those concluded between the parties in this case.

It would not then be necessary to reply to the third question referred by the national court. However, the answer which I propose to the first question may, perhaps in combination with remarks which the Court may wish to make in its judgment regarding clauses of the agreement which do not restrict competition, enable the national court to decide which of the provisions of the agreement referred to in the third question must be considered relevant for the application of Article 85(1).

JUDGMENT

[1] By order dated 15 May 1984, received by the court on the 25 June following, the Bundesgerichtshof, in accordance with Article 127 of the EEC Treaty, asked a number of questions relating to the interpretation of Article 85 EEC and of Commission Regulation 67/67 of 22 March 1967 concerning the application of Article 85(3) to categories of exclusive dealing agreements,[26] so that it should be determined whether these provisions apply to franchise agreements.

[2] These questions have arisen in the course of proceedings between the firm Pronuptia de Paris GmbH of Frankfurt am Main (hereinafter called the 'franchisor'), a subsidiary of a French company of the same name, and Mrs Schillgallis of Hamburg who runs a business under the name Pronuptia de Paris (hereinafter called the 'franchisee'). The litigation concerns the obligation of the franchisee to pay the franchisor arrears of fees based on its sales figures for 1978 to 1980.

[3] The French parent company of the franchisor distributes under the name 'Pronuptia de Paris' wedding dresses and other clothes worn at weddings. Distribution of these products in the Federal Republic of Germany is carried out in part through shops run directly by its subsidiary and in part through shops belonging to independent retailers tied to the subsidiary by franchise agreements, executed in its name by the subsidiary acting both on behalf of the parent company and on its own behalf.

[4] By three agreements signed on 24 February 1980 the franchisee obtained a franchise for three separate areas, Hamburg, Oldenburg and Hanover. The terms of these three agreements are for practical purposes identical. More precisely, they include the following provisions:

[5] The franchisor:

— grants to the franchisee the exclusive right to use the mark 'Pronuptia de Paris' for sale of its products and services for a particular territory outlined in a map attached to the agreement, as well as the right to advertise in that territory;
— agrees not to open another Pronuptia shop in the territory in question and not to provide any product or service to third parties in that territory;
— agrees to assist the franchisee in the commercial and promotional aspects of his business, in the setting up and designing of the shop, in the training of personnel, sales techniques, in fashion and product advice, sales, marketing, and generally in all respects in which, in the experience of the franchisee, it could contribute towards the improvement of the turnover and profitability of the franchisee.

[6] The franchisee, who remains the sole proprietor of its business and bears the associated risks, is required:

— to use the name Pronuptia de Paris and sell merchandise under that name only in the shop specified in the agreement. The shop must be arranged and decorated principally for sale of wedding-related products, according to the directions of the franchisor, with the purpose of protecting the worth of the mark used by the Pronuptia distribution chain. The shop may not be transferred to another site or redesigned without the franchisor's approval.
— to purchase from the franchisor 80 per cent of its requirements of wedding dresses and accessories as well as a proportion to be determined by the franchisor himself of cocktail dresses and formal wear and to obtain the remainder only from suppliers approved by the franchisor;
— to pay to the franchisor, in consideration of the benefits provided, an initial payment for the contract territory of 15,000 DM and, for the duration of the contract, a royalty equalling 10 per cent of the turnover realised by the sale of both Pronuptia products and all other merchandise; evening dresses purchased

26 JO 849/67, [1967] OJ Spec. Ed. 10.

from suppliers other than Pronuptia are not, however, included in this figure;

— to take account, without prejudice to its freedom to fix its own retail prices, of the recommended resale prices proposed by the franchisor;

— to advertise in the licensed territory only with the consent of the franchisor and in any case to make such advertising conform to that carried out on a national or international level by the franchisor, to disseminate as conscientiously as possible the catalogues and other promotional aids supplied by the franchisor, and generally to use the commercial methods communicated by the franchisor to the franchisee;

— to make its principal objective the sale of wedding articles;

— to refrain from any act of competition with a Pronuptia business, and in particular not to open any business with an identical or similar purpose to that covered by the agreement nor to participate, directly or indirectly, in such a business in the territory of the Federal Republic of Germany inclusive of West Berlin or in any territory where Pronuptia is represented in any way whatsoever, for the duration of the agreement and for one year following termination;

— not to transfer to third parties the rights and obligations arising out of the contract nor to sell the business without prior agreement of the franchisor, it being understood that the franchisor will grant his approval if the transfer is required for health reasons and the new contracting party can establish that he is solvent and prove that he is not in any form whatsoever a competitor of the franchisor.

[7] The first instance court ruled that the franchisee must pay 158,502 DM arrears of royalties due on its turnover in the years 1978–1980. The franchisee appealed against this judgment in the Oberlandesgericht, Frankfurt am Main, claiming it was not required to pay the arrears because the agreement infringed Article 85(1) of the Treaty and did not benefit from the group exemption for exclusive dealing agreements provided by Regulation 67/67. In a judgment of 2 December 1982, the Oberlandesgericht accepted the franchisee's arguments. It found that the reciprocal obligations of exclusivity constituted restrictions on competition within the Common Market, since the franchisor could only purchase and resell other merchandise from other member states in a very limited way. Since no exemption under Article 85(3) applied to them, held the Oberlandesgericht, these agreements must be considered void under Article 85(2). With respect to the issue of exemption, the Oberlandesgericht considered in particular that it was not necessary for it to decide if franchise agreements are in principle excluded from the application of Regulation 67/67. In fact, according to the Oberlandesgericht, the agreements at issue in any event involved undertakings going beyond the scope of Article 1 of the regulation and constituted restrictions on competition not covered by Article 2.

[8] The franchisor applied for review of this judgment to the Bundesgerichtshof, requesting reinstatement of the first instance court's judgment. The Bundesgerichtshof concluded that its judgment on the application depended on an interpretation of Community law. It requested, therefore, that the Court issue a preliminary ruling on the following questions:

1. Is Article 85(1) of the EEC Treaty applicable to franchise agreements such as the contracts between the parties, which have as their object the establishment of a special distribution system whereby the franchisor provides to the franchisee, in addition to

goods, certain trade names, trade marks, merchandising material and services?

2. If the first question is answered in the affirmative: Is Regulation No. 67/67/EEC of the Commission of 22 March 1967 on the application of Article 85(3) of the Treaty to certain categories of exclusive dealing agreements (block exemption) applicable to such contracts?

3. If the second question is answered in the affirmative:

(a) Is Regulation No. 67/67/EEC still applicable if several undertakings which, though legally independent, are bound together by commercial ties and form a single economic entity for the purposes of the contract participate on one side of the agreement?

(b) Does Regulation 67/67/EEC, and in particular Article 2(2)(c) thereof, apply to an obligation on the part of the franchisee to advertise solely with the prior agreement of the franchisor and in a manner that is in keeping with the latter's advertising, using the publicity material supplied by him, and in general to use the same business methods? Is it relevant in this connection that the franchisor's publicity material contains price recommendations which are not binding?

(c) Does Regulation No. 67/67/EEC, and in particular Articles 1(1)(b), 1(1)(a) and 2(b) thereof, apply to an obligation on the part of the franchisee to confine the sale of the contract goods exclusively or at least for the most part to particular business premises specially adapted for the purpose?

(d) Does Regulation 67/67/EEC, and in particular Article 1(1)(b) thereof, apply to an obligation on the part of a franchisee – who is bound to purchase most of his supplies from the franchisor – to make the rest of his purchases of goods covered by the contract solely from suppliers approved by the franchisor?

(e) Does Regulation No. 67/67/EEC sanction an obligation on the franchisor to give the franchisee commercial, advertising and professional support?

On the first question

[9] The firm Pronuptia de Paris GmbH of Frankfurt am Main, the franchisor, has argued that a system of franchise agreements makes it possible to combine the advantages of a form of distribution which presents a homogeneous face to the public (like that of subsidiaries) with distribution by independent retailers themselves bearing the risks of sale. This system, made up of a network of vertical agreements intended to guarantee a uniform image to the outside world, reinforces the franchisor's ability to compete on the horizontal plane, that is to say in relation to other forms of distribution. The system thus makes it possible for an enterprise that otherwise would not have the necessary financial means at its disposal to create a supra-regional distribution network, a network comprising, as franchisees, small enterprises which keep their autonomy. In view of these advantages Article 85(1) cannot apply unless the franchise agreements involve restrictions on the freedom of the contracting parties which go beyond those demanded by the nature of a franchise system. Exclusive supply and stocking provisions, to the degree that they aim to ensure a uniform range of goods, obligations to use uniform promotional materials, uniform layout of the business premises and the prohibition on selling in other shops the products delivered under the agreement are inherent in the very nature of the franchise agreement and are thus outwith the scope of Article 85(1).

[10] Mrs Schillgallis, the franchisee, proposes that the first question should be answered in the affirmative. The contracts in question are characterised by territorial protection given to the

318 EUROPEAN FRANCHISING

franchisee. They cannot be assimilated to agreements with commercial agents, given that unlike the latter franchisees act in their own name and on their own account and shoulder the marketing risks. The system of franchise agreements in question involves noticeable restrictions on competition, given the fact that Pronuptia is, as it itself proclaims, the French world leader in the wedding dress and accessory market.

[11] The French government, for its part, contends that Article 85(1) can be applied to franchise agreements which are contracts concerning distribution of a product concluded with independent businessmen, but that it does not necessarily apply, given the positive aspects of such agreements.

[12] The Commission maintains that the scope of Article 85(1) is not limited to specific types of contracts. When its conditions are met, therefore, Article 85(1) applies equally to those agreements which, apart from delivery of merchandise, have as their object the licensing of a trade name and trade mark, whether registered or not, or of the provision of services.

[13] We should begin by noting that franchise agreements, whose legality has not hitherto been considered by this Court, present enormous diversity. From the arguments before the Court, it is necessary to distinguish between different types of franchise, particularly: service franchise agreements, by which the franchisee offers services under the sign and the trade name, or indeed the trade mark, of the franchisor and complies with the franchisor's directives; production franchise agreements by which the franchisee himself manufactures, according to the instructions of the franchisor, products which he sells under the franchisor's trade mark; and finally, distribution franchise agreements by which the franchisee restricts himself to the sale of certain products in a shop carrying the mark of the franchisor. The Court will only consider this third type of agreement which conforms to that expressly referred to in the question from the national court.

[14] It should next be observed that the compatibility of distribution franchise agreement with Article 85(1) cannot be assessed in the abstract but depends on the clauses contained in such contracts. In order to give a fully useful response to the national court this Court will consider those contracts which have a content similar to that decribed above.

[15] In a distribution franchise system such as this, an enterprise which has established itself as a distributor in a market and which has thus been able to perfect a range of commercial methods gives independent businessmen the chance, at a price, of establishing themselves in other markets by using its mark and the commercial methods that created the franchisor's success. More than just a method of distribution, this is a manner of exploiting financially a body of knowledge, without investing the franchisor's own capital. At the same time this system gives businessmen who lack the necessary experience access to methods which they could otherwise only acquire after prolonged effort and research and allows them also to profit from the reputation of the mark. Distribution franchise agreements are thus different from either dealership agreements or those binding approved resellers appointed under a system of selective distribution which involve neither use of a single mark nor application of uniform commercial methods nor payment of royalties in consideration of the advantage thus conferred. Such a system, which permits the franchisor to take advantage of his success, is not by itself restrictive of competition. For it to function two conditions must be satisfied.

[16] First, the franchisor must be able to communicate his know-how to the franchisees and provide them with the necessary assistance in putting his methods into effect, without running the risk that this know-how and assistance will aid his competition, even indirectly. It thus follows that those clauses which are essential to prevent this risk do *not* constitute restrictions of competition in the sense of Article 85(1). These include the prohibition on the franchisee opening, for the duration of the franchise or for a reasonable period after its termination, a shop with an identical or similar purpose in an area where he could be in competition with one of the members of the network. The same applies to the obligation on the franchisee not to sell his shop without the prior approval of the franchisor: this clause serves to ensure that the benefit of the know-how and assistance provided does not go indirectly to a competitor.

[17] Secondly, the franchisor must be able to take appropriate measures to preserve the identity and reputation of the network which is symbolised by the mark. It thus follows that those clauses which provide a basis for such control as is indispensable for this purpose also do *not* constitute restrictions of competition in the sense of Article 85(1).

[18] This covers then the obligation on the franchisee to apply the commercial methods developed by the franchisor and to utilise the know-how provided.

[19] This is also the case with the franchisee's obligation only to sell the merchandise covered by the agreement in premises set up and decorated according to the franchisor's specifications, which have as their purpose to guarantee a uniform image corresponding to specified requirements. The same requirements apply to the location of the shop, the choice of which is apt to affect the reputation of the network. This explains why the franchisee cannot transfer his shop to another location without the consent of the franchisor.

[20] The prohibition on the franchisee assigning the rights and obligations under the contract without the assent of the franchisor safeguards the franchisor's right freely to choose its franchisees, whose qualifications as traders are essential for establishing and preserving the reputation of the network.

[21] Thanks to the control exercised by the franchisor over the selection of goods offered by the franchisee, the public can find at each franchisee's shop merchandise of the same quality. It can be impractical in certain cases, such as the field of fashion goods, to formulate objective quality specifications. Enforcing such specifications can also, because of the large number of franchisees, impose too great a cost on the franchisor. A clause prescribing that the franchisee can *only* sell products provided by the franchisor or by suppliers selected by him must, in these circumstances, be considered *necessary for the protection of the reputation of the network*. It must not, however, operate to prevent the franchisee from obtaining the products from other franchisees.

[22] Finally, since advertising contributes to defining the image which the public has of the mark, which symbolises the network, a clause which requires all advertising by the franchisee to be submitted for the approval of the franchisor is likewise essential for the preservation of the identity of the network, provided that the approval only relates to the nature of the advertising.

[23] It should on the other hand be stressed that, far from being necessary for the protection of the know-how provided or for the preservation of the identity and reputation of the network, certain clauses *do restrict competition between its members*. That is the case with clauses which effect a division of markets between the franchisor and franchisees or between franchisees or which prevent price competition between them.

[24] The attention of the national court should, in this regard, be drawn to the clause which requires the franchisee to sell the merchandise covered by the agreement *only* at the location designated in the contract. This clause prohibits the franchisee from opening a second shop. Its real significance emerges if one juxtaposes it with the undertaking by the franchisor to the franchisee, to ensure to him exclusivity of use of the licensed mark in a given territory. In order to honour the promise thus made to a franchisee the franchisor must not only refrain from establishing itself in the territory but must also secure undertakings from the other franchisees not to open another shop outside their own. The juxtaposition of clauses of this type results in a kind of market partitioning between the franchisor and the franchisees or among the franchisees and thus restricts competition within the network. As follows from the judgment in *Consten and Grundig* v. *EEC Commission*,[27] this type of restriction constitutes a restriction on competition in the sense of Article 85(1), since it concerns a mark that is already widely known. It is certainly possible that a prospective franchisee may not want to take the risk of joining the chain and making his investment, paying a relatively high entry fee and agreeing to pay a considerable annual fee, if he were not in a position to hope that his business would be profitable thanks to a certain amount of protection from competition by the franchisor and other franchisees. This consideration can, however, be significant only in the context of an examination of the agreement in the light of the conditions of Article 85(3).

[25] Although the clauses which restrict the franchisee's ability to fix his own prices in complete freedom are restrictive of competition, it is not so where the franchisor has merely communicated to the franchisees recommended prices, on condition however that there is no concerted practice between the franchisor and the franchisee or between franchisees with a view to the actual application of such prices. It is for the national court to determine whether this condition has been satisfied.

[26] Finally, it should be said that distribution franchise agreements which contain clauses effecting a partioning of markets between franchisor and franchisees or between franchisees are *per se* capable of affecting trade between member states, even if they are concluded between enterprises established in the same member state, to the extent that they prevent the franchisees from setting themselves up in another member state.

[27] In view of the above considerations, the first question must be answered as follows:

1. The compatibility of distribution franchise agreements with Article 85(1) depends on the clauses contained in the agreements and on the economic context in which they are included;

2. The clauses that are indispensable to prevent the know-how and assistance provided by the franchisor from benefiting competition do not constitute restrictions of competition within the meaning of Article 85(1);

3. The clauses which implement the control essential for the preservation of the identity and the reputation of the organisation represented by the trade mark also do not constitute restrictions on competition within the meaning of Article 85(1);

4. The clauses which effect a partitioning of markets between franchisor and franchisee or between franchisees constitute restrictions of competition within the meaning of Article 85(1);

5. The fact that the franchisor has communicated suggested prices to the franchisees does not constitute a restriction on competition, on condition that there has not been a concerted practice between franchisor and franchisees or between the franchisees with a view to effective application of these prices;

6. Distribution franchise agreements which contain clauses effecting a partitioning of markets between franchisor and franchisee or between franchisees are capable of affecting trade between member states.

On the second question

[28] The second question, which was only asked in the event of an affirmative reply to the first, deals with the question whether Commission Regulation 67/67 of 22 March 1967 on the application of Article 85(3) of the Treaty to certain categories of exclusive dealing agreements comes into play in distribution franchise agreements. In light of the considerations set out above regarding those clauses which effect a partitioning of the market between franchisor and franchisees and between franchisees, this question retains some relevance and we should therefore consider it.

[29] The firm Pronuptia de Paris, the franchisor, urges the Court to answer the second question in the affirmative. Regulation 67/67 should apply to exclusive distribution and supply undertakings regardless of whether such undertakings occur in agreements which also license a trade mark or other distinctive marks of the enterprise. In a franchise agreement, the exclusive purchase and distribution obligations offer the very advantages set out in the sixth recital of Regulation 67/67. Clauses other than those envisaged by Article 2 of Regulation 67/67 would present no obstacle to application of the exemption, since they did not restrain competition within the meaning Article 85(1).

[30] Mrs Schillgallis, the franchisee, argues that Regulation 67/67 does not apply to franchise agreements. First, this regulation was devised by the Commission on the basis of its experience in the period before its adoption, experience which was limited to dealership agreements. Second, the franchisor has clearly more powers over the franchisee than the grantor of a dealership over his distributor. Third, the restriction on competition inherent in franchise agreements also occurs on the horizontal level, since the franchisor itself generally operates its own subsidiaries which function at the same stage of the economic process as the franchisees.

[31] The French government confines itself to stating that Regulation 67/67 does not appear to be applicable to this type of contract.

[32] The Commission admits that it does not have sufficient experience to define the concept of a franchise agreement. It adds that the purpose of Regulation 67/67 was not to exempt restrictions on competition contained in agreements licensing trade marks, trade names or symbols, licences which, with the communication of know-how and commercial assistance, appear to it to be the essential element in a franchise agreement. However, if licensing agreements of this sort contain accords on the supply of goods for resale, and if these supply accords can be severed from the licensing accords, Regulation 67/67 could apply to supply agreements, insofar as its conditions are met. In this respect the exclusive dealer cannot, in that capacity, submit to restrictions on competition other than those specified in Article 1(1) or Article 2(1) of the regulation. In the agreements the subject of the Bundesgerichtshof's questions, the location clause contained in the franchise agreement establishes such a close relationship between the elements of exclusive distribution and of licensing in the franchise agreement that these elements constitute an indivisible whole, making the group exemption inapplicable

27 Cases 56 and 58/64, [1966] ECR 299, [1966] CMLR 418.

even to that part of the contract relating to the grant of exclusive selling rights.

[33] It is appropriate in this regard to note several elements in the text of Regulation 67/67. First, the category of agreements benefiting from the group exemption is defined by reference to reciprocal (or non-reciprocal) undertakings for distribution and purchase and not by reference to elements such as the use of a common mark, the application of uniform commercial methods and the payments of royalties in consideration of the benefits granted, which are characteristic of distribution franchise agreements. Second, the very terms of Article 2 expressly deal only with exclusive sales agreements, the nature of which, as set out above, is different from that of a distribution franchise agreement. Third, the same Article lists the restrictions and obligations which can be imposed on an exclusive distributor without referring to those which can be stipulated as obligations of the other contracting party; while in the case of a distribution franchise agreement the obligations assumed by the franchisor, especially the obligations to communicate know-how and to assist the franchisee, assume a very special importance. Fourth, the list of obligations burdening an exclusive distributor set out in Article 2(2) permits inclusion of neither the obligation to pay royalties nor the clauses which set up the control system indispensible for preserving the identity and reputation of the network.

[34] We may conclude therefore that Regulation 67/67 is not applicable to distribution franchise agreements such as those examined in the course of these proceedings.

On the third question
[35] In view of the answers provided to the national court's question, the third question has become irrelevant.

Costs
[36] The costs incurred by the French Government and by the Commission of the European Communities, which have submitted observations to the Court, are not recoverable. As these proceedings are, in so far as the parties to the main action are concerned, in the nature of a step in the action pending before the national court, the decision as to costs is a matter for that court.

On these grounds, THE COURT, in answer to the questions referred to it by the Bundesgerichtshof, by order dated 15 May 1984, *hereby rules*:

1. (a) The compatibility of distribution franchise agreements with Article 85(1) depends on the clauses contained in the contracts and on the economic context in which they have been included;

(b) Clauses that are indispensable to prevent the know-how and assistance provided to the franchisee by the franchisor from benefiting the franchisor's competitors do not constitute restrictions of competition within the meaning of Article 85(1);

(c) Clauses which implement the control indispensable for preservation of the identity and the reputation of the system symbolised by the trade mark also do not constitute restrictions on competition within the meaning of Article 85(1);

(e) The fact that the franchisor has transmitted suggested prices to the franchisees does not constitute a restriction of competition, on condition that there has not been a concerted practice between franchisor and franchisees or between franchisees regarding putting these prices into effect;

(f) Distribution franchise agreements which contain clauses effecting a division of markets between franchisor and franchisee or between franchisees are capable of affecting trade between member states.

2. Regulation 67/67 is not applicable to distribution franchise agreements such as those which have been considered in this proceeding.

Re the Agreements of Davide Campari-Milano SpA

Before the Commission of the European Communities
(78/253/EEC) [1978] 2 CMLR 397

Signed by Mr Commissioner Vouel, 23 December 1977*

Restrictive practices. Trade marks. Exclusive licences. An exclusive trade mark licence is a restriction of competition under Article 85(1) EEC. [51]

Restrictive practices. Exclusive licensees. Competing products. An obligation on exclusive licensees not to handle competing products for the duration of the licensing agreement restricts competition within Article 85(1) EEC. [53]

Restrictive practices. Exclusive licensees. Territorial restrictions. Active and passive sales. A ban on the grantor and grantees of exclusive licences engaging in active sales outside their allotted territories restricts competition under Article 85(1) EEC, even though passive sales are permitted. [54]

Restrictive practices. Licensees. Diplomatic customers. An obligation on the licensees of an alcoholic drink, Campari, to supply not their own product but that of the grantor to diplomatic customers, ships' victuallers and other organisations with duty-free facilities restricts competition under Article 85(1) EEC. [55]

Restrictive practices. Export prohibition. A prohibition on licensees of a product exporting that product outside the Common Market does not affect competition under Article 85(1) EEC where reimportation into the EEC of previously exported goods seems unlikely because of the economic factors applicable to the situation. [60]

Restrictive practices. Export prohibition. EFTA states. A prohibition on licensees exporting to Free Trade Agreement countries is permissible unless there is a practical likelihood of the exported goods being reimported into the Common Market. [60]

Restrictive practices. Quality control measures. Restriction of a manufacturing licence to those plants which are capable of guaranteeing the quality of the product are not covered by Article 85(1) EEC so long as it does not go beyond a legitimate concern for quality control, especially where the maintenance of quality is linked to trade mark right. [61]

Restrictive practices. Quality control. Secret manufacturing process. The obligation on licensees of a manufacturing process and related trade mark to follow the licensor's instructions relating to the manufacture of the product and the quality of the ingredients and to buy certain secret raw materials from the licensor is compatible with Article 85(1) EEC. Where the composition of the components is the factor which determines the particular characteristics of the end product and is a trade secret, the licensor cannot be required under Community law to reveal the secret to its licensees. [62]

Restrictive practices. Trade secrets. Know-how. An obligation on licensees not to divulge the licensed manufacturing process to third parties is compatible with Article 85(1) EEC. [63]

Restrictive practices. Promotion obligations. An obligation on licensees to maintain continuous contact with customers and to spend a standard minimum sum on advertising the licensed product is compatible with Article 85(1) EEC where it is not unduly restrictive on the other activities of the licensees. [64]

Restrictive practices. Licences. Assignment. A prohibition on licensees assigning their licence is compatible with Article 85(1) EEC. By banning assignments, the licensor is simply safeguarding its freedom to select its licensees; when it enters into an agreement the identity of the other party is highly material to it and it must remain free to decide with whom it will deal. [65]

Restrictive practices. Arbitral awards. The EC Commission, in granting an exemption under Article 85(3) EEC, required to be informed of any relevant arbitral awards 'as there is a risk that the agreements might be interpreted without regard for this decision, so that the Commission might have to amend it. There is a greater risk at arbitration than in the ordinary courts that interpretation of the agreement may go beyond the limits imposed by the exemption, particularly where the arbitrators, whose function is to produce an amicable settlement, are not bound by the substantive law. Furthermore, review of arbitral awards for their compatibility with Article 85 and 86, inasmuch as these fail to be regarded as part of EEC public policy, is not necessarily available in non-member states.' [87]

The EC Commission held that certain conditions imposed on licensees of the trade mark in and manufacture of the drink Campari infringed Article 85(1) EEC but exempted them under Article 85(3) subject to the obligation to submit annual returns on certain trading matters to the Commission.

DECISION

The Commission of the European Communities, in the light of the Treaty establishing the European Economic Community (especially Article 85) and of Council Regulation 17 of 6 February 1962 (especially Articles 4 to 8), received applications for negative clearance and notifications made on 20 and 27 October 1962 in respect of the trade mark licensing agreements entered into by Davide Campari-Milano SpA, with its registered office at Milan, Italy (hereinafter Campari-Milano), on 19 September 1957 with Ognibeni & Co., Amsterdam, the Netherlands on 1 January 1960 with Hans Prang, Hamburg, Germany, on 8 January 1962 with Soval, now called Campari-France SA, Nanterre, France, and on 11 October 1962 with Sovinac SA, Brussels, Belgium; it also received a notification on 27 June 1973 of the trade mark licensing agreement with Campari-Milano entered into on 14 April 1966 with Johs. M. Klein & Co., Copenhagen, Denmark.

The parties made amendments to the agreements during the proceedings in order to comply with the requirements of Article 85(3).

* Published in [1978] OJ L70/89 (13 March 1978). The authentic texts are in Danish, Dutch, French, German and Italian.

A summary of the notifications was published in accordance with Article 19(3) of Regulation 17 in the *Official Journal* No. C198 of 19 August 1977.

The Advisory Committee on Restrictive Practices and Dominant Positions delivered its opinion in accordance with Article 10 of Regulation 17 on 25 November 1977.

1. The Facts

[1] Campari-Milano is the holder of the international trademarks, Bitter Campari and Cordial Campari, which are carried by aperitifs in the manufacture of which secret concentrates (special mixtures of crushed herbs) are used.

[2] In order to promote these brands abroad, Campari-Milano set up a network of licensees to manufacture and sell its products. The network covers all the EEC countries with the exception of the United Kingdom and Ireland. Campari-Milano granted F. S. Matta Ltd an exclusive right to import and distribute its aperitifs in these two countries; the present version of the agreement qualifies for the block exemption given by Commission Regulation 67/67/EEC of 22 March 1967.

[3] A. Within the Common Market the business of the parties involved is regulated by the licensing agreements mentioned above, which have been notified to the Commission and which contain, in the version in force since 1 November 1977, the provisions described below.

[4] 1. Campari-Milano grants to the following firms an exclusive right to use its trademarks for the manufacture of its aperitifs using its secret processes and its concentrates, and for their sale in the following territories:

— Ognibeni & Co.: Netherlands,
— Hans Prang: Germany,
— Campari France SA: France, Monaco and certain French overseas territories,
— Sovinac SA: Belgium and Luxembourg,
— Johs M. Klein & Co.: Denmark.

[5] Campari-Milano undertakes not to manufacture its aperitifs itself in these territories during the validity of the agreements.

[6] 2. The licensees undertake that during the currency of the agreements they will not handle competing products, notably certain beverages called Bitter and aerated drinks similar to Campari Soda.

[7] 3. The licensees and Campari-Milano undertake not to carry on any active sales policy, not to set up any branches and not to advertise, the licensees outside their respective allotted territories, and Campari-Milano within these territories.

[8] However, the licensees and Campari-Milano will do all they can to meet unsolicited export orders for delivery within the EEC for Campari products manufactured according to the specifications as to alcoholic strength, labelling, bottle content, etc . . . applicable, in the case of a licensee, in its allotted territory, and, of Campari-Milano, in Italy. Such sales will be at the prices and on the conditions obtaining in its own exclusive territory in the case of an exporting licensee, and on the conditions obtaining on the Italian market in the case of Campari-Milano; where Campari-Milano is exporting, its prices will be increased by the royalties and advertising costs normally borne by the licensees.

[9] Where unsolicited orders are received for Bitter manufactured according to the specifications obtaining on the market to which the goods are to be exported, the parties are free to accept or refuse; the primary requirement is that the exclusive territories, or in Campari-Milano's case the Italian market, must not be under-supplied, and in the case of the licensees Campari-Milano must first be asked for the formulae required to manufacture the products. Campari-Milano has the right to meet orders addressed directly to it by members of the diplomatic corps or foreign armed forces.

[10] The licensees and Campari-Milano undertake to do all they can to help buyers of their products who wish to export the products within the EEC to obtain drawback of taxes or duties on alcohol to the extent permitted by the national fiscal regime in question.

[11] Lastly, each licensee undertakes not to export Campari products directly or indirectly outside the EEC, and, in the case of Campari-France, outside those non-member countries forming part of its allotted territory.

[12] All the contracts contain an obligation on the licensees to supply the original Italian product, rather than their own, to the diplomatic corps, to ships' victuallers, to foreign armed forces and in general to all bodies exempt from payment of duties.

[13] 5. The French, Belgian, Danish and Dutch licensees are to manufacture Campari products in their plant at Nanterre, Brussels, Copenhagen and Amsterdam.

[14] Campari-Milano is to be informed of any change in plant location, and may object if the new plant is not such as to ensure that the products will be of the right quality.

[15] 6. The licensees must comply exactly with the licensor's instructions for the manufacture of products, must ensure that the quality of the raw materials used meets the licensor's specifications, must purchase certain raw materials (secret mixtures of herbs and colouring matters) from the licensor, must submit for the licensor's approval a sample of each manufacturing run giving the date of filtering and the serial number of the boxes of herbs used, and may not divulge the manufacturing processes.

[16] 7. The licensees undertake to promote sales as far as possible and, in particular, to engage in suitable advertising, each spending the same fixed amount per litre bottle of Bitter sold.

[17] 8. The licensees are required to inform Campari-Milano of any trade mark infringements or passing-off which comes to their knowledge. Campari-Milano may instruct the licensees to take action against the infringers, giving the licensees the necessary power to do this.

[18] 9. In no case may the benefit of the contracts be assigned to third parties.

[19] 10. All disputes as to the interpretation and performance of the agreements are to be settled by three arbitrators, whose function is to produce an amicable settlement. As a rule arbitration will take place in Milan, but one agreement makes provision for arbitration outside the Community, in Switzerland.

[20] 11. Whereas the French agreement requires the licensee to pay royalties per bottle sold in return for use of the trade mark, the other agreements provide that royalties be included in the price of raw materials supplied by Campari-Milano.

[21] 12. The contracts are automatically renewable from year to year, or every two years, unless one side or the other gives prior notice of termination.

[22] B. In the form originally notified, the agreements contained an obligation on the licensees to manufacture only in certain plants and to purchase certain non-secret raw materials from the licensor; there was also a ban on exports by the licensees to other EEC countries and on exports by Campari-Milano to the licensees' allotted territories. However, when the Commission informed them in its statement of objections of 27 July 1976 that

it considered these obligations incompatible with Article 85(1) of the EEC Treaty, the parties changed them so that their agreements could qualify for exemption under Article 85(3). In particular, they replaced the ban on exports within the EEC by the undertaking to do everything possible to meet unsolicited orders inside the EEC, the Commission having stated in its objections that it would impose an obligation to that effect.

[23] C. Other considerations which arose during examination of the case are the following:

[24] 1. The exclusive arrangements made by Campari-Milano date from before the war as regards Campari-France, Sovinac and Ognibeni and from between 1949 and 1953 as regards Hang Prang and Klein. There is no financial link between the firms concerned.

[25] Bitter Campari is currently the only Campari product to be manufactured by the licensees. The volume of Bitter manufactured annually at present, according to the licensees, is between one and three million bottles. All the licensees have increased their production capacities considerably over the last few years by the construction of new factories and by plant extensions already carried out or in course of construction. The sale of Bitter Campari is at present the only activity carried on by the French licensee, who until recently regularly imported wine and vermouth, and accounts for the bulk of the business of the Dutch, German and Belgian licensees; these firms and the Danish licensee distribute a whole range of beverages (notably spirituous liquors, gin and wine) manufactured by themselves or imported, in general from France and Italy. Small quantities of Campari Soda and Cordial Campari are imported direct by some licensees.

[26] 2. Apart from the secret herbal mixtures, bitter orange essence and albumin, the licensees use locally bought sugar, alcohol and distilled water in manufacturing Bitter. The dosage of each of the ingredients of Bitter varies with the alcoholic strength to be given; at present this stands at 20° for Bitter manufactured and sold in France by the French licensee, 21.5° and 25° for Bitter manufactured by the Belgian licensee for sale in Belgium and Luxembourg respectively, 25° for Bitter manufactured by Dutch and Danish licensees and by Campari-Milano for sale on the Italian and British markets and 30° for Bitter sold in Germany. Detailed instructions for manufacture are supplied so that the dosages for the different markets can be achieved while keeping the quality and presentation as close as possible to the original Italian product.

[27] Campari bottles are manufactured according to Campari-Milano designs and models.

[28] According to the Commission's information, before the manufacture can be profitable, whatever the alcoholic strength, a vat of 28,000 litres at the very least is necessary. Like the alcoholic strength, bottle sizes for Bitter vary from one member state to another. Bottles are of one litre in Italy and France, 98 cl. in Luxembourg, 70 cl. in Germany, 72 cl. in Denmark and 75 cl. in the Netherlands, Belgium and the United Kingdom. Miniatures are also used. Finally, bottles supplied by Campari-Milano for sale to embassies and victuallers are always of 92 cl. with an alcoholic strength of 28.5 degrees.

[29] 3. Up to now licensees have sold Campari products in their respective allotted territories only. In these territories and in Italy, Bitter for ordinary consumption (i.e. with payment of duties and taxes) is sold by the manufacturers themselves or through independent distributors subject only to the general terms of sale imposed by the manufacturers. The terms of sale do not now oblige buyers to refrain from exporting. Sales in Luxembourg are carried out by an exclusive importer. The licensees were formerly required to sell a certain minimum quantity each year. This obligation ended in the course of 1977.

[30] Campari-Milano has no say in its licensees' price policies. The prices at which the licensees supply dealers on the domestic or export market are determined on the whole by identical cost factors, notably as regards raw materials, and there are no substantial differences. There is currently no longer any resale price maintenance, retail prices being generally the same in France, Belgium and the Netherlands and somewhat higher in Germany and Denmark, where the tax burden is heavier. In Luxembourg, on the other hand, retail prices are lower in consequence of the lower tax in that country. During recent years these prices have hardly changed, notwithstanding the considerable increases in salaries and the cost of the raw materials.

[31] Sales of Bitter in the Community have increased steadily over recent years, as a result both of the setting-up of a widespread distribution network, which has considerably increased the number of retailers, and of the stimulation of demand from major customers and supermarkets; between 1970 and 1977 sales doubled, in some case trebled, in Benelux and Germany. The average cost of the advertising campaigns carried out each year by the licensees is much the same for all of them. Campari-Milano's own expenditure on advertising, however, is lower by as much as a half.

[32] Sales for duty-free and tax-free consumption, i.e. sales to the diplomatic corps, to foreign armed forces or similar organisations enjoying extraterritorial rights, to ships and aircraft travelling abroad directly and to duty-free shops in ports and airports are for the most part carried out through victuallers. The agreements between the victuallers and licensees or Campari-Milano have not been notified to the Commission and are not dealt with in this proceeding. Sales of duty-free products represent only a small part of the total sales of most of the licensees.

[33] Over the last few years, Bitter Campari has been imported and sold by parallel importers, notably in Belgium and the Netherlands; these importers have paid the duties and taxes required in those countries. They have been supplied partly by victuallers and partly by wholesalers carrying on duty-free sales.

[34] In the Common Market, Bitter Campari is subject to the tax arrangements applying to alcohol and must conform to the regulations concerning the particulars which must appear on bottles, and to public health regulations.

[35] (a) In each member state duties and taxes are payable on Bitter Campari; these are calculated on the equivalent in pure alcohol of the product, so that the higher the alcoholic content the heavier the duty. The duties and taxes levied on imports are the same as on domestic products; for the most part they amount to slightly less than a half to two-thirds of the ex-works price. Since they are so heavy, it is not profitable to export Bitter manufactured in one member state to another unless duty exemption or drawback is possible in the member state of origin.

[36] Under national regulations, if the alcohol used in the manufacture of Bitter is to be exempted from duty and tax, it must be declared for export when the manufacturer buys it. Exports are deemed to include sales for duty-free and tax-free consumption.

[37] According to the Commission's information, in all EEC countries except France and the United Kingdom, both of which have a system for suspension of consumer taxes, all duties on Bitter not declared for export are payable when it leaves the place of manufacture or when seals or bands certifying payment of duty

are affixed. In general, once duty has been paid, there is no drawback for subsequent export. Only in Italy and France can duties already paid be remitted if the goods are exported, and in the latter country only through the manufacturer, to whom the Directorate-General for Taxation reimburses duty corresponding to declarations supplied by the exporter.

[38] It is to be noted that, with a view to the elimination of obstacles to the free circulation of alcoholic products between member states under undistorted competitive conditions, the Commission has made a proposal to the Council for a directive to harmonise excise duties on alcohol, and notably the terms on which dealers may stock sprituous liquors.* According to the proposal dealers could in certain circumstances stock spirituous liquors without paying excise duties and engage in parallel exports.

[39] (b) National regulations on public health and on the marketing of beverages subject to duties and taxes on alcohol require a number of particulars to appear on bottles when sold. These generally include the name of the product, the name and address of the manufacturer or importer, and the alcoholic strength (certain member states further require the words 'spirituous liquour' to appear, and a statement as to the content, ingredients and added products).

[40] (c) In certain member states the law requires beverages such as Bitter Campari to have an alcoholic strength of not less than a specified minimum (17° in France, 20° in Denmark and 30° in Germany).

[41] As the alcoholic strength required by German regulations is greater than that of Bitter Campari in the other member states, there is in effect a ban on imports to Germany, unless of course a consignment has been specially manufactured for the German market.

[42] However, it is worth noting that following complaints from importers the Commission addressed a reasoned opinion to the Federal Republic of Germany under Article 169 of the EEC Treaty, and Germany then cancelled the provisions applying to certain alcoholic products with an alcoholic strength of less than 30°; the products did not include Bitter.

[43] Other national legal provisions govern advertising of alcoholic drinks, restrict the number of licensed premises, prohibit the sale of aperitifs and bitters exceeding a specified alcoholic strength (e.g. in Belgium) or specify the actual content of bottles (in France, for instance, the authorised units are 35 cl., 50 cl., 70 cl., and 1 litre, the 75 cl. bottles used by Belgian and Dutch licensees not being allowed there.

[44] According to the explanations provided by Campari-Milano, the obligation on licensees to inform Campari-Milano of trade mark infringements coming to their knowledge does not apply to imports into each alloted territory of the original Italian product or of products manufactured under licence in another member state.

[45] 6. In the allotted territories, Bitter Campari is in competition with a number of substitute products, including Punt e Mes Carpano, Bitter Cinzano, Bitter Gambarotta, Bitter Negroni, Bitter Moroni, Bitter San Pellegrino, Bitter Rossi, Amer Picon, Suze, Amer Khuri, Cynar and Amer Claquesin.

[46] It has not been possible to establish Bitter Campari's exact market share. What is clear, however, is that the brand has acquired an international reputation and that the turnover attained by Campari-Milano and its licensees is a substantial one.

[47] 7. Following publication of summaries of the notification, no observations from third parties have been received by the Commission.

* [1972] JO C43/25.

II. Applicability of Article 85(1) of the EEC Treaty

[48] Article 85(1) of the EEC Treaty prohibits as incompatible with the Common Market all agreements between undertakings which may affect trade between member states and which have as their object or effect the prevention, restriction or distortion of competition within the Common Market.

[49] The agreements in question are between undertakings and include provisions (see points 1 to 4 under 1A above) which have as their object and their effect an appreciable restriction of competition within the Common Market.

[50] 1. The exclusive rights given to the licensees prevent Campari-Milano from granting trade mark licences for its products to other parties in the Netherlands, Germany, France, Belgium, Luxembourg and Denmark and also from itself manufacturing those products in these countries.

[51] The proprietor of a trade mark has the exclusive right to use the distinctive mark on first sale and to protect the product against infringement of the mark. The proprietor of the trade mark may by licence authorise the use of the protected mark by third parties. However, if he undertakes only to allow one single undertaking to use his trade mark in a particular territory and to refrain himself from manufacturing products bearing his trade mark then he loses his freedom to respond to other requests for licences and the competitive advantage to be gained from manufacture by himself in this territory.

[52] In the case in point, the exclusive nature of the licence entails a restriction upon Campari-Milano's freedom to use its marks as well as preventing third parties, particularly manufacturers of alcoholic beverages, from using them as licensees, however much they may find it in their interests to do so.

[53] 2. The non-competition clause (Point 1. A 2 above) prevents the licensees from manufacturing or selling products for the whole duration of the agreements. They may not buy such products, nor acquire licences to manufacture or sell them. The effect of the restriction is appreciable, since at present all the licensees, except the French one, are already distributing a whole range of beverages other than Bitter Campari and all have a substantial turnover on their total business.

[54] 3. The ban preventing Campari-Milano and its licensees from engaging in an active sales policy outside their respective territories prevents the licensees and the licensor from seeking custom in the territories of the other parties. They are therefore excluded from actively competing on those territories, while benefiting from a degree of protection within their own territory, where the only imports made must be in response to unsolicited orders. This ban must be considered as having an appreciable effect, since not only Campari-Milano but also all the licensees have considerable production capacity, which would enable them to supply other markets in the EEC. While such deliveries would primarily be of products manufactured according to the specifications in respect of alcoholic strength, bottle content, and labelling required on the manufacturer's home market, they could also be for Bitter manufactured according to other specifications required on the export market, for manufacturers can buy the alcohol without being taxed, in order to export the finished product. Furthermore, they may change the alcoholic strength or presentation of the product where they judge that the size of an order or at any rate the possibility of steady sales makes the manufacture of such a product and the use of new labels or bottles profitable.

[55] 4. The obligation to supply the original Italian product to diplomatic corps, ship's victuallers, foreign armed forces and generally speaking all organisations with duty-free facilities prevents the licensees from supplying Bitter which they have

manufactured themselves to these consumers. In view of the licensees' production capacities, this restriction also has an appreciable effect.

[56] B. The exclusive rights granted by Campari-Milano prevent Campari-Milano from granting other licences which would enable other parties to use its trade marks in the allotted territories and to export from these territories to other parts of the Common Market. They also prevent Campari-Milano itself from manufacturing Bitter in these territories and consequently from exporting from such territories. The exclusion of competing products prevents the licensees from marketing such products across borders between member states, or from making licence agreements in relation to such products with undertakings in other member states. The ban on engaging in an active sales policy outside their respective territories prevents Campari-Milano and its licensees from freely disposing throughout the Common Market of the Bitter they have manufactured, restricting them to their exclusive territories, and thus affects international trade in the product. The obligation to supply certain consumers with the original Italian product rather than that which they themselves manufacture means that the licensees have to obtain supplies of Bitter Campari from Italy and thus affects international trade in the product.

[57] These restrictions must be regarded as liable to affect trade between member states inasmuch as their effect is that trade between member states develops otherwise than it would have done without them, until at the same time they have a substantial degree of influence on market conditions.

[58] The agreements are therefore caught by Article 85(1) of the Treaty.

[59] C. The other provisions of the agreements entered into by Campari-Milano and its licensees are not in this case covered by Article 85(1), because they have neither the object nor the effect of appreciably restricting competition within the Common Market. This is so for the following provisions, in particular:

[60] — the obligation upon each licensee to refrain from exporting Bitter Campari directly or indirectly outside the Common Market. It is true that this obligation not only eliminates the freedom of the licensees and their trade customers to do business in the relevant product outside the EEC, but also prevents any distributor in a non-member country from buying the product from the licensees or from a previous purchaser for resale in the Common Market. However, any purchaser within the Community may obtain supplies of the products covered by the agreements not only directly from the licensee in his own territory but also, directly or indirectly, from other licensees or from Campari-Milano itself. Given these possibilities, reimportation into the Common Market of Bitter previously exported outside the Community by licensees or their trade customers would seem unlikely, in view of supplementary economic factors such as the accumulation of trade margins and of excise duties and taxes on alcohol levied by importing countries as well as the duties charged on crossing the European Economic Community borders. This assessment also applies to states with which the EEC has entered into free trade agreements, particularly as trade between the Community and these states in alcoholic beverages such as Bitter Campari is still subject to customs duties.

[61] — restrictions of the licence to those plants which are capable of guaranteeing the quality of the product. The effect of this restriction on the licensees' freedom of choice does not go beyond a legitimate concern for quality controls; further, this obligation upon the licensee does not constitute an absolute limitation of production to any particular place, since it only

gives Campari-Milano the right to oppose a change in the place of manufacture in cases where the new establishment proposed might adversely affect the quality of the products; this type of agreement as to quality control is very important for the licensor, since the maintainance of quality is referable to the existence of the trade mark right,

[62] — the licensees are obliged to follow the licensor's instructions relating to the manufacture of the product and the quality of the ingredients, and to buy certain secret raw materials from the licensor itself. Here again, control over the quality of the products manufactured under licence and over their similarity to the original Italian product is in the present case very important for the licensor, in the sense that it is again bound up with its interest in the maintenance of quality, which is referable to the existence of the trade mark right. According to information provided by the parties, the standards enforced do not oblige the licensees to obtain supplies of albumin or bitter orange essence from any particular source, but only to choose between different products on the basis of objective quality considerations. This does not, however, apply to the colouring matter and the herbal mixtures, where the licensor's legitimate concern to ensure that the product manufactured under licence has the same quality as the original product can be protected only if the licensees obtain all their supplies from it. The composition of the products in question which is the factor that determines the particular characteristics of Bitter Campari is a trade secret which the licensor cannot be required under Community law to reveal to its licensees,

[63] — the licensees are required to refrain from divulging the manufacturing processes to third parties. This obligation is essential if secret techniques or recipes are to be passed on for use by other undertakings,

[64] — the licensees are obliged to maintain continuous contact with customers and to spend a standard minimum sum on advertising Bitter Campari. In the present case there is nothing to suggest that the amount of the sum in question would prevent the licensees from engaging in other activities or carrying on their own advertising also,

[65] — the licensees are prohibited from assigning the benefit of the agreement. By banning assignments, the licensor is simply safeguarding its freedom to select its licensees. When it enters into an agreement the identity of the other party is highly material to it and it must remain free to decide with whom it will deal.

III. Applicability of Article 85(3) of the EEC Treaty

[66] Under Article 85(3) the provisions of Article 85(1) may be declared inapplicable to agreements between undertakings which contribute to improving the production and distribution of goods or to promoting technical or economic progress, while allowing consumers a fair share of the resulting benefit, and which do not:

(a) impose on the undertakings concerned restrictions which are not indispensable to the attainment of these objectives;

(b) afford such undertakings the possibility of eliminating competition in respect of a substantial part of the products in question.

[67] A. The restrictions on competition mentioned at points 1 to 4 of item II A satisfy the tests of Article 85(3).

[68] 1. The exclusivity granted by Campari-Milano contributes to improving the production and distribution of the products. By giving each licensee a guarantee that no other undertaking will obtain a licence within its allocated territory, and that in that territory neither Campari-Milano nor any other

licensee may manufacture products bearing the licensor's trade mark this commitment confers upon each licensee an advantage in its allotted territory. This territorial advantage is such as to permit a sufficient return on the investment made by each licensee for the purpose of manufacturing the product bearing the trade mark under conditions acceptable to the licensor and holder of the trade mark, and it enables the licensee to increase its production capacity and constantly to improve the already long-established distribution network.

[69] In practice the exclusivity granted has allowed each licensee to improve its existing plant and to build new plant. It has also enabled each licensee to strengthen its efforts to promote the brand, doubling the total volume of sales in the Benelux countries and Germany over the last six years, and, by establishing a multistage distribution network, to secure a constantly increasing number of customers and thus to ensure supplies throughout the allotted territory.

[70] 2. The ban on dealing in competing products also contributes to improving distribution of the licensed products by concentrating sales efforts, encouraging the build-up of stocks and shortening delivery times.

[71] The restriction on the licensees' freedom to deal in other products at the same time as the products here in question prevents the licensees from neglecting Campari in the event of conflict between the promotion of Campari sales and possible interest in another product. Although a non-competition clause in a licensing agreement concerning industrial property rights based on the result of a creative activity, such as a patent, would constitute a barrier to technical and economic progress by preventing the licensees from taking an interest in other techniques and products, this is not the case with the licensing agreements under consideration here. The aim pursued by the parties, as is clear from the agreement taken as a whole, is to decentralise manufacture within the EEC and to rationalise the distribution system linked to it, and thus to promote the sale of Campari-Milano's Bitter, manufactured from the same concentrates provided by Campari-Milano, according to the same mixing process and using the same ingredients, and bearing the same trade mark, as that of the licensor.

[72] The prohibition on dealing in competing products, therefore, makes for improved distribution of the relevant product in the same way as do exclusive dealing agreements containing a similar clause, which are automatically exempted by Regulation 67/67/EEC; a declaration that the prohibition in Article 85(1) is inapplicable to this clause is accordingly justified.

[73] 3. Distribution will also be improved by the prohibition against the parties engaging in an active sales policy outside their respective territories. This restriction on the licensees will help to concentrate their sales efforts, and provide a better supply to consumers in their territories for which they have particular responsibility, without preventing buyers elsewhere in the Community from securing supplies freely from any of the licensees. Application of the same restriction to Campari-Milano encourages the efforts made by each territory allotted; the licensees thus have the benefit of a certain protection relative to Campari-Milano's strong market position.

[74] 4. The obligation on licensees to supply the original Italian product rather than that which they themselves manufacture, when selling to diplomatic corps, ships' victuallers, foreign armed forces and generally speaking all organisations with duty-free facilities, also helps to promote sales of Campari-Milano's Bitter. By restricting licensees' freedom to supply the products they manufacture themselves it makes sure that particular categories of consumers,

who are deemed to be outside the licensee's territory and are usually required to move frequently from one territory to another, can always purchase the same original product with all its traditional features as regards both composition and outward appearance. Even though quality standards are observed, it is impossible in particular to avoid differences in taste between the products of the various manufacturers. This obligation is thus designed to prevent these consumers from turning to other competing products and to ensure that they continue to buy Bitter Campari, with the facility of being able to obtain stocks from their local dealer. Further, such consumers are not prevented from freely obtaining the licensees' own products even though any such purchase would be on the normal trading conditions applicable to non-duty-free purchasers.

[75] B. The licensing agreements have increased the quantities of Bitter Campari available to consumers and improved distribution, so that consumers benefit directly. There are other producers of bitter on the market, and effective competition will be strengthened by the growing quantities produced by Campari-Milano's licensees, so that it can be assumed that the improvements resulting from the agreements and the benefits which the licensees obtain from them are shared by consumers.

[76] As buyers may secure supplies of Bitter from other territories through unsolicited orders, they are in a position to exert pressure on the prices charged by the exclusive licensee in their territory if these should be too high.

[77] C. The restrictions of competition imposed on the parties involved must be considered indispensable to the attainment of the benefits set out above. None of the restrictions could be omitted without endangering the parties' object of promoting sales of Bitter Campari by concentrating the activities of the licensees on the product and offering the same original product to certain customers. In particular, none of the licensees and in all probability no other undertaking in the spirituous liquors industry would have been prepared to make the investment necessary for a significant increase in sales of Bitter if it were not sure of being protected from competition from other licensees or Campari-Milano itself.

[78] D. The licensing agreements which are the subject of the Decision do not give Campari-Milano, or its licensees the possibility of eliminating competition in respect of a substantial part of the Bitter products in question. In the EEC there exists a fairly large number of other well-known brands of bitter, which are all able to compete against Bitter Campari. Campari-Milano's licensees and Campari-Milano itself are also free to sell the Campari products in question within the Common Market but outside their territory for which they have particular responsibility.

[79] As things stand at present, all the tests for a decision applying Article 85(3) to the licensing agreements entered into by Campari Milano with Ognibeni & Co., Hans Prang, Campari-France SA, Sovinac SA and Johs. M. Klein and Co. are satisfied.

IV. Application of Articles 6, 7 and 8 of Regulation 17

[80] 1. In the form in which they were originally notified in the Commission and which prompted the statement of objections (see item I. B. above), the five licensing agreements entered into by Campari-Milano did not satisfy the tests of Article 85(3). The clauses listed above, contained in the agreement then in force, significantly restricted competition, and the restrictions could not be considered as being referable to the existence of the licensed trade marks, or as contributing to the production or distribution of the products, or to promoting technical or economic progress. The clauses which prevented application of Article 85(3) were deleted on 1 November 1977 at the Commission's request. It is

therefore possible, under Article 6(1) of Regulation 17, for the Decision applying Article 85(3) to take effect from the date on which the agreements were amended, which is to say 1 November 1977.

[81] In determining the period of validity of the Decision, as required by Article 8(1) of Regulation 17, account should be taken of the fact that the restrictions on competition covered by this Decision do not prevent the free movement of the goods in question between EEC member states, and in particular that the parties have undertaken, as from 1 November 1977, to do every-thing possible to meet unsolicited orders from within the EEC. The period allowed must be sufficient to permit the amended agreements to produce the effects intended; a period of nine years would seem reasonable.

[82] 2. The exclusive licensing agreements entered into by Campari-Milano with Ognibeni & Co., Hans Prang, Campari France SA, and Sovinac SA satisfy the tests of Article 7(1) of Regulation 17.

[83] The agreements were in existence at the date of entry into force of Regulation 17 on 13 March 1962, although the agree-ment with Sovinac SA existed in a previous version to that which was notified. The agreements were notified within the periods provided for under Article 5(1) of Regulation 17. They did not at that time satisfy the tests of Article 85(3), but have since been amended so that they do satisfy those requirements, as has been explained above.

[84] As regards the agreements in their version before amendment, the prohibition contained in Article 85(1) applies only for a period fixed by the Commission. The Commission must take into account the fact that the parties spontaneously amended the agreements, or agreed to amend them, in accordance with suggestions made by the Commission. These circumstances justify exemption from the prohibition of Article 85(1) for the whole of the period preceding the effective date of the Decision declaring Article 85(1) inapplicable to all of the agreements.

[85] The preceding observations apply also in the case of the agreement of 14 April 1966 with Johs. M. Klein and Co. An export ban imposed on a firm established in a country outside the EEC and aimed against deliveries into the EEC can constitute a restriction of competition capable of affecting trade between member states. However, in the present case such a ban was not an appreciable restriction before Denmark joined the EEC because the difficulties of importation arising from customs and tax regulations in practice prevented exports of Bitter Campari to the Community. Accordingly, pursuant to Article 25 of Regulation 17, the agreement made between Campari-Milano and Johs. M. Klein and Co. and duly notified on 27 June 1973 also satisfies the conditions for application of Article 7(1) of that Regulation.

[86] 3. In view of the importance and international reputation of the Campari brand, of the restrictive effects on the circulation of Bitter Campari between member states resulting from existing national legislation, and lastly the fact that exports by manu-facturers of Bitter Campari between member states resulting from existing national legislation, and lastly the fact that exports by manufacturers of Bitter Campari or by their customers depend ultimately on the willingness of the manufacturers themselves, the Commission should have the opportunity to assess in good time the situation resulting from the amended agreements on the relevant market. Consequently, in accordance with Article 8(1) of Regulation 17, Campari-Milano and each of its licensees should be required to send to the Commission annually, beginning on 15 December 1978, a report containing all inform-ation necessary for an assessment of developments resulting from the application of the agreements, especially from the point of

view of the free movement of Bitter within the EEC. This applies in particular to exports within the Community.

[87] Arrangements should also be made to ensure that the Commission is informed of any awards made under the arbitration clause, as there is a risk that the agreements might be interpreted without regard for this Decision, so that the Commission might have to amend it. There is a greater risk at arbitration than in the ordinary courts that interpretation of the agreement may go beyond the limits imposed by the exemption, particularly where the arbi-trators, whose function, as in this case, is to produce an amicable settlement, are not bound by the substantive law. Furthermore, review of arbitral awards for their compatibility with Articles 85 and 86, inasmuch as these fail to be regarded as part of EEC public policy, is not necessarily available in non-member states.

THE COMMISSION, for these reasons,
HAS ADOPTED THIS DECISION:

Article 1
The provisions of Article 85(1) of the Treaty establishing the European Economic Community are, pursuant to Article 85(3), declared inapplicable to the trade mark licensing agreements, as amended on 1 November 1977, entered into by Davide Campari-Milano SpA, Milan, on 19 September 1957 with Ognibeni & Co., Amsterdam, on 1 January 1960 with Hans Prang, Hamburg, on 8 January 1962 with Soval, now Campari-France SA, Nanterre, on 11 October 1962 with Sovinac SA, Brussels, and on 14 April 1966 with Johs. M. Klein & Co., Copenhagen.

Article 2
This Decision shall have effect from 1 November 1972 and shall apply until 1 November 1986.

Article 3
The abovementioned undertakings shall inform the Commission immediately of all awards made under the arbitration clause. Every year, beginning on 15 December 1978, they shall notify to the Commission:

1. the volume of their exports of Bitter Campari within the EEC;
2. the cases where they have refused:

(a) to meet export orders for delivery of Bitter Campari within the EEC;
(b) to seek a refund of the taxes corresponding to declarations made by customers who have exported Campari products within the EEC.

Article 4
The prohibition in Article 85(1) does not apply to the licensing agreements entered into by Davide Campari-Milano with Ognibeni & Co., Hans Prang, Soval (now Campari-France SA), Sovinac SA and Johs. M. Klein in their versions which were in force before the date, as indicated in Article 2 thereof, on which this Decision takes effect.

Article 5
This Decision is addressed to:

— Davide Campari-Milano SpA, Milan, Italy,
— Ognibeni & Co., Amsterdam, Netherlands,
— Hans Prang, Hamburg, Germany,
— Campari-France SA, Nanterre, France,
— Sovinac SA, Brussels, Belgium,
— Johs. M. Klein & Co., Copenhagen, Denmark.

Commission Decisions on Franchise Agreements

RE THE FRANCHISE AGREEMENTS OF YVES ROCHER

(Case IV/31.428-31.432) [1988] 4 CMLR 592
Before the Commission of the European Communities
(87/14/EEC)
(Signed by Mr. Comissioner Sutherland)

17 December 1986*.
[Gaz: EC861217]

Application for negative clearance.

Restrictive practices, Franchise agreements. Inasmuch as the members of a retail franchise network are bound together by close *de facto* commercial tics, the franchise contracts are the expression of a closely integrated form of distribution. They nevertheless constitute agreements between undertakings under Article 85(1) EEC, since the franchisees are the proprietors of their businesses, of which they bear the start-up costs and which they operate at their own risk. [38]

Restrictive practices, Franchise agreements, Competition, Industrial property. Obligations imposed by a franchisor on its franchisees to ensure that they exploit its proprietary industrial property rights and know-how in a manner in keeping with their subject matter are inherent in the very existence of its right in its intellectual creations and fall outside the scope of the contractual and concerted practice provisions of Article 85(1) EEC. Consequently, restrictions on the commercial freedom of franchisees, without which the franchisor's distribution know-how would not be transferred, do not constitute restrictions of competition under Article 85(1) [40]

Restrictive practices, Franchise agreements, Exclusive territorial rights. Where the franchisor appoints only one franchisee for a given territory (within which the franchisee has an exclusive right to use the franchisor's identifying marks and know-how and undertakes not itself to establish a shop in the territory of its franchisees and, in addition, franchisees are forbidden to open a second shop, the result is a degree of market-sharing between the franchisor and its franchisees or between the latter which restricts competition within the distribution network and brings the contracts within Article 85(1) EEC. [54]–[55]

Restrictive practices, Franchise agreements, Distribution, Block exemption. The block exemption regulations on exclusive dealing and exclusive distribution (67/67 and 1983/83) do not apply to distribution franchise contracts where the franchisor grants rights to use its identifying marks and its proven trading methods with a view to the application of an original and changing distribution formula. [57]

Restrictive practices, Franchise agreements, Prices. Resale price maintenance clauses in franchise agreements and the

prohibition on cross supplies between franchisees, which prevent the machinery for correcting price differences within the network from operating, preclude the grant of an exemption under Article 85(3) EEC to the franchise agreements. [63]

Restrictive practices, Franchise agreements, Inter-State trade. Where a franchisor prevents or hinders recourse by franchisees to transnational cross supplies which the price differences between certain member-states are likely to encourage, especially in the case of franchisees operating near national frontiers, an exemption under Article 85(3) for the franchise agreements will be refused. [64]

In relation to a network of franchised retail outlets for Yves Rocher cosmetics in seven EEC countries, the Commission *held that* the following features of the standard-form franchise contract were not caught by Article 85(1) EEC: (a) selection of franchisees in terms of the personal qualities and business qualifications which the franchisor requires for the application of its trading formula; (b) control by the franchisor of the location of the franchisee's shop in terms of the maintenance of the network's reputation; (c) requirement that the shop be fitted out and decorated in accordance with the franchisor's plans and specifications; (d) requirement that the franchisee use know-how and trading methods provided by the franchisor; (e) the franchisor's control of any local publicity undertaken by the franchisee on his own account; (f) requirement that the franchisee sell only products bearing the franchisor's trade mark; (g) prohibition on resale by franchisees of franchise products to resellers outside the network; (h) prohibition on the franchisee carrying on competing activities for the duration of the contract; (i) prohibition on the assignment or transfer of the franchise contract without the franchisor's approval; (j) prohibition for one year after termination of the franchise on the former franchisee carrying on a retail cosmetics business in his former exclusive territory; (k) requirement that the franchisee devote all his energy and as much time as necessary to promoting the sale of the franchisor's products; (l) right of the franchisor to inspect franchisees' stock levels, accounts and balance sheets (but not so as to affect the freedom of the franchisees to fix their selling prices); (m) the inclusion of recommended prices in the franchisor's catalogues. The Commission *held that* the following features were caught by Article 85(1): (a) exclusive territorial protection for each franchisee; (b) resale price maintenance; (c) prohibition on cross supplies between franchisees. Of the latter, (b) and (c) were *deleted* from the contracts after negotiation with the Commission. The Commission *held that* distribution block exemptions in Regulations 67/67 and 1983/83 did not apply, but *granted* an individual exemption under Article 85(3) to the standard form franchise contract until 14 January 1992 subject to the condition that the franchisor communicate annually to the Commission its current recommended sales prices and prices charged to its franchisees.

The following case was referred to in the decision:

* Published in [1987] O.J. L8/49 (10 January 1987). The authentic text is in French.

Pronuptia de Paris GmbH v. *Pronuptia de Paris Irmgard Shillgallis* (161/84), 29 January 1986; [1986] 1 C.M.L.R. 414. Gaz:161/84 [Reprinted in Appendix 6 above]

Decision

The Commission of the European Communities, in the light of the Treaty establishing the European Economic Community (especially Article 85) and of Council Regulation 17 (especially Articles 6 and 8) received a notification and application for negative clearance submitted on 15 January 1985 by Yves Rocher, of La Gacilly (France), concerning a system of standard form franchise contracts for the retailing of cosmetics covering France, Germany, Belgium, Luxembourg, the Netherlands, the United Kingdom and Spain.

A summary of the notification was published* pursuant to article 19(3) of Regulation 17. The Advisory Committee on Restrictive Practices and Dominant Positions was consulted.

I Facts

A. *The undertaking*

(1) Société d'Etudes de Chimie et de Thérapie Appliquées (SECTA) Laboratoires de Cosmétologie Yves Rocher, whose registered office is in La Gacilly, France, is one of the leading European producers of cosmetics. Its equity capital is held 35 per cent by the Yves Rocher family and 65 per cent by Sanon, a subsidiary of Elf Aquitaine, whose cosmetics production accounts for a quarter of its total turnover.

(2) Yves Rocher markets its products in 50 countries and has 15 wholly-owned marketing subsidiaries abroad. It originally sold its products by mail order but, starting in 1970, has set up in seven Community member states (France, Germany, Belgium, Luxembourg, the Netherlands, the United Kingdom and Spain) a network of franchised retail outlets known as 'Yves Rocher Beauty Centres'. These Centres sell only Yves Rocher products. The Yves Rocher group now has some 10 million mail-order customers. Its network of shops consists of about a thousand franchise businesses of which a little over 600 are in France. Their average annual turnover is less that 300,000 ECUs. Yves Rocher also operates a number of pilot schemes on its own account.

B. *The product and the market*

(3) Cosmetics in the broad sense, i.e. that of substances used in beauty care, can be broken down into 42 groups comprising some 100,000 different products. This extreme diversity reflects the public's many requirements, the creativity of perfumers and cosmeticians, and the high level of technical expertise attained which makes it possible to satisfy those requirements.

(4) Nevertheless, the general statistics published by the business circles concerned all distinguish between four main categories of products:

— beauty products (make-up and skin-care products),
— alcohol-based perfumes,
— hair-care products,
— toiletries.

(5) In all the member-states in which the Yves Rocher network is established cosmetics are a growth market, albeit to differing degrees for each of the four segments referred to above. Most customers are women (90 per cent of sales).

* [1986] O.J. C95/3, [1986] 2 C.M.L.R.95.

(6) On the supply side, the number of both producers and distributors of cosmetics is fairly large. The industry is characterised by the presence of subsidiaries of major industrial groups, being an attractive means of diversification for many groups whose principal line of business is technically similar (pharmaceutical groups in particular). The financial ties between cosmetics manufacturers are therefore global and complex.

(7) The degree of concentration in the industry is comparatively low. The largest European firm holds a 15 per cent share of the Community market, and none of the others has a share exceeding 5 per cent.

(8) If one compares the ranking, over a period of time, of producers in terms of market share, a fair amount of movement is apparent, which is itself an indication of the effort made by each firm to promote its image, and of the severity of competition between suppliers.

(9) In the cosmetics sector as a whole, Yves Rocher holds 7.5 per cent of the Fench market, 6 per cent of the Belgian market, and a share of less than 5 per cent in every other member-state in which the network is established. Unlike some producers who specialise in one or other of the above mentioned four categories of cosmetics, Yves Rocher is active in every segment of the market. Its business is oriented more towards the production of beauty products and alcohol-based perfumes, but even in France, the country in which the Yves Rocher network is most extensive, its sales to do not exceed 15 per cent of total sales in any particular category of products.

(10) The channels through which cosmetics are distributed are many in number and complementary in character in every member-state in which the Yves Rocher chain is established. A distinction may be drawn between general retail outlets and specialist (or selective, exclusive or franchise) retail outlets.

(11) In France, about half the cosmetics sold are marketed through some 100,000 general retail outlets (stores selling household products and cosmetics – *drogueries*), grocers' shops, self-service stores, etc.). A third of all sales are made through some 7,500 specialist retail outlets, including about a thousand franchise shops. Direct selling by the manufacturer (selling by mail order, door-to-door sales or own shops) and sales in chemist's shops each account for about 10 per cent of the industry's total turnover. The respective share of sales accounted for by various forms of distribution varies, however, according to the market segment, as can be seen from the table below showing the proportion of each category of products sold by each distribution method.*

Channels	Product					
	Alcohol-based perfumes	Beauty products	Toiletries	Hair-care products	Others	Total
General retailers	6.6	7.8	12.3	21.8	–	48.5
Specialist retailers	15.9	14.0	1.7	0.4	0.4	32.4
Direct selling	2.7	5.1	1.4	1.0	0.4	10.6
Sale in chemist's shops	0.1	5.4	1.2	1.7	–	8.4
Miscellaneous	0.1	–	–	–	–	0.1
Total	25.4	32.3	16.6	24.9	0.8	100.0

* Taken from a survey by DAFSA entitled 'The world perfume and cosmetic industry'.

(12) The percentage of overall cosmetics sales effected by general retailers is comparable in the other member-states concerned.

(13) Retail selling prices vary considerably from one member state in which the network is established to another. Compared with the prices charged by its competitors, Yves Rocher, whose marketing method is a combination of selling by mail order and specialist retailing, fixes its prices at a level somewhere between those of specialist retailers and those of general retailers.

Yves Rocher sells its products to its franchisees at an average discount of 30 per cent. on its recommended selling prices as published in its catalogues, excluding VAT.

C. The system of notified agreements

(14) As well as selling by mail order, the Yves Rocher group markets its products in the seven member-states concerned through a thousand or so franchised retailers, supplied, in France, direct from the Yves Rocher company and, in the other member-states by the marketing subsidiaries wholly owned by the company.

(15) The notified standard form franchise contracts are geared mainly to retailing; the beauty treatments that franchisees undertake to give under the notified contracts account for only a small proportion of their turnover.

The notified contracts all display basically the same features, with the exception of special arrangements for Belgian franchisees, particular provisions based on local commercial practice and the presence in the first few franchise contracts, concluded when the network was originally set up, of clauses prescribing resale prices and prohibiting cross supplies between Yves Rocher franchisees.

Methods of Choosing franchisees used by Yves Rocher

(16) Yves Rocher selects its franchisees in the light of their personality, their apparent overall aptitude for running a cosmetics retailing business, and their performance in a training programme.

Contracts are concluded with the franchisee personally and may not be assigned or transferred either in whole or in part without Yves Rocher's previous written consent, otherwise the agreement is cancelled without prior notice.

The franchisee undertakes to employ at his Centre a sufficient number of qualified staff.

Legal independence of franchisees

(17) All Yves Rocher franchisees are proprietors of their business, which they carry on at their own risk. They are responsible for the cost of fitting out their premises in accordance with plans and specifications which Yves Rocher causes to be drawn up at its own expense.

All commercial documents issued by the franchisee must carry the franchisee's name and the words 'Yves Rocher Beauty Centre'. Yves Rocher has circulated a directive to franchisees requiring them to display an appropriate notice indicating their status of independent franchisees within the Yves Rocher chain.

Franchisees are required to take out insurance covering their civil liability and employer's liability throughout the period of the contract.

Clause concerning the location of the Beauty Centre

(18) Each contract defines the exact location of the franchisee's shop. In practice, Yves Rocher carries out a preliminary market and location study and proposes to the franchisee the most promising shopping district, within which the franchisee determines the exact location of his beauty centre with the franchisor's consent. The contract stipulates that the shop may not be transferred to another place without Yves Rocher's consent and that the use of Yves Rocher identifying marks is not authorised in any other place.

Exclusive territory of the franchisee

(19) Yves Rocher grants the franchisee an exclusive right within an area defined in the contract to use the franchisor's identifying marks and know-how with a view to selling its products through a retail outlet. The franchisor undertakes not to authorise third parties to open another Yves Rocher Beauty Centre in that territory and not to establish such Centres there itself.

Yves Rocher reserves the right to sell its products to consumers by other means (in particular by mail order).

Grant by Yves Rocher of the right to use its idenitifying marks (shop sign, trade marks, symbols), and its designs and models

(20) Yves Rocher grants the franchisee the right to use the sign, trade marks, symbols, designs and models of which it is the owner, in particular for the bottles, packages and furnishings of the Beauty Centre.

(21) These rights may be exercised only in connection with the operation of the Beauty Centre and its purpose; the franchisee may not exercise them in any other place or for any other purpose and recognises moreover that the right to use the present and future trade name, marks and symbols of Yves Rocher belong exclusively to the company. The contract does not however restrict the right of franchisees to contract the franchisor's industrial property rights.

The grant by Yves Rocher of the above rights ceases on termination of the contract.

Transfer by Yves Rocher to the franchisee of commercial and beauty treatment know-how

(22) The know-how Yves Rocher undertakes to communicate to the franchisee encompasses every aspect of the franchise business, and in particular technical, commercial, promotional, publicity, administrative and financial matters, staff training and general administration.

Before the Centre is opened, Yves Rocher arranges training sessions for the franchisee on the organisation and running of a Centre and on the beauty products and treatments available there. It provides further training from time to time during the currency of the contract.

The franchisee undertakes not to divulge any confidential information and instructions to third parties, and not to use Yves Rocher's commercial secrets in any place or for any purpose other than the Beauty Centre.

Provision of technical and commercial assistance to the franchisee by Yves Rocher

(23) When the Centre is opened, Yves Rocher provides the franchisee with all the aid it considers appropriate in order that the Centre be established and operated in accordance with its policy and image, and places at the franchisee's disposal all its technical knowledge.

During the currency of the contract, the company advises and assists the franchisee on request in the operation of the Beauty Centre: procedures, purchase of products and supplies, publicity (publicity campaign at the time of launch, and periodical sales support and promotion activities, either in the shop or aimed directly at the consumer).

Financial obligations of the franchisee towards the franchisor

(24) In all countries, the franchisee must pay an initial licence fee. In the Netherlands, in addition to an initial licence fee at a lower amount, he must pay an annual royalty of 1 per cent of his turnover net of tax, excluding beauty treatment services.

The franchisee also pays Yves Rocher at regular intervals a fixed proportion of publicity costs.

Use by franchisees of uniform trading methods under Yves Rocher's supervision

(25) The method contracts require franchisees to employ uniform trading methods. The franchisee undertakes to operate his Centre in accordance with the procedures laid down by the company in an operating manual. This covers the following aspects of running the business: decor, lighting, fitting-out in accordance with plans and specifications which Yves Rocher causes to be drawn up at its own expense, layout and furnishing of Centres, presentation of products, sales techniques, publicity campaigns, nature and quality of beauty treatment services, accounts, insurance, etc.

The franchisee is obliged to submit for the prior approval of Yves Rocher all forms of publicity and promotion which he wishes to undertake on his own account. The control exercised by the franchisor extends only to the nature of the publicity and not to the retail prices quoted therein.

The franchisee also undertakes to operate one or more beauty treatment cabines in which only products and treatments authorised by the company may be used or given.

The franchisor reserves the right to carry out checks on stock levels and obtain from the franchisee a copy of his accounts or balance sheet.

Non-compeition covenant

(1) During the lifetime of the contract

(26) The franchisee is expressly forbidden to carry on either directly or indirectly, whether in return for payment or not, any business which competes with an Yves Rocher Beauty Centre. The franchisee is free to acquire financial interests in the capital of a competitor of Yves Rocher, provided this investment does not involve him personally in carrying on competing activities.

He is obliged to sell only products bearing the Yves Rocher trade mark, although he may sell accessories (brushes, tweezers, nail scissors, etc.) with Yves Rocher's previous consent.

(2) On termination of the contract

(27) The franchisee is forbidden to compete with Yves Rocher, whether directly or indirectly, even as an employee, for a period of one year within the exclusive territory, whether on his own account or with the help of a rival firm.

Supply arrangements

(28) The franchisee may purchase Yves Rocher products not only from Yves Rocher but allso from other franchisees, whether or not the latter are located in the same member-state.

He may buy approved accessories, shop furnishings and products for beauty treatments purposes from any supplier.

Sales promotion obligation

(29) The franchisee undertakes to devote all his energy and as much time as necessary to promoting the sale of Yves Rocher products and beauty treatments and agrees not to carry on any activities incompatible with those of a Beauty Centre.

Franchisees selling prices

(30) Yves Rocher circulates to its franchisees a list of recommended resale prices. All franchisees, including those in Belgium, are free to fix their retail selling prices at a lower or higher level, it being understood that it is recommended to them not to sell at a higher price than that given in the catalogue.

As a result of observations made by the Commission, Yves Rocher has expressly deleted with effect from 1 December 1986 the resale price maintenance provisions – which were not applied in practice – contained in the first contracts concluded when the network was originally set up.

Cross supplies between Yves Rocher franchisees

(31) The franchisee is prohibited from selling, whether directly or indirectly, Yves Rocher products to resellers other than Yves Rocher franchisees.

The first contracts forbade the franchisee to sell products even to other Yves Rocher franchisees. This provision has been deleted with effect from 1 December 1986 as a result of observations made by the Commission. Yves Rocher now authorises in all its contracts cross supplies, both national and transnational, between its franchisees.

Duration of contracts

(32) All Yves Rocher contracts are normally concluded and renewed for not more than five years.

Legal status of the Belgian franchisees

(33) Yves Rocher franchisees resell Yves Rocher products and approved accessories (*cf.* point 26) and give beauty treatments entirely in their own name and for their own account.

However, under the terms of their contracts, the Belgian franchisees sell, in Yves Rocher's name and for its account, Yves Rocher products supplied by the franchisor or by the other Belgian franchisees by way of cross supplies (*cf.* point 31) and receive a commission.

In each case, Belgian franchisees are free to fix their selling price to consumers (*cf.* point 30), it being understood that the amount of the 30 per cent commission owed to them by the franchisor when they sell in its name and on its account, varies accordingly.

Third parties' observations

(34) In response to publication of a notice pursuant to Article 19(3) of Regulation 17 the Commission received comments from several third parties. Some approved in substance the exemption of the notified standard form contracts, subject to certain objections of principle to the practice of recommending maximum resale prices, the effect of which could be to bring consumer prices to a uniform level. For the purpose of clarification, Yves Rocher has, at the request of the Commission, issued a circular to franchisees stressing that the recommended prices are purely guidelines and has undertaken to avoid any reference in its circulars to the notion of a maximum price. From now on the catalogues circulated by Yves Rocher will mention that the prices are recommended prices.

II. Legal Assessment

A. Article 85(1)

(35) Article 85(1) prohibits as incompatible with the Common Market all agreements between undertakings which may affect trade between member-states and which have as their object or

effect the prevention, restriction or distortion of competition within the Common Market.

Characteristics of the franchise contracts at issue

(36) By the notified standard form retail franchise contracts, Yves Rocher grants to its franchisees the exclusive right within an area defined in the contract, to use in a retail shop Yves Rocher identifying marks (sign, trade mark and trade name) and its designs and models for the sale of its products.

Yves Rocher transfers to them know-how, consisting in a body of technical and commercial knowledge, previously tested by the franchisor itself, which is not divulged to third parties and therefore constitutes a competitive advantage. This know-how, which is set out in an operating manual and backed up by continuing technical and commercial assistance, is constantly updated in the light of experience gained by the franchisor through its mail-order business and pilot schemes.

The close association between these two forms of support provided by the franchisor helps create an original formula for the retailing of a range of cosmetics based on the theme of natural beauty from plants and sold under a single branch which franchisees agree to promote exclusively.

(37) These rights of user are not granted unconditionally. Franchisees may exploit the industrial property rights granted and the knowledge communicated only in strict accordance with their subject matter: the original and constantly evolving formula for the retailing of Yves Rocher products using the franchisor's proven trading methods.

(38) Inasmuch as the members of the Yves Rocher network are thus bound together by close *de facto* commercial ties, the franchise contracts at issue are the expression of a closely integrated form of distribution. They nonetheless constitute agreements between undertakings within the meaning of Article 85(1), since the franchisees are the proprietors of their businesses, of which they bear the start-up costs and which they operate at their own risk.

Contractual obligations not restrictive of competition

(39) The original distribution formula translated into action by the contracts at issue does not in itself interfere with competition having regard to existing structures of production and supply in the relevant market.* It enables Yves Rocher to establish a uniform distribution network without investing its own capital in the fitting-out of retail shops and at the same time gives non-specialists access to the use of well-known identifying marks and proven trading methods.

(40) The obligations imposed by the franchisor on its franchisees to ensure that they exploit its proprietary industrial property rights and know-how in a manner in keeping with their subject matter are inherent in the very existence of its right in its intellectual creations and fall outside the scope of the contractual and concerted practice of Article 85(1). Consequently, the restrictions on the commercial freedom of franchisees, without which the transfer of the distribution formula concerned could not be envisaged, do not constitute restrictions of competition within the meaning of Article 85(1).

(41) The absence of any contractual obligation on the part of Yves Rocher to apply selection criteria in the choice of its franchisees is explained by the fact that Yves Rocher itself trains franchisees during an induction course with a view to setting up new franchise shops. It is logically entitled to choose its partners freely and turn down applicants who do not, in its view, have the personal qualities and business qualifications which it requires for the application of the formula it has developed.

(42) The franchisor must also be able to participate in determining the location of the Beauty Centre with the franchisee, in their mutual interest; a bad choice might cause the franchisee to fail in business and indirectly damage the network's reputation. In practice, Yves Rocher carries out a preliminary market and location survey, and proposes to the franchisee the most promising area. The exact location of the shop is determined by the franchisee with the franchisor's consent. In any event, the shop's location is agreed upon in the general interest of all members of the chain. For the same reasons, any change in the Beauty Centre's location is subject to Yves Rocher's consent. Article 85(1) is not applicable to this clause to the extent that the relocation of a Beauty Centre may only be refused for reasons of the network's reputation.

(43) The obligation on the part of the franchisee to sell Yves Rocher products only in a Beauty Centre fitted out and decorated in accordance with plans and specifications which Yves Rocher causes to be drawn up at its own expense is also intended to ensure compliance with the original distribution formula communicated by the franchisor. The exterior appearance and interior lay-out of a Beauty Centre and the presentation of products are not factors which can be divorced from the methods and procedures transmitted by Yves Rocher or from the network's brand image.

The same is true of the franchisee's obligation to use know-how transferred by the franchisor and to apply the trading methods developed by the franchisor.

(44) The clause whereby any local publicity undertaken by the licensee on his own account must be submitted for the prior approval of Yves Rocher is, so far as it concerns only the nature of the publicity to the exclusion of selling prices, intended to ensure a qualitative control by the franchisor over individual publicity measures in order to avoid any possible deviation from the theme of natural beauty from plants, on which the network's image is based.

(45) The obligation on the franchisee to sell only products bearing the Yves Rocher trade mark — except in the case of accessories previously approved by the franchisor — is inherent in the very nature of the Yves Rocher distribution formula, the purpose of which is to enable independent traders to sell the complete range of Yves Rocher products using a sign, a trade mark and symbols, as well as trading methods which have proved effective. The retailing of products bearing trade marks other than that of the franchisor exposes Yves Rocher to the risk of the use of their know-how for the benefit of competing producers and would detract from the identity of the network, which is symbolised by the Yves Rocher sign.

This implies that the franchisee may obtain supplies only from Yves Rocher or from other franchisees.

(46) The prohibition on the resale by franchisees of Yves Rocher products to resellers who do not belong to the Yves Rocher network is in this case inherent in franchisees' obligations to comply with the franchisor's procedures and methods and to offer products for sale under the Yves Rocher sign. These obligations would be made meaningless if Yves Rocher franchisees could freely pass over the goods covered by the contract to resellers who by definition have no access to the Yves Rocher know-how and are not bound by the same obligations, which are necessary in order to establish and maintain the originality and reputation of the network and its identifying marks.

---

* See Case 161/84, PRONUPTIA: [1986] 1 C.M.L.R. 414, at para. [15].

(47) The provision under which the franchisee agrees not to carry on competing activities for the duration of the contract, in the same way as the prohibition on the assignment or transfer in whole or in part of the franchise contract, without the prior written consent of the franchisor, and on the divulgence of the know-how made available, is indispensible to protect the know-how and assistance provided by the franchisor. By their nature, the know-how and assistance provided are of a kind which could be used for the benefit of other beauty products or services, which would, even if only indirectly, enable competitors to benefit from the trading methods employed. Other means to avoid the same risks might not be as effective.

The clause which requires that the acquisition of a financial interest in the capital of an undertaking competing with Yves Rocher should not involve the franchisee in personally taking part in competing acitivities pursues the same aim and is considered in the same way.

(48) The same is true of the clause forbidding former Yves Rocher franchisees from carrying on a retail cosmetics business in their former exclusive territories for one year after the contract's termination. This is simply intended to prevent Yves Rocher's competitors from benefiting from the know-how which has been communicated by Yves Rocher to the former franchisee, and from the clientele acquired as a result of that know-how and Yves Rocher's identifying marks at a time when owing to the exclusivity of the territory allotted to the franchisee during the currency of the contract. Yves Rocher has no retail outlet in that territory after the contract's expiry and must therefore be allowed a reasonable period in which to establish a new Beauty Centre.

In the present case, the clause does not go beyond what is strictly necessary to achieve its purpose, since a former franchisee can compete with Yves Rocher as soon as the contract expires by setting up in business outside his former exclusive territory, possibly in the territory of other Yves Rocher franchisees. Under the circumstances, this provision cannot be considered as restrictive of competition under Article 85(1).

This assessment is without prejudice to the rights of franchisees under national law on termination of contract.

(49) The general sales promotion obligation imposed on franchisees, in that they undertake to devote all their energy and as much time as necessary to promoting the sale of Yves Rocher products and beauty treatments, and agree in consequence not to carry on any activities incompatible with those of their Centre does not in this case amount to a restriction of competition. The success of the distribution formula adopted by Yves Rocher depends on the presence and the personal commitment of the franchisee in the operation of the business, the franchisee being selected on the basis of his/her personal qualities after having undergone appropriate training by Yves Rocher. Subject to this reservation, the clause does not prohibit the franchisee from carrying on a non-competing business provided the franchisee's personal commitment to the distribution of the Yves Rocher products is ensured.

(50) The right which the franchisor reserves to inspect franchisees' stock levels, accounts and balance sheets, is to enable the franchisor to verify, if the need arises, whether franchisees are discharging their obligations. In so far as this right serves only to enable checks to be carried out on franchisees' compliance with obligations not covered by Article 85(1), it likewise cannot be considered restrictive of competition without prejudice to any legal consequences under national law or interference by the franchisor.

In particular, the franchisor's right to inspect stock levels allows him to avoid the unduly long stocking of products which could affect their quality.

The Commission reserves its right to intervene should these controls be used by the franchisor to affect the freedom of the franchisees to fix their selling prices.

(51) The recommended prices shown on the catalogues issued by Yves Rocher to franchisees are legitimate, since franchisees remain entirely free to determine their own prices and since, during the proceedings, no evidence has been found of any concerted practice between the franchisor and franchisees, or among franchisees, to the effect that the recommended prices should be applied.*

No anti-competitive effects from the points of view of competing producers and distributors

(52) From the point of view of competing producers and distributors, the Yves Rocher network cannot have appreciable horizontal anti-competitive effects as against other brands in view of the large number of both producers and distributors of cosmetics.

(53) Although it is one of the leading European producers Yves Rocher holds just over 5 per cent of the entire cosmetics market in only two member-states, and in its principal geographical market it controls no more than 15 per cent of one of the four market segments. Its 600 or so franchised retail outlets in France cannot, with the approximately 7,000 specialist retailers in that country, have the effect of freezing the structures of distribution and rendering access to the market appreciably more difficult for competing producers compared with the 100,000 general retail outlets in that country and the relatively large volume of their sales in each of the four categories of cosmetics. The same holds true for the other member-states, where the total number of Yves Rocher sales outlets is less than 500 and non-specialist retailers' account for a similar proportion of the industry's sales.

Contractual obligations restrictive of competition

(54) On the other hand, Yves Rocher's selection of only one franchisee for a given territory within which the franchisee has an exclusive right to use the franchisor's identifying marks and know-how for the sale of Yves Rocher products in a Beauty Centre, the franchisor undertaking not to establish a shop itself in the territory of each of its franchisees, combined with the prohibition on the opening by franchisees of a second shop stemming from the prohibition on using Yves Rocher's identifying marks in a location other than that specified in the contract, results in a degree of sharing of markets between the franchisor and the franchisees or between franchisees, thereby restricting competition within the distribution network.

(55) By virtue of such clauses, Yves Rocher's franchise contracts prevent franchisees from setting up in business in another member-state and may thus affect trade between member-states to an appreciable extent in view of the size of the Yves Rocher group, its market share — greater than 5 per cent in two of the member-states concerned — the reputation of its products, the expansion of the Yves Rocher chain of shops throughout a substantial part of the Common Market and the existence alongside that chain of a highly developed mail-order business. The notified contracts therefore fall within Article 85(1).

* *Ibid*, at para. [25].

B. Article 85(3)

(56) Under Article 85(3), the provisions of Article 85(1) may be declared inapplicable in the case of any agreement which contributes to improving the production or distribution of goods or to promoting technical or economic progress, while allowing consumers a fair share of the resulting benefit, and which does not:

(a) impose on the undertakings concerned restrictions which are not indispensable to the attainment of these objectives;

(b) afford such undertakings the possibility of eliminating competition in respect of a substantial part of the products in question.

(57) Commission Regulations 67/67 and 1983/83, as last amended by the Act of Accession of Spain and Portugal, on the block exemption of exclusive dealing and exclusive distribution agreements are not applicable to the standard form franchise at issue, the legal nature of which is different.* The franchise contracts go beyond mere distribution agreements, for the franchisor undertakes to grant rights to use its identifying marks and its proven trading methods with a view to the application of an original and changing distribution formula. It must therefore be decided whether the contracts at issue qualify for an individual exemption under Article 85(3).

(58) Yves Rocher's franchise contracts contribute to improving the distribution of the goods in question, since they help the producer to penetrate new markets by enabling him to expand his network without having to undertake any investment in the fitting-out of new shops. Moreover, the development of a chain of identical retail outlets stenghtens competition *vis-à-vis* large retail organisations with a branch network. By its policy of selection and training, directed mainly at prospective franchisees with no experience of running a retail establishment selling beauty products, whose sales outlets thus supplement existing specialist sales outlets, Yves Rocher increases interbrand competition and accordingly improves the structure of cosmetics distribution.

(59) The close intergration of independent traders within the Yves Rocher network leads to a rationalisation of distribution through a standardisation of trading methods covering every aspect of retailing. The direct nature — there being no wholesalers — of the relationship between franchisor and franchisees facilitates consumer feedback and the adjustment of supply to a constantly changing demand, the fickleness of which is a feature of the market concerned.

(60) The grant to franchisees of an exclusive territory, combined with the prohibition on setting up outside this territory, enables them to pursue a more intensive policy of selling Yves Rocher products by concentrating on their allotted territory, helped in this by the fact that the Yves Rocher retailing formula is based on a single brand. Territorial exlusivity also simplifies planning and ensures the continuity of supplies.

(61) The agreements at issue allow consumers a fair share of the benefit resulting from these improvements in distribution, as a wide range of the same cosmetics is more readily available in a number of member-states. Moreover, because they are running their own business and are therefore motivated by the desire for maximum efficiency, franchisees make dynamic and hard-working retailers, which is to the consumer's advantage. The homogeneity of the network, the standardisation of trading methods and the direct link between franchisor and franchisee all ensure that the consumer benefits in full from the know-how

* *Ibid*, at paras. [15] & [33].

passed on by the franchisor and ensure the quality and freshness of the products, which are liable to deteriorate rapidly with time. Lastly, Yves Rocher's policy of charging prices mid-way between those of specialist and non-specialist retailers helps to widen the circle of cosmetics users.

(62) Finally, the commercial practice of the Yves Rocher network and the civil liability insurance taken out by the Yves Rocher group and by franchisees ensure that any product which may be defective is replaced and that any damage which might be sustained as a result of using an Yves Rocher product or undergoing beauty treatment by a franchisee with be covered. Further, consumers will be in a position to know that they are dealing with independent traders whose individual liability may be called upon.

(63) Yves Rocher's contracts have not imposed any restrictions which are not indispensable to the attainment of the above mentioned objective since the resale price maintenance clauses and the prohibition on cross supplies between franchisees, which prevented the machinery for correcting price differences within the network from operating, were deleted from old contracts. The remaining obligations caught by Article 85(1) are indispensable to the establishment of the network; none of the Yves Rocher franchisees would, in all probability, have agreed to undertake the investment needed to set up an independent business had he not been certain of receiving a degree of protection against competition from another Centre set up in his territory by the franchisor or another franchisee.

(64) The agreement between Yves Rocher and each of its franchisees does not afford them the possibility of eliminating competition in respect of a substantial part of cosmetics, as competition between franchisees is sufficiently ensured by the smallness of the exclusive territory allotted and the possibility for each franchisee to sell to any customer, from whatever area, entering his shop.

The loosening up of the system, adjusted by Yves Rocher at the Commission's request, has brought about a degree of price competition within the network in that franchisees can now freely obtain supplies from any other franchisee and profit from any difference between the selling prices which Yves Rocher fixes in each member-state at a level somewhere between those charged by its major local competitors. Yves Rocher will be unable to prevent or hinder, on pain of revocation of the exemption pursuant to Article 8(3) of Regulation 17, recourse by franchisees to the transnational cross supplies which the price differences between certain member-states are likely to encourage, especially in the case of franchisees operating near national frontiers.

(65) Even the combined effect of all Yves Rocher franchise contracts is not enough to afford the network the possibility of eliminating competition between brands, in view of the breadth and competitive structure of the supply side and the modest share of the cosmetics market held by Yves Rocher.

(66) The provisions of article 85(1) may therefore be declared not applicable to the standard form Yves Rocher franchise contracts, under the terms of Article 85(3). Accordingly it is not necessary to examine further the legal status of the Belgian franchisees. Assuming that they fall within the scope of Article 85(1) they benefit from the exemption in any event.

C. Articles 6 and 8 of Regulation 17

(67) The first franchise contracts concluded by Yves Rocher when its network was originally set up did not satisfy the requirements of Article 85(3) in the form in which they were

notified, in that they contained resale-price-maintenance clauses and a prohibition on cross supplies between Yves Rocher franchisees. These obligations have been deleted with effect from 1 December 1986 at the Commission's request. It is therefore possible, by virtue of Article 6(1) of Regulation 17, to make the date on which the exemption takes effect with regard to the old, amended contracts coincide with the date of coming into force of the amendments, namely 1 December 1986.

(68) The other contracts fulfilled the exemption conditions from the date on which they were notified, namely 15 January 1985. In accordance with the second sentence of Article 6(1) of Regulation 17, the exemption may take effect on that date with regard to these contracts.

(69) In view of the novel character of the notified standard form contracts and the speed at which the structure and methods of cosmetics distribution are liable to change, it is desirable to limit the period of validity of this Decision to 14 January 1992.

(70) Furthermore, it is appropriate that an obligation should be attached to the decision under Article 8(1) of Regulation 17, requiring Yves Rocher to communicate to the Commission each year the recommended sale prices and prices charged to franchisees for Yves Rocher products on the date of such communication in each member-state where the network is established. This obligation will permit the Commission to assess the economic interest of franchisees in making transnational cross sales which should in the normal course of things be brought about by price differences between member-states, and thus contribute, allowing a reduction in these differences, to allowing consumers a fair share of the benefit resulting from the improvement in distribution. The obligation imposed should also permit the Commission to evaluate the risk of direct or indirect obstacles, whether concerted or unilateral, to transnational cross deliveries, with a view to the possible application of Article 8(3) of Regulation 17.

THE COMMISSION, for these reasons,
HAS ADOPTED THIS DECISION:

Article 1
Pursuant to Article 85(3) of the EEC Treaty, the provisions of Article 85(1) are hereby declared inapplicable to the standard-form franchise contracts concluded by the Yves Rocher group for the retailing of its cosmetics within the Community.

Article 2
This Deceision shall apply with effect from 15 January 1985. However, it shall apply only with effect from 1 December 1986 in the case of those standard-form contracts which, until that date, contained resale-price-maintenance clauses and clauses prohibiting cross supplies between franchisees. It shall be valid until 14 January 1992.

Article 3
Société d'Etudes de Chimie et de Thérapie Appliquées (SECTA) Laboratoires de Cosmétologie Yves Rocher shall send the Commission on 1 September each year its current recommended retail prices and prices payable by franchisees in the member-states in which the network is established.

Article 4
This Decision is addressed to Société d'Etudes de Chimie et de Thérapie Appliquées (SECTA) Laboratoires de Cosmétologie Yves Rocher, F-56201 La Gacilly.

RE THE AGREEMENTS OF PRONUPTIA DE PARIS SA (Case IV/30.937)

**Before the Commission of the European Communities
(87/17/EEC)
[1989] 4 CMLR 355**

(Signed by Mr. Commissioner Sutherland)

17 December 1986*
[Gaz: EC861217B]

Application for negative clearance or exemption,

Restrictive practices, Franchise agreements, Competition. The following clauses in a standard-form franchise contract between franchisor and franchisees did not fall within Article 85(1) EEC: (a) obligation of the franchisor to assist the franchisee in selecting the site and premises, shopfitting, promotion and advertising, training etc.; (b) prohibition on the franchisee engaging in any similar business in the same area or in any other area where he would be competing with another franchisee both during the contract period and for one year thereafter; (c) prohibition on the franchisee transferring the franchised business or its management to another person; (d) obligation on the franchisee to carry on the business in the manner prescribed by the franchisor and to use the latter's know-how and expertise; (e) obligation on the franchisee to carry on the business from the premises approved by the franchisor and fitted out according to the latter's instructions; (f) submission of the franchisee's local advertising to the franchisor for approval; (g) requirement that the franchisee obtain his core goods 'connected with the essential object of the franchise business' exclusively from the franchisor or suppliers nominated by him, including other franchisees, (h) franchisor's right to vet *ex post* the quality of peripheral goods stocked by the franchisee to ensure they are not damaging to the brand image of the franchise; (i) franchisee only to use the franchise trade mark or logo in combination with his own business name and identifying him as a franchisee; (j) franchisee to pay royalties; (k) franchisee to contribute to an advertising and promotional fund; (l) circulation of retail prices to franchisees and franchisor's recommendation of maximum retail prices; (m) payment of minimum royalties annually; (n) requirement to advance order, and to hold minimum stocks. [25]-[27]

Restrictive practices, Franchise agreements, Retail. Retail franchise agreements are different in nature and in content from the bilateral obligations accepted by the parties in exclusive distribution contracts and dealerships in a selective distribution system. [27]

Restrictive practices, Franchise agreements, Market sharing. The following clauses in a retail franchise standard-form contract fell within Article 85(1) as involving market sharing: (a) exclusivity granted to franchisee to operate under the franchisor's name in a given sales area; (b) obligation on the franchisee to carry on the franchise business exclusively from the premises approved for that purpose. [28]

The Commission *held that* most of the clauses in Pronuptia's standard-form franchise agreement with its franchisees were not covered by Article 85(1) EEC, *that* two clauses related to market

---

* Published in [1987] O.J. L13/39 (15 January 1987). The authentic text is in French.

sharing and therefore were so covered, *and that* Regulation 1983/83 did not apply, *but granted* individual exemption for the period 1983 to 1991.

The following case was referred to by the Commission in its decision:

Pronuptia De Paris GmbH v. *Pronuptia De Paris Irmgard Schillgallis* (161/84), 29 January 1986; [1986] 1 C.M.L.R. 414, Gaz: 161/84 [Reprinted in Appendix 6 above.]

Decision

The Commission of the European Communities, in the light of the EEC Treaty and of Council Regulation 17 (especially Articles 6 and 8), received an application for negative clearance or exemption filed on 22 April 1983 by Pronuptia de Paris SA, of Paris, of its standard form of retail franchise agreement which it proposed to sign with all its franchisees.

A summary of the agreement was published* in accordance with Article 19(3) of Regulation 17. The Advisory Committee on Restrictive Practices and Dominant Positions was consulted.

I. Facts

A. Pronuptia de Paris

(1) Pronuptia de Paris (Pronuptia) is a French public limited company incorporated in 1958 which has a registered capital of 3.3 million FF. Pronuptia specialises in the sale of bridal wear and accessories. On 9 December 1985 financial difficulties forced the company to apply to the Paris Tribunal de Commerce for temporary protection from its creditors, during which it was allowed to continue its operations.

(2) Pronuptia carries on business mainly in France and other European countries, but is also represented outside Europe in countries such as Canada, Japan, Lebanon and the United States.

(3) In France, its distribution network numbers 148 of which 135 are franchised, five are subsidiaries and eight are branches.

(4) In the other member-states (Germany, Belgium, Spain, Greece, Ireland, Luxembourg and the United Kingdom) in which Pronuptia uses franchising to distribute its products, it has a little over 100 franchised outlets. In Germany, Spain and the United Kingdom it also has subsidiaries.

(5) The total turnover of the Pronuptia network throughout the world in 1985 was about 250 million FF.

(6) Pronuptia claims to have the biggest chain of shops offering formal wear in the world, and to be the only network specialising in bridal wear in France, where there is no similarly organised competition.** In France, Pronuptia holds about 30 per cent of the bridal wear market. Against this, it holds only more modest shares in other member-states.

B. The relevant products and market***

(7) The Pronuptia network sells and hires not only wedding dresses but also wedding attire for attendants and guests, including men's formal wear, and a full range of accessories such as hats, veils, tights, gloves, shoes, handbags, garters, scarves,

---

* [1986] O.J. C178/2.
** Pronuptia Operations Manual, Vol. 1, Section I, p.1, and Section II, pp.1 and 3.
*** The services offered by the Pronuptia chain (honeymoons, photographers, receptions, etc.) are disregarded as they are at present only offered in France and only if the franchisee wishes. Their economic impact is therefore probably insignificant.

and lingerie. Its collection in any year numbers around 1,000 items of all types.

(8) The articles offered from Pronuptia outlets fall into three categories which also differ as to their sourcing.

(a) fashion goods, of Pronuptia's own design, which are manufactured for it by subcontractors, such as its wedding dress designs which are registered and bear the 'Pronuptia' trade mark;

(b) other fashion goods, not of Pronuptia's design but of designs commissioned or selected 'off-the-shelf' from other suppliers, which Pronuptia buys in and on which it also puts its trade mark;

(c) goods not designed by or for Pronuptia which are purchased by franchisees directly from the supplier of their choice and invoiced to them by the supplier.

The articles in categories (a) and (b) which are supplied and invoiced to franchisees by Pronuptia itself account for about two-thirds of the goods traded through the network. Pronuptia sells at the same prices to all franchisees.

(9) There are many other manufacturers of bridal fashions in France and other EEC countries. In France, there are, to name but a few, 'Les Mariées de Christina', 'Les Mariées de Marcelle', (Maggy Rouff), 'Les Mariées de France', 'Les Mariées de Rêve', Claude Hervé, and 'Les Mariées Laura'; in Germany, there are Vera Mont, Pagels and Horrn, and the Team Brantude International chain. These manufacturers generally do not use the franchising route to sell their products. There is also competition from small dressmakers' shops and from the large fashion houses, all of which also design wedding dresses.

C. The Pronuptia franchise agreement

(10) Pronuptia proposes to sign the notified franchise agreement with all its franchisees both in France and in other EEC and non-EEC countries. It wishes the Commission to take a formal decision on its application for exemption of the agreement.

(11) The main provisions of the standard form agreement are as follows:

— The franchisor, Pronuptia, grants the franchisee the exclusive right to use the 'Pronuptia de Paris' trade mark in a defined sales territory, where the franchisee agrees to run a retail outlet dealing primarily in bridal wear and accessories under the Pronuptia name and logo or a derived logo approved by the franchisor. The franchisor undertakes to credit the franchisee with 10 per cent of any mail-order sales it makes to customers in the territory involving products normally sold by the franchisee (clause 1).

— The franchisor undertakes to assist the franchisee with, in particular, selecting the site and the premises, shopfitting and stocking, regular training of the franchisee and his staff, promotion and advertising (for which the franchisor will provide point-of-sale material and will check that the franchisee's advertising is consistent with the network's brand image), and with continuing information and advice on innovations, promotions, market analysis, purchasing, etc. (clause 3).

— The franchisee undertakes not to use the Pronuptia trade mark and logo other than in conjunction with his own business name followed by the words 'Franchisee of Pronuptia de Paris' (clause 2).

— The franchisee agrees to carry on the franchise business in the particular manner developed by the franchisor and to use the know-how and expertise the franchisor has made available (clause 4, second paragraph, first indent).

— The franchisee is required to carry on the franchised business exclusively from the premises approved by the franchisor and fitted and decorated according to its instructions (clause 4, second paragraph, second indent).

— The franchisee must obtain the franchisor's approval for his local advertising (clause 4, second paragraph, third indent).

— In consideration of the rights and services received, the franchisee agrees to pay the franchisor an initial non-recurring fee* and monthly royalties of between 4 and 5 per cent of his total turnover from the direct sale of the franchise goods to customers from the franchised shop (clause 5).

— The franchisee agrees to contribute a further sum, equal to his monthly royalty payment, to an advertising and promotional fund. This fund is managed by the franchisor, who however consults with franchisees on how to obtain the maximum benefit from the advertising budget (clause 6).

— The franchisee agrees to pay a minimum amount of royalties each year (clause 7).

— The franchisee agrees to order the goods traded from the franchised business exclusively from the franchisor, and may be required to obtain them exclusively from the franchisor if the franchisor is able to supply all the franchisee's requirements (clause 8, first and third paragraphs). However, the franchisee may obtain goods not connected with the essential object of the franchise business from the supplier of his choice, subject to the franchisor's right to vet such goods afterwards and to forbid the franchisee to market them from the franchised outlet if it judges them to be out of keeping with the brand image (clause 8, fourth and fifth paragraphs).

The franchisee undertakes to order at least 50 per cent of his estimated sales, based on those of the previous year, in advance according to a fixed timetable and to have the articles shown in the catalogue in stock (clause 8, seventh and eight paragraphs).

The franchisee is free to obtain Pronuptia products from any other franchise in the network (clause 8, ninth paragraph).

— The franchisee is free to set his own retail prices, the prices circulated by the franchisor in internal literature being only suggestions. However, the franchisee is recommended not to exceed the maximum prices quoted by the franchisor in advertising and promotions (clause 9).

— The franchisee may not assign the franchised business in law or in fact to another person without the written consent of the franchisor. In the event of the sale or assignment of the management of the franchised business, or the death or incapacity of the franchisee, or any other circumstance which prevents the franchisee from carrying on the franchise normally, the franchisor is entitled to terminate the contract (clause 10). The contract may also be determined if the franchisee files for bankruptcy, goes into liquidation, ceases trading, or if either party breaches its obligations (clause 13).

— The agreement has a term of five years, which is automatically renewed for further one-year periods unless terminated upon at least six months' notice before the end of any period (clause 11).

— The franchisee agrees not to engage, directly or indirectly, during the currency of the agreement and for one year after its expiry or termination, in any similar business in the same area or in any other area where he would be in competition with another Pronuptia outlet. However, the franchisee may continue to carry on the business in the allotted territory after the agreement has ended if he

(i) has exercised the franchise for more than 10 years,

(ii) has discharged his contractual obligations, and

(iii) does not put the know-how and experience he has accumulated at the service of a competing network (clause 12)

(12) At the Commission's request, Pronuptia has amended the standard form agreement to put into writing certain rights which the franchisee allegedly had in practice already, namely the rights

(a) to purchase Pronuptia products from other franchisees,

(b) to purchase goods not connected with the essential object of the franchise business from suppliers of their choice, subject to *ex post* qualitative vetting by the franchisor, and

(c) to set their own retail prices, the prices circulated by the franchisor being only suggestions and the franchisee merely being recommended not to exceed the maximum prices quoted by the franchisor in advertising and promotions. Pronuptia has abolished the clause which requires the franchisee not to harm the brand image of the franchisor by his pricing level.

D. The legal proceedings between Pronuptia and one of its German franchises

(13) Following legal proceedings in 1981, on the subject of a franchise contract and taken by Pronuptia's German subsidiary, Pronuptia GmbH, against one of its franchisees, the Federal Supreme Court asked the Court of Justice of the European Communities for a preliminary ruling on the following questions (*inter alia*):

(i) whether franchise agreements such as those before it fell within the scope of Article 85(1), and, if so,

(ii) whether such agreements could be covered by Commission Regulation 67/67, and, if so,

(iii) whether particular clauses found in the agreements before the Court were covered by Regulation 67/67.

The Court of Justice gave judgment* on 28 January 1986.

(14) In this judgment the Court of Justice defined retail franchises, with which the case and the present proceedings are concerned, as systems whereby 'a firm which has established itself in a certain business in one market, and has developed a system for carrying on that business, licenses independent traders, in return for payment, to use its name and proven formula for the business in other markets. Rather than a method of distribution, the system is a way of exploiting a body of expertise financially without having to invest the firm's own capital' (ground 15 of the judgment).

(15) The use of the same name and a uniform business system, and the payment of royalties for the advantages received, were typical features which set franchise agreements apart, the Court said, from exclusive distribution agreements or dealerships in a selective distribution system (ground 15).

(16) The Court acknowledged that for such a retail franchise operation to work the franchisor had to be able to

(a) 'make its know-how available to the franchisees and give them the assistance they require to be able to apply its business system', without running the risk of the know-how and assistance benefiting competitors (ground 16), and to

(b) 'take measures to preserve the common identity and reputation of the network trading under its names' (ground 17).

---

* The initial entry fee depends on the population of the allotted sales territory and varies between 0.15 and 0.20 FF per resident. The average population of a territory is about 300,000. The average entry fee is thus between 45,000 and 60,000 FF.

* Case 161/84: [1986] 1 C.M.L.R. 414.

(17) After having noted in ground 15 that a retail franchise operation 'does not in itself restrict competition', the Court held in the operative part of the judgment that 'the compatibility of retail franchise contracts with Article 85(1) is a function of the clauses such contracts contain and the economic context in which they occur.'

(18) It further held not to be restrictions of competition falling within Article 85(1) 'clauses that are indispensable to prevent the know-how made available and the assistance given by the franchisor from benefiting competitors' and 'clauses that provide for the control essential to preserve the common identity and reputation of the network trading under the name'.

(19) It held on the other hand that 'clauses that involve market sharing between frnachisor and franchisee or between franchisees constitute restrictions of competition within the meaning of Article 85(1) . . . and are capable of affecting trade between member states'.

(20) The Decision in the present proceedings is inspired by the principles established and guidance given by the Court in the above judgment.

(21) Following the publication of a notice pursuant to Article 19(3) of Regulation 17, the Commission has received several comments from third parties. These ask the Commission, before adopting a favourable decision, to be particularly careful in its examination of the legal and factual background of this standard agreement. In addition, they express concern over certain clauses of the contract, notably those that concern indicative prices and the prohibition of competition, and those which result in a partitioning of the market. In this respect, it is sufficient to point out that these clauses have been considered in the light of the principles set out in the judgment of the Court in the 'PRONUPTIA' case, already discussed, and taking very careful account of the factual background.

II. Legal Assessment

A. Article 85(1)

(22) Article 85(1) prohibits as incompatible with the Common Market all agreements between undertakings, decisions by associations of undertakings and concerted practices which may affect trade between member-states and which have as their object or effect the prevention, restriction or distortion of competition within the Common Market.

(23) The standard form of retail franchise agreement that Pronuptia proposes to sign with all its franchises is an agreement between business undertakings within the meaning of Article 85.

(a) Clauses not falling within Article 85(1)

(24) First, the obligation on the franchisor to assist the franchisee with selecting the site and premises, shopfitting, promotion and advertising, training, news of products, innovations, etc. (clause 3 of the contract) does not fall within the scope of Article 85(1) because it forms part of the basic services the franchisor provides to the franchisee.

(25) The clauses in the contract that serve the following purposes are also not restrictions of competition falling with Article 85(1) according to the Court's judgment (see also paragraph 18), in which many of these clauses were specifically mentioned;

(i) clauses that are essential to prevent the know-how made available and the assistance given by the franchisor from benefiting competitors, namely (*inter alia*):

— the prohibition on the franchisee from engaging, directly or indirectly during the currency of the agreement and for one year after its expiry or termination, in any similar business in the same area or in any other area where he would be in competition with another Pronuptia outlet (clause 12).

The ban on competition during the period of the contract is necessary to protect the know-how and other assistance supplied. These benefits lend themselves to use with other products which would benefit competitors, if only indirectly. Other ways of preventing this risk might not be as effective.

The period of one year after the ending of the contract during which the franchisee continues to be bound by the non-competition covenant can in the present case be regarded as reasonable, within the meaning of the court's judgment (ground 16), both for the purpose stated above and to allow Pronuptia to establish a new outlet in the territory of the former franchisee, which it is unable to do during the term of the contract because of the franchisee's exclusivity. It should also be noted that the post-term competition ban is relaxed in certain circumstances (clause 12, second paragraph).

Therefore, in this particular case, it should not be considered as restricting competition within the meaning of Article 85(1). The assessment of the clause in question does not prejudice any relief available to franchisees under national law at the end of the contract.

— the prohibition on the franchisee from selling the franchised business or assigning its management to another person, under penalty of termination by the franchisor (clause 10):

(ii) clauses that provide for the control essential to preserve the common identity and reputation of the network trading under the franchisor's name, namely (*inter alia*):

— the obligation on the franchisee to carry on the franchised business in the manner prescribed by Pronuptia and to use the know-how and expertise it makes available (clause 4, second paragraph, first indent),
— the obligation on the franchisee to carry on the franchised business from the premises approved by the franchisor and fitted and decorated according to its instructions (clause 4, second paragraph, second indent).
— the obligation on the franchisee to obtain the franchisor's approval for his local advertising (clause 4, second paragraph, third indent); it should be said that this control only concerns the nature of the advertisements with the object of ensuring conformity with the Pronuptia chain's brand image.
— the obligation on the franchisee, owing to the nature and quality of the products traded in the franchise business (fashion goods) and in order to preserve the consistency of the brand image, to order the goods connected with the essential object of the franchise business exclusively from the franchisor or suppliers nominated by the franchisor (clause 8, first paragraph). It is emphasised that the franchisee may purchase such goods from any other franchisee in the network (clause 8, ninth paragraph),
— the right of the franchisor to vet, *ex post*, the quality of products not connected with the essential object of the franchise business that the franchisee may purchase from the supplier of his choice and to forbid the franchisee to market them from the outlet if they are damaging to the brand image (clause 8, fourth and fifth paragraphs),
— the prohibition on the franchisee to assign their contract without the written agreement of the franchisor (clause 10).

(26) The Pronuptia standard form agreement also contains a number of other clauses which do not, by reason of their object, nature or effect, fall within Article 85(1). They include:

— the prohibition on the franchisee's using the Pronuptia trade mark or logo except in combination with his own business name followed by the words 'Franchisee of Pronuptia de Paris' (clause 2), which merely serves to identify the franchise relationship,

— the obligation on the franchisee to pay the franchisor an initial non-recurring fee and monthly royalties of between 4 and 5 per cent of his total turnover from the direct sale of the franchise goods to customers from the franchise shop (clause 5) because this is the franchisee's consideration for the rights and services obtained from the franchisor; it should be noted that no royalties are payable on goods that the franchisee sells to other franchisees in the Pronuptia network,

— the obligation on the franchisee to contribute a further sum, equal to his monthly royalty payment, to an advertising and promotional fund (clause 6); this obligation, while it restricts the commercial freedom of the franchisee as regards how much to spend on advertising, how to advertise and whether to advertise at all, does not appear in the present case likely appreciably to affect competition on the relevant market,

— the circulation of retail prices to franchisees and the recommendation to franchisees not to exceed the maximum prices quoted by the franchisor in his advertising and promotions (clause 9).

With regard to the circulation of retail prices by the franchisor, the Commission has no evidence of any concerted practice between the franchisor and franchisees or between franchisees *inter se* to maintain these prices. In these circumstances the mere suggestion of prices for the guidance of franchisees cannot be regarded as restrictive of competition, as is acknowledged by the Court in its judgment (see in particular paragraph 1(e) of the operative part of the judgement).

There is no more evidence of abuse to ground a conclusion other than that reached for the circulation of retail prices, *mutatis mutandis*, in the recommendation to franchisees not to exceed the prices quoted by the franchisor in advertising and promotions, since the recommendation to observe certain prices is not itself likely to restrict the licensee's freedom to determine his prices. The Commission reserves the right to intervene if the franchisor should seek to limit the franchisees' freedom to set their resale prices.

(27) Retail franchise agreements, as the Court acknowledged in its judgment (see paragraph 15), are different in nature and in content from the bilateral obligations accepted by the parties, both in cases of exclusive distribution contracts and dealerships in a selective distribution system.

This being so, the obligations on the franchisee

— to pay a minimum amount of royalties each year (clause 7),
— to order in advance according to a fixed time-table at least 50 per cent of his estimated sales, based on those of the previous year (clause 8, seventh paragraph), and
— to hold stocks (clause 8, eighth paragraph),

do not constitute in the present case, restrictions of competition falling within Article 85(1).

In a selective distribution system, such obligations could be regarded as restricting competition when they exclude from the network firms that fulfilled the uniform qualitative selection criteria but were unwilling to accept such further obligations, and when their affect was that distributors would be forced to push certain products to the detriment of other items. It is a different matter, however, in the systems of distribution franchises operated by Pronuptia in this particular case. In effect, the characteristics of such a system are such that the franchisor grants to the franchisee the exclusive right to use his brand marks and his commercial know-how in a defined territory, and that the franchisor is free to choose his franchisees. The exclusion of any others from the territory allotted to the franchisee is therefore a consequence which is inherent in the very system of franchising. Likewise, one may consider as a consequence inherent to this franchise system the fact that the franchisee, because of the use of the franchisor's exclusive mark and brand which identifies the franchised sales outlet, and because of the obligation not to compete, will in fact concentrate his promotional efforts on the particular products franchised.

In the circumstances, the real competitive situation in the market should not be influenced by the obligations in question as such.

(b) Clauses falling within Article 85(1)

(28) As the Court held in its judgment (ground 23 and 24 and operative part, paragraph 1(d)), 'Clauses that involve market sharing between franchisor and franchisee or between franchisees do constitute restrictions of competition within the meaning of Article 85(1).' This is the case with the following clauses, which were specifically mentioned by the Court:

— the exclusivity granted to the franchisee to operate under the franchisor's name in a given sales area (clause 1, first paragraph),
— the obligation on the franchisee to carry on the franchised business exclusively from the premises approved for that purpose (clause 4, second paragraph, second indent).

The combined effect of these clauses is to protect the franchisee against competition from other franchisees. Moreover, the further clause (clause 1, fifth paragraph) whereby the franchisor undertakes to pay the franchisee 10 per cent of any mail-order sales to customers in the franchisee's territory, on products normally sold by the franchisee, implies that the franchisor may not directly operate in the allocated territory.

(29) The Court also held that 'retail franchise agreements containing clauses that involve market sharing between franchisor and franchisee or between franchisees are inherently likely to affect trade between member-states, even if they are between parties resident in the same member-state, because they prevent the franchisees setting up in another member-state' (ground 26). An effect on trade is all the more likely in the present case as Pronuptia holds a significant share of the French market for the relevant products and its network covers several EEC countries (see paragraphs 4 and 6).

(30) Consequently, the clauses referred to in paragraph 28 are restrictions of competition falling within Article 85(1) and are likely to affect trade between member-states.

B. Article 85(3)

(31) Article 85(3) allows the provisions of Article 85(1) to be declared inapplicable to any agreement or category of agreements between undertakings which contributes to improving the production or distribution of goods or to promoting technical or economic progress, while allowing consumers a fair share of the resulting benefit, and which does not:

(a) impose on the undertakings concerned restrictions which are not indispensable to the attainment of these objectives;

(b) afford such undertakings the possibility of eliminating competition in respect of a substantial part of the products in question.

(32) The Court ruled in the judgment that Regulation 67/67 was inapplicable to retail franchise agreements such as those concerned in the present case. After noting that retail franchise agreements displayed features which distinguished them from exclusive distribution agreements (see paragraph 15), the Court stated that Article 2 of the regulation expressly referred only to exclusive distribution agreements and did not include among the obligations that could be imposed on the exclusive distributor either an obligation to pay royalties, obligations designed to preserve the common identity and reputation of the network, or obligations to transfer know-how and provide assistance. The standard form agreement is therefore not covered by the block exemption granted by Regulation 67/67.

(33) On 1 July 1983 a new block exemption for exclusive distribution agreements, Commission Regulation 1983/83, entered into force, replacing Regulation 67/67 for such agreements. The content of the new regulation is such that the same reasons as the Court gave for holding that Regulation 67/67 was inapplicable to agreements like that concerned in the present case could be adduced for saying that Regulation 1983/83 was also not applicable. Like the old regulation, Regulation 1983/83 only refers to exclusive distributorships and does not mention any of the above clauses that are typical of retail franchise agreements.

There are then grounds for examination of the standard form agreement in question to see if an individual exemption under Article 85(3) can be given.

(34) The standard form of franchise agreement that forms the basis of the Pronuptia distribution network contributes, through the combined effect of all its provisions, to improving the production and distribution of the products concerned, for the following reasons. It enables:

— the franchisor to extend its distribution network without the level of investment it would need to open its own retail network, which for a relatively small company like Pronuptia might not be possible, at least not so quickly. The investment involved in setting up the new outlets is undertaken by the prospective franchisees, in return for which they receive the benefit not only of the franchisor's established name and reputation, but also of its expertise, commercial know-how and marketing, which enables it to achieve a larger volume of business at lower cost and with less risk.

The franchise, in which the complementary interests of the franchisor and the franchisee converge, opens up the market to new competitors, intensifying inter-brand competition and increasing the competition faced by firms distributing their products through a branch network using a standard business format and product range;
— the franchisor to set up a distribution network using a standard business format and product range;
— the franchisor to keep in touch, thanks to its close and direct business relationship with the franchisees, with changes in consumer tastes and preferences and to reflect such changes in its production;
— the franchisee to concentrate his sales effort on a given area and to be more active in cultivating a clientèle there, thanks to the exclusivity which the combined effect of the clauses referred to in paragraph 28 gives him for that area, although consumers resident in the area are not prevented from purchasing the product outside the area and franchisees may freely buy and sell the products among themselves;
— the franchisee, thanks to his enjoyment of territorial exclusivity and his closeness to the marketplace, to make

confident forecasts of his future sales, which help the franchisor to plan his production better and to guarantee regular supplies of the products.

(35) The standard form of franchise agreement which forms the basis of the Pronuptia distribution network allows consumers a fair share of the benefit resulting from these improvements in productions and distribution.

Consumers may be expected to benefit, first of all, from a coherent distribution network offering uniform product quality and a comprehensive range of the articles and accessories available in the trade. Consumers will also benefit from the efficient and attentive service the franchisee will be encouraged to provide as a self-employed businessman who has a personal and direct interest in the success of his business, since he alone bears the financial risks. Consumers will further directly benefit from the continuity of supplies of products which satisfy their wants and reflect changes in tastes and fashion emerging in the market. Finally, the competitiveness of the market (see paragraph 9), and the freedom consumers have to purchase the products elsewhere in the network, will tend to force franchisees to pass a reasonable part of the benefits of the rationalisation of production and distribution on to consumers. Post-finally, consumers can tell that they are dealing with independent traders (see paragraph 11 above, third indent), who can be held responsible.

(36) The Pronuptia standard form agreement does not contain restrictions that are not indispensable to the attainment of the said benefits. The clauses referred to in paragraph 28, which restrict competition by giving the franchisee territorial exclusivity, can be considered, in the circumstances, to be indispensable in that prospective franchisees would probably be unwilling to undertake the necessary investment and to pay a substantial initial fee to enter the franchise system if they were not provided with some protection against competition from other franchisees and from the franchisor in the allotted territory. It should be noted that franchisees are free to buy and sell the products among themselves.

(37) Pronuptia's standard form of franchise agreement and the resulting self-contained franchising operation do not give the firms concerned the possibility of eliminating competition for a substantial part of the products in question. As noted above (paragraph 9), the Pronuptia network faces competition from a number of other manufacturers and suppliers in the EEC countries who do not use the franchising route to distribute their products.

Franchisees also compete with one another, because they can sell to any customer whether resident in the allotted territory or coming from outside it, and to any other franchisee. Furthermore, they are entirely free to determine their own sales prices.

(38) The agreement therefore meets all the requirements for exemption laid down by Article 85(3).

C. Articles 6 and 8 of Regulation 17

(39) Under Article 6 of Regulation 17, the Commission is required to specify the date from which an exemption decision takes effect. This date may not be earlier than the date of notification.

(40) Under Article 8 of Regulation 17, the Commission is also required to state the period of exemption.

(41) The notified standard form of Pronuptia retail franchise agreement, as it is applied, meets the requirements for exemption laid down in Article 85(3). An exemption may therefore be granted to take effect from the date of notification, 22 April 1983. It is reasonable in this case, in view of the five-year term of the

agreement and the date on which this decision takes effect, to grant the exemption for eight years.

THE COMMISSION, for these reasons,
HAS ADOPTED THIS DECISION.

Article 1
Pursuant to Article 85(3) of the EEC Treaty, the provisions of Article 85(1) are hereby declared inapplicable from 22 April 1983 until 21 April 1991 to the standard form of retail franchise agreement which Pronuptia signs with all its franchisees in the EEC.

Article 2
This Decision is addressed to Pronuptia de Paris SA, 8 Place de l'Opéra, F-75009 Paris.

RE THE FRANCHISE AGREEMENTS OF COMPUTERLAND EUROPE SA (CASE IV/32.034)

**Before the Commission of the European Communities
(87/407/EEC)
[1989] 4 CMLR 259**

(Signed by Mr. Commissioner Sutherland)

13 July 1987*
[Gaz: EC870713]

Restrictive practices, Agreements, Franchise agreements. Franchise agreements are agreements within the meaning of Article 85(1) EEC since the franchisees are proprietors of their own business and carry out economic and commercial activities at their own risk. [19]

Restrictive practices, Competition, Franchise agreements. A franchise agreement is not itself caught by Article 85(1) EEC where competitive market conditions prevail and its applicability cannot be determined in the abstract but depends on the specific provisions concerned. [20]

Restrictive practices, Franchise agreements, Non-competition clause. Provisions in a franchise agreement aimed at preventing the know-how and other assistance given by the franchisor from benefiting competitors are not caught by Article 85(1) EEC provided that any non-competition clause is not so restrictive as to prevent the franchisee acquiring financial interests in the capital of competing undertakings short of that necessary to give him control of those undertakings and in addition, any post-term non-competition clause is not unreasonably broad as regards both duration and geographical extent. [22]

Restrictive practices, Franchise agreements, Control of business methods. Provisions in franchise agreements which allow the franchisor to safeguard the identity and reputation of the network bearing his business name or symbol are not caught by Article 85(1) EEC where former franchisees are expressly entitled to continue using innovations or improvements they developed which are demonstrably separable from the

* Published in [1987] O.J. L222/12 (10 August 1987). The authentic text is in French.

franchisor's system, and given that no minimum purchasing requirement is imposed on the franchisees who are free to procure products, once approved by the franchisor, from any source of supply they wish. [23]

Restrictive practices, Franchise agreements. The following provisions of a franchise agreement were held to be irrelevant to competition and excluded from the scope of Article 85(1) EEC: (a) the franchisee's obligation to pay an entrance fee and subsequent royalty payments and advertisement contributions, where applied in a non-discriminatory manner, and given that inter-franchisee sales are exempt from royalty payments; (b) the franchisee's obligation to form a corporation; (c) the franchisee's obligation to post a sign on the premises indicating that he is the independent owner thereof operating under a franchise; (d) the franchisee's obligation to indicate his name and address on each product he sells; (e) provisions relating to the term and renewal of agreements and the assignment of the franchisee's lease to the franchisor. [24]

Restrictive practices, Franchise agreements, Exclusive territorial rights. Where a franchisee is obliged to operate only from the premises specified in the franchise contract and is assured of a protected zone in which no other outlet can be established either by the franchisor or by other franchisees, a certain degree of market-sharing between the franchisor and the franchisees, or between the latter, ensues which restricts competition in the distribution network and brings the agreements within Article 85(1) EEC. [25]

Restrictive practices, Franchise agreements, Sale restrictions. A franchisee's obligation to sell only to end users or to other franchisees within the distribution network, unless otherwise authorised, constitutes a restriction of competition where the name and trade mark of the franchisor only cover the business format and not the products sold, which bear the name and trade mark of each individual manufacturer. This restriction is mitigated where a retailer may operate both in the franchise network and within the selective distribution system of one or more manufacturers. [26]

Restrictive practices, Franchise agreements, Inter-State trade. Where a franchise distribution network is unique in its comprehensive cover of the Common Market and is likely to expand substantially, given that the products sold are those of the most important European and worldwide manufacturers, restrictions of competition maintained in the network are liable appreciably to affect trade between the member-states and will fall within Article 85(1) EEC. [27]

Restrictive practices, Franchise agreements, Block exemption. The characteristics which are typical of distribution franchise agreements such as the right to use the franchisor's business name and symbol in return for certain financial contributions and the obligation to adhere to uniform business standards developed by the franchisor are not referred to in the block exemption regulations on exclusive dealing and exclusive distribution (67/67 and 1983/83) and they are therefore not applicable. [29]

Restrictive practices, Franchise agreements, Exemption. Where a franchise system improves and rationalises the distribution of products, promotes intra-brand competition and leaves franchisees free to compete with each other as regards prices, to the direct benefit of consumers, and given that the restrictions in competition which the system entails are indispensable to ensure the existence of the network and that the system does not afford its members the possibility of eliminating competition in respect of a substantial part of the products concerned, the conditions of Article 85(3) EEC are fulfilled. [30]–[36]

The Commission *held that* a network of standard-form franchising agreements developed for the retailing of micro-computer products in all EEC countries except Ireland violated Article 85(1) EEC in so far as it provided for market sharing within the network and obliged retailers to sell only to end users or other franchisees unless otherwise authorised, *that* the distribution block exemptions in Regulations 67/67 and 1983/83 did not apply *but granted* individual exemption under Article 85(3) EEC, applicable also to other notified agreements once adapted so as to be in line with the standard form, until 31 December 1997 subject to the conditions that the franchisor, Computerland Europe SA of Luxembourg, should submit to the Commission an overview of the number of outlets per member-state and the market and market share of the network in the Community as a whole and in each individual member-state on 31 December 1992 and, in addition, should communicate any substantial changes in the franchise system to the Commission on an *ad hoc* basis.

The following cases were referred to by the Commission in its decision:

1. *Pronuptia de Paris Gmbh* v. *Pronuptia de Paris Irmgard Schillgallis* (161/84), 29 January 1986: [1986] 1 CMLR 414, Gaz: 161/84

2. *Re The Franchise Agreements of Yves Rocher* (87/14/EEC), 17 December 1986: [1987] O.J. L8/49, [1988] 4 CMLR 592, Gaz: EC861217

3. *Re The Agreements of Pronuptia de Paris SA* (87/17/EEC), 17 December 1986: [1987] O.J. L13/39 Gaz: EC861217A

Decision

The EC Commission, in the light of the Treaty establishing the European Economic Community and of Council Regulation 17 (especially Articles 6 and 8), received a notification and ap-plication for negative clearance submitted on 18 September 1986 by Computerland Europe SA of Luxembourg concerning its standard form franchise agreement developed for the retailing of Microcomputer products in Europe.

A summary of the notification was published* pursuant to Article 19(3) of Regulation 17. The Advisory Committee on Restrictive Practices and Dominant Positions was consulted.

I. Facts

A. General description of the Computerland franchise system
(1) CLE is a wholly-owned subsidiary of the Computerland Corporation of California (USA). CLE has subsidiaries in France, Spain, the United Kingdom and Italy with varying responsibilities, a subsidiary in Luxembourg which handles the distribution of products for the franchise network, and various branches, called regional offices, which handle marketing, advertising and public relations and provide on the spot support to franchisees, such as assistance in recruiting personnel. The Computerland group has approximately 850 retail stores worldwide. Its operations in Europe started in the late 1970s.

* [1987] O.J. C114/2, [1987] 2 CMLR 389

Since then, 100 outlets have been established in Western Europe, of which there are approximately 85 in all of the member-states except Ireland; the largest number of Computerland stores are found in France, the UK and Germany. According to CLE's prognosis, the number of outlets will more than double over the next three years. The average turnover of a Computerland store in the Community is 1.5 million ECUs. The turnover of the Computerland group worldwide in 1986 was over 1,000 million US dollars.

(2) Using the Computerland name, trade marks and the Computerland system, Computerland franchisees sell to end-users (predominantly business-users as opposed to home-users) numerous different brands of microcomputer products (hard-ware, software and peripheral products), and provide pre- and after-sales service and usually, training facilities. CLE assists franchisees in setting up and running their stores, providing both commercial and technical know-how. Its continuing support services include training, information, advice, guidance and know-how regarding the Computerland methods in store management, operation, financing, advertising, sales and inventory, based on Computerland's extensive empirical experience in the area of retail sales of microcomputer products through the world. CLE procures advance information on numerous brands of new products and how they can be used together, and passes this on to franchisees, as well as advice as to which among the many new products are likely to succeed on the market. Franchisees can thus offer their customers a broad range of up-to-date products and well-researched technical advice. In return, franchisees make various financial contributions and are bound by obligations aimed at preserving the uniformity and quality standards of the system.

(3) There are approximately 20 major manufacturers of microcomputer products in the world, of which five are estimated to account for the top five market shares of the European market. They use various ways of marketing these products, some of which overlap. Sales can be divided broadly into direct sales by the manufacturers to end-users, on the one hand, which account for 20 per cent of total sales in Europe, and sales through various types of intermediaries on the other. While some manufacturers use non-specialised outlets such as retailers of consumer electronics, many others, believing that for the time being these sophisticated technical products can only be sold effectively by specialised dealers capable of offering pre- and post-sales service and generally fulfilling certain standards of quality, have chosen to sell through authorised dealers. Such dealers can be independent retailers authorised by one or more manufacturers, or part of a dealer chain offering a broad range of products of different brands, pre-sales advice and after-sales service; some of these dealer chains, such as Computerland, are in the form of franchise networks.

Computerland stores sell the products of approximately half of the major manufacturers, including the five biggest on the European market. Their competitors are thus all retailers of whatever form selling the same or similar products. Leaving aside non-specialised retailers, statistics indicate that there are approximately 10,000 authorised microcomputer dealers in Western Europe, of which fewer than 1 per cent are Computerland stores. Although Computerland is the only pan-European chain, there are half a dozen multi-country chains (franchised or not), of which the largest after CLE has some 50 outlets in four countries. Furthermore, there are several single-country chains. In the three member-states in which CLE has its greatest number of outlets (France: 22, United Kingdom: 16,

Germany: 12), it is competing with at least half a dozen dealer chains, some having a comparable number of outlets.

In 1985, Computerland stores accounted for less than 3.3 per cent of retail sales in the Community as a whole, while in 1986 the largest market share in any given member-state was approximately 4 per cent. Worldwide, the Computerland group has much larger market shares, for example going even beyond 20 per cent in the United States, Canada, Australia and Japan.

B. Relevant features of the notified standard-form agreement

Choice and legal form of franchisees

(4) Franchisees are chosen on the basis of their personal and financial standing and their prior experience in the retail trade, and subject to successful completion of a training programme organised by CLE, employees are also expected to be fully trained in the Computerland system. Every franchisee is obliged to form a corporation for the purpose of running his Computerland store business, and a sign indicating that the franchisee independently owns and operates the business under a franchise from Computerland must be conspicuously posted in the store. The products sold must likewise bear labels indicating the franchisee's name, address and telephone number.

Use of the Computerland names, trade marks and system

(5) The franchisee is given the non-assignable right to use the Computerland names, marks and system in connection with the operation of the Computerland store and for no other purpose. In signing the agreement, the franchisee acknowledges the validity of the names and marks and CLE's ownership thereof, but there is no restriction of his right to contest CLE's industrial property rights.

The franchisee agrees to adhere to the standard business operating methods (set out in an 'Operator's Manual') and respect the confidentiality of the information he receives from CLE and to divulge it only, if necessary, to his employees, subject to a written statement in which the latter likewise acknowledge the confidential nature thereof. The franchisee must report to CLE any innovations or improvements he makes, and grants to CLE a worldwide, royalty-free non-exclusive right to use these during the term of the agreement. Upon termination for whatever reason, the franchisee must stop using the Computerland names, marks and system, and return the Operator's Manual and any other copyrighted material, but he may continue using any innovations or improvements he has developed which are demonstrably separable from the operation of the Computerland store and system.

Best personal efforts

(6) The franchisee undertakes to devote his best personal efforts to the day-to-day operation of his store; he may not engage in any other type or business at the store without prior written approval by CLE.

Location clause and protected area

(7) The franchisee must operate his Computerland store exclusively at the location approved in advance by CLE, but he is not obliged to make 'over-the-counter' sales, ie customers do not actually have to buy the products in the store itself. He must adhere to CLE's instructions regarding the interior and exterior of the premises and may not relocate without its prior approval.

Each location is surrounded by a 'protected area' having a radius of less than one kilometre after the first year of the agreement (during the first year it is double that distance) in which no other Computerland outlet may be established.

The protected area is not one of marketing or clientèle exclusivity, which means that any franchisee can sell to any end-user customer, wherever the customers may reside or do business. They can also set up so-called 'satellites', which offer showroom and selling facilities and can be inside or outside the 'mother store's' protected area, but not in the protected area of another Computerland franchisee. For stocking and servicing purposes and other operational support, such satellite outlets remain dependent on the Computerland store to which they are contractually attached.

Products and services – advertising/pricing policy

(8) The franchisee may only sell those products and perform those services specifically authorised in the Operator's Manual or in other instructions from CLE, or products and services of equivalent quality, subject to prior approval by CLE, which will not be unreasonably withheld. Franchisees play an active role in establishing the range of products they sell, *inter alia* by participating in regular meetings of the 'European Network Product Council', where proposals can be made to CLE to authorise new products.

Advertising material must be made or approved by CLE, but approval may not be withheld or withdrawn because of the franchisee's pricing policy, for which he bears sole responsibility.

Franchisees may purchase their requirements from CLE, which exercises a central purchasing function, but they are not obliged to do so, nor are there any minimum purchasing requirements. Franchisees are thus free to buy approved products from any supplier they choose.

CLE leaves franchisees free to determine their own resale prices; franchisees may, of course, receive recommended resale price lists from their other sources of supply.

Training facilities

(9) Most franchisees provide training facilities at the approved location, although there is no obligation to do so. Customers may sign up for training courses even without purchasing any of the franchisee's products. In general, the revenue derived from operating these training facilities, over which the monthly royalty must be paid, represents a very limited percentage of the franchisee's overall turnover.

Sales to end-users

(10) The Computerland system has been devised and developed to promote sales of microcomputer products at retail level. Franchisees are accordingly required to sell to end-users, unless otherwise authorised. Sales to other Computerland franchisees are expressly allowed. Furthermore, the obligation to sell to end-users does not prevent a franchisee from carrying out his obligations or exercising his rights under agreements he may have with any manufacturer as its authorised dealer.

Financial obligations/reporting requirements/right to inspect

(11) In return for being admitted into the Computerland franchise network, the franchisee must pay an initial entrance fee which varies between 250,000 Lfrs (5,800 ECUs) and 1,250,000 Lfrs (28,750 ECUs), depending on the type of outlet. Subsequently, a monthly royalty payment amounting to 3.5 per

cent of the preceding month's gross revenue, which is any income, from which certain items, such as VAT and inter-franchisee sales, are deducted. Normally, a monthly payment is also made as an advertising contribution. Franchisees must submit regular financial statements including balance sheets and profit-and-loss statements, and CLE's representatives must be allowed into the premises during working hours in order to inspect the operation of the store, including the quality of the goods being sold, the supplies on hand and the services rendered.

Non-competition clauses

(12) During the term of the agreement, the franchisee may not engage or have an interest in any business whose activities include the sale or service, at retail or wholesale level, of computer hardware, software and related products and services offered by Computerland stores. The franchisee must, however, remain free to acquire financial interests in the capital of a competing enterprise, provided such investment does not enable him effectively to control such a business.

Under the agreement as notified, the above non-competition obligation continued for three years after termination of the agreement at a given distance from the ex-franchisee's former outlet, for two years after termination at a given distance from any Computerland store and for one year after termination at any location. Following discussions with the Commission in the course of the notification procedure, CLE decided that a non-competition obligation of one year after termination of the agreement within a radius of 10 kilometres of the ex-franchisee's former outlet would be sufficient to safeguard the confidentiality of the know-how transmitted to the ex-franchisee during the term of the agreement and to allow a new Computerland store to be established and start accumulating good-will and clientèle in the ex-franchisee's former zone of business activities.

Guarantees

(13) CLE will only agree to sell a manufacturer's products if they are covered by a Europe-wide guarantee of at least six months. Products which franchisees acquire from other sources, for example directly from the manufacturer, must be covered by each manufacturer's respective guarantee, otherwise approval by CLE will be withheld.

Term and renewal

(14) The terms of the agreement is 10 years, unless terminated by mutual consent. Both franchisor and franchisee have the right to terminate unilaterally 'for good cause', with regard to which a non-exhaustive list of examples is given in the agreement.

Renewal for a further 10-year period is possible subject to certain conditions, including payment of a renewal fee.

Transfer of the agreement to third parties must be consented to by CLE.

On termination for whatever reason, CLE may choose to have assigned to it the franchisee's lease.

C. Other Computerland agreements

(15) Some Computerland franchisees have chosen not to re-place their existing contracts with the notified standard form agreement which was introduced in 1983, for varying reasons, such as the royalty level, the size of the protected area or other reasons not relevant for the present purposes. CLE has under-taken to ensure that to the extent these agreements, which are not standard, contain obligations which might be considered as being more restrictive of competition than their counterparts in the notified standard agreement, the necessary adaptation will take place.

(16) The same undertaking applies with respect to the special standard franchise agreement developed in 1986 for the German market in order to facilitate state-backed financing arrangements for the franchisees, which entails prior approval of the agreement by the lending bank.

(17) For Denmark and the Italian province of Tuscany, CLE has devised a slight variation to the standard agreement, 'Development Area Agreements', whereby a single enterprise is granted the exclusive right to open a fixed number of Computerland stores in a designated area over a limited period of time. This form of agreement is chosen for areas in which there are no existing Computerland stores and a franchisee is willing to take on the high economic risk of single-handedly setting up several stores in an undeveloped market. In return, he receives the above mentioned exclusivity, unless the timetable is not met, in which case CLE is again free to grant third parties the right to open stores in the area. These special agreements are an exception to the rule that a franchisee normally operates only one shop, and also offer a wider protected area to the successful developing franchisee. The Development Area Agreements do not impose any obstacles to export or imports.

D. Third parties' observations

(18) The Commission did not receive any observations from interested third parties following publication of the notice required by Article 19(3) of Regulation 17.

II. Legal Assessment

A. Article 85(1)

(19) The standard franchising agreement notified by CLE is an agreement within the meaning of Article 85(1) of the EEC Treaty. The individual franchisees who have entered into the standard agreement with CLE, a corporation under Luxembourg law, are the proprietors of their business and carry out economic and commercial activities at their own risk; the agreement is an instrument legally binding upon the parties.

(20) Both the Court of Justice* and the Commission** have been called upon to assess the applicability of Article 85 to distribution franchises, that is, franchise agreements under which the franchisee offers certain products and ancillary services, using the franchisor's business name and applying uniform business methods developed by the franchisor, usually subject to certain financial contributions. The main principle established by the Court, and followed by the Commission in its subsequent decisions, is that such franchise systems, which on the one hand allow a franchisor to profit from its success and expand into new geographical markets without making significant investments and on the other hand enable interested candidates to use the franchisor's name and reputation to set up a new business more easily and rapidly than if they had to acquire the necessary expertise independently, are not in themselves caught by Article 85(1) where competitive market conditions prevail. The appli-cability of Article 85(1) can, however, not be determined in the abstract, but depends on the specific provisions concerned.

An effective transfer of the business formula can only take place:

---

* *Pronuptia* (161/84); [1986] 1 CMLR, 414.
** *Yves Rocher* [1987] O.J. L8/49, [1988] 4 CMLR 592 and *Pronuptia* [1987] O.J. L13/39.

(i) if the franchisor is able to communicate his know-how to the franchisees and provide the necessary assistance without running the risk that competitors may benefit therefrom.

(ii) if the franchisor is able to take the necessary measures for maintaining the identity and reputation of the network bearing his business name or symbol.

All contractual provisions which are necessary to ensure that these conditions are met can be deemed to fall outside the scope of Article 85(1). Other provisions, in particular those which may lead to market sharing between the franchisor and the franchisees, or between the latter, or those which interfere with the franchisees' individual pricing policies, may on the contrary be considered restrictions of competition.

(21) The franchise network set up by CLE by means of the notified standard franchise agreement is a distribution franchise; the franchisor has devised an original method for selling microcomputer products and accessories to end-users, which in the interest of expansion it is willing to share with others, the franchisees. In return for receiving the package of Computerland's specifically developed commercial and technical know-how and the use of the franchisor's business name, trade marks, symbols and business methods, franchisees must make certain financial contributions and adhere to the standards of operation, devised by the franchisor. Although franchisees offer pre- and after-sales advice and make product repairs, such services are ancillary to their main task, which is the sale of products to the public. Furthermore, some franchisees may also choose to offer training facilities, not necessarily in connection with the sale of products. This service normally represents a minor part of their activities and can be viewed as a means of developing goodwill.

Having thus established that the Computerland system is a distribution franchise, the following tests can be applied.

PROVISIONS NOT FALLING WITHIN THE SCOPE OF ARTICLE 85(1)

In the specific circumstances of this case, the following provisions are not caught by Article 85(1).

(a) Provisions aimed at preventing the know-how and other assistance given by the franchisor from benefiting competitors

(22)(i) The franchisee's obligation to respect the confidentiality of the information received and to ensure that his employees do the same.

(ii) The franchisee's obligation not to carry on competing activities during the term of the agreement; at the Commission's request, the scope of the non-competition clause was adjusted so as to allow franchisees to acquire financial interests in the capital of competing undertakings, although not to the extent that such participation would enable them to control those undertakings.

(iii) The franchisee's obligation not to engage in competing activities for one year after termination of the agreement within a radius of 10 kilometres of his previous outlet. The post-term non-competition obligation which was included in the agreement as notified was considered to be unreasonably broad as regards both duration and geographical extent, but as amended the clause is deemed sufficient to prevent the ex-franchisee from using the know-how and clientele he has acquired to the benefit of CLE's competitiors. Also, given the time it takes CLE to choose, train and establish a new franchisee and for the latter to start acquiring goodwill and clientèle, the clause as modified is a reasonable compromise between the franchisor's concern to protect the confidentiality of his business formula and to open a new outlet in the ex-franchisee's former exclusive territory on the one hand,

and the ex-franchisee's legitimate interest in continuing to operate in the same field on the other hand. In view of the fact that, during the term of the agreement, a franchisee is not bound to over-the-counter sales and is furthermore free to sell anywhere, he can develop goodwill and clientèle far beyond his own protected area; during the one year in which the post-term non-competition obligation is in force, he can thus continue to reap the benefits of the efforts he has made as a franchisee, only being prevented from competing during that period in the vicinity of his former outlet.

The post-term non-competition clause is thus in the particular circumstances of this case not considered to be restrictive of competition within the meaning of Article 85(1). This assessment does not prejudice any provisions of national law which may bestow certain rights on franchisees upon termination of the contract.

(b) Provisions which allow the franchisor to safeguard the identity and reputation of the network bearing his business name or symbol

(23)(i) The criteria which CLE applies in selecting franchisees and their obligation to follow training courses and to familiarise employees with the Computerland system are justified means of ensuring that every Computerland outlet is managed in keeping with the business standards developed by the franchisor; the same concern underlies the provision that transfer of the agreement to third parties can only take place with CLE's consent;

(ii) The franchisee's obligation to use the Computerland names, trade marks and system only for the operation of the Computerland store and to stop using them immediately upon leaving the network are aimed at ensuring that the network image is not tarnished by activities not developed specifically by the franchisor; at the Commission's request, however, ex-franchisees are now expressly entitled to continue using innovations or improvements they have developed which are demonstrably separable from the Computerland system;

(iii) The franchisee's obligation to adhere to the franchisor's standard business methods is an inherent part of the franchise system and ensures the standards of uniformity and quality of the network;

(iv) The franchisee's obligation to devote his best personal efforts to the day-to-day operation of his store is necessary to ensure that the business methods developed by the franchisor are properly and fully applied; his obligation in principle not to engage in any activities in his store which are not included in the business formula transmitted by the franchisor is acceptable in the light of the concern to preserve the reputation and uniform identity of the network;

(v) The franchisee's obligation to obtain the franchisor's prior approval for the location of his store, and to adhere to the franchisor's instructions, regarding its interior and exterior aspects, is aimed at ensuring the reputation of the network, which is a concern not only of the franchisor but of every franchisee. In the Operator's Manual, CLE outlines the objective criteria it uses in site approval, such as the structure and dimensions of the building, its location in relation to key intersections and business centres, its accessibility for customers and the nature of the surrounding business centres. The main objective in setting up these criteria for site approval is to ensure that the success of the outlet is not hampered because of a possibly unfavourable location.

(vi) The franchisee's obligation to sell only the products and provide the services authorised by CLE, or products and services of equivalent quality is necessary to preserve the network's reputation as a source of high-quality microcomputer products mainly for the business community, sales of sub-standard products which do not meet the technical norms applied by CLE would damage the reputation of the network, thereby harming not only the franchisor but all other franchisees as well.

The franchisor's prior approval of the goods and services offered in Computerland stores ensures buyers that they will be able to obtain goods of the same quality from all franchisees, regardless of their location. In the case at hand, given the wide product range (there are over 3,000 items on CLE's product list) and the very rapid technological evolution in this product market, it would be impracticable to ensure the necessary quality control by establishing objective quality specifications which franchisees could apply themselves. In fact, laying down objective standards could be detrimental to the franchisees' freedom to sell the most up-to-date products, unless the specifications were constantly updated, an overly burdensome if not impossible task. In the present system, franchisees have a substantial voice in proposing products for approval, in bilateral contacts with CLE as well as collectively in the 'European Network Product Councils', which meet regularly; most products aimed at business users will be approved, and such approval covers all relevant accessories and future improvements; furthermore, should a manufacturer introduce new products of a higher standard than an existing range which has been approved, franchisees do not require prior approval to sell such new products. Also, as CLE's main source of income is derived from royalties on sales of all products by franchisees, it is in its interest to allow franchisees to sell products which are expected to be commercially successful, as long as they are technically suitable for the customers for which the Computerland network caters.

One essential element in assessing this provision under Article 85(1) is the fact that once a given product has been approved by CLE, franchisees are free to procure it from any source of supply they wish. Although franchisees may purchase their requirements from CLE, they are not obliged to do so, nor are there any minimum purchasing requirements if they do.

Furthermore, in selecting products which it will itself sell to franchisees, as well as in approving products which franchisees can procure from any source, CLE ensures that a Europe-wide guarantee is given. This policy is in line with the Commission's concern for market integration and consumer protection.*

(vii) The franchisee's obligation to use only advertising material made or approved by CLE.

Advertising plays an essential role in the development of a network's reputation. A franchisor therefore has a legitimate interest in ensuring that publicity undertaken by the franchisees will not adversely affect the reputation established by the franchisor. In the present case, the policy regarding advertising is clearly based on a justifiable concern for quality control and not aimed at interfering with the franchisee's freedom to determine his own prices; the notified agreement expressly states that approval of advertising material will not be conditional on, or subject to any change in, the pricing policy or the price quotations of the franchisee.

(viii) The franchisee's obligation to submit to inspections of the premises by CLE's representatives and to present financial statements allows the franchisor to verify whether the franchisee is operating in accordance with the Computerland business format and fulfilling his financial commitments.

* See for example *Twelfth Report on Competition Policy*, points 77 and 78, and *Commission Regulation 123/85*, recital 12.

(c) Other provisions

(24) The franchise system includes a number of provisions which are not relevant to competition and can therefore by their very nature in the present case be excluded from the scope of Article 85(1):

(i) The franchisee's obligation to pay an entrance fee and subsequent monthly royalty payments and advertising contributions; the financial commitment, which is applied on a non-discriminatory basis, is merely the consideration which the franchisee must pay for being admitted into the network and receiving the resulting rights and benefits; to ensure the possibility of inter-franchisee sales, the agreement now specifies that royalties are not payable on such transactions;

(ii) The franchisee's obligation to form a corporation, which is based on the consideration that his business dealings will thus be facilitated;

(iii) The franchisee's obligation to post a sign on the premises indicating that he is the independent owner thereof, operating under a franchise from CLE, which ensures that the public is in no way misled as to the true ownership of and responsibility for each individual outlet;

(iv) The franchisee's obligation to indicate on each product he sells his name and address, which is required solely for the purpose of directing end-users to sales and service assistance;

(v) The provisions relating to the term and renewal of the agreement, and the assignment of the franchisee's lease to the franchisor.

The assessment of these provisions is without prejudice to any relevant constraints under national law.

Provisions which constitute restrictions of competition within the meaning of Article 85(1)

(25) The conjunction of the location clause, which obliges the franchisee to operate from the premises specified in his contract and thus prevents him from opening further stores, and the exclusivity clause, which assures him of a protected zone in which no other Computerland outlets can be established, either by the franchisor or by other franchisees, results in a certain degree of market-sharing between the franchisor and the franchisees or between the latter, thus restricting competition in the network in which the Computerland business format is exploited.

In the present case, it is particularly the prohibition from opening further outlets which interferes with franchisee's commercial independence; in this context, it is important to take into account the fact that Computerland outlets are generally not one-man operations, but medium-sized enterprises employing on average ten to twenty persons and sometimes even substantially more. For such entrepreneurs, for whom expansion may be a logical and desirable development, the limitation to one outlet unless otherwise authorised is clearly restrictive.

Although franchisees are allowed to operate 'satellite shops' for display and selling purposes, also outside their protected areas, this freedom is only relative, in that prior approval by CLE and payment of a fee similar to the usual entrance fee, albeit reduced, are required. Also, such outlets may not be located in another franchisee's protected area.

(26) Under the specific circumstances of this case, the franchisee's obligation to sell only to end-users or to other Computerland franchisees unless otherwise authorised is likewise deemed to be a restriction of competition. In certain franchise systems, for example where franchisees sell products

bearing the franchisor's name and/or trade mark, the prohibition on resale by franchisees to resellers who do not belong to that franchise network is based on the legitimate concern that the name, trade mark or business format could be damaged if the contract products were sold by resellers who do not have access to the franchisor's know-how and are not bound by the obligations aimed at preserving the reputation and unity of the network and its identifying marks.

In the case at hand, however, the Computerland name and trade mark cover the business format as such, but not the micro-computer products being sold, which bear the name and trade mark of each individual manufacturer. The prohibition on Computerland franchisees to sell the products to otherwise qualified resellers is thus restrictive, both as regards the franchisees themselves, who while being independent entre-preneurs are thereby limited in their freedom in deciding to whom to sell, and as regards third party resellers, who are thereby deprived of a possible source of supply.

In the present case, this restriction is mitigated by a charac-teristic which is peculiar to sales in the microcomputer field, namely the fact that retailers can be part of a franchise network such as Computerland and at the same time be appointed an authorised dealer in a selective distribution system established by a manufacturer to ensure that his products are handled only by qualified resellers. A Computerland franchisee who thus operates simultaneously in two or more different networks must be in a position to fulfil the obligations and exercise the rights which flow from each one. In this context, the Commission has sought to ensure that a Computerland franchisee who is at the same time authorised by one or more manufacturers, can function both within the Computerland network and within the selective distribution network(s) to which he belongs.

(27) The provisions which lead to market sharing within the network and the obligation to sell to end-users are liable to affect intracommunity trade, because franchisees are not free to expand their operations to other member-states, either at retail or wholesale level. This effect on trade between member-states is liable to be appreciable, in view of:

— the expanse of the existing Computerland network, which is the ony one of its kind having outlets in all member-states except Ireland (where two outlets are, however, planned for the near future).
— the growth of the network: although the market share has not yet reached the 5 per cent mark in the EEC, the rate of growth which the network has experienced already in its first years of existence in Europe should lead to substantial expansion in the years to come. Indeed, sales by the network will probably increase more rapidly than the current trends, in view of the expected increase in the total number of outlets before 1990 to more than 150,
— the fact that the products sold by Computerland stores are those of the most important European and worldwide manufacturers.

In view of the above considerations, the notified standard agreement is deemed to fall within Article 85(1).

(28) The 'Development Area Agreements' referred to above under point 17, which contain similar provisions to the standard form agreement regarding location clause, protected area and sales to end-users, are accordingly likewise deemed to be restrictive of competition.

B. Article 85(3)

(29) The block exemption regulations relating to exclusive dealing and exclusive distribution agreements* are not applicable to distribution franchise agreements, such as the one at hand, which go beyond the category of agreements covered by those regulations.** The characteristics which are typical of distri-bution franchises, such as the franchisee's right to use the franchisor's business name and symbol in return for certain financial contributions and the obligations to adhere to uniform business standards developed by the franchisor, are not referred to in either block exemption regulation. The notified agreement must therefore be examined in the light of the conditions laid down in Article 85(3) for exemption on an individual basis.

(30) Distribution in the field of microcomputer products is improved by the Computerland system, since the franchisor, who acts as a link between the main microcomputer producers and the franchisees, is able to establish outlets throughout the Com-munity without any major financial investments, while fran-chisees are closely assisted in rapidly setting up and operating retail outlets in which a wide range of products and services are offered. Given the technical nature of the products in question and the fact that they are normally not sold as single items but as part of a range, potential buyers attach particular importance to trying out different systems and receiving pre-sales advice regarding possible applications and configurations and post-sales repair and maintenance services. Furthermore, the franchise system promotes both intra-brand and interbrand competition: the products offered are also sold via specialised dealer networks set up by the manufacturers as well as various other types of outlets, and the Computerland stores thus offer an alternative source of supply which stimulates competition, and thereby distribution, at retail level. Moreover, Computerland franchisees are free to compete with each other, also as regards the prices at which they sell to customers, which equally enhances the distribution of the products concerned.

(31) The Computerland system also contributes to rational-ising distribution: CLE takes orders from franchisees, buys the products from manufacturers or other sources of supply and resells them to the franchisees, thereby rapidly channelling the products concerned to the Computerland outlets. This central purchasing function enables CLE to negotiate favourable terms for its franchisees, with respect to prices and quantities supplied, and often allows franchisees to procure the products in question much sooner than other retail sellers.

(32) The benefits resulting from the improvement and ration-alisation of distribution accrue directly to consumers, which in this case are mainly professional end-users.

In the first place, the Computerland stores provide a single location at which customers can compare the prices and characteristics of a wide range of different brands of up-to-date microcomputer products and benefit from the advice of specially trained personnel especially as regards the possibility of using different brands of products together, and the training facilities offered. Customers who decide to buy their products at the Computerland outlet are ensured of further advice, maintenance and repair services and if necessary further training possibilities.

Secondly, the Computerland system offers consumers an expanding network of outlets at which they can buy micro-computer products. Computerland stores compete directly with

---

* Commission Regulation 67/67 and its successors, Commission Regulation 1983/83.
** Case 161/84 (*Pronuptia*), points 15 and 33.

the numerous other outlets selling the same products, with the result that all retailers should, because of the pressures of heightened competition, offer better quality, services and prices.

(33) The restrictions of competition which the Computerland system entails are indispensable to ensure the existence of the network: potential franchises would not be willing to make the investments necessary for opening up a new outlet if they were not assured that no other Computerland outlets will be established in their near vicinity. Aside from the restrictions which are thus the necessary cornerstone of the franchise system, franchisees are free as to the sources from which they procure approved products, the prices at which they wish to sell those products, the territories in which they operate, and the clientele they cater to.

(34) The franchisee's obligation to sell to end-users only, unless otherwise authorised by the franchisor, is a direct consequence of the fact that the basic concept underlying the franchisor's business formula is the operation of a network of retail stores in which products and services are offered to final consumers. The training and support services given to franchisees, who are willing to pay a fee in return, are therefore specifically aimed at helping them to become and remain efficient and profitable retail sellers. The Computerland business formula and all the efforts put into making it successful would be diluted if franchisees were free to divert their efforts to activities other than retail sales and servicing. In order for the benefits relating to improved and rationalised distribution to accrue and be passed on to consumers, in this case business users, it is therefore indispensable that franchisees accept the obligation to operate as retail sellers and not, for example, as wholesalers.

An important relaxation of this rule is the express freedom of franchisees to sell to other franchisees within the network; no royalties are due in the case of such inter-franchisee sales.

(35) The Computerland franchising system does not afford its members the possibility of eliminating competition in respect of a substantial part of the products concerned.

Computerland franchisees offer products which are at the same time sold by a very large number of competing outlets. Even in the member-states in which the greatest number of Computerland stores are located, they are faced by competing chains having a comparable number of outlets. Finally, given the overall competitive structure of this market, there is no danger that the Computerland network will reduce or otherwise distort competition between competing brands and distribution outlets.

Furthermore, there is a substantial amount of competition within the network itself; the protected zone surrounding each franchisee is relatively small, and does not entail any marketing or clientèle exclusivity, which means that franchisees are free actively to seek and to sell to any customers. CLE does not in any way impose or recommend prices at which the franchisees sell to customers which, combined with the franchisees' freedom as to their sources of supply, results in a substantial degree of price competition within the network.

Under these circumstances, the agreements between CLE and its franchisees do not individually or collectively afford the parties the possibility of eliminating competition with respect to the goods concerned.

(36) Consequently, the provisions of Article 85(1) may, under the terms of Article 85(3), be declared inapplicable to the standard form Computerland franchise agreement. The same arguments referred to in points 29 to 35 apply *mutatis mutandis* to the 'Development Area Agreements' and other existing franchise agreements which are equally or less restrictive of competition than the standard form agreement.

C. Articles 6 and 8 of Regulation 17

(37) The agreement as notified by CLE on 18 September 1986 contained a number of provisions which stood in the way of a favourable decision, in particular the clauses relating to the non-competition obligation both during the term of the agreement and after termination thereof, which was considered to be unreasonably broad. Following the discussions with the Commission during the course of the notification procedure, CLE has re-drafted the standard franchise agreement taking into account the comments made.

Pursuant to Article 6(1) of Regulation 17, the Commission is required to specify the date from which an exemption is granted. As the notified agreement did not fulfil the requirements for exemption, the date on which the exemption takes effect is not the date of the notification, but the date on which the franchisees were informed by CLE of the amended version of the agreement.

(38) According to Article 8(1) of Regulation 17, a decision in application of Article 85(3) must be issued for a specified period. Given the 10-year term of the standard franchise agreement, a corresponding period would seem appropriate. In view of the changeable nature of the retail market for microcomputer products as a whole and the expanding tendency of the Computerland network, the exemption should, however, not be more than 10 years either. CLE should be obliged, pursuant to Article 8(1) of Regulation 17, to communicate any substantial changes in the franchise system to the Commission and furthermore, halfway through the period of exemption, to inform the Commission of the number of outlets per member-state and the market share of the network in the Community as a whole and in each member-state individually.

(39) Finally, to the extent CLE maintains franchise agreements which differ from the standard agreements, provisions which are more restrictive of competition will be adapted to be in line with the standard agreement as amended.

THE COMMISSION, for these reasons,
HAS ADOPTED THIS DECISION:

Article 1
Pursuant to Article 85(3) of the EEC Treaty, the provisions of Article 85(1) are hereby declared inapplicable to the Computerland standard-form franchise agreement, including the 'Development Area Agreements' devised for the sale of microcomputer products at retail level in the common market, and to the other notified Computerland franchise agreements which have been adapted to the standard form agreement.

Article 2
With respect to the standard form agreement, including the 'Development Area Agreements', this Decision shall apply with effect from 10 July 1987 and shall be valid until 31 December 1997. With respect to other notified Computerland franchise agreements containing provisions which were more restrictive of competition than those contained in the standard form, this Decision shall take effect as of the date Computerland confirms to the Commission that those provisions have been adapted to be in line with their counterparts in the standard form agreement, and shall be valid until 31 December 1997.

Article 3
On 31 December 1992, CLE shall submit to the Commission an overview of:

— the number of outlets per member-state,

— the market share of the network in the Community as a whole and in each individual member-state.

Any substantial changes in the franchise system shall be communited to the Commission on an *ad hoc* basis.

Article 4
This Decision is addressed to:
Computerland Europe SA,
Zone Industrielle,
Route de Trèves,
L-2632 Findel.

RE THE APPLICATIONS OF THE SOCIETE ANONYME DES CHAUSSURES SEDUCTA CHARLES JOURDAN ET FILS, CHARLES JOURDAN HOLDING AG AND XAVIER DANAUD SA
(Case IV/31.697)

Before the Commission of the European Communities
(89/94/EEC)
[1989] 4 CMLR 591

2 December 1988*
[EC881202]

Application for negative clearance/exemption.

Restrictive practices, Franchising, Corner franchising, Know-how. Clauses in a franchise agreement or corner franchise agreement which are essential to prevent the know-how supplied and assistance provided by the franchisor from benefiting competitors and which provide for the control that is essential for preserving the common identity and reputation of the franchise network operating under the shop sign do not constitute restrictions of competition within the meaning of Article (1) EEC. [26] & [31]

Pronuptia de Paris GmbH v. *Pronuptia de Paris Irmgard Schillgallis* (161/84); [1986] ECR 353, [1986] 1 CMLR 414, applied; *Re the Agreements of Pronuptia de Paris SA* (87/17/EEC); [1987] O.J. L13/39, [1989] 4 CMLR 355; *Re The Franchise Agreements of Yves Rocher* (87/14/EEC); [1987] O.J. L8/49, [1988] 4 CMLR 592; *Re The Franchise Agreements of Computerland Europe SA* (87/407/EEC); [1987] O.J. L222/12 [1989] 4 CMLR 259, followed.

Restrictive practices, Franchising, Prices. The mere communication of recommended prices by affiliated companies within one group to their retailers, including those within the group's franchise network, cannot be regarded as restricting competition provided that it does not result in concerted practices between retailers in the network or between retailers and the group. [29]

Restrictive practices, Franchising, Franchisee selection. A franchisor is under no obligation to define and abide by selection criteria in choosing franchisees and is entitled, of his own accord, to choose traders which seem most suitable for maintaining the cohesion of the franchise network. [30]

* Published in [1989] O.J. L35/31 (7 February 1989). The authentic text is in French.

Restrictive practices, Franchising, Territorial protection, Inter-State trade. Clauses in a standard form franchise agreement, offered by several affiliated companies within a group as well as the holding company and providing for market sharing between them by granting the franchisee an exclusive right to operate under the group's trade marks in a given sales area and obliging the franchisee to carry on his business activities exclusively from premises approved for that purpose, constitute restrictions of competition within the meaning of Article 85(1) EEC since they have the combined effect of affording each franchisee a degree of protection against competition from other franchisees within its sales area, notwithstanding this is restricted since there may be several corner franchisees or traditional retailers selling the product concerned in the area. Inter-State trade may be affected where the agreements constitute the basis of a network which is bound to spread over the whole Community and franchisees are not allowed to become established in another member-state. [32]–[33]

Restrictive practices, Corner franchising, Competition, Inter-State trade. Article 85(1) EEC does not apply to a standard form corner franchise agreement, which gives the shopowner the exclusive right to display an internal shop sign within the shop, where it does not exclude branch shops of the franchisor or franchisee shops, which also have external shop signs, within the territory and does not exclude the display of the franchisor's trade marks in traditional retailers and given that the number of such agreements is very low and no significant increase is likely. [34]–[35]

Restrictive practices, Franchising, Group exemption. Commission Regulation 1983/83 does not apply to franchise agreements since their legal nature is different from that of distribution agreements. In addition to being distribution agreements, they are agreements under which the franchisor grants the franchisee the right to operate a shop using an original and evolving distribution formula. [36]

Pronuptia de Paris GmbH v. *Pronuptia de Paris Irmgard Schillgallis* (161/84); [1986] ECR 353, [1986] 1 CMLR 414, applied.

In relation to a franchise network, operated by several companies within the same group together with the holding company, and concerning the distribution of shoes and handbags in member-states the Commission *held that* the following provisions of the standard form franchise agreement were not caught by Article 85(1) EEC: (a) a non-competition obligation imposed on the franchisee for the duration of the agreement; (b) the prohibition on the franchisee from transferring the franchise agreement, sub-letting the shop, setting up a sub-franchise, placing the business under management by a third party or appointing a salaried shop manager without the franchisor's express approval; (c) the franchisee's obligation to carry on his business activity from premises fitted out according to the franchisor's advice; (d) the franchisee's obligation to co-operate with the franchisor in respect of advertising; (e) the ban on the franchisee from reselling the franchisor's goods to traders other than those already members of the group's distribution network and the obligation, unless otherwise authorised, to order goods connected with the essential object of the franchise business only from the same sources; (g) the franchisee's obligation to submit to checks by the franchisor; (h) the recommendation of sales prices by the franchisor. The Commission *held that* clauses granting the franchisee the exclusive right to operate under the franchisor's trade mark in a given sales area and obliging the franchisee to carry on the business activity exclusively from the premises approved for that purpose were caught by Article 85(1) EEC and *that* the group exemption on exclusive distribution agreements (Regulation 1983/83) did not apply, *but granted* an individual exemption under Article 85(3) for the period from 17 December 1986 until 16 December 1996 and *granted* negative clearance to a related standard form corner franchise agreement.

The following cases were referred to in the decision:

1. *Pronuptia de Paris GmbH* v. *Pronuptia de Paris Irmgard Schillgallis* (161/84), 29 January 1986: [1986] ECR 353, [1986] 1 CMLR 414. Gaz: 161/84

2. Re *The Agreements of Pronuptia de Paris SA* (EC Commission − 87/17/EEC), 17 December 1986: [1987] O.J. L13/39, [1989] 4 CMLR 355, Gaz: EC861217B.

3. Re *The Franchise Agreements of Yves Rocher* (EC Commission − 87/14/EEC), 17 December 1986: [1987] O.J. L8/49, [1988] 4 CMLR 592. Gaz: EC861217A.

4. Re *The Franchise Agreements of Computerland Europe SA* (EC Commission − 87/407/EEC), 13 July 1987: [1987] O.J. L222/12, [1989] 4 CMLR 259, Gaz: EC870713.

Decision

The Commission of the European Communities, in the light of the Treaty establishing the European Economic Community and of Regulation 17 (especially Articles 6 and 8), received an application for negative clearance and a notification submitted on 5 November 1985 by Société Anonyme des Chaussures Seducta Charles Jourdan et Fils of 1 Boulevard Voltaire, Romans (France), Charles Jourdan Holding AG, Spielhof 3, Glarus (Switzerland) and Xavier Danaud SA of Zone Industrielle de Charnas, Annonay (France) in respect of standard form franchise and corner franchise distribution agreements covering or intended to cover the member-states.

A summary of the notification was published* pursuant by Article 19(3) of Regulation 17. The advisory Committee on Restrictive Practices and Dominant Positions was consulted.

I. The Facts

A. The undertakings

(1) Charles Jourdan Holding AG is a company constituted under Swiss law whose registered office is situated at Spielhof 3, 8750 Glarus (Switzerland). It is itself owned by the Swiss holding company Portland Cement Works (PCW). Charles Jourdan AG with its affiliates, hereinafter referred to as the Charles Jourdan Group, owns, in whole or in part, a large number of companies in France, in the rest of the Community and outside the Community. These include in particular Société Anonyme des Chaussures Seducta Charles Jourdan et Fils and Société Anonyme Xavier Danaud, which together with Charles Jourdan AG, have notified the agreements which are the subject of this Decision.

— Société Anonyme des Chaussures Seducta Charles Jourdan et Fils notified the franchise and franchise-corner agreements relating to the Charles Jourdan trade mark (shoes and handbags) in France.
— Société Anonyme Xavier Danaud notified the franchise agreements covering the Xavier Danaud trade marks (shoes and

handbags) in France and the franchise-corner agreements covering the Xavier Danaud trade mark (shoes and handbags) in France.
— Charles Jourdan Holding AG notified the franchise agreements covering the Charles Jourdan trade mark (shoes and handbags) and the Xavier Danaud trade mark (shoes and handbags) outside France.

(2) The Charles Jourdan Group mainly manufactures and distributes shoes and leather goods (some 80 per cent of its turnover) and handbags (9 per cent of its turnover). It also distributes ready-to-wear clothing and accessories under its own trade mark, and these account for the remainder of its turnover.

In 1984, the Group achieved 55 per cent of its turnover in France and sold 1,685,000 pairs of shoes and 136,000 handbags. In 1987 the Group sold 1.1 million pairs of shoes.

The Group's turnover amounted to 896,943,000 FF in 1984 and 941,774,000 FF in 1985. In 1987 the turnover amounted to about 700,000,000 FF.

The turnover of Portland Cement Werke amounted to 568,000,000 Sfr. in 1985.

B. The product and the market

(3) The Group's main activity is the production and sale of shoes, in particular medium and top quality shoes. The articles in the middle of the range lie roughly within a retail price range of 400 FF to 700 FF, while the top quality articles cost over 700 FF. On the basis of this distinction, although approximate, articles bearing the Seducta trade mark may be regarded as top category and those bearing the Charles Jourdan, Christian Dior or Xavier Danaud trade marks as falling within the second category. A proportion of the Group's shoe production (around 10 per cent) is sub-contracted. The shoe trade marks distributed by the Charles Jourdan Group are Charles Jourdan, Seducta, Christian Dior and Xavier Danaud.

Another of the Group's activities is the production, partly through sub-contracting, and the sale of leather goods (handbags, but also belts, luggage, gloves, etc.).

The accessories marketed by the group are generally produced through sub-contracting. These include umbrellas, scarves, glasses, perfumes, tights, socks, ties, hats, watches, pens and jewellery. They are designed by the Charles Jourdan Group's stylists.

Lastly, the Charles Jourdan Group distributes under its trade mark a collection of ready-to-wear clothing for men and women that is produced entirely through sub-contracting.

(4) *The shoe market:*
Community production amounted to some 1,200 million pairs of shoes in 1986, almost half of which were manufactured in Italy and some 200 million of which were manufactured in France. In 1986, Community imports amounted to 345 million pairs and exports to 260 million pairs. In the case of France, manufacturers exported a quarter of their production, but more than one in every two pairs of shoes (54 per cent) worn in France is imported. The Community market, and in particular the French market, is therefore amply open to exports and imports.

There are a large number of smaller producers: out of a total of 423 French firms in 1982, only 15 employed more than 500 persons. However, the latter firms accounted for 25 per cent of total French production, with Eram and GEP heading the field.

Charles Jourdan's European competitors in the production of top-of-the-range shoes include Bally, Kelian, Carel, Manfield, Pinet, Clergerie, Maud Frison and Céline.

---

* [1988] O.J. C220/2, [1988] 4 CMLR 810.

Its European competitors in the production of middle-of-the-range shoes include Mirelli, France Arno, Salamander, Heyraud, Raoul and Dressoir.

Competition from producers within the Community (Italy and Spain), though also from non-Community countries (Hong Kong, Taiwan, Singapore and South Korea), is very strong.

These comments also apply to distribution, where competition is fierce not only among sales outlets, but also among distribution networks.

In France, the bulk of footwear products is still distributed by independent retailers. Some independent retailers have formed themselves into joint buying pools (e.g. Cédaf, UCF, etc.) or operate on a franchise basis (e.g. Eram, GEP, Labelle, Charles Jourdan).

Shoes are also sold through the subsidiaries of manufacturing firms (e.g. Bata, Bally, Eram, Myris, André and Charles Jourdan) and purely distributive firms (e.g. Raoul, France Arno and Manfield).

Lastly, shoes are also sold through a number of non-specialist outlets, such as supermarkets, mail order firms and department stores.

In the case of leather goods the number of individual French and European manufacturers is even larger, since this sector includes craft industry as well as industry proper. Competition from Asian countries is very keen in the case of medium quality products. Distribution is widely scattered amongst specialised shops, bazaars, supermarkets, etc.

In the case of leather goods, the Charles Jourdan Group is the third largest French producer.

(5) The Charles Jourdan Group's share of the French shoe market as a whole is around 1 per cent. Its share of the Community market is negligible. However, if one takes the market in medium and top quality shoes, the Group's market share may be estimated at nearly 10 per cent of the French market and around 2 per cent of the Community market. This market definition is not rigorous but it allows non-leather shoes and cheap shoes to be excluded.

The market share of the other products marketed by the group is insignificant both in France and at the Community level.

C. Distribution of the Group's products

(6) The distribution of the Charles Jourdan Group's products has to meet a number of requirements specific to the products and to the Group. Firstly, it is carried out by traders capable of dealing with a demanding clientele having above-average purchasing power. Secondly, close links are kept up between retailers and the Group so as to maintain a uniform style and approach to customers.

(7) Distribution is carried out through four types of shops:

— branches: these are owned and managed by the Group and display the Charles Jourdan or Xavier Danaud shop sign. They constitute the shop window of the group's activities. In general, they also market all the products in the Charles Jourdan range.
— franchised shops: these are independent of the Group, but have signed a franchise distribution agreement with it, allowing them to display the Charles Jourdan or Xavier Danaud shop sign on the outside of their shop premises in respect of the whole of the shop and allocating them a specified territory.
— franchise-corner retailers: these are independent traders who have signed a distribution agreement with the Group, allowing them to represent the Charles Jourdan or Xavier Danaud trade marks within a specified territory in a separate part of the shop premises, the articles in question being in competition with those

of other brands. The shop sign must be displayed within the shop and not on the outside, as in the case of franchised shops.

Because of the franchise-corner retailer's more limited commitment to the Group compared with franchised retailers, there is a difference in the rights and duties of each of the partners. The franchise-corner formula, which combines certain characteristics of franchise retailing and conventional retailing, is intended either, if chosen by the retailer, to allow the franchise-corner retailer to maintain greater independence from the group or, if chosen by the Group, to test the franchise-corner retailer's personal and professional capacity before giving him a franchise.
— traditional retailers: they have no legal link with the Group apart from agreements to sell articles bearing the trade mark. Such retailers are selected by the Charles Jourdan Group on the basis of objective considerations, namely the shop in which the activity is carried out, the quality of the products distributed and the retailer himself, his competence and reputation.

D. Main features of the standard-form agreements notified

(8) *Procedure for choosing the Group's franchisees and franchise-corner retailers*

The agreements are concluded *intuito personae* on the basis of the candidate's personal and professional qualities. The agreement may not be transferred to a third party without the approval of the Group. Any manager employed to run a shop must be approved in advance by the Group.

(9) *Legal independence of franchisees and franchise-corner retailers*

Franchisees and franchise-corner retailers are the owners of, and legally and financially responsible for, their businesses and fittings.

However, any change in the geographical location or in the internal or external fittings of the shop must be approved in advance by the Group.

(10) *Exclusive territory*

Each agreement defines the exact territory of the franchisee or franchise-corner retailer.

Within the franchisee's territory, the franchisee is allowed to operate his shop, under the external shop sign of one of the Group's trade marks and may distribute the relevant products only on the premises defined in the agreement.

Within the franchise-corner retailer's territory, the franchise-corner retailer is allowed to operate part of his shop under the internal shop sign of one of the Group's trade marks and may distribute the relevant products only on the premises defined in the agreement. There may be several traditional retailers and/or franchise-corner retailers within the territory of a franchisee. However, there cannot be more than one franchisee within one and the same territory.

(11) *Transfer of know-how from the Charles Jourdan Group to franchisees and franchise-corner retailers*

Franchisees receive know-how and continuous assistance from the Charles Jourdan Group in the following areas:

— purchasing (season's collection; standard order; trends; colours and materials in fashion), with information being provided to the retailer on the latest fashion trends.
— supply of the general decoration concept, with help being provided on the decoration or redecoration of the shop.
— establishment and maintenance of stock and management information, with assistance being provided on the internal management of the shop.

— provision of information on the sale of products in the 'affiliates and franchisees' networks, with information being given on the business activity of sales outlets distributing the same products.

— advertising, with material help or advice being provided on the advertising policy of franchisees.

The know-how thus made available is primarily commercial although it also covers management aspects. It is substantial and gives the trader a clear advantage over competitors. It is this, in addition to the prestige of the trade mark, which prompts actual or would-be independent traders to conclude such agreements with the Charles Jourdan Group.

Franchise-corner retailers only receive information on purchasing and fashion trends from the Charles Jourdan Group. Such information is both more limited and covers fewer fields than that provided for franchisees. No provision is made for management assistance.

All the information supplied to franchisees or franchise-corner retailers is confidential.

(12) *Industrial property rights*

The Charles Jourdan Group remains the owner of its registered trade marks and of its designs, trade names, signs, emblems, symbols and other distinctive commercial marks. It alone may decide on the use made of them.

(13) *Right of inspection by the Charles Jourdan Group*

Franchisees and franchise-corner retailers must make their accounts available to the Group and must each month send in a statement of sales and quantities sold for the previous month. They must allow inspections to be carried out of their staff and business premises, including premises for storage. The inspection may also relate to whether the franchisee is meeting the quality standards associated with the name and reputation of the goods.

(14) *Financial obligations to the Charles Jourdan Group*

In exchange for the franchisor supplying the general decoration concept, the overall building plan, samples of materials, the specification, and the assistance of the decorator, the franchisee has to pay an entry free of 20,000 FF to 30,000 FF depending on the trade mark involved. The costs of fitting out and equipping the shop are borne by the franchisee or the franchise-corner retailer. No entry fee is required from franchise-corner retailers, who have to pay only a guarantee deposit.

In return for the rights granted and the services supplied, the franchisee must also pay the franchisor, depending on the trade mark involved, a franchise fee of 1.5 or 2 per cent of the total amount of net sales, excluding tax, for the shop. In the case of franchise-corner retailers, the fee is set at 1 per cent of the shop's total sales, excluding tax. In practice, at least 50 per cent of such sales are accounted for by products bearing the Group's trade marks.

(15) *Non-competition clause*

In the case of franchise agreements, the non-competition clause prohibits the franchisee from operating within the allocated territory any other shop franchised by companies other than those of the Charles Jourdan Group, unless such other shop sells articles which because of their price and style cannot be regarded as competing with Charles Jourdan products.

Within the shop itself, the franchisee may distribute only products bearing the trade marks covered by the agreement and the Group's other trade marks. The franchisee may, however, be authorised by the Group to distribute other articles originating outside the Group.

In the case of agreements with franchise-corner retailers, there is a clause prohibiting them from displaying or selling products which, because of their trade mark, name or presentation, would be likely to detract from the Charles Jourdan Group's brand image.

Upon expiry of the agreements, the trader is not subject to any restrictions in his subsequent activities. Where a franchised shop is to be sold, the first offer must be made to the franchisor, who has a period of one month in which to decide whether to buy it.

(16) *Supply arrangements*

The trader may obtain direct supplies of products bearing the Charles Jourdan Group's trade marks either from the group itself, or from a Group branch shop, or from another member of the network, whether such a member is a franchisee or franchise-corner retailer, or even from a traditional retailer of products bearing the Group's trade marks, whether or not such supplies are established, in the same member-state. As a general rule, cross-supplies between distributors of products bearing the Group's trade marks are allowed, provided that the principal activity of the franchisee or franchise-corner retailer is not that of wholesaler. This possibility was granted to these Charles Jourdan Group retailers at the Commission's request.

(17) *Purchase prices*

Within one and the same member-state purchase prices are the same for all franchisees, franchise-corner retailers and traditional retailers. However, quantity rebates may be granted.

Variations in purchase prices from one member-state to another are due to the costs of distribution, transit, exchange, etc. involved in export operations.

(18) *Selling prices*

The Charles Jourdan Group draws up price lists every season. The price lists are intended for guidance purposes and retailers are not required to abide by them. This freedom for retailers to determine their selling prices was expressly specified in the agreements at the Commission's request.

(19) *Duration of the agreements*

All the agreements are concluded for an initial term of five years.

(20) *Termination of the agreements*

The Charles Jourdan Group may terminate a franchise agreement or an agreement with a franchise-corner retailer if the trader's assets are placed in the hands of the receiver or the trader goes into liquidation, if the shop is transferred to other premises or altered, or if sales are insufficient. In the event of breach of any of the clauses of the agreements, the Charles Jourdan Group or its partner, the franchisee or the franchise-corner retailer, may terminate the contract.

(21) *Effects of termination or expiry of the agreement*

Franchisees or franchise-corner retailers are not subject to any restrictions on the exercise of their future activities. They may continue to distribute similar or competing products within the same geographical area and in the same shop.

They are merely required to remove all shop signs and advertising displays from their shops, to modify the fittings associated with the activity of franchisee or franchise-corner retailer and to hand over to the Charles Jourdan Group all printed matter, labels, packing materials, etc. bearing the trade marks, excluding any supplies necessary for the disposal for remaining merchandise in stock.

(22) *Observations from third parties*
The Commission received no observations following its publication of a notice in accordance with Article 19(3) of Regulation 17.

II. Legal Assessment

A. Article 85(1)
(23) Through the standard-form distribution agreements notified the Charles Jourdan Group:

— grants to its franchisees and franchise-corner retailers, within a territory specified in the agreement, the exclusive right to use in a retail shop its identifications (shop signs, trade mark, business name) and its designs and models for the purposes of selling. This results in a uniform presentation of the products marketed within the network. The exclusive right applies to the shop sign on the outside of the shop and to the shop sign inside the shop in the case of franchise-corner retailers.
— transfers to its franchisees and its franchise-corner retailers know-how consisting of a body of commercial and management knowledge previously tried and tested by the Charles Jourdan Group itself and not divulged to third parties and of continuous assistance. The technical and business know-how is updated in the light of the results of the experience acquired by the Charles Jourdan Group.

(24) The Charles Jourdan Group is able to develop a coherent and efficient sales network without massive investments, while at the same time maintaining control over the activity of the sales outlets.
This formula allows franchise retailers not already experienced in the distribution of articles bearing the trade mark to benefit from the franchisor's know-how and experienced franchise retailers, in addition to this advantage, to concentrate all their efforts on marketing the products of the Charles Jourdan Group, whose reputation is enough to guarantee them a clientele.
The formula enables franchise-corner retailers to benefit from the Group's know-how and from the reputation of the Charles Jourdan Group's trade marks, while at the same time maintaining a large degree of business autonomy thanks to the distribution of competing trade marks in their shops.

(25) The standard-form franchise agreements or franchise-corner retailer agreements which the Charles Jourdan Group has signed or intends to sign with its franchisees or franchise-corner retailers are agreements between undertakings within the meaning of Article 85, the Charles Jourdan Group and each of its partners remaining independent undertakings.

(a) *Clauses not covered by Article 85(1)*

Franchise agreements
(26) The Court of Justice in the *Pronuptia* judgment,* and the Commission in the *Pronuptia*,** *Yves Rocher**** and *Computerland**** decisions, took the view that clauses which

* Case 161/84; [1986] ECR 353, [1986] 1 CMLR 414.
** [1987] O.J. L13/39, [1989] 4 CMLR 355.
*** [1987] O.J. L8/49, [1988] 4 CMLR 592.
**** [1987] O.J. L222/12, [1989] 4 CMLR 259.

are essential to prevent the know-how supplied and assistance provided by the franchisor from benefiting competitors and clauses which provide for the control that is essential for preserving the common identity and reputation of the network, operating under the shop sign do not constitute restrictions of competition within the meaning of Article 85(1).

(27) The clauses that are essential to prevent the know-how made available from benefiting competitors are the following:

— the clause providing for non-competition during the term of the agreement prohibits the franchisee from operating any other franchised shop within the allocated territory, unless such other shop sells products that are unrelated to the products of the Charles Jourdan Group. This clause is justified for the franchisee by the fact that the know-how provided could easily be used for the benefit of other products and other trade marks under another franchise system. The franchisee is not bound by any non-competition clause once the agreement has expired. Such a non-competition clause would not be justified first as the know-how provided includes a large element of general commercial techniques, and second, as this type of franchise is primarily granted to retailers who are already experienced in selling shoes.
— the provision prohibiting the franchisee from transferring its franchise contract, sub-letting its shop, setting up a sub-franchise, placing its business under management by a third party or appointing a salaried shop manager without the express approval of the Charles Jourdan Group to ensure that the franchisee possesses the professional qualities necessary for the exercise of its functions, but also that persons not belonging to the Charles Jourdan network do not benefit from the advantages inherent in the distribution system being examined here.

(28) The clauses that provide for the control essential to preserve the common identity and reputation of the network trading under the franchisor's name are as follows:

— obligation on the franchisee to carry on his business activity from premises fitted out according to the indications and advice of the group. This makes it possible to ensure the consistency, commercial homogeneity and reputation of the sales outlets of the Charles Jourdan Group's network.
— obligation on the franchisee to co-operate with the Charles Jourdan Group. This obligation relates principally to advertising, which must be carried out in agreement with the Charles Jourdan Group so as to maintain the Group's brand image and the quality of the management of the sales outlet, so as to prevent bad management from harming the interests of the trade marks represented.
— ban on the franchisee reselling the Charles Jourdan Group's goods to traders other than franchisees, franchise-corner retailers or retailers supplied by the Group. This clause is intended to maintain the unity of the network and the link, in the consumer's mind, between the Charles Jourdan Group's product and the place where it is sold.
— obligation on the franchisee unless otherwise authorised by the Group, in view of the nature of the products concerned (fashion goods) and in order to preserve the consistency of the brand image, to order the goods connected with the essential object of the franchise business exclusively from the Charles Jourdan Group or from suppliers designated by it. The franchisee may purchase the goods in question from any other franchisee, franchise-corner retailer or traditional retailer belonging to the Charles Jourdan network.
— obligation on the franchisee to submit to checks by the Charles Jourdan Group. The Group's right of scrutiny of the management

of its retailers is a counterpart to the responsibilities delegated by the Charles Jourdan Group to its partners.

(29) As regards retail prices, which are only recommended, it should be emphasised that the mere communication of recommended prices by the group to its retailers cannot be regarded as restricting competition, provided that it does not result in concerted practices between retailers in the network or between retailers and the Charles Jourdan Group.

(30) The lack of any obligation on the Group to define and abide by selection criteria in choosing its franchisees is due to the desire to establish an integrated and interdependent distribution network to which each trader, with his professional and personal capacities, has chosen to belong. The continuous assistance which the franchisee receives during the term of the agreement implies a significant involvement of the Group's representatives with each of the traders. The members of the distribution network must therefore be limited in number. Consequently, the Group can of its own accord choose the traders which seem to it most suitable for maintaining the cohesion of the network.

Franchise-corner retailer agreements

(31) The clauses not covered by Article 85(1) are firstly those which provide the Group with the essential control needed to preserve the common identity and reputation of the network symbolised by the shop sign within the shop: the franchise-corner retailer must carry out his activity in the part fitted out in accordance with the Group's directives. He must also co-operate with the Group in matters of advertising and management. He cannot purchase the goods from or resell the goods to traders other than those who are already members of the Group's distribution network. Lastly, the franchise-corner retailer must submit to checks by the Charles Jourdan Group.

The franchise-corner retailer is not subject to any non-competition obligation. Nevertheless he cannot display or sell in his shop products liable to detract from the Charles Jourdan Group's brand image. He is free to market other trade marks. This clause is justified by the quality of the Charles Jourdan Group's products, necessitating proper presentation. In view of the highly competitive situation in the sector, this restriction is not likely to have any significant effect on competition.

The agreement is automatically terminated in the event of transfer, management by a third party, control of the company by a third party or appointment of a salaried shop manager without the express approval of the Charles Jourdan Group, so as to ensure that the franchise-corner retailer has the necessary qualities and the advantages of the formula do not benefit a third party.

(b) *Clauses covered by Article 85(1)*

Franchise agreements

(32) The clauses that involve market sharing between the Charles Jourdan Group and its partners or between its partners themselves constitute restrictions of competition within the meaning of Article 85(1). This applies to:

— the exclusivity granted to the franchisee to operate under the franchisor's trade marks in a given sales area, and
— the obligation on the franchisee to carry on his business activity exclusively from the premises approved for that purpose.

The combined effect of these clauses is to afford each franchisee relative protection against competition from other franchisees within its sales area. However, such protection is restricted by the fact that, while there may be only one franchisee within a given area, there may be several franchise-corner retailers and traditional retailers within the area.

(33) The franchise agreements may affect trade between member-states as they constitute the basis of a network which is bound to spread over the whole Community and as the franchisees are not allowed to become established in another member-state.

Franchise-corner retailer agreements

(34) The exclusive right to display an internal shop sign within the shop, does not, within the territory, exclude either branch shops or franchise shops, which have, in addition, an external shop sign. Nor does such exclusive right exclude the display of Charles Jourdan Group trade marks in traditional retail shops. The contracts only restrict the retailer a little and, on a highly competitive market, offer very limited protection against competition within the network.

(35) Since, in addition, the number of franchise-corner retailers was very low on the date when the agreements were notified and since the number of franchise-corner retailers is not, according to the Charles Jourdan Group, going to increase significantly, they are not likely to affect trade between member-states, or significantly to prevent, restrict or distort competition within the Common Market. The provisions of Article 85(1) do not therefore appy to the franchise-corner agreements.

B. Article 85(3)

(36) Commission Regulation 1983/83* on the block exemption of exclusive distribution agreements does not apply to the standard-form franchise agreements in question, since their legal nature is different.** In addition to being distribution agreements they are agreements under which the franchisor grants the franchisee the right to operate a shop using an original and evolving distribution formula. It should therefore be examined whether the agreements in question are eligible for individual exemption under Article 85(3).

(37) Through the combined effect of their provisions as a whole, the standard-form franchise agreements governing the Charles Jourdan distribution network contribute to improving the distribution of the products concerned within the meaning of Article 85(3). They enable:

— the Charles Jourdan Group to extend its distribution network without carrying out investment in the material fitting out of new branches, investment which it would perhaps otherwise not be able to carry out, or to carry out as rapidly, since it is the prospective franchisees which are responsible for the necessary investment.
— the Charles Jourdan Group to make available to consumers a distribution network which is uniform in the business methods used and the range of products offered. Such uniformity makes it possible to rationalise business methods by standardising them.
— the Charles Jourdan Group, given the close and direct links which it has with its partners, to be rapidly informed by them of any changes in consumers' habits and tastes and thus to be able to take account of this in its forward plans on sales and production.
— the franchisee, who enjoys exclusive rights to use the external shop sign within the allocated territory, to concentrate his sales efforts on that territory and on the Group's trade marks.

* [1982] O.J. L173/1, [1983] 1 *Commercial Laws of Europe* 255.
** Case 161/84, *Pronuptia* at paras. [15] and [33].

— the franchisee to enjoy the commercial benefits of the brand image of the products and the tried and tested know-how and continuous assistance of the Charles Jourdan Group.

(38) The agreements governing the Charles Jourdan distribution network allow consumers a fair share of the benefit resulting from these improvements in distribution:

— consumers can acquire products from the Charles Jourdan Group's range in a larger number of sales outlets and countries.
— the know-how transmitted and the assistance provided by the Group to its partners ensure that consumers receive high-quality service.
— the fact that the retailers remain the owners of their businesses ensures commercial dynamism and diligence on the part of the trader.

The pressure of competition within the sector and the freedom which consumers have to purchase the products at any shop within the network will tend to force franchisees to pass on to consumers a reasonable share of the advantages resulting from the rationalisation of distribution.

(39) The Charles Jourdan Group's standard-form agreements do not contain restrictions that are not indispensable to the attainment of the said benefits. The restrictive clauses that provide for some territorial exclusivity may be considered, in the circumstances, to be indispensable in that few prospective franchisees would be willing to undertake the necessary investment, to pay an initial lump-sum fee or a guarantee deposit and to pay royalties in proportion to their tunrover in order to belong to such a distribution system, if they did not enjoy some territorial protection against competition from other franchisees and from the Charles Jourdan Group itself. It should be noted that the franchisees are free to buy and sell the relevant products among themselves or to sell them to and buy them from other independent retailers of the trade mark.

(40) The Charles Jourdan standard-form agreements and the system resulting from their implementation are not such as to afford the undertakings concerned the possibility of eliminating competition in respect of a substantial part of the products in question. With regard to producers and distributors that are competitors of the Charles Jourdan Group, the Charles Jourdan network cannot produce any significant horizontal anti-competitive effects outside of the trade mark, given the dispersal of the supply of products both at production level and at distribution level.

(41) The production and distribution of Charles Jourdan Group shoes, which is the Group's main activity, account for only a modest share of the French market and an even smaller share of the Community market. On the sub-market for medium and top quality shoes, the Charles Jourdan Group accounts for some 10 per cent of the French total and only around 2 per cent of the Community market. Its turnover, which amounted to less that 1,000 million FF in 1985, is relatively modest compared with that of its European competitors. In addition, the footwear market, like the market for leather goods, accessories or ready-to-wear clothing is buoyant and very keenly competitive.

(42) The franchisees are, in addition, in competition with one another, since they are allowed to sell to any consumer resident within or outside the allotted territory and to any other franchisee, franchise-corner retailer or retailer of the trade mark, subject to the condition of not acting as a wholesaler by way of principal activity. Furthermore, they are entirely free to set their selling prices. The distribution network, which covers several different systems of marketing, creates a healthy rivalry between retailers, thus allowing the consumer the widest choice and hence the best purchasing conditions.

Lastly, there is no provision for any no-competition clause upon expiry or after termination of the agreements, and this enables any franchisee to continue to carry on his business activity in his own shop without any restriction once he has ended his relationship with the Group.

(43) All the conditions for the application of Article 85(3) are thus met.

(44) The exemption decision will take effect as from the date on which the most recent amendments were made to the standard-form agreements, i.e. 17 December 1986. Exemption may be granted for a period of 10 years. This period seems justified given the limited restriction of competition resulting from the agreements and the competitive context in question.

THE COMMISSION, for these reasons,
HAS ADOPTED THIS DECISION:

Article 1
Pursuant to Article 85(3) of the EEC Treaty, the provisions of Article 85(1) are hereby declared inapplicable for the period from 17 December 1986 to 16 December 1996 to the standard-form of retail franchise agreements which the Charles Jourdan Group concludes with its franchisees in the Community.

Article 2
Pursuant to Article 2 of Regulation 17, the Commission hereby certifies that there are no grounds under Article 85(1) of the Treaty for action in respect of the standard-form, 'franchise-corner retailer' agreements which the Charles Jourdan Group concludes with its 'franchise-corner retailers'.

Article 3
This Decision is addressed to:

1. La Société des Chaussures Seducta Charles Jourdan et Fils,
   1 boulevard Voltaire,
   F-26071 Romans
2. Charles Jourdan Holding AG,
   Spielhof 3,
   CH-8750 Glarus
3. La Société Xavier Danaud,
   Zone Industrielle de Charnas,
   F-07100 Annonay

RE THE FRANCHISE AGREEMENTS OF SERVICEMASTER LIMITED
(Case IV/32.358)

Before the Commission of the European Communities
(88/604/EEC) [1989] 4 CMLR 581
(Signed by Mr Commissioner Sutherland)

14 November 1988*
[Gaz: EC881114]

Application for negative clearance or exemption.

Restrictive practices. Franchising. Services. Competition rules. Application. Service franchises show strong similarities

* Published in [1988] O.J. L332/38 (3 December 1988). The authentic text is in English.

to distribution franchises and can therefore be treated in basically the same way as the distribution franchises already exempted by the Commission, given that the competition rules apply to both products and services without distinction. This does not prevent the Commission from taking into account certain specific characteristics relating to the provision of services, e.g. the relative importance of know-how and the fact that they are often provided at the customer's premises. [6]

Restrictive practices. Franchising. Services. Know-how. Prices. Provisions of a service franchise agreement aimed at preventing the know-how and other assistance given by the franchisor from benefiting competitors and which allow the franchisor to safeguard the common identity and reputation of the franchise network do not fall within Article 85(1) EEC. Nor does the mere recommendation of sales prices or a provision obliging the franchisee to resell products connected with the service only to customers serviced by the franchisee. [7]–[21]

Restrictive practices. Franchising. Services. Territorial protection. Market sharing. The combined effect of clauses in a service franchise agreement which, on the one hand, prohibit the franchisee from setting up further outlets outside his own territory and, on the other, prevent the franchisee from actively seeking customers outside his territory is a certain degree of market sharing and they fall within Article 85(1) EEC. [22]

Restrictive practices. Franchising. Inter-State trade. In assessing whether restrictions of competition contained in a standard-form franchising agreement affect trade between member states appreciably it is necessary to take into account the likely future development of the franchise network concerned throughout the Community as well as its present extent. [23]

Restrictive practices. Franchising. Territorial protection. Intra-brand competition. Exemption. Provisions in franchise agreements relating to territorial protection which exclude any intra-brand competition between franchisees preclude the grant of an exemption under Article 85(3) EEC. [29]

In relation to a franchise network concerning the supply of housekeeping, cleaning and maintenance serrvices to commercial and domestic customers throughout the Community the Commission *held that* the following provisions of the standard-form franchise contract were not caught by Article 85(1) EEC:

(a) the requirement that the franchisee keep secret all know-how and information received, even after expiry of the agreement, and impose the same obligation on employees;

(b) a field of use restriction imposed on the franchisee in respect of the know-how and intellectual property rights licensed;

(c) a post-term use ban imposed on the franchisee in respect of know-how;

(d) a non-competition obligation imposed on the franchisee for the duration of the contract;

(e) a post-term non-competition and non-solicitation obligation imposed on the franchisee in respect of the franchise territory and applicable for one year;

(f) the prohibition on the franchisee selling the franchised business or assigning the franchise agreement to a third party without the franchisor's approval;

(g) the requirement that the franchisee use the franchisor's know-how and trading methods;

(h) the franchisee's grant back obligation in respect of improvements made in the operation of the business;

(i) the need for the franchisor's prior approval on the location of the franchise premises;

(j) the requirement that the franchisee devote the necessary time and attention to the franchise business and endeavour to increase turnover;

(k) the requirement that the franchisee purchase certain necessary equipment and chemicals from the franchisor or other suppliers nominated or approved by the franchisor;

(l) the requirement that the franchisee obtain the franchisor's approval for advertising;

(m) the requirement that the franchisee submit to inspections of premises by the franchisor and present financial statements;

(n) the recommendation of sales prices by the franchisor;

(o) the requirement that the franchisee resell home care products only with the consent of the franchisor and only to customers serviced by the franchisee.

The Commission *held that* provisions granting territorial protection to franchisees, albeit to a limited extent since, after negotiations with the Commission, they were amended so as not totally to exclude intra-brand competition between the franchisees by allowing the franchisees to provide services to non-solicited customers resident outside their own territory, were caught by Article 85(1) EEC *but granted* an individual exemption under Article 85(3) EEC with effect from the date of the communication of the amended contract for a period of 10 years ending 9 May 1998.

The following cases were referred to in the decision:

1. Re the franchise agreements of *Computerland Europe SA* (EC Commission 87/407/EEC), 13 July 1987; [1987] O.J. L222/12, [1989] 4 CMLR 259. Gaz: EC870713.

2. Re the franchise agreements of *Yves Rocher* (EC Commission 87/14/EEC), 17 December 1986: [1987] O.J. L8/49, [1988] 4 CMLR 592. Gaz: EC861217A.

3. Re the agreements of *Pronuptia de Paris SA* (EC Commission 87/17/EEC), 17 December 1986: [1987] O.J. L13/39, [1989] 4 CMLR 355. Gaz: EC861217B.

Decision

The Commission of the European Communities, in the light of the Treaty establishing the European Economic Community and of Regulation 17 (especially Articles 4, 6 and 8), received an application for negative clearance and notification submitted by ServiceMaster Ltd. of a standard form franchise agreement concerning the provision of housekeeping, cleaning and maintenance services in the Community.

A summary of the application and notification was published* pursuant to Article 19(3) of Regulation 17. The Advisory Committee on Restrictive Practices and Dominant Positions was consulted.

I. The Facts

(1) ServiceMaster has notified a standard form service franchise agreement for use in all the EEC member states. The agreement concerns the supply of housekeeping, cleaning and maintenance services to both commercial and domestic customers. Service-Master has applied for a negative clearance or alternatively an exemption decision under Article 85(3) of the Treaty.

(2) Following observations made by the Commission. ServiceMaster has agreed to make certain amendments to its notified agreement. The amended agreement was communicated to the Commission on 10 May 1988.

* [1988] O.J. L218/3, [1988] 4 CMLR 895.

(3) Reference is made to the notice published pursuant to Article 19(3) of Regulation 17*, for a more extensive description of the ServiceMaster franchise system and its relevant clauses which are mentioned or discussed hereinafter only in so far as is necessary for the reasoning of the Commission. The facts set out in the Article 19(3) notice form part of this decision.

(4) The Commission did not receive any observations from interested third parties following publication of the said notice.

II. Legal Assessment

A. Article 85(1)

(5) The franchise network set up by ServiceMaster by means of the notified standard form agreement is a service franchise; it concerns the supply of housekeeping, cleaning and maintenance services to commercial and domestic customers according to the instructions of ServiceMaster and, on an ancilliary basis, the supply of goods directly linked to the provision of those services. The ServiceMaster franchise includes a uniform presentation of the contract services based on the use of a common name, a substantial package of technical, commercial and administrative know-how relating to the provision of the services and continuing assistance provided by ServiceMaster. The franchisees are proprietors of their businesses, which they operate for their own account and at their own risk. In exchange for the right to exploit a ServiceMaster franchise and certain ServiceMaster intellectual property rights related to trade marks and copyrights, the franchisees have to make various financial contributions and are bound by obligations aimed at preserving the uniformity and quality standards of the ServiceMaster system.

(6) The Commission considers that, despite the existence of specific matters, service franchises show strong similarities to distribution franchises and can therefore basically be treated in the same way as the distribution franchises already exempted by the Commission**. This basic premise relies on the fact that the EEC competition rules apply without distinction to both products and services. This does not prevent the Commission from taking into account in individual cases certain specific characteristics relating to the provision of services.

In particular, know-how is often more important in the supply of services than in the supply of goods because each service requires the execution of particular work and creates a close personal relationship between the provider of the service and the receiver of the service. Therefore, the protection of the franchisor's know-how and reputation can be even more essential for service franchises than for distribution franchises where mainly the goods advertise the business by carrying the trade mark of the producer or distributor. Also certain services, as for instance the ServiceMaster services, are executed at the customer's premises, while goods are usually sold at the premises of the retailer. Services of this type further reinforce the link between the provider of the services and the customer.

Provisions not falling within Article 85(1)

The following provisions of the ServiceMaster franchise agreement do not fall within Article 85(1):

* *Ibid.*
** *See Commission decisions 87/407/EEC, Computerland:* [1987] O.J. L222/12, [1989] 4 CMLR 259; 87/14/EEC, *Yves Rocher:* [1987] O.J. L8/49, [1988] 4 CMLR 592; 87/17/EEC, *Pronuptia:* [1987] O.J. L13/39, [1989] 4 CMLR 355.

(a) *Provisions aimed at preventing the know-how and other assistance given by the franchisor from benefiting competitors*

(7) The franchisee's obligation to preserve, before and after the termination of the agreement, the secrecy of all information and know-how and to impose a similar obligation on his employees. The commercial value of know-how is dependent on its secrecy. The obligation not to disclose the know-how is a necessary condition for maintaining such value and for enabling ServiceMaster to grant it to other potential franchisees.

(8) The franchisee's obligation to use the know-how and intellectual property rights licensed solely for the purpose of exploitation of the ServiceMaster franchise. This field-of-use restriction is necessary to protect the franchisor's know-how because it lends itself to use with competitive services provided by either the franchisee or other competitors.

(9) The franchisee's obligation, after termination of the agreement, to cease using the know-how package of ServiceMaster unless this know-how package as a whole has fallen into the public domain otherwise than in breach of obligation. This post-term use ban on know-how is essential for the protection of the franchisor's right to this know-how. As long as its know-how has not become accessible to the public, the franchisor has the right to limit the transfer thereof to a fixed period of time, in this case to the lifetime of the franchise agreement. If the franchisor lost the exclusive right to make use of its know-how after expiry of the franchise agreement, it could not prevent competitors from using its know-how.

(10) The franchisee's obligation, during the term of the agreement, not to be engaged in a competing business, except through the acquisition of a financial interest not exceeding five per cent in the capital of a publicly-quoted company. This non-competition obligation is necessary to avoid the risk that the know-how supplied by ServiceMaster to its franchisees might benefit competitors, even indirectly. The limitation of the acquisition of a financial interest in a publicly-quoted company to five per cent of the share capital is intended to ensure that the franchisees do not become involved in the operation of such a company, with the risk of transferring know-how to a competing business. Although the prohibition against acquiring non-controlling financial interest in the capital of a competing publicly-quoted company can be a restriction of competition falling with Article 85(1), in this particular case it is not considered to be an appreciable restriction because the franchisees are generally small undertakings for which the prohibition against acquiring more than five per cent of a publicly-quoted company does not normally constitute a real hindrance in the development of their own activities. Furthermore, the franchisees are completely free in the acquisition of financial interests in non-competing companies.

(11) The franchisee's obligation, after the termination of the agreement, not to be engaged, for a period of one year, in a competing business within any territory within which he has provided services prior to the termination of the agreement. In addition, the franchisee may not solicit, for a period of one year, customers who have been, during the period of two years prior to the termination of the agreement, his customers.

This post-term non-competition and non-solicitation obligation is acceptable both as regards its duration and its geographical extent. This obligation is necessary to prevent the ex-franchisee from using the know-how and clientele he has acquired for his own benefit or for the benefit of ServiceMaster's competitors. It is further necessary to allow ServiceMaster a limited time period to establish a new outlet in the ex-franchisee's territory. This assessment does not prejudice any relief available to franchisees under national law upon termination of the contract.

(12) The prohibition on the franchisee against selling the franchised business or against assigning the franchise agreement to a third party without ServiceMaster's approval. The prohibition is clearly indispensable to protect the know-how and assistance provided by the franchisor.

(b) *Provisions which allow the franchisor to safeguard the common identity and reputation of the franchise network.*

(13) The franchisee's obligation to use ServiceMaster's know-how and to apply the trading methods developed by Service-Master is an obligation which is inherent in the franchise system and ensures the standards of uniformity and quality of the franchise network.

(14) The franchisee's obligation to communicate to Service-Master any improvements he makes in the operation of the business. This grant-back obligation is made on a non-exclusive and reciprocal basis. It will improve the efficiency of the ServiceMaster franchise network by creating a free interchange of improvements between all franchisees.

(15) The franchisee's obligation to obtain ServiceMaster's prior approval for the location of his franchise premises. This obligation is necessary to ensure that a bad choice does not damage the reputation of the network which is a concern of the whole franchise network.

(16) The franchisee's obligation to devote the necessary time and attention to the ServiceMaster business and to use his best endeavours to promote and increase the turnover of that business. This promotion obligation is intended to oblige the franchisee to concentrate his efforts on the development of his business. This obligation is acceptable in the light of the concern to preserve the reputation and uniform identity of the network by creating an efficient franchise system devoting all its efforts to the provision of the ServiceMaster services.

(17) The franchisee's obligation to purchase certain cleaning equipment and certain chemicals used in the operation of the business from ServiceMaster or other suppliers nominated or approved by ServiceMaster. This purchase obligation is essential for the efficient working of the business and acts as a form of quality control. The obligation does not prevent franchisees from obtaining supplies of equipment and goods of equivalent quality from third-party suppliers. ServiceMaster will not withhold its approval of suppliers proposed by franchisees if those suppliers' chemicals meet the requirements of safety, non-toxicity, biodegradeability and effectiveness. The franchisee is also free to purchase the required goods from any other ServiceMaster franchisee.

(18) The franchisee's obligation to obtain the approval of ServiceMaster for the carrying-out of advertising. This control concerns the nature of advertisements, but not selling prices, with the object of ensuring conformity with the ServiceMaster brand image.

(19) The franchisee's obligation to submit to inspections of his premises by ServiceMaster and to present financial statements. This obligation allows the franchisor to verify whether the franchisee is operating in accordance with the ServiceMaster methods of operation and is fulfilling his financial obligations. In so far as this right of inspection is not abused to discipline franchisees in their sales activities outside their own territory or in the determination of their sales prices, it cannot be considered restrictive of competition.

(c) *Other provisions*

(20) The recommendation of sales prices to franchisees is not a restriction of competition since franchisees remain entirely free to determine their own prices for the supply of services and home-care products.

(21) The franchisee's obligation to resell home-care products only with the consent of ServiceMaster and only to customers serviced by the franchisee. This restriction on the resale of home-care products is based on the legitimate concern that the franchisee must concentrate on his primary business which is the provision of services, rather than the resale of goods.

Provisions falling within Article 85(1)
The following provisions of the ServiceMaster franchise agreement fall within Article 85(1).

(22) The combined effect of the clause which prohibits the franchisee from setting up further outlets outside his own territory, and the territorial protection clause which prevents the franchisee from actively seeking customers outside his territory, results in a certain degree of market-sharing between the franchisees, thus restricting competition within the Service-Master network.

This territorial protection is, however, limited by two elements: the franchisee holds a non-exclusive right only within his territory with regard to ServiceMaster itself and each franchisee is entitled to provide services to non-solicited customers outside his territory.

(23) The trade between member states is affected by the prohibition imposed upon franchisees against setting up outlets in other member states and against actively seeking customers in territories of franchisees of other member states. These prohibitions lead to market-sharing between the franchisees of the different member states. This effect on intra-Community trade is likely to be appreciable. ServiceMaster has notified a standard form agreement which it will use for the establishment of a European-wide franchise network. However, when assessing the appreciable effect on trade between member states the Commission must also take into account the likely future development of such a network. In this respect it must be considered that ServiceMaster is an important competitor in the market which is capable of setting up a great number of outlets throughout the EEC as it has done before in the United States and Canada where ServiceMaster has over 2,900 franchisees. ServiceMaster already has a six per cent market share in the United Kingdom and reckons that its EEC market share will exceed five per cent in the near future. Given this context, the Commission considers that there exists a sufficient probability that the restrictions contained in the notified standard form agreement are, at the least, such as to affect intra-Community trade appreciably. The notified standard form franchise agreement therefore falls within Article 85(1). It is thus necessary to examine whether that agreement can be granted an exemption under Article 85(3).

B. Article 85(3)
(24) The ServiceMaster standard form franchise agreement contributes, through the combined effect of all its provisions to improving the supply of the services concerned for the following reasons:

— it helps ServiceMaster rapidly to penetrate new markets with only limited investments, in this case the markets of all 12 member-states.

— this rapid development of a European-wide service network increases inter-brand competition with other service providers in the various markets concerned.
— it helps a great number of small undertakings to enter a new market by allowing them to set up outlets more rapidly and with a higher chance of success because they receive the benefit of ServiceMaster's name and reputation, and of its technical, commercial and administrative know-how.
— it permits an intensive servicing of customers through the personal commitment of independent traders.

(25) The ServiceMaster standard form franchise agreement allows consumers a fair share of the benefit resulting from the above improvements in the supply of services. First, the network as a whole is intended to provide a better and uniformly high-quality service to consumers. Secondly, as already mentioned in the preceding paragraph, consumers will benefit from the efficient service which the franchisee will be encouraged to provide as an independent trader who has a personal and direct interest in the success of his business. Thirdly, the freedom which consumers enjoy to obtain services elsewhere in the network will force franchisees to pass on to consumers a reasonable part of the benefits of this intra-brand competition. Finally, because of strong inter-brand competition, the franchisees can be expected to offer better services and prices.

(26) The provisions falling within Article 85(1) are indispensable to the establishment and existence of the franchise network; the limited territorial protection granted to the franchisees is necessary to obtain and protect their investment, comprising *inter alia* the cost of the establishment and maintenance of the business premises, the payment of the initial franchise fee, the acquisition of the necessary means of transport for the carrying out of the services at the customers' premises and the acquisition of special equipment. The limited territorial protection is also necessary to ensure that the franchisees will concentrate their service activity on their own territory. On the other hand, the franchisees retain passive service rights in other territories and remain free in the determination of their sales prices.

(27) The ServiceMaster standard form franchise agreement does not afford its members the possibility of eliminating competition in respect of a substantial part of the services concerned.

The inter-brand competition in the market concerned is both very strong and open; the market for cleaning, housekeeping and maintenance services is highly competitive, with a large number of firms supplying similar or identical services. It is also a market with no barriers to entry, with the result that new suppliers can at any time challenge any attempt by ServiceMaster or its franchisees to increase their prices.

Intra-brand competition within the ServiceMaster network itself is also preserved: the limited territorial protection does not grant the franchisees any marketing or customer exclusivity. Franchisees are free to provide services to non-solicited customers resident outside their own territory. This brings about a certain degree of price competition between franchisees, who are free to determine their sales prices.

(28) The notified agreement therefore meets all the requirements for an exemption under Article 85(3).

C. Articles 6 and 8 of Regulation 17
(29) The agreement as notified by ServiceMaster on 3 June 1987 contained a number of provisions which did not fulfill the conditions for an exemption, in particular provisions relating to

the territorial protection which originally excluded any intra-brand competition between franchisees. Following observations made by the Commission, ServiceMaster agreed to make a certain number of amendments to its agreement. ServiceMaster communicated the amended agreement to the Commission on 10 May 1988. Therefore, the date on which the exemption can take effect is the date of communication of the amended agreement.

(30) It is appropriate in this case, in view of the highly competitive nature of the market concerned and the absence of any barriers to entry to that market, to grant the exemption for a period of 10 years.

THE COMMISSION, for these reasons,
HAS ADOPTED THIS DECISION:

Article 1
Pursuant to Article 85(3) of the EEC Treaty, the provisions of Article 85(1) are hereby declared inapplicable from 10 May 1988 until 9 May 1998 to the standard form service franchise agreement which ServiceMaster concludes with its franchisees within the EEC.

Article 2
This Decision is addressed to ServiceMaster Ltd, 50 Commercial Square, Freeman's Common, Leicester LE2 7SR, United Kingdom.

COMMISSION DECISION

of 23 March 1990
Relating to a proceeding under Article 85 of the EEC Treaty
(IV/32.736 – Moosehead/Whitbread)
(Only the English text is authentic)
(90/186/EEC)

The Commission of the European Communities

Having regard to the Treaty establishing the European Economic Community,

Having regard to Council Regulation No 17 of 6 February 1962, First Regulation implementing Articles 85 and 86 of the Treaty*, as last amended by the Act of Accession of Spain and Portugal and, in particular, Articles 6 and 8 thereof,

Having regard to the notification dated 2 June 1988 by Whitbread and Company plc and Moosehead Breweries Limited, concerning the grant by Moosehead to Whitbread of an exclusive licence to brew and sell beer under Mooshead's trademarks within the United Kingdom,

Having regard to the summary of the notification** as published pursuant to Article 19(3) of Regulation No 17,
After consulting the Advisory Committee on Restrictive Practices and Dominant Positions,
Whereas:

I. Facts

The notification
(1) On June 1988, pursuant to Article 4 of Regulation No 17, Moosehead Breweries Limited, New Brunswick, Canada, and

* O.J. No 13, 21.2.1962, p.204/62.
** O.J. No C 179, 15.7.1989, p.13.

Whitbread and Company plc, London, notified to the Commission a number of agreements concluded between them dated 12 May 1987, and 1 May 1988.

(2) The parties have applied for negative clearance or, failing that, exemption pursuant to Article 85(3) of the Treaty.

The parties
(3) Moosehead is a wholly-owned subsidiary of Sevenacres Holding Limited and based in New Brunswick, Canada, Moosehead is principally engaged in the manufacture, sale and distribution of beer, and owns no brewing interests within the Community.

(3) Whitbread, a company incorporated in England, is a brewer and operates approximately 6,000 managed or tenanted public houses. The turnover of Whitbread in 1987 was £1,554 million.

The product and the market
(5) The agreements concern the manufacture of a beer in the United Kingdom which is sold by Moosehead in Canada and other countries under the trademark 'Moosehead' (henceforth referred to as 'the Product'. The Product is similar in nature and alcoholic strength to other 'non-premium lagers' presently sold in the United Kingdom, although according to the notifying parties, it has a particular taste typical of Canadian lagers.

(6)1. As was explained in Commission Decision 84/381/EEC (Carlsberg)* the following factors distinguish the United Kingdom beer market from other European markets:

2. Most beer sold in the United Kingdom is sold in draught form in public houses licenced for the consumption of liquor; 81%** of all beer consumed in the United Kingdom is sold in on-licenced premises and 75% of all beer sold in the United Kingdom is in draught form. In 1987 lager represented 45% of the beer consumption in the United Kingdom***. In order to achieve substantial sales of a new beer in the United Kingdom it is therefore necessary for the seller to have access to a certain number of public houses.

3. Brewers largely distribute their beer in the United Kingdom using their own lorries. No large-scale independent distribution facility therefore exists for beer in the United Kingdom.

4. The majority of public houses in the United Kingdom are operated by tenants who are 'tied' by contract to purchase beer from one brewer alone. They are, in fact, owned by the brewer with which they sign such agreements. Since almost all draught beer, which accounts for over 75% of total beer sales, is sold in public houses and 57% of all on-licensed premises in the United Kingdom are owned by brewers and 'tied', it is very useful, if not indispensable, for a foreign brewer wishing to enter the United Kingdom market to gain the assistance of a large national brewer.

The number of tenants of on-licensed premises that are required to purchase from one brewer alone is likely to decrease by 1 November 1992 when, as a result of implementation of The Supply of Beer Order, all national brewers with more than 2,000 licensed premises must release from all product ties one half of their premises above the 2,000 threshold. Also, all on-licensed tenants tied by national brewers will be free to choose a guest beer as well as to purchase other non-alcoholic drinks from any source by 1 May 1990. Nevertheless, a substantial part of total United Kingdom beer consumption will continue to pass through 'tied' outlets.

5. The six major United Kingdom brewers*, which in 1987 held approximately 82% of the United Kingdom beer market, sell between them many different types of beers and also many different brands of lager. Whitbread held 12% of the United Kingdom retail sales of beer in 1987.

The agreements

General provisions
(7)1. The agreement in question is set out in three contracts: the Marketing and Technical Agreement; the Trade Mark User Agreement dated 12 May 1987, and the Assignment Agreement dated 1 May 1988. The Commission considers that these three contracts form part of a single agreement henceforth referred to as 'the Agreement'.

2. Under the Agreement, Moosehead grants to Whitbread the sole and exclusive right to produce and promote, market, and sell beer manufactured for sale under the name 'Moosehead' in the licenced territory (the United Kingdom, the Channel Islands and the Isle of Man, henceforth referred to as 'the Territory'), using Moosehead's secret know-how. Whitbread pays to Moosehead a royalty for this exclusive right.

3. Whitbread agrees that the quality of the beer and the type and quality of the raw materials shall comply with Moosehead specifications.

4. Whitbread agrees that it will neither seek customers, nor establish any branch or maintain any distribution depot for distribution of the Product, outside the Territory. It may, however, fill unsolicited orders from purchasers in the member states.

5. During the term of the Agreement, Whitbread agrees not to produce or promote within the Territory any other beer identified as a Canadian beer.

Trade mark provisions
(8)1. Under the Agreement, Whitbread agrees to sell the Product only under the trademark 'Moosehead'. Whitbread also agrees to use the trademark Moosehead only on or in relation to the Product.

The property rights in the trademarks in the United Kingdom are assigned to Whitbread and Moosehead jointly. This assignment is intended, according to the parties, to give Whitbread a stronger guarantee of its right to use the trademarks during the term of the Agreement. Moosehead grants to Whitbread the exclusive licence to use the trademarks in relation to the Product in the Territory during the term of the Agreement.

2. The Agreement stipulates that Moosehead shall not, without the consent of Whitbread, register or use, nor shall Whitbread apply to register, any trademark which resembles, or may reasonably be confused with, any of Moosehead trademarks in the Territory.

3. Furthermore, Whitbread acknowledges the title of Moosehead to the trademarks and the validity of the registrations of Moosehead as proprietor thereof. Whitbread undertakes to observe all conditions which may be prescribed by the terms of the registration of the trademarks and also not to do any act which would, or may, invalidate such registration or title, not apply to vary or cancel any registration of the trademarks.

4. The Agreement provides that upon its termination Whitbread shall reassign to Moosehead all its rights, title and interest

---

* O.J. No 1, 207, 2.8.1984, p.26.
** The statistics in this section are estimates of Whitbread.
*** MMC Report p.10.

* Allied, Bass, Elders, Grand Metropolitan, Scottish & Newcastle and Whitbread.

in the trademarks and in the goodwill associated therewith, and shall join with Moosehead in any application to register Moosehead as sole proprietor of the trademarks. Thereafter Whitbread shall desist from all use of the trademarks.

Know-how provisions

(9)1. Moosehead agrees to provide Whitbread with all the relevant know-how necessary to produce the Product, and furthermore agrees to supply Whitbread with all yeast which may be necessary.

2. Whitbread agrees to comply with the directions and specifications of Moosehead in relation to the know-how, and to purchase yeast only from Moosehead or a third party designated by Moosehead.

3. Whitbread agrees to use the know-how only for the manufacture of the Product and agrees to keep all know-how provided by Moosehead confidential.

(10) The marketing strategy for the promotion of the Product, the brand plans and sales forecast in the Territory must be jointly agreed by the parties. Whitbread, however, is solely responsible for implementing that policy and bearing its costs.

Duration of the Agreement

(11) The Agreement came into force on 1 May 1987, and operates for an indefinite period unless terminated pursuant to the following provisions:

— either party may terminate by giving notice to the other party varying from one to ten years, if specified amounts of the Product have not been sold by Whitbread;
— either party may terminate the Agreement by giving a shorter notice if a party commits a breach of any of its contractual obligations or if there is a substantial change in the ownership or control of either party.

(12) On termination of the Agreement, Whitbread is obliged to cease producing the Product, to return all know-how to Moosehead, and not to use this know-how in future. Furthermore, Whitbread may not use the trademarks following termination and must assign to Moosehead any right title and interest that it has acquired in the trademarks. Whitbread is also obliged to keep this know-how secret from any third party.

The parties' submissions

The parties have made the following submissions,

(13)1. As Moosehead has no branch in Europe and neither Moosehead nor any of its associate companies has a manufacturing facility in the Community, a distribution network for beer, or any experience of marketing beer in the United Kingdom, it would not, over the short term, be commercially feasible for Moosehead to set up its own manufacturing facility for the product. In view of the nature of the retail market for beer and given the distance and the scale on which sales would be established, it would not be economic for Moosehead to establish its own distribution network or to sell through independent wholesalers.

2. Whitbread has limited experience of Canadian lagers and, in particular, has no access to the unique culture yeast that gives Moosehead lager a particular taste that distinguishes it from the other lagers, nor to the technical information held by Moosehead necessary to manufacture the Product to which the Agreement relates. Whitbread, therefore, lacks the expertise to manufacture the Product for the United Kingdom market without assistance

from Moosehead. However, its general brewing facilities and experience mean that it is capable of producing Moosehead beer for sale in the Territory if this assistance is given by Moosehead. Furthermore, Whitbread does not possess a well-known Canadian trademark.

3. The parties argue that as a result of these facts the Agreement contributes towards improving production/distribution of the Product because (i) in the absence of the Agreement, the Product could not have been made available as quickly, or over as wide an area, and would thus have been available to fewer customers and at a later date; and (ii) the Agreement enables the Product to be produced in the Territory, which means it is likely to be fresher and cheaper, since it would be transported over a shorter distance.

The fierce competition in the lager sector of the beer market will ensure that the benefits of the Agreement are passed on to consumers and, furthermore, will prevent the Agreement from eliminating competition in respect of a substantial part of the products in question.

The clauses to the Agreement which are restrictive of competition are indispensable in order to give Whitbread sufficient confidence to invest substantial sums in the launch of a new beer onto an already competitive market, and to enable Moosehead to entrust the brewing and sale of the Product to another brewer in full knowledge that the licensee will concentrate its efforts, concerning the promotion and sale of Canadian lagers, exclusively on the Product.

4. The obligation upon Whitbread not to sell certain competing beers during the Agreement is indispensable to its objective.

(14) Third parties have made no objections subsequent to the publication made under Article 19(3) of Regulation No 17.

II. Legal Assessment

Article 85(1)

(15)1. The exclusive trademark licence for the production and marketing of the Product, the prohibition of active sales outside the Territory and the non-competition clause, as listed respectively in the last sentence of (8)1, and at (7)2, (7)4 and (7)5 above, fall under the prohibition of Article 85(1) since they have as their object or effect an appreciable restriction of competition within the common market.

In this case, the exclusive character of the licence has, as a consequence, the exclusion of third parties, namely the five other large brewers in the Territory, from the use, as licensees, of the Moosehead trademark, in spite of their potential interest and their ability to do so.

Likewise, the prohibition of active sales outside the Territory by the licensee and the ban on marketing competing brands of beer are appreciable restrictions of competition since Whitbread, because of its large production capacity, would be able to supply other markets within the Common Market and to distribute other Canadian brands.

These restrictions of competition may affect trade between member states to an appreciable extent because their effect will be that trade will develop between member states in conditions different from those which would have prevailed without the restrictions and, given the size of the parties to the Agreement, their influence on market conditions is appreciable. This is the case, in particular, for the prohibition of active sales outside the Territory.

2. The other clauses of the Agreement do not fall within Article 85(1) because they do not have as their object or effect an appreciable restriction of competition within the common market. This applies to Whitbread's obligation to maintain certain qualitative standards, to the know-how clauses, and to the trademark no-challenge clause.

3. The know-how provisions set out in paragraphs (9)1, (9)2 and (9)3 do not fall under Article 85(1) because the grant of know-how is not exclusive and the obligations imposed on the licensee are simply ancillary to the grant of the trademark licence and enable the licence to take effect.

In particular the exclusive purchasing obligation regarding yeast set out in paragraph (9)2, does not fall under Article 85(1) because it is necessary to ensure technically satisfactory exploitation of the licenced technology and a similar identity between the lager produced originally by Moosehead and the same lager produced by Whitbread.

4. In relation to the trademark non-challenge clause:

(a) in general terms, a trademark non-challenge clause can refer to the ownership and/or the validity of the trademark:

— The ownership of a trademark may, in particular, be challenged on grounds of the prior use or prior registration of an identical trademark.

A clause in an exclusive trademark licence agreement obliging the licensee not to challenge the ownership of a trademark, as specified in the above paragraph, does not constitute a restriction of competition within the meaning of Article 85(1). Whether or not the licensor or licensee has the ownership of the trademark, the use of it by any other party is prevented in any event, and competition would thus not be affected.

— The validity of a trademark may be contested on any ground under national law, and in particular on the grounds that it is generic or descriptive in nature. In such an event, should the challenge be upheld, the trademark may fall into the public domain and may thereafter be used without restriction by the licensee and any other party.

Such a clause may constitute a restriction of competition within the meaning of Article 85(1), because it may contribute to the maintenance of a trademark that would be an unjustified barrier to entry into given market.

Moreover in order for any restriction of competition to fall under Article 85(1), it must be appreciable. The ownership of a trademark only gives the holder the exclusive right to sell products under that name. Other parties are free to sell the product in question under a different trademark or tradename. Only where the use of a well-known trademark would be an important advantage to any company entering or competing in any given market and the absence of which therefore constitutes a significant barrier to entry, would this clause which impedes the licensee to challenge the validity of the trademark, constitute an appreciable restriction of competition within the meaning of Article 85(1).

(b) In the present case Whitbread is unable to challenge both the ownership and the validity of the trademark.

As far as the validity of the trademark is concerned it must be noted that the trademark is comparatively new to the lager market in the Territory. The maintenance of the 'Moosehead' trademark will thus not constitute an appreciable barrier to entry for any other company entering or competing in the beer market in the United Kingdom. Accordingly, the Commission considers that

the trademark non-challenge clause included in the Agreement, in so far as it concerns its validity (see the second indent of point 15.4 above), does not constitute an appreciable restriction of competition and does not fall under Article 85(1).

Furthermore, in so far as this clause concerns ownership, it does not constitute a restriction of competition within the meaning of Article 85(1) for the reasons stated in the first indent of point 15.4 above.

Article 85(3)

(16)1. The block exemption provided by Commission Regulation (EEC) No 556/89* applies to agreements combining know-how and trademark licenses where, as stated in Article 1(1), the trademark license is ancillary to that of the know-how. In the present case the principal interest of the parties lies in the exploitation of the trademark rather than of the know-how. The parties view the Canadian origin of the mark as crucial to the success of the marketing campaign, which promotes the Product as a Canadian beer. Under these circumstances, the provision of the agreement relating to the trademarks is not ancillary and Regulation 556/89 therefore does not apply.

2. In the light of the particularities of the United Kingdom beer market, described at points 6.1 to 6.5 above, the Commission considers that the Agreement is likely to contribute to the improvement of the production and distribution of the Product in the Territory and to promote economic progress. In particular, the following considerations are pertinent in this regard:

— The turnover presently achieved by Moosehead would not justify the capital costs involved in building custom production facilities for sales in the Territory. Thus, as the Agreement provides for Whitbread to brew the beer in its existing facilities, it is likely to improve the production of the Product in the common market. Furthermore, production will be at the point-of-sale and the beer need no longer be imported from Canada. The Agreement will thereby reduce transport costs and thus contribute to economic progress.
— Through the Agreement, the Product will automatically benefit from Whitbread's comprehensive distribution network. In the light of a market characterized by a paucity of independent distribution facilities, the Commission considers that the Agreement is likely to contribute to the improvement in the distribution of the Product in the Territory.
— Whitbread owns a number of 'tied-houses'. The Agreement will therefore enable Moosehead to guarantee immediate access for the Product to a wider number of retail outlets without expending the time and expense of approaching a large number of independent retailers. The Commission considers that, in this manner, the Agreement is also likely to contribute to the improvement in the distribution of the Product in the Territory.

Consumers will also benefit from the Agreement since they will have a wide choice with the entry of the Product in the market of the Territory.

Taking account of the existence of many similar competing beers and of the ability of the parties to sell the Product to other parties for export to other member states, the parties to the Agreement will not have the possibility of eliminating competition in respect of a substantial part of the products in question.

In examining the compatibility of the Agreement with these two requirements of Article 85(3), the Commission has paid particular attention to the liberalising measures that the United Kingdom Government is implementing in relation to the United

---

* O.J. No L 61, 4.3.1989, p.1.

Kingdom beer market. These measures are expected to become fully effective during the course of the exemption granted by the presented Decision.

After having considered the favorable effects for the production and marketing of beer resulting from the clauses which are restrictive of competition, and in particular the non-competition clause, the Commission considers that they are deemed to be indispensable to the attainment of the objectives of Article 85(3). A decision pursuant to Article 85(3) may, therefore, be adopted.

3. The Agreement remains in force until it is terminated by either party. The Agreement was notified to the Commission on 2 June 1988. It appears appropriate, pursuant to Articles 6(1) and 8(1) of Regulation No 17, to adopt such a decision for a period of 10 years.

Has adopted this Decision

Article 1
Pursuant to Article 85(3) of the EEC Treaty, the provisions of Article 85(1) are hereby declared inapplicable for the period from 3 June 1988 to 2 June 1998 to the Agreement notified to the Commission on 2 June 1988 by Moosehead Breweries Limited and by Whitbread and Company plc.

Article 2
This Decision is addressed to:

1. Moosehead Breweries Limited
   89, Main Street,
   Saint John West,
   New Brunswick, E2M 3M2,
   Canada.

2. Whitbread and Company plc,
   The Brewery,
   Chiswell Street,
   London EC1Y 6SD,
   United Kingdom.

Done at Brussels, 23 March 1990.

For the Commission
Leon BRITTAN
Vice-President

Commission Regulation (EEC) No 4087/88

of 30 November 1988
on the application of Article 85(3) of the Treaty to categories of franchise agreements
(OJ 1988 L 359/52)

The Commission of the European Communities

Having regard to the Treaty establishing the European Economic Community,

Having regard to Council regulation No 19/65/EEC of 2 March 1965 on the application of Article 85(3) of the Treaty to certain categories of agreements and concerted practices*, as last amended by the Act of Accession of Spain and Portugal, and in particular Article 1 thereof,

Having published a draft of this Regulation**,

Having consulted the Advisory Committee on Restrictive Practices and Dominant Positions,

Whereas:

(1) Regulation No 19/65/EEC empowers the Commission to apply Article 85(3) of the Treaty by Regulation to certain categories of bilateral exclusive agreements falling within the scope of Article 85(1) which either have as their object the exclusive distribution or exclusive purchase of goods, or include restrictions imposed in relation to the assignment or use of industrial property rights.

(2) Franchise agreements consist essentially of licences of industrial or intellectual property rights relating to trade marks or signs and know-how, which can be combined with restrictions relating to supply or purchase of goods.

(3) Several types of franchise can be distinguished according to their object; industrial franchise concerns the manufacturing of goods, distribution franchise concerns, the sale of goods, and service franchise concerns the supply of services.

(4) It is possible on the basis of the experience of the Commission to define categories of franchise agreements which fall under Article 85(1) but can normally be regarded as satisfying the conditions laid down in Article 85(3). This is the case for franchise agreements whereby one of the parties supplies goods or provides services to end users. On the other hand, industrial franchise agreements should not be covered by this Regulation. Such agreements, which usually govern relationships between producers, present different characteristics than the other types of franchise. They consist of manufacturing licences based on patents and/or technical know-how, combined with trade-mark licences. Some of them may benefit from other block exemptions if they fulfil the necessary conditions.

(5) This Regulation covers franchise agreements between two undertakings, the franchisor and the franchisee, for the retailing of goods or the provision of services to end users, or a combination of these activities, such as the processing or adaptation of goods to fit specific needs of their customers. It also covers cases where the relationship between franchisor and franchisee is made through a third undertaking, the master franchisee. It does not cover wholesale franchise agreements because of the lack of experience of the Commission in that field.

---

* OJ No 36, 6. 3. 1965, p. 533/65.
** OJ No C 229, 27. 8. 1987, p.3.

(6) Franchise agreements as defined in this Regulation can fall under Article 85(1). They may in particular affect intra-Community trade where they are concluded between undertakings from different member states or where they form the basis of a network which extends beyond the boundaries of a single member state.

(7) Franchise agreements as defined in this Regulation normally improve the distribution of goods and/or the provision of services as they give franchisors the possibility of establishing a uniform network with limited investments, which may assist the entry of new competitors on the market, particularly in the case of small and medium-sized undertakings, thus increasing interbrand competition. They also allow independent traders to set up outlets more rapidly and with higher chance of success than if they had to do so without the franchisor's experience and assistance. They have therefore the possibility of competing more efficiently with large distribution undertakings.

(8) As a rule, franchise agreements also allow consumers and other end users a fair share of the resulting benefit, as they combine the advantage of a uniform network with the existence of traders personally interested in the efficient operation of their business. The homogeneity of the network and the constant cooperation between the franchisor and the franchisees ensures a constant quality of the products and services. The favourable effect of franchising on interbrand competition and the fact that consumers are free to deal with any franchisee in the network guarantees that a reasonable part of the resulting benefits will be passed on to the consumers.

(9) This Regulation must define the obligations restrictive of competition which may be included in franchise agreements. This is the case in particular for the granting of an exclusive territory to the franchisees combined with the prohibition on acitively seeking customers outside that territory, which allows them to concentrate their efforts on their allotted territory. The same applies to the granting of an exclusive territory to a master franchisee combined with the obligation not to conclude franchise agreements with third parties outside that territory. Where the franchisees sell or use in the process of providing services, goods manufactured by the franchisor or according to its instructions and or bearing its trade mark, an obligation on the franchisees not to sell, or use in the process of the provision of services, competing goods, makes it possible to establish a coherent network which is identified with the franchised goods. However, this obligation should only be accepted with respect to the goods which form the essential subject-matter of the franchise. It should notably not relate to accessories or spare parts for these goods.

(10) The obligations referred to above thus do not impose restrictions which are not necessary for the attainment of the above mentioned objectives. In particular, the limited territorial protection granted to the franchisees is indispensable to protect their investment.

(11) It is desirable to list in the Regulation a number of obligations that are commonly found in franchise agreements and are normally not restrictive of competition and to provide that if,

because of the particular economic or legal circumstances, they fall under Article 85(1), they are also covered by the exemption. This list, which is not exhaustive, includes in particular clauses which are essential either to preserve the common identity and reputation of the network or to prevent the know-how made available and the assistance given by the franchisor from benefiting competitors.

(12) The Regulation must specify the conditions which must be satisfied for the exemption to apply. To guarantee that competition is not eliminated for a substantial part of the goods which are the subject of the franchise, it is necessary that parallel imports remain possible. Therefore, cross deliveries between franchisees should always be possible. Furthermore, where a franchise network is combined with another distribution system, franchisees should be free to obtain supplies from authorized distributors. To better inform consumers, thereby helping to ensure that they receive a fair share of the resulting benefits, it must be provided that the franchisee shall be obliged to indicate its status as an independent undertaking, by any appropriate means which does not jeopardize the common identity of the franchised network. Furthermore, where the franchisees have to honour guarantees for the franchisor's goods, this obligation should also apply to goods supplied by the franchisor, other franchisees or other agreed dealers.

(13) The Regulation must also specify restrictions which may not be included in franchise agreements if these are to benefit from the exemption granted by the Regulation, by virtue of the fact that such provisions are restrictions falling under Article 85(1) for which there is no general presumption that they will lead to the positive effects required by Article 85(3). This applies in particular to market sharing between competing manufacturers, to clauses unduly limiting the franchisee's choice of suppliers or customers, and to cases where the franchisee is restricted in determining its prices. However, the franchisor should be free to recommend prices to the franchisees, where it is not prohibited by national laws and to the extent that it does not lead to concerted practices for the effective application of these prices.

(14) Agreements which are not automatically covered by the exemption because they contain provisions that are not expressly exempted by the Regulation and not expressly excluded from exemption may nonetheless generally be presumed to be eligible for application of Article 85(3). It will be possible for the Commission rapidly to establish whether this is the case for a particular agreement. Such agreements should therefore be deemed to be covered by the exemption provided for in this Regulation where they are notified to the Commission and the Commission does not oppose the application of the exemption within a specified period of time.

(15) If individual agreements exempted by this Regulation nevertheless have effects which are incompatible with Article 85(3), in particular as interpreted by the administrative practice of the Commission and the case law of the Court of Justice, the Commission may withdraw the benefit of the block exemption. This applies in particular where competition is significantly restricted because of the structure of the relevant market.

(16) Agreements which are automatically exempted, pursuant to this Regulation need not be notified. Undertakings may nevertheless in a particular case request a decision pursuant to Council Regulation No 17(*) as last amended by the Act of Accession of Spain and Portugal.

* OJ No 13, 21. 2. 1962, p. 204/62.

(17) Agreements may benefit from the provisions either of this Regulation or of another Regulation, according to their particular nature and provided that they fulfil the necessary conditions of application. These may not benefit from a combination of the provisions of this Regulation with those of another block exemption Regulation.

Has adopted this Regulation:

Article 1

1. Pursuant to Article 85(3) of the Treaty and subject to the provisions of this Regulation, it is hereby declared that Article 85(1) of the Treaty shall not apply to franchise agreements to which two undertakings are party, which include one or more of the restrictions listed in Article 2.

2. The exemption provided for in paragraph 1 shall also apply to master franchise agreements to which two undertakings are party. Where applicable, the provisions of this Regulation concerning the relationship between franchisor and franchisee shall apply *mutatis mutandis* to the relationship between franchisor and master franchisee and between master franchisee and franchisee.

3. For the purposes of this Regulation:

(a) 'franchise' means a package of industrial or intellectual property rights relating to trade marks, trade names, shop signs, utility models, designs, copyrights, know-how or patents, to be exploited for the resale of goods or the provision of services to end users;

(b) 'franchise agreement' means an agreement whereby one undertaking, the franchisor, grants the other, the franchisee, in exchange for direct or indirect financial consideration, the right to exploit a franchise for the purposes of marketing specified types of goods and/or services; it includes at least obligations relating to:

— the use of a common name or shop sign and a uniform presentation of contract premises and/or means of transport,
— the communication by the franchisor to the franchisee of know-how,
— the continuing provision by the franchisor to the franchisee of commercial or technical assistance during the life of the agreement;

(c) 'master franchise agreement' means an agreement whereby one undertaking, the franchisor, grants the other, the master franchisee, in exchange of direct or indirect financial consideration, the right to exploit a franchise for the purposes of concluding franchise agreements with third parties, the franchisees;

(d) 'franchisor's goods' means goods produced by the franchisor or according to its instructions, and/or bearing the franchisor's name or trade mark;

(e) 'contract premises' means the premises used for the exploitation of the franchise or, when the franchise is exploited outside those premises, the base from which the franchisee operates the means of transport used for the exploitation of the franchise (contract means of transport);

(f) 'know-how' means a package of non-patented practical information, resulting from experience and testing by the franchisor, which is secret, substantial and identified;

(g) 'secret' means that the know-how, as a body or in the precise configuration and assembly of its components, is not generally known or easily accessible; it is not limited in the narrow sense that each individual component of the know-how should be totally unknown or unobtainable outside the franchisor's business:

(h) 'substantial' means that the know-how includes information which is of importance for the sale of goods or the provision of services to end users, and in particular for the presentation of goods for sale, the processing of goods in connection which the provision of services, methods of dealing with customers, and administration and financial management; the know-how must be useful for the franchisee by being capable at the date of conclusion of the agreement, of improving the competitive position of the franchisee, in particular by improving the franchisee's performance or helping or helping it to enter a new market;

(i) 'identified' means that the know-how must be described in a sufficiently comprehensive manner so as to make it possible to verify that it fulfils the criteria of secrecy and substantiality; the description of the know-how can either be set out in the franchise agreement or in a separate document or recorded in any other appropriate form.

Article 2

The exemption provided for in Article 1 shall apply to the following restrictions of competition:

(a) an obligation on the franchisor, in a defined area of the common market, the contract territory, not to:

— grant the right to exploit all or part of the franchise to third parties,
— itself exploit the franchise, or itself market the goods or services which are the subject-matter of the franchise under a similar formula,
— itself supply the franchisor's goods to third parties;

(b) an obligation on the master franchisee not to conclude franchise agreement with third parties outside its contract territory;

(c) an obligation on the franchisee to exploit the franchise only from the contract premises;

(d) an obligation on the franchisee to refrain, outside the contract territory, from seeking customers for the goods or the services which are the subject-matter of the franchise;

(e) an obligation on the franchisee not to manufacture, sell or use in the course of the provision of services, goods competing with the franchisor's goods which are the subject-matter of the franchise; where the subject-matter of the franchise is the sale or use in the course of the provision of services both certain types of goods and spare parts or accessories therefor, that obligation may not be imposed in respect of these spare parts or accessories.

Article 3

1. Article 1 shall apply notwithstanding the presence of any of the following obligations on the franchisee, in so far as they are necessary to protect the franchisor's industrial or intellectual property rights or to maintain the common identity and reputation of the franchised network;

(a) to sell, or use in the course of the provision of services, exclusively goods matching minimum objective quality specifications laid down by the franchisor;

(b) to sell, or use in the course of the provision of services, goods which are manufactured only by the franchisor or by third parties designed by it, where it is impracticable, owing to the nature of the goods which are the subject-matter of the franchise, to apply objective quality specifications;

(c) not to engage, directly or indirectly, in any similar business in a territory where it would compete with a member of the franchised network, including the franchisor; the franchisee may be held to this obligation after termination of the agreement, for a reasonable period which may not exceed one year, in the territory where it has exploited the franchise;

(d) not to acquire financial interests in the capital of a competing undertaking which would give the franchisee the power to influence the economic conduct of such undertaking;

(e) to sell the goods which are the subject-matter of the franchise only to end users, to other franchisees and to resellers within other channels of distribution supplied by the manufacturer of these goods or with its consent;

(f) to use its best endeavours to sell the goods or provide the services that are the subject-matter of the franchise; to offer for sale a minimum range of goods, achieve a minimum turnover, plan its orders in advance, keep minimum stocks and provide customer and warranty services;

(g) to pay to the franchisor a specified proportion of its revenue for advertising and itself carry out advertising for the nature of which it shall obtain the franchisor's approval.

2. Article 1 shall apply notwithstanding the presence of any of the following obligations on the franchisee:

(a) not to disclose to third parties the know-how provided by the franchisor; the franchisee may be held to this obligation after termination of the agreement;

(b) to communicate to the franchisor any experience gained in exploiting the franchise and to grant it, and other franchisees, a non-exclusive licence for the know-how resulting from that experience;

(c) to inform the franchisor of infringements of licensed, industrial or intellectual property rights, to take legal action against infringers or to assist the franchisor in any legal actions against infringers;

(d) not to use know-how licensed by the franchisor for purposes other than the exploitation of the franchise; the franchisee may be held to this obligation after termination of the agreement;

(e) to attend or have its staff attend training courses arranged by the franchisor;

(f) to apply the commercial methods devised by the franchisor, including any subsequent modification thereof, and use the licensed industrial or intellectual property rights;

(g) to comply with the franchisor's standards for the equipment and presentation of the contract premises and/or means of transport;

(h) to allow the franchisor to carry out checks of the contract premises and/or means of tansport, including the goods sold and the services provided, and the inventory and accounts of the franchisee;

(i) not without the franchisor's consent to change the location of the contract premises;

(j) not without the franchisor's consent, to assign the rights and obligations under the franchise agreement.

3. In the event that, because of particular circumstances, obligations referred to in paragraph 2 fall within the scope of Article 85(1), they shall also be exempted even if they are not accompanied by any of the obligations exempted by Article 1.

Article 4

The exemption provided for in Article 1 shall apply on condition that:

(a) the franchisee is free to obtain the goods that are the subject matter of the franchise from other franchisees; where such goods are also distributed through another network of authorised distributors, the franchisee must be free to obtain the goods from the latter;

(b) where the franchisor obliges the franchisee to honour guarantees for the franchisor's goods, that obligation shall apply in respect of such goods supplied by any member of the franchised network or other distributors which give a similar guarantee, in the common market;

(c) the franchisee is obliged to indicate its status as an independent undertaking; this indication shall however, not interfere with the common identity of the franchised network resulting in particular from the common name or shop sign and uniform appearance of the contract premises and/or means of transport.

Article 5

The exemption granted by Article 1 shall not apply where;

(a) undertakings producing goods or providing services which are identical or are considered by users as equvalent in view of their characteristics, price and intended use, enter into franchise agreements in respect of such goods or services;

(b) without prejudice to Article 2(e) and Article 3(1)(b) the franchisee is prevented from obtaining supplies of goods of a quality equivalent to those offered by the franchisor;

(c) without prejudice to Article 2(e), the franchisee is obliged to sell, or use in the process of providing services, goods manufactured by the franchisor or third parties designated by the franchisor and the franchisor refuses, for reasons other than protecting the franchisor's industrial or intellectual property rights, or maintaining the common identity and reputation of the franchised network, to designate as authorised manufacturers third parties proposed by the franchisee;

(d) the franchisee is prevented from continuing to use the licensed know-how after termination of the agreement where the know-how has become generally known or easily accessible, other than by breach of an obligation by the franchisee;

(e) the franchisee is restricted by the franchisor, directly or indirectly, in the determination of sale prices for the goods or services which are the subject matter of the franchise, without prejudice to the possibility for the franchisor of recommending sale prices;

(f) the franchisor prohibits the franchisee from challenging the validity of the industrial or intellectual property rights which form part of the franchise, without prejudice to the possibility for the franchisor of terminating the agreement in such a case;

(g) franchisees are obliged not to supply within the common market the goods or services which are the subject-matter of the franchise to end users because of their place of residence.

Article 6

1. The exemption provided for in Article 1 shall also apply to franchise agreements which fulfil the conditions laid down in Article 4 and include obligations restrictive of competition which are not covered by Articles 2 and 3(3) and do not fall within the scope of Article 5, on condition that the agreements in question are notified to the Commission in accordance with the provisions of Commission Regulation No 27* and that the Commission does not oppose such exemption within a period of six months.

2. The period of six months shall run from the date on which the notification is received by the Commission. Where, however,

* OJ No 35, 10. 5. 1962, p. 1118/62.

the notification is made by registered post, the period shall run from the date shown on the postmark of the place of posting.

3. Paragraph 1 shall apply only if:

(a) express reference is made to this Article in the notification or in a communication accompanying it, and

(b) the information furnished with the notification is complete and in accordance with the facts.

4. The benefit of paragraph 1 can be claimed for agreements notified before the entry into force of this Regulation by submitting a communication to the Commission referring expressly to this Article and to the notification. Paragraphs 2 and 3(b) shall apply *mutatis mutandis*.

5. The Commission may oppose exemption. It shall oppose exemption if it receives a request to do so from a member state within three months of the forwarding to the member state of the notification referred to in paragraph 1 or the communication referred to in paragraph 4. This request must be justified on the basis of considerations relating to the competition rules of the Treaty.

6. The Commission may withdraw its opposition to the exemption at any time. However, where that opposition was raised at the request of a member state, it may be withdrawn only after consultation of the Advisory Committee on Restrictive Practices and Dominant Positions.

7. If the opposition is withdrawn because the undertakings concerned have shown that the conditions of Article 85(3) are fulfilled, the exemption shall apply from the date of the notification.

8. If the opposition is withdrawn because the undertakings concerned have amended the agreement so that the conditions of Article 85(3) are fulfilled, the exemption shall apply from the date on which the amendments take effect.

9. If the Commission opposes exemption and its opposition is not withdrawn, the effects of the notification shall be governed by the provisions of Regulation No 17.

Article 7

1. Information acquired pursuant to Article 6 shall be used only for the purposes of this Regulation.

2. The Commission and the authorities of the member states, their officials and other servants shall not disclose information acquired by them pursuant to this Regulation of a kind that is covered by the obligation of professional secrecy.

3. Paragraphs 1 and 2 shall not prevent publication of general information or surveys which do not contain information relating to particular undertakings or associations of undertakings.

Article 8

The Commission may withdraw the benefit of this Regulation, pursuant to Article 7 of Regulation No 19/65/EEC, where it finds in a particular case that an agreement exempted by this Regulation nevertheless has certain effects which are incompatible with the conditions laid down in Article 85(3) of the EEC Treaty, and in particular where territorial protection is awarded to the franchisee and:

(a) access to the relevant market, or competition therein is significantly restricted by the cumulative effect of parallel networks of similar agreements established by competing manufacturers or distributors;

(b) the goods or services which are the subject-matter of the franchise do not face, in a substantial part of the common market, effective competition from goods or services which are identical or considered by users as equivalent in view of their characteristics, price and intended use;

(c) the parties, or one of them prevent end users, because of their place of residence, from obtaining, directly or through intermediaries, the goods or services which are the subject-matter of the franchise within the common market, or use differences in specifications concerning those goods or services in different member states, to isolate markets;

(d) franchisees engage in concerted practices relating to the sale prices of the goods or services which are the subject-matter of the franchise;

(e) the franchisor uses its right to check the contract premises and means of transport, or refuses its agreement to requests by the franchisee to move the contract premises or assign its rights and obligations under the franchise agreement, for reasons other than protecting the franchisor's industrial or intellectual property rights, maintaining the common identity and reputation of the franchised network or verifying that the franchisee abides by its obligations under the agreement.

Article 9

This Regulation shall enter into force on 1 February 1989.

It shall remain in force until 31 December 1999.

This Regulation shall be binding in its entirety and directly applicable in all member states.

Done at Brussels, 30 November 1988.

For the Commission
Peter SUTHERLAND
Member of the Commission

Commission Regulation (EEC) No 556/89

of 30 November 1988
on the application of Article 85(3) of the Treaty to certain categories of know-how licensing agreements
(OJ 1989 L 61/1)

The Commission of the European Communities

Having regard to the Treaty establishing the European Economic Community.

Having regard to Council Regulation No 19/65/EEC of 2 March 1965 on the application of Article 85(3) of the Treaty to certain categories of agreements and concerted practices*, as last amended by the Act of Accession of Spain and Portugal, and in particular to Article 1 thereof.

Having published a draft of this Regulation**,

After consulting the Advisory Committee on Restrictive Practices and Dominant Positions.

Whereas:

(1) Regulation No. 19/65/EEC empowers the Commission to apply Article 85(3) of the Treaty by Regulation to certain categories of bilateral agreements and concerted practices falling within the scope of Article 85(1) which include restrictions imposed in relation to the acquisition or use of industrial property rights, in particular patents, utility models, designs or trade marks, or to the rights arising out of contracts for assignment of, or the right to use, a method of manufacture or knowledge relating to the use or application of industrial processes.

The increasing economic importance of non-patented technical information (e.g. descriptions of manufacturing processes, recipes, formulae, designs or drawings), commonly termed 'know-how', the large number of agreements currently being concluded by undertakings including public research facilities solely for the exploitation of such information (so-called 'pure' know-how licensing agreements) and the fact that the transfer of know-how is, in practice, frequently irreversible make it necessary to provide greater legal certainty with regard to the status of such agreements under the competition rules, thus encouraging the dissemination of technical knowledge in the Community. In the light of experience acquired so far, it is possible to define a category of such know-how licensing agreements covering all or part of the common market which are capable of falling within the scope of Article 85(1) but which can normally be regarded as satisfying the conditions laid down in Article 85(3) where the licensed know-how is secret, substantial and identified in any appropriate form ('the know-how'). These definitional requirements are only intended to ensure that the communication of the know-how provides a valid justification for the application of the present Regulation and in particular for the exemption of obligations which are restrictive of competition.

A list of definitions for the purposes of this Regulation is set out in Article 1.

(2) As well as pure know-how agreements, mixed know-how and patent licensing agreements play an increasingly important role in the transfer of technology. It is therefore appropriate to include within the scope of this Regulation mixed agreements which are not exempted by Commission Regulation (EEC) No. 2349/84 (Article 1, 2 or 4)*** and in particular the following:

— mixed agreements in which the licensed patents are not necessary for the achievement of the objects of the licensed technology containing both patented and non-patented elements; this may be the case where such patents do not afford effective protection against the exploitation of the technology by third parties;
— mixed agreements which, regardless of whether or not the licensed patents are necessary for the achievement of the objects of the licensed technology, contain obligations which restrict the exploitation of the relevant technology by the licensor or the licensee in member states without patent protection in so far and as long as such obligations are based in whole or in part on the exploitation of the licensed know-how and fulfil the other conditions set out in this Regulation.

It is also appropriate to extend the scope of this Regulation to pure or mixed agreements containing ancillary provisions relating to trade marks and other intellectual property rights where there are no obligations restrictive of competition other than those also attached to the know-how and exempted under the present Regulation.

However, such agreements, too, can only be regarded as fulfilling the conditions of Article 85(3) for the purposes of this Regulation where the licensed technical knowledge is secret, substantial and identified.

(3) The provisions of the present Regulation are not applicable to agreements covered by Regulation (EEC) No. 2349/84 on patent licensing agreements.

(4) Where such pure or mixed know-how licensing agreements contain not only obligations relating to territories within the common market but also obligations relating to non-member countries, the presence of the latter does not prevent the present Regulation from applying to the obligations relating to territories within the common market.

However, where know-how licensing agreements for non-member countries or for territories which extend beyond the frontiers of the Community have effects within the common market which may fall within the scope of Article 85(1), such agreements should be covered by the Regulation to the same extent as would agreements for territories within the common market.

(5) It is not appropriate to include within the scope of the Regulation agreements solely for the purpose of sale, except where the licensor undertakes for a preliminary period before the licensee himself commences production using the licensed technology to supply the contract products for sale by the licensee. Also excluded from the scope of the Regulation are agreements relating to marketing know-how communicated in the context of franchising arrangements* or to know-how agreements entered into in connection with arrangements such as joint ventures or patent pools and other arrangements in which

---

* OJ No. 36, 6.3.1965, p. 533/65.
** OJ No. C 214, 12.8.1987, p. 2.
*** OJ No. L 219, 16.8.1984, p. 15.

* Commission Regulation (EEC) No. 4087/88 of 30 November 1988 on the application of Article 85(3) of the Treaty to categories of franchising agreements (OJ No. L 359, 28.12.1988, p. 46).

the licensing of the know-how occurs in exchange for other licences not related to improvements to or new applications of that know-how, as such agreements pose different problems which cannot at present be dealt with in one Regulation (Article 5).

(6) Exclusive licensing agreements, i.e. agreements in which the licensor undertakes not to exploit the licensed technology in the licensed territory himself or to grant further licences there, may not be in themselves incompatible with Article 85(1) where they are concerned with the introduction and protection of a new technology in the licensed territory, by reason of the scale of the research which has been undertaken and of the increase in the level of competition, in particular interbrand competition, and in the competitiveness of the undertakings concerned resulting from the dissemination of innovation within the Community.

In so far as agreements of this kind fall in other circumstances within the scope of Article 85(1), it is appropriate to include them in Article 1, in order that they may also benefit from the exemption.

(7) Both these and the other obligations listed in Article 1 encourage the transfer of technology and thus generally contribute to improving the production of goods and to promoting technical progress, by increasing the number of production facilities and the quality of goods produced in the common market and expanding the possibilities of further development of the licensed technology. This is true, in particular, of an obligation on the licensee to use the licensed product only in the manufacture of its own products, since it gives the licensor an incentive to disseminate the technology in various applications while reserving the separate sale of the licensed product to himself or other licensees. It is also true of obligations on the licensor and on the licensee to refrain not only from active but also from passive competition, in the licensed territory, in the case of the licensor, and in the territories reserved for the licensor or other licensees in the case of the licensee. The users of technologically new or improved products requiring major investment are often not final consumers but intermediate industries which are well informed about prices and alternative sources of supply of the products within the Community. Hence, protection against active competition only would not afford the parties and other licensees the security they needed, especially during the initial period of exploitation of the licensed technology when they would be investing in tooling up and developing a market for the product and in effect increasing demand.

In view of the difficulty of determining the point at which know-how can be said to be no longer secret, and the frequent licensing of a continuous stream of know-how, especially where technology in the industry is rapidly evolving, it is appropriate to limit to a fixed number of years the periods of territorial protection, of the licensor and the licensee from one another, and as between licensees, which are automatically covered by by the exemption. Since, as distinguished from patent licences, know-how licences are frequently negotiated after the goods or services incorporating the licensed technology have proved successful on the market, it is appropriate to take for each licensed territory the date of signature of the first licence agreement entered into for that territory by the licensor in respect of the same technology as the starting point for the permitted periods of territorial protection of the licensor and licensee from one another. As to the protection of a licensee from manufacture, use, active or passive sales by other licensees the starting point should be the date of signature of the first licence agreement entered into by the licensor within the EEC. The exemption of the territorial

protection shall apply for the whole duration of such allowed periods as long as the know-how remains secret and substantial, irrespective of when the member states in question joined the Community and provided that each of the licensees, the restricted as well as the protected one, manufactures the licensed product himself or has it manufactured.

Exemption under Article 85(3) of longer periods of territorial protection, in particular to protect expensive and risky investment or where the parties were not already competitors before the grant of the licence, can only be granted by individual decision. On the other hand, parties are free to extend the term of their agreement to exploit any subsequent improvements and to provide for the payment of additional royalties. However, in such cases, further periods of territorial protection, starting from the date of licensing of the improvements in the EEC, may be allowed only by individual decision, in particular where the improvements to or new applications of the licensed technology are substantial and secret and not of significantly less importance than the technology initially granted or require new, expensive and risky investment.

(8) However, it is appropriate in cases where the same technology is protected in some member states by necessary patents within the meaning of recital 9 of Regulation (EEC) No. 2349/84 to provide with respect to those member states an exemption under this Regulation for the territorial protection of the licensor and licensee from one another and as between licensees against manufacture, use and active sales in each other's territory for the full life of the patents existing in such member states.

(9) The obligations listed in Article 1 also generally fulfil the other conditions for the application of Article 85(3). Consumers will as a rule be allowed a fair share of the benefit resulting from the improvement in the supply of goods on the market. Nor do the obligations impose restrictions which are not indispensable to the attainment of the above mentioned objectives. Finally, competition at the distribution stage is safeguarded by the possibility of parallel imports, which may not be hindered by the parties in any circumstances. The exclusivity obligations covered by the Regulation thus do not normally entail the possibility of eliminating competition in respect of a substantial part of the products in question. This also applies in the case of agreements which grant exclusive licences for a territory covering the whole of the common market where there is the possibility of parallel imports from third countries, or where there are other competing technologies on the market, since then the territorial exclusivity may lead to greater market integration and stimulate Community-wide interbrand competition.

(10) It is desirable to list in the Regulation a number of obligations that are commonly found in know-how licensing agreements but are normally not restrictive of competition and to provide that in the event that because of the particular economic or legal circumstances they should fall within Article 85(1), they also would be covered by the exemption. This list, in Article 2, is not exhaustive.

(11) The Regulation must also specify what restrictions or provisions may not be included in know-how licensing agreements if these are to benefit from the block exemption. The restrictions, which are listed in Article 3, may fall under the prohibition of Article 85(1), but in their case there can be no general presumption that they will lead to the positive effects required by Article 85(3), as would be necessary for the granting of a block exemption, and consequently an exemption can be granted only on an individual basis.

(12) Agreements which are not automatically covered by the exemption because they contain provisions that are not expressly exempted by the Regulation and not expressly excluded from exemption, including those listed in Article 4(2) of the Regulation, may nonetheless generally be presumed to be eligible for application of the block exemption. It will be possible for the Commission rapidly to establish whether this is the case for a particular agreement. Such agreements should therefore be deemed to be covered by the exemption provided for in this Regulation where they are notified to the Commission and the Commission does not oppose the application of the exemption within a specified period of time.

(13) If individual agreements exempted by this Regulation nevertheless have effects which are incompatible with Article 85(3), the Commission may withdraw the benefit of the block exemption (Article 7).

(14) The list in Article 2 includes among others obligations on the licensee to cease using the licensed know-how after the termination of the agreement ('post-term use ban') (Article 2(1)(3)) and to make improvements available to the licensor (grant-back clause) (Article 2(1)(4)). A post-term use ban may be regarded as a normal feature of the licensing of know-how as otherwise the licensor would be forced to transfer his know-how in perpetuity and this could inhibit the transfer of technology. Moreover, undertakings by the licensee to grant back to the licensor a licence for improvements to the licensed know-how and/or patents are generally not restrictive of competition if the licensee is entitled by the contract to share in future experience and inventions made by the licensor and the licensee retains the right to disclose experience acquired or grant licences to third parties where to do so would not disclose the licensor's know-how.

On the other hand, a restrictive effect on competition arises where the agreement contains both a post-term use ban and an obligation on the licensee to make his improvements to the know-how available to the licensor, even on a non-exclusive and reciprocal basis, and to allow the licensor to continue using them even after the expiry of the agreement. This is so because in such a case the licensee has no possibility of inducing the licensor to authorise him to continue exploiting the originally licensed know-how, and hence the licensee's own improvements as well, after the expiry of the agreement.

(15) The list in Article 2 also includes an obligation on the licensee to keep paying royalties until the end of the agreement independently of whether or not the licensed know-how has entered into the public domain through the action of third parties (Article 2(1)(7)). As a rule, parties do not need to be protected against the foreseeable financial consequences of an agreement freely entered into and should therefore not be restricted in their choice of the appropriate means of financing the technology transfer. This applies especially where know-how is concerned since here there can be no question of an abuse of a legal monopoly and, under the legal systems of the member states, the licensee may have a remedy in an action under the applicable national law. Furthermore, provisions for the payment of royalties in return for the grant of a whole package of technology throughout an agreed reasonable period independently of whether or not the know-how has entered into the public domain, are generally in the interest of the licensee in that they prevent the licensor demanding a high initial payment up front with a view to diminishing his financial exposure in the event of premature disclosure. Parties should be free, in order to facilitate payment by the licensee, to spread the royalty payments for the use of the licensed technology over a period extending beyond the entry of the know-how into the public domain. Moreover, continuous payments should be allowed throughout the term of the agreement in cases where both parties are fully aware that the first sale of the product will necessarily disclose the know-how. Nevertheless, the Commission may, where it was clear from the circumstances that the licensee would have been able and willing to develop the know-how himself in a short period of time, in comparison with which the period of continuing payments in excessively long, withdraw the benefit of the exemption under Article 7 of this Regulation.

Finally, the use of methods of royalties calculation, which are unrelated to the exploitation of the licensed technology or the charging of royalties on products whose manufacture at no stage includes the use of any of the licensed patents or secret techniques would render the agreement ineligible for the block exemption (Article 3(5)). The licensee should also be freed from his obligation to pay royalties, where the know-how becomes publicly known through the action of the licensor. However, the mere sale of the product by the licensor or an undertaking connected with him does not constitute such an action (Article 2(1)(7) and Article 3(5)).

(16) An obligation on the licensee to restrict his exploitation of the licensed technology to one or more technical fields of application ('fields of use') or to one or more product markets is also not caught by Article 85(1) (Article 2(1)(8)). This obligation is not restrictive of competition since the licensor can be regarded as having the right to transfer the know-how only for a limited purpose. Such a restriction must however not constitute a disguised means of customer sharing.

(17) Restrictions which give the licensor an unjustified competitive advantage, such as an obligation on the licensee to accept quality specifications, other licences or goods and services that the licensee does not want from the licensor, prevent the block exemption from being applicable. However, this does not apply where it can be shown that the licensee wanted such specifications, licences, goods or services for reasons of his own convenience (Article 3(3)).

(18) Restrictions whereby the parties share customers within the same technological field of use or the same product market, either by an actual prohibition on supplying certain classes of customer or an obligation with an equivalent effect, would also render the agreement ineligible for the block exemption (Article 3(6)).

This does not apply to cases where the know-how licence is granted in order to provide a single customer with a second source of supply. In such a case, a prohibition on the licensee from supplying persons other than the customer concerned may be indispensable for the grant of a licence to the second supplier since the purpose of the transaction is not to create an independent supplier in the market. The same applies to limitations on the quantities the licensee may supply to the customer concerned. It is also reasonable to assume that such restrictions contribute to improving the production of goods and to promoting technical progress by furthering the dissemination of technology. However, given the present state of experience of the Commission with respect to such clauses and the risk in particular that they might deprive the second supplier of the possibility of developing his own business in the fields covered by the agreement, it is appropriate to make such clauses subject to the opposition procedure (Article 4(2)).

(19) Besides the clauses already mentioned, the list of restrictions precluding application of the block exemption in

Article 3 also includes restrictions regarding the selling prices of the licensed product or the quantities to be manufactured or sold, since they limit the extent to which the licensee can exploit the licensed technology and particularly since quantity restrictions may have the same effect as export bans (Article 3(7) and (8)). This does not apply where a licence is granted for use of the technology in specific production facilities and where both a specific know-how is communicated for the setting-up, operation and maintenance of these facilities and the licensee is allowed to increase the capacity of the facilities or to set up further facilities for its own use on normal commercial terms. On the other hand, the licensee may lawfully be prevented from using the licensor's specific know-how to set up facilities for third parties, since the purpose of the agreement is not to permit the licensee to give other producers access to the licensor's know-how while it remains secret (Article 2(1)(12)).

(20) To protect both the licensor and the licensee from being tied into agreements whose duration may be automatically extended beyond their initial term as freely determined by the parties, through a continuous stream of improvements communicated by the licensor, it is appropriate to exclude agreements with such a clause from the block exemption (Article 3(10)). However, the parties are free at any time to extend their contractual relationship by entering into new agreements concerning new improvements.

(21) The Regulation should apply with retroactive effect to know-how licensing agreements in existence when the Regulation comes into force where such agreements already fulfil the conditions for application of the Regulation or are modified to do so (Articles 8 to 10). Under Article 4(3) of Regulation No. 19/65/EEC, the benefit of thse provisions may not be claimed in actions pending at the date of entry into force of this Regulation, nor may it be relied on as grounds for claims for damages against third parties.

(22) Agreements which come within the terms of Articles 1 and 2 and which have neither the object nor the effect of restricting competition in any other way need no longer be notified. Nevertheless, undertakings will still have the right to apply in individual cases for negative clearance under Article 2 of Council Regulation No. 17* or for exemption under Article 85(3).

Has adopted this Regulation:

Article 1

(1) Pursuant to Article 85(3) of the Treaty and subject to the provisions of this Regulation, it is hereby declared that Article 85(1) of the Treaty shall not apply to pure know-how licensing agreements and to mixed know-how and patent licensing agreements not exempted by Regulation (EEC) No. 2349/84, including those agreements containing ancillary provisions relating to trade marks or other intellectual property rights, to which only two undertakings are party and which include one or more of the following obligations:

1. an obligation on the licensor not to license other undertakings to exploit the licensed technology in the licensed territory;

2. an obligation on the licensor not to exploit the licensed technology in the licensed territory himself;

3. an obligation on the licensee not to exploit the licensed technology in territories within the common market which are reserved for the licensor;

* O.J. No. 13, 21. 2. 1962, p.204/62.

4. an obligation on the licensee not to manufacture or use the licensed product, or use the licensed process, in territories within the common market which are licensed to other licensees;

5. an obligation on the licensee not to pursue an active policy of putting the licensed product on the market in the territories within the common market which are licensed to other licensees, and in particular not to engage in advertising specifically aimed at those territories or to establish any branch or maintain any distribution depot there;

6. an obligation on the licensee not to put the licensed product on the market in the territories licensed to other licensees within the common market;

7. an obligation on the licensee to use only the licensor's trademark or the get-up determined by the licensor to distinguish the licensed product during the term of the agreement, provided that the licensee is not prevented from identifying himself as the manufacturer of the licensed products;

8. an obligation on the licensee to limit his production of the licensed product to the quantities he requires in manufacturing his own products and to sell the licensed product only as an integral part of or a replacement part for his own products or otherwise in connection with the sale of his own products, provided that such quantities are freely determined by the licensee.

(2) The exemption provided for the obligations referred to in paragraph 1(1)(2) and (3) shall extend for a period not exceeding for each licensed territory within the EEC 10 years from the date of signature of the first licence agreement entered into by the licensor for that territory in respect of the same technology.

The exemption provided for the obligations referred to in paragraph 1(4) and (5) shall extend for a period not exceeding 10 years from the date of signature of the first licence agreement entered into by the licensor within the EEC in respect of the same technology.

The exemption provided for the obligation referred to in paragraph 1(6) shall extend for a period not exceeding five years from the date of the signature of the first licence agreement entered into by the licensor within the EEC in respect of the same technology.

(3) The exemption provided for in paragraph 1 shall apply only where the parties have identified in any appropriate form the initial know-how and any subsequent improvements to it, which become available to the parties and are communicated to the other party pursuant to the terms of the agreement and for the purpose thereof, and only for as long as the know-how remains secret and substantial.

(4) In so far as the obligations referred to in paragraph 1(1) to (5) concern territories including member states in which the same technology is protected by necessary patents, the exemption provided for in paragraph 1 shall extend for those member states as long as the licensed product or process is protected in those member states by such patents, where the duration of such protection exceeds the periods specified in paragraph 2.

(5) The exemption of restrictions on putting the licensed product on the market resulting from the obligations referred to in paragraph 1(2), (3), (5) and (6) shall apply only if the licensee manufactures or proposes to manufacture the licensed product himself or has it manufactured by a connected undertaking or by a subcontractor.

(6) The exemption provided for in paragraph 1 shall also apply where in a particular agreement the parties undertake obligations of the types referred to in that paragraph but with a more limited scope than is permitted by the paragraph.

(7) for the purposes of the present Regulation the following terms shall have the following meanings:

1. 'know-how' means a body of technical information that is secret, substantial and identified in any appropriate form;

2. the term 'secret' means that the know-how package as a body or in the precise configuration and assembly of its components is not generally known or easily accessible, so that part of its value consists in the lead-time the licensee gains when it is communicated to him; it is not limited to the narrow sense that each individual component of the know-how should be totally unknown or unobtainable outside the licensor's business;

3. the term 'substantial' means that the know-how includes information which is of importance for the whole or a significant part of (i) a manufacturing process or (ii) a product or service, or (iii) for the development thereof and excludes information which is trivial. Such know-how must thus be useful, i.e. can reasonably be expected at the date of conclusion of the agreement to be capable of improving the competitive position of the licensee, for example by helping him to enter a new market or giving him an advantage in competition with other manufacturers or providers of services who do not have access to the licensed secret know-how or other comparable secret know-how.

4. the term 'identified' means that the know-how is described or recorded in such a manner as to make it possible to verify that it fulfils the criteria of secrecy and substantiality and to ensure that the licensee is not unduly restricted in his exploitation of his own technology. To be identified the know-how can either be set out in the licence agreement or in a separate document or recorded in any other appropriate form at the latest when the know-how is transferred or shortly thereafter, provided that the separate document or other record can be made available if the need arises;

5. 'pure know-how licensing agreements' are agreements whereby one undertaking, the licensor, agrees to communicate the know-how, with or without an obligation to disclose any subsequent improvements, to another undertaking, the licensee, for exploitation in the licensed territory;

6. 'mixed know-how and patent licensing agreements' are agreements not exempted by Regulation (EEC) No. 2349/84 under which a technology containing both non-patented elements and elements that are patented in one or more member states is licensed;

7. the terms 'licensed know-how' or 'licensed technology' mean the initial and any subsequent know-how communicated directly or indirectly by the licensor to a licensee by means of pure or mixed know-how and patent licensing agreements; however, in the case of mixed know-how and patent licensing agreements the term 'licensed technology' also includes any patents for which a licence is granted besides the communication of the know-how;

8. the term 'the same technology' means the technology as licensed to the first licensee and enhanced by any improvements made thereto subsequently, irrespective of whether and to what extent such improvements are exploited by the parties or the other licensees and irrespective of whether the technology is protected by necessary patents in any member states;

9. 'the licensed products' are goods or services the production or provision of which requires the use of the licensed technology;

10. the term 'exploitation' refers to any use of the licensed technology in particular in the production, active or passive sales in a territory even if not coupled with manufacture in that territory, or leasing of the licensed products;

11. 'the licensed territory' is the territory covering all or at least part of the common market where the licensee is entitled to exploit the licensed technology;

12. 'territory reserved for the licensor' means territories in which the licensor has not granted any licences and which he has expressly reserved for himself;

13. 'connected undertakings' means:

(a) undertakings in which a party to the agreement, directly or indirectly:

— owns more than half the capital or business assets, or
— has the power to exercise more than half the voting rights, or
— has the power to appoint more than half the members of the supervisory board, board of directors or bodies legally representing the undertaking, or
— has the right to manage the affairs of the undertaking;

(b) undertakings which directly or indirectly have in or over a party to the agreement the rights or powers listed in (a);

(c) undertakings in which an undertaking referred to in (b) directly or indirectly has the rights or powers listed in (a);

(d) undertakings in which the parties to the agreement or undertakings connected with them jointly have the rights or powers listed in (a); such jointly controlled undertakings are considered to be connected with each of the parties to the agreement.

Article 2

(1) Article 1 shall apply notwithstanding the presence in particular of any of the following obligations, which are generally not restrictive of competition:

1. an obligation on the licensee not to divulge the know-how communicated by the licensor; the licensee may be held to this obligation after the agreement has expired;

2. an obligation on the licensee not to grant sub-licences or assign the licence;

3. an obligation on the licensee not to exploit the licensed know-how after termination of the agreement in so far and as long as the know-how is still secret;

4. an obligation on the licensee to communicate to the licensor any experience gained in exploiting the licensed technology and to grant him a non-exclusive licence in respect of improvements to or new applications of that technology, provided that:

(a) the licensee is not prevented during or after the term of the agreement from freely using his own improvements, in so far as these are severable from the licensor's know-how, or licensing them to third parties where licensing to third parties does not disclose the know-how communicated by the licensor that is still secret; this is without prejudice to an obligation on the licensee to seek the licensor's prior approval to such licensing provided that approval may not be withheld unless there are objectively justifiable reasons to believe that licensing improvements to third parties will disclose the licensor's know-how, and

(b) the licensor has accepted an obligation, whether exclusive or not, to communicate his own improvements to the licensee and his right to use the licensee's improvements which are not severable from the licensed know-how does not extend beyond the date on which the licensee's right to exploit the licensor's know-how comes to an end, except for termination of the agreement for breach by the licensee; this is without prejudice to an obligation on the licensee to give the licensor the option to continue to use the improvements after that date, if at the same time he relinquishes the post-term use ban or agrees, after having had an opportunity to examine the licensee's improvements, to pay appropriate royalties for their use;

5. an obligation on the licensee to observe minimum quality specifications for the licensed product or to procure goods or services from the licensor or from an undertaking designated by the licensor, in so far as such quality specifications, products or services are necessary for;

(a) a technically satisfactory exploitation of the licensed technology, or

(b) for ensuring that the production of the licensee conforms to the quality standards that are respected by the licensor and other licensees,

and to allow the licensor to carry out related checks.

6. obligations:

(a) to inform the licensor of misappropriation of the know-how or of infringements of the licensed patents, or

(b) to take or to assist the licensor in taking legal action against such misappropriation or infringements;

provided that these obligations are without prejudice to the licensee's right to challenge the validity of the licensed patents or to contest the secrecy of the licensed know-how except where he himself has in some way contributed to its disclosure:

7. an obligation on the licensee, in the event of the know-how becoming publicly known other than by action of the licensor, to continue paying until the end of the agreement the royalties in the amounts, for the periods and according to the methods freely determined by the parties, without prejudice to the payment of any additional damages in the event of the know-how becoming publicly known by the action of the licensee in breach of the agreement;

8. an obligation on the licensee to restrict his exploitation of the licensed technology to one or more technical fields of application covered by the licensed technology or to one or more product markets;

9. an obligation on the licensee to pay a minimum royalty or to produce a minimum quantity of the licensed product or to carry out a minimum number of operations exploiting the licensed technology;

10. an obligation on the licensor to grant the licensee any more favourable terms that the licensor may grant to another undertaking after the agreement is entered into;

11. an obligation on the licensee to mark the licensed product with the licensor's name;

12. an obligation on the licensee not to use the licensor's know-how to construct facilities for third parties; this is without prejudice to the right of the licensee to increase the capacity of its facilities or to set up additional facilities for its own use on normal commercial terms, including the payment of additional royalties.

(2) In the event that, because of particular circumstances, the obligations referred to in paragraph 1 fall within the scope of Article 85(1) they shall also be exempted even if they are not accompanied by any of the obligations exempted by Article 1.

(3) The exemption provided for in paragraph 2 shall also apply where in an agreement the parties undertake obligations of the types referred to in paragraph 1 but with a more limited scope than is permitted by that paragraph.

Article 3
Articles 1 and 2(2) shall not apply where:

1. the licensee is prevented from continuing to use the licensed know-how after the termination of the agreement where the know-how has meanwhile become publicly known, other than by the action of the licensee in breach of the agreement;

2. the licensee is obliged either:

(a) to assign in whole or in part to the licensor rights to improvements to or new applications of the licensed technology;

(b) to grant the licensor an exclusive licence for improvements to or new applications of the licensed technology which would prevent the licensee during the currency of the agreement and/or thereafter from using his own improvements in so far as these are severable from the licensor's know-how, or from licensing them to third parties, where such licensing would not disclose the licensor's know-how that is still secret; or

(c) in the case of an agreement which also includes a post-term use ban, to grant back to the licensor, even on a non-exclusive and reciprocal basis, licences for improvements which are not severable from the licensor's know-how, if the licensor's right to use the improvements is of a longer duration than the licensee's right to use the licensor's know-how, except for termination of the agreement for breach by the licensee;

3. the licensee is obliged at the time the agreement is entered into to accept quality specifications or further licences or to procure goods or services which he does not want, unless such licenses, quality specifications, goods or services are necessary for a technically satisfactory exploitation of the licensed technology or for ensuring that the production of the licensee conforms to the quality standards that are respected by the licensor and other licensees;

4. the licensee is prohibited from contesting the secrecy of the licensed know-how or from challenging the validity of licensed patents within the common market belonging to the licensor or undertakings connected with him, without prejudice to the right of the licensor to terminate the licensing agreement in the event of such a challenge;

5. the licensee is charged royalties on goods or services which are not entirely or partially produced by means of the licensed technology or for the use of know-how which has become publicly known by the action of the licensor or an undertaking connected with him;

6. one party is restricted within the same technological field of use or within the same product market as to the customers he may serve, in particular by being prohibited from supplying certain classes of user, employing certain forms of distribution or, with the aim of sharing customers, using certain types of packaging for the products, save as provided in Article 1(1) (7) and Article 4(2);

7. the quantity of the licensed products one party may manufacture or sell or the number of operations exploiting the licensed technology he may carry out are subject to limitations, save as provided in Article 1(1) (8) and Article 4(2);

8. one party is restricted in the determination of prices, components of prices or discounts for the licensed products;

9. one party is restricted from competing with the other party, with undertakings connected with the other party or with other undertakings within the common market in respect of research and development, production or use of competing products and their distribution, without prejudice to an obligation on the licensee to use his best endeavours to exploit the licensed technology and without prejudice to the right of the licensor to terminate the exclusivity granted to the licensee and cease communicating improvements in the event of the licensee's engaging in any such competing activities and to require the licensee to prove that the licensed know-how is not used for the production of goods and services other than those licensed;

10. the initial duration of the licensing agreement is automatically prolonged by the inclusion in it of any new improvements communicated by the licensor, unless the licensee has the right to refuse such improvements or each party has the right to terminate the agreement at the expiry of the initial term of the agreement and at least every three years thereafter;

11. the licensor is required, albeit in separate agreements, for a period exceeding that permitted under Article 1(2) not to license other undertakings to exploit the same technology in the licensed territory, or a party is required for periods exceeding those permitted under Articles 1(2) or 1(4) not to exploit the same technology in the territory of the other party or of other licensees;

12. one or both of the parties are required:

(a) to refuse without any objectively justified reason to meet demand from users or resellers in their respective territories who would market products in other territories within the common market;

(b) to make it difficult for users or resellers to obtain the products from other resellers within the common market, and in particular to exercise intellectual property rights or take measures so as to prevent users or resellers from obtaining outside, or from putting on the market in the licensed territory products which have been lawfully put on the market within the common market by the licensor or with his consent; or do so as a result of a concerted practice between them.

Article 4

(1) The exemption provided for in Articles 1 and 2 shall also apply to agreements containing obligations restrictive of competition which are not covered by those Articles and do not fall within the scope of Article 3, on condition that the agreements in question are notified to the Commission in accordance with the provisions of Commission Regulation No. 27* and that the Commission does not oppose such exemption within a period of six months.

(2) Paragraph 1 shall in particular apply to an obligation on the licensee to supply only a limited quantity of the licensed product to a particular customer, where the know-how licence is granted at the request of such a customer in order to provide him with a second source of supply within a licensed territory.

This provision shall also apply where the customer is the licensee and the licence, in order to provide a second source of supply, provides for the customer to make licensed products or have them made by a sub-contractor.

(3) The period of six months shall run from the date on which the notification is received by the Commission. Where, however, the notification is made by registered post, the period shall run from the date shown on the postmark of the place of posting.

(4) Paragraphs 1 and 2 shall apply only if:

(a) express reference is made to this Article in the notification or in a communication accompanying it, and

(b) the information furnished with the notification is complete and in accordance with the facts.

(5) The benefit of paragraphs 1 and 2 may be claimed for agreements notified before the entry into force of this Regulation by submitting a communication to the Commission referring expressly to this Article and to the notification. Paragraphs 3 and 4(b) shall apply *mutatis mutandis.*

(6) The Commission may oppose the exemption. It shall oppose exemption if it receives a request to do so from a member

* O.J. No. 35, 10.5.1962, p. 1118/62.

state within three months of the transmission to the member state of the notification referred to in paragraph 1 or of the communication referred to in paragraph 5. This request must be justified on the basis of considerations relating to the competition rules of the Treaty.

(7) The Commission may withdraw the opposition to the exemption at any time. However, where the opposition was raised at the request of a member state and this request is maintained, it may be withdrawn only after consultation of the Advisory Committee on Restrictive Practices and Dominant Positions;

(8) If the opposition is withdrawn becuase the undertakings concerned have shown that the conditions of Article 85(3) are fulfilled, the exemption shall apply from the date of notification.

(9) If the opposition is withdrawn because the undertakings concerned have amended the agreement so that the conditions of Article 85(3) are fulfilled, the exemption shall apply from the date on which the amendments take effect.

(10) If the Commission opposes exemption and the opposition is not withdrawn, the effects of the notification shall be governed by the provisions of Regulation No. 17.

Article 5

(1) This Regulation shall not apply to:

1. agreements between members of a patent or know-how pool which relate to the pooled technologies:

2. know-how licensing agreements between competing undertakings which hold interests in a joint venture, or between one of them and the joint venture, if the licensing agreements relate to the activities of the joint venture.

3. agreements under which one party grants the other a know-how licence and the other party, albeit in separate agreements or through connected undertakings, grants the first party a patent, trademark or know-how licence or exclusive sales rights, where the parties are competitors in relation to the products covered by those agreements;

4. agreements including the licensing of intellectual property rights other than patents (in particular trademarks, copyright and design rights) or the licensing of software except where these rights or the software are of assistance in achieving the object of the licensed technology and there are no obligations restrictive of competition other than those also attached to the licensed know-how and exempted under the present Regulation;

(2) However, this Regulation shall apply to reciprocal licences of the types referred to in paragraph 1(3) where the parties are not subject to any territorial restriction within the common market on the manufacture, use or putting on the market of the products covered by the agreements or on the use of the licensed technologies.

Article 6

This Regulation shall also apply to:

1. pure know-how agreements or mixed agreements where the licensor is not the developer of the know-how or the patentee but is authorised by the developer or the patentee to grant a licence or a sub-licence;

2. assignments of know-how or of know-how and patents where the risk associated with exploitation remains with the assignor, in particular where the sum payable in consideration of the assignment is dependent upon the turnover attained by the assignee in respect of products made using the know-how or the patents, the quantity of such products manufactured or the

number of operations carried out employing the know-how or the patents;

    3. pure know-how agreements or mixed agreements in which rights or obligations of the licensor or the licensee are assumed by undertakings connected with them.

Article 7

The Commission may withdraw the benefit of this Regulation, pursuant to Article 7 of Regulation No. 19/65/EEC, where it finds in a particular case that an agreement exempted by this Regulation nevertheless has certain effects which are incompatible with the conditions laid down in Article 85(3) of the Treaty, and in particular where:

    1. such effects arise from an arbitration award;

    2. the effect of the agreement is to prevent the licensed products from being exposed to effective competition in the licensed territory from identical products or products considered by users as equivalent in view of their characteristics, price and intended use;

    3. the licensor does not have the right to terminate the exclusivity granted to the licensee at the latest five years from the date the agreement was entered into and at least annually thereafter if, without legitimate reason, the licensee fails to exploit the licensed technology or to do so adequately;

    4. without prejudice to Article 1(1) (6), the licensee refuses, without objectively valid reason, to meet unsolicited demand from users or resellers in the territory of other licensees;

    5. one or both of the parties:

    (a) without objectively justified reason, refuse to meet demand from users or resellers in their respective territories who would market the products in other territories within the common market; or

    (b) make it difficult for users or resellers to obtain the products from other resellers within the common market, and in particular where they exercise intellectual property rights or take measures so as to prevent resellers or users from obtaining outside, or from putting on the market in the licensed territory products which have been lawfully put on the market within the common market by the licensor or with his consent;

    6. the operation of the post-term use ban referred to in Article 2(1)(3) prevents the licensee from working an expired patent which can be worked by all other manufacturers;

    7. the period for which the licensee is obliged to continue paying royalties after the know-how has become publicly known by the action of third parties, as referred to in Article 2(1)(7), substantially exceeds the lead time acquired because of the head-start in production and marketing and this obligation is detrimental to competition in the market;

    8. the parties were already competitors before the grant of the licence and obligations on the licensee to produce a minimum quantity or to use his best endeavours as referred to in Article 2(1)(9) and Article 3(9) have the effect of preventing the licensee from using competing technologies.

Article 8

(1) As regards agreements existing on 13 March 1962 and notified before 1 February 1963 and agreements, whether notified or not, to which article 4(2) (2)(b) of Regulation No. 17 applies, the declaration of inapplicability of Article 85(1) of the Treaty contained in this Regulation shall have retroactive effect from the time at which the conditions for application of this Regulation were fulfilled.

(2) As regards all other agreements notified before this Regulation entered into force, the declaration of inapplicability of Article 85(1) of the Treaty contained in this Regulation shall have retroactive effect from the time at which the conditions for application of this Regulation were fulfilled, or from the date of notification, whichever is the later.

Article 9

If agreements existing on 13 March 1962 and notified before 1 February 1963 or agreements to which Article 4(2) (2)(b) of Regulation No. 17 applies and notified before 1 January 1967 are amended before 1 July 1989 so as to fulfil the conditions for application of this Regulation, and if the amendment is communicated to the Commission before 1 October 1989 the prohibition in Article 85(1) of the Treaty shall not apply in respect of the period prior to the amendment. The communication shall take effect from the time of its receipt by the Commission. Where the communication is sent by registered post, it shall take effect from the date shown on the postmark of the place of posting.

Article 10

(1) As regards agreements to which Article 85 of the Treaty applies as a result of the accession of the United Kingdom, Ireland and Denmark, Articles 8 and 9 shall apply except that the relevant dates shall be 1 January 1973 instead of 13 March 1967 and 1 July 1973 instead of 1 February 1963 and 1 January 1967.

(2) As regards agreements to which Article 85 of the Treaty applies as a result of the accession of Greece, Articles 8 and 9 shall apply except that the relevant dates shall be 1 January 1981 instead of 13 March 1962 and 1 July 1981 instead of 1 February 1963 and 1 January 1967.

(3) As regards agreements to which Article 85 of the Treaty applies as a result of the accession of Spain and Portugal, Articles 8 and 9 shall apply except that the relevant dates shall be 1 January 1986 instead of 13 March 1962 and 1 July 1986 instead of 1 February 1963 and 1 January 1967.

Article 11

(1) Information acquired pursuant to Article 4 shall be used only for the purposes of the Regulation.

(2) The Commission and the authorities of the member states, their officials and other servants shall not disclose information acquired by them pursuant to this Regulation of the kind covered by the obligation of professional secrecy.

(3) The provisions of paragraphs 1 and 2 shall not prevent publication of general information or surveys which do not contain information relating to particular undertakings.

Article 12

This Regulation shall enter into force on 1 April 1989.

It shall apply until 31 December 1999.

This Regulation shall be binding in its entirety and directly applicable in all member states.

Done at Brussels, 30 November 1988.

For the Commission
Peter SUTHERLAND
Member of the Commission

Commission Regulation (EEC) No. 1983/83

of 22 June 1983
on the application of Article 85(3) of the Treaty to categories of exclusive distribution agreements
(OJ 1983 L 173/1)

The Commission of the European Communities

Having regard to the Treaty establishing the European Economic Community, and in particular Article 87 thereof,

Having regard to Council Regulation No. 19/65/EEC of 2 March 1965 on the application of Article 85(3) of the Treaty to certain categories of agreements and concerted practices*, as last amended by the Act of Accession of Greece, and in particular Article 1 thereof,

Having published a draft on this Regulation**,

Having consulted the Advisory Committee on Restrictive Practices and Dominant Positions,

(1) Whereas Regulation No. 19/65/EEC empowers the Commission to apply Article 85(3) of the Treaty by regulation to certain categories of bilateral exclusive distribution agreements and analogous concerted practices falling within Article 85(1);

(2) Whereas experience to date makes it possible to define a category of agreements and concerted practices which can be regarded as normally satisfying the conditions laid down in Article 85(3),

(3) Whereas exclusive distribution agreements of the category defined in Article 1 of this Regulation may fall within the prohibition contained in Article 85(1) of the Treaty; whereas this will apply only in exceptional cases to exclusive agreements of this kind to which only undertakings from one member state are party and which concern the resale of goods within that member state; whereas, however, to the extent that such agreements may affect trade between member states and also satisfy all the requirements set out in this Regulation there is no reason to withhold from them the benefit of the exemption by category;

(4) Whereas it is not necessary expressly to exclude from the defined category those agreements which do not fulfil the conditions of Article 85(1) of the Treaty;

(5) Whereas exclusive distribution agreements lead in general to an improvement in distribution because the undertaking is able to concentrate its sales activities, does not need to maintain numerous business relations with a larger number of dealers and is able, by dealing with only one dealer, to overcome more easily distribution difficulties in international trade resulting from linguistic, legal and other differences;

(6) Whereas exclusive distribution agreements facilitate the promotion of sales of a product and lead to intensive marketing and to continuity of supplies while at the same time rationalising distribution; whereas they stimulate competition between the products of different manufacturers; whereas the appointment of an exclusive distributor who will take over sales promotion, customer services and carrying of stocks is often the most effective way, and sometimes indeed the only way, for the manufacturer to enter a market and compete with other manufacturers already present; whereas this is particularly so in the case of small and medium-sized undertakings; whereas it must be left to the contracting parties to decide whether and to what extent they

consider it desirable to incorporate in the agreements terms providing for the promotion of sales;

(7) Whereas, as a rule, such exclusive distribution agreements also allow consumers a fair share of the resulting benefit as they gain directly from the improvement in distribution, and their economic and supply position is improved as they can obtain products manufactured in particular in other countries more quickly and more easily;

(8) Whereas this Regulation must define the obligations restricting competition which may be included in exclusive distribution agreements; whereas the other restrictions on competition allowed under this Regulation in addition to the exclusive supply obligation produce a clear division of functions between the parties and compel the exclusive distributor to concentrate his sales efforts on the contract goods and the contract territory; whereas they are, where they are agreed only for the duration of the agreement, generally necessary in order to attain the improvement in the distribution of goods sought through exclusive distribution; whereas it may be left to the contracting parties to decide which of these obligations they include in their agreements; whereas further restrictive obligations and in particular those which limit the exclusive distributor's choice of customers or his freedom to determine his prices and conditions of sale cannot be exempted under this Regulation;

(9) Whereas the exemption by category should be reserved for agreements for which it can be assumed with sufficient certainty that they satisfy the conditions of Article 85(3) of the Treaty;

(10) Whereas it is not possible, in the absence of a case-by-case examination, to consider that adequate improvements in distribution occur where a manufacturer entrusts the distribution of his goods to another manufacturer with whom he is in competition; whereas such agreements should, therefore, be excluded from the exemption by category; whereas certain derogations from this rule in favour of small and medium-sized undertakings can be allowed;

(11) Whereas consumers will be assured of a fair share of the benefits resulting from exclusive distribution only if parallel imports remain possible; whereas agreements relating to goods which the user can obtain only from the exclusive distributor should therefore be excluded from the exemption by category; whereas the parties cannot be allowed to abuse industrial property rights or other rights in order to create absolute territorial protection; whereas this does not prejudice the relationship between competition law and industrial property rights, since the sole object here is to determine the conditions for exemption by category;

(12) Whereas, since competition at the distribution stage is ensured by the possibility of parallel imports, the exclusive distribution agreements covered by this Regulation will not normally afford any possibility of eliminating competition in respect of a substantial part of the products in question; whereas this is also true of agreements that allot to the exclusive distributor a contract territory covering the whole of the common market;

---

* OJ No. 36, 6. 3. 1965, p.533/65.
** O.J. No. C 172, 10.7.1982, p. 3.

(13) Whereas, in particular cases in which agreements or concerted practices satisfying the requirements of this Regulation nevertheless have effects incompatible with Article 85(3) of the Treaty, the Commission may withdraw the benefit of the exemption by category from the undertakings party to them;

(14) Whereas agreements and concerted practices which satisfy the conditions set out in this Regulation need not be notified; whereas an undertaking may nonetheless in a particular case where real doubt exists, request the Commission to declare whether its agreements comply with this Regulation;

(15) Whereas this Regulation does not affect the applicability of Commission Regulation (EEC) No. 3604/82 of 23 December 1982 on the application of Article 85(3) of the Treaty to categories of specialisation agreements*; whereas it does not exclude the application of Article 86 of the Treaty,

Has adopted this Regulation

Article 1
Pursuant to Article 85(3) of the Treaty and subject to the provisions of this Regulation, it is hereby declared that Article 85(1) of the Treaty shall not apply to agreements to which only two undertakings are party and whereby one party agrees with the other to supply certain goods for resale within the whole or a defined area of the common market only to that other.

Article 2
1. Apart from the obligation referred to in Article 1 no restriction on competition shall be imposed on the supplier other than the obligation not to supply the contract goods to users in the contract territory.

2. No restriction on competition shall be imposed on the exclusive distributor other than;

(a) the obligation not to manufacture or distribute goods which compete with the contract goods;

(b) the obligation to obtain the contract goods for resale only from the other party;

(c) the obligation to refrain, outside the contract territory and in relation to the contract goods, from seeking customers, from establishing any branch, and from maintaining any distribution depot.

3. Article 1 shall apply notwithstanding that the exclusive distributor undertakes all or any of the following obligations:

(a) to purchase complete ranges of goods or minimum quantities;

(b) to sell the contract goods under trademarks, or packed and presented as specified by the other party;

(c) to take measures for promotion of sales, in particular:

— to advertise,
— to maintain a sales network or stock of goods,
— to provide customer and guarantee services,
— to employ staff having specialised or technical training.

Article 3
Article 1 shall not apply where:

(a) manufacturers of identical goods or of goods which are considered by users as equivalent in view of their characteristics, price and intended use enter into reciprocal exclusive distribution agreements between themselves in respect of such goods;

* OJ No. L 376, 31.12.1982, p. 33

(b) manufacturers of identical goods or of goods which are considered by users as equivalent in view of their characteristics, price and intended use enter into a non-reciprocal exclusive distribution agreement between themselves in respect of such goods unless at least one of them has a total annual turnover of no more than 100 million ECU,

(c) users can obtain the contract goods in the contract territory only from the exclusive distributor and have no alternative source of supply outside the contract territory;

(d) one or both of the parties makes it difficult for intermediaries or users to obtain the contract goods from other dealers inside the common market or, in so far as no alternative source of supply is available there, from outside the common market, in particular where one or both of them:

1. exercises industrial property rights so as to prevent dealers or users from obtaining outside, or from selling in, the contract territory properly marked or otherwise properly marketed contract goods;

2. exercises other rights or take other measures so as to prevent dealers or users from obtaining outside, or from selling in, the contract territory contract goods.

Article 4
1. Article 3(a) and (b) shall also apply where the goods there referred to are manufactured by an undertaking connected with a party to the agreement.

2. Connected undertakings are:

(a) undertakings in which a party to the agreement, directly or indirectly:

— owns more than half the capital or business assets, or
— has the power to exercise more than half the voting rights, or
— has the power to appoint more than half the members of the supervisory board, board of directors or bodies legally representing the undertaking, or
— has the right to manage the affairs;

(b) undertakings which directly or indirectly have in or over a party to the agreement the rights or powers listed in (a);

(c) undertakings in which an undertaking referred to in (b) directly or indirectly has the rights or powers listed in (a).

3. Undertakings in which the parties to the agreement or undertakings connected with them jointly have the rights or powers set out in paragraph 2(a) shall be considered to be connected with each of the parties to the agreement.

Article 5
1. For the purpose of Article 3(b), the ECU is the unit of account used for drawing up the budget of the Community pursuant to Articles 207 and 209 of the Treaty.

2. Article 1 shall remain applicable where during any period of two consecutive financial years the total turnover referred to in Article 3(b) is exceeded by no more than 10%.

3. For the purpose of calculating total turnover within the meaning of Article 3(b), the turnovers achieved during the last financial year by the party to the agreement and connected undertakings in respect of all goods and services, excluding all taxes and other duties, shall be added together. For this purpose, no account shall be taken of dealings between the parties to the agreement or between these undertakings and undertakings connected with them or between the connected undertakings.

Article 6

The Commission may withdraw the benefit of this Regulation, pursuant to Article 7 of Regulation No. 19/65/EEC, when it finds in a particular case that an agreement which is exempted by this Regulation nevertheless has certain effects which are incompatible with the conditions set out in Article 85(3) of the Treaty, and in particular where:

(a) the contract goods are not subject, in the contract territory, to effective competition from identical goods or goods considered by users as equivalent in view of their characteristics, price and intended use;

(b) access by other suppliers to the different stages of distribution within the contract territory is made difficult to a significant extent;

(c) for reasons other than those referred to in Article 3(c) and (d) it is not possible for intermediaries or users to obtain supplies of the contract goods from dealers outside the contract territory on the terms there customary;

(d) the exclusive distributor:

1. without any objectively justified reason refuses to supply in the contract territory categories of purchasers who cannot obtain contract goods elsewhere on suitable terms or applies to them differing prices or conditions of sale;

2. sells the contract goods at excessively high prices.

Article 7

In the period 1 July 1983 to 31 December 1986, the prohibition in Article 85(1) of the Treaty shall not apply to agreements which were in force on 1 July 1983 or entered into force between 1 July and 31 December 1983 and which satisfy the exemption conditions of Regulation No. 67/67/EEC*.

Article 8

This Regulation shall not apply to agreements entered into for the resale of drinks in premises used for the sale and consumption of beer or for the resale of petroleum products in service stations.

Article 9

This Regulation shall apply *mutatis mutandis* to concerted practices of the type defined in Article 1.

Article 10

This Regulation shall enter into force on 1 July 1983.

It shall expire on 31 December 1997.

This Regulation shall be binding in its entirety and directly applicable in all member states.

Done at Brussels, 22 June 1983.

For the Commission
Frans ANDRIESSEN
Member of the Commission

COMMISSION REGULATION (EEC) No. 1984/83

of 22 June 1983
on the application of Article 85(3) of the Treaty to categories of exclusive purchasing agreements
(OJ 1983 L 173/5)

The Commission of the European Communities

Having regard to the Treaty establishing the European Economic Community,

Having regard to Council Regulation 19/65/EEC of 2 March 1965 on the application of Article 85(3) of the Treaty to certain practices*, as last amended by the Act of Accession of Greece, and in particular Article 1 thereof.

Having published a draft of this Regulation**,

Having consulted the Advisory Committee on Restrictive Practices and Dominant Positions,

(1) Whereas Regulation No. 19/65/EEC empowers the Commission to apply Article 85(3) of the Treaty by regulation to certain categories of bilateral exclusive purchasing agreements entered into for the purpose of the resale of goods and corresponding concerted practices falling within Article 85;

(2) Whereas experience to date makes it possible to define three categories of agreements and concerted practices which can be regarded as normally satisfying the conditions laid down in Article 85(3); whereas the first category comprises exclusive purchasing agreements of short and medium duration in all sectors of the economy; whereas the other two categories comprise long-term exclusive purchasing agreements entered into for the resale of beer in premises used for the sale and consumption (beer supply agreements) and of petroleum products in filling stations (service-station agreements);

(3) Whereas exclusive purchasing agreements of the categories defined in this Regulation may fall within the prohibition contained in Article 85(1) of the Treaty; whereas this will often be the case with agreements concluded between undertakings from different member states; whereas an exclusive purchasing agreement to which undertakings from only one member state are party and which concerns the resale of goods within that member state may also be caught by the prohibition; whereas this is in particular the case where it is one of a number of similar agreements which together may affect trade between member states;

(4) Whereas it is not necessary expressly to exclude from the defined categories those agreements which do not fulfil the conditions of Article 85(1) of the Treaty;

(5) Whereas the exclusive purchasing agreements defined in this Regulation lead in general to an improvement in distribution; whereas they enable the supplier to plan the sales of his goods with greater precision and for a longer period and ensure that the reseller's requirements will be met on a regular basis for the duration of the agreement; whereas this allows the parties to limit the risk to them of variations in market conditions and to lower distribution costs;

(6) Whereas such agreements also facilitate the promotion of the sales of a product and lead to intensive marketing because the supplier, in consideration for the exclusive purchasing obligation, is as a rule under an obligation to contribute to the

* OJ No. 57, 25.3.1967, p.849/67

* OJ No 36, 6.3.1965, p. 533/65.
** OJ No C 172, 10.7.1982, p. 7.

improvements of the structure of the distribution network, the quality of the promotional effort or the sales success; whereas, at the same time, they stimulate competition between the products of different manufacturers; whereas the appointment of several resellers, who are bound to purchase exclusively from the manufacturer and who take over sales promotion, customer service and carrying of stock, is often the most effective way, and sometimes the only way, for the manufacturer to penetrate a market and compete with other manufacturers already present; whereas this is particularly so in the case of small and medium-sized undertakings; whereas it must be left to the contracting parties to decide whether and to what extent they consider it desirable to incorporate in their agreements terms concerning the promotion of sales;

(7) Whereas, as a rule, exclusive purchasing agreements between suppliers and resellers also allow consumers a fair share of the resulting benefit as they gain the advantages of regular supply and are able to obtain the contract goods more quickly and more easily;

(8) Whereas this Regulation must define the obligations restricting competition which may be included in an exclusive purchasing agreement; whereas the other restrictions of competition allowed under this Regulation in addition to the exclusive purchasing obligation lead to a clear division of functions between the parties and compel the reseller to concentrate his sales efforts on the contract goods; whereas they are, where they are agreed only for the duration of the agreement, generally necessary in order to attain the improvement in the distribution of goods sought through exclusive purchasing; whereas further restrictive obligations and in particular those which limit the reseller's choice of customers or his freedom to determine his prices and conditions of sale cannot be exempted under this Regulation;

(9) Whereas the exemption by categories should be resolved for agreements for which it can be assumed with sufficient certainty that they satisfy the conditions of Article 85(3) of the Treaty;

(10) Whereas it is not possible, in the absence of a case-by-case examination, to consider that adequate improvements in distribution occur where a manufacturer imposes an exclusive purchasing obligation with respect to his goods on a manufacturer with whom he is in competition; whereas such agreements should, therefore, be excluded from the exemption by categories; whereas certain derogations from this rule in favour of small and medium-sized undertakings can be allowed;

(11) Whereas certain conditions must be attached to the exemption by categories so that access by other undertakings to the different stages of distribution can be ensured; whereas, to this end, limits must be set to the scope and to the duration of the exclusive purchasing obligation; whereas it appears appropriate as a general rule to grant the benefit of a general exemption from the prohibition on restrictive agreements only to exclusive purchasing agreements which are concluded for a specified product or range of products and for not more than five years;

(12) Whereas, in the case of beer supply agreements and service-station agreements, different rules should be laid down which take account of the particularities of the markets in question;

(13) Whereas these agreements are generally distinguished by the fact that, on the one hand, the supplier confers on the reseller special commercial or financial advantages by contributing to his financing, granting him or obtaining for him a loan on favourable terms, equipping him with a site or premises for conducting his business, providing him with equipment or fittings, or undertaking other investments for his benefit and that, on the other hand, the reseller enters into a long term exclusive purchasing obligation which in most cases is accompanied by a ban on dealing in competing products;

(14) Whereas beer supply and service-station agreements, like the other exclusive purchasing agreements dealt with in this Regulation, normally produce an appreciable improvement in distribution in which consumers are allowed a fair share of the resulting benefit;

(15) Whereas the commercial and financial advantages conferred by the supplier on the reseller make it significantly easier to establish, modernise, maintain and operate premises used for the sale and consumption of drinks and service stations; whereas the exclusive purchasing obligation and the ban on dealing in competing products imposed on the reseller incite the reseller to devote all the resources at his disposal to the sale of the contract goods; whereas such agreements lead to durable co-operation between the parties allowing them to improve or maintain the quality of the contract goods and of the services to the customer and sales efforts of the reseller; whereas they allow long-term planning of sales and consequently a cost effective organisation of production and distribution; whereas the pressure of competition between products of different makes obliges the undertakings involved to determine the number and character of premises used for the sale and consumption of drinks and service stations, in accordance with the wishes of customers;

(16) Whereas consumers benefit from the improvements described, in particular because they are ensured supplies of goods of satisfactory quality at fair prices and conditions while being able to choose between the products of different manufacturers;

(17) Whereas the advantages produced by beer supply agreements and service-station agreements cannot otherwise be secured to the same extent and with the same degree of certainty; whereas the exclusive purchasing obligation on the reseller and the non-competition clause imposed on him are essential components of such agreements and thus usually indispensable for the attainment of these advantages; whereas, however, this is true only as long as the reseller's obligation to purchase from the supplier is confined in the case of premises used for the sale and consumption of drinks to beers and other drinks of the types offered by the supplier, and in the case of service stations to petroleum-based fuel for motor vehicles and other petroleum-based fuels; whereas the exclusive purchasing obligation for lubricants and related petroleum-based products can be accepted only on condition that the supplier provides for the reseller or finances the procurement of specific equipment for the carrying out of lubrication work; whereas this obligation should only relate to products intended for use within the service station;

(18) Whereas, in order to maintain the reseller's commercial freedom and to ensure access to the retail level of distribution on the part of other suppliers, not only the scope but also the duration of the exclusive purchasing obligation must be limited; whereas it appears appropriate to allow drinks suppliers a choice between a medium-term exclusive purchasing agreement covering a range of drinks and a long term exclusive purchasing agreement for beer; whereas it is necessary to provide special rules for those premises used for the sale and consumption of drinks which the supplier lets to the reseller; whereas, in this case, the reseller must have the right to obtain, under the conditions specified in this Regulation, other drinks, except beer, supplied under the agreement or of the same type but bearing a different trademark;

whereas a uniform maximum duration should be provided for service-station agreements, with the exception of tenancy agreements between the supplier and the reseller, which takes account of the long-term character of the relationship between the parties;

(19) Whereas to the extent that member states provide, by law or administrative measures, for the same upper limit of duration for the exclusive purchasing obligation upon the reseller as in service-station agreements laid down in this Regulation but provide for a permissible duration which varies in proportion to the consideration provided by the supplier or generally provide for a shorter duration than that permitted by this Regulation, such laws or measures are not contrary to the objectives of this Regulation which, in this respect, merely sets an upper limit to the duration of service-station agreements; whereas the application and enforcement of such national laws or measures must therefore be regarded as compatible with the provisions of this Regulation;

(20) Whereas the limitations and conditions provided for in this Regulation are such as to guarantee effective competition on the markets in question; whereas, therefore, the agreements to which the exemption by category applies do not normally enable the participating undertakings to eliminate competition for a substantial part of the products in question;

(21) Whereas, in particular cases in which agreements or concerted practices satisfying the conditions of this Regulation nevertheless have effects incompatible with Article 85(3) of the Treaty, the Commission may withdraw the benefit of the exemption by category from the undertakings party thereto;

(22) Whereas agreements and concerted practices which satisfy the conditions set out in this Regulation need not be notified; whereas an undertaking may nonetheless, in a particular case where real doubt exists, request the Commission to declare whether its agreements comply with this Regulation;

(23) Whereas this Regulation does not affect the applicability of Commission Regulation (EEC) No. 3604/82 of 23 December 1982 on the appliction of Article 85(3) of the Treaty to categories of specialisation agreements*; whereas it does not exclude the application of Article 86 of the Treaty,

Has adopted this Regulation:

Title 1

General provisions

Article 1
Pursuant to Article 85(3) of the Treaty, and subject to the conditions set out in Articles 2 to 5 of this Regulation, it is hereby declared that Article 85(1) of the Treaty shall not apply to agreements to which only two undertakings are party and whereby one party, the reseller, agrees with the other, the supplier, to purchase certain goods specified in the agreement for resale only from the supplier or from a connected undertaking or from another undertaking which the supplier has entrusted with the sale of his goods.

Article 2
1. No other restriction of competition shall be imposed on the supplier than the obligation not to distribute the contract goods or goods which compete with the contract goods in the reseller's principal sales area and at the reseller's level of distribution.

* OJ No. L 376, 31. 12. 1982, p.33.

2. Apart the obligation described in Article 1, no other restriction of competition shall be imposed on the reseller than the obligation not to manufacture or distribute goods which compete with the contract goods.

3. Article 1 shall apply notwithstanding that the resellers undertakes any or all of the following obligations;

(a) to purchase complete ranges of goods;

(b) to purchase minimum quantities of goods which are subject to the exclusive purchasing obligation;

(c) to sell the contract goods under trademarks, or packed and presented as specified by the supplier;

(d) to take measures for the promotion of sales, in particular;
— to advertise,
— to maintain a sales network or stock of goods,
— to provide customer and guarantee services,
— to employ staff having specialised or technical training.

Article 3
Article 1 shall not apply where:

(a) manufacturers of identical goods or of goods which are considered by users as equivalent in view of their characteristics, price and intended use enter into reciprocal exclusive purchasing agreements between themselves in respect of such goods;

(b) manufacturers of identical goods or of goods which are considered by users as equivalent in view of their characteristics, price and intended use enter into a non-reciprocal exclusive purchasing agreement between themselves in respect of such goods, unless at least one of them has a total annual turnover of no more than 100 million ECU;

(c) the exclusive purchasing obligation is agreed for more than one type of goods where these are neither by their nature nor according to commercial usage connected to each other;

(d) the agreement is concluded for an indefinite duration or for a period of more than five years.

Article 4
1. Article 3(a) and (b) shall also apply where the goods there referred to are manufactured by an undertaking connected with a party to the agreement.

2. Connected undertakings are:

(a) undertakings in which a party to the agreement, directly or indirectly:

— owns more than half the capital or business assets, or
— has the power to exercise more than half the voting rights, or
— has the power to appoint more than half the members of the supervisory board, board of directors or bodies legally representing the undertaking, or
— has the right to manage the affairs;

(b) undertakings which directly or indirectly have in or over a party to the agreement the rights or powers listed in (a);

(c) undertakings in which an undertaking referred to in (b) directly or indirectly has the rights or powers listed in (a).

3. Undertakings in which the parties to the agreement or undertakings connected with them jointly have the rights or powers set out in paragraph 2(a) shall be considered to be connected with each of the parties to the agreement.

Article 5
1. For the purpose of Article 3(b), the ECU is the unit of account used for drawing up the budget of the Community pursuant to Articles 207 and 209 of the Treaty.

2. Article 1 shall remain applicable where during any period of two consecutive financial years the total turnover referred to in Article 3(b) is exceeded by no more than 10%.

3. For the purpose of calculating total turnover within the meaning of Article 3(b), the turnovers achieved during the last financial year by the party to the agreement and connected undertakings in respect of all goods and services, excluding all taxes and other duties, shall be added together. For this purpose, no account shall be taken of dealings between the parties to the agreement or between these undertakings and undertakings connected with them or between the connected undertakings.

Title II
Special provisions for beer supply agreements

Article 6

1. Pursuant to Article 85(3) of the Treaty, and subject to Articles 7 to 9 of this Regulation, it is hereby declared that article 85(1) of the Treaty shall not apply to agreements to which only two undertakings are party and whereby one party, the reseller, agrees with the other, the supplier, in consideration for according special commercial or financial advantages, to purchase only from the supplier, an undertaking connected with the supplier or another undertaking entrusted by the supplier with the distribution of his goods, certain beers, or certain beers and certain other drinks, specified in the agreement for resale in premises used for the sale and consumption of drinks and designated in the agreement.

2. The declaration in paragraph 1 shall also apply where exclusive purchasing obligations of the kind described in paragraph 1 are imposed on the reseller in favour of the supplier by another undertaking which is itself not a supplier.

Article 7

1. Apart from the obligation referred to in Article 6, no restriction on competition shall be imposed on the reseller other than:

(a) the obligation not to sell beers and other drinks which are supplied by other undertakings and which are of the same type as the beers or other drinks supplied under the agreement in the premises designated in the agreement;

(b) the obligation, in the event that the reseller sells in the premises designated in the agreement beers which are supplied by other undertakings and which are of a different type from the beers supplied under the agreement, to sell such beers only in bottles, cans or other small packages, unless the sale of such beers in draught form is customary or is necessary to satisfy a sufficient demand from consumers;

(c) the obligation to advertise goods supplied by other undertakings within or outside the premises designated in the agreement only in proportion to the share of these goods in the total turnover realised in the premises.

2. Beers or other drinks of the same type are those which are not clearly distinguishable in view of their composition, appearance and taste.

Article 8

1. Article 6 shall not apply where:

(a) the supplier or a connected undertaking imposes on the reseller exclusive purchasing obligations for goods other than drinks or for services;

(b) the supplier restricts the freedom of the reseller to obtain from an undertaking of his choice either services or goods for which neither an exclusive purchasing obligation nor a ban on dealing in competing products may be imposed;

(c) the agreement is concluded for an indefinite duration or for a period of more than five years and the exclusive purchasing obligation relates to specified beers and other drinks;

(d) the agreement is concluded for an indefinite duration or for a period of more than 10 years and the exclusive purchasing obligation relates only to specified beers;

(e) the supplier obliges the reseller to impose the exclusive purchasing obligation on his successor for a longer period than the reseller would himself remain tied to the supplier.

2. Where the agreement relates to premises which the supplier lets to the reseller or allows the reseller to occupy on some other basis in law or in fact, the following provisions shall also apply:

(a) notwithstanding paragraphs (1)(c) and (d), the exclusive purchasing obligations and bans on dealing in competing products specified in this Title may be imposed on the reseller for the whole period for which the reseller in fact operates the premises;

(b) the agreement must provide for the reseller to have the right to obtain:

— drinks, except beer, supplied under the agreement from other undertakings where these undertakings offer them on more favourable conditions which the supplier does not meet;
— drinks, except beer, which are of the same type as those supplied under the agreement but which bear different trade marks, from other undertakings where the supplier does not offer them.

Article 9

Articles 2(1) and (3), 3(a) and (b), 4 and 5 shall apply *mutatis mutandis.*

Title III
Special provisions for service-station agreements

Article 10

Pursuant to Article 85(3) of the Treaty and subject to Articles 11 to 13 of this Regulation, it is hereby declared that Article 85(1) of the Treaty shall not apply to agreements to which only two undertakings are party and whereby one party, the reseller, agrees with the other, the supplier, in consideration for the according of special commercial or financial advantages, to purchase only from the supplier, an undertaking connected with the supplier or another undertaking entrusted by the supplier with the distribution of his goods, certain petroleum-based motor-vehicle fuels or certain petroleum-based motor-vehicle and other fuels specified in the agreement for resale in a service station designated in the agreement.

Article 11

Apart from the obligation referred to in Article 10, no restriction on competition shall be imposed on the reseller other than:

(a) the obligation not to sell motor-vehicle fuel and other fuels which are supplied by other undertakings in the service station designated in the agreement:

(b) the obligation not to use lubricants or related petroleum-based products which are supplied by other undertakings within the service station designated in the agreement where the supplier or a connected undertaking has made available to the reseller or financed, a lubrication bay or other motor-vehicle lubrication equipment;

(c) the obligation to advertise goods supplied by other undertakings within or outside the service station designated in the agreement only in proportion to the share of these goods in the total turnover realised in the service station;

(d) the obligation to have equipment owned by the supplier or a connected undertaking or financed by the supplier or a connected undertaking serviced by the supplier or an undertaking designated by him.

Article 12
1. Article 10 shall not apply where:

(a) the supplier or a connected undertaking imposes on the reseller exclusive purchasing obligations for goods other than motor-vehicle and other fuels or for services, except in the case of the obligations referred to in Article 11(b) and (d);

(b) the supplier restricts the freedom of the reseller to obtain, from an undertaking of his choice, goods or services, for which under the provisions of this Title neither an exclusive purchasing obligation nor a ban on dealing in competing products may be imposed;

(c) the agreement is concluded for an indefinite duration or for a period of more than 10 years;

(d) the supplier obliges the reseller to impose the exclusive purchasing obligation on his successor for a longer period than the reseller would himself remain tied to the supplier.

2. Where the agreement relates to a service station which the supplier lets to the reseller, or allows the reseller to occupy on some other basis, in law or in facts, exclusive purchasing obligations or prohibitions of competition indicated in this Title may, notwithstanding paragraph 1(c), be imposed on the reseller for the whole period for which the reseller in fact operates the premises.

Article 13
Articles 2(1) and (3), 3(a) and (b), 4 and 5 of this Regulation shall apply *mutatis mutandis*.

Title IV
Miscellaneous provisions

Article 14
The Commission may withdraw the benefit of this Regulation, pursuant to Article 7 of Regulation No. 19/65/EEC, when it finds in a particular case that an agreement which is exempted by this Regulation nevertheless has certain effects which are incompatible with the conditions set out in Article 85(3) of the Treaty, and in particular where:

(a) the contract goods are not subject, in a substantial part of the common market, to effective competition from identical goods or goods considered by users as equivalent in view of their characteristics, price and intended use;

(b) access by other suppliers to the different stages of distribution in a substantial part of the common market is made difficult to a significant extent;

(c) the supplier without any objectively justified reason:

1. refuses to supply categories of resellers who cannot obtain the contract goods elsewhere on suitable terms or applies to them differing prices or conditions of sale;

2. applies less favourable prices or conditions of sale to resellers bound by an exclusive purchasing obligation as compared with other resellers at the same level of distribution.

Article 15
1. In the period 1 July 1983 to 31 December 1986, the prohibition in Article 85(1) of the Treaty shall not apply to agreements of the kind described in Article 1 which either were in force on 1 July 1983 or entered into force between 1 July and 31 December 1983 and which satisfy the exemption conditions under Regulation No. 67/67/EEC*.

2. In the period 1 July 1983 to 31 December 1988, the prohibition in Article 85(1) of the Treaty shall not apply to agreements of the kinds described in Articles 6 and 10 which either were in force on 1 July 1983 or entered into force between 1 July and 31 December 1983 and which satisfy the exemption conditions of Regulation No. 67/67/EEC.

3. In the case of agreements of the kinds described in Articles 6 and 10, which were in force on 1 July 1983 and which expire after 31 December 1988, the prohibition in Article 85(1) of the Treaty shall not apply in the period from 1 January 1989 to the expiry of the agreement but at the latest to the expiry of this Regulation to the extent that the supplier releases the reseller, before 1 January 1989, from all obligations which would prevent the application of the exemption under Titles II and III.

Article 16
The Regulation shall not apply to agreements by which the supplier undertakes with the reseller to supply only to the reseller certain goods for resale, in the whole or in a defined part of the Community, and the reseller undertakes with the supplier to purchase these goods only from the supplier.

Article 17
This Regulation shall not apply where the parties or connected undertakings, for the purpose of resale in one and the same premises used for the sale and consumption of drinks or service station, enter into agreements both of the kind referred to in Title I and of a kind referred to in Title II or III.

Article 18
This Regulation shall apply *mutatis mutandis* to the categories of concerted practices defined in Articles 1, 6 and 10.

Article 19
This Regulation shall enter into force on 1 July 1983.
   It shall expire on 31 December 1997.

This Regulation shall be binding in its entirety and directly applicable in all member states.

Done at Brussels, 22 June 1983.

For the Commission
Frans ANDRIESSEN
Member of the Commission

* OJ No. 57, 25. 3. 1967, p.849/67.

Council Regulation 17 of February 6, 1962

First Regulation implementing Articles 85 and 86 of the Treaty
(O.J. 1962, 204; O.J. 1959–1962, 87)

The Council of the European Economic Community

Having regard to the Treaty establishing the European Economic Community, and in particular Article 87 thereof:

Having regard to the proposal from the Commission;

Having regard to the Opinion of the Economic and Social Committee;

Having regard to the Opinion of the European Parliament;

Whereas in order to establish a system ensuring that competition shall not be distorted in the common market, it is necessary to provide for balanced application of Articles 85 and 86 in a uniform manner in the member states;

Whereas in establishing the rules for applying Article 85(3) account must be taken of the need to ensure effective supervision and to simplify administration to the greatest possible extent;

Whereas it is accordingly necessary to make it obligatory, as a general principle, for undertakings which seek application of Article 85(3) to notify to the Commission their agreements, decisions and concerted practices;

Whereas, on the one hand, such agreements, decisions and concerted practices are probably very numerous and cannot therefore all be examined at the same time and, on the other hand, some of them have special features which may make them less prejudicial to the development of the common market;

Whereas there is consequently a need to make more flexible arrangements for the time being in respect of certain categories of agreements, decisions and concerted practices without prejudging their validity under Article 85;

Whereas it may be in the interest of undertakings to know whether any agreements, decisions or practices to which they are party, or propose to become party, may lead to action on the part of the Commission pursuant to Article 85(1) or Article 86;

Whereas, in order to secure uniform application of Articles 85 and 86 in the common market, rules must be made under which the Commission, acting in close and constant liaison with the competent authorities of the member states, may take the requisite measures for applying those Articles;

Whereas for this purpose the Commission must have the co-operation of the competent authorities of the member states and be empowered, throughout the common market, to require such information to be supplied and to undertake such investigations as are necessary to bring to light any agreement, decision or concerted practice prohibited by Article 85(1) or any abuse of a dominant position prohibited by Article 86;

Whereas in order to carry out its duty of ensuring that the provisions of the Treaty are applied, the Commission must be empowered to address to undertakings or associations of undertakings recommendations and decisions for the purpose of bringing to an end infringements of Articles 85 and 86;

Whereas compliance with Articles 85 and 86 and the fulfilment of obligations imposed on undertakings and associations of undertakings under this regulation must be enforceable by means of fines and periodic penalty payments;

Whereas undertakings concerned must be accorded the right to be heard by the Commission, third parties whose interests may be affected by a decision must be given the opportunity of submitting their comments beforehand, and it must be ensured that wide publicity is given to decisions taken;

Whereas all decisions taken by the Commission under this regulation are subject to review by the Court of Justice under the conditions specified in the Treaty; whereas it is moreover desirable to confer upon the Court of Justice, pursuant to Article 172, unlimited jurisdiction in respect of decisions under which the Commission imposes fines or periodic penalty payments;

Whereas this regulation may enter into force without prejudice to any other provisions that may hereafter be adopted pursuant to Article 87,

Has adopted this Regulation:

Article 1: Basic Provision

Without prejudice to Articles 6, 7 and 23 of this regulation, agreements, decisions and concerted practices of the kind described in Article 85(1) of the Treaty and the abuse of a dominant position in the market, within the meaning of Article 86 of the Treaty, shall be prohibited, no prior decision to that effect being required.

Article 2: Negative Clearance

Upon application by the undertakings or associations of undertakings concerned, the Commission may certify that, on the basis of the facts in its possession, there are no grounds under Article 85(1) or Article 86 of the Treaty for action on its part in respect of an agreement, decision or practice.

Article 3: Termination of Infringements

1. Where the Commission, upon application or upon its own initiative, finds that there is infringement of Article 85 or Article 86 of the Treaty, it may by decision require the undertakings or associations of undertakings concerned to bring such infringement to an end.

2. Those entitled to make application are:

(a) member states;
(b) natural or legal persons who claim a legitimate interest.

3. Without prejudice to the other provisions of this regulation, the Commission may, before taking a decision under paragraph (1), address to the undertakings or associations of undertakings concerned recommendations for termination of the infringement.

Article 4: Notification of New Agreements, Decisions and Practices

1. Agreements, decisions and concerted practices of the kind described in Article 85(1) of the Treaty which come into existence after the entry into force of this regulation and in respect of which the parties seek application of Article 85(3) must be notified to the Commission. Until they have been notified, no decision in application of Article 85(3) may be taken.

2. Paragraph (1) shall not apply to agreements, decisions or concerted practices where:

(i) the only parties thereto are undertakings from one member state and the agreements, decisions or practices do not relate either to imports or to exports between member states;

(ii) not more than two undertakings are party thereto, and the agreements only:

(a) restrict the freedom of one party to the contract in determining the prices for or conditions of business on which the goods which he has obtained from the other party to the contract may be resold; or,

(b) impose restrictions on the exercise of the rights of the assignee or user of industrial property rights — in particular patents, utility models, designs or trade marks — or of the person entitled under a contract to the assignment, or grant, of the right to use a method of manufacture or knowledge relating to the use and to the application of industrial processes;

(iii) they have as their sole object:

(a) the development or uniform application of standards or types;

(b) joint research and development;

(c) specialisation in the manufacture of products, including agreements necessary for the achieving this:

— where the products which are the objects of specialisation do not, in a substantial part of the common market, represent more than 15 per cent of the volume of business done in identical products or those considered by the consumers to be similar by reason of their characteristics, price and use, and

— where the total annual turnover of the participating undertakings does not exceed 200 million units of accounts.

These agreements, decisions and concerted practices may be notified to the Commission.

Article 5: Notification of Existing Agreements, Decisions and Practices

1. Agreements, decisions and concerted practices of the kind described in Article 85(1) of the Treaty, which are in existence at the date of entry into force of this regulation and in respect of which the parties seek application of Article 85(3) shall be notified to the Commission before 1 November 1962. However, notwithstanding the foregoing provisions any agreements, decisions and concerted practices to which not more than two undertakings are party shall be notified before 1 February 1963.

2. Paragraph (1) shall not apply to agreements, decisions or concerted practices falling within Article 4(2); these may be notified to the Commission.

Article 6: Decisions Pursuant to Article 85(3)

1. Whenever the Commission takes a decision pursuant to Article 85(3) of the Treaty, it shall specify therein the date from which the decision shall take effect. Such date shall not be earlier than the date of notification.

2. The second sentence of paragraph (1) shall not apply to agreements, decisions or concerted practices falling within Article 4(2) and Article 5(2), nor to those falling within article 5(1) which have been notified within the time limit specified in Article 5(1).

Article 7: Special Provisions for Existing Agreements, Decisions and Practices

1. Where agreements, decisions and concerted practices in existence at the date of entry into force of this regulation and notified within the limits specified in Article 5(1) do not satisfy the requirements of Article 85(3) of the Treaty and the undertakings or associations of undertakings concerned cease to give effect to them or modify them in such manner that they no longer fall within the prohibition contained in Article 85(1) or that they satisfy the requirements of Article 85(3), the prohibition contained in Article 85(1) shall apply only for a period fixed by the Commission. A decision by the Commission pursuant to the foregoing sentence shall not apply as against undertakings and associations of undertakings which do not expressly consent to the notification.

2. Paragraph (1) shall apply to agreements, decisions and concerted practices falling within Article 4(2) which are in existence at the date of entry into force of this regulation if they are notified before 1 January 1967.

Article 8: Duration and Revocation of Decisions under Article 85(3)

1. A decision in application of Article 85(3) of the Treaty shall be issued for a specified period and conditions and obligations may be attached thereto.

2. A decision may on application be renewed if the requirements of Article 85(3) of the Treaty continue to be satisfied.

3. The Commission may revoke or amend its decision or prohibit specified acts by the parties:

(a) where there has been a change in any of the facts which were fundamental in the making of the decision;

(b) where the parties commit a breach of any obligation attached to the decision;

(c) where the decision is based on incorrect information or was induced by deceit;

(d) where the parties abuse the exemption from the provisions of Article 85(1) of the Treaty granted to them by the decision.

In cases to which sub-paragraphs (b), (c) or (d) apply, the decision may be revoked with retroactive effect.

Article 9. Powers

1. Subject to review of its decision by the Court of Justice, the Commission shall have sole power to declare Article 85(1) inapplicable pursuant to Article 85(3) of the Treaty.

2. The Commission shall have power to apply Article 85(1) and Article 86 of the Treaty; this power may be exercised notwithstanding that the time limits specified in Article 5(1) and in Article 7(2) relating to notification have not expired.

3. As long as the Commission has not initiated any procedure under Articles 2, 3 or 6, the authorities of the member states shall remain competent to apply Article 85(1) and Article 86, in accordance with Article 88 of the Treaty; they shall remain competent in this respect notwithstanding that the time limits specified in Article 5(1) and in Article 7(2) relating to notification have not expired.

Article 10: Liaison with the Authorities of the Member States

1. The Commission shall forthwith transmit to the competent authorities of the member states a copy of the applications and notifications together with copies of the most important documents lodged with the Commission for the purpose of establishing the existence of infringements of Articles 85 or 86 of the Treaty or of obtaining negative clearance or a decision in application of Article 85(3).

2. The Commission shall carry out the procedure set out in paragraph (1) in close and constant liaison with the competent authorities of the member states; such authorities shall have the right to express their views on that procedure.

3. An Advisory Committee on Restrictive Practices and Monopolies shall be consulted prior to the taking of any decision following upon a procedure under paragraph (1), and of any decision concerning the renewal, amendment or revocation of a decision pursuant to Article 85(3) of the Treaty.

4. The Advisory Committee shall be composed of officials competent in the matter of restrictive practices and monopolies. Each member state shall appoint an official to represent it who, if prevented from attending, may be replaced by another official.

5. The consultation shall take place at a joint meeting convened by the Commission; such meeting shall be held not earlier than fourteen days after dispatch of the notice convening it. The notice shall, in respect of each case to be examined, be accompanied by a summary of the case together with an indication of the most important documents, and a preliminary draft decision.

6. The Advisory Committee may deliver an opinion notwithstanding that some of its members or their alternates are not present. A report of the outcome of the consultative proceedings shall be annexed to the draft decision. It shall not be made public.

Article 11: Requests for Information

1. In carrying out the duties assigned to it by Article 89 and by provisions adopted under article 87 of the Treaty, the Commission may obtain all necessary information from the Governments and competent authorities of the member states and from undertakings and associations of undertakings.

2. When sending a request for information to an undertaking or association of undertakings, the Commission shall at the same time forward a copy of the request to the competent authority of the member state in whose territory the seat of the undertaking or association of undertakings is situated.

3. In its request the Commission shall state the legal basis and the purpose of the request and also the penalties provided for in Article 15(1)(b) for supplying incorrect information.

4. The owners of the undertakings or their representatives and, in the case of legal persons, companies or firms, or of associations having no legal personality, the persons authorised to represent them by law or by their constitution shall supply the information requested.

5. Where an undertaking or association of undertakings does not supply the information requested within the time limit fixed by the Commission, or supplies incomplete information, the Commission shall by decision require the information to be supplied. The decision shall specify what information is required, fix an appropriate time limit within which it is to be supplied and indicate the penalties provided for by Article 15(1)(b) and Article 16(1)(c) and the right to have the decision reviewed by the Court of Justice.

6. The Commission shall at the same time forward a copy of its decision to the competent authority of the member state in whose territory the seat of the undertaking or association of undertakings is situated.

Article 12: Inquiry into Sectors of the Economy

1. If in any sector of the economy the trend of trade between member states, price movements, inflexibility of prices or other circumstances suggest that in the economic sector concerned competition is being restricted or distorted within the common market, the Commission may decide to conduct a general inquiry into that economic sector and in the course thereof may request undertakings in the sector concerned to supply the information necessary for giving effect to the principles formulated in Articles 85 and 86 of the Treaty and for carrying out the duties entrusted to the Commission.

2. The Commission may in particular request every undertaking or association of undertakings in the economic sector concerned to communicate to it all agreements, decisions and concerted practices which are exempt from notification by virtue of Article 4(2) and Article 5(2).

3. When making inquiries pursuant to paragraph (2), the Commission shall also request undertakings or groups of undertakings whose size suggests that they occupy a dominant position within the common market or a substantial part thereof to supply to the Commission such particulars of the structure of the undertakings and of their behaviour as are requisite to an appraisal of their position in the light of Article 86 of the Treaty.

4. Article 10(3) to (6) and Articles 11, 13 and 14 shall apply correspondingly.

Article 13. Investigations by the Authorities of the Member States

1. At the request of the Commission, the competent authorities of the member states shall undertake the investigations which the Commission considers to be necessary under Article 14(1), or which it has ordered by decision pursuant to Article 14(3). The officials of the competent authorities of the member states responsible for conducting these investigations shall exercise their powers upon reproduction of an authorisation in writing issued by the competent authority of the member state in whose territory the investigation is to be made. Such authorisation shall specify the subject-matter and purpose of the investigation.

2. If so requested by the Commission or by the competent authority of the member state in whose territory the investigation is to be made, the officials of the Commission may assist the officials of such authority in carrying out their duties.

Article 14: Investigating Powers of the Commission

1. In carrying out the duties assigned to it by Article 89 and by provisions adopted under Article 87 of the Treaty, the Commission may undertake all necessary investigations into undertakings and associations of undertakings. To this end the officials authorised by the Commission are empowered:

(a) to examine the books and other business records;
(b) to take copies of or extracts from the books and business records;
(c) to ask for oral explanations on the spot;
(d) to enter any premises, land and means of transport of undertakings.

2. The officials of the Commission authorised for the purpose of these investigations shall exercise their powers upon production of an authorisation in writing specifying the subject-matter and purpose of the investigation and the penalties provided for in Article 15(1)(c) in cases where production of the required books or other business records is incomplete. In good time before the investigation, the Commission shall inform the competent authority of the member state in whose territory the same is to be made, of the investigation and of the identity of the authorised officials.

3. Undertakings and associations of undertakings shall submit to investigations ordered by decision of the Commission. The decision shall specify the subject-matter and purpose of the investigation, appoint the date on which it is to begin and indicate the penalties provided for in Article 15(1)(c) and Article 16(1)(d) and the right to have the decision reviewed by the Court of Justice.

4. The Commission shall take the decisions referred to in paragraph 3 after consultation with the competent authority of the member state in whose territory the investigation is to be made.

5. Officials of the competent authority of the member state in whose territory the investigation is to be made may, at the request of such authority or of the Commission, assist the officials of the Commission in carrying out their duties.

6. Where as undertaking opposes an investigation ordered pursuant to this Article, the member state concerned shall afford the necessary assistance to the officials authorised by the Commission to enable them to make their investigation. Member states shall, after consultation with the Commission, take the necessary measures to this end before 1 October 1962.

Article 15: Fines

1. The Commission may by decision impose on undertakings or associations of undertakings fines of from one hundred to five thousand units of account where, intentionally or negligently:

(a) they supply incorrect or misleading information in an application pursuant to Article 2 or in a notification pursuant to Articles 4 or 5; or

(b) they supply incorrect information in response to a request made pursuant to Article 11(3) or (5) or to Article 12, or do not supply information within the time limit fixed by a decision taken under Article 11(5); or

(c) they produce the required books or other business records in incomplete form during investigations under Article 13 or 14, or refuse to submit to an investigation ordered by decision issued in implementation of Article 14(3).

2. The Commission may by decision impose on undertakings or associations of undertakings fines of from one thousand to one million units of account, or a sum in excess thereof but not exceeding 10 per cent. of the turnover in the preceding business year of each of the undertakings participating in the infringement where either intentionally or negligently:

(a) they infringe Article 85(1) or Article 86 of the Treaty; or

(b) they commit a breach of any obligation imposed pursuant to Article 8(1).

In fixing the amount of the fine, regard shall be had both to the gravity and to the duration of the investigation.

3. Article 10(3) to (6) shall apply.

4. Decisions taken pursuant to paragraphs (1) and (2) shall not be of a criminal law nature.

5. The fines provided for in paragraph (2)(a) shall not be imposed in respect of acts taking place:

(a) after notification to the Commission and before its decision in application of Article 85(3) of the Treaty, provided they fall within the limits of the activity described in the notification;

(b) before notification and in the course of agreements, decisions or concerted practices in existence at the date of entry into force of this regulation, provided that notification was effected within the time limits specified in Article 5(1) and Article 7(2).

6. Paragraph (5) shall not have effect where the Commission has informed the undertakings concerned that after preliminary examination it is of opinion that Article 85(1) of the Treaty applies and that application of Article 85(3) is not justified.

Article 16: Periodic Penalty Payments

1. The Commission may by decision impose on undertakings or associations of undertakings periodic penalty payments of from fifty to one thousand units of account per day, calculated from the date appointed by the decision, in order to compel them:

(a) to put an end to an infringement of Article 85 or 86 of the Treaty, in accordance with a decision taken pursuant to Article 3 of this regulation;

(b) to refrain from any act prohibited under Article 8(3);

(c) to supply complete and correct information which it has requested by decision taken pursuant to Article 11(5);

(d) to submit to an investigation which it has ordered by decision taken pursuant to Article 14(3).

2. Where the undertakings or associations of undertakings have satisfied the obligation which it was the purpose of the periodic penalty payment to enforce, the Commission may fix the total amount of the periodic payment at a lower figure than that which would arise under the original decision.

3. Article 10(3) to (6) shall apply.

Article 17: Review by the Court of Justice

The Court of Justice shall have unlimited jurisdiction within the meaning of Article 172 of the Treaty to review decisions whereby the Commission has fixed a fine or periodic penalty; it may cancel, reduce or increase the fine or periodic penalty payment imposed.

Article 18: Unit of Account

For the purposes of applying Articles 15 to 17 the unit of account shall be that adopted in drawing up the budget of the Community in accordance with Articles 207 and 209 of the Treaty.

Article 19: Hearing of the Parties and of Third Persons

1. Before taking decisions as provided for in Articles 2, 3, 6, 7, 8, 15 and 16, the Commission shall give the undertakings or associations of undertakings concerned the opportunity of being heard on the matters to which the Commission has taken objection.

2. If the Commission or the competent authorities of the member states consider it necessary, they may also hear other natural or legal persons. Applications to be heard on the part of such persons shall, where they show a sufficient interest, be granted.

3. Where the Commission intends to give negative clearance pursuant to Article 2 or take a decision in application of Article 85(3) of the Treaty, it shall publish a summary of the relevant application or notification and invite all interested third parties to submit their observations within a time limit which it shall fix being not less than one month. Publication shall have regard to the legitimate interest of undertakings in the protection of their business secrets.

Article 20: Professional Secrecy

1. Information acquired as a result of the application of Articles 11, 12, 13 and 14 shall be used only for the purpose of the relevant request for investigation.

2. Without prejudice to the provisions of Articles 19 and 21, the Commission and the competent authorities of the member states, their officials and other servants shall not disclose information acquired by them as a result of the application of this regulation and of the kind covered by the obligation of professional secrecy.

3. The provisions of paragraphs (1) and (2) shall not prevent publication of general information or surveys which do not contain information relating to particular undertakings or associations of undertakings.

Article 21: Publication of Decisions

1. The Commission shall publish the decisions which it takes pursuant to Articles 2, 3, 6, 7 and 8.

2. The publication shall state the names of the parties and the main content of the decision; it shall have regard to the legitimate interest of undertakings in the protection of their business secrets.

Article 22: Special Provisions

1. The Commission shall submit to the Council proposals for making certain categories of agreement, decision and concerted practice falling within Article 4(2) or Article 5(2) compulsorily notifiable under Article 4 or 5.

2. Within one year from the date of entry into force of this regulation, the Council shall examine, on a proposal from the Commission, what special provisions might be made for exempting from the provisions of this regulation agreements, decisions and concerted practices falling within Article 4(2) or Article 5(2).

Article 23: Transitional Provisions Applicable to Decisions of Authorities of the Member States

1. Agreements, decisions and concerted practices of the kind described in Article 85(1) of the Treaty to which, before entry into force of this regulation, the competent authority of a member state has declared Article 85(1) to be inapplicable pursuant to Article 85(3) shall not be subject to compulsory notification under Article 5. The decision of the competent authority of the member state shall be deemed to be a decision within the meaning of Article 6; it shall cease to be valid upon expiration of the period fixed by such authority but in any event not more than three years after the entry into force of this regulation.

Article 8(3) shall apply.

2. Applications for renewal of decisions of the kind described in paragraph (1) shall be decided upon by the Commission in accordance with article 8(2).

Article 24: Implementing Provisions

The Commission shall have the power to adopt implementing provisions concerning the form, content and other details of applications pursuant to Articles 2 and 3, and of notifications pursuant to Articles 4 and 5, and concerning hearings pursuant to Article 19(1) and (2).

Article 25

1. As regards agreements, decisions and concerted practices to which Article 85 of the Treaty applies by virtue of accession, the date of accession shall be substituted for the date of entry into force of this regulation in every place where reference is made in this regulation to this latter date.

2. Agreements, decisions and concerted practices existing at the date of accession to which Article 85 of the Treaty applies by virtue of accession shall be notified pursuant to Article 5(1) or Article 7(1) and (2) within six months from the date of accession.

3. Fines under Article 15(2)(a) shall not be imposed in respect of any act prior to notification of the agreements, decisions, and practices to which paragraph (2) applies and which have been notified within the period therein specified.

4. New member states shall take the measures referred to in Article 14(6) within six months from the date of accession after consulting the Commission.

5. The provisions of paragraphs (1) to (4) above still apply in the same way in the case of accession of the Hellenic Republic, the Kingdom of Spain and of the Portuguese Republic.

This regulation shall be binding in its entirety and directly applicable in all member states.

Done at Brussels, February 6, 1962.

B. TEXT OF REGULATION 27/62

Commission Regulation 27 of May 3, 1962
First Regulation implementing Council Regulation 17
of February 6, 1962
(O.J. 1962 p.1118, Amended by O.J. 1968 L 189/1,
O.J. 1975 L 172/7, O.J. 1985 L 240/1)

The Commission of the European
Economic Community

Having regard to the provisions of the Treaty establishing the European Economic Community, and in particular Articles 87 and 155 thereof,

Having regard to Article 24 of Council Regulation 17 of 6 February 1962 (First Regulation implementing Articles 85 and 86 of the Treaty),

Whereas under Article 24 of Council Regulation 17 the Commission is authorised to adopt implementing provisions concerning the form, content and other details of applications under Articles 2 and 3 and of notifications under Articles 4 and 5 of that Regulation;

Whereas the submission of such applications and notifications may have important legal consequences for each of the undertakings which is party to an agreement, decision or concerted practice; whereas every undertaking should accordingly have the right to submit an application or a notification to the Commission; whereas, furthermore, an undertaking exercising this right must inform the other undertakings which are parties to the agreement, decision or concerted practice, in order to enable them to protect their interests;

Whereas it is for the undertakings and associations of undertakings to transmit to the Commission information as to facts and circumstances in support of applications under Article 2 and of notifications under Articles 4 and 5;

Whereas it is desirable to prescribe forms for use in applications for negative clearance relating to implementation of Article 85(1) and for notifications relating to implementation of Article 85(3) of the Treaty in order to simplify and accelerate consideration by the competent departments, in the interests of all concerned;

Has adopted this Regulation:

Article 1: Persons entitled to submit applications and notifications

1. Any undertaking which is party to agreements, decisions or practices of the kind described in Articles 85 and 86 of the Treaty may submit an application under Article 2 or a notification under Articles 4 and 5 of Regulation 17. Where the application or notification is submitted by some, but not all, of the undertakings concerned, they shall give notice to the others.

2. Where applications and notifications under Articles 2, 3(1), 3(2)(b), 4 and 5 of Regulation 17 are signed by representatives of undertakings, or associations of undertakings, or natural or legal persons such representatives shall produce written proof that they are authorised to act.

3. Where a joint application or notification is submitted a joint representative should be appointed.

Article 2: Submission of applications and notifications

1. Thirteen copies of each application and notification shall be submitted to the Commission.

2. The supporting documents shall be either original or copies; copies must be certified as true copies of the original.

3. Applications and notifications shall be in one of the official languages of the Community. Supporting documents shall be submitted in their original language. Where the original language is not one of the official languages, a translation in one of the official languages shall be attached.

Article 3: Effective date of submission of applications and registrations

The date of submission of an application or notification shall be the date on which it is received by the Commission. Where, however, the application or notification is sent by registered post, it shall be deemed to have been received on the date shown on the postmark of the place of posting.

Article 4: Content of applications and notifications

1. Applications under Article 2 of Regulation 17 relating to the applicability of Article 85(1) of the Treaty and notifications under Article 4 or Article 5(2) of Regulation 17 shall be submitted on Form A/B, in the manner prescribed in the Form and in the Complementary Note thereto, as shown in the Annex to this Regulation.

2. Applications and notifications shall contain the information asked for in Form A/B and the Complementary Note.

3. Several participating undertakings may submit an application or notification on a single form.

4. Applications under Article 2 of Regulation 17 relating to the applicability of Article 86 of the Treaty shall contain a full statement of the facts, specifying, in particular, the practice concerned and the position of the undertaking or undertakings within the common market or a substantial part thereof in regard to products or services to which the practice relates. Form A/B may be used.

Article 5: Transitional Provisions

1. Applications and notifications submitted prior to the date of entry into force of this Regulation otherwise than on the prescribed forms shall be deemed to comply with Article 4 of this Regulation.

2. The Commission may require a duly completed form to be submitted to it within such time as it shall appoint. In that event, applications and notifications shall be treated as properly made only if the forms are submitted within the prescribed period and in accordance with the provisions of this Regulation.

Article 6

This Regulation shall enter into force on the day following its publication in the *Official Journal of the European Communities*.

This Regulation shall be binding in its entirety and directly applicable in all member states.

CHAPTER 13

Convention on the Law Applicable to Contractual Obligations

(19 June 1980)

PREAMBLE

The High Contracting Parties to the Treaty establishing the European Economic Community,

ANXIOUS to continue in the field of private international law the work of unification of law which has already been done within the Community, in particular in the field of jurisdiction and enforcement of judgments,

WISHING to establish uniform rules concerning the law applicable to contractual obligations,

HAVE AGREED AS FOLLOWS:

TITLE I. SCOPE OF THE CONVENTION

Article 1. Scope of the Convention.

(1) The rules of this Convention shall apply to contractual obligations in any situation involving a choice between the laws of different countries.

(2) They shall not apply to:

(a) questions involving the status or legal capacity of natural persons, without prejudice to Article 11;

(b) contractual obligations relating to:

— wills and succession,
— rights in property arising out of a matrimonial relationship,
— rights and duties arising out of a family relationship, parentage, marriage or affinity, including maintenance obligations in respect of children who are not legitimate;

(c) obligations arising under bills of exchange, cheques, and promissory notes and other negotiable instruments to the extent that the obligations under such other negotiable instruments arise out of their negotiable character;

(d) arbitration agreements and agreements on the choice of court;

(e) questions governed by the law of companies and other bodies corporate or unincorporate such as the creation, by registration or otherwise, legal capacity, internal organisation, or winding-up of companies and other bodies corporate or unincorporate and the personal liability of officers and members as such for the obligations of the company or body;

(f) the question whether an agent is able to bind a principal, or an organ to bind a company or body corporate or unincorporate, to a third party;

(g) the constitution of trusts and the relationship between settlors, trustees and beneficiaries;

(h) evidence and procedure, without prejudice to Article 14.

(3) The rules of this Convention do not apply to contracts of insurance which cover risks situated in the territories of the member states of the European Economic Community. In order to determine whether a risk is situated in these territories the court shall apply its internal law.

(4) The preceding paragraph does not apply to contracts of reinsurance.

Article 2. Application of Law of Non-contracting States.

Any law specified by this Convention shall be applied whether or not it is the law of a Contracting State.

TITLE II. UNIFORM RULES

Article 3. Freedom of Choice.

(1) A contract shall be governed by the law chosen by the parties. The choice must be expressed or demonstrated with reasonable certainty by the terms of the contract or the circumstances of the case. By their choice the parties can select the law applicable to the whole or a part only of the contract.

(2) The parties may at any time agree to subject the contract to a law other than that which previously governed it, whether as a result of an earlier choice under this article or of other provisions of this Convention. Any variation by the parties of the law to be applied made after the conclusion of the contract shall not prejudice its formal validity under Article 9 or adversely affect the rights of third parties.

(3) The fact that the parties have chosen a foreign law, whether or not accompanied by the choice of a foreign tribunal, shall not, where all the other elements relevant to the situation at the time of the choice are connected with one country only, prejudice the application of rules of the law of that country which cannot be derogated from by contract, hereinafter called 'mandatory rules'.

(4) The existence and validity of the consent of the parties as to the choice of the applicable law shall be determined in accordance with the provisions of Articles 8, 9 and 11.

Article 4. Applicable Law in the Absence of Choice

(1) To the extent that the law applicable to the contract has not been chosen in accordance with Article 3, the contract shall be governed by the law of the country with which it is most closely connected. Nevertheless, a severable part of the contract which has a closer connection with another country may by way of exception be governed by the law of that other country.

(2) Subject to paragraph 5 of this article, it shall be presumed that the contract is most closely connected with the country where the party who is to effect the performance which is characteristic of the contract has, at the time of conclusion of the contract, his habitual residence or, in the case of a body corporate or unincorporate, its central administration. However, if the contract is entered into in the course of that party's trade or profession, that country shall be the country in which the principal place of business is situated or, where under the terms of the contract the performance is to be effected through a place of business other

than the principal place of business, the country in which that other place of business is situated.

(3) Notwithstanding the provisions of paragraph 2 of this article, to the extent that the subject matter of the contract is a right in immovable property or a right to use immovable property, it shall be presumed that the contract is most closely connected with the country where the immovable property is situated.

(4) A contract for the carriage of goods shall not be subject to the presumption in paragraph (2). In such a contract if the country in which, at the time the contract is concluded, the carrier has his principal place of business is also the country in which the place of loading or the place of discharge or the principal place of business of the consignor is situated, it shall be presumed that the contract is most closely connected with that country. In applying this paragraph, single voyage charter parties and other contracts the main purpose of which is the carriage of goods shall be treated as contracts for the carriage of goods.

(5) Paragraph (2) shall not apply if the characteristic performance cannot be determined, and the presumptions in paragraphs (2), (3) and (4) shall be disregarded if it appears from the circumstances as a whole that the contract is more closely connected with another country.

Article 5. Certain Consumer Contracts.

(1) This article applies to a contract the object of which is the supply of goods or services to a person 'the consumer' for a purpose which can be regarded as being outside his trade or profession, or a contract for the provision of credit for that object.

(2) Notwithstanding the provisions of Article 3, a choice of law made by the parties shall not have the result of depriving the consumer of the protection afforded to him by the mandatory rules of the law of the country in which he has his habitual residence:

— if in that country the conclusion of the contract was preceded by a specific invitation addressed to him or by advertising, and he had taken in that country all the steps necessary on his part for the conclusion of the contract, or
— if the other party or his agent received the consumer's order in that country, or
— if the contract is for the sale of goods and the consumer travelled from that country to another country and there gave his order, provided that the consumer's journey was arranged by the seller for the purpose of inducing the consumer to buy.

(3) Notwithstanding the provisions of Article 4, a contract to which this article applies shall, in the absence of choice in accordance with Article 3, be governed by the law of the country in which the consumer has his habitual residence if it is entered into in the circumstances described in paragraph 2 of this article.

(4) This article shall not apply to:

(a) a contract of carriage;
(b) a contract for the supply of services where the services are to be supplied to the consumer exclusively in a country other than that in which he has his habitual residence.

(5) Notwithstanding the provisions of paragraph 4, this article shall apply to a contract which, for an inclusive price, provides for a combination of travel and accommodation.

Article 6. Individual Employment Contracts.

(1) Notwithstanding the provisions of Article 3, in a contract of employment a choice of law made by the parties shall not have the result of depriving the employee of the protection afforded to him by the mandatory rules of the law which would be applicable under paragraph 2 in the absence of choice.

(2) Notwithstanding the provisions of Article 4, a contract of employment shall, in the absence of choice in accordance with Article 3, be governed:

(a) by the law of the country in which the employee habitually carries out his work in performance of the contract, even if he is temporarily employed in another country; or
(b) if the employee does not habitually carry out his work in any one country, by the law of the country in which the place of business through which he was engaged is situated;

unless it appears from the circumstances as a whole that the contract is more closely connected with another country, in which case the contract shall be governed by the law of that country.

Article 7. Mandatory Rules.

(1) When applying under this convention the law of a country, effect may be given to the mandatory rules of the law of another country with which the situation has a close connection, if and in so far as, under the law of the latter country, those rules must be applied whatever the law applicable to the contract. In considering whether to give effect to those mandatory rules, regard shall be had to their nature and purpose and to the consequences of their application or non-application.

(2) Nothing in this Convention shall restrict the application of the rules of the law of the forum in a situation where they are mandatory irrespective of the law otherwise applicable to the contract.

Article 8. Material Validity.

(1) The existence and validity of a contract, or of any term of a contract, shall be determined by the law which would govern it under this Convention if the contract or term were valid.

(2) Nevertheless, a party may rely upon the law of the country in which he has his habitual residence to establish that he did not consent if it appears from the circumstances that it would not be reasonable to determine the effect of his conduct in accordance with the law specified in the preceding paragraph.

Article 9. Formal Validity.

(1) A contract concluded between persons who are in the same country is formally valid if it satisfies the formal requirements of the law which governs it under this Convention or of the law of the country where it is concluded.

(2) A contract concluded between persons who are in different countries is formally valid if it satisfies the formal requirements of the law which governs it under this Convention or of the law of one of those countries.

(3) Where a contract is concluded by an agent, the country in which the agent acts is the relevant country for the purposes of paragraphs 1 and 2.

(4) An act intended to have legal effect relating to an existing or contemplated contract is formally valid if it satisfies the formal requirements of the law which under this Convention governs or would govern the contract or of the law of the country where the act was done.

(5) The provisions of the preceding paragraphs shall not apply to a contract to which Article 5 applies, concluded in the circumstances described in paragraph 2 of Article 5. The formal validity of such a contract is governed by the law of the country in which the consumer has his habitual residence.

(6) Notwithstanding paragraphs 1 to 4 of this article, a contract the subject matter of which is a right in immovable property or a right to use immovable property shall be subject to the mandatory requirements of form of the law of the country where the property is situated if by that law those requirements are imposed irrespective of the country where the contract is concluded and irrespective of the law governing the contract.

Article 10. Scope of the Applicable Law.

(1) The law applicable to a contract by virtue of Articles 3 to 6 and 12 of this Convention shall govern in particular:

(a) interpretation,
(b) performance,
(c) within the limits of the powers conferred on the court by its procedural law, the consequences of breach, including the assessment of damages in so far as it is governed by rules of law,
(d) the various ways of extinguishing obligations, and prescription and limitation of actions,
(e) the consequences of nullity of the contract.

(2) In relation to the manner, of performance and the steps to be taken in the event of defective performance regard shall be had to the law of the country in which performance takes place.

Article 11. Incapacity.

In a contract concluded between persons who are in the same country, a natural person who would have capacity under the law of that country may invoke his incapacity resulting from another law only if the other party to the contract was aware of this incapacity at the time of the conclusion of the contract or was not aware thereof as a result of negligence.

Article 12. Voluntary Assignment.

(1) The mutual obligations of assignor and assignee under a voluntary assignment of a right against another person ('the debtor') shall be governed by the law which under this Convention applies to the contract between the assignor and assignee.

(2) The law governing the right to which the assignment relates shall determine its assignability, the relationship between the assignee and the debtor, the conditions under which the assignment can be invoked against the debtor, and any question whether the debtor's obligations have been discharged.

Article 13. Subrogation.

(1) Where a person ('the creditor') has a contractual claim upon another ('the debtor') and a third person has a duty to satisfy the creditor, or has in fact satisfied the creditor in discharge of that duty, the law which governs the third person's duty to satisfy the creditor shall determine whether the third person is entitled to exercise against the debtor the rights which the creditor had against the debtor under the law governing their relationship and, if so, whether he may do so in full or only to a limited extent.

(2) The same rule applies where several persons are subject to the same contractual claim and one of them has satisfied the creditor.

Article 14. Burden of Proof, Etc.

(1) The law governing the contract under this Convention applies to the extent that it contains, in the law of contract, rules which raise presumptions of law or determine the burden of proof.

(2) A contract or an act intended to have legal effect may be proved by any mode of proof recognised by the law of the forum or by any of the laws referred to in Article 9 under which that contract or act is formally valid, provided that such mode of proof can be administered by the forum.

Article 15. Exclusion of Renvoi.

The application of the law of any country specified by this Convention means the application of the rules of law in force in that country other than its rules of private international law.

Article 16. 'Ordre Public'.

The application of a rule of the law of any country specified by this Convention may be refused only if such application is manifestly incompatible with the public policy (*ordre public*) of the forum.

Article 17. No Retrospective Effect.

This Convention shall apply in a Contracting State to contracts made after the date on which this Convention has entered into force with respect to that State.

Article 18. Uniform Interpretation.

In the interpretation and application of the preceding uniform rules, regard shall be had to their international character and to the desirability of achieving uniformity in their interpretation and application.

Article 19. States with More Than One Legal System.

(1) Where a State comprises several territorial units each of which has its own rules of law in respect of contractual obligations, each territorial unit shall be considered as a country for the purposes of identifying the law applicable under this Convention.

(2) A State within which different territorial units have their own rules of law in respect of contractual obligations shall not be bound to apply this Convention to conflicts solely between the laws of such units.

Article 20. Precedence of Community Law.

This Convention shall not affect the application of provisions which, in relation to particular matters, lay down choice of law rules relating to contractual obligations and which are or will be contained in acts of the institutions of the European Communities or in national laws harmonised in implementation of such acts.

Article 21. Relationship with Other Conventions.

This Convention shall not prejudice the application of international conventions to which a Contracting State is, or becomes, a party.

Article 22. Reservations.

(1) Any Contracting State may, at the time of signature, ratification, acceptance or approval, reserve the right not to apply:

(a) the provisions of Article 7(1);
(b) the provisions of Article 10(1)(e).

(2) Any Contracting State may also, when notifying an extension of the Convention in accordance with Article 27(2), make one or more of these reservations, with its effect limited to all or some of the territories mentioned in the extension.

(3) Any Contracting State may at any time withdraw a reservation which it has made; the reservation shall cease to have effect on the first day of the third calendar month after notification of the withdrawal.

TITLE III. FINAL PROVISIONS

Article 23. [Derogations by Contracting States]

(1) If, after the date on which this Convention has entered into force for a Contracting State, that State wishes to adopt any new choice of law rule in regard to any particular category of contract within the scope of this Convention, it shall communicate its intention to the other signatory States through the Secretary-General of the Council of the European Communities.

(2) Any signatory State may, within six months from the date of the communication made to the Secretary-General, request him to arrange consultations between signatory States in order to reach agreement.

(3) If no signatory State has requested consultations within this period or if within two years following the communication made to the Secretary-General no agreement is reached in the course of consultations, the Contracting State concerned may amend its law in the manner indicated. The measures taken by that State shall be brought to the knowledge of the other signatory States through the Secretary-General of the Council of the European Communities.

Article 24. [Accession to Other Conventions]

(1) If, after the date on which this Convention has entered into force with respect to a Contracting State, that State wishes to become a party to a multilateral convention whose principal aim or one of whose principal aims is to lay down rules of private international law concerning any of the matters governed by this Convention, the procedures set out in Article 23 shall apply. However, the period of two years, referred to in paragraph 3 of that article, shall be reduced to one year.

(2) The procedure referred to in the preceding paragraph need not be followed if a Contracting State or one of the European Communities is already a party to the multilateral convention, or if its object is to revise a convention to which the state concerned is already a party, or if it is a convention concluded within the framework of the Treaties establishing the European Communities.

Article 25. [Consultations on Prejudicial Agreements]

If a Contracting State considers that the unification achieved by this Convention is prejudiced by the conclusion of agreements not covered by Article 24(1), that State may request the Secretary-General of the Council of the European Communities to arrange consultations between the signatory States of this Convention.

Article 26. [Revision of Convention]

Any Contracting State may request a revision of this Convention. In this event, a revision conference shall be convened by the President of the Council of the European Communities.

Article 27. [Territorial Application]

(1) This Convention shall apply to the European territories of the Contracting States, including Greenland, and to the entire territory of the French Republic.

(2) Notwithstanding paragraph 1:

(a) this Convention shall not apply to the Faroe Islands, unless the Kingdom of Denmark makes a declaration to the contrary;

(b) this Convention shall not apply to any European territory situated outside the United Kingdom for the international relations of which the United Kingdom is responsible, unless the United Kingdom makes a declaration to the contrary in respect of any such territory;

(c) this Convention shall apply to the Netherlands Antilles, if the Kingdom of the Netherlands makes a declaration to that effect.

(3) Such declarations may be made at any time by notifying the Secretary-General of the Council of the European Communities.

(4) Proceedings brought in the United Kingdom on appeal from courts in one of the territories referred to in paragraph 2(b) shall be deemed to be proceedings taking place in those courts.

Article 28. [Signature and Ratification]

(1) This Convention shall be open from June 19, 1980, for signature by the States party to the Treaty establishing the European Economic Community.

(2) This Convention shall be subject to ratification, acceptance or approval by the signatory States. The instruments of ratification, acceptance or approval shall be deposited with the Secretary-General of the Council of the European Communities.

Article 29. [Entry into Force]

(1) This Convention shall enter into force on the first day of the third month following the deposit of the seventh instrument of ratification, acceptance or approval.

(2) This Convention shall enter into force for each signatory State ratifying, accepting or approving at a later date on the first day of the third month following the deposit of its instrument of ratification, acceptance or approval.

Article 30. [Duration of Convention]

(1) This Convention shall remain in force for ten years from the date of its entry into force in accordance with Article 29(1), even for States for which it enters into force at a later date.

(2) If there has been no denunciation it shall be renewed tacitly every five years.

(3) A Contracting State which wishes to denounce shall, not less than six months before the expiration of the period of ten or five years, as the case may be, give notice to the Secretary-General of the Council of the European Communities. Denunciation may be limited to any territory to which the Convention has been extended by a declaration under Article 27(2).

(4) The denunciation shall have effect only in relation to the State which has notified it. The Convention will remain in force as between all other Contracting States.

Article 31. [Notification to Signatory States]

The Secretary-General of the Council of the European Communities shall notify the States party to the Treaty establishing the European Economic Community of:

(a) the signatures;

(b) the deposit of each instrument of ratification, acceptance or approval;

(c) the date of entry into force of this Convention;

(d) communications made in pursuance of Articles 23, 24, 25, 26, 27 and 30;

(e) the reservations and withdrawals of reservations referred to in Article 22.

Article 32. [Annexed Protocol]

The Protocol annexed to this Convention shall form an integral part thereof.

Article 33. [Deposit of Convention]

This Convention, drawn up in a single original in the Danish, Dutch, English, French, German, Irish and Italian languages, these texts being equally authentic, shall be deposited in the archives of the Secretariat of the Council of the European Communities. The Secretary-General shall transmit a certified copy thereof to the Government of each signatory State.

In witness whereof the undersigned, being duly authorised thereto, have signed this Convention.

Done at Rome on the nineteenth day of June in the year one thousand nine hundred and eighty.

[Signatures]

PROTOCOL

The High Contracting Parties have agreed upon the following provision which shall be annexed to the Convention:

Notwithstanding the provisions of the Convention, Denmark may retain the rules contained in Soloven (Statute on Maritime Law) paragraph 169 concerning the applicable law in matters relating to carriage of goods by sea and may revise these rules without following the procedure prescribed in Article 23 of the Convention.

[Signatures]

JOINT DECLARATION

At the time of the signature of the Convention on the law applicable to contractual obligations, the Governments of the Kingdom of Belgium, the Kingdom of Denmark, the Federal Republic of Germany, the French Republic, Ireland, the Italian Republic, the Grand Duchy of Luxembourg, the Kingdom of the Netherlands and the United Kingdom of Great Britain and Northern Ireland:

I. anxious to avoid, as far as possible, dispersion of choice of law rules among several instruments and differences between these rules;

— express the wish that the institutions of the European Communities, in the exercise of their powers under the Treaties by which they were established will, where the need arises, endeavour to adopt choice of law rules which are as far as possible consistent with those of this Convention;

II. declare their intention as from the date of signature of this Convention until becoming bound by Article 24, to consult with each other if any one of the signatory States wishes to become a party to any convention to which the procedure referred to in Article 24 would apply;

III. having regard to the contribution of the Convention on the law applicable to contractual obligations to the unification of choice of law rules within the European Communities, express the view that any State which becomes a member of the European Communities should accede to this Convention.

[Signatures]

JOINT DECLARATION

The Governments of the Kingdom of Belgium, the Kingdom of Denmark, the Federal Republic of Germany, the French Republic, Ireland, the Italian Republic, the Grand Duchy of Luxembourg, the Kingdom of the Netherlands, and the United Kingdom of Great Britain and Northern Ireland,

On signing the Convention on the law applicable to contractual obligations;

Desiring to ensure that the Convention is applied as effectively as possible;

Anxious to prevent differences of interpretation of the Convention from impairing its unifying effect;

Declare themselves ready:

1. to examine the possibility of conferring jurisdiction in certain matters on the Court of Justice of the European Communities and, if necessary, to negotiate an agreement to this effect;

2. to arrange meetings at regular intervals between their representatives.

[Signatures]

Council Regulation (EEC) No. 2423/88

of 11 July 1988
on protection against dumped or subsidised imports from countries not members of the
European Economic Community
(OJ 1988 L 209/1)

The Council of the European Communities

Having regard to the Treaty establishing the Euopean Economic Community, and in particular Article 113 thereof,

Having regard to the Regulations establishing the common organisation of agricultural markets and the Regulations adopted under Article 235 of the Treaty applicable to goods manufactured from agricultural products, and in particular the provisions of those Regulations which allow for derogation from the general principle that protective measures at frontiers may be replaced solely by the measures provided for in those Regulations,

Having regard to the proposal from the Commission.

Whereas by Regulation (EEC) No. 2176/84*, as amended by Regulation (EEC) No. 1761/87**, the Council adopted common rules for protection against dumped or subsidised imports from countries which are not members of the European Economic Community;

Whereas these rules were adopted in accordance with existing international obligations, in particular those arising from Article VI of the General Agreement on Tariffs and Trade (hereinafter referred to as 'GATT'), from the Agreement on implementation of Article VI of the GATT (1979 Anit-Dumping Code) and from the Agreement on Interpretation and Application of Articles VI, XVI and XXIII of the GATT (Code on Subsidies and Countervailing Duties);

Whereas in applying these rules it is essential, in order to maintain the balance of rights and obligations which these Agreements sought to establish, that the Community take account of their interpretation by the Community's major trading partners, as reflected in legislation or established practice;

Whereas it is desirable that the rules for determining normal value should be presented clearly and in sufficient detail; whereas it should be specifically provided that where sales on the domestic market of the country of export or origin do not for any reason form a proper basis for determining the existence of dumping, recourse may be had to a constructed normal value; whereas it is appropriate to give examples of situations which may be considered as not representing the ordinary course of trade, in particular where a product is sold at prices which are less than the cost of production, or where transactions take place between parties which are associated or which have a compensatory arrangement; whereas it is appropriate to list the possible methods of determining normal value in such circumstances;

Whereas it is expedient to define the export price and to enumerate the necessary adjustments to be made in those cases where reconstruction of this price from the first open-market price is deemed appropriate;

Whereas, for the purpose of ensuring a fair comparison between export price and normal value, it is advisable to establish guidelines for determining the adjustments to be made in respect of differences in physical characteristics, in quantities, in conditions and terms of sale and to draw attention to the fact that the burden of proof falls on any person claiming such adjustments;

* OJ No. L 201, 30.7.1984, p.1.
** OJ No. L 167, 26.6.1987, p.9.

Whereas the term 'dumping margin' should be clearly defined and the Community's established practice for methods of calculation, where prices or margins vary, codified;

Whereas it seems advisable to lay down, in adequate detail, the manner in which the amount of any subsidy is to be determined;

Whereas it seems appropriate to set out certain factors which may be relevant for the determination of injury;

Whereas it is necessary to lay down the procedures for anyone acting on behalf of a Community industry which considers itself injured or threatened by dumped or subsidised imports to lodge a complaint; whereas it seems appropriate to make it clear that in the case of withdrawal of a complaint, proceedings may, but need not necessarily, be terminated;

Whereas there should be co-operation between the member states and the Commission, both as regards information about the existence of dumping or subsidisation and injury resulting therefrom, and as regards the subsequent examination of the matter at Community level; whereas, to this end, consultations should take place within an advisory committee;

Whereas it is appropriate to lay down clearly the rules of procedure to be followed during the investigation, in particular the rights and obligations of the Community authorities and the parties involved, and the conditions under which interested parties may have access to information and may ask to be informed of the essential facts and considerations on the basis of which it is intended to recommend definitive measures;

Whereas it is desirable to state explicitly that the investigation of dumping or subsidisation should normally cover a period of not less than six months immediately prior to the initiation of the proceeding and that final determinations must be based on the facts established in respect of the investigation period.

Whereas to avoid confusion, the use of the terms 'investigations' and 'proceeding' in this Regulation should be clarified;

Whereas it is necessary to require that when information is to be considered as being confidential, a request to this effect must be made by the supplier, and to make clear that confidential information which could be summarised but of which no non-confidential summary has been submitted may be disregarded.

Whereas, in order to avoid undue delays and for administrative convenience, it is advisable to introduce time limits within which undertakings may be offered;

Whereas it is necessary to lay down more explicit rules concerning the procedure to be followed after withdrawal or termination of undertakings;

Whereas it is necessary that the Community's decision-making process permit rapid and efficient action, in particular through measures taken by the Commission, as for instance the imposition of provisional duties;

Whereas, in order to discourage dumping, it is appropriate to provide, in cases where the facts as finally established show that there is dumping and injury, for the possibility of definitive collection of provisional duties even if the imposition of a definitve anti-dumping duty is not decided on, on particular grounds;

Whereas it is essential, in order to ensure that anti-dumping and countervailing duties are levied in a correct and uniform manner, that common rules for the application of such duties be laid down; whereas, by reason of the nature of the said duties, such rules may differ from the rules for the levying of normal import duties;

Whereas experience gained from the implementation of Regulation (EEC) No. 2176/84 has shown that assembly in the Community of products whose importation in a finished state is subject to anti-dumping duty may give rise to certain difficulties;

Whereas in particular:

— where assembly or production is carried out by a party which is related or associated to any of the manufacturers whose exports of the like product are subject to an anti-dumping duty, and
— where the value of the parts or materials used in the assembly or production operation and originating in the country of origin of the product subject to an anti-dumping duty exceeds the value of all other parts or materials used,

such assembly or production is considered likely to lead to circumvention of the anti-dumping duty;

Whereas, in order to prevent circumvention, it is necessary to provide for the collection of an anti-dumping duty on products thus assembled or produced;

Whereas it is necessary to lay down the procedures and conditions for the collection of duty in such circumstances;

Whereas the amount of anti-dumping duty collected should be limited to that necessary to prevent circumvention;

Whereas provision should be made for the review of regulations and decisions to be carried out, where appropriate, in part only;

Whereas, in order to avoid abuse of Community procedures and resources, it is appropriate to lay down a minimum period which must elapse after the conclusion of a proceeding before such a review may be conducted, and to ensure that there is evidence of a change in circumstances sufficient to justify a review;

Whereas it is necessary to provide that, after a certain period of time, anti-dumping and countervailing measures will lapse unless the need for their continued existence can be shown;

Whereas appropriate procedures should be established for examining applications for refunds of anti-dumping duties; whereas there is a need to ensure that refund procedures apply only in respect of definitive duties or amounts of any provisional duty which have been definitively collected, and to streamline the existing procedures for refunds;

Whereas this Regulation should not prevent the adoption of special measures where this does not run counter to the Community's obligations under the GATT;

Whereas agricultural products and products derived therefrom might also be dumped or subsidised; whereas it is, therefore, necessary to supplement the import rules generally applicable to these products by making provision for protective measures against such practices;

Whereas, in addition to the above considerations, which, in essence, led to the adoption of Regulation (EEC) No. 2176/84, experience has shown that it is necessary to define more precisely certain of the rules to be applied and the procedures to be followed in the context of anti-dumping proceedings;

Whereas, for the determination of normal value, it is appropriate to ensure that when this is based on domestic prices, the price should be that actually paid or payable in the ordinary course of trade in the exporting country or country of origin and, therefore, the treatment of discounts and rebates should be clarified, in particular, with regard to deferred discounts which may be recognised if evidence is produced that they were not

introduced to distort the normal value. It is also desirable to state more explicitly how normal value is established on the basis of constructed value, in particular, that the selling, general and administrative expenses and profit should be calculated, depending on the circumstances, by reference to the expenses incurred and the profit realised on profitable sales made by the exporter concerned or by other producers or exporters or on any reasonable basis. In addition, it is appropriate to state that, where the exporter neither produces nor sells the like product in the country or origin, the normal value shall normally be established by reference to the prices or costs of the exporter's supplier. Finally, it is considered necessary to define more precisely the conditions under which sales at a loss may be considered as not having been made in the ordinary course of trade;

Whereas, for the determination of export prices, it is advisable to ensure that this is based on the price actually paid or payable and, therefore, the treatment of discounts and rebates should be clarified. In cases where the export price has to be reconstructed, it is necessary to state that the costs to be used in this reconstruction include those normally borne by an importer but paid by any party which appears to be associated with the importer or exporter;

Whereas, for the comparison of normal value and export prices, it is necessary to ensure that this is not distorted by claims for adjustments relating to factors which are not directly related to the sales under consideration or by claims for factors already taken into account. It is therefore appropriate to define precisely the differences which affect price comparability and to lay down more explicit rules on how any adjustment should be made, in particular, for differences in physical characteristics, transport, packing, credit, warranties and other selling expenses. With regard to such selling expenses, it is appropriate, for reasons of clarity, to specify that no allowance should be made for general selling expenses since such expenses are not directly related to the sales under consideration with the exception of salesmen's salaries which should not be treated differently to commissions paid. For reasons of administrative convenience, it is also appropriate to specify that claims for individual adjustments which are insignificant should be disregarded;

Whereas, it is expedient to clarify Community practice with regard to the use of averaging and sampling techniques;

Whereas, in order to avoid undue disruption to proceedings, it is advisable to clarify that the supply of false or misleading information may lead to such information being disregarded and any claims to which it refers being disallowed;

Whereas experience has shown that it is necessary to prevent the effectiveness of anti-dumping duties being eroded by the duty being borne by exporters. It is appropriate to confirm that, in such circumstances, additional anti-dumping duties may be imposed, where necessary retroactively;

Whereas, experience has also shown that the rules relating to the expiry of anti-dumping and countervailing measures should be clarified. For this purpose and in order to facilitate the administration of these rules, provision should be made for the publication of a notice of intention to carry out a review;

Whereas, it is appropriate to state more explicitly the methods to be used in the calculation of the amount to any refund, thus confirming the consistent practice of the Commission, as regards refunds and the relevant principles countained in the notice which the Commission has published concerning the reimbursement of anti-dumping duties*;

* OJ No. C 266, 22.10.1986, p.2.

Whereas, it is appropriate to take advantage of this opportunity to proceed to a consolidation of the provisions in question,

Has adopted this Regulation

Article 1
APPLICABILITY

This Regulation lays down provisions for protection against dumped or subsidised imports from countries not members of the European Economic Community.

Article 2
DUMPING

A. Principle

1. An anti-dumping duty may be applied to any dumped product whose release for free circulation in the Community causes injury.

2. A product shall be considered to have been dumped if its export price to the Community is less than the normal value of the like product.

B. Normal Value

3. For the purposes of this Regulation, the normal value shall be:

(a) the comparable price actually paid or payable in the ordinary course of trade for the like product intended for consumption in the exporting country or country of origin. This price shall be net of all discounts and rebates directly linked to the sales under consideration provided that the exporter claims and supplies sufficient evidence that any such reduction from the gross price has actually been granted. Deferred discounts may be recognised if they are directly linked to the sales under consideration and if evidence is produced to show that these discounts were based on consistent practice in prior periods or on an undertaking to comply with the conditions required to qualify for the deferred discount.

(b) when there are no sales of the like product in the ordinary course of trade on the domestic market of the exporting country or country of origin, or when such sales do not permit a proper comparison:

(i) the comparable price of the like product when exported to any third country, which may be the highest such export price but should be a representative price; or

(ii) the constructed value, determined by adding cost of production and a reasonable margin of profit. The cost of production shall be computed on the basis of all costs, in the ordinary course of trade, both fixed and variable, in the country of origin, of materials and manufacture, plus a reasonable amount for selling, administrative and other general expenses. The amount for selling, general and administrative expenses and profit shall be calculated by reference to the expenses incurred and the profit realised by the producer or exporter on the profitable sales of like products on the domestic market. If such data is unavailable or unreliable or is not suitable for use they shall be calculated by reference to the expenses incurred and the profit realised by other producers or exporters in the country of origin or export on profitable sales of the like product. If neither of these two methods can be applied the expenses incurred and the profit realised shall be calculated by reference to the sales made by the exporter or other producers or exporters in the same business sector in the country of origin or export or on any other reasonable basis.

(c) Where the exporter in the country of origin neither produces nor sells the like product in the country of origin, the normal value shall be established on the basis of prices or costs of other sellers or producers in the country of origin in the same manner as mentioned in subparagraphs (a) and (b). Normally the prices or costs of the exporter's supplier shall be used for this purpose.

4. Whenever there are reasonable grounds for believing or suspecting that the price at which a product is actually sold for consumption in the country of origin is less than the cost of production as defined in paragraph 3(b)(ii), sales at such prices may be considered as not having been made in the ordinary course of trade if they:

(a) have been made in substantial quantities during the investigation period as defined in Article 7(1)(c), and

(b) are not at prices which permit recovery, in the normal course of trade and within the period referred to in paragraph (a), of all costs reasonably allocated.

In such circumstances, the normal value may be determined on the basis of the remaining sales on the domestic market made at a price which is not less than the cost of production or on the basis of export sales to third countries or on the basis of the constructed value or by adjusting the sub-production-cost price referred to above in order to eliminate loss and provide for a reasonable profit. Such normal value calculations shall be based on available information.

5. In the case of imports from non-market economy countries and, in particular, those to which Regulations (EEC) No. 1765/82* and (EEC) No. 1766/82** apply, normal value shall be determined in an appropriate and not unreasonable manner on the basis of one of the following criteria:

(a) the price at which the like product of a market economy third country is actually sold:

(i) for consumption on the domestic market of that country; or
(ii) to other countries, including the Community;

or
(b) the constructed value of the like product in a market economy third country;

(c) if neither price nor constructed value as established under (a) and (b) provides an adequate basis, the price actually paid or payable in the Community for the like product, duly adjusted, if necessary, to include a reasonable profit margin.

6. Where a product is not imported directly from the country of origin but is exported to the Community from an intermediate country, the normal value shall be the comparable price actually paid or payable for the like product on the domestic market of either the country of export or the country of origin. The latter basis might be appropriate *inter alia*, where the product is merely transhipped through the country of export, where such products

---

* OJ No. L 195, 5.7.1982, p.1.
** OJ No. L 195, 5.7.1982, p.23.

are not produced in the country of export or where no comparable price for it exists in the country of export.

7. For the purpose of determining normal value transactions between parties which appear to be associated or to have a compensatory arrangement with each other may be considered as not being in the ordinary course of trade unless the Community authorities are satisfied that the prices and costs involved are comparable to those involved in transactions between parties which have no such link.

C. Export Price

8.(a) The export price shall be the price actually paid or payable for the product sold for export to the Community net of all taxes, discounts and rebates, actually granted and directly related to the sales under consideration. Deferred discounts shall also be taken into consideration if they are actually granted and directly related to the sales under consideration.

(b) In cases where there is no export price or where it appears that there is an association or a compensatory arrangement between the exporter and the importer or a third party, or that for other reasons the price actually paid or payable for the product sold for export to the Community is unreliable, the export price may be constructed on the basis of the price at which the imported product is first resold to an independent buyer, or if the product is not resold to an independent buyer, or not resold in the condition imported, on any reasonable basis. In such cases, allowance shall be made for all costs incurred between importation and resale and for a reasonable profit margin. These costs shall include those normally borne by an importer but paid by any party either in or outside the Community which appears to be associated or to have a compensatory arrangement with the importer or exporter.

Such allowances shall include, in particular, the following:

(i) usual transport, insurance, handling, loading and ancillary costs;

(ii) customs duties, any anti-dumping duties and other taxes payable in the importing country by reason of the importation or sale of the goods;

(iii) a reasonable margin for overheads and profit and/or any commission usually paid or agreed.

D. Comparison

9(a) The normal value, as established under paragraphs 3 to 7, and the export price, as established under paragraph 8, shall be compared as nearly as possible at the same time. For the purpose of ensuring a fair comparison, due allowance in the form of adjustments shall be made in each case, on its merits, for the differences affecting price comparability, i.e. for differences in:

(i) physical characteristics;
(ii) import charges and indirect taxes;
(iii) selling expenses resulting from sales made:

— at different levels of trade, or
— in different quantities, or
— under different conditions and terms of sale.

(b) Where an interested party claims an adjustment it must prove that its claim is justified.

10. Any adjustments to take account of the differences affecting price comparability listed in paragraph 9(a) shall, where warranted, be made pursuant to the rules specified below.

(a) Physical characteristics:
The normal value as established under paragraphs 3 to 7 shall be adjusted by an amount corresponding to a reasonable estimate of the value of the difference in the physical characteristics of the product concerned.

(b) Import charges and indirect taxes:
Normal value shall be reduced by an amount corresponding to any import charges or indirect taxes, as defined in the notes to the Annex, borne by the like product and by materials physically incorporated therein, when destined for consumption in the country of origin or export and not collected or refunded in respect of the product exported to the Community.

(c) Selling expenses (i.e.):
(i) Transport, insurance, handling, loading and ancillary costs:
Normal value shall be reduced by the directly related costs incurred for conveying the product concerned from the premises of the exporter to the first independent buyer. The export price shall be reduced by any directly related costs incurred by the exporter for conveying the product concerned from its premises in the exporting country to its destination in the Community. In both cases these costs comprise transport, insurance, handling, loading and ancillary costs.

(ii) Packing:
Normal value and export price shall be reduced by the respective, directly related costs of the packing for the product concerned.

(iii) Credit:
Normal value and export price shall be reduced by the cost of any credit granted for the sales under consideration.

The amount of the reduction shall be calculated by reference to the normal commercial credit rate applicable in the country of origin or export in respect of the currency expressed on the invoice.

(iv) Warranties, guarantees, technical assistance and other after-sales services:
Normal value and export price shall be reduced by an amount corresponding to the direct costs of providing warranties, guarantees, technical assistance and services.

(v) Other selling expenses:
Normal value and export price shall be reduced by an amount corresponding to the commissions paid in respect of the sales under consideration. The salaries paid to salesmen, i.e. personnel wholly engaged in direct selling activities, shall also be deducted.

(d) Amount of the adjustment
The amount of any adjustment shall be calculated on the basis of relevant data for the investigation period or the data for the last available financial year.

(e) Insignificant adjustments:
Claims for adjustments which are insignificant in relation to the price or value of the affected transactions shall be disregarded. Ordinarily, individual adjustments having an *ad valorem* effect of less than 0.5% of that price or value shall be considered insignificant.

E. Allocation of Costs

11. In general, all cost calculations shall be based on available accounting data, normally allocated, where necessary, in

proportion to the turnover for each product and market under consideration.

F. Like Product

12. For the purposes of this Regulation, 'like product' means a product which is identical, i.e. alike in all respects, to the product under consideration, or, in the absence of such a product, another product which has characteristics closely resembling those of the product under consideration.

G. Averaging and Sampling Techniques

13. Where prices vary:

— normal value shall normally be established on a weighted average basis,
— export prices shall normally be compared with the normal value on a transaction by transaction basis except where the use of weighted averages would not materially affect the results of the investigation.
— sampling techniques, e.g. the use of the most frequently occurring or representative prices may be applied to establish normal value and export prices in cases in which a significant volume of transactions is involved.

H. Dumping Margin

14.(a) 'Dumping margin' means the amount by which the normal value exceeds the export price.

(b) Where dumping margins vary, weighted averages may be established.

Article 3
SUBSIDIES

1. A countervailing duty may be imposed for the purpose of offsetting any subsidy bestowed, directly or indirectly, in the country of origin or export, upon the manufacture, production, export or transport of any product whose release for free circulation in the Community causes injury.

2. Subsidies bestowed on exports include, but are not limited to, the practices listed in the Annex.

3. The exemption of a product from import charges or indirect taxes, as defined in the notes to the Annex, effectively borne by the like product and by materials physically incorporated therein, when destined for consumption in the country of origin or export, or the refund of such charges or taxes, shall not be considered as a subsidty for the purposes of this Regulation.

4.(a) The amount of the subsidy shall be determined per unit of the subsidised product exported to the Community.

(b) In establishing the amount of any subsidy the following elements shall be deducted from the total subsidy:

(i) any application fee, or other costs necessarily incurred in order to qualify for, or receive benefit of, the subsidy;

(ii) export taxes, duties or other charges levied on the export of the product to the Community specifically intended to offset the subsidy.

Where an interested party claims a deduction, it must prove that the claim is justified.

(c) Where the subsidy is not granted by reference to the quantities manufactured, produced, exported or transported, the amount shall be determined by allocating the value of the subsidy, as appropriate, over the level of production or exports of the products concerned during a suitable period. Normally this period shall be the accounting year of the beneficiary.

Where the subsidy is based upon the acquisition or future acquisition of fixed assets, the value of the subsidy shall be calculated by spreading the subsidy across a period which reflects the normal depreciation of such assets in the industry concerned. Where the assets are non-depreciating, the subsidy shall be valued as an interest-free loan.

(d) In the case of imports from non-market economy countries and in particular those to which Regulations (EEC) No. 1765/82 and (EEC) No. 1766/82 apply, the amount of any subsidy may be determined in an appropriate and not unreasonable manner, by comparing the export price as calculated in accordance with Article 2(8) with the normal value as determined in accordance with Article 2(5). Article 2(10) shall apply to such a comparison.

(e) Where the amount of subsidisation varies, weighted averages may be established.

Article 4
INJURY

1. A determination of injury shall be made only if the dumped or subsidised imports are, through the effects of dumping or subsidisation, causing injury i.e. causing or threatening to cause material injury to an established Community industry or materially retarding the establishment of such an industry. Injuries caused by other factors, such as volume and prices of imports which are not dumped or subsidised, or contraction in demand, which, individually or in combination, also adversely affect the Community industry must not be attributed to the dumped or subsidised imports.

2. An examination of injury shall involve the following factors, no one or several of which can necessarily give decisive guidance:

(a) volume of dumped or subsidised imports, in particular whether there has been a significant increase, either in absolute terms or relative to production or consumption in the Community;

(b) the prices of dumped or subsidised imports, in particular whether there has been a significant price undercutting as compared with the price of a like product in the Community;

(c) the consequent impact on the industry concerned as indicated by actual or potential trends in the relevant economic factors such as:

— production,
— utilisation of capacity,
— stocks,
— sales,
— market share,
— prices (i.e. depression of prices or prevention of price increases which otherwise would have occurred),
— profits,
— return on investment,
— cash flow,
— employment.

3. A determination of threat of injury may only be made where a particular situation is likely to develop into actual injury. In this regard account may be taken of factors such as:

(a) rate of increase of the dumped or subsidised exports to the Community;

(b) export capacity in the country of origin or export, already in existence or which will be operational in the foreseeable future, and the likelihood that the resulting exports will be to the Community;

(c) the nature of any subsidy and the trade effects likely to arise therefrom.

4. The effect of the dumped or subsidised imports shall be assessed in relation to the Community production of the like product when available data permit its separate identification. When the Community production of the like product has no separate identity, the effect of the dumped or subsidised imports shall be assessed in relation to the production of the narrowest group or range of production which includes the like product for which the necessary information can be found.

5. The term 'Community industry' shall be interpreted as referring to the Community producers as a whole of the like product or to those of them whose collective output of the products constitutes a major proportion of the total Community production of those products except that:

— when producers are related to the exporters or importers or are themselves importers of the allegedly dumped or subsidised product the term 'Community industry' may be interpreted as referring to the rest of the producers;
— in exceptional circumstances the Community may, for the production in question, be divided into two or more competitive markets and the producers within each market regarded as a Community industry if,

(a) the producers within such market sell all or almost all their production of the product in question in that market, and

(b) the demand in that market is not to any substantial degree supplied by producers of the product in question located elsewhere in the Community.

In such circumstances injury may be found to exist even where a major proportion of the total Community industry is not injured, provided there is a concentration of dumped or subsidised imports into such an isolated market and provided further that the dumped or subsidised imports are causing injury to the producers of all or almost all of the production within such market.

Article 5
COMPLAINT

1. Any natural or legal person, or any association not having legal personality, acting on behalf of a Community industry which considers itself injured or threatened by dumped or subsidised imports may lodge a written complaint.

2. The complaint shall contain sufficient evidence of the existence of dumping or subsidisation and the injury resulting therefrom.

3. The complaint may be submitted to the Commission, or a member state, which shall forward it to the Commission. The Commission shall send member states a copy of any complaint it receives.

4. The complaint may be withdrawn, in which case proceedings may be terminated unless such termination would not be in the interest of the Community.

5. Where it becomes apparent after consultation that the complaint does not provide sufficient evidence to justify initiating an investigation, then the complainant shall be so informed.

6. Where, in the absence of any complaint, a member state is in possession of sufficient evidence both of dumping or subsidisation and of injury resulting therefrom for a Community industry, it shall immediately communicate such evidence to the Commission.

Article 6
CONSULTATIONS

1. Any consultations provided for in this Regulation shall take place within an Advisory Committee, which shall consist of representatives of each member state, with a representative of the Commission as chairman. Consultations shall be held immediately on request by a member state or on the initiative of the Commission.

2. The Committee shall meet when convened by its chairman. He shall provide the member states, as promptly as possible, with all relevant information.

3. Where necessary, consultation may be in writing only; in such case the Commission shall notify the member states and shall specify a period within which they shall be entitled to express their opinions or to request an oral consultation.

4. Consultation shall in particular cover:

(a) the existence of dumping or of a subsidy and the methods of establishing the dumping margin or the amount of the subsidy;

(b) the existence and extent of injury;

(c) the causal link between the dumped or subsidised imports and injury;

(d) the measures which, in the circumstances, are appropriate to prevent or remedy the injury caused by dumping or the subsidy and the ways and means for putting such measures into effect.

Article 7
INITIATION AND SUBSEQUENT INVESTIGATION

1. Where, after consultation it is apparent that there is sufficient evidence to justify initiating a proceeding the Commission shall immediately:

(a) announce the initiation of a proceeding in the *Official Journal of the European Communities*; such announcements shall indicate the product and countries concerned, give a summary of the information received, and provide that all relevant information is to be communicated to the Commission; it shall state the period within which interested parties may make known their views in writing and may apply to be heard orally by the Commission in accordance with paragraph 5;

(b) so advise the exporters and importers known to the Commission to be concerned as well as representatives of the exporting country and the complainants;

(c) commence the investigation at Community level, acting in co-operation with the member states; such investigations shall cover both dumping or subsidisation and injury resulting therefrom and shall be carried out in accordance with paragraphs 2 to 8; the investigation of dumping or subsidisation shall normally cover a period of not less than six months immediately prior to the initiation of the proceeding.

2.(a) The Commission shall seek all information it deems to be necessary and, where it considers it appropriate, examine and verify the records of importers, exporters, traders, agents, producers, trade associations and organisations.

(b) Where necessary the Commission shall carry out investigations in third countries, provided that the firms concerned give their consent and the government of the country in question has been officially notified and raises no objection. The Commission shall be assisted by officials of those member states who so request.

3.(a) The Commission may request member states:

— to supply information,
— to carry out all necessary checks and inspections, particularly amongst importers, traders and Community producers,
— to carry out investigations in third countries, provided the firms concerned give their consent and the government of the country in question has been officially notified and raises no objection.

(b) Member states shall take whatever steps are necessary in order to give effect to requests from the Commission. They shall send to the Commission the information requested together with the results of all inspections, checks or investigations carried out.

(c) Where this information is of general interest or where its transmission has been requested by a member state, the Commission shall forward it to the member states, provided it is not confidential in which case a non-confidential summary shall be forwarded.

(d) Officials of the Commission shall be authorised, if the Commission or a member state so requests, to assist the officials of member states in carrying out their duties.

4.(a) The complainant and the importers and exporters known to be concerned; as well as the representatives of the exporting country, may inspect all information made available to the Commission by any party to any investigation as distinct from internal documents prepared by the authorities of the Community or its member states, provided that it is relevant to the defence of their interests and not confidential within the meaning of Article 8 and that it is used by the Commission in the investigation. To this end, they shall address a written request to the Commission indicating the information required.

(b) Exporters and importers of the product subject to investigation and, in the case of subsidisation, the representatives of the country of origin, may request to be informed of the essential facts and considerations on the basis of which it is intended to recommend the imposition of definitive duties or the definitive collection of amounts secured by way of a provisional duty.

(c)(i) requests for information pursuant to (b) shall:

(aa) be addressed to the Commission in writing.

(bb) specify the particular issues on which information is sought,

(cc) be received, in cases where a provisional duty has been applied, not later than one month after publication of the imposition of that duty;

(ii) the information may be given either orally or in writing as considered appropriate by the Commission. It shall not prejudice any subsequent decision which may be taken by the Commission or the Council. Confidential information shall be treated in accordance with Article 8;

(iii) information shall normally be given no later than 15 days prior to the submission by the Commission of any proposal for final action pursuant to Article 12. Representations made after the information is given shall be taken into consideration only if received within a period to be set by the Commission in each case, which shall be at least 10 days, due consideration being given to the urgency of the matter.

5. The Commission may hear the interested parties. It shall so hear them if they have, within the period prescribed in the notice published in the *Official Journal of the European Communities*, made a written request for a hearing showing that they are an interested party likely to be affected by the result of the proceeding and that there are particular reasons why they should be heard orally.

6. Furthermore the Commission shall, on request, give the parties directly concerned an opportunity to meet, so that opposing views may be presented and any rebuttal argument put forward. In providing this opportunity the Commission shall take account of the need to preserve confidentiality and of the convenience of the parties. There shall be no obligation on any party to attend a meeting and failure to do so shall not be prejudicial to that party's case.

7.(a) This Article shall not preclude the Community authorities from reaching preliminary determinations or from applying provisional measures expeditiously.

(b) In cases in which any interested party or third country refuses access to, or otherwise does not provide, necessary information within a reasonable period, or significantly impedes the investigation, preliminary or final findings, affirmative or negative, may be made on the basis of the facts available. Where the Commission finds that any interested party or third country has supplied it with false or misleading information, it may disregard any such information and disallow any claim to which this refers.

8. Anti-dumping or countervailing proceedings shall not constitute a bar to customs clearance of the product concerned.

9.(a) An investigation shall be concluded either by its termination or by definitive action. Conclusion should normally take place within one year of the initiation of the proceeding.

(b) A proceeding shall be concluded either by the termination of the investigation without the imposition of duties and without the acceptance of undertakings or by the expiry or repeal of such duties or by the termination of undertakings in accordance with Articles 14 or 15.

Article 8
CONFIDENTIALITY

1. Information received pursuant to this Regulation shall be used only for the purpose for which it was requested.

2.(a) Neither the Council, nor the Commission, nor member states, nor the officials of any of these, shall reveal any information received pursuant to this Regulation for which confidential treatment has been requested by its supplier, without specific permission from the supplier.

(b) Each request for confidential treatment shall indicate why the information is confidential and shall be accompanied by a non-confidential summary of the information, or a statement of the reasons why the information is not susceptible of such summary.

3. Information will ordinarily be considered to be confidential if its disclosure is likely to have a significantly adverse effect upon the supplier or the source of such information.

4. However, if it appears that a request for confidentiality is not warranted and if the supplier is either unwilling to make the information public or to authorise its disclosure in generalised or summary form, the information in question may be disregarded.

The information may also be disregarded where such request is warranted and where the supplier is unwilling to submit a non-confidential summary, provided that the information is susceptible of such summary.

5. This Article shall not preclude the disclosure of general information by the Community authorities and in particular of the reasons on which decisions taken pursuant to this Regulation are based, or disclosure of the evidence relied on by the Community authorities in so far as necessary to explain those reasons in court proceedings. Such disclosure must take into account the legitimate interest of the parties concerned that their business secrets should not be divulged.

Article 9
TERMINATION OF PROCEEDINGS WHERE PROTECTIVE MEASURES ARE UNNECESSARY

1. If it becomes apparent after consultation that protective measures are unnecessary, then, where no objection is raised within the Advisory Committee referred to in Article 6(1), the proceeding shall be terminated. In all other cases the Commission shall submit to the Council forthwith a report on the results of the consultation, together with a proposal that the proceeding be terminated. The proceeding shall stand terminated if, within one month, the Council, acting by a qualified majority, has not decided otherwise.

2. The Commission shall inform any representatives of the country of origin or export and the parties known to be concerned and shall announce the termination in the *Official Journal of the European Communities*, setting forth its basic conclusions and a summary of the reasons therefor.

Article 10
UNDERTAKINGS

1. Where, during the course of an investigation, undertakings are offered which the Commission, after consultation, considers acceptable, the investigation may be terminated without the imposition of provisional or definitive duties.

Save in exceptional circumstances, undertakings may not be offered later than the end of the period during which representations may be made under Article 7(4)(c)(iii). The termination shall be decided in conformity with the procedure laid down in Article 9(1) and information shall be given and notice published in accordance with Article 9(2). Such termination does not preclude the definitive collection of amounts secured by way of provisional duties pursuant to Article 12(2).

2. The undertakings referred to under paragraph 1 are those under which:

(a) the subsidy is eliminated or limited, or other measures concerning its injurious effects taken, by the government of the country of origin or export; or

(b) prices are revised or exports cease to the extent that the Commission is satisfied that either the dumping margin or the amount of the subsidy, or the injurious effects thereof, are eliminated. In case of subsidisation the consent of the country of origin or export shall be obtained.

3. Undertakings may be suggested by the Commission, but the fact that such undertakings are not offered or an invitation to do so is not accepted, shall not prejudice consideration of the case. However, the continuation of dumped or subsidised imports may be taken as evidence that a threat of injury is more likely to be realised.

4. If the undertakings are accepted, the investigation of injury shall nevertheless be completed if the Commission, after consultation, so decides or if request is made, in the case of dumping, by exporters representing a significant percentage of the trade involved or, in the case of subsidisation, by the country of origin or export. In such a case, if the Commission, after consultation, makes a determination of no injury, the undertaking shall automatically lapse. However, where a determination of no threat of injury is due mainly to the existence of an undertaking, the Commission may require that the undertaking be maintained.

5. The Commission may require any party from whom an undertaking has been accepted to provide periodically information relevant to the fulfilment of such undertakings, and to permit verification of pertinent data. Non-compliance with such requirements shall be construed as a violation of the undertaking.

6. Where an undertaking has been withdrawn or where the Commission has reason to believe that it has been violated and where Community interests call for such intervention, it may, after consultations and after having offered the exporter concerned an opportunity to comment, apply provisional anti-dumping or countervailing duties forthwith on the basis of the facts established before the acceptance of the undertaking.

Article 11
PROVISIONAL DUTIES

1. Where preliminary examination shows that dumping or a subsidy exists and that there is sufficient evidence of injury caused thereby and the interests of the Community call for intervention to prevent injury being caused during the proceeding, the Commission, acting at the request of a member state or on its own initiative, shall impose a provisional anti-dumping or countervailing duty. In such cases, release of the products concerned for free circulation in the Community shall be conditional upon the provision of security for the amount of the provisional duty, definitive collection of which shall be determined by the subsequent decision of the Council under Article 12(2).

2. The Commission shall take such provisional action after consultation or, in cases of extreme urgency, after informing the member states. In this latter case, consultations shall take place 10 days at the latest after notification to the member states of the action taken by the Commission.

3. Where a member state requests immediate intervention by the Commission, the Commission shall within a maximum of five working days of receipt of the request, decide whether a provisional anti-dumping or countervailing duty should be imposed.

4. The Commission shall forthwith inform the Council and the member states of any decision taken under this Article. The Council, acting by a qualified majority, may decide differently. A decision by the Commission not to impose a provisional duty shall not preclude the imposition of such duty at a later date, either at the request of a member state, if new factors arise, or on the initiative of the Commission.

5. Provisional duties shall have a maximum period of validity of four months. However, where exporters representing a significant percentage of the trade involved so request or, pursuant to a notice of intention from the Commission, do not object, provisional anti-dumping duties may be extended for a further period of two months.

6. Any proposal for definitive action, or for extension of provisional measures, shall be submitted to the Council by the Commission not later than one month before expiry of the period of validity of provisional duties. The Council shall act by a qualified majority.

7. After expiration of the period of validity of provisional duties, the security shall be released as promptly as possible to the extent that the Council has not decided to collect it definitively.

Article 12
DEFINITIVE ACTION

1. Where the facts as finally established show that there is dumping or subsidisation during the period under investigation and injury caused thereby, and the interests of the Community call for Community intervention, a definitive anti-dumping or countervailing duty shall be imposed by the Council, acting by qualified majority on a proposal submitted by the Commission after consultation.

2.(a) Where a provisional duty has been applied, the Council shall decide, irrespective of whether a definitive anti-dumping or countervailing duty is to be imposed, what proportion of the provisional duty is to be definitively collected. The Council shall act by a qualified majority on a proposal from the Commission.

(b) The definitive collection of such amount shall not be decided upon unless the facts as finally established show that there has been dumping or subsidisation, and injury. For this purpose, 'injury' shall not include material retardation of the establishment of a Community industry, nor threat of material injury, except where it is found that this would, in the absence of provisional measures, have developed into material injury.

Article 13
GENERAL PROVISIONS ON DUTIES

1. Anti-dumping or countervailing duties, whether provisional or definitive, shall be imposed by Regulation.

2. Such Regulation shall indicate in particular the amount and type of duty imposed, the product covered, the country of origin or export, the name of the supplier, if practicable, and the reasons on which the Regulation is based.

3. The amount of such duties shall not exceed the dumping margin provisionally estimated or finally established or the amount of the subsidy provisionally estimated or finally established; it should be less if such lesser duty would be adequate to remove the injury.

4.(a) Anti-dumping and countervailing duties shall be neither imposed nor increased with retroactive effect. The obligation to pay the amount of these duties is incurred in accordance with Directive 79/623/EEC*.

(b) However, where the Council determines:

(i) for dumped products:

— that there is a history of dumping which caused injury or that the importer was, or should have been, aware that the exporter practices dumping and that such dumping would cause injury, and
— that the injury is caused by sporadic dumping i.e. massive dumped imports of a product in a relatively short period, to such an extent that, in order to preclude it recurring, it appears necessary to impose an anti-dumping duty retroactively on those imports;
or

(ii) for subsidised products:

— in critical circumstances that injury which is difficult to repair is caused by massive imports in a relatively short period of a product benefiting from export subsidies paid or bestowed inconsistently with the provisions of the GATT and of the Agreement on interpretation and Application of Articles VI, XVI and XXIII of the GATT, and
— that it is necessary, in order to preclude the recurrence of such injury, to assess countervailing duties retroactively on these imports;
or

(iii) for dumped or subsidised products:

— that an undertaking has been violated,

the definitive anti-dumping or countervailing duties may be imposed on products in relation to which the obligation to pay import duties under Directive 79/623/EEC has been or would have been incurred not more than 90 days prior to the date of application of provisional duties, except that in the case of violation of an undertaking such retroactive assessment shall not apply to imports which were released for free circulation in the Community before the violation.

5. Where a product is imported into the Community from more than one country, duty shall be levied at an appropriate amount on a non-discriminatory basis on all imports of such product found to be dumped or subsidised and causing injury, other than imports from those sources in respect of which undertakings have been accepted.

6. Where the Community industry has been interpreted as referring to the producers in a certain region; the Commission shall give exporters an opportunity to offer undertakings pursuant to article 10 in respect of the region concerned. If an adequate undertaking is not given promptly or is not fulfilled, a provisional or definitive duty may be imposed in respect of the Community as a whole.

7. In the absence of any special provisions to the contrary adopted when a definitive or provisional anti-dumping or countervailing duty was imposed, the rules on the common

* OJ No. L 179, 17.7.1979, p.31.

definition of the concept of origin and the relevant common implementing provisions shall apply.

8. Anti-dumping or countervailing duties shall be collected by member states in the form, at the rate and according to the other criteria laid down when the duties were imposed, and independently of the customs duties, taxes and other charges normally imposed on imports.

9. No product shall be subject to both anti-dumping and countervailing duties for the purpose of dealing with one and the same situation arising from dumping or from the granting of any subsidy.

10.(a) Definitive anti-dumping duties may be imposed, by way of derogation from the second sentence of paragraph 4(a), on products that are introduced into the commerce of the Community after having been assembled or produced in the Community, provided that:

— assembly or production is carried out by a party which is related or associated to any of the manufacturers whose exports of the like product are subject to a definitive anti-dumping duty,
— the assembly or production operation was started or substantially increased after the opening of the anti-dumping investigation,
— the value of parts or materials used in the assembly or production operation and originating in the country of exportation of the product subject to the anti-dumping duty exceeds the value of all other parts or materials used by at least 50%.

In applying this provision, account shall be taken of the circumstances of each case, and, *inter alia*, of the variable costs incurred in the assembly or production operation and of the research and development carried out and the technology applied within the Community.

In that event the Council shall, at the same time, decide that parts or materials suitable for use in the assembly or production of such products and originating in the country of exportation of the product subject to the anti-dumping duty can only be considered to be in free circulation in so far as they will not be used in an assembly or production operation as specified in the first subparagraph.

(b) Products thus assembled or produced shall be declared to the competent authorities before leaving the assembly or production plant for their introduction into the commerce of the Community. For the purposes of levying an anti-dumping duty, this declaration shall be considered to be equivalent to the declaration referred to in Article 2 of Directive 79/695/EEC*.

(c) The rate of the anti-dumping duty shall be that applicable to the manufacturer in the country of origin of the like product subject to an anti-dumping duty to which the party in the Community carrying out the assembly or production is related or associated. The amount of duty collected shall be proportional to that resulting from the application of the rate of the anti-dumping duty applicable to the exporter of the complete product on the cif value of the parts or materials imported; it shall not exceed that required to prevent circumvention of the anti-dumping duty.

(d) The provisions of this Regulation concerning investigation, procedure, and undertakings apply to all questions arising under this paragraph.

11.(a) Where the exporter bears the anti-dumping duty, an additional anti-dumping duty may be imposed to compensate for the amount borne by the exporter.

* OJ No L 205, 13.8.1989, p. 19.

(b) When any party directly concerned submits sufficient evidence showing that the duty has been borne by the exporter, e.g. that the resale price to the first independent buyer of the product subject to the anti-dumping duty is not increased by an amount corresponding to the anti-dumping duty, the matter shall be investigated and the exporters and importers concerned shall be given an opportunity to comment.

Where it is found that the anti-dumping duty has been borne by the exporter, in whole or in part, either directly or indirectly and where Community interests call for intervention, an additional anti-dumping duty shall, after consultation, be imposed in accordance with the procedures laid down in Articles 11 and 12.

This duty may be applied retroactively. It may be imposed on products in relation to which the obligation to pay import duties under Directive 79/625/EEC has been incurred after the imposition of the definitive anti-dumping duty, except that such assessment shall not apply to imports which were released for free circulation in the Community before the exporter bore the anti-dumping duty.

(c) Insofar as the results of the investigation show that the absence of a price increase by an amount corresponding to the anti-dumping duty is not due to a reduction in the costs and/or profits of the importer for the product concerned then the absence of such price increase shall be considered as an indicator that the anti-dumping duty has been borne by the exporter.

(d) Article 7(7)(b) applies within the context of investigations under this paragraph.

Article 14
REVIEW

1. Regulations imposing anti-dumping or countervailing duties and decisions to accept undertakings shall be subject to review, in whole or in part, where warranted.

Such review may be held either at the request of a member state or on the initiative of the Commission. A review shall also be held where an interested party so requests and submits evidence of changed circumstances sufficient to justify the need for such review, provided that at least one year has elapsed since the conclusion of the investigation. Such requests shall be addressed to the Commission which shall inform the member states.

2. Where, after consultation, it becomes apparent that review is warranted, the investigation shall be re-opened in accordance with Article 7, where the circumstances so require. Such re-opening shall not *per se* affect the measures in operation.

3. Where warranted by the review, carried out either with or without re-opening of the investigation, the measures shall be amended, repealed or annulled by the Community institution competent for their introduction. However, where measures have been taken under the transitional provisions of an Act of Accession the Commission shall itself amend, repeal or annul them and shall report this to the Council; the latter may, acting by a qualified majority, decide that different action be taken.

Article 15

1. Subject to the provisions of paragraphs 3, 4 and 5, anti-dumping or countervailing duties and undertakings shall lapse after five years from the date on which they entered into force or were last modified or confirmed.

2. The Commission shall normally, after consultation and within six months prior to the end of the five year period, publish in the *Official Journal of the European Communities* a notice of the impending expiry of the measure in question and inform the Community industry known to be concerned. This notice shall state the period within which interested parties may make known their views in writing and may apply to be heard orally by the Commission in accordance with Article 7(5).

3. Where an interested party shows that the expiry of the measure would lead again to injury or threat of injury, the Commission shall, after consultation, publish in the *Official Journal of the European Communities* a notice of its intention to carry out a review of the measure. Such notice shall be published prior to the end of the relevant five year period. The measure shall remain in force pending the outcome of this review.

However, where the initiation of the review has not been published within six months after the end of the relevant five year period the measure shall lapse at the end of that six month period.

4. Where a review of a measure under Article 14 is in progress at the end of the relevant five year period, the measure shall remain in force pending the outcome of such review. A notice to this effect shall be published in the *Official Journal of the European Communities* before the end of the relevant five year period.

5. Where anti-dumping or countervailing duties and undertakings lapse under this Article the Commission shall publish a notice to that effect in the *Official Journal of the European Communities*. Such notice shall state the date of expiry of the measure.

Article 16
REFUND

1. Where an importer can show that the duty collected exceeds the actual dumping margin or the amount of the subsidy, consideration being given to any application of weighted averages, the excess amount shall be reimbursed. This amount shall be calculated in relation to the changes which have occurred in the dumping margin or the amount of the subsidy which were established in the original investigation for the shipments to the Community of the importer's supplier. All refund calculations shall be made in accordance with the provisions of Articles 2 or 3 and shall be based, as far as possible, on the same method applied in the original investigation, in particular, with regard to any application of averaging or sampling techniques.

2. In order to request the reimbursement referred to in paragraph 1, the importer shall submit an application to the Commission. The application shall be submitted via the member state in the territory of which the products were released for free circulation and within three months of the date on which the amount of the definitive duties to be levied was duly determined by the competent authorities or of the date on which a decision was made definitively to collect the amounts secured by way of provisional duty.

The member state shall forward the application to the Commission as soon as possible, either with or without an opinion as to its merits.

The Commission shall inform the other member states forthwith and give its opinion on the matter. If the member states agree with the opinion given by the Commission or do not object to it within one month of being informed, the Commission may decide in accordance with the said opinion.

In all other cases, the Commission shall, after consultation, decide whether and to what extent the application should be granted.

Article 17
FINAL PROVISIONS

This Regulation shall not preclude the application of:

1. any special rules laid down in agreements concluded between the Community and third countries;

2. the Community Regulations in the agricultural sector and of Regulation (EEC) No. 1059/69*, (EEC) No. 2730/75**; and (EEC) No. 2783/75***; this Regulation shall operate by way of complement to those Regulations and in derogation from any provisions thereof which preclude the application of anti-dumping or countervailing duties;

3. special measures, provided that such action does not run counter to obligations under the GATT.

Article 18
REPEAL OF EXISTING LEGISLATION

Regulation (EEC) No. 2176/84 is hereby repealed.

References to the repealed Regulation shall be construed as references to this Regulation.

Article 19
ENTRY INTO FORCE

This Regulation shall enter into force on the third day following its publication in the *Official Journal of the European Communites*.

It shall apply to proceedings already initiated.

This Regulation shall be binding in its entirety and directly applicable in all member states.
Done at Brussels, 11 July 1988.

For the Council
The President
P. ROUMELIOTIS

ANNEX
ILLUSTRATIVE LIST OF EXPORT SUBSIDIES

(a) The provision by governments of direct subsidies to a firm or an industry contingent upon export performance.

(b) Currency retention schemes or any similar practices which involve a bonus on exports.

(c) Internal transport and freight charges on export shipments, provided or mandated by governments, on terms more favourable than for domestic shipments.

* OJ No. L 141, 12.6.1969, p.1.
** OJ No. L 281, 1.11.1975, p.20.
*** OJ No. L 282, 1.11.1975, p.104.

(d) The delivery by governments or their agencies of imported or domestic products or services for use in the production of exported goods, on terms or conditions more favourable than for delivery of like or directly competitive products or services for use in the production of goods for domestic consumption, if (in the case of products) such terms or conditions are more favourable than those commercially available on world markets to their exporters.

(e) The full or partial exemption, remission, or deferral specifically related to exports, of direct taxes or social welfare charges paid or payable by industrial or commercial enterprises. Notwithstanding the foregoing, deferral of taxes and charges referred to above need not amount to an export subsidy where, for example, appropriate interest charges are collected.

(f) The allowance of special deductions directly related to exports or export performance, over and above those granted in respect to production for domestic consumption, in the calculation of the base on which direct taxes are charged.

(g) The exemption or remission in respect of the production and distribution of exported products, of indirect taxes in excess of those levied in respect of the production and distribution of like products when sold for domestic consumption. The problem of the excessive remission of value added tax is exclusively covered by this paragraph.

(h) The exemption, remission or deferral or prior stage cumulative indirect taxes on goods or services used in the production of exported products in excess of the exemption, remission or deferral or like prior stage cumulative indirect taxes on goods or services used in the production of like products when sold for domestic consumption; provided, however, that prior stage cumulative indirect taxes may be exempted, remitted or deferred on exported products even when not exempted, remitted or deferred on like products when sold for domestic consumption, if the prior stage cumulative indirect taxes are levied on goods that are physically incorporated (making normal allowance for waste) in the exported product. This paragraph does not apply to value added tax systems and border tax adjustments related thereto.

(i) The remission or drawback of import charges in excess of those levied on imported goods that are physically incorporated (making normal allowance for waste) in the exported product; provided, however, that in particular cases a firm may use a quantity of home market goods equal to, and having the same quality and characteristics as, the imported good as a substitute for them in order to benefit from this provision if the import and the corresponding export operations both occur within a reasonable time period, normally not to exceed two years. This paragraph does not apply to value added tax systems and border tax adjustments related thereto.

(j) The provision by governments (or special institutions controlled by governments) of export credit guarantee or insurance programmes, of insurance or guarantee programmes against increases in the costs of exported products or of exchange risk programmes, at premium rates, which are manifestly inadequate to cover the long-term operating costs and losses of the programmes.

(k) The grant by governments (or special institutions controlled by and/or acting under the authority of governments) of export credits at rates below those which they actually have to pay for the funds so employed (or would have to pay if they borrowed on international capital markets in order to obtain funds of the same maturity and denominated at the same currency as the export credit), or the payment by them of all or part of the costs incurred by exporters or financial institutions in obtaining credits, in so far as they are used to secure a material advantage in the field of export credit terms.

Provided, however, that if the country of origin or export is a party to an international undertaking on official export credits to which at least 12 original signatories to the Agreement on Interpretation and Application of Articles VI, XVI and XXIII of the GATT are parties as of 1 January 1979 (or a successor undertaking which has been adopted by those original signatories), or if in practice the country of origin or export applies the interest rate provisions of the relevant undertaking, an export credit which is in conformity with those provisions shall not be considered an export subsidy.

(l) Any other charge on the public account constituting an export subsidy in the sense of Article XVI of the GATT.

Notes

For the purposes of this Annex the following definitions apply;
1. The term 'direct taxes' shall mean taxes on wages, profits, interest, rents, royalties, and all other forms of income, and taxes on the ownership of real property.
2. The term 'import charges' shall mean tariffs, duties, and other fiscal charges not elsewhere enumerated in these notes that are levied on imports.
3. The term 'indirect taxes' shall mean sales, excise, turnover, value added, franchise, stamp, transfer, inventory and equipment taxes, border taxes and all taxes other than direct taxes and import charges.
4. 'Prior stage' indirect taxes are those levied on goods or services used directly or indirectly in making the product.
5. 'Cumulative' indirect taxes are multi-staged taxes levied where there is no mechanism for subsequent crediting of the tax if the goods or services subject to tax at one stage of production are used in a succeeding stage of production.
6. 'Remission' of taxes include the refund or rebate of taxes.

Regulation (EEC) No. 802/68 of the Council

of 27 June 1968
on the common definition of the concept of the origin of goods
(OJ 1968 L 148/1)

The Council of the European Communities

Having regard to the Treaty establishing the European Economic Community, and in particular Articles 111, 113, 155, 227 and 235 thereof;

Having regard to the proposal from the Commission;

Having regard to the Opinion of the European Parliament;

Having regard to the Opinion of the Economic and Social Committee;

Whereas member states have to determine or verify the origin of imported goods whenever application of the Commons Customs Tariff, of quantitative restrictions or of any other provisions applicable to trade so requires;

Whereas member states have to certify the origin of exported goods in all cases where such certification is required by the authorities of the importing countries, in particular where advantages derive from that certification;

Whereas, in either case, in the absence of any international definition of the concept of the origin of goods, member states at present apply their own rules for the determination, verification and certification or origin; whereas the differences between such national rules are likely to lead to differences in applying the Common Customs Tariff, quantitative restrictions and other provisions applicable to trade with third countries, and also in the preparation and issue of certificates of origin for goods exported to third countries;

Whereas, it is therefore necessary to draw up on the subject rules common to all the member states;

Whereas goods produced wholly in a particular country and not containing products imported from other countries are to be considered as originating in that country, and the goods belonging to this category must accordingly be specified;

Whereas, as a result of the development of international trade and of greater international division of labour, the manufacture of any one product tends increasingly to be carried out by undertakings located in different countries; whereas it must therefore be determined which of those countries is to be considered as the country of origin of the product in question;

Whereas there are good grounds for accepting as the country of origin that in which the last substantial process or operation that was economically justified was performed;

Whereas it is impossible at present to define the concept of origin in respect of petroleum products;

Whereas the origin of a product is usually established by means of a certificate of origin prepared and issued by an authority or agency duly authorised for this purpose; the conditions with which the certificate is required to comply, so that it may be used as evidence, must therefore be specified;

Whereas the concept of Community origin should be defined, but where the needs of the export trade so require, the certificate of origin may specify that the goods in question originated in a particular member state;

Whereas uniform application of the provisions of this Regulaltion should be ensured and it is essential to provide for a Community procedure for adopting the necessary implementing

provisions; whereas, for this purpose and with the object of organising close and effective co-operation between the Commission and the member states, a committee should be set up;

Whereas the provisions of this Regulation relate both to commercial policy with regard to third countries and to free movement of goods within the Community, and in particular to uniform application of the Common Customs Tariff; whereas, with regard to the latter, the relevant Articles of the Treaty do not confer on the institutions of the Community the power to adopt binding provisions with regard to a common definition of the concept of the origin of goods; the provisions of this Regulation must therefore also be based on Article 235;

Has adopted this Regulation:

Article 1
This Regulation defines the concept of the origin of goods for purposes of:

(a) the uniform application of the Common Customs Tariff, of quantitative restrictions, and of all other measures adopted, in relation to the importation of goods, by the Community or by member states;

(b) the uniform application of all measures adopted, in relation to the exportation of goods, by the Community or by member states;

(c) the preparation and issue of certificates of origin.

Article 2
The provisions of this Regulation shall not affect the special rules concerning trade between the Community or member states, on the one hand, and the countries to which the Community or member states are bound by agreements which derogate from the most favoured-nation clause, on the other, and in particular those establishing a customs union or a free-trade area.

Article 3
The Regulation shall not apply to the petroleum products listed in Annex 1. The concept of origin in respect of those products will be defined later.

Article 4
1. Goods wholly obtained or produced in one country shall be considered as originating in that country.

2. The expression 'goods wholly obtained or produced in one country' means:

(a) mineral products extracted within its territory;

(b) the vegetable products harvested therein;

(c) live animals born and raised therein;

(d) products derived from live animals raised therein;

(e) products of hunting or fishing carried on therein;

(f) products of sea-fishing and other products taken from the sea by vessels registered or recorded in that country and flying its flag;

(g) goods obtained on board factory ships from the products referred to in (f) originating in that country, if such factory ships are registered or recorded in that country and flying its flag;

(h) products taken from the sea-bed or beneath the sea-bed outside territorial waters, if that country has, for the purposes of exploitation, exclusive rights to such soil or subsoil;

(i) waste and scrap products derived from manufacturing operations and used articles, if they were collected therein and are only fit for the recovery of raw materials;

(j) goods which are produced therein exclusively from goods referred to in subparagraphs (a) to (f) or from their derivatives, at any stage of production.

Article 5

A product in the production of which two or more countries were concerned shall be regarded as originating in the country in which the last substantial process or operation that is economically justified was performed, having been carried out in an undertaking equipped for the purpose, and resulting in the manufacture of a new product or representing an important stage of manufacture.

Article 6

Any process or work in respect of which it is established, or in respect of which the facts as ascertained justify the presumption, that its sole object was to circumvent the provisions applicable in the Community or the member states to goods from specific countries shall in no case be considered, under Article 5, as conferring on the goods thus produced the origin of the country where it is carried out.

Article 7

Accessories, spare parts or tools delivered with any piece of equipment, machine, apparatus or vehicle which form part of its standard equipment shall be deemed to have the same origin as that piece of equipment, machine, apparatus or vehicle.

The circumstances in which the presumption of origin referred to in the preceding paragraph shall also apply to essential spare parts for use with any piece of equipment, machine, apparatus or vehicle dispatched beforehand, shall be determined in accordance with the procedure laid down in Article 14.

Article 8

For purposes of application of Article 4 to 7, the member states shall be considered as constituting a single territorial unit.

Article 9

1. When the origin of a product has to be proved on importation by the production of a certificate of origin, that certificate shall fulfil the following conditions:

(a) It must be prepared by a reliable authority or agency duly authorised for that purpose by the country of issue;

(b) It must contain all the particulars necessary for identifying the product to which it relates, in particular

— the number of packages, their nature, and the marks and numbers they bear,
— the kind of product, and its gross and net weight,
— the name of the consignor;

(c) It must certify unambiguously that the product to which it relates originated in a specific country.

2. Notwithstanding the production of a certificate of origin which fulfils the conditions prescribed by paragraph 1, the competent authorities may, if there is cause for serious doubt, demand any additional proof with the object of ensuring that the indication of origin conforms to the rules laid down in this Regulation and to the provisions adopted for its implementation.

Article 10

1. Certificates of origin for goods originating in and exported from the Community must comply with the conditions prescribed by Article 9(1)(a) and (b).

2. Such certificates of origin shall certify that the goods originated in the Community.

However, when the needs of the export trade so require, they may certify that the goods originated in a particular member state.

If the conditions of Article 5 are fulfilled only as a result of a series of operations or processes carried out in different member states, the goods may only be certified as being of Community origin.

3. Member states shall take the requisite steps to ensure that by the end of the transitional period at the latest the certificates of origin issued by their authorities or authorised agencies are prepared and issued in accordance with the provisions of Annex II, in so far as the needs of the export trade do not otherwise require.

Article 11

Each member state shall inform the Commission of the steps taken by its central administration for the purposes of applying this Regulation, and of any problems which have arisen in connection with its application. The Commission shall forthwith communicate this information to the other member states.

Article 12

1. A Committee on Origin (hereinafter called the 'Committee') shall be set up and shall consist of representatives of the member states, with a representative of the Commission acting as Chairman.

2. The Committee shall draw up its own rules of procedure.

Article 13

The Committee may examine all questions relating to the application of this Regulation referred to it by its Chairman, either on his own initiative or at the request of a representative of a member state.

Article 14

1. The provisions required for applying Articles 4 to 7, 9 and 10 shall be adopted in accordance with the procedure laid down in paragraphs 2 and 3 of this Article.

2. The representative of the Commission shall submit to the Committee a draft of the provisions to be adopted. The Committee shall deliver an Opinion on the draft within a time limit set by the Chairman having regard to the urgency of the matter. Decisions shall be taken by a majority of twelve votes, the votes of the member states being weighted as provided in Article 148(2) of the Treaty. The Chairman shall not vote.

3.(a) The Commission shall adopt the envisaged provisions if they are in accordance with the Opinion of the Committee.

(b) If the envisaged provisions are not in accordance with the Opinion of the Committee, or if no Opinion is delivered, the Commission shall without delay submit to the Council a proposal with regard to the provisions to be adopted.

The Council shall act by a qualified majority.

Article 15

If the provisions in force in a member state for the issue of certificates of origin for exports are so altered by the provisions referred to in Article 14 that an economic activity is affected, the Commission may authorise the member state in question at the request thereof to defer the application of the provisions referred to in Article 14 in respect of a specific product for a period not exceeding one year from the entry into force of those provisions.

This Article shall remain in force for a period of five years from the date of entry into force of this Regulation.

Article 16

This Regulation shall be applicable in the French overseas departments.

Article 17

This Regulation shall enter into force on 1 July 1968.

ANNEX I

List of Petroleum Products (Article 3)

CCT heading No	*Description of goods*
ex. 27.07 B1	Aromatic oils as defined in Note 2 to Chapter 27, of which more than 65% by volume distils at temperatures up to 250°C (including mixtures of petroleum spirit and benzole) for use as power or heating fuels.
27.09	Petroleum oils and oils obtained from bituminous minerals, crude
27.10	Petroleum oils and oils obtained from bituminous minerals, other than crude; preparations not elsewhere specified or included, containing not less than 70% by weight of petroleum oils or of oils obtained from bituminous minerals, these oils being the basic constituents of the preparations
27.11	Petroleum gases and other gaseous hydrocarbons
27.12	Petroleum jelly
27.13	Paraffin wax, micro-crysalline wax, slack wax, ozokerite, lignite wax, peat wax and other mineral waxes, whether or not coloured
27.14	Petroleum bitumen, petroleum coke and other residues of petroleum oils or of oils obtained from bituminous minerals
27.15	Bitumen and asphalt, natural; bituminous shale, asphaltic rock and tar sands
27.16	Bituminous mixtures based on natural asphalt, on natural bitumen, on petroleum bitumen, on mineral tar or on mineral tar pitch (for example, bituminous mastics, cut-backs)

CCT heading No	*Description of goods*
29.01 AI	Hydrocarbons, acyclic, for use as power or heating fuels
29.01 BII(a)	Cyclanes and cyclenes, for use as power or heating fuels
29.01 DI(a)	Benzene, toluene, xylenes, for use as power or heating fuels
ex.34.03 A	Lubricating preparations containing less than 70% by weight of petroleum oils or of oils obtained from bituminous minerals
ex.34.04	Artificial waxes (including water-soluble waxes); prepared waxes, not emulsified or containing solvents, with a basis of paraffin wax, micro-crystalline wax, slack wax, or other mineral waxes
38.14 BI(a)	Anti-knock preparations, oxidation inhibitors, gum inhibitors, viscosity improvers, anti-corrosive preparations and similar prepared additives for mineral oils, for lubricants containing petroleum oils or oils obtained from bituminous minerals
38.19 E	Mixed alkylenes

ANNEX II

Provisions concerning the preparation and issue of certificates of origin

1. The certificate of origin shall be issued upon written request of the applicant.

If the circumstances justify it, in particular where the applicant maintains a regular flow of exports, member states may decide not to require a request for each export operation, on condition that the provisions of this Regulation are complied with.

2. The application form shall be printed in the official language or in one or more of the official languages of the exporting member state. The form of certificate of origin shall be printed in one or more of the official languages of the Community or, depending on the practice and requirements of trade, in any other language.

3. The application form and the certificate of origin shall be completed in typescript or by hand, in an identical manner, in one of the official languages of the Community or, depending on the practice and requirements of trade, in any other language. Where forms are completed by hand, they shall be written in block letters in ink.

4. The format of the certificate shall be 21×30cm. The paper used shall be free of mechanical pulp, dressed for writing purposes and weigh at least 64 grammes per square metre. It shall have printed on it a sepia-coloured guilloche pattern that will reveal any forgery by mechanical or chemical means.

5. Member states may print the forms of certificate of origin themselves, or have them produced by printers whom they have duly appointed. In the latter case, each form shall make reference to the appointment, and bear the printer's distinguishing mark.

Commission Proposal

for a Council Directive on the liability of suppliers of services
COM(90) 482 final – SYN 308
(Submitted by the Commission on 9 November 1990)

The Council of the European Communities

Having regard to the Treaty establishing the European Economic Community, and in particular Article 100a thereof,

Having regard to the proposal from the Commission,

In co-operation with the European Parliament,

Having regard to the opinion of the Economic and Social Committee,

Whereas the Council Resolution of 9 November 1989 stressed the priority nature of the implementation at Community level of means of promoting the safety of services as part of the re-launching of the consumer protection policy,

Whereas there is a Community dimension to the market in services;

Whereas, although the laws of the member states concerning the liability of the suppliers of services for the damage caused by their services all seek to provide greater protection for persons for whom the services are intended and for third parties, they continue to differ in content and as regards the degree of protection provided; whereas such differences may create barriers to trade and unequal conditions in the internal market in services; whereas they do not guarantee the same degree of protection for the injured person against all damage caused to the person, nor to the consumer against damage caused to movable or immovable property by a service;

Whereas action at Community level is the most appropriate in view of these divergences and the Community dimension of services;

Whereas the principle of reversing the burden of proof of a fault on the part of the supplier of the defective service is the most suitable in view of the level of protection afforded by national law in the member states; whereas such a principle already exists in several national legislations, but should be formalised and applied in a standard manner;

Whereas the characteristics of services, including their 'one-off' nature, which is sometimes intangible, the fact that the service 'disappears' at the moment that damage is caused, and the respective positions of the injured person with no specific technical knowledge and the trader who possesses such knowledge, justify a reversal of the burden of proof of the fault on the part of the supplier of the service in favour of the injured person;

Whereas a fault on the part of the supplier of the service must be assessed in relation to the reasonable expectation that the service should not cause damage to the physical integrity of persons and of movable or immovable property, including the persons or property which were the object of the service;

Whereas the mere fact that a better service existed or might have existed at the moment of performance or subsequently does not constitute a fault;

Whereas, having regard to the diversity of services on the one hand and the existence of Council Directive 85/374/EEC* concerning product liability on the other, a broad definition of

service should be adopted based on the traditional distinction between service and the manufacture of goods, services and the transfer of rights *in rem*; whereas, on account of their special nature, public services intended to maintain public safety should be excluded from this Directive; whereas package travel services and waste services already governed by specific Community legislation should also be excluded; whereas the same applies for damage already covered by liability arrangements governed by international agreements ratified by the member states or by the Community;

Whereas the object of protecting consumers and compensating persons injured by defective services does not justify a distinction between private and public suppliers of services; whereas, however, only services provided by commercial traders should be covered and not those rendered by one individual to another;

Whereas protection of the injured person requires compensation for the damage to the health or physical integrity of persons; whereas protection of the consumer requires compensation for the damage to the physical integrity of their movable or immovable property; whereas any material damage resulting therefrom should also be compensated for;

Whereas it falls to the injured person to provide proof of the damage and of the causal relationship between that damage and the service supplied;

Whereas the respective positions of the parties provide justification that there be no reduction in the supplier's liability where damage is caused jointly by the fault of the supplier and the intervention of a third party, but that such liability may be reduced (or even waived) in the event of a joint fault on the part of the injured person.

Whereas the protection of the injured person implies that the supplier of the services should not be able to limit or exclude his liability in relation to the former;

Whereas when liability for a given damage is shared by several persons, protection of the injured person requires that they have joint and several liability;

Whereas the position of the consumer with regard to the franchisor giving his name to the services undertaking and the franchisee to whom he applies justifies joint and several liability of the franchisor, the franchisee and the master franchisee;

Whereas the Directive is without prejudice to the application of Council Directive 89/391/EEC of 12 June 1989 on the introduction of measures to encourage improvements in the safety and health of workers at work* and the specific Directives deriving therefrom;

Whereas the system of liability established by this Directive and the nature of the services justify reasonably short limitation periods for bringing proceedings for the recovery of damages and the termination of liability, except where services relating to the design and construction of immovable property are concerned,

Has adopted this Directive:

---

* OJ No L 210, 7.8.1985, p. 29.

* OJ No L 183, 29.6.1989, p. 1.

Article 1
Principle

1. The supplier of a service shall be liable for damage to the health and physical integrity of persons or the physical integrity of movable or immovable property, including the persons or property which were the object of the service, caused by a fault committed by him in the performance of the service.

2. The burden of proving the absence of fault shall fall upon the supplier of the service.

3. In assessing the fault, account shall be taken of the behaviour of the supplier of the service, who, in normal and reasonably foreseeable conditions, shall ensure the safety which may reasonably be expected.

4. Whereas the mere fact that a better service existed or might have existed at the moment of performance or subsequently shall not constitute a fault.

Article 2
Definition of service

For the purpose of this Directive, 'service' means any transaction carried out on a commercial basis or by way of a public service and in an independent manner, whether or not in return for payment, which does not have as its direct and exclusive object the manufacture of moveable property or the transfer of rights *in rem* or intellectual property rights.

This Directive shall not apply to public services intended to maintain public safety. It shall not apply to package travel or to waste services.

Nor shall it apply to damage covered by liability arrangements governed by international agreements ratified by the member states or by the Community.

Article 3
Definition of supplier of services

1. The term 'supplier of services' means any natural or legal person governed by private or public law who, in the course of his professional activities or by way of a public service, provides a service referred to in Article 2.

2. Any person who provides a service by using the services of a representative or other legally independent intermediary shall continue to be deemed to be a supplier of services within the meaning of this Directive.

3. If the supplier of the service referred to in paragraph 1 is not established within the Community, and without prejudice to his liability, the person carrying out the service in the Community shall be considered as the supplier of that service for the purpose of this Directive.

Article 4
Definition of damage
The term 'damage' means:

(a) death or any other direct damage to the health or physical integrity of persons;

(b) any direct damage to the physical integrity of movable or immovable property, including animals, provided that this property:

(i) is of a type normally intended for private use or consumption, and

(ii) was intended for or used by the injured person, principally for his private use or consumption;

(c) any financial material damage resulting directly from the damage referred to at (a) and (b).

Article 5
Proof
The injured person shall be required to provide proof of the damage and the causal relationship between the performance of the service and the damage.

Article 6
Third parties and joint liability

1. The liability of the supplier of the service shall not be reduced where the damage is caused jointly by a fault on his part and by the intervention of a third party.

2. The liability of the supplier of the service may be reduced, or even waived, where the damage is caused jointly by a fault on his part and by the fault of the injured person, or a person for whom the injured person is responsible.

Article 7
Exclusion of liability
The supplier of a service may not, in relation to the injured person, limit or exclude his liability under this Directive.

Article 8
Joint and several liability

1. If, in applying this Directive, several people are liable for a given damage, they shall be jointly liable, without prejudice to the provisions of national law relating to the law of recourse of one supplier against another.

2. The franchisor, the master franchisee and the franchisee, within the meaning of Commission Regulation (EEC) No 4087/88 of 30 November 1988 on the application of Article 85(3) of the Treaty to categories of franchise agreements* shall be deemed to be jointly and severally liable within the meaning of paragraph 1.

However, the franchisor and the master franchisee may absolve themselves of liability if they can prove that the damage is due to a product which, on the basis of Regulation (EEC) No 4087/88, they themselves had not been able to supply or impose.

Article 9
Extinction of rights
The member states shall provide in their legislation that the rights conferred upon the injured person pursuant to this Directive shall be extinguished upon the expiry of a period of five years from the date on which the supplier of services provided the service which caused the damage, unless in the meantime the injured person has instituted legal, administrative or arbitration proceedings against that person.

Hoever, this period shall be extended to 20 years where the service relates to the design or construction of immovable property.

Article 10
Limitation period

1. Member states shall provide in their legislation that a limitation period of three years shall apply to proceedings for the recovery of damages as provided for in this Directive, beginning on the day on which the plaintiff became aware or should reasonably have become aware of the damage, the service and the identity of the supplier of the service.

However, this period shall be extended to 10 years where the service relates to the design or construction of immovable property.

* OJ No L 359, 28.12.1988, p. 46.

2. The laws of member states regulating suspension or interruption of the limitation period shall not be affected by this Directive.

Article 11
Transitional provision
This Directive shall not apply to services provided before the date on which the provisions referred to in Article 12(1) enter into force.

Article 12
Implementing provisions
1. Member states shall adopt the laws, regulations and administrative provisions necessary to comply with this Directive by 31 December 1992.

They shall immediately inform the Commission thereof.

When member states adopt these provisions, they shall contain a reference to this Directive or shall be accompanied by such reference at the time of their official publication. The procedure for such reference shall be adopted by member states.

2. Member states shall communicate to the Commission the provisions of national law which they adopt in the area governed by this Directive.

Article 13
Final provision
This Directive is addressed to the member states.

The Loi Doubin

Law no. 89-1008 dated 31 December 1989 in respect of the development of commercial and craft businesses and the improvement of their economic legal and social environment.
The National Assembly and the Senate have adopted,
The President of the Republic promulgates the Law of which the terms are as follows:

Provisions in favour of business

Article 1
Any person who places a commercial name, a trade mark or sign at the disposal of another person in consideration for an undertaking of exclusivity or quasi-exclusivity for the exercise of his business, is obliged, prior to the signature of any contract concluded in the common interests of the two parties, to provide the other party with a document detailing honest information which will allow the other party to contract in full knowledge of the facts.

This document, of which the contents are prescribed by statutory order, will in particular provide details of the history and experience of the business, the current state and prospects for development of the market in question, the size of the network of concessionaries, the period and conditions of renewal, termination and assignment of the contract as well as the extent of the exclusivity.

Where the payment of a sum of money is required prior to the signature of the contract referred to above; in particular in order to reserve a zone, the services granted in consideration of this sum as well as the reciprocal obligations of both parties in such a case must be defined in writing.

The document provided for in the first paragraph as well as the draft contract must be provided a minimum of 21 days before the signature of the contract or, in any event, before the payment of the sum referred to in the paragraph above.

(English translation by Martin Wilson, Field Fisher Waterhouse)

STATUTORY ENACTMENT OF ARTICLE 1 OF THE LOI DOUBIN

Statutory order number 91—337 dated 4 April 1991 in respect of the application of Article 1 of the law number 89—1008 dated 31st December 1989 relating to the development of commercial and craft businesses and the improvement of their economic, legal and social environment.

The Prime Minister,
Following the report of the Minister of Justice, the Minister of Industry and of Territorial Organisation as well as the Minister responsible for business and crafts,

In the light of the penal code, particularly Article R25;

In the light of Article 1 of Law no. 89—1008 dated 31st December 1989 in respect of the development of commercial and craft businesses and the improvement of their economic, legal and social environment;

The financial section of the Council of State being in agreement,

Decrees:
Article 1
— The document provided for in the first paragraph of Article 1 of the law dated 31st December 1989 referred to above should contain the following information:

1. The address of the seat of the business and the nature of its activities together with an indication of its legal form and the identity of its managing director if the managing director is a physical person or its managing company together with the amount of the capital;

2. The registration number at the commercial registry or the reference number on the register of professions and, where the trademark which is the subject of the contract has been acquired following an assignment or a licence, the date and registration number at the national register of trademarks, and for licences an indication of the term for which the licence has been granted;

3. The addresses of the business's bankers. This information can be limited to the addresses of the five principal banks;

4. The date of incorporation of the company, with a summary of the principal stages of its development, including the development of its network of outlets, if appropriate, as well as all information allowing an appreciation of the professional experience acquired by the business or its directors. The information referred to in the above paragraph may only refer to the five years preceding the provision of the document. It must be completed by a presentation of the general and local state of the market in respect of the products or services which are subject to the contract as well as the prospects of development of this market.

The annual accounts in respect of the two last financial years must be annexed to this part of the document and public companies must exhibit the report established during the last two financial years in accordance with the third paragraph of Article 341.1 of Law No. 66—537 dated 24th June 1966 in respect of commercial companies.

5. A presentation of the network of concessionaries, which must include:

(a) A list of the companies which make up the network together with an indication of the means of exploitation in respect of each company;

(b) The address of the company established in France with whom the person proposing the contract is linked by means of contracts of a similar nature to the contract envisaged and the date of conclusion or renewal of those contracts;

Where the network consists of more than 50 outlets, the information referred to in the previous paragraph is only required in respect of the companies closest to the area where trading is envisaged by the other party;

(c) The number of companies which, being linked to the network by contracts of the same nature as that which is envisaged, have ceased to form part of the network during the year preceding the delivery of the document. The document should state whether their contracts simply expired or whether they were terminated or rescinded;

(d) If appropriate, the presence, in the trading area of the outlet envisaged by the proposed contract, of any establishment in which the same products or services are offered as those which form the subject of this contract, with the express agreement of the person proposing to contract;

(e) An indication of the terms of the proposed contract, the conditions of renewal, termination and assignment as well as the area of exclusivity.

The document should further detail the nature and amount of expense and investment specific to the trademark or to the label which the person receiving the draft contract will have to incur before commencing trading.

Article 2

Any person who places a commercial name, trademark or sign at the disposal of another person whilst requiring an undertaking of exclusivity or quasi-exclusivity in relation to the exercise of its activity without having provided the information document and the draft contract referred to at Article 1 of the Law dated 31st December 1989 referred to above, will be liable to a fine applicable to offences of the fifth class.

In cases where an offender re-offends, the penalty of fines applicable to re-offenders in respect of offences of the fifth class will be imposed.

Article 3

The Minister of Justice, the Minister of Industry and of Territorial Organisation, together with the Minister responsible for Commerce and Crafts are charged with the implementation of this order which will be published in the official journal of the French Republic.

Signed in Paris on the 4th April 1991

By the Prime Minister: *Michel Rocard*

The Minister responsible for Commerce and Craft:
                                                François Doubin

The Minister of Justice: *Henri Nallet*

The Minister of Industry and Territorial Organisation:
                                                Roger Fauroux

(English translation by Martin Wilson, Field Fisher Waterhouse)

Council Directive

of 18 December 1986
on the co-ordination of the laws of the Member States relating to self-employed commercial agents
(86/653/EEC) — (OJ 1986 L 382/17)

The Council of the European Communities

Having regard to the Treaty establishing the European Economic Community, and in particular Articles 57(2) and 100 thereof,

Having regard to the proposal from the Commission*,

Having regard to the opinion of the European Parliament**,

Having regard to the opinion of the Economic and Social Committee***,

Whereas the restrictions on the freedom of establishment and the freedom to provide services in respect of activities of intermediaries in commerce, industry and small craft industries were abolished by Directive 64/224/EEC****;

Whereas the differences in national laws concerning commercial representation substantially affect the conditions of competition and the carrying-on of that activity within the Community and are detrimental both to the protection available to commercial agents *vis-à-vis* their principals and to the security of commercial transactions; whereas moreover those differences are such as to inhibit substantially the conclusion and operation of commercial representation contracts where principal and commercial agent are established in different member states;

Whereas trade in goods between member states should be carried on under conditions which are similar to those of a single market, and this necessitates approximation of the legal systems of the member states to the extent required for the proper functioning of the common market; whereas in this regard the rules concerning conflict of laws do not, in the matter of commercial representation, remove the inconsistencies referred to above, nor would they even if they were made uniform, and accordingly the proposed harmonisation is necessary notwithstanding the existence of those rules;

Whereas in this regard the legal relationship between commercial agent and principal must be given priority;

Whereas it is appropriate to be guided by the principles of Article 117 of the Treaty and to maintain improvements already made, when harmonising the laws of the member states relating to commercial agents;

Whereas additional transitional periods should be allowed for certain member states which have to make a particular effort to adapt their regulations, especially those concerning indemnity for termination of contract between the principal and the commercial agent, to the requirements of this Directive,

Has adopted this Directive:

Chapter 1

Scope

Article 1

1. The harmonisation measures prescribed by this Directive shall apply to the laws, regulations and administrative provisions of the member states governing the relations between commercial agents and their principals.

2. For the purposes of this Directive, 'commercial agent' shall mean a self-employed intermediary who has continuing authority to negotiate the sale or the purchase of goods on behalf of another person, hereinafter called the 'principal', or to negotiate and conclude such transactions on behalf of and in the name of that principal.

3. A commercial agent shall be understood within the meaning of this Directive as not including in particular:

— a person who, in his capacity as an officer, is empowered to enter into commitments binding on a company or association,
— a partner who is lawfully authorised to enter into commitments binding on his partners,
— a receiver, a receiver and manager, a liquidator or a trustee in bankruptcy.

Article 2

1. This Directive shall not apply to:

— commercial agents whose activities are unpaid,
— commercial agents when they operate on commodity exchanges or in the commodity market, or
— the body known as the Crown Agents for Overseas Governments and Administrations, as set up under the Crown Agents Act 1979 in the United Kingdom, or its subsidiaries.

2. Each of the member states shall have the right to provide that the Directive shall not apply to those persons whose activities as commercial agents are considered secondary by the law of that member state.

Chapter II

Rights and obligations

Article 3

1. In performing his activities a commercial agent must look after his principal's interests and act dutifully and in good faith.

2. In particular, a commercial agent must:

(a) make proper efforts to negotiate and, where appropriate, conclude the transactions he is instructed to take care of;

(b) communicate in his principal all the necessary information available to him;

(c) comply with reasonable instructions given by his principal.

Article 4

1. In his relations with his commercial agent a principal must act dutifully and in good faith.

2. A principal must in particular:

(a) provide his commercial agent with the necessary documentation relating to the goods concerned;

* OJ No. C 13, 18.1.1977, p.2; OJ No. C 56, 2.3.1979, p.5.
** OJ No. C 239, 9.10.1978, p.17.
*** OJ No. C 59, 8.3.1978, p.31.
**** OJ No. 56, 4.4.1964, p.869/64.

(b) obtain for his commercial agent the information necessary for the performance of the agency contract, and in particular notify the commercial agent within a reasonable period once he anticipates that the volume of commercial transactions will be significantly lower than that which the commercial agent could normally have expected.

3. A principal must, in addition, inform the commercial agent within a reasonable period of his acceptance, refusal, and of any non-execution of a commercial transaction which the commercial agent has procured for the principal.

Article 5
The parties may not derogate from the provisions of Articles 3 and 4.

Chapter III

Remuneration

Article 6
1. In the absence of any agreement on this matter between the parties, and without prejudice to the application of the compulsory provisions of the member states concerning the level of remuneration, a commercial agent shall be entitled to the remuneration that commercial agents appointed for the goods forming the subject of his agency contract are customarily allowed in the place where he carries on his activities. If there is no such customary practice a commercial agent shall be entitled to reasonable remuneration taking into account all the aspects of the transaction.
2. Any part of the remuneration which varies with the number or value of business transactions shall be deemed to be commission within the meaning of this Directive.
3. Articles 7 to 12 shall not apply if the commercial agent is not remunerated wholly or in part by commission.

Article 7
1. A commercial agent shall be entitled to commission on commercial transactions concluded during the period covered by the agency contract:

(a) where the transaction has been concluded as a result of his action, or
(b) where the transaction is concluded with a third party whom he has previously acquired as a customer for transactions of the same kind.

2. A commercial agent shall also be entitled to commission on transactions concluded during the period covered by the agency contract:

— either where he is entrusted with a specific geographical area or group of customers,
— or where he has an exclusive right to a specific geographical area or group of customers,

and where the transaction has been entered into with a customer belonging to that area or group.
Member states shall include in their legislation one of the possibilities referred to in the above two indents.

Article 8
A commercial agent shall be entitled to commission on commercial transactions concluded after the agency contract has terminated:

(a) if the transaction is mainly attributable to the commercial agent's efforts during the period covered by the agency contract and if the transaction was entered into within a reasonable period after that contract terminated; or
(b) if, in accordance with the conditions mentioned in Article 7, the order of the third party reached the principal or the commercial agent before the agency contract terminated.

Article 9
A commercial agent shall not be entitled to the commission referred to in Article 7, if that commission is payable, pursuant to Article 8, to the previous commercial agent, unless it is equitable because of the circumstances for the commission to be shared between the commercial agents.

Article 10
1. The commission shall become due as soon as and to the extent that one of the following circumstances obtains:

(a) the principal has executed the transaction; or
(b) the principal should, according to his agreement with the third party, have executed the transaction; or
(c) the third party has executed the transaction.

2. The commission shall become due at the latest when the third party has executed his part of the transaction or should have done so if the principal had executed his part of the transaction, as he should have.
3. The commission shall be paid not later than on the last day of the month following the quarter in which it became due.
4. Agreements to derogate from paragraphs 2 and 3 to the detriment of the commercial agent shall not be permitted.

Article 11
1. The right to commission can be extinguished only if and to the extent that:

— it is established that the contract between the third party and the principal will not be executed, and
— that fact is due to a reason for which the principal is not to blame.

2. Any commission which the commercial agent has already received shall be refunded if the right to it is extinguished.
3. Agreements to derogate from paragraph 1 to the detriment of the commercial agent shall not be permitted.

Article 12
1. The principal shall supply his commercial agent with a statement of the commission due, not later than the last day of the month following the quarter in which the commission has become due. This statement shall set out the main components used in calculating the amount of commission.
2. A commercial agent shall be entitled to demand that he be provided with all the information, and in particular an extract from the books, which is available to his principal and which he needs in order to check the amount of the commission due to him.
3. Agreements to derogate from paragraphs 1 and 2 to the detriment of the commercial agent shall not be permitted.
4. This Directive shall not conflict with the internal provisions of member states which recognise the right of a commercial agent to inspect a principal's books.

Chapter IV

Conclusion and termination of the agency contract.

Article 13

1. Each party shall be entitled to receive from the other on request a signed written document setting out the terms of the agency contract including any terms subsequently agreed. Waiver of this right shall not be permitted.

2. Notwithstanding paragraph 1 a member state may provide that an agency contract shall not be valid unless evidenced in writing.

Article 14

An agency contract for a fixed period which continues to be performed by both parties after that period has expired shall be deemed to be converted into an agency contract for an indefinite period.

Article 15

1. Where an agency contract is concluded for an indefinite period either party may terminate it by notice.

2. The period of notice shall be one month for the first year of the contract, two months for the second year commenced, and three months for the third year commenced and subsequent years. The parties may not agree on shorter periods of notice.

3. Member states may fix the period of notice at four months for the fourth year of the contract, five months for the fifth year and six months for the sixth and subsequent years. They may decide that the parties may not agree to shorter periods.

4. If the parties agree on longer periods than those laid down in paragraphs 2 and 3, the period of notice to be observed by the principal must not be shorter than that to be observed by the commercial agent.

5. Unless otherwise agreed by the parties, the end of the period of notice must coincide with the end of a calendar month.

6. The provisions of this Article shall apply to an agency contract for a fixed period where it is converted under Article 14 into an agency contract for an indefinite period, subject to the proviso that the earlier fixed period must be taken into account in the calculation of the period of notice.

Article 16

Nothing in this Directive shall affect the application of the law of the member states where the latter provides for the immediate termination of the agency contract:

(a) because of the failure of one party to carry out all or part of his obligations;

(b) where exceptional circumstances arise.

Article 17

1. Member states shall take the measures necessary to ensure that the commercial agent is, after termination of the agency contract, indemnified in accordance with paragraph 2 or compensated for damage in accordance with paragraph 3.

2.(a) The commercial agent shall be entitled to an indemnity if and to the extent that:

— he has brought the principal new customers or has significantly increased the volume of business with existing customers and the principal continues to derive substantial benefits from the business with such customers, and

— the payment of this indemnity is equitable having regard to all the circumstances and, in particular, the commission lost by the commercial agent on the business transacted with such customers. Member states may provide for such circumstances also to include the application or otherwise of a restraint of trade clause, within the meaning of Article 20;

(b) The amount of the indemnity may not exceed a figure equivalent to an indemnity for one year calculated from the commercial agent's average annual remuneration over the preceding five years and if the contract goes back less than five years the indemnity shall be calculated on the average for the period in question;

(c) The grant of such an indemnity shall not prevent the commercial agent from seeking damages.

3. The commercial agent shall be entitled to compensation for the damage he suffers as a result of the termination of his relations with the principal.

Such damage shall be deemed to occur particularly when the termination takes place in circumstances:

— depriving the commercial agent of the commission which proper performance of the agency contract would have procured him whilst providing the principal with substantial benefits linked to the commercial agent's activities,

— and/or which have not enabled the commercial agent to amortise the costs and expenses that he had incurred for the performance of the agency contract on the principal's advice.

4. Entitlement to the indemnity as provided for in paragraph 2 or to compensation for damage as provided for under paragraph 3, shall also arise where the agency contract is terminated as a result of the commercial agent's death.

5. The commercial agent shall lose his entitlement to the indemnity in the instances provided for in paragraph 2 or to compensation for damage in the instances provided for in paragraph 3, if within one year following termination of the contract he has not notified the principal that he intends pursuing his entitlement.

6. The Commission shall submit to the Council, within eight years following the date of notification of this Directive, a report on the implementation of this Article, and shall if necessary submit to it proposals for amendments.

Article 18

The indemnity or compensation referred to in Article 17 shall not be payable:

(a) where the principal has terminated the agency contract because of default attributable to the commercial agent which would justify immediate termination of the agency contract under national law;

(b) where the commercial agent has terminated the agency contract, unless such termination is justified by circumstances attributable to the principal or on grounds of age, infirmity or illness of the commercial agent in consequence of which he cannot reasonably be required to continue his activities;

(c) where, with the agreement of the principal, the commercial agent assigns his rights and duties under the agency contract to another person.

Article 19

The parties may not derogate from Articles 17 and 18 to the detriment of the commercial agent before the agency contract expires.

Article 20

1. For the purposes of this Directive, an agreement restricting the business activities of a commercial agent following termination of the agency contract is hereinafter referred to as a restraint of trade clause.

2. A restraint of trade clause shall be valid only if and to the extent that:

(a) it is concluded in writing; and

(b) it relates to the geographical area or the group of customers and the geographical area entrusted to the commercial agent and to the kind of goods covered by his agency under the contract.

3. A restraint of trade clause shall be valid for not more than two years after termination of the agency contract.

4. This Article shall not affect provisions of national law which impose other restrictions on the validity or enforceability of restraint of trade clauses or which enable the courts to reduce the obligations on the parties resulting from such an agreement.

Chapter V

General and final provisions

Article 21

Nothing in this Directive shall require a member state to provide for the disclosure of information where such disclosure would be contrary to public policy.

Article 22

1. Member states shall bring into force the provisions necessary to comply with this Directive before 1 January 1990. They shall forthwith inform the Commission thereof. Such provisions shall apply at least to contracts concluded after their entry into force. They shall apply to contracts in operation by 1 January 1994 at the latest.

2. As from the notification of this Directive, member states shall communicate to the Commission the main laws, regulations and administrative provisions which they adopt in the field governed by this Directive.

3. However, with regard to Ireland and the United Kingdom, 1 January 1990 referred to in paragraph 1 shall be replaced by 1 January 1994.

With regard to Italy, 1 January 1990 shall be replaced by 1 January 1993 in the case of the obligations deriving from Article 17.

Article 23

This Directive is addressed to the member states.

Done at Brussels, 18 December 1986.

For the Council
The President
M. JOPLING

Franchisors to whom the questionnaire was sent
(CHAPTER 7)

FRANCE

M Philippe Sabran
Intermer
21 Du Bois De Leuze
13310 St-Martin-de-Crau
France

M Welsch
Actuel Club
33 Champs-Elysées
75008 Paris
France

M Alain Constant
FA1
107 Rue de Courcelles
75107 Paris
France

M Frederic Creutzer
Alain Manoukian SA
104 Rue Réaumur
75002 Paris
France

M Chancerel
Alufast
Rue des Chauffours
Imm Les Bureaux de Cergy
95002 Cergy-Pontoise
France

M Claude Caplain
Groupe André
28 Rue de Flandre
75940 Paris Cedex 19
France

M Gerard Peyrichoux
Laines Anny Blatt
50 Rue de L'Epideme
BP300
59203 Tourcoing Cedex

M Bergeaud
Actua Sa
16 Cité Joly
75011 Paris
France

M Quiniou/Mlle Naudan
Michel Quiniou
97 Rue de Rennes
75006 Paris
France

M Henry Bertieux
SA Alain Afflelou
3 Rue des Quatre Cheminées
92100 Boulogne-Billancourt
France

M Jean-Claud Mantion
International Logistic-System
36 Rue Roux de Brignoles
13006 Marseille
France

M Bernard Pruvot
SA Maxiam
15 Avenue de la Résistance
Centre Cial Croix de
Chavaux
93100 Montreuil
France

M Jacques Gauthier
Offemont SA
226 Rue de Rivoli
75001 Paris
France

Mme Veronique Batier
Jean Laporte Artisan
Parfumeur
8 Rue de la Boétie
75008 Paris
France

M Jacques Bigey
Atebat
Zone Artisanale
68990 Heimsbrunn
France

MM Boulon/Frick
Athena Club Sa
Immeuble Forentin
71 Chemin du Moulin
Carnot
69570 Dardilly
France

M JC Violet
A G A V
22 rue Audibert Lavirotte
69008 Lyon
France

M Hagron
B 3 Services
57 Boulevard de la Villette
75010 Paris
France

M Michel Enee
Chaussures Bally-France
95 Bis Boulevard Richard
Lenoir
75011 Paris
France

M Luthy/M Lemaire
Dans un Jardin Exploitation Sa
12 Rieu
1208 Génève

M Philippe Ledru
Supermarché Doc
94 Rue Albert Calmette
78350 Juoy-En-Josas
France

MM Favier/Tahar
Marshall SA
3 rue Rougemont
75009 Paris
France

M Jean-Jacques Schott
Bidegain SA
Avenue Montardon
64000 Pau
France

MM Grosz/Mortier
Barter Associés Intern SA
24 Cours Evrard de Fayolle
33000 Bordeaux
France

M Rouveyre
Bata SA
Tour Eve
1 Place Tour Sud, la
Défense
92806 Puteaux
France

Mme Figeac
Hygiène Diffusion
ZI des Fournels
34400 Lunel-Viel
France

M Jacques Berdy
Berdy
13 rue Labie
75017 Paris
France

M R Cahn
Betco
14 Avenue de Vendome
BP 822
41008 Blois Cedex
France

M Jean-Charles Chekroun
Spiral SA
101 rue du Mas Saint-Pierre
Zac de Tournezy Bat 12
34000 Montpellier
France

M Tiberghien
Compobaie SA
ZA la Vialette
81150 Marssac
France

M Bernard Cohen
Bonpoint Sa
67 rue de L'Université
75007 Paris
France

M Franck Grignon
Disco – Groupe Printemps
7 Allée du Cdt Mouchotte
91550 Paray-Vieille-Poste
France

M Regnault
Franchise Concepts et
Develop
BP 136
Avenue D'Avignon
84962 le Pontet Cedex
France

M Maestripieri
Hervillier
50 rue de L'Epideme
59200 Tourcoing
France

M Dulaurier
Bijouterie du Medoc
Centre Commercial
Meriadeck
33092 Bordeaux Cedex
France

M Subercazes
Sarl BJS Franchise
166 rue Frère
33000 Bordeaux
France

Mme De La Maisonneuve
Sarl Bonnefête
134 Avenue Achille Peretti
92200 Neuilly
France

M Henri Griffon
La Boutique Griffon SA
93 Boulevard Haussmann
75008 Paris
France

M Edmond Bouville
Centrale Service Pro
Centre D'Affaires Cap –
Ouest
6 rue Eugène Thomas
17000 La Rochelle
France

M Gerard Colas
Buffalo Grill Sa
RN 20
91630 Avrainville
France

Mme Bineau
Carel
4 rue Tronchet
75008 Paris
France

M Gerard Poisson
Carrosserie de France
1 rue de Paris
94470 Boissy-Saint-Leger
France

M Andre Regard
Catena France
13/15 rue de la Verrerie
75004 Paris
France

M Patrick Gasselin
Caverne des Particuliers SA
12 rue des Etats Généraux
78000 Versailles
France

M Xavier Carette
Catteau SA
45 rue D'Isbergues
62120 Aire S/Lys
France

MM Venturini/Coutant
But International
BP 82
77312 Marne-la-Valée
Cedex 2
France

M Henri Briancon
Dinofran et Cie
38 Boulevard Gallieni
92390 Villeneuve-la-Garenne
France

M Eric Saiz
Caroll International
14 rue Chapon
75003 Paris
France

M Yannick Fruchet
SA Catimini
94 rue Choletaise
BP 67
49450 Saint-Macaire-en-
Mauges
France

M Michel Salzard
Sarl Caves du Val D'Or
71640 Mercurey
France

M Barret
Invest Center
Mauriane Parc D'Activité
Chemin du Littoral
13016 Marseille
France

M Pierre Marcorelles
Marcorel
Z1
34880 Laverune
France

M Jean-Pierre Mongon
Cerruti 1881 SA
3 Place de la Madeleine
75008 Paris
France

M Daniel Maitre
Promodes France
Tour Avenir Ouest
64 rue du 8 Mai 1945
92000 Nanterre
France

M Majonchi/Mlle Fraenkel
Chantegrill Sarl
28 Route de Versailles
78430 Louveciennes
France

M Raduszynski
Franck Mickael
30 rue de Berri
75008 Paris
France

Mme Martine Robion
PRM SA
30 rue des Saints-Pères
75007 Paris
France

M Didier Halphen
Chaussac
66 Avenue Paul Doumer
92500 Rueil Malmaison
France

M Bertrand Evrard
Aldeta Conseils SA
3-5 rue Saint-Génois
BP 111
59001 Lille Cedex
France

Mme Durand/M di Pierro
Chacok
1050 Route de la Mer
06410 Biot
France

Mme Tryoen
Chantal Thomass Studio
100 rue du Cherche Midi
75006 Paris
France

M Jean Maurice Rosaye
Charles Jourdan
28 Avenue de New York
75016 Paris
France

M Chatillon
Chatillon Sarl
6 rue Victor Hugo
29200 Brest
France

M Leclerc/M Lepoutre
Chausport
27 rue Claude Lorrain
59100 Roubaix
France

M Benazech
Cheminees Juval
RN 117
31800 Labarthe Inard
France

M Layani
SEBH
31 rue de la Gare
Bat 334
93001 Aubervilliers
France

M Akil
Chrysalia Orfèvre
1 Allée Verte
75001 Paris
France

M Chavanon
5 A Sec France
7 rue Vallon Jourdan
13007 Marseille
France

Mle Maxime/Mme Farci
Claude Maxime Rive
Gauche
16 rue de L'Abbaye
75006 Paris
France

Mme Sadock Francine
Cocon
25 rue Quentin Bauchart
75008 Paris
France

M Housset
Franchise Comptoirs
Modernes
1 Place du Gue de Maulny
72100 Le Mans
France

M Francis Lacroix
Comtesse du Barry Sa
Route de Touget
32200 Gimont
France

M Journault
Chouette un Tonneau Sa
6 Place Notre Dame
38000 Grenoble
France

M R Boudot
Chinna Sa
BP 1
01470 Briord
France

M Sabourin
Clairbois France
117 Route de Poitiers
86280 Saint-Bénoit
France

M Francois Picq
Climat de France Sa
14 Avenue des Andes
BP 93
91943 Les Ulis Cedex
France

M Georges L Hauguel
Coffea Sa
70 rue Dumont D'Urville
76600 le Havre
France

M Bruno Lemoine
Computerland France
52 rue de la Boëtie
75008 Paris
France

M Michel Spinelli
Corextel Sa
173 Bureaux de la Colline
92213 Saint-Cloud Cedex
France

Service Franchise
Connexion SA
82 Boulevard de Picpus
75012 Paris
France

M Frederic Nouailhac
Coste Diffusion
15 Rue Des Cerisiers
91090 Lisses
France

Mme Suzanne Boucher
Creations Yves Saint Brice
47 Bis Rue Bouvreuil
76000 Rouen
France

M Thierry Tombret
Cuir Center France
176-182 Boulevard De
Charonne
75020 Paris
France

M Nicolet
Plus International
312 Route De Benodet
29000 Quimper
France

M Stephane Levalois
Dal'Alu
Beautiran
33640 Portets
France

M Yonnel Balez
De Maison Pierre
19 Rue Jules Ferry
38100 Grenoble
France

M Divry
Copy 2000 SA
39 rue D'Amsterdam
75008 Paris
France

M Daniel Ansart
Courrèges SA
40 rue François 1ER
75008 Paris
France

M Montredon
Conseil Technique
Immobilier
10 rue Ordener
75018 Paris
France

M Georges Benyaich
France Chauffage
61 Boulevard Bessieres
75017 Paris
France

M Ponchon
Culasse
23 Avenue Des Vieux
Moulins
BP 380 – ZI De Vovray
74012 Annecy
France

M Regis Maquet
S I P C
4 Ter Avenue Hoche
75008 Paris
France

Mlle Bertrand
Sarl Prodec
La Croix Blanche
74330 Sillingy
France

M Alain Dufour
Delta Protection
Parc D'Affaires De Dardilly
BP 70
69543 Champagne Au Mont
D'or
France

M Frederic Dansette
Descamps
88 rue de Rivoli
6BIS/10 Av Ledru Rollin
75012 Paris
Cedex 04
France

M Alain Puel
Aux Ducs De Gascogne
Route De Mauvezin
82200 Gimont
France

M Brun
Elegance Canine
4 Avenue Gambetta
06600 Antibes
France

M Paris
EPVM Partenariat
6 rue Rogier
51100 Reims
France

Mme Payard
Espace Loggia
5 Bis Faubourg Bretagne
41220 La Ferté-St-Cyr
France

Melle Daneluzzi
Etoffe Et Maison Expansion
74 rue de Rennes
75006 Paris
France

M Jean-Paul Cervin
Arta Creation
101 rue Lesage
51100 Reims
France

M Christian Gouron
Ste Gle Revetements
Dominotier
4 Avenue du Maine
75015 Paris
France

M JP Saulnier
Ecotel Sa
Min
Route De Marseille
84000 Avignon
France

M Charles Seroude
Epac International
60 rue Michel-Ange
75016 Paris
France

M Jeanpierre
Groupe Printemps Prisunic
102 rue de Provence
75009 Paris
France

Mm Garnier/Barny
Etam Sa
6 Square De L'Opera L
Jouvet
75009 Paris
France

M Salin
Europ'Yachting
Port de Plaisance de Paris
11 Boulevard de la Bastille
75012 Paris
France

Mireille Barreau
Felicitas
58 avenue des Vosges
67000 Strasbourg
France

M Bertrand Evrard
Aldeta Conseis Sa
3-5 rue Saint-Génois
BP 111
59001 Lille Cedex
France

M Prost
La Foir'Fouille Sa
1000 route de Nimes
BP 3
34170 Castelnau Le Lez
France

Genevieve Schloesser
Diffusion France Foulards
3 Quai au Sable
67000 Strasbourg
France

M Pierre Rousseau
Le Fournil de Pierre
214 Avenue du Président
Wilson
93210 La Plaine-Saint-Denis
France

M Jean-Louis Arnoux
Meijac Sa
BP 237
34506 Béziers Cedex
France

M Chretiennot
Geant Service
Plan de Campagne
13480 Cabries
France

M Portes
Flash One France
29 rue Bayen
75017 Paris
France

M Bisch
Fly Mobilier Europeen
14 Avenue de Colmar
BP 1308
680-56 Mulhouse Cedex
France

M Armandeh
Global France
2 C rue de L'Epine
Prolongee
Bureau de la Noue
93541 Bagnolet Cedex
France

JP Laurent Atthalin
Fountain Industries France
ZI Cantimpre
Fontaine N D
59400 Cambrai
France

M Philippe de Nombel
Francesco Smalto
International
29 rue Marbeuf
75008 Paris
France

Mme Gaby Ache
Garage de France
248 Avenue
De Thouars
33400 Talence
France

M Denis Marque
Genevieve Lethu SA
BP 1037
17007 La Rochelle Cedex
France

M Regis Macquet
Soceite Georges Rech
112 rue Réaumur
75002 Paris
France

Mme Claudine Orsini
Gisele Delorme SA
29 rue Louis Blanc
75010 Paris
France

M Francis Laffay
Guillemets Expansion
Zone Civile de la Base
RN 330
60100 Creil
France

M Marc Lafourcade
Pluri Publi SA
33 Avenue Mozart
75016 Paris
France

M Yvon Binet
Promodes France
Route de Paris
14120 Mondeville
France

M D Lerouge
Gram
Rue des Saumonieres
44300 Nantes
France

M Bourdeau/M Ruetsy
SARL SMG
Rue de L'Aiguefou
49230 St-Germain-
Sur-Moine
France

M Pierre de Lagarde
Groupe Informatique
Marquet
105 Avenue de la
République
BP 21
59561 La Madeleine
France

Mme Pawsci
SA Evasion Et Loisirs
17 rue de Puebla
29200 Brest
France

M Denis Grenouiller
SARL HLP
24 rue du 11 Novembre
42100 Saint-Etienne
France

M Daniel Kauz
D F C
1 rue du Bois
92140 Clamart
France

M Edmond David
Infinitif SA
26 rue du Caire
75002 Paris
France

M Lucien Gleyzes
ITA France
54 Boulevard Gabriel
Koenigs
31300 Toulouse
France

M Pascal Birer
Jacadi SA
132 rue de Billancourt
92100 Boulogne
France

Dominique Gireil
SARL C & G
54 Port Saint-Sauveur
3100 Toulouse
France

M Philippe Dassie
Un Jardin En Plus SA
82 rue de Montigny
95100 Argenteuil
France

M Serge Gros
Gerome Coiffure SA
5 rue Cambon
75001 Paris
France

M Jean-Marc Athuil
Atelson SA
12 Bis rue du Plateau
92500 Rueil Malmaison
France

M Garnier/M Barny
Kiosk (Groupe Etam)
6 Square de L'Opéra Louis
Jouvet
75009 Paris
France

M Christian Salisson
Lasserre Pret-A-Porter
SARL
19 Chemin de la Garonne
31200 Toulouse
France

M Michel Cauvin
Franklin Holding SA
37 Avenue Franklin
Roosevelt
75008 Paris
France

M Bruno Coquelin
STE Tripode
26 rue de la Maison Rouge
Lognes
77323 Marne La Vallee
Cedex 2
France

M Jean-Paul Reffet
SA Jean Barnasson Et Cie
116 rue Saint-Dominique
75007 Paris
France

M JF Lazartique
CTRC JF Lazartique
3 rue Faubourg Saint-
Honoré
75008 Paris
France

M Jean Marie Effosse
Bijoutiers de France
20 rue des Quatre Fils
75003 Paris
France

MM Carpentier/Deruelle
Kodokan Sport Sa
Zone Industrielle N 1
BP 91
62290 Noeux Les Mines
France

M Mondolfo
Club Franchise Distribution
54/56 rue de Guingand
92300 Levallois
France

M Montfollet
Groupe Levitan
BP 12
60290 Rantigny
France

Mme Louise Bitau
Karil − M
175 rue du Temple
75003 Paris
France

M Roland Escargnel
ETS Escargnel
9 rue Fauchier
13002 Marseille
France

M Philippe Roger
LPO
438 Avenue de la Division
Leclerc
92290 Chatenay Malabry
France

Mme Colombet
Madura SA
11 rue de Poissy
75005 Paris
France

M Bernard Hipeau
Vieux Chene Expansion
9 Route De Saint Leu
95360 Montmagny
France

Mme Texte
ECL Entreprise Construc.
Loire
12-18 Avenue De La
Jonchere
Elysee II
78170 La Celle St-Cloud
France

M Lamielle
Roset SA
BP 9
Briord
91470 Serrières De Briord
France

Mme Bassement
Création Loisir
Développement
13 Quai Georges V
76600 Le Havre
France

M Georges Drouin
Lovefrance SA
Route De Vannes
BP 414
44819 St Herblain Cedex
France

Mme Michelle Geneton
Madison
20 Rue Du Morvan
94620 Rungis
France

M Michel Goldenberg
La Maison D'Eloise
18 Bis Avenue Clemenceau
94170 Le Perreux
France

M Daniel Chambourdon
Kiteco
1401 Chemin De Cleres
76230 Bois Guillaume
France

M Paumard/M Poirier
Sonkad SA
4 Rue Des Ridelleries
53000 Laval
France

M Monpetit
Marese
17 Rue De La Poterne
38100 Grenoble
France

M Patrice Vassy
Aquarius SA
1 Rue De Seguret Saincric
12000 Rodez
France

Mm Malet/Breville
Hotels Mercure
7 Allee Du Brevent
91021 Evry Cedex
France

M Michel Brault
Ste Tourangelle De
Commerce
28 Quai Foch
17230 Marans
France

M Rosaz
Mobis SA
107 Rue Edith Cavell
94400 Vitry
France

M Gilles Martin
SA Kit Diffusion
ZA Les Calsades
BP 2
12340 Bozouls
France

M Johannes Wilhelm
Mastok International
100 Route De Thionville
57050 Metz
France

Mm J Domas/P Gueugneau
Profrance SA
4 Rue Felix Jacquier
BP 6013
69466 Lyon Cedex 06
France

M Michel Rady
Mercatique Et Distribution
58110 Brinay
France

M Luc Thevenin
Le Silencieux SA
96 Avenue Paul Doumer
BP 226
92503 Rueil Malmaison
Cedex
France

Mme Valerie Dillmann
DDM
46 Avenue De Segur
75015 Paris
France

Melle Chaillou
Mod's Hair SARL
9 Rue Saint-Sabin
75011 Paris
France

M Le Roy
ANPF
2-4 Rue Pierre Et Marie
Curie
45140 Ingre
France

M Jacques Bidon
Discount Club
89 Route De Laghet
06340 La Trinité
France

Melle Weil
Natalys
18 Avenue Gallieni
92000 Nanterre
France

M H Foare
Jacques Jaunet SA
51 Avenue Du Marechal
Leclerc
49300 Cholet
France

M Yves Portrat
Nuggets SA
4 Quai De Seine
93400 Saint-Ouen
France

Mm Pommier/Casenave
SARL L'Onglerie
54 Quai De Brazza
BP 107
33105 Bordeaux Cedex
France

M Lucien Roucaute
Roucaute SA
Numero 3.589
Première Avenue
06510 Carros
France

Mme Fabienne Mesnier
Petit Bateau SA
8 Rue Brey
75017 Paris
France

M Lecine
Myrys
Route D'Alet
11300 Limoux
France

Mm Ribas/Van Durme
Sagam
4 Allée Verte
75011 Paris
France

Mme Proust
Norgil
51 Rue De L'Alcazar
59800 Lille
France

M Olivier Desforges
SA Des Ets Olivier
Desforges et Cie
40 Rue De L'Abbé Lemire
BP 203
59561 La Madeleine Cedex
France

M Caribaux
Camad
12 Rue Du Sergent Maginot
75016 Paris
France

M Michel Carron
Parapharm SA
27 Avenue Jean Baptiste Le
Bas
59480 La Bassée
France

M Bernard Boutin
Desmazieres SA
Chemin Des Coteaux
64800 Nay
France

M Bernard Becue
Les Fils De Louis Muilliez
112 Rue Du Collège
59100 Roubaix
France

MM Maroni/Enjolras
Photorush
12 Rue Charles De Mangou
18340 Levet
France

M Stany
Pierre Laroche Diffusion
108 Rue Réaumur
75002 Paris
France

Patrice Skoupsky
Davtex SA
28 Rue Desseaux
76100 Rouen Cedex
France

M JP Matras
Ste Financiere Jolimat
13 Rue Principale
21110 Bretenieres
France

M Michel Vial
Jardineries Expansion
3 Avenue De Romans
26000 Valence
France

M Rosenberg
Soprovi SA
15 Route De Beaune
21300 Chenove
France

M Tribalat
Photoflash SARL
10 Faubourg Saint Pierre
03100 Montlucon
France

M H De Tregomain
Ets Pierbe
28 Avenue Barthelemy
Thimonnier
69300 Caluire
France

M Henri Schu
Groupe Pigier SA
114 Rue Marius Aufan
92300 Levallois-Perret
France

M Vercleven
Lainieres De Roubaix
149 Rue D'Oran
59100 Roubaux
France

M Ruhlmann
Société M Phi SA
4 Route De Pfulgriesheim
67370 Griesheim S/Souffel
France

Mme Morgeaux
Sofoga
166 Avenue Georges
Clemenceau
92000 Nanterre
France

Melle Graff/M Cousin
Point Nature
70 Avenue De La
Republique
94700 Maisons-Alfort
France

M B Vaillant
SA Bretonniere
173 Rue Saint-Martin
75003 Paris
France

Marc-Andre De Gorgue
Sodireg
ZI De Fosse Saint-Witz
95470 Fosses
France

M Thevent
Sodigral
ZI De Bissy
BP 409
73000 Chambéry
France

M Hervé Haezebrouck
SA Pronuptia De Paris
8 Place De L'Opéra
75009 Paris
France

Valerie Monnier
Les Facadiers Qualitec
21 Rue Du Chai Des Farines
33000 Bordeaux
France

Mme Sarreau
Le Relais Des Caves
BP 185
69822 Belleville Cedex
France

MM Pux/Beasse
Renov'Car SARL
BP 515
Zac Des Vergers –
Collegien
77090 Collegien
France

M Scoffier
La Porcelaine Blanche
32 Rue Des Renaudes
75017 Paris
France

Mle Carmona/M Balazun
Presto Pizza
115 Avenue Saint-Medard
33320 Eysines
France

M Jeanpierre
Groupe Printemps-Prisunic
102 Rue de Provence
75009 Paris
France

Mme Galy-Ache
Pneus Service France
ZA De Thouars
248 Avenue De Thouars
33400 Talence
France

M Daniel Terrier
Inhotel SA
20 Rue Du Pont Des Halles
94656 Rungis Cedex
France

M Daviau
SARL Le Relais Du
Vigneron
Le Clos Martigneau
49130 Juigne S/Loire
France

M Labreuille
RTM France
24 Rue Auguste Chabrieres
75015 Paris
France

M Monge
SARL es Cinq M
31 Avenue De L'Océan
33930 Montalivet
France

M Laurent Pincon
SARL Sodereve
5 Rue De La Folie Regnault
75011 Paris
France

M Himbaut/M Turfait
Turfait Compagnie SA
38-39 Rue Louis Armand
ZI Aix-En-Provence
13763 Les Milles Cedex
France

MM Juffroy/Le Tannou
Saint Algue Enterprise
14 Rue Des Deux Gares
75010 Paris
France

M Frederic Yelkovanian
San Marina
ZI Les Paluds
155 Avenue Du Dirigeable
13685 Aubagne Cedex
France

J Bougon/P Wecksteen
Shop Photo Video Groupe
16 Rue au Pain
78000 Versailles
France

M Christian Simon
SA Cofipar
31 Cours Langlet
51100 Reims
France

M Andre Retif
Retif SA
RN 7 Les Deux Rives
06270 Villeneuve Loubet
France

M Claude Girardin
Intexal
1 Rue Du Parc
92300 Levallois Perret
France

Mme Annino
Rural
57 Bld De La Villette
75010 Paris
France

M Revel
GTI
9 Rue Des Alpes
69120 Vaulx-En-Vélin
France

M Paul Zemmour
Major
11 Bis Rue Rabelais
93100 Montreuil
France

M Yvon Binet
Promodes France
ZI Route De Paris
14120 Mondeville
France

M Canet
Laboratoire Simone Malher
106 Quai Des Chartrons
33082 Bordeaux Cedex
France

M Michel Briol
Futura-France/Singer
41-43 Rue Pergolese
75116 Paris
France

M G Wacrenier
Ets Jules De Surmont
47 Rue De Bradford
59200 Tourcoing
France

M Bruno Escur
Soho
20 Avenue Sommer
ZI D'Antony
92167 Antony
France

M Philippe Verger
SOS Service
28 Rue Pascal
75005 Paris
France

M B Herlin
FBH
74 Avenue Du General De
Gaulle
72000 Le Mans
France

Mme Legendre
Stefanel France
43 Rue Des Francs
Bourgeois
75004 Paris
France

Nicole David
STP Groupe
ZI Des Yvaudieres
Rue Du Colombier
37705 St-Pierre-Des-Corps
France

Paul Roux
Sipeg
Grange De Malassis CD 40
91400 Gometz La Ville
France

Mme Millot
Accor-Sofitel
5 Rue Du Venoux
91021 Evry Cedex
France

M Vaudo/DPT Franchise
SARL Depot Vinicole
Route Nationale 19
77171 Sourdun
France

Mme Colette Lebenbojm
Tecmodis SA
142 Boulevard Diderot
75012 Paris
France

M Carpentier
CSI SARL
27 Rue Eugène Pelletan
94100 Saint-Maur-Des-
Fosses
France

M Abrial
SA Stephane Kelian
Avenue R Schuman
BP 88
26302 Bourg-De-Péage
France

M JF Mouton
Les Structures Francaises
61 Boulevard Bessières
75017 Paris
France

Nathalie Noguera
Studios Du Chesnay
6 Rue Mazière
78000 Versailles
France

M Andre Regard
Catena France
13/15 Rue De La Verrerie
75004 Paris
France

Mme Helene Prazowski
Ste Nvelle D'Exp La
Sweaterie
6 Rue Desire Granet
ZI Du Val D'Argent
95105 Argenteuil
France

M Rosenfeld
Sym SA
8 Rue Du Chemin Vert
75011 Paris
France

M Berthelot
Dermagne SA
5 Avenue Caroline
92210 Saint-Cloud
France

Mme Geraldine Thibault
Tartine Et Chocolat
99 Rue De La Verrerie
75004 Paris
France

Monique Pawlak
Franchinor Expansion
230 Avenue Jean Jaurès
59790 Ronchin
France

M Philippe Bonnal
Sunset Ice Cream
33 Avenue Du Maine
Tour Maine Montparnasse
75755 Paris Cedex 15
France

M Claude Rouquet
Alpha Service
8 Rue Porte Basse
33000 Bordeaux
France

M Daniel Lefebvre
SA Les Mag. Sylvain
Lefebvre
4 Rue Chaubaud
51100 Reims
France

M Cretin
Tandy France
C Cial Les 3 Fontaines
BP 147
95022 Cergy Cedex
France

M Guy Loiseaux
Tapis Nord SARL
47 Route De Mons
59600 Bettignies
France

M Dominique Montlaur
La Taste De Provence
ZA Les Chalus
04300 Forcalquier
France

M Bernard
TSF
Rue Jean De France
60650 Villers-Saint-
Barthélémy
France

M Didier Gheza
Tempera Diffusion
8 Route De Galice
13090 Aix En Provence
France

M Franck Grignon
Disco – Groupe Printemps
7 Allee Du CDT Mouchotte
91550 Paray-Vieille-Poste
France

Hughes De La Taille
Tousalon France
2508 – RN 20
BP 112 Saran
45400 Fleury-Les-Aubrais
France

M Gassot
Central Sports
ZA Nord
Avenue Du Meyrol
26200 Montélimar
France

M Luc Delforge
SA Herbaut
57 Rue De La Liberté
BP 9
62119 Dourges
France

M Robert Eymeric
Le Tuc Immobilier
4 Rue De Tourre
84100 Orange
France

M Paul Dudon
SA Dudon-Larquier
7 Avenue Maréchal Foch
64000 Pau
France

M Ferreux
Tissus Guy Patrice
4 Rue Aristide Briand
90000 Belfort
France

MM Barthalot/Hazan
D.E.C.O.R. 17 SA
17 Avenue Des Ternes
75017 Paris
France

Mme Susperregui
C.N.C.F.
Le Peyret – St Medard
D'Eyrans
BP 2
33650 Labrede
France

M Pascal Lescouzeres
Franchi-Troc
33 Boulevard Solferino
35000 Rennes
France

M Brunet
ETS Horticoles G Truffaut
Ferme De La Maison Neuve
91220 Bretigny-Sur-Orge
France

M Roland Jallot
Aurelien SA
6 Cité Paradis
75010 Paris
France

Mm Garnier/Barny
Etam SA
6 Square De L'Opéra L
Jouvet
75009 Paris
France

M Jean-Luc Ferre
Uni Centre Promotion SA
5 Avenue Jean Laigret
41000 Blois
France

M Henri Masson
Unicis
16 Rue Faidherbe
BP 237
69002 Lille Cedex
France

Mme Cordier
Union Conseil
18 Rue Kléber
92400 Courbevoie
France

Mme Caput
SA Ena
5/7 Chemin Des Tuileries
13015 Marseille Saint-
Antoine
France

M Roger Autaa
Roger Autaa Distribution
SARL
10 Rue Bourg Mayou
64160 Morlaas
France

Caroline Vandenbroucke
Aluminium Systemes
42 Route De Deulemont
59560 Warneton
France

M Regis Macquet
Societe Georges Rech
112 Rue Réaumur
75002 Paris
France

Mme Janine Crepet
Uni Inter SA
26 Rue Thomassin
BP 2051
69226 Lyon Cedex 02
France

Mme Michele D'Amico
Unideal
23 Route De Cannes
06650 Opio
France

M Hervé Labouree
Sté Internationale Du Siège
50 Rue Du Faubourg Saint-
Antoine
75012 Paris
France

M Dugas
Sodifra
3 Avenue Paul Séjourne
31000 Toulouse
France

M Alain Arnauld
Ste Du Vernet
36 Boulevard Pasteur
63000 Clermont-Ferrand
France

M De Colonges
Gle De Transports & Ind
GTI
Tour Europe
92080 Paris La Défense
CX7
France

Mme Balgan
La Vie Claire SA
70 Avenue De La
Republique
94700 Maisons Alfort
France

M Millet Lage
A Link SARL
25 Rue Du Grand Saint-Jean
24000 Montepellier
France

M Jacques Richebois
Weinberg SA
31 Rue Des Jeuneurs
75002 Paris
France

M JP Fischer
E.P.I.B.
BP 57
ZAC Le Plateau De Biere
77192 Dammarie-les-Lys
France

M Guy Rabuel
Z – Groupe Zannier
3 Boulevard Saint Martin
75003 Paris
France

M Humbert
Accore-Franchise
6 Quai Pierre Scize
69009 Lyon
France

Mme Levavasseur
Victoire
12 Place Des Victoires
75002 Paris
France

M Gerard Denise
S.E.A.V.T.
106 Rue Danton
BP 325
92306 Levallois Perret
Cedex
France

Pascal Marechal
Weiber France
72 Quai Des Carrières
94220 Charenton-Le-Pont
France

M Chelly
S.C.H.
48 Rue Alphonse Penud
75020 Paris
France

M Alain Bertrand
Lab Bio Végétale Yves
Rocher
6 Avenue Kléber
75116 Paris
France

M Patrice Vassy
Aquarius SA
1 Rue Seguret Saincric
12000 Rodez
France

M Jean-Yves Vigouroux
Ada SA
69 Avenue De Fontainebleau
94270 Le Kremlin-Bicetre
France

RA Dalloz
Euromarket France
BP 56
73800 Montmelian Cedex
France

Jean-Francois Recoules
SARL Segag
RN 88
Terssac
81150 Marssac/Tarn
France

M Gasser
Creation Diffusion France
11 Rue Lambert
68100 Mulhouse
France

M Serge Raulic
Aquatonic
Grand Hotel Des Ternes
100 Bd Hebert
35401 Saint-Malo
France

M Jacques Bigey
Atebat
Zone Artisanale
68990 Heimsbrunn
France

M Thierry Viguier
S.A.C.G.E.
36 Rue Emeriau
75015 Paris
France

Brigitte Gouere
Soficar
Le Central
6 Rue Albert Einstein
94006 Créteil L'Chat
France

Patricia Fauvel
Vecteur A
21 Rue De Miromesnil
75008 Paris
France

M Trojman
Alice Lange SA
1 Rue Des Dominicains
67000 Strasbourg
France

M Jean-Didier Astruc
Groupe Aquarius
126 Rue Réaumur
75002 Paris
France

M Mennessiez
C.E.S. SA
5 Rue Des Trois Moulins
77000 Melun
France

Bertrand De Sainte Marie
Dynamique Services
10 Rue De Meric
57050 Metz
France

M Bernard Hipeau
Vieux Chene Expansion
9 Route De Saint-Leu
95360 Montmagny
France

M Vincent David
Nouvelle Donne
BP 19
35130 La Guerche
France

M Philippe Mergaux
Autonet Diffusion
12 Rue Gustave Eiffel
94510 La Queue En Brie
France

Mmes Ciolek/Bouvard
Avis Immobilier SA
68 Boulevard De Sebastopol
75003 Paris
France

M C Dross
Balladins SA
20 Rue Du Pont Des Halles
94656 Rungis Cedex
France

M Charles Bernardini
Bazar De L'Hôtel De Ville
55 Rue De La Verrerie
75004 Paris
France

Mme Helene Heking
SARL Camhi Et Fils
5 Rue Du Dr Michel
Rosanoff
06000 Nice
France

M Deniaux
Sodial
Rue Des Cooperateurs
59220 Denain
France

M Jean-Pierre Torck
SA Camaieu
162 Bd De Fourmies
59100 Roubaix
France

M Sylvain Favard
A S M
75 Ter Rue Du Point Du
Jour
92100 Boulogne
France

M Le Roy
Plus International
Centre Commercial Rallye
312 Route De Benodet
29000 Quimper
France

M Gilles Msallan
Bausalon
14 Avenue De Colmar
BP 1308
68056 Mulhouse Cedex
France

M Charles
Bijell
39 Place Des Otages
26000 Morlaix
France

M Urbiha
Burgode SA
6 Ter Rue De Nachey
21240 Tallant
France

MM Beaumanoir/Gigou
Cache-Cache
Centre Commercial
La Madeleine
35400 Saint-Malo
France

M Martinaud
SA Echelle
113 RN 6
69720 Saint-Bonnet-
De-Mure
France

Mme Fantoni
Caroline Rohmer
75 Bis Avenue Marceau
75016 Paris
France

Mme Guirao/M Dulaurier
Societe Quatror
Des 4 Pavillons
33310 Lormont
France

M Sebastien Mele
Aspac SA
29 Rue De Léningrad
75008 Paris
France

Helene Gale
SA Centres Helene Gale
22 Cours Du Chapeau Rouge
33000 Bordeaux
France

M Lorashi/M Drieniourt
Groupe Hermes
4 Rue Emile Billoquet
76350 Oissel
France

Mme Haioun/M Driffort
Jean Cacharel SA
51 Rue Etienne Marcel
75001 Paris
France

M Alain Lemaire
Christiaensen SA
10 Rue De La Maison Rouge
Lognes
77323 Marne-La-Vallée
Cedex 2
France

M Lewinger/M Tournon
Promo Textiles
36 Rue E Noirot
42300 Roanne
France

M Bester
Maison Centmil Chemises
112 Rue De Richelieu
75002 Paris
France

M Alain Delacroix
Robert Bosch France SA
32 Avenue Michelet
93404 Saint-Ouen
France

Martine Hollender
Century Frances SA
CE 1701
91017 Evry Cedex Lisses
France

M Favennec
Plus international
312 Route De Benodet
29000 Quimper
France

M Moutet
SARL Chez Le Gaulois
Moriond
73120 Courchevel
France

Mm J Nachim/A Bornstein
Nachim
246 Rue Saint-Denis
75002 Paris
France

Mme Rebull/M Meneboeuf
Clayeux 08 Sa
Avenue Du Marechal
Leclerc
BP 91
71304 Montceau Cedex
France

M Laurent
F.I.C.
9 Rue De La Plaine
77360 Vaires S/Marne
France

M Michel Coursault
Dame Nature Sa
8 Avenue Du Marechal De
Saxe
69006 Lyon
France

Mme Chantal Konrad
De Neuville Sa
12 Rue De La Maison Route
Lognes
77323 Marne-La-Vallée
Cedex 2
France

Mme Azouze
Charles Dexter
100 Bld De Sebastopol
75003 Paris
France

M Philippe Schuller
Hypromat France
15 Rue Du Travail
67720 Hoerdt
France

Mme Rajon
SARL Equip-Club
21 Avenue Alsace Lorraine
38300 Bourgoin-Jallieu
France

M Remy Camous
Promodes France
Route Nationale 13
78240 Chambourcy
France

M D Lerouge
Gimac
Rue Des Saumonieres
44300 Nantes
France

Marianne Pinon
Daniel D SA
Route De Lavaur
BP 36
81301 Graulhet Cedex
France

M F Mathieu
Elif SA
5 Rue Sainte Lucie
31300 Toulouse
France

M C Giovannetti
O.M.I.
23 Bld Des Capucines
75002 Paris
France

M Olivier Gicquel
Avenue Placement
1 Rue De La Pepiniere
75008 Paris
France

M Marques
R Jourdain Sa
Rue Des Margats
BP 45
77521 Coulommiers Cedex
France

Service Franchise
S.E.R.G.H.
14 Rue Pièrre Ier De Serbie
75008 Paris
France

M J Gaulin
La Foire Aux Tissus
2 Bis Boulevard De La
République
47000 Agen
France

M Fournier
Fourniplast SARL
291 Route Balguerie
Stuttemberg
33000 Bordeaux
France

M Gimbert
Gimbert-Surgeles
Avenue Du Corps Franc
Pommies
32500 Fleurance
France

M JB Blanchemain
S.E.R.C.
143 Avenue Charles De
Gaulle
92200 Neuilly S/Seine
France

Mm Esnault/Tremblay
Inter Caves
ZI La Haie Griselle
94470 Boissy Saint-Leger
France

M Vidalin
Nixdorf Computer
14 Avenue Des Beguines
95802 Cergy-Pontoise
France

M JG D'Echallens
Florida International SA
Route De La Cassette
86000 Poitiers
France

Mle Jursza/M Gamel
Moly Sa
Farrou BP 113
12200 Villefranche De
Rouergue
France

M Michel Gal
French Connection
2 Rue Du Cygne
75002 Paris
France

Mme Garnier
La Fromenterie
Zone Industrielle De Grezan
Route De Beaucaire
3000 Nimes
France

M Thierry Froment
Gamm Vert Sa
83/85 Avenue De La Grande
Armée
75782 Paris Cedex 16
France

M Rozenblum
Rozex SA
7/9 Rue Du Frenier St-
Lazare
75003 Paris
France

M Grant
T.F.D./B.F. Intl
85 Rue La Fayette
75009 Paris
France

M Serge Glories
Hildegarde's Nails
Combes Dels Martyrs
BP 5
11570 Palaja-Cazilhac
France

M Lanowith
DMC
50 Bld Sebastopol
75003 Paris
France

M Lebroussais
Interior's
144 Boulevard Jules Durand
76600 Le Havre
France

M Jacky Beline
Jackson Burger
7 Rue Travot
49300 Cholet
France

M Blanc
Vigoplant Franchise
BP 32
ZI Des Charriers
17102 Saintes
France

M Richard Wagner
Cinderella
20 Rue Des Sablons
75016 Paris
France

MM Martin/Gay
GTI
9 Rue Des Alpes
69120 Vaulx En Velin
France

M Kaszuk
Sopac SA
Rue Du 3EME Souave
68130 Altkirch
France

Mme Delille
Diffujambes
87 Rue Saint-Lazare
75009 Paris
France

M Desigaud
Investissement Loisirs
38 Route De Vienne
69007 Lyon
France

M Eric Postulka
Flora Partner
23 Rue Milot
33000 Bordeaux
France

Mme Annie Marie
SARL Jardins De
Mediterranee
21 Rue Alexis Alquier
66000 Perpignan
France

M Aurelien
Desforges Franchising
Group
71 Bld Richard Lenoir
75011 Paris
France

Mme Selan
Cocidac
59 Rue De L'Ourcq
75019 Paris
France

M David Bitton
U F C
35 Rue De Turbigo
75003 Paris
France

Mme Blum Benzacar
Kookai
82 Rue Réaumur
75002 Paris
France

M Richard
Covemat
1-3 Rue Rouget De L'Isle
69604 Villeurbanne
France

Mle Frederique Merer
Lynx Optique Sa
6 Place De Stalingrad
92150 Suresnes
France

M Michel Claude
SARL Boutique Maison
L'Alsace
39 Champs-Elysées
75008 Paris
France

M Belmont/M Pierquin
S.A.D.C.
4 Bis Rue Gustave-Geffroy
75013 Paris
France

MM Rybaka/Miller
H.E.T. Entrepot Franchise
16 Rue Ledru Rollin
94100 Saint-Maur
France

M Mouralis
BCS
ZI Nord
Rue Copernic
13200 Arles
France

M Le Gall
SARL L'Italie Gourmande
26 Rue De Nemours
35000 Rennes
France

M Jean-Pierre Fischer
LMR
BP 57
ZAC Le Plateau De Bière
77192 Dammarie-Les-Lys
Cedex
France

Mle Valerie Quintana
SARL Madrilene Diffusion
17/19 Rue De La Moulinatte
33130 Begles
France

M Didier Boivin
Polyprotec
8 Place De La Madeleine
75008 Paris
France

M Rene Boissin
Gesfra
ZA Saint-Vincent
73190 Challes-Les-Eaux
France

M Desplanques
Baticonseil SA
26600 Granges-Lès-
Beaumont
France

M Philippe Lafon
Marcelle Griffon
ZI De Riorges
42309 Roanne
France

M Thauvin
Mid
131 Rue Cardinet
75017 Paris
France

M Vincent Mousseigne
Nicolas SA
252 Avenue Du Général
Leclerc
94700 Maisons Alfort
France

M Francois Picq
Nuit D'Hotel
14 Avenue Des Andes
BP 93
91943 Les Ulis Cedex
France

M Philippe Brocart
S.F.A.T.D.
99 Rue De Lyon
13015 Marseille
France

M Bigret
SMCB
9 Ter/11 Rue Carnot
94270 Le Kremlin 7
Bicetre
France

M Xavier Durand
SARL Marison Becal
Rue Courteline
BP 13
66750 Saint-Cyprien
France

M Chesnot
SVPHR
64 Rue Du Maréchal Foch
78000 Versailles
France

M Christian Herry
Texindis SA
3 Avenue De Romans
26000 Valence
France

M Alfredo Julio
Les Nouvelles Boulangeries
1 Rue Auguste Perret
BAT B − Ilot 7 − Silic 310
94588 Rungis Cedex
France

M Alain Levi
Office Des Particuliers (L')
1 Place Joachim Gasquet
13100 Aix-En-Provence
France

M Velluet/M Blau
SARL L'Ourson Joyeux
6/10 Rue Guillaume
Bertrand
75011 Paris
France

M Dufour
Pentasonic
20 Rue Perier
92120 Montrouge
France

M Andre-Noel Lopez
Ste Francaise De
Boulangerie
Le Ligoures −
Place Romee De Villeneuve
13090 Aix-En-Provence
France

M Roger Guiguet
All Systems
BP 51
38170 Seyssinet
France

M Barrieres
Plaxicolor
169 Avenue De Muret
21300 Toulouse
France

Directeur Commercial
Pela Diffusion
3 Rue Saint-Clair
69300 Caluire
France

M Laviale
SARL Lama
6 Place Saint Silain
24000 Perigueux
France

M Creuzeau
Sodial
Rue Des Cooperateurs
59220 Denain
France

M Thierry Demaegdt
Projet Enterprises
1 Rue Jacquart
27000 Evreux
France

M Jean Roussotte
Gagmi Services
57 Boulevard De La Villette
75010 Paris
France

M Celard
Plasmovital
8 Rue Bossuet
21000 Dijon
France

M Dumilieu
Multi Conseil
8 Place Des Terreaux
69001 Lyon
France

M Didier Berger
Pop Bijoux
151 Rue Du Temple
75003 Paris
France

M Hipeau Bernard
Vieux Chene Expansion
9 Route De Saint-Leu
95360 Montmagny
France

M Chapaux/M Dumas
Primagaz
Direct Reg Sud Est
Park La Cristole RN7
84011 Avignon
France

M Vincent David
Nouvelle Donne
BP 19
35130 La Guerche
France

M Martin/Mme Lasnet
Seddac Sa
36 Rue Raymond Marcheron
92170 Vanves
France

M Benoit Guerin
S.F.A.T.D.
99 Rue De Lyon
13015 Marseille
France

Mm Driencourt-Loraschi
Ste Sciv
Chateau Saint Martin
4 Rue Emile Billoquet
76350 Oissel
France

M Daniel Wanono
Rene Derhy
6 Rue Du Faubourg
Poisson-Niere
75010 Paris
France

M Campanini/M Roizot
SARL Rhumex
67 Route De Beaune
BP 46
31300 Chenove
France

M Alain Levy
Chocolats & Confiserie Luxe
SA
Route Du Pont Au Péage
BP 136
67404 Illkirch Cedex
France

Mm Soulard/Bakli
Francincom
RN 1 − BP 22
La Mare D'Ouillers
60570 Mortefontaine En
Thelle
France

M Michel Gintzburger
France Quick SA
40 Rue Jean Jaures
93170 Bagnolet
France

Yvon Le Riboter
SARL Creafor
44 Rue Gourien
22000 Saint-Brieuc
France

M Jean-Louis Arnoux
Memas SA
BP 237
34506 Bézière Cedex
France

M Jean-Luc Perez
SA Primevere Hotels
Lieu Dit Les Champceuils
RN 447 − BP 66
91220 Bretigny-Sur-Orge
France

M Kammer
Sacha
24 Rue De Buci
75006 Paris
France

M Franck Grignon
Disco − Groupe Printemps
7 Allée Du Commandant
Mouchotte
91550 Paray-Vieille-Poste
France

M Strauss
Inter Centre
24 Rue Du Pont Mouja
54000 Nancy
France

M Jerome Logre
SHS Laser
63 Bld Des Batignolles
75008 Paris
France

M Dumas
S.D.B.M. SARL
4 Rue Gonod
63000 Clermont-Ferrand
France

M Marconnet
Status
5 Bis Rue Froissart
75003 Paris
France

Serge Bellulo
Super Forme
11 Rue De Cambrai
75019 Paris
France

Mm Costes/Gabet
Prodecum Service Expansion
202 Rue Leon Blum
69100 Lyon Villeurbanne
France

M Valentin
Tarte Julie Diffusion
38 Rue Des Poissonniers
92200 Neuilly-Sur-Seine
France

M Saint-Jours/Mme Neyrad
SARL Thermes
19 Rue Des Cordeliers
64000 Pau
France

M Bernard Hipeau
Sieges Center
9 route De Saint Leu
95360 Montmagny
France

M A Richard
Covemat
1/3 Rue Rouget De Lisle
69100 Villeurbanne
France

M Dominique Lerouge
Story France
Rue Des Saumonieres
44300 Nantes
France

M Alonzo
Sylvette Page
12 Impasse Du Bourrelier
CP 1518
44806 Saint-Herblain Cedex
France

M Philippe Pons
Tambour Tattant
42 Avenue Franklin
Roosevelt
30000 Nimes
France

M Jacques Maillot
Telem
16 Rue De L'Etang
BP 1
38610 Gières
France

M Benichou
Tony Boy
11 Rue Du Faubourg St-
Martin
75010 Paris
France

M Panazol
ETS Gilles Panazol
ZI La Borie
24110 St-Astier-En-Périgord
France

M Jean Jacques Herry
Novodis
354 Avenue De Chabeville
26000 Valence
France

Marie Therese Comte
Aquarius SA
1 Rue Seguret Saincric
12000 Rodez
France

Mme Kowalsi
SA Segers
ZI Des Marichelles
62800 Lievin
France

Mle Carmona/M Balazun
Presto Pizza
115 Avenue De Saint-
Medard
33320 Eysines
France

M Ouillet/Mme Vivier
Sodima International SA
170 Bis Boulevard
Montparnasse
75014 Paris
France

M Feroldi
Le Forum Des Animaux
Centre Commercial
Barneoud
Magnan
Plan De Campagne
13480 Cabries
France

Mme De Rouard
Ste Phyto Diffusion
07130 Soyons
France

M Pierre Chemin
Cejibe SA
Chemin De l'Ile Piot
84000 Avignon
France

M Cornet
Ste Serrucolor
6 Rue Des Bigos
BP 43 – ZI
34744 Vendargues
France

M Jean Roussotte
Gagmi Services
57 Boulevard De La Villette
75010 Paris
France

M Daniel Celerier
Voyage Pour Tous
26 Quai De Bacalan
33300 Bordeaux
France

M Hoinville
Bidermann SA Dpt Y St
Laurent
114 Rue De Turenne
75003 Paris
France

BELGIUM
J L Dewinter
S A Christiaensen Int'l NV
Morettestraat 11
1740 Ternat
Belgium

A Wilmet
EPECE
Rue des Champs 30
5590 Ciney
Belgium

H Ruijs
GB-INNON-BM –
Bricocenter
Avenue des Olympiades 20
1140 Bruxelles
Belgium

P Vandenwijngaerden
GB-INNON-BM – Divisie
UNIC
PB 999
1000 Brussel
Belgium

G Heytens
Heytens Decor NV
Hengstenberg 111/113
3090 Overijse
Belgium

J Groos
Hubo Belgie NV
Hubo Belgique SA
Avenue E Plasky-laan 114 b
10
Bruxelles
1040 Brussel
Belgium

Duchesne
Intertan Belgium (Tandy)
A Division of Intertan
Canada Ltd
Rue des Pieds d'Alouette 39
5100 Naninne
Belgium

J P Tihon
Motorest NV Div "Quick"
1F
Grote Steenweg 224 Bus 5
2600 Berchem/Antwerpen
Belgium

P Iserbyt
Nopri SA
Rue d'Argent 8
1000 Bruxelles
Belgium

L Pauwels
Postland NV
2160 Wommelgem
Belgium

Mme B Schmidt
Premaman SA
Avenue L Mommaerts 6/8
1140 Bruxelles
Belgium

J Stievenart
Societe Benelux Des Laines
de France SA
Bld de l'Empereur 14
1000 Bruxelles
Belgium

Ph Painer
Superbois
Anc Ets R Collette SA
Ile Monsin 60
4020 Liège 2
Belgium

Mme P Hupez
Tonton Tapis
Zoning Industriel
4671 Barchon
Belgium

Bertrand
Univers Du Cuir
Chaussée de Waterloo 39
1600 Rhode-St-Genese
Belgium

Achtergael
Agimmo NV
Kortrijkse Steenweg 267
9000 Gent
Belgium

B Van De Sijpe
Alain Henry Sprl
Avenue des Villas 85
1060 Bruxelles
Belgium

Peter A McEwan
Arthur Pierre International
SA
Steenweg op Brussel 344
3090 Overijse
Belgium

Maître André Lombart
Ballon Buyle Lagasse
Maingain et Philippe
Bld Reyers 103 Bte 30
1040 Bruxelles
Belgium

Norbert Horsmans
Benelux Self Auto Wash SA
rue de l'Industrie
B-3895 Foetz
Belgium

A Quaresme
Robert Bosch SA
Chaussée de Mons 130
1070 Bruxelles
Belgium

R Creutz
Cegeco SA
rue Libon 35
4800 Verviers
Belgium

De Heer Marcel Coppens (F
+ N)
De Broquevillelaan 5
1150 Brussel
Belgium

Maurice Wilkin
Decoration Design Sprl
Avenue Blonden 42
4000 Liège 1
Belgium

J De Rijbel
Eismann NV
Industriezone Klein Gent
2200 Herentals
Belgium

H Ruijs
GB Autocenter – Auto 5
Avenue des Olympiades 20
1140 Bruxelles
Belgium

J Van Mol
Generale De Banque SA
(F + N)
Montague de Parc 3
1040 Bruxelles
Belgium

W Vanlandeghem
Groselec NV
Ringlaan 6
8520 Kuurne
Belgium

W Anderson
Les Petits Riens asbl
rue Américaine 101
1050 Bruxelles
Belgium

Meester Guy Meyns
Ch Woestlann 57
1090 Brussel
Belgium

Van Campenhout
Modex SA (PicPus)
rue de Naples 18
1050 Bruxelles
Belgium

A Decraene
Outboard Marine Belgium
NV
Pathoekeweg 120
8000 Brugge
Belgium

Brenig
Parfumerie ICI Paris XL SA
Avenue Van Volxem 229
1190 Bruxelles
Belgium

Meester Oliver Vaes
Donnet Vaes & Wouters
Mechelsesteenweg 195
2018 Antwerpen 1
Belgium

Meester Stephan Wagner
Tabalevest 9/2
2000 Antwerpen 1
Belgium

Yves Duquesne
Watchwatch Belgium SA
rue de Marais Rouge 160
9600 Renaix
Belgium

DENMARK
Bianco Danmark ApS
Ambolten 23
6000 Kolding
Denmark

BP Danmark A/S
Hasselager Centervej 13-15
8260 Viby J
Denmark

Budstikken A/S
Niels Ebbesensvej 17
9911 Frederiksberg C
Denmark

Dagrofa Detail
Gammelager 13
2605 Brøndby
Denmark

Danica Køkkenet A/S
Heimdalsvej 8
8850 Bjerringbro
Denmark

Form & Figur A/S
Sjællandsbroen 2
2450 København SV
Denmark

HTH Køkkener A/S
Industrivej 6
6870 Ølgod
Denmark

Nyborg Vaskerimaskiner
A/S
Østerbro 4
5690 Tommerup
Denmark

Nynorm A/S
Kratholmvej 27
5260 Odense S
Denmark

Pakke-Trans Amba
Albuen 5-7
6000 Kolding
Denmark

Radio/TV Booking A/S
Kong Georgsvej 46
2000 Frederiksberg
Denmark

Rent a Tent
Energivej 14
2750 Ballerup
Denmark

Tidy Car Danmark
Dag Hammarskjölds Allé 29
2100 Købenavn Ø
Denmark

VVS Comfort A/S
Scandiagade 15
2450 København SV
Denmark

Civiløkonom Henning
Hvidberg
Tjørnebakken 5
3540 Lynge
Denmark

Knud Petersen
Dansk
Ejendomsmæglerforening
Stormgade 16
1470 København K
Denmark

Dansk Shell A/S
Kampmannsgade 2
1604 København V
Denmark

Eksperto A/S
Himmelev Bygade 57-59
4000 Roskilde
Denmark

Erhvervs-Gruppen Danmark
A/S
Gydevang 24-26
3450 Allerød
Denmark

GreenMark
Toftevej 15 B
3450 Allerød
Denmark

Group Fox
Kalverhave 2
4100 Ringsted
Denmark

Korsdalsvej 101
2610 Rødovre
Denmark

Japan Photo
Maren Turisgade 1
9000 Alborg
Denmark

Johnson International
Grundkær 5
1650 Hvidovre
Denmark

Kvik Køkkenet A/S
Østerbro 14
6933 Kibæk
Denmark

Hæstved Handelsskole
Farimagsgade 65
4700 Næstved
Denmark

Oticon A/S
Mileparken 20 E
2740 Skovlunde
Denmark

Pasta Basta Delikatesse
Valkendorfsgade 22, 2
1151 København K
Denmark

Photo Team A/S
Jens Juulsvej 18
8260 Viby J
Denmark

Proff Clean
Box 67
2630 Tastrup
Denmark

Revisionsfirmaet Preben
Larsen
Østergade 17-19
1011 København K
Denmark

Roskilde Banke A/S
Algade 14
4000 Roskilde
Denmark

SFI Scandinavian Franchise
Inst
Box 4082
S-181 04 Lidingo
Denmark

Sign Text A/S
Mosetoften 20
8722 Hedensted
Denmark

Statoil A/S
Skt. Annæ Plads 13
1298 København K
Denmark

PORTUGAL
Teresa Catarino
Cenoura
Rua Rodrigo da Fonseca
24-2° 1200 Lisbon
Portugal

Gonçalves Pereira
Materna
Estrada da Circunvalação
Quinta do Figo Maduro
No 3 1700 Lisboa
Portugal

Ronald Brodheim
Rodier
Rua Alexandre Herculano 9
1000 Lisboa
Portugal

José Theotonio
Lanidor
Av Columbano Bordalo
Pinheiro 97
1000 Lisboa
Portugal

Mondi
Rua Alexandre Herculano
9 r/c 1000 Lisboa
Portugal

Antonio Verissimo
Italus
Rua do Cemitério
Lote 3 Quinta da Ponte
Povoa de Sto Adrião
2675 Odivelas
Portugal

Ruy Peterle
Boticario
Av Eng Duarte Pacheco
Torre 2 Piso 7o Sala 3
Edificio Amoreiras
1000 Lisboa
Portugal

Nelson Outeiro
Saviotti & Esaguy
Rua Marques da Fronteira
73 7o C
1000 Lisboa
Portugal

José Luis
Il Fornaio
Miguens Cardoso
Boutique de Pão
Triunfo Franchising
Av do Forte
2795 Linda A Velha
Portugal

José Rodriques
Màquinas de Encadernar
Rua Luis de Camões
58
2490 Vila Nova de Ourem
Portugal

Fernando Henriques
Technal Portuguesa
Rua da Guiné 33
Prior Velho
2670 Sacavem
Portugal

Costa Ramos
Maconde
Apartado 9 Regufe
4481 Vila Do Conde Codex
Portugal

Franklim Chagas
Quelhas
Mundiserviços
Rua Braamcamp 9 – 7o
1200 Lisboa
Portugal

Joao Jardim de Queiroz
Seguros
Mundial Confiança
Largo do Chiado 8
1200 Lisboa
Portugal

UNITED KINGDOM
The Managing Director
A1 Damproofing (UK) Ltd
Charnley Fold Lane
Bamber Bridge
Preston PR5 6AA

The Managing Director
Timberguard (UK) Ltd
40 Lune Street
Preston
Lancs

The Managing Director
Pass & Company
Timber Preservation UK Ltd
Passco House
635 High Road
Leytonstone
London E11 4RD

The Managing Director
Jet-Rod Franchising Ltd
Irwell House
89 Barton Lane
Eccles
Manchester M30 0EY

The Managing Director
Bathcare
207a Linketty Lane East
Crownhill
Plymouth PL6 5JX

The Managing Director
The Bath Wizard Ltd
Victory House
Somers Road North
Portsmouth PO1 1PJ

The Managing Director
Cico Chimney Linings
Westleton
Saxmundham
Suffolk

The Managing Director
British Damp Proofing
The School House
Fleetwood Road
Esprick
Preston PR4 3JH

The Managing Director
Dampcure Woodcure/30 Ltd
Darley House
Cow Lane
Garston
Watford
Herts WD2 6PH

The Managing Director
Dyno Rod Plc
143 Maple Road
Surbiton
Surrey KT6 4BJ

The Managing Director
Metro Rod Services Ltd
Metro House
Churchill Way
Macclesfield
Cheshire SK11 6AY

The Managing Director
The Bath Doctor
Suite 5
Britannia House
Leagrove Road
Luton
Beds LU3 1RJ

The Managing Director
Brick-Tie Services Ltd
Yorkshire House
Easy Road
Leeds LS9 8SQ

The Managing Director
Complete Weed Control Ltd
Langston Priory Mews
Station Road
Kingham
Oxon OX7 6UW

The Managing Director
Countrywide Garden
Maintenance Services Ltd
164-200 Stockport Road
Cheadle
Cheshire SK8 2DP

The Managing Director
Crimesecure Ltd
Ivatt Way
Westwood Industrial Estate
Peterborough PE3 7PB

The Managing Director
Dyno Locks
Dyno Rod Developments
143 Maple Road
Surbiton
Surrey KT6 4BJ

The Managing Director
Evvacote Franchise Ltd
24-26 Friern Park
Finchley
London N12 9DA

The Managing Director
Garden Building Centres Ltd
Jardinerie Garden Centre
Kenilworth Road
Hampton-in-Arden
Warwicks

The Managing Director
Gun-Point Ltd
Thavies Inn House
3/4 Holborn Circus
London EC1N 2PL

The Managing Director
Lockmasters Mobile Ltd
Security House
The Windmills
Turk Street
Alton
Hampshire GU34 1EF

The Managing Director
Cobblestone Paving Co (UK)
Ltd
Auckland House
Perry Road
Witham
Essex CM8 3SX

The Managing Director
Dyno Electrics
Dyno Rod Developments
143 Maple Road
Surbiton
Surrey KT6 4BJ

The Managing Director
The Garage Door Company
Unit 7
Russell Road Industrial
Estate
Edinburgh EH11 2NN

The Managing Director
Graffiti Management
5 The Hamiltons
Torquay Road
Shaldon
Devon TQ14 OAY

The Managing Director
Leadstyle Ltd
2 Sparken Hill
Worksop
Notts S80 1AP

The Managing Director
The Marley Paving Co Ltd
Lichfield Road
Branston
Burton-on-Trent
Staffs DE14 3HD

The Managing Director
Master Thatchers Ltd
29 Nine Mile Ride
Finchampstead
Wokingham
Berks RG11 4QD

The Managing Director
Mortar Mason Ltd
Westleton
Saxmundham
Suffolk 1P17 3BS

The Managing Director
National Security
Britannia House
Leacombe Road
Luton LU3 1RJ

The Managing Director
Potholes Ltd
Prospect Road
Airesford
Hampshire SO24 9QF

The Managing Director
Servowarm Ltd
199 The Vale
Acton
London W3 7RB

The Managing Director
Alpine Windows
Alpine House
Honeypot Lane
Kingsbury
London NW9 9RU

The Managing Director
Fersina Windows Ltd
Fersina House
Industry Road
Carlton Industrial Estate
Barnsley
South Yorks S70 3NH

The Managing Director
Mixamate Holdings Ltd
Beddington Lane
Croydon
Surrey CR9 4QD

The Managing Director
Mr Fixit
Bay House
Bramham
Wetherby
Yorks LS23 9JS

The Managing Director
Newlook Bath Services Ltd
Oaklands
Dorstone
Hereford HR3 6AR

The Managing Director
Re-Nu Ltd
130 Stoneleigh Avenue
Worcester Park
Surrey KT4 8XZ

The Managing Director
Stained Glass Overley UK
Ltd
23 Hurricane Way
Norwich NR6 6EJ

The Managing Director
Curadraft (GB) Ltd
Delmae House
Unit 1
Home Farm
Ardington
Nr. Wantage
Oxon

The Managing Director
Quattro Seal
Suite 1
New Mansion House
Wellington Road
South Stockport SK1 3UA

The Managing Director
Trident Warehouse Co
Units 6-9
Venturebank
Claybank Road
Portsmouth
Hants PO3 5NH

The Managing Director
Dial-A-Dino's
Empire House
Hanger Green
London W5 3BD

The Managing Director
Gino's Dial-A-Pizza Ltd
4a Mill Street
Cannock
Staffordshire WS11 3DL

The Managing Director
Snappy Tomato Pizza (UK)
Ltd
17 Mercia Business Village
Torwood Close
Westwood Business Park
Coventry CV4 8HX

The Managing Director
Burger King UK Ltd
20 Kew Road
Richmond
Surrey TW9 2NA

The Managing Director
Chicken George Food
Systems Ltd
Shirley Lodge
470 London Road
Slough SL3 8QY

The Managing Director
Don Millers Hot Bread
Kitchens Ltd
166 Bute Street Mall
Luton
Beds LU1 2TL

The Managing Director
Ventrolla Ltd
51 Tower Street
Harrogate
North Yorks HG1 1HS

The Managing Director
Domino's Pizza
Unit 10
Maryland Road
Tongwell
Milton Keynes MK15 8HF

The Managing Director
Perfect Pizza
65 Staines Road
Hounslow
Middlesex TW3 3HW

The Managing Director
Berni
Oxford House
97 Oxford Road
Uxbridge UB8 1HX

The Managing Director
Chantegrill
24 Kingly Street
London W1

The Managing Director
Dixy Fried Chicken (GB)
Ltd
123 Clapton Common
London E5 9AB

The Managing Director
Grandma Batty's
Wondercourt Ltd
Yorkshire House
Vulcan Street
Birds Royd Lane
Brighouse
West Yorks HD6 1LQ

The Managing Director
Kansas Fried Chicken
130A Wilmslow Road
Handforth
Cheshire SK9 3LQ

The Managing Director
McDonalds Hamburgers Ltd
11-59 High Road
East Finchley
London NW8

The Managing Director
Mister Donut
353 North End Road
Fulham
London SW6 1NN

The Managing Director
Mr Cod Ltd
6-7 High Street
Woking
Surrey GU21 1BG

The Managing Director
Pancake Place
Clydesdale Bank House
20 New Road
Milnathort
Kinross KY13 7XT

The Managing Director
Pizza Piazza
Little Dudley House Ltd
B30 Barwell Business Park
Leatherhead Road
Chessington
Surrey KT9 2NY

The Managing Director
Wimpy International
10 Windmill Road
London W4 1SD

The Managing Director
Kentucky Fried Chicken
(Great Britain) Ltd
88-97 High Street
Brentford
Middlesex TW8 8BG

The Managing Director
Merryweathers
109 Hersham Road
Walton-on-Thames
Surrey KT12 1RN

The Managing Director
Morley's (Fast Foods) Ltd
162 Clapham High Street
Clapham
London SW4

The Managing Director
Olivers (UK) Ltd
Eagle Works
Harpur Street
Bedford MK40 1JZ

The Managing Director
PizzaExpress Ltd
29 Wardour Street
Soho
London W1V 3HB

The Managing Director
Poppins Restaurants
28 Sudley Road
Bognor Regis
West Sussex PO21 1ER

The Managing Director
Winstons Pizza
10 Lune Street
Preston
Lancs PR1 2NL

The Managing Director
Baskin-Robbins
Glacier House
Old Field Lane
Greenford
Middlesex UB6 OBA

The Managing Director
Toasty Kitchens
2 Castle Street
Salisbury SP1 1BB

The Managing Director
Rainbow International
Mansfield Franchising Ltd
Phoenix House
Mansfield Road
Sutton-in-Ashfield
Notts NG17 4HR

The Managing Director
Global Franchise Services
Ltd
8-10 High Street
Sutton
Surrey

The Managing Director
VDU Services Franchising
Ltd
VDU House
Old Kiln Lane
Churt
Farnham GU10 2JH

The Managing Director
Dial A Char
DAC Ltd
77 London Road
East Grindstead
West Sussex RH19 1EQ

The Managing Director
Dinkum Dog
Plumcourt Ltd
88-92 Wallis Road
London E9 5LN

The Managing Director
Chem-Dry Southern Services
The Weltech Centre
The Ridgeway
Welwyn Garden City
Herts AL7 2AA

The Managing Director
Safeclean
D G Cook Ltd
Delmae House
Unit 1 Home Farm
Ardington
Nr Wantage
Oxon

The Managing Director
Coverall
Stanley House
Stanley Gardens
London W3 7SY

The Managing Director
ServiceMaster Ltd
308 Melton Road
Leicester LE4 7SL

The Managing Director
Country Cousins
26 High Street
Merstham
Surrey RH1 3EA

The Managing Director
The Maids Ltd
Venture House
7 Leicester Road
Loughborough
Leics LE11 2AE

The Managing Director
Odd-Jobs (UK) Ltd
5 Bridge Street
Macclesfield SK11 6EG

The Managing Director
Square 1 Cleaning Services
Ltd
221c South Coast Road
Peacehaven
East Sussex BN10 8LB

The Managing Director
Coffeeman Management Ltd
73 Woodsbridge Industrial
Park
Wimborne
Dorset BH21 6SU

The Managing Director
Lambourn Court
International Business Centre
1 Lambourn Court
Emerson Valley
Milton Keynes MK4 2DA

The Managing Director
Allied Dunbar
Parliament House
North Row
London W1R 1DL

The Managing Director
Homebuyers Advice Centre
Plc
Suite 401
India Buildings
Water Street
Liverpool L2 ORB

The Managing Director
Molly Maid UK
Hamilton Road
Slough
Berks SL1 4QY

The Managing Director
Poppies (UK) Ltd
31 Houndgate
Darlington DL1 5RH

The Managing Director
Catermat Fresh Drinks Ltd
13 Redhills Road
Eastern Industrial Area
South Woodham Ferrers
Chelmsford
Essex CM3 5UJ

The Managing Director
Krograb
Springleader Beverage
Services Ltd
Chelford
Macclesfield
Cheshire SK11 9BD

The Managing Director
OTSS Business Centres Ltd
3 Spencer Parade
Northampton NN1 5AA

The Managing Director
The Commercial
(Brokerage) House Ltd
261/269 Ecclesall Road
Sheffield S11 8NX

The Managing Director
Mortgage Advice Centre
(Franchise) Ltd
Jacobs Well
Ground Floor
20 Hook Road
Epsom
Surrey KT19 8TH

The Managing Director
Swinton Group Ltd
Swinton House
6 Great Marlborough Street
Manchester M1 5SW

The Managing Director
Future Training &
Recruitment
Future Centres (Franchise)
Sandhurst Lane
Whydown
East Sussex TN39 4RH

The Managing Director
RT Computer Training
15 Victoria Street
Wetherby
West Yorks LS22 4RE

The Managing Director
The Accounting Centre
Elscot House
Arcadia Avenue
Finchley
London N3 2JE

The Managing Director
Cab Glazing Services
Unit 6
Clifton Industrial Estate
Cherryhinton Road
Cambridge CB1 4WG

The Managing Director
The Compleat Engraver and
Colourist
TC Graphics Ltd
Valley House
Needham
Nr Harleston
Norfolk IP20 9LG

The Managing Director
Data Maid Ltd
47 First Avenue
Deeside Industrial Park
Deeside
Clwyd CH5 2NU

The Managing Director
William Green Financial
Services Ltd
Ashton House
467 Silbury Boulevard
Central Milton Keynes
MK9 2AH

The Managing Director
Priority Management
Systems (UK)
Trent House
Dallow Road
Luton
Beds LU1 1LY

The Managing Director
Wetherby Office Training
Flockton House
Audby Lane
Wetherby
West Yorks LS22 4FD

The Managing Director
Anicare
23 Buckingham Road
Shoreham-by-Sea
West Sussex BN4 5UA

The Managing Director
Culligan International
Blenheim Road
Cressex Industrial Estate
High Wycombe
Bucks HP12 3RS

The Managing Director
Countrywide Interior
Landscapes Ltd
164-200 Stockport Road
Cheadle
Cheshire SK8 2DP

The Managing Director
First Impressions
1 Dover Street
Cambridge CB1 1DY

The Managing Director
The Hall of Names Ltd
London House
Suite 323
26-40 Kensington High
Street
London W8 4PF

The Managing Director
Infopoint
205 Cowley Road
Oxford OX4 1XH

The Managing Director
Marketing Methods Ltd
1 Buxton Road West
Disley
Stockport SK12 2AF

The Managing Director
National Vacuum Cleaner
Services
Richmond House
1 Richmond Street
Herne Bay
Kent CT6 5LU

The Managing Director
The Quill Group
Harbro House
Okell Street
Runcorn
Cheshire WA7 5AP

The Managing Director
Red Letters
2 Mews Court
Newton Avenue
East Grinstead
West Sussex RH19 4SW

The Managing Director
House of Colour
4 Dudrich House
Princes Lane
London N10 3LU

The Managing Director
Kwik Strip (UK) Ltd
PO Box 1087
Summerleaze
Church Road
Winscombe
Avon BS25 1BH

The Managing Director
Mastersharp
P A Research Ltd
28 Glen Road
Boscombe
Bournemouth BH5 1HS

The Managing Director
Nationwide Investigations
86 Southwark Bridge Road
London SE1 OEX

The Managing Director
Sketchley Recognition
Express Ltd
PO Box 7
Rugby Road
Hinckley
Leics LE10 2NE

The Managing Director
Safeway Motoring School
Ltd
PO Box 325
Bristol BS99 7XE

The Managing Director
Stockcheck
The Courtyard
Harewood Estate
Harewood
Leeds LS17 9LS

The Managing Director
Time and Place Marketing
Services
8 Beatrice Road
Worsley
Manchester M28 4TN

The Managing Director
The UK School of Motoring
39 Dee Street
Aberdeen
Scotland

The Managing Director
Val-U-Pak
Valuefuture Plc
Harpenden Hall
Southdown Road
Harpenden
Herts AL5 1PT

The Managing Director
Autela Components Ltd
Regal House
Birmingham Road
Stratford-upon-Avon
Warks CV37 OBN

The Managing Director
Cordon Alloys (UK) Ltd
Codon House
Clifton Road
Marton
Blackpool
Lancs FY4 4QA

The Managing Director
Direct Salon Services
Newport Way
Cannon Park
Middlesbrough
Cleveland TS1 5JW

The Managing Director
Kendall Oil
C.A.N. Trading Ltd
2-3 Bacchus House
Calleva Park
Aldermaston
Reading RG7 4QW

The Managing Director
Tumble Tots (UK) Ltd
Cannons Sports Club
Cousin Lane
London EC4R 3TE

The Managing Director
Uticolor
Acton Workshops
School Road
London NW10

The Managing Director
Vinyl Master (UK) Ltd
Unit 2a
Vulcan Works
205 Leckhampton Road
Cheltenham GL53 OAL

The Managing Director
Chemcial Express
Ninian Way
Tame Valley Industrial
Tamworth
Staffs B77 5DZ

The Managing Director
The Cookie Coach Company
Division of Carrs Food Ltd
Southside
Bredbury Industrial Park
Stockport
Cheshire SK6 2SP

The Managing Director
G&T Video Services
(Franchise) Ltd
35 Balena Close
Creekmoor Industrial Estate
Creekmoor
Poole
Dorset BH17 7EB

The Managing Director
Motabitz
27-37 Craven Street
Northampton NN1 3EZ

The Managing Director
Snap-on-Tools Ltd
Palmer House
150-154 Cross Street
Sale
Cheshire M33 1AQ

The Managing Director
Team Audio
The Diamond Stylus Co Ltd
Mochdre Industrial Estate
Colwyn Bay
Clwyd LL28 5HD

The Managing Director
Trust Parts Ltd
Unit 7
Groundwell Industrial Estate
Crompton Road
Swindon SN2 5AY

The Managing Director
Circles
Modernideas Ltd
786 London Road
Larkfield
Maidstone
Kent ME20 6BE

The Managing Director
Alfred Marks
Adia House
84-86 Regent Street
London W1A 1AL

The Managing Director
EPC (European Personnel
Counsellors) Ltd
Owl's Barn
Dorney Wood Road
Burnham
Bucks SL1 8EH

The Managing Director
Travail Employment Group
24 Southgate Street
Gloucester GL1 2DP

The Managing Director
Spaceage Plastics Ltd
Spaceage House
85 Ringwood Road
Poole
Dorset BH14 ORH

The Managing Director
Trafalgar Cleaning
Chemicals
Unit 14
Fenlake Industrial Estate
Fenlake Road
Bedford MK42 OHB

The Managing Director
Betterware Sales Ltd
Fairview Estate
Kingsbury Road
Curdworth
Sutton Coldfield
West Midlands B76 9EH

The Managing Director
Roman Spa Health and
Leisure Products Ltd
30 Princess Victoria Street
Bristol BS8 4BZ

The Managing Director
Ashfield Personnel
(Franchising) Ltd
21 Bridge Street
Hemel Hempstead
Herts HP1 1EG

The Managing Director
KPR Recruitment Ltd
Crispin House
Maldon Road
Witham
Essex CM8 2UR

The Managing Director
Banson Tool Hire
Pellon Lane
Halifax HX1 5SB

The Managing Director
Hire Technicians Group Ltd
Chalk Hill House
8 Chalk Hill
Watford
Herts WD1 4BH

The Managing Director
Balforth, Alliance and
Leicester Property Services
10 Bank Street
Norwich NR2 4SE

The Managing Director
Century 21 Real Estate
Agency Ltd
Station House
Darkes Lane
Potters Bar
Herts EN6 1AJ

The Managing Director
Country Business Sales Ltd
9a Churchgate Street
Soham
Ely
Cambs CB7 5DS

The Managing Director
Donald Storrie Estate
Agency
40 Cadzow Street
Hamilton ML3 6DG

The Managing Director
The Flat Shop
119 The Promenade
Cheltenham
Glos GL50 1NW

The Managing Director
Quest Estates International
15 Saint Thomas Street
Lymington
Hants SO4 9NB

The Managing Director
M & B Marquees
Unit 16
Swinborne Court
Burnt Mills Industrial Estate
Basildon
Essex SS13 1QA

The Managing Director
Britannia Business Sales
Britannia Buildings
Park Gate
Bradford
West Yorkshire BD1 5BS

The Managing Director
Cornerstone
Abbey National Estate
Agency Ltd
Abbey House
Baker Street
London NW1 6XL

The Managing Director
Country Rose
Country Properties
41 High Street
Baldock
Herts SG7 5NP

The Managing Director
Everett Masson & Furby Ltd
18 Walsworth Road
Hitchin
Herts SG4 9SP

The Managing Director
Link & Company
(Franchise) Plc
The Estate House
High Road
Chigwell IG7 5BJ

The Managing Director
Saunders of Kensington Ltd
40 Gloucester Road
South Kensington
London SW7 4QU

The Managing Director
Seekers
Thornganby Ltd
234-236 The Broadway
London NW9 6AG

The Managing Director
Your Move
Deanpeak Enterprises Ltd
51 New Bedford Road
Luton
Beds LU1 1HR

The Managing Director
In-toto Ltd
Wakefield Road
Gildersome
Leeds LS27 OQW

The Managing Director
Strachan Studio
George Strachan & Son Ltd
Cross Green Way
Leeds
West Yorks LS9 ORS

The Managing Director
The Bread Roll Co.
Unit 6
Veniam Industrial Estate
224 London Road
St. Albans
Herts AL1 1JF

The Managing Director
Northern Dairies
3 Baine Lane
Wakefield
Yorks WF2 ODL

The Managing Director
Alan Paul Hairdressing
164 New Chester Road
Birkenhead
Merseyside

The Managing Director
Swinton The Estate Agents
24-26 Park Green
Macclesfield
Cheshire SK11 7NA

The Managing Director
H-Plan Manufacturing Co
Ltd
Dallow Road
Luton
Beds LU11 1SP

The Managing Director
Texas Homecare Installation
Services Ltd
Home Charm House
Park Farm
Wellingborough
Northants NN8 3XA

The Managing Director
Alpine Soft Drinks (UK) Ltd
Richmond Way
Chelmsley Wood
Birmingham B37 7TT

The Managing Director
Coca-Cola Export
Corporation
Pemberton House
Wrights Lane
London W8 5SN

The Managing Director
Unigate Dairies Ltd
14/40 Victoria Road
Aldershot
Hants GU11 1TH

The Managing Director
Blinkers Franchising Ltd
Consort Court
High Street
Fareham
Hampshire PO16 7AL

The Managing Director
Command Performance
256 High Street
Slough
Berks SL1 1JU

The Managing Director
Essanelle Ltd
27-37 St Georges Road
London SW19 4DS

The Managing Director
Keith Hall Franchising Ltd
119-121 Derby Road
Long Eaton
Nottingham NG10 4LA

The Managing Director
Votre Beaute (Franchise) Ltd
Cattespoole Mill
Tardebigge
Nr Bromsgrove
Worcs BS60 1LZ

The Managing Director
Quality International
2 Valentine Place
London SE1 8QH

The Managing Director
Laser Sporting Leisure Ltd
South Thames Studios
5-11 Lavington Street
London SE1 ONZ

The Managing Director
Spice (UK) Ltd
18 Henrietta Street
Old Trafford
Manchester M16 9GA

The Managing Director
Das Haar (Franchises) Ltd
Dundas House
166 Buchanan Street
Glasgow G1

The Managing Director
Francesco Group (Holdings)
Ltd
Woodings Yard
Bailey Street
Stafford ST17 4BG

The Managing Director
Saks Hair (Holdings) Ltd
57 Coniscliffe Road
Darlington
Co Durham DL3 7EH

The Managing Director
The Great Adventure Game
Unit 16
Smiths' Yard
Summerley Street
London SW18 5HR

The Managing Director
Skirmish (Europe) Ltd
The Warehouse
Sandy Lane
Oxted
Surrey

The Managing Director
Splatoon
Licensed to Thrill (UK) Ltd
The Hunting Lodge
Standbridge Lane
Kettlethorpe
Sandal
Wakefield WF2 7NT

The Managing Director
Autosheen Car Valeting
Services (UK) Ltd
Everitt Close
Denington Industrial Estate
Wellingborough
Northants NN8 2QE

The Managing Director
Professional Appearance
Services Ltd
3 Avon Reach
Chippenham SN15 1EE

The Managing Director
Wash'N'Wax Ltd
11 Randolph Place
Edinburgh EH3 7TA

The Managing Director
Arrow Car, Van & Truck
Rental Ltd
Unit 3
26 Maybole Road
Ayr KA7 2QA

The Managing Director
Budget Rent a Car
International Inc
41 Marlowes
Hemel Hempstead
Herts HP1 1LD

The Managing Director
Practical Used Car Rental
137-145 High Street
Bordesley
Birmingham B12 0JU

The Managing Director
National Car Care Club
Wilmslow House
Southend Road
Woodord Green
Essex IG8 8HJ

The Managing Director
Suds Ltd
Hine House
Randlesdown Road
Bellingham
London SE6 3BT

The Managing Director
AI Fullers International Rent
a Car
240 Burlington Road
New Malden
Surrey KT3 4NN

The Managing Director
Avis Rent-A-Car Ltd
Trident House
Station Road
Hayes
Middlesex UB3 4DJ

The Managing Director
Hertz Rent A Car
Radnor House
1272 London Road
Norbury
London SW16 4XW

The Managing Director
Multilink Leasing Ltd
1 St John's Road
Hove
East Sussex BN3 2FB

The Managing Director
Thrifty Car Rental
City Rentals Ltd
City House
14/16 Temple End
High Wycombe
Bucks HP13 5DR

The Managing Director
Venture Hire Ltd
Wincanton House
333 Western Avenue
London W3 OTS

The Managing Director
Hometune (UK)
77 Mount Ephraim
Tunbridge Wells
Kent TN4 8BS

The Managing Director
Tune-Up Ltd
23 High Street
Bagshot
Surrey GU19 5AF

The Managing Director
Colourmatch
P A Research Ltd
28 Glen Road
Boscombe
Bournemouth
Dorset BH5 1HS

The Managing Director
Magic Windshields UK
12 Beehive Lane
Ilford
Essex IG1 3RG

The Managing Director
Novus Windscreen Repair
The Glass Doctor Ltd
11 Darwin House
Dudley Innovation Centre
Dudley Road
Kingswinford
West Midlands DY6 8XZ

The Managing Director
Stop Thief (UK) Ltd
Unit 9
Avenue 1
Business Park
Letchworth
Herts SG6 2BB

The Managing Director
Computa Tune
9 Petra Road
Clayton Park
Clayton-le-Moors
Accrington
Lancs BB5 5JB

The Managing Director
Mobiletuning Ltd
The Gate House
Lympne Industrial Park
Lympne
Kent CT21 4LR

The Managing Director
Auto Armour
P A Research Ltd
28 Glen Road
Boscombe
Bournemouth
Dorset BH5 1HS

The Managing Director
Highway Windscreens (UK)
Ltd
Arodene House
41-55 Perth Road
Gants Hill
Ilford
Essex IG2 6BX

The Managing Director
Mr. Clutch
20 Lower Coombe Street
Croydon
Surrey CR0 1AA

The Managing Director
Silver Shield Screens Ltd
Wheler Road
Off Humber Road
Whitley
Coventry CV3 4LA

The Managing Director
Truseal Car Care
After Market Specialists
AMS (UK) Ltd
Panalpina House
1a Knoll Rise
Orpington
Kent BR6 0LR

The Managing Director
Amtrak
Company House
Tower Hill
Bristol BS2 0EQ

The Managing Director
Business Post Ltd
Express House
8 Galleymead Road
Colnbrook SL3 0ER

The Managing Director
City Link Transport
Holdings Ltd
Batavia Road
Sunbury-on-Thames
Middlesex TW16 5LR

The Managing Director
Duty Driver Ltd
42a Station Road
Twyford
Berks RG10 9NT

The Managing Director
Hornets Network Ltd
26 High Street
Merstham
Surrey RH1 3EA

The Managing Director
Interlink Express Parcels
Brunswick Court
Brunswick Square
Bristol BS2 8PE

The Managing Director
Panic Link Ltd
Control Sortation Centre
Melbourne Road
Lount
Ashby-de-la-Zouch
Leics LE6 5RS

The Managing Director
Brewer & Turnbull
Removals
Holme Road
Bamber Bridge
Preston
Lancs PR5 6BP

The Managing Director
Captain Cargo Ltd
Wetherby Road
Ascot Drive Industrial Estate
Derby DE2 8HL

The Managing Director
Classic Carriages
Limousines Ltd
Desborough Street
High Wycombe
Bucks HP11 2NF

The Managing Director
G-Force Couriers Ltd
Old Smithfield
Industrial Estate
Aston Street
Shifnal
Shropshire TF11 8DT

The Managing Director
Intacab Ltd
Service House
West Mayne
Basildon
Essex SS15 6RW

The Managing Director
Nexday Ltd
Sunrise House
Bedford Road
Northampton NN1 5NW

The Managing Director
TNT Parcel Office
TNT Express (UK) Ltd
TNT House
Abeles Way
Atherstone
Warks CV9 2RY

The Managing Director
Transam Express Courier
Parcels Ltd
Creswick House
9 Small Street
The Centre
Bristol BS1 1DB

The Managing Director
EuroSpeedy Printing Centres
(SW) Ltd
Smythen Street
Exeter
Devon EX1 1BN

The Managing Director
Kall-Kwik Printing
Kall-Kwik House
206 Prembroke Road
Ruislip
Middlesex HA4 8NQ

The Managing Director
PIP Printing
FranPrint Ltd
Black Arrow House
2 Chandos Road
London NW10 6NF

The Managing Director
Prontaprint Plc
Coniscliffe House
Coniscliffe Road
Darlington DL3 7EX

The Managing Director
The Body and Face Place
Alan Paul Plc
Alan Paul House
164 New Chester Road
Birkenhead
Merseyside L64 9BG

The Managing Director
Body Shop International Plc
Nairn House
Dominion Way
Rustington
West Sussex BN16 3LR

The Managing Director
AlphaGraphics Printshops of
The Future (UK) Ltd
Ryedale Building
58-60 Piccadilly
York YO1 1NX

The Managing Director
Kalamazoo Franchising Ltd
Northfield
Birmingham B31 2RW

The Managing Director
PDC Copyprint
PDC International Plc
1 Church Lane
East Grinstead
West Sussex RH19 3AZ

The Managing Director
Printdesigns Ltd
Reliance Works
Chester Road
Kelsall
Cheshire CW6 ORJ

The Managing Director
The Barry 'M' Shop
1 Bittacy Business Centre
Bittacy Hill
Mill Hill East
London NW7 1BA

The Managing Director
Body Reform
Natural Beauty Products Ltd
Western Avenue
Bridgend Industrial Estate
Bridgend
Mid Glamorgan CF31 3RT

The Managing Director
Copy Cats Ltd
46 Kansas Avenue
Salford Quays
Greater Manchester M5 2GL

The Managing Director
Goodebodies Natural Beauty
International Body Centres
Ltd
Osborne House
20 Victoria Avenue
Harrogate
North Yorks HG1 5QY

The Managing Director
Nectar Cosmetics Ltd
Carrickfergus Industrial
Estate
Belfast Road
Carrickfergus
Northern Ireland BT38 8PH

The Managing Director
The Soap Shop Ltd
44 Sidwell Street
Exeter EX4 6NS

The Managing Director
Beanfreaks Ltd
3 St Mary Street
Cardiff CF1 2AF

The Managing Director
Circle C Stores
24 Fitzalan Road
Roffey
Horsham
West Sussex RH13 6AA

The Managing Director
Holland & Barrett
Canada Road
Byfleet
Surrey KT14 7JL

The Managing Director
Natural Life Health Foods
Ltd
15 Queens Street
Salisbury
Wilts SP1 1EY

The Managing Director
Herbal World
Suite 16-17
Teme Street
Tenbury Wells
Worcs WR15 8AA

The Managing Director
Secret Garden Plc
153 Regent Street
London W1

The Managing Director
Yves Rocher (London) Ltd
664 Victoria Road
South Ruislip
Middlesex HA4 ONY

The Managing Director
Bellina
31 Knightsdale Road
Ipswich
Suffolk IP1 4JJ

The Managing Director
Circle K
Fareham Point
Wickham Road
Fareham
Hants PO16 7BU

The Managing Director
The Late Late Supershop
(UK) Ltd
132-152 Powis Street
Woolwich
London SE18 6NL

The Managing Director
Rusts Ltd
17 Covingham Square
Swindon
Wilts SN3 5AA

The Managing Director
Scoop-A-Market
Bonnington Road Lane
Edinburgh EH6 5PX

The Managing Director
Weigh and Save
3rd Floor
Bridgewater House
Whitmarsh Street
Manchester M1 6LU

The Managing Director
Muggins (UK) Ltd
JLA Group
Meadowcroft Lane
Halifax Road
Ripponden
West Yorkshire HX6 4AJ

The Managing Director
Bumpsadaisy Ltd
3 The Bayer Building
211 Lower Bristol Road
Bath BA2 7DQ

The Managing Director
Clarks Shoes Ltd
PO Box 106
40 High Street
Street
Somerset BA16 OYA

The Managing Director
Coppernob
95 Great Portland Street
London W1N 5RA

The Managing Director
Just for the Night
80 Sandridge Road
St Albans
Herts AL1 4AR

The Managing Director
Thorntons
Derwent Street
Belper
Derbyshire DE5 1WP

The Managing Director
Euroclean
13 The Office Village
4 Romford Road
London E15 4BZ

The Managing Director
Bow Belles
Brunswick Suite
Colwick Hall
Colwick Park
Nottingham NG2 4BH

The Managing Director
Cinderella Designer Gowns
Ltd
Lochrin
Coatbridge ML5 3SS

The Managing Director
Clothesline
248 Seaward Street
Glasgow G41 1NG

The Managing Director
Dash
PO Box 5
Rowdell Road
Northolt
Middlesex UB5 5QT

The Managing Director
Levi Strauss (UK) Ltd
Moulton Park Industrial
Estate
Northampton NN3 1OQ

The Managing Director
Mamanbebe
40 Station Road Industrial
Estate
Hailsham
East Sussex BN27 2EW

The Managing Director
Snips in Fashion
Eurobe Ltd
Station Approach
St Mary Cray Station
Orpington
Kent BR5 2NB

The Managing Director
Young's Formal Wear
(Youngs Franchise Ltd)
70-78 York Way
Kings Cross
London N1 9AG

The Managing Director
The Blind Spot (Franchising)
Ltd
805 Lincoln Road
Peterborough PE1 3HG

The Managing Director
Colour Counsellers Ltd
3 Dovedale Studios
465 Battersea Park Road
London SW11 4LR

The Managing Director
Decorating Den
Decorating Systems
(Scotland) Ltd
Alva Industrial Estate
Alva
Clackmannanshire
Scotland FK12 5DQ

The Managing Director
Athena
Pentos Retailing Group Ltd
Berwick House
Livery Street
Birmingham B3 2PB

The Managing Director
Pronuptia de Paris
(Youngs Franchise Ltd)
70-78 York Way
Kings Cross
London N1 9AG

The Managing Director
Tie Rack Plc
Capital Interchange Way
Brentford
Middlesex TW8 OEX

The Managing Director
Apollo Window Blinds Ltd
Johnstone Avenue
Glasgow G52 4YH

The Managing Director
Carpetlink Ltd
63-65 Boughton
Chester CH3 5AF

The Managing Director
Curtain Dream
30 Nesfield Street
Bradford
West Yorks BD1 3ET

The Managing Director
Home Chose Carpets
Jubilee House
Jubilee Court
Dersingham
Kings Lynn PE31 6HH

The Managing Director
Fastframe Franchises Ltd
International Centre
Netherton Park
Stannington
Northumberland NE61 6EF

The Managing Director
The Frame Factory
Franchise Ltd
67 Vivian Avenue
Hendon
London NW4 3XE

The Managing Director
The Moviebank
The Automated Retailer Co
Ltd
21 Greycaine Road
Bushey Mill Lane
Watford WD2 4QT

The Managing Director
Bike
31 Kensington Church Street
London W8 4LL

The Managing Director
Compleat Cookshop
Compleat Franchise Services
Ltd
Enterprise House
Buckingham Road
Aylesbury
Bucks HP19 3QQ

The Managing Director
Crown Optical Centre
Crown Eyeglass Plc
Glenfield Park
Northrop Avenue
Blackburn
Lancs BB1 5QF

The Managing Director
Fires and Things
Heat House
4 Brighton Road
Horsham
West Sussex RH13 5BA

The Managing Director
Flower Stop Ltd
35 Cranleigh Close
Sanderstead
Surrey CR2 9LH

The Managing Director
The Original Art Shops Ltd
12 Southchurch Road
Southend-on-Sea
Essex SS1 2NE

The Managing Director
Video Cube (UK) Ltd
23 Harley House
Marylebone Road
London NW1 5HE

The Managing Director
Capricci
CMT International
Bridge House
Salcotes Road
Lytham St Annes
Lancs FY8 4HN

The Managing Director
Computerland Europe SA
Crown House
7 Windsor Road
Slough
Berks SL1 2DX

The Managing Director
Descamps Ltd
197 Sloane Street
London SW1X 9QX

The Managing Director
The Flower Express
20 Theresa Avenue
Bishopstown
Bristol B57 9EP

The Managing Director
Foto Inn Plc
35 South Molton Street
London W1Y 1HA

The Managing Director
In-Style Optical Centres
Home Optical Services Ltd
50 Houghton Avenue
Bacup
Lancs OL13 9RD

The Managing Director
Inter-Teddy Worldwide Ltd
13 Manor Court
Leigham Avenue
London SW16 2DH

The Managing Director
Kwik-Silver Print
(Franchising) Ltd
263 Commercial Road
Portsmouth
Hampshire PO1 4BP

The Managing Director
Memories Plc
5 Cambridge Street
Manchester M1 5GF

The Managing Director
Pandel Tiles
Proctor & Lavender Ltd
Unit 38 Forge Lane
Minworth Industrial Park
Sutton Coldfield
West Midlands B76 8AH

The Managing Director
Robin Hood Golf Centre
196-202 Robin Hood Lane
Hall Green
Birmingham B28 OLG

The Managing Director
Singer
91 Colman Road
Leicester LE5 4LE

The Managing Director
Insport
1d Saxeway
Chartridge Lane
Chartridge
Chesham
Bucks

The Managing Director
Knobs & Knockers
Franchising Ltd
Hathaway House
7d Woodfield Road
London W9 3EA

The Managing Director
Mainly Marines
6 Trojan Way
Croydon CRO 4XL

The Managing Director
The Open Fire Centres
Cattespoole Mill
Tardebigge
Nr Bromsgrove
Worcs B60 1LZ

The Managing Director
Phone-In (UK) Ltd
Enterprise House
Valley Street North
Darlington
Co Durham DL1 5GY

The Managing Director
Ryman
Pentos Retailing Group Ltd
35 Livery Street
Birmingham B3 2PB

The Managing Director
Snappy Snaps (UK) Ltd
Glenthorne Mews
115 Glenthorne Road
London W6 OLJ

The Managing Director
Tandy
Intertan (UK) Ltd
Tandy Centre
Leamore Lane
Walsall WS2 7PS

The Managing Director
National Slimming Centres
3 Trinity House
161 Old Christchurch Road
Bournemouth

The Managing Director
Sweatbox UK Ltd
10 Barnstaple Close
Thorpe Bay
Southend
Essex SS1 3PD

The Managing Director
Body Sense Ltd
The Chestnuts
18 East Street
Farnham
Surrey GU9 7SD

The Managing Director
Splash Dance
143a North Street
Romford
Essex RM1 1ED

Nectar Beauty Shops Ltd
Carrickfergus
Co. Antrim
Northern Ireland BT38 8XX

IRELAND

Priority Management
Kiltartan House
Foster Street
Galway
Telephone: 091/64224
Mr. James Storan

Ceiling Doctor
Dublin Executive Office
Centre
Maas Road
Dublin 22
Telephone: 01/593481
Mr. Richard Farrelly

Enoura
50 Pembroke Road
Dublin 4
Telephone: 01/609066
Mr. Pedro Reynolds

THE NETHERLANDS

The Managing Director
Boerenbond & Bouwmarkt
Cehave NV
Postbus 200
5460 BC Veghel
The Netherlands

The Managing Director
Arie Schoon
Schoon Bakkerij Support BV
Berenkoog 14
1822 BJ Alkmaar
The Netherlands

The Managing Director
Jamin
Jamin Winkelbedrijf BV
Postbus 148
4900 AC Oosterhout
The Netherlands

The Managing Director
Melvin Winkelgroep
Maalderij 30
1185 ZC Amstelveen
The Netherlands

The Managing Director
Multi-Vlaai
Maxi-Vlaai BV
Postbus 6822
5900 ZG Sevenum
The Netherlands

The Managing Director
Simons Vers Bakkerij BV
Kerkbuurt 42
3361 BJ Sliedrecht
The Netherlands

The Managing Director
Stop Shopp BV
Postbus 602
7000 AP Doetinchem
The Netherlands

The Managing Director
Lampenier BV
Postbus 241
5680 AE Best
The Netherlands

The Managing Director
Blankhout Ned. Franchising
BV
Peppelkade 16
3992 AK Houten
The Netherlands

The Managing Director
HaBe Nijverdal BV
Jan Van Galenlaan 14
7441 JD Nijverdal
The Netherlands

The Managing Director
Moto Franchise-Organisatie
BV
Postbus 153
6600 AD Wijchen
The Netherlands

The Managing Director
Palthe NV
Postbus 17
7600 AA Almelo
The Netherlands

The Managing Director
Ako BV
Postbus 562
1000 AN Amsterdam
The Netherlands

The Managing Director
De Boekelier
Friendchise BV
Postbus 122
3454 ZJ De Meern
The Netherlands

The Managing Director
Bruna BV
Meidoornkade 12
3900 AE Houten
The Netherlands

The Managing Director
Media Expresse
Medianet BV
Postbus 6298
2001 HG Haarlem
The Netherlands

The Managing Director
Meneer Kees
Friendchise BV
Postbus 122
3400 ZJ De Meern
The Netherlands

The Managing Director
Milo Beheer BV
Rigaweg 1
9723 TE Groningen
The Netherlands

The Managing Director
Multishop Boden vof
Postbus 2
4174 ZG Hellouw (Gld)
The Netherlands

The Managing Director
Portas
Franciscushof 59
4133 BB Vianen
The Netherlands

The Managing Director
Prénatal "Moeder & Kind"
BV
Postbus 30004
1303 AA Almere-De Vaart
The Netherlands

The Managing Director
Cieba BV
Postbus 20
2350 AA Leiderdorp
The Netherlands

The Managing Director
Brilmij BV
Amersfoortsestraat 84 A
3769 AM Soesterberg
The Netherlands

The Managing Director
Hans Anders Pris-optiek
Franchise BV
Hoge Bergen 16-20
4704 RH Roosendaal
The Netherlands

The Managing Director
Pharma Medical
International BV
Europalaan 20
3526 KS Utrecht
The Netherlands

The Managing Director
Capi BV
Postbus 2298
8203 AG Lelystad
The Netherlands

The Managing Director
Libel Bruidsmode
Creatie Libel BV
Spoorstraat 100
4702 VM Roosendaal
The Netherlands

The Managing Director
All-Port Spanplafonds
All-Port P.V.B.A.
Boomsesteenweg 496
2610 Wilrijk/Belgium

The Managing Director
Bouwmaat
Intergamma BV
Postbus 44
3750 GA Bunschoten
The Netherlands

The Managing Director
Creteprint
Cobblestone Paving Holland
Postbus 137
9600 AC Hoogezand
The Netherlands

The Managing Director
Formido
Houthandel "Utrecht" BV
Postbus 222
3512 GE Utrecht
The Netherlands

The Managing Director
Maars BV
Postbus 1000
3840 BA Harderwijk
The Netherlands

The Managing Director
Praxis Doe-Het-Zelf Center
BV
Postbus 268
1110 AG Diemen
The Netherlands

The Managing Director
Foto + BV
Postbus 350
7940 AJ Meppel
The Netherlands

The Managing Director
Foto-Quelle Nederland BV
Postbus 128
2130 BA Hoofddorp
The Netherlands

The Managing Director
Mr Photo
Handelsond Ijsselland BV
Postbus 66
7770 AB Hardenberg
The Netherlands

The Managing Director
Foto Print Express BV
Burgwal 5
5341 CP Oss
The Netherlands

The Managing Director
Lijst-in BV
Bredaseweg 41
4844 CK Terheyden
The Netherlands

The Managing Director
MultiCopy International BV
Weesperstraat 65
1018 VN Amsterdam
The Netherlands

The Managing Director
Pinky
Stella Zoetwaren BV
Postbus 1639
6201 BP Maastricht
The Netherlands

The Managing Director
Sweetheart Candyshops
Franchise BV
Prins Hendrikplein 14
2518 JC Den Haag
The Netherlands

The Managing Director
Automat Franchise BV
Postbus 188
7900 AD Hoogeveen
The Netherlands

The Managing Director
Auto-tronics vof
Koudenhor 54-56
2011 JD Haarlem
The Netherlands

The Managing Director
BoVo AutoAdmie BV
Minckelersstraat 19
5916 PE Venlo
The Netherlands

The Managing Director
Dregema
Weerdingerstraat 255 B
7811 CM Emmen
The Netherlands

The Managing Director
Cartoon Nederland BV
Kalverstraat 8
1012 PC Amsterdam
The Netherlands

The Managing Director
Albert Heijn Franchising BV
Postbus 33
1500 EA Zaandam
The Netherlands

The Managing Director
Amax
Groothandel P Karsten BV
1695 ZG Blokker
The Netherlands

The Managing Director
De Boer Supermarkten
Postbus 25000
9400 HG Assen
The Netherlands

The Managing Director
Edah
Vendex Food Groep BV
Postbus 217
5700 AE Helmond
The Netherlands

The Managing Director
Eismann BV
Postbus 279
6940 AG Dieren
The Netherlands

The Managing Director
De Groene Winkel Ned BV
Postbus 2082
2400 CB Alphen a/d Rijn
The Netherlands

The Managing Director
De Natuurwinkel BV
Waterput 19
1511 JA Oostzaan
The Netherlands

The Managing Director
De Kaasspecialist BV
Postbus 243
3760 AE Soest
The Netherlands

The Managing Director
Etos Beauty Case
Etos BV
Postbus 500
1500 EM Zaandam
The Netherlands

The Managing Director
Aspens Holland BV
Vendelier 31
3900 PB Veenendaal
The Netherlands

The Managing Director
DiDi Fashion
Coltex BV
Postbus 134
1700 AC Heerhugowaard
The Netherlands

The Managing Director
Marc O'Polo Benelux BV
Karveelweg 15
6222 NJ Maastricht
The Netherlands

The Managing Director
Oilily
Olly's BV
Postbus 8077
1802 KB Alkmaar
The Netherlands

The Managing Director
Pulls
Van de Wijk Mode Beheer
BV
Postbus 847
7400 AT Deventer
The Netherlands

The Managing Director
Unigro NV
Postbus 230
3992 GA Houten
The Netherlands

The Managing Director
Boedelbak BV
(Carrier-trailers)
Herengracht 472
1017 CA Amsterdam
The Netherlands

The Managing Director
Getifix Nederland BV
(Cleaning Equipment)
Postbus 107
1620 AC Hoorn
The Netherlands

The Managing Director
Rentex Nederland BV
(Textile, Clothing, Medical
Instruments)
Diedenweg 94
6717 KV Ede
The Netherlands

The Managing Director
Assuring Nederland BV
(Insurance)
Postbus 1800
8901 CC Leeuwarden
The Netherlands

The Managing Director
NV Bouwfonds Ned
Gemeenten
Postbus 15
3870 DA Hoevelaken
The Netherlands

City Courier Amsterdam BV
Nieuwe Hemweg 4 C
1013 BG Amsterdam
The Netherlands

The Managing Director
Free Record Shops BV
Postbus 155
2900 AD Capelle a/d Ijssel
The Netherlands

The Managing Director
Microland BV
Reaal 5
2300 TK Leiderdorp
The Netherlands

The Managing Director
Nashua
Nacom BV
Postbus 93150
5203 MB Den Bosch
The Netherlands

The Managing Director
Tandy Holland
Postbus 3130
5203 DC Den Bosch
The Netherlands

The Managing Director
Beauty Care International
Postbus 179
2060 AD Bloemendaal
The Netherlands

The Managing Director
Maasdam Beauty Salons
Parfumerie J Maasdam BV
Postbus 337
2300 AH Leiden
The Netherlands

The Managing Director
Door Praktijkrainers BV
Postbus 281
3940 AG Doorn
The Netherlands

The Managing Director
Financieel Dienstencentrum
Rijswijk (ZH) BV
Postbus 1082
2280 CB Rijswijk
The Netherlands

The Managing Director
Helping Hand Services Ned
Postbus 995
1200 AZ Hilversum
The Netherlands

The Managing Director
De Hypothekers Associatie
BV
Stavorenweg 4
2803 PT Gouda
The Netherlands

The Managing Director
Instituut Meditel (Ned) NV
(Prevention Health Care)
Kon Julianaplein 30
2595 AA Den Haag
The Netherlands

The Managing Director
Mail & More BV
(Postal Services &
Communication)
Gebouw London
Burg Stramanweg 102
1101 AA Amsterdam-ZO
The Netherlands

The Managing Director
Rotation Marketing BV
(Promotion & Marketing)
Insulindestraat 1 C
5013 BA Tilburg
The Netherlands

The Managing Director
Flower Fashion Franchise
Twelloseweg 79
7300 BM Terwolde
The Netherlands

The Managing Director
C'Est Bon
C.I.V. Nespec UA
Postbus 1139
1000 BC Amsterdam
The Netherlands

The Managing Director
Herma
Aangesloten Bedrijven
Organisatie Hema BV
Postbus 2145
1000 CC Amsterdam
The Netherlands

The Managing Director
Decorette BV
Postbus 1000
2800 CB Gouda
The Netherlands

The Managing Director
Gamma
Intergamma BV
Postbus 44
3750 GA Bunschoten
The Netherlands

The Managing Director
B-1 Gebr Van Bree BV
Kerkstraat 46
5701 PM Helmond
The Netherlands

The Managing Director
Forma Natura BV
Lange Jansstraat 12-14
3512 BB Utrecht
The Netherlands

The Managing Director
Nimco Schoenbedrijven BV
Tooropstraat 16-26
6521 NP Nijmegen
The Netherlands

The Managing Director
De Voetenvriend Nederland
BV
Postbus 185
7580 AD Losser
The Netherlands

The Managing Director
Nauticring (Acquatics)
Verkooporganisatie
Nauticring
Postbus 532
8200 AM Leystad
The Netherlands

The Managing Director
Degalux International BV
Postbus 607
3900 AP Veenendaal
The Netherlands

The Managing Director
Philips International BV
Corp Centre TDS-PID
Postbus 245
7300 AD Apeldoorn
The Netherlands

The Managing Director
Handymay Nederland BV
Postbus 3361
4800 DJ Breda
The Netherlands

The Managing Director
Happy Hobby BV
Postbus 97
Houthandel "Utrecht" BV
Postbus 222
3500 GE Utrecht
The Netherlands

The Managing Director
Karwei Holland Nationaal
BV
Laagraven 3
3400 LG Nieuwegein
The Netherlands

The Managing Director
Plus Klus BV
Postbus 37
7590 AA Denekamp
The Netherlands

The Managing Director
Cor Vingerhoed Witgoed
White-Line Apparaten BV
Oosteinde 5
2900 LG Barendrecht
The Netherlands

The Managing Director
Laarhoven Design BV
Postbus 67
2380 AB Zoeterwoude
The Netherlands

The Managing Director
Barnies Kipcorners
Kapteynstraat 1
3771 CA Barneveld
The Netherlands

The Managing Director
De Blok Trendhandel BV
Burg de Zeeuwstraat 296
2981 AJ Ridderkerk
The Netherlands

The Managing Director
Harmanni Reizen
Reisburo Harmanni BV
Postbus 207
9400 AE Assen
The Netherlands

The Managing Director
All Star Travel BV
Westkadijk 2
3861 MB Nijkerk
The Netherlands

The Managing Director
Bubbels Modesieraden BV
Postbus 502
3330 AM Zwijndrecht
The Netherlands

The Managing Director
Vide Photo Film
Videoland Nederland BV
Postbus 188
2200 AB Noordwijk
The Netherlands

The Managing Director
O'Sign Studio
O Harris Import Company
BV
Postbus 1025
1300 BA Almere
The Netherlands

The Managing Director
Covin BV
Postbus 416
5201 AK Den Bosch
The Netherlands

The Managing Director
Ben Cotto Pizza
Spinveld 15 A
4815 HR Breda
The Netherlands

The Managing Director
Bram Ladage
Staaldiepseweg 11
3231 ND Brielle
The Netherlands

The Managing Director
Coffee Club Franchise BV
Beurspassage 4
1000 LW Amsterdam
The Netherlands

The Managing Director
Het Station
Servex BV
Postbus 19208
3500 DE Utrecht
The Netherlands

The Managing Director
Florado Franchise BV
Postbus 233
4905 AA Oosterhout
The Netherlands

The Managing Director
De Tuinier
Groenland Combinatie
Nederland BV
Postbus 490
7900 AL Hoogeveen
The Netherlands

The Managing Director
Impodra BV
Postbus 390
4879 AJ Eten-Leur
The Netherlands

The Managing Director
Naturo Kurkexperts BV
Postbus 190
1000 AD Amsterdam
The Netherlands

The Managing Director
Parketstudio
Overmat Industries BV
Postbus 83
5165 ZH Waspik
The Netherlands

The Managing Director
Rowi Parket Nederland BV
Constructieweg 1
3400 NM Nieuwegein
The Netherlands

The Managing Director
Greenshop Franchising BV
Postbus 524
6040 AM Roermond
The Netherlands

The Managing Director
D'Ouwe Moestuin
Cevem BV
Postbus 113
4100 AC Leerdam
The Netherlands

The Managing Director
Tunivers BV
Generatorstraat 23
3903 LH Veenendaal
The Netherlands

The Managing Director
"De Twee Gebroeders" BV
Dorpsstraat 23
1689 EP Zwaag
The Netherlands

The Managing Director
John Martens
de Tapijtspecialist BV
Postbus 63
3850 AB Ermelo
The Netherlands

IP Benelux BV
Postbus 48
7090 AA Dinxperlo
The Netherlands

The Managing Director
Lederland Holland BV
Postbus 1100
3400 BC Nieuwegein
The Netherlands

The Managing Director
Oase
Slaapkamerspeciaalzaken
Postbus 122
2665 ZJ Bleiswijk
The Netherlands

The Managing Director
De Tuinier
Groenland Combinatie
Nederland BV
Postbus 490
7900 AL Hoogeveen
The Netherlands

The Managing Director
Keramos Design VOF
Postbus 8295
3503 RG Utrecht
The Netherlands

The Managing Director
Cosmo Hairstyling
Hairhold
Achter de Kamp 2
3811 JG Amersfoort
The Netherlands

The Managing Director
Happy Hobby BV
Postbus 97
7500 AB Enschede
The Netherlands

The Managing Director
VNR-Binorm Franchising
BV
Postbus 76
6710 BB Ede
The Netherlands

The Managing Director
Days West Europe BV
IBC-weg 2
5600 PK Best
The Netherlands

The Managing Director
Blokker BV
Postbus 4072
1009 AB Amsterdam
The Netherlands

The Managing Director
Marskramer BV
Postbus 126
2800 AC Gouda
The Netherlands

The Managing Director
Selectshop BV
Harderwijkweg 3A
2803 PW Gouda
The Netherlands

Mr. J A I M Burgers
Mitex – Ned Vereniging van
Ondernemers in de
Textieldetailhandel
Voldelstraat 172
1054 GV Amsterdam
The Netherlands

R van Horssen
RetailPlan Holland BV
Restyling Planontwikkeling
en Bouwbegeleiding
Postbus 29173
3001 GC Rotterdam
The Netherlands

The Managing Director
Keller Keukenfabriek BV
Postbus 112
4700 BC Roosendaal
The Netherlands

The Managing Director
SieMatic Benelux BV
Postbus 711
5000 AS Tilburg
The Netherlands

The Managing Director
Phildar BV
Postbus 72
5000 AB Hilvarenbeek
The Netherlands

The Managing Director
Pingouin Nederland
Hildo Kropstraat 8 A
3431 CC Nieuwegein
The Netherlands

The Managing Director
Hunkermöler
Vroom & Dreesmann Ned
BV
Postbus 386
1200 AJ Hilversum
The Netherlands

The Managing Director
Ladbroke Totalisator
(STDR)
Postbus 17260
2502 CG Den Haag
The Netherlands

The Managing Director
Kelly Fashion BV
Asterweg 3
1031 HL Amsterdam
The Netherlands

G L Bouwman
Van de Velden Groep CCV
Postbus 9226
6800 KH Arnhem
The Netherlands

GERMANY

An den Direktor
Mode-Schröder
Einkaufs-u-Vertriebs KG
Mühlenstrasse 11
2887 Elsfleth
Germany

An den Direktor
Straunch Pohl Kersten Lieser
& Partner
Bayenthalgürtel 31
5000 Köln 51
Germany

An den Direktor
Karl Thomas
Möbelwerkstätten
GmbH & Co KG
Walkmühlenstr 93
2740 Bremervörde
Germany

An den Direktor
TOP MAGAZIN Verlags
GmbH
Alt Niederkassel 78
4000 Düsseldorf 11
Germany

An den Direktor
Treppenmeister GmbH
Ringstrasse 4-6
7047 Jettingen
Germany

An den Direktor
Yves Rocher GmbH
Postfach 80 11 30
7000 Stuttgart 80
Germany

An den Direktor
Picobello Service GmbH
Weidtmannweg 5
4030 Ratingen
Germany

An den Direktor
PLUSS
Unternehemsberatung GmbH
Himmelstr 12-16
2000 Hamburg 60
Germany

An den Direktor
Pro Fashion
Modevertriebs GmbH
Postfach 330469
4000 Düsseldorf
Germany

An den Direktor
Prontaprint
Steinstrasse 15
2000 Hamburg 1
Germany

An den Direktor
Rentex Vertriebs GmbH &
Co KG
Postfach 2865
5800 Hagen 1
Germany

An den Direktor
Ring Deutscher Baubetreuer
GmbH & Co Verw KG
Bavariaring 20
8000 München 2
Germany

An den Direktor
ServiceMaster Operations
Germany GmbH
Lange Str 33
7239 Pfalzgrafenweiler
Germany

An den Direktor
AFRA GmbH (Pingouin)
Kossmannstr. 43
6600 Saarbrücken
Germany

An den Direktor
AQUELLA Heimdienst
GmbH
Postfach 60 01 07
4630 Bochum 6
Germany

An den Direktor
AUFINA Verwaltungs-und
Treuhand GmbH
Hagenauer Str. 42
6200 Wiesbaden
Germany

An den Direktor
Axel Weiss Agentur KG
Grazer Strasse 46
2850 Bremerhaven

An den Direktor
Oskar D Biffar GmbH & Co
KG
Postfach 140
6732 Edenkoben/Pfalz
Germany

An den Direktor
H G Becker GmbH
Goebelstr 55-57
2804 Lilienthal
Germany

An den Direktor
Bleyle-Franchise-GmbH
Hoferstrasse 9
7140 Ludwigsburg
Germany

An den Direktor
SELEX-Zentralverwaltungs
und Beratungs GmbH
Postfach 2408
7600 Offenburg
Germany

An den Direktor
Sixt Aktiengesellschaft
Postfach
8023 München-Pullach
Germany

An den Direktor
SOFTAWARIS
''Studienkreis'' für
Informatik sowie Programm
und Computergestütze
Sprachkurse GmbH
Kurt-Schumacher-Platz 8
4630 Bochum 1
Germany

An den Direktor
Spinnard Versandhandel
GmbH
Ruhrstrasse 10-12
4650 Gelsenkirchen
Germany

An den Direktor
SYNCON GmbH
Südi Auffahrstallee 76
8000 München 19
Germany

An den Direktor
Ekkehard Brysch & Partner
Postfach 11 62
2930 Varel 1
Germany

An den Direktor
Clean Park GmbH
Amselweg 6/1
7057 Winnenden
Germany

An den Direktor
Cosy-Wasch Autoservice-
Betriebe GmbH
Postfach 1147
1000 Berlin 30
Germany

Dank IS Björn
Franchisegesellschaft mbH
Lembekstrasse 36
2000 Hamburg 54
Germany

An den Direktor
Zentrale Gelsenkirchener
Schülerhilfe
J Birkner + J Gratze GbR
Steinmetzstr 4
4650 Gelsenkirchen-Buer
Germany

An den Direktor
Agewa GmbH & Co KG
(VALHAL)
Postfach 12 60
4740 Oelde 4 – Stromberg
Germany

An den Direktor
Autoradioland GmbH
Uerdinger Str 2-8
4150 Krefeld
Germany

An den Direktor
DR BABOR GmbH & Co
KG
Postfach 207
5100 Aachen
Germany

An den Direktor
DER TEELADEN
Gebr. Gschwendlner GmbH
Postfach 51 46
5303 Bornheim
Germany

An den Direktor
DESCAMPS GmbH
Postfach 47
7640 Kehl-Kork
Germany

An den Direktor
Diamant Technik Herdecke
GmbH
Postfach 1 60
5800 Herdecke/Ruhr
Germany

An den Direktor
Die Günther Bureau Service
System
Büroservice GmbH
Leopoldstr. 28 a/II
8000 München 40
Germany

An den Direktor
Döhle Inclusiv
Beraten & Machen
Löffelstrasse 1
2160 Stade
Germany

An den Direktor
Domicil-Möbel GmbH
7987 Weingarten
Germany

An den Direktor
Baumann Creative
Carl-Zeiss-Str 8
7080 Aalen
Germany

An den Direktor
Blumenauer Holding GmbH
Am Haag 33
6232 Bad Soden 2
Germany

An den Direktor
CAP Call a Pizza
Schnellrestaurant Betriebs
GmbH
Kraillerstr 62a
8000 München 80
Germany

An den Direktor
H CARLTON Konsumguter-
Vertriebs GmbH
Margetschöchheimer Str 200
8702 Zell
Germany

An den Direktor
CAVALLO Exclusiv
Autovermietung GmbH
Schulstrasse 14
8062 Odelzhausen
Germany

An den Direktor
CAR WASH PLACE
Verwaltungs GmbH
International
Kronprinzstr 54
2000 Hamburg 55
Germany

An den Direktor
Eismann Tiefkühl-
Heimservice GmbH
Seibelstrasse 38
4020 Mettmann
Germany

An den Direktor
Ellingstedter Eisfabrik
GmbH
(Janny's Eis)
2381 Ellingstedt
Germany

An den Direktor
FORMA-PLUS Bauelemente
GmbH
Postfach 12 08
8596 Mitterteich
Germany

An den Direktor
Foto-Quelle Schickedanz &
Co
Thomas-Mann-Str 50
8500 Nürnberg 50
Germany

An den Direktor
Getifix Reiningungstechnik
& Miet-Service GmbH
Haferwende 1
2800 Bremen 33
Germany

An den Direktor
Goodyear Reifen + Auto
Service
Josef Kempen GmbH
Postfach 600465
5000 Köln 60
Germany

An den Direktor
CR Computer-Vermietung
und Unternehmensberatung
GmbH
Pirazzistr 41
6050 Offenbach
Germany

An den Director
DEKORENO
Einzelhandelsvertriebs-und
Beteiligungs-GmbH
Max-Volmer-Strasse 1
4010 Hilden 1
Germany

An den Direktor
"Deutsche EIG" Einkaufs-
und Importges. f. das
Gastgewerbe mbH
(Mövenpick)
Mörickestr 67
7000 Stuttgart 1
Germany

An den Direktor
Dia Commerz Werbe GmbH
& Co KG
Friedrich-Ebert-Platz 2
4400 Münster
Germany

An den Direktor
EDUSCHO GmbH & Co
KG
Postfach 10 79 60
2800 Bremen 1
Germany

An den Direktor
ELAN Kfz-Service Ges
mbH
KarlstraBe 104
4000 Düsseldorf 1
Germany

An den Direktor
Haus für Sicherheit
Zingel 9
3200 Hildesheim
Germany

An den Direktor
Ihr platz GmbH & Co
Postfach 3740
4500 Osnabrück
Germany

An den Direktor
INTEXAL (Rodier)
Textil-Vertriebs GmbH
Riesstrasse 15
8000 München 50
Germany

An den Direktor
ip20 Inbau
Innenausbausysteme
Vertriebs-AG
Usedomstrasse 23
2000 Hamburg 70
Germany

An den Direktor
Kerz Haarmode
H Kerz GmbH
Schützenstr 33
6450 Hanau
Germany

An den Direktor
Flora Loggia
Marketing-und Service
GmbH
Osterwiesenstr 15
7071 Iggingen-Brainkofen
Germany

An den Direktor
Foto-Lippka OHG
Siebeneickerstr 90
5620 Velbert 15
Germany

An den Direktor
FRAHMTEX GmbH
Im Buckleberg 9
7519 Karlsbad-Auerbach
Germany

An den Direktor
FTT-Fertigteil-Technik
GmbH & Co KG
Flensburger Hagen 14A
2000 Norderstedt
Germany

An den Direktor
Getränkeland 2000
Postfach 1350
4352 Herten
Germany

An den Direktor
Goldschatz Juwelier GmbH
Bruppenweg 8/1
7450 Hechingen 11
Germany

An den Direktor
Hacienda Mexicana
Restaurantbetriebe GmbH
Wilhelmstrasse 3
8720 Schweinfurt
Germany

An den Direktor
LIESEGANG & RINKE
Wall 39
5600 Wuppertal 1
Germany

An den Direktor
Manpower Planen + Leisten
GmbH
Sonnenstrasse 17
8000 München 2
Germany

An den Direktor
Marc O'Polo Textilvertrieb
Werner Böck GmbH
Hochsühlstr 32
8200 Stepahnskirchen
Germany

An den Direktor
Mod's Hair C.F.S. Coiffure
Franchising System GmbH
Bettrather Str 73
4050 Mönchengladbach 1
Germany

An den Direktor
OBI Heimwerker- u
Freizeitbedarf
Handels GmbH & Co KG
Systemzentrale
Postfach 1270
5600 Wermelskirchen 1
Germany

An den Direktor
Optima Zentrale Nord
AKTUAL GmbH & Co KG
Postfach 1203
2084 Rellingen 1
Germany

An den Direktor
Optima Zentrale Süd
Wilhelm Harzmann GmbH
& Co KG
Göggingen
7482 Krauchenwies 3
Germany

An den Direktor
HEKA Kunststoffechnik
Beteiliguns GmbH
Waldstrasse 3
4434 Ochtrup
Germany

An den Direktor
HOBBYmade Ges Für
kreative
Freizeitgestaltung
Konzeption
und Franchising mbH
Hochstrasse 13
4250 Bottrop
Germany

An den Direktor
HYGAN Chemie & service
GmbH & Co KG
Robert-Bosch-Str 18
2200 Elmshorn
Germany

An den Direktor
ISOTEC Franchise-Systeme
GmbH
Johan-Wilhelm-Lindlar-Str 9
5060 Bergisch Gladbach 2
Germany

An den Direktor
JEDE Deutschland GmbH
Buchenstrasse 9
5470 Andernach
Germany

An den Direktor
KAJ Chemietechnik GMBH
& Co KG
Neunkirchener Str 38
8560 Lauf
Germany

An den Direktor
KAMINO Kamin-und
Ofenhaus
Verwaltungs-u Beteiligungs
GmbH
Loyerberstr 83
2902 Rastede
Germany

An den Direktor
Ott Franchise Vertriebsges
mbH
(fil à fil)
Königsallee 80
4000 Düsseldorf 1
Germany

An den Direktor
Marc Picard Franchise-
Marketing
GmbH & Co Vertriebs KG
Siedlungsstr 3
6981 Altenbuch
Germany

An den Direktor
PORTSA Deutschland
GmbH
Dieselstrasse 1-3
6000 Dietzenbach-Steinberg
Germany

An den Direktor
PORST AG
Postfach 1660
8540 Schwabach
Germany

An den Direktor
Pro image Strategisches
Management
Taterberg 8
2217 Rosdorf
Germany

An den Direktor
Ramp & Mauer GmbH &
Co KG
Reifenberger Str 1
6238 Hofheim/Ts
Germany

An den Direktor
KLEENOTHEK
Franchise-Zentrale
Römerstrasse 183
4134 Rheinberg
Germany

An den Direktor
KVM (Asmo Küchen
Center)
Küchen Vertrieb &
marketing
Freisinger Str 3
8057 Eching
Germany

An den Direktor
Mäc Würstl
Nordkanalstr 58
2000 Hamburg 1
Germany

An den Direktor
Mandarina Duck GmbH
Feldstrasse 37
4000 Düsseldorf 30
Germany

An den Direktor
McChinese GmbH
Postfach 5261
7800 Freiburg
Germany

An den Direktor
McSun Sonnenstudio GmbH
Schulweg 3
4715 Acheberg-Herbern
Germany

An den Direktor
SIMA GmbH
Industriestrasse 21
6720 Speyer
Germany

An den Direktor
VAT Baustrofftechnik
GmbH
Postfach 701726
2000 Hamburg
Germany

An den Direktor
VOSSEN GmbH
Postfach 3154
4800 Gütersloh
Germany

An den Director
Wab's Wasserbetten GmbH
Brüderweg 16
4600 Dortmund 1
Germany

An den Direktor
WALKERS Deutschland
Hägenstrasse 12
3000 Hannover 73
Germany

An den Direktor
WEST AIR Courier
Marketing GmbH
Kölner Weg 20
5000 Köln 40
Germany

An den Direktor
MCI-Club
Verbraucherdienst GmbH
Postfach 1919
6550 Bad Kreuznach
Germany

An den Direktor
MIT-Wohnen
Möbelvertriebsges mbH
Postfach 52
7968 Saulgau
Germany

An den Direktor
NEFF Gewindespindeln
GmbH
Postfach 1229
7035 Waldenbuch
Germany

An den Direktor
Novus GmbH
Im Langgewann 10
6238 Hotheim a Ts
Germany

An den Direktor
Nynorm Handelsges mbH &
Co
Islandstr 7A
2000 Hamburg 73
Germany

An den Direktor
Obs Optik-Brillen-Shop
GmbH
Postfach 72
3100 Celle
Germany

An den Direktor
Photocard Deutschland
Rietig/Kock Ringstr 8
6116 Eppertshausen
Germany

ITALY
Administratore Delegato
AI Box S.p.A.
Servizio rapido di
manutenzione autoveicoli
Via Pinerolo, 19
10152 Torino
Italy

Administratore Delegato
Arnoldo Mondadori Ed
Divisione Mondadori per
Voi
Libri e riviste
20090 Segrate/MI
Italy

Administratore Delegato
Casakit S.r.l.
Arredeamento casa
Via Di Vittorio, 15
20068 Peschiera B./MI
Italy

Administratore Delegato
Coin S.r.l.
Grandi Magazzini
Via Terraglio, 17
30174 Mestre/VE
Italy

Administratore Delegato
Compar S.p.A. − BATA
Organizzazione per la
produzione
e vendita di calzature
Via Volta, 2
35010 Limena/PD
Italy

Administratore Delegato
Consorzio A&O Italiana
Distribuzione organizzata
alimentari
Via C. Colombo, 51
20090 Tezzano S.N./MI
Italy

Administratore Delegato
Gruppo Pam S.p.A.
Supermercati alimentari
Via delle Industrie, 8
30038 Spinea/Ve
Italy

Administratore Delegato
IP − Italiana Petroli S.p.A.
Prodotti petroliferi
Piazza della Vittoria, 1
16121 Genova
Italy

Administratore Delegato
Maniffatura Lane G.
Marzotto & Figli S.p.A.
Tessuti ed abbigliamento
signora
Via Giuriolo, 1
36071 Arzignano/VI
Italy

Administratore Delegato
Miraglia S.p.A.
Abbigliamento intimo ed
esterno
uomo e donna
Via U. La Malfa, 64
90146 Palermo
Italy

Administratore Delegato
Natura Holding Italiana
S.p.A.
Prodotti alimentari, cosmesi
e della salute naturali
Via Cavour, 20
10048 Vinovo/To
Italy

Administratore Delegato
Portofino's Trading
Administration S.p.A.
Servizi per salute e bellezza
Via Molino Nuovo, 1
16030 Avegno/GE
Italy

Administratore Delegato
Consorzio Gigad S.r.l.
Distribuzione organizzata
alimentari
Viale Italia 3
20094 Corsico/MI
Italy

Administratore Delegato
Consorzio Vegetale Italia
Via Caldera 21
20153 Milano
Italy

Administratore Delegato
Eurocasa S.p.A.
Mobili per arredamento
Via Dante, 14
20121 Milano
Italy

Administratore Delegato
F.LLI Ferretti Di Ferretto
S.p.A.
Produzione cucine,
arredamenti
ed edifici prefabbricati
Via Volterrana, 60
56033 Capannoli/PI
Italy

Administratore Delegato
G. Ricordi & C. S.p.A.
Strumenti musicali,
pianoforti
edizioni musicali e dischi
Via Salomone, 77
20138 Milano
Italy

Administratore Delegato
Grimaldi S.p.A.
Intermediazione immobiliare
Corso Re Umberto, 54
10128 Torino
Italy

Administratore Delegato
Buzzoni S.r.l.
Industria arredamento negozi
Via Roma, 44
45038 Polesella/RO
Italy

Administratore Delegato
Co.GE.S. S.r.l.
Arredamento in legno o
metallo di negozi
Via Belgio, 1
35020 Padova
Italy

Administratore Delegato
Comir S.p.A. − c/o Centro
Commerciale
Centri commerciali
Via Nazionale
83013 Mercogliano/AV
Italy

Administratore Delegato
Hair Diffusion S.a.s.
di Egidio Marino & C
Parrucchiere per signora
Piazza Ricci, 8
18100 Imperia
Italy

Administratore Delegato
I.D.S. − Impressa
Distribuzione
Specializzata S.p.A.
Abbigliamento uomo e
giovane
Via Egeo, 18
10134 Torino
Italy

Administratore Delegato
I.L.F.I. S.r.l.
Intermediazione immobiliare
Via Cherubini, 3
20145 Milano
Italy

Administratore Delegato
I Pellettieri D'Italia S.p.A.
Abbigliamento, calzature,
accessori
Via Melzi d'Eril, 30
20154 Milano
Italy

Administratore Delegato
Kenny S.p.A.
Risttorazione rapido
Via A. Manuzio, 15
2000 Milano
Italy

Administratore Delegato
La Rinascente S.p.A.
Grandi Magazzini
Direzione Franchising
Palazzo Z − Milanofiori
20089 Rozzani/MI
Italy

Administratore Delegato
Luigi Buffetti S.p.A.
Forniture per ufficio
Via Aurelia, 1100
00166 Roma
Italy

Administratore Delegato
Frisina G. Remo
Avvocato in Reggio Calabria
C. so V. Emanuele, 109
89100 Reggio Calabria
Italy

Administratore Delegato
Jeanne Perego R.P. S.r.l.
Consulenza di relazioni
pubbliche
Via Maria Teresa, 8
20123 Milano
Italy

Administratore Delegato
Karl Steiner S.p.A.
Progettazione e arredo
punti vendita
Via Gallinao, 28
20051 Limbiate/MI
Italy

Administratore Delegato
Milan Arredamenti S.r.l.
Arredamento su misura
negozi
V. le del Lavoro, 28
45100 Rovigo
Italy

Administratore Delegato
Passeri Maurizio
Consulenza in franchising e
organizzazione aziendale
Via Fontana, 15
20122 Milano
Italy

Administratore Delegato
Presco S.r.l.
Societa di ingegneria per la
distribuzione organizzata
Via P. Sarpi, 41
20154 Milano
Italy

Administratore Delegato
Naj-Oleari S.r.l.
Tessuti, abbigliamento
oggettistica
Via Filelfo, 5
20145 Milano
Italy

Administratore Delegato
Omnia S.r.l.
Abbigliamento e biancheria
Via Valcatoio, 20
03056 Isola Liri/Fr
Italy

Administratore Delegato
Orsogril S.p.A.
Grigliati, recinzioni,
cancelli,
serramenti in PVC, scale e
porte di sicurezza
Via Milano, 51
22063 Cantu'/Co

Administratore Delegato
Pirola Maggioli S.p.A.
Stampati, articoli e libri
per ufficio
Via Portogallo, 5
47037 Rimini/FO
Italy

Administratore Delegato
Plastimoda S.p.A. –
Mandarina Duck
Produzione borse, valigie ed
accessori
Via Don Minzoni, 36/38
40057 Cadriano Di
Granarolo/BO
Italy

Administratore Delegato
Ufficio Internzionale
Brevetti
Ing. C. Gregorj S.p.A.
Brevetti e marchi
Via Dogano, 1
20123 Milano
Italy

Administratore Delegato
Quattroci S.r.l. – Bagatt
Calzature ed accessori in
pelle
Corso Cavour, 43
28041 Arona/No
Italy

Administratore Delegato
Standa S.p.A.
Grandi Magazzini
Strada 4 – Palazzo Q1
Milanofiori
20089 Rozzano/MM
Italy

Administratore Delegato
Trussardi S.p.A.
Abbigliamento, pelletteria
consulenza stilistica
Piazza Duse, 4
20122 Milano
Italy

Administratore Delegato
Centri Di Bellezza Yves
Rocher Italia
Iram S.r.l.
Cosmetica e Profumeria
Via Emilia, 10
20090 Buccinasco/MI
Italy

Administratore Delegato
Cagip S.r.l.
Profumeria e prodotti per la
casa
via Gozzi, 1
20129 Milano
Italy

Administratore Delegato
Despar Italia a.r.l.
Distribuzione organizzata
alimentari
V. le Puglie, 15
20137 Milano
Italy

Administratore Delegato
Diffusione Moro Mare
In Franchising S.r.l.
Pizzerie
via Rosselli, 4/6
16145 Genova
Italy

SPAIN
A/a Sr Francisco Caudali
Benetton
Poligono Industrial Santa
Rita
08755 Castellbisbal
Spain

A/a Sr Juan Ledesma
Creaciones Al SA
Poligono La Ermita
29600 Marbella
Spain

A/a Sra Fina Paula
Adolfo Domiquez
Po1 Industrial Ciprian de
Vinas
Apartado 1.160
32080 Orense
Spain

A/a Sr Pierre Bouvier
Almanes SA
Serrano 82 2o dcha
28006 Madrid
Spain

A/a Sra Amparo Soler
Alambique SA
Pza Encarnacion 2
28013 Madrid
Spain

A/a Sr Rafael Rubio
IFA Espanola SA
Sepulveda 4 Po1 Ind
Alcobendas
28100 Madrid
Spain

A/a Sr Jorge Piguer
Alphagrafics Espana SA
c/ Ricardos 7
04001 Almeria
Spain

A/a Sr Francisco Lamy
Euro Franchise SA
c/ Lagasca 27
28001 Madrid
Spain

A/a Sr Diego Linares
Laboro Seguridad SA
c/ Alonso de Ojeda 5
21002 Huelva
Spain

A/a Sr Juan Garcia Illa
Hilabor SA
c/ Colon 114
08222 Terrasa
Spain

A/a Sr José Luis Gastello
Lanas Katia SA
Ctra Les Fonts a Terrassa
km22
08194 Les Fonts Terrassa
Spain

A/a Sra Cristina Famies
Gruppo Investmenti Moda
SA
Avda Diagonal 433 Bis 4o
1a
08036 Barcelona
Spain

A/a Sr Jesus Gallego
Mundipaper SA
c/ Cromo 107
08907 L'Hospitalet De
Llobregat
Spain

A/a Sr Leopoldo Gonzalez
Romans
Operadora Hotelera Azca SA
Pza de Carlos Trias Bortran
4
28020 Madrid
Spain

A/a Sr José de Ynclàn
Giraldo
Amarras
c/ Lagasca 33
28001 Madrid
Spain

A/a Sr José de Ynclan
Amazonia SA
c/ Lagasca 70
28001 Madrid
Spain

A/a Sr Juan Carlos Amich
Amichi
c/ Penuelas 12
28005 Madrid
Spain

A/a Sr Amando Lasauca
Buli 88 SA
c/ Diagonal 333 bajos
08037 Barcelona
Spain

A/a Sr Amando Belicha
Commercial Antojos SA
Hermanos de Andrés 14
28029 Madrid
Sapin

A/a Sra Carmen Almagro
Cosmenatura SA
Nunez de Balboa 114 3o
28006 Madrid
Spain

A/a Snr Philippe Debeaupte
Godhor Europe Expansion
SA
Av Intanta Carlota 123 7o
08029 Barcelona
Spain

A/a Sra Rosa Millet
Parbella SA
c/ Mallorca 272 6o 6a
08037 Barcelona
Spain

A/a Sr Xavier Irizar
Imagine
c/ Caspe 30
Barcelona
Spain

A/a Sr José M Borras
Unisport So Coop
(Coop Detallistas Artic
Deporte)
Po1 Cova Solera Parela 45
08191 Rubi
Spain

A/a Sr Andrés Bellido
Bellido SA
San Bernardo 110
28015 Madrid
Spain

A/a Sr Luis Guillen
Luis Guillen SA
c/ Vallés 70-72
08303 Mataro
Spain

A/a Sr Carlos Picas
Jeans Jobs
c/ Duràn y Bas 12
08091 Rubi
Spain

A/a Sr Joaquim Massaqué
Vestuario Profesional SA
c/ Doctor Crehueras 18-20
08201 Sabadell
(Barcelona)
Spain

A/a Sr Giancarlo Cavattoni
Buffetti SA
Gtra de Viladecans km 1
08849 Sant Climent de
Llobregat
Spain

A/a Sr Fernando Rodriguez
Induyco SA
c/ Tomà Breton 60-62
28005 Madrid
Sapin

A/a Sr Josep Madi
Orfil SA
c/ Camp 28-30
08022 Barcelona
Spain

A/a Sr Manuel Prado
Galecon Club SA
Claudio Coello 102
28006 Madrid
Spain

A/a Sr José Martinez
Cia General De Zapateria
SA
Apartado 120
07300 Inca
Spain

A/a Sr Gerhard Thedens
Blitz Candy SA
C/ Fuencarral 33 1o 8a
28004 Madrid
Spain

A/a Sr Luciano Ortiz de
Latierro
Smuack SA
c/ Paz 9
CC Dendaraba
01004 Vitoria
Spain

A/a Sr Francisco Mendiola
Penta
General Yague 57 1o
28020 Madrid
Spain

A/a Sr José Luis Nunez
Industrias De Fibras Textiles
SA
Plaza de Europa 7
26003 Logrono
Spain

A/a Sr Ramon Gorina
Gorina Y Sauquet SA
c/ Sant Cugat 111
08201 Sabadell
Spain

A/a Sr Pedro Luis Cadenas
Leda
Calabria 205 bis
08029 Barcelona
Spain

A/a Sr Manuel Jiménez
Montesinos
Letrayon SA
c/ Aragoneses 9
Po1 Ind Alcobendas
28100 Alcobendas
(Madrid)
Spain

A/a Sr Julio Royo Burillo
Distributors Gimenex Y
Compania SA
(Digsa)
Po1 Malpica c/ F
Parcelas 46-47
50016 Zaragoza
Spain

A/a Sr So1 Monge
Trip Difusion SA
Pau Claris 97 bajos
08009 Barcelona
Spain

A/a Sr Agusti Bonavia
5 a Sec Difusion Espana SA
Via Layetana 13 2o 3a
08009 Barcelona
Spain

A/a Sr Luis Rodriguez
Blanco
Cinco Y Pico
c/ Salvador Moreno 42 4 P
36001 Pontevedra
Spain

A/a Sr Javier Rodriguez
Arague
Trezano SA
c/ Vivero 7
28040 Madrid
Spain

A/a Sr Joaquin Saez-Merino
Martinez
SAM SA
c/ Correos 3 3o
46002 Valencia
Spain

A/a Sr José Pedro Orio
Dipan
Torres Quevedo 6
Po1 Ind
28100 Alcobendas
Spain

A/a Sr Luis Araujo
Macavi
General Peron
40 (moda-Shopping L-49)
28006 Madrid
Spain

A/a Sra Inma Domenech
Inma Premama SA
c/ Descartes 22-24
08021 Barcelona
Spain

A/a Sr Jean Martin Gautier
Magic Moment SA
c/ Paris 184
08036 Barcelona
Spain

A/a Sr Vicente Villalba
Mamandel
Avda Eduardo Boscà 33 1o
46023 Valencia
Spain

A/a Sr Francisco Coch
Isna SA
c/ Bruch 25
08010 Barcelona
Spain

A/a Sr Juan Miquel
Mendez-Laiz
Congelados Artico
Nueve de Mayo
2 1o 13 Edificio Salesas
33002 Oviedo
Spain

A/a Sr Urbano Blanes
Auto Bake Iberica SA
Via de los Poblados 10
planta 5a nave 8
28033 Madrid
Spain

A/a Sr Francesc Roca
Tot Sport Iberica SA
c/ Muntaner 374 5o 1a
08000 Barcelona
Spain

A/a Sr Manzanares
Daper SA
Jorge Juan 19
28001 Madrid
Spain

A/a Srta Nieves Martinez
Nesgran SA
Avda Paises Catalanes 33-49
08950 Esplugas de Llobregat
Spain

A/a Sr Manuel Tarrida
Commercial Espanola
Arama SA
c/ Ramon y Caoal
s/n Po1 Industrial "El Pla"
08750 Molins De Rei
Barcelona
Spain

A/a Sr Emilio Diaz
Empresa Nacional de
Artesania SA
c/ Oquendo 23
28006 Madrid
Spain

A/a Sr Aron Cohen Auday
Manufacturas Arfor
Valgrande 27
PO1 Ind Alcobendas
28020 Madrid
Spain

A/a Sr Armando Lasauca
Sport 84 SA
c/ Diagonal 333 bajos
08037 Barcelona
Spain

A/a Sr Miquel Legaés
Mayffred SA
c/ Padre A Soler 10 12
17800 Olot
Spain

A/a Sra ma Teresa Elosequi
Medistock SA
c/ Antonio Maura 6 lo 1sq
28014 Madrid
Spain

A/a Sr José Mir
Querol SA
c/ Benicarlo 25-28
46020 Valencia
Spain

A/a Sr Manuel Mondéjar
Bata SA Espanola
c/ Profesor Manuel Sala 5
03003 Alicante
Spain

A/a Sr Julià Torres
Indas SA
c/ Segundo Mata 6
28033 Pozuelo de Alarcon
Spain

A/a Sr Pedro Franco
Espanola De1 Descanso SA
c/ Coso 102 Oficina 12
50001 Zaragoza
Spain

A/a Sr Joaquin Gil
Frankfurt SA
c/ Lauria 5
08010 Barcelona
Spain

A/a Sr Sanchez Guadrado
Mayoristas Asociados de
Espana SA
Hilarion Eslava 27 bis
28015 Madrid
Spain

A/a Sra Amparo Anquela
Farmabel SA
Po1 Ind de Bayas parcela 79
09200 Miranda de Ebro
Spain

A/a Sr Rafael Alvàrez de
Espejo
Papelar SA
Dr Esquerdo 18
28028 Madrid
Spain